HANDBOOK OF PSYCHOLINGUISTICS

HANDBOOK OF PSYCHOLINGUISTICS

Edited by

MORTON ANN GERNSBACHER

DEPARTMENT OF PSYCHOLOGY
UNIVERSITY OF WISCONSIN–MADISON
MADISON, WISCONSIN

ACADEMIC PRESS
A Division of Harcourt Brace & Company

SAN DIEGO NEW YORK BOSTON LONDON SYDNEY TOKYO TORONTO

Academic Press, Inc.
525 B Street, Suite 1900, San Diego, California 92101-4495

United Kingdom Edition published by
Academic Press Limited
24–28 Oval Road, London NW1 7DX

Library of Congress Cataloging-in-Publication Data

Handbook of psycholinguistics / edited by Morton Ann Gernsbacher.
     p.   cm.
  Includes bibliographical references and index.
  ISBN 0-12-280890-8
  1. Psycholinguistics--Handbooks, manuals, etc. I. Gernsbacher,
Morton Ann.
P37.H335 1994
401'.9--dc20   93-23396
                                                CIP

PRINTED IN THE UNITED STATES OF AMERICA
94 95 96 97 98 99   QW   9 8 7 6 5 4 3 2 1

CONTENTS

CHAPTER 1   METHODS IN READING RESEARCH

KARL HABERLANDT

CHAPTER 2   WHY STUDY SPOKEN LANGUAGE?

FERNANDA FERREIRA AND MICHAEL ANES

CHAPTER 9 VISUAL WORD RECOGNITION: THE JOURNEY FROM FEATURES TO MEANING
DAVID A. BALOTA

CHAPTER 10 CONTEXT AND THE PROCESSING OF AMBIGUOUS WORDS
GREG B. SIMPSON

CHAPTER 11 SENTENCE PARSING
DON C. MITCHELL

CHAPTER 19 UNDERSTANDING EXPOSITORY TEXT: BUILDING MENTAL STRUCTURES TO INDUCE INSIGHTS
BRUCE K. BRITTON

CHAPTER 20 RESOLVING SENTENCES IN A DISCOURSE CONTEXT: HOW DISCOURSE REPRESENTATION AFFECTS LANGUAGE UNDERSTANDING
SIMON C. GARROD AND A. J. SANFORD

CHAPTER 21 SELECTIVE PROCESSING IN TEXT UNDERSTANDING
A. J. SANFORD AND S. C. GARROD

CHAPTER 22 THE PSYCHOLOGY OF DISCOURSE PROCESSING
WALTER KINTSCH

CHAPTER 23 RECENT CONTROVERSIES IN THE STUDY OF LANGUAGE ACQUISITION
PAUL BLOOM

CHAPTER 24 CHILD PHONOLOGY: PAST RESEARCH, PRESENT QUESTIONS, FUTURE DIRECTIONS
LOUANN GERKEN

CHAPTER 34 FUTURE DIRECTIONS
ALAN GARNHAM

CONTRIBUTORS

Numbers in parentheses indicate the pages on which the authors' contributions begin.

MICHAEL ANES (33), Department of Psychology, Michigan University, East Lansing, Michigan 48824

DAVID A. BALOTA (303), Department of Psychology, Washington University, St. Louis, Missouri 63130

PAUL BLOOM (741), Department of Psychology, University of Arizona, Tucson, Arizona 85721

KATHRYN BOCK (945), Department of Psychology, University of Illinois at Urbana-Champaign, Urbana, Illinois 61801

BRUCE K. BRITTON (641), Department of Psychology, Institute for Behavioral Research, University of Georgia, Athens, Georgia 30602

CRISTINA CACCIARI (447), Dipartimento di Psicologia, Università di Bologna, I-40127 Bologna, Italy

DAVID CAPLAN (1023), Neuropsychology Laboratory, Massachusetts General Hospital, Boston, Massachusetts 02114

PATRICIA A. CARPENTER (1075), Department of Psychology, Carnegie-Mellon University, Pittsburgh, Pennsylvania 15213

HERBERT H. CLARK (985), Department of Psychology, Stanford University, Stanford, California 94305

FERNANDA FERREIRA (33), Department of Psychology, Michigan State University, East Lansing, Michigan 48824

CHARLES R. FLETCHER (589), Department of Psychology, University of Minnesota, Minneapolis, Minnesota 55455

ALAN GARNHAM (1123), Laboratory of Experimental Psychology, School of Biological Sciences, University of Sussex, Brighton BN1 9QG, United Kingdom

S. C. GARROD (675, 699), Human Communication Research Centre, Department of Psychology, University of Glasgow, Glasgow G12 9YR, United Kingdom

LouAnn Gerken (781), Department of Psychology and Cognitive Science Center, State University of New York, Buffalo, Buffalo, New York 14260

Raymond W. Gibbs, Jr. (411), Department of Psychology, University of California, Santa Cruz, Santa Cruz, California 95064

Arthur M. Glenberg (609), Department of Psychology, University of Wisconsin–Madison, Madison, Wisconsin 53706

Sam Glucksberg (447), Department of Psychology, Princeton University, Princeton, New Jersey 08544

Stephen D. Goldinger (265), Department of Psychology, Arizona State University, Tempe, Arizona 85287

Arthur C. Graesser (517), Department of Psychology, Memphis State University, Memphis, Tennessee 38152

Karl Haberlandt (1), Department of Psychology, Trinity College, Hartford, Connecticut 06106

Brenda K. Johnson (517), Department of Psychology, Memphis State University, Memphis, Tennessee 38152

Marcel Adam Just (1075), Department of Psychology, Carnegie-Mellon University, Pittsburgh, Pennsylvania 15213

Kerry Kilborn (917), Department of Psychology, University of Glasgow, Glasgow G12 9YR, United Kingdom

Walter Kintsch (721), Department of Psychology, University of Colorado, Boulder, Colorado 80309

Keith R. Kluender (173), Department of Psychology, University of Wisconsin–Madison, Madison, Wisconsin 53706

Peter Kruley (609), Department of Psychology, University of Wisconsin–Madison, Madison, Wisconsin 53706

Marta Kutas (83), Department of Neurosciences, University of California, San Diego, La Jolla, California 92093

William E. Langston (609), Department of Psychology, University of Wisconsin–Madison, Madison, Wisconsin 53706

Willem Levelt (945), Max-Planck-Institut für Psycholinguistik, NL 6525 XD Nijmegen, The Netherlands

Scott E. Lively (265), Department of Psychology, Indiana University, Bloomington, Indiana 47405

Dominic W. Massaro (219), Department of Psychology, University of California, Santa Cruz, Santa Cruz, California 95064

Cathy L. McMahen (517), Department of Psychology, Memphis State University, Memphis, Tennessee 38152

Don C. Mitchell (375), Department of Psychology, University of Exeter, Exeter, Devon EX4 4QG, United Kingdom

Akira Miyake (1075), Department of Psychology, Carnegie-Mellon University, Pittsburgh, Pennsylvania 15213

Jane Oakhill (821), Laboratory of Experimental Psychology, University of Sussex, Brighton BN1 9QG, United Kingdom

Richard K. Olson (895), Department of Psychology and Institute of Behavioral Genetics, University of Colorado, Boulder, Colorado 80302

Charles A. Perfetti (849), Department of Psychology, University of Pittsburgh, Pittsburgh, Pennsylvania 15260

David B. Pisoni (265), Speech Research Laboratory, Indiana University, Bloomington, Indiana 47405

Keith Rayner (57), Department of Psychology, University of Massachusetts, Amherst, Massachusetts 01003

Robert E. Remez (145), Department of Psychology, Barnard College, New York, New York 10027

A. J. Sanford (675, 699), Department of Psychology, University of Glasgow, Glasgow G12 9YR, United Kingdom

Sara C. Sereno (57), Department of Psychology, University of Oregon, Eugene, Oregon 97403

Greg B. Simpson (359), Department of Psychology, University of Kansas, Lawrence, Kansas 66045

Murray Singer (479), Department of Psychology, University of Manitoba, Winnipeg, Manitoba, Canada R3T 2N2

David Swinney (1055), Department of Psychology, Center for Human Information Processing, University of California, San Diego, La Jolla, California 92093

Paul van den Broek (539), Center for Research in Learning, Perception, and Cognition, University of Minnesota, Minneapolis, Minnesota 55455

Cyma K. Van Petten (83), Department of Psychology, University of Arizona, Tucson, Arizona 85721

Edgar Zurif (1055), Department of Psychology and Center for Complex Systems, Brandeis University, Waltham, Massachusetts, 02254, and Aphasia Research Center, Boston University School of Medicine, Boston, Massachusetts, 02215

PREFACE

Editing a handbook on any topic is, by definition, a daunting task. Handbooks are defined as reference manuals—compendia of necessary information that place crucial resources into the hands of their readers. The task seems even more daunting when the information to be amassed comes from a field as broad as psycholinguistics.

Indeed, when I first mentioned the idea of editing a handbook of psycholinguistics to a colleague, he asked if I were on drugs. After I shook my head—horizontally, of course—he predicted that by the time I finished the project, I would be. But my initial reasoning was that the field of psycholinguistics had come of age. Although into its third decade, the field had no handbook. My goal in editing the *Handbook of Psycholinguistics* was to compile state-of-the-art descriptions of the research and theory of many of the subareas of psycholinguistics. The chapters, written by leading experts, would each contribute to a broad and deep coverage of the field.

I was admittedly biased when I chose the topics to be included in the *Handbook,* and equally biased when I invited authors to write on each topic. I take responsibility for these biases, but I do not apologize for them. The resulting *Handbook* should be an excellent resource for researchers, graduate students, university and college teachers, and other professionals in the fields of psycholinguistics, language comprehension, reading, neuropsychology of language, linguistics, language development, and computational modeling (of language). The *Handbook* should also serve as an excellent overview of psycholinguistics for readers in the broader disciplines of cognitive psychology, education, and computer science.

I am grateful to my graduate students, my laboratory personnel, and several scientists who visited my laboratory during the time that I was compiling the *Handbook.* Manuel de Vega, Manuel Carreiras, Jose Miguel Diaz, and Adelina Esteves, all from the Universidad de la Laguna; and Matthew Traxler, Jennifer Deaton, Victor Villa-Good, Bruce McCandliss, and Julie Foertsch, graduate students at the University of Oregon and the University of Wisconsin–Madison, helped me read through the bulk of the chapters and provide insightful comments to the authors. Caroline Bolliger and Sara Glover spent countless hours cataloging the chapters, photocopying the manuscripts, downloading electronic files, and air expressing various communications. As always, Rachel R. W. Robertson, director of our Language Comprehension Laboratory, was the backbone of our endeavor. She single-handedly oversaw the monumental task of proofreading each chapter and contacting authors about countless queries. I also thank the staff at Academic Press, in particular, Joe Ingram, Nikki Fine, and Diane Scott.

Finally, I am indebted to the authors who penned these chapters. This is their handbook, and I have served only as the editor. From my initial plea for ''Helf,'' through my reminder limericks (to which I received several back that eclipsed my wit), to the final, draconian deadlines, these authors persevered—despite disk crashes, new babies, cross-country moves, and exotic sabbaticals. These authors believed in this project, and to them I am extremely grateful. Their chapters coalesce into a manual describing the fascinating field of psycholinguistics; this manual should remain resourceful until I get another drug-induced idea and edit a second edition.

Morton Ann Gernsbacher

CHAPTER 1

METHODS IN READING RESEARCH

KARL HABERLANDT

I. INTRODUCTION

Theories and methods in cognitive science depend on one another; in reading research too, methods serve theoretical goals while research paradigms are based on theoretical assumptions. Theoretical frameworks of reading derive their assumptions from cognitive psychology; this is true both for global assumptions like the activation hypothesis and for specific ones, such as the hypothesis that subjects adopt strategies in decision tasks. Reading theories assume processes, representations, and outcomes of comprehension. Researchers seek to identify processes at different levels of linguistic structure and to document the representations while minimizing confounds in the reading materials and task-specific strategies.

The technological advances of the past two decades have improved the methods of reading research, which in turn has contributed to broader and more detailed theories. There are better eye trackers and more powerful mini-computers and statistical packages, all of which have greatly improved data collection and analysis. The number of observations possible per session and per subject, the resolution, and statistical sophistication have all increased. Although these improvements are impressive, the key issue in methodology and in research remains the problem of interpretation: What do the data mean?

This chapter discusses methods used to assess comprehension of written language ranging from individual words to full texts. The choice of a particular method depends on the specific theoretical issue an investigator is interested in. In general, experimental methods are constrained by theoretical assumptions about comprehension processes and representations; I review these in the first section. We will see that theorists emphasize comprehension PROCESSES and that, as a result, chronometric techniques dominate among methods of reading research. In the remaining sections, I review three such paradigms: the reading, decision, and naming methods. For each I describe the general procedure and rationale with illustrative applications and selected results. I also discuss criticisms and responses from the advocates of each method. The most common criticism is that a particular task introduces task-specific confoundings. The challenge for proponents of the task is to identify and control for such confoundings. The review of research paradigms suggests there is no single perfect method and that researchers should evaluate hypotheses in terms of several techniques. Other methodological issues involve the potential interactions between stimuli, tasks, reader goals, and individual readers as well as issues of data analysis, such as the use of the F' test, multiple regression, and other linear modeling techniques (e.g., Kieras & Just, 1984; Lorch & Myers, 1990). No single chapter could handle all these issues; they are best treated in the context of individual theoretical contributions (see also Ferreira & Anes, this volume; Garnham, this volume).

II. THEORETICAL ISSUES

A. Assumptions on Reading Comprehension

1. Comprehension Processes

For the mature reader, reading usually appears to be an instantaneous and unified process. Under the scrutiny of research, however, this impression is inaccurate. Reading is not a single mental operation; rather, theorists distinguish among component processes of reading at the word, sentence, and text level. These component processes are implicated in the generation of meaning representations of the text at different levels of abstractness (e.g., Balota, Flores d'Arcais, & Rayner, 1990; Haberlandt & Graesser, 1985; Just & Carpenter, 1980; van Dijk & Kintsch, 1983).

Each of the component processes of reading is thought to consist of subprocesses. Word-level processes, for example, include encoding and lexical access. Encoding operations transform the visual characters of a word into a mental representation that forms the basis for word recognition. Lexical access refers to the process of recovering the word's meaning from memory. Researchers isolate subprocesses like encoding and lexical access by documenting that each is sensitive to manipulations of specific stimulus factors and independent of others. Manipulations in word length, for example, are assumed to affect encoding but not lexical access, whereas familiarity affects lexical access but not encoding (Bower & Clapper, 1989; Just & Carpenter, 1987).

Sentence-level processes include syntactic parsing processes. Using surface markers, word class, word position, and punctuation, these processes organize the words of sentences into a syntactic structure. Drawing on information from across the text, text-level processes establish links between a sentence and the previous text. This is achieved via a range of inferences including anaphoric, backward, and elaborative inferences. Inferences take advantage of causal connections in the text and of a reader's general knowledge of the world.

A critical issue in reading research is the extent to which processes at different levels operate independently. Interactive theories (e.g., Just & Carpenter, 1987; McClelland, 1991) assume collaboration among component processes, whereas modular theories postulate independence (e.g., Fodor, 1983). This debate surfaces in theoretical treatments of lexical access and syntactic processes. For example, are parsing operations subject to the impact of textual and pragmatic constraints? According to an influential view, readers' initial parsing decisions are independent of semantic considerations (e.g., Frazier,

1987). According to interactive theories, readers use all sources of information, including semantic ones, to guide early parsing processes (e.g., Taraban & McClelland, 1988).

The quest to identify specific word-, sentence-, and text-level operations and the relations between them has motivated the research methodologies under discussion here. It turns out that the basic research methods, including reading, decision, and naming methods, are equally applicable to research at each of these levels. Decision methods, for example, are employed to examine word-, sentence-, and text-level processes.

Comprehension unfolds in real time as the reader understands the words and sentences of a text. The goal of chronometric methods is to monitor these processes (see, e.g., Posner, 1978); it is assumed that longer processing times reflect a greater processing load. The transient processing load depends on the accessibility of representations needed for comprehension, on their activation level, and on the current demands on working memory. For example, when the reader has to keep several referents in mind, the working memory load increases and reading is expected to slow down.

Reading researchers have adopted the distinction between automatic and controlled processes common in cognitive research. An automatic reading process takes place without the deliberate intervention of the reader as in, for example, lexical access or sentence parsing. Controlled processes depend on the subject's knowledge of the experimental design, including the distribution of different types of trials in an experiment (e.g., Tweedy, Lapinski, & Schvaneveldt, 1977). Controlled processes are also a function of the reading goal; a reader controls the base rate of comprehension, adjusting it to the specific task, whether verbatim recall or question answering (Aaronson & Ferres, 1984; Haberlandt, Graesser, & Schneider, 1989; Just & Carpenter, 1987; Kieras & Just, 1984).

2. Representations

Processes generate representations that differ in their duration; representations based on surface features are short-lived. Semantic representations of sentences and texts last longer, and global representations like the text-base model and the situation model are the most durable (Glenberg, Meyer, & Lindem, 1987; Johnson-Laird, 1983; van Dijk & Kintsch, 1983). Both explicit information in the text and reader inference contribute to text representations. Detecting the locus and type of inferences is a major research issue (see Kintsch, Welsch, Schmalhofer, & Zimny, 1990; Speelman & Kirsner, 1990). The involvement of representations in reading is assessed by the activation of critical target concepts; patterns of reading times and latencies presumably reflect the underlying representation.

The activation assumption is fundamental in cognitive psychology; in experimental psychology it dates back to Marbe's Law, which was popular over a century ago (Corballis, 1967). Theories of memory, semantic network and feature models, models of episodic memory, and the major frameworks of reading comprehension are based on the activation concept. According to network theories, concepts form nodes in semantic memory; the nodes are related via semantic, episodic, or textual pathways (e.g., Collins & Quillian, 1969; Meyer & Schvaneveldt, 1976). When a concept is mentioned or inferred, its node becomes active and the activation is assumed to spread automatically to other nodes (see also Anderson, 1983; Chang, 1980; Fletcher, 1981; Glenberg et al., 1987; McKoon & Ratcliff, 1980, 1984). In feature theories and connectionist models, evidence of a concept accumulates up to a threshold and activates the concept (e.g., McClelland, 1991; Morton, 1979; Ratcliff, Hockley, & McKoon, 1985).

Comprehension depends on activation of information; as the reader processes the sentences of a passage, new information is integrated with the existing representation. Information is linked with antecedents; linkage requires that the antecedents be active in working memory or be reinstated if they are inactive (e.g., Dell, McKoon, & Ratcliff, 1983; Fletcher, 1981; Gernsbacher, 1990; Just & Carpenter, 1987; van Dijk & Kintsch, 1983). Activation theories imply an inhibitory or dampening mechanism that prevents swamping the text representation and the rest of memory with activation; once a referent is activated and the new information is integrated, new concepts are activated. Whether they displace previous concepts or actively suppress them remains unresolved (e.g., Gernsbacher, 1990). The activation concept is ubiquitous in reading research; its measurement, however, is controversial and far from simple, regardless of the measurement technique used.

Reading research deals with representations at different levels of abstractness and with the processes that generate and operate on them. The objective of specific theories is to identify component processes as they take place on line. Neither representations nor processes are phenomenologically penetrable; the research methods reviewed here were developed to make them transparent.

B. What Is Natural Reading?

Reading theories are evaluated using a wide range of laboratory tasks to illuminate NATURAL reading. This is the issue of ecological validity; it is periodically raised in cognitive psychology (e.g., Banji & Crowder, 1989; Klatzky, 1991; Neisser, 1978). This issue rarely surfaces in the quotidian laboratory research of reading researchers but nevertheless influences their choice of paradigms, stimuli, and analyses. The following three questions capture the ecological concern:

1. What is natural reading?
2. What is a natural sentence or text?
3. How natural is a particular method?

There are no short and certainly no single answers to these questions, and no attempt will be made here to offer them. Yet it is useful to keep these questions in mind as we examine the methods of reading research. According to its textbook definition, reading involves component processes that extract the meaning of a text and generate a representation in the reader's mind. This definition does not capture the natural reading situation, if indeed there is one. Naively, one may view natural reading as taking in words and sentences printed on paper, perhaps while relaxing in an easy chair. This situation is referred to as an "unconstrained" reading situation, a sort of baseline (see Dixon, 1984). Is it appropriate, however, to invoke a reading baseline? After all, readers process texts in very different ways; they skim, summarize, read for entertainment and other purposes. Increasingly, reading takes place without print and involves video terminals, especially in education and the workplace. Here, the reader presses a key to advance text segments, scroll back, and highlight phrases (Bromley, Jarvella, & Lundberg, 1985; Granaas, McKay, Laham, Hurt, & Juola, 1984; Wright, 1987). Although there is no commonly accepted standard of natural reading, it stands nevertheless as an implicit standard of reading research (e.g., Danks, 1986; Rayner & Pollatsek, 1989; Seidenberg, Waters, Sanders, & Langer, 1984).

The response to the imperative of natural reading varies; some researchers seek to maximize the naturalness of overt reading behavior in the laboratory but use artificial reading materials. Others emphasize natural reading materials but are less concerned about the naturalness of the testing methods. Every research method can be taken to task on its naturalness, whether because subjects are asked to process up to 100 mini-passages like those in Tables I–III during a single lab session, or because readers are interrupted with tests during and after reading passages. Reading research techniques are necessarily intrusive, as is true for experimental research in general. Science knows no alternative to the controlled experiment, and the science of language is no different "from the rest of science, where nature has to be pushed or pulled out of its normal course before it reveals its secrets" (Singer, 1990, p. 23). Acknowledging the fact that our methods may intrude on the process of natural reading, however, does not license every method. Criteria need to be developed to constrain intrusiveness while taking into account the tradeoff between scientific gain and artificiality.

C. Reading Materials

Because language is a rich and multifaceted stimulus, every research report in psycholinguistics, including those in this handbook, features a section describing and justifying the choice of stimulus materials. The goal of experimental science to isolate variables, a daunting task anywhere, is particularly difficult when texts are involved. The choice of stimulus materials and the detection and control of confounds is both a theoretical and a methodological problem.

There is no set of explicit a priori principles to guide a researcher in the selection of stimulus materials other than the objective of uncovering confounds at all levels of text. What constitutes a confound is difficult to say in the abstract; it depends on a specific theory or hypothesis. In general, stimulus materials are said to be confounded when factors other than the one intended by the experimenter influence the dependent variable. Suppose a researcher seeks to investigate the effects of syntactic structure on reading times. She constructs two sentences she believes to be equivalent except for their syntactic structure. If the sentences were to differ in terms of meaning too, there would be a confounding. The problem is that the latter might contribute to changes in reading times without being detected.

Sometimes confounds are easy to spot and quantify as, for example, between the occurrence frequency and length of words, or between the amount of new information in a sentence and its serial position in the text. In other cases, discovering a confound is not so straightforward; for example, semantic acceptability and syntactic structure may covery in simple sentences (e.g., Ferreira & Henderson, 1990; Taraban & McClelland, 1988), and word-based associations may correlate with sentence-level inferences (Keenan, Potts, Golding, & Jennings, 1990; McKoon & Ratcliff, 1986). Frequently, there is a debate over which factors produce confoundings and how to remove or control for them. Noting the panoply of confounds, Cutler (1981) even wondered whether psycholinguistic research is possible at all. Reading researchers have voted in the affirmative by continuing their research.

When choosing stimulus materials, there is a continuum of options ranging from the use of existing texts to using texts specifically written by the experimenter to isolate the variable(s) of theoretical interest. Neither extreme can fully overcome the problem of confoundings. Consider some studies that employed experimenter-generated stimuli: the first is a pair of studies that sought to control for lexical factors, the other is a case that illustrates confounding between syntactic and semantic factors.

1. Control of Lexical Factors

The first study is typical of reading experiments in which lexical factors are successfully controlled by using the same words for different sentence structures (e.g., King & Just, 1991). Here the structure of relative clauses was the variable of interest; the researchers wanted to compare the processing of object relatives (1) and subject relatives (2) and used the same set of words for each version.

(1) *The reporter that the senator attacked admitted the error.*
(2) *The reporter that attacked the senator admitted the error.*

Object relatives like (1) should take longer to read because neither *reporter* nor *senator* can be thematically assigned until the verb *attacked* is encountered. Therefore, both of these arguments must be held in working memory. In subject relatives, however, the thematic assignment of *the reporter* is possible as soon as *attacked* is read, thus permitting immediate assignment of *the senator*.

The second example is McKoon and Ratcliff's (1986) study to assess text-level inferences in reading. McKoon and Ratcliff (1986) had subjects read inference sentences like the one shown in Table I. A recognition test followed to investigate whether readers made specific inferences—for example, the inference that the actress was dead. The potential confound is that the words in the inference sentence in Table I might be related lexically to the target word *dead* and thus evoke the inference by lexical association (see McKoon & Ratcliff, 1990a). McKoon and Ratcliff wrote the control sentence shown in Table I. The

TABLE I
Control for Lexical Priming in an Inference Study

Inference: *The director and the cameraman were ready to shoot closeups when suddenly the actress fell from the 14th story.*
Test word: *dead*
Word Control: *Suddenly the director fell upon the cameraman, demanding closeups of the actress on the 14th story.*
Test word: *dead*

control sentence contains the words of the inference sentence that might be associated with the target word but do not predict that anyone is dead. This control condition, however, did not satisfy every critic. Keenan and her colleagues noted that the two text versions were similar only at the word level, not at the propositional level; the test word is implied at the propositional level and one cannot control for this (see Keenan et al., 1990).

2. Confounding Syntactic Structure and Semantic Acceptability

The comprehension of structurally ambiguous sentences is one of the most fertile topics in psycholinguistic and reading research. Debates over confounds in ambiguous sentences are characteristic of this research. During the last decade, researchers have investigated the minimal attachment principle in order to elucidate the modularity of syntactic parsing processes. According to the minimal attachment principle, readers interpret successive words of a sentence so as to generate the minimum number of nodes in the syntactic structure. For example, readers interpret the phrase *the answer* in the sentence *The girl knew the answer by heart* as a direct object. When subsequent information overrules the initial interpretation, however, as it does in *The girl knew the answer was wrong*, readers pause in the ambiguous region to generate the extra node representing the sentence complement *the answer was wrong* (e.g., Frazier, 1987; Frazier & Rayner, 1982; Rayner, Carlson, & Frazier, 1983). The minimal attachment principle inspired much research in which researchers varied the type of sentence complement, sentence length, and the choice of surface markers (e.g., Ferreira & Henderson, 1990; Kennedy, Murray, Jennings, & Reid, 1990).

Typically, sentences with verb-phrase attachments like (3a) are more easily understood than sentences with noun-phrase attachment like (3b).

(3a) *The spy saw the cop with binoculars.*
(3b) *The spy saw the cop with a revolver.*

Taraban and McClelland (1988) noted that sentence structure and semantic naturalness are difficult to separate. They had subjects rate the set of sentences developed by Rayner and Frazier for their semantic acceptability and found that the raters judged the sentences with verb-phrase attachment more sensible than those with noun-phrase attachment. Next, Taraban and McClelland invented a set of sentences in which the opposite was true: Sentences with noun-phrase attachment met the raters' expectations more often than their counterparts with verb-phrase attachment. Consider sentences (4a) and (4b).

(4a) *I read the article in the bathtub.*
(4b) *I read the article in the magazine.*

Raters judged (4b) more likely and, not surprisingly, another group of subjects comprehended them more quickly. As a result, Taraban and McClelland questioned the syntactic assumptions of the minimal attachment principle. They did not have the last word on this issue, however; Frazier (e.g., 1990) was quick to respond (see also Ferreira & Henderson, 1990; Mitchell, Corley, & Garnham, 1992). The specifics of the criticism and response, although important in the original theoretical context, are almost incidental here; this argument illustrates debates about stimulus materials typical in reading research.

3. Uniformity and Unit Length of Stimuli

In reading experiments, subjects usually see dozens of experimental sentences like (1)–(4) interspersed among filler sentences. Their presentation is usually carefully counterbalanced within and across subjects. The narrowness and uniformity of stimulus materials within and across experiments calls into question the validity of statistical tests, including the F' test, however. This test purports to assess the generalizability of results over subjects and stimulus materials. Selection of subjects and materials, however, must be random; this presents a problem when the experimenter composes, edits, and norms sentences and texts to meet the goals of the study. Though this problem was noted long ago (Keppel, 1976), it has not been sufficiently addressed (see also Garnham, this volume).

One aspect of the ecological issue concerns the use of individual words and sentences in the study of reading comprehension. Normally we read intact texts rather than words, sentences, or minipassages like those in Tables II and III. Most theorists assume that research with smaller units has valid implications for normal reading because results obtained with such segments have, in some cases, been validated against reading patterns observed in full-length texts (e.g., Just & Carpenter, 1980, 1987). Other researchers, however, use intact texts in the laboratory (e.g., Haberlandt & Graesser, 1989; Just & Carpenter, 1987; Olson, Duffy, & Mack, 1984; Rothkopf & Billington, 1983). While these researchers may not face questions of validity, their work usually lacks the experimental controls necessary to assess specific hypotheses, for example, about syntactic parsing or inference processes. Furthermore, even in long texts, the number of critical sentences exhibiting a specific syntactic structure is too small to permit reliable interpretations. Haberlandt and Graesser (1989) used unedited magazine articles of 2000–2600 words which contained confoundings. Their research strategy was to partial identifiable confoundings using multiple regression analyses (e.g., Graesser & Riha, 1984; Just & Carpenter, 1987; Lorch & Myers, 1990). Word-level variables like word length and occurrence frequency; sentence-level variables such as phrase and clause boundaries; and text-level variables such as the number of propositions, arguments, or causal links were quantified and entered as predictor variables (e.g., Bloom, Fletcher, van den Broek, Reitz, & Shapiro, 1990; Haberlandt & Graesser, 1989; Just & Carpenter, 1980).

I have now sketched the basic assumptions of reading research on processes and representations and reviewed issues in the choice of stimulus materials. The remainder of the chapter treats three general methods of data collection: the reading time methodologies, decision-making tasks, and naming latency paradigms. These are chronometric techniques; they reflect the goal of reading research to capture the dynamic changes in mental load as a person reads, and the activation of representations as the reader's focus shifts from topic to topic.

III. READING-TIME METHODS

Self-paced reading-time methods are based on the assumption that a subject reads a passage "at a pace that matches the internal comprehension processes," and therefore an analysis of the reading rate will uncover "the comprehension processes themselves" (Just & Carpenter, 1980). The interpretation of reading times is based on two additional hypotheses, the immediacy and the eye–mind assumptions. According to the immediacy hypothesis, the reader tries to comprehend a unit of text, usually a word, as soon as possible rather than waiting until the end of a clause or sentence. The eye–mind hypothesis states that the mind processes the word currently fixated by the eye. In other words, there is no delay between the word being fixated and the mental processes devoted to that word. Self-paced timing techniques include eye-tracking methods, key-press methods such as the moving window and stationary window methods, and the pointing method.[1]

Critics of reading-time methods concede that reading times reflect changes in the processing load. They note, however, that reading times do not reveal the source of the changes in processing (see also Altmann & Steedman, 1988; McKoon & Ratcliff, 1980). Rather, the reading time for a word or a sentence is the result of several components, and it is unclear how to apportion the aggregate time to these subprocesses. Even if the processes were known, there are different theories about how they might affect reading times. The processes could be additive and serial, they might interact, or they might operate in parallel.

There are other interpretational problems in reading-time data; one problem is that the immediacy assumption may not always hold. Researchers have discovered spillover effects: Readers continue to process a previous sentence or word while inspecting new text (Haberlandt & Bingham, 1978; Rayner, Sereno, Morris, Schmauder, & Clifton, 1989). Readers may also preview a text segment and begin processing it prior to fully fixating on it (Rayner et al., 1989).

Researchers have acknowledged problems involved in interpreting reading times. They have validated reading times by correlating them with empirically or theoretically based measures of comprehension difficulty. For example, passages are rated for their difficulty, familiarity, or narrativity, and these ratings are used as a predictor of reading times (e.g., Graesser, Hoffman, & Clark, 1980; see also Olson et al., 1984). Theoretical measures are based on structural text models (Kintsch, Kozminsky, Streby, McKoon, & Keenan, 1975; O'Brien, Duffy, & Myers, 1986), simulation models (Just & Carpenter, 1980, 1987), and linguistic models of the syntactic structure of sentences (e.g., Rayner et al., 1983).

Researchers typically assess reading outcomes using recognition, recall, or comprehension tests. The type of comprehension test used influences the reader's goal and reading time: When verbatim recall as opposed to question-answering is required, the reader slows down and may change his or her reading pattern (e.g., Aaronson & Ferres, 1984; Haberlandt et al., 1989).

A. Eye-Tracking Methods

In eye-tracking methods, a text is exposed on a computer screen and the subject's eye movements and fixations are recorded. An invisible beam of light

---

[1] Reading researchers have designed sophisticated experimenter-paced reading methods to investigate comprehension. In one such technique, successive words of a text are flashed in rapid succession on a screen (e.g., Potter, 1984).

is projected to the cornea of one eye; the light is reflected and recorded by a video camera. Vertical and horizontal positions of the eye are sampled up to 1000 (!) times per second; head movements are eliminated using a bite bar (Just & Carpenter, 1980; McConkie, Hogaboam, Wolverton, Zola, & Lucas, 1979; Rayner et al., 1989). The eye-tracking recordings reveal what the reader is looking at and for how long. They show that the eyes do not move smoothly and continuously; rather there are ballistic movements called saccades, usually from left to right; fixations; and regressions to previous locations in the text. The mean fixation lasts about 250 ms, excluding extremely long or short fixations (>1000 ms, <40 ms). Several measures of eye fixations are available for each region on the screen, including the duration of the first fixation, the sum of the total fixations excluding regressions, and the aggregate duration of all fixations and regressions. The latter is referred to as the gaze duration. The eye-tracking method may be altered to allow for many experimental variations, including a contingent technique in which the text is changed according to the position of the eye (e.g., Rayner & Pollatsek, 1989).

1. Applications

Eye-movement data are used in research ranging from studies on intra-word effects to inferences at the text level. Inhoff (e.g., 1987) investigated the effect of word structure on eye-movement patterns. He found reading was facilitated when readers were able to preview the initial three letters of the word to the immediate right of their current fixation. Using gaze durations, Just and Carpenter (1980) found independent effects of word length and familiarity on processing: Familiar and short words were read faster. Zola (1984) found that readers process words more quickly when they are predictable given the sentence context (see also Schustack, Ehrlich, & Rayner, 1987). Patterns of eye fixations reveal syntactic processing at clause boundaries and in structurally ambiguous regions. Using unedited texts and controlling for differences between words using regression analysis, Just and Carpenter (e.g., 1980) reported longer gaze durations at clause-final words, especially at sentence boundaries. Rayner et al. (1989) confirmed the clausal effect in control sentences using identical target words.

Investigating elaborative inferences, O'Brien, Shank, Myers, and Rayner (1988) concluded from gaze durations that readers make elaborative inferences only when the context strongly implies the inference. These investigators manipulated the extent to which the context suggested an inference and the explicitness of a target concept. The target concept was referred to twice; the first reference was either implicit or explicit, whereas the second reference was explicit. When the context barely suggested the concept, readers' gaze durations on the target were longer, suggesting that they had not inferred it initially. Readers made the inference more quickly, however, when the context was highly suggestive, as indicated by the absence of differences in gaze durations (see also Garrod, O'Brien, Morris, & Rayner, 1990).

2. Evaluation

According to critics, the eye-tracking method is problematic; because there are several fixation measures it is difficult to identify THE eye fixation. Should researches sum fixations for a given word? Should they include return gazes in an aggregate measure such as the gaze duration? If fixations are not aggregated for a word, it is not clear which fixation to use and what to do if each produces a different interpretation (e.g., Clifton, Speer, & Abney, 1991). Usually, researchers do not analyze processing during saccades; such processing, however, may contribute 10–15% of reading times (Aaronson & Ferres, 1984).

There are also specific criticisms of each of the measures outlined above. Kliegl, Olson, and Davidson (1982), for example, noted that gaze durations only include accumulated intraword fixation durations and do not allow researchers to distinguish between the duration and the number of fixations. Because of multiword viewing, peripheral preview, spillover effects, and regressions, these measures do not permit an unambiguous evaluation of the cognitive processing of words (Aaronson & Ferres, 1984; Hogaboam & McConkie, 1981; Rayner et al., 1989).

Eye-tracking researchers have met the critics head on. They consider the abundance of eye fixation measures on reading patterns like preview, spillover, intraword fixations, and regressions an advantage; they believe that these are naturally occurring processes and that comprehension theories should, therefore, account for them. In response to questions about the most appropriate eye-fixation measure to use, they recommend using several of them: for example, first-fixation time, gaze duration, and the probability of fixating on a word. Even though each eye-fixation record cannot be interpreted, it is important to acknowledge gaps in interpretability and encourage further research (see Rayner & Sereno, this volume).

B. Window Methods

In window methods, a text appears on a video terminal and the reader exposes successive segments of the text, the windows, by pressing a key. The intervals between presses are defined as the reading times for the window. The window may display the entire text or individual sentences, phrases, or words. While I focus here on word-reading times, passage- and sentence-reading times are also useful; many of the effects based on these more global measures, for example, the passage-type and new-argument effects, were first described by Kintsch et al. (1975) and subsequently replicated using more fine-grained research methods (see also Garrod & Sanford, 1990; Goldman & Saul, 1990; Singer, Revlin, & Halldorson, 1990). Global methods are limited because they do not reveal the location of critical processes within a sentence or passage.

Several word-reading methods are available to track the transient processing load within sentences (e.g., Aaronson & Ferres, 1984; Just, Carpenter, & Woolley, 1982). One of the most popular is the moving window method. At the beginning of a trial, the subject views a computer screen filled with patterns of dashes and spaces in place of text; dashes correspond to letters, and spaces correspond to spaces between words. Successive words are revealed by pressing a key; except for the current word the screen remains masked with dashes. With each subsequent key press, the previous word is masked and a new word appears. Words appear to march across the screen at a pace set by the reader's key presses (e.g., Altmann & Steedman, 1988; Bromley et al., 1985; Dixon, 1984; Ferreira & Clifton, 1986; Haberlandt & Graesser, 1985; Just et al., 1982; Taraban & McClelland, 1988).

1. Applications

The window methods are comparable in their resolution to the eye-tracking method except for intraword effects and regressive eye movements. At the word level, these methods are sufficiently sensitive to detect frequency and length effects (Haberlandt & Graesser, 1985; Just et al., 1982; Mitchell, 1984) as well as spillover effects (Haberlandt & Graesser, 1990; Mitchell, 1984). At the sentence level, clausal and structural effects have been uncovered. Word-reading times are longer at clause-final words, especially at the sentence boundary, indicating sentence wrap-up processes (Aaronson & Ferres, 1984; Just et al., 1982). As for structural effects, Clifton et al. (1991) reported that word-reading times were faster for verb-attachment sentences than for noun-attachment sentences (Section II,C,1); this finding was in agreement with the minimal attachment principle. The moving window method has also yielded results disconfirming Frazier's principle. These results are attributable to the choice of stimulus materials rather than to the moving window technique, however (see also Altmann & Steedman, 1988; Ferreira & Clifton, 1986; Taraban & McClelland, 1988).

Text-level factors have been identified including effects attributable to the causal structure of narratives: Reading times at clause boundaries increase when readers infer causal links between clauses and when they reinstate causal antecedents at sentence boundaries (Bloom et al., 1990). Because the typical exposition depends less on causal links, it takes readers relatively longer to read expository passages; this is manifest at the level of individual words, including function words (e.g., Haberlandt, 1984). Processing new information requires more resources than reading repeated arguments; this is true when a concept is first introduced in the passage (Haberlandt & Graesser, 1989) and at clausal boundaries (e.g., Haberlandt & Graesser, 1990; Just et al., 1982). Reading times for clause- and sentence-final words increase as a function of the number of new arguments present in the current clause, thus reflecting text-level integration at these locations (e.g., Haberlandt & Graesser, 1990).

2. Evaluation

Using eye-tracking data as a standard, critics of the moving window method note quantitative and qualitative differences between eye fixations and reading times. The correlation between reading times and gaze durations is only $r = .57$ (see Just et al., 1982), and reading times are about 80% longer in the moving window task than in eye-tracking situations, giving rise to the possibility that this task involves additional processes (e.g., Clifton et al., 1991; Danks, 1986; Mitchell, 1987). Danks (1986) argued that readers cannot press the response key as fast as their eyes move. "Thus, they tend to press the key relatively rapidly, retaining each word in a short-term buffer, until they reach an opportune time to pause and comprehend, usually at the end of a sentence or clause" (Danks, 1986).

In contrast to gaze duration patterns, the largest predictors of reading time are sentence boundaries. According to Danks (1986), the large effects at sentence boundaries suggest that readers use a reading strategy specific to the push-button task. Furthermore, this strategy is heavily constrained by the physical limitations of the presentation conditions (see also Mitchell, 1987).

The reader sees text units that are predefined by the experimenter, whether they are words, phrases, or sentences. Finally, the moving window method does not permit regressive eye movements. Such regressions occur frequently in syntactically difficult sentences, according to Kennedy and Murray (1984), but cannot be detected using this method.

Acknowledging limitations of the moving window method, its proponents point out that the method has important features of natural reading: Words appear on the screen as they do in texts. Using peripheral vision, the reader can estimate the length of the upcoming word, and the eye moves from left to right and makes return sweeps when advancing to the next line (Graesser & Haberlandt, 1986; Just & Carpenter, 1984). Proponents of this method cite the correlation of $r = .57$ between reading times and gaze duration patterns as support for the paradigm rather than as a criticism. In qualitative aspects too, reading time patterns collected in the moving window paradigm are more similar to the eye-fixation patterns than its critics admit. This is true at the level of words (Just et al., 1982), sentences (Ferreira & Clifton, 1986; Taraban & McClelland, 1988), and text-level processing (Haberlandt, Graesser, Schneider, & Kiely, 1986; but see Magliano, Graesser, Eymard, Haberlandt, & Gholsen, 1993). The qualitative similarities between reading time and eye-fixation patterns detract from criticisms of the moving window method. For example, word-reading times are sensitive to word-level factors such as occurrence frequency; this indicates that readers process the current word rather than pushing the button mechanically. Reading pauses at clause and sentence boundaries are not the result of particular reading strategies, either. Rayner et al. (1989) report increased eye-fixation times at clause and sentence boundaries in an experiment where each word served as its own control. Backtracking and previewing are not possible in the conventional window methods. However, as listeners, people are familiar with comprehension situations that do not allow backtracking and previewing. Furthermore, window methods may be augmented to permit backtracking by using additional buttons that allow forward and backward reading mode (Bromley et al., 1985).

3. Variations of the Moving Window Method

There are variations of the window technique, including the stationary and cumulative window methods and the pointing method. In the stationary window condition, words are presented successively in the same location on the screen (Aaronson & Ferres, 1984).

In the cumulative window method, unlike in the moving window method, words are exposed through a button press and remain on the screen. This technique was developed to allow reader regressions. Subjects tended, however, to expose words quickly until a clause or sentence was exposed and then they read the entire sentence (Just et al., 1982). In addition, parsing effects at the sentence level differed from those obtained in the eye-fixation and moving window situations: In the latter two Ferreira and Henderson (1990) found support for the minimal attachment model of parsing that they did not find using the cumulative method (see also Ferreira & Clifton, 1986).

In the pointing method, the reader points to a screen location with a device like a mouse, exposing the current word. Other words are partially masked; the mask reveals word length and shape but obscures its letters. Readers can point forward and regress to previous words. According to Dixon (1984), reading-time patterns using this method were similar to those in the eye-tracking and moving window paradigms. As in eye-tracking, regressions to prior words were relatively rare; only about 10% of the words were reread.

At every level of structure, including entire texts, sentences, and words, the key-press methods have yielded useful information about comprehension processes. Global passage-reading times reveal effects of text type and argument structure (e.g., Kintsch et al., 1975); sentence- and word-reading times reflect many of the same effects that eye-tracking data do. Button-press methods are less costly than eye-tracking methods and can be implemented on any microcomputer (Ferreira & Clifton, 1986). They are readily available as part of a comprehensive laboratory system of experiments in cognition, the MEL package (e.g., Schneider, 1990). These methods, therefore, play a vital role in research when resolution at the intraword level is not critical, and reading times have been validated by eye-fixation methods. When eye-fixation data and reading times yield different results, the former are preferred. For the typical reading experiment, the reader's oculomotor system and reading are better coupled than button pressing and reading (Ferreira & Henderson, 1990). The moving window method, however, is useful in exploratory research, and when necessary, the eye-tracking technique can produce more detailed findings.

Reading-time methods continuously assess comprehension load as subjects read a passage. The assumption that these methods can track the changing mental load during reading has been called into question. Researchers have at their disposal an arsenal of additional techniques subsumed under the classes of decision-making methods and naming-latency paradigms. These techniques involve explicit and discrete testing episodes. Their goal is to assess the transient activation or the workload of the reader. Typically, reading and probing alternate: a subject reads a text; a signal is given to alert her to the test, followed by the test probe. A response is made, feedback on speed and accuracy is given, and then reading resumes. Response latency is the dependent measure in the decision and naming tasks.

IV. DECISION METHODS

It is almost axiomatic that as readers process a text, they focus on and activate different concepts, much like successive lights are lit up on an electronic billboard. Theorists use different terms to describe this idea, including focus (Sidner, 1983), staging (Chafe, 1987), and foregrounding (e.g., Glenberg et al., 1987). It would be convenient if reading researchers could tap active concepts *directly*. Decision and naming tasks were developed to accomplish this goal.

As their name indicates, the decision methods call for a speeded decision from the subject in response to a target item; responses include *Yes* or *No*, *New* or *Old*, or *Same* or *Different*. The most widely used decision tasks are the lexical decision and item-recognition paradigms. Other techniques include same/different judgments (e.g., Morrow, Bower, & Greenspan, 1990), sentence verification, and question-answering (Reder, 1987).

In decision tasks, response latency is the dependent variable. The latency of targets is compared to that of neutral controls, for example, a word like *ready* or a string of letters. The latency is thought to reflect the activation of the target information both explicit and inferred. The interpretation of the latency depends on the specific experimental design. In the simplest case, the latency is inversely proportional to the activation of the information; the greater the activation, the faster the response. Other experimental designs induce inter- ference (e.g., Glucksberg, Kreuz, & Rho, 1986) or assess inferences by using negative probes slowing down the target latency (e.g., McKoon & Ratcliff, 1986). Decision tasks are widely used because they afford experimenters control in the choice, placement, and timing of probes. They have yielded a rich harvest of results ranging from lexical access to text-level inference processes. Decision methods are not without problems, however, and much of an investigator's ingenuity is needed to detect and surmount them. In the following sections, I discuss aspects of methodological control in decision methods and review some general problems inherent in these methods. Then I describe the lexical decision and item-recognition paradigms in detail.

A. Experimenter Control over Stimuli in the Decision Paradigm

Decision methods have a number of advantages over reading-time methods in detecting activation and in tracking its time course. Because decision methods permit greater experimenter control over the testing situation, they provide an opportunity to monitor the dynamic changes in activation. This can be done by placement of probes in different locations in the text (e.g., Dell et al., 1983; Gernsbacher, 1990; McKoon & Ratcliff, 1984; Swinney & Osterhout, 1990), as well as by presenting successive probes in the priming paradigm.

1. The Priming Paradigm

In the priming paradigm, the subject reads sentences and then sees succes- sive pairs of test items. The first member of the pair is known as the prime and the second as the target. The prime is assumed to make contact with its representation in memory, activate it, and spread activation to other concepts in the representation. From the pattern of response latencies of targets compared to control words, researchers infer the structure of the representation. Facilita- tion is reflected by a shorter latency for target than for neutral items. Longer latencies reflect inhibition; inhibition is observed when context and target stimuli are based on different representations, whether they are semantic categories (Neely, 1977), sentences (Ratcliff & McKoon, 1981), or referents (Gernsbacher, 1990).

2. Stimulus Onset Asynchrony

To the extent that priming is automatic, it is a useful measure of text structure. Strategic processing, however, influences priming too, namely when the subject engages in overt rehearsal or develops expectations and biases about the construction of the stimulus materials and the distribution of different types of test trials (e.g., Neely, 1977; Tweedy et al., 1977). One technique used to separate automatic from strategic processes uses the time course of activation. By manipulating the interval between the onset of the prime and the onset of the target, the stimulus onset asynchrony (SOA), researchers have identified automatic components at the shorter end and strategic components at the longer end of a given SOA continuum. For example, using individual concepts and propositions as stimulus materials, the automatic and strategic components start at about 150 and 600 ms, respectively (e.g., Posner & Snyder, 1975; Ratcliff & McKoon, 1981).

The factors that occasion automatic and strategic processes depend on the stimulus materials and on the experimental context. Ratcliff and McKoon (1981), for example, attributed automatic activation to priming from the meaning of repeated arguments in working memory. They attributed slow-onset activation to the reinstatement of antecedents from long-term memory. In research on lexical access, the SOA between the context stimulus and the target has been used to track the time course of the lexical access of polysemous words: Typically, at short intervals, multiple access is followed by selection at longer intervals (e.g., Onifer & Swinney, 1981; Simpson & Burgess, 1985; Simpson & Krueger, 1991).

B. General Problems with Decision Methods

Decision testing methods have been criticized from two different perspectives: one deals with interpreting activation, and the other with strategies that subjects are assumed to use in decision tasks. Consider first the assessment of activation: Finding that a target is activated does not reveal the reasons for the activation. For one, it is difficult to distinguish between the level of activation and the memory strength (Wickelgren, Corbett, & Dosher, 1980). Memory strength refers to the relative permanence of information over time. A representation like one's name or telephone number has been repeatedly strengthened in multiple encodings and therefore has a strong trace. Representations are weak if they have not been recently rehearsed. Activation strength refers to the transitory retrieval state of the target; any information can be temporarily active without having great memory strength. In reading, activation may also result from different sources, including a high base level of activation in the lexicon, contextual facilitation, or an inference (McKoon & Ratcliff, 1990b; Swinney & Osterhout, 1990). Finally, the idea that spreading activation can be measured has been questioned; activation may dissipate too quickly to be detected by conventional on-line methods (e.g., Ratcliff & McKoon, 1981).

Ideally, a decision task should be nonintrusive and assess reading processes, such as lexical access and inferences, in their normal state. Unfortunately, test procedures may introduce extraneous mental operations. For example, subject strategies intended to enhance response accuracy (Balota & Chumbley, 1984) and inferences to integrate the test stimulus with the text (e.g., Potts, Keenan, & Golding, 1988) may be problematic. Presentation of the probe may also interrupt those reading processes the researcher seeks to study, especially when the target is shown as the person processes a sentence. In any case, decision methods involve concurrent task demands; the subject must repeatedly shift from comprehending sentences to responding to a target.[2] Each of these tasks

[2] The concurrent task technique can also be used to a researcher's advantage. This technique, widely used in attention research, is based on the principle of resource allocation. The person reads a passage and performs a concurrent task, for example, monitoring an external event or looking for typographical errors. Performance on the secondary task reflects the comprehension load: When the reader gets very absorbed by the text, he pays less attention to the secondary task

is resource-demanding and may thus interfere with the other task (e.g., Kellas, Paul, Martin, & Simpson, 1991). In short, decision methods entail possible confounding between reading processes that produce activation and the testing situation; both influence response speeds. The typical way of dealing with confounds is to use controls designed to eliminate unwanted effects. There is an abundance of studies that assess and presumably remove confounds (e.g., Balota et al., 1990; Foss, 1988; Graesser & Bower, 1990). I describe a sample of these studies in the following sections on the lexical decision and recognition paradigms.

C. Lexical Decision Task

1. Applications

In the lexical decision task, the subject sees a string of letters like *candles* or *assintart* and decides whether or not the string represents an English word. The latency of pressing one of two keys is assumed to reflect the access time of the word; typically, latencies are faster for more familiar words (e.g., Gordon, 1983) and are primed by semantically related and associated contexts (e.g., Schuberth & Eimas, 1977; West & Stanovich, 1982). Lexical decision latencies are also influenced by text-level variables, as illustrated by Sharkey and Mitchell's (1985) study. They presented passages like (5) followed by test words that had not appeared in the passage.

(5) *The children's birthday party was going quite well.*
They all sat round the table and prepared to sing.
Decision word: *candles*

Passage (5) describes activities typical of a birthday party, an event familiar to most of us. Readers' knowledge of such events has been represented in terms of schematic representations, known as scripts. A script is a flexible collection of objects, characters, and activities of common events, including birthdays, going to a restaurant, and attending a lecture. Readers presumably infer events and concepts not mentioned in script-based passages like (5). In support of this theory, Sharkey and Mitchell found facilitation for script-related targets such as *candle*.

The lexical decision task has also been used to investigate text-level priming and elaborative inferences (e.g., Potts et al., 1988). These researchers found no facilitation for words implied by inference sentences like those in Table I.

In the cross-modal lexical decision task, a subject listens to sentences that semantically bias one of the meanings of polysemous words (e.g., *bug*) while strings of letters are presented visually and simultaneously with specific words for a lexical decision (e.g., Swinney, 1979). Typically, facilitation is observed for words related to the target whether they are relevant or irrelevant to the context. This indicates multiple access: Both meanings of ambiguous words

---

(Britton, Glynn, Meyer, & Penland, 1982; Britton, Holdredge, Curry, & Westbrook, 1979; Healy, Conboy, & Drewnoski, 1987). The concurrent task technique is also used in spoken language comprehension (e.g., Cutler, Butterfield, & Williams, 1987; Foss & Blank, 1980; Pitt & Samuel 1990).

are activated, at least for SOAs up to 200 ms. After that, the related meaning is selected and remains active. Gernsbacher and Faust (1990) attributed the loss in activation of the unrelated meaning to suppression rather than a decay process. These authors varied the cross-modal task by presenting sentences in the center of the computer screen and test words at the top of the screen in capital letters. Results of multiple access support the position that lexical access is modular, independent of context (e.g., Lucas, 1987; Onifer & Swinney, 1981; Tanenhaus, Leiman, & Seidenberg, 1979; Till, Mross, & Kintsch, 1988).

2. Evaluation

The lexical decision task is widely criticized because of its decision component (e.g., Balota & Chumbley, 1984; Balota et al., 1990; Balota & Lorch, 1986; Forster, 1981; Seidenberg et al., 1984). Forster (1981) expressed a concern that subjects check the relation between the prime and the target after lexical access. He observed that subjects may respond *No* to a target word simply because it is not predicted by the context. This response, however, is not based on the subject's failure to discriminate between words and nonwords, but on the strategy of responding in terms of context. According to this view, in Sharkey and Mitchell's (1985) experiment, subjects may have accessed the meaning of *candle* and THEN checked its relation to the context sentences. Because *candle* was related to the context, post-access integration was faster and the response was facilitated. Thus facilitation may have nothing to do with context-priming. Subjects use any information available that helps them distinguish between words and nonwords; this adds a confounding with text-level processes like inferencing or script activation.

According to Glucksberg et al. (1986), the cross-modal lexical decision task entails a special pitfall, namely the possibility of backward priming. Acoustically presented items remain in echoic memory and may coincide with an ambiguous target presented visually several hundred milliseconds later. As a result, the nominal target could function backward as a biasing context for the ambiguous prime. To prevent such backward priming, Glucksberg et al. (1986) employed a lexical decision procedure in which INTERFERENCE rather than facilitation was used as a measure of activation. Here, pronounceable nonwords like *piamoe* and *kidnea* were included as targets. It takes longer to reject such nonwords than nonpronounceable strings like *xpqj*. Glucksberg and his colleagues reasoned that semantic context would make pronounceable strings like *pimey* more wordlike and thus slow down the *No* response. For example, hearing the sentence *He took a long walk through the words, and the fragrance of the balsam and fir trees perfumed the air* might remind subjects of the word *piny*. As a result, subjects would take longer to arrive at the nonword decision when presented with *pimey*. Based on the interference version of the cross-modal decision task, Glucksberg concluded that discourse-level context can influence lexical access.

Arguing in defense of the cross-model paradigm, Swinney and Osterhout (1990) noted that backward priming does not operate in every type of test. These investigators used the cross-modal paradigm to evaluate activation of anaphoric references. They used test sentences introducing several antecedents, for example, *doctor, boxer,* and *swimmer,* one of which was referred to later by a pronoun. Test sentences were presented via headphones, and prior to and immediately after presenting the target pronoun, a test string was flashed on a computer screen. Facilitation would indicate activation of the referent. According to Swinney and Osterhout, there is nothing to backward-prime from in these cases, and the pronoun is not a source of information for activation (Swinney & Osterhout, 1990; see also Burgess, Tanenhaus, & Seidenberg, 1989).

D. Recognition Methods

In the item-recognition paradigm, one or more target words are presented during or immediately after reading a passage. Subjects must indicate with a button press whether or not the target appeared in the passage (e.g., Chang, 1980; Dell et al., 1983). The reader receives feedback on the accuracy and sometimes on the speed of his response. The dependent variables include the recognition latency of correct hit responses to target words and, depending on the design of the study, the probability of hits, correct rejections, and false alarms. Except for the encoding time of the test word, the recognition latency for the target word is assumed to reflect the activation of the concept represented by the target word (Dell et al., 1983; McKoon & Ratcliff, 1984; see also Gillund & Shiffrin, 1984). Negative targets, which are words NOT found in the context passage, are used to detect inferences: Here, the correct response is *no,* but if the reader infers the concept, she may hesitate responding *no,* thus increasing the latency.

1. Applications

In a series of seminal studies, Ratcliff and McKoon (1978) used the priming paradigm to examine a variety of important effects. These researchers mapped the memory structure underlying sentences and interpreted their data in terms of a propositional representation; they found that concepts within a proposition prime each other independent of their physical distance in the surface structure of the sentence. McKoon and Ratcliff (1980) demonstrated that the priming effect was a function of the distance between concepts in the propositional structure of paragraphs. Glenberg et al. (1987) used the item-recognition task to demonstrate the involvement of mental models in reading propositionally identical texts. They used associated and disassociated passages as illustrated in Table II and presented target words, for example *sweatshirt,* as recognition probes. Subjects responded faster when targets were spatially associated, indicating that the concept remained foregrounded. Glenberg attributed this facilitation to a mental model in which the main actor of the narrative was central (see also Morrow et al., 1990). Dell et al. (1983) examined the activation of antecedent information when the reader encounters an anaphoric reference

TABLE II
Sample Passage in Glenberg et al. (1987) Study

John was preparing for a marathon in August. After doing a few warm-up exercises, he (put on) [took off] his sweatshirt and went jogging. He jogged halfway around the lake without too much difficulty. Further along his route, however, John's muscles began to ache.
Target word: *sweatshirt*
Disassociated version included phrase enclosed in brackets rather than in parentheses.

---

during reading. They presented short paragraphs, one word at a time, and recognition probes at one of several locations in the sentence, as illustrated in Table III. Dell and his colleagues found that when the reader encounters the anaphoric reference *criminal,* she activates both the antecedent *burglar* and its companion *garage,* indicating that the embedding proposition was reactivated. Testing at successive locations, Dell observed that the antecedent remained active while other arguments dropped out (see also Gernsbacher, 1989; O'Brien et al., 1986; Speelman & Kirsner, 1990).

McKoon and Ratcliff (1986) used the item-recognition technique to assess whether readers infer predictable events as they encode a text. For example, would readers infer that the actress was dead when reading the inference sentence in Table I? Subjects read inference and control sentences followed 500 ms later by the presentation of target words (e.g., *dead*). The correct response was *no.* In their first experiment, subjects took somewhat longer to respond in the inference than in the control condition. In subsequent research, however, there were no differences. These results were also observed using other tasks like the lexical decision and naming tasks. Based on several studies and different methodologies, McKoon and Ratcliff (e.g., 1990a) concluded, therefore, that readers only minimally encode elaborative inferences.

2. Evaluation

The item-recognition paradigm has been the target of criticism; critics note the possibility of backward inferences and diverse subject strategies. Backward inferences may have operated, for example, in the study by Dell and his colleagues; it is possible that the probe words were more compatible with the test sentences than the control words were. Probe words were, therefore, integrated more quickly and facilitated. The possibility of backward integration also exists in the McKoon and Ratcliff (1986) study; even if no inference was made, the latency in testing may be influenced by the compatibility of the test word with the text. In such a compatibility check, the latency of positive test words would be speeded and that of negative test words slowed. The item-recognition latencies are therefore ambiguous, at least without further controls (O'Brien et al., 1986; Potts et al., 1988; Seidenberg, Tanenhaus, Leiman, & Bienkowski, 1982). McKoon and Ratcliff (1990b) countered these reservations empirically, noting that compatibility, measured by subjects' ratings, did not predict recogni-

---

TABLE III
Sample Passage Used in Anaphoric Reference Experiment of Dell et al. (1983)

A burglar surveyed the garage set back from the street. Several milk bottles were piled at the curb. The banker and her husband were on vacation.
Test (anaphor) The_1 $criminal_2$ $slipped_3$ $away_4$ *from* the_5 $streetlamp._6$
Test (no anaphor) The_1 cat_2 $slipped_3$ $away_4$ *from* the_5 $streetlamp._6$
Target (referent of anaphor): *burglar*
Companion word: *garage*
Control word: *bottles*

Note: The subscripts indicate probe positions.

tion performance for individual items (McKoon & Ratcliff, 1989, 1990a, 1990b; Balota et al., 1990). McKoon and Ratcliff (1989) argued that compatibility checking occurs in lexical decision situations (Forster, 1981) but has not been demonstrated for any other situation, as Potts et al. (1988) claim.

Another potential methodological problem is that performance in recognition testing involves such mixed subject heuristics as direct-retrieval strategies and plausibility judgments (Albrecht & O'Brien, 1991; Reder, 1987). When making a plausibility judgment, a subject does not necessarily activate the text representation at the propositional level but rather evaluates how compatible the test probe is with the gist of the text. Reder (e.g., 1987) described the plausibility strategy in recognition experiments. The subject's choice of strategy in recognition experiments depends on the nature of the distractors. When foils include passage-unrelated items, subjects use the plausibility strategy. When foils are related to the passage, subjects tend to use a direct-retrieval strategy (Albrecht & O'Brien, 1991; Keenan et al., 1990).

According to McKoon and Ratcliff (1986, 1990a), strategic processes are minimized in a speeded recognition test which involves "automatic, not strategic, retrieval processes." These processes reflect the text representation generated during reading rather than confounding inferences generated during testing. The speeded item-recognition procedure includes a study and test phase as before, except a prime word, for example, *ready,* is flashed for a brief interval, typically less than 500 ms, before the test word is displayed. The speeded recognition paradigm and lexical decision tasks revealed that subjects took no longer to reject the target in the inference condition than in the control condition. McKoon and Ratcliff took this as confirmation that predictable events are only minimally encoded (see also Singer & Ferreira, 1983). O'Brien and Albrecht (1991) note, however, that speeded response procedures may force subjects to respond on the basis of partial information and therefore encourage, rather than eliminate, strategic processing (see also Keenan et al., 1990).

Let us note a final interpretational problem with recognition latencies: The speed of response depends on several structures generated by the reader, including verbatim information, the propositional textbase, and the situation model. Recognition tests usually tap the verbatim trace; however, propositional and situational information influence the decision as well (e.g., Reder, 1987; Schmalhofer & Glavanov, 1986). Indeed, it is important to isolate the contribution of each of these representations to recognition performance. By varying reader's study goals, Schmalhofer and Glavanov (1986) differentially emphasized text-based or situation-based representations. Then they assessed retrieval processes by using a modified speed–accuracy trade-off procedure in a sentence recognition test; for every test, the subject made several successive *yes–no* decisions paced by experimenter prompts. The dependent variable in this procedure is the accuracy profile as a function of total processing time. Schmalhofer and Glavanov found that situational information influenced recognition performance at the earliest testing intervals.

The item-recognition paradigm is widely used to study inference, understanding of anaphoric references, and a variety of text representations including propositional and situational representations. The success of the paradigm rests equally on the choice of appropriate control stimuli and on validating findings using different paradigms (see also Section VI). In general, decision methods are widely used in reading research; they permit close experimental control over a variety of parameters, including the placement of targets at different locations in the text, manipulation of the SOA between prime and target, and the assessment of activation.

V. NAMING METHODS

In naming methods, subjects read the study passage followed by the visual presentation of a target. The subject makes a vocal response such as naming the target item (e.g., Baluch & Besner, 1991; Warren, 1977), giving a one-word answer (Albrecht & O'Brien, 1991), or naming a color in the Stroop test (Tanenhaus, Flanigan, & Seidenberg, 1980). The latency of the response is the dependent variable. Like the decision methods, naming methods are based on activation theory; the assumption underlying the naming methods is that highly active concepts are more available for pronunciation, and thus positive targets are named more quickly (Potts et al., 1988; Seidenberg et al., 1982, 1984). Because naming methods do not involve decisions, the criticisms of the decision methods do not apply here. Presumably, these techniques do not elicit strategies like the plausibility strategy and criterion shifts (Albrecht & O'Brien, 1991; Keenan et al., 1990; Potts et al., 1988; Tanenhaus et al., 1980). Naming methods also have an advantage in terms of the criterion of naturalness; pronouncing a word is more natural to subjects than having to decide whether a target is actually a word or not (Forster, 1981). The incidence of errors is relatively small (<3%; see Warren, 1977). Finally, naming assesses availability in working memory as opposed to strength in long-term memory (O'Brien, 1987).

The most widely used naming method is the word-naming technique; the subject is seated at a video terminal and reads the stimulus item(s). A test is signaled by a visual prompt such as a row of Xs presented for 500 ms followed by the target item. The subject must read the item aloud as quickly as possible. The initial vocal response activates a voice key, records the elapsed time from the onset of the target, and erases the screen (e.g., O'Brien & Albrecht, 1991).

1. Applications

The naming method has been applied in research on processes from the word to the text level. At the word level, effects of word occurrence frequency have been observed (e.g., Baluch & Besner, 1991; West & Stanovich, 1982). Naming latencies were facilitated in associative priming, for example, when pairs like *Uncle–Aunt* were shown; the facilitation increased as the duration of the prime was increased (Warren, 1977). Research results showing the effect of sentence context are ambiguous; Simpson and Krueger (1991) found facilitation, but Forster (1981) did not. This divergence, however, is attributable to differences other than the naming method; the researchers used different designs and stimulus materials. At the sentence level, Ferreira (1991) found that latencies to initiate speech were a function of the structure of sentences that subjects had memorized; the more complex the underlying phrase structure tree of the sentence, the longer it took subjects to initiate speech.

At the text level, naming methods have been successfully used to illuminate a variety of processes, including reinstatement searches, anaphoric references, the centrality of concepts, and elaborative inferences. Reinstatement of a previous concept reactivates the concept (O'Brien, 1987), as well as related concepts which were not mentioned in the study passage (O'Brien & Albrecht, 1991). Access to an anaphoric reference depends on its recency and on its membership in the same category of referents (e.g., O'Brien, Plewes, & Albrecht, 1990). Central concepts in a passage are more accessible than peripheral ones, presumably because they are more interconnected with the remainder of the passage (Albrecht & O'Brien, 1991). Finally, the pattern of naming latencies found in this research supports McKoon and Ratcliff's (1986) original hypothesis that readers only minimally encode predictable inferences (Potts et al., 1988).

2. Evaluation

Critics have observed that naming procedures may be of limited use in detecting inferences for theoretical and methodological reasons. To the extent that naming involves lexical access, and access is modular relative to text-level processes (Fodor, 1983; Keenan et al., 1990), there is no effect of the latter on naming, and thus naming is not a useful index of inferences. Problems may result from the fact that naming procedures are based on the articulatory system and its specific mechanisms. Articulations, including naming, tend to have short latencies and entail the possibility of floor effects. Unless target words across conditions are identical, researchers must be mindful of what Steinberg and his colleagues have called ARTICULATORY UNPACKING AND EXECUTION (e.g., Sternberg, Monsell, Knoll, & Wright, 1980). According to Sternberg, articulations are planned in working memory; the more complex the structure of the articulation, the longer it takes to initiate it (see also Ferreira, 1991; Klapp, 1974). Appropriate control words must therefore be chosen to match the syllabic structure of experimental target words.

Another potential limit of the naming paradigm is that strings can be pronounced according to rules of grapheme–phoneme correspondence without retrieving meaning (e.g., Forster, 1981; Halle, 1990). One approach to circumventing this problem involves an adaptation of the Stroop color-naming task in order to assess comprehension processes (e.g., Paul, Kellas, Martin, & Clark, 1992). Typically, the subject reads a context sentence or passage and is presented with several test items, for example, words implied by the passage. The kicker is that the test words are printed in different colors, and the subject's task is to name the colors rather than pronouncing the words. The rationale of the modified Stroop test is as follows: When a target word is inferred by the reader it becomes active, and there should be a tendency to pronounce it, and as a result the time to name its color would be slowed down. The pattern of color-naming latencies is used to indicate comprehension processes. Imaginative as the naming paradigm is, including the modified Stroop task, it shares the drawback of the decision and recognition tasks; the reading process is frequently interrupted and we do not know what the effects of the interruptions are on reading. Decision and naming techniques would be strengthened if such task characteristics were understood more fully. It is to be hoped that this issue will become part of the future agenda of comprehension research.

VI. CONCLUSION

When analyzing context effects in lexical access, Seidenberg et al. (1984) noted that the lexical decision task should be used with "extreme caution." The review of methods in this chapter suggests that caution is appropriate for any method. Reading-time methods, while they reflect modulations in workload as a reader processes a text on line, do not reveal the underlying processes. They are usually free, however, from confounds like backward integration and plausibility checking which have been shown to influence latencies in decision tasks. Decision methods can potentially assess activation directly; given an appropriate experimental design and careful control of stimuli, they can also illuminate the structure of representations generated in comprehension. Decision methods, however, are plagued by confounds such as backward integration and decision strategies during testing. The naming methods have the same advantage as decision methods. In addition, researchers do not need to worry about subject strategies. They too, however, represent interruptions of the reading process. In sum, there is no single perfect method.

It would be wrong to conclude from this review that experiments in reading research are impossible. On the contrary, the experiment is the only tool we have to uncover reading processes. Fortunately, investigators have been sensitive to confoundings in both materials and tasks and have become as ingenious in addressing methodological problems as they are at inventing techniques and discovering confoundings. A general recommendation for researchers is to use multiple methods, including neuropsychological techniques, to assess theoretical predictions (e.g., Carpenter, 1984; Rayner, Flores d'Arcais, & Balota, 1990; Rayner & Pollatsek, 1987; Singer, 1990). While this makes research more costly, it strengthens the results and their interpretation. Researchers increasingly use multiple methods, illustrated here by a few representative projects. For example, Albrecht and O'Brien (1991) used decision and naming methods to evaluate activation of central text concepts. Clifton et al. (1991) used two different reading-time methods, a window method and eye-tracking, to investigate the effects of syntactic structure on comprehension. In these cases, differences between methods were relatively minor and the results converged.

Frequently, interpretations of data collected in different techniques differ. What should the investigator do in such cases, and how should differences be arbitrated? When results differ, researchers tend to favor one of the methods. These preferences usually emerge within a particular context; they should not be interpreted as a general verdict on a technique. For example, in an investigation of on-line processing of ambiguous sentences, Ferreira and Henderson (1990) used three different reading-time methods: eye-tracking, moving window, and cumulative moving window. There was agreement in the reading-time patterns of the first two methods, but not the third. As a result, these investigators favored the noncumulative reading techniques. Employing the lexical decision and naming tasks, Potts et al. (1988) studied inferential processing; they found evidence of inferences in the lexical decision task, but not in the naming task. For specific theoretical and for methodological reasons, Potts and his colleagues favored the latter task; their results were also in agreement with those observed in the item-recognition task (e.g., McKoon & Ratcliff, 1990b). McNamara and Healy (1988) used the lexical decision task and a self-paced reading-time method in an investigation of spreading activation among concepts related by semantic and rhyming relations. While similar priming effects were observed across tasks, the authors noted that lexical decision latencies depended on the nature of the nonword distractors. Consequently, these investigators favored the reading-time method.

The choice of stimulus materials and of specific controls remains as important as choosing an appropriate technique of collecting data. After all, the reading material chosen engages the reading processes we seek to investigate. Researchers have made every effort to control confounds, and by using filler materials, they seek to avoid the preponderance of many homogeneous items. Even if all precautions are taken in the selection of stimulus materials and data collection, it is unlikely that an experiment can be fully confound-proof. This review suggests two ways of compensating for this limitation: one is to evaluate a hypothesis in successive experiments using different tasks; the other is to recognize that confoundings result from specific performance characteristics as the subject responds in a test. Any effort to illuminate performance in the task at a theoretical level advances methods of reading research and our understanding of comprehension processes.

ACKNOWLEDGMENTS

Part of the work reported here was presented at the 25th International Congress of Psychology in Brussels, 1992. I thank Morti Gernsbacher and Judy Kiely for their valuable suggestions and advice on earlier versions of this chapter. Preparation of the chapter was supported in part by the Charles A. Dana Foundation and Trinity College.

REFERENCES

Aaronson, D., & Ferres, S. (1984). The word-by-word reading paradigm: An experimental and theoretical approach. In D. Kieras & M. Just (Eds.), *New methods in reading comprehension research* (pp. 31–68). Hillsdale, NJ: Erlbaum.

Albrecht, J. E., & O'Brien, E. J. (1991). Effects of centrality on retrieval of text-based concepts. *Journal of Experimental Psychology: Learning, Memory, and Cognition, 17,* 932–939.

Altmann, G., & Steedman, M. (1988). Interaction with context during human sentence processing. *Cognition, 30,* 191–238.

Anderson, J. R. (1983). *The architecture of cognition.* Cambridge, MA: Harvard University Press.

Balota, D. A., & Chumbley, J. I. (1984). Are lexical decisions a good measure of lexical access? The role of word frequency in the neglected decision stage. *Journal of Experimental Psychology: Human Perception and Performance, 10,* 340–357.

Balota, D. A., Flores d'Arcais, G. B., & Rayner, K. (Eds.). (1990). *Comprehension processes in reading.* Hillsdale, NJ: Erlbaum.

Balota, D. A., & Lorch, R. F. (1986). Depth of automatic spreading activation: Mediated priming effects in pronunciation but not in lexical decision. *Journal of Experimental Psychology: Learning, Memory, and Cognition, 12,* 336–345.

Baluch, B., & Besner, D. (1991). Visual word recognition: Evidence for strategic control of lexical and nonlexical routines in oral reading. *Journal of Experimental Psychology: Learning, Memory, and Cognition, 17,* 644–652.

Banji, M. R., & Crowder, R. G. (1989). The bankruptcy of everyday memory. *American Psychologist, 44,* 1185–1193.

Bloom, C. P., Fletcher, C. R., van den Broek, P., Reitz, L., & Shapiro, B. P. (1990). An on-line assessment of causal reasoning during comprehension. *Memory & Cognition, 18,* 65–71.

Bower, G. H., & Clapper, J. P. (1989). Experimental methods in cognitive science. In M. Posner (Ed.), *Foundations of cognitive science* (pp. 245–300). Cambridge, MA: MIT Press.

Britton, B. K., Glynn, S. M., Meyer, B. J. F., & Penland, M. J. (1982). Effects of text structure on use of cognitive capacity during reading. *Journal of Educational Psychology, 74*, 51–61.

Britton, B. K., Holdredge, T. S., Curry, C., & Westbrook, R. D. (1979). Use of cognitive capacity in reading identical texts with different amounts of discourse level meaning. *Journal of Experimental Psychology: Human Learning and Memory, 5*, 262–270.

Bromley, H. J., Jarvella, R. J., & Lundberg, I. (1985). From LISP machine to language lab. *Behavior Research Methods, Instruments, & Computers, 17*, 399–402.

Burgess, C., Tanenhaus, M. K., & Seidenberg, M. S. (1989). Context and lexical access: Implications of nonword interference for lexical ambiguity resolution. *Journal of Experimental Psychology: Learning, Memory, and Cognition, 15*, 620–632.

Carpenter, P. A. (1984). The influence of methodologies on psycholinguistic research: A regression to the Whorfian hypothesis. In D. Kieras & M. Just (Eds.), *New methods in reading comprehension research* (pp. 3–11). Hillsdale, NJ: Erlbaum.

Chafe, W. L. (1987). Cognitive constraints on information flow. In R. S. Tomlin (Ed.), *Coherence and grounding in discourse: Outcome of a symposium* (pp. 21–51). Amsterdam: Benjamins.

Chang, F. R. (1980). Active memory processes in visual sentence comprehension: Clause effects and pronominal reference. *Memory & Cognition, 8*, 58–64.

Clifton, C., Speer, S., & Abney, S. P. (1991). Parsing arguments: Phrase structure and argument structure as determinants of initial parsing decisions. *Journal of Memory and Language, 30*, 251–272.

Collins, A. M., & Quillian, M. R. (1969). Retrieval time from semantic memory. *Journal of Verbal Learning and Verbal Behavior, 8*, 240–247.

Corballis, M. C. (1967). Serial order in recognition and recall. *Journal of Experimental Psychology, 74*, 99–105.

Cutler, A. (1981). Making up materials is a confounded nuisance, or: Will we be able to run any psycholinguistic experiments at all in 1990? *Cognition, 10*, 65–70.

Cutler, A., Butterfield, S., & Williams, J. N. (1987). The perceptual integrity of syllabic onsets. *Journal of Memory and Language, 26*, 406–418.

Danks, J. H. (1986). Identifying component processes in text comprehension: Comment on Haberlandt and Graesser. *Journal of Experimental Psychology: General, 115*, 193–197.

Dell, G. S., McKoon, G., & Ratcliff, R. (1983). The activation of antecedent information during the processing of anaphoric reference in reading. *Journal of Verbal Learning and Verbal Behavior, 22*, 121–132.

Dixon, P. (1984). A new technique for measuring word processing time in reading. *Behavior Research Methods, Instruments, & Computers, 16*, 109–114.

Ferreira, F. (1991). Effects of length and syntactic complexity on initiation times for prepared utterances. *Journal of Memory and Language, 30*, 210–233.

Ferreira, F., & Clifton, C. (1986). The independence of syntactic processing. *Journal of Memory and Language, 25*, 348–368.

Ferreira, F., & Henderson, J. M. (1990). Use of verb information in syntactic parsing: Evidence from eye movements and word-by-word self-paced reading. *Journal of Experimental Psychology: Learning, Memory, and Cognition, 16*, 555–568.

Fletcher, C. R. (1981). Short-term memory processes in text comprehension. *Journal of Verbal Learning and Verbal Behavior, 20*, 564–574.

Fodor, J. A. (1983). *The modularity of mind*. Cambridge, MA: MIT Press.

Forster, K. I. (1981). Priming and the effects of sentence and lexical contexts on naming time: Evidence for autonomous lexical processing. *Quarterly Journal of Experimental Psychology, 33A*, 465–495.

Foss, D. J. (1988). Experimental psycholinguistics. *Annual Review of Psychology, 39*, 301–348.

Foss, D. J., & Blank, M. A. (1980). Identifying the speech codes. *Cognitive Psychology, 12*, 1–31.

Frazier, L. (1987). Sentence processing: A tutorial review. In M. Coltheart (Ed.), *Attention and performance XII: The psychology of reading* (pp. 559–586). Hillsdale, NJ: Erlbaum.

Frazier, L. (1990). Exploring the architecture of the language system. In G. Altman (Ed.), *Cognitive models of speech processing: Psycholinguistics and computational perspectives* (pp. 409–433). Cambridge, MA: MIT Press.

Frazier, L., & Rayner, K. (1982). Making and correcting errors during sentence comprehension:

Eye movements in the analysis of structurally ambiguous sentences. *Cognitive Psychology, 14,* 178–210.

Garrod, S., O'Brien, E. J., Morris, R. K., & Rayner, K. (1990). Elaborative inferencing as an active or passive process. *Journal of Experimental Psychology: Learning, Memory, and Cognition, 16,* 250–269.

Garrod, S., & Sanford, A. (1990). Referential processing in reading: Focusing on roles and individuals. In D. A. Balota, G. B. Flores d'Arcais, & K. Rayner (Eds.), *Comprehension processes in reading* (pp. 465–485). Hillsdale, NJ: Erlbaum.

Gernsbacher, M. A. (1989). Mechanisms that improve referential access. *Cognition, 32,* 99–156.

Gernsbacher, M. A. (1990). *Language comprehension as structure building.* Hillsdale, NJ: Erlbaum.

Gernsbacher, M. A., & Faust, M. (1990). The role of suppression in sentence comprehension. In G. B. Simpson (Ed.), *Understanding word and sentence* (pp. 97–128). Amsterdam: North-Holland.

Gillund, G., & Shiffrin, R. M. (1984). A retrieval model for both recognition and recall. *Psychological Review, 91,* 1–67.

Glenberg, A. M., Meyer, M., & Lindem, K. (1987). Mental models contribute to foregrounding during text comprehension. *Journal of Memory and Language, 26,* 69–83.

Glucksberg, S., Kreuz, R. J., & Rho, S. (1986). Context can constrain lexical access: Implications for models of language comprehension. *Journal of Experimental Psychology: Learning, Memory, and Cognition, 12,* 323–335.

Goldman, S. R., & Saul, E. U. (1990). Applications for tracking reading behavior on the Macintosh. *Behavior Research Methods, Instruments, & Computers, 22,* 526–532.

Gordon, B. (1983). Lexical access and lexical decision: Mechanism of frequency sensitivity. *Journal of Verbal Learning and Verbal Behavior, 22,* 24–44.

Graesser, A. C., & Bower, G. H. (1990). *Inferences and text comprehension.* San Diego, CA: Academic Press.

Graesser, A. C., & Haberlandt, K. F. (1986). Research on component processes in reading: Reply to Danks. *Journal of Experimental Psychology, General, 115,* 198–200.

Graesser, A. C., Hoffman, N. L., & Clark, L. F. (1980). Structural components of reading time. *Journal of Verbal Learning and Verbal Behavior, 19,* 135–151.

Graesser, A. C., & Riha, J. R. (1984). An application of multiple regression techniques to sentence reading times. In D. Kieras & M. Just (Eds.), *New methods in reading comprehension research* (pp. 183–218). Hillsdale, NJ: Erlbaum.

Granaas, M. M., McKay, T. D., Laham, R. D., Hurt, L. D., & Juola, J. F. (1984). Reading moving text on a CRT screen. *Human Factors, 26,* 97–104.

Haberlandt, K. F. (1984). Components of sentence and word reading times. In D. E. Kieras & M. A. Just (Eds.), *New methods in reading comprehension research* (pp. 219–252). Hillsdale, NJ: Erlbaum.

Haberlandt, K. F., & Bingham, G. (1978). Verbs contribute to the coherence of brief narratives: Reading related and unrelated sentence triples. *Journal of Verbal Learning and Verbal Behavior, 17,* 419–425.

Haberlandt, K. F., & Graesser, A. C. (1985). Component processes in text comprehension and some of their interactions. *Journal of Experimental Psychology: General, 114,* 357–374.

Haberlandt, K. F., & Graesser, A. C. (1989). Processing of new arguments at clause boundaries. *Memory & Cognition, 17,* 186–193.

Haberlandt, K. F., & Graesser, A. C. (1990). Integration and buffering of new information. In A. Graesser & G. Bower (Eds.), *Inferences and text comprehension* (pp. 71–87). San Diego, CA: Academic Press.

Haberlandt, K. F., Graesser, A. C., & Schneider, N. J. (1989). Reading strategies of fast and slow readers. *Journal of Experimental Psychology: Learning, Memory, and Cognition, 15,* 815–823.

Haberlandt, K. F., Graesser, A. C., Schneider, N. J., & Kiely, J. (1986). Effects of task and new arguments on word reading times. *Journal of Memory and Language, 25,* 314–322.

Halle, M. (1990). Phonology. In D. N. Osherson & H. Lasnik (Eds.), *Language: An invitation to cognitive science* (pp. 43–68). Cambridge, MA: MIT Press.

Healy, A. F., Conboy, G. L., & Drewnowski, A. (1987). Characterizing the processing units of reading. In B. Britton & S. Glynn (Eds.), *Executive control processes in reading* (pp. 279–296). Hillsdale, NJ: Erlbaum.

Hogaboam, T. W., & McConkie, G. W. (1981). *The rocky road from eye fixations to comprehension* (Tech. Rep. No. 207). Urbana: University of Illinois, Center for the Study of Reading.

Inhoff, A. W. (1987). Parafoveal word perception during eye fixations in reading: Effects of visual salience and word structure. In M. Coltheart (Ed.), *Attention and performance XII: The psychology of reading* (pp. 403–418). Hove, England: Erlbaum.

Johnson-Laird, P. N. (1983). *Mental models: Towards a cognitive science of language, inference, and consciousness.* Cambridge, MA: Harvard University Press.

Just, M. A., & Carpenter, P. A. (1980). A theory of reading: From eye fixations to comprehension. *Psychological Review, 87,* 329–354.

Just, M. A., & Carpenter, P. A. (1984). Using eye fixations to study reading comprehension. In D. Kieras & M. Just (Eds.), *New methods in reading comprehension research* (pp. 151–182). Hillsdale, NJ: Erlbaum.

Just, M. A., & Carpenter, P. A. (1987). *The psychology of reading and language comprehension.* Newton, MA: Allyn & Bacon.

Just, M. A., Carpenter, P. A., & Woolley, J. D. (1982). Paradigms and processes in reading comprehension. *Journal of Experimental Psychology: General, 111,* 228–238.

Keenan, J. M., Potts, G. R., Golding, J. M., & Jennings, T. M. (1990). Which elaborative inferences are drawn during reading? A question of methodologies. In D. A. Balota, G. B. Flores d'Arcais, & K. Rayner (Eds.), *Comprehension processes in reading* (pp. 377–402). Hillsdale, NJ: Erlbaum.

Kellas, G., Paul, S. T., Martin, M., & Simpson, G. B. (1991). Contextual feature activation and meaning access. In G. Simpson (Ed.), *Understanding word and sentence* (pp. 47–71). Amsterdam: Elsevier.

Kennedy, A., & Murray, W. S. (1984). Inspection times for words in syntactically ambiguous sentences under three presentation conditions. *Journal of Experimental Psychology: Human Perception and Performance, 10,* 833–849.

Kennedy, A., Murray, W. S., Jennings, F., & Reid, C. (1990). Parsing complements: Comments on the generality of the principle of minimal attachment. *Language and Cognitive Processes, 4,* 51–74.

Keppel, G. (1976). Words as random variables. *Journal of Verbal Learning and Verbal Behavior, 15,* 263–266.

Kieras, D. E., & Just, M. A. (1984). *New methods in reading comprehension research.* Hillsdale, NJ: Erlbaum.

King, J., & Just, M. A. (1991). Individual differences in syntactic processing: The role of working memory. *Journal of Memory and Language, 30,* 580–602.

Kintsch, W., Kozminsky, E., Streby, W. J., McKoon, G., & Keenan, J. M. (1975). Comprehension and recall of text as a function of content variables. *Journal of Verbal Learning and Verbal Behavior, 14,* 196–214.

Kintsch, W., Welsch, D., Schmalhofer, F., & Zimny, S. (1990). Sentence memory: A theoretical analysis. *Journal of Memory and Language, 29,* 133–159.

Klapp, S. T. (1974). Syllable-dependent pronounciation latencies in number naming, a replication. *Journal of Experimental Psychology, 102,* 1138–1140.

Klatzky, R. L. (1991). Let's be friends. *American Psychologist, 46,* 43–45.

Kliegl, R., Olson, R. K., & Davidson, B. J. (1982). Regression analyses as a tool for studying reading processes: Comment on Just and Carpenter's eye fixation theory. *Memory & Cognition, 10,* 287–296.

Lorch, R. F. J., & Meyers, J. L. (1990). Regression analyses of repeated measures data in cognitive research. *Journal of Experimental Psychology: Learning, Memory, and Cognition, 16,* 149–157.

Lucas, M. (1987). Frequency effects on the processing of ambiguous words in sentence context. *Language and Speech, 30,* 25–46.

Magliano, J. P., Graesser, A. C., Eymard, L. A., Haberlandt, K., & Gholson, B. (1993). The locus of interpretive and inference processes during text comprehension: A comparison of gaze durations and word reading times. *Journal of Experimental Psychology: Learning, Memory, and Cognition, 19,* 704–709.

McClelland, J. L. (1991). Can connectionist models discover the structure of natural language? In R. Morelli, D. Anselmi, M. Brown, K. F. Haberlandt, & D. Lloyd (Eds.), *Minds, brains, and computers: Perspectives in cognitive science and artificial intelligence* (pp. 168–189). Norwood, NJ: Albex.

McConkie, G. W., Hogaboam, T. W., Wolverton, G. S., Zola, D., & Lucas, P. A. (1979). Toward the use of eye movements in the study of language processing. *Discourse Processes, 2,* 157–177.

McKoon, G., & Ratcliff, R. (1980). Priming in item recognition: The organization of propositions in memory for text. *Journal of Verbal Learning and Verbal Behavior, 19,* 369–386.

McKoon, G., & Ratcliff, R. (1984). Priming and on-line text comprehension. In D. Kieras & M. Just (Eds.), *New methods in reading comprehension research* (pp. 119–128). Hillsdale, NJ: Erlbaum.

McKoon, G., & Ratcliff, R. (1986). Inferences about predictable events. *Journal of Experimental Psychology: Learning, Memory, and Cognition, 12,* 82–91.

McKoon, G., & Ratcliff, R. (1989). Semantic associations and elaborative inference. *Journal of Experimental Psychology: Learning, Memory, and Cognition, 15,* 326–338.

McKoon, G., & Ratcliff, R. (1990a). Dimensions of inference. In A. C. Graesser & G. H. Bower (Eds.), *Inferences and text comprehension* (pp. 313–328). San Diego, CA: Academic Press.

McKoon, G., & Ratcliff, R. (1990b). Textual inferences: Models and measures. In D. A. Balota, G. B. Flores d'Arcais, & K. Rayner (Eds.), *Comprehension processes in reading* (pp. 403–421). Hillsdale, NJ: Erlbaum.

McNamara, T. P., & Healy, A. F. (1988). Semantic, phonological, and mediated priming in reading and lexical decisions. *Journal of Experimental Psychology: Learning, Memory, and Cognition, 14,* 398–409.

Meyer, D. E., & Schvaneveldt, R. W. (1976). Meaning, memory structure, and mental processes. *Science, 192,* 27–33.

Mitchell, D. C. (1984). An evaluation of subject-paced reading tasks and other methods for investigating immediate processes in reading. In D. Kieras & M. Just (Eds.), *New methods in reading comprehension research* (pp. 69–89). Hillsdale, NJ: Erlbaum.

Mitchell, D. C. (1987). Lexical guidance in human parsing: Locus and processing characteristics. In M. Coltheart (Ed.), *Attention and performance XII: The psychology of reading* (pp. 601–618). Hove, England: Erlbaum.

Mitchell, D. C., Corley, M. M. B., & Garnham, A. (1992). Effects of context in human sentence parsing: Evidence against a discourse-based proposal mechanism. *Journal of Experimental Psychology: Learning, Memory, and Cognition, 18,* 69–88.

Morrow, D. G., Bower, G. H., & Greenspan, S. L. (1990). Situation-based inferences during narrative comprehension. In A. Graesser & G. Bower (Eds.), *Inferences and text comprehension* (pp. 123–135). San Diego, CA: Academic Press.

Morton, J. (1979). Word recognition. In J. Morton & J. C. Marshall (Eds.), *Psycholinguistics 2: Structures and processes* (pp. 107–156). Cambridge, MA: MIT Press.

Neely, J. H. (1977). Semantic priming and retrieval from lexical memory: Roles of inhibitionless spreading activation and limited-capacity attention. *Journal of Experimental Psychology: General, 106,* 226–254.

Neisser, U. (1978). Memory: What are the important questions? In M. M. Gruneberg, P. Morris, & R. N. Sykes (Eds.), *Practical aspects of memory* (pp. 3–24). London: Academic Press.

O'Brien, E. J. (1987). Antecedent search processes and the structure of text. *Journal of Experimental Psychology: Learning, Memory, and Cognition, 13,* 278–290.

O'Brien, E. J., & Albrecht, J. E. (1991). The role of context in accessing antecedents in text. *Journal of Experimental Psychology: Learning, Memory, and Cognition, 17,* 94–102.

O'Brien, E. J., Duffy, S. A., & Myers, J. L. (1986). Anaphoric inference during reading. *Journal of Experimental Psychology: Learning, Memory, and Cognition, 12,* 346–352.

O'Brien, E. J., Plewes, P. S., & Albrecht, J. E. (1990). Antecedent retrieval processes. *Journal of Experimental Psychology: Learning, Memory, and Cognition, 16,* 241–249.

O'Brien, E. J., Shank, D. M., Myers, J. L., & Rayner, K. (1988). Elaborative inferences during reading: Do they occur on-line? *Journal of Experimental Psychology: Learning, Memory, and Cognition, 14,* 410–420.

Olson, G. M., Duffy, S. A., & Mack, R. L. (1984). Thinking out-loud as a method for studying real-time comprehension processes. In D. Kieras & M. Just (Eds.), *New methods in reading comprehension research* (pp. 253–286). Hillsdale, NJ: Erlbaum.

Onifer, W., & Swinney, D. A. (1981). Accessing lexical ambiguities during sentence comprehension: Effects of frequency of meaning and contextual bias. *Memory & Cognition, 9,* 225–236.

Paul, S. T., Kellas, G., Martin, M., & Clark, M. B. (1992). Influence of contextual features on the activation of ambiguous word meanings. *Journal of Experimental Psychology: Learning, Memory, and Cognition, 18,* 703–717.

Pitt, M. A., & Samuel, A. G. (1990). Attentional allocation during speech perception: How fine is the focus? *Journal of Memory and Language, 29,* 611–632.

Posner, M. I. (1978). *Chronometric explorations of mind.* Hillsdale, NJ: Erlbaum.

Posner, M. I., & Snyder, C. R. (1975). Attention and cognitive control. In R. Solso (Ed.), *Information processing and cognition: The Loyola symposium* (pp. 55–85). Hillsdale, NJ: Erlbaum.

Potter, M. C. (1984). Rapid serial visual presentation (RSVP): A method for studying language processing. In D. Kieras & M. Just (Eds.), *New methods in reading comprehension research* (pp. 91–119). Hillsdale, NJ: Erlbaum.

Potts, G. R., Keenan, J. M., & Golding, J. M. (1988). Assessing the occurrence of elaborative inferences: Lexical decision versus naming. *Journal of Memory and Language, 27,* 399–415.

Ratcliff, R., Hockley, W., & McKoon, G. (1985). Components of activation: Repetition and priming effects in lexical decision and recognition. *Journal of Experimental Psychology: General, 114,* 435–450.

Ratcliff, R., & McKoon, G. (1978). Priming in item recognition: Evidence for the propositional structure of sentences. *Journal of Verbal Learning and Verbal Behavior, 17,* 403–417.

Ratcliff, R., & McKoon, G. (1981). Automatic and strategic priming in recognition. *Journal of Verbal Learning and Verbal Behavior, 20,* 204–215.

Rayner, K., Carlson, M., & Frazier, L. (1983). The interaction of syntax and semantics during sentence processing: Eye movements in the analysis of semantically biased sentences. *Journal of Verbal Learning and Verbal Behavior, 22,* 358–374.

Rayner, K., Flores d'Arcais, G. B., & Balota, D. A. (1990). Comprehension processes in reading: Final thoughts. In D. A. Balota, G. B. Flores d'Arcais, & K. Rayner (Eds.), *Comprehension processes in reading* (pp. 631–638). Hillsdale, NJ: Erlbaum.

Rayner, K., & Pollatsek, A. (1987). Eye movements in reading: A tutorial review. In M. Coltheart (Ed.), *Attention and performance XII: The psychology of reading* (pp. 327–362). Hove, England: Erlbaum.

Rayner, K., & Pollatsek, A. (1989). *The psychology of reading.* Englewood Cliffs, NJ: Prentice-Hall.

Rayner, K., Sereno, S. C., Morris, R. K., Schmauder, A. R., & Clifton, C. J. (1989). Eye movements and on-line language comprehension processes. *Language and Cognitive Processes, 4,* SI21–SI49.

Reder, L. M. (1987). Strategy selection in question answering. *Cognitive Psychology, 19,* 90–138.

Rothkopf, E. Z., & Billington, M. J. (1983). Passage length and recall with test size held constant: Effects of modality, pacing, and learning set. *Journal of Verbal Learning and Verbal Behavior, 22,* 667–681.

Schmalhofer, F., & Glavanov, D. (1986). Three components of understanding a programmer's manual: Verbatim, propositional, and situational representations. *Journal of Memory and Language, 25,* 279–294.

Schneider, W. (1990). *MEL User's Guide: Computer techniques for real time psychological experimentation.* Pittsburgh: Psychology Software Tools.

Schuberth, R. E., & Eimas, P. D. (1977). Effects of context on the classification of words and nonwords. *Journal of Experimental Psychology: Human Perception and Performance, 3,* 27–36.

Schustack, M., Ehrlich, S. F., & Rayner, K. (1987). The complexity of contextual facilitation in reading: Local and global influences. *Journal of Memory and Language, 26,* 322–340.

Seidenberg, M. S., Tanenhaus, M. K., Leiman, J. M., & Bienkowski, M. (1982). Automatic access of the meanings of ambiguous words in context: Some limitations of knowledge-based processing. *Cognitive Psychology, 14,* 489–537.

Seidenberg, M. S., Waters, G. S., Sanders, M., & Langer, P. (1984). Pre- and postlexical loci of contextual effects on word recognition. *Memory & Cognition, 12,* 315–328.

Sharkey, N. E., & Mitchell, D. C. (1985). Word recognition in a functional context: The use of scripts in reading. *Journal of Memory and Language, 24,* 253–270.

Sidner, C. L. (1983). Focusing and discourse. *Discourse Processes, 6,* 107–130.

Simpson, G. B., & Burgess, C. (1985). Activation and selection processes in the recognition of ambiguous words. *Journal of Experimental Psychology: Human Perception and Performance, 11,* 28–39.

Simpson, G. B., & Krueger, M. A. (1991). Selective access of homograph meanings in sentence context. *Journal of Memory and Language, 30,* 627–643.

Singer, M. (1990). *Psychology of language: An introduction to sentence and discourse processes.* Hillsdale, NJ: Erlbaum.

Singer, M., & Ferreira, F. (1983). Inferring consequences in story comprehension. *Journal of Verbal Learning and Verbal Behavior, 22,* 437–448.

Singer, M., Revlin, R., & Halldorson, M. (1990). Bridging-inferences and enthymemes. In A. Graesser & G. Bower (Eds.), *Inferences and text comprehension* (pp. 35–51). San Diego, CA: Academic Press.

Speelman, C. P., & Kirsner, K. (1990). The representation of text-based and situation-based information in discourse comprehension. *Journal of Memory and Language, 29,* 119–132.

Sternberg, S., Monsell, S., Knoll, R. L., & Wright, C. E. (1980). The latency and duration of rapid movement sequences: Comparisons of speech and typewriting. In R. A. Cole (Ed.), *Perception and production of fluent speech* (pp. 469–505). Hillsdale, NJ: Erlbaum.

Swinney, D. A. (1979). Lexical access during sentence comprehension: (Re)consideration of context effects. *Journal of Verbal Learning and Verbal Behavior, 18,* 645–659.

Swinney, D. A., & Osterhout, L. (1990). Inference generation during auditory language comprehension. In A. C. Graesser & G. H. Bower (Eds.), *Inferences and text comprehension* (pp. 17–33). San Diego, CA: Academic Press.

Tanenhaus, M. K., Flanigan, H. P., & Seidenberg, M. S. (1980). Orthographic and phonological activation in auditory and visual word recognition. *Memory & Cognition, 8,* 513–520.

Tanenhaus, M. K., Leiman, J. M., & Seidenberg, M. S. (1979). Evidence for multiple stages in the processing of ambiguous words in syntactic contexts. *Journal of Verbal Learning and Verbal Behavior, 18,* 427–440.

Taraban, R., & McClelland, J. L. (1988). Constituent attachment and thematic role assignment in sentence processing: Influences of content-based expectations. *Journal of Memory and Language, 27,* 597–632.

Till, R. E., Mross, E. F., & Kintsch, W. (1988). Time course of priming for associate and inference words in a discourse context. *Memory & Cognition, 16,* 283–299.

Tweedy, J. R., Lapinski, R. H., & Schvaneveldt, R. W. (1977). Semantic-context effects on word recognition: Influence of varying the proportion of items presented in an appropriate context. *Memory & Cognition, 5,* 84–89.

van Dijk, T. A., & Kintsch, W. (1983). *Strategies of discourse comprehension.* New York: Academic Press.

Warren, R. E. (1977). Time and the spread of activation in memory. *Journal of Experimental Psychology: Human Learning and Memory, 3,* 458–466.

West, R. F., & Stanovich, K. E. (1982). Source of inhibition in experiments on the effect of sentence context on word recognition. *Journal of Experimental Psychology: Learning, Memory, and Cognition, 8,* 385–399.

Wickelgren, W. A., Corbett, A. T., & Dosher, B. A. (1980). Priming and retrieval from short-term memory: A speed accuracy trade-off analysis. *Journal of Verbal Learning and Verbal Behavior, 19,* 387–404.

Wright, P. (1987). Reading and writing for electronic journals. In B. Britton & S. Glynn (Eds.), *Executive control processes in reading* (pp. 23–55). Hillsdale, NJ: Erlbaum.

Zola, D. (1984). Redundancy and word perception during reading. *Perception & Psychophysics, 36,* 277–284.

CHAPTER 2

WHY STUDY SPOKEN LANGUAGE?

FERNANDA FERREIRA AND MICHAEL ANES

I. INTRODUCTION

The linguistic input we received during the developmentally crucial ages between two and five was almost exclusively auditory. Even as adults, most of
our linguistic experience comes from encounters with spoken language. Yet
this asymmetry in the amount of exposure to spoken versus written language
is not mirrored in the scientific study of language comprehension. Instead, most
studies of comprehension, whether at the level of word recognition, sentence
comprehension, or text processing, have employed visually presented materials.
Typically, it is tacitly (and sometimes explicitly) assumed that results obtained
from reading paradigms will generalize fairly straightforwardly to spoken language. The general view seems to be that reading and spoken language processing differ only in the modality through which word information is acquired,
so that after lexical access, the two forms of processing converge. However,
as we describe below, language processing in the two modalities differs on
other dimensions as well, so that auditory language processing warrants its
own independent line of study.

In this chapter, we begin with a discussion of some of the differences
between spoken and written language processing and consider some of the
reasons the latter has been investigated more thoroughly than the former. Next,
in the largest section of the chapter, we review some of the methodologies that
have been used to examine spoken language processing. We only consider
studies that used sentences as materials or that examined some aspect of sentence processing (that is, we do not discuss auditory word recognition). This
review of methodologies is divided into two subsections, one considering off-
line tasks such as click detection, sentence recall, sentence continuation, and
the gating paradigm, and the other considering reaction time tasks (some of
which are also off-line) such as picture–sentence verification, phoneme monitoring, cross-modal priming, and end-of-sentence comprehension measures. In the
final section we discuss some potentially promising new methodologies for
studying auditory sentence comprehension. We do not, unfortunately, announce the discovery of an auditory analogue of the eye movement monitoring

technique—a technique as sensitive and unobtrusive as that for recording eye movements still eludes us.

II. DIFFERENCES BETWEEN SPOKEN LANGUAGE PROCESSING AND READING

One important difference between spoken and written language is that during reading, the comprehender can control the rate at which information is taken in—readers can slow down or speed up the input to suit their level of comprehension. Rayner and his colleagues (Rayner, 1978; Rayner & Pollatsek, 1989; Rayner, Sereno, Morris, Schmauder, & Clifton, 1989) have found that the average duration of a fixation on a word is about a quarter of a second. However, there is a great deal of variability around this average. Some words receive fixations of around one second; at the other extreme, some words are skipped, particularly words that are frequent, predictable, and short. Carrithers and Bever (1984) noted that a process comparable to word-skipping during reading occurs in spoken language: Function words (words such as *the* and *of*), the majority of which are short and frequent, tend to be spoken quickly and with little stress. However, the two processes might not be as comparable as at first appears. Hayduk (1990) found that, with character length and frequency controlled, function and content words are equally likely to be skipped during reading. In contrast, in spoken language, content words all receive main word stress and thus tend not to be drastically shortened (Nespor & Vogel, 1987; Selkirk, 1984), no matter how frequent or short. Thus, word-skipping during reading and phonological reduction in spoken sentences do not seem to be controlled by the same linguistic variables. More generally, the comprehender can control the rate of information acquisition during reading; spoken language must be processed at whatever speech rate is adopted by the speaker.

A second important difference between spoken and written language concerns the segmentation information available in the perceptual input. In alphabetically written visual language, word boundaries are clearly marked by spaces and sentence boundaries are marked by periods. Even sentence-internal clause boundaries are sometimes marked by commas, although this punctuation is often optional (Frazier & Rayner, 1982). Word and phrasal boundaries are not so clearly marked in spoken language. As has been noted for many years, word boundaries are not acoustically indicated; often a pause will occur within a word and not between two adjacent words (for recent discussions of this issue, see Cutler, 1990; Shillcock, 1990). Clause and sentence boundaries sometimes do have acoustic correlates (Cooper & Paccia-Cooper, 1980; Ferreira, 1991; Gee & Grosjean, 1983). However, the production of these boundaries varies somewhat across idiolects and dialects, and the boundary markings tend to be blurred in faster speech.

Up to this point, the differences we have mentioned favor visual language. However, auditory language is richer than visual language in at least one important respect, and that is the availability of prosodic information. In spoken language, as was mentioned above, variations in word duration, the location and duration of pauses, and pitch carry important information about the structural organization of a sentence. For example, a sentence such as (1) contains a temporary syntactic ambiguity as it is written here.

(1) *Because Bill left the room seemed empty.*

Auditorily, however, the ambiguity would be far less apparent, or even eliminated. The clause boundary after *left* would be marked by lengthening of *left,* a dramatic fall followed by a rise in pitch, and possibly also a pause. These cues may be used by the syntactic processor to prevent a garden path sentence (Beach, 1991; Slowiaczek, 1981), or at least to make recovery from a garden path far easier.

In visual language, whatever prosodic information is available must be created by the comprehender through phonological recoding and subvocalization. Research has shown that readers tend to recode visually presented sentences into an auditory format, a process that includes both the accessing of phonological representations for words (e.g., Carr & Pollatsek, 1985; Van Orden, Johnston, & Hale, 1988) and the creation of sentence prosody (Slowiaczek & Clifton, 1980). A visually presented sentence such as (1) might not initially be subvocalized with the correct prosody, because on the first pass through the sentence the speaker would not know the correct location of the syntactic boundary and thus could not place the prosodic markings in the correct location. Reanalysis would thus require a revision of both the sentence's syntactic and prosodic structures.

Given the differences between spoken language processing and reading, as well as the greater frequency of exposure to spoken language, why would it be that reading has been studied more extensively than spoken language processing? As researchers who are guilty of this emphasis, we can think of three not entirely independent reasons. First, it is easier and less expensive to study written language. For example, to conduct an experiment on sentence processing using the moving window technique (Just, Carpenter, & Woolley, 1982), all that is required is a personal computer and some software for collecting button-press times. The stimuli for presentation to subjects are simply typed into a text file, and the experiment is pretty much ready to go. To study auditory language processing, one requires not just computer equipment and software, but also equipment for auditorily recording sentences and playing them to subjects (tape player, microphone, speakers, headphones), and ideally also hardware and software for digitizing speech and manipulating speech files.

Second, if stimuli are to be presented auditorily, the investigator must decide what the prosodic characteristics of the sentences will be, and those characteristics either have to be equated across conditions (if the experimental hypotheses do not involve prosodic variables) or manipulated systematically (if prosody is under investigation). However, we do not know enough about the prosodic structure of sentences of different types to know what prosodic variables may turn out to be important. Consider a recent study by Beach (1991), who examined sentences such as (2) and (3).

(2) *The city council argued the mayor's position forcefully.*
(3) *The city council argued the mayor's position was incorrect.*

Both sentences are ambiguous up to the word *position* and are then disambiguated by the subsequent context. In (2), the sentence is disambiguated toward a simpler syntactic structure than in (3), according to the minimal attachment principle (Frazier, 1978; Frazier & Rayner, 1982; see also Mitchell, this volume), and studies have shown that (3) is harder to comprehend in the disambiguating region than is (2). However, almost all these studies were done using visually presented materials.

If one were interested in exploring the relative difficulty of these two sentences in the auditory domain, which prosodic variables would it be necessary to hold constant, and which manipulate? Where in the sentence should those manipulations occur? One place to look for insight is the work of Cooper (Cooper & Paccia-Cooper, 1980), who has extensively examined how the prosodic characteristics of a sentence are affected by its syntactic structure. Cooper has found that words at the ends of phrases and clauses tend to be lengthened and followed by a pause. Cooper argues that the right bracket of a syntactic phrase or clause is the locus of word lengthening and pausing; left brackets (phrase/clause beginnings) have little effect on sentence prosody. The syntactic bracketings of (2) and (3) are shown as (2′) and (3′).

(2′) [$_{NP}$The city council]$_{NP}$ [$_{VP}$argued [$_{NP}$the mayor's position]$_{NP}$ forcefully]$_{VP}$
(3′) [$_{NP}$The city council]$_{NP}$ [$_{VP}$argued [$_{S}$[$_{NP}$the mayor's position]$_{NP}$ [$_{VP}$was incorrect]$_{VP}$]$_{S}$

Because these sentences do not differ in the number or location of RIGHT brackets, Cooper's theory of the mapping from syntax to prosody does not predict any differences in their prosodic characteristics. Therefore, one might conclude that they cannot be prosodically disambiguated. However, Beach (1991) examined the possibility that the presence of LEFT syntactic brackets could affect the prosodic phrasing of a sentence. Note that in (3′), the word *argued* precedes two left brackets, but in (2′), the same word precedes just one left bracket. She varied the length of the word *argued* in sentences such as (2) and (3) and found that when the word was lengthened, subjects predicted that the sentence would turn out as in (3), with a sentential complement; if the word *argued* had a short duration, subjects predicted the sentence would continue as in (2), with a direct object. The presence of a left bracket thus does seem to affect how a sentence should be prosodically phrased. The moral is that much work needs to be done on the relation between prosody and other levels of representation in language processing before researchers will know what are the important variables that affect the prosodic structure of a sentence.

Finally, perhaps the most important reason why spoken language is studied less than reading has to do with the availability of appropriate tasks, particularly in the area of sentence comprehension and parsing (the process of assigning syntactic structure to a sentence). In this research area, an important question has been how and when various linguistic and nonlinguistic sources of information are used during comprehension. As the differences between various theories of sentence comprehension become more and more subtle (e.g., Frazier, 1990, vs. Tanenhaus, Garnsey, & Boland, 1990), extremely sensitive tasks are required to distinguish between their predictions. Currently, it is widely believed that the best task for studying sentence comprehension is eye-movement monitoring, because it allows the experimenter to examine moment-by-moment changes in processing load continuously and unobtrusively (Ferreira & Henderson, 1990; Rayner et al., 1989; see also Haberlandt, this volume). A close second choice is the moving window technique, using a window size of one word (Ferreira & Henderson, 1990; Haberlandt, this volume). Unfortunately, there is no comparably sensitive task for examining spoken language processing.

On the other hand, it is important to note that many research questions in sentence comprehension, whether auditory or visual, do not require the use of an "on-line" task such as eye-movement monitoring—a task which provides a record of moment-by-moment changes in processing load. For example, as we will see later, the processes involved in assigning antecedents to overt anaphors and "gaps" have been profitably studied using activation methodologies such as cross-modal lexical decision and naming. In addition, often one is interested in first establishing that a certain source of information influences linguistic processing at some stage, without necessarily determining what stage that is. For that purpose, off-line tasks (tasks that do not measure changes in processing load) may work just as well. And finally, if one's goal is to examine reanalysis processes—that is, how the comprehender recovers from errors made during initial processing—then again an on-line technique might not be necessary (Ferreira & Henderson, 1991). As will be apparent in the next section, the problems in the general area of spoken language processing on which the field of psycholinguistics has made some progress are the problems suited to the currently available methodologies. Much is known, for example, about coreference processes during auditory sentence comprehension, but far less about how spoken sentences are syntactically processed, and how nonsyntactic sources of information, particularly prosodic information, influence syntactic parsing decisions.

III. METHODOLOGIES FOR STUDYING SPOKEN LANGUAGE PROCESSING

This section is divided into two parts, based on distinguishing between tasks that involve the collection of some non–time-based measure (e.g., recording a subject's subjective judgment of a stimulus) and those that involve collection of reaction times (e.g., measuring the time it takes a subject to make some subjective judgment). How does this distinction relate to the contrast drawn above between on-line and off-line tasks? To answer this question, it may be useful to conceptualize this contrast as a continuum rather than a dichotomy. At one end are virtually all non–reaction-time tasks, because none measure processing load at any point during sentence comprehension (although they of course provide other sorts of valuable information). Reaction-time measures fall at various points along the on-line/off-line continuum. For example, measuring the time it takes subjects to make a judgment at the end of a sentence is pretty much an off-line task, because processing load is not measured until the end of the sentence, and changes in load are not assessed at all. At the other extreme, the eye-movement monitoring recording technique is about the most on-line measure we currently have available, as it provides a record of processing load in a sentence on virtually a character-by-character basis.

A. Non–Reaction-Time Methods

A classic methodology that has been used to investigate language processing is the click detection task, pioneered by J. A. Fodor, Bever, and Garrett (e.g., J. A. Fodor & Bever, 1965; Garrett, Bever, & Fodor, 1965; for a general discussion of this research, see J. A. Fodor, Bever, & Garrett, 1974). The subject listens to a sentence and at the same time monitors for a click or some

other extraneous (nonlinguistic) sound. The fundamental assumption on which
the task is based is that perceptual units of any type resist interruption, and so
if syntactic phrases are perceptual units, clicks will tend to be perceived as
occurring at constituent boundaries even when they actually occur in the middle
of a constituent. Consistent with this assumption, the work cited above has
indicated that clicks tend to migrate perceptually to clause boundaries. Geers
(1978) used the click detection task to investigate how syntactic and prosodic
cues might combine to influence subjects' segmentation of sentences. Sentences
were recorded with an intonational break at either a clause boundary or a minor
phrasal boundary. Clicks were then placed either at the clause boundary or in
other less appropriate locations (including the minor phrasal boundary). Geers
found that subjects tended to report clicks as occurring at the clause boundary,
and this effect was exaggerated when a prosodic boundary occurred at the
same location.

These results suggest that listeners' segmentation of a sentence into constituents might be facilitated by a correspondence between prosodic and syntactic
structures. However, the click detection task does not allow the determination
of when the prosodic information is used by the sentence processor. But, as
argued above, even though off-line tasks such as this one may not provide
clear-cut answers to questions concerning the timing of information use from
syntactic versus prosodic sources, this experiment does suggest that comprehenders may reinforce their syntactic hypotheses about a sentence with prosodic
evidence (or, perhaps, prosodic hypotheses are confirmed with syntactic evidence—the task does not allow us to distinguish between these possibilities).
One implication is that subjects given a sentence such as (1), repeated as (4),
with a strong prosodic boundary after *left* would not be garden-pathed, because:
prosodic information would first suggest the existence of a syntactic boundary
after the first verb, that hypothesis would then be confirmed by the ultimate
form of the sentence, and the correspondence between prosodic and syntactic
cues might strengthen that interpretation of the sentence.

(4) *Because Bill left the room seemed empty.*

Of course, the click detection task used by Geers is subject to the criticisms
that were raised against it many years ago regarding establishing the point in
processing at which click migration occurs. Displacement may occur during
early sentence perception, as argued by Fodor, Bever, and Garrett in their
early work, or perhaps the displacement occurs later when the subject marks
on paper the apparent location of the click—that is, the effect may be perceptual
or postperceptual. As noted by Clark and Clark (1977), it is impossible to decide
between these two possibilities.

A second non–reaction-time task that has been used to examine the interaction between prosodic and syntactic information is what we term the sentence-
gating task, used most recently by Beach (1991). Beach presented subjects with
only a portion of a locally ambiguous sentence, and subjects had to indicate
how they believed the sentence would continue. Thus, we call this a gating
task because the subject receives only part of the input and then has to predict
the remainder. She presented either just the first noun phrase and verb of the
sentence (e.g., *Jay believed*) or the first NP, verb, and postverbal NP (*Jay
believed the gossip*). In addition to manipulating the amount of the sentence
received by the subjects, Beach also varied the prosodic characteristics of the

main verb (*believed*). In one version, the word had a short duration, and fundamental frequency (the acoustic correlate of pitch, abbreviated as F0) did not vary across the word; in the other version, the word had a much longer duration and ended with a dramatic fall in F0. Pitch rose again on the word after the verb, but this cue was only available in the condition in which subjects received a longer portion of the sentence, because only that condition included material after the verb.

The subjects' task was to indicate whether the sentence would continue as either (5a) or (5b).

(5)a. *Jay believed the gossip about the neighbors right away.*
   b. *Jay believed the gossip about the neighbors wasn't true.*

Beach found that subjects predicted the sentence would continue as in (5b) if the sentence portion they received contained a verb with a short duration and no variation in F0; subjects predicted the sentence would continue as in (5a) if they received the other version. It appears that speakers sometimes announce that a clause is imminent by lengthening the word immediately before the clause's left boundary, and listeners are sensitive to that prosodic cue. From this finding, Beach argued that prosodic information can affect how listeners structure a spoken sentence and that prosodic information could be used by listeners to avoid a syntactic garden path.

These results are extremely interesting and important, because they demonstrate the utility of prosodic information for the resolution of syntactic ambiguity. And as with the click detection study described above, this work suggests a number of experiments that should be done to explore the finding further. However, it is important to keep in mind the limits of this type of paradigm for resolving some of the outstanding questions in the area of sentence parsing. Beach wishes to argue that the results show that prosodic cues influence syntactic decisions, and that therefore the language processing system is an interactive rather than a modular system. As argued by J. A. Fodor (1983), modules are cognitive structures that have access to a limited range of information; that is, they are "informationally encapsulated." Beach's argument is that if the parser were a module, then it would presumably have access only to syntactic information when making syntactic decisions and not, say, prosodic information. Because her results show that prosodic information can influence subjects' decisions about the ultimate syntactic form of a sentence, the modularity thesis is compromised.

However, there are two problems with this argument. The first is that the task Beach used is not appropriate for distinguishing between the use of prosodic information to inform normal syntactic decisions, and the use of prosodic information to facilitate guesses about upcoming sentence content and structure. To draw an analogy, we have little doubt that subjects given the fragment in (6) (whether auditorally or visually) would provide a continuation in which *the answer* constituted the subject of an embedded clause (as in *Bill hoped the answer would turn out to be right*).

(6) *Bill hoped the answer*

This prediction would be based on English speakers' knowledge that the verb *hoped* takes a sentence complement and rarely if ever a direct object. However, research examining visually presented sentences such as *Bill hoped the answer would turn out to be right* and employing the eye-movement monitoring technique has demonstrated that such sentences still garden-path the syntactic parser, indicating that information about verb preferences is not used initially by the parser to aid in syntactically structuring the input (Ferreira & Henderson, 1990; but see Trueswell, Tanenhaus, & Kello, 1992). The point of this analogy is that information used to make overt syntactic predictions and that used to make normal parsing decisions sometimes diverge. Finding that subjects use some type of information to make a conscious decision about a sentence does not make the case that they will use that information during normal on-line sentence processing.

The second problem with Beach's argument concerns the assumption that the use of prosodic information to inform syntactic decisions would be inconsistent with the modularity thesis. It is true that a module is "a special-purpose computer with a proprietary database" (J. A. Fodor, 1985, p. 3), and it is reasonable to assume that any syntactic module would have as its proprietary database information stated in a syntactic vocabulary. Therefore, the syntactic module's computations would not be expected to have access to prosodic information. However, Frazier (1990) has argued that the language processing system is actually a sequence of modules, and that any one module has access both to its proprietary database and to the output of modules placed earlier in the information processing sequence. Thus, the syntactic module can consult information stated in a syntactic vocabulary (e.g., category information such as "noun" and "verb" as well as phrase structure rules such as "Sentence → Noun Phrase plus Verb Phrase") as well as the output of earlier modules. Likely candidates for these earlier modules include the lexical module, which provides the syntactic module with information about syntactic categories, and a prosodic module, which provides information about prosodic groupings such as phonological and intonational phrases. Of course, at this point it is a hypothesis—although in our view, a quite reasonable one—that prosodic information is processed in a module situated earlier in the information processing sequence than the syntactic module.

Turning now to a different methodology, Jakimik and Glenberg (1990) recently used a sentence memory task to examine auditory language comprehension. They examined the comprehension of what they term "temporal anaphors" such as *former* and *latter*. For comprehenders to locate the antecedent of a temporal anaphor, they must retain a representation of the temporal order in which information was conveyed and then match that order to the appropriate anaphor. Jakimik and Glenberg's intriguing hypothesis was that temporal anaphors would be better understood in spoken than in written discourse, because information about temporal order is better retained in the auditory modality. (This prediction is based on Glenberg and Swanson's, 1986, temporal distinctiveness theory, which we will not discuss here.)

To examine this prediction, subjects were presented either auditorily or visually with three-sentence texts, the final line of which contained either a temporal anaphor (e.g., *the first call,* in a passage about loon calls) or a semantic anaphor (e.g., *the sad call,* from a similar passage). Subjects listened to or read the passages normally up to the anaphor, and at the anaphor, they were prompted to recall its antecedent. The rest of the passage was then presented, and the subject ended the trial by responding to a comprehension question. As predicted, Jakimik and Glenberg found that antecedents were better recalled when the text was presented auditorily rather than visually. Interestingly, this effect was not limited to temporal anaphors—antecedents for semantic anaphors were also more accurately recalled in the auditory modality.

This study makes two important points. First, auditory language processing can be fruitfully investigated using this sort of recall task, particularly if one wishes to examine antecedent–anaphor relations. Second, it is important to investigate and compare the two modalities, because modality seems to affect linguistic processing. Jakimik and Glenberg in fact suggest that written language is "a poor relative of the original" (1990, p. 588), because written language does not represent and maintain information about temporal order or prosody as effectively as does spoken language. They suggest that researchers should pay more attention specifically to the processing of spoken language, a conclusion which concurs with the general theme of this chapter. Unfortunately, their task may only be suitable for investigating questions of coreference between antecedent and anaphor and not so useful to researchers considering other aspects of language processing such as the timing of use of information from various linguistic sources. In addition, Jakimik and Glenberg examined only proportion correct recall, but did not measure the time it took subjects to recall the antecedent. We do not know from their experiment whether antecedents more often correctly recalled were also recalled more quickly. If a researcher wanted to examine whether the inappropriate antecedent is actively inhibited or instead has less initial activation than the appropriate antecedent, some sort of reaction time methodology would be necessary.

A task similar in spirit to this sentence recall task was used by Gernsbacher and Shroyer (1989) to investigate cataphoric processing. A cataphor is a part of speech such as *this guy* which signals that the associated concept is likely to be mentioned later in the text. Gernsbacher and Shroyer proposed that concepts mentioned with the indefinite article *this* are more accessible than concepts mentioned with the indefinite article *a*. Subjects in their experiment listened to texts in which a concept was introduced either with *this* or *a,* as in *She found this egg* versus *She found an egg*. The subjects' task was to continue the text after the critical concept. Consistent with the notion that cataphors make a concept more accessible, Gernsbacher and Shroyer found that subjects referred sooner and more often to a concept introduced by *this* than a concept introduced by *a*. Another interpretation of this finding is that subjects are sensitive to the linguistic constraints on the use of anaphors and cataphors and so know that it is ill-formed to use a phrase such as *this guy* unless the corresponding concept becomes the dominant theme of the remainder of the discourse. The technique of eliciting story continuations does not allow us to distinguish between these two interpretations.

As we hope this section makes clear, many of the classic non–reaction-time methodologies can still fruitfully be used to explore spoken language processing. These tasks can be used, for example, to demonstrate that a variable or source of information influences linguistic decisions, both conscious and unconscious. For example, the sentence gating task demonstrates clearly that prosodic information can be used to influence syntactic decisions—but whether the information influences the initial parse of the sentence or just the subject's conscious decision about what seems plausible is impossible to tell. The continuation task used by Gernsbacher indicates that phrases such as *this guy* are typically the topic of later discourse. But again, we do not know whether the effect occurs because the corresponding concept is highly active or because subjects try to make their productions conform to linguistic conventions, nor do we know precisely how the cataphor and its referent are eventually linked. Off-line tasks, then, are useful for answering research questions that take a yes/no form; for example, Does prosodic information influence syntactic parsing? Do speakers make a cataphor the topic of later discourse? But to answer questions concerning when and how information sources are coordinated during linguistic processing, on-line tasks are required.

B. Reaction Time Methods

As mentioned above, reaction time tasks as a whole are more on line than the types of tasks reviewed in the previous section. However, reaction time tasks differ a great deal in the extent to which they are on line. We begin with a reaction time technique that is at the off-line end of the continuum and currently very rarely used, the picture–sentence verification task (for some recent studies using the task, see Chen & Peng, 1990; Kim, Shatz, & Akiyama, 1990; Marquer & Pereira, 1990; Merrill & Mar, 1987; Sokolov, 1988). The subject listens to a sentence and then examines a picture to determine whether it is a truthful representation of the sentence's content. Reaction time (and accuracy) to make the true/false decision is the dependent measure. Early studies demonstrated that listeners take longer to (a) judge that a statement is false rather than true of a picture (Clark & Chase, 1972, 1974); (b) make a decision about a statement containing negation (Clark & Chase, 1972); and (c) judge a picture with respect to a passive compared to an active sentence (Gough, 1965, 1966; Slobin, 1966). In addition, subjects are less accurate at determining that a picture is false of a sentence if the given information in the sentence (the information presumed to be shared by speaker and listener) is contradicted rather than the new information (novel information of which the speaker wishes to make the listener aware) (Hornby, 1974; this study used visual rather than auditory presentation of the sentences). A generalization that emerges from this work is that complex sentences are more difficult to verify than (syntactically and propositionally) simpler sentences.

This task has a number of clear limitations. First, while it may allow the researcher to show that a syntactically complex construction such as a passive takes longer to verify than an active, it does not permit the specification of where within the sentence the difficulty arises or what precisely about the relation between the sentence and picture causes the difficulty. Second, the task has the obvious limitation that it can be used only to explore the processing of quite concrete, imageable sentences. For instance, it would be difficult to examine the processing of passives involving stimulus–experiencer verbs such as *embarrassed* (as in *Mary was embarrassed by Bill's actions*), despite the theoretical interest in comparing the processing of such passives and more standard agent–patient passives (Huitema, 1992). It would also be difficult to compare the processing of sentences with different propositional content, because the characteristics of the pictures would be so radically different.

Third, the task does not isolate linguistic processing, but rather the processes involved in understanding sentences, understanding pictures, and comparing the two. This aspect of the task was demonstrated by Olson and Filby (1972). They had subjects listen to passives, focus on either the agent or patient of the action in the picture, and then verify the sentence with respect to the picture. They found that when subjects were told to focus on the object, passives were easier than actives, and when told to focus on the agent, actives were easier than passives. These results indicate that the manner in which a picture is encoded affects sentence verification. On the other hand, the fact that the sentence–picture verification task taps into our ability to compare linguistic and visual information could be viewed as a strength rather than a limitation if one were interested in studying how language is used to convey information about the visual world. And this is in fact a critical question about language processing, because a fundamental purpose of language is to convey information about the world, and a fundamental task for the listener is to use language to learn about the characteristics of the environment.

The next methodology we consider is also a classic technique, phoneme monitoring. The subject listens to a word or sentence and attempts to locate a particular phoneme. When the target phoneme is detected, the subject pushes a button and reaction times are recorded. Phoneme monitoring has been used to explore both lexical and sentence processing in the auditory modality. It appears that phoneme monitoring is still widely used to examine auditory lexical processing (Cutler, Butterfield, & Williams, 1987; Cutler, Mehler, Norris, & Segui, 1986, 1987; Dupoux & Mehler, 1990; Frauenfelder, Segui, & Dijkstra, 1990; Schriefers, Zwitserlood, & Roelofs, 1991) but has virtually disappeared from the field of sentence processing.

The earliest studies of sentence comprehension using the phoneme monitoring task were designed to examine the question of whether context influences the accessing of different meanings of ambiguous words (see Cairns & Hsu, 1980; Cairns & Kamerman, 1975; Foss, 1969; Mehler, Segui, & Carey, 1978; among others). Some of the studies found multiple access, and others selective access (see Simpson, this volume), and so research eventually was directed toward trying to track down the reasons for the discrepancies in the results. Eventually, the task was abandoned in favor of techniques such as cross-modal lexical decision and naming, which test the availability of word meanings more directly (Seidenberg, Tanenhaus, Leiman, & Bienkowski, 1982) and are not subject to the same influences as phoneme monitoring. It turned out that a large number of variables influenced phoneme detection time, and that the interpretation of phoneme detection times is far from straightforward. Considering the first point, studies have shown that the time to detect the initial phoneme of a target word is longer when the target word is preceded by a word that is infrequent (Foss, 1969) or long (Mehler et al., 1978), or when preceded by a word beginning with a similar phoneme (Dell & Newman, 1980; Foss & Gernsbacher, 1983). The properties of the target word also make a difference: Phoneme detection times are greater the longer (Foss & Gernsbacher, 1983) and less predictable (Swinney & Prather, 1980) the vowel following the target phoneme. Reaction times are also longer the earlier the position of the target word in the sentence (Cutler, 1976; Foss, 1969; Holmes & Forster, 1970; Shields, McHugh & Martin, 1974).

These findings suggest that anyone who wished to use the phoneme monitoring task today would be faced with a difficult challenge. The sentences being compared would have to contain the target word in the same position in all conditions; the target word ideally would be the same in all versions; and the word preceding the target word ideally would not differ either. What sort of experiment could meet all these conditions? Cutler and Fodor (1979) provide one interesting example. Based on Cutler's previous work, Cutler and Fodor predicted that detection times for a target phoneme would be faster in focused compared with nonfocused words. A neutrally spoken sentence such as (7) was preceded with a question that focused either the word *corner* (*Which man was wearing the hat?*) or the word *blue* (*Which hat was the man wearing?*).

(7) *The man on the corner was wearing the blue hat.*

Thus, in this experiment, the sentence versions being compared were identical. Position effects were not a concern either, because the prediction was that detection times for /k/ would be fast given the first question and slow given the second; conversely, detection times for /b/ would be slow given the first question and fast given the second. These predictions were supported, indicating that listeners at some stage of sentence processing are sensitive to the focus structure of the sentence, so that a target phoneme in a focused word is responded to quickly.

The constraints described above would also still permit the examination of garden-path sentences using the phoneme monitoring technique, particularly pairs such as (8).

(8)a. *Kim knows Leslie bakes tasty cakes.*
   b. *Kim knows that Leslie bakes tasty cakes.*

Because previous studies using visual materials have shown that processing time is elevated on the disambiguating word in sentences such as (8a), one might want to have subjects monitor for the /b/ in *bakes* and predict longer phoneme detection times in (8a) than in (8b). In fact, a study much like this one was done by Hakes (1972). He had subjects monitor for the /o/ in a sentence such as (9) and found that detection times were longer when the complementizer *that* was absent.

(9) *The world-famous physicist forgot* (*that*) *his old professor had been the first to suggest the crucial experiment to him.*

This finding is somewhat different from the prediction outlined above. The Hakes study showed that phoneme monitoring times on the ambiguous region of a garden-path sentence are long; the prediction above was that times would be long on the disambiguating word. A study by Hakes and Foss (1970) suggests that this prediction might be borne out: They found that with a sentence such as (10a), detection time for the target phoneme /b/ was long compared to a version of the same sentence containing relative pronouns, (10b).

(10)a. *The puzzle the youngster the tutor taught devised bewildered the mathematicians.*
    b. *The puzzle that the youngster that the tutor taught devised bewildered the mathematicians.*

The word *bewildered* could possibly be considered the (or perhaps a) disambiguating word in sentence (10a).

The need to control the lexical characteristics of the preceding and target word as well as the target word's sentential position are not the only problems associated with the phoneme monitoring technique. One serious concern surrounds the assumptions underlying the use of dual tasks to infer processing load. Here we must be careful, because phoneme monitoring is used both to understand phoneme identification itself and as a secondary load task to investigate sentence processing. The use of phoneme monitoring to study phoneme identification is illustrated in the work of most of the researchers cited above who use the task to study lexical processing. Such researchers ask whether it is easier to detect a phoneme given various sorts of lexical variables, such as lexical stress pattern. This question, while interesting and important, is beyond the scope of this chapter. (For the same reason, we have chosen not to discuss research in which subjects are presented with an acoustically ambiguous phoneme and decide the identity of the phoneme given lexical and sentential constraints [e.g., Connine, 1987; Connine, Blasko, & Hall, 1991; McQueen, 1991].)

The logic underlying the use of phoneme monitoring as a secondary load task was given by Foss (1969), who states that "as decision difficulty concerning the identification of entities at one level increases, speed and accuracy of decisions concerning other entities should decrease since the difficult decisions utilize the bulk of S's limited-capacity mechanisms" (p. 457). The decisions in question are the primary task of identifying the lexical, syntactic, and semantic structure of the sentence, and the secondary task of identifying a particular phoneme. The more "processing resources" required to make linguistic decisions at a particular point in a sentence, the fewer resources will be available to identify the target phoneme. Navon and Gopher (1979) and Friedman and Polson (1981) list some of the difficulties with this logic. First, this logic assumes a single pool of resources, but some research favors a multiple resources view (e.g., Friedman & Polson, 1981; Hellige & Longstreth, 1981; Hellige & Wong, 1983) based on the brain's hemispheric asymmetries. However, given that the primary and secondary tasks involved in phoneme monitoring are both linguistic, it may be reasonable to assume that both draw on the same resource pool.

But even granting the single-pool assumption, a second assumption of the logic is problematic: the assumption that the supply of resources is fixed, and that therefore a decrease in supply available for one task implies an increase for the other. This assumption is problematic because it is possible that the conjoining of the two tasks leads to an increase in the total amount of available resources, or that as either the primary or secondary task becomes difficult the pool of resources correspondingly increases.

Third, the logic assumes that the demands of the two tasks are additive, and that performance on the two tasks is independent. There is no reason to treat this assumption as a priori plausible, and under some experimental conditions, it is highly implausible. For example, imagine that one did a study such as Beach's, in which garden-path sentences were enriched with prosodically disambiguating material. The subject's task would be to monitor for a phoneme in the disambiguating word, and one might find that phoneme monitoring times were facilitated by prosodic information. But because phonemic segments and prosodic variations are both types of phonological information, subjects might become extra-sensitive to the prosodic characteristics of the sentence when they must monitor for a phoneme. This hypersensitivity would occur because the two tasks might not be independent, but instead might combine into a higher level task in which subjects carefully monitor the phonological characteristics of the sentence and perhaps distort their processing of information at other (e.g., syntactic and semantic) levels.

A second problem with the use of the phoneme monitoring technique to study sentence processing concerns the requirement that subjects make a conscious decision about the identity of a phoneme. Thus, phoneme detection may be facilitated by various sorts of sentential constraints because the information provided by those constraints allows more processing resources to be freed up for phoneme detection, or it could be that resource allocation to the two tasks does not change, but rather the conscious decision to push a button is influenced by syntactic and semantic information. The decision could be facilitated because congruence between information from all sources of information makes subjects more likely to say yes to the presence of a phoneme than would incongruence (the general argument here is adapted from those made by Seidenberg, Waters, Sanders, & Langer, 1984). This would not necessarily be a problem if one were simply using phoneme monitoring to examine the processing of, say, garden-path sentences. One might find slower detection times on the disambiguating word of such sentences and not worry about distinguishing between the two possible interpretations of such a result. The difficulty comes when the researcher introduces a source of information that could potentially aid in the comprehension of garden-path sentences. Then there is ambiguity about whether the constraining source of information facilitated decisions about the syntactic structure of the sentence or facilitated the decision component of the phoneme detection task. In other words, it is impossible to know whether the two sources of information interacted during syntactic processing or remained independent. Consequently, the phoneme monitoring technique could not be used to decide between modular and interactive models of auditory sentence processing.

A task similar to the phoneme monitoring technique is the word monitoring task, used by Marslen-Wilson, Tyler, and their colleagues. Early studies (Marslen-Wilson & Tyler, 1980) demonstrated that word monitoring times were faster the later the position of the target word in a sentence, and as was mentioned earlier, this finding was also obtained using phoneme monitoring. Recently, Tyler and Warren (1987) used word monitoring to explore the effects of disruptions in what they termed the local and global structures of spoken sentences. The local structure of a sentence concerns the internal structure of individual phrases; the global structure refers to the overall well-formedness of the sentence. A "sentence" such as *book the reading was man the* contains both local and global syntactic disruptions, because the order of elements within phrases is inconsistent with the grammer of English (articles must precede, not follow, nouns) and the order of phrases within the sentence is semantically inappropriate (books do not read people). In contrast, a sentence such as *the book was reading the man* is globally disrupted but locally intact. Tyler and Warren also manipulated the well-formedness of local and prosodic structures at the prosodic level by varying whether phonological and intonational phrase boundaries occurred at prosodically appropriate or inappropriate locations. They found that syntactic disruptions slowed down word monitoring times only when they were local; in contrast, both local and global prosodic disruptions were detrimental. From these results they argued that speakers construct local syntactic structures for phrases and a global prosodic structure for a sentence, but never compute a global syntactic structure. Syntax is used only to establish the internal structure of phrases (and presumably also to establish the sentence's prosodic organization).

Unfortunately, these arguments must be taken with some caution because of the nature of the task. Word monitoring has many of the same weaknesses as phoneme monitoring. In addition, it is difficult to know whether listeners normally do not construct a global syntactic structure for a sentence, or simply do not construct a global syntactic structure (a resource-demanding task) when engaged in a task that does not require one (word monitoring). Similarly, word monitoring as a dependent variable taps primarily into the lexical level of processing and so may be predominantly affected by variables which affect the lexical level. Finally, it might be useful to have subjects answer comprehension questions about the sentences. Subjects may not have been paying attention to the global structure of the sentence in the Tyler and Warren experiment because the task did not require them to comprehend the sentences' overall meaning.

Next we consider the cross-modal lexical decision and naming tasks, which have been used to investigate the activation levels of concepts at various points in the processing of a sentence. Subjects in these experiments listen to a sentence and at some critical point are interrupted with a visual probe word. Their task is either to make a lexical decision (e.g., Shapiro, Zurif, & Grimshaw, 1987, 1989) or to name the word (e.g., Seidenberg et al., 1982), and reaction times are recorded. These tasks have been used to investigate the processing of lexical ambiguity in sentences (Blutner & Sommer, 1988; Onifer & Swinney, 1981; Seidenberg et al., 1982; Swinney, 1979; Tabossi, 1988; Tanenhaus, Leiman, & Seidenberg, 1979), with the majority of studies showing multiple access of meanings for ambiguous words immediately after encountering the word, and selective access a few hundred milliseconds later. Zwitserlood (1989) recently used cross-modal lexical decision to examine the cohort model of spoken word recognition (Marslen-Wilson, 1984; Marslen-Wilson & Tyler, 1980; Marslen-Wilson & Welsh, 1978). She found that multiple word candidates were not activated during spoken language processing until the listener had received some sensory activation of the word. In addition, both contextually appropriate and inappropriate candidates were initially activated, so that sentence context selected only after lexical access.

The cross-modal technique has also been used to investigate coreference processes, and in particular, the activation of potential antecedents for an anaphor. Recently, MacDonald and MacWhinney (1990) had subjects listen to sentences and then, at various points within a sentence, verify whether a visually presented probe word appeared in the sentence. Subjects were also asked questions after the sentences to ensure that they were processing for meaning. Among other findings, it turned out that assignment of antecedents was quite slow for ambiguous pronouns (taking longer than half a second), and not immediate even for gender-disambiguated pronouns. In addition, pronouns appeared to inhibit inappropriate potential referents. In related work, Swinney, Ford, Frauenfelder, and Bresnan (1988) found evidence that only structurally appropriate antecedents for pronouns (as given by the binding theory; Chomsky, 1981) were activated upon encountering a pronoun, and similar results were obtained by Nicol (1988) with both pronouns and reflexives (e.g., *himself*).

A number of researchers have used the cross-modal technique to investigate in spoken sentences the activation of antecedents of "traces" (Chomsky, 1981), which in the sentence-processing literature tend to be called "gaps" (J. D. Fodor, 1978, 1989). For example, according to both the government and binding framework of Chomsky and his colleagues as well as the framework of head-driven phrase structure grammar (HPSG; Pollard & Sag, 1992), sentence (11) contains a trace in the direct object position, marked with a *t*.

(11) *Which boxer did Tom see* t *yesterday?*

Swinney et al. (1988) found that the antecedent of a *wh*-trace was reactivated immediately upon encountering the trace, suggesting that listeners understand sentences with moved elements by associating or coindexing the trace and its antecedent. (The Swinney et al. study was done using sentences with relative clauses rather than with *wh*-questions, but the same logic applies in the two cases.) The government and binding framework (but not HPSG) also states that a passive sentence such as *The dentist was invited* t *to the party* contains a trace in postverbal position, indicating the position from which the verb's object was moved. Osterhout and Nicol (1988) found a tendency (unfortunately, nonsignificant) for the concept of *dentist* in such a sentence to be reactivated at the trace (see also Bever & McElree, 1988; MacDonald, 1989, who obtained significant activation of the antecedent at the gap location but used visual presentation of sentences). These studies raise the intriguing possibility that gaps and explicit anaphors display similar coreference patterns.

The cross-modal technique has also been used recently to examine verb complexity effects during sentence processing. Shapiro et al. (1987, 1989) had subjects listen to sentences and then immediately after the critical verb make a lexical decision to an unrelated word. The critical verb was either relatively simple or complex, as defined by the number of argument frames the verb permitted. An example is shown in (12).

(12)a. *John fixed the car.* (simple verb)
    b. *John lent the car.* (complex verb)

The cross-modal technique is used here as a secondary load task—the more complex a verb, the more resources its processing requires, so fewer resources will be available to make the lexical decision. Shapiro et al. found that lexical decisions were longer after the more complex verbs. However, Schmauder (1991) could not replicate this finding using either the cross-modal task or eye-movement monitoring (of visually presented sentences). Shapiro, Brookins, Gordon, and Nagel (1991) and Schmauder, Kennison, and Clifton (1991) exchanged ideas about what the boundary conditions might be on the verb complexity effect, but it is clear, as Schmauder et al. point out, that the effect is quite delicate (perhaps in part because of the difficulties outlined earlier with the assumptions underlying the dual-task paradigm) and the conditions under which it can be elicited are not well understood.

Generally, cross-modal techniques are useful for examining the reactivation of a concept at a critical location within a sentence—for example, the availability of meanings for an ambiguous word, or the activation level of a hypothesized antecedent (or nonantecedent) for an anaphor. However, not all psycholinguistic questions lend themselves to predictions about activation levels of concepts. For example, to examine whether a word in a spoken sentence is difficult to process or integrate with the ongoing sentence representation, what is needed is a measure of processing difficulty, not a measure of activation level for a concept. One might attempt to use the cross-modal priming task as a dual task, as did Shapiro and his colleagues, with the logic that the more difficult a sentence is to process at a particular point, the longer lexical decision (or naming) times will be to an irrelevant word. However, the debate between Shapiro, Schmauder, and their respective colleagues is quite illustrative of the difficulties that can arise from using secondary load tasks to measure processing difficulty.

Finally, the last reaction-time paradigm we consider is end-of-sentence comprehension time. Here, a subject listens to a sentence and then pushes a button to indicate when the sentence has been understood. This task was used by Slowiaczek (1981) and Speer and Slowiaczek (1992) to examine the processing of garden-path sentences with different prosodic structures (either appropriate, neutral, or misleading). In both studies, appropriate prosodic information helped subjects process the garden-path sentences, but not enough to eliminate completely the standard garden-pathing effect. Although this task may be useful for examining some questions in language processing, it is not sensitive enough to indicate precisely when various sources of information have their effect. We cannot tell whether listeners first are garden-pathed and then use prosodic information to aid in their recovery of the correct structure, or whether the prosodic information is available in time to prevent the garden path from happening altogether. Both possibilities are consistent with a modular model of sentence processing (see Section III,A and Mitchell, this volume) but clearly diverge on the matter of how different information sources are integrated.

This completes our survey of the different methodologies used to study spoken language processing. Undoubtedly we have left out some paradigms, but this survey should serve to give a flavor for the kinds of tasks that have been used and the kinds of questions that have been examined using those tasks. The main points may be summarized as follows: First, offline tasks can profitably be used to examine global questions about language processing (for example, can prosodic information be used to inform syntactic decisions at some stage of processing?). Second, the cross-modal lexical decision and naming tasks are useful for exploring the (re)activation of concepts during sentence processing. Third, however, no published work describes the use of a technique that would be suitable for the study of sentence parsing, especially the timing of use of information from various sources. No unobtrusive, on-line technique for measuring processing load throughout a sentence is currently being used in our field.

IV. FUTURE DIRECTIONS

In this section we discuss some potentially promising methodologies for study-ing auditory language processing. Townsend and Bever (1991) have recently developed a new dual-task paradigm. They had subjects listen to three-sentence texts and perform two tasks: report on the cohesiveness of the text and deter-mine when the speaker's voice changed from male to female. Their primary dependent variables were the percentage of occasions on which subjects failed to notice a voice change (misses) and the time it took subjects to detect speaker changes. They argued that it is critical to have subjects perform tasks that require both higher and lower levels of linguistic processing (such as monitoring both for text cohesiveness and changes in voice characteristics). Otherwise, if subjects simply have to monitor, for example, for a particular phoneme, they can decide to shift all their processing resources to that task. As a result, a finding that subjects perform better on the phoneme detection task given some higher level linguistic constraint may only reflect listeners' ability to shift pro-cessing resources toward low-level processing tasks when resources are freed up at higher levels. Subjects in the Townsend–Bever task cannot simply shift processing resources to the lower level task, because to do so would compromise processing at the higher level. Using their technique, Townsend and Bever found that subjects could detect a speaker change faster and more accurately at the end of a sentence (where syntactic and semantic constraints are presum-ably the greatest) compared to the sentence beginning. This finding is similar to that obtained with word and phoneme monitoring: Subjects are faster and more accurate toward the end of a sentence. (Townsend and Bever also found that discourse constraints had the opposite effect from sentence constraints, but we will not describe here their explanation of this pattern.)

It is not clear to us that the logic of this paradigm is radically different from that employed in other studies. It is important to heed their caution that subjects be made to process sentences to the level of meaning in experiments which require them to monitor for some comparatively lower level feature of the linguistic stimulus. For instance, in any monitoring paradigm subjects should be asked to answer a comprehension question, or make a semantically or pragmatically based judgment about the stimulus after the stimulus is presented, to prevent the simple shift of resources to lower level processing that Townsend and Bever describe. In addition, Townsend and Bever's task of having subjects monitor for a voice change is original and may be promising. This task may be less objectionable than the phoneme or word monitoring tasks, because it does not require the subject to monitor consciously for a linguistic/representational aspect of the sentence. Voice changes do not constitute linguistic variations, but the acoustic features of voices figure importantly in later stages of linguistic processing (i.e., identifying phonemes, which in turn influence lexical and sen-tential processing). But given that the logic of dual-task paradigms is so problem-atic, it might be best to put our resources into developing a more direct and unobtrusive on-line technique for measuring processing load during spoken language comprehension.

One such technique is the recording of event-related brain potentials (ERPs) during sentence processing. This technique is described in detail by Kutas and Van Petten (this volume), so we will be brief here. The technique involves having subjects examine some stimulus while at the same time monitoring ERPs from the subject's scalp. The task is unobtrusive, since the subject does not have to perform any extraneous task, and it provides a continuous measure of processing over the entire sentence. Thus, this task would be extremely useful to someone wanting to study on-line processing of auditorily presented sentences. The main limitation of the task is that, at least to our knowledge, it has been necessary in most work to present each word of a sentence quite slowly (e.g., Van Petten & Kutas, 1990, visually presented each word of a sentence for 200 ms followed by a blank interval of 700 ms), in order to associate ERP waveforms and the eliciting stimulus accurately. On the other hand, perhaps there is a way around this limitation (for example, Garnsey, Tanenhaus, & Chapman, 1989, presented words visually at a rate of two per second, which is closer to a natural presentation rate), as discussed by Kutas and Van Petten (this volume). One possibility would be to use words that are relatively long (e.g., a four-syllable word could take about 0.5 s to say). Such words could be presented with no pause between them but still with enough of a stimulus–onset asynchrony to allow accurate association of the ERP profile and the words of the sentence.

Finally, we describe a task that we are currently developing in our laboratory and that we hope will turn out to be promising. We have set up an auditory version of the moving window technique (Just et al., 1982). Sentences are naturally spoken, recorded, and digitized, and then markers are placed in front of each prosodic word in the sentence. For example, a sentence might be marked as shown in (13), where a slash indicates the location of a marker.

(13) *Because/Bill/left/the room/seemed/empty.*

The subject begins by pushing a button to initiate the trial. The waveform is presented over speaker or headphones up to the location of the first marker, and the subject must push the button to receive the next word of the sentence. The subject continues in this fashion until the entire sentence is presented and then answers a comprehension question. The logic is obvious—if subjects encounter a portion of the sentence which is difficult to process (for example, the disambiguating word *seemed*) in (13), they will wait longer to press the button for the next word compared to a condition in which that portion of the sentence is easy to integrate. Our software allows us to manipulate the prosody of the sentence, so we can compare processing of versions of (13) containing different degrees of prosodic disambiguation.

We have found in pilot testing of this technique that subjects quickly learn how to push the button so that the sentence sounds smooth and normal. We are conducting studies to determine whether the technique is sensitive to linguistic variables that should affect processing time (as indicated by reading studies) and to see what sorts of variables can be manipulated using this task. We will undoubtedly encounter difficulties and possibly even pitfalls as we continue calibrating this task. To take just one concern, we worry about how prosodic variables should be manipulated, given that some of the manipulations we will want to employ as independent variables (e.g., lengthening of a critical word, inserting a pause after it) exactly mirror our dependent variable. However, we believe the task has enough promise that it is worth exploring.

V. CONCLUSIONS

All of us working in psycholinguistics know that we need to devote more experimental attention to the study of spoken language processing. In fact, the early days (the 1960s and 1970s) were dominated by studies using auditory presentation of sentences and techniques such as click detection and phoneme monitoring. Visual presentation gained ascendency when problems with these techniques became too obvious to ignore and when psycholinguistics shifted from the study of low-level processes such as parsing to high-level "reading" processes such as inferencing and text integration. As a result, even after these thirty years of study we know little about spoken language processing, particularly how processing decisions are made on-line. Perhaps, however, one of the tasks we describe in Section IV will turn out to be useful and appropriate. The discovery of an on-line auditory task would be quite timely, because the field of psycholinguistics seems recently to have acquired a strong interest in prosody and its relation to language processing and acquisition (see, e.g., Beach, 1991; Ferreira, 1991; Gerken, 1991; Levelt, 1989). The questions and the interest are out there; what the field now requires is a solid methodology.

REFERENCES

Beach, C. M. (1991). The interpretation of prosodic patterns at points of syntactic structure ambiguity: Evidence for cue trading relations. *Journal of Memory and Language, 30,* 644–663.

Bever, T. G., & McElree, B. (1988). Empty categories access their antecedents during comprehension. *Linguistic Inquiry, 19,* 35–43.

Blutner, R., & Sommer, R. (1988). Sentence processing and lexical access: The influence of the focus-identifying task. *Journal of Memory and Language, 27,* 359–367.

Cairns, H. S., & Hsu, J. R. (1980). Effects of prior context on lexical access during sentence comprehension: A replication and reinterpretation. *Journal of Psycholinguistic Research, 9,* 319–326.

Cairns, H. S., & Kamerman, J. (1975). Lexical information processing during sentence comprehension. *Journal of Verbal Learning and Verbal Behavior, 14,* 170–179.

Carr, T. H., & Pollatsek, A. (1985). Recognizing printed words: A look at current models. In D. Besner, T. G. Waller, & G. E. MacKinnon (Eds.), *Reading research: Advances in theory and practice* (Vol. 5). Orlando, FL: Academic Press.

Carrithers, C., & Bever, T. G. (1984). Eye fixation patterns during reading confirm theories of language comprehension. *Cognitive Science, 8,* 157–172.

Chen, Y., & Peng, R. (1990). An experimental study on sentence comprehension. *Acta Psychologica Sinica, 22,* 225–231.

Chomsky, N. (1981). *Lectures on government and binding.* Dordrecht: Foris.

Clark, H. H., & Chase, W. G. (1972). On the process of comparing sentences against pictures. *Cognitive Psychology, 3,* 472–517.

Clark, H. H., & Chase, W. G. (1974). Perceptual coding strategies in the formation and verification of descriptions. *Memory & Cognition, 2,* 101–111.

Clark, H. H., & Clark, E. V. (1977). *Psychology and language: An introduction to psycholinguistics.* New York: Harcourt Brace Jovanovich.

Connine, C. M. (1987). Constraints on interactive processes in auditory word recognition: The role of sentence context. *Journal of Memory and Language, 26,* 527–538.

Connine, C. M., Blasko, D. G., & Hall, M. (1991). Effects of subsequent sentence context in auditory word recognition: Temporal and linguistic constraints. *Journal of Memory and Language, 30,* 234–250.

Cooper, W. E., & Paccia-Cooper, J. M. (1980). *Syntax and speech.* Cambridge, MA: Harvard University Press.

Cutler, A. (1976). Phoneme-monitoring reaction time as a function of preceding intonation contour. *Perception & Psychophysics, 20,* 55–60.

Cutler, A. (1990). Exploiting prosodic probabilities in speech segmentation. In G. T. M. Altmann (Ed.), *Cognitive models of speech processing.* Cambridge, MA: MIT Press.

Cutler, A., Butterfield, S., & Williams, J. N. (1987). The perceptual integrity of syllabic onsets. *Journal of Memory and Language, 26,* 406–418.

Cutler, A., & Fodor, J. A. (1979). Semantic focus and sentence comprehension. *Cognition, 7,* 49–59.

Cutler, A., Mehler, J., Norris, D., & Segui, J. (1986). The syllable's differing role in the segmentation of French and English. *Journal of Memory and Language, 25,* 385–400.

Cutler, A., Mehler, J., Norris, D., & Segui, J. (1987). Phoneme identification and the lexicon. *Cognitive Psychology, 19,* 141–177.

Dell, G. S., & Newman, J. E. (1980). Detecting phonemes in fluent speech. *Journal of Verbal Learning and Verbal Behavior, 19,* 608–623.

Dupoux, E., & Mehler, J. (1990). Monitoring the lexicon with normal and compressed speech: Frequency effects and the prelexical code. *Journal of Memory and Language, 29,* 316–335.

Ferreira, F. (1991). Effects of length and syntactic complexity on initiation times for prepared utterances. *Journal of Memory and Language, 30,* 210–233.

Ferreira, F., & Henderson, J. M. (1990). The use of verb information in syntactic parsing: A comparison of evidence from eye movements and word-by-word self-paced reading. *Journal of Experimental Psychology: Learning, Memory, and Cognition, 16,* 555–568.

Ferreira, F., & Henderson, J. M. (1991). Recovery from misanalyses of garden-path sentences. *Journal of Memory and Language, 30,* 725–745.

Fodor, J. A. (1983). *The modularity of mind.* Cambridge, MA: MIT Press.

Fodor, J. A. (1985). Precis of *The modularity of mind. Behavioral and Brain Sciences, 8,* 1–42.

Fodor, J. A., & Bever, T. G. (1965). The psychological reality of linguistic segments. *Journal of Verbal Learning and Verbal Behavior, 4,* 414–420.

Fodor, J. A., Bever, T. G., & Garrett, M. (1974). *The psychology of language.* New York: McGraw Hill.

Fodor, J. D. (1978). Parsing strategies and constraints on transformations. *Linguistic Inquiry, 9,* 427–473.

Fodor, J. D. (1989). Empty categories in sentence processing. *Language and Cognitive Processes, 4*(3/4), 155–209.

Foss, D. J. (1969). Decision processes during sentence comprehension: Effects of lexical item difficulty and position upon decision times. *Journal of Verbal Learning and Verbal Behavior, 8,* 457–462.

Foss, D. J., & Gernsbacher, M. A. (1983). Cracking the dual code: Toward a unitary model of phoneme identification. *Journal of Verbal Learning and Verbal Behavior, 22,* 609–632.

Frauenfelder, U. H., Segui, J., & Dijkstra, T. (1990). Lexical effects in phonemic processing: Facilitatory or inhibitory? *Journal of Experimental Psychology: Human Perception and Performance, 16,* 77–91.

Frazier, L. (1978). On comprehending sentences: Syntactic parsing strategies. Ph.D. Dissertation, University of Connecticut. Distributed by Indiana University Linguistics Club.

Frazier, L. (1990). Exploring the architecture of the language-processing system. In G. T. M. Altmann (Ed.), *Cognitive models of speech processing.* Cambridge, MA: MIT Press.

Frazier, L., & Rayner, K. (1982). Making and correcting errors during sentence comprehension: Eye movements in the analysis of structurally ambiguous sentences. *Cognitive Psychology, 14,* 178–210.

Friedman, A., & Polson, M. C. (1981). Hemispheres as independent resource systems: Limited capacity processing and cerebral specialization. *Journal of Experimental Psychology: Human Perception and Performance, 7,* 1031–1058.

Garnsey, S. M., Tanenhaus, M. K., & Chapman, R. M. (1989). Evoked potentials and the study of sentence comprehension. *Journal of Psycholinguistic Research, 18,* 51–60.

Garrett, M., Bever, T. G., & Fodor, J. A. (1965). The active use of grammar in speech perception. *Perception & Psychophysics, 1,* 30–32.

Gee, J. P., & Grosjean, F. (1983). Performance structures: A psycholinguistic and linguistic appraisal. *Cognitive Psychology, 15,* 411–458.

Geers, A. E. (1978). Intonation contour and syntactic structure as predictors of apparent segmentation. *Journal of Experimental Psychology: Human Perception and Performance, 4*, 273–283.

Gerken, L. (1991). The metrical basis for children's subjectless sentences. *Journal of Memory and Language, 30*, 431–451.

Gernsbacher, M. A., & Shroyer, S. (1989). The cataphoric use of the indefinite *this* in spoken narratives. *Memory & Cognition, 17*, 536–540.

Glenberg, A. M., & Swanson, N. C. (1986). A temporal distinctiveness theory of recency and modality effects. *Journal of Experimental Psychology: Learning, Memory, and Cognition, 12*, 3–15.

Gough, P. B. (1965). Grammatical transformations and speed of understanding. *Journal of Verbal Learning and Verbal Behavior, 4*, 107–111.

Gough, P. B. (1966). The verification of sentences: The effects of delay of evidence and sentence length. *Journal of Verbal Learning and Verbal Behavior, 5*, 492–496.

Hakes, D. T. (1972). Effects of reducing complement constructions on sentence comprehension. *Journal of Verbal Learning and Verbal Behavior, 11*, 278–286.

Hakes, D. T., & Foss, D. J. (1970). Decision processes during sentence comprehension: Effects of surface structure reconsidered. *Perception & Psychophysics, 8*, 413–416.

Hayduk, S. J. (1990). *Do people process content and function words differently?* Unpublished honour's thesis, University of Alberta, Edmonton, Canada.

Hellige, J. B., & Longstreth, L. E. (1981). Effects of concurrent hemisphere-specific activity on unimanual tapping rate. *Neuropsychologia, 19*, 395–405.

Hellige, J. B., & Wong, T. M. (1983). Hemisphere-specific interference in dichotic listening: Task variables and individual differences. *Journal of Experimental Psychology: General, 112*, 218–239.

Holmes, V. M., & Forster, K. I. (1970). Perceptual complexity and understanding sentence structure. *Journal of Verbal Learning and Verbal Behavior, 11*, 148–156.

Hornby, P. A. (1974). Surface structure and presupposition. *Journal of Verbal Learning and Verbal Behavior, 13*, 530–538.

Huitema, J. S. (1992). *Comprehending sentences containing traces.* Unpublished manuscript, University of Illinois, Urbana-Champaign.

Jakimik, J., & Glenberg, A. (1990). Verbal learning meets psycholinguistics: Modality effects in the comprehension of anaphora. *Journal of Memory and Language, 29*, 582–590.

Just, M. A., Carpenter, P. A., & Woolley, J. (1982). Paradigms and processes in reading comprehension. *Journal of Experimental Psychology: General, 10*, 833–849.

Kim, J. L., Shatz, M., & Akiyama, M. M. (1990). Effects of language and task on children's patterns of sentence verification and denial. *Developmental Psychology, 26*, 821–829.

Levelt, W. (1989). *Speaking.* Cambridge, MA: MIT Press.

MacDonald, M. C. (1989). Priming effects from gaps to antecedents. *Language and Cognitive Processes, 4*, 35–56.

MacDonald, M. C., & MacWhinney, B. (1990). Measuring inhibition and facilitation from pronouns. *Journal of Memory and Language, 29*, 469–492.

Marquer, J., & Pereira, M. (1990). Reaction times in the study of strategies in sentence–picture verification: A reconsideration. *Quarterly Journal of Experimental Psychology, 42A*, 147–168.

Marslen-Wilson, W. D. (1984). Function and process in spoken-word recognition. In H. Bouma & D. G. Bouwhuis (Eds.), *Attention and performance X: Control of language processes* (pp. 125–150). Hillsdale, NJ: Erlbaum.

Marslen-Wilson, W. D., & Tyler, L. K. (1980). The temporal structure of spoken language understanding. *Cognition, 8*, 1–71.

Marslen-Wilson, W. D., & Welsh, A. (1978). Processing interaction and access during word recognition in continuous speech. *Cognitive Psychology, 10*, 29–63.

McQueen, J. M. (1991). The influence of the lexicon on phonetic categorization: Stimulus quality in word-final ambiguity. *Journal of Experimental Psychology: Human Perception and Performance, 17*, 433–443.

Mehler, J., Segui, J., & Carey, P. (1978). Tails of words: Monitoring ambiguity. *Journal of Verbal Learning and Verbal Behavior, 17*, 29–35.

Merrill, E. C., & Mar, H. H. (1987). Differences between mentally retarded and nonretarded persons' efficiency of auditory sentence processing. *American Journal of Mental Deficiency, 91*, 406–414.

Navon, D., & Gopher, D. (1979). On the economy of the human processing system. *Psychological Review, 86,* 214–255.

Nespor, M., & Vogel, I. (1987). *Prosodic phonology.* Dordrecht: Foris.

Nicol, J. (1988). *Coreference processing during sentence comprehension.* Doctoral dissertation, Massachusetts Institute of Technology, Cambridge.

Olson, D. R., & Filby, N. (1972). On the comprehension of active and passive sentences. *Cognitive Psychology, 3,* 361–381.

Onifer, W., & Swinney, D. A. (1981). Accessing logical ambiguities during sentence comprehension: Effects of frequency-of-meaning and contextual bias. *Memory & Cognition, 9,* 225–236.

Osterhout, L., & Nicol, J. (1988). *The time-course of antecedent activation following empty subjects.* Unpublished manuscript.

Pollard, C., & Sag, I. A. (1992). Anaphors in English and the scope of binding theory. *Linguistic Inquiry, 23,* 261–304.

Rayner, K. (1978). Eye movements in reading and information processing. *Psychological Bulletin, 85,* 618–660.

Rayner, K., & Pollatsek, A. (1989). *The psychology of reading.* Englewood Cliffs, NJ: Prentice-Hall.

Rayner, K., Sereno, S. C., Morris, R. K., Schmauder, A. R., & Clifton, C. (1989). Eye movements and on-line language comprehension processes. *Language and Cognitive Processes, 4,* S121–S149.

Schmauder, A. R. (1991). Argument structure frames: A lexical complexity metric? *Journal of Experimental Psychology: Learning, Memory, and Cognition, 17,* 49–65.

Schmauder, A. R., Kennison, S. M., & Clifton, C. (1991). On the conditions necessary for obtaining argument structure complexity effects. *Journal of Experimental Psychology: Learning, Memory, and Cognition, 17,* 1188–1192.

Schriefers, H., Zwitserlood, P., & Roelofs, A. (1991). The identification of morphologically complex spoken words: Continuous processing or decomposition? *Journal of Memory and Language, 30,* 26–47.

Seidenberg, M. S., Tanenhaus, M. K., Leiman, J. M., & Bienkowski, M. (1982). Automatic access of the meanings of ambiguous words in context: Some limitations of knowledge-based processing. *Cognitive Psychology, 14,* 489–537.

Seidenberg, M. S., Waters, G. S., Sanders, M., & Langer, P. (1984). Pre- and postlexical loci of contextual effects on word recognition. *Memory & Cognition, 12,* 315–328.

Selkirk, E. O. (1984). *Phonology and syntax: The relation between sound and meaning.* Cambridge, MA: MIT Press.

Shapiro, L. P., Brookins, B., Gordon, B., & Nagel, N. (1991). Verb effects during sentence processing. *Journal of Experimental Psychology: Learning, Memory, and Cognition, 17,* 983–996.

Shapiro, L. P., Zurif, E., & Grimshaw, J. (1987). Sentence processing and the mental representation of verbs. *Cognition, 27,* 219–246.

Shapiro, L. P., Zurif, E., & Grimshaw, J. (1989). Verb processing during sentence comprehension: Contextual impenetrability. *Journal of Psycholinguistic Research, 18,* 223–243.

Shields, J., McHugh, A., & Martin, J. (1974). Reaction time to phoneme targets as a function of rhythmic cues in continuous speech. *Journal of Experimental Psychology, 102,* 250–255.

Shillcock, R. (1990). Lexical hypotheses in continuous speech. In G. T. M. Altmann (Ed.), *Cognitive models of speech processing.* Cambridge, MA: MIT Press.

Slobin, D. I. (1966). Grammatical transformations and sentence comprehension in childhood and adulthood. *Journal of Verbal Learning and Verbal Behavior, 5,* 219–227.

Slowiaczek, M. L. (1981). *Prosodic units as language processing units.* Doctoral dissertation, University of Massachusetts, Amherst.

Slowiaczek, M. L., & Clifton, C. (1980). Subvocalization and reading for meaning. *Journal of Verbal Learning and Verbal Behavior, 19,* 573–582.

Sokolov, J. L. (1988). Cue validity in Hebrew sentence comprehension. *Journal of Child Language, 15,* 129–155.

Speer, S. R., & Slowiaczek, M. L. (1992). *The influence of syntactic structure on comprehending sentences with temporary syntactic ambiguities.* Unpublished manuscript, Northeastern University, Boston.

Swinney, D. A. (1979). Lexical access during sentence comprehension: (Re)-consideration of context effects. *Journal of Verbal Learning and Verbal Behavior, 18*, 645–660.

Swinney, D. A., Ford, M., Frauenfelder, U., & Bresnan, J. (1988). On the temporal course of gap-filling and antecedent assignment during sentence comprehension. In B. Grosz, R. Kaplan, M. Macken, & I. Sag (Eds.), *Language structure and processing*. Stanford, CA: Center for the Study of Language and Information.

Swinney, D. A., & Prather, P. (1980). Phoneme identification in a phoneme monitoring experiment: The variable role of uncertainty about vowel contexts. *Perception & Psychophysics, 27*, 104–110.

Tabossi, P. (1988). Accessing lexical ambiguity in different types of sentential contexts. *Journal of Memory and Language, 27*, 324–340.

Tanenhaus, M. K., Garnsey, S. M., & Boland, J. (1990). Combinatory lexical information and language comprehension. In G. T. M. Altmann (Ed.), *Cognitive models of speech processing*. Cambridge, MA: MIT Press.

Tanenhaus, M. K., Leiman, J. M., & Seidenberg, M. S. (1979). Evidence for multiple stages in the processing of ambiguous words in syntactic contexts. *Journal of Verbal Learning and Verbal Behavior, 18*, 427–440.

Townsend, D. J., & Bever, T. G. (1991). The use of higher-level constraints in monitoring for a change in speaker demonstrates functionally distinct levels of representation in discourse comprehension. *Language and Cognitive Processes, 6*(1), 49–77.

Trueswell, J. C., Tanenhaus, M. K., & Kello, C. (1992). Verb-specific constraints in sentence processing: Separating effects of lexical preference from garden-paths. *Journal of Experimental Psychology: Learning, Memory, and Cognition, 19*, 528–553.

Tyler, L. K., & Warren, P. (1987). Local and global structure in spoken language comprehension. *Journal of Memory and Language, 26*, 638–657.

Van Orden, G. C., Johnston, J. C., & Hale, B. L. (1988). Word identification in reading proceeds from spelling to sound to meaning. *Journal of Experimental Psychology: Learning, Memory, and Cognition, 14*, 371–386.

Van Petten, C., & Kutas, M. (1990). Interactions between sentence context and word frequency in event-related brain potentials. *Memory & Cognition, 18*, 380–393.

Zwitserlood, P. (1989). The locus of the effects of sentential-semantic context in spoken-word processing. *Cognition, 32*, 25–64.

CHAPTER 3

EYE MOVEMENTS IN READING
PSYCHOLINGUISTIC STUDIES

KEITH RAYNER AND SARA C. SERENO

I. INTRODUCTION

Many psycholinguists are interested in the immediate, on-line processes which occur during reading (see, e.g., Balota, Flores d'Arcais, & Rayner, 1990; Besner & Humphreys, 1991; Marslen-Wilson, 1989). In exploring normal silent reading, researchers have developed many techniques in order to make appropriate inferences about moment-to-moment language processes. These methods include (a) word-by-word reading (subjects control the rate of presentation by pressing a button), (b) rapid serial visual presentation (RSVP) of sentences (subjects are presented words at a set rate in the same spatial location), and (c) completion responses (subjects silently read a passage and then make a standard word recognition response, such as naming or lexical decision, to a subsequent target word). While these techniques have yielded interesting findings, there are problems that accompany each of them. For example, all these tasks are somewhat unnatural (i.e., readers do not usually do such things), and the reading rate that emerges from such paradigms, when compared to normal reading, is often atypical. Some of the tasks disrupt the flow of reading, while others involve a secondary task. A fourth technique involves measuring the total reading time for a larger segment of text (such as a phrase, clause, or sentence). This is simply a variation of the word-by-word reading paradigm, with the unit of presentation enlarged to include a number of words. What this paradigm gains in terms of naturalness in reading, it loses in terms of its ability to register the precise time needed for processing individual words and, hence, provides a pale reflection of moment-to-moment processes.

In this chapter, we argue that one of the best ways to study language comprehension is to record subjects' eye movements as they read. Eye-movement measurement, in comparison to other available techniques, provides a relatively natural, on-line method for investigating critical psycholinguistic issues, with certain advantages over the techniques mentioned above. Making eye movements while reading is not an artificially induced task. In addition, monitoring subjects' eye movements as they read does not perturb their normal reading rate. On the other hand, recording of eye position generally requires that the position of the head be fixed (by use of a bitebar or chin rest) as well as that of the text (usually displayed on a cathode ray tube, CRT, or video monitor). These constraints are sometimes viewed as introducing an unnatural component to the reading situation. However, we contend that subjects in eye-movement experiments read quite normally. Our introspections concur with Tinker's (1939) demonstration many years ago that reading rate and comprehension do not significantly differ when subjects read text in laboratory versus normal conditions (i.e., without fixed head or text).

We would not want to argue that the ONLY way to study reading is by examining the eye-movement record. In building a theory of language processing, it is necessary to obtain converging evidence from various sources. The tasks mentioned at the outset undoubtedly probe the nature of readers' mental representations and often yield accurate inferences about on-line processing. Among current methodologies, however, the eye-movement technique excels in revealing moment-to-moment processes in reading.

II. EYE MOVEMENTS: SOME BASIC FACTS

For every eye fixation that a reader makes, a given line of text can be divided into three regions based on the reader's visual acuity: the FOVEAL, PARAFOVEAL, and PERIPHERAL regions. The foveal region includes the central 2° of visual angle around the point of fixation (for text at a normal viewing distance, 1° of visual angle is equivalent to three or four letters). The fovea is specialized for processing detail. Beyond the fovea, acuity drops off markedly. Thus, words presented to locations further from the fovea are more difficult to identify. The parafoveal region of a line of text extends from the foveal region out to about 5° of visual angle on each side of fixation. Readers are able to acquire some useful information from this region (as discussed in more detail later). The peripheral region includes everything beyond the parafoveal region. Although readers are aware of the ends of lines and other gross aspects of the text, information in peripheral vision tends to be of little use during reading.

The general characteristics of eye movements during reading have been known for some time. Typically, readers fixate for about 200–250 ms and saccade (move their eyes) forward about eight character spaces.[1] About 10–15% of fixations are regressions (i.e., readers look back to reread material). An important fact, however, is that there is considerable variability within each of these measures both between and within subjects. A given subject may fixate for less than 100 ms to over 500 ms within the same passage and make saccades of as little as 1 character space or as much as 15 or more character spaces (such long saccades usually initiate or follow a regression). It has been documented that the variability associated with each of these measures is related to cognitive processing during reading (Rayner, 1978; Rayner & Pollatsek, 1987, 1989). For example, when text is difficult, readers tend to make longer fixations,

---

[1] In reading, the appropriate metric of how far readers move their eyes is character spaces and not visual angle (see Morrison & Rayner, 1981).

shorter saccades, and more regressions (Rayner, Sereno, Morris, Schmauder, & Clifton, 1989).

Most of the research on eye movements and language processing has focused on fixation time on a word, although researchers have also examined the frequency of regressions. The variability in saccade length can lead to a situation in which a word is skipped (i.e., it does not receive a fixation even though it is perceived and processed). There is, however, a systematic relationship between the characteristics of a word and the probability with which it is skipped. Short words (three letters or less) are much more likely to be skipped than longer words (six letters or more). Words six letters long are almost always fixated and words eight letters or longer are rarely if ever skipped (Rayner & McConkie, 1976). Carpenter and Just (1983) reported that content words were fixated 83% of the time while function words (which are much shorter) were fixated only 38% of the time. Rayner and Duffy (1988) reported that a content word (from five to nine letters long) was fixated 84% of the time while the function word *the* which preceded it was fixated only 19% of the time.

While eye-movement data are informative with respect to understanding reading, they are not perfect reflections of the mental activities associated with comprehension. There is a purely motoric component involved in fixation time (Kowler & Anton, 1987; Rayner, Slowiaczek, Clifton, & Bertera, 1983). Low-level visual and perceptual factors also influence the fixation time on a word and the saccade length to a subsequent word (O'Regan & Levy-Schoen, 1987). Any of these factors may influence the measure taken to gauge immediate comprehension processes. Nevertheless, useful information can still be obtained from the resulting data.

III. METHODOLOGICAL ISSUES

Before we move to topics more central to psycholinguistic studies, a number of issues inherent in the eye-movement methodology first need to be addressed. We discuss four issues that are relevant in using eye-movement data to investigate on-line language processes: (a) the size of the perceptual span, (b) the eye–mind span, (c) eye-movement control, and (d) eye-movement measures of processing time. Each of these is discussed in turn.

A. The Perceptual Span

The PERCEPTUAL SPAN can be defined as that portion of the text from which useful information is obtained during a single fixation in reading. Knowing the size of this region is important. For example, if the region encompasses several words, eye-movement data would not be a very good indicator of on-line processing because it could not be determined which word was being processed at any point in time. In an ideal situation, the reader would identify only the fixated word and then, on the ensuing saccade, move to the next word to identify it. Fortunately, it turns out that this is frequently the case.

The most definitive research on the size of the perceptual span has utilized the eye-contingent display change techniques introduced by McConkie and Rayner (1975) and Rayner (1975) (reviews of this research can be found in

Rayner, 1978, and Rayner & Pollatsek, 1987, 1989). Eye-contingent display changes are accomplished with the use of a highly accurate eye-tracking system that monitors a reader's eye movements. The eye-tracking system is interfaced with a computer which samples the eye position every millisecond. The computer is also interfaced to a CRT on which text is presented. Changes in the text are then made contingent on the reader's eye position. We briefly describe two eye-contingent techniques, the MOVING WINDOW and BOUNDARY paradigms. The moving window paradigm (McConkie & Rayner, 1975) allows the perceptual span to be functionally approximated. In this paradigm, an experimenter-defined region of text around the point of fixation is presented normally, while the text beyond this "window" is altered in some way (e.g., letters are replaced with Xs). With each new fixation, a new window is established—hence the term moving window. The basic premise is that reading will proceed normally (i.e., it will not be disrupted) when the window size is as large as the region from which a reader usually acquires information.

In the moving window paradigm, a display change is associated with each eye movement. In the boundary paradigm (Rayner, 1975), by contrast, only one display change occurs as the text is read. The boundary paradigm makes it possible to determine how much and what kinds of parafoveal information the reader is able to acquire from a target word before it is fixated. In this paradigm, a word or nonword letter string initially occupies the critical target location in the text. An invisible (to the subject) boundary is placed just to the left of the target location. When the reader makes an eye movement that crosses this boundary, the initially displayed stimulus (i.e., the parafoveal preview) is replaced by the target word. The parafoveal preview could be, for example, visually, phonologically, or semantically related to the succeeding target. Fixation time on the target is examined as a function of the relationship between the parafoveal preview and the target. The effect of distance from the pre-boundary fixation to the target word is also examined.

Studies using eye-contingent display paradigms have revealed that the perceptual span on a given fixation is quite limited. For readers of English, useful information is extracted from a region extending from the beginning of the currently fixated word (but no more than 3 or 4 character spaces to the left of fixation) to about 15 character spaces to the right of fixation (McConkie & Rayner, 1975, 1976; Rayner, Inhoff, Morrison, Slowiaczek, & Bertera, 1981; Rayner, Well, & Pollatsek, 1980). Information used to identify a word, however, is generally confined to a region extending no more than about five to seven character spaces to the right of fixation. The word identification span is, thus, smaller than the perceptual span, and it is more affected by word boundaries (Rayner, Well, Pollatsek, & Bertera, 1982). Functionally, this means that the reader generally identifies the currently fixated word, then fixates the next word. Nevertheless, if two short words (or even three very short words) fall within the word identification span, they may all be identified during a single fixation. When a reader fixates a content word, if a short function word follows that content word, both words can usually be identified on the same fixation.

In many cases, when the parafoveal word cannot be identified, some processing of that word occurs before it is eventually fixated. This preprocessing, however, does not reach a semantic level (Rayner, Balota, & Pollatsek, 1986; Rayner & Morris, 1992). A fair amount of research has documented a PREVIEW

EFFECT in which only the first few letters of the parafoveal word are processed (see Rayner & Pollatsek, 1987). The first few letters of a word are encoded in either an abstract letter (Rayner et al., 1982) or phonological code (Pollatsek, Lesch, Morris, & Rayner, 1992). The existence of the preview effect, on the one hand, and word-skipping, on the other, are concerns that must be addressed when interpreting the eye-movement record. Both parafoveal preview and word-skipping are natural aspects of a reader's processing activities, but neither is insurmountable. By controlling contexts across experimental conditions, for example, such problems can be minimized.

Two other aspects of the perceptual span—namely, its asymmetry and size—are relevant. The specifics of a language's orthography affect the asymmetry of the perceptual span, in terms of both the direction and the extent of the asymmetry. Whereas the span is asymmetric (larger) to the right of fixation for readers of English, it is asymmetric to the left of fixation for readers of text that is written from right to left, such as Hebrew. When native readers of Hebrew who are bilingual in English read English, however, their span is asymmetric to the right of fixation (Pollatsek, Bolozky, Well, & Rayner, 1981). The asymmetry of the perceptual span is thus determined by attentional factors related to the predominant direction of eye movements. The size of the span is affected by spatial characteristics of the orthography as well. The perceptual span is smaller for readers of Japanese and Chinese (Ikeda & Saida, 1978; Osaka, 1987), languages which are largely logographic in nature. The difficulty of the text, of course, also influences how much useful information is acquired on a fixation (Henderson & Ferreira, 1990; Inhoff, Pollatsek, Posner, & Rayner, 1989; Rayner, 1986). When the text (Rayner, 1986) or fixated word (Henderson & Ferreira, 1990; Inhoff et al., 1989) is difficult to process, little useful information to the right of fixation is acquired. Finally, the perceptual span seems to be confined to the line of text that is being read—that is, no useful information is obtained below the currently fixated line (Inhoff & Briihl, 1991; Pollatsek, Raney, LaGasse, & Rayner, 1993).

B. The Eye–Mind Span

As the name implies, the EYE–MIND SPAN refers to the linkage between the eyes (where they fixate and for how long) and the mind (what it is processing) in reading. The eye–mind span can be described as the lag between visual and cognitive processing. If the eyes lead the mind by an appreciable amount, eye-movement data would not be a particularly sensitive measure of the processing time associated with a given word because it would be unclear which word was being processed during a particular eye fixation. On the other hand, if the eye–mind span is well defined, then eye-movement data can provide a good reflection of the moment-to-moment cognitive processes associated with reading.

Just and Carpenter (1980), in their IMMEDIACY HYPOTHESIS, argued that there is effectively no eye–mind span. By this account, all processing for a given word (up to that point in the text) is accomplished before the eyes move on. While there is now clear evidence that the ease or difficulty of processing a word influences how long the reader looks at that word, the relationship is not perfect (Rayner et al., 1989). There are two problems in claiming that fixation time on a word is a pure reflection of the processes associated with comprehension of that word. The first is the parafoveal preview effect which has already been discussed—that is, some of the processing associated with a word is accomplished on the prior fixation. The second problem has to do with the SPILLOVER EFFECT. The spillover effect is exemplified in (1) and (2).

(1) *The concerned steward calmed the child.*
(2) *The concerned student calmed the child.*

These two sentences differ only in the initial noun that is used. The two nouns are matched on word length and number of syllables, but differ in how frequently they appear in print. By such a measure, *steward* is a low-frequency word and *student* is a high-frequency word. Rayner and Duffy (1986) and Inhoff and Rayner (1986) found that fixation times were 30–90 ms longer on low-frequency than on high-frequency words. They also found that fixation time on a following word (*calmed* in the example) was 30–40 ms longer when it was preceded by a low-frequency compared to a high-frequency word. This finding suggests that the reader's analysis of the low-frequency word may have spilled over onto the processing of the following word. Such spillover effects are quite pervasive and have been observed in a number of studies dealing with eye movements and language processing. Some portion of the spillover effect may be due to the lack of preview, as mentioned earlier. For example, when a word that is difficult to process is encountered, so much attention is devoted to processing that word that preview information from the next word is not acquired (Henderson & Ferreira, 1990; Inhoff et al., 1989; Rayner, 1986; Rayner et al., 1989).

When spillover effects are coupled with preview effects, questions arise about the extent to which fixation time on a word reflects the processing time for that word. Ultimately, we will need a theory that specifies what processing is completed during a fixation on a word and what processing is done when the eyes are not directly fixating the word. As a practical solution for the present, however, careful control of the context in which target words appear (e.g., identical preceding contexts) allows us to make safe conclusions based on differences observed in the eye-movement record.

C. Eye-Movement Control

Much evidence suggests that the two major components of eye movements during reading—saccade length and fixation duration—are controlled by different mechanisms. That is, the decision of where to fixate next and when to make an eye movement are largely independent of each other (Rayner & McConkie, 1976; Rayner & Pollatsek, 1981, 1987). The decision of where to look next is in large part determined by the length of words to the right of fixation (Morris, Rayner, & Pollatsek, 1990; O'Regan, 1979, 1980; Rayner, 1979; Rayner & Morris, 1992; Rayner & Pollatsek, 1987; cf. McConkie, Kerr, Reddix, & Zola, 1988). The decision of when to move the eyes to another word seems to be based on more complex processes (Rayner & Pollatsek, 1989; Sereno, 1992). However, it is clear that the ease or difficulty of understanding the fixated word does influence this decision.

Morrison (1984) proposed an elegant model of eye movement control in reading. In his model, successful access of the meaning of the fixated word

(word *n*) gives rise to an attentional shift to the next word (word *n* + 1). Eye movements follow attentional movements in a more or less time-locked fashion by means of motor programs. However, there is a lag between the time an eye movement is programmed and the time it is initiated. Because of this delay, Morrison proposed that access of the meaning of word *n* + 1 may occur before the saccade is executed. This is especially likely to happen if word *n* + 1 is a short function word. In some cases, when word *n* + 1 is accessed well before a saccade to it occurs, the saccade may be reprogrammed and word *n* + 1 will be skipped. On other occasions, the motor program for the saccade to word *n* + 1 may be so far advanced that it cannot be canceled or modified. In such a case, another saccade is programmed in parallel to word *n* + 2. The result is either a short fixation on word *n* + 1 followed by a fixation on word *n* + 2, or a fixation of normal duration at a position intermediate between the two saccade targets. Morrison's model provides mechanisms that account for a variety of phenomena observed in the eye-movement record—for example, word-skipping, very short fixations (<100 ms), and less than optimal landing sites (see Morrison, 1984, for details).

While Morrison's model accounts for a number of characteristics of eye movements in reading, it does not offer an explanation for certain other aspects. A crucial claim of the Morrison model is that a decision to move attention is dependent on lexical access of the fixated word. Thus, there should be a direct relationship between lexical access times and fixation times for words in text. The assumption that lexical access triggers an eye movement to a following word poses two problems. First, the common occurrence of refixations on words suggests that the eyes are directed to move before lexical access is complete. Second, the idea that lexical access alone orients attention, and hence eye movements, seems too simplistic to account for the likely influence of higher order processes. Although it has been shown that integration processes (e.g., conceptual combination) can spill over onto a subsequent fixation (Rayner & Duffy, 1986; Rayner et al., 1989), it is clear that these processes are reflected as well in the fixation time on the word itself (Schustack, Ehrlich, & Rayner, 1987; Rayner & Frazier, 1989; Rayner et al., 1989). Fixation time on a word is also influenced by processes involved in determining sentence structure (Clifton & Ferreira, 1989; Ferreira & Clifton, 1986; Frazier & Rayner, 1982; see also Mitchell, this volume) and integrating sentences into the discourse (O'Brien, Shank, Myers, & Rayner, 1988; Schustack et al., 1987).

Recent research has subsequently addressed many problems in Morrison's model in various ways (Henderson & Ferreira, 1990; Pollatsek & Rayner, 1990; Rayner & Balota, 1989; Rayner & Pollatsek, 1987; Sereno, 1992). It is beyond the scope of the present chapter to go into further detail about the exact mechanisms that control eye movements in reading. The prior discussion, however, does raise the following question: If eye fixations reflect integration and higher level processes as well as lexical access, is it possible to ascertain precisely what fixation times represent? Some researchers (e.g., Altmann, 1988; Altmann & Steedman, 1988) have argued that this uncertainty reduces the value of eye-movement data, given the cost and difficulty involved in using the eye-tracking methodology. In our view, it seems preferable to have the moment-to-moment record that eye-movement data provide with the opportunity to perform finer grained analyses in determining the critical variables involved in language processing. Finally, although we are not able to completely delineate the processes reflected in EVERY eye fixation, valuable data can still be obtained from the eye-movement record. In many studies, the ease or difficulty of processing can be evaluated by manipulating various properties of the text. With clear hypotheses and knowing where to look in the eye-movement record, useful conclusions can be drawn about on-line processing.

D. Measures of Processing Time

Choosing the appropriate measure of processing time to be used with eye-fixation data has been a controversial topic (see Blanchard, 1985; Inhoff, 1984; Just & Carpenter, 1980; McConkie, Hogaboam, Wolverton, Zola, & Lucas, 1979; Rayner & Pollatsek, 1987). The issues of concern differ depending on whether the unit of analysis is a single word or a larger region of text, and we consider each in turn.

1. Measures for Words

If readers made only one fixation on each and every word, there would be little to discuss. Sometimes words are fixated more than once, however, and sometimes they are skipped. The matter of multiple fixations on a word (before moving to another word) has received widely different treatments in terms of data analysis. For example, some researchers only use data in which a single fixation is made on the target word. This approach avoids possible problems associated with multiple fixations on a word. The disadvantage of the approach is that some target words in an experiment may receive multiple fixations. Using only single-fixation instances typically means that much data have been discarded. The fact that the reader needs to refixate a word undoubtedly contains important information about the processing associated with that word.

A second way of dealing with the issue of multiple fixations on a word is to use the FIRST FIXATION DURATION on a word (i.e., the only fixation, or the first of multiple fixations) as a measure of lexical access. The assumption here is that additional fixations reflect higher order processing or are noise (Inhoff, 1984). Some other researchers make an opposite assumption, arguing that the second fixation is more diagnostic of lexical access (O'Regan, 1990; O'Regan & Levy-Schoen, 1987; Vitu, O'Regan, & Mittau, 1990). By this account, when the eyes initially land in a "bad" position, a second fixation is made to a more informative position in the word. However, Sereno (1992) demonstrated that significant word frequency effects (indicating that lexical access has been achieved) are present in the first fixations of words receiving more than one fixation (see also Inhoff & Rayner, 1986). Thus, while multiple fixations on a word may be due in part to low-level visual acuity factors, their occurrence can also reflect the processing difficulty associated with the word (Rayner & Pollatsek, 1987).

Another solution to the problem of multiple fixations on a word is to use the GAZE DURATION measure. Gaze duration represents the sum of consecutive fixations on a word before making a saccade to another word. If only one fixation is made on a word, then the first fixation and gaze duration measures are equivalent. Some researchers favor gaze duration as the best measure of processing time (Just & Carpenter, 1980), while others view it with skepticism

(Hogaboam & McConkie, 1981; Kliegl, Olson, & Davidson, 1982). The distinction between first fixation and gaze duration has been discussed elsewhere in more detail (see Rayner & Pollatsek, 1987). We believe that first fixation and gaze duration reflect related processes. When readers encounter difficulty processing a word, they either maintain their initial fixation or make a second fixation on the word. Low-frequency words, for example, are more likely to be refixated than high-frequency words (Inhoff & Rayner, 1986). If a word is particularly difficult (e.g., a very long word), readers may make three or four fixations on the word. In most of the data that we are familiar with, comparable results have been obtained for first fixation and gaze duration measures. The word frequency effect discussed above (e.g., Rayner & Duffy, 1986) is one such example—first fixation duration was 37 ms longer and gaze duration 87 ms longer on low-frequency words than on high-frequency words. Both effects were highly significant and supported the same conclusion, namely, that low-frequency words are more difficult to process in text than high-frequency words.

We will not discuss word skipping in detail here (see Rayner & Pollatsek, 1987). However, an important question arises in determining the appropriate measure of processing time for a word that is skipped. Words that are skipped are usually identified on the prior fixation (i.e., the fixation to the left of the word that is skipped), resulting in a longer duration on this fixation (Hogaboam, 1983; Pollatsek, Rayner, & Balota, 1986). Simply omitting skipped words in the data analysis (Blanchard, 1985; Carpenter & Just, 1983) or assigning a zero value to them (Just & Carpenter, 1980) lessens the probability of attaining an accurate assessment of processing time. One solution is to report measures of first fixation and gaze duration conditioned on there being a fixation on the word along with the probability that the word is fixated. We have also adopted an alternative scoring procedure for words that are skipped. If there is a fixation in the region to the left of the target word (within three character spaces), this fixation is coded as the fixation time for the target word.

A final measure of processing time that is sometimes used is the TOTAL FIXATION TIME on a target word. This measure is the sum of the gaze duration on the word and the fixation time resulting from any regressions made to that word. Thus, total time includes the time for reanalysis when the word was not completely processed on an initial encounter.

Our general conclusion is that as much information as possible should be examined in inferring cognitive activities associated with word processing. Recording first fixation duration, gaze duration, the probability of fixating a word, and the frequency of regressions to a word provides vital information about how words in context are processed. Clearly, the ease or difficulty in understanding a particular word influences all these measures.

2. Measures for Regions

When the unit of analysis is larger than a single word, it is also important to examine multiple measures obtained from the eye-movement record. Typically, researchers divide a sentence into different target regions and examine processing times for each region. The measures often adopted include (a) first pass reading time, (b) second pass reading time, (c) total reading time, and (d) the probability of a regression into a region (see Frazier & Rayner, 1982).

FIRST PASS READING TIME is obtained by summing all fixations that occur within a region before a saccade out of that region is made. SECOND PASS READING TIME includes any time spent rereading a region. TOTAL READING TIME for a region, as its name suggests, is the sum of first and second pass reading times. Since various experimental manipulations may result in regions that differ in terms of absolute number of words (or contain words that differ in word length), the reading time for a region is often divided by the number of character spaces in the region to yield a READING TIME PER CHARACTER measure. While the reading time per character measure smooths out differences due to the number of words in a region, there are potential problems associated with it. One obvious problem is the assumption that reading time increases linearly as a function of the number of letters in a region. This measure also ignores possible confounds arising from differences in the number of words, word lengths, and word frequencies.

In our laboratory, we have written computer programs that score the data in all the ways that have been discussed here both when the unit of analysis is a region and when it is a word. Our strategy is to examine all the measures to provide a consistent picture of what is happening as sentences are read.

Having considered some of the critical methodological issues in using eye movements, we now turn to research that has been conducted to investigate language processing. In our review, we focus primarily (but not exclusively) on studies from our laboratory. We discuss evidence showing that eye fixations reveal a great deal of information about (a) word processing, (b) syntactic processing (how words are assigned to appropriate constituent units), and (c) discourse processing (how text information is integrated during comprehension).

IV. WORD PROCESSING

Recent eye-movement studies have examined a number of variables which can influence lexical access for a given word. In this section we examine how the lexical properties of a word are reflected in the fixation time on that word (see Balota & Rayner, 1991, for a detailed discussion of parafoveally vs. foveally acquired information). We have classified these variables on three different levels: (a) intraword variables (e.g., word-initial letter information); (b) word variables (e.g., word frequency and length, semantic complexity, and ambiguity); and (c) extraword variables (e.g., constraints provided by the sentence or discourse in which the word occurs).

A. Intraword Variables

Many studies have indicated that the initial letters of a word play an important role in word recognition. For example, Lima and Pollatsek (1983) demonstrated (with words in isolation) that there was more interference in recognizing a word when the presentation of the beginning segment of the word was delayed compared to when the final segment was delayed. As we noted earlier, in reading there is a preview benefit obtained from the first few letters of the word to the right of fixation (Blanchard, Pollatsek, & Rayner, 1989; Rayner et al.,

1982). In a reading study, Lima and Inhoff (1985) varied word-initial bigram and trigram frequency of target words while equating overall word frequency. For example, *dwarf* and *clown* have the same word frequency, but very few words begin with *dwa-* (a low-frequency trigram) whereas many words begin with *clo-* (a high-frequency trigram). Lima and Inhoff (1985) found that readers spent less time on words that began with more familiar letters, although such words provided no differential parafoveal preview benefits.

Other studies have investigated whether word-initial morphological information has a special status in word identification processes (see, e.g., Taft, 1985). In a study by Lima (1987), subjects read sentences that contained words, matched in word length and frequency, that were either prefixed (e.g., *remind*) or pseudoprefixed (e.g., *relish*). As in the Lima and Inhoff (1985) study, there was no parafoveal preview benefit for prefixed as compared to pseudoprefixed words, but prefixed words were (foveally) fixated for less time than pseudoprefixed words. A study by Inhoff (1989) also examined word-initial morphological information. Subjects read sentences that contained either a six-letter compound, pseudocompound, or control word (e.g., *cowboy, carpet,* and *mirror,* respectively). Although the words were matched in overall word frequency, the subword constituents of the pseudocompound words (*car, pet*) were significantly higher in frequency than those of the compound words (*cow, boy*). Inhoff (1989) found that the pseudocompound words were fixated for less time than the compound words. Thus, while both Lima (1987) and Inhoff (1989) found a standard preview benefit overall (i.e., shorter fixations on a target word when parafoveal information was available), they found differential morphological effects only during foveal processing.

B. Word Variables

There are a number of dimensions that measure a word's complexity. As previously indicated, the frequency of a word influences the fixation time on that word (Inhoff, 1984; Inhoff & Rayner, 1986; Just & Carpenter, 1980; Kliegl et al., 1982; Rayner, 1977; Rayner & Duffy, 1986; Rayner et al., 1989; Sereno, 1992). Although the early demonstrations of this finding tended to confound word length with word frequency (low-frequency words are, on average, longer words, and longer words receive more fixations), more recent studies have controlled for word length as well as the number of syllables. It is also possible that sublexical processes are involved with the word frequency effect, but Rayner and Duffy (1986) controlled for bigram and trigram frequency and still obtained significant frequency effects.

Rayner and Duffy (1986) also varied the semantic complexity of verbs. Readers spent no more time on verbs that were causative (e.g., *kill*), factive (e.g., *regret*) or negative (e.g., *doubt*) compared to control verbs (see also Inhoff, 1985). More recently, Schmauder (1991) failed to find differences in fixation times between verbs that have many possible argument structure frames (e.g., *detect*) and verbs that have few (e.g., *cherish*). Although there do not appear to be any salient differences due to semantic complexity across different types of verbs in the eye-movement record, there is evidence that verbs as a class, when compared to nouns, for example, are more difficult to process, and this is reflected in fixation times (Rayner, 1977).

Ambiguity is another source of complexity associated with a word. Some words belong to more than one syntactic category (e.g., *pardon* can be a noun or a verb). It seems that readers delay category assignment of such words until disambiguating information is obtained (Frazier & Rayner, 1987). Other words may have more than one meaning (e.g., *boxer* can be a fighter or a type of dog). Such words are read more slowly than unambiguous words under circumstances in which the two meanings are equally available and there is no prior disambiguating context. The question of most interest about semantically ambiguous words, however, is whether context guides access of the appropriate meaning (selective access) or whether all meanings are automatically accessed and context only affects later post-access selection processes (multiple access). This topic is discussed in the next section.

C. Extraword Variables

The degree of constraint imposed by a discourse context on a subsequent target can influence the fixation time on that target. A number of studies have shown that fixation times are significantly shorter on targets that are predictable from the preceding context (Balota, Pollatsek, & Rayner, 1985; S. F. Ehrlich & Rayner, 1981; Inhoff, 1984; Schustack et al., 1987) or are semantically related to words occurring earlier in the text (Carroll & Slowiaczek, 1986; Duffy & Rayner, 1990; Morris, in press; Schustack et al., 1987; Zola, 1984).

A recent study by Sereno and Rayner (1992) introduced a new paradigm to investigate word processing and priming effects during reading. We refer to it as FAST PRIMING. It utilizes the boundary paradigm described earlier. When the eyes are to the left of the boundary, a random letter string occupies the target location (to neutralize parafoveal preview). When the eyes cross the boundary, a prime word is first briefly presented (timed from the onset of the fixation, not when the boundary is crossed) and then replaced by the target word (which remains on the CRT until the subject finishes the text). When the prime was presented for 30 ms, Sereno and Rayner (1992) found that fixation times were significantly faster for targets preceded by semantically related primes compared to targets preceded by unrelated primes. We are presently conducting experiments using fast priming to examine the automatic activation of phonological codes (cf. Pollatsek et al., 1992) and the processing of lexically ambiguous words.

Researchers have used lexical ambiguity resolution as a tool in understanding how words in general are integrated into a discourse context. A number of studies have been conducted in our laboratory investigating the processing of lexically ambiguous words during reading in an attempt to tease apart lexical effects from postlexical contextual effects (Dopkins, Morris, & Rayner, 1992; Duffy, Morris, & Rayner, 1988; Frazier & Rayner, 1988; Rayner & Duffy, 1986; Sereno, Pacht, & Rayner, 1992). The results of these studies indicate that fixation times on ambiguous words are influenced by three factors. The first is the type of context in which the word appears—disambiguating information can either precede the ambiguous word (biasing context) or follow it (neutral context). The second factor is the meaning that the context instantiates—context can support the more frequent (dominant) meaning or the less frequent (subordinate) meaning. The third factor is the type of ambiguous word—the word can have two equally likely meanings (balanced ambiguous word) or it can have one highly dominant meaning and one or more subordinate meanings (biased ambiguous word). To account for the results from eye-movement ambiguity experiments, two different models, namely the reordered access model (Duffy et al., 1988) and the integration model (Rayner & Frazier, 1989), have been proposed. It is beyond the scope of the present chapter to discuss these or other models of lexical ambiguity resolution (see Sereno et al., 1992, for a review; see also Simpson, this volume). The important point for the current discussion is that research on lexical ambiguity provides further evidence that the fixation time on a word varies in a meaningful way as a function of the characteristics of that word and its relation to the context.

The research described above clearly indicates that time spent on a word is a sensitive measure of processing difficulty. The question remains, however, whether fixation times primarily reflect lexical access processes, postlexical integration processes, or both. It could be the case, for example, that high-frequency words and predictable words are fixated for less time because lexical access is easier for high-frequency words and context facilitates access to related concepts. Alternatively, high-frequency and predictable words may be easier to integrate into the current discourse representation. Recent findings (Rayner et al., 1989; Schustack et al., 1987) suggest a difficult path to the resolution of the question—fixation time on a word reflects both lexical access and integration processes.

V. Syntactic Processing

A great deal of empirical evidence suggests that readers perform an on-line structural analysis of text, constructing a grammatical representation of sentences as they read. Eye-movement research, both in our laboratory (Britt, Perfetti, Garrod, & Rayner, 1992; Clifton, 1992, 1993; Clifton, Speer, & Abney, 1991; Ferreira & Clifton, 1986; Ferreira & Henderson, 1990; Frazier & Rayner, 1982, 1987, 1988; Rayner, Carlson, & Frazier, 1983; Rayner & Frazier, 1987; Rayner, Garrod, & Perfetti, 1992) and in other laboratories (Altmann, Garnham, & Dennis, 1992; Holmes, Kennedy, & Murray, 1987; Holmes & O'Regan, 1981; Kennedy & Murray, 1984; Kennedy, Murray, Jennings, & Reid, 1989; Mehler, Bever, & Carey, 1967; Tanenhaus, Carlson, & Trueswell, 1989; Trueswell, Tanenhaus, & Kello, 1993), has led to precise insights into the initial stages of sentence comprehension. Three issues that have emerged from this research are (a) the nature of the principles underlying structural analysis, (b) the proper measure of syntactic complexity, and (c) the parameters of semantic or pragmatic information in initial syntactic analysis. We deal with each of these with regard to the eye-movement record.

A. Parsing Principles

Various strategies have been proposed to describe how a reader determines the proper structural analysis of a sentence. We focus on principles that have been developed and tested by Frazier and her colleagues. Frazier (1987) argued the reader builds an initial (unique) analysis of a sentence on the basis of syntactic knowledge (e.g., phrase structure rules). In this way, the words of a sentence are assigned to phrasal constituents whose organization is determined—a process called PARSING. Because a text sometimes contains temporary syntactic ambiguities and because only a single analysis is initially constructed, there are occasions in which information encountered at a later point requires the reader to revise her/his initial analysis. In such cases, the reader is said to have been "led down the garden path." The model of parsing put forward by Frazier and colleagues has thus come to be known as the garden path theory.

Two psychologically motivated principles of the garden path theory which have received the most experimental attention are MINIMAL ATTACHMENT and LATE CLOSURE (Frazier, 1979; Frazier & Rayner, 1982):

1. *Minimal Attachment:* Attach each incoming lexical item into the existing structure, adding the smallest possible number of new nodes (in a syntactic tree).
2. *Late Closure:* Attach incoming lexical items, when grammatically permissible, into the phrase currently being processed.

These principles guide the reader in making initial attachment decisions. Both assume that grammatical information about a word, including its part of speech and the phrase structure rules associated with that part of speech, are needed to incorporate the word into the unfolding sentence structure. There is some disagreement among researchers, however, as to whether other sources of grammatical information (e.g., subcategorization, argument structure, thematic role, or animacy information) can constrain parsing decisions (cf. Clifton, 1992; Clifton et al., 1991; Mitchell, 1987; Tanenhaus et al., 1989; see also Mitchell, this volume). That is, information associated with a particular lexical item (e.g., whether a verb is transitive or not) may or may not affect the initial parse.

Because minimal attachment and late closure are general principles, they can be applied to a variety of syntactic constructions. They also make clear predictions in terms of when reading will be disrupted. Early evidence that eye-movement measures were sensitive to garden path effects was provided by Frazier and Rayner (1982) and Rayner, Carlson, and Frazier (1983). Consider sentences (3)–(4).

(3) *We knew John well.*
(4) *We knew John left.*

Both sentences begin with the string *We knew John*. Minimal attachment entails an initial analysis of the noun *John* as object of the verb *knew*. This is consistent with the continuation *well* in (3) but inconsistent with the continuation *left* in (4).[2] In (4), *John* is subject of the complement clause rather than object of the main verb. When *left* is read, the initial analysis has to be revised at some cost in processing, if the reader has been garden-pathed. Such a disruption is evident in the eye-movement record—the initial fixation on *left* (the critical word indicating that the preferred analysis may be wrong) is significantly longer than that on *well* even though these words are matched for word length and frequency (Frazier & Rayner, 1982).

Other baselines of comparison have been used. For example, the first fixation on a disambiguating word in a temporarily ambiguous sentence can be compared to the first fixation on that same word in a sentence made unambiguous by the insertion of the complementizer *that,* as in (5).

(5) *The clairvoyant predicted (that) the effects of the earthquake would be quite minimal.*

Rayner and Frazier (1987; see also Ferreira & Henderson, 1990) found longer initial fixations on *would* when it was temporarily ambiguous (no *that*) compared to when it was disambiguated (*that* included).

Eye-movement measures other than the first fixation in a region also provide evidence in support of claims that parsing is disrupted with certain syntactic constructions. Frequent regressions from the disambiguating region, or lengthened reading times in the disambiguating region (e.g., first or second pass reading times), can indicate disruption. Such measures, however, are not maximally diagnostic in pinpointing when and where a misanalysis is noted. Differences across conditions may reflect not only the initial garden path, but also differences between initial and revised syntactic analyses or the plausibility of alternative competing analyses.

B. Syntactic Complexity

From the above discussion, it is clear that eye-movement research can help to evaluate theories of how the reader identifies and resolves temporary syntactic ambiguities. A major issue that has recently received attention in eye-movement studies of parsing concerns the effect of syntactic complexity in its own right, in the absence of any ambiguity.

Holmes et al. (1987) and Kennedy et al. (1989) have claimed that differences attributed to garden-pathing and reanalysis are actually due to discrepancies in complexity among syntactic forms. They argued that a sentence complement, as in (4), for example, is more complex than a noun phrase (NP) object, as in (3), and therefore more difficult to process even when a complementizer is present. There is much evidence, however, indicating that sentence complements are easier to process when the complementizer is present than when it

---

[2] The tree structures for minimal (3) and nonminimal (4) attachment sentences are diagrammed as follows.

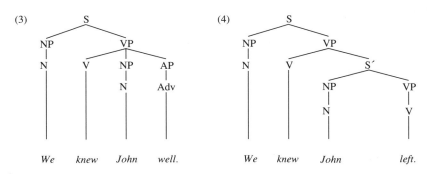

Minimal attachment posits that (3) is structurally preferred to (4) because fewer nodes are necessary to attach *John* into the tree.

is not (Ferreira & Henderson, 1990; Mitchell & Holmes, 1985; Rayner & Frazier, 1987). In addition, Rayner and Frazier (1987) found that sentences containing unambiguous complements, as in (6), were no more difficult to process than those with direct object NPs, as in (7).

(6) *The drug dealer discovered that an undercover FBI agent was living next door.*

(7) *The drug dealer discovered an undercover FBI agent in the house next door.*

This last finding, however, should be taken cautiously because reading times on different words were compared. While it is not definitive evidence against the claim that structural complexity per se contributes to processing difficulty, neither does it support the claim that such structural complexity is responsible for the processing difficulty of sentence complement sentences.[3]

C. The Role of Semantic Information in Parsing

Over the last decade, eye-movement studies have taken center stage in a debate concerning the extent to which semantic and pragmatic information influence initial parsing decisions (i.e., on-going syntactic construction). Inferences about such decisions are made on the basis of differences in fixation times in carefully controlled experiments. Rayner, Carlson, and Frazier (1983) presented sentences containing temporary syntactic ambiguities. They reported that although pragmatic information biasing the structurally less preferred (i.e., nonminimal attachment) reading was present, this did not influence initial parsing decisions but only the ease of reanalysis. In other words, the pragmatic information that was available did not prevent the garden path. Ferreira and Clifton (1986), likewise, found that initial parsing decisions for nonminimal attachment sentences were not influenced by preceding biasing semantic contexts.

More recently, these studies have been challenged (see, e.g., Altmann & Steedman, 1988; Tanenhaus et al., 1989; Trueswell, 1993; Taraban & McClelland, 1988). Taraban and McClelland (1988) constructed materials semantically biased toward the nonminimal attachment interpretation and, in fact, found faster reading times for nonminimal, as in (8), than for minimal, as in (9), attachment sentences.

(8) *The thieves stole all the paintings in the museum while the guard slept.*

(9) *The thieves stole all the paintings in the night while the guard slept.*

However, it is possible that the self-paced reading technique they used may not have had the temporal resolution to detect an early minimal attachment advantage. Altmann and others (Altmann, 1988; Altmann & Steedman, 1988; Altmann et al., 1992; Crain & Steedman, 1985) have claimed that parsing diffi-

---

[3] It is unclear how to reconcile the Holmes et al. (1987) and the Kennedy et al. (1989) results (that the presence of overt complementizers did not facilitate the processing of sentences with complement clauses) with those of Rayner and Frazier (1987) and Ferreira and Henderson (1990). Most of the Holmes–Kennedy data come from self-paced reading tasks, which can distort the reading process, as we have argued (see also Clifton & Ferreira, 1989). However, some of their data come from eye-movement monitoring. Thus, methodological factors apparently do not account for the differences between their studies and ours.

culty (measured in terms of reading time) attributed to nonminimal attachment is actually due to presuppositional complexity (i.e., the number of propositions which must be added to a text to satisfy its semantic requirements). They claim that minimal versus nonminimal attachment sentences should be compared only when they are preceded by contexts that are referentially supportive. Early studies provided some evidence that presenting sentences in a supportive or biasing context could override a minimal attachment advantage, but these studies used self-paced reading and off-line techniques. The results of eye-movement studies using these preconditions have been mixed. Some studies have not found contextual override effects on initial parsing decisions (Ferreira & Clifton, 1986; Rayner et al., 1992), while others have (Altmann et al., 1992; Britt et al., 1992). It appears that research on this issue needs to be focused on establishing the conditions under which context does and does not exert an early effect on parsing.[4]

VI. Discourse Processing

In understanding text, a reader must not only be able to integrate information within sentences but must also make connections across sentences to form a coherent discourse representation. To what extent can eye-movement data reflect higher order comprehension processes in reading? The basic issue here is whether effects associated with these processes can be localized to specific eye fixations. In this section, we focus on experiments from our laboratory that deal with three different aspects of comprehension processes: (a) sentence and clause wrap-up, (b) antecedent search, and (c) elaborative inference. In each case, fixation time on a target word is examined as a function of a higher order manipulation occurring in the text. Our goal is to determine how readers integrate the current word with information obtained earlier in the text.

A. Sentence and Clause Wrap-Up

Just and Carpenter (1980) reported that fixation times on words that occurred at the end of a sentence were unusually long. They compared fixation times on words which ended a sentence, however, to fixation times on different words that were not sentence-final. Rayner et al. (1989) reported a study in which subjects read passages containing a target word that occurred either at the end of a sentence or at the end of a clause. Gaze duration on the target word was longer when it was sentence-final than when it was clause-final. Although this result replicated Just and Carpenter's (1980) finding, the magnitude of the effect was not nearly so large. In a second experiment reported by Rayner et al. (1989), subjects read sentences in which the target word either ended a clause

---

[4] Altmann et al. (1992) recently argued that different conclusions about a set of data can be reached depending on whether or not a REGRESSION-CONTINGENT ANALYSIS is used. They argued that when trials on which regressions occurred were eliminated from an analysis, there was evidence favoring contextual override. However, we (Rayner & Sereno, in press) found that when regressions were eliminated from the data set of Rayner et al. (1992), the garden path effect was even stronger. Thus, we are skeptical about the generalizability and usefulness of regression-contingent analyses.

or did not. Fixation times were longer on the target word when it was clause-final than when it was not.

The Just and Carpenter (1980) and Rayner et al. (1989) experiments suggest that readers attempt to integrate information from within a clause or sentence and that these additional processing demands are reflected in longer fixations occurring at the end of the clause or sentence. In order to successfully comprehend a discourse, however, readers must also integrate current information with prior information on an on-going basis. In the next two sections, we discuss several studies that investigate where and when such connections are made.

B. Antecedent Search

The process of establishing a connection between an anaphoric element and its antecedent in a text has been termed ANTECEDENT SEARCH. Pronominal reference and noun-to-noun reference are two such instances in which the correct linkage between discourse elements is required for text comprehension.

In the case of pronominal reference, when a pronoun like *she* is encountered in the course of reading a passage, the reader must identify an antecedent that matches in gender and number. Sometimes this process is trivially easy and no disruption is observed in the eye-movement record (Blanchard, 1987). Clifton and Ferreira (1987) presented self-paced reading data suggesting that the process becomes substantially more difficult when the antecedent is not the sentence topic or, perhaps more accurately, not an argument of the main clause of the previous sentence (cf. also Graesser, 1981; Sanford & Garrod, 1981). In an eye-movement study, K. Ehrlich and Rayner (1983) varied the distance (e.g., near, far) between a pronoun and its prior antecedent. In the far condition, a new topic was introduced between antecedent and pronoun. They compared the duration of fixations in the vicinity of the pronoun across distance conditions. They found that fixation durations were longer in the far compared to the near condition but, interestingly, reading times did not diverge until at least one fixation after the pronoun. K. Ehrlich and Rayner (1983) concluded that antecedent search is initiated while the reader is fixating the pronoun, but may not be completed until one or two fixations following the pronoun when the antecedent is difficult to recall.

Just as a pronoun requires an antecedent, a definite NP that does not directly refer to something outside the text requires a coreferring antecedent in the text. For example, if a reader encounters the NP *the bird* which is not identifiable from the extralinguistic context (as the NP *the sky* would be), a search for an appropriate antecedent is initiated. Pronouns carry little semantic information beyond gender and number and therefore, under some conditions, require an extensive antecedent search extending over several fixations. In contrast, nouns typically have more semantic content, which presumably facilitates the search for an antecedent. Duffy and Rayner (1990) presented passages containing anaphoric NPs to investigate antecedent search. They indeed found evidence that, with anaphoric NPs, antecedent search time was primarily localized on the target noun (i.e., there were no major spillover effects) (see also Garrod & Sanford, this volume).

C. Elaborative Inference

Within a discourse representation, the simplest kind of connection is one in which one word gains its reference through another word in the text. However, information that has not been explicitly stated up to a given point in the text may also be inferred by the reader. This is called ELABORATIVE INFERENCE. Current models of discourse comprehension assume that a reader activates relevant world knowledge in order to comprehend text (see, e.g., Glenberg, Kruley, & Langston, this volume; Kintsch, this volume; and Singer, this volume). Thus, the resulting text representation incorporates what the reader infers or "fills in" (implicit knowledge) as well as what is actually found in the text (explicit knowledge). Evidence for on-line elaborative inferences is relatively scarce, since much of the data used to demonstrate such processes is open to an alternative explanation—that an inference is made only when it is probed for. If on-line inferences are critical in text comprehension, it is important to demonstrate their existence empirically.

Results from recent eye-movement experiments have confirmed the notion that elaborative inferences do occur on-line. These data have also served to differentiate between conditions in which the reader makes an inference and those in which the reader waits for more explicit information. In a study by O'Brien et al. (1988), fixation time was examined on a target word (e.g., *knife*) in the final sentence of a passage (10).

(10) *He threw the knife into the bushes, took her money, and ran away.*

The target word was previously either explicitly mentioned in the text (e.g., by the phrase *stabbed her with his **knife***) or only strongly suggested (e.g., by the phrase ***stabbed** her with his weapon*). O'Brien et al. (1988) found no difference in gaze duration on the target word across these conditions. It thus appears that the concept 'knife' had been inferred from the prior context. In contrast, when the text did not strongly suggest the concept 'knife' (e.g., by the phrase ***assaulted** her with his weapon*), gaze duration on *knife* in the final sentence was longer compared to conditions when *knife* was explicitly mentioned or strongly suggested earlier in the passage. This finding suggests that the longer gaze duration on *knife* was due to a memory search for its antecedent. The finding also indicates that the process of searching for the antecedent begins immediately.

Although the O'Brien et al. (1988) study provides evidence for on-line elaborative inferences, other studies they reported clearly demonstrate that such inferences occur under rather restricted circumstances. They found evidence for elaborative inferences only when the context was sufficiently constraining or when there was a "demand sentence" (which invited the reader to make the inference) just prior to the final sentence which contained the target word. A subsequent study by Garrod, O'Brien, Morris, and Rayner (1990) further constrained the conditions under which elaborative inferences are thought to occur. Garrod et al. (1990) found evidence for elaborative inferences only when there was an anaphoric relationship between two nouns (e.g., . . . *she saw a cute red-breasted bird . . . She hoped **the** robin would . . .* ; compared to . . . *she saw a cute red-breasted bird . . . She hoped **a** robin would . . .*).

They found that gaze duration on the target word (*robin*) was equivalent in explicit (*robin . . . robin*) and implicit (*bird . . . robin*) conditions when there was an anaphoric relationship, but longer in the implicit condition than explicit condition when there was not.

The research we have described dealing with clause and sentence wrap-up, antecedent search, and elaborative inference shows quite clearly that fixation times on a target word can be influenced by higher order processes. In all three cases, variations in fixation time on the target word could only be due (given the control conditions provided in the experiments) to readers using information obtained earlier in the text to process the target word.

VII. SUMMARY

The studies we have reviewed here reinforce our belief that eye-movement data provide an excellent means to study word, sentence, and discourse processing in reading. The primary characteristic of most of the work reviewed is that specific locations in the text are identified in advance where processing can be experimentally manipulated. This research has demonstrated that cognitive activity is reflected in the pattern of eye movements, in particular, fixation times. The advantage of this method is that data can be collected on-line as subjects read text. It is not necessary to draw inferences about comprehension processes from end-of-sentence tasks or global measures such as total reading time (where one is unable to pinpoint critical areas of the sentence that actually lead to changes in reading time). Subjects can read at their own pace, secondary tasks need not be employed, and the experimental situation is relatively normal.

This is not to say that eye movements are a perfect reflection of cognitive processes in reading. There are many serious problems that need to be addressed, and we have touched on some of them here (see also Rayner & Pollatsek, 1987). In addition, there are some inconsistent results in the literature. Some of the inconsistency is perhaps due to characteristics of the particular studies and methods of data scoring and analysis. Undoubtedly, some processes at the syntactic, semantic, or discourse level are not confined to single fixations in the eye-movement record, but instead extend across a number of fixations. We have had the experience of devising seemingly appropriate materials to probe a certain type of comprehension process only to find no obvious or immediate effect in eye-fixation times. In such cases, though, overall reading times often reflect processing complexity.

We believe that a paramount goal of research using eye movements to study comprehension ought to be the delineation of conditions under which individual fixation times do and do not reflect such processing. When processing difficulty is not readily apparent in individual fixations, we need theories which make strong predictions about where and when it can be made to appear in order to allow an interpretation, using measures with a resolution finer than global reading time. Recent eye-movement research on comprehension processes has been very informative, and we suspect that answers to many questions about on-line language processing will yet be unveiled by examining in greater detail the spatial and temporal record left by the eyes during reading.

Acknowledgments

Preparation of this chapter was supported by Grant DBS-9121375 from the National Science Foundation and by Grant HD17246 from the National Institute of Child Health and Human Development. We would like to thank Chuck Clifton and Morti Gernsbacher for their helpful comments on an earlier draft of this chapter.

References

Altmann, G. T. M. (1988). Ambiguity, parsing strategies, and computational models. *Language and Cognitive Processes, 3,* 73–97.

Altmann, G. T. M., & Steedman, M. (1988). Interaction with context during human sentence processing. *Cognition, 30,* 191–238.

Altmann, G. T. M., Garnham, A., & Dennis, Y. (1992). Avoiding the garden path: Eye movements in context. *Journal of Memory and Language, 31,* 685–712.

Balota, D. A., Flores d'Arcais, G. B., & Rayner, K. (Eds.). (1990). *Comprehension processes in reading.* Hillsdale, NJ: Erlbaum.

Balota, D. A., Pollatsek, A., & Rayner, K. (1985). The interaction of contextual constraints and parafoveal visual information. *Cognitive Psychology, 17,* 364–390.

Balota, D. A., & Rayner, K. (1991). Word recognition processes in foveal and parafoveal vision: The range of influence of lexical variables. In D. Besner & G. W. Humphreys (Eds.), *Basic processes in reading: Visual word recognition* (pp. 198–232). Hillsdale, NJ: Erlbaum.

Besner, D., & Humphreys, G. W. (Eds.). (1991). *Basic processes in reading: Visual word recognition.* Hillsdale, NJ: Erlbaum.

Blanchard, H. E. (1985). A comparison of some processing time measures based on eye movements. *Acta Psychologica, 58,* 1–15.

Blanchard, H. E. (1987). Pronoun processing during fixations: Effects of the time course of information utilization. *Bulletin of the Psychonomic Society, 25,* 171–174.

Blanchard, H. E., Pollatsek, A., & Rayner, K. (1989). The acquisition of parafoveal word information in reading. *Perception & Psychophysics, 46,* 85–94.

Britt, M. A., Perfetti, C. A., Garrod, S., & Rayner, K. (1992). Parsing in discourse: Context effects and their limits. *Journal of Memory and Language, 31,* 293–314.

Carpenter, P. A., & Just, M. A. (1983). What your eyes do while your mind is reading. In K. Rayner (Ed.), *Eye movements in reading: Perceptual and language processes* (pp. 275–307). New York: Academic Press.

Carroll, P., & Slowiaczek, M. L. (1986). Constraints on semantic priming in reading: A fixation time analysis. *Memory & Cognition, 14,* 509–522.

Clifton, C., Jr. (1992). Tracing the course of sentence comprehension: How lexical information is used. In K. Rayner (Ed.), *Eye movements and visual cognition: Scene perception and reading* (pp. 397–414). New York: Springer-Verlag.

Clifton, C., Jr. (1993). The role of thematic roles in sentence parsing. *Canadian Journal of Experimental Psychology, 47,* 222–246.

Clifton, C., Jr., & Ferreira, F. (1987). Discourse structure and anaphora: Some experimental results. In M. Coltheart (Ed.), *Attention and performance XII: The psychology of reading* (pp. 635–654). London: Erlbaum.

Clifton, C., Jr., & Ferreira, F. (1989). Ambiguity in context. *Language and Cognitive Processes, 4,* SI77–SI103.

Clifton, C., Jr., Speer, S., & Abney, S. (1991). Parsing arguments: Phrase structure and argument structure as determinants of initial parsing decisions. *Journal of Memory and Language, 30,* 251–271.

Crain S., & Steedman, M. (1985). On not being led up the garden path: The use of context by the psychological syntax processor. In D. R. Dowty, L. Karttunen, & A. M. Zwicky (Eds.), *Natural language parsing: Psychological, computational, and theoretical perspectives* (pp. 320–358). Cambridge: Cambridge University Press.

Dopkins, S., Morris, R. K., & Rayner, K. (1992). Lexical ambiguity and eye fixations in reading:

A test of competing models of lexical ambiguity resolution. *Journal of Memory and Language, 31*, 461–476.

Duffy, S. A., Morris, R. K., & Rayner, K. (1988). Lexical ambiguity and fixation times in reading. *Journal of Memory and Language, 27*, 429–446.

Duffy, S. A., & Rayner, K. (1990). Eye movements and anaphor resolution: Effects of antecedent typicality and distance. *Language and Speech, 33*, 103–119.

Ehrlich, K., & Rayner, K. (1983). Pronoun assignment and semantic integration during reading: Eye movements and immediacy of processing. *Journal of Verbal Learning and Verbal Behavior, 22*, 75–87.

Ehrlich, S. F., & Rayner, K. (1981). Contextual effects on word perception and eye movements during reading. *Journal of Verbal Learning and Verbal Behavior, 20*, 641–655.

Ferreira, F., & Clifton, C., Jr. (1986). The independence of syntactic processing. *Journal of Memory and Language, 25*, 348–368.

Ferreira, F., & Henderson, J. M. (1990). The use of verb information in syntactic parsing: Evidence from eye movements and word-by-word self-paced reading. *Journal of Experimental Psychology: Learning, Memory, and Cognition, 16*, 555–568.

Frazier, L. (1979). *On comprehending sentences: Syntactic parsing strategies*. Bloomington: Indiana University Linguistics Club.

Frazier, L. (1987). Sentence processing: A tutorial review. In M. Coltheart (Ed.), *Attention and performance XII: The psychology of reading* (pp. 559–586). Hillsdale, NJ: Erlbaum.

Frazier, L., & Rayner, K. (1982). Making and correcting errors during sentence comprehension: Eye movements in the analysis of structurally ambiguous sentences. *Cognitive Psychology, 14*, 178–210.

Frazier, L., & Rayner, K. (1987). Resolution of syntactic category ambiguities: Eye movements in parsing lexically ambiguous sentences. *Journal of Memory and Language, 26*, 505–526.

Frazier, L., & Rayner, K. (1988). Parameterizing the language processing system: Left- vs. right-branching within and across languages. In J. A. Hawkins (Ed.), *Explaining language universals* (pp. 247–279). Oxford: Basil/Blackwell.

Garrod, S., O'Brien, E. J., Morris, R. K., & Rayner, K. (1990). Elaborative inferencing as an active or passive process. *Journal of Experimental Psychology: Learning, Memory, and Cognition, 16*, 250–257.

Graesser, A. C. (1981). *Prose comprehension beyond the word*. New York: Springer-Verlag.

Henderson, J. M., & Ferreira, F. (1990). The effects of foveal processing difficulty on the perceptual span in reading: Implications for attention and eye movement control. *Journal of Experimental Psychology: Learning, Memory, and Cognition, 16*, 417–429.

Hogaboam, T. W. (1983). Reading patterns in eye movement data. In K. Rayner (Ed.), *Eye movements in reading: Perceptual and language processes* (pp. 309–332). New York: Academic Press.

Hogaboam, T. W., & McConkie, G. W. (1981). *The rocky road from eye fixations to comprehension* (Tech. Rep. No. 207). Urbana: University of Illinois, Center for the Study of Reading.

Holmes, V. M., Kennedy, A., & Murray, W. S. (1987). Syntactic structure and the garden path. *Quarterly Journal of Experimental Psychology, 39A*, 277–294.

Holmes, V. M., & O'Regan, J. K. (1981). Eye fixation patterns during the reading of relative clause sentences. *Journal of Verbal Learning and Verbal Behavior, 20*, 417–430.

Ikeda, M., & Saida, S. (1978). Span of recognition in reading. *Vision Research, 18*, 83–88.

Inhoff, A. W. (1984). Two stages of word processing during eye fixations in the reading of prose. *Journal of Verbal Learning and Verbal Behavior, 23*, 612–624.

Inhoff, A. W. (1985). The effect of factivity on lexical retrieval and postlexical processing during eye fixations in reading. *Journal of Psycholinguistic Research, 14*, 45–56.

Inhoff, A. W. (1989). Lexical access during eye fixations in reading: Are word access codes used to integrate lexical information across interword fixations? *Journal of Memory and Language, 28*, 444–461.

Inhoff, A. W., & Briihl, D. (1991). Semantic processing of unattended text during selective reading: How the eyes see it. *Perception & Psychophysics, 49*, 289–294.

Inhoff, A. W., Pollatsek, A., Posner, M. I., & Rayner, K. (1989). Covert attention and eye movements during reading. *Quarterly Journal of Experimental Psychology, 41A*, 63–89.

Inhoff, A. W., & Rayner, K. (1986). Parafoveal word processing during eye fixations in reading: Effects of word frequency. *Perception & Psychophysics, 40*, 431–439.

Just, M. A., & Carpenter, P. C. (1980). A theory of reading: From eye fixations to comprehension. *Psychological Review, 87,* 329–354.

Kennedy, A., & Murray, W. S. (1984). Inspection times for words in syntactically ambiguous sentences under three presentation conditions. *Journal of Experimental Psychology: Human Perception and Performance, 10,* 833–849.

Kennedy, A., Murray, W. S. Jennings, F., & Reid, C. (1989). Parsing complements: Comments on the generality of the principle of minimal attachment. *Language and Cognitive Processes, 4,* SI51–SI76.

Kliegl, R., Olson, R. K., & Davidson, B. J. (1982). Regression analysis as a tool for studying reading processes: Comment on Just and Carpenter's eye fixation theory. *Memory & Cognition, 13,* 107–111.

Kowler, E., & Anton, S. (1987). Reading twisted text: Implications for the role of saccades. *Vision Research, 27,* 45–60.

Lima, S. D. (1987). Morphological analysis in reading. *Journal of Memory and Language, 26,* 84–99.

Lima, S. D., & Inhoff, A. W. (1985). Lexical access during eye fixations in reading: Effects of word-initial letter sequence. *Journal of Experimental Psychology: Human Perception and Performance, 11,* 272–285.

Lima, S. D., & Pollatsek, A. (1983). Lexical access via an orthographic code? The Basic Orthographic Syllable Structure (BOSS) reconsidered. *Journal of Verbal Learning and Verbal Behavior, 22,* 310–332.

Marslen-Wilson, W. (Ed.). (1989). *Lexical representation and process.* Cambridge, MA: MIT Press.

McConkie, G. W., Hogaboam, T. W., Wolverton, G. S., Zola, D., & Lucas, P. A. (1979). Toward the use of eye movements in the study of language processing. *Discourse Processes, 2,* 157–177.

McConkie, G. W., Kerr, P. W., Reddix, M. D., & Zola, D. (1988). Eye movement control during reading: I. The location of initial eye fixations on words. *Vision Research, 28,* 1107–1118.

McConkie, G. W., & Rayner, K. (1975). The span of the effective stimulus during an eye fixation in reading. *Perception & Psychophysics, 17,* 578–586.

McConkie, G. W., & Rayner, K. (1976). Asymmetry of the perceptual span in reading. *Bulletin of the Psychonomic Society, 8,* 365–368.

Mehler, J., Bever, T. G., & Carey, P. (1967). What we look at when we read. *Perception & Psychophysics, 2,* 213–218.

Mitchell, D. C. (1987). Lexical guidance in human parsing: Locus and processing characteristics. In M. Coltheart (Ed.), *Attention and performance XII: The psychology of reading* (pp. 601–618). Hillsdale, NJ: Erlbaum.

Mitchell, D. C., & Holmes, V. M. (1985). The role of specific information about the verb in parsing sentences with local structural ambiguity. *Journal of Memory and Language, 24,* 542–559.

Morris, R. K. (in press). Lexical and message-level sentence context effects on fixation times in reading. *Journal of Experimental Psychology: Learning, Memory, and Cognition.*

Morris, R. K., Rayner, K., & Pollatsek, A. (1990). Eye guidance in reading: The role of parafoveal letter and space information. *Journal of Experimental Psychology: Human Perception and Performance, 16,* 268–281.

Morrison, R. E. (1984). Manipulation of stimulus onset delay in reading: Evidence for parallel programming of saccades. *Journal of Experimental Psychology: Human Perception and Performance, 10,* 667–682.

Morrison, R. E., & Rayner, K. (1981). Saccade size in reading depends upon character spaces and not visual angle. *Perception & Psychophysics, 30,* 395–396.

O'Brien, E. J., Shank, D. M., Myers, J. L., & Rayner, K. (1988). Elaborative inferences during reading: Do they occur on-line? *Journal of Experimental Psychology: Learning, Memory, and Cognition, 14,* 410–420.

O'Regan, J. K. (1979). Eye guidance in reading: Evidence for the linguistic control hypothesis. *Perception & Psychophysics, 25,* 501–509.

O'Regan, J. K. (1980). The control of saccade size and fixation duration in reading: The limits of linguistic control. *Perception & Psychophysics, 28,* 112–117.

O'Regan, J. K. (1990). Eye movements and reading. In E. Kowler (Ed.), *Reviews of oculomotor research: Vol. 4. Eye movements and their role in visual and cognitive processes* (pp. 395–453). New York: Elsevier.

O'Regan, J. K., & Levy-Schoen, A. (1987). Eye-movement strategy and tactics in word recognition and reading. In M. Coltheart (Ed.), *Attention and performance XII: The psychology of reading*, (pp. 363–383). London: Erlbaum.

Osaka, N. (1987). Effect of peripheral visual field size upon eye movements during Japanese text processing. In J. K. O'Regan & A. Levy-Shoen (Eds.), *Eye movements: From physiology to cognition* (pp. 421–430). Amsterdam: North-Holland.

Pollatsek, A., Bolozky, S., Well, A. D., & Rayner, K. (1981). Asymmetries in the perceptual span for Israeli readers. *Brain and Language, 14,* 174–180.

Pollatsek, A., Lesch, M., Morris, R. K., & Rayner, K. (1992). Phonological codes are used in the integration of information across saccades in word identification and reading. *Journal of Experimental Psychology: Human Perception and Performance, 18,* 148–162.

Pollatsek, A., Raney, G. E., LaGasse, L., & Rayner, K. (1993). *The use of information below fixation in reading and in visual search. Canadian Journal of Experimental Psychology, 47,* 179–200.

Pollatsek, A., & Rayner, K. (1990). Eye movements and lexical access in reading. In D. A. Balota, G. B. Flores d'Arcais, & K. Rayner (Eds.), *Comprehension processes in reading* (pp. 143–163). Hillsdale, NJ: Erlbaum.

Pollatsek, A., Rayner, K., & Balota, D. A. (1986). Inferences about eye movement control from the perceptual span in reading. *Perception & Psychophysics, 40,* 123–130.

Rayner, K. (1975). The perceptual span and peripheral cues in reading. *Cognitive Psychology, 7,* 65–81.

Rayner, K. (1977). Visual attention in reading: Eye movements reflect cognitive processes. *Memory & Cognition, 4,* 443–448.

Rayner, K. (1978). Eye movements in reading and information processing. *Psychological Bulletin, 85,* 618–660.

Rayner, K. (1979). Eye guidance in reading: Fixation locations within words. *Perception, 8,* 21–30.

Rayner, K. (1986). Eye movements and the perceptual span in beginning and skilled readers. *Journal of Experimental Child Psychology, 41,* 211–236.

Rayner, K., & Balota, D. A. (1989). Parafoveal preview effects and lexical access during eye fixations in reading. In W. Marslen-Wilson (Ed.), *Lexical representation and process* (pp. 261–290). Cambridge, MA: MIT Press.

Rayner, K., Balota, D. A., & Pollatsek, A. (1986). Against parafoveal semantic preprocessing during eye fixations in reading. *Canadian Journal of Psychology, 40,* 473–483.

Rayner, K., Carlson, M., & Frazier, L. (1983). The interaction of syntax and semantics during sentence processing: Eye movements in the analysis of semantically biased sentences. *Journal of Verbal Learning and Verbal Behavior, 22,* 358–374.

Rayner, K., & Duffy, S. A. (1986). Lexical complexity and fixation times in reading: Effects of word frequency, verb complexity, and lexical ambiguity. *Memory & Cognition, 14,* 191–201.

Rayner, K., & Duffy, S. A. (1988). On-line comprehension processes and eye movements during reading. In M. Daneman, G. E. MacKinnon, & T. G. Waller (Eds.), *Reading research: Advances in theory and practice* (Vol. 6, pp. 13–66). San Diego, CA: Academic Press.

Rayner, K., & Frazier, L. (1987). Parsing temporarily ambiguous complements. *Quarterly Journal of Experimental Psychology, 39A,* 657–673.

Rayner, K., & Frazier, L. (1989). Selection mechanisms in reading lexically ambiguous words. *Journal of Experimental Psychology: Learning, Memory, and Cognition, 15,* 779–790.

Rayner, K., Garrod, S., & Perfetti, C. A. (1992). Discourse influences during parsing are delayed. *Cognition, 45,* 109–139.

Rayner, K., Inhoff, A. W., Morrison, R. E., Slowiaczek, M. L., & Bertera, J. H. (1981). Masking of foveal and parafoveal vision during eye fixations in reading. *Journal of Experimental Psychology: Human Perception and Performance, 7,* 167–179.

Rayner, K., & McConkie, G. W. (1976). What guides a reader's eye movements? *Vision Research, 16,* 829–837.

Rayner, K., & Morris, R. K. (1992). Eye movement control in reading: Evidence against semantic preprocessing. *Journal of Experimental Psychology: Human Perception and Performance, 18,* 163–172.

Rayner, K., & Pollatsek, A. (1981). Eye movement control in reading: Evidence for direct control. *Quarterly Journal of Experimental Psychology, 33A,* 351–373.

Rayner, K., & Pollatsek, A. (1987). Eye movements in reading: A tutorial review. In M. Coltheart

(Ed.), *Attention and performance XII: The psychology of reading* (pp. 327–362). London: Erlbaum.

Rayner, K., & Pollatsek, A. (1989). *The psychology of reading.* Englewood Cliffs, NJ: Prentice-Hall.

Rayner, K., & Sereno, S. C. (in press). Regressive eye movements and sentences parsing: On the use of regression contingent analyses. *Memory & Cognition.*

Rayner, K., Sereno, S. C., Morris, R. K., Schmauder, A. R., & Clifton, C., Jr. (1989). Eye movements and on-line language comprehension processes. *Language and Cognitive Processes, 4,* SI21–SI49.

Rayner, K., Slowiaczek, M. L., Clifton, C., Jr., & Bertera, J. H. (1983). Latency of sequential eye movements: Implications for reading. *Journal of Experimental Psychology: Human Perception and Performance, 9,* 912–922.

Rayner, K., Well, A. D., & Pollatsek, A. (1980). Asymmetry of the effective visual field in reading. *Perception & Psychophysics, 27,* 537–544.

Rayner, K., Well, A. D., Pollatsek, A., & Bertera, J. H. (1982). The availability of useful information to the right of fixation in reading. *Perception & Psychophysics, 31,* 537–550.

Sanford, A. J., & Garrod, S. C. (1981). *Understanding written language: Explorations in comprehension beyond the sentence.* New York: Wiley.

Schmauder, A. R. (1991). Argument structure frames: A lexical complexity metric? *Journal of Experimental Psychology: Learning, Memory, and Cognition, 17,* 49–65.

Schustack, M., Ehrlich, S. F., & Rayner, K. (1987). The complexity of contextual facilitation in reading: Local and global influences. *Journal of Memory and Language, 26,* 322–340.

Sereno, S. C. (1992). Early lexical processes when fixating a word in reading. In K. Rayner (Ed.), *Eye movements and visual cognition: Scene perception and reading* (pp. 304–316). New York: Springer-Verlag.

Sereno, S. C., Pacht, J. M., & Rayner, K. (1992). The effect of meaning frequency on processing lexically ambiguous words: Evidence from eye fixations. *Psychological Science, 3,* 296–300.

Sereno, S. C., & Rayner, K. (1992). Fast priming during eye fixations in reading. *Journal of Experimental Psychology: Human Perception and Performance, 18,* 173–184.

Taft, M. (1985). The decoding of words in lexical access: A review of the morphological approach. In D. Besner, T. G. Waller, & G. E. MacKinnon (Eds.), *Reading research: Advances in theory and practice* (Vol. 5, pp. 83–123). Orlando, FL: Academic Press.

Tanenhaus, M. K., Carlson, G., & Trueswell, J. C. (1989). The role of thematic structure in interpretation and parsing. *Language and Cognitive Processes, 4,* SI211–SI234.

Taraban, R., & McClelland, J. L. (1988). Constituent attachment and thematic role assignment in sentence processing: Influence of content-based expectations. *Journal of Memory and Language, 27,* 597–632.

Tinker, M. A. (1939). Reliability and validity of eye-movement measures of reading. *Journal of Experimental Psychology, 19,* 732–746.

Trueswell, J. C., Tanenhaus, M. K., & Kello, C. (1993). Verb-specific constraints in sentence processing: Separating effects of lexical preference from garden-paths. *Journal of Experimental Psychology: Learning, Memory, & Cognition, 19,* 528–551.

Vitu, F., O'Regan, J. K., & Mittau, M. (1990). Optimal landing position in reading isolated words and continuous text. *Perception & Psychophysics, 47,* 583–600.

Zola, D. (1984). Redundancy and word perception during reading. *Perception & Psychophysics, 36,* 277–284.

CHAPTER 4

PSYCHOLINGUISTICS ELECTRIFIED
EVENT-RELATED BRAIN POTENTIAL INVESTIGATIONS

MARTA KUTAS AND CYMA K. VAN PETTEN

I. INTRODUCTION

There are those who would argue that there is no more to be learned about mental faculties from monitoring the patterns of electrical activity at the scalp than there was from palpating the various and sundry bumps on skulls of talented individuals or hysterical widows in the heyday of phrenology. But the contributions of various schools of thought often outlast the schools themselves or the techniques that they espoused. For example, the important distinction between perceptual and reflective knowledge, and the idea that cognition can be divided into separable mental faculties—both very much a part of modern-day psychology—were first emphasized by Gall and his followers. The discipline of cognitive electrophysiology seeks to provide a view of various of these perceptual and cognitive processes as they unfold in real time. The brain's electrophysiology can serve as a framework for extending the much sought after links between psychological and neurobiological levels of analysis. More-over, as neuroscientists begin to appreciate the importance of correlated neuronal activity throughout the central nervous system, there is obviously much to be gained from mapping the regularities in external stimuli or events onto the regularities in brain activity time-locked to those events. Already there is ample evidence showing that these perceptual and cognitive regularities are mirrored, in part, in the modulations of electrical activity referred to as the evoked potential (EP) or event-related brain potential (ERP).

II. GENERAL DESCRIPTION OF THE ELECTROENCEPHALOGRAM AND EVENT-RELATED BRAIN POTENTIALS

A. Electroencephalogram

Given our current state of technology, there are two relatively unobtrusive methods for looking at brain activity associated with both sensory and cognitive functioning. Both of these methods allow measurement of the electrical activity of the brain, taking advantage of the fact that transmission of information in the brain involves the flow of ions. Ion flow across a neuronal membrane produces a voltage field around each active neuron. The activity of a single neuron can be monitored during invasive intracranial recordings, but the electrical fields around neighboring neurons also sum geometrically to produce a field that can be detected as far away as the scalp.

Scalp electrodes can thus be used to record the voltage fluctuations produced by large populations of neurons; the resulting trace of voltage across time is known as the electroencephalogram (EEG). Any given tracing reflects the differences in electric potential (i.e., voltage) between two recording sites. One glimpse at the underlying mental processes is provided by the differential EEG patterns observed while a subject is engaged in various tasks which presumably engage different neural systems (for review, see Butler & Glass, 1976). Such studies typically focus on the relative amount of "alpha"—EEG power in the frequency band between 8 and 12 Hz—although similar analyses can be applied to other frequency bands as well (e.g., beta, gamma, theta, etc.).[1] Because high alpha power is generally associated with rest and relaxation, alpha suppression is presumed to reflect increased mental activity. Most EEG studies of language, therefore, have been aimed at showing that during "verbal" tasks there is less alpha over the left but not the right hemisphere and that the converse holds for "nonverbal" tasks (J. Doyle, Ornstein, & Galin, 1974; Ehrlichman & Wiener, 1980; Galin & Ornstein, 1972). Although there has been modest support for this differential-activation hypothesis, many of the studies have been criticized on a number of methodological grounds (Gevins et al., 1979).

B. Event-Related Brain Potentials

The emphasis of the present chapter is on a different aspect of the scalp-recorded electrical activity, namely activity that is time-locked or synchronized to some external event. At any given moment the EEG is likely to reflect the activity of a number of functionally distinct neuronal populations. With the advent of computer averaging, it became possible to obtain an estimate of activity which is time-locked to an arbitrary point, such as the onset of a stimulus. At the scalp an ERP (5–10 μV) is substantially smaller in amplitude than the background EEG (50–100 μV) and must, therefore, be extracted by an averaging procedure. This involves recording ERPs to repeated presentations

---

[1] There has been a recent upsurge of interest in gamma or 40 Hz band activity, correlated brain activity, and its role in binding the various attributes of a visual stimulus into a coherent object (Engel, Konig, Kreiter, Schillen, & Singer, 1992; Gray, Engel, Konig, & Singer, 1992; Lowel & Singer, 1992; Singer, 1990).

of "similar" stimuli. Voltage fluctuations generated by neurons which are not involved in processing the stimuli of interest will be random with respect to the time of stimulus onset and thus cancel each other, to leave a record of the event-related activity (ERP) that was time-locked to stimulus presentation. Averaging improves the signal-to-noise ratio of the evoked signal in proportion to the square root of the number of responses included. The number of stimuli needed for a reliable (i.e., "clean") average is a function of the amplitude of the ERP component under study. The smaller the component, the more trials are needed to extract it from the "noise" or spontaneous EEG. Which stimuli are defined as "similar" for the purposes of repetition and averaging depends on the goals of the experiment and is established a priori by the experimenter. For example, we could investigate the factor of word frequency by averaging across many different words from each of several different frequency ranges. If some part of the waveform recorded was sensitive to variation in word frequency, the ERP "frequency" effect could then be used to test alternative proposals on the role of frequency in word recognition for words in isolation or in sentence context (see Van Petten & Kutas, 1990, 1991a).

The major statistical assumption in averaging is that the signal is indeed time-locked to the averaging trigger whereas the noise is not. Time-locked noise typically occurs only in the case of electrical artifacts generated by the laboratory equipment which presents the stimulus (e.g., vibration from a headphone speaker or a tactile stimulator). For the early "sensory" portion of the ERP elicited by the stimulus, the time-locking assumption is well supported. In the case of later portions of the ERP which are instead elicited by higher-level "cognitive" analyses of the stimulus, the latency of the signal may not be invariant with regard to stimulus onset. Under these circumstances there are a variety of pattern recognition techniques such as cross-correlation (e.g., Woody adaptive filter) and discriminant analysis that can be used to characterize and re-align the signal for subsequent averaging (for details of these procedures, see Coles, Gratton, Kramer, & Miller, 1986).

1. Peaks and Components

The ERP waveform of voltage plotted against post-stimulus time typically includes a series of positive and negative peaks. In reading a report of an ERP experiment it is essential to note the polarity markings on figures, as some investigators plot positive upward on the page and others "negative up." It is also important to remember that both the amplitude and the polarity of these peaks are relative. Voltage is, by definition, the difference in electrical charge between two spatial locations, whether the two locations are the two poles of a battery or two recording sites on a human head. In ERP recording, one site is typically used as the reference or "inactive" site for all others, so that the choice of reference location will determine both the polarity and amplitude of the recordings. The amplitude/voltage of the peaks in an ERP is relative in a second sense as well. Because our interest is in brain activity elicited by particular stimuli rather than spontaneous activity, we need a comparison with some neutral time period. The ERP average will thus typically include a pre-stimulus baseline, that is a short (100–200 ms) record of activity (or preferably inactivity) immediately preceding each experimental stimulus. Post-stimulus activity is then evaluated relative to the pre-stimulus portion of the recording epoch, so that voltages are only negative or positive with respect to the zero provided by the baseline. Given the relativity of this "zero," ERP researchers are often more concerned with whether a portion of the waveform is "negative-going" or "positive-going" (i.e., becoming more negative or positive with increasing time) than whether it is above or below the baseline pre-stimulus epoch per se.

The peaks of an ERP are typically labeled according to their polarity (negative [N] or positive [P]) and latency in milliseconds relative to stimulus onset (e.g., N100, P230, P300). On occasion, the peaks are designated by their polarity and ordinal position in the waveform (e.g., N1, P1, N2). Sometimes, albeit less often, the labels denote a functional description (e.g., readiness potential, RP; mismatch negativity, MMN) or refer to the brain area which is presumed to be the neural generator of a component (e.g., auditory brainstem response, ABR). Which brings us to the distinction between a peak in a waveform, readily observed by the eye, and the more theoretical concept of a "component" (see also Allison, Wood, & McCarthy, 1986; Donchin, Ritter, & McCallum, 1978).

Asking a group of cognitive psychophysiologists to define "component" may sometimes seem like opening Pandora's box. The basic concept is clear: The processing of any external stimulus occurs over some period of time, so that different parts of the nervous system are invoked at different points and perform different analyses. The ERP is an extended record of this processing, so that different temporal intervals of the waveform will reflect different anatomical locations and different functional processes, although any particular interval may involve more than one temporally overlapping brain region/functional process. Thus, while investigators differ as to the relative importance granted different factors, all use some combination of two sets of factors to identify some portion of an ERP as a unitary component. One set of factors is visible in a single ERP waveform and bears some, although usually unknown, relationship to the anatomy of the underlying neural generators: polarity, latency from stimulus onset, and relative amplitude across a number of scalp locations (i.e., scalp distribution). The second set of factors involves comparisons between two or more experimental conditions to determine what experimental manipulations will influence one temporal region of the waveform.

Susceptibility to SOME experimental manipulation is essential for component identification, making "peak" nonsynonymou with "component." However, the experimental manipulations may take very different forms: (a) variations of the physical attributes of the stimuli, such as size, luminance, or color for a visual stimulus; (b) varying the psychological attributes of the stimuli, such as using words which are known or unknown to the subject; (c) varying the physiological state of the subject, by drug administration, selecting a population with a particular type of brain damage, etc.; or (d) varying the psychological state of the subject via task instructions.

The functional characterization offered by the sort of stimulus and task manipulations used by psychologists and the neural characterization that might be offered by a physiologist are thus all part of the definition of an ERP component, under ideal circumstances. However, circumstances are rarely ideal. A functional characterization is most easily carried out via experiments involving large numbers of healthy human subjects, whereas a neural characterization typically requires converging evidence from animal models, neurological pa-

tients undergoing invasive clinical procedures, and scalp recordings from patients with defined brain damage (Arezzo, Vaughan, Kraut, Steinschneider, &
Legatt, 1986; Buchwald & Squires, 1982; Halgren, 1990; Knight, Scabini,
Woods, & Clayworth, 1989; McCarthy, Wood, Williamson, & Spencer, 1989;
Pineda, Foote, & Neville, 1989; Pineda, Swick, & Foote, 1991; Smith & Halgren, 1989). In the absence of such converging evidence, only a few general
principles of neurophysiology constrain the possible generators of a scalp-
recorded component.

It is generally believed that the electrical activity recorded at the scalp
is a summation of graded post-synaptic potentials (PSPs) generated by the
depolarization and hyperpolarization of brain cells (see Nunez, 1981, 1990;
Wood & Allison, 1981). The electrical conductivity of the skull separating the
brain from scalp electrodes is low enough that potentials recorded at the scalp
must be a reflection of the activity of a relatively large number of neurons, on
the order of 10^3–10^4 cells. Pyramidal cells in the cortical layers are likely
candidates for most ERP components because they are large and because their
dendritic processes are organized in parallel; such an organization leads to
the summation of the associated currents, especially when these neurons are
synchronously activated in relation to the eliciting event. Negativity or positivity
at the scalp reflects the direction of current flow between the active neurons
and the recording site. The direction of current flow is determined by a combination of the orientation of the neurons to the recording site, the active areas of
the neuronal membrane (basal dendrites, apical dendrites, or cell bodies), and
whether the membrane is being excited (depolarized) or inhibited (hyperpolar-
ized). It is thus not possible to equate scalp positivity with neuronal excitation
or inhibition unless one has advance knowledge of the other relevant factors.

As a general rule, the amplitudes, latencies, and scalp distributions of the
earlier components of the ERP (with latencies of less than 100 ms) are highly
reproducible from session to session within an individual (Halliday, 1982).
Moreover, systematic variations in the physical parameters of the evoking
stimulus (e.g., intensity, frequency, duration) lead to predictable changes in
these early components reflecting the altered activation of the sensory pathways. Hence, the earlier evoked components are considered to be "exogenous"
or stimulus-bound; they are generally impervious to a subject's state of alertness
or attentiveness. It is this invariance in the face of changing psychological states
that makes the exogenous components an excellent diagnostic tool for certain
sensory and neurologic disorders (Chiappa, 1983; Cracco & Bodis-Wollner,
1986).

For present purposes, however, given our interest in the neural bases of
cognition in general, and language in particular, the more informative brain
waves are the so-called endogenous components, which may precede or follow
a triggering event by many hundreds of milliseconds. An "event" in this case
refers to a stimulus, a response, a voluntary movement, or a cognitive operation
for which an external timing marker can be specified so that time-locked electrical brain activity (ERP) can be examined. The relative insensitivity of endogenous components to variations in the physical stimulus parameters contrasts
with their exquisite responsivity to task demands, instructions, and subjects'
intentions, decisions, expectancies, strategies, mentl set, and so on. In other
words, endogenous ERP components are not "evoked" by a stimulus but are

elicited by the perceptual and cognitive operations that are engendered by that stimulus. The same physical stimulus may or may not be followed by a particular endogenous component depending on how the subject chooses to process that stimulus. The term "late" component is often used interchangeably with "endogenous" component because most potentials in this class occur with a latency beyond 100 ms.

2. Recording Parameters

It is important to note that there are well-reasoned rules for determining the characteristics of the amplifiers, bandpass, digital sampling rate, number of stimulus repetitions, time between repetitions, et cetera for the recording of ERPs (see Regan, 1989).[2] No amount of elegance in experimental design or theoretical framework can override an inappropriate recording bandpass or a low signal-to-noise ratio from an insufficient number of trials. A psycholinguist new to ERP research might believe that presenting the same syntactic construction more than 10–20 times will alter the subject's processing strategies and therefore limit the number of trials to five or six. This is clearly too few for any but the largest of electrical signals, but the problem can usually be handled by including a large number of experimental trials supplemented by an even larger number of filler stimuli. Alternatively, some experimenters have chosen to deal with this problem by trading off numbers of trials and subjects (see Garnsey, Tanenhaus, & Chapman, 1989). Fewer than 25–30 trials in an average usually does not provide a good signal-to-noise ratio. Similarly, fewer than 15–20 subjects does not give a true picture of between-subject variability. Moreover, optimal recording parameters will differ depending on whether one is interested in early or late components. This issue is one that may trip up a psycholinguist who teams up with a clinical ERPer or hospital researcher who is accustomed to recording the higher frequency early components and not the lower frequency components and therefore uses a low-pass filter setting of 0.3 Hz instead of 0.01 Hz, or is not sensitive to low-frequency artifacts in the recording.

To date almost all the investigations employing ERPs as indices of language processing have been based on analyses of the voltage waveforms in time. However, in principle there is no reason that such analyses must be restricted to measurements of the voltage waveform. Indeed it may be quite informative to examine the consequences of the experimental manipulations for other estimates of the electrical activity, such as various moments of the voltage field.

Distribution or topography across the scalp recording array has always been one of the criteria for component identification. Because each "active" scalp site is referred to a common reference site, scalp distribution will depend on the location of the reference. An ideal reference site is immune to brain activity (i.e., "inactive") yet is susceptible to the same electrical noise from the external environment as the scalp sites of interest. Reference sites are typically on or close to the head for the latter reason. However, it is also clear

---

[2] We touch only a few topics in recording procedures here, and briefly at that. The interested reader should consult reference works (Coles et al., 1986; Regan, 1989) for more detailed information.

that none of the more commonly used reference sites, mastoid (bony process right behind the ear), earlobe, chin, nose, vertex, inion, or sternum-vertebra, is completely insulated from brain activity. Until recently the most common reference was linked left and right mastoids. However, Nunez (1981, 1990) showed that linking the mastoids could actually distort the shape of the field at the scalp by forcing the voltage at the two mastoids to be equipotential. Thus, many researchers switched to using an off-line average of the recordings at the two mastoids as a reference. This procedure requires that during the recording session one mastoid be used as a reference for all sites and the other mastoid be included as an active site. The underlying reason for using both mastoids as a reference is, of course, some suspicion that the left and right mastoids may not be equivalent because they pick up more activity from one side of the brain. But if there is good reason to believe that the mastoids are asymmetrically active in a particular paradigm, then it is probably a good idea to use a reference site somewhere along the midline. The best of these is a noncephalic sterno-vertebral reference (Nunez, 1981, 1990; Van Petten & Kutas, 1988).

Recently, much effort has gone into the development of procedures for obtaining reference-free estimates of the ERP. One solution that has been suggested has been to use a so-called average reference together with many electrodes that cover the surface of the head evenly; in this case, the reference for any given site is the average activity across all the other recording sites (Bertrand, Perrin, & Pernier, 1985; Spitzer, Cohen, Fabrikant, & Hallett, 1989). Clearly, the average reference is very sensitive to the total number of electrodes use, as well as to their spatial layout across the head (see Tomberg, Noel, Ozaki, & Desmedt, 1990). The best coverage is afforded by many electrodes (around 26 or more), evenly spaced. The average reference procedure still provides a voltage waveform in time.

Another reference-free procedure provides, instead of the standard voltage measure, an estimate of the instantaneous electrical current flowing into and out of the scalp at each recording site. Current source density (CSD) analysis comes from the second spatial derivative of the voltage surface at the scalp (see Nunez, 1981, 1990; Pernier, Perrin, & Bertrand, 1988). CSD is often used in combination with a spherical spline function to interpolate data recorded from irregularly spaced electrodes and infer current sources and sinks that are not directly beneath a recording site (Perrin, Pernier, Bertrand, Giard, & Echallier, 1987). CSD, like the average reference procedure, requires good spatial sampling of the scalp surface (often 64 sites or more) with precisely defined loci.

3. Measurement and Analysis

There is a sufficiently large number of techniques for data reduction and analysis to make it impossible to cover either all of them or any of them to any depth. Thus what follows is a brief description of the most common ones (but for more details and procedures, see Gevins & Remond, 1987; Lehmann & Skrandies, 1984; Regan, 1989). However, we cannot overemphasize our belief that the choice of analysis method should be motivated as much as possible by some experimental rationale—the nature of the ERP comparisons determined by the questions asked and the hypotheses and predictions which led to the experimental design. As in all other areas, fancy analytic technique cannot make up for poor experimental design.

The most common ERP measures within electrified psycholinguistics are the amplitude (in microvolts) and the latency from stimulus onset (in milliseconds) of a peak in the average waveform. Typically, peak identification involves selecting either the largest or smallest voltage within some prespecified time window. The amplitude of the peak is calculated relative to a baseline; the baseline is presumed to be a time of inactivity and has most often been some period (50–200 ms) prior to stimulus onset.[3] Thus, the resulting measure is referred to as base-to-peak measure; in this way, a peak in the ERP is reduced to the amplitude and latency of a single point. This can be constrasted with a peak-to-peak measure taken between successive peaks of opposite polarity rather than from an inactive baseline (see Coles et al., 1986, for a discussion of other techniques for measuring peaks). Peak-to-peak measurements have serious drawbacks (see Regan, 1989), the most obvious being that a difference between two conditions may reflect a change in the positive peak, the negative peak, or both. It is important to note that neither base-to-peak nor peak-to-peak measures confer a privileged psychological or physiological status to a peak relative to other points in the ERP waveform. As points of highest voltage, peaks are convenient landmarks.

Since peak measurements are inaccurate estimates of long-lasting effects in the ERP that may span multiple peaks and are also quite sensitive to residual noise in the average, many researchers use MEAN amplitude measures—the average voltage during some time window which may span several hundred milliseconds. Such area measurements are taken relative to the mean amplitude in a presumably inactive baseline region. Area measures are less affected by noise and latency jitter than peak measures but are equally dependent on the choice of baseline and do not circumvent the problem of component overlap. There are two approaches to choosing the boundaries for areal integration. For previously documented experimental effects, the limits of the window are those used in prior experiments. When characterizing novel experimental effects, or for researchers who find a particular time window too arbitrary, area measurements are taken across the entire waveform in successive increments 30–100 ms in duration. If the waveforms to be compared are noisy, it may be as important to say that some time windows are not statistically different as to say that others are.

Both peak and mean amplitude measures are usually subjected to a multivariate analysis of variance or an analysis of variance with repeated measures, in some cases followed up by Tukey or Scheffe contrasts.

The most common multivariate technique for ERP analysis that has been advocated and used by some researchers is principal components analysis (PCA). PCA, which is closely related to factor analysis, is a procedure for

---

[3] Choosing a good baseline is by no means an easy task, especially in the case of ERPs to words within written text or natural speech, where the interval preceding sentence-intermediate words is clearly not inactive. Whenever the choice of a baseline is uncertain, a safe procedure is to make measurements relative to several and assess the extent to which the interpretation of the effects would be altered by the different choices. Obviously, the best outcome is if the choice of baseline does not alter the conclusions one would draw.

extracting a small number of components from the total variance of the ERP. The variance in most ERP data to date can be accounted for by no more than eight factors. A discussion of the limits of PCA analysis of ERPs can be found in McCarthy and Wood (1985).

Over the past few years, there has been a significant decrease in the cost of computers and graphics programs as well as an increase in the number of electrode locations from which data are recorded. Thus, it has become necessary to develop a variety of techniques to display multichannel data. The choice of procedures for displaying multidimensional data from a round head on a two-dimensional medium is not without its problems and consequences (see Duffy, 1986; Gevins & Bressler, 1988). A variety of such procedures exist, with some clearly better than others. It is critical to note that most of these are means of DISPLAYING data only, and have nothing to do with data ANALYSIS. In fact, there are very few statistical procedures currently available for comparing two or more experimental conditions with multichannel recordings. Within a standard ANOVA, a typical approach is to include electrode site as a multilevel factor or factors.[4] In this case, some correction procedure must be used to compensate for violations of sphericity of variance (see Vasey & Thayer, 1987, for discussion and suggestions).

4. Magnetic Event-Related Fields

Where there are electric currents and electric fields there are also magnetic fields; electric current generates a magnetic field whose field lines follow the "right hand rule."[5] Until recently this knowledge about the relation between electric and magnetic fields was of little use in the neurosciences, but with the recent advances in superconductors—materials that lose all electrical resistance when cooled below a critical temperature—it has become possible to measure the neuronal magnetic fields (the magnetoencephalogram, MEG) in much the same way as the EEG. Measurement of MEG requires a superconducting quantum interference device (SQUID), in conjunction with pickup or detection coils all of which are immersed in a bath of liquid helium. The system works because a magnetic field interferes with the flow of a superconducting current within a SQUID; the stronger the field the larger the interference. Thus, in the same way that it is possible to present stimuli and record the voltage waveforms at various locations over the head, it is possible to record the magnetic fields associated with the active neurons. By recording from many locations over the scalp it is possible to get a spatiotemporal map of the brain's electrical activity associated with an eliciting stimulus.

Although a large population of neurons, organized side by side and firing simultaneously, is a must for both electric and magnetic scalp recordings, the ERP and MEG provide somewhat different views of the underlying brain activity (Hari & Lounasmaa, 1989; Regan, 1989; Williamson & Kaufman, 1987). Mag-

---

[4] For instance, one might use two factors, one for laterally (left vs. right) and another to represent the anterior/posterior dimension. It is best not to include midline electrodes in ANOVAs using laterality as a factor, since the midline amplitudes are almost always larger than those recorded more laterally.

[5] If the thumb of the right hand is put along the direction of the moving charge of an electric current, then the magnetic field lines fall along the direction of the other fingers of the hand.

netic recordings are relatively more sensitive to neural activity which is close to the surface of the brain because the strength of a magnetic field decreases proportional to the cube of the distance from the current flow, whereas an electrical field decreases only with the square of the distance. This means that pickup coils a few millimeters above the scalp are likely to be sensitive to activity within the cerebral cortex only. Second, SQUID devices detect only magnetic fields produced by current flow oriented tangentially to the skull, not radially. This means that only neurons tangential to the skull, namely those within cortical sulci rather than gyri, will contribute to the magnetic field. Third, the relations between direction of current flow and orientation of the resulting magnetic field suggest that magnetic recording devices are more sensitive to intracellular than extracellular current flow. Given a single active zone in a neuron, say the apical dendrites, intracellular current will flow in only one direction, whereas extracellular "volume" currents will arrive from both ends of the neuron and produce canceling magnetic fields. Finally, the skull and other tissues are completely transparent to magnetic fields, in sharp contrast to the low electrical conductivity of bone. While magnetic recordings are thus limited in scope, it is substantially easier to estimate where a magnetic event-related field (MERF) source is located. This is in contrast to the ERP, which reflects currents both perpendicular and tangential to the skull, is sensitive to variations in skull thickness and electrical conductivity, is distorted by large holes like the eyeball or ear canal, and gets a contribution from volume current. This is at least one reason that it is generally not safe to say that where an ERP component is biggest in amplitude is necessarily the place to look for its generator. In summary, the MEG mostly provides information about the synchronous firing of pyramidal cells located superficially within cortical sulci. The ERP provides a broader picture of underlying neuronal activity, which includes both superficial and deep sources to various orientations relative to the scalp. To date only one study has employed the MEG to localize a component of the ERP elicited in language-processing paradigms (Schmidt, Arthur, Kutas, George, & Flynn, 1989).

III. WHY USE ERPs TO STUDY LANGUAGE?

There are two distinct uses to which ERPs have been put in the study of language. The ERP technique occupies a privileged but precarious position on the boundary between psychology and neuroscience. The ERP is both a correlate of behavior, much like a button-push, and a direct reflection of brain activity, much like a spike in a single-cell recording. On the one hand, electrophysiological measures have been used to address questions specifically related to the structure and processes of language. To this end, investigators have sought various markers of specific linguistic processes and evidence for the existence of different hypothesized levels of linguistic representations. We refer to this as the psycholinguistic ERP approach. On the other hand, however, ERPs are also a physiological measure of mass neuronal activity which can be used to examine the functional organization of the brain for language and language processing. The majority of studies adopting this approach compare not only the ERPs elicited by two different experimental conditions but also how the pattern of differences is altered across the course of normal development or in the face of unusual early experiences such as congenital deafness or bilingualism (see, e.g., Holcomb, Coffey, & Neville, 1992; Neville, Kutas, & Schmidt, 1982).

Before discussing the specific ways in which ERPs have been used, we examine the advantages and disadvantages of using the electrical activity of the brain in investigations of language processing.

A. Advantages

1. Lots of Data

One of the indisputableadvantages of the ERP technique is that the EEG/ERP can be recorded in synchrony with all events of interest. Every word flashed on a CRT or played through a speaker will elicit an ERP, and the response begins within a few milliseconds of the stimulus. The measure is as close to immediate and on-line as is now technically possible. As long as there is a time-locking point, an ERP can be extracted for every event in an experiment. In sentence processing research, this enables the experimenter to track processes throughout the course of a sentence within a single subject. It also means that with appropriate stimulus coding, one can examine more than one issue within a single study. Theoretically, one could investigate semantic context, word frequency, lexical class, clause boundary, word repetition, and verb subcategorization effects in one grand experiment, although in practice the standard requirements for matching stimuli on extraneous factors would probably preclude looking at more than two issues in a single study (although less pristine pilot data can be gathered on several others as well).

In addition to the sheer number of ERP averages that can be formed from a single data set divided into different stimulus categories, each averaged waveform is itself a multidimensional measure. An ERP waveform provides information about early sensory and perceptual processes as well as some of the later cognitive processes. Thus, without much additional effort it is possible to guarantee that none of the observed effects are a consequence of abnormal or differential perceptual processes. Insofar as the componential analysis of ERPs is successful and different components are validated against specific linguistic or nonlinguistic operations, an ERP analysis will aid in delineating the different subprocesses engaged during the performance of any given task. There is thus the possibility of monitoring the activity of a specific mental process via an ERP signature across tasks or stimulus configurations with very different characteristics. For instance, the presence of a negativity (N400) whose amplitude is sensitive to semantic relations in both lexical decision and categorization tasks and in both sentences and word lists supports the idea that there is some mechanism of semantic analysis common to sentences and lists which can be tapped into by a variety of tasks.

Of course, there is no free lunch—comparing components across experiments is a difficult matter and sometimes leads to heated discussion among ERP researchers. It is thus important to note that there are ways of analyzing ERPs to yield useful information which do not require a componential analysis. Given a well-characterized problem, it is sometimes theoretically sufficient to determine whether two waveforms elicited in conditions differing in one and only one factor are statistically identical or not. Such an identity/nonidentity strategy is analogous to reaction time (RT) research, wherein milliseconds are not, in and of themselves, an interesting unit of analysis, but similar or different RTs across conditions are. However, a caveat is in order here: It is much safer to conclude that the ERPs associated with two conditions differ than that they are the same. It is possible that adding another recording site or two would reveal a distributional difference that was unobservable with sparser spatial sampling. Thus, statements about ERP identity across conditions are particularly worrisome if they are based on only a few midline sites [such as frontal along nasion-inion line (Fz), central along nasion-inion line (Cz), and parietal along nasion-inion line (Pz)]. Recent work by Nobre and McCarthy (1992) suggests that even 12–16 recording sites may be too few to identify all the different loci of activity in a language processing task. If this finding generalizes, and 50 electrodes are indeed needed to make even identity/nonidentity judgements, we may be well advised to set up regional centers with such facilities, conduct initial experiments at such testing sites, and perform the more restricted follow-up studies at facilities with fewer resources.

Additionally, issues that revolve around questions of timing do not always require the identification of specific ERP components. For example, if one was interested in the relative timing of processes sensitive to word frequency and those sensitive to semantic context, it might be sufficient to ask which effect has the earlier onset latency (see Van Petten & Kutas, 1991a). However, while it might be valid to ignore the question of whether the two ERP effects surfaced in the same component, this strategy should remain tentative until more information accrues about the temporal relationship between different scalp components and underlying neurophysiological activity. Finally, another experimental strategy requires a componential analysis within a single experiment, but does not require comparisons across experiments. We might call this final strategy "counting the experimental effects." As an illustration, one might find an amplitude difference in Component X as a consequence of manipulating Factor A, but find amplitude differences in Components X and Y as a consequence of manipulating Factor B. No doubt, this pattern of results would stimulate further work on what cognitive processes are reflected in Components X and Y. However, it can also be taken as a hint that Factor B is not unitary but involves distinct subprocesses, at least one of which is shared with Factor A.

2. Freedom from Extraneous Task Demands

Another appealing characteristic of the ERP methodology for language research is that task demands do not need to be imposed on the subject unless they are experimentally interesting. Often in psycholinguistic research, the task assigned to a subject is not an inherent subcomponent of natural language processing (i.e., lexical decision), but is instead necessary as an index of some aspect of natural language processing. Substantial task analysis and numerous experiments are then required to evaluate the relationship between the underlying linguistic process and the experimental index and to determine what aspects of performance variability are specific to the experimental task rather than general to the linguistic process (Balota, 1990; de Groot, 1990). In ERP research, there is still, of course, an inferential chain between data and conclusions, but the chain can be shortened by one link since responses can be obtained without imposing what is essentially a secondary task requiring some motor response. Simply reading or listening for comprehension or memory is sufficient to elicit different ERPs as a consequence of some psycholinguistic manipulation.

For pragmatic reasons, we have sometimes included a secondary task in many of the experiments wherein subjects' primary task was to read a number of unrelated sentences. Having a button to press every now and then serves to reassure some subjects that they are really participating in an experiment, and the behavioral responses provide the experimenter with an easy way to monitor a subject's alertness during a long session. Such secondary tasks have included detecting an occasional repeated sentence, indicating whether or not a subsequent probe word occurred in the preceding sentence, making a true/ false response to a question about the preceding sentence, and indicating whether or not a particular letter of the alphabet occurred in a probe word following each sentence. These tasks all were constructed in such a way that subjects were neither required to make overt responses while reading nor, with the exception of the repeated sentence task (wherein the repeated sentences were excluded from analysis), to recognize task-related stimuli while reading (in the recognition probe and letter detection tasks, subjects did not know which word or which letter would be their target until some time after the completion of the sentence and did not know what constituent of a sentence would be questioned). Thus far there has been little variability in the pattern of ERP results as a function of which secondary task was used. Other investigators have employed sentence acceptability ratings (Neville, Nicol, Barss, Forster, & Garrett, 1991; Osterhout & Holcomb, 1992) or lexical decisions to the final words (Roesler, Friederici, Puetz, & Hahne, 1992) to similar effect. Thus we think that the ERP results common to all these experiments reflect general mechanisms of word recognition and sentence comprehension rather than task-specific factors.

The ubiquity of some ERP results across a range of secondary tasks should not be taken to suggest that an appropriately designed task cannot be used to augment the ERP data. An experimental condition might be subdivided to reveal different ERPs elicited during trials which received correct or incorrect subsequent responses from a subject. Or, instead of classifying **trials,** one might classify **subjects** according to their accuracy in the experimental task. We have recently observed that an ERP index of the utilization of sentence context is correlated with how well a subject does in the task of deciding whether or not a subsequent probe word appeared in an experimental sentence, suggesting a possible link between the ability to use sentence context and working memory capacity (Van Petten, in press).

Yet another approach is to include secondary stimuli without adding a secondary task. For example, Papanicolaou (1980) developed an ERP version of the "secondary probe" reaction time (Posner & Boies, 1971). Photic probe stimuli (i.e., brief light flashes used as processing probes) were presented to subjects as they processed speech for acoustic, phonetic, or semantic targets. Papanicolaou found that the N1 component of the ERP to the visual probe was asymmetric during performance of the phonetic and semantic but not acoustic tasks. Unlike the RT probe paradigms, the ERP probes are very unobtrusive. It is, however, important to control for interactions between the ERPs to the probes and the ERPs to the speech across experimental conditions.

3. Modality Neutral

Some experimental tasks in the psycholinguist's battery are tied to a particular input modality. Phoneme monitoring and shadowing, for example, have been useful techniques for investigating spoken word processing (Foss & Ross, 1983; Marslen-Wilson & Tyler, 1980), but it is difficult to say what would constitute analogous results in reading. Because one can use very general tasks such as "read/listen for meaning" in ERP experiments, it is easier to compare results across presentation modalities to determine which processes might indeed be amodal. Although the early sensory components of the waveform are unique to the input modality, the later cognitive components are apparent (although not identical) across stimulus modalities. Below, we briefly review the results of similar paradigms using spoken, written, and signed language.

4. A Link to the Brain

As noted earlier in this chapter, the exact relationship between any scalp-recorded ERP and the neuronal activity which generated it is not obvious from visual inspection of the ERP. A number of laboratories are engaged in defining this relationship for various components of the ERP using intracranial recordings in both humans and animals, correlation of human brain lesions identified in magnetic resonance images with abnormalities in the scalp potentials, animal lesion experiments, and the use of pharmacological agents specific to some neural systems (Buchwald, 1990; Johnson, Rohrbaugh, & Parasuraman, 1987; Knight, 1990; Paller, Zola-Morgan, Squire, & Hillyard, 1988; Pineda et al., 1989, 1991; Williamson & Kaufman, 1987). This research endeavor is far from complete but has met with significant progress over the last 15 years. We will not review these results here since these investigators have only recently turned their attentions to the ERPs elicited in psycholinguistic paradigms.

In addition to the various empirical methods for discovering ERP generators, there has recently been a great deal of interest in analytical techniques for constraining the possible neural generators given the scalp-recorded data (Balish & Muratore, 1990; Dale & Sereno, 1993; van Oosterom, 1991). It is well known that it is not possible to uniquely determine the distribution of current flows inside the head that lead to an external electrical or magnetic field; for any external field, there is more than one intracranial state capable of producing it. However, certain assumptions (some more problematic than others) can reduce the number of possible solutions. Initially, a mathematical model must reduce the activity of millions of individual neurons to a small set of equivalent electrical dipoles. The head is modeled as a set of concentric spherical shells (brain, meninges, skull) of differing electrical conductivity. One can then compare the predictions of a model with particular dipole locations with empirical results. For magnetic ERP data, a topographic map of the magnetic fields around the head can be constructed given enough recording sites. A "perfect" magnetic field distribution corresponding to one intracranial current dipole would have two extrema, where the field enters and leaves the head. From the strength of the field and the separation of the extrema, one can get a first-order approximation of the location of the dipole. Then by tweaking the parameters of the spherical model (including depth, orientation, and strength of the hypothetical dipole) it is possible to see how much error variance remains between the model and the real data. The parameters of this model then become the best guess as to the generator of the field recorded. The hypothesis so generated can then be tested via the empirical methods noted above. To date, much of the work with MERFs has focused on the early sensory components of the ERP for which a general vicinity was already known from anatomical, physiological, and neuropsychological data. The other simplifying factor for the localization of these early components is that a single brain area may dominate activity soon after the stimulus is delivered, so that one dipole may account for most of the scalp field. In the time region that cognitive electrophysiologists are most interested in, hundreds of milliseconds later, information has had time to diverge to a number of brain areas. Thus far, there has been little success at using such models for localizing more than one simultaneous dipole source. But this endeavor is only a few years old, and future prospects look bright.

A similar modeling approach can be taken with maps of electric fields (Berg & Scherg, 1991a, 1991b). This is a more difficult problem because electrical recordings are sensitive to a larger volume of the brain (deep as well as superficial sources) and are also more subject to distortion from the resistivity of intervening tissues.

B. Some Disadvantages and Some Limitations of Current Data

1. Artifacts

As is true of any experimental technique, the ERP technique has some drawbacks. For example, one experimental constraint on the recording of ERPs is a limit on concurrent motor activity that the subject can be allowed to engage in. Eye movements, activity of facial muscles, and tongue movements each produce electrical artifacts which may obscure the record of ongoing EEG (Grozinger, Kornhuber, Kriebel, Szirtes, & Westphal, 1980; Picton & Stuss, 1984; Stuss, Sarazin, Leech, & Picton, 1983). In practice this means that the best ERP recordings are obtained when the subject stays relatively still; this is also the case for magnetic recordings although for different reasons. It follows that it is difficult to record an ERP during natural reading (i.e., in association with saccadic eye movements across text on a page) and during pronunciation tasks. This particular limitation can in principle be overcome by the development of analytic techniques which tease apart the contributions of different electrical generators; in combination with dipole modeling techniques such as Brain Electric Source Analysis (BESA), this is a real possibility (Berg & Scherg, 1991a, 1991b).

More typically, EEG trials contaminated by biological, but nonneural, electrical activity such as electro-oculographic artifacts from eye movements and blinks, excessive muscle activity, tongue movements, large electrocardiographic potentials, and changes in skin conductance are rejected. Artifact rejection is not a conceptually difficult matter, but it does require a visual distinction between EEG and these other sources of electrical activity. A few examples of artifacts are illustrated in Figure 1. It is best if these distinctions can be made on line so that the problem can be corrected, rather than relying on subsequent computer algorithms to reject contaminated trials. Low-frequency artifacts are of particular concern since most of the energy in the late cognitive

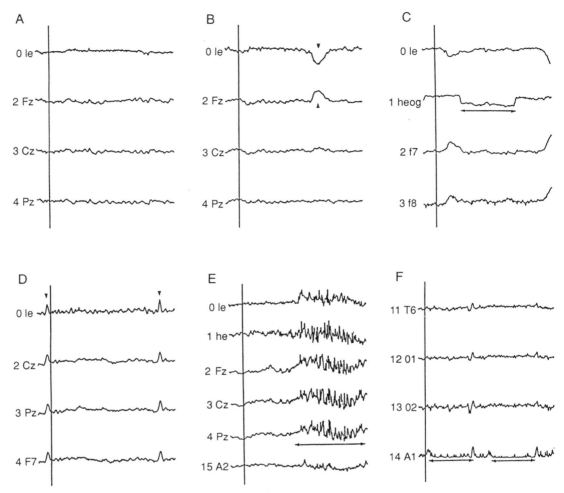

Fig. 1 Six panels representing single-trial EEG. The vertical line in each case represents stimulus onset. (A) clean EEG from below the lower eye and at three midline locations; (B) eye blink marked by an arrow; note the reversal of polarity for the blink above (*frontal site*) and below the eye; (C) lateral eye movement most noticeable in the horizontal electro-oculogram recording; this is a bipolar record between electrodes placed at the left and right external canthus of the eye; includes two sites over left and right frontal sites; (D) heartbeat (*arrow*) in lower eye record, two midline sites, and left frontal site; (E) excessive muscle (*underlining*) in lower eye, horizontal eye, three midline sites, and at right mastoid; (F) amplifier blocking (*underlining*) in left mastoid recording. Abbreviations: le, below the eye; heog or he, horizontal eye, bipolar left to right canthi recording; F7, frontal left hemisphere; F8, frontal right hemisphere; T6, posterior temporal right hemisphere; O1, occipital left hemisphere; O2, occipital right hemisphere; A2, right mastoid process; A1, left mastoid process.

components of the ERP also tends to be in the low frequencies. Of this category, skin potentials are the most frequent and the most difficult to reject via computer algorithms. Proper electrode application and instruction of subjects can reduce most sources of artifact to near zero. The exception to this rule is eye blinks, where one can only try to set up the experiment so that subjects have pre-defined intervals (between sentences for example) to blink. A few adaptive filter techniques for subtracting eye artifacts from the EEG have been developed, although no one technique has been widely adopted and there are some good arguments that every filter will be associated with some distortion of the data (O'Toole & Iacono, 1987). Eye movement artifacts are also less of a problem for current source density (i.e., second spatial derivative of potential field) maps.

2. Overlapping Components

In addition to artifacts, ERP interpretation can be complicated by the elicitation of multiple ERP components in the same latency range. Thus, some ingenuity in experimental design is called for to circumscribe cognitive activity and avoid overlapping endogenous ERP components. For instance, a well-studied large positive ERP component named the P300 or P3b generally appears in any task in which the subject is required to make a binary decision, as in go/no-go tasks or cases where the subject must press one of two buttons (Donchin, 1981; Donchin & Coles, 1988; Johnson, 1988; Kutas & Hillyard, 1989; Pritchard, 1981; Verleger, 1988). Thus, tasks such as lexical decision which require an on-line decision of this type are likely to yield overlapping P300 and N400 components within the same latency window. Because the latency of the P300 varies with the time required to make the decision, and its amplitude may reflect the subject's confidence in their decision, the P300 elicited across experimental conditions may not be constant. Such variations in P300 latency and/or amplitude can then obscure experimental effects in other components. In a semantic priming paradigm, Bentin and colleagues dealt with this problem by comparing the effect of semantic relationship in subaverages of the target ERPs sorted according to lexical decision times (Bentin, McCarthy, & Wood, 1985). They were able to show an N400 priming effect in all subaverages despite variation in P300 latency. Kutas and colleagues have argued that the difficulties in disentangling these two components can be avoided altogether by eliminating the necessity for a task-related decision within the post-stimulus epoch of interest. Kutas and Hillyard (1989), for instance, showed that it was possible to obtain semantic priming effects on the N400 component of the ERP with no overt behavioral responses required of the subject. This experiment asked for a decision that both was orthogonal to the priming manipulation and could not be made until after all the stimuli for a given trial had been given. Specifically, subjects had to indicate whether a letter flashed approximately one second later had been present in either (or both) words in related and unrelated pairs. Other sets of overlapping components may still create interpretive difficulties in some experiments, but the P300 at least can usually be eliminated by some attention to experimental design.

A problem related to overlapping components elicited by the same stimulus is that of overlapping responses to two or more stimuli. If a second stimulus is presented before the ERP to a preceding stimulus has played out, the ERP synchronized to the presentation of either stimulus will contain some portion of the response to the preceding or following stimulus. If stimulus presentation rate is constant, there will be no certain means of uniquely assigning aspects of the ERP within the overlap region to one or the other stimulus (see Woldorff, 1993, for a more detailed analysis of this issue). Most ERP studies of language have been conducted in the visual modality for stimuli presented at relatively slow rates (e.g., one word every 600–900 ms) in order to reduce the amount of overlap from adjacent responses and isolate the response to a single word. However, the overlap problem is tractable, such that recent work has utilized presentation rates of 200–400 ms per word. A generally cautious approach will always be to examine responses from slow presentation rates before turning to faster rates. Figure 2 illustrates an example of this approach.

Aside from the impact of presentation rate, the serial word presentation (SVP) format is itself different from normal self-paced reading. Some investigators have presented frames including two or three words at a time; in this case the ERP is elicited by the combination of words so that responses to single words are not isolable (Fischler, Bloom, Childers, Arroyo, & Perry, 1984). A couple of labs have also worked on multiword presentations using the subjects' saccades as time-lock points for the averaging procedure, rather than the computer's signal of stimulus onset. The data have been very similar to that seen with SVP, suggesting that SVP presentation is not overly disruptive of the normal reading process (Marton & Szirtes, 1988a, 1988b; Marton, Szirtes & Breuer, 1985; Marton, Szirtes, Donauer, & Breuer, 1985).

Besides its potential impact on subjects' reading strategies, we should also remember that SVP presentation with standard averaging procedures provides a restricted window on what we might be able to observe in the ERP. In the most standard situation, one will see one second's worth of ERP time-locked

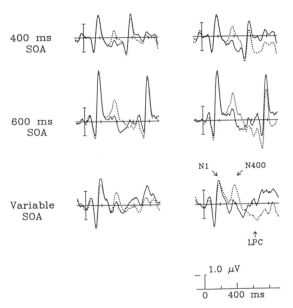

FIG. 2   Word repetition effects at a left parietal-temporal electrode site, at three different stimulus presentation rates. Both high- (*left column*) and low-frequency (*right column*) words show a smaller N400 amplitude for repeated (*solid line*) than new (*dotted line*) words. Low-frequency words additionally show a reduced late positivity (LPC) upon repetition, beginning about 500 ms post-stimulus. With a 400 ms stimulus–onset asynchrony (SOA), this repetition effect began after the presentation of the next word; note that it begins after the N1 elicited by this next word. With an SOA of 600 ms, the repetition effect still begins at around 500 ms, but it is now clear that the positivity was elicited by the word presented at time 0 and not the subsequent word. In the third row, a variable SOA was used (320–680 ms), so that the ERP to the second word is not time-locked to time 0 in the figure. The similar latency of the LPC repetition effect in this case provides further evidence that it is elicited by the word presented at time 0. Data from Van Petten et al. (1991).

to the onset of each word in a set. It might be difficult to observe, for example, slower processes which occur over the course of an entire sentence if they are not strictly synchronized to any single word. This particular problem can be surmounted by forming long-epoch averages which encompass a larger portion of a sentence, as shown in Figure 3. This figure also illustrates why we believe that it is a good idea to examine such long-epoch averages.

A

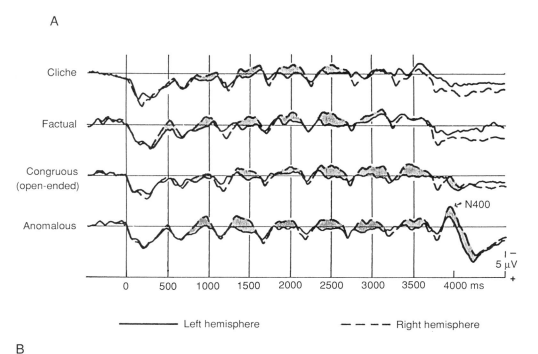

B

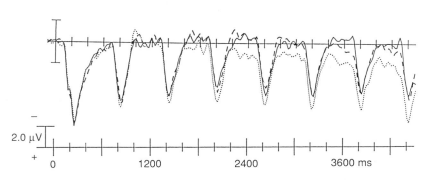

FIG. 3 Long-epoch averages showing the ERPs elicited by sequential words in sentences presented one word at a time. (A) ERPs to seven-word sentences preceded by a stimulus. Recorded at a midline parietal site. Figure from Kutas, Van Petten, and Besson (1988). (B) ERPs to the first seven words of congruent sentences (*solid line*), syntactically structured but semantically anomalous sentences (*dashed line*), and random word strings (*dotted line*). Note the slow positive potential elicited in random word strings which is superimposed on the ERPs elicited by individual words. The slow positive shift was difficult to visualize in shorter recording epochs. Recorded at a left central site (C3); data from Van Petten and Kutas (1991a).

Spoken language brings its own complications for establishing a time-lock point to synchronize the ERP averaging process. In connected speech, there are rarely silent pauses between words. Only in the last few years have there been many studies using words or sentences rather than single phonemes or syllables (D. L. Molfese, 1980; Wood, 1975). One technique has been to perform minor editing of the stimulus set so that each word has an easily defined onset point (Holcomb & Neville, 1991). Even more recent work has suggested that ERPs to natural unedited speech can be reliable; these will be a very effective way of studying the breakdown of language in aphasics and other patient populations (P. Hagoort, personal communication).

IV. OVERVIEW OF LANGUAGE-SENSITIVE COMPONENTS

An exhaustive review of ERP studies relevant to language research would occupy more space than available. We aspire only to give the reader some background, a flavor of active research topics, and enough citations to search for relevant information. We begin with an overview of potentially useful ERP components and the impact of general cognitive factors on these components. Because the concept of "component" is intimately tied to the demonstration of one or more experimental effects, any such lists of components will need to be constantly updated. We focus first and foremost on those that are fairly well characterized and clearly relevant to the study of language processing, with other components which have been less well characterized described in subsequent sections. This general background section is followed by summaries of the impact of some biological and psycholinguistic factors on particular components.

A. N400

The N400 was first described in an experiment contrasting semantically predictable with semantically incongruent sentence completions (Kutas & Hillyard, 1980c). Subjects in this experiment (as in most of those described here) silently read sentences presented one word at a time on a CRT. Incongruous final words elicited a negative wave which was largest over posterior scalp locations and somewhat larger over the right than the left hemisphere. Congruous endings elicited a positive-going wave instead. The separation between the congruous and incongruous waveforms occurred at about 200 ms after the onset of the visual word; the difference peaked at about 400 ms post-stimulus, as shown in Figure 4 (Kutas & Hillyard, 1980a, 1980b, 1980c, 1982; Kutas, Van Petten, & Besson, 1988). Since the initial experiment, it has become clear that the positivity elicited by a wholly predictable word is the exceptional case; most words elicit an N400 whose amplitude and latency vary with experimental manipulation.

The largest and most robust N400 is elicited by an open-class word that is semantically anomalous within its context and not associated with any task-related decision. This general finding holds whether the anomalous word occurs at the end or in the middle of a sentence (see Fig. 5; Kutas & Hillyard, 1983). In both cases, the anomalous word elicits a significantly larger negativity which

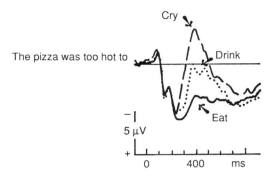

FIG. 4 ERPs elicited by sentence-final words at a midline central site, showing the positivity (*solid line*) for a predictable word, N400 elicited by an incongruous word (*dashed line*). When the final word is semantically incongruent but related to the expected final word (*dotted line*), it elicits a smaller N400 than an unrelated incongruity. Sample endings are for illustrative purposes only, since the same sentence frames were never repeated in this experiment. Figure from Kutas et al. (1984). Copyright Raven Press. Reprinted with permission.

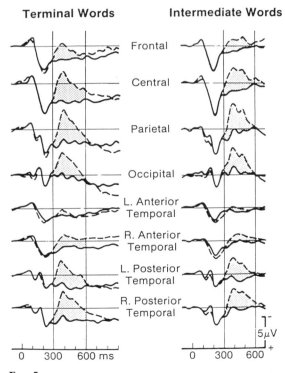

FIG. 5 ERPs to semantically incongruous words at intermediate and terminal positions of sentences (*dashed lines*). The superimposed waveforms (*solid lines*) are ERPs to semantically congruent words at corresponding positions. From Kutas and Hillyard (1983). Copyright 1983 by the Psychonomic Society. Reprinted by permission.

diverges from the response to a semantically appropriate word in the same ordinal position at about 200 ms, peaks between 350 and 400 ms, and in the averaged waveform, has a duration of 300–400 ms. It is unknown whether this relatively long duration in the average is a consequence of the averaging procedure, or whether each single-trial N400 also has a long duration. Analytic procedures for extracting single-trial ERPs are difficult even for ERP components with very large amplitudes (15 μV), and the N400 is not one of these (most N400s are in the 5–8 μV range). N400 amplitude differences between conditions are of shorter duration for some experimental contrasts than others, suggesting that "the" N400 may be composed of overlapping subcomponents whose characterization will require further research.

The fact that an N400 effect is apparent shortly after the appearance of an anomalous/congruent word, regardless of its ordinal position in a sentence, is most consistent with those models of sentence processing that emphasize the immediate and on-line nature of comprehension (Gernsbacher & Hargreaves, 1988; Just & Carpenter, 1980).[6] The sentence N400 data do not support models in which information is largely buffered for inferential and elaborative processing at clause or sentence boundaries. This is not to deny that there is substantial interpretation and integration at the ends of sentences and probably other syntactic boundaries as well. Indeed it is likely that most structural boundaries are regions of higher than average processing load. Eye-movement data, click displacement studies, and ERP data all attest to the sense of such a view (Fodor & Bever, 1965; Garrett, Bever, & Fodor, 1966; Just & Carpenter, 1980; D. C. Mitchell & Green, 1978). The nature and timing of processes at clause boundaries is ripe for good ERP research. The late positive wave elicited by terminal words at sentence boundaries is invariably larger and more prolonged than that elicited by intermediate words. The long duration of this positivity is one reason that we generally provide subjects with an interval between sentences that is three or four times as long as that between words. The additional time between sentences also gives subjects enough time to blink without contaminating the data—it usually requires some instruction and feedback to encourage subjects to delay blinking for close to a second after the final word of a sentence.

While the initial discovery of the N400 was during sentence processing, our current understanding is most consistent with the idea that it is the default response to words (see Section IV,A,4 for the exceptions). When letter strings are presented in lists or pairs rather than sentences, the following pattern of results has emerged: words which are unrepeated and semantically unrelated to previous words elicit the largest N400; orthographically legal, pronounceable nonwords (pseudowords) also elicit large N400s; and unpronounceable nonwords elicit little or no N400 activity (Bentin, 1987; Bentin et al., 1985; Holcomb, 1988; Rugg & Nagy, 1987; Smith & Halgren, 1987). In various studies using different materials, the pseudoword N400 has been either somewhat larger or

---

[6] An N400 or any ERP component is most obvious in a contrast between two waveforms where one has a small amplitude component and the other a large one. It is important however, to maintain a distinction between the component per se, and the EFFECT, or amplitude difference between two waveforms.

somewhat smaller than that elicited by real words. It is not yet clear how the amplitude of the pseudoword N400 will compare to that of the largest possible N400 elicited by real words, namely that to a set of words which are unrepeated, unrelated to previous words, and low in frequency of usage. In any case, the difference between pseudowords and nonwords gives a starting point for thinking about the fundamental process reflected in the N400. If the component were produced only after the meaning of a word had been accessed, there should be no N400 for pseudowords. On the other hand, if N400 amplitude reflected simply the ''wrongness'' of a letter string, there should be a sizable N400 for illegal nonwords. The results for the two classes of nonwords thus is more consistent with the view that the N400 reflects some of the earlier processes in word recognition, wherein illegal nonwords can be quickly rejected, but pseudowords require some additional processing to determine that they are not, in fact, words and therefore do not fit with their present context.

1. Scalp Distribution

The prototypic N400 semantic incongruity effect is broadly distributed across the scalp but is larger over parietal, posterior temporal, and occipital sites than frontal sites. It is also larger over the right than the left hemisphere. The hemispheric asymmetry is not a strong effect, but clearly a real one. A survey of 30+ experiments shows perhaps 60% with statistically significant right-greater-than-left asymmetries, a number with insignificant tendencies in the same direction, some bilaterally symmetrical N400 effects, and a very small number of left-greater-than-right asymmetries (Kutas & Hillyard, 1982; Kutas, Van Petten, & Besson, 1988; M. Kutas, unpublished observations). Typically, the responses to both congruent and incongruent words are asymmetric as well, although both the size and the direction of the asymmetry vary considerably across subjects. Thus, the N400 elicited by incongruous words is often but not always larger over the right hemisphere sites. Perhaps the degree of asymmetry is task-dependent, although this observation has not been investigated systematically. Additionally, the positivity elicited by highly predictable sentence-final words is usually larger over the right when linked or averaged mastoids are used as the reference.

We should note that ''right hemisphere distribution'' does not imply ''right hemisphere generation''; in fact the weight of evidence favors a left hemisphere generator (see Section V,A). A posterior right hemisphere distribution characterizes the N400 elicited by printed words delivered at a relatively slow rate. A smaller number of observations have consistently indicated that when the SOA between words drops below 400 ms, the N400 effect shows a more frontal distribution than at slower rates (Kutas, 1987; Van Petten & Kutas, 1987; M. Kutas, unpublished observations). Similarly, the distribution of the N400 elicited by spoken words may be distinct from the visual topography (see Section IV,A,3).

2. Latency

Although the N400 (difference) is elicited in close synchrony with an anomalous word, the peak latency is slightly later (by about 30 ms) for semantic anomalies occurring in the middle rather than at the ends of sentences. We take this as an indication that intermediate anomalies are appreciated more slowly than terminal anomalies. A similar but larger delay has been observed when sentences are presented at the rapid rate of 10 words per second (Kutas, 1987; see also Gunter, Jackson, & Mulder, 1992). In contrast to slower rates (1–4 words per second), these N400s both begin and peak 50–100 ms later. Because the same subjects and the same stimuli (counterbalanced) were included in the ERPs obtained at different rates, we are confident in labeling all the incongruity effects as N400 effects despite the change in scalp distribution with the rate manipulation. The general waveshape, duration, and lateral distribution of the incongruity effects were unchanged by rate, but this still presents a case of conflict between a top-down functional definition of a component and a bottom-up data-driven definition. The change in scalp distribution with rate may reflect the overlap of an additional process needed to read material presented at faster than normal reading rates. It clearly underscores our need to know more about what changes in cellular physiology can produce such a shift in scalp distribution. Nonetheless, the similarity of results across rates suggests that it is reasonable to draw inferences about normal reading processes from slower than normal presentation speeds. The advantage of allowing more time between words is that it is possible to visualize the entire sequence of ERP components elicited by single words without overlapping responses from previous and subsequent words.

While we refer to the N400 (and other ERP components) in terms of its peak latency, this should be taken as an easy reference point rather than as an indication that 400 ms is a critical processing point. In most experiments, N400 amplitude differences are apparent by 200 ms post-stimulus. At present, neither the cellular events underlying word processing nor those underlying the N400 are known. It is possible, for instance, that the N400 is elicited at the offset of the relevant process(es), thereby reflecting activity which began earlier than either the peak or the onset. Because the physiology of the cortex is marked by interactions between cell types in each lamina, feedback between laminae within a single cortical area, and feedback between areas, neural activity continues well beyond what one might think of as the "important" processing done by any particular subpopulation of cells. In the retina, a more peripheral and thus better understood neural system, delays between "critical" cellular events and evoked potentials have been better characterized. The earliest (0.1–30 ms) components of the electroretinogram (ERG, the ERP of the retina) are generated by the photoreceptors after they absorb light. A larger later component, the B-wave, is generated not by neurons, but rather by current flowing along Mueller (glial) cells in response to the release of potassium by active neurons upstream from the photoreceptors. The amplitude of the B-wave is thus tied to the initial event in the retina, light striking photoreceptors, without receiving any direct contribution from those cells. Later yet, changes in the distribution of potassium ions cause the hyperpolarization of the pigment epithelium at the back of the eye; this event generates the C-wave of the ERG, which can last for 5 s (Berson, 1981; Kline, Ripps, & Dowling, 1978). Similarly, we suspect that the relevant cognitive operations **precede** the N400 rather than being coincident with it. In any case, N400 is a convenient label rather than a specific moment of recognition, comprehension, or integration (assuming that such events occur at moments rather than across intervals of time).

3. Modality of Presentation

N400 effects have been observed in the visual modality in a variety of languages including English (see Kutas & Van Petten, 1988, for a previous review), Dutch (Gunter et al., 1992), French (Ardal, Donald, Meuter, Muldrew, & Luce, 1990; Besson & Macar, 1987; Spanish (Kutas, Bates, Kluender, Van Petten, Clark, & Blesch, in preparation) and Japanese (Koyama et al., 1991). In the auditory modality, N400 effects appear both in comparisons of congruous versus incongruous sentence terminations, and for semantically related versus unrelated words in lists (Bentin, Kutas, & Hillyard, 1993; Connolly, Stewart, & Phillips, 1990; Herning, Jones, & Hunt, 1987; Holcomb & Neville, 1990, 1991; McCallum, Farmer, & Pocock, 1984; O'Halloran, Isenhart, Sandman, & Larkey, 1988). Both the initial auditory experiment of McCallum et al. and the recent thorough investigations of Holcomb and Neville hint at differences between the auditory and visual N400. The data suggest that the auditory N400 effect begins earlier and is longer in duration. Additionally, the auditory N400 seems to be larger over the left than the right hemisphere, and more frontally distributed than the analogous visual effects. Each of these are issues which need to be systematically investigated. Given our previous statement that the N400 belongs to the class of late/cognitive/endogenous ERP components rather than the early/sensory/exogenous class, it may seem surprising to find differences contingent on the modality of input. However, the extraction of linguistic information from a printed word is likely to exhibit a very different time course than for a spoken word: A printed word can usually be captured in one visual fixation whereas an auditory signal is extended in time. Moreover, a reader can control the rate of stimulus input via longer or shorter gaze durations whereas a listener is obliged to keep up with the speaker. Given these disparities, the similarities between auditory and visual N400s are more striking than the differences.

Another example of the relative independence of the N400 from surface form comes from the work of Neville and colleagues with congenitally deaf adults (Kutas, Neville, & Holcomb, 1987; Neville, 1985). Her studies yield clear N400s in response to semantic incongruities in American Sign Language (ASL). Such data show that the N400 effect reflects a level of analysis beyond the individual letters in a written word, the phonemes or syllables in a spoken word, or the handshapes and movements in a signed word.

Also in line with this general view are data comparing semantic incongruities in the form of line drawings versus words. Figure 6 shows the ERPs elicited by words and line drawings completing written sentences in a congruous or incongruous way (Kutas & Van Petten, 1990). In this experiment, subjects saw 160 sentences one word at a time; their task was to attend for a subsequent recognition memory test. One-fourth of the sentences were completed by a line drawing, half of which were semantically incongruent. The remaining sentences were terminated by words, one-sixth of which were incongruent. Despite the differences in waveforms elicited by words and drawings, there is a remarkable similarity in the relative difference between congruent and incongruent stimuli. In this data set, the congruity effect at the parietal site peaked earlier for line drawings than words. Perhaps this finding argues that drawings provide a faster route to meaning than written words. However it is that our semantic concepts

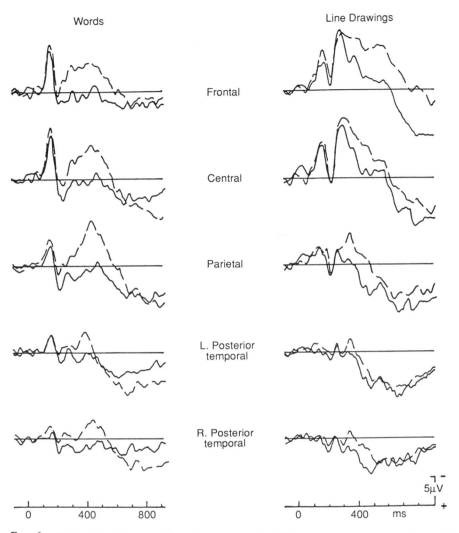

FIG. 6 ERPs elicited by semantically congruent (*solid lines*) and incongruent (*dashed lines*) sentence terminal words are shown in the left column. On the right are ERPs to line drawings which completed sentence fragments in a congruous or incongruous way. Copyright 1990 by Elsevier Science Publishers. Reprinted by permission.

develop, they are based more on objects in the visual world than on decoding orthography. But the present data are not clean enough to allow such interpretations. For one thing, the concepts represented in the words versus drawings were not matched for imageability; while those depicted by the drawings were imageable by definition, those represented by words may not all have been. Also, because the majority of sentences ended with words, pictures (regardless of their congruity) were relatively unexpected; this difference might be manifest in the large frontal negativity and/or P3-like components seen in the ERPs to pictures. Experiments of this sort, properly done, would contribute to our understanding of whether words and visual objects are represented via a common conceptual system or separate systems (Glucksberg, 1984; Kolers & Brison, 1984; Kroll & Potter, 1984; Paivio, 1991; Pylyshyn, 1973). There has been amazingly little ERP research directed at this question (but see a recent study by Nigam, Hoffman, & Simons, 1992).

4. Task Sensitivity

As noted above, sentence incongruity effects have been obtained across a range of tasks, none of which conflicted with subjects' primary instructions to read for comprehension (see Section III,A). Semantic relationship effects have also been observed in N400s collected in word list or pair experiments using lexical decision, semantic categorization, semantic rating, or letter search tasks (Bentin et al., 1985; Holcomb, 1986; Holcomb & Neville, 1990; Kutas & Hillyard, 1989; McCallum et al., 1984; Rugg, 1985b, 1987). However, in list/pair experiments, the degree to which the assigned task encourages semantic analysis has a clear impact on the ERPs. Kutas and Hillyard manipulated this factor by contrasting a letter search task with one where subjects rated the strength of each pair's semantic relationship. Holcomb (1986) varied the proportion of related pairs in a lexical decision task together with instructions which alerted subjects to the semantic relationships in the high-proportion condition (see Kutas & Van Petten, 1988, for review). In these cases, additional attention to semantic relationships had little impact on the amplitude of the N400 elicited by the unrelated words, but the positivity elicited by related words was enhanced and thus so was the N400 effect, or difference between related and unrelated words. This sort of data has led us to consider the N400 as the standard response to words, whereas the relative lack of an N400 is reflective of contextual constraint.

The differing task sensitivity of the N400 effect in sentence and word list paradigms is probably best explained by common sense. When instructed to sit quietly in a sound-attenuated chamber which is relatively featureless except for the presence of a CRT displaying sentences, subjects spontaneously read for comprehension, which entails a fairly detailed level of semantic analysis for each incoming word. The secondary tasks assigned thus far have not been so demanding as to interfere with this tendency. Word lists or pairs do not naturally engender as high a level of semantic analysis, so that it is only under tasks which enforce this strategy that the list/pair effects begin to approach the sentence effects in amplitude.

More recently, investigators have begun to examine more extreme attentional manipulations than those utilized by Kutas and Holcomb, such as presenting words outside the spatial focus of attention in the visual modality (Nobre & McCarthy, 1987, 1992, personal communication; Otten, Rugg, & Doyle, in press), or in an unattended ear in the auditory modality (Bentin, Kutas, & Hillyard, 1993). In these situations, the subject is actively prevented from analysis of these words due to the demands of attending to other words which are within the focus of attention. In these situations, the typical N400 semantic effects are absent. A more thorough review of this interesting research domain will have to wait a few years; at present we can only suggest that semantic effects on N400 amplitude are present under a wide variety of conditions but do demand attentional processing (see Kutas, 1993, for an expanded discussion of this topic).

Two studies have investigated the impact of visual masking in a word pair priming paradigm (Brown & Hagoort, 1993; Neville, Pratarelli, & Forster, 1989). In these experiments, related and unrelated word pairs were used, but the first (prime) word was masked to a level which precluded better than chance performance in forced choice identification. Both studies yielded no sign of the typical centro-parietal N400 difference between related and unrelated second words, although Neville et al. observed a small effect at frontal sites. Under the same masking conditions, small priming effects were found in lexical decision times, whereas larger reaction time effects (12 vs. 70 ms in Brown and Hagoort, 12 vs. 90 ms in Neville et al.) and typical N400 effects were observed under unmasked conditions. These data suggest that obtaining an N400 effect requires conscious perception of the stimuli. At face value, the dissociation between reaction time and ERP measures would indicate that lexical decision indexes some priming process(es) that the N400 does not. One caveat is in order here, however. There has been little work explicitly comparing the signal-to-noise ratio of ERP and behavioral measures of the same process. In any psychological experiment, one includes multiple trials in each condition to overcome random variability or "noise" in the data. It is not clear how to compare the sources of variability in reaction time to those in an ERP measure. We do know, however, that it typically requires more trials to obtain a clean ERP average than a reliable RT, perhaps because some of the spontaneous EEG that must be averaged out has no correlate in reaction time. Additionally, "outlying" reaction times are typically trimmed before calculating a mean RT, and there is no similar procedure in common use before forming an average ERP. If indeed the signal-to-noise ratio is lower for the ERP than for RTs, it will be difficult to determine whether or not processes that result in very small RT differences also influence ERPs.

B. The Contingent Negative Variation and the Readiness Potential

The contingent negative variation (CNV) is a slow, negative potential that develops on the scalp when a person prepares to process sensory information or take a motor action (Donchin, Gerbrandt, Leifer, & Tucker, 1972; Hillyard, 1973; Irwin, Knott, McAdam, & Rebert, 1966; McAdam, Irwin, Rebert, & Knott, 1966; Rohrbaugh & Gaillard, 1983; Walter, Cooper, Aldridge, McCallum, & Winter, 1964). It was first described as the negativity between a warning stimulus and a later imperative stimulus requiring a motor response. Subsequently, it was observed that the CNV could be elicited prior to perceptual judgments as well as motor acts, although its amplitude is generally larger when overt movements are involved. In fact, it is probably most accurate to regard the classic CNV paradigm as one which elicits at least two components that overlap and sum to yield the CNV: a negativity before an anticipated stimulus or the CNV per se, and a second negativity related to planning a movement. The second negativity has been labeled the readiness potential or Bereitschafts-potential. The readiness potential is clearly related to preparation to act, as it is apparent before muscle activity in self-paced movement paradigms where there is neither a warning nor an imperative stimulus, and it has a scalp distribution consistent with the organization of motor cortex. Thus, most formulations of the cognitive events underlying the CNV characterize them as anticipation or preparation to process incoming information, whereas the RP is an index of the preparation of specific muscle groups which will be called on to make a response.

The RP[7] has been put to good use in a variety of paradigms to track the time course of stimulus analysis (de Jong, Coles, Logan, & Gratton, 1990; Gratton et al., 1990; Gratton, Coles, Sirevaag, Eriksen, & Donchin, 1988; Miller & Hackley, 1992; Osman, Bashore, Coles, Donchin, & Meyer, 1992). The most useful attributes of the RP for a cognitive psychologist are that it indexes motor preparation rather than the final command to contract a muscle and is larger over the hemisphere contralateral to the responding hand. If different categories of stimuli are assigned responses from different hands, one can then observe preparation of one response hand, whether or not this preparation culminates in an actual movement. RP investigators have thus been able to track subjects' partial or interim analyses of stimuli prior to their settling on a final decision which manifests in an overt movement. The recording of RPs is both technically demanding and requires experimental design and analyses distinct from those of the other ERPs discussed here. To date, the "partial-information" paradigm has thus been used primarily with stimulus arrays involving geometrical shapes or letters of the alphabet. We can hope, however, that further development of RP paradigms will allow their application to psycholinguistic issues. What if one could actually monitor which parse of a garden-path sentence a subject was following at various points in the sentence?

The CNV, like the RP, is clearly not specific to language processing. However, it has been used to investigate differential preparation of the two hemispheres for either receptive processing or language production (Butler, Glass, & Heffner, 1981; Donchin, Kutas, & McCarthy, 1977; Donchin, McCarthy, & Kutas, 1977; Picton & Stuss, 1984). The design of these experiments is very similar to those using alpha power in the EEG to assess differential hemispheric activation.

C. P300

The P300 falls somewhere between the N400 and the CNV as far as the generality of the cognitive process(es) it reflects. There is an enormous literature concerning the P300 family of potentials, so we will include here only the most basic of descriptions (for reviews, see Donchin, 1981; Donchin & Coles, 1988; Donchin et al., 1978; Johnson, 1988; Pritchard, 1981; Verleger, 1988). P300s are elicited by any stimuli requiring a binary decision (yes/no, go/no-go, left-button/right-button, etc.). The decision need not involve an overt motor response; for instance, maintaining a silent count of target stimuli presented among nontargets is sufficient to elicit a large centro-parietal positive wave. The P300 is thus sensitive to the "task-relevance" of a stimulus. The amplitude of the P300 is also sensitive to the degree of confidence a subject has in his or her classification of the stimuli.

---

[7] Actually, most of the psychological work has focused on that part of the readiness potential that is asymmetric—the so-called lateralized readiness potential (LRP), although we use the term RP to encompass all RP–related studies.

While a binary decision between two equiprobable events is sufficient to elicit a P300, its amplitude is particularly sensitive to fluctuations in stimulus probability (at least at interstimulus stimulus intervals of <3 s). For example, increasing the proportion of randomly occurring deviations within a Bernoulli sequence has been shown to yield P300s of linearly decreasing amplitude (Duncan-Johnson & Donchin, 1977). Indeed, one of the more influential views of the P300 component, the expectancy model, is based on the relation between P300 amplitude and subjective probability (Squires, Wickens, Squires, & Donchin, 1976). In many experiments, it appears that subjects spontaneously take note of stimulus probability, so that low-frequency events elicit larger P300s even if no experimental task is assigned. Like the N400, the P300 is modality-neutral, so that either a red light among a series of blue lights or a high-pitched tone occurring unpredictably among a sequence of low-pitched tones will yield a larger P300 than the standard stimuli, although P300s in different modalities have slightly different scalp distributions and developmental timecourses (G. Barrett, Neshige, & Shibasaki, 1987; Johnson, 1989a, 1989b; Simson, Vaughan, & Ritter, 1977; Snyder, Hillyard, & Galambos, 1980).

Like its amplitude, the latency of the P300 has been found to be highly but systematically variable. The more complex the stimulus evaluation phase of the decision process leading to the P300, the longer is its measured peak latency, which can vary from 300 to 1000+ ms (Donchin et al., 1978; Kutas, McCarthy, & Donchin, 1977; Magliero, Bashore, Coles, & Donchin, 1984; McCarthy & Donchin, 1981; Ritter, Simson, & Vaughan, 1972).

The P300 is not language-specific, but since its amplitude and latency are reflective of some general process(es) of stimulus evaluation and classification (see Donchin & Coles, 1988; Verleger, 1988), it can be harnessed to the study of psycholinguistic issues (see, e.g., Polich, McCarthy, Kramer, Wang, & Donchin, 1983).

There are, however, some disjunctions between the general conditions which elicit P300s and the outcome of psycholinguistic paradigms. The most obvious example of this occurred in the first N400 experiment of Kutas and Hillyard (1980c). Given the database described above, these researchers reasoned that unpredictable sentence endings embedded in a series of meaningful sentences would be low-probability events, and if the subjects were reading for comprehension, they would also be task-relevant events—a perfect recipe for a P300 to semantically incongruent words. This, of course, is not how the experiment turned out, since the incongruities elicited N400s instead. Surprises such as this illustrate that while our ability to predict stimulus and task configurations that will elicit P300s is generally quite good, our concepts are still somewhat inadequate.

The P300 has thus far not proved useful in sentence processing paradigms (but see Section VI,B), but a psycholinguist needs to be aware of the general circumstances which will yield P300s and cognizant that they may appear in situations where they serve as confounds in data interpretation. P300s will be apparent in any task requiring a binary decision, with a latency corresponding to the time at which the decision is made. Such task-induced P300s of variable latency may overlap other components which are sensitive to the psycholinguistic manipulations of interest. The probability sensitivity of the P300 also suggests that the occurrence of stimuli in one or another experimental condition be made as equiprobable as possible.

D. Very Slow Potentials

Over the past five years or so, there has been a resurgence of interest in the use of direct current (DC) recording in investigations of various cognitive phenomena.[8] This revived interest is based on the belief that measurement of DC shifts provides one of the best means for online monitoring of relatively long lasting, sustained cognitive processes, as in learning and memory. Negative DC shifts on the scalp have been shown to covary with potentials recorded at the cortical surface and with the firing patterns of cortical single neurons (e.g., Caspers, Speckmann, & Lehmenkuhler, 1980). In addition, it has been shown that those cortical areas which exhibit an increase in regional cerebral blood flow also give rise to an increase in DC shifts (Goldenberg et al., 1989; Uhl, Goldenberg et al., 1990). Thus, it is assumed that these scalp-recorded DC shifts can be used to assess varying cerebral activation patterns. The majority of these studies have focused on learning and memory in general rather than language processes per se (Lang et al., 1988; Ruchkin, Johnson, Grafman, Canoune, & Ritter, 1992; Uhl, Franzen et al., 1990; Uhl, Lang, Lindinger, & Deecke, 1990; Uhl, Lang, Spieth, & Deecke, 1990). However, it has consistently been observed that learning and memory tasks involving verbal materials, as opposed to nonverbal materials such as faces or music, are characterized by negative DC potential shifts that are largest over left frontal areas. This left lateralization is evident during both acquisition and retrieval phases of these experiments. The processing of nonlinguistic stimuli also leads to steady potential shifts but with a different topographical profile (e.g., Ruchkin et al., 1992). Indeed, Ruchkin and his colleagues have been using these slow potential shifts to evaluate the neurological reality of the hypothesized subsystems within working memory such as visuospatial scratch pad, phonological buffer, and so on. Although there are clear benefits to DC recording, it is appreciably more difficult than most AC recordings and should, therefore, be undertaken only if the psycholinguistic question requires it (see Rugg, Kok, Barrett, & Fischler, 1986).

V. BIOLOGICAL FACTORS

A. Handedness and Lateralization for Language

Although it leaves much to be desired as a description of the neural substrates for language processing, an asymmetric cortical organization for many language processing abilities has been well documented. In right-handers (or in subject groups unselected for handedness and thus dominated by right-handers), several components of the ERP including the N400, CNV, and P300 have shown amplitude asymmetries in language processing studies (Butler et al., 1981; Kutas, Van Petten, & Besson, 1988; Neville, 1974, 1980; Neville, Mills, & Lawson, 1992). The CNV and P300 are larger at recording sites over the left hemisphere, while the N400 is larger over the right hemisphere. The asymmetry of the N400 might be regarded as paradoxical until one remembers that scalp distribution is determined by the orientation of neuronal current flow and not by the location

---

[8] Note that the majority of work discussed so far has been recorded with alternating current (AC) amplifiers with time constants ranging from 3 to 10 s. DC amplifiers have an infinite time constant.

of neurons per se. Such "paradoxical lateralization" has been observed in an early component of the visual pattern-reversal ERP: This P1 is larger over the hemisphere ipsilateral to stimulus presentation, in contrast to the known projections of the right and left visual fields onto contralateral visual cortex. This pattern of results has been explained as a consequence of the generating neurons being close to the medial surface of the hemisphere and oriented such that their dipoles point toward the scalp overlying the opposite hemisphere (G. Barrett, Blumhardt, Halliday, Halliday, & Kriss, 1976). A similar line of reasoning has been used to explain the paradoxical lateralization of the readiness potential prior to foot movements (Brunia, 1984).

The best evidence to date on the hemisphere responsible for the generation of scalp-recorded N400s comes from a study including commissurotimized ("split-brain") subjects (Kutas, Hillyard, & Gazzaniga, 1988). While subjects who have their corpus callosum (and often anterior commissure) severed for relief of epilepsy can never be regarded as equivalent to normal subjects, divided visual field studies in such patients provide a relatively unambiguous technique for restricting stimuli to one or the other hemisphere. In this experiment, sentence fragments (omitting the final word) were presented aurally so that both hemispheres had access to the context, but the final words were presented in the visual half-fields to limit access to a single hemisphere. There were four conditions: (a) congruent final word displayed in both left (LVF) and right visual field (RVF); (b) incongruent final word to LVF and RVF; and (c) and (d) congruent word to one visual field, incongruent word to the opposite visual field. The critical comparison is thus between the last two conditions: Only a hemisphere receiving an incongruent word should generate an N400, IF that hemisphere has the capability. The five split-brain subjects all showed some degree of receptive language ability in both hemispheres. In a pre-test, they were able to judge with greater than 70% accuracy whether or not a word presented to the LVF (right hemisphere) formed a sensible completion to the auditory sentence, and of course showed higher accuracies for the RVF. However, while all five of the left hemispheres generated N400s when presented with incongruous words, only two of the right hemispheres did so. The critical distinction between the two groups of subjects proved to be right hemisphere control of expressive language. At the time of testing, one of the two subjects with right hemisphere N400s could control overt speech with that hemisphere, whereas the other subject showed a high degree of generative capacity with respect to written output. Some six months after the ERP experiment, this subject began to show a right hemisphere speech capability which was fully developed two years later. While this study raises interesting questions about the role of speech capability in hemispheric specialization for language (discussed in the original report), it also suggests that only a hemisphere with full language capability will generate an N400. Thus, the typical right-greater-than-left asymmetry of the N400 should probably be taken as reflective of the dipole orientation of a left hemisphere generator.

The relationship between handedness and asymmetric organization for language has received a fair amount of attention in anatomical and behavioral studies, with the general conclusion that some 60–80% of left-handers show a left hemisphere dominance equivalent to that of right-handers, but a substantial minority show a reversed asymmetry or a greater degree of bilaterality (for reviews, see Bradshaw & Nettleton, 1981; Kolb & Whishaw, 1990; Perecman,

1983). Relatively few ERP studies using words or sentences as stimuli have contrasted left- and right-handed groups of subjects to see if they yield opposing patterns of asymmetry. S. E. Barrett and Rugg (1989) examined handedness and phonological priming but found no group difference.

In work with both healthy and brain-damaged subjects, family history of left-handedness has sometimes proved as important as the handedness of the subjects themselves, so that right-handers with left-handed family members appear to have a more bilateral language representation than those without (Bever, Carrithers, Cowart, & Townsend, 1989; Bradshaw & Nettleton, 1981; Hardyck & Petrinovich, 1977; but see also Orsini, Satz, Soper, & Light, 1985). There are slightly more ERP data in this domain, as it takes little additional effort to query one's subjects about family handedness in the regular course of an experiment. We have consistently observed that the typical right-greater-than-left asymmetry of the visual N400 is absent or reduced in right-handers with left-handed family members. This is true not only for the N400 incongruity effect, but also for the smaller N400 elicited by congruent, intermediate sentence words (Kutas & Hillyard, 1980b; Kutas, Van Petten, & Besson, 1988). Whether the laterality of the auditory N400 is also sensitive to familial left-handedness is unknown. It would also be interesting to find out if the reduced asymmetry associated with familial sinistrality holds equally for young children, or in ASL.

B. Development and Aging

Babies and children are likely to be less compliant than adults to standard instructions to sit still, pay attention, and refrain from eye movements, so that obtaining clean ERPs from these populations requires a patient and ingenious experimenter. On the other hand, as ERPs do not require an overt response, many of the problems inherent in the more traditional assessments of a child's language capabilities are bypassed. Electrophysiological data related to language processing have begun to appear only over the last few years (although see Kurtzberg, 1985, for a description of ERPs to stop-consonant CV syllables in infants up to 24 months old). For example, Mills, Coffey, and Neville (1993) collected ERPs from 20 month old infants as they listened to sets of words including ten whose meaning they knew, ten whose meaning they did not know, plus ten words played backward in time (also see Molfese, 1989, 1990). Two aspects of the procedure helped increase the amount of artifact-free data. First, the words were presented from a speaker located behind a moving puppet in a puppet theater, although the movements of the puppet's mouth were not synchronized to the word presentation. Moreover, after the child sat still for approximately ten trials, a battery-operated toy attached to the puppet theater was activated as the experimenter praised the child. This procedure led to a major reduction in the percentage of trials lost due to artifacts. Different patterns of ERPs were elicited by the three types of stimuli. Specifically, two negative peaks (N200 and N350) were elicited primarily by normally spoken and not by backward words (which do not conform to the articulatory/phonological constraints of English; this is probably true of most languages). The amplitude of N200 further distinguished the known and unknown words, especially over temporal-parietal regions of the left hemisphere.

Neville's laboratory has also studied older children in various language tasks. For example, Holcomb et al. (1992) studied children and young adults aged 5–26 years as they heard or read sentences that ended with either a highly expected ending or a semantically anomalous word (in the reading version, the minimum age was 7). They found that a host of early and late components of the ERP decreased in amplitude and latency with age. More relevant for present purposes, they observed that while all age groups showed an N400 effect in both modalities, the size of the effect was inversely correlated with age. The results were interpreted as consistent with other reports showing that children rely less on semantic context as they acquire good language skills. It should be noted, however, that with more complex language materials than predictable versus incongruous sentences, we have observed that some N400 effects are positively correlated with language skills (Van Petten, in press).

Although outside the domain of this chapter, the reader should note that there exist ERP data on language and non-language tasks from a number of different populations of children characterized by their abnormal language skills, such as those with Williams syndrome and language-impaired children (Neville, Coffey, Holcomb, & Tallal, 1993: Neville, Mills, & Bellugi, in press).

In experiments contrasting congruous and incongruous sentence completions, or related and unrelated words in lists, young adults generate larger, more peaked, and shorter peak latency N400s in the visual modality than do elderly adults (Gunter et al., 1992; Hamberger & Friedman, 1989; Harbin, Marsh, & Harvey, 1984). Pooling the developmental data with the aging data shows that there is a linear reduction in the amplitude of the N400 incongruity effect from 5 years (or earlier) to 80 years of age (Holcomb et al., 1992; Kutas, Mitchiner, & Iragui-Madoz, 1992). It will be interesting to see if all N400 effects exhibit a similar linear decline. Preliminary evidence suggests that N400s elicited by spoken words may not reflect aging processes as directly (P. Hagoort, C. Brown, & T. Swaab, personal communication).

C. Deafness and Language History

Congenitally deaf individuals who learn ASL as their first language have been something of a proving ground for theories about the abilities of the two hemispheres underlying the left dominance for language. Since the right hemisphere is generally superior in visuospatial abilities and both lexical and syntactic information is conveyed by modulations of handshape, location, and motion in ASL, one might think that native signers would show a right hemisphere dominance for language. However, studies of brain-damaged signers have shown that it is left hemisphere damage which is most likely to lead to aphasia and that the syndromes are remarkably similar to spoken language aphasias (Bellugi, Klima, & Poizner, 1988; Poizner, Bellugi, & Klima, 1991).

The work of Neville and colleagues with healthy signers has complemented the sign aphasia studies by showing that the N400 sentence incongruity effect shows the typical right-greater-than-left asymmetry in congenitally deaf individuals tested in either ASL or written English (Kutas et al., 1987; Neville, 1991; Neville et al., 1992). For English sentences, however, deaf and hearing native-speaking subjects do not exhibit identical ERPs (Neville et al., 1992). The basic N400 to congruent open-class words in intermediate sentence positions is larger over the right only at occipital sites in the deaf subjects, as opposed to the more widespread asymmetry in the hearing subjects. Similarly, the typical asymmetries observed at frontal sites for closed-class words are reduced in the deaf subjects. The deaf ERPs to both classes of words are also marked by a large positive offset beginning about 100 ms after stimulus onset. At present, it is difficult to determine if the other apparent differences are due to the presence of this overlapping positivity or independent from it. In either case, preliminary evidence suggests that these deaf/hearing differences may have little to do with deafness per se, or the fact that ASL and English are learned in different modalities. This is because English is the second language of these subjects, and they are often not fully fluent in written English. Deaf subjects who perform the best on tests of English grammar show a pattern of ERPs and ERP asymmetries more like native English speakers (Neville, 1991).

However, Neville et al. have found that the acquisition of acoustic versus spatial language does have some consequences for the asymmetry of cortical organization (Neville & Lawson, 1987a, 1987b, 1987c). In a nonlinguistic visuo-spatial task requiring the detection of motion and directionality in the periphery, native English speakers are more accurate for stimuli in the left visual field, whereas deaf signers show the reverse asymmetry. This reversed asymmetry can be attributed to the acquisition of ASL (rather than auditory deprivation), since hearing children of deaf parents show the same pattern. So, rather than the visuospatial superiority of the right hemisphere engendering right hemisphere language, acquisition of a visuospatial language seems to have improved some aspects of the left hemisphere's performance in this domain. The ERPs collected during the motion detection task also showed differences in scalp distributions (in both the lateral and the anterior–posterior dimensions), some of which could be attributed to auditory deprivation, and others to the acquisition of ASL.

While native signers are a unique population, Neville's results have hinted that some of the hearing/deaf differences in language processing experiments reflect the difference between a first and second language. In studies including spoken language bilinguals, it is clear that the N400 sentence incongruity effect peaks later in the less fluent language (Ardal et al., 1990; Kutas et al., in preparation; Neville et al., 1992). The effects of experimental manipulations which are more syntactic in nature show qualitative differences depending not only the fluency of the subject in that language, but the particular language being tested. Both syntactic manipulations and inter-language comparisons are relatively recent trends in psycholinguistic ERP research; we note some of those results below.

VI. PSYCHOLINGUISTIC FACTORS

A. Lexical and Semantic Manipulations

1. Isolated Words

Isolated words can be sorted on a number of dimensions to determine whether or not these have ERP signatures. Orthographic and phonological characteristics are two obvious dimensions which have received little attention. For instance, we do not know if there is any difference between regularly and irregularly pronounced words. Such a comparison might shed light on the relative timings and obligatory/optional status of various routes by which a word can be retrieved. Similarly, number of orthographic neighbors influences pronunciation time for words, rejection times for nonwords, and masked priming effects for words (Coltheart, Davelaar, Jonasson, & Besner, 1977; Forster, 1987; Patterson & Coltheart, 1987). We do not know if there is an ERP correlate which can be used to further understand neighborhood effects, although this is a topic under investigation (P. Michie & M. Coltheart, personal communication). Finally, the impact of a word's inflectional status has not been investigated in lists of unrelated words, although we have compared inflected to uninflected words in text, and other investigators have investigated priming between forms of the same word (M. C. Doyle & Rugg, 1991; C. Van Petten, R. Kluender, & M. Kutas, unpublished).

The dimension of concreteness has been given a modicum of attention. Paller and colleagues found that concrete words elicited more negative ERPs than abstract words from about 300 to 900 ms (Paller, Kutas, Shimamura, & Squire, 1987). However, the dimension of concreteness was incidental to the design of this memory experiment; a rating of concreteness was the task assigned to subjects during the study phase of the experiment as a prelude to subsequent tests of recall and priming. The difference between concrete and abstract words may then have been a consequence of how subjects construed the task; for instance they may have considered abstract words to be the "targets." Smith and Halgren (1987) used a lexical decision task in which the concreteness of the words was irrelevant to the task and observed no ERP difference between abstract and concrete words. In contrast, Kounios and Holcomb (in press) found that concrete words elicited more negativity between 300 and 500 ms than did abstract words with the difference being more pronounced over the right than the left hemisphere. Since this concreteness effect was smaller during lexical decision than during an abstract/concrete judgment, the three studies do seem to form a consistent pattern. Kounious and Holcomb also noted different ERP repetition effects for the two word types and interpreted their overall findings as converging evidence of the dual coding theory's structural account of concreteness effects in semantic processing. In a subsequent study, these investigators used concrete and abstract words to complete sentences (Holcomb, Kounious, & Anderson, submitted). They found no difference when the words were predictable, high cloze probability completions eliciting little N400 activity. As low cloze endings however, concrete words elicited larger N400s than abstract words. The factor of concreteness/abstractness is thus one where a few more experiments may present a clear picture.

Frequency of usage is a lexical factor which has been examined in priming paradigms using lists of words, in sentences, and in text. We thus devote a separate section to it below, together with the related phenomena of word repetition effects.

2. Sentences

Thus far, we have mentioned only the most basic of N400 effects obtained in sentences, the difference between congruent and incongruent words. The amplitude of the N400 elicited by words in a sentence reflects finer gradations of the semantic constraints placed on that word. One a priori metric of the amount of semantic constraint imposed on a terminal word by the preceding sentence fragment can be obtained via the off-line technique of cloze probability, e.g., what proportion of subjects will fill in a particular word as being the most likely completion of a sentence fragment (Taylor, 1953). Cloze probability proportions and N400 amplitude have been shown to be inversely correlated at a level above 90%. It is important to note, however, the subtle distinction between the cloze probability of a terminal word and the contextual constraint of the sentence fragment per se. For example, the fragment *The bill was due at the end of the* . . . is of high contextual constraint in that most people will fill in *month,* while *He was soothed by the gentle* . . . is of low contextual constraint because there are a number of acceptable endings, no one of which is clearly preferred over the others (Bloom & Fischler, 1980). But both fragments can be completed by words of equal (low) cloze probability as in *The bill was due at the end of the hour* and *He was soothed by the gentle wind.* The results of experiments which crossed several levels of contextual constraint with several levels of cloze probability showed that N400 amplitude was correlated with the cloze probability of the final word but generally independent of the contextual constraint of the preceding sentence fragment (Kutas & Hillyard, 1984; Kutas, Lindamood, & Hillyard, 1984). This result was critical in establishing that N400 amplitude does not index the violation of previously established expectancies for a particular word which was not presented, but rather is sensitive to the degree to which the sentence fragment prepared the way for the word which actually followed. Note, however, that in the absence of an explicit attempt to dissociate cloze probability and contextual constraint, the two factors are generally correlated. In what follows we use the term "contextual constraint" in reference to this more typical situation.

Given the cloze probability results for sentence-final words, we wanted to determine if N400 amplitude also reflected gradations of semantic constraint for intermediate words. One can use the cloze probability for intermediate words, but obtaining useful measures for relatively unconstrained intermediate words requires an enormous number of subjects. We used a pragmatic shortcut instead. With a set of unrelated stimulus sentences, the subject/reader must begin each sentence with no information concerning the topic, but as it progresses he or she should begin building a mental model of the concept expressed by the sentence and have more available information concerning what sorts of words might occur next. The strength of the correlation between degree of semantic constraint and word position will naturally vary from sentence to sentence, but an average across a large number of sentences (100–240 in these experiments) should reveal the correlation. Intermediate words sorted according to sentence position yielded a linear decrement in N400 amplitude with increasing position (Kutas, Van Petten, & Besson, 1988). We subsequently verified that the decrement was due to a sentence-level factor via the observation that it did not occur in random word strings of equal length, and we have replicated the effect for congruent sentences in several other data sets (Van Petten & Kutas, 1990, 1991a, 1991b, unpublished observations). The correlation between N400 amplitude and sentence position holds only for the open-class words of a sentence; while closed-class words elicit N400s, these are not sensitive to overall sentence position. Although the hypothesis has not been explicitly tested, it seems likely that the constraints on closed-class words do not develop over an entire sentence but are instead more local and bound within a single phrase or clause.

3. Semantic Relationships in Lists or Pairs of Words

Studies using lexical decision, letter search, and category judgment tasks have shown that words elicit smaller N400s if semantically related to the previous word than if not (Bentin et al., 1985; Boddy, 1981; Boddy & Weinberg, 1981; Harbin et al., 1984; Holcomb & Neville, 1990; Kutas, in press; Polich, Vanasse, & Donchin, 1981; Rugg, 1985b, 1987). In many of the studies using semantic categories as stimuli, these were a convenient means of defining "related" and "unrelated" words *a priori,* and it was found that an out-of-category word following several from the same category elicited a larger N400 than another word from the established category. Other studies have used phrases or sentence fragments to establish a semantic category (e.g., *a type of fish,* or *an apple is a . . .*). These have similarly observed that words which do not fit the category elicit larger N400s than those which do (Fischler, Bloom, Childers, Roucos, & Perry, 1983; Neville, Kutas, Chesney, & Schmidt, 1986).

Recent work has shown that among words which fit an established category, atypical members (*a type of bird: ostrich*) elicit larger N400s than typical members (Heinze, Muente, & Kutas, 1993; M. Kutas, unpublished observations; Stuss, Picton, & Cerri, 1988). The ERP categorization and typicality effects are immune to larger list-context effects observed in reaction time measures of category judgments. For instance, the use of false but related trials such as *a fish: whale* or *a bird: bat* produces slower reaction times for the true trials than when the false trials are unrelated (*a fish: window*). The impact of the related lures is more pronounced for atypical category judgments than typical. The N400 measure, however, shows no effect of list context, and no interaction between list context and typicality, suggesting that the list-context effect may be due to decision-related processes occurring subsequent to those indexed by the N400 (Heinze et al., 1993).

The typicality effect might be considered one manifestation of contextual constraint, so that the size of the N400 is dependent on how predictable the target word is. Kounios and Holcomb (1992) have noted that it matters whether a categorial statement begins with the superordinate (*Some fruits are apples*) or the subordinate term (*All apples are fruits*). Words at the end of a superordinate sentence elicited larger N400s, perhaps because the terminal word was less predictable given the one-to-many mapping between a category name and its exemplars. Kutas and her colleagues have also found that the size and the latency of the N400 effect are influenced by whether the prime consists of a category or an antonym. Across a series of experiments they used statements like *The opposite of black* and *A type of animal* as primes and found that the N400 difference between words that matched or did not match the prime was larger, more peaked, and of earlier peak latency in the antonym than in the category conditions. As can be seen in Figure 7, this effect is due to an earlier and larger positivity to congruent words, and a slightly earlier rise and peak of the N400 is due to incongruent words in the antonym condition. In fact, the typicality effect on the N400 appears to fall on the continuum from the early positivity for the highly predictable, congruent exemplars primed by a small category (antonyms) to the large N400 elicited by unpredictable, incongruent nonmembers primed by a larger category.

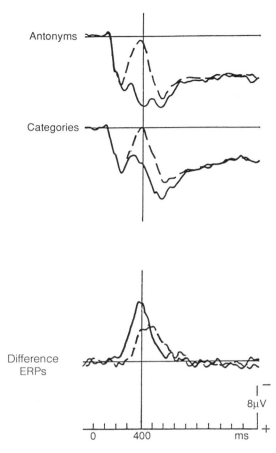

FIG. 7 Grand average ERPs elicited by positive (*solid line*) and negative (*dashed line*) instances of antonym and category conditions. The bottom half shows the difference ERPs derived from a point-by-point subtraction of the positive from negative instance ERP for the antonym (*solid line*) and category (*dashed line*) conditions, respectively, overlapped (M. Kutas, unpublished data).

4. Associative versus Sentence-Level Semantics

When the stimuli for these category experiments have been in the form of sentences, there has been a dissociation between the truth or falsity of the sentence and the semantic relationship between the content words of the sentence. Fischler and colleagues (1983) found that *An apple is a **weapon*** elicited the same N400 as *An apple is not a **weapon***, both of which were smaller than *An apple is/**is not** a fruit*. Kounios and Holcomb (1992) similarly observed an effect of relatedness on N400 amplitude, but no effect of whether the quantifier made the sentence true or false: *fruits* elicited the same size N400 in *All apples are fruits* and *No apples are fruits*.

The absence of a sentence validity effect in category experiments may seem to be in conflict with the evidence tying the N400 to sentence-level context effects (see above), unless one considers that these equation-like statements probably do not fully engage the same sentence-processing mechanisms used in normal discourse. We have recently contrasted lexical/associative semantic relationships to sentence-level semantic relationships and observed that both independently influence N400 amplitude (Kutas, in press; Van Petten, in press; Van Petten & Kutas, 1991a; see also Fischler, Boaz, Childers, & Perry, 1985, for a similar conclusion).

A somewhat different paradigm for comparing lexical and sentence-level semantic context is one of the traditional paradigms for examining lexical ambiguity. In this type of study, an ambiguous word is placed at the end of a sentence which clearly disambiguates it. The ambiguous word is then followed by one of three types of probe words which are related to the sententially appropriate sense of the ambiguity, the inappropriate sense, or neither. We have replicated the standard reaction time result in this paradigm to find that both of the related probes elicit faster responses than the unrelated word. However, on the basis of a large latency difference between the N400 priming effect for contextually appropriate and inappropriate probe words, we have argued that sentential context guides the initial interpretation of words which are ambiguous in isolation. These results are detailed elsewhere (Van Petten & Kutas, 1987, 1991a).

5. Nonsemantic Relationships in Word Pairs

We have seen that semantic relationships influence N400 amplitude under a variety of experimental tasks, probably because semantic processing is the default mode for analyzing relationships between items. A handful of studies have shown that if subjects are assigned a rhyme-judgment task, then nonrhyming words elicit larger N400s than rhyming (Rugg, 1984, 1985a; Sanquist, Rohrbaugh, Syndulko, & Lindsley, 1980). In Rugg's studies, most of the rhyming pairs were orthographically dissimilar (e.g., *moose–juice*), so that the reduced N400 could be attributed to the phonemic similarity. Polich and colleagues investigated the interactions between phonemic and orthographic similarity by crossing these two factors to yield four types of word pairs, and varying the task between rhyme and visual similarity judgments (Polich et al., 1983; see also the discussion of this study in Kutas and Van Petten 1988). For rhyme judgments, they found that both phonemic and orthographic similarity influenced the amplitude of the N400 elicited by second word. For visual similarity judgments, orthographic but not phonemic similarity influenced N400 amplitude. These data thus indicate that phonemic priming effects on the N400 occur only when the task demands this sort of analysis and are also consistent with behavioral reports that subjects are unable to ignore orthographic information during a rhyme-judgment task (Seidenberg & Tanenhaus, 1979).

6. Word Frequency and Repetition

Frequency and repetition are logically related, but one refers to a subject's life history of encounters with a particular word (necessarily estimated from normative frequency counts), and the other to the frequency of a word within a particular experiment. Both factors have been part of active research programs, some of which are primarily concerned with memory rather than language processing. For these reasons, we will not be able to review all the frequency/repetition studies in great detail here (for more extensive reviews, see Besson, Kutas, & Van Petten, 1992; P. F. Mitchell, Andrews, & Ward, 1993; Van Petten, Kutas, Kluender, Mitchiner, & McIsaac, 1991). Both frequency and repetition influence multiple components of the ERP, some of which are affected by both factors.

Repeating a word in a list or in text, or repeating an entire sentence, yields a smaller amplitude N400 for the second than the first presentation of open-class words (Besson et al., 1992; Karayanadis, Andrews, Ward, & McConaghy, 1991; Nagy & Rugg, 1989; Rugg, 1985b, 1987, 1990; Rugg, Furda, & Lorist, 1988; Rugg & Nagy, 1987, 1989; Smith & Halgren, 1987; Van Petten et al., 1991). This repetition effect occurs both within and across the visual and auditory modalities (Feldstein, Smith, & Halgren, 1987; Rugg, 1992). Rugg's work suggests, however, that there is a latency difference for cross-modal repetition depending on whether the spoken word occurs first or second. The N400 repetition effect is also sensitive to the lag between occurrences of the word. The influence of lag time has been fairly well characterized in word lists, where the repetition effect is not apparent beyond about 45 minutes (see citations above, and Fischler, Boaz, McGovern, & Ransdell, 1987). In sentences or text, a limit has not yet been established. The N400 repetition effect seems fairly impervious to experimental task, provided that both presentations are within the focus of attention.[9]

Analogously to the repetition effect, high-frequency words tend to elicit smaller N400s than low-frequency words. The frequency effect on N400 amplitude is, however, qualified by interactions with both repetition and semantic constraint. When words are repeated in lists, or when entire sentences are repeated, the frequency effect disappears for the second presentation (Besson et al., 1992; Rugg, 1990; Smith & Halgren, 1987). In other words, low-frequency words show a disproportionate repetition effect so that N400 amplitude is equalized by repetition. Sentence and text processing experiments show that semantic context is also capable of wiping out the N400 frequency effect. Above, we described the decrement in N400 amplitude with increasing sentence position. These experiments also show that low-frequency words elicit larger N400s than high-frequency words early in a sentence, but later there is no such difference, as shown in Figure 8. Like the basic word position effect, the position by frequency interaction is due to semantic factors, since it is not apparent either in random word strings or in syntactically legal but semantically anomalous sentences (Van Petten & Kutas, 1990, 1991a, 1991b). In contrast to the independent sentences used in these experiments, semantic constraints in connected discourse span sentences; in text we observe little sign of any N400 frequency effect (Van Petten et al., 1991).

The N400 effects are thus fairly well characterized and orderly: We have seen that amplitude is influenced by frequency, repetition, and semantic constraints, and all three factors interact as if operating through a common mechanism (see also Kotz, Holcomb, & Kounios, 1992). The two(?) other ERP components sensitive to repetition and frequency are less well understood at present. There have been some reports of a repetition effect preceding the N400, in the

---

[9] We refer to selective attention paradigms where multiple words are presented simultaneously, or words are presented individually at a very high rate, and subjects are instructed to attend only to words in one spatial location or one color. As described earlier, these manipulations yield different patterns of effects than the standard situation where the subject has no conflicting attentional demands.

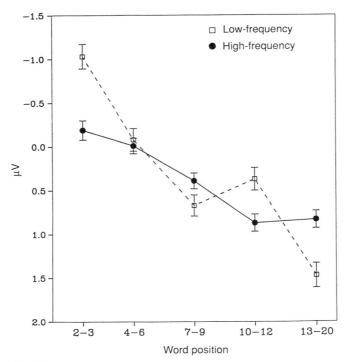

FIG. 8 Amplitude of the N400 elicited by intermediate open-class words in different ordinal positions of congruent sentences, averaged across electrode sites. Data from Van Petten (in press).

latency range of the P2 (200–250 ms, primarily at frontal scalp sites; Rugg, 1987; Van Petten et al., 1991; Young & Rugg, 1992). However, this early effect has been ephemeral, visible or not visible in apparently similar experimental designs (Bentin & Peled, 1990; Karayanadis et al., 1991; Nagy & Rugg, 1989; Rugg et al., 1988; Rugg & Nagy, 1987, 1989). Moreover, the direction of the repetition effect has been variable, sometimes an apparent enhancement of the P2 with repetition, sometimes an apparent diminution. The P2 effect has appeared often enough to suggest that it is a real phenomenon, but obviously we do not have a grasp of it at present.

The third repetition-sensitive component of the ERP is a late positivity. In word lists, this LPC is larger for the second than the first presentation of a word, and further is specific to low- rather than high-frequency words (Rugg, 1990; Rugg & Doyle, 1992; Young & Rugg, 1992). However, when we have compared initial versus subsequent presentations of words in connected discourse, we have observed that the late positivity is decreased rather than enhanced by repetition (Van Petten et al., 1991). The list and text effects are likely to be the same phemomenon, since both are most evident for low-frequency words, larger over the left than the right hemisphere, and have a latency range of 500–900 ms post-stimulus. Like the N400, the LPC is thus sensitive to both frequency and repetition. Finally, when entire sentences are repeated, the LPC repetition effect is most prominent for incongruous rather than congruous sentence completions (Besson et al., 1992). We have speculated that the LPC frequency/repetition effect reflects the retrieval of episodic information, but this is clearly a complex pattern of results calling for further research (for further discussion, see Besson et al., 1992; P. F. Mitchell et al., 1993; Van Petten et al., 1991).

7. Vocabulary Class

Kutas and Hillyard (1983) first noted that open-class or "content" words (nouns, verbs, most adjectives, -*ly* adverbs) elicited different ERPs than closed-class or "function" words (pronouns, articles, conjunctions, prepositions, etc.) in sentences. However, they did not attempt to determine which aspects of the vocabulary distinction (word length, frequency of usage, repetition, contextual constraint, abstractness of meaning, referentiality, syntactic role, etc.) were responsible for the ERP differences. The difference between open- and closed-class words is highly replicable (see Fig. 9 for a representative example) but

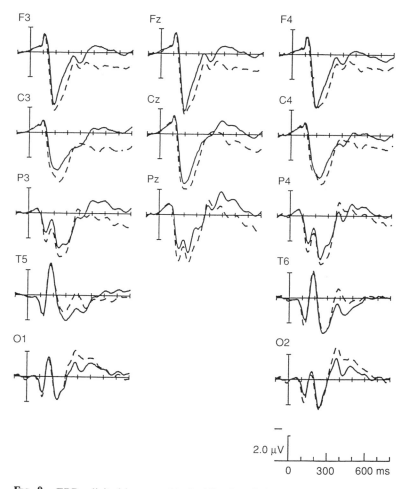

FIG. 9 ERPs elicited by open (*dashed lines*) and closed (*solid lines*) class words in sentences, excluding the initial and final words. F, frontal; C, central; P, parietal; T, temporal; O, occipital. Odd numbers denote sites over the left hemisphere; even numbers, sites over the right hemisphere. Data from Van Petten and Kutas (1990).

probably consists of variance due to more than one of the possible factors mentioned above. Closed-class words in sentences invariably elicit smaller N400s than open-class words. Van Petten and Kutas (1991b) suggested that this is due to the converging influences of higher frequency of usage, higher repetition rate, and greater predictability of closed class items in sentences.

A second difference between open- and closed-class words is a late ramp-shaped negativity over frontal scalp sites, dubbed the N400–700 (see Fig. 9, and Neville et al., 1992). Van Petten and Kutas observed variability in this component when comparing closed-class words in random word strings, syntactically legal but semantically anomalous sentences, and congruent sentences as in (1)–(3).

(1) *To prided the bury she room she of peanut the had china.*
(2) *He ran the half white car even though he couldn't name the raise.*
(3) *He was so wrapped up in the past that he never thought about the present.*

The frontal N400–700 proved sensitive to both sentence type and word position, as shown in Figure 10. Early in a sentence, the N400–700 was essentially absent in all three conditions but developed in amplitude over the course of congruent sentences. The N400–700 also seems to be absent when open- and closed-class words are presented in a list format for lexical decision (Garnsey, 1985). This finding suggests that the N400–700 does not distinguish between open- and closed-class words *per se* but is instead tied to the development of a coherent sentence structure. This together with other characteristics of the N400–700 effect is consistent with its being a member of the CNV family of potentials (Van Petten & Kutas, 1991b).

The N400 and N400–700 effects probably do not exhaust the ways that

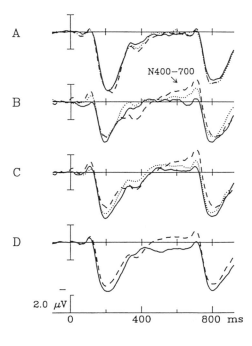

FIG. 10 (A) ERPs to closed-class words in the first and second ordinal positions of congruent sentences (*solid line*), syntactically structured but semantically anomalous sentences (*dotted line*), and random word strings (*dashed line*). (B) ERPs to closed-class words in the ninth and tenth positions of the same three conditions, showing the larger N400–700 in Congruent sentences. The Syntactic sentences appear to fall midway between the Congruent and Random conditions, but they were not statistically different from Random. (C) Closed-class words in the 3rd and 4th (*solid line*), 5th and 6th (*dotted line*), and 9th and 10th (*dashed line*) positions of Congruent sentences, showing the development of the N400–700 across the course of a sentence. (D) ERPs to all intermediate open (*solid line*) and closed (*dashed line*) class words from the congruent sentences. Data from Van Petten and Kutas (1991a).

open and closed ERPs differ. Indeed, the ERP correlates of vocabulary class and variability within each class are being actively pursued in several laboratories (Garnsey, 1985; Kluender & Kutas, 1993, in press; Neville et al., 1992; Van Petten & Kutas, 1991b).

B. Syntactic Manipulations

The history of N400 research demonstrates that VIOLATIONS have been a good way of eliciting large and robust ERP effects. However, the fact that this is the case does not imply that ERP components are specific or unique reflections of any given linguistic violation. For example, the N400 was originally viewed as a semantic violation detector, but numerous studies since have demonstrated that a violation is neither necessary nor sufficient to yield an N400 component. Instead, the semantic anomalies which elicit the largest N400 effects have proved to be derivable from an interaction of lexical properties (such as frequency of occurrence and vocabulary class) with contextual constraints at the sentence and discourse levels. ERP research on syntactic processing is only a few years old and has been focused on violations of syntactic structure as a first-pass strategy for obtaining ERP effects. As this research matures, it may prove possible to characterize many of the "syntactic" ERP effects as more general reflections of language processing rather than responses specific to linguistic errors (see Kutas & Kluender, in press, for a more extended discussion of the role of violations in ERP research).

Garnsey and colleagues constructed their stimulus sentences so that the presence or absence of an ERP violation response would provide the answer to the question of whether or not subjects use verb argument preferences as an on-line aid to sentence parsing (Garnsey et al., 1989). They used sentences with embedded questions to determine when subjects would assign a questioned item (i.e., filler) to a possible gap, as in (4)–(7).

(4) *The babysitter didn't know which **door** the child PUSHED _____ carelessly at the store.*

(5) *The babysitter didn't know which **name** the child PUSHED _____ carelessly at the store.*

(6) *The tour operator wondered which **visitor** the guide WALKED _____ briskly down the hall.*

(7) *The tour operator wondered which **topic** the guide WALKED _____ briskly down the hall.*

Because *push* usually takes a direct object, both a flexible parsing strategy based on verb argument preferences and an inflexible "first resort" strategy would assign *door* and *name* to the first possible gap location after the verb. Either strategy would thus result in a semantic incongruity at *pushed* in (5), as indexed by a large N400 relative to the control sentence (4). However, the two strategies predict different outcomes when the verb does not preferentially take an object, as in (6) and (7). Strict adherence to a "first resort strategy" would result in a large N400 following the verb *walked* in (7) but not in (6). On the other hand, if the parser was sensitive to verb argument preference, then neither (6) nor (7) would be anomalous at the verb and no N400 effect would be observed. This is indeed what the results showed.

Garnsey used the N400 semantic incongruity effect as a vehicle for examining questions about syntactic processing. Other studies have been more directly aimed at determining whether or not there is any ERP reflection of a syntactic violation *per se*. The first of these was performed by Kutas and Hillyard (1983), who incorporated morphological violations of verb number, noun number, and verb tense in written text. These morphological violations did not yield an N400 with the same amplitude and distribution as that elicited by semantic violations in the same texts, but there was nonetheless an enhanced negativity in the 300–500 ms range relative to control words. Additionally, there was a hint of an enhanced late positivity following the violaton (see Fig. 11).

This positivity was late enough to appear mostly in the recording epoch for the subsequent word in the sentence and so was not noted in the original report. A replication with another group of monolingual English speakers has shown that both the enhanced negativity and positivity were real effects, and that the different morphological violations are associated with different ERP changes (Kutas et al., in preparation). Comparisons with bilingual Spanish/ English speakers reading the same materials and analogous materials in Spanish showed that the exact pattern of negative and positive ERP violation effects was dependent both on the stimulus language and the subject's language history; for example, bilinguals who learned English relatively late (after 8 years) showed the largest late positivities to verb tense violations (see Fig. 12). Hagoort, Brown, and Groothusen (in press) have likewise observed an enlarged positivity in response to agreement errors in Dutch.

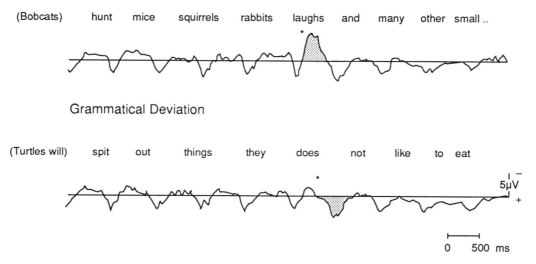

FIG. 11   Grand average ERPs to semantic violations and grammatical (morphological) violations embedded in text. Recordings are from a midline parietal site. Data from Kutas and Hillyard (1983).

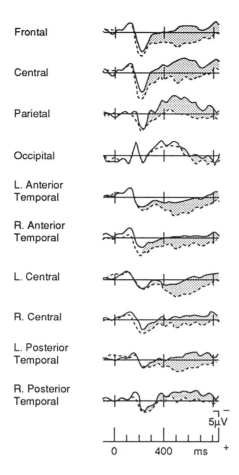

Frontal

Central

Parietal

Occipital

L. Anterior
Temporal

R. Anterior
Temporal

L. Central

R. Central

L. Posterior
Temporal

R. Posterior
Temporal

FIG. 12   Grand average ERPs elicited by verb tense violations (*dashed lines*) and control words (*solid lines*) embedded in Spanish text from Spanish-speaking individuals who had learned English after the age of eight. Data from Kutas et al. (in preparation).

Osterhout (1990; Osterhout & Holcomb, 1992) sought an ERP sign of syntactic violations by manipulating verb argument structure in a manner similar to Garnsey's work. In one experiment, he contrasted sentences like (8)–(9).

(8) *The broker hoped **to** sell the stock.*
(9) *The broker persuaded **to** sell the stock.*

Since *persuaded* in its active form requires an object, (9) becomes an unusual sentence construction at the word *to*, whereas (8) continues to be a common construction. [10] Osterhout observed that between 300 and 900 ms after the onset of the word *to*, the ERP in (9) was more positive, primarily over the frontal sites; the response was dubbed P600. The similarity between this P600 and the late positivity elicited by agreement violations is worth noting (Kutas et al., in preparation; Kutas & Hillyard, 1983), as is its possible relation to the N400–

[10] Note that (9) is not ungrammatical at *to*, as the sentence could continue *The broker persuaded to sell the stock was sent to jail*. Osterhout investigated this condition in a subsequent experiment.

700 effect described above.[11] More recording sites and greater scrutiny will be required to ascertain the relationships between the positivity elicited by agreement violations, Osterhout's P600, and the N400–700.

In a subsequent experiment, Osterhout used verbs which follow a gradient in the preference to take an object, as in (10)–(13).

(10) Pure intransitive: *The doctor hoped the patient **was** lying.*
(11) Biased intransitive: *The doctor believed the patient **was** lying.*
(12) Biased transitive: *The doctor charged the patient **was** lying.*
(13) Pure transitive: *The doctor forced the patient **was** lying.*

As in the first experiment, subjects performed a sentence acceptability task. The four sentence types showed a gradient of acceptability, but fairly similar ratings for the two intransitive conditions (91% vs. 84% vs. 66% vs. 4%, respectively). The ERPs elicited by the word *was* followed a similar gradient, showing the highest amplitude positivity in the Pure Transitive condition, intermediate amplitude positivity in the Biased Transitive condition, and little difference between the two intransitive conditions. Relative to Osterhout's previous report, this P600 began somewhat later (about 500 ms) and was larger over more posterior recording sites.

Both the scalp distribution and general appearance of the P600 in Osterhout's second experiment[12] are similar to those of the P300 component. Since subjects were performing a sentence-acceptability task where the word *was* delivered the task-relevant information, the conditions fit those which typically elicit decision-related P300s. Additionally, fewer sentences were judged unacceptable (about 40%) than acceptable, so that unacceptable sentences were lower in experimental probability, a second factor known to influence P300 amplitude. However, Hagoort and colleagues (in press) have also obtained centro-parietal positivities in response to syntactic errors when subjects were only asked to read for comprehension. One could still contend that language is so over-learned that the experimenter does not have control over what a subject considers "task-relevant," and that across a subject's life history with his or her language, an error is always a low-frequency event. However, it still remains to be sorted out why some "errors" elicit parietal P3-like positivities, some frontal positivities, and others N400s. Only after we understand this variability can a viable functional characterization of the processing systems handling various aspects of sentence structure be developed. We believe this will be one of the major challenges of psycholinguistic research using ERPs in the next decade. Whatever the ultimate solution, it is clear that comparisons among experiments conducted in different laboratories will be greatly facilitated if the contribution of specific experimental tasks, and the P300s likely to be elicited by those tasks, can be adequately controlled.

---

[11] The absence of the normal N400–700 would manifest as a relative positivity with a frontal distribution. If the P600 and N400–700 did prove to be the presence/absence of the same ERP component, it would suggest a link between normal sentence processing and the collapse of such processing in the face of certain types of ungrammatical sentences.

[12] We have described only two of six experiments in Osterhout's dissertation. See Osterhout (1990) for a more complete discussion.

Neville and colleagues (1991) also investigated a variety of syntactic errors in sentences. One condition included phrase structure violations which can be viewed as violations of normal word order. Subjects were asked to make grammaticality judgments on sentences like (14)–(15).

(14) *The scientist criticized a proof **of** the theorem.*
(15) *The scientist criticized Max's **of** proof the theorem.*

The erroneous word *of* in (15) was associated with a number of ERP effects relative to (14), including a pronounced negativity between 300 and 500 ms over temporal regions of the left hemisphere, and a bilaterally distributed late positivity.

In another condition, the "specified subject constraint" (Chomsky, 1973; Fiengo & Higginbotham, 1981; Huang, 1982) was violated, rendering questions like (17) ungrammatical.

(16) *The scientist criticized Max's **proof** of the theorem.*
(17) *What did the scientist criticize Max's **proof** of?*

Over left anterior sites in particular, the ERP to the word *proof* in (17) showed a sustained negativity relative to the control sentence. The earliest portion of this effect (starting at word onset) is too early to reflect differential processing of the word *proof* and must instead be a remnant of differential processing of the previous word. Given the high correlation in the stimulus set between (a) a question's eventual ungrammaticality and (b) the presence of a proper name in a question, the subjects may have begun differential processing before the occurrence of the word that actually rendered the question ungrammatical. Although the negative difference recorded at *proof* did begin early, the 300–500 ms latency band showed the largest amplitude, suggesting that this portion of the effect may indeed have been elicited by the ungrammatical word.

Kluender and Kutas (in press) have also reported negativities in the 300–500 ms latency band which are most prominent over left anterior regions (LAN). However, these were recorded at a number of word positions in questions that were unequivocally grammatical. ERPs were recorded as subjects read a variety of yes/no and *wh-* questions. Comparisons made at various points in the questions suggested that words elicited an enhanced LAN whenever there was an unresolved filler–gap dependency, so that the same lexical items in different question types, or at different points within the same question, would elicit LANs of different amplitudes. The LAN seemed to reflect the presence of an unassigned filler (presumably held in working memory) regardless of whether or not the filler–gap dependency was a grammatical one. Kluender and Kutas (1993) also found that the amplitude of the LAN was modulated by lexical factors at some locations within the questions. They have hypothesized that the amplitude of this left anterior negativity indexes the use of working memory during sentence comprehension. In this scheme, the LAN is most prominent during difficult-to-process or flat-out ungrammatical questions when a working memory system becomes overburdened from trying to maintain both lexical and filler–gap information simultaneously.

The application of ERPs to the study of sentence parsing and various syntactic structures is a field in its infancy. There are other very recent studies that we have not reviewed here (Hagoort et al., in press; King & Kutas, 1992;

Roesler et al., 1992), but those we discussed have been sufficient to illustrate the diversity of ERP effects elicited by syntactic manipulations. There is clearly ERP variability associated with syntactic variability, so that investigators have something to work with, a first step in any scientific endeavor. Moreover, there is an obvious difference between N400 effects which have been associated with semantic processing, word frequency, and repetition, and many of the other effects evident in studies of syntactic processing. We believe that a clear picture of the ERP concomitants of syntactic analysis will emerge as comparisons are made across a large number of studies from different labs, conducted in different languages, given some sensitivity to the following design considerations.

1. *Stimulus repetition.* Word repetition can elicit N400 and/or late positive ERP differences depending on the frequency of the eliciting word, the type of context, and the temporal interval since the last occurrence of the word. Repetition is thus best avoided unless it is the topic of interest.

2. *Task relevance.* Information concerning the subjects' assigned task will elicit P300s whose amplitude and latency will vary with the difficulty of the judgment and the confidence level associated with the decision. Unless this is a desired factor in the design, task-related decisions should be eliminated, postponed until after the recording epoch, or made orthogonal to the linguistic variables of interest.[13]

3. *Correlations between experimental conditions and incidental aspects of the stimulus set* may induce special strategies specific to the stimulus set.

4. *Pre-stimulus baselines for comparing two ERPs.* Activity from the preceding word may spill over into the recording epoch for the current word, so that the preceding words in different conditions should be as similar as possible.

5. *Ordinal position of the critical words in a sentence.* We have seen that the ERPs to both open and closed class words vary systematically (but differently) as a function of the position of the words in sentences, suggesting that this factor should be equated if it is not of interest. The differences between immediately adjacent words are, however, small in amplitude, so that contrasting words in slightly different positions may not have great impact on the data. However, the ERPs to initial and final words in sentences differ dramatically from one another, and from the ERPs elicited by intermediate words, so that it will never be reasonable to conduct comparisons across initial, intermediate, and final words.

VII. Conclusions

This chapter has been a review of the methods and data in the domain of the electrophysiology of psycholinguistics. It is aimed at the psycholinguist who wants to better understand experimental reports in which ERPs are the primary dependent measure and/or the brave souls who may wish to use ERPs to address certain psycholinguistic questions. Almost any question is game—all

---

[13] For example, Roesler and colleagues used a lexical decision task in a study comparing the ERPs to syntactically correct and incorrect sentences (Roesler et al., 1992). Although this yielded P300s, there was no reason to believe that their amplitudes or latencies would vary across the experimental conditions.

that is required is a good experimental design and a knowledge of the strengths and weaknesses of the ERP methodology. While we chose to organize the chapter around the methods and measures rather than the issues, it is the desire to answer the various questions concerned with the representation and timing of language processes at both psychological and physiological levels that has yielded the data that were reviewed and will no doubt drive the researchers of tomorrow farther into the wavy frontiers of comprehension and perhaps where almost no electrophysiologist has yet dared to venture—production.

ACKNOWLEDGMENTS

M. Kutas and some of the research described herein were supported by an RSDA from NIMH (MH00322) and grants from NICHD (HD22614) and NIA (AG08313). Cyma Van Petten was supported in part by NINDS NS30825. We thank Susan Garnsey for her organizational comments and Eve Wilhite for secretarial assistance.

REFERENCES

Allison, T., Wood, C. C., & McCarthy, G. (1986). The central nervous system. In M. G. H. Coles, E. Donchin, & S. W. Porges (Eds.), *Psychophysiology: Systems, processes, and applications* (pp. 5–25). New York: Guilford Press.

Ardal, S., Donald, M. W., Meuter, R., Muldrew, S., & Luce, M. (1990). Brain responses to semantic incongruity in bilinguals. *Brain and Language, 39,* 187–205.

Arezzo, J. C., Vaughan, H. G., Kraut, M. A., Steinschneider, M., & Legatt, A. D. (1986). Intercranial generators of event-related potentials in the monkey. In R. Q. Cracco & I. Bodis-Wollner (Eds.), *Evoked potentials: Frontiers of clinical neuroscience* (pp. 174–189). New York: Liss.

Balish, M., & Muratore, R. (1990). The inverse problem in electroencephalography and magnetoencephalography. *Advances in Neurology, 34,* 79–88.

Balota, D. A. (1990). The role of meaning in word recognition. In D. A. Balota, G. B. Flores d'Arcais, & K. Rayner (Eds.), *Comprehension processes in reading* (pp. 9–32). Hillsdale, NJ: Erlbaum.

Barrett, G., Blumhardt, L., Halliday, A. M., Halliday, E., & Kriss, A. (1976). A paradox in the lateralization of the visual evoked response. *Nature (London) 261,* 253–255.

Barrett, G., Neshige, R., & Shibasaki, H. (1987). Human auditory and somatosensory event-related potentials: Effects of response condition and age. *Electroencephalography and Clinical Neurophysiology, 66,* 409–419.

Barrett, S. E., & Rugg, M. D. (1989). Asymmetries in event-related potentials during rhyme-matching: Confirmation of the null effects of handedness. *Neuropsychologia, 27*(4), 539–548.

Bellugi, U., Klima, E. S., & Poizner, H. (1988). Sign language and the brain. In F. Plum (Ed.), *Language, communication, and the brain* (pp. 39–56). New York: Raven Press.

Bentin, S. (1987). Event-related potentials, semantic processes, and expectancy factors in word recognition. *Brain and Language, 31,* 308–327.

Bentin, S., Kutas, M., & Hillyard, S. A. (1993). *Semantic processing of attended and unattended words in dichotic listening: Behavioral and electrophysiological evidence.* Manuscript submitted for publication.

Bentin, S., Kutas, M., & Hillyard, S. A. (1993). Electrophysiological evidence for task effects on semantic priming in auditory word processing. *Psychophysiology, 30,* 161–169.

Bentin, S., McCarthy, G., & Wood, C. C. (1985). Event-related potentials associated with semantic priming. *Electroencephalography and Clinical Neurophysiology, 60,* 343–355.

Bentin, S., & Peled, B. S. (1990). The contribution of task-related factors to ERP repetition effects at short and long lags. *Memory & Cognition, 18,* 359–366.

Berg, P., & Scherg, M. (1991a). Dipole modelling of eye acuity and its application to the removal of eye artifacts from the EEG and MEG. *Clinical Physics and Physiological Measurement*, *12*, 49–54.

Berg, P., & Scherg, M. (1991b). Dipole models of eye movements and blinks. *Electroencephalography and Clinical Neurophysiology*, *79*(1), 36–44.

Berson, E. L. (1981). Electrical phenomena in the retina. In R. A. Moses (Ed.), *Adler's physiology of the eye: Clinical application*. St. Louis, MO: Mosby.

Bertrand, O., Perrin, F., & Pernier, J. (1985). A theoretical justification of the average reference in topographic evoked potential studies. *Electroencephalography and Clinical Neurophysiology*, *62*, 462–464.

Besson, M., Kutas, M., & Van Petten, C. (1992). An event-related potential (ERP) analysis of semantic congruity and repetition effects in sentences. *Journal of Cognitive Neuroscience*, *4*(2), 132–149.

Besson, M., & Macar, F. (1987). An event-related potential analysis of incongruity in music and other nonlinguistic contexts. *Psychophysiology*, *24*, 14–25.

Bever, T. G., Carrithers, C., Cowart, W., & Townsend, D. J. (1989). Language processing and familial handedness. In A. M. Galaburda (Ed.), *From reading to neurons* (pp. 331–357). Cambridge, MA: MIT Press.

Bloom, P. A., & Fischler, I. S. (1980). Completion norms for 329 sentence contexts. *Memory & Cognition*, *8*, 631–642.

Boddy, J. (1981). Evoked potentials and the dynamics of language processing. *Biological Psychology*, *13*, 125–140.

Boddy, J., & Weinberg, H. (1981). Brain potentials, perceptual mechanism and semantic categorization. *Biological Psychology*, *12*, 43–61.

Bradshaw, J. L., & Nettleton, N. C. (1981). The nature of hemispheric specialization in man. *Behavioral and Brain Sciences*, *4*, 51–91.

Brown, C. M., & Hagoort, P. (1993). The processing nature of the N400: Evidence from masked priming. *Journal of Cognitive Neuroscience*, *5*(1), 34–44.

Brunia, C. H. M. (1984). Contingent negative variation and readiness potential preceding foot movements. *Annals of the New York Academy of Sciences*, Vol. 425, (pp. 403–406) New York: Academy of Sciences.

Buchwald, J. S. (1990). Animal models of cognitive event-related potentials. In J. W. Rohrbaugh, R. Parasuraman, & R. Johnson, Jr. (Eds.), *Event-related brain potentials* (pp. 57–75). New York: Oxford University Press.

Buchwald, J. S., & Squires, N. S. (1982). Endogenous auditory potentials in the cat: A P300 model. In C. Woody (Ed.), *Conditioning: Representation of involved neural function* (pp. 503–515). New York: Raven Press.

Butler, S. R., & Glass, A. (1976). EEG correlates of cerebral dominance. In A. H. Riesen & R. F. Thompson (Eds.), *Advances in psychobiology* (pp. 219–272). New York: Wiley.

Butler, S. R., Glass, A., & Heffner, R. (1981). Asymmetries of the contingent negative variation (CNV) and its after positive wave (APW) related to differential hemispheric involvement in verbal and non-verbal tasks. *Biological Psychology*, *13*, 157–171.

Caspers, H., Speckmann, E. J., & Lehmenkuhler, A. (1980). Electrogenesis of cortical DC potentials. In H. H. Kornhuber & L. Deecke (Eds.), *Motivation, motor, and sensory processes of the brain: Electrical potentials, behavior, and clinical use* (pp. 3–16). Amsterdam: Elsevier.

Chiappa, K. H. (1983). *Evoked potentials in clinical medicine*. New York: Raven Press.

Chomsky, N. (1973). Conditions on transformations. In S. Anderson & P. Kiparsky (Eds.), *A festschrift for Morris Halle*. New York: Holt, Rinehart, & Wilson.

Coles, M. G. H., Gratton, G., Kramer, A. F., & Miller, G. A. (1986). Principles of signal acquisition and analysis. In M. G. H. Coles, E. Donchin, & S. W. Porges (Eds.), *Psychophysiology: Systems, processes, and applications*. New York: Guilford Press.

Coltheart, M., Davelaar, E., Jonasson, J. T., & Besner, D. (1977). Access to the internal lexicon. In S. Dornic (Ed.), *Attention and performance VI*. London: Academic Press.

Connolly, J. F., Stewart, S. H., & Phillips, N. A. (1990). The effects of processing requirements on neurophysiological responses to spoken sentences. *Brain and Language*, *39*, 302–318.

Cracco, R. Q., & Bodis-Wollner, I. (1986). *Evoked potentials: Frontiers of clinical neuroscience*. New York: Liss.

Dale, A. M., & Sereno, M. I. (1993). Improved localization of cortical activity by combining EEG and MEG with MRI cortical surface reconstruction: A linear approach. *Journal of Cognitive Neuroscience, 5*(2), 162–176.

de Groot, A. M. B. (1990). The locus of the associative-priming effect in the mental lexicon. In D. A. Balota, G. B. Flores d'Arcais, & K. Rayner (Eds.), *Comprehension processes in reading* (pp. 101–124). Hillsdale, NJ: Erlbaum.

Donchin, E. (1981). Surprise! . . . Surprise? *Psychophysiology, 18,* 493–513.

Donchin, E., & Coles, M. G. H. (1988). Is the P300 component a manifestation of context updating? *Behavioral and Brain Sciences, 11,* 357–374.

Donchin, E., Gerbrandt, L. K., Leifer, L., & Tucker, L. (1972). Is the contingent negative variation contingent on a motor response. *Psychophysiology, 9,* 178–188.

Donchin, E., Kutas, M., & McCarthy, G. (1977). Electrocortical indices of hemispheric utilization. In S. Harnad, R. W. Doty, L. Goldstein, J. Jaynes, & G. Krauthamer (Eds.), *Lateralization in the nervous system* (pp. 339–384). New York: Academic Press.

Donchin, E., McCarthy, G., & Kutas, M. (1977). Electroencephalographic investigations of hemispheric specialization. In J. E. Desmedt (Ed.), *Language and hemispheric specialization in man: Cerebral event-related potentials. Progress in clinical neurophysiology (Vol. 3).* (pp. 212–242). Basel: Karger.

Donchin, E., Ritter, W., & McCallum, W. C. (1978). Cognitive psychophysiology: The endogenous components of the ERP. In E. Callaway, P. Tueting, & S. H. Koslow (Eds.), *Event-related brain potentials in man* (pp. 349–441). New York: Academic Press.

Doyle, J., Ornstein, R. E., & Galin, D. (1974). Lateral specialization of cognitive mode: An EEG study. *Psychophysiology, 16,* 247–252.

Doyle, M. C., & Rugg, M. D. (1991). *Investigating formal and derivational priming using ERPs.* Poster presented at New Developments in Event-related Potentials, Hanover, Germany.

Duffy, F. H. (1986). *Topographic mapping of brain electrical activity.* Boston: Butterworth.

Duncan-Johnson, C. C., & Donchin, E. (1977). On quantifying surprise: The variation of event-related potentials with subjective probability. *Psychophysiology, 14,* 456–467.

Ehrlichman, H., & Wiener, M. (1980). EEG asymmetry during covert mental activity. *Psychophysiology, 17,* 228–236.

Engel, A. K., Konig, P., Kreiter, A. K., Schillen, T. B., & Singer, W. (1992). Temporal coding in the visual cortex: New vistas on integration in the nervous system. *Trends in Neurosciences, 15*(6), 218–226.

Feldstein, P., Smith, M. E., & Halgren, E. (1987, June). *Cross-modal repetition effects on the N400.* Paper presented at the Fourth International Conference on Cognitive Neurosciences, Paris-Dourdan, France.

Fiengo, R., & Higginbotham, J. (1981). Opacity in NP. *Linguistic Analysis, 7,* 395–421.

Fischler, I. S., Bloom, P. A., Childers, D. G., Arroyo, A. A., & Perry, N. W. (1984). Brain potentials during sentence verification: Late negativity and long-term memory strength. *Neuropsychologia, 22,* 559–568.

Fischler, I. S., Bloom, P. A., Childers, D. G., Roucos, S. E., & Perry, N. W. (1983). Brain potentials related to stages of sentence verification. *Psychophysiology, 20,* 400–409.

Fischler, I. S., Boaz, T., Childers, D. G., & Perry, N. W. (1985). Lexical and propositional components of priming during sentence comprehension. *Psychophysiology, 22,* 576. (Abstract)

Fischler, I. S., Boaz, T. L., McGovern, J., & Ransdell, S. (1987). An ERP analysis of repetition priming in bilinguals. In R. Johnson, Jr., J. W. Rohrbaugh, & R. Parasuraman (Eds.), *Current trends in event-related potential research: Electroencephalography and clinical neurophysiology, Supplemt 40* (pp. 388–393). Amsterdam: Elsevier.

Fodor, J. A., & Bever, T. G. (1965). The psychological reality of linguistic segments. *Journal of Learning and Verbal Behavior, 4,* 414–420.

Forster, K. I. (1987). Form-priming with masked primes: The best match hypothesis. In M. Coltheart (Ed.), *Attention and performance XII. The psychology of reading* (pp. 127–146). London: Erlbaum.

Foss, D. J., & Ross, J. R. (1983). Great expectations: Context effects during sentence processing. In G. B. Flores d'Arcais & R. J. Jarvella (Eds.), *The process of language understanding* (pp. 169–192). New York: Wiley.

Galin, D., & Ornstein, R. E. (1972). Lateral specialization of cognitive mode. II. EEG frequency analysis. *Psychophysiology, 9,* 412–418.

Garnsey, S. M. (1985). *Function and content words: Reaction time and evoked potential measures of word recognition* (Tech. Rep. No. URCS-29). Rochester, NY: University of Rochester.

Garnsey, S. M., Tanenhaus, M. K., & Chapman, R. M. (1989). Evoked potentials and the study of sentence comprehension. *Journal of Psycholinguistic Research, 18,* 51–60.

Garrett, M. F., Bever, T. G., & Fodor, J. (1966). The active use of grammar in speech perception. *Perception & Psychophysics, 1,* 30–32.

Gernsbacher, M. A., & Hargreaves, D. J. (1988). Accessing sentence participants: The advantage of first mention. *Journal of Memory and Language, 27,* 699–711.

Gevins, A. S., & Bressler, S. L. (1988). Functional topography of the human brain. In G. Pfurtscheller & F. H. Lopes da Silva (Eds.), *Functional brain imaging* (pp. 99–116). Toronto, Canada: Hans Huber.

Gevins, A. S., & Remond, A. (Eds.). (1987). *Methods of analysis of brain electrical and magnetic signals. Handbook of electroencephalography and clinical neurophysiology* (Revised Series, Vol. 1). Amsterdam: Elsevier.

Gevins, A. S., Zeitlin, G. M., Doyle, J. C., Yingling, C. D., Schaffer, R. E., Callaway, E., & Yeager, C. L. (1979). Electroencephalogram correlates of higher cortical functions. *Science, 203,* 665–667.

Glucksberg, S. (1984). Commentary: The functional equivalence of common and multiple codes. *Journal of Verbal Learning and Verbal Behavior, 23,* 100–104.

Goldenberg, G., Podreka, I., Uhl, I., Steiner, M., Willmes, K., & Deecke, L. (1989). Cerebral correlates of imagining colours, faces, and a map: I. SPECT of regional cerebral blood flow. *Neuropsychologia, 27*(11 & 12), 1315–1328.

Gratton, G., Bosco, C. M., Kramer, A. I., Coles, M. G., Wickens, C. D., & Donchin, E. (1990). Event-related brain potentials as indices of information extraction and response priming. *Electroencephalography and Clinical Neurophysiology, 75*(5), 415–432.

Gratton, G., Coles, M. G. H., Sirevaag, E. J., Eriksen, C. W., & Donchin, E. (1988). Pre- and post-stimulus activation of response channels: A psychophysiological analysis. *Journal of Experimental Psychology: Human Perception and Performance, 14,* 331–344.

Gray, C. M., Engel, A. K., Konig, P., & Singer, W. (1992). Synchronization of oscillatory neuronal responses in cat striate cortex: Temporal properties. *Visual Neuroscience, 8*(4), 337–347.

Grozinger, B., Kornhuber, H. H., Kriebel, J., Szirtes, J., & Westphal, K. T. P. (1980). The Bereitschaftspotential preceding the act of speaking: Also an analysis of artifacts. In H. H. Kornhuber & L. Deecke (Eds.), *Progress in brain research: Motivation, motor and sensory processes of the brain: Electrical potentials, behavior and clinical use* (pp. 798–804). Amsterdam: Elsevier.

Gunter, T. C., Jackson, J. L., & Mulder, G. (1992). An electrophysiological study of semantic processing in young and middle-aged academics. *Psychophysiology, 29*(1), 38–54.

Hagoort, P., Brown, C., & Groothusen, J. (1993). The syntactic positive shift as an ERP-measure of syntactic processing. *Language and Cognitive Processes, 8*(4), 439–483.

Halgren, E. (1990). Insights from evoked potentials into the neuropsychological mechanisms of reading. In A. B. Scheibel & A. F. Wechsler (Eds.), *Neurobiology of higher cognitive function* (pp. 103–149). New York: Guilford Press.

Halliday, A. M. (1982). *Evoked potentials in clinical testing.* New York: Churchill-Livingstone.

Hamberger, M. J., & Friedman, D. (1990). Age-related changes in semantic activation: Evidence from event-related potentials. In C. H. M. Brunia, A. W. K. Gaillard, & A. Toc (Eds.), *Psychophysiological brain research* (pp. 279–284). Tilburg, Netherlands: Tilburg University Press.

Harbin, T. J., Marsh, G. R., & Harvey, M. T. (1984). Differences in the late components of the event-related potential due to age and to semantic and non-semantic tasks. *Electroencephalography and Clinical Neurophysiology, 59,* 489–496.

Hardyck, C., & Petrinovich, L. (1977). Left-handedness. *Psychology Bulletin, 84,* 385–404.

Hari, R., & Lounasmaa, O. V. (1989). Recording and interpretation of cerebral magnetic fields. *Science, 244,* 432–436.

Heinze, H.-J., Muente, T. F., & Kutas, M. (1993). *Context effects in a category verification task as assessed by event-related brain potential (ERP) measures.* Manuscript submitted for publication.

Herning, R. I., Jones, R. T., & Hunt, J. S. (1987). Speech event-related potentials reflect linguistic content and processing level. *Brain and Language, 30,* 116–129.

Hillyard, S. A. (1973). The CNV and human behavior. In W. C. McCallum & J. R. Knott (Eds.),

Event-related slow potentials of the brain: Their relation to behavior. Electroencephalography and Clinical Neurophysiology, Supplement (pp. 161–171).

Holcomb, P. J. (1986). ERP correlates of semantic facilitation. *Electroencephalography and Clinical Neurophysiology, Supplement, 38,* pp. 320–322.

Holcomb, P. J. (1988). Automatic and attentional processing: An event-related brain potential analysis of semantic processing. *Brain and Language, 35,* 66–85.

Holcomb, P. J., Coffey, S. A., & Neville, H. J. (1992). Visual and auditory sentence processing: A developmental analysis using event-related brain potentials. *Developmental Neuropsychology, 8*(2 & 3), 203–241.

Holcomb, P. J., Kounios, J., & Anderson, J. (1993). *Dual coding, context availability and concreteness effects in sentence comprehension: An electrophysiological investigation.* Manuscript submitted for publication.

Holcomb, P. J., & Neville, H. J. (1990). Auditory and visual semantic priming in lexical decision: A comparison using event-related brain potentials. *Language and Cognitive Processes, 5,* 281–312.

Holcomb, P. J., & Neville, H. J. (1991). Natural speech processing: An analysis using event-related brain potentials. *Psychobiology, 19*(4), 286–300.

Huang, C. T. J. (1982). *Logical relations in Chinese and the theory of grammar.* Doctoral dissertation, Massachusetts Institute of Technology, Cambridge.

Irwin, D. A., Knott, J. R., McAdam, D. W., & Rebert, C. S. (1966). Motivational determinants of the 'contingent negative variation.' *Electroencephalography and Clinical Neurophysiology, 21,* 538–543.

Johnson, R., Jr. (1988). The amplitude of the P300 component of the event-related potential: Review and synthesis. In P. K. Ackles, J. R. Jennings, & M. G. H. Coles (Eds.), *Advances in psychophysiology* (pp. 69–138). Greenwich, CT: JAI Press.

Johnson, R., Jr. (1989a). Auditory and visual P300s in temporal lobectomy patients: Evidence for modality-dependent generators. *Psychophysiology, 26,* 633–650.

Johnson, R., Jr. (1989b). Developmental evidence for modality-dependent P300 generators: A nominative study. *Psychophysiology, 26,* 651–657.

Johnson, R., Jr., Rohrbaugh, J. W., & Parasuraman, R. (Eds.). (1987). *Current trends in event-related potential research: Electroencephalography and clinical neurophysiology, Supplement 40.* Amsterdam: Elsevier.

Just, M. A., & Carpenter, P. A. (1980). A theory of reading: From eye fixations to comprehension. *Psychological Review, 87,* 329–354.

Karayanadis, F., Andrews, S., Ward, P. B., & McConaghy, N. (1991). Effects of inter-item lag on word repetition: An event-related potential study. *Psychophysiology, 28,* 307–318.

King, J., & Kutas, M. (1992). ERPs to sentences varying in syntactic complexity for good and poor comprehenders. *Psychophysiology, 29*(4A), S44.

Kline, R., Ripps, H., & Dowling, J. E. (1978). Generation of B-wave currents in the skate retina. *Proceedings of the National Academy of Sciences of the U.S.A., 75,* 5727–5731.

Kluender, R., & Kutas, M. (in press). *Interaction of lexical and syntactic effects in the processing of unbounded dependencies. Language and cognitive processes.*

Kluender, R., & Kutas, M. (1993). Bridging the gap: Evidence from ERPs on the processing of unbounded dependencies. *Journal of Cognitive Neuroscience, 5*(2), 196–214.

Knight, R. T. (1990). Neural mechanisms of event-related potentials: Evidence from human lesion studies. In J. W. Rohrbaugh, R. Parasuraman, & R. Johnson, Jr. (Eds.), *Event-related brain potentials* (pp. 3–18). New York: Oxford University Press.

Knight, R. T., Scabini, D., Woods, D. L., & Clayworth, C. C. (1989). Contributions of temporal-parietal junction to the human auditory P3. *Brain Research, 502,* 109–116.

Kolb, B., & Whishaw, I. Q. (Eds.). (1990). *Fundamentals of human neuropsychology.* San Francisco: Freeman.

Kolers, P. A., & Brison, S. J. (1984). Commentary: On pictures, words, and their mental representation. *Journal of Verbal Learning and Verbal Behavior, 23,* 105–113.

Kotz, S. A., Holcomb, P. J., & Kounios, J. (1992). A comparison of semantic and repetition priming: Event-related potential evidence. *Psychophysiology, 29*(4A), S46.

Kounios, J., & Holcomb, P. (1992). Structure and process in semantic memory: Evidence from event-related potentials and reaction times. *Journal of Experimental Psychology, 121*(4), 460–480.

Kounios, J., & Holcomb, P. J. (in press). *Concreteness effects in semantic processing: ERP evidence supporting dual-coding theory. Journal of Experimental Psychology: Learning, Memory, and Cognition.*

Koyama, S., Nageishi, Y., Shimokochi, M., Hokama, M., Miyazato, Y., Miyatani, M., & Ogura, C. (1991). The N400 component of event-related potentials in schizophrenic patients: A preliminary study. *Electroencephalography and Clinical Neurophysiology, 78,* 124–132.

Kroll, J. F., & Potter, M. C. (1984). Recognizing words, pictures and concepts: A comparison of lexical, object, and reality decisions. *Journal of Verbal Learning and Verbal Behavior, 23,* 39–66.

Kurtzberg, D. (1985). Late auditory evoked potentials and speech sound discrimination by infants. Symposium presented at the meeting of the Society for Research in Child Development, Toronto.

Kutas, M. (1987). Event-related brain potentials (ERPs) elicited during rapid serial visual presentation of congruous and incongruous sentences. *Electroencephalography and Clinical Neurophysiology, Supplement 40,* 406–411.

Kutas, M. (1993). In the company of other words: Electrophysiological evidence for single word versus sentence context effects. *Language and Cognitive Processes, 8*(4), 533–572.

Kutas, M., Bates, E., Kluender, R., Van Petten, C., Clark, V., & Blesch, F. (in preparation). *What's critical about the critical period? Effects of early experience in the language processing of bilinguals.*

Kutas, M., & Hillyard, S. A. (1980a). Event-related brain potentials to semantically inappropriate and surprisingly large words. *Biological Psychology, 11,* 99–116.

Kutas, M., & Hillyard, S. A. (1980b). Reading between the lines: Event-related brain potentials during natural sentence processing. *Brain and Language, 11,* 354–373.

Kutas, M., & Hillyard, S. A. (1980c). Reading senseless sentences: Brain potentials reflect semantic incongruity. *Science, 207,* 203–205.

Kutas, M., & Hillyard, S. A. (1982). The lateral distribution of event-related potentials during sentence processing. *Neuropsychologia, 20,* 579–590.

Kutas, M., & Hillyard, S. A. (1983). Event-related brain potentials to grammatical errors and semantic anomalies. *Memory & Cognition, 11,* 539–550.

Kutas, M., & Hillyard, S. A. (1984). Brain potentials during reading reflect word expectancy and semantic association. *Nature (London), 307,* 161–163.

Kutas, M., & Hillyard, S. A. (1989). An electrophysiological probe of incidental semantic association. *Journal of Cognitive Neuroscience, 1,* 38–49.

Kutas, M., Hillyard, S. A., & Gazzaniga, M. S. (1988). Processing of semantic anomaly by right and left hemispheres of commissurotomy patients. *Brain, 111,* 553–576.

Kutas, M., & Kluender, R. (in press). What is who violating: A reconsideration of linguistic violations in light of event-related brain potentials. In H. Heinze, T. Muente, & G. R. Mangun (Eds.), *Cognitive electrophysiology.* La Jolla, CA: Birkhauser Boston, Inc.

Kutas, M., Lindamood, T. E., & Hillyard, S. A. (1984). Word expectancy and event-related brain potentials during sentence processing. In S. Kornblum & J. Requin (Eds.), *Preparatory states and processes* (pp. 217–237). Hillsdale, NJ: Erlbaum.

Kutas, M., McCarthy, G., & Donchin, E. (1977). Augmenting mental chronometry: The P300 as a measure of stimulus evaluation time. *Science, 197,* 792–795.

Kutas, M., Mitchiner, M., & Iragui-Madoz, V. (1992). Effects of aging on the N400 component of the ERP in a semantic categorization task. *Psychophysiology, 29*(4A), 47.

Kutas, M., Neville, H. J., & Holcomb, P. J. (1987). A preliminary comparison of the N400 response to semantic anomalies during reading, listening, and signing. *Electroencephalography and Clinical Neurophysiology, Supplement 39,* 325–330.

Kutas, M., & Van Petten, C. (1988). Event-related brain potential studies of language. In P. Ackles, J. R. Jennings, & M. G. H. Coles (Eds.), *Advances in psychophysiology* (pp. 139–187). Greenwich, CT: JAI Press.

Kutas, M., & Van Petten, C. (1990). Electrophysiological perspectives on comprehending written language. In P. M. Rossini & F. Mauguiere (Eds.), *Electroencephalography and clinical neurophysiology: Supplement 41. New trends and advanced techniques in clinical neurophysiology.* Amsterdam: Elsevier.

Kutas, M., Van Petten, C., & Besson, M. (1988). Event-related potential asymmetries during the reading of sentences. *Electroencephalography and Clinical Neurophysiology, 69,* 218–233.

Lang, W., Lang, M., Uhl, F., Kornhuber, A., Deecke, L., & Kornhuber, H. H. (1988). Left frontal lobe in verbal associative learning: A slow potential study. *Experimental Brain Research, 70,* 99–109.

Lehmann, D., & Skrandies, W. (1984). Spatial analysis of evoked potentials in man—A review. *Progress in Neurobiology, 23,* 227–250.

Lowel, S., & Singer, W. (1992). Selection of intrinsic horizontal connections in the visual cortex by correlated neuronal activity. *Science, 255,* 209–212.

Magliero, A., Bashore, T. R., Coles, M. G. H., & Donchin, E. (1984). On the dependence of P300 latency on stimulus evaluation processes. *Psychophysiology, 21,* 171–186.

Marslen-Wilson, W., & Tyler, L. G. (1980). The temporal structure of spoken language understanding. *Cognition, 8,* 1–71.

Marton, M., & Szirtes, J. (1988a). Context effects on saccade-related brain potentials to words during reading. *Neuropsychologia, 26*(3), 453–463.

Marton, M., & Szirtes, J. (1988b). Saccade-related brain potentials during reading correct and incorrect versions of proverbs. *International Journal of Psychophysiology, 6,* 273–280.

Marton, M., Szirtes, J., & Breuer, P. (1985). Electrocortical signs of word categorization in saccade-related brain potentials and visual evoked potentials. *International Journal of Psychophysiology, 3,* 131–144.

Marton, M., Szirtes, J., Donauer, N., & Breuer, P. (1985). Saccade-related brain potentials in semantic categorization tasks. *Biological Psychology, 20,* 163–184.

McAdam, D. W., Irwin, D. A., Rebert, C. S., & Knott, J. R. (1966). Cognitive control of the contingent negative variation. *Electroencephalography and Clinical Neurophysiology, 21,* 194–195.

McCallum, W. C., Farmer, S. F., & Pocock, P. V. (1984). The effects of physical and semantic incongruities on auditory event-related potentials. *Electroencephalography and Clinical Neurophysiology, 59,* 477–488.

McCarthy, G., & Donchin, E. (1981). A metric for thought: A comparison of P300 latency and reaction time. *Science, 211,* 77–80.

McCarthy, G., & Wood, C. C. (1985). Scalp distributions of event-related potentials: An ambiguity associated with analysis of variance models. *Electroencephalography and Clinical Neurophysiology, 62,* 203–208.

McCarthy, G., Wood, C. C., Williamson, P. D., & Spencer, D. D. (1989). Task-dependent field potentials in human hippocampal formation. *Journal of Neuroscience, 9,* 4253–4268.

Miller, J., & Hackley, S. A. (1992). Electrophysiological evidence for temporal overlap among contingent mental processes. *Journal of Experimental Psychology: General, 121*(2), 195–209.

Mills, D. L., Coffey, S. A., & Neville, H. J. (1993). Language acquisition and cerebral specialization in 20-month-old infants. *Journal of Cognitive Neuroscience, 5,* 317–334.

Mitchell, D. C., & Green, D. W. (1978). The effects of context and content on immediate processing in reading. *Quarterly Journal of Experimental Psychology, 30,* 609–636.

Mitchell, P. F., Andrews, S., & Ward, P. B. (1993). An event-related potential study of semantic congruity and repetition in sentence-reading task: Effects of context change. *Psychophysiology, 30,* 496–509.

Molfese, D. L. (1980). The phoneme and the engram: Electrophysiological evidence for the acoustic invariant in stop consonants. *Brain and Language, 9,* 372–376.

Molfese, D. L. (1989). Electrophysiological correlates of word meanings in 14-month-old human infants. *Developmental Neuropsychology, 5,* 70–103.

Molfese, D. L. (1990). Auditory evoked responses recorded from 16-month-old human infants to words they did and did not know. *Brain and Language, 38,* 345–363.

Nagy, M. E., & Rugg, M. D. (1989). Modulation of event-related potentials by word repetition: The effects of inter-item lag. *Psychophysiology, 26*(4), 431–436.

Neville, H. J. (1974). Electrographic correlates of lateral asymmetry in the processing of verbal and nonverbal auditory stimuli. *Journal of Psycholinguistic Research, 3,* 151–163.

Neville, H. J. (1980). Event-related potentials in neuropsychological studies of language. *Brain and Language, 11,* 300–318.

Neville, H. J. (1985). Effects of early sensory and language experience on the development of the human brain. In J. Mehler & R. Fox (Eds.), *Neonate cognition: Beyond the blooming buzzing confusion.* Hillsdale, NJ: Erlbaum.

Neville, H. J. (1991). Whence the specialization of the language hemisphere? In I. G. Mattingly & M. Studdert-Kennedy (Eds.), *Modularity and the motor theory of speech perception* (pp. 269–294). Hillsdale, NJ: Erlbaum.

Neville, H. J., Coffey, S., Holcomb, P., & Tallal, P. (1993). The neurobiology of sensory and language processing in language-impaired children. *Journal of Cognitive Neuroscience, 5*(2), 235–253.

Neville, H. J., Kutas, M., Chesney, G., & Schmidt, A. (1986). Event-related brain potentials during the initial encoding and subsequent recognition memory of congruous and incongruous words. *Journal of Memory and Language, 25,* 75–92.

Neville, H. J., Kutas, M., & Schmidt, A. (1982). Event-related potential studies of cerebral specialization during reading. II. Studies of congenitally deaf adults. *Brain and Language, 16,* 316–337.

Neville, H. J., & Lawson, D. (1987a). Attention to central and peripheral visual space in a movement detection task. I. Normal hearing adults. *Brain Research, 405,* 253–267.

Neville, H. J., & Lawson, D. (1987b). Attention to central and peripheral visual space in a movement detection task: An event-related potential and behavior study. II. Congenitally deaf adults. *Brain Research, 405,* 268–283.

Neville, H. J., & Lawson, D. (1987c). Attention to central and peripheral visual space in a movement detection task: An event-related potential and behavior study. III. Separate effects of auditory deprivation and acquisition of a visual language. *Brain Research, 405,* 284–294.

Neville, H. J., Mills, D. L., & Lawson, D. (1992). Fractionating language: Different neural subsystems with different sensitive periods. *Cerebral Cortex, 2*(3), 244–258.

Neville, H. J., Mills, D. L., & Bellugi, U. (in press). Effects of altered auditory sensitivity and age of language acquisition on the development of language-relevant neural systems: Preliminary studies. In S. Broman (Ed.), *Atypical cognitive deficits in developmental disorders: Implications for brain function.* Hillsdale, NJ: Erlbaum.

Neville, H. J., Nicol, J. L., Barss, A., Forster, K. I., & Garrett, M. F. (1991). Syntactically based sentence processing classes: Evidence from event-related brain potentials. *Journal of Cognitive Neuroscience, 3,* 151–165.

Neville, H. J., Pratarelli, M. E., & Forster, K. A. (1989). Distinct neural systems for lexical and episodic representations of words. *Neuroscience Abstracts, 15,* 246.

Nigam, A., Hoffman, J. E., & Simons, R. F. (1992). N400 to semantically anomalous pictures and words. *Journal of Cognitive Neuroscience, 4*(1), 15–22.

Nobre, A. C., & McCarthy, G. (1987). Visual selective attention to meaningful text: An analysis of event-related potentials. *Society for Neuroscience Abstracts, 13,* 852.

Nobre, A. C., & McCarthy, G. (1992, June). *Attention to interleaved stories in the absence of physical cues.* Poster presented at the Fifth International Conference on Cognitive Neurosciences, Jerusalem, Israel.

Nunez, P. L. (1981). *Electric fields of the brain.* New York: Oxford University Press.

Nunez, P. L. (1990). Physical principles and neurophysiological mechanisms underlying event-related potentials. In J. W. Rohrbaugh, R. Parasuraman, & R. Johnson, Jr. (Eds.), *Event-related brain potentials* (pp. 19–36). New York: Oxford University Press.

O'Halloran, J. P., Isenhart, R., Sandman, C. A., & Larkey, L. S. (1988). Brain responses to semantic anomaly in natural, continuous speech. *International Journal of Psychophysiology, 6,* 243–254.

Orsini, D. L., Satz, P., Soper, H. V., & Light, R. K. (1985). The role of familial sinistrality in cerebral organization. *Neuropsychologia, 23,* 223–231.

Osman, A., Bashore, T., Coles, M. G. H., Donchin, E., & Meyer, D. (1992). On the transmission of partial information: Inferences from movement-related brain potentials. *Journal of Experimental Psychology, 18*(1), 217–232.

Osterhout, L. (1990). *Event-related brain potentials elicited during sentence comprehension.* Unpublished doctoral dissertation, Tufts University, Medford, MA.

Osterhout, L., & Holcomb, P. J. (1992). Event-related brain potentials elicited by syntactic anomaly. *Journal of Memory and Language, 31*(6), 785–806.

O'Toole, D. M., & Iacono, W. G. (1987). An evaluation of different techniques for removing eye-blink artifact from visual evoked potential recordings. *Psychophysiology, 24,* 487–497.

Otten, L. J., Rugg, M. D., & Doyle, M. C. (in press). Modulation of event-related potentials by word repetition: The role of selective attention. *Psychophysiology.*

Paivio, A. (1991). Dual coding theory: Retrospect and current status. *Canadian Journal of Psychology, 45,* 255–287.

Paller, K. A., Kutas, M., Shimamura, A. P., & Squire, L. R. (1987). Brain responses to concrete and abstract words reflect processes that correlate with later performance on tests of recall and stem-completion priming. In R. Johnson, Jr., J. W. Rohrbaugh, & R. Parasuraman (Eds.), *Current trends in event-related brain potentials: Electroencephalography and clinical neurophysiology, Supplement 40* (pp. 360–365). Amsterdam: Elsevier.

Paller, K. A., Zola-Morgan, S., Squire, L. R., & Hillyard, S. A. (1988). P3-Like brain waves in normal monkeys and monkeys with medial temporal lesions. *Behavioral Neuroscience, 102,* 714–725.

Papanicolaou, A. C. (1980). Cerebral excitation profiles in language processing: The photic probe paradigm. *Brain and Language, 9,* 269–280.

Patterson, K., & Coltheart, V. (1987). Phonological processes in reading: A tutorial review. In M. Coltheart (Ed.), *Attention and performance XII. The psychology of reading* (pp. 421–448). London: Erlbaum.

Perecman, E. (Ed.). (1983). *Cognitive processing in the right hemisphere.* New York: Academic Press.

Pernier, J., Perrin, F., & Bertrand, O. (1988). Scalp current density fields: Concept and properties. *Electroencephalography and Clinical Neurophysiology, 69,* 385–389.

Perrin, F., Pernier, J., Bertrand, O., Giard, M. H., & Echallier, J. F. (1987). Mapping of scalp potentials by surface spline interpolation. *Electroencephalography and Clinical Neurophysiology, 66,* 75–81.

Picton, T. W., & Stuss, D. T. (1984). Event-related potentials in the study of speech and language: A critical review. In D. N. Caplan, A. R. Lecours, & A. M. Smith (Eds.), *Biological perspectives on language* (pp. 303–360). Cambridge, MA: MIT Press.

Pineda, J. A., Foote, S. L., & Neville, H. J. (1989). Effects of Locus Coeruleus lesions on auditory, long-latency, event-related potentials in monkeys. *Journal of Neuroscience, 9,* 81–93.

Pineda, J. A., Swick, D., & Foote, S. L. (1991). Noradrenergic and cholinergic influences on the genesis of P3-like potentials. In C. H. M. Brunia (Ed.), *Event-related brain research* (pp. 165–172). Amsterdam: Elsevier.

Poizner, H., Bellugi, U., & Klima, E. S. (1991). Brain function for language: Perspectives from another modality. In I. G. Mattingly & M. Studdert-Kennedy (Eds.), *Modularity and the motor theory of speech perception* (pp. 145–174). Hillsdale, NJ: Erlbaum.

Polich, J. M., McCarthy, G., Wang, W. S., & Donchin, E. (1983). When words collide: Orthographic and phonological interference during word processing. *Biological Psychology, 16,* 155–180.

Polich, J. M., Vanasse, L., & Donchin, E. (1981). Category expectancy and the N200. *Psychophysiology, 18,* 142.

Posner, M. I., & Boies, S. J. (1971). Components of attention. *Psychology Review, 78,* 391–408.

Pritchard, W. S. (1981). Psychophysiology of P300: A review. *Psychological Bulletin, 89,* 506–540.

Pylyshyn, Z. W. (1973). What the mind's eye tells the mind's brain: A critique of mental imagery. *Psychological Bulletin, 80,* 1–24.

Regan, D. (1989). *Human brain electrophysiology: Evoked-potentials and evoked magnetic fields in science and medicine.* New York: Elsevier.

Ritter, W., Simson, R., & Vaughan, H. G. (1972). Association cortex potential and reaction time in auditory discrimination. *Electroencephalography and Clinical Neurophysiology, 33,* 547–555.

Roesler, F., Friederici, A. D., Puetz, P., & Hahne, A. (1992). Event-related brain potentials (ERPs) during linguistic processing: Semantic and syntactic priming effects. *Journal of Clinical and Experimental Neuropsychology, 14,* 33.

Rohrbaugh, J. W., & Gaillard, A. W. K. (1983). Sensory and motor aspects of the contingent negative variation. In A. W. K. Gaillard & W. Ritter (Eds.), *Tutorials in ERP research: Endogenous components* (pp. 269–310). Amsterdam: North-Holland.

Ruchkin, D., Johnson, R., Grafman, J., Canoune, H., & Ritter, W. (1992). Distinctions and similarities among working memory processes: An event-related potential study. *Cognitive Brain Research, 1,* 53–66.

Rugg, M. D. (1984). Event-related potentials and the phonological processing of words and non-words. *Neuropsychologia, 22,* 435–443.

Rugg, M. D. (1985a). The effects of handedness on event-related potentials in a rhyme matching task. *Neuropsychologia, 23,* 765–775.

Rugg, M. D. (1985b). The effects of semantic priming and word repetition on event-related potentials. *Psychophysiology, 22,* 642–647.

Rugg, M. D. (1987). Dissociation of semantic priming, word and nonword repetition by event-related potentials. *Quarterly Journal of Experimental Psychology, 39A,* 123–148.

Rugg, M. D. (1990). Event-related brain potentials dissociate repetition effects of high- and low-frequency words. *Memory & Cognition, 18,* 367–379.

Rugg, M. D. (1992, June). *Electrophysiological studies of human memory.* Paper presented at the Fifth International Conference on Cognitive Neurosciences, Jerusalem, Israel.

Rugg, M. D., & Doyle, M. C. (1992). Event-related potentials and recognition memory for low- and high-frequency words. *Journal of Cognitive Neuroscience, 4,* 69–79.

Rugg, M. D., Furda, J., & Lorist, M. (1988). The effects of task on the modulation of event-related potentials by word repetition. *Psychophysiology, 25,* 55–63.

Rugg, M. D., Kok, A., Barrett, G., & Fischler, I. S. (1986). ERPs associated with language and hemispheric specialization. In W. C. McCallum, R. Zapolli, & F. Denoth (Eds.), *Cerebral psychophysiology: Studies in event-related potentials* (pp. 273–300). Amsterdam: Elsevier.

Rugg, M. D., & Nagy, M. E. (1987). Lexical contribution to nonword-repetition effects: Evidence from event-related potentials. *Memory & Cognition, 15,* 473–481.

Rugg, M. D., & Nagy, M. E. (1989). Event-related potentials and recognition memory for words. *Electroencephalography and Clinical Neurophysiology, 72,* 395–406.

Sanquist, T. F., Rohrbaugh, J. W., Syndulko, K., & Lindsley, D. B. (1980). Electrocortical signs of levels of processing: Perceptual analysis and recognition memory. *Psychophysiology, 17,* 568–576.

Schmidt, A. L., Arthur, D. L., Kutas, M., George, J., & Flynn, E. (1989). Neuromagnetic responses evoked during reading meaningful and meaningless sentences. *Psychophysiology, 26,* S6.

Seidenberg, M. S., & Tanenhaus, M. K. (1979). Orthographic effects on rhyme monitoring. *Journal of Experimental Psychology: Human Learning and Memory, 5,* 546–554.

Simson, R., Vaughan, H. G., & Ritter, W. (1977). The scalp topography of potentials in auditory and visual discrimination tasks. *Electroencephalography and Clinical Neurophysiology, 42,* 528–535.

Singer, W. (1990). The formation of cooperative cell assemblies in the visual cortex. *Journal of Experimental Biology, 153,* 177–197.

Smith, M. E., & Halgren, E. (1987). Event-related potentials during lexical decision: Effects of repetition, word frequency, pronounceability, and concreteness. In R. Johnson, Jr., J. W. Rohrbaugh, & R. Parasuraman (Eds.), *Current trends in event-related potential research: Electroencephalography and Clinical Neurophysiology, Supplement 40* (pp. 417–421). Amsterdam: Elsevier.

Smith, M. E., & Halgren, E. (1989). Dissociation of recognition memory components following temporal lobe lesions. *Journal of Experimental Psychology: Learning, Memory, and Cognition, 15,* 50–60.

Snyder, E., Hillyard, S. A., & Galambos, R. (1980). Similarities and differences among the P3 waves to detected signals in three modalities. *Psychophysiology, 17,* 112–122.

Spitzer, A. R., Cohen, L. G., Fabrikant, J., & Hallett, M. (1989). A method for determining optimal interelectrode spacing for topographic mapping. *Electroencephalography and Clinical Neurophysiology, 72,* 355–361.

Squires, K., Wickens, C., Squires, N., & Donchin, E. (1976). The effect of stimulus sequence on the waveform of the cortical event-related potential. *Science, 193,* 1142–1146.

Stuss, D. T., Picton, T. W., & Cerri, A. M. (1988). Electrophysiological manifestations of typicality judgement. *Brain and Language, 33*(2), 260–272.

Stuss, D. T., Sarazin, F. F., Leech, E. E., & Picton, T. W. (1983). Event-related potentials during naming and mental rotation. *Electroencephalography and Clinical Neurophysiology, 56,* 133–146.

Taylor, W. L. (1953). "Cloze" procedure: A new tool for measuring readability. *Journalism Quarterly, 30,* 415–417.

Tomberg, C., Noel, P., Ozaki, I., & Desmedt, J. E. (1990). Inadequacy of the average reference for the topographic mapping of focal enhancements of brain potentials. *Electroencephalography and Clinical Neurophysiology, 77*(4), 259–265.

Uhl, F., Franzen, P., Serles, W., Lang, W., Lindinger, G., & Deecke, L. (1990). Anterior frontal cortex and the effect of proactive interference in paired associate learning: A DC potential study. *Journal of Cognitive Neuroscience, 2*(4), 373–382.

Uhl, F., Goldenberg, G., Lang, W., Lindinger, G., Steiner, M., & Deecke, L. (1990). Cerebral correlates of imaging colours, faces and a map. II. Negative cortical DC potentials. *Neuropsychologia, 28*(1), 81–93.

Uhl, F., Lang, W., Lindinger, G., & Deecke, L. (1990). Elaborative strategies in word pair learning: DC-Potential correlates of differential frontal and temporal lobe involvement. *Neuropsychologia, 28*(7), 707–717.

Uhl, F., Lang, W., Spieth, F., & Deecke, L. (1990). Negative cortical potentials when classifying familiar and unfamiliar faces. *Cortex, 26*, 157–161.

van Oosterom, A. (1991). History and evolution of methods for solving the inverse problem. *Journal of Clinical Neurophysiology, 8*, 371–380.

Van Petten, C. (1993). A comparison of lexical and sentence-level context effects in event-related potentials. *Language and Cognitive Processes, 8*(4).

Van Petten, C., & Kutas, M. (1987). Ambiguous words in context: An event-related potential analysis of the time course of meaning activation. *Journal of Memory and Language, 26*, 188–208.

Van Petten, C., & Kutas, M. (1988). The use of event-related potentials in the study of brain asymmetries. *International Journal of Neuroscience, 39*, 91–99.

Van Petten, C., & Kutas, M. (1990). Interactions between sentence context and word frequency in event-related brain potentials. *Memory and Cognition, 18*, 380–393.

Van Petten, C., & Kutas, M. (1991a). Electrophysiological evidence for the flexibility of lexical processing. In G. Simpson (Ed.), *Word and sentence* (pp. 129–184). Amsterdam: North-Holland.

Van Petten, C., & Kutas, M. (1991b). Influences of semantic and syntactic context on open and closed class words. *Memory & Cognition, 19*, 95–112.

Van Petten, C., Kutas, M., Kluender, R., Mitchiner, M., & McIsaac, H. (1991). Fractionating the word repetition effect with event-related potentials. *Journal of Cognitive Neuroscience, 3*, 131–150.

Vasey, W. V., & Thayer, J. F. (1987). The continuing problem of false positives in repeated measures ANOVA in psychophysiology: A multivariate solution. *Psychophysiology, 24*, 479–486.

Verleger, R. (1988). Event-related potentials and cognition: A critique of the context updating hypothesis and an alternative interpretation of P3. *Behavioral and Brain Sciences, 11*, 343–427.

Walter, W. G., Cooper, R., Aldridge, V. J., McCallum, W. C., & Winter, A. L. (1964). Contingent negative variation: An electric sign of sensorimotor association and expectancy in the human brain. *Nature (London), 203*, 380–384.

Williamson, S. J., & Kaufman, L. (1987). Analysis of neuromagnetic signals. In A. S. Gevins & A. Remond (Eds.), *Methods of analysis of brain electrical and magnetic signals. Handbook of electroencephalography and clinical neurophysiology* (Revised series, Vol. 1). (pp. 405–448). Amsterdam: Elsevier.

Woldorff, M. (1993). Distortion of ERP averages due to overlap from temporally adjacent ERPs: Analysis and correction. *Psychophysiology, 30*, 98–119.

Wood, C. C. (1975). Auditory and phonetic levels of processing in speech perception: Neurophysiological and information-processing analysis. *Journal of Experimental Psychology, 104*, 3–20.

Wood, C. C., & Allison, T. (1981). Interpretation of evoked potentials: A neurophysiological perspective. *Canadian Journal of Psychology, 35*, 113–135.

Young, M. P., & Rugg, M. D. (1992). Word frequency and multiple repetition as determinants of the modulation of ERPs in a semantic classification task. *Psychophysiology, 29*(6), 664–676.

CHAPTER 5

A GUIDE TO RESEARCH ON THE PERCEPTION OF SPEECH

ROBERT E. REMEZ

I. INTRODUCTION

"Turn up your funk motor!" said OVE. Its dictum, borrowed from singer James Brown, was a result of a graduate school assignment, circa 1975, to match the acoustic pattern of a natural utterance using a speech synthesizer known as OVE (for Orator Verbis Electris: Fant & Martony, 1962); and, in the process, to study the acoustic currency redeemable as phonetic properties. The impression that OVE spoke intelligibly resulted from the accuracy of the spectral analyses that were used to set its parameters; that it sounded like a plausible voice was a consequence of its precise simulation of glottal impulses and its production of stately, five-format resonance patterns. And both the intelligibility and naturalness of this synthetic signal depended, as natural signals do, on the receptivity of the listener, which is the topic of the present chapter. Because the recognition of speech is a subject of study by diverse disciplines, even brief exposure to this variegated literature can produce vertigo. One potential antidote offered here is a perceptual perspective on speech, which takes an account of human speech perception as its principal aim. Of course, we are farther from a complete account than the easy success with OVE had implied. The overarching questions remain: What is speech perception? How does the listener know what the talker is saying?

The objectives of this chapter must be modest. Rather than presenting an enumeration of the work that now occupies the field of speech perception, this essay describes several differences among contemporary approaches, exposing the uniquely perceptual issues about spoken communication. First, we examine the ontology of speech perception, reviewing along the way the research on gestural, auditory, and linguistic claims about the nature of speech perception. Second, we consider the issue of perceptual mode and of modularity. Third, we contrast the study of the perceptual basis for speech sounds with the study of the perception of speech. Last, we speculate about perceptual organization of speech. Overall, the chapter tries to point the way, as a guide does, and must leave aside much of the rich detail that would appear in a field manual.

II. On the Ontology of Phonetic Categories

No guide to the varieties of research on speech can overlook the great differences that characterize the contending conceptualizations of speech perception. MacNeilage (1971) once amusingly indicated these differences by contrasting the metatheoretical influences deriving from neurophysiology, from linguistics, from empiricism, or from materialism. Today, the different conceptualizations do not rest only on different traditions or inspirations. There appear to be substantial disagreements a priori about the basic nature of speech perception and disunity in defining the phenomena to be explained in a perceptual account. In familiar terms, these accounts mainly diverge in designating the distal objects of perception.

What are the distal objects of phonetic perception? This question invokes a general paradigm for framing perceptual hypotheses which originated with the earliest adventures in physiological optics (N. Pastore, 1971) but which was codified in our time by Gestalt psychology. It stipulates that objects existing at some remove from the perceiver impart a pattern to an energy field, which mediates the contact between objects and perceiver. The senses then transduce proximal effects of the patterned medium; and, perception creates knowledge of DISTAL OBJECTS by detecting and differentiating the properties of PROXIMAL STIMULATION. This much is axiomatic for contemporary views of perception, but in the case of speech, the problem of designating the distal objects is set in three very different ways. One way proceeds literally, admitting that the vocal anatomy forms the sound. From this observation, it has seemed appropriate to take the tongue, lips, jaw, and so on as the distal objects perceived through an analysis of the transduced acoustic medium. In this account, perception brings about an experience of the articulatory causes of sounds that strike the ear. This first kind of perceptual theory aims to explain such phenomena.

These days, the straightforward equation between distal object and articulator is opposed in two different ways. One opposing view ignores the talker altogether in favor of the listener's auditory processes. In this conceptualization, the perceptual objects are defined as types of auditory qualities, by the premise that the sounds of speech self-evidently evoke a sufficient auditory process. Each distinctive phonetic element is cast as an auditory type, requiring reference neither to a talker's phonetic intentions nor to an elevated tongue-tip. Here, the theory aims to explain the projection from auditory type to phonetic type.

The other way that perceptual accounts have sidestepped a literal-minded designation of distal objects asserts that the cause of spoken proximal stimulation is a talker, and not merely a talker's vocal anatomy. In this framework, the talker's linguistic intentions govern tongue movements and lip protrusions and so on and are the ultimate causes of the proximal stimulation. Therefore, the distal objects in this view of speech perception are linguistic and abstract, each drawn from a set of markers that compose a matrix of contrasts at one or more levels of language. Accordingly, the movements of the vocal anatomy figure as components of an articulatory medium that precedes the acoustic medium in conveying the talker's linguistic intentions to the listener (see Studdert-Kennedy, 1986). In this formulation, the perceptual account aims to explain the listener's awareness of a talker's linguistic intent.

At this juncture, rather different versions of speech perception follow from the premise that the listener perceives either movements of the vocal anatomy, or a succession of psychoacoustic tokens, or linguistic intentions that rule the production of speech. Although some contemporary research supports one or another premise by delineating its theoretical advantages, there are also a variety of reports examining phonetic perceptual experience directly. These studies have sought to test whether phonetic perception includes articulatory or psychoacoustic representations along with phonetic properties. In the past few years of such research, the theoretical fog that caused this difference in definition seems to be lifting, and by reviewing the evidence favoring each view, we can resolve the ontological issues in speech perception more clearly. We will eliminate two of the three alternatives and frame the discussion of other current issues.

A. Gestural Themes in Speech Perception

Appeals to articulation in the perception of speech have been made in one form or another since the earliest psychological studies (Washburn, 1916), and it must be acknowledged that the pivotal conceptualization of speech perception for the past 35 years—as model and as lightning rod—has been the motor theory (A. M. Liberman, 1957; A. M. Liberman, Cooper, Shankweiler, & Studdert-Kennedy, 1967). The heart of the classic motor theory is a hypothetical solution ot the INVERSE PROBLEM in speech perception, in which the perceiver is said to determine the causes of the acoustic spectra incident at the ear by covertly modeling the articulation of speech. Here, the listener is conceptualized as a talker who produces the same kinds of spectra as those comprised in speech signals and who therefore listens in a special way. A key premise of this approach is a claim of a one-to-one correspondence between motor signal and phonetic segment, though the correspondence between acoustic manifestations and underlying phonetic segments is many-to-one. To cope with the indeterminacy of a perceptual projection from auditory effect to phonetic cause, the listener instead recreates the articulations covertly that might have produced the spectra incident at the ear, by special cognitive recourse to the small stock of motor plans that express phonetic segments. In short, the perceiver makes the best of the situation in which a condition of isomorphism exists only between motor signal and phonetic segment, and not between phonetic segment and acoustic effect.

The motor theory in its classic form was undone by several lines of study. First, the presumed isomorphism between motor signal and phonetic segment proved to be false. On closer examination, there seemed to be as many motor manifestations of a given consonant as there were acoustic manifestations (MacNeilage, 1972). In other words, the perceiver who somehow achieved access to the efferent neural component of an utterance would find no core of phonetic invariance in the signals after all. Furthermore, key demonstrations that speech perception survived despite motor incapacity weakened the case. The motor theory is only true if perception is contingent on production (MacNeilage,

Rootes, & Chase, 1967). Much convincing evidence opposing a special perceptual role for motor signals or articulatory modeling also stemmed from a remarkable efflorescence of research on infants in the past two decades. The greater part of this work showed that subjects of tender and inarticulate age exhibit an uncanny prodigiousness as phonetic listeners, as if neither proficient articulation nor even much experience is requisite for speech perception (Eimas, Miller, & Jusczyk, 1987).

Nonetheless, the claim of specialization and the focus on speech production survives due to two theoretical developments that drew on the luster of the classic motor theory, each in very different ways. First, an explicit formulation of the autonomy of speech perception from other kinds of auditory or visual perception was made under a novel rubric of MODULARITY (Fodor, 1983), the idea that cognitive systems are composed in part of parallel, independent input mechanisms, or modules. At the same time that a claim of modularity expressed the specialized nature of speech perception—Fodor's version was argued from studies of speech as well as from philosophy and neurology—it did so by designating the perception of speech as a dedicated domain of perception, rather than by stipulating unique perceptual functions. The independence of phonetic perception from auditory analysis which had seemed so attractive in the efference gambit was thereby asserted, without claiming special principles of phonetic perception. In a separate development, the distinction between mediated and DIRECT PERCEPTION (Gibson, 1979), which had been introduced to describe the visual sense, was appropriated in some explanations of phonetic perception (Fowler, 1986; Fowler & Smith, 1986). Direct perception occurs by registering information about objects without intellectual mediation; any appeal to principles of direct perception in accounts of speech necessarily excludes cognitive recourse to motor signals.

In consequence, one of today's offspring of motor theory emphasizes abstract phonetic gestures detected through modular and specialized processes. In the version of A. M. Liberman and Mattingly (1985), no mediating representation of motor signals is invoked for the projection from acoustic spectra to phonetic segments. Nevertheless, gestures are favored as distal objects in the direct-realist rendition which happens to oppose the modularity of speech perception. Fowler and Rosenblum (1991) wrote that phonetic perception is a typical rather than a special process, yielding knowledge of distal objects and events: In the case of speech, these are coordinated movements of vocal tract structures.

A report by Fowler (1984) affirms the primacy of gestures in the perception of speech. She posed the problem along familiar lines: At any moment, the acoustic spectrum of speech bears the influence of several phonetic segments at once. The perceiver detects the phonetic sequence despite this contextual variation in the acoustic manifestations of consonants and vowels, through two possible routes: (a) the speech signal is parsed into a series of "context-sensitive allophones," a sequence of acoustic moments bearing the significant influence of a single segment; or (b) the acoustic pattern is represented as temporally imbricated phonetic gestures (see Fig. 1 for a graphic representation of the alternatives). To distinguish the alternatives empirically, this study exploited a digital editing technique in which consonantal release bursts—which are always specific to the vowels with which they occur (Dorman, Studdert-

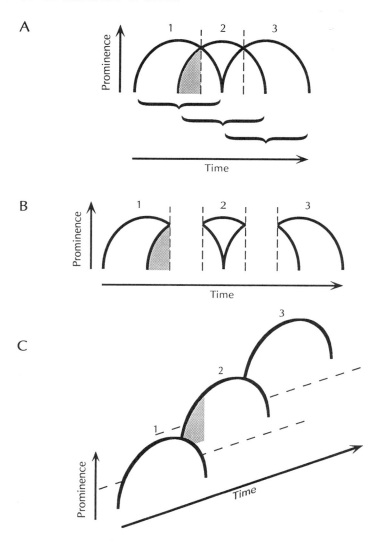

FIG. 1 A schematic view of perceptual segmentation, from Fowler (1984). (A) Gestures of speech production occur in sequence; the effects of successive segments coincide temporally, though at differing levels of prominence. (B) One segmentation strategy preserves the linearity of the signal by isolating acoustic moments in which individual intended segments (*numbers*) achieve relative prominence. (C) Alternative segmentation strategy represents coarticulation as the temporal coincidence of gestures with independent phonetic effect free from contextual influence. In all three panels, the gray portion of segment 2 occurs when segment 1 is hypothetically the most prominent source of motoric and acoustic effect.

Kennedy, & Raphael, 1977)—were paired with appropriate and inappropriate vowels. Although these pastiche syllables were identified perfectly well, Fowler's view predicted that listeners would hear subtle gestural differences between allophonically matched and mismatched syllables (also see Whalen, 1984). The listeners in her study judged that two acoustically identical [g]-consonants, one of which occurred in a mismatched syllable, were less similar perceptually than two acoustically different [g]-consonants occurring within allophonically appropriate signals.

This outcome was explained by claiming that similarity judgments were based on underlying gestures; in no case would this have occurred were perception based on a faithful representation of the literal sensory attributes of the signal. Of course, control tests provided assurance that the effects were not due to different levels of identifiability, nor to acoustic artifacts, leaving the perceived articulatory similarity of the consonantal gestures to explain the findings. Fowler concluded that the perceiver extracts information from the acoustic signal to separate temporally coincident articulations in a realistic manner.

Shall we conclude that the distal objects are movements of the articulators? Despite the appeal of articulatory principles to explain the phenomena of Fowler (1984), the claim seems unwarranted. Though the dynamics of articulation are embodied in a movement system responsive to grammatical expression, the details of articulation are not manifest in speech perception in the way that the details of distal objects—tables and chairs—are in vision. For any articulatory perspective, it is troubling that ordinary listeners who perceive a full range of phonetic contrasts generally know rather little about vocal anatomy; a chronicle of mistaken intuitions and useless Gedankenexperiments about articulation is provided by Ladefoged (1967), attesting to the perceptual obscurity of phonetically governed gestures through the ages. In the laboratory today, articulatory synthesizers create speech sounds by deliberately modeling the movements of articulators, though the intuitions of the operators (who repeatedly speak, listen, and feel themselves speak in service of the synthesis task) often take second place to cinefluorographic, microbeam, or magnetometric records of natural articulations (Rubin, Baer, & Mermelstein, 1981; Rubin & Vatikiotis-Bateson, in press). The sounds of speech do not appear to be as obscure at first glance as vocal gestures are, and we turn next to the proposal that the objects of phonetic perception are complex auditory impressions.

B. Auditory Themes in Speech Perception

Emphasis on the auditory qualities of speech sounds has an antique history, antedating the discovery of formants. In this designation of perceptual objects, the sound itself is said to compose the perceptual stuff; for the theory that a vowel is a tone-quality of fixed pitch, a kind of elementary sensation, the precedent is claimed by Wheatstone (1837, cited in Helmholtz, 1877/1885/1954). The latest echoes of this view assert that a speech sound is a complex experience of pitch, loudness, or timbre (for instance, Jakobson, Fant, & Halle, 1952; Kuhl, Williams, & Meltzoff, 1991).

Because a concern for auditory mechanism is natural in studying the perception of speech, a simple distinction must guide our quest here for the distal object. On one hand, auditory principles are often implicated in accounting for the perception of linguistic or articulatory properties, in which case the distal objects are obviously not designated as a succession or collection of complex sounds. Explicit auditory models have been applied to explain phenomena within linguistic phonetics (Lindblom, 1984), to improve automatic recognition (Blomberg, Carlson, Elenius, & Granström, 1984), or to fashion a computational approximation of perception (for example, Patterson & Holdsworth, in press), usually with the candid expectation that a good model of an auditory system assures a perceptually legitimate glimpse of a speech signal. In such studies, though, the common objective is to rationalize the phonetic properties of speech. On the other hand, some have claimed precisely that the objects of speech perception are auditory impressions (Kluender, Diehl, & Wright, 1988), and that speech perception is a matter of apprehending speech as sound (Sawusch, 1991).

To support an argument for auditory objects, Ohala (1986) marshals five kinds of evidence. First, the vowel [ɚ] occurs in multiple articulatory forms, all of which are acoustically identical. This neatly illustrates an arrangement in which a perceptual representation of sound serves as an acoustic target to the production system and can incorporate little of the specific articulatory causes of any individual phone. Second, a ventriloquist produces the requisite acoustic properties of speech through an articulatory organization that fixes the jaw and lips. The intelligibility of speech produced in this manner suggests again that the perceiver is indifferent to the peculiarities of articulation, though certainly not to the acoustic effects. Third, the mynah replicates speech sounds by means of syrinx and beak, rather than larynx, tongue and lips; but we understand the bird without forming a distinct perceptual impression of its anatomical differences from human talkers. Fourth, several key diachronic phenomena in phonetic inventories are well explained by appealing to the acoustic similarity of historically related phonetic manifestations, as if the transformation were only weakly constrained by articulation. Last, the clinical literature shows that talkers compensate for disorders of articulation by approximating the sounds of speech, not the articulation. If the objects of perception were articulatory, we would expect compensation to aim at typical articulation and not at agreeable acoustic effects.

To this list we can add the evidence of Kluender, Diehl, and Killeen (1987), in whose training study a group of quail learned to distinguish and to generalize natural instances of voiced stop consonants. Because these avian subjects must know nothing about human vocal articulation, nor about the linguistic attributes of speech—and because nothing in the quail's world readily resembled [b], [d] and [g]—an appeal to auditory properties alone seemed plausible to explain the categorization performance. To justify the study, Kluender et al. (1987) noted that the categorization of speech by human listeners is similar to categorization by quail, arguing that neither the articulatory nor the linguistic experience unique to human listeners is absolutely necessary for categorizing voiced stops; calling on the principle of parsimony, Kluender et al. conjectured that speech perception occurs through whatever auditory resources are held in common by humans and quail.

Contrary to Kluender et al. (1987), the claim that distal objects are auditory need not rely on hypothetical sensory mechanisms shared by humans and ground-foraging birds. A different defense of auditory distal objects was offered by Kuhl (1991), based on a direct test of vowel perception in which the performance of human adults and infants contrasted sharply with that of adult macaques. A designation of auditory perceptual objects rested here on the particular psychophysical criteria that were exposed through experimental measures. All the listeners in Kuhl's study were tested with synthetic five-formant tokens of [i], designed to differ according to the plan shown in Figure 2. Two groups of variants were fashioned from designated center points, along equi-interval radii and equi-interval concentric orbits lying in an acoustic plane framed by the frequencies of the first and second formants. In one group of [i] tokens (*open circles*), the central item was a good example of the vowel; in the other group (*filled circles*), the center was 120 mels eccentric from the good [i] along the radius at 135° clockwise and was a poorer instance of [i]. In perceptual tests of "goodness," the same acoustic item was chosen as the best [i] whether it was the center among the variants, or eccentric to the tokens in the test set; there were no range effects on perceptual goodness judgments, in other words. In the critical discrimination tests, Kuhl measured the success with which subjects noticed differences between the center [i] and items from the group; each group of vowels was tested separately. Human adults and infants did not discriminate differences from the better [i] as well as they discriminated differences from the poorer; monkeys performed well regardless of the vowel group.

To explain this pattern of results, Kuhl argued that both goodness and discrimination judgments are mediated in humans by an auditory prototype representing the typical sensory effects of [i]. The assimilation of variants to the prototype (cf. Posner & Keele, 1968) impeded discrimination when the standard was fixed on the better [i], but not when it was fixed on the poorer. More generally, Kuhl alleged that the categories of phonetic perception were structured by prototypes, each one a "hot spot" of acoustic or auditory typicality which together act as internalized standards for evaluating auditory sensations (see Massaro, 1987b; Samuel, 1982).

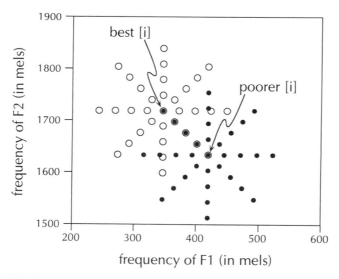

FIG. 2 Variants of the vowel [i] employed in a study of perceptual goodness and discrimination by Kuhl (1991). When the discrimination standard was fixed on the best [i], it assimilated its neighbors (*open circles*); when the set was fixed on a poorer [i] (*filled circles*), performance of human adults and infants improved. Macaques were indifferent to this effect of vowel-set and discriminated well regardless of the center item.

Shall we concede that the distal objects are auditory representations of speech? It hardly needs mentioning that the perception of speech accompanies psychoacoustic impressions of the loudness, duration, and pitch of an utterance, along with more complex auditory attributes like roughness, noisiness, and the like (Hirsh, 1988). In characterizing the distal objects of speech perception, the problem is to determine whether psychoacoustic attributes of speech sounds bring about the perception of consonants and vowels or are equivalent to the perception of consonants and vowels. This topic has received substantial attention in the past decade, and the evidence weighs heavily against a designation of auditory perceptual objects.

An equation between auditory representations and perceptual objects seems possible only if two implied premises of the claim prove true: (a) listeners are able to identify auditory attributes of familiar spoken distal objects, much as they identify tables and chairs as familiar objects of visual perception; and (b) phonetic impressions do not occur when auditory impressions are not speechlike. Neither of these premises is true.

To paraphrase the first, it must be true that the listener who understands an utterance by relying on its auditory properties can identify the auditory attributes or forms associated with phonetic segments. Here, the evidence is clear that variations in duration, power, and frequency of components of the speech signal are not registered as such but affect the linguistic attributes of utterances (e.g., House & Fairbanks, 1953; Klatt, 1976; Mermelstein, 1978; Silverman, 1985). Phonetic distinctions often exhibit multiple acoustic correlates (Lisker, 1978), yet the listener can rarely determine the precise auditory properties underlying the phonetic attributes (Repp, 1982). In order to apprehend the phonetically relevant parts of speech signals as attributes of auditory form, the crucial acoustic components must be removed from the context in which they evoke phonetic effects (e.g., Mann & Liberman, 1983; Mattingly, Liberman, Syrdal, & Halwes, 1971; Rand, 1974; Samuel, 1981); however, this suggests that perceiving a signal phonetically is antagonistic to its auditory representation (also see Repp, 1987). The elusiveness of purely auditory impressions of speech necessitates a special plea if this level of analysis is to be equated with the perceptual objects. No other distal objects are similarly occult.

The second premise says that phonetic perception must not accompany unspeechlike auditory impressions. This derives straight from the essentialism of the auditory claim, namely that phonetic perception is based on auditory attributes which typify the manifestations of particular consonants and vowels. To put it plainly, the auditory view says that the vowel [i] is a particular sound each talker makes when producing that segment; the perturbations of speaking rate, or phonetic environment, or anatomical differences between talkers, or paralinguistic goals drive the auditory manifestations of the segment from an ideal appearance, though not so far that the essential acoustic attributes are obscured. The core of invariance in the correspondence between signal and perceived consonant or vowel is to be sought in the typical auditory attributes that are evoked by the acoustic properties of each phonetic segment. A test of this premise is reported by Remez, Rubin, Pisoni, and Carrell (1981), who found that speech perception survived the replacement of natural acoustic components with impossible ones. By fitting time-varying sinusoids to the frequency pattern of formant centers, a signal was created that was not perceived to be a voice and for which the auditory impressions were clearly not of vocal signals. (A spectrographic comparison of a natural sentence and a sinewave replica is shown in Fig. 3.) In fact, listeners reported that the sinewave analogs of utterances that they readily transcribed did not sound like natural or even synthetic speech (Remez & Rubin, in press). Most listeners hear tones accompanied by phonetic impressions (Remez, Pardo, & Rubin, 1991). Evidently, phonetic perception can occur even when the acoustic elements composing the signal depart hugely from the kinds of spectra that issue from a talker's vocal tract. The specific local auditory attributes of speech on which assertions of typicality are based appear less important to perception if the modulation of the signal occurs in a speechlike way.

With respect to ordinary speech, the findings with tonal analogs suggest that the spectral and auditory details of speech signals are responsible for impressions of vocal timbre, and studies of this aspect of perception are surely important for understanding why utterances sound the way they do. Neverthe-

A

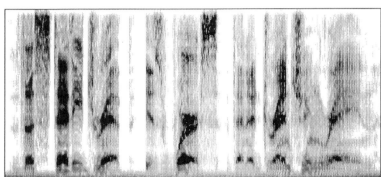

ðə s t ɛl i d rɪ   p ɪz wɚ s   ðənə drɛnčɪ ŋ rɛi   n

B

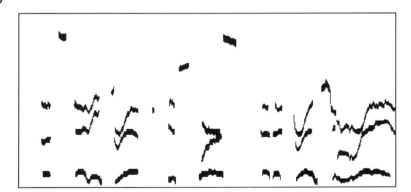

FIG. 3 Spectrograms of two versions of the sentence *The steady drip is worse than a drenching rain*. (A) Natural speech. (B) A replica made by setting a time-varying sinusoid equal to the frequency and amplitude pattern of each of the three lowest formant centers, and a fourth sinusoid equal to the frequency and amplitude of the intermittent fricative formant. See Remez, Rubin, Nygaard, and Howell (1987) for a technical description of sinewave replication of utterances.

less, if time-varying characteristics of the spectrum sustain the perception of phonetic properties, then this prompts a shift in emphasis away from the psycho-acoustic evaluation of individual spectral elements toward studies of the coherence of the signal elements composing the time-varying pattern. At this level of abstraction, in which the superficial acoustic properties of speech are abandoned, we may discover characteristic modulations typifying individual phonetic features, consonants and vowels, diphones, particular talkers, rates of speech, or paralinguistic goals.

For now, these phenomena are counterevidence to many proposals that assert that a consonant or vowel is an essential momentary spectrum or auditory quality. In the absence of convincing evidence that the perceptual objects are gestures of the vocal anatomy, or are auditory essences, the claims favoring linguistic objects intended by the talker hold great appeal.

C. Linguistic Themes in Speech Perception

Linguistic distal objects are amply represented in speech research, following Jakobson and Halle (1956): "An efficacious physiological, physical and psychological analysis of speech sounds presupposes their linguistic interpretation" (p. 33). Approaches differ in the level of linguistic analysis alleged to be primary in perception, and the field is far from consensus. The preferred units have ranged from the distinctive feature, to the phonetic segment, to the context-sensitive allophone, to the syllable, to the word (see Remez, 1987).

Overviews of the perception of speech according to linguistic themes are plentiful (Darwin, 1976; Jusczyk, 1986; Klatt, 1989; J. L. Miller, 1990; Pisoni & Luce, 1986). For the narrow purpose of contrasting the approaches to the distal object in perceptual accounts, a complete directory of views is hardly necessary. Here, we simply expose the empirical grounds for linguistic distal objects. While the dominant approach within psychology has emphasized the perception of distinctive contrasts within a set of phonetic segments, some evidence also supports a perceptual role played by a subordinate constituent, the phonetic feature, and some a superordinate constituent, the syllable. We will briefly illustrate each of these cases before turning to other issues in current research.

One setting of the problem of speech perception has employed the framework of the distinctive feature, appropriated from linguistic phonetics. In this fashion, the sound pattern of a language is conceptualized as a set of contrasts, some in VOICING (as in the English contrast VOICED vs. VOICELESS, which distinguishes /b/ from /p/, /d/ from /t/, and /g/ from /k/), some in MANNER of production (as in the English contrasts ORAL vs. NASAL vs. FRICATIVE, which distinguish /b/ from /m/ from /v/ and /d/ from /n/ from /z/, etc.), and some in PLACE of articulation (as in the English contrasts LABIAL vs. ALVEOLAR vs. VELAR, which distinguish /b/ from /d/ from /g/ and /p/ from /t/ from /k/, etc.). Phonetic segments, then, are viewed as bundles of contrastive rather than characteristic attributes, and the perceiver accordingly identifies the instantaneous state of linguistically governed contrasts from available acoustic attributes.

An account of this kind is offered by Stevens and Blumstein (1981), who claimed, based on acoustic modeling of speech production and perceptual tests, that the phonetic features on which segmental contrasts depend exhibit reliable acoustic effects. Applied to features of articulatory place, this approach favors the gross shape of the brief (25 ms) acoustic spectrum evident at the moment of release of a consonant closure. Templates intended to approximate the listener's sensitivity to such critical acoustic junctures succeed reasonably well in categorizing place features at levels approaching the human listener (Blumstein & Stevens, 1980; also see Lahiri, Gewirth, & Blumstein, 1984, and Walley & Carrell, 1983, for a discussion of the limitations of this conceptualization). Such studies argue for a primary role of distinctive features in perception, and in a recent extension of this view, Stevens (1990, 1991) suggests that lexical access is achieved via an asynchronous sequential representation of distinctive features.

A great mixture of findings upholds the phonetic segment as a unit of perception (and production). Graded variation along many acoustic dimensions is perceived in a context supplied by phonetic segments (see A. M. Liberman, Harris, Hoffman, & Griffith, 1957); segment-size speech errors are common, though admittedly single feature errors do occur (Shattuck-Hufnagel, 1983); orthographies thrive by approximating segmental descriptions (I. Y. Liberman, Shankweiler, Liberman, Fowler, & Fischer, 1977); diachronic phenomena suggest that the segment is a critical unit of language change (Fowler, 1986). While these corroborate the reality of the phonetic segment indirectly, there can be no question that the consonants and vowels, if not primary perceptual objects, are readily obtained from whatever grain of linguistic analysis is preeminent in cognition.

Strong evidence favoring the syllable as a basic unit of speech perception comes from psychological studies of recognition using the targeting paradigm. In this sort of test, a listener is asked to respond as quickly as possible when an attribute designated by the experimenter occurs in an utterance. For example, Segui, Frauenfelder, and Mehler (1981) compared the relative latencies for detecting segmental or syllabic targets in disyllabic utterances, some of which were words, some were not. (The nonwords were phonotactically regular.) Syllable targets (/ba/, /pi/, /dɛ/) were reported more rapidly than were phoneme targets (/b/, /p/, /d/), at 284 ms versus 346 ms, and no advantage was observed for words over nonwords. Most generally, evidence of this kind has been taken to indicate that the syllable is directly available from an auditory analysis and is represented at first in a unitary form. Subsequent analysis is undertaken to resolve the syllabic representation into its consonantal and vocalic attributes, as the situation demands.

We have seen that linguistically designated distal objects presently come in various sizes, and it might be supposed that the field awaits a definitive set of experiments to spotlight an ultimate level from which all others are derived. Alternatively, let us suppose that the attention of the competent listener is plastic, adjustable: (a) to the scale of the immediate phenomena, (b) to endogenous perceptual intentions, and (c) to the performance goals assigned by an experimenter. A comparison of recent studies suggests as much. In one, Nygaard (1993) assessed the spectrotemporal discrepancy tolerated by subjects when fusing dichotically presented constituents of a speech signal. The success of dichotic coherence was observed as an effect on phonetic identity in nonsense syllables. This kind of fusion is held to be a low-level process originating early in the auditory analysis of an incident acoustic signal (Hirsh, 1988). However, when the phonetic alteration occasioned by auditory fusion affected lexical status—word or nonword—Nygaard observed changes in the threshold for fusion, as if a subject listened to speech through the lexicon in those test conditions. It was essential to use synthetic speech in conducting this study, to say nothing of the listening circumstances which differed from the ideal of carefully articulated natural speech heard binaurally in a quiet environment. Such extreme measures are justified by the need to expose the component capabilities of speech perception.

Nonetheless, a study by Burton, Baum, and Blumstein (1989) would urge the conclusion that the subtle facility exhibited by Nygaard's subjects may have been a special adaptation to exotic listening conditions. In their study, a test was used that also allowed the observation of lexical effects on phonetic categorization of acoustic signals. When synthetic speech was used, lexical biases on the perception of ambiguous phonetic segments were observed, as Nygaard reported. In contrast, when natural speech was used to compose the test materials through digital editing, Burton et al. observed that the phonetic ambiguities held fast, and were not resolved as familiar words. No lexical bias was expressed in the natural speech conditions.

Which finding do we accept: one that found a lexical effect, or one that showed that a lexical effect can be ameliorated by changing the acoustic properties of the speech sounds? Both studies reveal aspects of the resourcefulness of perceivers at the same time that they suggest, in combination, that the linguistic units of perception are not fixed. Moreover, linguistically specified perceptual objects are better considered the results of perception, not the reified corpuscles of processing. To conclude otherwise risks committing the EXPERIENCE ERROR (Köhler, 1947), a special failure of method in which different physical correlates are sought for each attribute of a perceptual object. The key to a complete picture of the perception of linguistic distal objects is a conceptualization of scale variation in perception and attention, of magnification and minification while listening (see Eimas, Marcovitz-Hornstein, & Payton, 1990).

III. MODE AND MODULE

The culmination of 19th-century neurology characterized language as a distinct component of human endowment, and our less homuncular view today sees clustered contributions of peri-Sylvian and subcortical components devoted to language. This embodiment provides the context for our discussion that, over the years, has converged on three related questions: Is speech a part of language? Is there a mode of perception unique to speech? Is there a specialized module that achieves perception in a speech mode? To answer the first, consider that the evolutionary arguments and evidence of Negus (1949) and Lieberman (1973) are well established despite controversy now and then in interpreting particular fossil remains. It is certain that evolution induced in humans an enhanced phonetic repertoire relative to the apes. The coordination and control of vocal structures, unquestionably a linguistic function supplementing respiration and deglutition, is bound historically to speech production and perception, and some have argued that linguistic intentions take their particular shape precisely though a capacity to form sensible sound patterns (Fowler, Rubin, Remez, & Turvey, 1980). Though this conceptualization places speech squarely within language phylogenetically, speech is apparently no longer necessary for language, a conclusion urged by research on American Sign Language. Visual–manual linguistic communication provides a stark contrast with speech, and cross-linguistic study of speech and sign promises to demarcate universal aspects of language from specific accommodations to its form of expression. Reports of sign babbling in infancy suggest no less. Though speech may have been the motor of evolution for language, it is now better understood as the most natural form of expression of a general linguistic disposition that can use the peripheral vehicle necessitated by circumstance (Petitto & Marentette, 1991).

A. A Speech Mode

The possibility that speech evokes a unique mode of perception has received wide attention. Commonly, the notion of perceptual mode has retained an intuitive likeness to an anatomically defined sense—vision or hearing, for example—and at issue is whether the perception of speech is achieved similarly, via special resources reserved for that function. In an alternative conceptualization, speech is perceived through hearing or vision (Massaro, 1987b). The greater part of this inquiry about mode has aimed to delineate special processes assigned to speech, as if the operators as well as the arguments of a phonetic mode must be unlike any other. The likelihood that speech perception is independent of other concurrent perceptual inflow regardless of its intrinsic processes has only been addressed more recently.

This empirical campaign began with psychophysical tests that contrasted phonetic perception with the resolution of subordinate auditory forms (A. M. Liberman et al., 1957; A. M. Liberman, Harris, Kinney, & Lane, 1961). Initially, research distinguished phonetic perception by exposing departures from Weber's law in the discrimination of consonants. Most recently, the reliance on categorization of a simple acoustic test series as an index has been supplanted with more elaborate methods. One line of research has exploited the listener's failure to detect an aspect of the correspondence of acoustic and phonetic attributes, under the banner of PHONETIC TRADING RELATIONS. In natural speech, acoustic sources of information about a single phonetic attribute can be diverse: the duration of silence, the spectrum of a release burst, the fundamental and formant frequencies, and so on. Experimental investigations of the perceptual convergence of acoustically dissimilar signal elements have manipulated such parameters, to measure the perception of stop MANNER, for example, when it is promoted a bit by each of several acoustic elements. Experiments on trading relations have asked, How much of a phonetic attribute does a given acoustic element buy?

First, judicious synthesis or editing of natural speech is used to compose two different assortments of acoustic elements that make the same phonetic sum. This is easy to calibrate, by determining that two different ensembles of acoustic elements elicit the same phonetic label with the same probability or confidence. Then, these are placed within a graded series in which some of the acoustic elements contributing to the manner attribute add up to different phonetic sums. Last, the listener is asked to distinguish the differences. In such tests, the perceiver acts as if it does not matter whether a phonetic quarter is purchased for two acoustic dimes and an acoustic nickel, or for five acoustic nickels, so to speak. Accordingly, listeners are unable to discriminate syllables when the strength of the phonetic effects are equated, despite inequalities in the specific acoustic manifestations (Fitch, Halwes, Erickson, & Liberman, 1980; cf. Hary & Massaro, 1982; Massaro & Hary, 1984).

Perhaps no less significant is the ability of listeners to determine implicitly which aspect of a single continuous acoustic property, the fundamental frequency for instance, is pertinent to consonantal voicing; which to the vowel, relative to its intrinsic pitch; which to lexical stress; which to clausal accent; and which to the sentence-initial upsweep, downdrift, or terminal fall. The facts of trading and of many-to-one relations between acoustic and phonetic attributes led Repp (1982) to conclude that such effects are probably mediated by familiarity with the consistent albeit diverse acoustic products of phonetically governed articulation, a facility that is surely specific to speech. Auditory integration proves insufficiently supple and insufficiently specialized with respect to acoustic mechanics to motivate the necessary trades. Moreover, the intermodal integration that occurs in audio-visual perception of speech, to which we turn in Section V, gives credibility to the conclusion that auditory integration mechanisms alone can hardly be responsible for phonetic trading relations or for the perception of speech.

Forsaking an appeal to special process, researchers have also considered the independence of phonetic perception as a way to discern a phonetic mode. Digital techniques have been used to create patterns simultaneously perceivable as auditory forms and as phonetic impressions. This phenomenon has been termed DUPLEX PERCEPTION (Isenberg & Liberman, 1979; A. M. Liberman, Isenberg, & Rakerd, 1981; cf. R. E. Pastore, Schmuckler, Rosenblum, & Szczesiul, 1983) and provides evidence of the distinctiveness of perception in a speech mode. In a typical instance, the acoustic pattern of a consonant–vowel syllable is fractured into two portions; one is a formant frequency transition, which in isolation sounds like a pitch glide, lacking phonetic attributes; the other is the remainder of the syllable pattern, which in isolation seems to begin with an indeterminate consonant. When presented dichotically, the listener fuses the dispersed elements into a proper syllable and more. The components combining across the ears relieve the ambiguity in the syllable-initial consonant and gravitate spatially toward the ear that received the major portion of the formant pattern. Remarkably, the isolated formant frequency transition contributing to the consonant percept is also heard as a pitch sweep at the opposite ear. In short, the same formant frequency transition is perceived in two ways: (a) phonetically, following integration with the rest of the speech signal; and (b) as an auditory form without phonetic effect. Wholly apart from the issues of process, such evidence reveals the autonomy of phonetic perception from auditory analysis. In other words, even were the operating principles alike in an auditory mode and a phonetic mode, these concurrent and phenomenally discrepant effects can be taken as evidence of functional separation. An aspect of the biological preparation for language is the precociousness of this separate sensitivity to speech and auditory form (Eimas & Miller, 1992).

Overall, the differentiation of the premises underlying tests of the speech mode shows great promise. For one reason, the search continues for perceptual processes that exist solely within a phonetic realm, any of which would count as a clear marker of specialization. But this traditional route into the problem is only one. If, as Fowler and Rosenblum (1991) allege, perception of speech bears close resemblance to other kinds of object perception, then we may expect the efforts to identify unique phonetic functions to prove fruitless. Nevertheless, the similarity of two processes does not warrant a claim that a single resource is responsible for both. The findings of duplex perception, of concurrent, divergent functions for speech and auditory perception, are prima facie evidence of independence regardless of the underlying processes. These studies begin to establish diagnostic criteria for distinguishing a phonetic mode of perception from other perceptual effects. However, evidence of an independent phonetic perceptual mode may not be evidence of embodiment in a phonetic module.

B. A Phonetic Module

The step from devoted function to module has seemed a small one to take. Certainly, the definitive attributes of modules elaborated by Fodor (1983) have reprised some of the principal characteristics of perception in a phonetic mode. Consider these aspects of modules: DOMAIN SPECIFICITY, meaning that the effective inputs are limited to a single kind; MANDATORY COMMITMENT, meaning that a module is constrained to act whenever it can, irresistibly, unless attention is held elsewhere; LIMITED ACCESS TO UNDERLYING REPRESENTATIONS, meaning that the ascending levels of representation—perceptual forms, in this case, rather than objects and events—are discarded during modular computation and are unavailable to cognitive processes; FAST ACTION, meaning that processes within an input module are concluded quickly; INFORMATIONAL ENCAPSULATION, meaning that modules are not influenced by knowledge or belief; SHALLOW OUTPUTS, meaning that multifaceted elaboration of an input is excluded from modular processes and is reserved for cognitive functions. In addition, Fodor speculated that modules are distinguished by their assignment to a FIXED NEURAL ARCHITECTURE, by the consistency of the effects of their failure in CHARACTERISTIC BREAKDOWNS; and by their STEREOTYPED PACE AND COURSE OF DEVELOPMENT. As a summary of research reports, these attributes of modules would do quite well. However, evidence from studies of tonal analogs of speech falsifies the claim that phonetic perception is necessarily modular.

Our project (Remez et al., 1981) employed sinewave replicas of sentences, in which three or four sinewaves reproduce oral, nasal, and fricative formants (see Fig. 3). In one test, we used an instructional condition in which the signals were played to naive listeners who were simply asked to characterize what they heard. In this case, listeners generally reported a variety of impressions without susceptibility to the phonetic properties of the tone patterns. They said they heard electronic sounds, radio interference, tape recorder problems, bad electronic music, and so on. Another group of listeners were asked instead to transcribe synthetic speech. Undaunted by the odd timbre of the tones, this group simply proceeded to write down the sentence. In the case of this second group, the impressions of words and tones derived simultaneously from a single signal, evidence of independence of phonetic and auditory perceptual analyses. This result is fully consistent with a modular view of each process. However, comparing this condition with the free identifications requested from the first group shows that the belief of the listener about the nature of the signal must be known in order to predict whether phonetic properties will be apparent in a sinewave sentence. The spectrotemporal properties of a sinewave replica were only sufficient when the listener was warned to expect synthetic speech. This evidence falsifies the modular criteria of mandatory commitment and of encapsulation, for sensory conditions alone did not determine the perceptual path independent of the knowledge or belief of the listener. In Fodor's view, the domain of modular operation must be defined on the raw sensory properties of the input. Mattingly and Liberman (1990) are more accommodating, stipulating that the specific acoustic or auditory properties are less significant than the resolution of the pattern into phonetic attributes. But all proponents of a modular view of speech perception hold to encapsulation, which our evidence falsifies by delineating a role of belief in the creation of a phonetic perceptual mode.

Clearly, the topic of modular status of the speech mode is far from settled. A pressing empirical issue is to determine the nature of the transition from (a) the perception of sinewave sentence replicas as auditory forms to (b) the perception of sinewave sentences as phonetic objects with simultaneous auditory forms. It is within the scope of such an investigation to determine whether the criteria of modularity survive or whether speech perception is identified as a mode of perceptual organization without modular standing.

IV. THE PERCEPTUAL BASIS OF PHONETIC CATEGORIES AND THE PERCEPTION OF SPEECH

In charting the varieties of research on speech, we cannot overlook the disproportionate emphasis placed on studies of the perceptual basis for phonetic categories. In such investigations, the goal has been to determine how phonetic distinctions arise perceptually. By opposing two segments that differ minimally—a single feature difference as defined within linguistic phonetics—researchers have catalogued (a) the acoustic elements that convey distinctions between the consonants or the vowels of a language and (b) the auditory sensitivities of careful listeners to such patterns. Whether the emphasis on this approach stems from the ready availability of psychophysical methods, which operate best with unidimensional problems, or whether it comes from the special focus on articulatory dynamics, which captured the attention of the field long ago and holds it to this day, or whether it derives from the immense fondness for probabilistic functionalism shared by cognitivists, which cherishes sources of information to sample, weigh, and categorize (Massaro, 1987a), the effect has been to feature threshold studies of simple phonetic contrasts for many years. The importance of this work cannot be denied. It has produced an inventory of acoustic correlates of the units stipulated by phonetic linguistics and went far beyond this by showing the relative sensitivities of the listener to the crucial ingredients composing the patterns. Moreover, the literature on the sensory and cognitive psychology of categorization contains many contributions by researchers whose immediate technical aims were more modest, set by the evaluation of stationary and transient spectra in cueing PLACE OF ARTICULATION in fricative consonants, for instance.

The unfortunate impact of this emphasis has been to focus the field singularly on studies of the perceptual basis of phonetic linguistics. At stake here is a kind of explanatory adequacy that stands apart from craftwork questions, for instance, of the replicability of categorization functions across different listeners or different speech samples. The phenomena of the VOICING contrast, to take an immensely popular topic as an example, are highly replicable over many different kinds of acoustic realizations—broadband, narrowband, passband, peak-clipped, and so on—and in many different laboratories and in different languages and with different listeners. These data are analogous to the grammaticality judgments in the theory of competence, and we know from these studies that a listener who is asked to play the role of connoisseur of syllable-length speech signals categorizes them consistently, despite the vicissitudes of instrumentation and listening conditions. Nonetheless, we cannot say whether the sensitivities exhibited by a test subject wearing the hat of the meticulous listener are those that support the perception of ordinary speech, though we may be certain that they bolster the intuitions of the phonetician. In fact, there are so few descriptive studies of the acoustics of fluent production that we can only speculate about a perceiver's performance with such signals. If the ideal talker speaks to be heard, to be understood, then the typical speech sample employed in perceptual research is obtained from an utterance that violates the bromide, for it is produced to be analyzed, to exemplify an instance justified by linguistic aims, or to be used in a test of perceptual categorization.

This issue has simmered in the background since Pickett and Pollack (1963) reported that words in isolation and words in context differed in perceptibility and since Lieberman (1963) reported that sentence contexts differed in the information they provide about the words they comprise. There are some harbingers that the field is readying to broach this subject. Recently, Hunnicutt (1985) showed that the talker continuously adjusts the production of speech, apparently balancing the information provided by the segmental structure against that provided globally by the context of the sentence. In a kindred study, Fowler and Housum (1987) showed that the perceiver's accommodation roughly matches the talker's articulatory variability, even across a discourse; but we need a method with which to press on with this investigation, and we need a measure of the principles of variability manifest in ordinary speech.

A preliminary if huge project along these lines was completed over the course of the past decade by Crystal and House (1988, 1990), and the data delivered a few good surprises. The durational and distributional characteristics of segments were analyzed in speech elicited from two brief (approximately 300 word) texts, read aloud by six talkers. Not much innovation was required for the measurements, which had been well conventionalized for carefully produced, isolated utterances by the field. The linguistic taxonomy used to represent phone classes or stress groups was likewise uncontroversial. The decision to examine only durational characteristics precludes a general assessment of the robustness of conventional descriptions of perceptually relevant acoustic correlates. Those limits in mind, and considering the cue value only of durational differences, then, Crystal and House provided a handy checklist of tests of claims in the literature against their fluent database. Of course, this counts as a first estimate of the fit between the perceptual account of perfect laboratory speech and the fluent speech of ordinary reading, if not spontaneous speech. The surprise is that half the predictions based on the phonetics literature failed to find support in the fluent database. Perhaps the most vexing finding was the small proportion of stop consonants that actually showed clear stop holds. There can be no more disappointing news for anyone who hopes to preserve a perceptual account of acoustic phonetic correspondences based on careful, exemplary utterances.

The picture of normal variability will become clearer with the development of perceptual research on loud speech (Schulman, 1989), clear speech (Picheny, Durlach, & Braida, 1986) and spontaneous speech (Remez, Berns et al., 1991). Meanwhile, appeals to typical acoustic manifestations of consonants and vowels must be greeted with some suspicion. In the proposal recently offered by Kuhl (1991), a particular five-formant, 500 ms steady-state [i] is offered as a prototype for instances of that vowel. On acoustic grounds, this proposal is unbelievable, for few vowels ever attain such great duration, and even isolated vowels show de-tensing or centralization over their extent (Nearey & Assmann, 1986). On perceptual grounds, vowels are readily identified when coarticulated with consonants, even in artificial signals lacking the syllable nuclei that come closest to the proposed phonetic prototype (Jenkins, Strange, & Edman, 1983). Given the varieties of phonetic environment, diction, and listening conditions in which speech perception fares well, the sensory effects of vowels must depart greatly from the ethereal archetypes in Kuhl's conceptualization. A cluster of archetypes of the nine or ten vowels of American English would resemble each other more closely than any archetype would resemble tokens of its type in fluent speech.

With accounts of speech perception changing to accommodate natural varieties of utterances, the attention of the field returns to the problem of the acoustic correlates of segmental attributes, with a difference this time. Once, an acoustic correlate seemed to be a kind of analytic entity, and research aimed to enumerate this stock of elements from which the talker drew in composing an utterance and which the perceiver registered in solving the inverse problem. Now, it seems unlikely that there are acoustic norms, or that the set of acoustic correlates is even finite and small. The last straw is the finding of intelligibility of sinewave analogs, which shows that the perception of speech is possible even when the elements, in detail, could not have originated in any talker's vocal tract. How then does a listener determine which acoustic properties are pertinent to phonetic perception and which are not? Although this question is deflected by most theories of recognition, which commonly assume rather than derive the acoustic ingredients relevant to perception, it has actually been approached by research on perceptual organization.

V. Perceptual Organization of Speech

An examination of the perceptual accounts of speech collected by Klatt (1989) reveals an assumption consistent across the batch. Whether a theory employs an analytic approach, analysis by synthesis, or cognitively guided heuristics, each begins with a speech signal ready to be perceived. The ordinary perceiver is not so fortunate. We live and listen in a world of talkers who often speak at the same time. It should go without saying that sources of acoustic activity are rarely limited to human voices. Any theory of speech perception that begins with a speech signal already identified as such presupposes an account of perceptual organization to explain how the preceiver sorts the excitation incident at the ear into separate streams, some of them phonetic, each indexed to a worldly source of sound and ready to analyze.

How does the perceptual organization of speech occur? Actually, two different proposals have been offered. In one, AUDITORY SCENE ANALYSIS, low-level auditory mechanisms are said to apply to an otherwise unanalyzed sensory representation of an auditory array (Bregman, 1990). These mechanisms constitute a set of elementary principles of auditory form deriving from Gestalt psychology (Julesz & Hirsh, 1972; Wertheimer, 1923) and effect a preliminary parsing of the auditory inflow into streams, each segregated from concurrent auditory activity. More complex schematic mechanisms may be invoked secondarily to adjudicate stream assignments based on knowledge or familiarity and therefore can amend the source assignments of particular elements. A remarkably consistent empirical base established by Bregman and colleagues shows that the limits of such schematic revision must be strict. Typically, listeners have great difficulty determining the detailed properties of two simultaneous sources in relation to each other, and we may conclude that source assignments made by the Gestalt-based mechanisms are difficult to undo.

Primary emphasis in the elaboration of auditory scene analysis has been placed on distinguishing multiple concurrent streams, preserving the original metaphor of auditory perceptual organization (Cherry, 1953). In this classic setting, the listener is said to isolate and hold the acoustic signals stemming from an individual talker amid the clamor of a cocktail party. The empirical approach taken by Bregman was to pose abstract listening problems for test subjects in which rapidly repeated patterns of tones, buzzes, and noises fractured into separate perceptual streams. A catalog of principles was thereby motivated through precise calibration of the disposition to segregate auditory forms. These studies support the specific claims that acoustic patterns are organized perceptually according to one or more elementary principles: of PROXIMITY (Bregman & Campbell, 1971), SIMILARITY (Bregman & Doehring, 1984; Dannenbring & Bregman, 1978; Steiger & Bregman, 1981), COMMON FATE (Bregman, Abramson, Doehring, & Darwin, 1985; Bregman & Pinker, 1978), and CLOSURE (G. A. Miller & Licklider, 1950), operating in the domains of frequency, amplitude, and spectrum. Bregman (1990) has claimed that these elementary principles of grouping facilitate the segregation of simultaneous talkers, and some perceptual tests have shown that the principles of scene analysis do apply with equal force to acoustic patterns that compose syllables (for example, Darwin, 1981; Dorman, Cutting, & Raphael, 1975; Lackner & Goldstein, 1974). In this conceptualization of organization, voices with different fundamental frequencies are split into separate streams on the basis of the similar harmonics shared by the formants of each talker. Glottal pulsing also serves to hold the components of a single signal together by amplitude comodulation of the voiced formants, a kind of common fate mechanism. Similarity in location (azimuth and elevation, and perhaps even range) also promotes grouping of the components of a single voice.

While it is hard to deny the success of the Gestalt rules in predicting the grouping tendencies of auditory forms, Remez (1987) argued that the combination of elementary rules and latterly asserted schemas would prove inadequate for the perceptual organization of speech, on theoretical grounds. Chief among the deficiencies of this view of organization based on auditory forms was a reliance of the Gestalt rules on grouping by physical similarity, which breaks complex signals into streams of like elements. In consequence, the easiest case for the listener to organize—a speech signal produced by a single talker in a quiet environment—is a defeat for the Gestalt rules, which break that signal into multiple perceptual streams. The problem can be exposed in reference to Hockett's (1955) analogy between phonetic segments and Easter eggs. Speech signals are structured as if an intended sequence of phonetic segments—brightly painted eggs, in the analogy—were realized acoustically in a coarticulated manner that blurred the ordinal discreteness of the phonetic intentions. Hockett described articulation as a clothes wringer that broke the eggs and mixed them into each other. The perceiver was conceived as an observer of a conveyor belt on which the broken and wrung eggs were carried whose job was to identify the original phonetic eggs from an acoustic mess of brightly colored shell, yolk, and albumin. Although scene analysis is intended to separate simultaneous processions of eggs with different sources (or, in C. J. Darwin's extension, to separate a stream of broken eggs from a rat who happens to fall onto the conveyor belt, a metaphor for an extraneous sound), Remez argued that the simple rules of scene analysis necessarily fracture the procession of a single stream of eggs into one stream of yolk, a second stream of shell, and a third stream of white. Or, to return to acoustic description, the parsing of elements by similarity would derive one stream for each of the vocalic formants, which change frequency and amplitude dissimilarly, reflecting the action of independently controlled articulators; another for the nasal formants, which appear and disappear from the spectrum suddenly; another for the fricative formants; another few for aspirate formants; and another for few consonantal release bursts of different spectral composition and duration.

In general, aperiodic and periodic, slowly and rapidly changing, similar and dissimilar elements would each be placed into separate perceptual streams by the application of the elementary rules. It would then be up to latterly occurring schematic knowledge to save the fractured streams, recombining the elements and justifying the reunion by resort to familiarity or knowledge of vocal production. Although a process in which resources are first applied to break up and then to reintegrate a signal is clearly less than optimal—after all, why divide something that has to be restored to be used?—it is not impossible to imagine processing limits of this kind. In engineered systems, optimization is a goal (Klatt, 1989), in contrast to biological adaptive systems, which do not optimize (Gould & Lewontin, 1979).

In an alternative to the organization of speech by auditory scene analysis, Remez, Rubin, Berns, Pardo, and Lang (in press) proposed that phonetic organization occurs early in the perceptual process by means of specific sensitivity to the time-varying properties of the constituents of vocal signals. Evidence of PHONETIC ORGANIZATION came from studies with sinewave replicas of sentences that were combined despite gross acoustic dissimilarities as well as dichotic presentation of components. Organization was indexed by the intelligibility of the phonetic message carried by the tones, which appeared to endure

(a) the absence of comodulation across the sinusoidal formant-analogs, (b) the dichotic separation of the tonal components of the sentence, and (c) the substitution of time-varying sinusoids for natural, familiar acoustic elements. At the same time that listeners exhibited phonetic organization of the sinusoidal copies of utterances, they also reported auditory organization of the tones, in the form of spatially arrayed counterpoint, revealing that auditory and phonetic organizations existed simultaneously and independently for these oddly synthesized sentences. This finding is evidence that auditory mechanisms of organization are not responsible for phonetic organization.

The perceptual functions revealed through application of such unusual techniques are probably not unique to instances in which a synthesizer speaks in sinusoidal sentences, due to the nature of the acoustic transformation that these sounds use. It seems likelier that this acoustic technique works as a phonetic signal because it satisfies a perceptual requirement on the structure of patterns composed by the elements of a speech signal. We would expect this to be the case following the premise that the set of acoustic realizations of speech signals is indefinitely large. In such circumstances, the perceiver could ground perception neither in memorization of the most typical acoustic manifestations of speech, nor in gauging the likeness of any particular sample to archetypal acoustic elements. Instead, the perceiver accepts all kinds of acoustic properties as ingredients for phonetic perception, and the sinewave sentences expose the basis for this prodigiousness in a sensitivity to the acoustic patterns that issue from phonetically governed vocal sources, whatever their superficial acoustic properties are. It is this sensitivity to vocal pattern that allows phonetic organization to occur for sinewave sentences, to be sure, and to occur in ordinary listening as well.

An independent consideration that threatens the plausibility of Gestalt grouping principles in the organization of speech comes from the literature on multisensory integration in speech perception. Much has been written about this topic, and this terrific and important domain of research is well summarized elsewhere (Bernstein, Coulter, O'Connell, Eberhardt, & Demorest, 1992; Kuhl & Meltzoff, 1988; Summerfield, 1987). This literature expresses a growing consensus that auditory, visual, vibrotactile, and haptic aspects of speech signals are organized conjointly in perception and do not appear to receive terminating analyses within each sensory modality previous to combination. To take an exemplary case, Green and Miller (1985) showed that changes in visually displayed articulatory rate affected the value of the critical voice onset time for perceiving the VOICING feature of a labial stop consonant. Here, the value of the phonetic feature depended on acoustically delivered information about which the visual information must have been neutral, locally; the voicing of a consonant cannot be determined from a visual display of a talker. But information about the articulatory rate, which influences the determination of apparent voicing when it is delivered acoustically, is easily delivered visually. Therefore, the perceptual effect on voicing of the visual display was not brought about by an impression of a rival feature but by the global context for evaluating the acoustic information. On such grounds, researchers have concluded that multisensory correspondences are resolved as a necessary condition for phonetic perception to proceed. The rules of perceptual organization in such cases cannot be ascribed to the automatic action of the Gestalt-based criteria of auditory scene analysis.

VI. CONCLUSION

In presenting the issues that move the field, I have adopted a particular point of view about theoretical and empirical challenges facing us. The conclusions deriving from this point of view, which are defended herein, may be summarized briefly.

1. The perception of speech begins with a linguistically intentioned talker and concludes with the perception of the linguistic distal objects along with the characteristics of the talker.

2. It is likely that the perception of speech is accomplished by resources reserved for determining phonetic attributes, though it is less likely that this perceptual mode operates in the manner of an orthodox module.

3. The province of the phonetic perceptual mode is to provide stable categories of signal elements and to find phonetic attributes in fluent speech.

4. Facing huge variability in the specific acoustic manifestations of individual talkers and in fluent speech, perception relies on specifically phonetic organization in lieu of general auditory principles by which to resolve the acoustic effects of phonetically governed articulation.

ACKNOWLEDGEMENTS

The author gratefully acknowledges the assistance of Jennifer Fellowes, Carol Fowler, Elizabeth Lynch, Jennifer Pardo, David Pisoni, Philip Rubin, and Pam Spritzer, and the support of the National Institute on Deafness and Other Communication Disorders (DC00308) in the preparation of this manuscript.

REFERENCES

Bernstein, L. E., Coulter, D. C., O'Connell, M. P., Eberhardt, S. P., & Demorest, M. E. (1992, June). *Vibrotactile and haptic speech codes*. Lecture presented at the 2nd International Conference on Tactile Aids, Hearing Aids, & Cochlear Implants, Royal Institute of Technology, Stockholm, Sweden.

Blomberg, M., Carlson, R., Elenius, K., & Granström, B. (1984). Auditory models as front ends in speech-recognition systems. In J. S. Perkell & D. H. Klatt (Eds.), *Invariance and variability in speech processes* (pp. 108–114). Hillsdale, NJ: Erlbaum.

Blumstein, S. E., & Stevens, K. N. (1980). Perceptual invariance and onset spectra for stop consonants in different vowel environments. *Journal of the Acoustical Society of America, 67*, 648–662.

Bregman, A. S. (1990). *Auditory scene analysis*. Cambridge, MA: MIT Press.

Bregman, A. S., Abramson, J., Doehring, P., & Darwin, C. J. (1985). Spectral integration based on common amplitude modulation. *Perception & Psychophysics, 37*, 483–493.

Bregman, A. S., & Campbell, J. (1971). Primary auditory stream segregation and perception of order in rapid sequences of tones. *Journal of Experimental Psychology, 89*, 244–249.

Bregman, A. S., & Doehring, P. (1984). Fusion of simultaneous tonal glides: The role of parallelness and simple frequency relations. *Perception & Psychophysics, 36*, 251–256.

Bregman, A. S., & Pinker, S. (1978). Auditory streaming and the building of timbre. *Canadian Journal of Psychology, 32*, 19–31.

Burton, M. W., Baum, S. R., & Blumstein, S. E. (1989). Lexical effects on the phonetic categorization of speech: The role of acoustic structure. *Journal of Experimental Psychology: Human Perception and Performance, 15*, 567–575.

Cherry, E. C. (1953). Some experiments on the recognition of speech, with one and with two ears. *Journal of the Acoustical Society of America, 25*, 975–979.

Crystal, T. H., & House, A. S. (1988). Segmental durations in connected-speech signals: Current results. *Journal of the Acoustical Society of America, 83,* 1553–1573.

Crystal, T. H., & House, A. S. (1990). Articulation rate and the duration of syllables and stress groups in connected speech. *Journal of the Acoustical Society of America, 88,* 101–112.

Dannenbring, G. L., & Bregman, A. S. (1978). Streaming vs. fusion of sinusoidal components of complex tones. *Perception & Psychophysics, 24,* 369–376.

Darwin, C. J. (1976). The perception of speech. In E. C. Carterette & M. P. Friedman (Eds.), *Handbook of perception* (pp. 175–226). New York: Academic Press.

Darwin, C. J. (1981). Perceptual grouping of speech components differing in fundamental frequency and onset-time. *Quarterly Journal of Experimental Psychology, 33A,* 185–207.

Dorman, M. F., Cutting, J. E., & Raphael, L. J. (1975). Perception of temporal order in vowel sequences with and without formant transitions. *Journal of Experimental Psychology: Human Perception and Performance, 1,* 121–129.

Dorman, M. F., Studdert-Kennedy, M., & Raphael, L. J. (1977). Stop consonant recognition: Release bursts and formant transitions as functionally equivalent, context-dependent cues. *Perception & Psychophysics, 22,* 109–122.

Eimas, P. D., Marcovitz-Hornstein, S., & Payton, P. (1990). Attention and the role of dual codes in phoneme monitoring. *Journal of Memory and Language, 29,* 160–180.

Eimas, P. D., & Miller, J. L. (1992). Organization in the perception of speech by infants. *Psychological Science, 3,* 340–345.

Eimas, P. D., Miller, J. L., & Jusczyk, P. W. (1987). On infant speech perception and the acquisition of language. In S. Harnad (Ed.), *Categorical perception: The groundwork of cognition* (pp. 161–195). New York: Cambridge University Press.

Fant, C. G. M., & Martony, J. (1962). Speech synthesis. *Quarterly Progress Report on Speech Research, 2,* 18–24.

Fitch, H. L., Halwes, T., Erickson, D. M., & Liberman, A. M. (1980). Perceptual equivalence of two acoustic cues for stop-consonant manner. *Perception & Psychophysics, 27,* 343–350.

Fodor, J. A. (1983). *The modularity of mind.* Cambridge, MA: MIT Press.

Fowler, C. A. (1984). Segmentation of coarticulated speech in perception. *Perception & Psychophysics, 36,* 359–368.

Fowler, C. A. (1986). An event approach to the study of speech perception from a direct-realist perspective. *Journal of Phonetics, 14,* 3–28.

Fowler, C. A., & Housum, J. (1987). Talkers' signaling of "new" and "old" words in speech and listeners' perception and use of the distinction. *Journal of Memory and Language, 26,* 489–504.

Fowler, C. A., & Rosenblum, L. D. (1991). The perception of phonetic gestures. In I. G. Mattingly & M. Studdert-Kennedy (Eds.), *Modularity and the motor theory of speech perception: Proceedings of a conference to honor Alvin M. Liberman* (pp. 33–59). Hillsdale, NJ: Erlbaum.

Fowler, C. A., Rubin, P. E., Remez, R. E., & Turvey, M. T. (1980). Implications for speech production of a general theory of action. In B. Butterworth (Ed.), *Language production: Vol. I. Speech and talk* (pp. 373–420). New York: Academic Press.

Fowler, C. A., & Smith, M. R. (1986). Speech perception as "vector analysis": An approach to the problems of invariance and segmentation. In J. S. Perkell & D. H. Klatt (Eds.), *Invariance and variability in speech processes* (pp. 123–139). Hillsdale, NJ: Erlbaum.

Gibson, J. J. (1979). *The ecological approach to visual perception.* Boston: Houghton Mifflin.

Gould, S. J., & Lewontin, R. C. (1979). The spandrels of San Marco and the Panglossian paradigm: A critique of the adaptationist programme. *Proceedings of the Royal Society of London, Series B, 205,* 581–598.

Green, K. P., & Miller, J. L. (1985). On the role of visual rate information in phonetic perception. *Perception & Psychophysics, 38,* 269–276.

Hary, J. M., & Massaro, D. W. (1982). Categorical results do not imply categorical perception. *Perception & Psychophysics, 32,* 409–418.

Helmholtz, H. L. F. (1954). *On the sensations of tone as a physiological basis for the theory of music.* New York: Dover. (2nd English edition of 1885, rendered conformal to the 4th German edition of 1877)

Hirsh, I. J. (1988). Auditory perception and speech. In R. C. Atkinson, R. J. Herrnstein, G. Lindzey, & R. D. Luce (Eds.), *Stevens' Handbook of experimental psychology* 2nd ed., Vol. 1. (pp. 377–408). New York: Wiley (Interscience).

Hockett, C. F. (1955). *A manual of phonology.* Baltimore, MD: Waverly Press.

House, A. S., & Fairbanks, G. (1953). The influence of consonant environment upon the secondary acoustical characteristics of vowels. *Journal of the Acoustical Society of America, 25,* 105–113.

Hunnicutt, S. (1985). Intelligibility versus redundancy—conditions of dependency. *Language and Speech, 28,* 47–56.

Isenberg, D., & Liberman, A. M. (1979). Speech and nonspeech perception from the same sound. *Journal of the Acoustical Society of America, 64,* S20.

Jakobson, R., Fant, G., & Halle, M. (1952). *Preliminaries to speech analysis* (Tech. Rep. No. 13). Cambridge: Massachusetts Institute of Technology, Acoustics Laboratory.

Jakobson, R., & Halle, M. (1956). *Fundamentals of language.* The Hague, The Netherlands: Mouton.

Jenkins, J. J., Strange, W., & Edman, T. R. (1983). Identification of vowels in ''vowelless'' syllables. *Perception & Psychophysics, 34,* 441–450.

Julesz, B., & Hirsh, I. J. (1972). Visual and auditory perception: An essay of comparison. In E. E. David, Jr. & P. B. Denes (Eds.), *Human communication: A unified view* (pp. 283–340). New York: McGraw-Hill.

Jusczyk, P. W. (1986). Speech perception. In K. R. Boff, L. Kaufman, & J. P. Thomas (Eds.), *Handbook of perception and human performance* (pp. 27-1–27-57). New York: Wiley.

Klatt, D. H. (1976). Linguistic uses of segmental duration in English: Acoustic and perceptual evidence. *Journal of the Acoustical Society of America, 59,* 1208–1221.

Klatt, D. H. (1989). Review of selected models of speech perception. In W. Marslen-Wilson (Ed.), *Lexical representation and process* (pp. 169–226). Cambridge, MA: MIT Press.

Kluender, K. R., Diehl, R. L., & Killeen, P. R. (1987). Japanese quail can learn phonetic categories. *Science, 237,* 1195–1197.

Kluender, K. R., Diehl, R. L., & Wright, B. A. (1988). Vowel-length differences before voiced and voiceless consonants: An auditory explanation. *Journal of Phonetics, 16,* 153–169.

Köhler, W. (1947). *Gestalt psychology.* New York: Liveright.

Kuhl, P. K. (1991). Human adults and human infants show a ''perceptual magnet effect'' for the prototypes of speech categories, monkeys do not. *Perception & Psychophysics, 50,* 93–107.

Kuhl, P. K., & Meltzoff, A. N. (1988). Speech as an intermodal object of perception. In A. Yonas (Ed.), *Perceptual development in infancy: The Minnesota symposia on child psychology* (Vol. 20, pp. 235–266). Hillsdale, NJ: Erlbaum.

Kuhl, P. K., Williams, K. A., & Meltzoff, A. N. (1991). Cross-modal speech perception in adults and infants using nonspeech auditory stimuli. *Journal of Experimental Psychology: Human Perception and Performance, 17,* 829–840.

Lackner, J. R., & Goldstein, L. M. (1974). Primary auditory stream segregation of repeated consonant–vowel sequences. *Journal of the Acoustical Society of America, 56,* 1651–1652.

Ladefoged, P. (1967). *Three areas of experimental phonetics.* Oxford: Oxford University Press.

Lahiri, A., Gewirth, L., & Blumstein, S. E. (1984). A reconsideration of acoustic invariance for place of articulation in diffuse stop consonants: Evidence from a cross language study. *Journal of the Acoustical Society of America, 76,* 391–404.

Liberman, A. M. (1957). Some results of research on speech perception. *Journal of the Acoustical Society of America, 29,* 117–123.

Liberman, A. M., Cooper, F. S., Shankweiler, D. P., & Studdert-Kennedy, M. (1967). Perception of the speech code. *Psychological Review, 74,* 431–461.

Liberman, A. M., Harris, K. S., Hoffman, H. S., & Griffith, B. C. (1957). The discrimination of speech sounds within and across phoneme boundaries. *Journal of Experimental Psychology, 54,* 358–368.

Liberman, A. M., Harris, K. S., Kinney, J. A., & Lane, H. (1961). The discrimination of relative onset-time of the components of certain speech and nonspeech patterns. *Journal of Experimental Psychology, 61,* 379–388.

Liberman, A. M., Isenberg, D., & Rakerd, B. (1981). Duplex perception of cues for stop consonants: Evidence for a phonetic mode. *Perception & Psychophysics, 30,* 133–143.

Liberman, A. M., & Mattingly, I. G. (1985). The motor theory of speech perception revised. *Cognition, 21,* 1–36.

Liberman, I. Y., Shankweiler, D. P., Liberman, A. M., Fowler, C. A., & Fischer, F. W. (1977). Explicit syllable and phoneme segmentation in the young child. In A. S. Reber & D. L. Scarborough (Eds.), *Toward a psychology of reading* (pp. 207–226). Hillsdale, NJ: Erlbaum.

Lieberman, P. (1963). Some effects of semantic and grammatical context on the production and perception of speech. *Language and Speech, 6,* 172–187.

Lieberman, P. (1973). On the evolution of language: A unified view. *Cognition, 2,* 59–94.

Lindblom, B. (1984). On the origin and purpose of discreteness and invariance in sound patterns. In J. S. Perkell & D. H. Klatt (Eds.), *Invariance and variability in speech processes* (pp. 493–510). Hillsdale, NJ: Erlbaum.

Lisker, L. (1978). Rabid vs. rapid: A catalog of acoustic features that may cue the distinction. *Haskins Laboratories Status Report on Speech Research, SR-54,* 127–132.

MacNeilage, P. F. (1971). Some observations on the metatheory of speech perception. *Language and Speech, 14,* 12–17.

MacNeilage, P. F. (1972). Speech physiology. In J. H. Gilbert (Ed.), *Speech and cortical functioning* (pp. 1–72). New York: Academic Press.

MacNeilage, P. F., Rootes, T. P., & Chase, R. A. (1967). Speech production and perception in a patient with severe impairment of somesthetic perception and motor control. *Journal of Speech and Hearing Research, 10,* 449–467.

Mann, V. A., & Liberman, A. M. (1983). Some differences between phonetic and auditory modes of perception. *Cognition, 14,* 211–235.

Massaro, D. W. (1987a). Psychophysics versus specialized processes in speech perception: An alternate perspective. In M. E. H. Schouten (Ed.), *The psychophysics of speech perception* (pp. 46–65). Dordrecht: Martinus Nijhoff.

Massaro, D. W. (1987b). *Speech perception by ear and eye: A paradigm for psychological inquiry.* Hillsdale, NJ: Erlbaum.

Massaro, D. W., & Hary, J. M. (1984). Categorical results, categorical perception and hindsight. *Perception & Psychophysics, 35,* 586–588.

Mattingly, I. G., & Liberman, A. M. (1990). Speech and other auditory modules. In G. M. Edelman, W. E. Gall, & W. M. Cowan (Eds.), *Signal and sense: Local and global order in perceptual maps* (pp. 501–520). New York: Wiley.

Mattingly, I. G., Liberman, A. M., Syrdal, A. K., & Halwes, T. (1971). Discrimination in speech and nonspeech modes. *Cognitive Psychology, 2,* 131–157.

Mermelstein, P. (1978). On the relationship between vowel and consonant identification when cued by the same acoustic information. *Perception & Psychophysics, 23,* 331–336.

Miller, G. A., & Licklider, J. C. R. (1950). The intelligibility of interrupted speech. *Journal of the Acoustical Society of America, 22,* 167–173.

Miller, J. L. (1990). Speech perception. In D. N. Osherson & H. Lasnik (Eds.), *Language: An invitation to cognitive science* (Vol. 1, pp. 69–93). Cambridge, MA: MIT Press/Bradford Books.

Nearey, T. M., & Assmann, P. F. (1986). Modeling the role of inherent spectral change in vowel identification. *Journal of the Acoustical Society of America, 80,* 1297–1308.

Negus, V. E. (1949). *The comparative anatomy and physiology of the larynx.* London: Heinemann.

Nygaard, L. C. (1993). Phonetic coherence in duplex perception: Effects of acoustic differences and lexical status. *Journal of Experimental Psychology: Human Perception and Performance, 19,* 268–286.

Ohala, J. J. (1986). Against the direct realist view of speech perception. *Journal of Phonetics, 14,* 75–82.

Pastore, N. (1971). *Selective history of theories of visual perception, 1650–1950.* New York: Oxford University Press.

Pastore, R. E., Schmuckler, M. A., Rosenblum, L., & Szczesiul, R. (1983). Duplex perception with musical stimuli. *Perception & Psychophysics, 33,* 469–474.

Patterson, R. D., & Holdsworth, J. (in press). A functional model of neural activity patterns and auditory images. In W. A. Ainsworth & E. F. Evans (Eds.), *Advances in speech, hearing and language processing* (Vol. 3). London: JAI Press.

Petitto, L. A., & Marentette, P. F. (1991). Babbling in the manual mode: Evidence for the ontogeny of language. *Science, 251,* 1493–1496.

Picheny, M. A., Durlach, N. I., & Braida, L. D. (1986). Speaking clearly for the hard of hearing. II: Acoustic characteristics of clear and conversational speech. *Journal of Speech and Hearing Research, 29,* 434–446.

Pickett, J. M., & Pollack, I. (1963). Intelligibility of excerpts from fluent speech: Effects of rate of utterance and duration of excerpt. *Language and Speech, 6,* 151–164.

Pisoni, D. B., & Luce, P. A. (1986). Speech perception: Research, theory, and the principal issues. In E. C. Schwab & H. C. Nusbaum (Eds.), *Pattern recognition by humans and machines* (pp. 1–50). New York: Academic Press.

Posner, M. I., & Keele, S. W. (1968). On the genesis of abstract ideas. *Journal of Experimental Psychology, 77,* 353–363.

Rand, T. C. (1974). Dichotic release from masking for speech. *Journal of the Acoustical Society of America, 55,* 678–680.

Remez, R. E. (1987). Units of organization and analysis in the perception of speech. In M. E. H. Schouten (Ed.), *The psychophysics of speech perception* (pp. 419–432). Dordrecht: Martinus Nijhoff.

Remez, R. E., Berns, S. M., Nutter, J. S., Lang, J. M., Davachi, L., & Rubin, P. E. (1991). On the perceptual differentiation of spontaneous and prepared speech. *Journal of the Acoustical Society of America, 89,* 2011–2012.

Remez, R. E., Pardo, J. S., & Rubin, P. E. (1991, November). *Making the (auditory) scene with speech.* Paper presented at the 32nd annual meeting of the Psychonomic Society, San Francisco.

Remez, R. E., & Rubin, P. E. (in press). Acoustic shards, perceptual glue. In J. Charles-Luce, P. A. Luce, & J. R. Sawusch (Eds.), *Theories in spoken language: Perception, production, and development.* Norwood, NJ: Ablex.

Remez, R. E., Rubin, P. E., Berns, S. M., Pardo, J. S., & Lang, J. M. (in press). *On the perceptual organization of speech. Psychological Review.*

Remez, R. E., Rubin, P. E., Nygaard, L. C., & Howell, W. A. (1987). Perceptual normalization of vowels produced by sinusoidal voices. *Journal of Experimental Psychology: Human Perception and Performance, 13,* 40–61.

Remez, R. E., Rubin, P. E., Pisoni, D. B., & Carrell T. D. (1981). Speech perception without traditional speech cues. *Science, 212,* 947–950.

Repp, B. H. (1982). Phonetic trading relations and context effects: New experimental evidence for a speech mode of perception. *Psychological Bulletin, 92,* 81–110.

Repp, B. H. (1987). The role of psychophysics in understanding speech perception. In M. E. H. Schouten (Ed.), *The psychophysics of speech perception* (pp. 3–27). Dordrecht: Martinus Nijhoff.

Rubin, P. E., Baer, T., & Mermelstein, P. (1981). An articulatory synthesizer for perceptual research. *Journal of the Acoustical Society of America, 70,* 321–328.

Rubin, P. E., & Vatikiotis-Bateson, E. (in press). Measuring and modeling speech production, In S. L. Hopp & C. S. Evans (Eds.), *Animal acoustic communication: Recent technical advances.* New York: Springer-Verlag.

Samuel, A. G. (1981). The role of bottom-up confirmation in the phonemic restoration illusion. *Journal of Experimental Psychology: Human Perception and Performance, 11,* 1124–1131.

Samuel, A. G. (1982). Phonetic prototypes. *Perception & Psychophysics, 31,* 307–314.

Sawusch, J. R. (1991). Invariant auditory attributes and a model of speech perception. In *Actes du XIIIième Congrès International des Sciences Phonetique* (Vol. 1, pp. 63–67). Aix-en-Provence: International Congress of Phonetic Sciences.

Schulman, R. (1989). Articulatory dynamics of loud and normal speech. *Journal of the Acoustical Society of America, 85,* 295–312.

Segui, J., Frauenfelder, U., & Mehler, J. (1981). Phoneme monitoring, syllable monitoring, and lexical access. *British Journal of Psychology, 72,* 471–477.

Shattuck-Hufnagel, S. (1983). Sublexical units and suprasegmental structure in speech production planning. In P. MacNeilage (Ed.), *The production of speech* (pp. 109–136). New York: Springer-Verlag.

Silverman, K. (1985). Vowel intrinsic pitch influences the perception of intonational prominence. *Journal of the Acoustical Society of America, 77,* S38.

Steiger, H., & Bregman, A. S. (1981). Capturing frequency components of glided tones: Frequency separation, orientation, and alignment. *Perception & Psychophysics, 30,* 425–435.

Stevens, K. N. (1990, December). *Lexical access from features.* Lecture presented at the Workshop on Speech Technology for Man-Machine Interaction, Tata Institute of Fundamental Research, Bombay, India.

Stevens, K. N. (1991). Acoustic links to phonetic units. In I. G. Mattingly & M. Studdert-Kennedy

(Eds.), *Modularity and the motor theory of speech perception: Proceedings of a conference to honor Alvin M. Liberman* (pp. 181–184). Hillsdale, NJ: Erlbaum.

Stevens, K. N., & Blumstein, S. E. (1981). The search for invariant acoustic correlates of phonetic features. In P. D. Eimas and J. L. Miller (Eds.), *Perspectives on the study of speech* (pp. 1–38). Hillsdale, NJ: Erlbaum.

Studdert-Kennedy, M. (1986). Two cheers for direct realism. *Journal of Phonetics, 14,* 99–104.

Summerfield, Q. (1987). Some preliminaries to a comprehensive account of audio-visual speech perception. In B. Dodd & R. Campbell (Eds.), *Hearing by eye: The psychology of lip-reading* (pp. 3–51). Hillsdale, NJ: Erlbaum.

Walley, A. C., & Carrell, T. D. (1983). Onset spectra and formant transitions in the adult's and child's perception of place of articulation in stop consonants. *Journal of the Acoustical Society of America, 73,* 1011–1022.

Washburn, M. F. (1916). *Movement and mental imagery: Outlines of a motor theory of the complexer mental processes.* Boston: Houghton Mifflin.

Wertheimer, M. (1923). Untersuchungen zur Lehre von der Gestalt. II. *Psychologische Forschung, 4,* 301–350. [Reprinted in translation as ''Laws of organization in perceptual forms.'' In W. D. Ellis (Ed.), *A sourcebook of Gestalt psychology* (pp. 71–88). London: Routledge & Kegan Paul, 1938.]

Whalen, D. H. (1984). Subcategorical phonetic mismatches slow phonetic judgments. *Perception & Psychophysics, 35,* 49–64.

CHAPTER 6

SPEECH PERCEPTION AS A TRACTABLE PROBLEM IN COGNITIVE SCIENCE

KEITH R. KLUENDER

I. INTRODUCTION: SPEECH PERCEPTION AS AN IDEAL PROBLEM FOR COGNITIVE SCIENCE

Whether they study perception or higher level processes of language or reasoning, all cognitive scientists are confronted with two basic and competing challenges. First, psychological theories must entail sufficient complexity to capture the richness of human abilities. Second, those theories must incorporate adequate constraints to provide falsifiable predictions and, hence, explanatory power. In general, this second challenge has proven more difficult than the former, and most researchers can share at least a handful of frustrating encounters with theories that, while attractive at first blush, proved unassailable by data, real or imaginary. In the face of these challenges, speech perception may well be an exemplary area of research in cognitive science because powerful and general constraints can be enlisted in its study.

There are several ways cognitive scientists can hope to constrain theory in a manner that yields falsifiable hypotheses. First, they may develop a studied appreciation for the natural bounds upon, and variation within, the environment with which the organism is confronted. For example, researchers of color vision have garnered very useful insights into processes of color constancy by surveying the spectral composition of a broad sample of natural objects under varying degrees of illumination (Dannemiller, 1992a,b; Maloney, 1986). In the study of speech perception, the domain is naturally circumscribed as the domain of all sounds used across languages to convey phonetic distinctions, and variation within that domain has been exquisitely described for hundreds of languages by legions of phoneticians.

A second useful source of constraint may be found in the study of the organism itself as researchers study the structure and function of neural hardware to better understand what sorts of processes are biologically possible. While the jury may still be out on the prospects for the broad and burgeoning field of cognitive neuroscience, recent progress in areas germane to speech perception suggest that this approach is quite promising. Auditory neurophysiologists have been making remarkable headway in describing neural encoding of speech sounds in auditory pathways (see, for example, Greenberg, 1988a). In addition, as more becomes known about neural processes for learning, important insights may be revealed about the processes by which an individual learns the phonetic categories specific to his or her language. Observations on each of these fronts are beginning to be sufficiently detailed to inspire testable hypotheses about perception of speech.

A third approach is to develop computational models and simulations that, prerequisite to their machine instantiation, require explicit constraints on both process and problem domain. This is not to say that either mathematical formalism or computational instantiation necessarily implies anything about psychological reality. It is simply the case that when modeling a process, the theorist is confronted with problems that are sometimes neglected in psychological theory. For example, efforts to model processes of categorization have often relied heavily on prior extraction of features, and feature extraction has frequently been assumed without question. An effort to computationally instantiate categorization processes must either include explicit description of features (hopefully, with some justification for how that set of features came to be) or abandon the notion of features in lieu of some more realistic input representation.

For over 40 years, there has been a sustained effort to develop machine speech recognition devices. Unfortunately, the bulk of this effort has been carried out with almost exclusive emphasis on engineering considerations; however, there is hope that as psychologically plausible processes become incorporated, the best of these models could be tested against human performance. It is interesting that in the absence of much consideration of how humans process speech, no engineering approach to speech perception has achieved the success of an average two-year old, and this fact nicely introduces one final potential constraint.

Ontogenetic considerations can lend further constraint because it is not enough simply to hypothesize cognitive processes; one must also consider how such processes make their way into the head. One may be able to evaluate competing models of cognitive processes on the basis of the relative plausibility of such processes being either a part of the infant's initial state and/or the result of subsequent learning. Again, researchers in speech perception are in the enviable position of having a wealth of data regarding infant abilities to discriminate and categorize speech sounds, and some of the most provocative recent data address the development of these abilities over the first year of life.

Given that the study of speech perception can benefit from this broad arsenal of scientific approaches, here it is argued that speech perception is an ideal topic of study for the cognitive scientist. Even if one does not accept this claim for speech perception's relatively exclusive status, one surely should appreciate the scientific benefits of such a diverse array of converging approaches to the problem. With such assets in hand, it must be made clear that a theory of speech perception still must be evaluated, like any scientific theory, by its predictive power, simplicity, and ability to unify seemingly disparate domains of phenomena. Of course, predictive power is the name of the game in science. A theory that predicts nothing (or everything) is of little use, and a theory has value to scientists only when it embodies claims that have the potential to be falsified by the data. It is true that parsimony is sometimes eschewed as impossible to define, and as a purely philosophical point, simplicity can be a slippery concept. However, in practice, it is only infrequently difficult to make judgments of the relative simplicity of competing models or theories. Simplicity is only half the story, as generality must also be cherished. A single general model that explains data that previously required a number of separate restricted models should be most valued.

This chapter serves as an introduction to an approach to the study of speech perception that is motivated by this scientific spirit while building on the constraints described above. Here, an effort will be made to lay the groundwork for a very conservative approach to modeling the perception and categorization of human speech. This approach relies on efforts from related fields in the service of developing simple general explanations for speech perception and categorization. In particular, this effort draws heavily on the linguistics literature on phonetic inventories, as well as on psychoacoustics and neurophysiology findings that bear on how auditory systems process complex sounds. Finally, it is very much inspired by what is known about simple general processes of learning and categorization.

II. WHAT NEEDS TO BE EXPLAINED BY A THEORY OF SPEECH PERCEPTION

A. Phylogeny and Ontogeny

A theory of speech perception must explain how listeners come to use the particular sounds of their language (phonemes) in the service of recognizing lexical units (morphemes). In keeping with the appeal to constraints made above, it is suggested that a good deal of the explanation of speech perception lies in understanding the PHYLOGENY and ONTOGENY of sound systems used by talkers and listeners. The use of the term phylogeny implies that a comprehensive theory ought to be informed by how and why languages come to use the particular set of speech sounds that they do. When one examines cross-language regularities—in much the same way that the comparative anatomist studies cross-species commonalities—it is apparent that phonologies share much in common, owing primarily to constraints imposed by the articulatory and auditory apparatus. By understanding how the sound inventories of languages have come to take the forms they do, much as the evolution biologist seeks to understand the adaptation of species, one may learn a great deal about processes that underlie speech production and perception. Here, the emphasis will be on the role auditory systems play in selecting the particular sets of phonemes used by languages. Out of hundreds of producible mouth sounds, some phonemes and combinations of phonemes are clearly favored, frequently in ways that exploit the discriminative abilities of listeners. As one develops an accurate specification of how speech sounds are encoded by the auditory system, speech sounds may be mapped into a perceptual space in a manner that reveals important insights about these phonetic regularities.

By itself, such a mapping does not constitute phonetic categorization. Experience plays a critical role in parceling the space into categories; after all, the fact that different languages partition the space differently implies that the categorization of speech sounds depends on linguistic experience. Consequently, a comprehensive model of speech perception should also address the ontogeny of sound systems. That is, it should illuminate the process by which the child, as an individual language user, learns the phonetic categories specific to his or her language. The aim of this chapter is to demonstrate how one can integrate findings from research in perception, linguistics, auditory neurophysiology, and computer science toward an explanation of speech perception that addresses both phylogeny and ontogeny.

One would be myopic to conclude that this is all there is to developing a complete model of speech perception. After all, phonemes exist only in the service of the morphemes they comprise. Toward the end of this chapter, there is a brief discussion of the relation between learning speech categories and lexical development; however, the reader is directed to other chapters in this volume (Massaro; Lively, Pisoni, and Goldinger) where processes of auditory lexical access are addressed more thoroughly.

B. Egon Brunswick and the Ecological Survey

While the theoretical approach described in this chapter is not wholly like that proposed by Egon Brunswick, several central issues in speech perception were perhaps best anticipated in his writing about visual perception a half century ago. Brunswick (1937, 1940, 1944, 1952) deeply appreciated the value of knowing well the scope and nature of objects and events to be perceived. He was most interested in visual perceptual constancies. Simplified somewhat here, Brunswick envisioned an object or event in the environment (distal stimulus) as giving rise to an array of proximal cues (properties of the retinal image for vision, or acoustic properties for speech perception). By this view, perception is the process by which multiple cues are combined to yield a unitary percept. The classic problem of visual perceptual constancy is that the proximal array varies as a function of changes in orientation, distance, illumination, and so on. By Brunswick's formulation, any single cue is, at best, reasonably well correlated with the object or event. Accepting the premise that there exist no proximal cues that by themselves are either necessary or sufficient to support veridical perception, Brunswick (1937, 1940) suggested that perceptual processes must use an array of proximal cues. He defined the strength of the correlation between a proximal cue and a distal property as its ECOLOGICAL VALIDITY and described the degree to which the distal physical property is correlated with the perceptual response as FUNCTIONAL VALIDITY (Brunswick, 1955; Postman & Tolman, 1959). For any cue, ecological validity could, in principle, be expressed as its experienced co-occurrence with the object or event in the world. In practice, of course, it is typically impossible to know an observer's complete experience with every cue and every object or event, so Brunswick argued that an ECOLOGICAL SURVEY needs to be carried out, from which the correlation of each proximal cue with the distal stimulus may be assessed. Understandably, the Augean task of actually conducting such an ecological survey has been carried out only rarely (Brunswick, 1944; Krinov, 1947), although the usefulness of such surveys has been amply demonstrated (see, e.g., Dannemiller, 1992a,b; Maloney, 1986).

The reader who is familiar with problems in speech perception will surely recognize the parallels between Brunswick's formulation of the problem of perceptual constancy and the notorious problem of lack of invariance in speech perception. Here, the use of multiple stimulus attributes for perception of speech is accepted as fact and is discussed at length in the section on ontogeny, but for now, consider the issue of ecological surveys and the phylogeny of phonetic inventories.

III. PHYLOGENY: SYSTEMATICITY IN THE FACE OF DIVERSITY

Happily, researchers in speech perception are the beneficiaries of what is doubtless the most extensive ecological survey ever conducted. Through over 100 years of study by phoneticians, the domain of speech sounds has been scrupulously catalogued. One very rich source of information is the UCLA Phonological Segment Inventory Database (UPSID), in which a representative sample of the phonological inventories of the world's languages has been characterized (Maddieson, 1984). From this database, one can answer questions such as: What is the most common number of vowels used by languages? Which vowels are favored across languages? For languages that use five vowels, which five are most typical? What is the most prevalent consonantal contrast? If a language uses three places of articulation, which three are favored?[1]

Now, it is true that one of the first things that becomes apparent to someone surveying language sound systems is the sheer diversity. To the English monolingual, the clicks of Zulu and the uvular plosives of Awiya seem strange, while the bilabial fricatives of Irish seem familiar but not linguistic. One finds similar diversity in vowel systems. The fact that Maddieson (1984) required 58 phonetic attributes to characterize all 558 consonants, 260 vowels, and 51 diphthongs in the UPSID sample is ample testament to the rich variety of sounds used by the world's languages. Not only is there a very large number of sounds used, but there is also ample heterogeneity in inventory size with as few as 11 (Rotokas, Mura) and as many as 141 (!Xū) phonemes used in any particular language.

However, upon systematic inspection, what becomes apparent even in the face of such diversity is the fact that phonetic inventories are anything but random. The vast majority of those 869 phonemes are relatively rare, while a handful are extremely common. For example, all known languages have stop consonants. The overwhelming majority of languages have three places of articulation for stop consonants which typically include bilabial, alveolar, and

---

[1] It bears note that the phonetic descriptions on which UPSID is based are not uniform in quality. Maddieson and his colleagues did re-analyze data according to a single set of criteria; however, variation in quality and level of detail remain. Fortunately for the discussion at hand, relative coarseness of description has not substantively obscured the description of phonetic contrasts (as compared with absolute description of phonetic segments). Kingston (1991) suggests that some degree of imprecision is, in fact, a virtue for statistical evaluation of what is and is not a typical phonetic contrast.

velar, as is the case for English. And, over 80% of languages utilize a distinction in voicing, usually at these three main places of articulation (Maddieson, 1984).

It is also true that over 90% of all languages include fricatives. While Maddieson lists 30 different fricatives, many are rare while a few are ubiquitous. Over 80% of languages have some version of /s/ (as in *sale*), with /ʃ/ and /f/ (as in *shale* and *fail*) being quite frequent as well. It seems to be no coincidence that all three of these prevalent fricatives are voiceless, as roughly a third as many fricatives are voiced as are voiceless. Without belaboring the point with further examples of regularities among nasals, liquids, and semivowels, suffice it to say that, when it comes to consonants, diversity does not imply entropy.

The structure of vowel systems is as orderly as or more orderly than that for consonants. Again, there is a good deal of variety in the particular number of vowels used by languages, as some languages use as few as three vowels while others use as many as 24. While 21.5% of the languages in Maddieson's sample have five vowels, other numbers of vowels appear to be relatively favored. Four is less common than either three or five, and eight is less common than seven or nine.

Especially for the five- to nine-vowel systems that predominate among phonological inventories, the particular sets of vowels used by languages with the same number of vowels have a good deal in common. The relatively large number of languages that use five vowels tend to use the same five vowels. There are also clear preferences for certain seven-vowel inventories, and although the sample begins to dwindle for systems with eight or more vowels, there remains a good deal of commonality among systems with the same number of vowels (Crothers, 1978).

A. Articulatory Constraints and Systematicity

What is one to make of powerful commonalities among phonetic inventories? What are the forces acting on languages that encourage the selection of some sounds and groups of sounds over others? One's first suggestion may be that some sounds are easier to produce than others. With a few notable exceptions (Kuhl, 1986, 1988; Lindblom, 1986; Ohala, 1974; K. N. Stevens, Keyser, & Kawasaki, 1986), phoneticians have typically attempted to explain phonetic regularities in terms of physical or physiological constraints on speech production. This has been especially true when a phonetic regularity occurs widely across languages, approximating a phonetic universal. For example, Keating, Linker, and Huffman (1983) recommend that plain voiceless stops are favored by virtue of aerodynamic and articulatory efficiency. Similarly, the prevalence of voiceless fricatives might be explained if one demonstrates that it is easier to sustain sufficient airflow for the turbulence required for fricatives when vocal cords are spread. The fact that children learn to produce voiced fricatives only after most other speech sounds have been mastered is also supportive of an explanation based on articulatory ease.

Of course, the human vocal tract is capable of generating only so many different sounds—some easy and some hard to produce—and articulatory constraints do play an important role in the selection of speech sounds. The role of articulatory ease is perhaps best evidenced by the fact that languages tend to use articulatorily less demanding consonants before incorporating more complex consonants. Lindblom and Maddieson (1988) classified consonants according to whether they required "basic" articulations, "elaborated" articulations, or combinations of elaborated articulations which they refer to as "complex." When inspecting the phonemic inventories for languages with increasing numbers of consonants, they found that languages have a strong tendency to exploit basic consonants before incorporating elaborated consonants, and to include elaborated consonants before complex consonants. Without fully explaining how Lindblom and Maddieson (1988) classified consonants in these three categories, suffice it to say that articulatory cost does play an influential role in the selection of consonant inventories. A least effort principle seems to guide not only the selection of segment inventories, but also to influence the on-line realization of phonetic segments in speech production (Lindblom & Engstrand, 1989).

Aside from these general observations, the degree to which producing some sounds may require more energy or greater coordination has proven very difficult to quantify. In principle, however, there is no reason that articulatory ease cannot eventually be quantified with precision sufficient to suggest testable hypotheses about the composition of language inventories. Locke (1980) has proposed that the order in which children learn to produce sounds reflects the degree of articulatory complexity. It seems true that articulatory ease should much affect the progression of production ability; however, one would suspect that perceptual distinctiveness and distributional characteristics of the child's phonetic experience also play no small role. In any event, the simple premise that children learn to produce sounds that are easy to articulate earlier because they are easier to articulate permits an analysis short of ideal as a metric for articulatory ease. In the future, richer conceptualizations of articulatory effort may yield valuable insights, but for now, all that can be claimed confidently with regard to the role of articulatory constraints on phonetic inventories is that such constraints must matter. The answers to exciting questions of how to quantify articulatory ease and how to explain specifically how articulatory constraints shape language inventories remain relatively unrefined. As will become clear in the following discussion, even precise definition of articulatory effort will greatly underdetermine a good many of the gestural covariation commonly observed in languages (Diehl & Kluender, 1989a; Kluender, Diehl, & Wright, 1988).

B. Auditory Constraints and Systematicity

No matter what form the eventual conceptualization of articulatory ease takes, it is quite clear that talkers are willing to expend effort for communicative robustness. For example, the tense vowels /i/ and /u/ (as in *beet* and *boot*) surely require more effort to produce relative to their lax counterparts /ɪ/ and /ʊ/ (as in *bit* and *book*), yet across languages, these tense vowels occur five times more frequently than the lax. One question that must be asked by the speech researcher is whether the relatively orderly composition of phonetic inventories can lend insights into processes of speech perception. And, can a theory of speech perception be capable of explaining and predicting the composition of phonological inventories? What is the nature of the relation between speech perception and phonological inventories?

Even in the face of foregoing arguments for parsimony, no theory ought to portray Nature as more simple than she really is, and there is at least one property of speech perception that is exceptional, this being the symmetry of communication. Talkers control their acoustic output with the listener "in mind." Aside from communication systems, music, and visual art, there may be no other instances of perceptual events being created with such deference to the perceiver's interests. Clear examples of talkers molding their utterances to the needs of the listener include instances in which conditions for communication are not optimal. Talkers speak more clearly to young or nonnative listeners for whom phonetic distinctions are not obvious; and when environments are noisy or reverberant, talkers strive to produce phonetic contrasts that are maximally distinctive. The present chapter's emphasis on parsimony need not be at odds with this recognition that humans talking are not like leaves rustling and turbines whining. In fact, significant progress may be made toward a model of speech perception based on an appreciation for the efforts of talkers to capitalize on the general auditory predisposition of listeners.

This argument can be extended with the claim that the sound systems of language communities have adapted to be fairly robust signaling devices by exploiting general characteristics of auditory systems whenever possible. An obvious way that a language community achieves such robustness is by developing an inventory of phonemes so as to optimize phonetic distinctiveness acoustically and auditorily. In the literature, this claim has been articulated as the AUDITORY ENHANCEMENT HYPOTHESIS (see, e.g., Diehl & Kluender, 1989a; Diehl, Kluender, & Walsh, 1990) and as the closely related hypothesis that Lindblom and his colleagues refer to as the DISPERSION PRINCIPLE (Liljencrantz & Lindblom, 1972; Lindblom, 1986, 1989). Importantly, it is suggested here that neither acoustic energy nor auditory stimulation are the objects of speech perception per se (see Kluender, 1991b; Remez, this volume). Instead, the claim is simply that spoken linguistic information is transmitted via an acoustic/auditory channel, and language users exploit the transmission characteristics of auditory systems in order to maintain the integrity of their linguistic message.

Inspection of regularities in vowel sounds used by languages provide some of the most illuminating examples of auditory processes operating as the driving force behind selection of phonetic inventories. Different languages use different sets of vowel sounds. A language ought to come to use the subset of vowels that are most easily discriminated from one another. In particular, those vowels favored for languages with five vowels ought to be the five vowels that, as a group, are as distant as possible from one another in perceptual space. In support of this claim, Liljencrants and Lindblom (1972) showed that for languages with six or fewer vowels, the vowel inventories are well predicted by a principle of maximal auditory distance in a simplified two-dimensional (F1–F2) space (see also Disner, 1984). As a general rule, the set of vowels selected by a language, whether it uses three or ten vowels, comprises sounds that tend toward maximal discriminability (see Fig. 1).

One may suggest that this dispersion is, instead, the product of languages having a tendency to use vowels that are as articulatorily extreme as possible and that acoustic distinctiveness is simply the physical consequence of maximally distinctive articulatory gestures (Fowler, 1989). However, a number of compelling observations of regularities in vowel production suggest that auditory, and

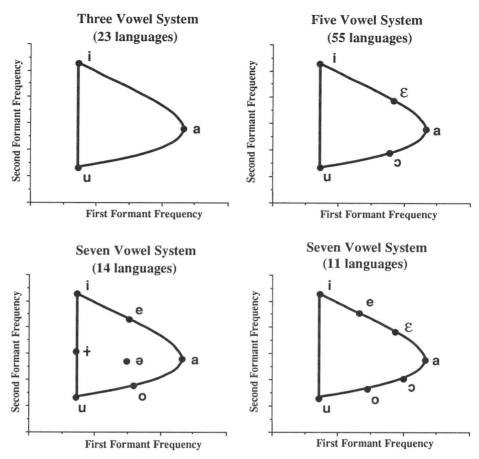

FIG. 1 Most common vowel inventories for languages with three to seven vowels are shown (based on cross-language survey by Crothers, 1978).

not articulatory, considerations are at work. The following examples represent cases of auditory enhancement in which talkers marshall two or more articulatorily independent gestures in the service of acoustic/auditory distinctiveness.

C. Auditory Enhancement for Vowels

Among the world's languages, the three "point" vowels /i/, /u/, and /a/ are the most common by far (Maddieson, 1984), each appearing almost twice as frequently as any nonpoint vowel. These vowels serve to define extremes in both the articulatory and acoustic space of potential vowels. The articulatory space can be generally described in terms of three dimensions, tongue height, tongue frontness/backness, and lip rounding. The vowels /i/ and /u/ are both HIGH vowels produced with the jaw and tongue body in a raised position, while /a/ is a LOW vowel produced with the jaw and tongue body lowered. High vowels /i/ and /u/ are distinguished by the fact that the tongue body is raised toward the front of the mouth for /i/, while it is raised toward the back for /u/.

One dominant tendency among languages is that back, but not front, vowels are produced with the lips rounded. In Maddieson's (1984) sample, there are 254 languages that have the high back rounded vowel /u/, but only 20 languages that have the high back unrounded vowel /ɯ/. Similarly, 271 languages in the sample have the high front unrounded vowel /i/, and only 21 have the high front rounded vowel /y/. No apparent articulatory constraint is involved, inasmuch as the tongue body and lips are not physiologically tethered. Consider, however, the acoustic/auditory consequences of tongue fronting and lip rounding. The vowels /i/ and /u/ can be distinguished for the most part by the frequency of the second formant (F2). While they both have relatively low frequency first formants (F1), production of /i/ results in a high F2 (near the third formant, F3), while production of /u/ results in a low F2 (near F1). Fronting the tongue results in a higher frequency F2, while lip rounding results in a lower F2. Quite clearly, the effect of lip rounding (lower F2) is to make vowels acoustically more backlike. For /u/ and other back vowels, rounding serves to make them acoustically and auditorily more distinct from front vowels, while rounding of front vowels such as /i/ serves the counterproductive role of making them less frontlike and hence less distinctive (Diehl & Kluender, 1989a; Diehl et al., 1990; K. N. Stevens et al., 1986). The cross-language tendency for back vowels to be rounded and front vowels to be unrounded is consistent with the view that talkers articulate in order to provide acoustic products that are maximally distinctive.

NASALIZATION—lowering of the velum in order to allow air and sound to escape via the nose—is another vowel feature that exhibits strong distributional tendencies. Across languages for which vowel nasalization is not phonemic, low vowels such as /a/, /æ/, and /ɔ/ (as in *cot, cat,* and *caught*) tend to be nasalized much more often than high vowels (Ohala, 1974). Again, any purely mechanical explanation of this tendency (e.g., based on some indirect coupling of the tongue and velum) appears to be ruled out, since there is clear electromyographic evidence (Lubker, 1968) of active velar raising (which reduces nasalization) during high vowels. The F1 of low vowels is at a relatively high frequency, and frequency of F1 serves to distinguish low from high vowels. One of several acoustic consequences of slight nasalization (nonphonemic) is to effectively raise the frequency of F1 (House & Stevens, 1956; Ohala, 1974; K. N. Stevens, Fant, & Hawkins, 1987). The auditory enhancement explanation for the general observation that low vowels are more nasalized than high vowels is that, by virtue of making a high F1 higher, nasalization serves to enhance the high–low distinction by further raising the high F1 of low vowels still higher. Perceptual studies in which listeners identify nasalized and nonnasalized vowels of varying vowel heights verify that nasalization serves to make vowels sound "lower" (Krakow, Beddor, Goldstein, & Fowler, 1988; Wright, 1975, 1986) and support the auditory enhancement explanation for the nasalization of predominantly low vowels.

Another parameter that covaries universally with vowel height is fundamental frequency (*f*ø): High vowels such as /i/ and /u/ tend to have higher values of *f*ø than low vowels such as /a/, /æ/, and /ɔ/ (Lehiste, 1970). Phoneticians have generally assumed that this *f*ø variation is an unavoidable physical consequence of vowel height differences, prompting the widespread use of the term INTRINSIC VOWEL PITCH. Ladefoged (1964) and Honda (1981) have proposed variations of a scenario by which an elevated tongue pulls on laryngeal structures in such a way as to place tension on the vocal folds and raise their frequency of vibration. A second hypothesis (Atkinson, 1973) is based on a hypothesized acoustic coupling between the laryngeal source and the vocal tract such that $f\emptyset$ is raised in the direction of F1. Each of these hypotheses is either incompatible with later data (Ewan, 1979; Lindau, Jacobson, & Ladefoged, 1972) or is subject to alternative explanation (Diehl et al., 1990).

Traunmüller (1981) found that listeners judge vowel height not on the basis of F1 frequency alone, but rather by the distance (in Bark units, an auditory transformation of frequency) between $f\emptyset$ and F1. The smaller this difference, the higher the perceived vowel (see also Syrdal, 1985; Syrdal & Gopal, 1986). It now seems apparent that talkers actively regulate $f\emptyset$, narrowing the F1/$f\emptyset$ difference for high vowels and expanding it for low vowels, in order to enhance perceptual distinctiveness. This hypothesis is supported by the observation that high vowels are produced with greater activation of the cricothyroid muscle, the primary muscle involved in active control of pitch (Dyhr, 1991; Vilkman, Aaltonen, Raimo, Arajärvi, & Oksanen, 1989). This result is predicted by the active auditory enhancement account and not by production-based explanations that appeal to passive interactions.

One final example of auditory enhancement of vowels may be found in cross-language regularities in gender differences in vowel production. Female formants are generally higher in frequency, mostly due to the fact that female vocal tracts are typically shorter than male vocal tracts. All things being equal, the acoustic consequence of shorter vocal tracts is higher formant frequency values, and a vocal tract that is 15% shorter will give rise to formants with frequency values 15% higher. Contrary to this simple scenario, not all vowels share the same scaling factor across gender (Fant, 1966, 1975); for example, formant values for female and male /u/ are on average relatively close while female and male formant values for /a/ are not (Henton, 1992; Yang, 1990). The female vowel space is expanded in such a manner as to make female vowels more acoustically/auditorily distinct even when formant values are scaled by a factor commensurate with differing vocal tract size. It is generally accepted that the degree to which the frequencies of female formants for vowel sounds are higher than those for males cannot be explained solely on the basis of anatomical differences in vocal tracts (Fant, 1966, 1975; Goldstein, 1980; Nordstrom, 1977). While some have suggested that non-anatomical vowel space differences may be attributable to sociolinguistic factors (Goldstein, 1980), Diehl and Lindblom (1990) suggest that the greater dispersion of female formant patterns results from an implicit strategy of female talkers to overcome the poorer resolution of spectral peaks afforded by the higher female $f\emptyset$. In support of this conclusion, Diehl, Lindblom, and Hoemeke (in preparation, cf. Diehl & Lindblom, 1990) demonstrated that vowel intelligibility is reduced at higher $f\emptyset$ values as the acoustic and perceptual distance between vowels tends to decrease.

D. Auditory Enhancement for Consonants

Instances of auditory enhancement are not limited to vowels, as there are a number of clear instances of auditory enhancement for consonants as well.

Consider the case for medial voicing contrasts such as that between voiced /b/ and voiceless /p/ as in *rabid* and *rapid*. Two of the most perceptually salient cues signaling this distinction are closure duration and presence or absence of glottal pulsing during the closure interval. Voiced labial stops are produced with shorter lip closure than voiceless stops, and the closure interval for voiced stops is likely to contain low-frequency periodic energy corresponding to vocal fold vibration. Each of these cues, closure duration and glottal pulsing, is capable of signaling the medial voicing distinction. It is clear that listeners use both acoustic cues when making judgments of medial voicing, as listeners require a significantly longer closure interval to perceive a stop as voiceless when the interval contains energy from glottal pulsing (Lisker, 1978). It is possible that listeners' sensitivity to both cues in their perception of voiced and voiceless medial stops is the result of their experience with the typical covariance of such cues for the voicing distinction; however, this seems not to be the whole story. In fact, the joint influence of closure duration and glottal pulsing on perception of medial voicing appears to be at least partially grounded in general auditory processes.

A general auditory contribution to the effects of closure duration and glottal pulsing has been demonstrated in experiments using nonspeech analogues of syllables such as /aba/ and /apa/. Parker, Diehl, and Kluender (1986) created stimuli consisting of two squarewave segments separated by an interval that had either no energy (silent) or had up to 60 ms of low-amplitude energy from glottal pulsing plus up to 60 ms of silence. Their stimuli mimicked the temporal properties and peak amplitudes of /aba/ and /apa/ stimuli, and the interval between the two squarewave segments varied from 20 to 120 ms in duration. Following training with endpoint stimuli, the task for subjects was to label these nonspeech stimuli as having a short or long interval between the two squarewave segments. A "short" judgment is analogous to a voiced or *b* judgment for speech stimuli. Analogous to the case for speech stimuli, when glottal pulsing was present, listeners required a longer interval between squarewave segments in order to judge the interval as long.

Interestingly, the interaction between glottal pulsing and interval duration was reliable only when the frequency of the squarewave segments decreased before the interval and increased following the interval, the same frequency contours that occur in both $f\phi$ and F1 for naturally produced medial voicing contrasts. While demonstrating a clear auditory interaction between glottal pulsing and closure duration under appropriate spectral conditions, Parker et al.'s experiments did not establish whether the effect of frequency contour was associated with analogous changes in $f\phi$ or in F1 for speech stimuli, for as the $f\phi$ of a square wave changes, the frequencies of all harmonics of the $f\phi$ change proportionately. It was unclear whether changes in the squarewave $f\phi$ and associated harmonics should be taken to correspond to changes in speech $f\phi$, changes in F1, or both. To answer this question, Kingston, Diehl, Kluender, and Parker (1990) used single format stimuli (F1) for which F1 and $f\phi$ frequencies were varied parametrically in a study demonstrating that the interaction between glottal pulsing and perceived interval duration is reliable only when the frequency of F1 follows the same pattern as occurs for naturally produced utterances (fall–rise). They found no reliable interaction between $f\phi$ changes and the effect of pulsing. From the Parker et al. and Kingston et al. studies, it can be concluded that the effect of glottal pulsing (voicing) on perceived closure duration is at least partly of a general auditory nature, and the F1 correlate of consonant voicing auditorily enhances the voicing contrast.

Another example of auditory enhancement can be found in the voicing contrast for syllable-initial stop consonants. In the production of the voicing distinction, the seemingly straightforward timing relation between the release of consonantal occlusion and vocal fold vibration gives rise to a broad array of acoustic cues. For English voiced stops, periodic energy resulting from vocal fold vibration either precedes or is nearly coincidental with release, whereas for English voiceless stops,[2] voice onset follows release by 40–100 ms (Lisker & Abramson, 1964). During the delay between release and voice onset, there is little or no energy in F1 (owing primarily to the presence of a low-frequency antiresonance introduced by tracheal coupling to the vocal cavities), and there is aperiodic energy (frication and aspiration) in the second and higher formants. This period between consonantal release and voicing onset during which there is no energy in F1 can be referred to as F1 CUTBACK, and as F1 cutback becomes longer, listeners are more likely to identify stimuli as voiceless /p/, /t/, or /k/. In natural articulation, one consequence of longer F1 cutback is a higher frequency of F1 onset, as the frequency of F1 increases following release as the articulators move away from occlusion. The longer the delay between release and the onset of voicing, the higher the frequency of F1 onset.

This natural covariance between duration of F1 cutback and F1 onset frequency is reflected in listeners' perception. In studies using synthetic speech stimuli varying in duration of F1 cutback, it has been demonstrated that for stimuli with higher F1 onset frequency, shorter durations of F1 cutback are required to produce a voiceless percept (Kluender, 1991a). Again, listeners' sensitivity to the natural covariance between these two acoustic correlates of voicing does not require use of tacit knowledge of articulatory covariation as the effects seem to be purely auditory. Experiments using nonspeech analogues of F1 cutback have found the same dependency between F1 cutback and F1 onset frequency (Parker, 1988). Furthermore, Japanese quail (*Coturnix coturnix japonica*) show the same effects of F1 onset frequency on their "labeling" of stop consonants varying in F1 cutback (Kluender, 1991a), and this interaction between F1 onset frequency and F1 cutback is not related to experience with natural covariance between the two acoustic cues (Lotto & Kluender, 1992).

The reader may note that, for the present example, auditory enhancement need not necessarily require active coordination of articulatory gestures. For some phonetic distinctions, a single articulatory act simply may give rise to multiple acoustic consequences that act synergistically auditorily. For syllable-initial voicing, the fact that F1 frequency is higher at longer durations of F1 cutback is a natural consequence of the time course of the opening gesture, and one may ask whether the auditory synergy between F1 cutback and F1 onset frequency is only a serendipitous convergence.

Are convergences between the correlated acoustic products of a gesture and auditory synergies necessarily serendipitous? No; in fact, articulatory acts for which acoustic products act synergistically auditorily are exactly what one

---

[2] While it is technically most correct to refer to syllable-initial English voiceless stops as "voiceless aspirated," they are referred to here as "voiceless."

would expect if the phonetic inventories of languages are selected on the basis of communicative robustness. Consequently, given the robust perceptual interactions observed for multiple acoustic products from voicing, it should come as no surprise that the vast majority of languages have more than one series of stops across place of articulation usually varying in characteristics of voicing (84.2% in the UPSID database; Maddieson, 1984). Although it is clear that the cases of auditory enhancement for vowel sounds due to lip rounding, nasalization, and $f\emptyset$ changes require active coordination by the talker, it is not a requirement of the auditory enhancement hypothesis that increased discriminability be the product of active coordination of gestures.

That being said, it is possible that the auditory interaction between F1 cutback and F1 frequency onset is, in fact, actively exploited in production. Consider the fact that there is significant variation in voice onset time (VOT) across the three places of articulation for syllable-initial stops: labial /b/, /p/, alveolar, /d/, /t/, and velar /g/, /k/. VOTs for both voiced and voiceless syllable-initial stops are significantly longer for velars than for alveolars, and somewhat longer for alveolars than for labials (Lisker & Abramson, 1964). Presumably, some difference in the duration of formant transitions (including F1) should be expected by virtue of articulatory constraints related to inertial constraints on the articulators involved. For velar stops, the more massive tongue body must move away from the velum, while for alveolars and labials, only the tongue tip and lips must move from the point of occlusion. By way of a production explanation, it may be the case that for vocal fold vibration to be initiated, air must be able to escape the oral cavity in order to allow a sufficient drop in transglottal pressure. Consequently, onset of voicing could be affected by the speed with which articulators can release closure and allow the required dissipation of oral pressure (Diehl & Kluender, 1987; Summerfield, 1974). By this explanation, the greater the inertia of the articulator, the longer the voicing lag. Although no reliable articulatory measures have demonstrated that this is the case, it remains a potential articulatory explanation of the differences in VOT observed across place of articulation.

The auditory enhancement hypothesis may provide an alternative, however. While it is true enough that a more massive articulator such as the tongue body may take longer to move from occlusion for velar stops, it would also be the case that F1 transitions would be longer as a consequence. Given the fact that a longer transition is manifested in a lower slope of F1 for any vowel environment, F1 onset frequency is lower for a longer transition at any duration of F1 cutback along the transition. This being true, could the explanation of longer VOTs for more massive articulators be due to talkers delaying voice onset because the longer the F1 cutback, the higher the F1 onset frequency? In this way, talkers could be actively exploiting the auditory synergy between F1 cutback duration and F1 onset frequency. This question has not been resolved; however, it is possible that syllable-initial VOT across place of articulation is another example of gestural organization in the service of auditory enhancement.

In addition to syllable-initial voicing, there are other clear instances whereby a single articulatory act has multiple physical acoustic consequences that combine perceptually in a synergistic manner. One example in which two acoustic consequences of the same articulatory gesture have mutually enhancing auditory effects can be found in the relation between amplitude rise time and transition duration for the distinction between stop–semivowel pairs such as /b/ and /w/. The facts of production are relatively simple. For stops, pressure builds up behind the point of occlusion prior to a rapid release of closure. Acoustically, the release results in rapidly changing formant transitions with a correspondingly rapid increase in energy escaping the mouth. For semivowels, little pressure builds up, as occlusion is often incomplete, and the articulator movement away from occlusion is gradual. Formant transitions change more slowly, and amplitude increases relatively gradually.

This covariation between transition duration and rise time in production is mirrored in the listener's categorization behavior, as both frequency and amplitude changes conspire in perception. For syllables varying in transition duration from /ba/ to /wa/, when onsets have short amplitude rise times, longer formant transitions are required for a syllable to be perceived as /wa/; that is, shorter rise times lead to more /ba/ responses (Shinn & Blumstein, 1984; Walsh & Diehl, 1991). Explanation of listeners' sensitivity to the natural covariance between frequency transition and rise time does not seem to require use of tacit knowledge of articulatory or acoustic covariation, however. Walsh and Diehl (1991) carried out an analogous experiment using nonspeech stimuli in which a single sine wave modeled the F1 center-frequency trajectories of a series of stimuli varying from /ba/ to /wa/. They created two such series, one with short and one with long amplitude rise times. When listeners were asked to judge whether the onsets of stimuli with varying durations of frequency glides were *abrupt* or *gradual,* they labeled more short-rise-time stimuli as *abrupt* and more long-rise-time stimuli as *gradual.* The mutually enhancing effects of frequency change and rise time are not limited to speech stimuli.

Finally, it may be noted that there is an analogous set of findings for the distinction between the affricate /tʃ/ and the fricative /ʃ/ (as in *chew* and *shoe*). Production of affricates such as /tʃ/ results in shorter amplitude rise times and shorter durations of fricative noise than does production of fricatives such as /ʃ/ (Gerstman, 1957). When amplitude rise time and duration of frication are independently covaried, listeners show the same sensitivity to the natural covariance between rise time and duration as was found for stops and semivowels (Kluender & Walsh, 1992).

The preceding examples of auditory enhancement illustrate a number of ways phonetic inventories are selected in a manner that exploits general characteristics of auditory systems. And these examples are but a few of a growing number of phonetic and phonological regularities that are being explained on the basis of auditory processes (for more examples, see Diehl & Kluender, 1989a, 1989b; Diehl, Kluender, & Walsh, 1990; Kingston & Diehl, 1993). Again, it should be noted that it is not being claimed that auditory predispositions will explain all there is to know about the selection of phonetic inventories, for constraints on articulation as well as sociolinguistic factors doubtless play no small role. More important is the fact that many regularities in phonetic inventories have the potential to illuminate the processes by which speech is perceived. Not only can a richer understanding of auditory perception yield insights into why phonological inventories come to take the forms that they do, but the structure of linguistic sound systems can inform theory in speech perception and, more generally, in auditory perception. When one observes phonetic tendencies that are universal or near universal, and those tendencies are not explainable in terms of articulatory constraints, there is good likelihood that such phonetic regularities have the potential to reveal auditory processes exploited by languages. The most extensive ecological survey ever conducted holds much promise for the study of speech perception as a paradigm for study of auditory perception in general.

IV. ONTOGENY OF SPEECH PERCEPTION AND CATEGORIZATION

A. The Initial State

Two decades of studies document the impressive abilities of human infants, some less than one week old, to discriminate a wide variety of consonants and vowels (for comprehensive reviews, see Eimas, Miller, & Jusczyk, 1987; Jusczyk, 1982; Kuhl, 1987). For example, it has been demonstrated that infants can distinguish voiced from voiceless stop consonants, and 1-month olds, 2-month olds, 4-month olds, and adults all respond best to differences at roughly the same durations of VOT (Eimas, Siqueland, Jusczyk, & Vigorito, 1971; Jusczyk, Rosner, Reed, & Kennedy, 1989). Infants are capable of discriminating changes in voicing for fricatives such as /s/ and /z/ by the age of 3 months (Eilers, 1977; Eilers, Wilson, & Moore, 1977). At least by the age of 6 months, infants also discriminate naturally produced syllables beginning with stop consonants that are either voiceless aspirated or breathy voiced (/tʰ/–/dʰ/), a voicing contrast used in Hindi (Werker, Gilbert, Humphrey, & Tees, 1981).

Infants can also discriminate stop consonants differing in cues to place of articulation when these cues are changes in formant transitions (Eimas, 1974; Moffitt, 1971; Morse, 1972; Till, 1976), frequency of release bursts (C. Miller, Morse, & Dorman, 1977), or both (Jusczyk, Bertoncini, Bijeljac-Babic, Kennedy, & Mehler, 1990; Williams & Bush, 1978). Infants also discriminate changes in place of articulation for fricatives, both voiced (Jusczyk, Murray, & Bayly, 1979) and voiceless (Eilers et al., 1977; Holmberg, Morgan, & Kuhl, 1977; Jusczyk et al., 1979), and infants are able to distinguish consonants varying in place of articulation for other manners of articulation such as nasals (Eimas & Miller, 1977), glides (Jusczyk, Copan, & Thompson, 1978), and liquids (Eimas, 1975). In addition to these place contrasts found in English, 6-month-old infants can discriminate unaspirated dental from retroflex voiced (/ḍ/–/d/) (Werker & Lalonde, 1988) and voiceless (/ṭ/–/t/) stops (Werker et al., 1981) and uvular from velar glottalized voiceless stops (/k̂/–/q̇/) (Werker & Tees, 1984a). Finally, Best, McRoberts, & Sithole (1988) found that 6-month olds easily discriminate voiceless unaspirated apical and lateral clicks used in Zulu.

Infants can also distinguish several other consonantal distinctions. J. L. Miller and Eimas (1983) found that infants can discriminate between stop and nasal consonants such as /b/ and /m/. And, 3-to-4-month olds can discriminate between stops and glides (Eimas & Miller, 1980; J. L. Miller & Eimas, 1983).

Perhaps unsurprising in light of their impressive performances with consonants, infants are also quite good at distinguishing vowel sounds, being capable of discriminating high from low vowels (Kuhl & Miller, 1975; Trehub, 1973), front from back vowels (Kuhl, 1978; Trehub, 1973), tense from lax vowels

(Jusczyk et al., 1990; Swoboda, Morse, & Levitt, 1976), and nasalized from oral vowels (Trehub, 1976). In fact, even newborn infants are sensitive to changes in vowel quality in the first week of life (Bertoncini, Bijeljac-Babic, Jusczyk, Kennedy, & Mehler, 1988; Jusczyk et al., 1990).

This plethora of positive findings indicates that infants have the discriminative capacity necessary for most or all of the phonetic distinctions they will need to use in their language. These studies stand not only as confirmation of the infant's sensory capacity, but also as further evidence that language sound inventories come to include primarily distinctions that are robust auditorily. The positive results from this broad range of experiments are consistent with more recent findings regarding infant psychoacoustic capacities (e.g., Olsho, Koch, Carter, Halpin, & Spetner, 1988; Olsho, Koch, & Halpin, 1987; Spetner & Olsho, 1990; Werner & Gillenwater, 1990). Early infant auditory abilities appear to be quite well developed, and by 3 months of age, the human auditory system is nearly adultlike in absolute sensitivity and frequency resolving power within the frequency range of most speech sounds (Werner & Bargones, in press).

The infant speech results are also consistent with the claim that languages would use few distinctions that are perceptually troublesome; consequently, it should come as little surprise that discriminating phonetic contrasts is generally not an insurmountable task for the infant. While the impressive abilities of infants to discriminate speech sounds have often been taken to be the signature of specialized innate predispositions, early speech discrimination abilities do not demand such conclusions. Of course, some phonetic distinctions will be easier than others, and the claim being made here is simply that in many cases, much of the evidence for infants' abilities to discriminate speech sounds may fall out gracefully from general properties of auditory systems.

As an extension of this claim, some investigators have suggested that languages have evolved to take advantage of existing gradients and discontinuities in audition (e.g., Kuhl, 1986, 1988; Kuhl & Miller, 1978; Kuhl & Padden, 1983; K. N. Stevens, 1989). With regard to consonants, for example, it appears that English and most (but not all) other languages use voicing distinctions that straddle discontinuities in auditory temporal resolution. As noted above, very young infants discriminate pairs of stimuli varying in VOT in a manner very much like English-speaking adults independent of whether their language environment is English (Eimas et al., 1971; Jusczyk et al., 1989) or a language such as Kikuyu (Streeter, 1976) or Spanish (Lasky, Syrdal-Lasky, & Klein, 1975) that uses VOTs of durations different from English.

As further evidence of general auditory predispositions, Pisoni (1977) found that adult listeners show similar boundaries when labeling two-tone stimulus complexes that vary in the duration by which the onset of the lower frequency tone lags behind the onset of the higher tone, and Jusczyk, Pisoni, Walley, and Murray (1980) found that $2^{1}/_{2}$-month-old infants discriminate these stimuli in a manner similar to adults, although infants required somewhat longer tone onset asynchronies. The cross-language infant findings and these nonspeech findings are strongly suggestive that general auditory factors are at work.

If infants' abilities to discriminate speech sounds are to rely largely on general auditory abilities, then one would expect nonhuman animals to do equally well on these same discrimination tasks. In studies designed to investigate the role of general auditory factors in perception of voicing, Kuhl and Miller (1975, 1978) trained chinchillas (*Chinchilla laniger*) to respond differentially to voiced (/ba/, /da/, /ga/) versus voiceless (/pa/, /ta/, /ka/) stops, and the animals' "labeling" performance was like that for human listeners, including the sharp division between categories characteristic of human identification functions. As is the case for human adults and infants, chinchilla discrimination was best at the category boundary and poorer within category (Kuhl, 1981). And boundary locations for VOT stimuli at the labial, alveolar, and velar places of articulation were at almost exactly the same VOT values for both chinchillas and humans. Analogous to the claims made by Pisoni (1977) and Jusczyk et al. (1980, 1989), Kuhl and Miller (1975, 1978) argued that this convergence between human and nonhuman labeling boundaries may be the result of a common limit on the ability to temporally resolve the onset of aspiration energy and onset of vocalic energy.

Using the same stimuli as Kuhl and Miller (1975, 1978), Dooling, Okanoya, and Brown (1988) found that budgerigars (*Melopsittacus undulatus*) group VOT stimuli in a fashion much like humans and chinchillas. Whatever the nature of the auditory discontinuity, it appears that the same process may be at work in the avian auditory system. Further support for this idea was found by Kluender (1991a) in studies using humans and Japanese quail (*Coturnix coturnix japonica*) as subjects. He found that labeling boundaries for humans and quail were strikingly similar, and that F1 characteristics affected labeling by human and avian subjects in the same fashion. This is particularly germane to discussion of infant phoneme discrimination, as J. L. Miller and Eimas (1983) had earlier shown that similar manipulations of F1 dramatically altered discrimination performance of 3- and 4-month-old infants. While they suggested that their infant findings "indicate that the infant possesses finely tuned linguistically-relevant perceptual abilities," (p. 135) it appears likely that the perceptual abilities in question lie in general operating characteristics of auditory systems.

A number of animal studies also support the notion that general processes of audition and learning are adequate to account for discrimination of place of articulation. Macaques (Kuhl & Padden, 1983) discriminate stimuli along a synthetic series ranging from /ba/ to /da/ to /ga/ in a manner very similar to human performance (Mattingly, Liberman, Syrdal, & Halwes, 1971).

Another important example of basic auditory processes giving rise to adult-like phonetic categorization is the stop–glide distinction between /b/ and /w/. This distinction is signaled primarily by the duration of the formant transitions, and for both adult (J. L. Miller & Liberman, 1979) and infant listeners (Eimas & Miller, 1980; J. L. Miller & Eimas, 1983), when the vowel following the stop or glide is longer, the duration of transition required to perceive a stimulus as changing from /ba/ to /wa/ becomes longer as well. This contextual effect of the following vowel also appears to have a general auditory basis. For both adults (Diehl & Walsh, 1989; Pisoni, Carrell, & Gans, 1983) and infants (Jusczyk, Pisoni, Reed, Fernald, & Myers, 1983), these results have been replicated using sinewave replicas of the J. L. Miller and Liberman (1979) stimuli that are not perceived as speech. In addition, E. B. Stevens, Kuhl, and Padden (1988) found that rhesus and Japanese macaques (*Macaca mulata* and *M. muscata*) exhibit the same effect of vowel duration in a study using the same speech stimuli as used by Eimas and Miller (1980).

It is appropriate to note that not all investigators find the results of speech studies with nonhumans to be compelling evidence that general auditory processes are at work, particularly for the case of infant abilities. One argument against interpreting nonhuman animal data as evidence against species-specific processes is that similar performance between humans and nonhumans does not necessarily imply that common mechanisms are at work (e.g., Jusczyk & Bertoncini, 1988; Remez, 1989). Of course, the inference is not logically necessary; however, it is in keeping with the principle of parsimony. It would be theoretically extravagant to insist that all the observed parallels are strictly accidental, and a compelling counterargument must also suggest why behavioral similarities exist.

One criticism of claims for common human and nonhuman processes has been that nonhuman performance with speech is only analogous to human performance (similar processes arising from disparate evolutionary sources), not homologous (similarities arising from common evolutionary sources). By way of example, one may suggest that the existence of evolutionary convergences (e.g., the chambered eye of octopi and vertebrates, the wings of birds and bats, the fins of fish and whales) presents sufficient reason to doubt that common auditory mechanisms underlie parallels in speech perception between humans and nonhumans. However, even in the case of analogous structures and processes, the similarities are almost never accidental. Rather, they reflect the fact that species from quite diverse evolutionary lineages sometimes come to occupy similar ecological niches and to face similar functional demands. Dawkins (1987) refers to this as similar "ways of life." As an example of convergence to analogous structures and functions, consider the fact that both fish and whales have fins. As mammals, cetaceans share an evolutionary history long ago separate from fish and later diverged from that mammalian lineage as they replaced legs with fins as an adaptation to aquatic life.

What is the likelihood that performance similarities among humans, Japanese and rhesus macaques, chinchillas, budgerigars, and quail reflect convergent evolution? If these diverse species can be said to share a common way of life, at least in respects relevant to possible convergent auditory capabilities, the commonalities must be very general. All these species do share an acoustic environment in which most of the energy occurs at frequencies below 6 or 7 kHz and in which sound is primarily airborne. And it is true that acoustic energy from many natural sources has a dominant periodicity having higher harmonics with successively lower amplitude, and that many acoustic sources have both resonances and antiresonances shaping the spectrum. But these same very general features of the acoustic environment would have been present at virtually all points along the evolutionary trajectories of these species, presumably as far back as their common ancestor. In other words, there is no reason to expect that the parallel selection pressures necessary for convergent evolution to take place would not have been present from the very beginning. In the absence of some rationale for divergence followed by some rationale for subsequent convergence, one is hard pressed to admit such parallels between humans and nonhumans as analogies, not homologies (Diehl & Kluender, 1989b).

Finally, to the extent that one can explain speech perception through an understanding of the representation of speech sounds in the neural hardware, and that hardware is consistent between species, the case for different processes between species is difficult to maintain. For example, Sinex and McDonald (1988, 1989) measured auditory nerve responses to VOT series in the auditory nerve of chinchillas, and, based on this work, Sinex, McDonald, and Mott (1991) have been able to predict human discrimination of VOT differences across place of articulation using computational simulations based on their neural recordings. This success seems unlikely to be a chance convergence across analogous systems.

Another example involving VOT comes from a series of studies by Kluender, Lotto, and Jenison (1992). Based on single-unit responses in cat auditory nerves (e.g., Jenison, Greenberg, Kluender, & Rhode, 1991), they made predictions about the effects of overall stimulus intensity on perception of voicing for stop consonants as a function of the frequency difference between F1 and F2. This interaction between F1, F2, and intensity was predicted only on the basis of neural responses in a nonhuman auditory system. When one can explain fairly complex perceptual interactions with general low-level auditory processes, it becomes unnecessary to appeal to less general or higher level processes.

It seems clear that nonhuman animal studies of perception of human speech can be quite informative in establishing the role of sensory capacities in perception of speech. And, in a less glamorous role for animal models, investigation of the neural representation of speech can provide important insights into speech perception. Neurophysiologists have made a great deal of progress describing the representation of speech in the auditory periphery (see Greenberg, 1988b, for review). For example, responses to vowels have been described for the auditory nerve (AN) (Delgutte & Kiang, 1984a, 1984d; Sachs & Young, 1979; Young & Sachs, 1979) and for the anteroventral cochlear nucleus (Blackburn & Sachs, 1986; Sachs, Blackburn, & Young, 1988). Responses in AN have been described for fricative and affricate consonants (Delgutte & Kiang, 1984b, 1984c) and for stop consonants (Delgutte & Kiang, 1984c; M. I. Miller & Sachs, 1983; Sinex & Geisler, 1983; Sinex & McDonald, 1988, 1989). In addition to this effort, a number of useful computational simulations of neural encoding of speech have been based on these empirical measurements (e.g., Deng, Geisler, & Greenberg, 1988; Ghitza, 1988; Jenison et al., 1991; Seneff, 1988; Shamma, 1988; Slaney & Lyon, 1990). While extended review of the impressive body of literature regarding the neural representation of speech sounds is not possible here, there is much confidence that a richer knowledge of auditory processing—both functionally and neurally—will lead to a better understanding of infant speech discrimination findings.

B. Learning Categories for Vowels

There are at least two compelling reasons to believe that not all infant performance must so nicely fall out of general predispositions of auditory systems. First, all the results demonstrating the remarkable ability of infants (or animals) to simply discriminate speech sounds may well be taken to be only powerful illustrations of sensory capacity. Importantly, the ability to discriminate speech sounds is not synonymous with the ability to form phonetic categories. While a relatively complete understanding of the auditory representation of speech sounds is an essential step in understanding how phonemes are recognized, by itself mapping acoustic phonetic information onto either neural representations or some more abstract perceptual space does not constitute phonetic categorization. Experience plays a critical role in parceling the speech sounds into categories; after all, the fact that different languages partition the domain of possible speech sounds differently implies that the categorization of speech sounds depends on linguistic experience.

A related reason to find speech categorization so important—in contrast to describing the sensory representation of speech—is the classic problem of LACK OF INVARIANCE. It is generally accepted that phonemes do not have invariant properties. That is, for most or all phonemes, there are no necessary and sufficient cues that uniquely identify the phonetic category. While there have been a good many efforts to identify invariant cues (e.g., Blumstein & Stevens, 1979; K. N. Stevens & Blumstein, 1981), these efforts have not been broadly successful. In accepting the requirement of multiple acoustic/auditory attributes, it becomes clear that even the most definitive description of auditory representations and processes will fall short of explaining how multiple attributes are combined into categories.

Curiously, the fact that multiple stimulus attributes need to be used for successful phonetic categorization has persisted to be deeply troubling to theorists in speech perception at least since Liberman, Cooper, Shankweiler, and Studdert-Kennedy's (1967) influential exposition on the problem of speech perception. It is not entirely clear why this is so. Philosophers have long noted that necessary and sufficient conditions rarely if ever exist for establishing membership in natural categories (Ryle, 1951; Wittgenstein, 1953). Among those who study categorization in other domains, it is almost universally accepted that multiple stimulus attributes are typically required for categorization (see Smith & Medin, 1981, for review).

Given the fact that multiple stimulus attributes must be used for categorization of phonemes, this leaves one with the question of how infants come to learn phonetic categories in the face of wide variation among acoustic attributes of phonetic categories. Some of the most important recent findings in the entire field of speech perception come from investigations of infant phonetic category structure and developmental change in speech perception/categorization by human infants over the first year of life. These studies of phonetic category acquisition and structure are beginning to reveal the manner in which stimuli that are potentially distinct perceptually come to be treated differentially by the listener when acoustic differences signal phonemic distinctions but are treated more or less equivalently when acoustic differences are irrelevant to such distinction.

One of the most challenging obstacles for the infant is to use acoustic information that distinguishes one phoneme from another in the face of sometimes widely varying acoustic properties that do not distinguish phonemes in their language. Acoustic differences that are large enough to convey a phonetic contrast in one language may be of little or no relevance to the phonetic categories of another language. Some of these differences may simply be unrelated to distinctions used in a particular language and would not occur in a language context. Other differences may surface as allophonic variants of phonemes that are used in the language but do not distinguish one phoneme from another. In addition, clearly audible differences such as gender of talker, speaking rate, stress, and other factors have profound effects on the acoustic signal, yet the language learner must learn to maintain phonetic categories across these variations. Careful study of the ways in which infants overcome such challenges can help to both constrain and inform theory for speech perception.

At least by the age of six months, infants have the ability to group stimuli by vowel category even when stimuli from different categories overlap considerably along acoustic dimensions (Kuhl, 1983).[3] In a reinforced head turn paradigm, Kuhl trained infants to turn their heads only when the vowel category of the background stimulus changed during presentation of the closely related vowels /a/ and /ɔ/ spoken by a male talker. When tested on novel vowels produced by women and children (adding random variation in pitch contour in addition to shifting absolute frequency of formants), infants provided the correct response on the first trial, demonstrating that they recognized the novel vowels as belonging to the same category despite talker and fø changes.

While these studies attest to the ability of infants to categorize vowels in the face of phonemically irrelevant variation, more recent studies by Grieser and Kuhl (1989; Kuhl, 1991) have investigated how vowel categories may be structured along acoustic/auditory dimensions that are directly relevant to vowel categorization. Members of the same vowel category that differ in acoustic/auditory dimensions seem not to be perceptually equivalent for either 6-month olds or adults, and Kuhl and her colleagues' studies suggest that vowel categories can be conceptualized as being organized around an ideal or prototypical version of the vowel.

One ubiquitous finding in the categorization literature is the fact that members of categories, whether dogs or birds or automobiles, are not equally good members. Thus categories can be said to have a graded structure, and this graded structure is often described as being centered around an ideal, or PROTOTYPICAL, instance of the category (Rosch, 1975, 1978). Here, the terms *prototype* and *prototypical* are used only for consistency with Kuhl's formulation of these issues. In the categorization literature, phenomena that have been attributed to the existence of prototypes have also been explained by various exemplar models that do not require that categories be defined by reference to a single representation of the category (see, e.g., Brooks, 1978; Knapp & Anderson, 1984; Medin & Schaffer, 1978; Nelson, 1974; Reed, 1972). While there are significant differences both within and between different prototype and exemplar models of categorization, for now it will be adequate to understand that, in general, categories exhibit an internal structure such that not all instances of a category constitute equally good category members. In addition, categories

---

[3] Kuhl refers to this ability as "perceptual constancy," not as categorization. In the speech literature, the problem of overcoming variation in acoustic properties among which none alone is necessary and sufficient for phoneme identification has been referred to as a problem of perceptual constancy (Eimas, 1982; Kuhl, 1979, 1980; Miller, 1981; Studdert-Kennedy, 1982) as well as a problem of categorization. These two terms are frequently used to refer to the same phenomenon in the speech perception literature; however, it is not true that most theorists studying perceptual constancy believe that they are studying a form of categorization, or vice versa. Kluender (1988) discusses the putative distinction between perceptual constancy and categorization at length and suggests that such a distinction may not be a helpful one, particularly for the case of speech perception. In any event, the term "categorization" will be used in the present discussion.

have the appearance of having a central tendency in some multidimensional space, and this central tendency will be referred to as the prototype without inferring that a prototype defines the category per se.

Using a reinforced head-turn paradigm, Grieser and Kuhl inferred the existence of vowel prototypes for the vowel /i/ by examining the extent to which 6-month-old infants responded to a change from a repeating background /i/ stimulus to another variant of /i/ drawn from the same category. They reasoned that, to the extent that the background stimulus was a good or prototypical example of the vowel category /i/, infants should be more likely to generalize (not respond) to a change in vowel token to another variant of /i/. By their reasoning, subjects should be less likely to respond to differences between prototypical vowels and nonprototypical vowels than to differences between a pair of nonprototypical vowels, assuming equal sensory distance between both types of pairs. In fact, the degree to which infants generalized from the background stimulus to another variant of the vowel category was greater when the background stimulus was a vowel judged by adult listeners to be near ideal. Kuhl (1991) conceptualizes this as a PERCEPTUAL MAGNET EFFECT, and she suggests that infants come to have vowel category prototypes similar to those for adults, and that variants of the vowel category are perceptually assimilated to the prototype to a greater degree than could be explained on psychophysical distance alone.

As might be expected, whether one of the comparison stimuli was a prototype or not, greater acoustic/auditory distance resulted in greater discriminability, and infants were generally more likely to respond when acoustic/auditory differences were greater. This fact makes the results a bit more difficult to interpret with regard to more detailed structure of infant vowel categories. In a sense, the paradigm pitted the infant's ability to discriminate two vowel tokens against the infant's tendency to equate discriminably different vowels as members of the same category. By analogy, one would not wish to suggest that infants were incapable of detecting gender and age differences in Kuhl's (1983) studies with the vowels /a/ and /ɔ/. In any event, the later prototype studies (Grieser & Kuhl, 1989; Kuhl, 1991) clearly demonstrate that infants were less likely to respond, indicating a stimulus change, when the background stimulus represented a relatively ideal example of the category.

Grieser and Kuhl's experimental paradigm served as an ingenious way to ask the very difficult question of whether infant subjects showed evidence of categories organized about something akin to prototypes. However, it leaves one in the perplexing position of inferring category structure from relatively flat response structure. The unavoidable confounding of infants' ability to discriminate with their ability to categorize makes it difficult to evaluate the structure of the category beyond inferring that the category shows evidence of being structured about a prototype. While it is at least theoretically possible to use this paradigm to infer the overall structure of a category by comparing infants' generalization from every category variant to every other category variant, this may be practically impossible to do with limitations inherent in testing infants.

Kuhl's persuasive evidence for vowel prototypes constitutes a very important step in understanding how infants learn to group the sounds of their language, and studies further elucidating the structure of infant vowel categories will be most valued. It will be important to know more about the overall structure of infant vowel categories (in contrast to establishing only the center or prototype) because, to a large extent, it is the hallmark of categorization that categories have a graded structure, with some stimuli (not only the prototype) being better examples of the category than others. For adult listeners, Kuhl (1991) demonstrated clearly that not only do vowel categories have the appearance of being structured around a prototype, but also that instances nearer to the prototype are better examples of the category—an archetypal category structure. This also appears to be the case for adult phonetic categories for consonants (e.g., Massaro, 1987; J. L. Miller, Connine, Schermer, & Kluender, 1983; J. L. Miller & Volaitis, 1989; Samuel, 1982).

What has become most apparent is that the degree to which infants treat members of the same vowel category equivalently is critically dependent on their experience with a particular language. Vowel category structure does not seem to fall out of any general auditory predisposition among primates, as rhesus monkeys do not provide much evidence that prototypical stimuli are perceived as any more similar to other vowels in the category than are nonprototypical stimuli when discriminating /i/ and /i/-like sounds in a task analogous to that used with infants (Kuhl, 1991).

Support for a learning explanation can be found in a recent study (Kuhl, Williams, Lacerda, Stevens, & Lindblom, 1992) using the same paradigm as Kuhl (1991) with infants from different language environments. Six-month-old infants raised in Swedish- and English-speaking environments exhibit quite different tendencies to respond to changes from a prototypical to nonprototypical vowel when the vowels are drawn from the category for the Swedish high front rounded vowel /y/ versus the category for the English vowel /i/. Again, for both groups of infants, larger acoustic differences were detected more easily for both native and nonnative[4] vowel categories. Importantly, however, English infants were much more likely to respond to differences between a prototypical high front rounded Swedish vowel /y/ and variants of /y/ than they were to respond to differences between the prototypical English /i/ and its variants. The complementary pattern was found for Swedish infants' responses. The fact that infants are much more likely to generalize across equal acoustic/auditory changes for vowels like those with which they have experience is evidence that, by 6 months of age, infants have begun to learn the equivalence classes for vowel categories from their language environment.

Here, it is suggested that the ability of 6-month olds to learn vowel categories appropriate to their language can be explained simply by general processes of learning. In Kuhl's (1991) study with monkeys, the animals did not have the benefit of earlier exposure to the distribution of English vowels prior to engaging in the discrimination task. Kluender and Lotto have recently completed the first of a series of studies designed to investigate whether nonhuman animals can learn vowel categories like those for human infants and adults when they are given the opportunity to learn the relative distributions of examples common to a category. In their first study, they investigated whether eight European starlings (*Sturnus vulgaris*) have the capacity to form categories for English

---

[4] The Swedish vowel system does include a variant of the vowel /i/; however, Swedish /i/ is substantially different acoustically from English /i/, and the /i/ prototype used in Kuhl et al.'s study was clearly not prototypical of Swedish /i/.

and Swedish vowels and whether the structure of those categories is like that for human infants. These birds were trained to form equivalence classes for vowel categories, in contrast to Kuhl's (1991) training of monkeys to discriminate category members. Half the birds were designated "English" birds and were trained to distinguish versions of the English vowels /i/ and /ɪ/. The other four birds were designated "Swedish" birds and were trained to distinguish versions of the Swedish vowels /ʉ/ and /y/. The Swedish vowel /ʉ/ is a high central rounded vowel somewhat intermediate between the English vowels /i/ and /u/. In Kluender and Lotto's experiment, each bird's data revealed that all starlings' responses generalized with facility to novel category examples. Each "English" starling generalized across /y/ and /ʉ/ tokens that were responded to differentially by "Swedish" birds, and each "Swedish" starling generalized across /i/ and /ɪ/ tokens that were reliably discriminated by "English" birds. In summary, every bird learned the vowel categories with which they were trained, as evidenced by generalization to novel examples that were discriminably different for other subjects.

Most important, response gradients indicated a graded structure about the central (prototypical) vowel of the training category. The data suggest that the animals truly learned humanlike categories for the vowels. Their responses generalize well to potentially discriminable novel stimuli, and their response patterns exhibit graded category structure.[5]

In order to better understand how such a relatively simple organism can come to learn vowel category structure that is similar to that for humans, a simple linear association network model was simulated using elementary matrix and vector operations (Jordan, 1986). This type of model can be considered to be an instantiation of the Hebbian synapse rule (Hebb, 1949) and is a tightly constrained model in which all operations are local and there is no need for the "back-propagation" of errors common to many current network models. The network model was exposed to training vowels represented as vectors of values indicating the amount of energy in each of 23 critical band filters. Following "experience" with these vowels that represent training stimuli assigned to each bird, this simple linear associative model accounted for 95% of the variance in mean peck rates for each of the 34 novel vowel tokens. It is clear not only that nonhuman animals have little difficulty learning categories for human vowels, and that those categories show evidence of gradient structure around prototypes, but also that the process of vowel category learning may be a remarkably simple one.

---

[5] It bears note that there is one property of the starlings' category structure that may not be characteristic of human vowel categories. Inspection of individual birds' response gradients revealed that the graded structures of the categories were skewed away from competing categories. While positive vowel examples at or near the prototype were generally responded to with greater vigor, strength of response did not fall away from the prototype symmetrically. For example, for an "English" starling trained to respond to /i/ but not /ɪ/, responses were generally stronger for /i/ variants that had lower F1 values and higher F2 values. This anisotropism may be an artifact of the birds doing a task that required them to divide the F1–F2 space in the most efficacious manner, thus encouraging them to simply respond as a monotonic function of F1 and F2 values varying in directions appropriate to the vowels with which they were trained. In order to assess this possibility, Kluender and Lotto are conducting studies to investigate whether the anisotropism decreases or disappears when the direct relation between formant frequency and reinforcement is attenuated.

C. Learning Categories for Consonants

Similar to the infant studies of vowel categorization across acoustic differences related to gender and age described above (Kuhl, 1983), Kuhl (1980) and Hillenbrand (1983, 1984) extended these findings to consonants in experiments of the same basic design. In these studies, 6-month-old infants were trained to respond to changes in CV syllables that differed in the initial consonant. Infants categorized syllables as beginning with the fricative consonant /s/ versus /ʃ/ when the fricatives preceded three different vowels (/a/, /i/, and /u/) and the syllables were produced by four different talkers (2 male, 2 female) (Kuhl, 1980). As with the study using the vowels /a/ and /ɔ/, there was substantial physical acoustic overlap among /s/ and /ʃ/ across the three vowel environments.

Again using syllables produced by male and female talkers and the /a/, /i/, /u/ contexts, Hillenbrand (1983) demonstrated infants' ability to distinguish syllables beginning with a nasal /m/, /n/, /ŋ/ from those with a nonnasal stop /b/, /d/, /g/. Infants' performance in this experiment was not simply due to an inability to discriminate syllables, for infants could also categorize syllables beginning with a labial nasal /m/ versus an alveolar nasal /n/. These studies are evidence of infants' ability to maintain phonetic equivalence classes for consonants in the face of significant intracategory acoustic variation and intercategory acoustic similarity.

This ability to neglect intracategory variation is fundamental to infants learning phonetic categories appropriate to their language, as intracategory variation for one language can be intercategory variation for another. Werker and her colleagues (Werker et al., 1981; Werker & Lalonde, 1988; Werker & Logan, 1985; Werker & Tees, 1983, 1984a, 1984b) have demonstrated that, as a function of learning consonant categories for one's native language, infants' tendency to respond to differences between some consonants that are not in their language begins to attenuate. The series of studies by Werker and Lalonde (1988) permits a relatively complete description of the phenomena Werker and her colleagues have investigated. They exploited the fact that speakers of English and Hindi use place of articulation somewhat differently for stop consonants. While for English, three places of articulation are used for voiced stop consonants: labial, alveolar, and velar (e.g., /b/, /d/, and /g/, respectively), in Hindi four places are used: labial, dental, retroflex, and velar (e.g., /b/, /d̪/, /ḍ/, and /g/, respectively.)[6] They created a synthetic continuum that varied perceptually from /b/ to /d/ (for native English-speaking adults) and from /b/ to /d̪/ to /ḍ/ (for native Hindi-speaking adults). Using the same reinforced head turn procedure used by Kuhl, they found that 6-to-8-month-old infants from English-speaking families responded to changes in stimulus tokens that crossed perceptually from the English categories /b/ to /d/ and also responded to changes from the Hindi categories /d̪/ to /ḍ/.[7] A different group of infants from

[6] Hindi uses voiceless plosive uvular and glottal stops as well, but not their voiced counterparts.

[7] Werker and Lalonde also included conditions in which the stimulus change was as great as that for either the English or Hindi contrasts yet did not bridge phonemic categories for any language. Infants showed little or no evidence of discriminating these nonphonemic contrasts, and this was taken as evidence that the performance of infants from English-speaking homes with Hindi contrasts could not be explained simply on the basis of sensory sensitivity. Although it is not known whether such a stimulus could actually be produced by a human vocal tract, the fact that no language uses the contrast contrived for the study could also be evidence that, in fact, the contrast may not be particularly salient perceptually.

English-speaking families aged 11–13 months responded reliably only to the English /b/–/d/ contrast, and not to the Hindi /ḍ/–/d̪/ contrast. Essentially, 6-to-8-month-old infants responded in a manner typical of phonetic categorization by native-Hindi adults, while 11-to-13-month olds responded like native-English adults, treating dental and retroflex stops as being the same.

This general finding appears to be robust, as Werker and her colleagues have found quite analogous results in studies with infant subjects from English-speaking homes responding to distinctions between naturally produced tokens of voiceless Hindi stops that were either dental or retroflex (/t̪/–/ṭ/), Hindi stops that were either voiceless aspirated or breathy voiced (/tʰ/–/dʰ/), as well as Interior Salish consonants that were either glottalized velar or uvular (/k'/–/q'/). In all cases, 6-to-8-month olds more reliably responded to nonnative distinctions than did 11-to-13-month olds, indicating that as infants learn the consonantal categories appropriate to their language, they are either unlikely or unable to respond to acoustic differences that do not differentiate sounds in their language.

As Werker and Lalonde (1988) noted, it cannot be ascertained whether the degree to which infants respond to changes within and between phonetic categories is a function of discrimination or categorization, the same concern as with Kuhl's vowel studies. What is clear is that distinctions that were once clearly discriminable become either relatively indiscriminable or ignored as the infant has greater experience with the distributions of phonetic segments in his or her language environment.

It is probably reasonable to conclude that most demonstrations of poor within-category discrimination by adult listeners do not indicate that discriminative ability is really lost. While poor within-category discrimination was once the hallmark of categorical perception by adult listeners (Wood, 1975), it has been amply demonstrated that adults can make within-category discriminations with facility when adequate methods of training or testing are used (e.g., Carney, Widen, & Viemeister, 1977; Jamieson & Morosan, 1986; Pisoni, Aslin, Perey, & Hennessy, 1982; Pisoni & Lazarus, 1974; Werker & Tees, 1984b). Not incidentally, virtually all of the studies demonstrating poor within-category discrimination used ABX or AXB tasks. Both of these tasks confound memory with discrimination, in a sense, encouraging categorization to play a role (see Massaro, this volume, for a more thoroughgoing discussion of categorical perception).

One particularly relevant demonstration that discriminative abilities may well be intact can be found in Werker and Logan's (1985) study of discrimination of naturally produced Hindi voiceless dental and retroflex stops. Using an AX task, they found that, after a very limited amount of experience without feedback (24 trials), native English-speaking subjects became proficient at discriminating syllables beginning with dental versus retroflex voiceless stops when inter-stimulus intervals (ISI) were short (250 ms). With only a few more trials of experience (48 total), native-English listeners discriminated dental from retroflex stops with a longer ISI (500 ms). More experience (96 trials) was required for competent discrimination at a longer ISI (1500 ms). It bears note that Werker and Lalonde (1988) used 1000 ms ISIs when testing adults in their study, and this may well have led to underestimating the ability of their subjects to discriminate the synthetic tokens.

Finally, experiments using more direct measures of consonant category structure (Massaro, this volume; J. L. Miller et al., 1983; J. L. Miller & Volaitis, 1989; Samuel, 1982) indicate that not all consonant category exemplars are equally good. Weak performance in discrimination tasks cannot necessarily be taken to imply that all tokens are equivalent.

D. Plausibility of Human-Specific Biological Predispositions for All Phonetic Categories

Some theorists (e.g., Eimas, 1975, 1991) recommend that Werker and her colleagues' data support the hypothesis that infants have a specialized biological predisposition to discriminate a universal set of phonetic contrasts. By this view, the process of learning a language involves either a decline in or reorganization of this universal sensitivity. There are two reasons to be skeptical about this hypothesis.

With regard to evolution, consider what is implied by the claim that all sounds of all languages are somehow hard-wired into the infant. Begin with the accepted fact that evolution does not give rise to structures and processes *de novo* (Jacob, 1977). Nature will either make do with existing structures or processes, or it will adapt existing processes, in which case there must be ample selective pressure to do so. Cross-linguistic phonetic data call into question whether there could ever have been adequate selective pressure for a universal set of phonetic segments to become supported by specialized biological predispositions. The reason for such doubt is that there is simply too much diversity in the phonetic inventories used in languages. Innately specified processes, as products of selective pressure, should instead give rise to much greater conformity in phonetic inventories, and languages would generally share a collection of speech sounds that have been primed by the biological substrate. Furthermore, one would suspect that this collection should be relatively modest in size, for after accommodating an inventory that is adequate for successful communication (e.g., Rotokas and Mura have only 11 phonemes), there would be little pressure to increment the size of the universal set of phonetic segments.

The fact that languages make use of so very many phonetic distinctions (although some are used rarely) can be seen in the use of place of articulation. Maddieson (1984) needed eight places of articulation (nine if one includes the double place for labial-velar) to describe stop consonants across languages. For individual languages, three and four places of articulation for stop consonants are most common (53.9% and 32.5% of languages, respectively), although a small number of languages use five or six places (11.0% and 1.9% respectively). If three or four places are sufficient for over 85% of languages (retroflex not typically among the three or four), why would one be specially predisposed for eight? Specifically, if retroflex stops occur in only about 11.4% of languages, how does one argue that there was adequate selective pressure to make 100% of infants specially prepared to discriminate them from all others?

One may wish, however, to make the more restricted claim that only some phonetic contrasts are innately endowed in the human infant. Presumably, the most nearly universal contrasts could be specially primed in the biological substrate. Unfortunately for this argument, it is just those contrasts that are so prevalent across languages—such as voicing and place of articulation for stop consonants—that are discriminated with facility by nonhuman animals.

And nonhuman animals have little difficulty discriminating a host of differences in vowel quality (Burdick & Miller, 1975; Kluender & Diehl, 1987).[8]

The argument regarding the sheer number of phonemes and phonological contrasts used by languages could be challenged by suggesting that it is not phonemes, but subphonemic features, that are selected. Of course, a relatively small number of features could give rise to a large number of phonemes. For example, only eight binary features could potentially give rise to 256 (2^8) phonemes. However, such reasoning only moves the question to putative selective pressures that would establish some number of necessary features. This reasoning fails by the realization that one needs at least 58 phonetic attributes to fully characterize phonetic inventories across languages (Maddieson, 1984). Even after sorting these attributes into separate classes for vowels and consonants, and after eliminating unpronounceable combinations, the number of potential phonemes is enormous.

All of this argues against hard-wired phonetic inventories and argues for a greater role for learning in the development of phonetic categories from the very beginning, as it is unlikely that selective pressures would give rise to so many phonemes across languages.

E. How Infants Can Learn Phonetic Categories

Before examining how general processes of category learning can account for infants learning phonetic categories, it may be helpful to get some idea about how infants learn nonlinguistic categories. A series of studies with infants carried out by Cohen and colleagues (Cohen, 1981; Cohen & Strauss, 1979; Husaim & Cohen, 1981; Younger, 1985; Younger & Cohen, 1983, 1985, 1986) over the last decade provides important insights into how the acquisition of categories may proceed from very early in the life of a child. Consider for now only the motivation for and results from one series of these studies (Younger & Cohen, 1983). Their experiments were founded on the observation that, while features vary across members of a category, each feature is more or less well correlated with the category. Consequently, features tend to cluster together, being, on average, reasonably well correlated with one another. Rosch and her colleagues (Rosch, 1978; Rosch, Mervis, Gray, Johnson, & Boyes-Braem, 1976) had suggested that categories can be defined as clusters of features that tend to co-occur. If correlations among features represent an important structural characteristic of categories (Rosch, 1978), it follows that categories should be learned through experience with the co-occurrence of features that are correlated with the category and with each other.

Note that this conceptualization is different from Brunswick's formulation of ecological validity and functional validity in his theory of perceptual constancy. Ecological validity was expressed as the correlation between some proximal stimulus attribute and the distal object. Functional validity was defined as the correlation between a distal property and the perceptual response. In

---

[8] One may ask whether the lack of conformity among languages must also undermine any appeal to auditory constraints in the selection of phonetic inventories. However, this would only be so if there existed no other forces on inventory selection such as articulatory ease or sociolinguistic factors. While one may appeal to the same forces as a caveat regarding species-specific dispositions, the nonhuman findings would remain as counterevidence.

contrast, here the emphasis is on correlations among stimulus attributes. In nature, attributes that are well correlated with a category will likely be well correlated with other attributes that are also well correlated with the category, so this may at first seem to be an unimportant distinction. However, when one considers how infants learn categories for phonemes or for other objects and events in the world, the distinction is a critical one. If correlations between attributes and categories are the basis for learning categories, one might assume the extreme nativist position that infants must come into the world with preconceived categories. In such a case, category learning would involve learning the correlations between attributes and innate category nodes. On the other hand, if infants learn categories on the basis of correlations between attributes in a manner abstractly analogous to principal components analysis, then there is no need to appeal to a priori categories.

Younger and Cohen (1983) demonstrated that 10-month-old infants could learn an artificial category that was defined only by the correlation between features. Their experiment was carried out with a visual habituation–dishabituation design quite analogous to that used in many infant speech perception studies. They assessed the extent to which presentation of a novel object elicited dishabituation, thus suggesting that the infant recognized that a change in category had taken place. Two groups of infants were shown line drawings of impossible animal forms that had different types of bodies, tails, feet, ears, and legs. In the first phase of the experiment (habituation), the first group of infants saw drawings in which the type of body, tail, and legs were correlated with each other (ears and legs varied freely), while the second group viewed drawings in which types of parts comprising the animal were uncorrelated. The first group of infants became habituated to presentations of stimuli for which body parts were correlated, and during the test phase they looked longer at only the uncorrelated and the novel drawings, treating the new correlated test stimuli as familiar. The second group of infants, however, could not habituate to the presentation of drawings in which parts were uncorrelated. For this second group, there apparently was insufficient commonality among stimuli with uncorrelated parts for habituation to occur. Quite clearly, when compared to the infants in the second control group, infants from the first group responded on the basis of correlation among features. At least by the time infants are 10 months old, they appear to have the ability to use correlations among visual features to establish a category following only brief laboratory experience with examples of the category and can extend that category to new instances that share the correlation among attributes.

Consider, then, how infants might learn phonetic categories relevant to their language given the benefit of many orders of magnitude more experience with category members. The problem for the infant learning the phonemes of his or her language may be quite adequately conceptualized as the general problem of category learning. One must learn to group objects or events across potentially discriminable physical/sensory differences that are uncorrelated with category-relevant differences. The challenge for the infant learning his or her native language is precisely this. Infants must learn how acoustic/auditory attributes tend to co-occur, and those clusters of correlated attributes define their phonetic categories.

In general, the correlated attributes that define one phonetic category will all be more correlated with each other than with attributes that are well correlated with other phonetic categories. Aside from attributes that are not well correlated with any sounds in the native language, discriminable acoustic differences that have the potential to define phonetic categories in some languages but in fact do not define the categories for an infant's language will come to be assimilated into the structure of categories that are relevant to the infant's language environment to the extent that they are correlated with attributes of categories in the infants' language experience. For a given phonetic contrast, there are three ways this can happen.

First, acoustic/auditory attributes of two contrasting nonnative phonetic categories can both be reasonably well correlated with attributes of a single native category. Consider the case for formant patterns contributing to categorization of stop consonants with varying place of articulation. For example, dental stops are acoustically realized in a manner quite similar to that for alveolar stops. Consequently, it should come as no surprise that very few languages use a dental/alveolar distinction (Aranda and Nunggubuyu are quite rare examples; Maddieson, 1984). Similarly, the relatively uncommon alveolar/retroflex distinction involves acoustically similar utterances.

Now, consider the acoustic realization of alveolar stops in English. Allophonic variation in alveolar stops may provide ample acoustic overlap with acoustic attributes associated with dental and retroflex stops. When [d] is produced in the environment of the retroflex continuant [r] as in *adroit*, the phonetic realization can be like that for the retroflex stop /ḍ/. Similarly, when [d] is produced in the environment of a dental fricative such as [θ] in words like *width*, the phonetic realization can be like that for the dental stop /d̪/ (Polka, 1991). There is likely a good deal of similar variation in the acoustic realization of most phonemes, especially when such variation does not compromise consonantal phonemic contrasts. Given the facts about the acoustic distribution of alveolar stops in fluent English, it would be the case that acoustic attributes consistent with dental or retroflex stops would be well correlated with those acoustic attributes most characteristic of alveolar stops. Dental-like or retroflexlike acoustic attributes would be assimilated within the covariance structures of alveolar categories. Werker and Lalonde's (1988) adult identification data are entirely consistent with this scenario. Stimuli that are identified by native-Hindi listeners as dental or retroflex are all assimilated into the set of stimuli identified as alveolar by native-English listeners. Anything less would make listeners less adroit with *adroit*.[9] Best et al. (1988) refer to a similar process as SINGLE-CATEGORY assimilation.

A related way nonnative contrasts can be assimilated with native contrasts involves cases in which attributes of one category of a two-category nonnative contrast can be well correlated with attributes of a single native category, while attributes of the other category of the nonnative contrast are less well correlated

---

[9] The occurrence of dental and retroflex stops in English does present yet another problem for notions of innate universal phonetic inventories because one must ask how innate contrasts between dental, alveolar, and retroflex stops should ever reduce to a single alveolar category for native-English listeners. Given the occurrence of dental and retroflex stops as allophonic variants of [d] in English, one cannot appeal to atrophy of processes due to disuse.

with attributes of the native category. One example of this is the Farsi distinction between velar and uvular stops. Native-English listeners do not lose the ability to discriminate Farsi velars from uvulars. Instead, they perceive the Farsi voiced velar and uvular stops as being good and poor instances, respectively, of the same English category /g/ (Polka, 1992). In this case, Farsi velar stops are perceived as relatively good English velar stops because they share most or all of the acoustic/auditory attributes that comprise the correlated structure of the English /g/ category. Farsi uvular stops would share fewer attributes with those for English /g/ or would have attributes that are similar but not identical to those for /g/. A related process has been referred to as CATEGORY-GOODNESS assimilation by Best et al. (1988). It should be noted how well the formulation of this second type of assimilation coincides with Rosch's theorization about prototypes and category formation (Rosch, 1978; Rosch et al., 1976). Although Best et al. make the distinction between single-category and category-goodness assimilation, these may be more appropriately considered to be variants of the same process. In the case of single-category assimilation, the degree to which nonnative exemplars are related to the native category structure is simply more nearly equal.

The third way native and nonnative contrasts can interact can be found in cases where the native language does not exactly share a contrast with a nonnative language, but the native language does have an analogous contrast that facilitates perception of the nonnative contrast. For example, French does not include a voicing distinction for dental fricatives such as /ð/–/θ/, yet native-French listeners can discriminate voiced from voiceless English fricatives, perceiving them as versions of French dental stops /d̪/ and /t̪/, respectively (Jamieson & Morosan, 1986). Best et al. (1988) label this type of assimilation TWO-CATEGORY because each phoneme of the nonnative contrast maps more or less onto a different category in the native language. Within the framework of correlated attributes, one would explain the fact that French listeners perceive the English fricatives as versions of French stops as because the acoustic/auditory attributes of the dental fricatives are reasonably well correlated with attributes of the French dental stops as produced with typical allophonic variation in fluent speech.

This scenario leaves one only with those distinctions such as Zulu clicks that are unrelated to phonemic, and hence lexical, distinctions in the English environment. Across the domain of producible mouth sounds, there will always remain some acoustic/auditory attributes that are not well correlated with any of the attributes for any phonetic categories within a given language. For example, acoustic/auditory attributes of the click sounds of Zulu are correlated with no sounds of English, and their perception should be (and is) relatively unaltered by the process of learning English phonemes (Best et al., 1988). To the extent that such utterances occur, they will not occur as natural covariation within any of the infant's phonetic categories. The process of phonemic and lexical development will leave such distinctions categorically and perceptually intact.

Finally, one may ask why 6-month-old American and Swedish infants in Kuhl et al.'s (1992) study displayed a clear effect of language environment in their responses to within-category changes in native and nonnative vowel sounds, while 6-to-8-month-old infants in Werker and her colleagues' studies showed little effect of language environment in their responses to consonant changes. The most obvious reason that vowel categorization should be advanced relative to consonant categorization lies in the nature of the speech signal itself. Vowels are longer and louder than consonants, and particularly in the case of stressed syllables, vowels undergo relatively less context-dependent variation and can be conceptualized as "islands of reliability" in the speech stream (Diehl, Kluender, Foss, Parker, & Gernsbacher, 1987). Notably, the fact that infants may learn vowel categories before consonant categories is consistent with the notions that the lexicon becomes organized by stressed vowel and that lexical access comes to be directed by stressed syllables (see, for example, Bradley, 1980; Cutler, 1976; Grosjean & Gee, 1987; Kluender, Walsh, & Gough, 1987), particularly in early development.

Admittedly, this general explanation for the learning of phonetic categories leaves a lot of work to be done by processes of learning; however, the processes required for it to be true may be among the simplest and most accepted in learning theory. It may require little more than Hebbian learning (Hebb, 1949) or some other form of simple unsupervised learning. Within unsupervised learning, all that is changed by virtue of experience is the degree to which connections between inputs are strengthened or weakened as a function of correlated or uncorrelated activation, respectively. This conceptualization of category learning is by no means novel (see, e.g., Anderson & Hinton, 1981; Anderson, Silverstein, Ritz, & Jones, 1977; Knapp & Anderson, 1984; Kohonen, 1977, 1987) and has the attraction of being neurally plausible (Bear & Cooper, 1989; Brown, Kairiss, & Keenan, 1990). This is not to say that the problem of computationally describing this learning is a trivial one. In the case of vowel categorization, for example, gender differences in spectral composition appear to require some nonlinear transform of the input (Kluender & Jenison, 1990; Morin & Nusbaum, 1990; but see Henton, 1992, for the alternative view).

Evidence that quite simple learning processes are adequate for learning phonetic categories can be found in studies demonstrating the ability of Japanese quail to learn consonant categories in the face of considerable acoustic variation. Kluender, Diehl, & Killeen (1987) tested whether Japanese quail could learn to form a category corresponding to syllable-initial /d/, a segment chosen because its acoustic properties are particularly variable as a function of the following vowel. Quail were first trained to discriminate syllables consisting of /d/ followed by /i/, /u/, /æ/, and /a/ from syllables with the same vowels preceded by /b/ and /g/. They were then given unreinforced generalization trials in which they correctly distinguished /d/ from /b/ and /g/ in syllables with the eight novel vowels /ɪ/, /ʊ/, /ɛ/, /ʌ/, /eʸ/, /oʸ/, /oʷ/, and /ɝ/. Responding was categorical, with peck rates more than ten times higher to positive than to negative stimuli. Acoustic analyses of the categorized syllables revealed no single acoustic property or pattern of acoustic properties that could support this generalization, suggesting that quail mastered a more complex mapping of stimuli into categories requiring multiple stimulus attributes. In follow-up experiments with the same birds, it was demonstrated that the animals easily generalized their categorization to other male talkers.

Kluender and Diehl (1987) proceeded to explore ways in which multiple acoustic properties can be used to learn categories by explicitly training quail to acquire a "polymorphous" category (Ryle, 1951). Again, natural categories—phonetic categories included—are almost always polymorphous with no single necessary or sufficient property. Instead, a sufficient subset of positive properties must be present for inclusion in the category. Kluender and Diehl used syllables produced by ten different talkers that varied on three dimensions: initial-consonant type (voiced vs. voiceless, velar vs. nonvelar), vowel type (front vs. back, high vs. low), and gender of talker. Two quail learned different categories based on these dimensions. For one bird (1539), the positive category properties were voiced stop, front vowel, and male talker, while for a second bird (1562), positive properties were velar stop, high vowel, and female talker. During training, birds were reinforced for pecking in the presence of stimuli that were positive on exactly two of the three dimensions, and were not reinforced in the presence of stimuli that were negative on two of the dimensions. As formidable a task as this may appear, both quail learned these categories, using all three constituent dimensions in mastering the task. Quail could categorize on the basis of vowel height and frontness/backness, consonantal place of articulation and voicing, as well as gender of talker (see Fig. 2).

Perhaps the most interesting outcome of this experiment was that the quail performance revealed an internal category structure that closely parallels that found in studies of human categorization. Each quail generalized to novel instances of its polymorphous category with facility, pecking significantly more to novel positive stimuli than to novel negative ones. This happened when the novel stimuli were positive on only two of the three dimensions, but the highest level of responding occurred when the novel stimulus was positive on all three dimensions (a situation never encountered during training). It appears, therefore, that the quail formed something like category prototypes for these syllables. As noted above, theories of human categorization have invoked prototypes to account for the fact that certain category instances seem more representative than others and are generally easier to learn and remember, even when they have never been directly experienced (Posner & Keele, 1968; Rosch, 1978). With the exception of the triple-positive stimuli, the quail did respond slightly more to stimuli used in training than to novel tokens. This is consistent with accounts of human category formation that emphasize experience with individual exemplars (Medin & Schaffer, 1978).

One final and reasonable objection to animal studies of categorization is the fact that animals receive reinforcement contingent on correct responses. When learning categories for speech or for other events in the world, infants do not need explicit reinforcement in order to categorize correctly. Yet infants learn phonetic categories with facility. There are reasons to suspect that this may not prove to be as serious an objection as one may first believe. Since the very early demonstrations of what learning theorists called "latent learning" (Tolman & Honzik, 1930), there have been a great many examples of incidental learning (see Thistlethwaite, 1951, for an early review). In fact, Tolman (1932), who interestingly enough anticipated the principles of Hebbian learning (Tolman, 1948), concluded that the mere experiencing of a stimulus is sufficient for learning to occur; the role of reinforcement is to allow this learning to be manifested in measurable performance. Kluender and Lotto presently have studies under way investigating the necessity of reinforcement contingencies in the formation of vowel categories. At this point, however, there is no reason to believe that general principles of learning, whether instantiated in nonhuman animals, in computational models using covariance matrices, or in connectionist networks, will be inadequate to explain the structure of phonetic categories.

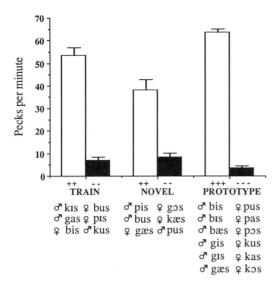

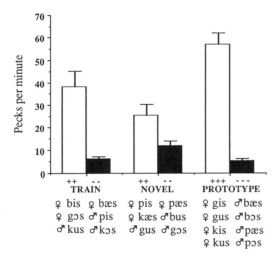

FIG. 2 Data are displayed for two Japanese quail who were trained to learn "polymorphous" categories for syllables for which there existed no necessary and sufficient conditions. Positive attributes of the syllables were: male talker, voiced stops, and front vowels for Bird 1539 (*top*); and female talker, velar stops, and high vowels for Bird 1562 (*bottom*). Both birds best distinguished novel syllables that were either positive or negative on all three stimulus dimensions (prototypes), whereas for stimuli that were positive or negative on only two of the three dimensions, they discriminated training stimuli better than novel stimuli. Error bars designate one standard error.

One type of information that will be critically important in the development of adequate learning models for speech perception will be richer characterization of the input to the learning process. Part of developing a better understanding of the input will take the form of more accurate sensory and neural descriptions of speech sounds as they pass through the auditory system (e.g., Jenison, 1991; Jenison et al., 1991). In addition, one needs to know the distributional tendencies of different speech sounds in the environment.

Not only will it be essential to know the relative frequencies of occurrence for different speech sounds in the child's environment, but it will be necessary to know how phonetic information is acoustically realized in fluent speech. In other words, while cross-language phonetic data contribute impressive *type* data about phonetic inventories, learning models will require extensive *token* data. As Lindblom (1990) and Remez (this volume) make clear, the acoustic realization of citation-form "laboratory speech" may at best be considered an abstraction of fluent conversational speech. Fortunately, ecological surveys that include more realistic appraisals of the acoustic information specifying phonemes are becoming available. Painstaking measurements of connected and conversational speech (e.g., Crystal & House, 1988a–1988e; Remez et al., 1991), together with large databases of fluent speech collected for computer speech recognition efforts (Price, Fisher, Bernstein, & Pallett, 1988), are welcome tools in the effort. Perhaps even more exciting are acoustic data on baby talk (e.g., Davis, 1991), as adult-to-child utterance data will provide some of the best insights into the child's input.

Hopefully, the reader is convinced that quite general processes of learning are up to the task of learning phonetic categories. As more becomes known about processes of category learning—in terms of both behavioral and neurophysiological measures—there is little doubt that models will mature in their sophistication and neural plausibility. One's best guess at what goes on in a relatively simple animal's brain when it learns to make seemingly complex categorizations will surely improve. Successful performance in speech categorization tasks by simple systems (both biological and computational) offers hope that relatively elegant and general models will continue to suffice.

V. SUMMARY

The goal of this chapter has been to cast the problem of speech perception and categorization as both general and tractable. Of course, developing a complete explanation requires the same sort of sustained effort required in any domain of cognitive science. The important point is that the study of speech perception, by virtue of having an almost ideal set of constraints at hand, is ripe for scientific success. The claims set out above are intended to be as parsimonious as possible, and many of the specific propositions set forth will surely see the fate that befalls most falsifiable hypotheses in science. To the extent that some of the simple general hypotheses favored here fall in the face of data, they will have served their purpose in the Popperian scheme. To the extent that they stand, speech scientists will find that they are much closer to solving their problem than they may have imagined.

ACKNOWLEDGMENTS

The author gratefully acknowledges the advice and assistance of Randy L. Diehl, Andrew J. Lotto, and John Kingston, and the support of the National Institute on Deafness and Other Communicative Disorders (DC00719) and of the Graduate School at the University of Wisconsin.

REFERENCES

Anderson, J. A., & Hinton, G. E. (1981). Models of information processing in the brain. In G. E. Hinton & J. A. Anderson (Eds.), *Parallel models of associative memory.* (pp. 9–48). Hillsdale, NJ: Erlbaum.

Anderson, J. A., Silverstein, J. W., Ritz, S. A., & Jones, R. S. (1977). Distinctive features, categorical perception, and probability learning: Some applications of a neural model. *Psychological Review, 84,* 413–451.

Atkinson, J. (1973). *Aspects of intonation in speech: Implications from experimental study of fundamental frequency.* Doctoral dissertation, University of Connecticut, Storrs.

Bear, M. F., & Cooper, L. N. (1989). Molecular mechanisms for synaptic modification in the visual cortex: Interaction between theory and experiment. In M. A. Gluck & D. E. Rumelhart (Eds.), *Neuroscience and connectionist theory* (pp. 65–93). Hillsdale, NJ: Erlbaum.

Bertoncini, J., Bijeljac-Babic, R., Jusczyk, P. W., Kennedy, L. J., & Mehler, J. (1988). An investigation of young infants' perceptual representations of speech sounds. *Journal of Experimental Psychology: General, 117,* 21–23.

Best, C. T., McRoberts, G. W., & Sithole, N. M. (1988). Examination of perceptual reorganization for nonnative speech contrasts: Zulu click discrimination by English speaking adults and infants. *Journal of Experimental Psychology: Human Perception and Performance, 14,* 345–360.

Blackburn, C. C., & Sachs, M. B. (1986). *The representation of the steady-state vowel sound [ε] in the temporal discharge patterns of cat anteroventral cochlear nucleus neurons.* 16th annual meeting of the Society for Neuroscience.

Blumstein, S. E., & Stevens, K. N. (1979). Acoustic invariance in speech production: Evidence from measurements of the spectral characteristics of stop consonants. *Journal of the Acoustical Society of America, 66,* 1001–1017.

Bradley, D. (1980). Lexical representation of derivational relation. In M. Aronoff & M. L. Kean (Eds.), *Juncture* (pp. 37–55). Saratoga, CA: Anma Libri.

Brooks, L. (1978). Nonanalytic concept formation and memory for instances. In E. Rosch & B. B. Lloyd (Eds.), *Cognition and categorization* (pp. 169–211). Hillsdale, NJ: Erlbaum.

Brown, T. H., Kairiss, E. W., & Keenan, C. L. (1990). Hebbian synapses: Biophysical mechanisms and algorithms. *Annual Review of Neuroscience, 13,* 475–511.

Brunswick, E. (1937). Psychology as a science of objective relations. *Philosophy of Science, 4,* 227–260.

Brunswick, E. (1940). Thing constancy as measured by correlation coefficients. *Psychological Review, 47,* 69–78.

Brunswick, E. (1944). Distal focussing of perception: Size constancy in a representative sample of situations. *Psychological Monographs, 56*(1,Whole No. 254).

Brunswick, E. (1952). The conceptual framework of psychology. In O. Neurath (Ed.), *International Encyclopedia of Unified Science,* Vol. 1(10), Chicago: University of Chicago.

Brunswick, E. (1955). Representative design and probabilistic functionalism: A reply. *Psychological Review, 62,* 236–242.

Burdick, C. K., & Miller, J. D. (1975). Speech perception by the chinchilla: Discrimination of sustained /a/ and /i/. *Journal of the Acoustical Society of America, 58,* 415–427.

Carney, A. E., Widen, G., & Viemeister, N. (1977). Noncategorical perception of stop consonants differing in VOT. *Journal of the Acoustical Society of America, 62,* 961–970.

Cohen, L. B. (1981). New issues are not always that new: A reply to Kemler. *Merrill-Palmer Quarterly, 27,* 465–470.

Cohen, L. B., & Strauss, M. S. (1979). Concept acquisition in the human infant. *Child Development, 7,* 419–424.

Crothers, J. (1978). Typology and universals of vowel systems. In J. H. Greenberg, C. A. Ferguson, & E. A. Moravcsick (Eds.), *Universals of human language (Vol. 2),* Stanford, CA: Stanford University Press.

Crystal, T. H., & House, A. S. (1988a). Segmental durations in connected-speech signals: Current results. *Journal of the Acoustical Society of America, 83,* 1553–1573.

Crystal, T. H., & House, A. S. (1988b). Segmental durations in connected-speech signals: Syllabic stress. *Journal of the Acoustical Society of America, 83,* 1574–1585.

Crystal, T. H., & House, A. S. (1988c). A note on the durations of fricatives in American English. *Journal of the Acoustical Society of America, 84*, 1932–1935.

Crystal, T. H., & House, A. S. (1988d). The duration of American-English vowels: An overview. *Journal of Phonetics, 16*, 263–284.

Crystal, T. H., & House, A. S. (1988e). The duration of American-English stop consonants: An overview. *Journal of Phonetics, 16*, 285–294.

Cutler, A. (1976). Phoneme monitoring reaction time as a function of preceding intonation contour. *Perception & Psychophysics, 20*, 55–60.

Dannemiller, J. L. (1992a). Rank orderings of photoreceptor photon catches from natural objects are nearly illuminant-invariant. *Vision Research, 33*, 131–140.

Dannemiller, J. L. (1992b). Spectral reflectance of natural objects: How many basis functions are necessary? *Journal of the Optical Society of America A, 9*, 507–515.

Davis, B. (1991). Phonetics of baby talk speech: Implications for infant speech perception. *Perilus, 14*, 157.

Dawkins, R. (1987). *The blind watchmaker*. New York: Norton.

Delgutte, B., & Kiang, N. Y.-S. (1984a). Speech coding in the auditory nerve: I. Vowel-like sounds. *Journal of the Acoustical Society of America, 75*, 866–878.

Delgutte, B., & Kiang, N. Y.-S. (1984b). Speech coding in the auditory nerve: III. Voiceless fricative consonants. *Journal of the Acoustical Society of America, 75*, 887–896.

Delgutte, B., & Kiang, N. Y.-S. (1984c). Speech coding in the auditory nerve: IV. Sounds with consonant-like dynamic characteristics. *Journal of the Acoustical Society of America, 75*, 897–907.

Delgutte, B., & Kiang, N. Y.-S. (1984d). Speech coding in the auditory nerve: V. Vowels in background noise. *Journal of the Acoustical Society of America, 75*, 908–918.

Deng, L., Geisler, C. D., & Greenberg, S. (1988). A composite model of the auditory periphery for the processing of speech. *Journal of Phonetics, 16*, 93–108.

Diehl, R. L., & Kluender, K. R. (1987). On the categorization of speech sounds. In S. Harnad (Ed.), *Categorical perception* (pp. 226–253). Cambridge: Cambridge University Press.

Diehl, R. L., & Kluender, K. R. (1989a). On the objects of speech perception. *Ecological Psychology, 1*, 121–144.

Diehl, R. L., & Kluender, K. R. (1989b). Reply to the commentators. *Ecological Psychology, 1*, 195–225.

Diehl, R. L., Kluender, K. R., Foss, D. J., Parker, E. M., & Gernsbacher, M. A. (1987). Vowels as islands of reliability. *Journal of Memory and Language, 26*, 564–573.

Diehl, R. L., Kluender, K. R., & Walsh, M. A. (1990). Some auditory bases of speech perception and production. In W. A. Ainsworth (Ed.), *Advances in Speech, Hearing and Language Processing* (pp. 243–268). London: JAI Press.

Diehl, R., & Lindblom, B. (1990, November). *Auditory phonetics*. 120th meeting of the Acoustical Society of America, San Diego, CA.

Diehl, R., Lindblom, B., & Hoemeke, K. A. (in preparation). *Effects of f0 on vowel identification accuracy*.

Diehl, R. L., & Walsh, M. A. (1989). An auditory basis for the stimulus-length effect in the perception of stops and glides. *Journal of the Acoustical Society of America, 85*, 2154–2164.

Disner, S. F. (1984). Insights on vowel spacing. In I. Maddieson (Ed.), *Patterns of sound* (pp. 136–155). Cambridge: Cambridge University Press.

Dooling, R. J., Okanoya, K., & Brown, S. D. (1988). Speech perception by budgerigars (*Melopsittacus undulatus*): The voiced–voiceless distinction. *Perception & Psychophysics, 46*, 65–71.

Dyhr, N. (1991). The activity of the cricothyroid muscle and the intrinsic fundamental frequency in Danish vowels. *Phonetica, 47*, 141–154.

Eilers, R. E. (1977). Context sensitive perception of naturally produced stops and fricative consonants by infants. *Journal of the Acoustical Society of America, 61*, 1321–1336.

Eilers, R. E., Wilson, W. R., & Moore, J. M. (1977). Developmental changes in speech discrimination in infants. *Journal of Speech and Hearing Research, 18*, 158–167.

Eimas, P. D. (1974). Auditory and linguistic processing of cues for place of articulation by infants. *Perception & Psychophysics, 16*, 564–570.

Eimas, P. D. (1975). Speech perception in early infancy. In L. B. Cohen & P. Salapatek (Eds.), *Infant perception: From sensation to cognition, Vol. II* (pp. 193–231). New York: Academic Press.

Eimas, P. D. (1982). Speech perception: A view of the initial state and perceptual mechanisms. In J. Mehler, E. C. T. Walker, & M. Garret (Eds.), *Perspectives on mental representations* (pp. 340–360). Hillsdale, NJ: Erlbaum.

Eimas, P. D. (1991). Comment: Some effects of language acquisition on speech perception. In I. G. Mattingly & M. Studdert-Kennedy (Eds.), *Modularity and the motor theory of speech perception* (pp. 111–116). Hillsdale, NJ: Erlbaum.

Eimas, P. D., & Miller, J. L. (1977). Discrimination of the information for manner of articulation by young infants. *Infant Behavior and Development, 3,* 247–252.

Eimas, P. D., & Miller, J. L. (1980). Contextual effects in infant speech perception. *Science, 209,* 1140–1141.

Eimas, P. D., Miller, J. L., & Jusczyk, P. W. (1987). On infant speech perception and the acquisition of language. In S. Harnad (Ed.), *Categorical perception* (pp. 161–195). Cambridge: Cambridge University Press.

Eimas, P. D., Siqueland, E. R., Jusczyk, P. W., & Vigorito, J. (1971). Speech perception in infants. *Science, 171,* 303–306.

Ewan, W. G. (1979). Can intrinsic vowel F0 be explained by source/tract coupling? *Journal of the Acoustical Society of America, 66,* 358–362.

Fant, G. (1966). A note on vocal tract size factors and non-uniform F-pattern scalings. *STL-QPSR, 4,* 22–30.

Fant, G. (1975). Non-uniform vowel normalization. *STL-QPSR, 2-3,* 1–19.

Fowler, C. A. (1989). Real objects of speech perception: A commentary on Diehl and Kluender. *Ecological Psychology, 1,* 145–160.

Gerstman, L. J. (1957). *Perceptual dimensions for the friction portions of certain speech sounds.* Unpublished doctoral dissertation, New York University.

Ghitza, O. (1988). Temporal non-place information in the auditory-nerve firing patterns as a front-end for speech recognition in a noisy environment. *Journal of Phonetics, 16,* 109–123.

Goldstein, U. (1980). *An articulatory model for the vocal tracts of growing children.* D.Sc. dissertation, Massachusetts Institute of Technology, Cambridge.

Greenberg, S. (Ed.). (1988a). Representation of speech in the auditory periphery [Theme issue]. *Journal of Phonetics, 16*(1).

Greenberg, S. R. (1988b). The ear as a speech analyzer. *Journal of Phonetics, 16,* 139–150.

Grieser, D., & Kuhl, P. K. (1989). Categorization of speech by infants: Support for speech-sound prototypes. *Developmental Psychology, 25,* 577–588.

Grosjean, F., & Gee, J. P. (1987). Prosodic structure and spoken word recognition. In U. H. Frauenfelder & L. K. Tyler (Eds.), *Spoken word recognition* (pp. 135–155). Cambridge, MA: MIT Press.

Hebb, D. (1949). *The organization of behavior.* New York: Wiley.

Henton, C. (1992). The abnormality of male speech. In G. Wolf (Ed.), *New departures in linguistics* (pp. 27–59). New York: Garland.

Hillenbrand, J. (1983). Perceptual organization of speech sounds by infants. *Journal of Speech and Hearing Research, 26,* 268–282.

Hillenbrand, J. (1984). Perception of sine-wave analogs of voice-onset time stimuli. *Journal of the Acoustical Society of America, 75,* 231–240.

Holmberg, T. L., Morgan, K. A., & Kuhl, P. K. (1977, December). *Speech perception in early infancy: Discrimination of fricative consonants.* 94th meeting of the Acoustical Society of America, Miami Beach, FL.

Honda, K. (1981). Relationship between pitch control and vowel articulation. In D. Bless & J. Abbs (Eds.), *Vocal-fold physiology* (pp. 286–297). San Diego, CA: College-Hill Press.

House, A. S., & Stevens, K. N. (1956). Analog studies of the nasalization of vowels. *Journal of Speech and Hearing Disorders, 21,* 218–232.

Husaim, J. S., & Cohen, L. B. (1981). Infant learning of ill-defined categories. *Merrill-Palmer Quarterly, 27,* 443–456.

Jacob, J. (1977). Evolution and tinkering. *Science, 196,* 1161–1166.

Jamieson, D. G., & Morosan, D. E. (1986). Training non-native speech contrasts in adults: Acquisition of the English /ð/–/θ/ contrast by francophones. *Perception & Psychophysics, 40,* 205–215.

Jenison, R. L. (1991). *A dynamic model of the auditory periphery based on the responses of single auditory-nerve fibers.* Unpublished doctoral dissertation, University of Wisconsin, Madison.

Jenison, R. L., Greenberg, S., Kluender, K. R., & Rhode, W. S. (1991). A composite model of the auditory periphery for the processing of speech based on the filter response functions of single auditory nerve fibers. *Journal of the Acoustical Society of America, 90,* 289–305.

Jordan, M. I. (1986). An introduction to linear algebra in parallel distributed processing. In D. E. Rumelhart & J. L. McClelland (Eds.), *Distributed processing: Explorations in the microstructure of cognition* (Vol. 1, pp. 365–422). Cambridge, MA: MIT Press.

Jusczyk, P. W. (1982). Auditory versus phonetic coding of signals during infancy. In J. Mehler, M. Garrett, & E. C. T. Walker (Eds.), *Perspectives in mental representation: Experimental and theoretical studies of cognitive processes and capacities* (pp. 361–387). Hillsdale, NJ: Erlbaum.

Jusczyk, P. W., & Bertoncini, J. (1988). Viewing the development of speech perception as an innately guided learning process. *Language and Speech, 3,* 217–236.

Jusczyk, P. W., Bertoncini, J., Bijeljac-Babic, R., Kennedy, L. J., & Mehler, J. (1990). The role of attention in speech perception by young infants. *Cognitive Development, 5,* 265–286.

Jusczyk, P. W., Copan, H. C., & Thompson, E. J. (1978). Perception by two-month olds of glide contrasts in multisyllabic utterances. *Perception & Psychophysics, 24,* 515–520.

Jusczyk, P. W., Murray, J., & Bayly, J. (1979, March). *Perception of place-of-articulation in fricatives and stops by infants.* The biennial meeting of the Society for Research in Child Development, San Francisco.

Jusczyk, P. W., Pisoni, D. B., Reed, M. A., Fernald, A., & Myers, M. (1983). Infants' discrimination of the duration of a rapid spectrum change in nonspeech signals. *Science, 222,* 175–177.

Jusczyk, P. W., Pisoni, D. B., Walley, A., & Murray, J. (1980). Discrimination of relative onset time of two-component tones by infants. *Journal of the Acoustical Society of America, 67,* 262–270.

Jusczyk, P. W., Rosner, B. S., Reed, M. A., & Kennedy, L. J. (1989). Could temporal order differences underlie 2-month-olds' discrimination of English voicing contrasts? *Journal of the Acoustical Society of America, 90,* 83–96.

Keating, P., Linker, W., & Huffman, M. (1983). Patterns of allophone distribution for voiced and voiceless stops. *Journal of Phonetics, 11,* 277–290.

Kingston, J. (1991). Phonetic underresolution in UPSID. In *XIIth International Congress of Phonetic Sciences* (pp. 359–362). Université de Provence: Aix-en-Provence, France.

Kingston, J., & Diehl, R. L. (1993). *Phonetic knowledge.* Manuscript submitted for publication.

Kingston, J., Diehl, R., Kluender, K., & Parker, E. (1990, November). *Resonance versus source characteristics in perceiving spectral continuity between vowels and consonants.* 120th meeting of the Acoustical Society of America, San Diego, CA.

Kluender, K. R. (1988). *Auditory constraints on phonetic categorization: Trading relations in humans and nonhumans.* Unpublished doctoral dissertation, University of Texas at Austin.

Kluender, K. R. (1991a). Effects of first formant onset properties on voicing judgements result from processes not specific to humans. *Journal of the Acoustical Society of America, 90,* 83–96.

Kluender, K. R. (1991b). Psychoacoustic complementarity and the dynamics of speech perception and production. *Perilus, 14,* 131–135.

Kluender, K. R., & Diehl, R. L. (1987, November). *Use of multiple speech dimensions in concept formation by Japanese quail.* 114th meeting of the Acoustical Society of America, Miami, FL.

Kluender, K. R., Diehl, R. L., & Killeen, P. R. (1987). Japanese quail can learn phonetic categories. *Science, 237,* 1195–1197.

Kluender, K. R., Diehl, R. L., & Wright, B. A. (1988). Vowel-length difference before voiced and voiceless consonants: An auditory explanation. *Journal of Phonetics, 2,* 153–169.

Kluender, K. R., & Jenison, R. L. (1990, November). *Perceptual categorization of vowel sounds: Representation in a self-organizing network with auditory inputs.* 120th meeting of the Acoustical Society of America, San Diego, CA.

Kluender, K. R., Lotto, A. J., & Jenison, R. L. (1992, October). *Perception of voicing in syllable-initial stops at different intensities: Does neural synchrony encode voice-onset?* 124th meeting of the Acoustical Society of America, New Orleans, LA.

Kluender, K. R., & Walsh, M. A. (1992). Amplitude rise time and the perception of the voiceless affricate/fricative distinction. *Perception & Psychophysics, 51,* 328–333.

Kluender, K. R., Walsh, M. A., & Gough, P. A. (1987, November). *Lexical stress influences naming latencies for disyllabic words.* 28th annual meeting of the Psychonomic Society, Seattle, WA.

Knapp, A. G., & Anderson, J. A. (1984). Theory of categorization based on distributed memory storage. *Journal of Experimental Psychology: Learning, Memory, and Cognition, 10*, 616–637.

Kohonen, T. (1977). *Associative memory: A system theoretic approach.* Berlin: Springer-Verlag.

Kohonen, T. (1987). *Self-organization and associative memory.* New York: Springer-Verlag.

Krakow, R. A., Beddor, P. S., Goldstein, L. M., & Fowler, C. A. (1988). Coarticulatory influences on the perceived height of nasal vowels. *Journal of the Acoustical Society of America, 83*(3), 1146–1158.

Krinov, E. L. (1947). Spectral reflectance properties of natural formations. *NRC Tech. Transl. NRC TT-439.*

Kuhl, P. K. (1978, May). *Perceptual constancy for speech-sound categories.* N.I.C.H.D. Conference on Child Phonology: Perception, Production, and Deviation, Bethesda, MD.

Kuhl, P. K. (1979). Speech perception in early infancy: Perceptual constancy for spectrally dissimilar vowel categories. *Journal of the Acoustical Society of America, 66*, 1668–1679.

Kuhl, P. K. (1980). Perceptual constancy for speech-sound categories in early infancy. In G. H. Yeni-Komshian, J. F. Kavanagh, & C. A. Ferguson (Eds.), *Child phonology: Vol. 2. Perception.* New York: Academic Press.

Kuhl, P. K. (1981). Discrimination of speech by nonhuman animals: Basic sensitivities conducive to the perception of speech-sound categories. *Journal of the Acoustical Society of America, 70*, 340–349.

Kuhl, P. K. (1983). Perception of auditory equivalence classes for speech in early infancy. *Infant Behavior and Development, 6*, 263–285.

Kuhl, P. K. (1986). Theoretical contributions of tests on animals to the special-mechanisms debate in speech. *Experimental Biology, 45*, 233–265.

Kuhl, P. K. (1987). Perception of speech and sound in early infancy. In P. Salapatek & L. Cohen (Eds.), *Handbook of infant perception* (Vol. 2, pp. 257–381). New York: Academic Press.

Kuhl, P. K. (1988). Auditory perception and the evolution of speech. *Human Evolution, 3*, 19–43.

Kuhl, P. K. (1991). Human adults and human infants show a ''perceptual magnet effect'' for the prototypes of speech categories, monkeys do not. *Perception & Psychophysics, 50*, 93–107.

Kuhl, P. K., & Miller, J. D. (1975). Speech perception by the chinchilla: Voiced-voiceless distinction in the alveolar-plosive consonants. *Science, 190*, 69–72.

Kuhl, P. K., & Miller, J. D. (1978). Speech perception by the chinchilla: Identification functions for synthetic VOT stimuli. *Journal of the Acoustical Society of America, 63*, 905–917.

Kuhl, P. K., & Padden, D. M. (1983). Enhanced discriminability at the phonetic boundaries for the place feature in macaques. *Journal of the Acoustical Society of America, 73*, 1003–1010.

Kuhl, P. K., Williams, K. A., Lacerda, F., Stevens, K. N., & Lindblom, B. (1992). Linguistic experience alters phonetic perception in infants six-months of age. *Science, 255*, 606–608.

Ladefoged, P. (1964). *A phonetic study of West African languages.* Cambridge: Cambridge University Press.

Lasky, R. E., Syrdal-Lasky, A., & Klein, R. E. (1975). VOT discrimination by four and six and a half month old infants from Spanish environments. *Journal of Experimental Child Psychology, 20*, 215–225.

Lehiste, I. (1970). *Suprasegmentals.* Cambridge, MA: MIT Press.

Liberman, A. M., Cooper, F. S., Shankweiler, D. P., & Studdert-Kennedy, M. (1967). Perception of the speech code. *Psychological Review, 74*, 431–461.

Liljencrantz, J., & Lindblom, B. (1972). Numerical simulation of vowel quality systems: The role of perceptual contrast. *Language, 48*, 839–862.

Lindau, M., Jacobson, L., & Ladefoged, P. (1972). The feature advanced tongue root. *UCLA Working Papers in Phonetics, 22*, 76–94.

Lindblom, B. (1986). Phonetic universals in vowel systems. In J. J. Ohala & J. J. Jaeger (Eds.), *Experimental phonology.* Orlando, FL: Academic Press.

Lindblom, B. (1989). Some remarks on the origin of the phonetic code. In C. von Euler, I. Linberg, & G. Lennerstrand (Eds.), *Brain and reading: Proceedings of the Seventh International Rodin Remediation Conference* (pp. 27–44). London: Macmillan.

Lindblom, B. (1990). On the notion of 'possible speech sound.' *Journal of Phonetics, 18*, 135–152.

Lindblom, B., & Engstrand, O. (1989). In what sense is speech quantal? *Journal of Phonetics, 17*, 107–121.

Lindblom, B., & Maddieson, I. (1988). Phonetic universals in consonant systems. In L. M. Hyman & C. N. Li (Eds.), *Language, speech and mind* (pp. 62–78). New York: Routledge.

Lisker, L. (1978). Rapid versus rabid: A catalogue of acoustical features that may cue the distinction. *Haskins Laboratories Status Report on Speech Research, SR-54,* 127–132.

Lisker, L., & Abramson, A. S. (1964). A cross-language study of voicing in initial stops: Acoustical measurements. *Word, 20*(3), 284–422.

Locke, J. (1980). Mechanisms of phonological development in children: Maintenance, learning, and loss. *Proceedings of the Chicago Linguistic Society, 16,* 220–238.

Lotto, A. J., & Kluender, K. R. (1992, October). *Effects of first formant onset frequency on voicing judgments result from auditory processes not specific to humans.* 124th meeting of the Acoustical Society of America, New Orleans, LA.

Lubker, J. F. (1968). An electromyographic-cinefluorographic investigation of velar function during normal speech production. *Cleft Palate Journal, 5,* 1–18.

Maddieson, I. (1984). *Patterns of sound.* Cambridge: Cambridge University Press.

Maloney, L. (1986). Evaluation of linear models of surface spectral reflectance with small numbers of parameters. *Journal of the Optical Society of America, 3,* 1673–1683.

Massaro, D. W. (1987). Categorical partition: A fuzzy logical model of categorization behavior. In S. Harnad (Ed.), *Categorical perception* (pp. 254–283). Cambridge: Cambridge University Press.

Mattingly, I. G., Liberman, A. M., Syrdal, A. K., & Halwes, T. (1971). Discriminating in speech and nonspeech modes. *Cognitive Psychology, 2,* 131–157.

Medin, D. L., & Schaffer, M. M. (1978). A context theory of classification learning. *Psychological Review, 85,* 207–238.

Miller, C., Morse, P., & Dorman, M. (1977). Cardiac indices of infant speech perception: Orienting and burst discrimination. *Quarterly Journal of Experimental Psychology, 29,* 533–545.

Miller, J. L. (1981). Effects of speaking rate on segmental distinctions. In P. D. Eimas & J. L. Miller (Eds.), *Perspectives on the study of speech* (pp. 39–74). Hillsdale, NJ: Erlbaum.

Miller, J. L., Connine, C. M., Schermer, T. M., & Kluender, K. R. (1983). A possible auditory basis for internal structure of phonetic categories. *Journal of the Acoustical Society of America, 73,* 2124–2133.

Miller, J. L., & Eimas, P. D. (1983). Studies on the categorization of speech by infants. *Cognition, 13,* 135–165.

Miller, J. L., & Liberman, A. M. (1979). Some effects of later occurring information on the perception of stop consonant and semivowel. *Perception & Psychophysics, 25,* 457–465.

Miller, J. L., & Volaitis, L. E. (1989). Effect of speaking rate on the perceptual structure of a phonetic category. *Perception & Psychophysics, 46,* 505–512.

Miller, M. I., & Sachs, M. B. (1983). Representation of stop consonants in the discharge patterns of auditory nerve fibers. *Journal of the Acoustical Society of America, 74,* 502–517.

Moffitt, A. R. (1971). Consonant cue perception by twenty- to twenty-four week old infants. *Child Development, 42,* 717–731.

Morin, T. M., & Nusbaum, H. C. (1990). Perceptual learning of vowels in a neuromorphic system. *Computer Speech and Language, 4,* 79–126.

Morse, P. A. (1972). The discrimination of speech and nonspeech stimuli in early infancy. *Journal of Experimental Child Psychology, 14,* 477–492.

Nelson, K. (1974). Concept, word and sentences: Inter-relations in acquisition and development. *Psychological Review, 81,* 267–285.

Nordstrom, P. E. (1977). Female and infant vocal tracts simulated from male area functions. *Journal of Phonetics, 5,* 81–92.

Ohala, J. J. (1974). Experimental historical phonology. In J. M. Anderson & C. Jones (Eds.), *Historical linguistics: II. Theory and description in phonology* (pp. 353–389). Amsterdam: North-Holland.

Olsho, L. W., Koch, E. G., Carter, E. A., Halpin, C. F., & Spetner, N. B. (1988). Pure-tone sensitivity of human infants. *Journal of the Acoustical Society of America, 84,* 1316–1324.

Olsho, L. W., Koch, E. G., & Halpin, C. F. (1987). Level and age effects in infant frequency discrimination. *Journal of the Acoustical Society of America, 82,* 454–464.

Parker, E. M. (1988). Auditory constraints on the perception of stop voicing: The influence of lower-tone frequency on judgements of tone-onset simultaneity. *Journal of the Acoustical Society of America, 83*(4), 1597–1607.

Parker, E. M., Diehl, R. L., & Kluender, K. R. (1986). Training relations in speech and nonspeech. *Perception & Psychophysics, 34,* 314–322.

Pisoni, D. B. (1977). Identification and discrimination of the relative onset time of two component tones: Implications for voicing perception in stops. *Journal of the Acoustical Society of America, 61,* 1352–1361.

Pisoni, D. B., Aslin, R. N., Perey, A. J., & Hennessy, B. L. (1982). Some effects of laboratory training on identification and discrimination of voicing contrasts in stop consonants. *Journal of Experimental Psychology: Human Perception and Performance, 8,* 297–314.

Pisoni, D. B., Carrell, T. D., & Gans, S. J. (1983). Perception of the duration of rapid spectrum changes in speech and nonspeech signals. *Perception & Psychophysics, 34,* 314–322.

Pisoni, D. B., & Lazarus, J. A. (1974). Categorical and noncategorical modes of speech perception along the voicing continuum. *Journal of the Acoustical Society of America, 55,* 328–333.

Polka, L. (1991). Cross-language speech perception in adults: Phonemic, phonetic, and acoustic contributions. *Journal of the Acoustical Society of America, 89,* 2961–2977.

Polka, L. (1992). Characterizing the influence of native language experience on adult speech perception. *Perception & Psychophysics, 52*(1), 37–52.

Posner, M. I., & Keele, S. W. (1968). On the genesis of abstract ideas. *Journal of Experimental Psychology, 73,* 28–38.

Postman, L., & Tolman, E. C. (1959). Brunswick's probabilistic functionalism. In S. Koch (Ed.), *Psychology: A study of a science: Vol. 1. Sensory, perceptual, and physiological formulations.* New York: McGraw Hill.

Price, P. J., Fisher, W. M., Bernstein, J., & Pallett, D. S. (1988). The DARPA 1000-word resource management database for continuous speech recognition. *IEEE Transactions ASSP-36,* 651–654.

Reed, S. K. (1972). Pattern recognition and categorization. *Cognitive Psychology, 3,* 382–407.

Remez, R. E. (1989). When the objects of perception are spoken. *Ecological Psychology 1*(2), 161–180.

Remez, R. E., Berns, S. M., Nutter, J. S., Lang, J. M., Davachi, L., & Rubin, P. E. (1991). On the perceptual differentiation of spontaneous and prepared speech. *Journal of the Acoustical Society of America, 89,* 2011–2012.

Rosch, E. H. (1975). Cognitive representations of semantic categories. *Journal of Experimental Psychology: General, 3,* 193–233.

Rosch, E. H. (1978). Principles of categorization. In E. Rosch & B. Lloyd (Eds.), *Cognition and categorization.* Hillsdale, NJ: Erlbaum.

Rosch, E. H., Mervis, C. B., Gray, W. D., Johnson, D., & Boyes-Braem, P. (1976). Basic objects in natural categories. *Cognitive Psychology, 8,* 382–439.

Ryle, G. (1951). *Thinking and language:* III. *Freedom, language and reality.* London: Harrison.

Sachs, M. B., Blackburn, C. C., & Young, E. D. (1988). Rate-place and temporal-place representations of vowels in the auditory nerve and anteroventral cochlear nucleus. *Journal of Phonetics, 16,* 37–53.

Sachs, M. B., & Young, E. D. (1979). Encoding of steady-state vowels in the auditory nerve: Representations in terms of discharge rate. *Journal of the Acoustical Society of America, 66,* 470–479.

Samuel, A. G. (1982). Phonetic prototypes. *Perception & Psychophysics, 31,* 307–314.

Seneff, S. (1988). A joint synchrony/mean rate model of auditory speech processing. *Journal of Phonetics, 16,* 55–76.

Shamma, S. (1988). The acoustic features of speech sounds in a model of auditory processing: vowels and voiceless fricatives. *Journal of Phonetics, 16,* 77–91.

Shinn, P., & Blumstein, S. E. (1984). On the role of the amplitude envelope for the perception of [b] and [t]. *Journal of the Acoustical Society of America, 75,* 1243–1252.

Sinex, D. G., & Geisler, C. D. (1983). Responses of auditory-nerve fibers to consonant–vowel syllables. *Journal of the Acoustical Society of America, 73,* 602–615.

Sinex, D. G., & McDonald, L. P. (1988). Average discharge rate representation of voice-onset time in the chinchilla auditory nerve. *Journal of the Acoustical Society of America, 83,* 1817–1827.

Sinex, D. G., & McDonald, L. P. (1989). Synchronized discharge rate representation of voice-onset time in the chinchilla auditory nerve. *Journal of the Acoustical Society of America, 85,* 1995–2004.

Sinex, D. G., McDonald, L. P., & Mott, J. B. (1991). Neural correlates of nonmonotonic temporal acuity for voice onset time. *Journal of the Acoustical Society of America, 90,* 2441–2449.

Slaney, M., & Lyon, R. F. (1990, November). *Visual representations of speech—A computer model based on correlation*. 120th meeting of the Acoustical Society of America, San Diego, CA.

Smith, E. E., & Medin, D. L. (1981). *Categories and concepts*. Cambridge, MA: Harvard University Press.

Spetner, N. B., & Olsho, L. W. (1990). Auditory frequency resolution in human infancy. *Child Development, 61,* 632–652.

Stevens, E. B., Kuhl, P. K., & Padden, D. M. (1988, November). *Macaques show context effects in speech perception*. 116th meeting of the Acoustical Society of America, Honolulu, Hawaii.

Stevens, K. N. (1989). On the quantal nature of speech. *Journal of Phonetics, 17,* 3–45.

Stevens, K. N., & Blumstein, S. E. (1981). The search for invariant acoustic correlates of phonetic features. In P. D. Eimas & J. L. Miller (Eds.), *Perspectives in the study of speech* (pp. 1–38). Hillsdale, NJ: Erlbaum.

Stevens, K. N., Fant, G., & Hawkins, S. (1987). Some acoustical and perceptual correlates of nasal vowels. In R. Channon & L. Shockey (Eds.), *In honor of Ilse Lihiste* (pp. 241–254). Dordrecht: Paris.

Stevens, K. N., Keyser, S. J., & Kawasaki, H. (1986). Toward a phonetic and phonological theory of redundant features. In J. S. Perkell & D. H. Klatt (Eds.), *Invariance and variability in speech processes* (pp. 426–429). Hillsdale, NJ: Erlbaum.

Streeter, L. A. (1976). Language perception of two-month old infants shows effects of both innate mechanisms and experience. *Nature (London) 259,* 39–41.

Studdert-Kennedy, M. (1982). A note on the biology of speech perception. In J. Mehler, M. Garrett, & E. Walker (Eds.), *Perspectives in mental representation* (pp. 329–338). Hillsdale, NJ: Erlbaum.

Summerfield, Q. (1974). Processing of cues and contexts in the perception of voicing contrasts. In G. Fant (Ed.), *Preprints of the 1974 Stockholm Speech Communication Seminar* (Vol. 3, pp. 77–86). Upsala, Sweden: Almqvist & Wiksell.

Swoboda, P. J., Morse, P. A., & Levitt, L. A. (1976). Continuous vowel discrimination in normal and at risk infants. *Child Development, 47,* 332–339.

Syrdal, A. K. (1985). Aspects of a model of the auditory representation of American English vowels. *Speech Communication, 4,* 121–135.

Syrdal, A. K., & Gopal, H. S. (1986). A perceptual model of vowel recognition based on the auditory representation of American English vowels. *Journal of the Acoustical Society of America, 79,* 1086–1100.

Thistlethwaite, D. (1951). A critical review of latent learning and related experiments. *Psychological Bulletin, 48,* 97–129.

Till, J. A. (1976, November). *Infants' discrimination of speech and nonspeech stimuli*. Annual meeting of the American Speech and Hearing Association, Houston.

Tolman, E. C. (1932). *Purposive behavior in animals and men*. New York: Appleton-Century.

Tolman, E. C. (1948). Cognitive maps in rats and men. *Psychological Review, 55,* 189–208.

Tolman, E. C., & Honzik, C. H. (1930). Introduction and removal of reward and maze performance in rats. *University of California, Berkeley, Publications in Psychology, 4,* 257–275.

Traünmuller, H. (1981). Perceptual dimension of openness in vowels. *Journal of the Acoustical Society of America, 69,* 1465–1475.

Trehub, S. E. (1973). *Auditory-linguistic sensitivity in infants*. Unpublished doctoral dissertation, McGill University, Montreal, Canada.

Trehub, S. E. (1976). The discrimination of foreign speech contrasts by infants and adults. *Child Development, 47,* 466–472.

Vilkman, E., Aaltonen, O., Raimo, I., Arajärvi, P., & Oksanen, H. (1989). Articulatory hyoid-laryngeal changes vs. cricothyroid activity in the control of intrinsic F0 of vowels. *Journal of Phonetics, 17,* 193–203.

Walsh, M. A., & Diehl, R. L. (1991). Formant transition and amplitude rise times as cues to the stop/glide distinction. *Quarterly Journal of Experimental Psychology, 43A,* 603–620.

Werker, J. F., Gilbert, J. H. V., Humphrey, K., & Tees, R. C. (1981). Developmental aspects of cross-language speech perception. *Child Development, 52,* 349–355.

Werker, J. F., & Lalonde, C. E. (1988). Cross-language speech perception: Initial capabilities and developmental change. *Developmental Psychology, 24,* 672–683.

Werker, J. F., & Logan, J. (1985). Cross-language evidence for three factors in speech perception. *Perception & Psychophysics, 37,* 35–44.

Werker, J. F., & Tees, R. C. (1983). Developmental change across childhood in the perception of non-native speech sounds. *Canadian Journal of Psychology, 37,* 278–286.

Werker, J. F., & Tees, R. C. (1984a). Cross-language speech perception: Evidence for perceptual reorganization during the first year of life. *Infant Behavior and Development, 7,* 49–63.

Werker, J. F., & Tees, R. C. (1984b). Phonemic and phonetic factors in adult cross-language speech perception. *Journal of the Acoustical Society of America, 75,* 1866–1878.

Werner, L. A., & Bargones, J. Y. (in press). Psychoacoustic development of human infants. In C. Rovee-Collier & L. Lipsitt (Eds.), *Advances in Infancy Research* (Vol. 7). Norwood, NJ: Ablex.

Werner, L. A., & Gillenwater, J. M. (1990). Pure-tone sensitivity of 2- to 5- week-old infants. *Infant Behavior and Development, 13,* 355–375.

Williams, L., & Bush, M. (1978). The discrimination by young infants of voiced stop consonants with and without release bursts. *Journal of the Acoustical Society of America, 63,* 1223–1225.

Wittgenstein, L. (1953). *Philosophical investigations* (G. E. M. Anscombe, Trans.). Oxford: Basil/Blackwell.

Wood, C. C. (1975). Auditory and phonetic levels of processing in speech perception: Neurophysiological and information-processing analyses. *Journal of Experimental Psychology: Human Perception and Performance, 104,* 3–20.

Wright, J. T. (1975). Effects of vowel nasalization on the perception of vowel height. In C. A. Ferguson, L. M. Hyman, & J. J. Ohala (Eds.), *Nasalfest: Papers from symposium on nasals and nasalization* (pp. 373–388). Stanford, CA: Stanford University, Language Universals Project.

Wright, J. T. (1986). The behavior of nasalized vowels in the perceptual vowel space. In J. J. Ohala & J. J. Jaeger (Eds.), *Experimental phonology.* Orlando, FL: Academic Press.

Yang, B. (1990). *A comparative study of normalized English and Korean vowels.* Unpublished doctoral dissertation, University of Texas at Austin.

Young, E. D., & Sachs, M. B. (1979). Representation of steady-state vowels in the temporal aspects of the discharge patterns of the populations of auditory-nerve fibers. *Journal of the Acoustical Society of America, 66,* 1381–1403.

Younger, B. A. (1985). The segregation of items into categories by 10-month-old infants. *Child Development, 56,* 1574–1583.

Younger, B. A., & Cohen, L. B. (1983). Infant perception of correlations among attributes. *Child Development, 54,* 858–867.

Younger, B. A., & Cohen, L. B. (1985). How infants form categories. In G. Bower (Ed.), *The psychology of learning and motivation: Advances in research and theory* (Vol. 19, pp. 211–247). Orlando, FL: Academic Press.

Younger, B. A., & Cohen, L. B. (1986). Developmental changes in infants' perception of correlations among attributes. *Child Development, 57,* 803–815.

CHAPTER 7

PSYCHOLOGICAL ASPECTS OF SPEECH PERCEPTION

IMPLICATIONS FOR RESEARCH AND THEORY

DOMINIC W. MASSARO

I. INTRODUCTION

In a psychology laboratory, a six-week-old infant in a baby chair has a pacifier in his mouth. As he sucks on the pacifier, the experimenter presents the sound /ba/ contingent on the infant's sucking. Given this feedback, the baby increases his sucking rate but soon becomes bored and sucks less. Now, however, the /ba/ sound is changed to /da/ and the infant increases his sucking rate again. The infant must have noticed the sound change from /ba/ to /da/.

A petite 3-year-old girl sits at a table of toy figures. She is told a short story and she must describe the story with the toy figures. To the child, she is playing a game, but to the psychologist and psycholinguist, she is displaying a remarkable ability to perceive and understand language. As an example, the child is told *The fence the horse kicks*. The child takes the horse and has it kick the fence.

A sophomore in college is studying Mandarin Chinese and learns that the syllable /ma/ has four possible meanings depending on its pitch. At first it is difficult to determine which is which. With practice, categorizing these variants becomes second nature.

A senior citizen is watching a talk show on television and is having trouble hearing the participants. He remembers he doesn't have his glasses, retrieves them, and puts them on. Surprisingly, seeing the show better allows him to hear the show better.

Spoken language is an inherent dimension of humanity from the crib to the grave. A worthwhile goal is to describe how we perceive and understand speech. The answer might take several different forms. It might be argued, for example, that a speech "organ" has evolved to carry out this function. A speech organ is necessary because speech is a highly specialized domain that necessarily requires a specialized processing system. In contrast, it might be hypothesized that understanding speech is just one domain of many that require discrimination, categorization, and understanding. We also discriminate, categorize, and interact with everyday objects and events. Why should speech be any different? Of course, other solutions between these two extreme alternatives are possible. We begin with this issue of whether speech perception is specialized.

II. Is Speech Perception Specialized?

A central issue in speech perception and psycholinguistics has been the so-called modularity of speech and language. Noam Chomsky (1980) has described language as an independent organ (or module), analogous to other organs such as our digestive system. This organ follows an independent course of development in the first years of life and allows the child to achieve a language competence that cannot be explained in traditional learning terms. Thus, a mental organ responsible for the human language faculty is viewed as responsible for our language competence. This organ matures and develops with experience, but the mature system does not simply mirror this experience. The language user inherits rule systems of highly specific structure. This innate knowledge allows us to acquire the rules of the language, which cannot be induced from normal language experience because (advocates argue) of the paucity of the language input. The data of language experience are so limited that no process of induction, abstraction, generalization, analogy, or association could account for our language competence. Somehow, the universal grammar given by our biological endowment allows the child to learn to use language appropriately without learning many of the formal intricacies of language. Other linguists, however, have documented that our language input is not as sparse as the nativists would have us believe (Sampson, 1989).

Although speech has not had an advocate as charismatic and influential as Chomsky, a similar description has been given for speech perception. Some theorists now assume that a speech module is responsible for speech perception (Liberman & Mattingly, 1989). The justification for this module has been analogous to the one for language more generally. Performance is not easily accounted for in terms of the language input. In speech, it is claimed that the acoustic signal is deficient and that typical pattern recognition schemes could not work. Put another way, it is argued that speech exceeds our auditory information processing capabilities. In terms of the modularity view, our speech perception system is linked with our speech production system—and our speech perception is somehow mediated by our speech production. For these theorists (and for the direct-realist perspective of Fowler, 1986), the objects of speech perception are articulatory events or gestures. These gestures are the primitives that the mechanisms of speech production translate into actual articulatory movements, and they are also the primitives that the specialized mechanisms of speech perception recover from the signal.

A. Evolutionary History of Speech

If speech perception were a highly unique and modular function, we would expect it to have a relatively long evolutionary history. That is, a unique process would be expected to have a unique evolutionary history. Speech as we know it, however, appears to be relatively recent in our evolutionary history. Before the artificial speech of the last few decades, speech could be produced only by biological entities. Our speech is critically dependent on the characteristics of our respiratory system and vocal tract. Thus, it is of interest to determine the evolutionary history of the biological system used for speech.

Lieberman (1991) provides a systematic analysis of the evolution of human speech. Using fossil records, he argues that speech as we know it was not possible just over 100,000 years ago. As can be seen in Figure 1, Neanderthal had a larynx positioned high, close to the entrance to the nasal cavity. The tongue was also positioned almost entirely in the mouth, as opposed to being half in the pharynx as it is in our mouths. Using computer modeling, it was discovered that the Neanderthal vocal tract would not form the configurations that are necessary to produce [i], [u], and [a] vowels. Its speech would also be necessarily nasalized (since the nasal cavity could not be blocked off), which would create a less discriminable signal because of the superimposed nasal sounds. The fossils of *Homo sapiens* of around 100,000 years ago appear to have skulls that contain a modern supralaryngeal vocal tract. From this, Lieberman concludes that language as we know it, in terms of having the supralaryngeal vocal tract to support it, is about 100 to 125 thousand years old. Given that speech is so recent in our evolutionary history, it seems unlikely that a unique skill has evolved to perceive speech and understand language. Independent of the issue of the uniqueness of speech perception, we cannot expect an evolutionary description of speech perception to be sufficient. As psycholinguists, we must also be concerned with proximal causes and influences, not just the distal influences described by evolutionary theory.

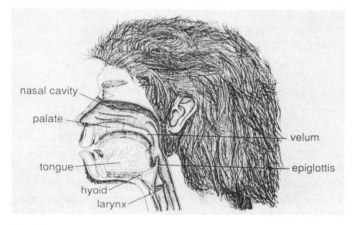

FIG. 1 The reconstructed airway of the La Chapelle-aux-Saints Neanderthal fossil (after Lieberman, 1991).

It appears that the astonishing brain growth of our ancestors occurred before the development of speech and language. This means that it is unlikely that specific brain structures evolved to enable speech production and speech perception. Our gift of language, thought, and culture must be due to exploiting the plasticity of the brain for communication. In addition, spoken language became the higher level programming language of human computer systems.

B. Lack of Invariance between Signal and Percept

One of the original arguments for the specialized nature of speech perception involved the uncertain relationship between properties of the speech signal and a given perceptual (read phonemic) category. It was stressed that, contrary to other domains of pattern recognition, one could not delineate a set of acoustic properties that uniquely defined a phoneme. The classic example involved the dramatic changes in the second-formant transitions of stop consonants in different vowel environments. Although there has been a small but continuous defense of the idea that phonemes do have invariant properties (Cole & Scott, 1974; Blumstein & Stevens, 1981), most investigators have accepted the tremendous variability of phonemes in different contexts (e.g., Wickelgren, 1969).

The argument for lack of invariance has always been articulated in a narrow sense and holds very little force with close scrutiny. First, there has been no questioning of the psychological reality of the phonetic units described in theoretical linguistics—even though the concept is even debatable in that domain. Second, it has been accepted without question that phonemes are perceived. However, a subject report of the syllable /ba/ does not necessarily imply that phoneme perception mediated this behavior. Third, research in many domains has shown that a strict correspondence between signal and perceived pattern is the exception rather than the rule in human pattern recognition. As we will see in more detail, the use of multiple sources of ambiguous information better characterizes pattern recognition in most domains, including speech. Fourth, enlarging the perceptual units of analysis to syllables of V, VC, and CV size greatly overcomes much of the invariance problem (where V is a vowel and C is a consonant or consonant cluster).

C. Nonlinearity of Segmental Units

The nonlinearity of phoneme segments in speech has also been used in the same argument for specialty as the lack of invariance. As dramatized by Hockett (1955), phonemes appear to be eggs run through a wringer so that it is difficult to discern at what point one egg ends and the next begins. This blurring and the contextual variance of phonemes is due to the articulation of one phoneme being influenced by the articulation of preceding and following phonemes. This co-articulation arises from physical necessity—even if the talker intended to articulate discrete phonemes, which can also be challenged. Once again, a strict linearity is not necessary for a nonspecialized pattern recognition process.

Perhaps the most comparable situation is handwriting, in which the visible characteristics of a letter are influenced by its adjacent neighbors.

D. Rate of Speech Processing

One traditional argument for a special processor for speech is that the transmission rate of the speech signal appears to exceed our perceptual capacity. Phonetic segments—the minimum linguistic units of speech that are approximated by the letters of the alphabet—occur at a rate of between 10 and 20 per second. Supposedly, humans cannot identify nonspeech signals at even half this rate. There are several counterarguments to the rate argument, however. First, speech has a fast rate only when phonetic segments are taken as the psychologically real unit of analysis. Although linguists have described the linguistic reality of these phonetic segments, there is no evidence that these segments are psychologically functional in speech perception. If syllables (V, CV, and VC) are assumed to be functional perceptual units in speech perception, then the rate of presentation of these signals is well within the range of our information processing capability.

A second problem with counting the rate of phonetic segments as an index of speech rate is that a word could be recognized without necessarily recognizing the phonetic segments that make it up. Some evidence for this idea has been obtained in the processing of nonspeech sounds (Warren, 1982). If a sequence of arbitrarily selected sounds is presented, listeners have trouble identifying the order of the elements that make up the sequence unless each sound is presented for 0.25 s or so. On the other hand, one sequence could be discriminated from another when the sounds are much shorter—in the range of 5–100 ms. Warren, Bashford, and Gardner (1990) found that subjects could discriminate different sequences of repeated vowels without identifying their order. The emergence of unique words with different words for different sequences was responsible for the discrimination. A conjunction of different sounds has the consequences of a unique percept emerging which can be informative for the perceptual system. Two different sequences of identical components are discriminated from one another because one arrangement sounds different from the other. One might sound "bubbly" and the other "shrill." Subjects can even learn to label these sequences as wholes if appropriate feedback is given. This research is consistent with research on language acquisition. Peters (1983) observed that the child acquires speech segments in terms of a variety of sizes: syllables, words, or even phrases. For example, the child learns to identify the word *through* not in terms of a sequence of three phonetic segments but as a CV syllable of a particular quality.

A final problem with the argument that the rate of speech processing is larger than other forms of auditory information processing is the positive contribution of context (see Section II,I). Our ability to process speech at a fast rate holds only for familiar speech. Even linguists have great difficulty transcribing a language that they do not know. Knowing a language allows us to perceive speech on the basis of a deficient signal or with little processing time. For example, we can perceive the first /s/ in the word *legislatures* even when the relevant segment has been replaced with a noise or a tone (Warren, 1970).

Similarly, we can perceive speech of a language we know when it is speeded up at two or three times its normal rate.

E. Speech Perception by Nonhumans

There is another source of evidence against the hypothesis that speech perception is carried out by a specialized module unique to humans. If speech perception were special and mediated in any way by speech production, then discrimination and recognition of fundamental speech categories should be impossible for nonhumans. However, some nonhuman animals can discriminate fundamental speech segments. Chinchillas (a small rodent with auditory capabilities close to humans) can discriminate fundamental distinctions such as the auditory difference signaling the difference between /ba/ and /pa/. More recently and more impressively, Kluender, Diehl, and Killeen (1987) have shown that quail can learn to discriminate the stop consonant /d/ from the stops /b/ and /g/ (occurring in different vowel environments). Given these results, it appears that there is information in the auditory speech signal that can be processed using normal perceptual processes.

F. Categorical Perception

One of the classic research findings used to support speech as a specialized modular process was categorical perception. Categorical perception occurs when changes along some dimension of the speech signal are not perceived continuously but in a discrete manner. Listeners are supposedly limited in their ability to discriminate differences between different sounds belonging to the same phoneme category. The sounds within a category are only identified absolutely, and discrimination is possible for only those sounds that can be identified as belonging to different categories. For example, small changes can be made in the consonant–vowel syllable /be/ (*bay*) to transform it in small steps into the syllable /de/ (*day*). These syllables are used in identification and discrimination tasks. The results seemed to indicate that subjects can discriminate the syllables only to the extent they recognize them as different categories. These results were contrasted with other forms of perception in which we can discriminate many more signals that we can categorize. Hence, speech perception seemed to qualify as a special type of performance.

There are severe weaknesses in the previous evidence for categorical perception. The results have been interpreted as showing categorical perception because discrimination performance was reasonably predicted by identification performance. It turns out that this relation between identification and discrimination provides no support for categorical perception, for two reasons. First, categorical perception usually provides an inadequate description of the relation between identification and discrimination, and has not been shown to provide a better description than continuous perception. Second, other explanations of the results are possible, and these explanations do not require any special processes for speech (Massaro, 1987, 1989b).

In fact, there is now an abundance of evidence that perceivers are very good at perceiving differences within a speech category. For example, subjects are very good at indicating the degree to which a speech stimulus represents a given speech category. In addition, reaction times of identification judgments illustrate that members within a speech category vary in ambiguity or the degree to which they represent the category (Massaro, 1987). These results indicate that subjects can discriminate differences within a speech category, and they are not limited to just categorical information. Decision processes can transform continuous sensory information into results usually taken to reflect categorical perception. A finding of categorical partitioning of a set of stimuli in no way implies that these stimuli were perceived categorically.

G. The Demise of Categorical Perception

Categorical perception is a belief that will not die or fade away easily. Many textbooks and tutorial articles also state that speech is perceived categorically (J. R. Anderson, 1990; Eimas, 1985; Flavell, 1985; Miller, 1981). However, I have argued in too many places that previous results and more recent studies are better described in terms of continuous perception—a relatively continuous relationship between changes in a stimulus and changes in perception (Massaro, 1987).

There are severe weaknesses in previous evidence for categorical perception. One approach—the traditional one used throughout the almost three decades of research on categorical perception—concerns the relation between IDENTIFICATION and DISCRIMINATION. In the typical experiment, a set of speech stimuli along a speech continuum between two alternatives is synthesized. Subjects identify each of the stimuli as one of the two alternatives. Subjects are also asked to discriminate among these same stimuli. The results have been interpreted as showing categorical perception because discrimination performance was reasonably predicted by identification performance (Studdert-Kennedy, Liberman, Harris, & Cooper, 1970). It turns out that this relation between identification and discrimination provides no support for categorical perception, for two reasons. First, the categorical model usually provides an inadequate description of the relation between identification and discrimination, and has not been shown to provide a better description than continuous models. Second, even if the results provided unequivocal support for the categorical model, explanations other than categorical perception are possible (Massaro, 1987; Massaro & Oden, 1980).

We saw that evidence against categorical perception comes from a direct experimental comparison between categorical and continuous models of perception. Subjects asked to classify speech events independently varying along two dimensions produce identification results consistent with the assumption of continuous information along each of the two dimensions. A model based on categorical information along each dimension gives a very poor description of the identification judgments. In other research, we asked subjects to make repeated ratings of how well a stimulus represents a given category (Massaro & Cohen, 1983). The distribution of the rating judgments to a given stimulus is better described by a continuous model than a categorical one. The best conclusion is to reject all reference to categorical perception of speech and to concentrate instead on the structures and processes responsible for categorizing the world of speech.

Most readers will remain unconvinced so long as no satisfying explanation is given for the sharp category boundaries found in speech perception research. However, it is only natural that continuous perception should lead to sharp category boundaries along a stimulus continuum. Given a stimulus continuum from A to *not* A that is perceived continuously, goodness(A) is an index of the degree to which the information represents the category A. The left panel of Figure 2 shows goodness(A) as a linear function of Variable A.

An optimal decision rule in a discrete judgment task would set the criterion value at 0.5 and classify the pattern as A for any value greater than 0.5. Otherwise, the pattern is classified as *not* A. Given this decision rule, the probability of an A response would take the form of the step-function shown in the right panel of Figure 2. That is, with a fixed criterion value and no variability, the decision operation changes the continuous linear function given by the perceptual operation into a step function. Although based on continuous perception, this function is identical to the idealized form of categorical perception in a speech identification task. It follows that a step function for identification is not evidence for categorical perception because it can also occur with continuous information.

If there is noise in the mapping from stimulus to identification, a given level of Variable A cannot be expected to produce the same identification judgment on each presentation. It is reasonable to assume that a given level of Variable A produces a normally distributed range of goodness(A) values with a mean directly related to the level of Variable A and a variance equal across all levels of Variable A. If this is the case, noise will influence the identification judgment for the levels of Variable A near the criterion value more than it will influence

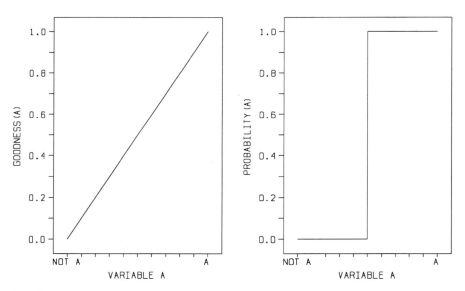

Fig. 2   *Left:* The degree to which a stimulus represents the category A, called goodness(A), as a function of the level along a stimulus continuum between *not* A and A. *Right:* The probability of an A response, probability(A), as a function of the stimulus continuum if the subject maintains a decision criterion at a particular value of goodness(A) and responds A if and only if the goodness(A) exceeds the decision criterion.

the levels away from the criterion value. Figure 3 illustrates the expected outcome for identification if there is normally distributed noise with the same criterion value assumed in Figure 2.

If the noise is normal and has the same mean and variance across the continuum, a stimulus whose mean goodness is at the criterion value will produce random classifications. The goodness value will be above the criterion on half of the trials and below the criterion on the other half. As the goodness value moves away from the criterion value, the noise will have a diminishing effect on the identification judgments. Noise has a larger influence on identification in the middle of the range of goodness values than at the extremes because variability goes in both directions in the middle and only inward at the extremes. This differential effect of noise across the continuum will produce an identification function that has a sharp boundary. Thus, our hypothetical subject giving this result appears to show enhanced discrimination across the category boundary when, in fact, discrimination was constant across the continuum. The shape of the function resulted from noise at the decision stage.

This example shows that categorical decisions made on the basis of continuous information produce identification functions with sharp boundaries, previously taken to indicate categorical perception. Strictly speaking, of course, categorical perception was considered present only if discrimination behavior did not exceed that predicted from categorization. However, one should not have been impressed with the failure of discrimination to exceed that predicted by categorization if the discrimination task resembled something more akin to categorization than discrimination. That is, subjects will tend to rely on identification labels in discrimination tasks if the perceptual memory is poor (Massaro, 1987).

At the theoretical level, it is necessary to distinguish between sensory and decision processes in the categorization task. What is central for our purposes is that decision processes can transform continuous sensory information into

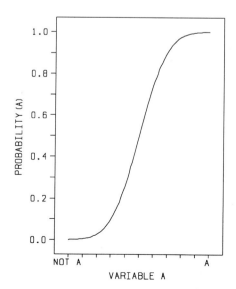

Fig. 3 Probability(A) as a function of Variable A given the linear relationship between goodness(A) and Variable A and the decision criterion represented in Figure 2, but with normally distributed noise added to the mapping of Variable A to goodness(A).

results usually taken to reflect categorical perception. A finding of relatively categorical partitioning of a set of stimuli in no way implies that these stimuli were perceived categorically. Tapping into the process in ways other than simply measuring the identification response reveals the continuous nature of speech perception. Perceivers can rate the degree to which a speech event represents a category, and they can discriminate among different exemplars of the same speech category. Werker (1991) has demonstrated remarkable changes in speech categorization as a function of development and native language. She and others (Kuhl, 1990) have found age-related changes in the sensitivity to nonnative contrasts. These changes are not necessarily evidence for categorical speech perception, however. As Werker (1991, p. 104) states, "However, the fact that adults can still discriminate the nonnative contrasts under certain testing conditions indicates that maintenance is operating at the level of linguistic categories rather than auditory abilities." In addition, reaction times (RT) of identification judgments illustrate that members within a speech category vary in ambiguity or the degree to which they represent the category (Massaro, 1987).

Although speech perception is continuous, there may be a few speech contrasts that qualify for a weak form of categorical perception. This weak form of categorical perception would be reflected in somewhat better discrimination between instances from different categories than between instances within the same category. As an example, consider an auditory /ba/ to /da/ continuum similar to one used in the current experiments. The F2 and F3 transitions were varied in linear steps between the two endpoints of the continuum. The syllable /ba/ is characterized by rising transitions and /da/ by falling transitions. Subjects might discriminate between a rising and falling transition more easily than between two rising or two falling transitions even though the frequency difference is identical in the two cases. Direction of pitch change is more discriminable than the exact magnitude of change. This weak form of categorical perception would arise from a property of auditory processing rather than a special characteristic of speech categories. Thus similar results would be found in humans, chinchillas, and monkeys as well as for nonspeech analogs (as they are, e.g., Kuhl, 1987; Pastore, 1987). However, it is important to note that discrimination between instances within a category is still possible; and although a weak form of categorical perception might exist for a few categories, most do not appear to have this property. We must hence explain continuous rather than categorical speech perception.

Psychology and the speech sciences seem reluctant to give up the notion of categorical perception perhaps, in part, because of phenomenal experience. Our phenomenal experience in speech perception is that of categorical perception. Listening to a synthetic speech continuum between /ba/ and /pa/ provides an impressive demonstration of this. Students and colleagues usually agree that their percept changes qualitatively from one category to the other in a single step or two with very little fuzziness in between. (This author has had similar experiences, hearing certain German phonological categories in terms of similar English ones.) Our phenomenal experience, however, is not enough to confirm the existence of categorical perception. As noted by Marcel (1983), phenomenal experience might be dependent on linking current hypotheses with sensory information. If the sensory information is lost very quickly, continuous information could participate in the perceptual process but might not be readily accessible to introspection. Reading a brief visual display of a word might lead to recognition even though the reader is unable to report certain properties of the type font or even a misspelling of the word. Yet the visual characteristics that subjects cannot report could have contributed to word recognition. Analogously, continuous information could have been functional in speech perception even if retrospective inquiry suggests otherwise. As in most matters of psychological inquiry, we must find methods to tap the processes involved in cognition without depending only on introspective reports.

Dennett (1991) has clarified an important distinction between filling and finding out. We report a variety of experiences such as the apparent motion in the phi phenomenon. The issue for Dennett is whether it is correct to say that the sensory system accomplishes these outcomes by filling in. That is, the sensory system accomplishes an identical outcome in the phi phenomenon that it does in continuous motion. It has been reported that the color of the moving object changes in midstream when a red dot at one location is alternated with a green dot at another location. Does the visual system fill in to give us the impression of a continuously moving dot that changes color? Dennett argues very forcefully that our impressions go beyond the information given, but that our sensory systems do not—that is, they do not fill in.

Dennett's philosophical argument is highly relevant to categorical perception. In the categorical perception viewpoint, there seems to be significant filling in. Categorical perception accomplishes at the sensory/brain level a direct correspondence between some representation and our impression. Categorical perception supposedly occurs because the sensory/perceptual system blurs any stimulus differences within a category and perhaps sharpens stimulus differences between categories. To describe categorical perception in the context of filling in, we perceive two different speech events as the same category because the speech-is-special module makes them equivalent at the sensory/perceptual level. Categorical perception also seems to predict filling in because sensory processing supposedly occurs in such a manner to render the stimuli within a category indiscriminable. This process would be analogous to filling in. On the other hand, it is possible that categorization is simply finding out (as I argue in several places). That is, the goal of speech perception is categorization, and we are able to find out which category best represents the speech event without necessarily modifying the sensory/perceptual representation of that event. In terms of the fuzzy logical model of perception (FLMP), we evaluate, integrate, and make a categorical decision if necessary without necessarily modifying the sensory/perceptual representations of the speech event.

Filling in might also appear to be an attractive explanation of our phenomenal experience of contradictory auditory and visual speech. We are told to report what we hear, and the visible speech biases our experience relative to the unimodal case. Because it is our auditory experience we are reporting, it seems only natural to believe that the representation of the auditory speech has been changed—filled in—by the visual. Another interpretation, however, is that we do not have veridical access of the auditory representation. As Marcel (1983) has pointed out, we report interpretations—finding out—and not representations. Thus, one must be careful about equating phenomenal reports with representations.

Categorical perception has been a popular assumption because it appeared to place certain constraints on the speech perception process—constraints that make speech perception possible and/or easier. If the infant were limited to perceiving only the discrete categories of his or her language, then acquisition of that language would be easier. However, an ability to discriminate within category differences could only hurt speech perception. We know that higher order sentential and lexical information contributes to speech perception. If categorical perception were the case, errors would be catastrophic in that perceivers would access the incorrect category. Categorical perception would also make it difficult to integrate sentential and lexical information with the phonetic information. Continuous information is more naturally integrated with higher order sources of information (Massaro, 1987).

One of the impediments to resolving the controversy is the term PERCEPTION. If perception simply refers to our reported experience, then we cannot deny categorical perception because we naturally attend to the different categories of language. If perception refers to the psychological processing, however, then it is clear that the processing system is not limited to categorical information. One possible reason why categorical perception has been viewed so positively is that scientists misinterpreted the outcome for the processes leading up to the outcome.

Despite our phenomenal experience and the three decades of misinterpreting the relationship between the identification and discrimination of auditory speech, we must conclude that speech is perceived continuously, not categorically. Our work shows that visible and bimodal speech are also perceived continuously. This observation also seems to pull the carpet from under current views of language acquisition that attribute discrete speech categories to the infant and child (Eimas, 1985; Gleitman & Wanner, 1982). Most important, the case for the modularity or specialization of speech is weakened considerably because of its reliance on the assumption of categorical perception. We are now faced with the bigger challenge of explaining how multiple continuous sources of information are evaluated and integrated to achieve a percept with continuous information.

H. Development of Speech Perception

The development of speech perception also speaks to the issue of modularity and the need to assume a specialized processor for speech. Modularity necessarily has a large nativistic component. About two decades ago, investigators presented evidence for this view based on studies of infant speech perception. Early studies seem to find that infants noticed changes between speech categories but not within speech categories (Eimas, 1985). For example, the infant appeared to discriminate an auditory change that changed the signal from /ba/ to /pa/ but not a similar auditory change within either of these two categories. These early studies were misleading, however, and more recent research has shown that infants can discriminate differences within, as well as between, categories (Massaro, 1987). Thus, research with infants reveals that they are capable of discriminating the multiple dimensions of the auditory speech signal, such as the loudness or duration of a speech segment. However, the role these differences play in the language must be learned, and infants are not prewired to categorize the signals into innate phonetic categories. In fact, infants and young children do not appear to discriminate and categorize the speech signal as well as adults. Their caregivers seem to be aware of this limitation because there is also a substantial amount of motherese during the first years of life. In MOTHERESE, the caregiver speaks clearly and slowly to the child. There is also experimental evidence of a slow acquisition of the fundamental distinctions of our spoken language. Children have more difficulty discriminating speech categories, and their ability to discriminate increases gradually across childhood. Even after the onset of schooling, American children have trouble discriminating the segments /v/ and /ð/ (as in *vat* and *that*) (Massaro, 1987).

I. Contextual Effects in Speech Perception

Another strong source of evidence against the modularity of speech perception involves the strong contribution of linguistic and situational context to speech perception. We perceive language more easily when we have some expectation of what the talker is going to say. Many of our conversations involve situations in which we find ourselves predicting exactly what the talker will say next. Experiments have shown that the first words of a sentence can facilitate the recognition of the next word. Another piece of evidence for the positive contribution of context is the finding that trained phoneticians are not able to transcribe a nonnative language accurately. Much of the original detail is lost in the transcription. Not knowing the language or the meaning of the message makes us poorer perceivers.

J. Conclusion

The research that I have reviewed weakens the claim that speech perception requires a specialized module. If speech perception were governed by a specialized module, we would expect no relationship between speech and other skills. However, there is a positive correlation between motor skills and language, and also one between cognitive functioning and vocabulary size. For example, there is a positive correlation between cognitive development and the learning of new words. It seems that speech perception can be considered as one of several perceptual/cognitive functions that can be understood in terms of more general perceptual and learning processes.

III. VARIOUS FORMS OF CONTEXT EFFECTS IN SPEECH PERCEPTION

There is considerable debate concerning how informative the acoustic signal actually is (Blumstein & Stevens, 1979; Cole & Scott, 1974; Liberman, Cooper, Shankweiler, & Studdert-Kennedy 1967; Massaro, 1975b; Massaro & Oden, 1980). Even if the acoustic signal was sufficient for speech recognition under ideal conditions, however, few researchers would believe that the listener relies on only the acoustic signal. It is generally agreed that the listener normally achieves good recognition by supplementing the information from the acoustic signal with information generated through the utilization of linguistic context. A good deal of research has been directed at showing a positive contribution of linguistic context (Cole & Jakimik, 1978; Marslen-Wilson & Welsh, 1978; Pollack & Pickett, 1963). We now review some of this research.

A. Detecting Mispronunciations

Abstracting meaning is a joint function of the independent contributions of the perceptual and contextual information available. In one experiment, Cole (1973) asked subjects to push a button every time they heard a mispronunciation in a spoken rendering of Lewis Carroll's *Through the Looking Glass*. A mispronunciation involved changing a phoneme by 1, 2, or 4 distinctive features (for example, *confusion* mispronounced as *gunfusion, bunfusion,* and *sunfusion,* respectively). The probability of recognizing a mispronunciation increased from 30% to 75% with increases in the number of feature changes, which makes the contribution of the perceptual information passed on by the primary recognition process. The contribution of contextual information should work against the recognition of a mispronunciation since context would support a correct rendering of the mispronounced word. In support of this idea, all mispronunciations were correctly recognized when the syllables were isolated and removed from the passage.

Cole and Jakimik (1978) extended Cole's (1973) mispronunciation task to evaluate how higher order contextual information can influence sentence processing. To the extent that a word is predicted by its preceding context, the listener should be faster at detecting a mispronunciation. This follows from the idea that the quickest way to detect a mispronunciation is to first determine what the intended word is and then notice a mismatch with what was said. Given the sentences *He sat reading a **book/bill** until it was time to go home for his tea,* mispronouncing the /b/ in *book* as /v/ should be detected faster than the same mispronunciation of *bill.* In fact, listeners were 150 ms faster detecting mispronunciations in highly predictable words than in unpredictable words.

In other experiments Cole and Jakimik (1978) demonstrated similar effects of logical implication. Consider the test sentence *It was the middle of the next day before the killer was caught,* with the /k/ in *killer* mispronounced as /g/. Detection of the mispronunciation should be faster when the text word is implied by the preceding sentence *It was a stormy night when the phonetician was murdered,* compared to the case in which the preceding sentence states that the phonetician merely died. Thematic organization also facilitated recognition of words in their stories. Given an ambiguous story, a disambiguating picture shortened reaction times to mispronunciations of thematically related words but not to mispronunciations of other words that were unrelated to the theme of the story.

Marslen-Wilson (1973) asked subjects to shadow (repeat back) prose as quickly as they heard it. Some individuals were able to shadow the speech at extremely close delays with lags of 250 ms, about the duration of a syllable or so. One might argue that the shadowing response was simply a sound-to-sound mapping without any higher order semantic-syntactic analyses. When subjects make errors in shadowing, however, the errors are syntactically and semantically appropriate given the preceding context. For example, given the sentence *He had heard at the Brigade,* some subjects repeated *He had heard that the Brigade.* The nature of the errors did not vary with their latency; the shadowing errors were always well formed given the preceding context.

B. Limitations of Results

Perceivers have been shown to be efficient exploiters of different types of context to aid in speech perception. However, it might be claimed that the context effects that were observed occurred AFTER speech perception. One might argue, for example, that the rapid shadowing errors observed by Marslen-Wilson (1973) occurred at the stage of speech production rather than speech perception. Analogous to research in other domains, it is essential to locate the stage of processing responsible for experimental findings. A new task has helped address this issue and, more important, the results can be used to reveal how stimulus information and context jointly contribute to word recognition.

C. Gating Task

The gating task (Grosjean, 1980, 1985) has been a recent method developed to assess speech perception and word recognition. As indicated by the name of the task, portions of the spoken message are eliminated or gated out. In a typical task with single words, only the first 50 ms or so of the word is presented. Successive presentations involve longer and longer portions of the word by increasing the duration of each successive presentation by 20 ms. Subjects attempt to name the word after each presentation. Warren and Marslen-Wilson (1987), for example, presented words such as *school* or *scoop*. Figure 4 shows that the probability of correct recognition of a test word increases as additional word information is presented in the gating task.

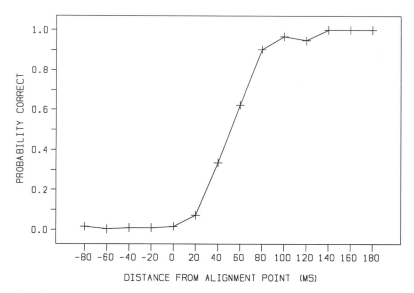

FIG. 4   Probability of correct recognition of the test word as a function of the distance from the alignment point in the test word. The alignment point corresponds to a point near the onset of the final consonant of the word (results adapted from Warren & Marslen-Wilson, 1987).

The gating task appears to have promise for the investigation of speech perception and spoken language understanding. Investigators have worried about two features of the gating task that may limit its external validity. The first feature task is that subjects hear multiple presentations of the test word on a given trial. The standard procedure is to present increasingly larger fragments of the same word on a given trial. The subject responds after each presentation of the fragment. The repeated presentations of the fragment may enhance recognition of the test word relative to the case in which the subject obtains only a single presentation of an item. In visual form perception, for example, it has been shown that repeated tachistoscopic presentations of a test form lead to correct recognition, even though the duration is not increased as it is in the gating task (Uhlarik & Johnson, 1978). The same short presentation of a test form that does not produce correct recognition on its initial presentation can give correct recognition if it is repeated three or four times in the task. This improvement in performance occurs even though the duration of the test stimulus was not increased. These repeated looks at the stimulus can lead to improved performance relative to just a single look. Information from successive presentations can be utilized to improve performance, and therefore multiple presentations lead to better performance than just a single presentation. Based on this result, performance in the gating task might reflect repeated presentations of the test word, in addition to the fact that the successive presentations increased in duration.

Cotton and Grosjean (1984) compared the standard multiple presentation format with the format in which subjects heard only a single fragment from each word in the task. Similar results were found in both conditions. Salasoo and Pisoni (1985) carried out a similar study and found that the average duration of the test word needed for correct identification was only 5 ms less in the task with multiple presentations on a trial than for a single presentation of the test word. Thus, using successive presentations in the gating task appears to be a valid method of increasing the duration of the test word to assess its influence on recognition.

A second question concerning gating tasks has to do with how quickly subjects are required to respond in the task. It could be the case that subjects, given unlimited time to respond in the task, will perform differently from their performance in the on-line recognition of continuous speech. That is, the gating task might be treated as a conscious problem-solving task in which subjects are very deliberate in making their decision about what word was presented. This deliberation would not be possible in a typical situation involving continuous speech, and therefore the results might be misleading. To assess performance under more realistic conditions, Tyler and Wessels (1985) employed a naming response in the gating task. Subjects were required to name the test word as quickly as possible on each trial. In addition, a given word was presented only once to a given subject. The results from this task were very similar to the standard gating test. The durations of the test words needed for correct recognition were roughly the same as that found in the standard gating task. Thus, the experiments exploring the external validity of the gating task have been very encouraging. The results appear to be generalizable to the on-line recognition of continuous speech.

D. Integrating Sentential Context

Tyler and Wessels (1983) used the gating paradigm to assess the contribution of various forms of sentential context to word recognition. Subjects heard a sentence followed by the beginning of the test word (with the rest of the word gated out). The word was increased in duration by adding small segments of the word until correct recognition was achieved. The sentence contexts varied in syntactic and semantic constraints. Some sentence contexts had minimal semantic constraints in that the target word was not predictable in a test given the sentence context and the first 100 ms of the target word. Performance in this condition can be compared to a control condition in which no sentential constraints were present. The experimental question is whether context contributes to recognition of the test word.

Figure 5 gives the probability of correct word recognition as a function of the number of segments in the test word and the context condition. Both variables had a significant influence on performance. In addition, the interaction between the two variables reveals how word information and context jointly influence word recognition. Context influences performance most at intermediate levels of word information. The contribution of context is most apparent when there is some but not complete information about the test word. The lines in Figure 5 give the predictions of the fuzzy logical model of perception

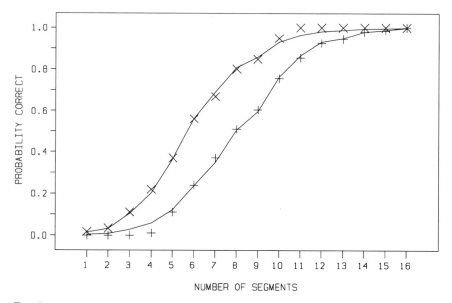

FIG. 5 Observed (*points*) and predicted (*lines*) probability of identifying the test word correctly as a function of the sentential context and the number of segments of the test word. The minimum context (*crosses*) refers to minimum semantic and weak syntactic constraints. The none context (*plusses*) refers to no semantic and weak syntactic constraints (results of Tyler & Wessels, 1983; predictions of the FLMP).

(see Section V,G). The FLMP describes word recognition in terms of the evaluation and integration of word information and sentential context followed by a decision based on the outcome. As can be seen in the figure, the model captures the exact form of the integration of the two sources of information.

A positive effect of sentence context in this situation is very impressive because it illustrates a true integration of word and context information. The probability of correct recognition is zero when context is given with minimum word information. Similarly, the probability of correct recognition is zero with three segments of the test word presented without context. That is, neither the context alone nor the limited word information permits word recognition; however, when presented jointly word recognition is very good. Thus, the strong effect of minimum semantic context illustrated in Figure 5 can be considered to reflect true integration of word and contextual sources of information.

The form of the interaction of stimulus information and context is relevant to the prediction of the cohort model. Marslen-Wilson (1987) assumes that some minimum cohort set must be established on the basis of stimulus information before context can have an influence. In terms of FLMP description, this assumption implies that the evaluation of context should change across different levels of gating. To test this hypothesis, another model was fitted to the results. In this model, context was assumed to have an influence only after some minimum gating interval. Because it is not known what this minimum interval should be, an additional free parameter was estimated to converge on the interval that gave the best description of the observed results. This model did not improve the description of the results, weakening the claim that context has its influence only after some minimum stimulus information has been processed. This result is another instance of the general finding that there are no discrete points in psychological processing. The system does not seem to work one way at one point in time (i.e., no effect of context) and another way in another point in time (i.e., an effect of context).

IV. INDEPENDENT VERSUS INTERACTIVE INFLUENCES OF CONTEXT

We have reached the stage of research in which context effects are well documented. What is important for the next stage is to understand how context and the speech signal come together to support speech perception. There are two general explanations. First, top-down context interacts with bottom-up sensory information to modify the latter's representation. This can be described as a sensitivity effect—context actually modifies the sensitivity of the relevant sensory system. For example, lexical context could change the perceiver's ability to distinguish some speech segment within the word. Second, context might simply provide an additional source of information that supplements the sensory information. In this case, bias is a more appropriate description of the contribution of top-down context. The lexical context biases the speech perception system to perceive some speech segment in the word, but the context does not change the workings of the relevant sensory system. We turn to three studies of context effects with the goal of distinguishing between these two explanations of context effects.

A. Phonemic Restoration

Samuel (1981) reported one of the few other existing experiments addressing sensitivity and bias effects in language processing. He employed a signal detection framework in a study of phonemic restoration. In the original type of phonemic restoration study (Warren, 1970), a phoneme in a word is removed and replaced with some stimulus, such as a tone or white noise. Subjects have difficulty indicating what phoneme is missing. Failure to spot the missing phoneme could be a sensitivity effect or a bias effect. Samuel addressed this issue by creating signal and noise trials. Signal trials contained the original phoneme with superimposed white noise. Noise trials replaced the original phoneme with the same white noise. Subjects were asked to indicate whether or not the original phoneme was present. Sensitivity is reflected in the degree to which the two types of trials can be discriminated and can be indexed by d' within the context of signal detection theory. Bias would be reflected in the overall likelihood of saying that the original phoneme is present.

To evaluate the top-down effects of lexical constraints, Samuel compared performance on phonemes in test words relative to performance on the phoneme segments presented in isolation. A bias was observed in that subjects were more likely to respond that the phoneme was present in the word than in the isolated segment. In addition, subjects discriminated the signal from the noise trials much better in the segment context than the word context. The d' values averaged about two or three times larger for the segment context than for the word context. In contrast to the results of the study of phonological context discussed in Section IV,B, there appears to be a large negative effect of top-down context on sensitivity (changes in sensitivity are equivalent to nonindependent effects of stimulus and context). However, the segment versus word comparison in the Samuel study confounds stimulus contributions with top-down contributions. An isolated segment has bottom-up advantages over the same segment presented in a word. Forward and backward masking may degrade the perceptual quality of a segment presented in a word relative to being presented alone. In addition, the word context might provide co-articulatory information about the critical phoneme which would not be available in the isolated segment.

Samuel carried out a second study that should have overcome the confounding inherent in comparing words and segments. In this study, a word context was compared to a pseudoword context. As an example, the word *living* might be compared to the pseudoword *lathing,* or *modern* might be compared to *madorn.* Samuel also reasoned that pseudowords might show a disadvantage relative to words, simply because subjects would not know what sequence of segments makes up a pseudoword. As an attempt to compensate for this disadvantage for pseudowords, each word or pseudoword was first spoken in intact form (primed) before its presentation as a test item. There was a d' advantage of primed pseudowords over primed words, which Samuel interpreted as a sensitivity effect. Analogous to the difference in the segment and word conditions, a stimulus confounding might also be responsible for the difference between pseudowords and words. Natural speech was used, and therefore an equivalence of stimulus information between the words and pseudowords could not be insured. In fact, the pseudowords averaged about 10%

longer in duration than the words. Longer duration is usually correlated with a higher quality speech signal, which might explain the advantage of the pseudowords over the words.

In a final experiment, Samuel placed test words in a sentence context. The test word was either predicted or not by the sentence context. The results indicated that the predictability of the test word had a significant influence on bias but not sensitivity. The influence of sentence predictability appears to be a valid comparison because there was no apparent stimulus confounding between the predictable and unpredictable contexts. Given the possibility of stimulus confoundings when sensitivity effects were found and no sensitivity effect with a sentence context, it seems premature to conclude that the phonemic restoration paradigm produces sensitivity effects. More generally, top-down effects on sensitivity have yet to be convincingly demonstrated, making the concept of top-down activation unnecessary to explain speech perception.

B. Phonological Context

To study how stimulus information and phonological constraints are used in speech perception, subjects were asked to identify a liquid consonant in different phonological contexts (Massaro, 1989c). Each speech sound was a consonant cluster syllable beginning with one of the three consonants /p/, /t/, or /s/ followed by a liquid consonant ranging (in five levels) from /l/ to /r/, followed by the vowel /i/. The five different levels along the /l/–/r/ continuum differed in terms of the frequency of the third formant (F3) at the onset of the liquid—which is higher for /l/ than /r/. (Formants are bands of energy in the syllable that normally result from natural resonances of the vocal tract in real speech.) There were 15 test stimuli created from the factorial combination of five stimulus levels combined with three initial consonant contexts. Eight elementary school children were instructed to listen to each test syllable and to respond whether they heard /li/ or /ri/.

Figure 6 gives the inverse logistic transform of the average probability of an /r/ response as a function of the two factors. As can be seen in the figure, both factors had a strong effect. The probability of an /r/ response increased systematically with decreases in the F3 transition. Phonological context also had a significant effect on the judgments. Subjects responded /r/ more often given the context /t/ than given the context /p/. Similarly, there were fewer /r/ responses given the context /s/ than given the context /p/. Finally, the significant interaction reflected the fact that the phonological context effect was greatest when the information about the liquid was ambiguous. As will be described in Section V,C, these two factors had independent influences on performance.

C. Lexical Context

Elman and McClelland (1988) carried out an ingenious demonstration of context effects in speech perception. Because of co-articulation—the influence of producing one speech segment on the production of another—a given speech segment has different acoustic forms in different contexts. The phonemes /s/ and /ʃ/ are necessarily produced differently and will differentially influence the production of the following speech segment. Perceivers not only recognize the

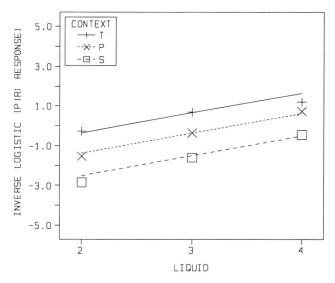

FIG. 6   Predicted (*lines*) and observed (*points*) inverse logistic transformation of the probability of an /r/ identification for the middle three levels of liquid. Context is the curve parameter (results of Massaro, 1989c).

different speech segments /s/ and /ʃ/; they apparently are able to compensate for the influence of these segments in recognizing the following speech segment. During production of speech, co-articulation involves the assimilation of the acoustic characteristics of one sound in the direction of the characteristics of the neighboring sound. The production of /s/ contains higher frequency energy than /ʃ/, and co-articulation will result in the sound following /s/ having higher frequency energy. The energy in /k/ is somewhat lower in frequency than that in initial /t/—the /t/ has a high burst. Thus, /s/ biases the articulation of a following stop in such a way that the stop segment has somewhat higher frequency energy. The segment /ʃ/, on the other hand, biases the articulation of a following stop in such a way that the stop segment has somewhat lower frequency energy. Perceivers apparently take this assimilative coarticulatory influence into account in their perceptual recognition of /t/ and /k/ (and /d/ and /g/) and show a contrast effect. Mann and Repp (1981) showed that recognition of the following segment as /t/ or /k/ is dependent on whether the preceding segment is /s/ or /ʃ/. Given a vowel–fricative syllable followed by a stop–vowel syllable, subjects were more likely to identify the stop as /k/ than /t/ if the preceding fricative was /s/ than if it was /ʃ/ (a contrast effect).

The goal of the Elman and McClelland (1988) study was to induce the same contrast effect but mediated by the lexical identity of a word rather than the acoustic structure of the preceding syllable. Using synthetic speech, a continuum of speech sounds ranging between *tapes* and *capes* was made by varying the onset properties of the sounds. These sounds were placed after the words *Christmas* and *foolish*. As expected from the Mann and Repp (1981) study, there were more judgments of *capes* following *Christmas* than following *foolish*. However, this dependency could have been triggered directly by the acoustic differences between /s/ and /ʃ/. To eliminate this possibility, Elman and McClelland (1988) created an ambiguous sound half way between /s/ and /ʃ/ and replaced the original fricatives in *Christmas* and *foolish* with this ambiguous sound. Given a lexical context effect first reported by Ganong (1980) and also replicated by Connine and Clifton (1987), we would expect that the ambiguous segment would tend to be categorized as /s/ when it occurs in *Christmas* and as /ʃ/ when it occurs in *foolish*. The empirical question is whether the same contrast effect would occur given the same ambiguous segment in the two different words. That is, Would just the lexical identity of the first word also lead to a contrast effect in the recognition of the following speech segment varying between *tapes* and *capes*? In fact, subjects were more likely to report the test word *capes* following the context word *Christmas* than following the context word *foolish*, and this effect was larger when the segmental information about the /k/–/t/ distinction in the test word was ambiguous.

How does an interactive activation model such as TRACE describe this effect? According to Elman and McClelland (1988), the contrast effect can be induced by assuming connections from the phoneme level in one time slice to the feature level in adjacent time slices (as in TRACE I, Elman & McClelland, 1986). In our example, the units corresponding to /s/ and /ʃ/ would be connected laterally and downward to feature units which in turn are connected upward to the phoneme units /t/ and /k/. The downward activation from the fricative phoneme to the feature level would modulate the upcoming upward activation from the feature level to the stop phonemes. To describe the lexical effect for the case in which the two words *Christmas* and *foolish* have the same ambiguous final fricative segment, top-down connections from the word level to the phoneme level would activate the appropriate phoneme unit—/s/ and /ʃ/ in *Christmas* and *foolish*, respectively. These units would then activate downward to the feature level, leading to a contrast effect. Because of the assumed top-down activation modulating the bottom-up activation, interactive activation is central to their explanation.

However, an adequate explanation of the Elman and McClelland results does not require interactive activation. The results simply show that top-down information from the lexical level can influence the amount of information transmitted at the sublexical level. It is the lexical context that disambiguates the final segment of the context word which, in turn, influences identification of the first segment of the following word. We already know that lexical context influences identification of the segments that make up a word (Ganong, 1980). In terms of the FLMP, the lexical context and the segmental information are integrated to achieve perceptual recognition and, therefore, identification of the ambiguous segment. Elman and McClelland (1988) have extended this phenomenon to an indirect measure of identification of the critical segment (/s/ or /ʃ/) by assessing its influence on a following segment (/t/ or /k/). Although this result contributes to the validity of top-down effects on perceptual processing by making the hypothesis of a postperceptual decision less likely, the result appears to be neutral with respect to the existence of interactive activation. In fact, Figure 7 gives the fit of the FLMP to the results (Elman & McClelland, 1988, Experiment 1). Nine free parameters were estimated to predict the 28 data points: seven for the seven levels along the *tapes–capes* continuum, one for /s/ or /ʃ/ in the intact context word condition, and one for

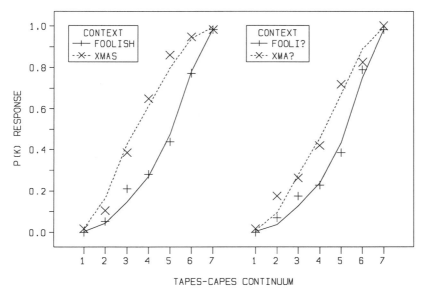

FIG. 7 Observed (*points*) and predicted (*lines*) probability of a /k/ identification as a function of stimulus and preceeding context for original and ambiguous preceding consonant. Results from Elman and McClelland (1988). The predictions are for the FLMP.

lexical context. The pure lexical context effect is seen in the right panel and the combined effect of lexical context and context segment (/s/ or /ʃ/) is shown in the left panel. It should be emphasized that the FLMP explanation is in terms of perceptual processes and is not simply a result of a postperceptual decision mechanism. We now consider extant theories of speech perception and word recognition and evaluate them within the context of empirical evidence.

V. THEORIES OF SPEECH PERCEPTION AND WORD RECOGNITION

Although there are several current theories of spoken word recognition, they can be classified and described fairly easily. All theories begin with the acoustic signal and usually end with access to a word or phrase in the mental lexicon. Six models of word recognition will be discussed to highlight some important issues in understanding how words are recognized. We review several important characteristics of the models to contrast and compare the models. Figure 8 gives a graphical presentation of these characteristics. One important question is whether word recognition is mediated or nonmediated. A second question is whether the perceiver has access to only categorical information in the word recognition process, or whether continuous information is available. A third consideration is whether information from the continuously varying signal is used on line at the lexical stage of processing, or whether there is some delay in initiating processing of the signal at the lexical stage. A fourth characteristic involves parallel versus serial access to the lexical representations in memory. The final characteristic we will consider is whether the word recognition process functions autonomously, or whether it is context-dependent.

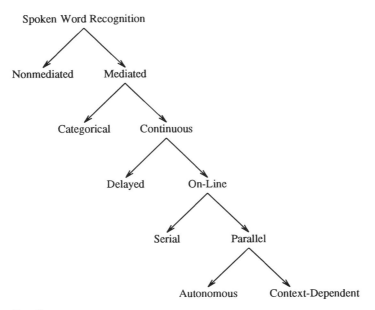

FIG. 8 Tree of wisdom illustrating binary oppositions central to the differences among theories of spoken word recognition.

A. Logogen Model

The logogen model described by Morton (1964, 1969) has had an important influence on how the field has described word recognition. Morton proposed that each word that an individual knows has a representation in long-term memory. To describe this representation, Morton used the term LOGO-GEN—*logos,* meaning 'word', and *genēs,* meaning 'born'. Each logogen has a resting level of activity, and this level of activity can be increased by stimulus events. Each logogen has a threshold—when the level of activation exceeds the threshold, the logogen fires. The threshold is a function of word frequency; more frequent words have lower thresholds and require less activation for firing. The firing of a logogen makes the corresponding word available as a response. Figure 9 gives a schematic diagram of the logogen model.

Morton's logogen model can be evaluated with respect to the five characteristics shown in Figure 8. The model is nonmediated because there is supposedly a direct mapping between the input and the logogen. That is, no provision has been made for smaller segments, such as phonemes or syllables, to mediate word recognition. The perceiver of language appears to have continuous information, given that the logogen can be activated to various degrees. On the other hand, one might interpret the theory as categorical because of the assumption of a threshold below which the logogen does not fire. Processing is on-line rather than delayed. With respect to the fourth issue, words are activated in parallel rather than serially. Finally, as can be seen in Figure 9, the logogen allows for the contribution of contextual information in word recognition. Contextual information activates logogens in the same way that information from the stimulus word itself activates logogens. The main limitation in the logogen model is

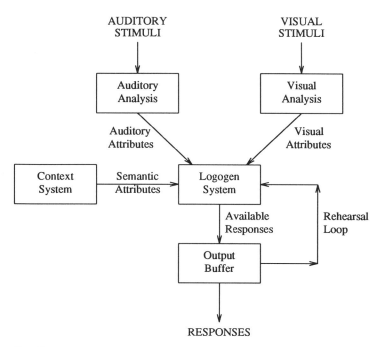

FIG. 9 A schematic diagram of the logogen model. Recognition occurs when the activation in a logogen exceeds a critical level and the corresponding word becomes available as a response (adapted from Morton & Broadbent, 1967).

its nonmediated nature. Thus, the model has difficulty explaining intermediate recognition of sublexical units (e.g., CV syllables) and how nonwords are recognized. However, an important feature of the logogen model is the assumed independence of stimulus information and context in speech perception.

B. Cohort Model

A recent influential model of word recognition is the COHORT model (Marslen-Wilson, 1984). According to this model, word recognition proceeds in a left-to-right fashion on line with the sequential presentation of the information in a spoken word. The acoustic signal is recognized phoneme by phoneme from left to right during the word presentation. Each phoneme is recognized categorically. Word recognition occurs by way of the elimination of alternative word candidates (cohorts). Recognition of the first phoneme in the word eliminates all words that do not have that phoneme in initial position. Recognition of the second phoneme eliminates all the remaining cohorts that do not have the second phoneme in second position. Recognition of phonemes and the elimination of alternative words continues in this fashion until only one word remains. It is at this point that the word is recognized. Figure 10 gives an example illustrating how the corhort model recognizes the word *elephant*.

The corhort model is easy to describe with respect to the five characteristics in Figure 8. The model is mediated, categorical, on-line, parallel, and contextu-

/ɛ/	/ɛl/	/ɛl ə /	/ɛl ə f/	/ɛl ə f ə /
aesthetic	elbow	elegiac	elephant	elephant
any	elder	elegy	elephantine	_____
.	eldest	element	_____	(1)
.	eleemosynary	elemental	(2)	
ebony	elegance	elementary		
ebullition	elegiac	elephant		
echelon	elegy	elephantine		
.	element	elevate		
.	elemental	elevation		
economic	elementary	elevator		
ecstacy	elephant	elocution		
.	elephantine	eloquent		
.	elevate	_____		
element	elevation	(12)		
elephant	.			
elevate	.			
.				
.	_____			
.	(28)			
entropy				
entry				
.				
.				
extraneous				
.				
_____				
(324)				

FIG. 10 "Illustration of how the word *elephant* is recognized, according to the cohort model (Marslen-Wilson, 1984). Phonemes are recognized categorically and on-line in a left-to-right fashion as they are spoken. All words inconsistent with the phoneme string are eliminated from the cohort. The number below each column represents the number of words remaining in the cohort set at that point in processing the spoken word. Note that the example is for British pronunciation in which the third vowel of *elephantine* is pronounced /æ/" (from Massaro, 1989a).

ally dependent to some extent. Word recognition is mediated by phoneme recognition, phonemes are recognized on-line categorically, words are accessed in parallel, and the word alternative finally recognized can be influenced by context. The primary evidence against the cohort model concerns the categorical recognition of phonemes. We have seen that phonemes are not perceptual units and the speech perception is not categorical.

As might be expected, the cohort model has not gone unmodified. Its advocates have acknowledged that the model's integrity is not critically dependent on phonemes as the unit of analysis. Thus, simpler features could be processed as they occur to establish a viable cohort. In addition, the features need not work in an all-or-none fashion, but could provide continuous activation—allowing a fuzzy boundary between words in and out of the cohort. Although the theory allows speech to be processed on line, it can also be modified to allow word recognition to occur somewhat later than the normatively ideal recognition point. These modifications are necessary to bring the model in line with empirical results, but they weaken the model considerably and make it more difficult to test against alternative models.

C. TRACE Model

The TRACE model of speech perception (McClelland & Elman, 1986) is one of a class of models in which information processing occurs through excitatory and inhibitory interactions among a large number of simple processing units. These units are meant to represent the functional properties of neurons or neural networks. Three levels or sizes of units are used in TRACE: feature, phoneme, and word. Features activate phonemes which activate words, and activation of some units at a particular level inhibits other units at the same level. In addition, an important assumption of interactive activation models is that activation of higher order units activates their lower order units; for example, activation of the /b/ phoneme would activate the features that are consistent with that phoneme.

With respect to the characteristics in Figure 8, the TRACE model is mediated, on-line, somewhat categorical, parallel, and context-dependent. Word recognition is mediated by feature and phoneme recognition. The input is processed on-line in TRACE, all words are activated by the input in parallel, and their activation is context-dependent. In principle, TRACE is continuous, but its assumption about interactive activation leads to a categorical-like behavior at the sensory (featural) level. According to the TRACE model, a stimulus pattern is presented, and activation of the corresponding features sends more excitation to some phoneme units than others. Given the assumption of feedback from the phoneme to the feature level, the activation of a particular phoneme feeds down and activates the features corresponding to that phoneme (McClelland & Elman, 1986, p. 47). This effect of feedback produces enhanced sensitivity around a category boundary, exactly as predicted by categorical perception. Evidence against phonemes as perceptual units and against categorical perception is, therefore, evidence against the TRACE model.

The TRACE model is structured around the process of interactive activation between layers at different levels and also competition within layers. Because of this process, the representation over time of one source of information is modified by another source of information. Contrary to independence predicted by the FLMP, TRACE appears to predict nonindependence of top-down and bottom-up sources of information. As discussed in Section IV,B, Massaro (1989c) varied a top-down and a bottom-up source of information in a speech identification task. An important question is whether the top-down context from the lexical level modified the representation at the phoneme level. The TRACE model accounts for the top-down effects of phonological constraints by assuming interactive activation between the word and phoneme levels. Bottom-up activation from the phoneme units activates word units, which in turn activate the phoneme units that make them up. Interactive activation appropriately describes this model because it is clearly an interaction between the two levels that is postulated. The amount of bottom-up activation modifies the amount of top-down activation, which then modifies the bottom-up activation, and so on.

In terms of the logistic results in Figure 6, an independent influence of context should simply change the spread among the curves, whereas a nonindependent effect should differentially influence their slopes. Thus, nonindependence effects would be seen in nonparallel functions, contrary to the results that are observed.

I claimed that the concept of interactive activation, as implemented in TRACE, should produce nonindependence effects (Massaro, 1989b). Take as an example a liquid phoneme presented after the initial consonant /t/. The liquid would activate both /l/ and /r/ phonemes to some degree; the difference in activation would be a function of the test phoneme. There are many English words that begin with /tr/ but none than begin with /tl/, and therefore there would be more top-down activation for /r/ than for /l/. Top-down activation of /r/ would add to the activation of the /r/ phoneme at the phoneme level. What is important for our purposes is that the amount of top-down activation is positively related to the amount of bottom-up activation. Now consider the top-down effects for the two adjacent stimuli along the /l/–/r/ continuum. Both test stimuli activate phonemes to some degree, and these phonemes activate words, which then activate these phonemes. Given that two adjacent syllables along the continuum are different, they have different patterns of bottom-up activation, and therefore, the top-down activation must also differ. The difference in the top-down activation will necessarily change the relative activation of the two phonemes. This relationship between top-down and bottom-up activation should be reflected in a nonindependent effect of top-down context.

Because the TRACE model, as originally formulated, cannot be tested directly against the results, a simulation of the experiment with TRACE was compared the observed results. A simulation allows a test of fundamental properties of TRACE rather than a concern with specific results that are primarily a consequence of the details of the implementation. Differences due to the makeup of the lexicon and specific parameter values are less important than systematic properties of the predictions. Within the current architecture of the TRACE model, the word level appears to play a fundamental role in the discrimination of alternatives at the phoneme level. The most straightforward test of this observation is to simulate results with the standard TRACE model and compare this simulation with the observed results. The simulation used the lexicon, input feature values, and parameter values given in McClelland and Elman (1986, Tables 1 and 3). Three levels of information about the liquid (*l, r,* and *L*) were used as three levels of input information. The phoneme /L/ refers to an intermediate level of a liquid phoneme with neutralized diffuse and acute feature specifications. The other feature specifications for /L/ are the same as those for /l/ and /r/. Thus, the input /L/ activates the two liquids more than the other phonemes but activates /l/ and /r/ to the same degree. These three liquids were placed after initial /t/, /p/, and /s/ contexts and followed by the vowel /i/. The simulations, therefore, involved a test of these nine stimulus conditions.

A simulation of TRACE involves presentation of a pattern of activation to the units at the feature level. The input is presented sequentially in successive time slices, as would be the case in real speech. The processing of the input goes through a number of cycles in which all the units update their respective activations at the same time, based on the activations computed in the previous update cycle. The TRACE simulation is completely deterministic; a single run is sufficient for each of the three initial consonant conditions. The activation of the /l/ and /r/ units at the phoneme level occurred primarily at the 12th time slice of the trace, and these values tended to asymptote around the 54th cycle of the simulation run. Therefore, the activations at the 12th time slice after the 54th cycle were taken as the predictions of the model. These activations cannot be taken as direct measures of the question of the independence of top-down and bottom-up sources of information. In order to assess this question, it is necessary to map these activation levels into predicted responses.

The predicted proportion of /l/ and /r/ responses is not given by the activations directly. McClelland and Elman (1986) assume that the activation a_i of a phoneme unit is transformed by an exponential function into a strength value S_i,

$$S_i = e^{ka_i} \qquad (1)$$

The parameter k is assumed to be 5. The strength value S_i represents the strength of alternative i. The probability of choosing an alternative i, $P(R_i)$, is based on the activations of all relevant alternatives, as described by Luce's (1959) choice rule.

$$P(R_i) = \frac{S_i}{\sum} \qquad (2)$$

where $\sum$ is equal to the sum of the strengths of all relevant phonemes, derived in the manner illustrated for alternative i. The activation values were translated into strength values by the exponential function given by Eq. (1). The constant k was set equal to 5. The probability of an /r/ judgment was determined from the strength values using Eq. (2).

To determine if top-down context makes an independent or nonindependent contribution, the response proportions were translated into logistic values. This analysis is analogous to the Braida and Durlach (1972) and Massaro (1979) analyses, except the logistic rather than the Gaussian transform is used. The two transforms are very similar to one another. In addition, the present analysis of independence versus nonindependence parallels the question of sensitivity versus bias in those previous studies and in Massaro (1989b). These logistic values are given in Figure 11. As can be seen in the figure, the predicted curves are not parallel. In terms of the present analysis, the contribution of top-down context is nonindependent. Thus the simulation is consistent with the intuition that interactive activation between the word and phoneme levels in TRACE produces nonindependent changes at the phoneme level (Massaro, 1988).

At first glance, the effect of the context /p/ seems strange, because there is a strong bias for /r/ rather than for /l/. One might have expected very little difference, because initial /p/ activates both /pr/ and /pl/ words. However, the makeup of the lexicon used in the simulation favored /r/ much more than /l/. In this case, the /p/ context functions more like the /t/ context.

The predictions of TRACE were also determined for other values of the constant k used in Eq. (1) that maps activations into strength values. Eight values of k were used, giving a total of eight simulated subjects. The values of k were 0.5, 1, 2, 3.5, 5, 7.5, 10, and 15. For each value of k, there was a nonindependent effect of context. Given that TRACE has been shown to predict

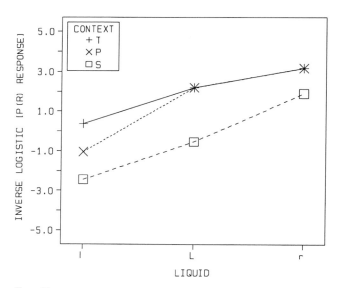

Fig. 11 Inverse logistic of the probability of an /r/ identification as a function of liquid and context. Predictions of the TRACE model (from Massaro, 1989c).

nonindependence of stimulus and context, the predictions are falsified by the actual results in Figure 6.

D. Autonomous Search Model

A fourth model is an autonomous search model that has been proposed to describe word recognition (Forster, 1979, 1981, 1985). The model involves two stages: an initial access stage and a serial search stage. This model was developed for the recognition of written words rather than for recognizing spoken words. However, advocates of the model have begun to apply its basic assumptions to spoken word recognition (Bradley & Forster, 1987). For ease of presentation, we present the model in terms of recognizing a written word.

The first stage in processing a written stimulus involves recognizing the letters that make up a word. The abstract representation of this information serves as an access code to select some subset of the lexicon. The distinctive feature of this model is that words within this subset must be processed serially. The serial order of processing is determined by the frequency of occurrence of the words in the language. After making a match in the search stage of processing, a verification or postsearch check is carried out against the full orthographic properties of the word. If a match is obtained at this stage, the relevant contents of the lexical entry are made available.

The autonomous search model can be described with respect to the five characteristics in Figure 8. The model is mediated, categorical, on-line, serial, and contextually independent. Written word recognition is mediated by letter recognition, letters are recognized on line categorically, final recognition of a word requires a serial search. All this processing goes on without any influence from the context at other levels, such as the sentence level. The autonomous

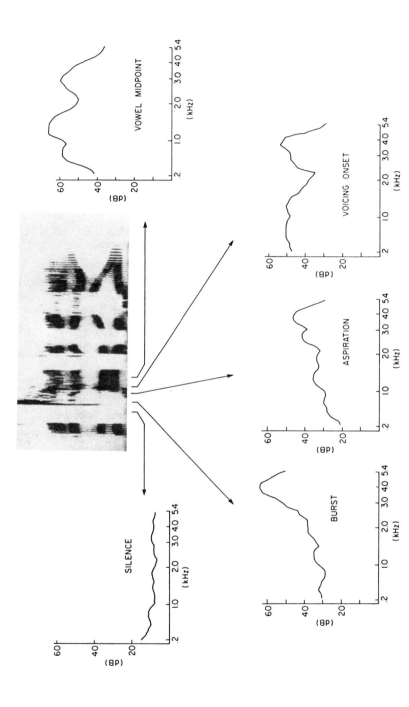

FIG. 12 "The phonetic transition from the middle of [t] to the middle of [a] . . . has been approximated by a sequence of five static critical-band spectra'' (from Klatt, 1989, p. 193).

search model appears to fail on at least two counts: categorical perception and contextually independent processing. We have reviewed evidence for continuous perception, and there is convincing evidence for the influence of context in word recognition (see section on Lexical Context).

E. Lexical Access from Spectra Model

Klatt (1979) developed a lexical access from spectra (LAFS) model that bypasses features and segments as intermediate to word recognition. The expected spectral patterns for words and for cross-word boundaries are represented in a very large decoding network of expected sequences of spectra. Figure 12 illustrates how each word is first represented phonemically, then all possible pronunciations are determined by phonetic recording rules specifying alterna-

STEP 1: LEXICAL TREE (PHONEMIC)

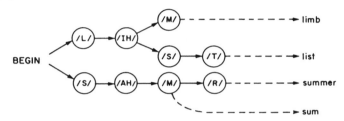

STEP 2: LEXICAL NETWORK (PHONETIC)

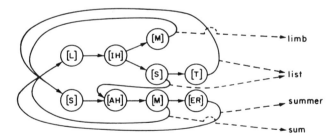

STEP 3: LEXICAL ACCESS FROM SPECTRA (SPECTRAL TEMPLATES)

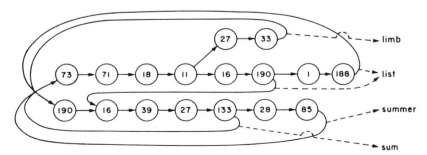

FIG. 13 The lexical tree, lexical network, and lexical access from spectra of the LAFS model (from Klatt, 1989, p. 195).

tive pronunciations within and across word boundaries, and these phonetic representations are converted to sequences of spectral templates like those shown in Figure 13. Figure 12 shows a sequence of 5 static critical-band spectra corresponding to the middle of [t] to the middle of [a].

Central to the LAFS model are the assumptions that running spectra fully represent speech and that the differences among spectra can differentiate among the meaningful differences in real speech. With respect to the five characteristics in Figure 8, the model is mediated, continuous, on line, parallel, and contextually independent. A goodness-of-match is determined for each word path based on the running spectra of the speech stimulus. The goodness-of-match provides continuous and not just categorical information. Multiple alternatives can be evaluated in parallel and on line as the speech signal arrives. Finally, the contextual dependencies built into the representation are phonologically based, and therefore there is no provision for semantic and syntactic constraints. That is, the contribution of linguistic context is limited to its effects on articulation and, therefore, properties of the speech signal. Constraints over and above this influence are not accounted for in the model. Thus, the model could not easily account for the positive contribution of linguistic context.

F. Lexical Access from Features (LAFF) Model

Stevens (1986; 1988, cited in Klatt, 1989) has articulated a model describing lexical access via acoustic correlates of linguistic binary phonetic features (LAFF). These features are language universal and binary (present or absent). The display in (1) includes a conventional featural representation of the word *pawn*. At the right it is modified to reflect expectations as to the temporal locations within the syllable of acoustic information important to the detection of feature values. In addition, features not specified by a plus or minus are deemed not critical to the lexical decision. This model is driven by parsimony in that the features are assumed to be binary and robust. Binary features allow the integration process to be shortcircuited in that multiple ambiguous sources of information do not have to be combined. With respect to the five characteristics in

(1) Conventional and Modified Lexical Representation (Stevens, 1988, cited in Klatt, 1989)

Features	Conventional			Modified		
	p	$ɔ$	n	p	$ɔ$	n
high	−	−	−		−	
low	−	+	−		+	
back	−	+	−		+	
nasal	−	−	+			+
spread glottis	+	−	−	+		
sonorant	−	+	+	−		
voiced	−	+	+	−		
strident	−	−	+			
consonantal	+	−	+	+		+
coronal	−	−	+	−		+
anterior	+	−	+	+		+
continuant	−	+	−	−		−

Figure 8, the model is mediated, categorical, delayed, parallel, and contextually independent. A goodness-of-match is determined for each word path based on the distinctive features assembled from the speech input. As we discussed in Section V,C, there is strong evidence against categorical information at the feature level. The goodness-of-match provides just categorical information with respect to each feature. Continuous information could be derived from the number of features that match each word in memory. Multiple alternatives can be evaluated in parallel, but the matching process cannot perform reliably until the complete word has been presented. Finally, the contextual dependencies built into the representation are phonologically based, and therefore there is no prescribed provision for linguistic constraints. Thus, the model has difficulty with the positive contribution of linguistic context.

G. Fuzzy Logical Model of Perception

The central thesis of this present framework is that there are multiple sources of information supporting speech perception, and the perceiver evaluates and integrates all these sources to achieve perceptual recognition. Within just the auditory signal, there are many different sources of information or cues that the listener uses to decode the message. For example, investigators have listed 16 different acoustic properties that distinguish /igi/ from /iki/. As noted earlier, perceivers also use situational and linguistic context to help disambiguate the signal. Finally, it has been repeatedly demonstrated that perceivers use information from other modalities in face-to-face communication. Both lip movements and hand gestures have been shown to aid in speech perception.

According to the fuzzy logical model of perception, well-learned patterns are recognized in accordance with a general algorithm, regardless of the modality or particular nature of the patterns (Massaro, 1987). Similar to other approaches, it is assumed that speech is processed through a sequence of processing stages (Pisoni & Luce, 1987). The model has received support in a wide variety of domains and consists of three operations in perceptual (primary) recognition: feature evaluation, feature integration, and decision. Continuously valued features are evaluated, integrated, and matched against prototype descriptions in memory, and an identification decision is made on the basis of the relative goodness-of-match of the stimulus information with the relevant prototype descriptions.

Central to the FLMP are summary descriptions of the perceptual units of the language. These summary descriptions are called prototypes, and they contain a conjunction of various properties called features. A prototype is a category, and the features of the prototype correspond to the ideal values that an exemplar should have if it is a member of that category. The exact form of the representation of these properties is not known and may never be known. However, the memory representation must be compatible with the sensory representation resulting from the transduction of the audible and visible speech. Compatibility is necessary because the two representations must be related to one another. To recognize the syllable /ba/, the perceiver must be able to relate the information provided by the syllable itself to some memory of the category /ba/.

Prototypes are generated for the task at hand. In speech perception, for example, we might envision activation of all prototypes corresponding to the perceptual units of the language being spoken. For ease of exposition, consider a speech signal representing a single perceptual unit, such as the syllable /ba/. The sensory systems transduce the physical event and make available various sources of information called features. During the first operation in the model, the features are evaluated in terms of the prototypes in memory. For each feature and for each prototype, featural evaluation provides information about the degree to which the feature in the speech signal matches the featural value of the prototype.

Given the necessarily large variety of features, it is necessary to have a common metric representing the degree of match of each feature. The syllable /ba/, for example, might have visible featural information related to the closing of the lips and audible information corresponding to the second and third formant transitions. These two features must share a common metric if they eventually are going to be related to one another. To serve this purpose, fuzzy truth values (Zadeh, 1965) are used because they provide a natural representation of the degree of match. Fuzzy truth values lie between zero and one, corresponding to a proposition being completely false and completely true. The value .5 corresponds to a completely ambiguous situation, whereas .7 would be more true than false, and so on. Fuzzy truth values, therefore, not only can represent continuous rather than just categorical information, they can also represent different kinds of information. Another advantage of fuzzy truth values is that they couch information in mathematical terms (or at least in a quantitative form). This allows the natural development of a quantitative description of the phenomenon of interest.

Feature evaluation provides the degree to which each feature in the syllable matches the corresponding feature in each prototype in memory. The goal, of course, is to determine the overall goodness of match of each prototype with the syllable. All the features are capable of contributing to this process, and the second operation of the model is called feature integration. That is, the features (actually, the degrees of matches) corresponding to each prototype are combined (or conjoined, in logical terms). The outcome of feature integration consists of the degree to which each prototype matches the syllable. In the model, all features contribute to the final value, but with the property that the least ambiguous features have the most impact on the outcome.

The third operation during recognition processing is decision. During this stage, the merit of each relevant prototype is evaluated relative to the sum of the merits of the other relevant prototypes. This relative goodness-of-match gives the proportion of times the syllable is identified as an instance of the prototype. The relative goodness-of-match could also be determined from a rating judgment indicating the degree to which the syllable matches the category. The pattern classification operation is modeled after Luce's (1959) choice rule. In pandemonium-like terms (Selfridge, 1959), we might say that it is not how loud some demon is shouting but rather the relative loudness of that demon in the crowd of relevant demons. An important prediction of the model is that one feature has its greatest effect when a second feature is at its most ambiguous level. Thus, the most informative feature has the greatest impact on the judgment.

Figure 14 illustrates the three stages involved in pattern recognition. The three stages are shown to illustrate their necessarily successive but overlapping processing. Different sources of information are represented by capital letters. The evaluation process transforms these into psychological values (indicated by lowercase letters) that are then integrated to give an overall value. The classification operation maps this value into some response, such as a discrete decision or a rating. The model confronts several important issues in describing speech perception. One fundamental claim is that multiple sources of information are evaluated in speech perception. The sources of information are both bottom-up and top-down. Two other assumptions have to do with the evaluation of the multiple sources of information. Continuous information is available from each source, and the output of evaluation of one source is not contaminated by the other source. The output of the integration process is also assumed to provide continuous information. With respect to the contrasts in Figure 8, spoken word recognition is mediated, continuous, on-line, serial and parallel, and both autonomous and context-dependent.

The theoretical framework of the FLMP has proven to be a valuable framework for the study of speech perception. Experiments designed in this framework have provided important information concerning the sources of information in speech perception and how these sources of information are processed to support speech perception. The experiments have studied a broad range of information sources, including bottom-up sources such as audible and visible characteristics of speech and top-down sources, including phonological, lexical, syntactic, and semantic constraints (Massaro, 1987).

Although the FLMP has not explicitly addressed the general problem of word recognition, its principles can easily be extended to describe spoken word recognition. The additional assumptions needed would resemble the properties already discussed in other models. Perhaps the most compatible is a neighborhood activation model (Luce, 1986), in which word recognition reduces to

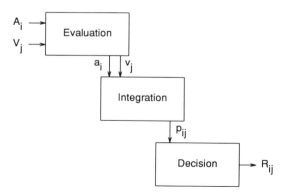

FIG. 14 Schematic representation of the three stages involved in perceptual recognition. The three stages are shown to illustrate their necessarily successive but overlapping processing. The sources of information are represented by capital letters. Auditory information is represented by A_i and visual information by V_j. The evaluation process transforms these sources of information into psychological values (indicated by lowercase letters a_i and v_j). These sources are then integrated to give an overall degree of support for a given alternative p_{ij}. The decision operation maps this value into some response R_{ij}, such as a discrete decision or a rating.

finding the best match in a set of activated word candidates (a process analogous to the decision process of the FLMP). This model is grounded in relative goodness-of-match (or activation) rather than absolute activation—again an important similarity between it and the FLMP.

H. Conclusion

We have reviewed seven current models of speech perception and word recognition. Models of speech perception are confronted with several characteristics of speech perception that are apparently easy for humans but difficult for models and machines. Some of these characteristics are listed in Table I. We now illustrate the simultaneous influence of multiple influences in a bimodal speech perception experiment.

VI. A PROTOTYPICAL EXPERIMENT

There is valuable and effective information afforded by a view of the speaker's face in speech perception and recognition by humans. Visible speech is particularly effective when the auditory speech is degraded because of noise, bandwidth filtering, or hearing impairment. As an example, the perception of short sen-

TABLE I
Aspects of Speech Perception That Cause Problems for Models but Not Listeners

Problem	FLMP solution
1. Context dependency of feature values. The value of a feature is not constant for different segments. For example, the voice onset time (VOT) for a voiced stop /gi/ is roughly equal to the VOT for the voiceless stop /pa/.	Prototypes represent V, CV, and VC syllables. The feature values for these units are relatively constant. A different VOT value can be specified for the syllables /gi/ and /pa/.
2. Spectral characteristics of speech segments are influenced by gender, age, rate of speaking, and background noise.	A prototype can consist of a disjunction of several descriptions of each syllable. There is evidence that a dozen or so descriptions could represent individuals of all ages and sexes, for example (Wilpon & Rabiner, 1985).
3. Characteristics of consonants change as a function of their vowel environment.	Same solution as 1.
4. The formant transitions of a CV vary as a function of the vowel preceding the CV.	This variation does not appear to be psychologically meaningful (Massaro & Oden, 1980).
5. Formant values for vowels change with the phonetic environment. For example, a lax front vowel (e.g., /ɪ/) changes dramatically when followed by /l/.	Same solution as 1.
6. Formant values for vowels depend on vowel duration.	There is experimental evidence that these two sources of information are processed independent of one another (Massaro, 1984).
7. Vowel duration is influenced by nonsegmental properties, such as rate of speaking, syntax, and semantics.	Parallel influences can be described by the fuzzy integration of the FLMP.

tences that have been bandpass-filtered improves from 23% correct to 79% correct when subjects are permitted a view of the speaker. This same type of improvement has been observed in hearing-impaired listeners and patients with cochlear implants (Massaro, 1987). The strong influence of visible speech is not limited to situations with degraded auditory input, however. A perceiver's recognition of an auditory-visual syllable reflects the contribution of both sound and sight (McGurk & MacDonald, 1976). If an auditory syllable /ba/ is dubbed onto a videotape of a speaker saying /da/, subjects often perceive the speaker to be saying /ða/.

To study how perceivers use both auditory and visual speech, we carried out an experiment manipulating auditory and visual information in a cross-linguistic speech perception task (Massaro, Tsusaki, Cohen, Gesi, & Heredia, 1993). Five levels of audible speech varying between /ba/ and /da/ were crossed with five levels of visible speech varying between the same alternatives. The audible and visible speech also are presented alone, giving a total of 25 + 5 + 5 = 35 independent stimulus conditions. This test procedure is called an expanded factorial design.

A five-step auditory /ba/ to /da/ continuum was synthesized by altering the parametric information specifying the first 80 ms of the consonant–vowel syllable. Using an animated face, control parameters are changed over time to produce a realistic articulation of a consonant–vowel syllable. By modifying the parameters appropriately, a five-step visible /ba/ to /da/ continuum was synthesized. The presentation of the auditory synthetic speech was synchronized with the visible speech for the bimodal stimulus presentations. All the test stimuli were recorded on videotape for presentation during the experiment. Six unique test blocks were recorded with the 35 test items presented in each block. Subjects were instructed to listen and to watch the speaker, and to identify the syllable as either /ba/ or /da/.

The points in Figure 15 give the average results for a group of Spanish-speaking subjects in the experiment (all instructions and the test were in Spanish for these subjects). As can be seen in the figure, both the auditory and visual sources influenced identification performance. There was also a significant interaction because the effect of one variable was larger to the extent that the other variable was ambiguous. The lines give the predictions of the FLMP. This model is able to capture the results of several influences on identification performance. The FLMP also predicts the results of individual subjects.

It is important to evaluate the results of individual subjects because group results can be misleading (Massaro & Cohen, 1993). All the model tests were carried out on individual subjects. The points in Figure 16 give the mean proportion of identifications for a typical Japanese-speaking subject in the same experiment. The identification judgments changed systematically with changes in the audible and visible sources of information. The likelihood of a /da/ identification increases as the auditory speech changes from /ba/ to /da/, and analogously for the visible speech. Each source has a similar effect in the bimodal conditions relative to the corresponding unimodal condition. In addition, the influence of one source of information is greatest when the other source is ambiguous.

To describe the results, the important assumption of the FLMP is that the auditory source supports each alternative to some degree and analogously for the visual source. Each alternative is defined by ideal values of the auditory

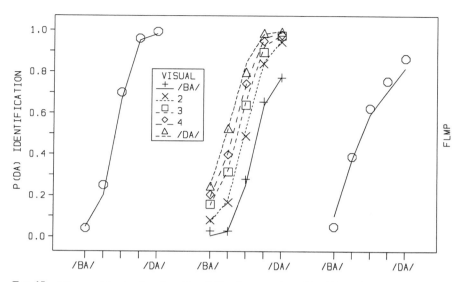

FIG. 15 Observed (*points*) and predicted (*lines*) proportion of /da/ identifications for the auditory-alone (*left*), the factorial auditory-visual (*center*), and visual-alone (*right*) conditions as a function of the five levels of the synthetic auditory and visual speech varying between /ba/ and /da/ (Spanish-speaking subjects). The lines give the predictions for the FLMP (after Massaro et al., 1993).

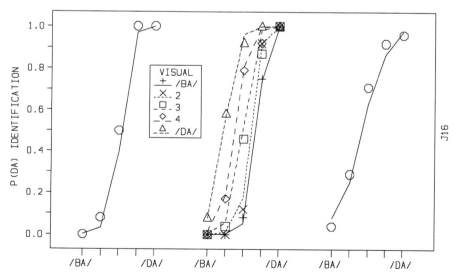

FIG. 16 The points give the mean proportion of /da/ identifications for a typical Japanese subject in the experiment as a function of the auditory and visual sources of information. The lines give the predictions of FLMP (after Massaro et al., 1993).

and visual information. Each level of a source supports each alternative to differing degrees represented by feature values. The feature values representing the degree of support from the auditory and visual information for a given alternative are integrated following the multiplicative rule given by the FLMP. The decision operation gives the response by determining the relative goodness-of-match of the relevant response alternatives. The formal model, as tested against the results, requires five parameters for the visual feature values and five parameters for the auditory feature values. The lines in Figures 15 and 16 give the predictions of FLMP. The model provides a good description of the identifications of both the unimodal and bimodal syllables.

VII. Conclusion

Our short review of research and theory indicates that speech perception might be best understood in terms of general perceptual, cognitive, and learning processes. The guiding assumption for the proposed framework is that humans use multiple sources of information in the perceptual recognition and under-standing of spoken language. In this regard, speech perception resembles other forms of pattern recognition and categorization because integrating multiple sources of information appears to be a natural function of human endeavor. Integration appears to occur to some extent regardless of the goals and motiva-tions of the perceiver. A convincing demonstration for this fact is the Stroop color-word test. People asked to name the color of the print of words that are color names printed in different colors become tongue-tied and have difficulty naming the colors. We cannot stop ourselves from reading the color word, and this interferes with naming the color of the print.

VIII. Synthetic Visible Speech and Computer Animation

Given the importance of visible speech and the perceiver's natural ability to integrate multiple sources of information, our current research goal is to develop an animation system for visible speech synthesis. A critical assumption concerns the experimental, theoretical, and applied value of synthetic speech. Auditory synthetic speech has proven to be valuable in all three of these domains. Much of what we know about speech perception has come from experimental studies using synthetic speech. Synthetic speech gives the experimenter control over the stimulus in a way that is not always possible using natural speech. Synthetic speech also permits the implementation and test of theoretical hypotheses, such as which cues are critical for various speech distinctions. The applied value of auditory synthetic speech is apparent in the multiple everyday uses for text-to-speech systems for both normal and visually impaired individuals.

We believe that visible synthetic speech will prove to have the same value as audible synthetic speech. Synthetic visible speech will provide a more fine-grained assessment of psychophysical and psychological questions not possible with natural speech. For example, testing subjects with synthesized syllables intermediate between several alternatives gives a more powerful measure of integration relative to the case of unambiguous natural stimuli. It is also obvious that synthetic visible speech will have a valuable role to play in alleviating some of the communication disadvantages of the deaf and hearing-impaired.

A main objective of our research is to identify the facial properties that are informative by evaluating the effectiveness of various properties in a synthetic animated face. Analogous to the valuable contribution of using auditory speech synthesis in speech perception research, visible speech synthesis permits the type of experimentation necessary to determine (a) what properties of visible speech are used, (b) how they are processed, and (c) how this information is integrated with auditory information and other contextual sources of information in speech perception. Our experimental and theoretical framework has been validated in several domains (Massaro, 1987), and it is ideal for addressing these questions about facial information in speech perception.

One attractive aspect of providing or using audible and visible speech jointly is the complementarity of audible and visible speech. Visible speech is usually most informative for just those distinctions that are most ambiguous auditorily. For example, places of articulation (such as the difference between /b/ and /d/) are difficult via sound but easy via sight. Voicing, on the other hand, is difficult to see visually but is easy to resolve via sound. Thus, audible and visible speech not only provide two independent sources of information; these two sources are often productively complementary. Each is strong when the other is weak.

The development of a realistic, high-quality facial display provides a powerful tool for investigation of a number of questions in auditory-visual speech perception. The analysis of the articulation of real speakers guides our development of the visible speech synthesis. In addition, perception experiments indicate how well the synthesis simulates real speakers. We expect that the results of our research will also have applications in the area of automatic lip-reading to enhance speech recognition by machine. If perceivers achieve robust recognition of speech by using multiple sources of information, the same should be true for machine recognition.

One applied value of visible speech is its potential to supplement other (degraded) sources of information. Visible speech should be particularly beneficial in poor listening environments with substantial amounts of background noise. Its use is also important for hearing-impaired individuals because it allows effective communication within speech—the universal language of the community. Just as auditory speech synthesis has proved a boon to our visually impaired citizens in human–machine interaction, visual speech synthesis should prove to be valuable for the hearing-impaired. We expect that lip-reading a stylized representation of the face is also possible. The successful use of stylized representations would make animation much easier and would allow the visible speech to be transmitted over a low-bandwidth channel such as a telephone line.

Finally, synthetic visible speech is an important part of building synthetic "actors" (Thalmann & Thalmann, 1991). We can also be confident that synthetic visible speech will play a valuable role in the exciting new sphere of virtual reality.

A. Other Channels for Speech

It is important to uncover other dimensions of input for supplementing the auditory signal in speech. One potential source of information is tactile, which appears to be naturally integrated with auditory or visual speech in the same way that auditory and visual speech are integrated. For example, deaf individuals benefit from both tactile and visual speech in the same way that hearing-impaired individuals benefit from both auditory and visual information. The value of tactile speech is also illustrated by deaf nonsighted individuals who can perceive speech by holding their hands on the speaker's face. This Tadoma method has proven to be a successful channel of communication, and it has even been demonstrated that hearing individuals can exploit this information in speech perception. Virtual reality gloves providing tactile information are now becoming commercially available. A promising line of inquiry would be to not only provide visible speech via animation, but to also transform the information into a tactile form that would be transmitted via a glove to the perceiver.

B. Psychological Theory and Technology

Although technology has outdistanced psychological theory, we believe that important applications of the former are critically dependent on the latter. We learned a lesson from human–computer interaction, in which early computer systems did not consider the psychology of the user. Now user-friendliness is a central feature of most systems. Analogously, the contributions of technology to communication will critically depend on applications that are based on sound psychological theory. I am optimistic about the contribution psycholinguistics can make to the optimal application of technological innovation.

ACKNOWLEDGMENTS

The writing of this paper was supported, in part, by grants from the Public Health Service (PHS R01 NS 20314) and the National Science Foundation (BNS 8812728).

REFERENCES

Anderson, J. R. (1990). *Cognitive psychology and its implications*. New York: Freeman.

Blumstein, S. E., & Stevens, K. N. (1979). Acoustic invariance in speech production: Evidence from measurements of the spectral characteristics of stop consonants. *Journal of the Acoustical Society of America, 66,* 1001–1017.

Blumstein, S. E., & Stevens, K. N. (1981). Phonetic features and acoustic invariance in speech. *Cognition, 10,* 25–32.

Bradley, D. C., & Forster, K. I. (1987). In U. H. Frauenfelder & L. K. Tyler (Eds.), *Spoken word recognition* (pp. 103–134). Cambridge, MA: MIT Press.

Braida, L. D., & Durlach, N. I. (1972). Intensity perception II: Resolution in one-interval paradigms. *Journal of the Acoustical Society of America, 51,* 483–502.

Chomsky, N. (1980). *Rules and representations*. Oxford: Blackwell.

Cole, R. A. (1973). Listening for mispronunciations: A measure of what we hear during speech. *Perception & Psychophysics, 13,* 153–156.

Cole, R. A., & Jakimik, J. (1978). Understanding speech: How words are heard. In G. Underwood (Ed.), *Strategies of information-processing* (pp. 67–116). London: Academic Press.

Cole, R. A., & Scott, B. (1974). Toward a theory of speech perception. *Psychological Review, 81*, 348–374.

Connine, C. M., & Clifton, C. (1987). Interactive use of lexical information in speech perception. *Journal of Experimental Psychology: Human Perception and Performance, 13*, 291–299.

Cotton, S., & Grosjean, F. (1984). The gating paradigm: A comparison of successive and individual presentation formats. *Perception & Psychophysics, 35*, 41–48.

Dennett, D. C. (1991). *Consciousness explained.* Boston: Little, Brown and Co.

Eimas, P. D. (1985, January). The perception of speech in early infancy. *Scientific American, 252*(1), 46–52.

Elman, J., & McClelland, J. (1986). Exploiting lawful variability in the speech wave. In J. S. Perkell & D. H. Klatt (Eds.), *Invariance and variability in speech processes.* Hillsdale, NJ: Erlbaum.

Elman, J., & McClelland, J. (1988). Cognitive penetration of the mechanisms of perception: Compensation for coarticulation of lexically restored phonemes. *Journal of Memory and Language, 27*, 143–165.

Flavell, J. H. (1985). *Cognitive development,* Englewood Cliffs, NJ: Prentice-Hall.

Forster, K. I. (1979). Levels of processing and the structure of the language processor. In W. Cooper & E. Walker (Eds.), *Sentence processing: Psycholinguistic studies presented to Merrill Garrett* (pp. 27–86). Hillsdale, NJ: Erlbaum.

Forster, K. I. (1981). Priming and the effects of sentence and lexical contexts on naming time: Evidence for autonomous lexical processing. *Quarterly Journal of Experimental Psychology, 33*, 465–495.

Forster, K. I. (1985). Lexical acquisition and the modular lexicon. *Language and Cognitive Processes, 1*, 87–108.

Fowler, C. (1986). An event approach to the study of speech perception from a direct-realist perspective. *Journal of Phonetics, 14*, 3–28.

Ganong, W. F. III. (1980). Phonetic categorization in auditory word recognition. *Journal of Experimental Psychology: Human Perception and Performance, 6*, 110–125.

Gleitman, L. R., & Wanner, E. (1982). Language acquisition: The state of the state of the art. In E. Wanner & L. R. Gleitman (Eds.), *Language acquisition: The state of the art* (pp. 3–48). Cambridge: Cambridge University Press.

Grosjean, F. (1980). Spoken word recognition processes and the gating paradigm. *Perception & Psychophysics, 28*, 267–283.

Grosjean, F. (1985). The recognition of words after their acoustic offset: Evidence and implications. *Perception & Psychophysics, 38*, 299–310.

Hockett, C. (1955). *Manual of phonology* (Publications in Anthropology and Linguistics, No. 11). Bloomington: Indiana University Press.

Klatt, D. H. (1979). Speech perception: A model of acoustic-phonetic analysis and lexical access. *Journal of Phonetics, 7*, 279–312.

Klatt, D. H. (1989). Review of selected models of speech perception. In W. Marslen-Wilson (Ed.), *Lexical representation and process* (pp. 169–226). Cambridge, MA: MIT Press.

Kluender, K. R., Diehl, R. L., & Killeen, P. R. (1987). Japanese quail can learn phonetic categories. *Science, 237*, 1195–1197.

Kuhl, P. K. (1987). The special-mechanisms debate in speech research: Categorization tests on animals and infants. In S. Harnad (Ed.), *Categorical perception: The groundwork of cognition* (pp. 355–386). Cambridge: Cambridge University Press.

Kuhl, P. K. (1990). Towards a new theory of the development of speech perception. *Proceedings of the 1990 International Conference on Spoken Language Processing, 2*, 745–748.

Liberman, A. M., Cooper, F. S., Shankweiler, D. P., & Studdert-Kennedy, M. (1967). Perception of the speech code. *Psychological Review, 74*, 431–461.

Liberman, A. M., Harris, K. S., Hoffman, H. S., & Griffith, B. C. (1957). The discrimination of speech sounds within and across phoneme boundaries. *Journal of Experimental Psychology, 54*, 358–368.

Liberman, A. M., & Mattingly, I. G. (1989). A specialization for speech perception. *Science, 243*, 489–494.

Lieberman, P. (1991). *Uniquely human.* Cambridge, MA: Harvard University Press.

Luce, P. A. (1986). *Neighborhoods of words in the mental lexicon* Tech. Rep. No. 6. Bloomington: Indiana University, Research on Speech Perception.

Luce, R. D. (1959). *Individual choice behavior*. New York: Wiley.

Mann, V. A., & Repp, B. H. (1981). Influence of preceding fricative on stop consonant perception. *Journal of the Acoustical Society of America, 69,* 548–558.

Marcel, A. J. (1983). Conscious and unconscious perception: An approach to the relations between phenomenal experience and perceptual processes. *Cognitive Psychology, 15,* 238–300.

Marslen-Wilson, W. D. (1973). Linguistic structure and speech shadowing at very short latencies. *Nature, 244,* 522–523.

Marslen-Wilson, W. D. (1984). Function and process in spoken word recognition: A tutorial review. In H. Bouma & D. G. Bouwhuis (Eds.), *Attention and performance X: Control of language processes* (pp. 125–150). Hillsdale, NJ: Erlbaum.

Marslen-Wilson, W. D. (1987). Functional parallelism in spoken word recognition. In U. H. Frauenfelder & L. K. Tyler (Eds.), *Spoken word recognition* (pp. 71–102). Cambridge, MA: MIT Press.

Marslen-Wilson, W. D., & Welsh, A. (1978). Processing interactions and lexical access during word recognition in continuous speech. *Cognitive Psychology, 10,* 29–63.

Massaro, D. W. (1975a). *Experimental psychology and information processing*. Chicago: Rand McNally.

Massaro, D. W. (Ed.). (1975b). *Understanding language: An information processing analysis of speech perception, reading, and psycholinguistics*. New York: Academic Press.

Massaro, D. W. (1979). Letter information and orthographic context in word perception. *Journal of Experimental Psychology: Human Perception and Performance, 5,* 595–609.

Massaro, D. W. (1984). Time's role for information, processing, and normalization. *Annals of the New York Academy of Sciences, Timing and Time Perception, 423,* 372–384.

Massaro, D. W. (1987). *Speech perception by ear and eye: A paradigm for psychological inquiry*. Hillsdale, NJ: Erlbaum.

Massaro, D. W. (1988). Ambiguity in perception and experimentation. *Journal of Experimental Psychology: General, 117,* 417–421.

Massaro, D. W. (1989a). *Experimental psychology: An information processing approach*. San Diego, CA: Harcourt Brace Jovanovich.

Massaro, D. W. (1989b). Multiple book review of *Speech Perception by Ear and Eye: A Paradigm for Psychological Inquiry. Behavioral and Brain Sciences, 12,* 741–794.

Massaro, D. W. (1989c). Testing between the TRACE model and the fuzzy logical model of perception. *Cognitive Psychology, 21,* 398–421.

Massaro, D. W., & Cohen, M. M. (1983). Evaluation and integration of visual and auditory information in speech perception. *Journal of Experimental Psychology: Human Perception and Performance, 9,* 753–771.

Massaro, D. W., & Oden, G. C. (1980). Speech perception: A framework for research and theory. In N. J. Lass (Ed.), *Speech and language: Advances in basic research and practice* (Vol. 3, pp. 129–165). New York: Academic Press.

Massaro, D. W., Tsuzaki, M., Cohen, M. M., Gesi, A., & Heredia, R. (1993). Bimodal speech perception: An examination across languages. *Journal of Phonetics, 21,* 445–478.

Mattingly, I. G., & Studdert-Kennedy, M. (Eds.). (1991). *Modularity and the motor theory of speech perception*. Hillsdale, NJ: Erlbaum.

McClelland, J. L. (1991). Stochastic interactive processes and the effect of context on perception. *Cognitive Psychology, 23,* 1–44.

McClelland, J. L., & Elman, J. L. (1986). The TRACE model of speech perception. *Cognitive Psychology, 18,* 1–86.

McGurk, H., & MacDonald, J. (1976). Hearing lips and seeing voices. *Nature (London), 264,* 746–748.

Miller, G. A. (1981). *Language and speech*. San Francisco: Freeman.

Morton, J. (1964). A preliminary functional model for language behavior. *International Audiology, 3,* 216–225.

Morton, J. (1969). Interaction of information in word recognition. *Psychological Review, 76,* 165–178.

Morton, J., & Broadbent, D. E. (1967). Passive versus active recognition models, or is your hommunculus really necessary? In W. Wathen-Dunn (Ed.), *Models for the perception of speech and visual form* (pp. 103–110). Cambridge, MA: MIT Press.

Pastore, R. E. (1987). Categorical perception: Some psychophysical models. In S. Harnad (Ed.), *Categorical perception: The groundwork of cognition* (pp. 29–52).

Peters, A. M. (1983). *The units of language acquisition.* Cambridge: Cambridge University Press.

Pisoni, D. B., & Luce, P. A. (1987). Acoustic-phonetic representations in word recognition. *Cognition, 25,* 21–52.

Pollack, I., & Pickett, J. M. (1963). The intelligibility of excerpts from conversation. *Language and Speech, 6,* 165–171.

Salasoo, A., & Pisoni, D. (1985). Interaction of knowledge sources in spoken word identification. *Journal of Memory and Cognition, 2,* 210–231.

Sampson, G. R. (1989). Language acquisition: Growth or learning? *Philosophical Papers, 18,* 203–240.

Samuel, A. G. (1981). Phonemic restoration: Insights from a new methodology. *Journal of Experimental Psychology: General, 110,* 474–494.

Selfridge, O. G. (1959). Pandemonium: A paradigm for learning. In *Mechanisation of thought processes, Proceedings of a symposium held at the National Physical Laboratory on 24–27 November 1958* (pp. 511–526). London: H. M. Stationery Office.

Stevens, K. N. (1986). Models of phonetic recognition II: A feature-based model of speech recognition. In P. Mermelstein (Ed.), *Proceedings of the Montreal satellite symposium on speech recognition, Twelfth International Congress on Acoustics.*

Studdert-Kennedy, M., Liberman, A. M., Harris, K. S., & Cooper, F. S. (1970). Motor theory of speech perception: A reply to Lane's critical review. *Psychological Review, 77,* 234–249.

Thalmann, N. M., & Thalmann, D. (1991). *Computer animation '91.* Heidelberg: Springer-Verlag.

Tyler, L. K., & Wessels, J. (1983). Quantifying contextual contributions to word-recognition processes. *Perception & Psychophysics, 34,* 409–420.

Tyler, L. K., & Wessels, J. (1985). Is gating an on-line task? Evidence from naming latency data. *Perception & Psychophysics, 38,* 217–222.

Uhlarik, J., & Johnson, R. (1978). Development of form perception in repeated brief exposures to visual stimuli. In R. D. Pick & H. L. Pick, Jr. (Eds.), *Perception and experience* (pp. 347–360). New York: Plenum.

Warren, P., & Marslen-Wilson, W. D. (1987). Continuous uptake of acoustic cues in spoken word recognition. *Perception & Psychophysics, 41,* 262–275.

Warren, R. M. (1970). Perceptual restoration of missing speech sounds. *Science, 167,* 392–393.

Warren, R. M. (1982). *Auditory perception: A new synthesis.* New York: Pergamon.

Warren, R. M., Bashford, J. A., & Gardner, D. A. (1990). Tweaking the lexicon: Organization of vowel sequences into words. *Perception & Psychophysics, 47,* 423–432.

Werker, J. (1991). The ontogeny of speech perception. In I. G. Mattingly & M. Studdert-Kennedy (Eds.), *Modularity and the motor theory of speech perception* (pp. 91–109). Hillsdale, NJ: Erlbaum.

Wickelgren, W. A. (1969). Context-sensitive coding, associative memory and serial order in speech behavior. *Psychological Review, 76,* 1–15.

Wilpon, J. G., & Rabiner, L. R. (1985). A modified k-means clustering algorithm for use in speaker-independent isolated word recognition. *IEEE Transactions ASSP-33,* 587–594.

Zadeh, L. A. (1965). Fuzzy sets. *Information and Control, 8,* 338–353.

CHAPTER 8

SPOKEN WORD RECOGNITION
RESEARCH AND THEORY

SCOTT E. LIVELY, DAVID B. PISONI, AND
STEPHEN D. GOLDINGER

I. INTRODUCTION

Spoken word recognition represents the interface between speech perception and higher levels of cognitive processing. In studying spoken word recognition, we hope to gain a better understanding of how human listeners translate acoustic signals into mental representations stored in long-term memory and how these representations are used to understand spoken language. Research on spoken word recognition is an interdisciplinary field that draws on the resources of psychologists, cognitive scientists, speech and hearing researchers, engineers, and computer scientists. Insights into spoken language processing will require many different sources of knowledge that cross a wide range of scientific disciplines. In the present chapter, we begin first by reviewing some of the basic problems of spoken language processing. Next, a number of tasks that are commonly used to study word recognition and lexical access are examined. This is followed by a brief review of different approaches to the mental lexicon and the types of mechanisms that are used to access words from memory. Finally, new directions in speech perception and spoken word recognition are discussed.

II. SPOKEN VERSUS VISUAL WORD RECOGNITION

Many current models of spoken word recognition have been developed as adaptations of models used in visual word recognition (Forster, 1976, 1979, 1987, 1989; Morton, 1969, 1970). However, important changes need to be incorporated to account for the uniqueness of speech as a temporal phenomenon. The difficulty of the translation problem can be illustrated by comparing spoken language to written language. The most obvious difference is that speech is distributed in time, whereas writing is distributed in space. This difference has two important consequences for perceptual analysis: First, a theoretical account must address how information is integrated across time. Typically, models of spoken word recognition have used a strategy that involves matching input signals to templates or static representations in memory. This template-based approach ignores the importance of the temporal distribution of information in spoken language. Second, the availability of the input differs substantially for written and spoken language. Under normal conditions, written material can be rescanned and reanalyzed when ambiguities are encountered. Spoken language, in contrast, is available to the listener only once and fades rapidly from the perceptual field. A theoretical account must address how listeners process speech so accurately, given the inherent transient nature of the signal.

In addition to differences in spatio-temporal distribution, written and spoken language also differ in several other ways. Consider the constancy of each signal. Written language demonstrates a certain amount of physical invariance: each time a writer presses a key on a typewriter, the same visual character is reproduced on the page. Spoken language, in contrast, is highly variable: each time a speaker produces a phoneme, a different acoustic form is generated. Moreover, the same word can have different acoustic realizations when it is produced by different talkers, at different speaking rates, or in different phonetic contexts (Chomsky & Miller, 1963; Lehiste, 1964; Liberman, Delattre, Cooper, & Gerstman, 1954).

The lack of acoustic-phonetic invariance in speech perception has serious consequences for models of spoken word recognition. Any model of spoken word recognition that operates via a strict template-matching strategy, or through attempts to find one-to-one correspondences between the physical signal and representations in memory, becomes very difficult to defend. Template matching would be painfully inefficient because instances of the same nominal word are never physically identical across successive productions. In general, models based on a template-matching strategy avoid the issue by allowing for partial matches and permitting confidence in the match to be proportional to the goodness of fit between the incoming signal and the item stored in memory (Klatt, 1979, 1980).

Another difference between spoken and written language deals with linearity of the message. Characters on a printed page have discrete boundaries and are linearly arrayed so that successive sounds are represented by strings of letters; speech fails to demonstrate such an orderly correspondence between the linguistic symbols used to transcribe an utterance and the speech waveform. Under conditions of linearity, a unique portion of the signal transmits information about each phoneme in the message. Thus, if phoneme X precedes phoneme Y in transcription, then the signal corresponding to X must also precede Y (Chomsky & Miller, 1963). In natural speech, phonemes overlap and are coarticulated in order to achieve transmission rates of up to 10 phonemes per second (Liberman, 1991; Liberman, Cooper, Shankweiler, & Studdert-Kennedy, 1967; Studdert-Kennedy, 1980). As a consequence, a simple invariant mapping between acoustic features and perceived phonemes has been difficult to find, despite intense research efforts over the last 45 years (Kewley-Port, 1982, 1983; Stevens & Blumstein, 1978, 1981).

The importance of the failure of linearity and invariance extends beyond issues of low-level phonetic perception. The linearity problem presents a challenge to models of spoken word recognition that assume words are recognized in a left-to-right manner by the serial activation of successive phonemes. By ignoring co-articulation, important predictive information about upcoming phonetic segments is minimized. Early commitment to a symbolic perceptual representation, like a linear string of phonemes, may lead to errors in the code that contacts the lexicon. These errors may be difficult to correct, given that important context-dependent information is lost. Klatt (1979, 1980) argued convincingly that as much acoustic information as possible should be brought to bear on the incoming signal and that commitment to any particular segmentation should be delayed. One consequence of this view is that the data-driven components of models of spoken word recognition should be sensitive to "the lawful variability in the speech waveform" (Elman & McClelland, 1986). If listeners behave according to a principle of optimality, then ignoring information in the signal may lead to suboptimal performance (Anderson, 1990).

   Another important difference between written and spoken language deals with segmentation. While letters and words are separated on the printed page, the same kind of orderly physical segmentation rarely occurs in spoken language. The lack of segmentation is illustrated in Figure 1 by comparing the upper and lower panels. Both panels show spectrograms of the sentence *I owe you a yo-yo*. Time is represented on the x-axis of each panel and frequency is represented on the y-axis. In the upper panel, the words in the sentence were spoken in isolation. In the lower panel, the words were produced fluently as a sentence. As shown here, physical boundaries do not exist between successive words composing the sentence. In fluent speech, segmentation is almost nonex-

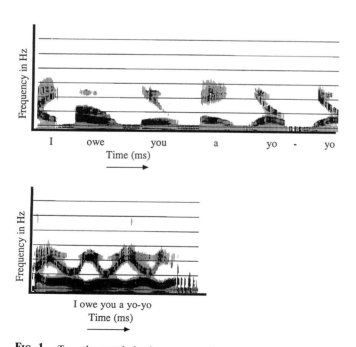

FIG. 1   *Top*, the words in the sentence *I owe you a yo-yo* spoken in isolation; *bottom*, a natural production of the same words in a sentence context.

istent and appears to be accomplished as a byproduct of the word recognition process. The lack of acoustic-phonetic segmentation creates another set of problems for theorists. If segmentation was present in speech, speaking would be tantamount to spelling, and the rapid transmission rate of spoken language would be lost (Liberman, 1991). Due to failures of linearity and invariance, simple segmentation strategies must be abandoned. Instead, context-sensitive cues for phonemes (Wicklegren, 1969), stress, and intonation contours must be used to aid in segmentation (Cutler, 1976; Cutler & Darwin, 1981; Nakatani & Schaffer, 1978).

The problems of linearity, invariance, and segmentation are summarized nicely by Hockett (1955).

> Imagine a row of Easter eggs carried along a moving belt; the eggs are of various sizes, and variously colored, but not boiled. At a certain point, the belt carries the row of eggs between the two rollers of a wringer, which quite effectively smash them and rub them more or less into each other. The flow of eggs before the wringer represents the series of impulses from the phoneme source; the mess that emerges from the wringer represents the output of the speech transmitter. At a subsequent point, we have an inspector whose task it is to examine the passing mess and decide, on the basis of the broken and unbroken yolks, the variously spread-out albumen, and the variously colored bits of shell, the nature of the flow of eggs which previously arrived at the wringer. (p. 210)

III. RESEARCH METHODS USED TO STUDY SPOKEN WORD RECOGNITION

As noted above, the inherent physical variability of the speech signal creates a number of problems for spoken word recognition. Despite the unique nature of the speech signal and the issues it raises for speech perception, the bulk of research has been conducted using auditory analogs of tasks that were originally developed to study visual word recognition. In this section, we briefly review several of the basic methods used to study spoken word recognition. We then consider some of the major empirical phenomena in spoken word recognition in the next section.

A. Perceptual Identification

PERCEPTUAL IDENTIFICATION is the simplest procedure used to study spoken word recognition. Subjects listen to isolated words and try to identify them as accurately as possible. In an open-set identification task, listeners may respond with any word; in a closed-set identification task, subjects are given a set of response alternatives prior to each trial. To reduce ceiling effects, a variety of techniques are typically used to degrade the signal. These include masking with broadband noise, signal-correlated noise, and speech babble (P. A. Luce, 1986).

Several properties of the perceptual identification task make it a useful tool for studying spoken word recognition. First, identification is assumed to be a natural extension of the processing operations that listeners normally engage in when they hear spoken words. Second, the task has proven to be useful for examining the structural relationships among words stored in the mental lexicon because it is sensitive to word frequency and lexical similarity effects (P. A. Luce, 1986). Finally, the open-response format allows for systematic examinations of the frequency and patterns of errors that subjects make under difficult listening conditions (Savin, 1963).

Despite its strengths, two problems with the perceptual identification task limit its usefulness. First, the task employs a postperceptual measure of performance, reflecting only the end product of spoken word recognition and lexical access (Levelt, 1978; Marslen-Wilson, 1987). This makes the task susceptible to postperceptual biases and guessing strategies. Second, the perceptual identification task typically requires the use of a degraded signal. Subjects may adopt sophisticated guessing strategies in response to degraded signals that do not reflect the processes normally used in spoken language comprehension (Catlin, 1969; Hasher & Zacks, 1984). As a consequence, the task may measure decision strategies rather than recognition processes.

B. Gating

Grosjean (1980) modified the standard perceptual identification task to capitalize on the temporal distribution of spoken language. In the GATING PARADIGM, only a portion of the stimulus item is presented on each trial. For example, on the first presentation, only the first 30 ms of a word is presented. During the second presentation, 60 ms of the word is presented. Stimuli are repeated in this manner until the word is recognized. In other versions of the task, the entire stimulus is masked by noise, and a proportion of the item is unmasked on each trial. Words may be gated either from their beginnings or endings (Salasoo & Pisoni, 1985). Subjects identify the stimulus after each presentation and rate the confidence of their responses.

The advantage of the gating task is that a number of dependent measures can be collected, including isolation points, recognition points, and confidence ratings. The isolation point for a stimulus occurs when sufficient acoustic-phonetic information is available to preclude all other possible candidates for recognition (Grosjean, 1980). The recognition point, in contrast, refers to the amount of stimulus information necessary to identify a stimulus word. Isolation and recognition points do not necessarily occur simultaneously. For example, recognition points can precede isolation points when words are presented in an appropriate semantic context. Interactions between the word recognition system and syntactic and semantic processors can be examined by measuring differences between isolation and recognition points.

Although the gating paradigm does take into account the temporal distribution of speech, it does not account for the failures of linearity and invariance. The acoustic phonetic information on which listeners base their responses is indeterminate because information about several phonemes may be transmitted in parallel. The criticisms of the standard perceptual identification task also apply to gating: the paradigm assesses the end product of the recognition process and is therefore susceptible to postperceptual biases and sophisticated guessing strategies. Thus, it may measure decision strategies rather than the recognition process itself.

C. Lexical Decision

In contrast to the perceptual identification and gating tasks, which use degraded stimuli, the auditory LEXICAL DECISION task requires subjects to respond to isolated stimuli presented at high signal-to-noise ratios. The task is a simple two-alternative, forced-choice procedure in which subjects classify stimuli as *words* or *nonwords*. In the auditory version of the task, subjects are presented with words and pronounceable pseudowords. (There is no auditory analog of the orthographically illegal nonword.) Both response latency and accuracy are measured. Given the simplicity of the task, response latency is typically the dependent variable of most interest, although Abrams and Balota (1991) have also used movement force and velocity as converging dependent measures.

One of the strengths of the lexical decision task is that it is very sensitive to word frequency and lexical similarity effects, two variables of primary interest. A second advantage is that it allows for the collection of response latencies in addition to accuracy measures. Finally, lexical decision is an immediate measure of processing activities and may not be susceptible to the same postperceptual biases as perceptual identification.

Although lexical decision is one of the most commonly used procedures to study spoken and visual word recognition, it is somewhat problematic. Balota and Chumbley (1984) showed that word frequency effects were inflated in lexical decision, relative to naming and semantic categorization. They argued that familiarity with stimulus items, in addition to processes involved in word recognition and lexical access, may affect decision processes. Grainger and Segui (1990) have also cautioned that the magnitude of effects observed in lexical decision can be modulated by the frequency of words that are similar to the stimulus items. They reported that response latencies and error rates increased when stimulus words were similar to at least one item that was higher in word frequency. This suggests that the composition of the stimulus set and the magnitude of lexical effects should be carefully examined before drawing any conclusions about the time-course of word recognition processes.

D. Naming

The auditory lexical decision task is a two-alternative, forced-choice procedure that was borrowed directly from the visual word recognition literature. Another task that was adapted from the visual word recognition literature is the NAMING PARADIGM. In this procedure, subjects are presented with spoken words and are asked to repeat them aloud as quickly as possible. Typically, response latencies and error rates are considered as the dependent measures. However, Balota, Boland, and Shields (1989) found that utterance durations are also reliably affected by some experimental manipulations. Thus, both the onset latency and utterance duration may provide information about the word recognition process.

Naming has become a popular task for studying word recognition for several reasons. First, the response is natural; subjects do not have to form artificial response categories, such as *word* and *nonword*. Second, the typical naming task does not require stimulus degradation in order to obtain lexical effects. Finally, the naming paradigm does not tend to overestimate the role of word frequency in the same way the lexical decision task does (Balota & Chumbley, 1984, 1985).

Despite its methodological simplicity, there has been considerable debate about the utility of the naming task in studies of visual word recognition. Balota and Chumbley (1985) have shown that naming yields word frequency effects even when the onset of production is delayed by over 1000 ms. This finding suggests that frequency effects are sensitive not only to lexical access but also to the production stage of the naming task. Thus, word frequency effects may be exaggerated by processes that are not directly related to lexical access.

With respect to visual word recognition, Paap, McDonald, Schvaneveldt, and Noel (1987) have argued further that naming may not reflect lexical access at all. Rather, they suggest that lexical and nonlexical sources of information race to provide a response (see Patterson & Coltheart, 1987). When stimulus items are orthographically regular, subjects engage a nonlexical set of grapheme-to-phoneme translation rules to complete the task. Under these conditions, naming latencies do not reflect access to the lexicon at all. Rather, response times indicate direct translation of orthographic input into phonetic output. P. A. Luce (1986) has made a similar argument concerning the auditory naming task. He suggests that naming latencies may reflect, in part, the translation of a phonological input code to an articulatory output code. Intermediate lexical processing may not be necessary. In defense of the naming task, however, Monsell, Doyle, and Haggard (1989; Monsell, 1990) have suggested that lexical effects may be masked by the output processes that are carried out in parallel with lexical access. They argue that the magnitude of lexical effects in naming are comparable to those observed in other word recognition tasks when the influence of nonlexical variables is controlled (see also Glushko, 1979).

E. Shadowing and Mispronunciation Detection

The auditory naming paradigm was an adaptation of the naming task used extensively in visual word recognition research. SHADOWING is an extension of the naming task to longer passages. In shadowing, subjects repeat spoken utterances in near synchrony with a talker. Typically, the task has been used to assess the interaction of different levels of language processing. For example, Marslen-Wilson (1985) has found that subjects actively engage in syntactic and semantic analysis of the input during shadowing. He reported that both error rates and shadowing latencies increased as syntactic, semantic, and lexical constraints in the stimulus materials were relaxed: performance decreased when stimulus materials were either syntactically, semantically, or lexically anomalous. These findings indicate that shadowers do not simply repeat the stimulus materials in an unanalyzed form. Rather, they make use of available linguistic structure.

The appeal of the shadowing task is its immediacy (Marslen-Wilson, 1985). Because subjects are required to repeat utterances as quickly as possible, the task is relatively free of postperceptual biases. However, the weakness of the task is that not all subjects perform the task in the same manner. Marslen-Wilson (1985) found that subjects were either *close* shadowers or *distant* shadowers. Close shadowers lag behind the speaker by 250 to 300 ms, while distant shadowers follow by more than 500 ms. Furthermore, distant shadowers do not become close shadowers with practice, suggesting that some strategic processing may be engaged in the task.

F. Phoneme Monitoring

Each of the tasks outlined so far has been an auditory analog of a task that was originally designed to study visual word recognition. None of these experimental techniques take into consideration the nature of segmental representations or the time course of spoken word recognition. In PHONEME MONITORING, however, access to acoustic-phonetic representations is critical. In this procedure, subjects make speeded responses whenever a target phoneme is present in a stimulus pattern. The task has been used to study the recognition of isolated spoken words (Eimas, Marcovitz-Hornstein, & Payton, 1990; Frauenfelder & Segui, 1989; Lively & Pisoni, 1990; Rubin, Turvey & van Gelder, 1976) and words embedded in semantically meaningful and anomalous sentences (Eimas & Nygaard, 1992; Foss, 1969; Foss & Blank, 1980; Foss & Gernsbacher, 1983).

The advantage of the phoneme monitoring task is that it is explicitly concerned with the dynamic unfolding of an acoustic-phonetic representation during spoken word recognition. The relative contributions of prelexical (e.g., phonemic) and lexical information can be examined over time by having subjects monitor for targets in different stimulus positions (Marslen-Wilson, 1984). The major disadvantage of the task is that the results are highly dependent on the manner in which the experiment is performed. Some studies have shown that subjects respond on the basis of a low-level acoustic-phonetic code (Foss & Blank, 1980; Foss & Gernsbacher, 1983): variables such as lexical status and word frequency do not affect response latencies. However, other findings suggest that subjects do access the mental lexicon during phoneme monitoring (Cutler, Mehler, Norris, & Segui, 1987; Eimas et al., 1990; Frauenfelder & Segui, 1989; Lively & Pisoni, 1990). These studies have shown reliable effects of word frequency, lexical status, lexical similarity, and semantic relatedness. Another difficulty with the task is that the response is unnatural. Subjects are asked to detect or categorize components of words rather than to explicitly name or identify them (McNeill & Lindig, 1973).

G. Phoneme Restoration

Another experimental procedure that has been used to study spoken word recognition is the PHONEME RESTORATION PARADIGM. In the original version of the task, Warren (1970) replaced phonemes in words with noise and found that listeners reported hearing an intact presentation of the stimulus. Samuel (1981) extended the method so that critical phonemes were either replaced by noise or had noise added to them. Subjects in Samuel's version of the task were asked to judge whether the stimuli had replaced or added noise components.

The utility of the phoneme restoration task is twofold. First, the "added versus replaced" technique allows for the separation of subjects' biases (β) and sensitivities (d') and can be used as a converging measure of the processes involved in spoken word recognition. Samuel (1981, 1986) has shown that the task is sensitive to word-initial information; words that have unique beginnings are more likely to undergo restorations in their early syllables than words that do not have unique beginnings. He has also shown that the task is sensitive to word/nonword manipulations and priming effects; d' is lower for words than for nonwords. Second, the method provides a means to study the interactions between the speech perception and word recognition systems. The drawback of the procedure is that it is a postperceptual task. Thus, only the end result of such interactions can be observed.

Taken together, the experimental methods outlined above provide several ways to study and measure access to the mental lexicon. However, each of these tasks is subject to a number of criticisms. It appears that no single task is sufficient to describe all the processes used in word recognition. Accurate accounts of the process may only be obtained after biasing and nonlexical factors are partialed out of the data. To remedy this situation, a number of theorists have emphasized the need to use converging measures from a variety of experimental procedures (Andrews, 1989, 1992; Balota & Chumbley 1984, 1985, 1990; Besner & McCann, 1987; P. A. Luce, 1986; Monsell, 1990; Monsell et al., 1989). As such, theoretical work must be developed outside the context of particular experimental tasks. Models that account for data from a single experimental paradigm are not likely to generate a complete understanding of the processes involved in spoken word recognition.

IV. SPOKEN WORD RECOGNITION PHENOMENA

A. Word Frequency Effects

The WORD FREQUENCY EFFECT is perhaps the most widely studied phenomenon in spoken word recognition. Although word counts have been almost universally obtained from written language (Kucera & Francis, 1967; Thorndike & Lorge, 1944), they are assumed to approximate the distribution of words in spoken language (see Carterette & Jones, 1974).[1]

High-frequency words are recognized faster and more accurately in almost all word recognition tasks. Savin (1963) provided one of the earliest demonstrations of the frequency effect in spoken word recognition. He presented subjects with high- and low-frequency words in white noise for perceptual identification and found that high-frequency words were recognized at lower signal-to-noise ratios than low-frequency words. Furthermore, when subjects made errors, they responded with words that were higher in frequency than the words that were actually presented. Using the gating task, Luce et al. (1984) reported that high-frequency words required less acoustic phonetic information for recognition than low-frequency words. P. A. Luce (1986) found that lexical decision times for spoken words were faster to high-frequency words than to low-frequency words. Under certain experimental conditions, the phoneme monitoring task is also sensitive to word frequency; phonemes in high-frequency words are detected faster than phonemes in low-frequency words (Eimas et al., 1990; Lively & Pisoni, 1990).

---

[1] However, it is interesting to note that the distribution of phonemes in high- and low-frequency words differs (Landuaer & Streeter, 1973). High-frequency words also tend to be shorter in duration than low-frequency words (Zipf, 1949).

A number of mechanisms have been proposed to account for the word frequency effect. The details of these mechanisms are reviewed in Section VI. For the present discussion, however, two basic approaches have been proposed: One approach suggests that frequency effects are the result of a bias; the other approach suggests that frequency effects reflect the sensitivity of the word recognition system. In his review of word frequency effects, P. A. Luce (1986) cites a number of different models that incorporate frequency as biasing information. For example, Savin (1963) proposed that subjects engage in a sophisticated guessing strategy that favors high-frequency words when stimuli are presented in noise. Guessing among alternatives is mediated by the number and frequency of the items that must be discriminated (P. A. Luce, 1986; Treisman, 1978a, 1978b). Balota and Chumbley (1984) and Broadbent (1967) have also proposed other bias-related accounts of frequency effects. Each of these approaches involves manipulating the criteria used to select a response in order to favor high-frequency words over low-frequency words.

An alternative to the bias approach is the assumption that frequency effects arise from changes in the sensitivity of the word recognition system. According to this account, the thresholds or resting activation levels of lexical representations are set in a frequency-sensitive manner (McClelland & Rumelhart, 1981; Morton, 1969). Thus, the selection criteria are the same for high- and low-frequency words, but less stimulus information is required to recognize high-frequency words.

B. Lexical Similarity Effects

While word frequency effects are assumed to reflect the statistical DISTRIBUTION of spoken words in the language, LEXICAL SIMILARITY EFFECTS reflect RELATIONSHIPS among phonetically similar words. In this case, the focus is on how the recognition of a given word is affected by the presence of other phonetically similar words in the language. One measure of similarity that has been used in the spoken word recognition literature is an adaptation of Coltheart, Develaars, Jonasson, and Besner's (1976) N-metric. The N-metric was developed to assess similarity effects in visual word recognition. Two words are considered to be visual NEIGHBORS if they differ from each other by only one letter. The auditory analog of the N-metric assumes that words are neighbors if they differ by only one phoneme (Greenberg & Jenkins, 1964; Landauer & Streeter, 1973). According to these definitions, *sand* and *wand* are visual neighbors, but not auditory neighbors; *vote* and *vogue* are auditory neighbors, but not visual neighbors; *bat* and *cat* are auditory and visual neighbors. Words that are similar to many other words come from *dense* neighborhoods: words that are similar to few other words come from *sparse* neighborhoods. Although the N-metric is only a gross measure of perceptual similarity, its use has led to a number of important findings.

Several experimental paradigms have produced consistent findings based on manipulations of lexical similarity. For example, although Savin (1963) did not explicitly manipulate perceptual similarity, he reported that misidentifications across subjects in perceptual identification were highly regular. The pattern of responses suggested that subjects were generating and selecting their responses from a set of phonetically similar alternatives. Luce found that identification accuracy was dependent on the number and frequency of neighbors of a stimulus word (P. A. Luce, 1986; see also Pisoni, Nusbaum, Luce, & Slowiaczek, 1985). Moreover, Pisoni et al. (1985) found that lexical similarity plays an important role in determining identification accuracy when stimulus words were controlled for frequency. They reanalyzed data originally collected by Hood and Poole (1980) and found that words from dense neighborhoods were identified less accurately than words from sparse neighborhoods, although all words were of equal frequency.

Treisman (1978a, 1978b) addressed the issue of lexical similarity and its effect on identification accuracy in his partial identification theory. He proposed that words can be represented as points in a multidimensional space and that identification accuracy is highly dependent on the discriminability of the items. As words become more discriminable, and thereby less similar to other words, identification accuracy increases. In the categorization literature, Krumhansl (1978) has also considered how identification of an object is affected by the presence of other similar objects. According to her DISTANCE–DENSITY MODEL, density changes the discriminability of objects in the space; objects in dense regions require finer discriminations than equally similar objects in sparse regions.

The evidence presented so far suggests that similarity effects are strictly inhibitory. That is, words from dense neighborhoods tend to be identified less accurately than words from sparse neighborhoods. However, other findings indicate that the role of similarity may depend on the nature of the task and the modality of presentation. In tasks such as auditory perceptual identification and lexical decision, a unique item must be discriminated from its competitors before a response can be provided. When a large number of alternatives must be discriminated, responses tend to be slow and inaccurate. However, when only a gross discrimination is required, responses are faster to words from dense neighborhoods. For example, words from dense neighborhoods are responded to faster than words from sparse neighborhoods in phoneme categorization (Lively & Pisoni, 1990). Similar advantages have been observed in the visual word recognition literature for words from dense neighborhoods. Andrews (1989, 1992) reported that naming and lexical decision responses to low-frequency words from dense neighborhoods were faster than responses to low-frequency words from sparse neighborhoods.

An important debate has developed in the word recognition literature concerning lexical similarity effects. One position proposes that the NUMBER of words in a neighborhood has an impact on recognition. For example, Andrews (1989, 1992) has shown advantages for words from dense neighborhoods in visual lexical decision and naming. A second position argues that similarity effects reflect the FREQUENCY of the items that must be discriminated. Grainger, O'Reagan, Jacobs, and Segui (1989; Grainger, 1990; Grainger & Segui, 1990) have shown that visual lexical decision and naming responses are slower when a stimulus word is similar to at least one word that is higher in frequency. A third position is that BOTH the number of words that must be discriminated AND their frequencies will have an impact on word recognition. P. A. Luce (1986) showed that both neighborhood size and neighborhood frequency accounted for significant and independent portions of the variance observed in auditory perceptual identification and lexical decision experiments.

C. Form-Based Priming Effects

Research on priming effects can be divided into two areas. One set of findings is concerned with relationships among the meanings of words. The other set is concerned with FORM-BASED PRIMING. In this case, researchers have been interested in how the phonetic and phonological relationships among the sound patterns of words affect recognition. Discussion here is limited to results from form-based priming studies in spoken word recognition. (For a recent review of the semantic priming literature, see Neely, 1991.)

Studies on form-based priming have been concerned with how target word recognition is affected by primes that share common phonemes or phonetic features. For example, phonological priming studies have examined how the recognition of a word such as *bull* is affected by the prior presentation of a word like *beer*. In this case, the prime and target share the phoneme /b/. Phonological priming may be contrasted with phonetic priming. In phonetic priming, the prime and target do not share any phonemes, but they do have phonetic features in common and are confusable in noise. For example, *veer* and *bull* do not share any phonemes, but are confusable in noise. *Gum* and *bull* do not share any phonemes either and are not confusable in noise. In a phonetic priming experiment, *veer* and *bull* would be presented as a trial in which the prime and target are related. *Gum* and *bull* would be presented as a trial in which the prime and target are unrelated. Subjects' speed and accuracy in recognizing *bull* are compared across conditions (Goldinger, Luce, Pisoni, & Marcario, 1992).

Several interesting findings have been reported in the form-based priming literature. Slowiaczek, Nusbaum, and Pisoni (1987) reported facilitation in perceptual identification for phonological prime–target pairs that varied in the number of overlapping phonemes. As the primes and targets became more similar, identification performance increased, relative to an unprimed baseline condition. Using a lexical decision task, however, Slowiaczek and Pisoni (1986) failed to find evidence of facilitation for phonological primes. These null results were attributed to the differing task demands of perceptual identification and lexical decision. Recently, Radeau, Morais, and Dewier (1989) reported similar null results and even inhibition in phonological priming using lexical decision and shadowing tasks. The literature is complicated further by the findings of Goldinger, Luce, and Pisoni (1989), who reported inhibition in perceptual identification when primes and targets were phonetically confusable (*bull–veer*) but did not share phonemes. Thus, it appears that phonological primes (*bull–beer*) produce facilitation when subjects are given a postperceptual task. When subjects participate in on-line tasks, however, no priming effects are observed. Further, when primes and targets are phonetically confusable, inhibition in perceptual identification is observed.

Recently, Goldinger et al. (1992) tried to account for the conflicting findings. They argued that the facilitation observed in phonological priming reflects the buildup of a bias across trials. On trials in which primes and targets were unrelated, subjects' responses were biased toward reporting items that shared phonemes with the primes. When the proportion of phonologically related items was reduced, the magnitude of the facilitatory priming effect was decreased. Furthermore, Goldinger et al. (1992) argued that while phonological priming reflects a bias, the inhibition effect in phonetic priming reflects the activation of lexical candidates. They point out that a number of models assume that activated words and phonemes inhibit similar items (P. A. Luce, 1986; McClelland & Elman, 1986). When a phonetically similar target occurs after a prime, the activation levels of its component phonemes should be inhibited, relative to the condition in which an unrelated prime was presented. Consequently, responses are slower and less accurate. Goldinger et al.'s proposal suggests that form-based priming manipulations are sensitive to both the on-line nature of lexical processing and the development of sophisticated response strategies over many experimental trials.

V. THE MENTAL LEXICON

Each of the models of spoken word recognition reviewed in this chapter assumes that contact is made with a MENTAL LEXICON when spoken words are identified. Several features of lexical representation and process must be considered before any specific models can be described. First, the mental lexicon of the average adult is very large. Oldfield (1966) estimated that adults may be familiar with 75,000 words or more. Second, words in the lexicon are accessed very quickly. For example, Oldfield (1966) claimed that words may be accessed in 500 ms, whereas Marslen-Wilson (1987) suggested that word recognition may require as little as 200 ms. Third, the mental lexicon is assumed to be represented in a specialized area of memory located in the brain's left hemisphere (Oldfield, 1966). In the remainder of this section, we discuss the traditional linguistic conception of lexical representations. Then we review several of the mechanisms that have been proposed to access words from the mental lexicon. Finally, in the last section we consider a revised view of the mental lexicon.

A. Representations

The most important issue in discussing the mental lexicon deals with the kinds of information that should be included in a lexical representation. Aitchison (1987) metaphorically describes the lexicon as a large collection of coins. Each coin represents a different lexical entry. Orthographic and phonological information are stored on one side of the coin; syntactic and semantic information are stored on the other side. These representations are assumed to be very flexible, given that speakers can alter their pronunciations and can extend the meanings of words to novel situations.

From a linguistic viewpoint, the assumption that phonological, orthographic, syntactic, and semantic information are all stored in one lexical entry is much too broad. For example, Chomsky and Halle (1968; Halle, 1985) have argued that the lexicon's purpose is to store irregular information that is not computable on the basis of syntactic or phonological rules. Halle (1985) explicitly states that

> one may speculate that space in our memory is at a premium and that we must, therefore, store in our memory as little information as possible about the

phonetic shape of each word, eliminating as many redundancies as possible and placing maximum reliance on our ability to compute the omitted information. (p. 105)

From this perspective, the lexicon serves a supporting role to the computational machinery of a generative grammar. We will see below that this approach is too rigid and that many aspects of spoken word recognition will require a more robust and flexible view of lexical representation and the role of the mental lexicon in spoken word recognition. Nevertheless, a substantial amount of research and theorizing has been done based on this view of the mental lexicon.

B. Processes I: Serial versus Parallel Processes in Word Recognition

Over the years, a number of processing mechanisms have been proposed to access and retrieve words from memory. Two aspects of these mechanisms have been of particular interest to researchers. First, there has been a concern with the nature of the comparison process. Some approaches assume a serial comparator (Forster, 1976, 1979; Paap et al., 1987; Paap, Newsome, McDonald, & Schvaneveldt, 1982), whereas others assume that the comparator handles multiple activated items in parallel (Marslen-Wilson, 1987; Morton, 1969, 1970). Second, there has been an interest in detailing the capacity limitations of the system. In other words, how many alternatives can be considered simultaneously without loss of speed or efficiency? For serial comparison models, a severe capacity limitation is imposed; only one alternative at a time is processed. In contrast, parallel models are much more flexible and powerful. One class of parallel models has no capacity limitations on the comparator (Morton, 1969, 1970). Theoretically, an infinite number of lexical items can be simultaneously considered without cost to the system. Another class of parallel models suggests that the comparator can process only a limited number of items a time (McClelland & Elman, 1986; Townsend & Ashby, 1983). Assumptions about the comparison process have important implications for predictions that different models make, particularly with respect to lexical similarity effects (Andrews, 1989).

The most restrictive class of models has assumed a limited capacity, serial comparator. Lexical entries are considered for recognition one at a time and each candidate adds to the overall processing cost. The strength of limited capacity, serial models lies in their ability to predict word frequency effects. If words are searched in a frequency-ordered way, high-frequency words will be encountered before low-frequency words (Forster, 1976, 1979). A tacit assumption of this type of mechanism is that the search is self-terminating rather than exhaustive. If the search process were exhaustive, all items would be considered prior to a response, and the advantage for high-frequency words would be lost (Forster & Bednall, 1976; Goldinger, 1989).

Several problems are apparent with a serial-ordered, self-terminating search procedure. Consider first how many items must be searched before a match is obtained. Marslen-Wilson (1985) reports that spoken words are recognized in 200–250 ms. In order to achieve this type of efficiency, the number of items that can be considered must be minimized (Feldman & Ballard, 1982). If the lexicon is divided into separate bins of lexical entries (Forster, 1976, 1979), then the size of each bin must be limited to allow for rapid search. However, this creates additional problems for serial-ordered, self-terminating models because the correct bin and item must now be selected. This forces a comparator to make two decisions in approximately 250 ms. Searching several bins in parallel would solve the problem but would also weaken the central assumption of this class of models.

A second problem for the serial-ordered, self-terminating model centers around its prediction of lexical similarity effects. In its current form, the model cannot predict effects of lexical density that are independent of word frequency. If similarity effects reflect the number of alternatives that must be considered, then the difference in processing times between two items should reflect the number of higher frequency alternatives. Thus, the model predicts that a low-frequency word with few high-frequency neighbors will be recognized more rapidly than a low-frequency item with many high-frequency neighbors. A number of findings from the visual word recognition literature contradict this prediction. Andrews (1989) reported evidence from lexical decision and naming tasks showing that low-frequency words from high-density neighborhoods are recognized faster than low-frequency words from low-density neighborhoods. Grainger's recent findings also contradict this prediction. He found that having more than one high-frequency neighbor is no more detrimental to processing than having only one higher frequency neighbor (Grainger, 1990; Grainger et al., 1989; Grainger & Segui, 1990).

Serial-ordered self-terminating models may be contrasted with unlimited capacity, parallel activation models. These models are the least restrictive; no costs are incurred by the system when multiple candidates are activated, so the system is free to consider all possible alternatives simultaneously. Frequency effects can easily be accommodated within the unlimited capacity parallel framework by a number of possible mechanisms. For example, Morton (1969, 1970) proposed that frequency is encoded into the resting activation levels of logogens—counting devices for words in memory, and Marslen-Wilson (1990) proposed activation functions of varying slopes for words differing in frequency.

Although word frequency effects can easily be accommodated in the unlimited capacity parallel framework, the effects of lexical similarity are more problematic. Because these models assume that words are activated independently of each other (Morton, 1969), they cannot predict effects of lexical similarity. Thus, the recognition of one lexical candidate should not be influenced by the activation of other candidates, in contrast to the lexical similarity effects reviewed above.

The unlimited capacity parallel models and the serial-ordered self-terminating models represent two extremes. Both types of models have difficulty in predicting the observed relationships between word frequency and lexical similarity. A third approach that can account for the findings is the limited capacity parallel models. Unlike the unlimited capacity models, these models assume that only a finite number of lexical alternatives are simultaneously considered for recognition (Townsend & Ashby, 1983).

A number of processing mechanisms can be used to produce a limited capacity model. For example, McClelland and Rumelhart (1981) and Rumelhart and McClelland (1982) functionally limited the processing capacity of their interactive activation model by assuming lateral inhibitory connections among processing units. Lateral inhibition modulates the activation level of a group of processing units; strongly activated nodes suppress the excitation levels of neighboring units. Another way of instantiating a limited capacity processing mechanism is to constrain the decision-making component. P. A. Luce (1986), for example, assumed that the number and frequency of activated candidates influences the selection of a candidate for recognition. Thus, the accuracy of the decision is affected by the number and nature of items that must be discriminated.

The power of the limited capacity parallel model lies in its ability to predict the effects of both frequency and lexical similarity. Word frequency effects can be incorporated into the model in a number of ways. For example, connectionist models assume that high-frequency words have higher resting activation levels than low-frequency words (McClelland & Rumelhart, 1981). Alternatively, connection strengths between sublexical and lexical processing units may be stronger for high-frequency words. Another possibility is to assume that frequency acts as a bias at the decision stage of word recognition (P. A. Luce, 1986).

Predictions about the effects of lexical density can also be derived directly from the limited capacity architecture. For example, these models predict a disadvantage for words from dense neighborhoods when a unique item must be identified (P. A. Luce, 1986). In this case, activation and competition among similar lexical alternatives cause responses to be slower and less accurate. Advantages for words from dense neighborhoods can also be predicted. In tasks that do not require the resolution of a unique lexical alternative, a large number of similar alternatives push the system toward a response. McClelland and Rumelhart (1981) describe this as a GANG EFFECT.

Andrews (1989) and Goldinger (1989) have argued that limited capacity, parallel activation models account for more data than either the serial self-terminating or the unlimited capacity models. However, limited capacity models may, in fact, be too powerful. Devising rigorous tests to limit this class of models is difficult. Thus, research that develops constraints on the limited capacity, parallel activation framework will provide an important contribution to our understanding of the underlying mechanisms.

C. Processes II: Autonomous versus Interactive Processes in Word Recognition

Another contemporary issue is whether language is processed by autonomous or interactive mechanisms. In the strictest form of autonomous models, the stages of linguistic processing are serial, and processing within the linguistic system is strictly unidirectional (Fodor, 1983; Garfield, 1987). High-level representations are built up from lower level representations. More important, high-level decisions cannot be used to influence the computations that take place at lower levels of representation. Thus, the incoming waveform is translated into an acoustic-phonetic representation at the first stage of processing (Studdert-Kennedy, 1980). This representation is used to access the mental lexicon. Lexical information drives processing within a syntactic module. Finally, the output of the syntactic processor is used to begin message-level computations (Forster, 1976, 1979; Garnham, 1985).

Modular models can be contrasted with interactive models. Interactive models treat comprehension as a problem in constraint satisfaction in which different levels of linguistic processing "conspire" to provide a plausible interpretation of the input (Garnham, 1985). As a consequence, syntactic and semantic information can be used to guide lexical processing.

The issue of autonomous versus interactive processing is an important problem for the models of spoken word recognition discussed below. Although most models assume that the lexicon is contacted initially via data-driven, bottom-up processes, modular and interactive models differ in how they use syntactic and semantic information during word recognition. Autonomous models claim that this information is available only after a word is recognized. In contrast, interactive models allow higher level representations to guide lexical processing.

VI. MODELS OF SPOKEN WORD RECOGNITION

Most accounts of spoken word recognition were originally derived from models of visual word recognition. The translation across modalities has not always demonstrated a concern for the basic problems of speech perception discussed earlier. Despite this oversight, three basic metaphors have been used to describe the processes involved in mapping an acoustic waveform onto a representation stored in long-term memory. One set of models assumes that words are retrieved from memory through a search process. In this case, the lexicon is endowed with special organizational properties that allow for the fast and efficient search through a large number of stored alternatives. The second class of models assumes that words are recognized through an activation process. In general, these models assume that lexical candidates are activated in proportion to their match to the incoming signal. The criteria for response selection vary from model to model, but generally items are selected on the basis of their relative activation levels. The third class of models combines assumptions from the first two types of models. These hybrid models assume that a number of candidates are initially activated and then a search process is engaged to find the proper entry. Examples of models from each class are considered here. We begin with the search model, followed by the pure activation models, and conclude with the hybrid models. Our goal is briefly to outline the design principles of each model and to point out their relative strengths and weaknesses.

A. Search Models

In its original form, Forster's AUTONOMOUS SEARCH MODEL (1976, 1979) made strong claims about the structure of the linguistic processing system and the subsystem dedicated to visual word recognition. Although the model has been revised in recent years (Forster, 1987, 1989), the original instantiation provides a pedagogically important example of an autonomous model of language processing.

According to Forster, the word recognition system is divided into several parts, as illustrated in Figure 2. One component, or peripheral access file, deals with information about how words are spelled; a second is devoted to acoustic-

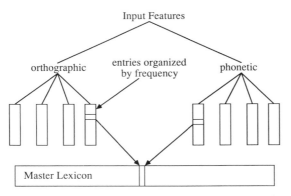

FIG. 2 The word recognition portion of Forster's autonomous search model (from Forster, 1979).

phonetic input. At the earliest stage of processing, an unrecognized pattern is submitted to the proper peripheral access file for analysis. Words in each file are arranged in a number of separate bins. Items within each bin are assumed to be arranged in descending order of frequency. Thus, high-frequency words are searched before low-frequency words. When an entry in one of the peripheral bins or access files is matched to the input, a pointer to an entry in the master lexicon is retrieved. Once the pointer has been traced into the master lexicon, properties of the word, such as its syntactic function and semantic composition are made available to the General Problem Solver (GPS). Because Forster (1976, 1979) assumes that linguistic processes operate independently of each other, word recognition is not influenced by syntactic or semantic computations. Information about the plausibility of the incoming message is sent to the GPS from the cognitive system that is responsible for extralinguistic conceptual knowledge. The role of the GPS is to collect and integrate the output from each processor and to decide how to act on that information. It serves as a control mechanism or executive to oversee the operations of the entire processing system.

Over the years, the search model has undergone extensive revision (Forster, 1987, 1989). The revised version of the search model is now similar to activation-based models discussed below. In the original model, a single comparator matched the incoming signal to lexical representations in the peripheral access files. This created a problem in terms of the number of bins that needed to be searched, relative to the observed speed of word recognition (Feldman & Ballard, 1982; Forster, 1989). In the revised model, Forster proposed a separate comparator for each bin. The addition of multiple comparators solves the problem of determining which bin to search first. As Forster points out, a logical extension of the model is to dedicate a comparator for each lexical entry. This addition, however, would effectively transform the model from a search-based model to an activation-based model and would abandon the frequency-ordered search mechanism that made the original version so appealing. A second addition to the model has been to assume different levels of activity among lexical entries (Forster, 1987). This change was motivated by a number of form-based priming findings that showed facilitation due to orthographic similarities among primes and targets. Although Forster contends that his notion of activation is qualitative rather than quantitative, these assumptions make the new model very similar to activation models (see also Grainger & Segui, 1990).

B. Activation Models

1. Morton's Logogen Model

Morton's LOGOGEN MODEL (1969, 1970, 1982) was one of the earliest examples of a direct access, activation-based model of word recognition. An overview of the logogen processing system is shown in Figure 3. Each word in the lexicon is represented by an independent, passive detecting unit called a *logogen* that contains orthographic, phonological, syntactic, and semantic information. Logogens monitor the input signal (auditory or visual) for relevant information. As information is gathered, the activation levels of the logogens rise. When a logogen has gathered enough information to cross a recognition threshold, the information contained in the logogen becomes available to the cognitive system.

The logogen model has several attributes that allow it to account for phenomena in the word recognition literature. First, the response thresholds for individual logogens can be modified by word frequency: logogens corresponding to high-frequency words have lower thresholds. This mechanism allows the model to predict word frequency effects in a task such as auditory perceptual identification because less acoustic phonetic information is required to cross the thresholds of logogens corresponding to high-frequency words.

Second, the logogen model is interactive: expectations generated from the syntactic and semantic structure of the input affect logogens' activation levels. Thus, words that are syntactically consistent with the input require less acoustic-phonetic information for recognition than they would if they were presented

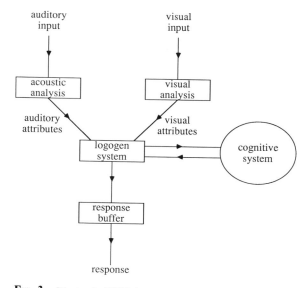

FIG. 3   Morton's (1970) logogen model of word recognition (from Morton, 1970).

in isolation. The interactive assumption also allows the model to account for semantic priming. Logogens that are semantically related to the prime are partially activated when the target is presented. Thus, when *doctor* is presented, the logogen corresponding to *nurse* also moves toward its threshold, given their semantic relation. This leads to the prediction that *nurse* should be recognized faster and/or more accurately than it would have been without the presentation of a prime.

Despite its simplicity, the logogen model has several problems. In its current instantiation, the model, like many others in the field of word recognition, is vague (Pisoni & Luce, 1987). The model is underspecified in three ways: First, the model does not specify the perceptual units that are used to map acoustic phonetic input onto logogens in memory. Second, the model does not specify how different sources of linguistic information are integrated. Finally, the model cannot account for lexical similarity effects. Because logogens are activated independently, they are unable to facilitate or inhibit the activation levels of other phonetically similar logogens. Thus, effects of lexical density cannot be accommodated by the logogen model in its present form.

2. Marslen-Wilson's Cohort Theory

Cohort theory (Marslen-Wilson, 1987, 1990; Marslen-Wilson & Welsh, 1978; Marslen-Wilson & Tyler, 1980) is example of an activation-based model that was directly motivated by several observations about spoken word recognition. First, spoken word recognition may be characterized by early selection of several hypothesized lexical candidates. Marslen-Wilson (1987) defined early selection as "the reliable identification of spoken words, in utterance contexts, before sufficient acoustic-phonetic information has become available to allow correct recognition on that basis alone" (p. 73). Second, listeners recognize words very quickly, in close to real time. Marslen-Wilson (1985, 1987) reported that word recognition occurs within 200–250 ms of the beginning of the word. Finally, spoken word recognition is a highly efficient process. Marslen-Wilson (1984, 1987, 1990) argues that listeners are very sensitive to the *recognition point* of a word—that is, the point at which the word diverges from all other possible candidates. Thus, only a minimal amount of acoustic-phonetic information is needed for accurate identification. As a consequence of these observations, Marslen-Wilson and his colleagues have proposed and developed an influential model that operates via a *contingent process*. According to cohort theory, spoken word recognition involves deciding what was presented and what was not. Thus, the recognition process involves both identification and discrimination (see P. A. Luce, 1986).

Marslen-Wilson (1987) divided spoken word recognition into three subprocesses. At the first level, the word recognition system makes contact with a low-level, acoustic-phonetic representation of the input signal. A set of lexical candidates is activated during this stage. Next, a selection process is used to choose a single item from the *word-initial cohort*. Finally, the highest level subprocessor takes the selected lexical item and integrates it into the available syntactic/semantic discourse.

For the purposes of this chapter, the access and selection mechanisms are of the most interest. Cohort theory assumes that the lexicon is initially contacted in a strictly bottom-up, data-driven manner. Abstract lexical representations stored in memory are accessed via acoustic-phonetic representations generated from the input signal. The lexical candidates generated by the access mechanism form the word-initial cohort. In the original version of the model, Marslen-Wilson and Welsh (1978) argued that each member of the word-initial cohort was assumed to have the same initial phoneme. In more recent instantiations of the model, however, the word-initial cohort for a word is assumed to contain words that have phonetically similar initial phonemes, thereby loosening the constraints on cohort membership (Marslen-Wilson, 1987).

After access, the word-initial cohort is then submitted to the selection mechanism. Unlike the access mechanism, the selection mechanism is sensitive to multiple sources of information, such as acoustic phonetic input, word frequency, and syntactic/semantic context. Marslen-Wilson (1990) suggested that the activation levels of items in the word-initial cohort change according to their overall consistency with the incoming signal. Items that are consistent with the input remain strongly activated, while the activation levels of inconsistent items drop off.

An important change has been made in the selection phase of the most recent version of cohort theory (Marslen-Wilson, 1990). Continuous activation functions have been added to the model. In early instantiations of the model, candidates were assumed to be either in or out of the cohort in a binary manner (Marslen-Wilson & Tyler, 1980; Marslen-Wilson & Welsh, 1978). With continuous activation functions, candidates can be judged relative to competitors. The change from binary to continuous activation functions now allows the model to account for word frequency effects. Marslen-Wilson (1987, 1990) assumes that high-frequency words receive more activation per unit of information than low-frequency words. This assumption predicts that low-frequency words will be harder to recognize in the context of high-frequency words because the activation levels of high-frequency words dominate, even after they are no longer consistent with the acoustic-phonetic input or the syntactic/semantic context. Thus, low-frequency words with high-frequency competitors may be recognized more slowly or less accurately due to the high activation levels of similar high-frequency words. P. A. Luce (1986) has made the same point concerning the importance of the relative frequencies of competitors in the recognition process (see also Grainger, 1990).

In evaluating cohort theory as a model of spoken word recognition, two desirable properties are apparent. First, the model is explicit concerning the time course of spoken word recognition. Unlike models derived from visual word recognition, cohort theory acknowledges the temporal nature of speech. The concept of the recognition point of a word gives the model considerable power in determining when a word can be discriminated from other lexical candidates and helps to account for the real-time nature of spoken word recognition. Second, the model acknowledges the importance of the beginnings of words and the left-to-right nature of spoken word recognition (Cole & Jakimik, 1980; Pisoni & Luce, 1987). For example, Marslen-Wilson and Welsh (1978) found that phonemes near the ends of words were restored more often during shadowing than phonemes at the beginnings of words. Similarly, Cole, Jakimik, and Cooper (1978) found that mispronunciations in word beginnings were detected more accurately than in word endings.

The importance attached to word-initial information in cohort theory is also a problem with the model. It is difficult to understand how listeners recover from errors caused by activating the wrong word-initial cohort. Marslen-Wilson

(1987) has attempted to make the model more flexible by assuming that items are represented featurally, rather than phonemically. In this case, all items in the new word-initial cohort share similar initial phonemes, but all the initial phonemes need not be the same. With this softening of assumptions, however, some mechanism needs to be provided to explain how the acoustic signal is transformed into phonetic features. And, it should be pointed out that recognition points are defined by left-to-right segmental structure, not a featural similarity metric. Although a bottom-up access phase is still plausible, the access mechanism needs to explain how the acoustic signal is mapped onto what is essentially an idealized symbolic, featural representation of speech.

3. McClelland and Elman's TRACE Model

The TRACE model of speech perception and spoken word recognition (Elman & McClelland, 1986; McClelland, 1991; McClelland & Elman, 1986) was designed to deal explicitly with the problems of variability, linearity, and segmentation. It is a connectionist model, based on McClelland and Rumelhart's interactive activation model of visual word recognition (1981; Rumelhart & McClelland, 1982). Individual processing units, or nodes, are dedicated to features, phonemes, and words. Nodes at each level of representation are highly interconnected. Feature nodes are connected to phoneme nodes, and phoneme nodes are connected to word nodes. In addition to between-level connections, units at the same level are also interconnected. Connections between levels are strictly facilitatory, symmetric, and bidirectional; connections within levels are inhibitory. This assumption lends interactivity to the model because higher level lexical information can influence the activation of phonemes at lower levels. Nodes influence each other in proportion to their activation levels and the strengths of their interconnections.

Unlike the logogen model, TRACE provides an explicit description of the time course of speech perception and spoken word recognition. The concept of a *trace,* which represents the working memory of the model, comes from assumptions about excitatory and inhibitory connections among processing units and temporal distribution of inputs. Activation levels of consistent units are increased as inputs are presented to the model, due to the excitatory connections between layers of nodes: activation levels among competing nodes are inhibited in proportion to their degree of overlap. As excitation and inhibition are passed among the network's nodes, a pattern of activation, or trace, is developed to represent the processing history of the input. The selection of a unique item for recognition from the activated candidates is governed by R. D. Luce's (1959) choice rule.

TRACE has several appealing properties as a model of speech perception and spoken word recognition. First, it is a dynamic model because the recognition process is viewed as a temporally extended event. Unlike logogen, TRACE gives an explicit account of the unfolding of spoken word recognition. Second, TRACE's use of bidirectional connections between levels of representation gives an explicit account of how data-driven and conceptually driven processes interact. Third, because of its architecture, TRACE deals with problems unique to spoken word recognition, such as linearity and segmentation. Fourth, TRACE can account for a number of phenomena in the speech perception and spoken word recognition literature without making ad hoc assumptions. For example, TRACE shows boundary shifts in categorical perception by using high-level lexical information to resolve ambiguous phoneme segments in favor of those that create words (Ganong, 1980). This falls naturally out of the inter-active activation architecture, with no additional assumptions required.

In spite of the model's strong points, two serious weaknesses of TRACE need to be considered. First, the model's treatment of time is unrealistic because each phoneme is assumed to have the same duration. Klatt (1989) has pointed out that this assumption ignores the inherent temporal variability of speech. Second, TRACE has only a very small lexicon of monosyllabic words. It is unclear how the model will perform if it is scaled up to a more realistic estimate of the size of the adult lexicon.

4. Luce's Neighborhood Activation Model

P. A. Luce's NEIGHBORHOOD ACTIVATION MODEL (NAM; Goldinger et al., 1989; P. A. Luce, 1986; Luce, Pisoni, & Goldinger, 1990) is an activation-based processing instantiation of R. D. Luce's (1959) biased choice rule. The fundamental principle underlying the model is that both frequency and percep-tual similarity affect recognition. According to NAM, the frequencies of items in a word's similarity neighborhood have an important impact on recognition.

The importance of neighborhood size and structure has been formalized using R. D. Luce's (1959) biased choice rule [Equation (1)]. As applied in NAM, the rule predicts that the probability of correctly identifying a stimulus word S_i is a frequency-weighted function of the probability that the stimulus word was presented versus the frequency-weighted probabilities that other similar words N_{ij} were presented. Similarity is estimated as a measure of confusability among consonant–vowel and vowel–consonant sequences that are independent of any word or its neighbors. It is quantified in Eq. (1) by the conditional probability terms, which represent the conditional probabilities of identifying segments in the stimulus word. Viewed this way, the similarity between two words is a conditional probability of confusing one sequence of conso-nant–vowel and vowel–consonant combinations with another.

$$p(\mathrm{ID}_{S_i}) = \frac{\left[\prod_{i=1}^{n} p(\mathrm{PS}_i/\mathrm{PS}_i)\right]\mathrm{Freq}\ S_i}{\left\{\left[\prod_{i=1}^{n} p(\mathrm{PS}_i/\mathrm{PS}_i)\right]\mathrm{Freq}\ S_i\right\} + \sum_{j=1}^{\#\ \mathrm{neighbors}} \left\{\left[\prod_{i=1}^{n} p(\mathrm{PN}_{ij}/\mathrm{PS}_i)\right]\mathrm{Freq}\ N_j\right\}} \quad (1)$$

By definition, similarity is a relationship among two or more objects. In contrast, bias is a measure applied to a single object (Nosofsky, 1991a). Word frequency is a bias term in NAM that modulates the importance of similarity among words. As Eq. (1) states, the probability of identifying a word with few neighbors is high. When a low-frequency word with several high-frequency neighbors is presented, the probability of identifying the stimulus is low, due to the frequency-weighted neighborhood similarity term in the denominator of Eq. (1). Similarly, a low-frequency word with many high-frequency neighbors will be even less accurately identified for the same reason. Thus, NAM predicts that the probability of correctly identifying a word will depend on the size and composition of the word's similarity neighborhood.

Lexical processing in NAM occurs by activating acoustic-phonetic patterns for the forms of words in memory and their corresponding decision units (P. A. Luce, 1986; P. A. Luce et al., 1990). During word recognition, decision units monitor the activity level of the acoustic-phonetic patterns. Initially, they are sensitive only to low-level acoustic phonetic activation and are completely data-driven. As the decision units become more active, they broaden the scope of information to which they are sensitive. Luce has suggested that decision units continue to monitor the incoming acoustic-phonetic signal, as well as the overall activity level of the other decision units and higher level lexical information (P. A. Luce, 1986; P. A. Luce et al., 1990). The strength of the set of candidate words proposed for recognition is assessed in each unit by the application of the frequency-biased choice rule.

In many respects, NAM is similar to cohort theory. Both are data-driven, bottom-up models that rely on acoustic-phonetic information for initial access to the lexicon. The use of activation levels that are proportional to the match with the incoming signal is a common property of all activation-based models of recognition. However, NAM also has several other properties that make it desirable as a model of spoken word recognition. First, NAM explicitly considers the size and structure of similarity neighborhoods in making predictions about the speed and accuracy of spoken word recognition (see also Treisman, 1978a, 1978b). Second, NAM displays generality. If the particular representations assumed by the model are ignored, then the model simply reduces to an instantiation of R. D. Luce's biased choice rule. The applicability of this rule extends far beyond problems in spoken word recognition. For example, Nosofsky (1986, 1987, 1988, 1991b) has applied the rule successfully to predict recognition, categorization, and identification performance with simple visual stimuli, and Townsend has applied the rule to problems in visual letter identification (Townsend & Ashby, 1982; Townsend & Landon, 1982). Viewed in a larger context, NAM is an attempt to move the study of spoken word recognition from a psycholinguistic subdiscipline into the mainstream of current research and theorizing in cognitive psychology.

C. Activation–Search Models

1. Paap's Activation–Verification Model

Paap et al.'s ACTIVATION–VERIFICATION MODEL combines aspects of the pure activation theories described above with the search model proposed by Forster (Becker & Killion, 1977; Paap et al., 1982, 1987). Although the model was originally designed to account for the word superiority effect in visual word recognition, it can be extended in a straightforward manner to address spoken word recognition.

The activation–verification model divides word recognition into three subprocesses. First, the physical stimulus is translated into a form that is used to activate items stored in the lexicon. Paap et al. assume that low-level visual features are used to activate letters. The activation level of letters is modulated by their confusability with other letters in isolation. *Mutatis mutandis,* acoustic-phonetic features activate phoneme patterns for spoken words. Second, the activation levels of the letters or phonemes are used to determine the activation of words in the lexicon. Many words may be contacted at the encoding stage by low-level input. Finally, a threshold limits the number of items that are passed on to the verification stage. Verification is similar to Forster's autonomous search model; candidates are considered serially and their order is determined by word frequency. During verification, a goodness-of-fit statistic is used by the decision subprocess to determine matches and mismatches between activated candidates and the input. If the statistic falls below a criterion established by the decision mechanism, the candidate is rejected. However, if it is sufficiently large, the candidate is recognized.

2. Klatt's Lexical Access from Spectra

The LEXICAL ACCESS FROM SPECTRA model (LAFS) is another example of a hybrid activation and search model (Klatt, 1979, 1980, 1989). Klatt argues that previous models of speech perception and spoken word recognition have failed to acknowledge the importance of variability in spoken language. He notes that these models have all assumed an intermediate level of representation (phonemes) that is removed from the physical signal. A generic representation of these traditional models is displayed in the left panel of Figure 4. Klatt proposes that phonemes may not be necessary for word recognition and lexical access. He rejects the assumption of phonetic representations on the grounds that they may be error-prone. If the representation used to search for candidates is errorful, there may be no graceful way to recover. Instead, Klatt assumes that spoken words are recognized directly from an analysis of the input spectrum using a large network of diphones, or phoneme–phoneme combinations (e.g. consonant–vowel and vowel–consonant sequences). His basic approach is illustrated in the right panel of Figure 4.

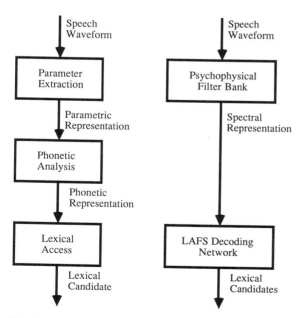

FIG. 4 *Left*, a traditional model of speech perception and word recognition in which an intermediate phonetic level is computed; *right*, the LAFS framework, which carries out lexical access directly, without any intermediate level of analysis (adapted from Klatt, 1979).

Klatt (1979, 1980) argues that diphones, which are measured from the center of one phoneme to the center of the next phoneme, are sufficiently invariant to provide accurate recognition directly from the incoming signal without computing an intermediate representation. Diphones are linked through connections that represent phonological rules. As shown in Figure 5, the interconnections of templates via phonological rules allows for the recognition of consecutive words such as *list some,* despite the deletion of the word-final /t/ in *list.* The combination of diphones and phonological rules creates a precompiled network of lexical information in memory.

When processing spoken language, inputs to the LAFS network are matched against the stored spectral templates in 10 ms intervals. Klatt (1979) suggests that this interval respects the limits on the rate of spectral change in speech and the psychophysical resolving powers of the human auditory system. LAFS delays commitment to a particular item until a beam search is conducted through the network of activated nodes. The beam search prunes away alternatives that are less consistent with the acoustic input. At the end of the beam search, the diphones for the best match to the input remain active. The use of

Step 1: lexical tree (phonemic)

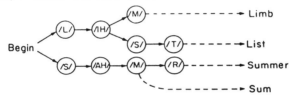

Step 2: lexical network (phonetic)

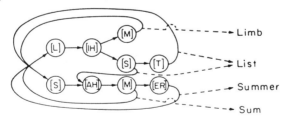

Step 3: lexical access from spectra (spectral templates)

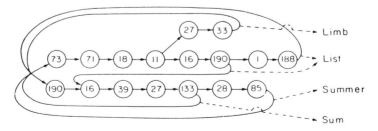

FIG. 5 A portion of the LAFS network showing phonemic, phonetic, and spectral templates (from Klatt, 1979).

the activation and beam search technique is similar to the recognition algorithm employed in the HARPY speech understanding system, an early computer-based speech recognition system (Lowerre, 1976; Lowerre & Reddy, 1978).

Since all lexical knowledge is precompiled in LAFS, Klatt had to propose a system for phonetic analysis in order to cope with the problem of recognizing unfamiliar words and nonwords. The phonetic analysis system, SCRIBER, is conceptually similar to LAFS. SCRIBER's output, however, is a phonetic transcription of the input signal. New words discovered by SCRIBER are submitted to processes of morphological decomposition and phonemic analysis. Relevant phonological rules are applied to the phonemic analysis, and a set of spectral diphone representations is derived. These templates are then added to the LAFS module. Future encounters with the unknown string are recognized directly from the acoustic spectrum.

In addition to using spectral representations as a means of direct lexical access, another important difference between LAFS and other models of spoken word recognition is that LAFS is a noninteractive model. Klatt argues that syntactic and semantic information is not used to constrain the set of activated lexical alternatives generated by the LAFS module. Thus, LAFS is a strictly feedforward word recognition network that determines which lexical items will be passed on for later syntactic and semantic analysis.

Another major difference between LAFS and other models of spoken word recognition concerns the model's assumptions about the relationship between speech perception and word recognition. LAFS was motivated by very specific problems in speech perception, such as the lack of segmentation and the acoustic-phonetic invariance problem. These issues are addressed through the use of phonological rules that concatenate spectral diphone sequences. Klatt also claims that, in addition to handling these problems, the model is capable of handling issues such as talker normalization, prosody (rhythm and stress), and changes in speaking rate. For example, talker normalization is accomplished by generating a set of templates that are talker-dependent. General knowledge about the talker's dialect can be obtained through an analysis of the connectivity patterns of the diphone sequences. Thus, the network represents both specific and general information about talkers (Klatt, 1979, 1980). The influence of prosody on word recognition can also be accounted for by considering patterns of connectivity among diphone sequences. For example, the words *CONduct* and *conDUCT* share templates in their second syllables. However, the paths taken to that shared representation differ between the two items. The beam search recovers different paths to distinguish the two items.

Normalization for speaking rate is handled in a different manner. The network activates templates in correspondence to their match with the incoming signal. If the signal does not change rapidly, as when a talker speaks slowly, then successive templates are activated slowly. Similarly, changes such as phonetic and phonological reduction and segment deletions that occur when a talker speaks rapidly are handled by the connectivity patterns among the spectral templates.

Although Klatt's model is impressive in terms of the way it approaches the acoustic and phonological properties of spoken language, several criticisms can be raised. First, the principle of delayed commitment creates problems when placed in the context of continuous discourse (Grosjean & Gee, 1987). If recognition is delayed until after a word's offset, then an unwieldy number of lexical candidates may rapidly become active. This problem could be constrained by allowing syntactic and semantic information to influence the activation of lexical alternatives. However, this solution violates the spirit of the model in at least two ways. First, it is not clear how this restriction would be implemented, making the model less quantifiable. Second, the current model is driven by acoustic information only; Klatt's goal was to see how well such a limited model could explain how acoustic signals are translated into lexical candidates. The addition of high-level, interactive processes would make the model less parsimonious. Another problem with LAFS concerns its ability to account for empirical data. It is not clear how frequency effects would be accounted for by LAFS. Although Klatt's model provides a promising engineering approach to spoken word recognition, its psychological implications are limited and need to be assessed in behavioral experiments with human listeners.

VII. NEW DIRECTIONS IN SPEECH PERCEPTION AND SPOKEN WORD RECOGNITION

In Section V,A, the traditional linguistic perspective on the mental lexicon was reviewed (Chomsky & Halle, 1968; Halle, 1985). This view is based on economy of storage and heavy reliance on the computational machinery of syntactic rules. However, a radically different view of the mental lexicon is suggested by several recent models in the human memory literature. These so-called EPISODIC or INSTANCE-BASED models suggest that a highly detailed representation of every stimulus pattern is encoded and retained in long-term memory (Eich, 1982, 1985; Gillund & Shiffrin, 1984; Hintzman, 1986; Humphreys, Bain, & Pike, 1989; Murdock, 1982; Raaijmakers & Shiffrin, 1981). Representations include the stimulus and information about its surrounding context. Retrieval is accomplished by comparing new inputs to all traces stored in long-term memory in parallel (Hintzman, 1986). Stored traces that are similar to the input are counted as strong evidence toward the recognition of the input. Forgetting occurs by assuming that memory traces cannot remain uncorrupted indefinitely, so traces decay over time (Hintzman, 1986) or are obscured by new traces (Eich, 1982). Thus, information about the fine details of a specific occurrence of a word may be lost over time.

Several lines of evidence suggest that human listeners retain more than just abstract, canonical forms of words in memory. First, a number of studies have shown that information about a talker's voice plays an important role in spoken word recognition. For example, Mullennix and Pisoni (1990) showed that source information is integrally perceived along with the phonetic form of a word in a Garner speeded classification task (Garner, 1974). Their findings suggest that voice information cannot be consciously ignored when recognizing spoken words. Memory experiments by Martin, Mullennix, Pisoni, and Summers (1989) and Goldinger, Pisoni, and Logan (1991) have shown that listeners encode detailed information about a talker's voice into long-term memory. Under certain experimental conditions, voice information can be used to facilitate recall. More recently, Palmeri, Goldinger, and Pisoni (1993) found that episodic information about a talker's voice is also available for explicit recognition judgments.

Finally, Goldinger (1992) showed that the perceptual similarity among voices affects the size of the repetition effect: stronger effects were observed for words repeated in the same voice or a perceptually similar voice than for words repeated in a dissimilar voice. Taken together, these studies demonstrate that detailed perceptual information is not lost or filtered out of lexical representations.

Second, recent findings on the perceptual effects of speaking rate have also provided important new information about the nature of lexical representations in spoken word recognition. Sommers, Nygaard, and Pisoni (1992) found that words produced at multiple speaking rates were less intelligible than the same words produced at a single rate. In another experiment, they found that words presented at different amplitudes were identified as accurately as words presented at a single amplitude. These findings suggest that some sources of variability may be more detrimental to word recognition than others. Finally, in a recent memory study, Nygaard, Sommers, and Pisoni (1992) found that lists of words produced at a single speaking rate were recalled more accurately than lists of the same words produced at multiple speaking rates. This difference was confined to the primacy portion of the serial position curve. Nygaard et al.'s results indicate that low-level variability in the speech signal due to speaking rate may affect both encoding and rehearsal processes.

Taken together, the findings on encoding of variability discussed above indicate that lexical representations may be far more detailed and robust than theorists have typically assumed in the past. Important sources of variability may be episodically encoded into long-term memory. Moreover, this information may be used to facilitate the recognition of new stimulus patterns (Jacoby & Brooks, 1984). Continued investigations of stimulus variability in speech perception and spoken word recognition should provide valuable information about the detailed nature of lexical representation and process.

VIII. SUMMARY AND CONCLUSIONS

In recent reviews of the word recognition literature, Marslen-Wilson (1990) and Forster (1989) have commented that current models of spoken word recognition are becoming increasingly similar to each other. In their original forms, many of the models considered in earlier sections made strong predictions about the effects of different lexical variables on speed and accuracy. As each of these proposals failed various empirical tests, the models were revised and tested again. Many of the core assumptions that differentiated the various models have been weakened or lost, and this revision process has led to a convergence of the models on a few basic principles. Below, we consider several general themes that are common among contemporary models of spoken word recognition.

A. Activation

A common theme adopted by almost all current models of word recognition is the activation of multiple candidates during the early recognition process. The assumption of a strict serial search through the entire lexicon becomes untenable when the size of the lexicon is compared to the speed and efficiency of word recognition (Feldman & Ballard, 1982; Forster, 1987, 1989). The plausibility of serial search is stretched even further when the demands on a comparison mechanism are considered. As a result, parallel activation and search mechanisms are a component of almost every model of word recognition, including Forster's (1989) revised search model.

Many of the proposals about the activation process converge on the same theme, namely, that the activation levels are graded, rather than binary. Marslen-Wilson (1990) has modified cohort theory so that the strengths of candidates' activations are assumed to decay continuously as they become inconsistent with the acoustic phonetic input. This change from the original version of cohort theory, which assumed all-or-none activation functions, makes the model strikingly similar to NAM, TRACE, and LAFS.

B. Selection Rules

Several models have also assumed a small set of selection rules which attempt to describe how a unique word is selected from a pool of possible candidates. Models such as NAM and TRACE have used versions of R. D. Luce's (1959) choice rule to decide among multiple candidates. In its pure form, the choice rule considers the activation level of a candidate relative to the activation levels of all other candidates in the set. Another selection rule adopts the best fitting candidate as the choice for recognition. For example, LAFS applies a beam search technique to prune away implausible lexical paths. Selection of an item is then made on the basis of the best fit among the remaining candidates. Similarly, Paap et al. (1982) use a goodness-of-fit statistic to select the best candidate for recognition.

C. Translation from Physical to Mental

Another metaphor shared by many models addresses the common problem of the translation of the physical signal into a form that can make contact with some symbolic code in lexical memory. With the exception of LAFS, models of spoken word recognition operate via a process that matches the input against stored representations based on the acoustic-phonetic structure of the word (Forster, 1979; P. A. Luce, 1986; Marslen-Wilson, 1987; McClelland & Elman, 1986). The assumption that the physical signal is translated into an abstract segmental representation prior to contact with the mental lexicon is one that requires further inquiry. The mechanisms responsible for this transformation have remained unspecified in most models. Furthermore, the size of the linguistic unit derived from this transformation is also problematic. Evidence for phonemic units can be cited for English, but support for larger units, such as syllables, can be drawn from word recognition studies performed in French (Segui, Frauenfelder, & Mehler, 1981). At the present time, there is little agreement among theorists about the size or number of the basic perceptual units in spoken word recognition. As Klatt points out, the issue of the linguistic unit of contact may be misguided, given that access to the lexicon could be initiated via a match to the neural, nonlinguistic translation of the physical signal. The issue of perceptual units in speech perception and spoken word recognition clearly remains an important theoretical problem for further study.

D. Word Recognition and Cognition

Although questions about the nature of linguistic representations and units of access are important to the study of spoken word recognition, there is a broader question that most models have failed to address. For the most part, contemporary models of spoken word recognition have been artificially divorced from the rest of cognition. In our view, the process of word recognition and lexical access should be viewed as an integral part of a coherent cognitive system that is employed in learning, memory, categorization, and countless other activities. None of these processes can be considered truly independent of one another. By definition, spoken word recognition involves matching an acoustic-phonetic pattern to a representation in long-term memory. Given the inherent variability of speech, the process of contacting items in long-term memory may be viewed as an act of categorization in which a token must be matched to a type stored in the mental lexicon. Clearly, issues relevant to memory and categorization apply to spoken word recognition as well: Is the recognized token discarded after contact with an abstract, canonical representation? Or, is the token and all of its contextual baggage stored in memory and then used in recognizing a later token? Although issues of prototype and examplar storage have been popular topics of debate in the recent memory and categorization literature (Smith & Medin, 1981), these topics are seldom touched on in the spoken word recognition literature (but see Goldinger, 1992; Jusczyk, 1992). In our view, research on spoken word recognition will advance only when the major theoretical issues are treated as specific subproblems of memory, categorization, and learning. The recent findings on the perceptual effects of talker and rate variability discussed above provide support for this conclusion.

A promising new direction is the research carried out by Grossberg and his colleagues, who have attempted to account for a diverse body of data spanning the fields of word recognition, memory, categorization, and even neuroscience within the framework of one global model, Adaptive Resonance Theory (ART) (Carpenter & Grossberg, 1986; Grossberg & Stone, 1986). ART is a self-organizing dynamic system that treats learning and memory as integral events. With respect to word recognition, ART has been applied to semantic priming, lexical decision results from a variety of experimental conditions, and numerous recognition and recall studies (Grossberg & Stone, 1986). The appeal of ART is that it incorporates a broad theoretical perspective and can be applied to problems in many different areas of research.

In summary, future progress in spoken word recognition will require taking a somewhat broader perspective than previous theoretical accounts of speech perception and spoken word recognition. In its current state, the spoken word recognition literature is filled with a number of very similar models, all containing slight variants of the same sets of ideas and principles. It is appropriate to reiterate Forster's (1989) concern that, in the future, researchers working on spoken word recognition will need to focus on developing a set of design principles for the next generation of models, rather than trying to decide whose interpretation of a particular model is the best. We believe that new models of spoken word recognition will be strengthened substantially by relating them directly to many of the current issues and theoretical efforts in learning, memory, and categorization.

References

Abrams, R. A., & Balota, D. A. (1991). Mental chronometry: Beyond reaction time. *Psychological Science, 2,* 153–157.

Aitchison, J. (1987). *Words in the mind: An introduction to the mental lexicon.* New York: Blackwell.

Anderson, J. R. (1990). *The adaptive character of thought.* Hillsdale, NJ: Erlbaum.

Andrews, S. (1989). Frequency and neighborhood effects on lexical access: Activation or search. *Journal of Experimental Psychology: Learning, Memory, and Cognition, 15,* 802–814.

Andrews, S. (1992). Frequency and neighborhood effects on lexical access: Lexical similarity or orthographic redundancy. *Journal of Experimental Psychology: Learning, Memory, and Cognition, 18,* 234–254.

Balota, D. A., Boland, J. E., & Shields, L. W. (1989). Priming in pronunciation: Beyond pattern recognition and onset latency. *Journal of Memory and Language, 28,* 14–36.

Balota, D. A., & Chumbley, J. I. (1984). Are lexical decisions a good measure of lexical access? The role of word frequency in the neglected decision stage. *Journal of Experimental Psychology: Human Perception and Performance, 10,* 340–357.

Balota, D. A., & Chumbley, J. I. (1985). The locus of word-frequency effects in the pronunciation task: Lexical access and/or production? *Journal of Memory and Language, 24,* 89–106.

Balota, D. A., & Chumbley, J. I. (1990). Where are the effects of frequency in visual word recognition tasks? Right where we said they were! Comment on Monsell, Doyle, and Haggard (1989). *Journal of Experimental Psychology: General, 119,* 231–237.

Becker, C. A., & Killion, T. H. (1977). Interaction of visual and cognitive effects in word recognition. *Journal of Experimental Psychology: Human Perception and Performance, 3,* 389–401.

Besner, D., & McCann, R. S. (1987). Word frequency and pattern distortion in visual word identification: An examination of four classes of models. In M. Coltheart (Ed.), *Attention and performance XII: The psychology of reading* (pp. 201–219). Hillsdale, NJ: Erlbaum.

Broadbent, D. E. (1967). Word-frequency effect and response bias. *Psychological Review, 74,* 1–15.

Carpenter, G. A., & Grossberg, S. (1986). Neural dynamics of category learning and recognition: Structural invariants, reinforcement, and evoked potentials. In M. L. Commons, S. M. Kosslyn, & R. J. Hernstein (Eds.), *Pattern recognition in animals, people, and machines.* Hillsdale, NJ: Erlbaum.

Carterette, E. C., & Jones, M. H. (1974). *Informal speech: Alphabetic and phonemic texts with statistical analyses and tables.* Los Angeles: University of California Press.

Catlin, J. (1969). On the word-frequency effect. *Psychological Review, 76,* 504–506.

Chomsky, N., & Halle, M. (1968). *The sound pattern of English.* New York: Harper & Row.

Chomsky, N., & Miller, G. (1963). Introduction to formal analysis of natural languages. In R. D. Luce, R. Bush, & E. Galanter (Eds.), *Handbook of mathematical psychology* (Vol. 2). New York: Wiley.

Cole, R. A., & Jakimik, J. (1980). A model of speech perception. In R. A. Cole (Ed.), *Perception and production of fluent speech.* Hillsdale, NJ: Erlbaum.

Cole, R. A., Jakimik, J., & Cooper, W. E. (1978). Perceptibility of phonetic features in fluent speech. *Journal of the Acoustical Society of America, 64,* 44–56.

Coltheart, M., Develaar, E., Jonasson, J. T., & Besner, D. (1976). Access to the internal lexicon. In S. Dornic (Ed.), *Attention and performance VI.* Hillsdale, NJ: Erlbaum.

Cutler, A. (1976). Phoneme monitoring reaction time as a function of preceding intonation contour. *Perception & Psychophysics, 20,* 55–60.

Cutler, A., & Darwin, C. J. (1981). Phoneme-monitoring reaction time and preceding prosody: Effects of stop closure duration and of fundamental frequency. *Perception & Psychophysics, 29,* 217–224.

Cutler, A., Mehler, J., Norris, D., & Segui, J. (1987). Phoneme identification and the lexicon. *Cognitive Psychology, 19,* 141–177.

Eich, J. E. (1982). A composite holographic associative memory model. *Psychological Review, 89,* 627–661.

Eich, J. E. (1985). Levels of processing, encoding specificity, elaboration and CHARM. *Psychological Review, 92,* 1–38.

Eimas, P. D., Marcovitz-Hornstein, S. B., & Payton, P. (1990). Attention and the role of dual codes in phoneme monitoring. *Journal of Memory and Language, 29,* 160–180.

Eimas, P. D., & Nygaard, L. C. (1992). Contextual coherence and attention in phoneme monitoring. *Journal of Memory and Language, 31,* 375–395.

Elman, J. L., & McClelland, J. L. (1986). Exploiting lawful variability in the speech waveform. In J. S. Perkell & D. H. Klatt (Eds.), *Invariance and variability in speech processes* (pp. 360–385). Hillsdale, NJ: Erlbaum.

Feldman, J. A., & Ballard, D. H. (1982). Connectionist models and their properties. *Cognitive Science, 6,* 205–254.

Fodor, J. A. (1983). *The modularity of mind.* Cambridge, MA: MIT Press.

Forster, K. I. (1976). Accessing the mental lexicon. In R. J. Wales & E. Walker (Eds.), *New approaches to language mechanisms.* Amsterdam: North-Holland.

Forster, K. I. (1979). Levels of processing and the structure of the language processor. In W. E. Cooper & E. C. T. Walker (Eds.), *Sentence processing: Psycholinguistic studies presented to Merill Garrett.* Hillsdale, NJ: Erlbaum.

Forster, K. I. (1987). Form-priming with masked primes: The best-match hypothesis. In M. Coltheart (Ed.), *Attention and performance XII: The psychology of reading.* Hillsdale, NJ: Erlbaum.

Forster, K. I. (1989). Basic issues in lexical processing. In W. Marslen-Wilson (Ed.), *Lexical representation and process* (pp. 75–107). Cambridge, MA: MIT Press.

Forster, K. I., & Bednall, E. S. (1976). Terminating and exhaustive search in lexical access. *Memory & Cognition, 4,* 53–61.

Foss, D. J. (1969). Decision processes during sentence comprehension: Effects of lexical item difficulty and position upon decision times. *Journal of Verbal Learning and Verbal Behavior, 8,* 457–462.

Foss, D. J., & Blank, M. A. (1980). Identifying the speech codes. *Cognitive Psychology, 12,* 1–31.

Foss, D. J., & Gernsbacher, M. A. (1983). Cracking the dual code: Toward a unitary model of phoneme identification. *Journal of Verbal Learning and Verbal Behavior, 22,* 609–632.

Frauenfelder, U. H., & Segui, J. (1989). Phoneme monitoring and lexical processing: Evidence for associative context effects. *Memory & Cognition, 17,* 134–140.

Ganong, W. F. (1980). Phonetic categorization in auditory word perception. *Journal of Experimental Psychology: Human Perception and Performance, 6,* 110–115.

Garfield, J. (1987). *Modularity in knowledge representation and natural-language understanding.* Cambridge, MA: MIT Press.

Garner, W. (1974). *The processing of information and structure.* Potomac, MD: Erlbaum.

Garnham, A. (1985). *Psycholinguistics: Central topics.* London: Methuen.

Gillund, G., & Shiffrin, R. M. (1984). A retrieval model for both recognition and recall. *Psychological Review, 91,* 1–67.

Glushko, R. J. (1979). The organization and activation of orthographic knowledge in reading aloud. *Journal of Experimental Psychology: Human Performance and Perception, 5,* 674–691.

Goldinger, S. D. (1989). *Neighborhood density effects for high frequency words: Evidence for activation-based models of word recognition. Research on speech perception* (Progress Report No. 15, pp. 163–186). Bloomington: Indiana University Press.

Goldinger, S. D. (1992). *Words and voices: Implicit and explicit memory for spoken words. Research on speech perception* (Tech. Rep. No. 7). Bloomington: Indiana University Press.

Goldinger, S. D., Luce, P. A., & Pisoni, D. B. (1989). Priming lexical neighbors of spoken words: Effects of competition and inhibition. *Journal of Memory and Language, 28,* 501–518.

Goldinger, S. D., Luce, P. A., Pisoni, D. B., & Marcario, J. K. (1992). Form-based priming in spoken word recognition: The roles of competition and bias. *Journal of Experimental Psychology: Learning, Memory, & Cognition, 18,* 1211–1238.

Goldinger, S. D., Pisoni, D. B., & Logan, J. S. (1991). On the locus of talker variability effects in recall of spoken word lists. *Journal of Experimental Psychology: Learning, Memory, and Cognition, 17,* 152–162.

Grainger, J. (1990). Word frequency and neighborhood frequency effects in lexical decision and naming. *Journal of Memory and Language, 29,* 228–244.

Grainger, J., O'Reagan, J. K., Jacobs, A. M., & Segui, J. (1989). On the role of competing word units in visual word recognition: The neighborhood frequency effect. *Perception & Psychophysics, 45,* 189–195.

Grainger, J., & Segui, J. (1990). Neighborhood frequency effects in visual word recognition: A comparison of lexical decision and masked identification latencies. *Perception & Psychophysics, 47,* 191–198.

Greenberg, J. H., & Jenkins, J. J. (1964). Studies in the psychological correlates of the sound system of American English. *Word, 20,* 157–177.

Grosjean, F. (1980). Spoken word recognition processes and the gating paradigm. *Perception & Psychophysics, 28,* 299–310.

Grosjean, F., & Gee, J. P. (1987). Prosodic structure and spoken word recognition. *Cognition, 25,* 135–155.

Grossberg, S., & Stone, G. (1986). Neural dynamics of word recognition and recall: Attentional priming, learning, and resonance. *Psychological Review, 93,* 46–74.

Halle, M. (1985). Speculations about the representation of words in memory. In V. Fromkin (Ed.), *Phonetic linguistics* (pp. 101–114). New York: Academic Press.

Hasher, L., & Zacks, R. (1984). Automatic processing of fundamental information. *American Psychologist, 39,* 1372–1388.

Hintzman, D. L. (1986). "Schema abstraction" in a multiple-trace memory model. *Psychological Review, 93,* 411–423.

Hockett, C. (1955). *Manual of phonology* (Publications in Anthropology and Linguistics, No. 11). Bloomington: Indiana University.

Hood, J. D., & Poole, J. P. (1980). Influence of the speaker and other factors affecting speech intelligibility. *Audiology, 19,* 434–455.

Humphreys, M. S., Bain, J. D., & Pike, R. (1989). Different ways to cue a coherent memory system: A theory for episodic, semantic, and procedural tasks. *Psychological Review, 96,* 208–233.

Jacoby, L. L., & Brooks, L. R. (1984). Nonanalytic cognition: Memory, perception, and concept learning. In G. Bower (Ed.), *The psychology of learning and motivation* (Vol. 18). Orlando, FL: Academic Press.

Jusczyk, P. (1992). Infant speech perception and the development of the mental lexicon. In H. C. Nusbaum & J. C. Goodman (Eds.), *The transition from speech sounds to spoken words: The development of speech perception.* Cambridge, MA: MIT Press.

Kewley-Port, D. (1982). Measurement of formant transitions in naturally produced consonant–vowel syllables. *Journal of the Acoustical Society of America, 72,* 379–389.

Kewley-Port, D. (1983). Time-varying features as correlates of place of articulation in stop consonants. *Journal of the Acoustical Society of America, 73,* 322–335.

Klatt, D. H. (1979). Speech perception: A model of acoustic-phonetic analysis and lexical access. *Journal of Phonetics, 7,* 279–312.

Klatt, D. H. (1980). Speech perception: A model of acoustic-phonetic analysis and lexical access. In R. A. Cole (Ed.), *Perception and production of fluent speech.* Hillsdale, NJ: Erlbaum.

Klatt, D. H. (1989). Review of selected models of speech perception. In W. Marslen-Wilson (Ed.), *Lexical representation and process* (pp. 169–226). Cambridge, MA: MIT Press.

Krumhansl, C. L. (1978). Concerning the applicability of geometric models to similarity data: The interrelationship between similarity and spatial density. *Psychological Review, 85,* 445–463.

Kucera, F., & Francis, W. (1967). *Computational analysis of present day American English.* Providence, RI: Brown University Press.

Landauer, T., & Streeter, L. A. (1973). Structural differences between common and rare words: Failure of equivalence assumptions for theories of word recognition. *Journal of Verbal Learning and Verbal Behavior, 12,* 119–131.

Lehiste, I. (1964). Acoustic characteristics of selected English consonants. *International Journal of American Linguistics, 30,* 10–115.

Levelt, W. J. M. (1978). A survey of studies of sentence perception. In W. J. M. Levelt & G. B. Flores d'Arcais (Eds.), *Studies in the perception of language.* New York: Wiley.

Liberman, A. M. (1991). *The relation of speech to reading and writing.* Unpublished manuscript.

Liberman, A. M., Cooper, F. S., Shankweiler, D. S., & Studdert-Kennedy, M. (1967). Perception of the speech code. *Psychological Review, 74,* 431–461.

Liberman, A. M., Delattre, P. C., Cooper, F. S., & Gerstman, L. H. (1954). The role of consonant–vowel transitions in the perception of the stop and nasal consonants. *Psychological Monographs, 68,* 1–13.

Lively, S. E., & Pisoni, D. B. (1990). *Some lexical effects in phoneme categorization: A first report. Research on speech perception,* (Progress Report No. 16). Bloomington: Indiana University, Speech Research Laboratory.

Lowerre, B. T. (1976). *The HARPY speech recognition system.* Unpublished doctoral dissertation, Carnegie Mellon University, Pittsburgh.

Lowerre, B. T., & Reddy, D. R. (1978). The HARPY speech understanding system. In W. A. Lea (Ed.), *Trends in speech recognition.* New York: Prentice-Hall.

Luce, P. A. (1986). *Neighborhoods of words in the mental lexicon.* Unpublished doctoral dissertation, Indiana University, Bloomington.

Luce, P. A., Pisoni, D. B., & Manous, L. M. (1984). *Isolation points and frequency effects in the gating paradigm: Predictions from an on-line data-base. Research on speech perception* (Progress Report No. 10). Bloomington: Indiana University, Speech Research Laboratory, 303–310.

Luce, P. A., Pisoni, D. B., & Goldinger, S. D. (1990). Similarity neighborhoods of spoken words. In G. T. M. Altmann (Ed.), *Cognitive models of speech processing: Psycholinguistic and computational perspectives.* Cambridge, MA: MIT Press.

Luce, R. D. (1959). *Individual choice behavior.* New York: Wiley.

Marslen-Wilson, W. D. (1984). Function and process in spoken word recognition. In H. Bouma & D. G. Bouwhuis (Eds.), *Attention and performance X: Control of language processes* (pp. 125–150). Hillsdale, NJ: Erlbaum.

Marslen-Wilson, W. D. (1985). Speed shadowing and speech comprehension. *Speech Communication, 4,* 55–73.

Marslen-Wilson, W. D. (1987). Functional parallelism in spoken word-recognition. *Cognition, 25,* 71–102.

Marslen-Wilson, W. D. (1990). Activation, competition, and frequency in lexical access. In G. T. M. Altmann (Ed.), *Cognitive models of speech processing: Psycholinguistic and computational perspectives.* Cambridge, MA: MIT Press.

Marslen-Wilson, W. D., & Tyler, L. K. (1980). The temporal structure of spoken language understanding. *Cognition, 8,* 1–71.

Marslen-Wilson, W. D., & Welsh, A. (1978). Processing interactions during word-recognition in continuous speech. *Cognitive Psychology, 10,* 29–63.

Martin, C. S., Mullennix, J. W., Pisoni, D. B., & Summers, W. V. (1989). Effects of talker variability on recall of spoken word lists. *Journal of Experimental Psychology: Learning, Memory, and Cognition, 15,* 676–684.

McClelland, J. L. (1991). Stochastic interactive processes and the effect of context on perception. *Cognitive Psychology, 23,* 1–44.

McClelland, J. L., & Elman, J. L. (1986). The TRACE model of speech perception. *Cognitive Psychology, 18,* 1–86.

McClelland, J. L., & Rumelhart, D. E. (1981). An interactive-activation model of context effects in letter perception: Part I. An account of basic findings. *Psychological Review, 88,* 375–407.

McNeill, D., & Lindig, L. (1973). The perceptual reality of phonemes, syllables, words and sentences. *Journal of Verbal Learning and Verbal Behavior, 12,* 419–430.

Monsell, S. (1990). Frequency effects in lexical tasks: Reply to Balota and Chumbley. *Journal of Experimental Psychology: General, 119,* 335–339.

Monsell, S., Doyle, M. C., & Haggard, P. N. (1989). Effects of frequency on visual word recognition tasks: Where are they? *Journal of Experimental Psychology: General, 118,* 43–71.

Morton, J. (1969). Interaction of information in word recognition. *Psychological Review, 76,* 165–178.

Morton, J. (1970). Word recognition. In J. Morton & J. D. Marshall (Eds.), *Psycholinguistics 2: Structure and processes* (pp. 107–156). Cambridge, MA: MIT Press.

Morton, J. (1982). Disintegrating the lexicon: An information processing approach. In J. Mehler, E. Walker, & M. Garrett (Eds.), *On mental representation.* Hillsdale, NJ: Erlbaum.

Mullennix, J. W., & Pisoni, D. B. (1990). Stimulus variability and processing dependencies in speech perception. *Perception & Psychophysics, 47,* 379–390.

Murdock, B. B., Jr. (1982). A theory for the storage and retrieval of item and associative information. *Psychological Review, 89,* 609–626.

Nakatani, L. H., & Schaffer, J. A. (1978). Hearing "words" without words: Prosodic cues for word perception. *Journal of the Acoustical Society of America, 63,* 234–245.

Neely, J. H. (1991). Semantic priming effects in visual word recognition: A selective review of current findings and theories. In D. Besner & G. Humphreys (Eds.), *Basic issues in reading: Visual word recognition* (pp. 264–336). Hillsdale, NJ: Erlbaum.

Nosofsky, R. M. (1986). Attention, similarity, and the identification–categorization relationship. *Journal of Experimental Psychology: General, 115,* 39–57.

Nosofsky, R. M. (1987). Attention and learning processes in the identification and categorization of integral stimuli. *Journal of Experimental Psychology: Learning, Memory, and Cognition, 14,* 700–708.

Nosofsky, R. M. (1988). Exemplar-based accounts of relations between classification, recognition and typicality. *Journal of Experimental Psychology: Learning, Memory, and Cognition, 14,* 700–708.

Nosofsky, R. M. (1991a). Stimulus bias, asymmetric similarity, and classification. *Cognitive Psychology, 23,* 94–140.

Nosofsky, R. M. (1991b). Tests of an exemplar model for relating perceptual classification and recognition memory. *Journal of Experimental Psychology: Human Perception and Performance, 17,* 3–27.

Nygaard, L. C., Sommers, M. S., & Pisoni, D. B. (1992). Effects of speaking rate and talker variability on the recall of spoken words. *Journal of the Acoustical Society of America, 91,* 2340.

Oldfield, R. C. (1966). Things, words, and the brain. *Quarterly Journal of Experimental Psychology, 18,* 340–353.

Paap, K. R., McDonald, J. E., Schvaneveldt, R. W., & Noel, R. W. (1987). Frequency and pronounceability in visually presented naming and lexical-decision tasks. In M. Coltheart (Ed.), *Attention and performance XII: The psychology of reading* (pp. 221–244). Hillsdale, NJ: Erlbaum.

Paap, K. R., Newsome, S. L., McDonald, J. E., & Schvaneveldt, R. W. (1982). An activation–verification model for letter and word recognition: The word-superiority effect. *Psychological Review, 89,* 573–594.

Palmeri, T. J., Goldinger, S. D., & Pisoni, D. B. (1993). Episodic encoding of voice attributes and recognition memory for spoken words. *Journal of Experimental Psychology: Learning, Memory and Cognition, 19,* 309–328.

Patterson, K., & Coltheart, V. (1987). Phonological processes in reading: A tutorial review. In M. Coltheart (Ed.), *Attention and performance XII: The psychology of reading* (pp. 421–447). Hillsdale, NJ: Erlbaum.

Pisoni, D. B., & Luce, P. A. (1987). Acoustic-phonetic representations in word recognition. *Cognition, 25,* 21–52.

Pisoni, D. B., Nusbaum, H. C., Luce, P. A., & Slowiaczek, L. M. (1985). Speech perception, word recognition, and the structure of the lexicon. *Speech Communication, 4,* 75–95.

Raaijmakers, J. G. W., & Shiffrin, R. M. (1981). Search of associative memory. *Psychological Review, 88,* 93–134.

Radeau, M., Morais, J., & Dewier, A. (1989). Phonological priming in spoken word recognition: Task effects. *Memory & Cognition, 17,* 525–535.

Rubin, P., Turvey, M. T., & van Gelder, P. (1976). Initial phonemes are detected faster in spoken words than in spoken nonwords. *Perception & Psychophysics, 19,* 394–398.

Rumelhart, D. E., & McClelland, J. L. (1982). An interactive model of context effects in letter perception: Part 2. The perceptual enhancement effect and some tests and extensions of the model. *Psychological Review, 89,* 60–94.

Salasoo, A., & Pisoni, D. B. (1985). Interaction of knowledge sources in spoken word identification. *Journal of Verbal Learning and Verbal Behavior, 24,* 210–234.

Samuel, A. G. (1981). Phonemic restoration: Insights from a new methodology. *Journal of Experimental Psychology: General, 110,* 474–494.

Samuel, A. G. (1986). The role of the lexicon in speech perception. In H. Nusbaum & E. Schwab (Eds.), *Pattern recognition by humans and machines: Speech perception* (Vol. 1, pp. 89–111). Orlando, FL: Academic Press.

Savin, H. B. (1963). Word-frequency effect and errors in the perception of speech. *Journal of the Acoustical Society of America, 35,* 200–206.

Segui, J., Frauenfelder, U., & Mehler, J. (1981). Phoneme monitoring, syllable monitoring, and lexical access. *British Journal of Psychology, 72,* 471–477.

Slowiaczek, L. M., Nusbaum, H. C., & Pisoni, D. B. (1987). Phonological priming in auditory word recognition. *Journal of Experimental Psychology: Learning, Memory, and Cognition, 13,* 64–75.

Slowiaczek, L. M., & Pisoni, D. B. (1986). Effects of phonological similarity on priming in auditory lexical decision. *Memory & Cognition, 14,* 230–237.

Smith, E. E., & Medin, D. L. (1981). *Categories and concepts.* Cambridge, MA: Harvard University Press.

Sommers, M. S., Nygaard, L. C., & Pisoni, D. B. (1992). The effects of speaking rate and amplitude variability on perceptual identification. *Journal of the Acoustical Society of America, 91,* 2340.

Stevens, K. N., & Blumstein, S. E. (1978). Invariant cues for place of articulation in stop consonants. *Journal of the Acoustical Society of America, 64,* 1358–1368.

Stevens, K. N., & Blumstein, S. E. (1981). The search for invariant acoustic correlates of phonetic feature. In P. D. Eimas & J. L. Miller (Eds.), *Perspectives on the study of speech* (pp. 1–38). Hillsdale, NJ: Erlbaum.

Studdert-Kennedy, M. (1980). Speech perception. *Language and Speech, 23,* 45–66.

Thorndike, E. L., & Lorge, I. (1944). *The teacher's word book of 30,000 words.* New York: Teacher's College Press.

Townsend, J. T., & Ashby, F. G. (1982). Experimental test of contemporary models of visual letter recognition. *Journal of Experimental Psychology: Human Perception and Performance, 8,* 834–864.

Townsend, J. T., & Ashby, F. G. (1983). *Stochastic modeling of elementary psychological processes.* Cambridge: Cambridge University Press.

Townsend, J. T., & Landon, D. E. (1982). An experimental and theoretical investigation of the constant-ratio rule and other models of visual letter confusion. *Journal of Mathematical Psychology, 25,* 119–162.

Treisman, M. (1978a). Space or lexicon? The word frequency effect and the error response frequency effect. *Journal of Verbal Learning and Verbal Behavior, 17,* 37–59.

Treisman, M. (1978b). A theory of the identification of complex stimuli with an application to word recognition. *Psychological Review, 85,* 525–570.

Warren, R. M. (1970). Perceptual restoration of missing speech sounds. *Science, 176,* 392–393.

Wicklegren, W. A. (1969). Context-sensitive coding, associative memory, and serial order in (speech) behavior. *Psychological Review, 76,* 1–15.

Zipf, G. (1949). *Human behavior and the principle of least effort.* Cambridge, MA: Addision-Wesley.

CHAPTER 9

VISUAL WORD RECOGNITION

THE JOURNEY FROM FEATURES TO MEANING

DAVID A. BALOTA

I. INTRODUCTION

A. The Word

Ah yes, the word! The word is as central to psycholinguists as the cell is to biologists. In the present chapter, I review some of the major issues that have been addressed in visual word recognition research; other chapters in this volume are devoted to auditory word recognition. At the onset, I should note that the present review is from the perspective of a cognitive psychologist, not a linguist. Moreover, the goal of the present review is not to provide in-depth reviews of every area addressed by word recognition researchers. This would far exceed space limitations. Rather, I will attempt to acquaint the reader with the richness and diversity of the empirical and theoretical issues that have been uncovered in this literature.

The organization of the chapter is as follows: First, I briefly outline why word recognition research has been central to a number of quite distinct developments in both cognitive psychology and psycholinguistics. Second, I review the evidence regarding letter recognition, sublexical organization, and lexical-level influences on word recognition. Interspersed within each of these sections is a discussion of some of the current theoretical developments and controversies. Third, I review the literature on context effects in word recognition, again highlighting major theoretical developments and controversies. Fourth, I conclude by discussing limitations regarding inferences that are possible based on the available data and suggest some avenues for future research in this area. However, before turning to the review of the literature, I begin by discussing why lexical-level analyses have been so central to developments in both cognitive psychology and psycholinguistics.

B. Why the Word?

In order to provide a framework for understanding the breadth of word recognition research, it is useful to list a few of the basic research issues that the word recognition literature has touched. For example, word recognition research has been central to notions regarding different levels/codes of analysis in language processing, attention, and memory (e.g., Craik & Lockhart, 1972; Posner, 1986). The lexical unit is ideally suited for such work because words can be analyzed at many different levels, e.g., features, letters, graphemes, phonemes, morphemes, semantics, among others. As we shall see below, much of the work in word recognition has been devoted to identifying functional roles of these different levels in the word recognition process.

A second domain where word recognition research has been a central player has been in the development of theories of automatic and attentional processes (e.g., Healy & Drewnowski, 1983; Laberge & Samuels, 1974; Neely, 1977; Posner & Snyder, 1975). Part of the reason for this emphasis is the natural relation between the development of reading skills and the development of automaticity. Here, one can see the extra impetus from education circles regarding the development of word recognition skills. Moreover, the notion that aspects of word recognition have been automatized and are no longer under conscious control of the reader has provided some of the major fuel for arguments regarding self-encapsulated linguistic processing modules (see Fodor, 1983).

Third, word recognition research has also been central to developments regarding basic pattern recognition processes. One of the most difficult problems in pattern recognition research has been in identifying the underlying subordinate critical features of a given pattern (e.g., Neisser, 1967). Written words are relatively well defined patterns. Historically, words have been the central unit of analysis in much of the verbal learning and memory research that dominated experimental psychology between the 1950s and 1960s. Because of this interest, there have been a number of important norming studies that are exemplified by Kucera and Francis's (1967) printed word frequency norms (counts of the frequency of occurrence of a given word in selected visual media), Noble's (1952) meaningfulness norms (a metric of the number of meanings generated to a given target), and Osgood, Suci, and Tannenbaum's (1957) semantic differential, among many others. In addition, there has been considerable recent interest in quantifying the characteristics of sublexical units, such as bigrams, trigrams, lexical neighbors, and others. Clearly, the centrality of the lexical unit in pattern recognition models is due in part to the efforts devoted to defining the stimulus.

Finally, because words are relatively well characterized patterns, they have been the focus of development of formal mathematical models of pattern recognition. For example, one of the first formal models in cognitive psychology was the Selfridge and Neisser (1960) Pandemonium model of letter recognition. Moreover, the interactive activation framework developed by McClelland and Rumelhart (1981) was central to nurturing the current widespread interest in formal connectionist models of cognitive performance. As we shall see below, word-level analyses appear to be ideally suited for the parallel distributed processing framework.

In sum, word recognition research has taken on so much importance because words are relatively well defined minimal units that carry many of the interesting codes of analysis (i.e., orthography, phonology, semantics, syntax) and processing distinctions (e.g., automatic vs. attentional) that have driven much of the work in cognitive psychology and psycholinguistics. Thus, although it would seem that the more important goal would be to pursue how individuals process language at higher levels such as clauses, sentences, and paragraphs, many researchers have pursued research at the level of the word because of its inherent tractability. As we shall see in the following review, although progress is being made, the ease of tracking the processes involved in word recognition may be more apparent than real.

II. CLASSIC VARIABLES OF INTEREST IN WORD RECOGNITION: WHAT DO WE KNOW?

In this section, I review some of the variables that have been pursued in word recognition research. First, I attempt to break the word down into smaller, more tractable bits. Second, I discuss the influence of variables that can be quantified at the whole word level, such as frequency, familiarity, meaningfulness, and contextual availability. Third, I provide an overview of the priming literature. Sprinkled within each of these sections is discussion of the major theoretical models and issues.

A. Breaking Down the Visual Word into Constituents

1. Features

One fundamental approach to pattern recognition is that a given pattern must first be broken down into features that are common to the set of patterns that one is interested in modeling. Some of the primary work in this area was developed by J. J. Gibson and Gibson (1955), who forcefully argued that feature-level analyses were an essential aspect of pattern recognition and, more generally, perceptual learning. The basic notion is that by identifying the primitive features, one has the building blocks for pattern recognition. This provided researchers with a well-specified problem: What are the primitive features used in letter recognition? The hunt was on!

Fortunately, it turns out that the feature analytic approach is ideally suited for letter recognition. Although there are differences across fonts, English orthography can be relatively well described by a limited set of features, such as horizontal lines, vertical lines, closed curves, open curves, intersections, cyclic redundancy, and others (see, for example, E. Gibson, Osser, Schiff, & Smith, 1963). Once researchers proposed such primitive features, both behavioral and neurological evidence began to accumulate that documented the role of such features in visual perception. On the behavioral side, there were studies of confusion matrices indicating that letters that shared features were more likely to be confused in degraded perceptual conditions, compared to letters that did not share many features (e.g., Kinney, Marsetta, & Showman, 1966). In addition, visual search studies by Neisser (1967), among others, indicated that subjects were relatively faster to find a given target letter (e.g., Z) when it was embedded in a set of letters that did not share many features with the target (e.g., O, J, U, Z, D), compared to a set of letters that did share many features with the target (e.g., F, N, K, Z, X).

In addition to the behavioral evidence, there was also exciting evidence accumulating during the same period that appeared to identify neural substrates that might subserve feature-like detection processes. Consider, for example, the pioneering work by Hubel and Wiesel (1962, 1968). In this work, Hubel and Wiesel used single cell recording techniques to investigate neural activity in areas of the striate cortex in alert cats. When different stimuli were presented to the retina of the cat, there were increases in neural activity in specific cortical areas. In fact, Hubel and Wiesel found evidence that there were cells that appeared to be especially sensitive to visual stimuli that mapped onto such things as vertical lines, horizontal lines, angles, and even motion. The importance of this work is very simple: It provided the neurological evidence that converged with the notion that pattern recognition ultimately depends on primitive feature analytic processes. More recent work by Petersen, Fox, Snyder, and Raichle (1990) using positron emission tomography has extended this work to humans in demonstrating significant blood flow changes in specific areas of the striate cortex corresponding to feature-like detection systems in alert humans.

One of the first well-specified feature analytic models of letter recognition was developed by Selfridge (1959; Selfridge & Neisser, 1960). This model is displayed in Figure 1. The basic notion is that when a stimulus is displayed it briefly resides in an iconic representation (referred to metaphorically as an Image Demon). A set of 28 feature decoders that are sensitive to specific features (Feature Demons) begin to analyze the iconic representation. For example, as shown in Figure 1, one can see that the first circle is blackened indicating that the iconic image entails one vertical line. (An additional circle would be blackened with each additional feature along a given dimension.) These letter units then feed or activate a cognitive decision system. The more consistent the feature analyses are with a given letter, the greater the activation for that letter representation. The decision system simply picks the letter unit with the greatest activation (i.e., the Cognitive Decision Demon "listens" to determine which Letter Demon is shouting the loudest).

An important aspect of the Pandemonium model is that it entailed some capacity for learning. For example, during the learning phase, the system first maps which features correspond to which letters by storing the results of these feature tests. Moreover, if a particular feature is especially important for discriminating between letters, then the weights associated with (i.e., the importance of) this feature might be incremented. In this way, the Pandemonium model can extract the critical features that are most powerful in discriminating among letters. As we shall see, the Pandemonium model predates by some 20 years some of the important letter recognition and word recognition models that have more recently been developed. It is quite amazing that the Pandemonium model worked so well given the computational hardware limitations of the late 1950s and early 1960s.

Although most models of word recognition assume a first step of primitive feature identification, there are still many unresolved questions in this initial stage of processing. First, what is the glue that puts the features together? Specifically, once vertical lines, horizontal lines, and intersections have been

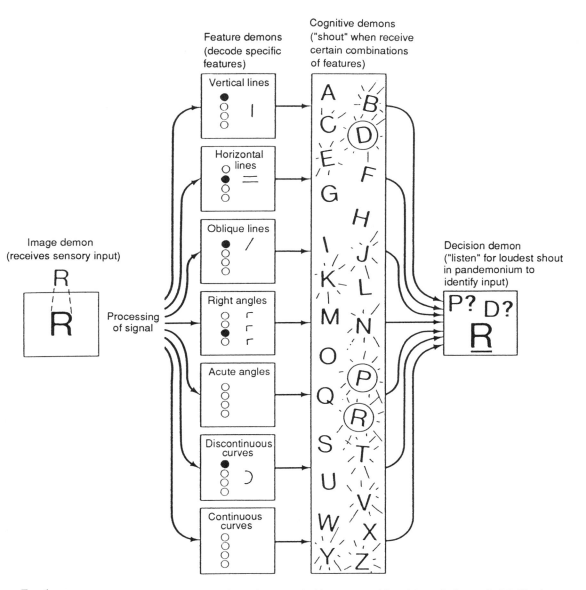

FIG. 1   Selfridge and Neisser's (1960) Pandemonium model of letter recognition. [From S. Coren, L. M. Ward, & J. T. Enns (1994). *Sensation and Perception, 4th Ed.* Ft. Worth: Harcourt Brace.

detected, how does one put the features together to identify a letter, e.g., the letter R? Obviously, we do not perceive free-floating features. Second, what happens in the feature analytic models when distortions occur that modify the feature (i.e., a 60° rotated vertical line is no longer a vertical line)? Third, and along the same lines, what are the critical features when the letters are distorted via different fonts or a novel style of handwriting? Reading still proceeds in an acceptable fashion even though there are considerable changes in the critical set of features (see Manso de Zuniga, Humphreys, & Evett, 1991, for a recent discussion of reading handwritten text). Fourth, are features across letters coded serially in reading, e.g., from left to right in English orthography, or is there a parallel coding of features? Based on the work by Treisman (1986), one might expect that there is an early parallel coding of features that is followed by a more capacity-demanding conjunction process (however, see G. L. Shulman, 1990). Although there is little evidence that necessitates the application of parallel coding of features to reading, most models of word recognition appear to support a parallel registration of features in letter recognition. Finally, are features within letters the critical level of analysis in word recognition or are there supraletter or even word-level features (e.g., Purcell, Stanovich, & Spector, 1978)? Thus, although feature analyses are the first step in most of the models of word recognition, it should be clear that a considerable number of questions still need to be answered in mapping features onto letters. However, in lieu of being bogged down in some of the more important fundamental aspects of visual perception, let's assume we have made it to the letter. Surely, things must get a bit more tractable there.

2. Letters

Assuming that features are critical in letter recognition, and letters are crucial in word recognition, then one might ask what variables are important in letter recognition. For example, does the frequency of a given letter in print influence its perceptibility? Fortunately, there seems to be a relatively straightforward answer to this question. Appelman and Mayzner (1981) reviewed 58 studies that entailed 800,000 observations from a variety of paradigms that spanned 100 years of research. The conclusion from their review is very straightforward: Letter frequency does appear to influence speeded tasks such as letter matching, naming, and classification tasks (e.g., is the letter a vowel or a consonant?). However, letter frequency does not appear to influence accuracy in perceptual identification tasks. The results from the Appelman and Mayzner study are intriguing for three reasons: First, a priori, one would clearly expect that frequency of ANY operation (perceptual, cognitive, and motoric) should influence performance, and hence it is unclear why there is not a letter frequency effect in identification tasks. Second, as we shall see below, there is a consistent word-level frequency effect in both response latency tasks and perceptual identification tasks, and hence there at least appears to be a difference between frequency effects at different levels within the processing system, that is, letters versus words. Third, this is our first exposure of a general theme that runs across the word recognition literature, that is, different tasks that a priori should tap the same level of analyses often yield different patterns of data.

Another question that one might ask regarding letter-level influences is whether there is a word length effect in word recognition tasks, as measured by the total number of letters in a given word. Obviously, if the letter is a crucial player in word recognition, then one should find consistent effects of letter length in word recognition tasks. Interestingly, there has been some disagreement on this topic. Although there is clear evidence that longer words take more time in perceptual identification (McGinnies, Comer, & Lacey, 1952) and pronunciation (Forster & Chambers, 1973) and produce longer fixation durations in reading (see Just & Carpenter, 1980), there has been some conflicting evidence regarding the lexical decision task (Henderson, 1982). In the lexical decision task, subjects are required to decide as quickly as possible whether a letter string is a word or nonword, with response latency and accuracy being the major dependent measures. Because the lexical decision task has been taken as a premier task for developing word recognition models, this is a troublesome finding. Interestingly, however, Chumbley and Balota (1984) reported relatively large length effects in the lexical decision task when the words and nonwords are equated on length and regularity. It is possible that inconsistent results with respect to past word length studies using the lexical decision task may have been due to subjects relying on any available dimensions that may be contaminated with length to bias their decisions in the lexical decision task. Thus, it appears safe to conclude at this point that there are consistent, albeit sometimes small, word length effects in virtually all word recognition tasks, when other variables are controlled.

More intriguing questions regarding letter recognition date back to questions that were originally posed by Cattell (1885). The interest here is basically, What is the perceptual unit in word recognition? A priori it would seem obvious that the letter should be the primary unit of analysis in visual word recognition, that is, words are made up of letters. However, Cattell (1885, 1886) reported a remarkable finding that was initially viewed as inconsistent with this notion. Cattell found that some words can be named more quickly than single letters. The problem this finding posed was very simple: How could the letter be the critical unit of analysis in word recognition, if words could be named more quickly than the letters that presumably make up the words? Along with the Cattell results, it was also reported that the exposure duration necessary to identify a word was in some cases less than the exposure duration necessary to identify a single letter. In fact, Erdmann and Dodge (1898) reported that the exposure duration necessary to identify four to five letters in a display was sufficient to read single words that could contain as many as 22 letters. Again, if words can be better perceived than letters, then how could letters be the basic unit of perception, since words are made up of letters?

Of course, an alternative account of this pattern of data is simply that subjects can use any available information regarding orthographic redundancy and lexical-level information to facilitate letter processing, and such information is unavailable when single letters are presented. This view was labeled the SOPHISTICATED GUESSING account of some of the initial findings. However, because of a seminal study by Reicher (1969), it appeared that there was more to this phenomenon than simply sophisticated guessing. In Reicher's study, on each trial, one of three stimuli was briefly flashed (e.g., a single letter, K, a word, WORK, or a nonword, OWRK), after which a patterned mask was presented. After the mask was presented, subjects were presented with two letters (e.g., D and K) adjacent to the position of the previous target letter for a forced-choice decision. The remarkable finding here is that subjects produced reliably higher accuracy when the first stimulus was a word than when it was a single letter or a nonword. Because both the letters D and K produce acceptable words within the WOR context, subjects could not rely on preexisting lexical knowledge to bias their response one way or the other (but see Krueger & Shapiro, 1979; Massaro, 1979, for an alternative view). This finding was termed the word superiority effect and was also reported in a study by Wheeler (1970).

There were two important subsequent findings that constrained the interpretation of the word superiority effect. First, the effect primarily appears under conditions of patterned masking (masks that involve letter-like features) and does not occur under conditions of energy masking (masks that involve high-luminous contrasts, e.g., Johnston & McClelland, 1973; Juola, Leavitt, & Choe, 1974). In fact, it appears that the interfering effect of the mask is primarily on performance in the letter alone condition and does not produce much of a breakdown in the word condition (Bjork & Estes, 1973). Second, letters are also better recognized when presented in pronounceable nonwords (e.g., MAVE), compared to unpronounceable nonwords or alone (e.g., Carr, Davidson, & Hawkins, 1978; McClelland & Johnston, 1977). Thus, the word superiority effect does not simply reflect a word-level effect.

The importance of the word superiority effect derives not only from the information that it provides about letter and word recognition, but also from its impact on the level of modeling that researchers began to use to influence their theory development. Specifically, this effect led to the development of a quantitative model of word and letter recognition developed by McClelland and Rumelhart (1981; Rumelhart & McClelland, 1982; also see Paap, Newsome, McDonald, & Schvaneveldt, 1982). As noted earlier, this type of modeling endeavor set the stage for the explosion of interest in connectionist models of cognitive processes (e.g., McClelland & Rumelhart, 1986; Rumelhart & McClelland, 1986; Seidenberg & McClelland, 1989).

Figure 2 provides an overview of the architecture of the McClelland and Rumelhart (1981) model. Here one can see three basic processing levels: feature detectors, letter detectors, and word detectors. These levels are attached by facilitatory (*arrowed lines*) and/or inhibitory (*knobbed lines*) pathways. As shown in Figure 2, there are inhibitory connections within the word level and within the letter level. Very simply, when a stimulus is presented, the flow of activation is from the feature level to the letter level and eventually onto the word level. As time passes, the letter-level representations can be reinforced, via the facilitatory pathways, by the word-level representations and vice versa. Also, as time passes, within both the letter- and word-level representations, inhibition from highly activated representations will decrease the activation at less activated representations, via the within-level inhibitory pathways.

How does the model account for the word superiority effect? The account rests heavily on the notion of cascadic processes in the information processing system (see Abrams & Balota, 1991; Ashby, 1982; McClelland, 1979). Specifically, a given representation does not necessarily need to reach some response threshold before activation patterns can influence other representations, but rather, there is a relatively continuous transferal of activation and inhibition across and within levels as the stimulus is processed. Consider the letter-alone condition in the Reicher paradigm, described earlier. When a letter is presented, it activates the set of features that are consistent with that letter. These featural detectors produce activation for the letter detectors that are consistent with those features and inhibition for the letter detectors that are inconsistent with those features. Although there is some activation for words that are consistent with the letter and some inhibition for words that are inconsistent with the letter, this effect is relatively small because there is little influence of a single letter producing activation at the word level. Now, consider the condition

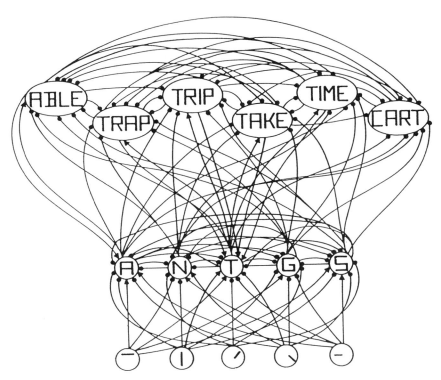

Fig. 2 McClelland and Rumelhart's (1981) interactive activation model of letter recognition. Copyright (1981) by the American Psychological Association. Reprinted by permission.

wherein the letter is embedded in a word context. In a word context there is now sufficient partial information from a set of letters to influence word-level activation patterns, and this will produce a significant top-down influence onto letter-level representations, that is, increase activation for consistent letters and decrease activation for the inconsistent letters. It is this higher level activation and inhibition that overrides the deleterious influence of the patterned mask.

In passing it is worth noting here that there is also evidence by Schendel and Shaw (1976) that suggests that features (e.g., lines) are better detected when the features are part of a letter than when presented alone. Hence, it is possible that there is also a letter superiority effect. This could easily be accommodated within the McClelland and Rumelhart model by assuming that there are also top-down influences from the letter level to the feature level.

Of course, one might ask at this point how this model could handle the pseudoword superiority effect. That is, letters are also better detected when embedded in pronounceable nonwords than when embedded in unpronounceable nonwords (Baron & Thurston, 1973; Carr et al., 1978) or presented in isolation (e.g., Carr et al., 1978; McClelland & Johnston, 1977). When letters are embedded in pronounceable nonwords, it is likely that there will be some overlap of spelling patterns between the pseudoword and acceptable lexical entries. For example, the pronounceable nonword MAVE activates 16 different four-letter words that share at least two letters within the McClelland and

Rumelhart network. Thus, the influence of orthographic regularity appears to naturally fall out of the interaction across multiple lexical entries that share similar spelling patterns within the language. As we shall see below, the influence of orthographic regularity on word recognition performance has been central to many of the more recent developments in word recognition research.

Although the influence of orthographic regularity appears to fall from this model, there are also some important limitations of orthographic regularity within the McClelland and Rumelhart model. Consider, for example, the impact of bigram frequency. For example, the vowel pair *ee* occurs in many more words than the cluster *oe*. The available evidence indicates that there is relatively little impact of bigram frequency on letter recognition within a Reicher-type paradigm (Manelis, 1974; McClelland & Johnston, 1977; Spoehr & Smith, 1975). McClelland and Rumelhart have successfully simulated this finding within their interactive activation framework. Although high-frequency letter clusters are more likely than low-frequency letter clusters to activate many word-level representations, this activation will be compensated by the fact that there will also be more word-level inhibition across those activated representations. Because, as noted above, there are influences of the number of lexical representations that share more than two letters, the lack of an influence of bigram frequency would appear to indicate that there may be a critical limit in the amount of overlap across lexical representations that is necessary to overcome the deleterious effects of within-level inhibition.

At this point, it is worth noting that there was some preliminary evidence that bigram frequency could influence word identification performance. For example, Broadbent and Gregory (1968) found that there was a clear influence of bigram frequency in word identification, but only for low-frequency words. In particular, for low-frequency words, low bigram frequency items produced an advantage over high bigram frequency items (also see Rice & Robinson, 1975). McClelland and Rumelhart suggested that this pattern might fall from their model if one assumes output from the word level is driving performance in the perceptual identification task. The presence of many neighbors (as in the high bigram frequency condition) produces considerable confusion for those words that are relatively difficult to identify to begin with, namely, the low-frequency words.

Unfortunately, the influence of bigram frequency on lexical-level performance has not produced consistent results in the literature. For example, Gernsbacher (1984) and Jastrzembski (1981) both failed to find any influence of bigram frequency in the lexical decision task, and Gernsbacher argued that previous findings were due to either response biases in the perceptual identification tasks or possible confoundings with familiarity of the letter string. Recently, Andrews (1992) again failed to find any influence of bigram frequency in either lexical decision or pronunciation performance. As we shall see below, one question that arises from this apparent lack of an influence of bigram frequency is, Why are there influences of neighbors primarily when the neighbors share more than two letters?

In addition to bigram frequency, one might ask whether positional frequency influences letter recognition. Positional frequency refers to the probability that a given letter(s) will occur in a given position within a word. Mayzner and Tresselt (1965) tabulated the summed positional frequency for single letters, bigrams, trigrams, tetragrams, and pentagrams (Mayzner et al., 1965a, 1965b, 1965c) across a set of 20,000 words. This metric should reflect the orthographic structure across words within a given language. In fact, one might expect influences of such a metric to fall quite nicely out of the McClelland and Rumelhart model. In fact, Massaro, Venezky, and Taylor (1979) reported evidence of a large impact of summed positional frequency within a Reicher-type paradigm. Their results indicated that both summed positional frequency and a rule-based metric of orthographic regularity (see discussion below) were found to influence letter recognition performance. Thus, at least at the level of letter recognition, there does appear to be an influence of positional letter frequency in a Reicher-type paradigm. Because letter position obviously must be coded in the McClelland and Rumelhart model, one might expect this effect to naturally fall from the combined facilitatory and inhibitory influences across lexical-level representations.

In sum, the interactive activation model provides a cogent quantitative account of what appears to be evidence of multiple levels within the processing system working in concert to influence letter recognition. A particularly important aspect of this model is the fact that ''other'' similar lexical-level representations appear to have an influence on the ease to recognize a given letter within a word. It appears that letter- or word-level representations do not passively accumulate information, as in a logogen-type model (see Morton, 1969), but letters and words appear to be recognized in the context of similar representations that either reinforce or diminish the activation at a given representation. We now turn to some discussion of the dimensions that define similarity in such networks.

III. GETTING FROM LETTERS TO WORDS: INFLUENCES OF SUBLEXICAL LEVELS OF ORGANIZATION

The journey from letters to words has been a central concern in word recognition models. Although there are many issues that are addressed in this area, one of the major theoretical issues has been the specification of the RULES that are useful in translating an orthographic pattern into an acceptable lexical/phonological representation. Unfortunately, as we shall see, such a translation process is far from easy in English orthography.

A. Specifying the Rules of Translation

One of the most evasive goals encountered in the analysis of English orthography is the specification of the FUNCTIONAL UNIT(S) of sublexical organization. An obvious spelling-to-sound mapping might involve a simple one-to-one correspondence between graphemic units (single letters or letter clusters) and phonemes. Obviously, such an analysis fails relatively quickly in English because some graphemes, like *ph,* can serve as one phoneme in words like *grapheme* and *phoneme,* and two phonemes in a word like *uphill.* Likewise, even single letters are quite ambiguous, such as the *c* in the words *cat* and *cider.* English orthography simply does not allow a one-to-one mapping of spelling to sound.

Although a simple mapping of spelling to sound may not work for all words, it is still possible that one may gain considerable insight into the vast majority of words via an analysis of the regularities in the orthography. Such an enterprise was undertaken in a number of large-scale studies of English orthography in the late 1960s and early 1970s (e.g., Haas, 1970; Hanna, Hanna, Hodges, & Rudorf, 1966; Venezky, 1970; Wijk, 1966). For example, Venezky coded the grapheme-to-phoneme correspondences across a set of 20,000 medium- to high-frequency words. Through an in-depth analysis of the consistency of grapheme-to-phoneme patterns, Venezky distinguished between two large classes of grapheme-to-phoneme correspondences. PREDICTABLE patterns are those which can be based on the regular graphemic, morphemic (minimal meaningful units, e.g., *redistribution* = *re* + *distribute* + *tion*), or phonemic features of the words in which they occur, whereas UNPREDICTABLE patterns are simply those patterns that do not appear to fit within any predictable class. The important question here is how many patterns are predictable when one considers similarities across words within the language. For example, some correspondences appear to be relatively invariant (predictable invariant patterns), as when the grapheme *f* always corresponds to the sound /f/ with the only exception being in the word *of*. On the other hand, other graphemes have many variations, each of which appear to be relatively predictable (predictable variant patterns). For example, the letter *c* most typically corresponds to the phoneme /k/ but corresponds to the phoneme /s/ in many words when it is succeeded by the letter *i, y,* or *e*.

As Henderson (1982) points out, there are a number of sublexical constraints within the grapheme-to-phoneme system in English, which are called phonotactic constraints. For example, because certain stop consonant sequences are not permissible in English (e.g., /bp/ and /pb/), whenever one is confronted with such a sequence of letters (e.g., *pb* or *bp*), the correspondence is such that the first phoneme is silent (e.g., *subpoena*). Thus, in this case, the phonological constraints of the language drive the grapheme-to-phoneme conversion of the spelling patterns. There also appear to be predictable constraints on the grapheme-to-phoneme mapping that are derived at the morphemic and syllabic levels. For example, the graphemic sequence *mb* corresponds to two separate phonemes when it segments syllables as in *ambulance* and *amber,* but only one phoneme at word-ending positions, as in *tomb* and *bomb*. Unfortunately, as Henderson points out, the situation becomes somewhat more complex when one considers that *mb* also only corresponds to one phoneme when it precedes inflectional affixes (e.g., *bombing*), but not when it precedes other morphemes (*bombard*). Moreover, there appear to be other constraints that are simply based on allowable grapheme-to-phoneme correspondences in particular positions within words. For example, the *ck* spelling pattern corresponds to the phoneme /k/, but the *ck* pattern does not occur at the beginning of words; in these later cases the *c* to /k/ correspondence or the *k* to /k/ correspondence occurs.

For demonstrative purposes, I have only touched on some of the problems that one encounters in attempting to understand the regularity of spelling-to-sound correspondences in English orthography. Although ultimately it may be possible to specify such grapheme-to-phoneme rules in English, it is noteworthy that even with the relatively complex rule systems developed by Venezky and others, Coltheart (1978) estimates that 10–15% of the words will still be unpredictable, that is, irregular. Likewise, Wijk notes that about 10% of the words will not fit his *Regularized Inglish*. This may be an underestimate, because, as Henderson points out, of the most common 3000 words, as many as 21% violate Wijk's regularization rules. More important, even if one had a fully developed rule-based system of spelling to sound in English, this would not necessarily indicate that such a rule-based system is represented in readers of English. In fact, even if such a rule-based system were represented, this would not be sufficient evidence to indicate that such rules play a role in fluent word recognition. Hence, instead of providing a detailed discussion of the enormously complex rule systems that have been developed, the present discussion focuses on the empirical evidence regarding how readers use sublexical information in word recognition. The interested reader is referred to Henderson (1982), Wijk (1966), and Venezky (1970) for excellent treatments of the search for rule-based translations of spelling-to-sound in English.

B. If Not Rules, Then What? The Controversy Regarding Dual-Route and Single-Route Models of Pronunciation

If it is unlikely that there will be a limited number of rules that specify the translation from spelling to sound in English (i.e., an ASSEMBLED route), it would appear likely that there is a second route (the LEXICAL or DIRECT route) to recognize words. In the second, lexical, route the reader may simply map the orthographic string onto a lexical representation and then access the programs necessary for pronouncing a given word aloud. Hence, we have the dual route model of word recognition (Coltheart, 1978; Humphreys & Evett, 1985), in which word pronunciation can be performed either by assembling phonology from orthography based on regularities within the language (e.g., as captured in the rules by Venezky, 1970) or by directly accessing a lexical representation via the whole-word orthographic input.

It is important to note here that because orthographies differ with respect to the regularity of spelling-to-sound correspondences, orthographies may also differ with respect to the weight placed on the assembled and lexical routes. For example, if the alphabetic system in a given language is unequivocal in mapping orthography to phonology, as in a language such as Serbo-Croatian, then one might find little or no influence of the lexical route in speeded pronunciation performance (Frost, Katz, & Bentin, 1987). The reader can rely totally on the assembled route, because it always produces the correct response. However, in English, and even to a greater extent in other languages such as Hebrew (e.g., Frost et al., 1987), the mapping between orthography and phonology is far less transparent. Hence, one should find increasing lexical effects in speeded pronunciation performance as one decreases the transparency of the spelling-to-sound correspondences (also referred to as orthographic depth). In support of this prediction, Frost et al. have reported larger frequency and lexicality effects in Hebrew compared to English, which in turn produced larger effects compared to Serbo-Croatian. Thus, comparisons across orthographies that differ with respect to the regularity of the spelling-to-sound correspondence support the notion that two routes are more likely in languages that have relatively deep orthographies.

If the inadequacy of a rule-based system demands a lexical route in English orthography, then one might ask what evidence there is for a role of an assembled route. Why would subjects ever use an assembled route to name a word aloud if, by necessity, there must be a lexical route? One piece of evidence that researchers originally identified as being consistent with an assembled route is the relative ease with which individuals can name nonwords aloud. Because nonwords do not have a direct lexical representation, it would appear that a nonlexical route is necessary for naming nonwords. However, this piece of evidence was soon disabled by evidence from activation synthesis approaches (e.g., Glushko, 1979; Kay & Marcel, 1981; Marcel, 1980), in which the pronunciation of a nonword could be generated by the activation of similarly spelled words. In fact, activation synthesis theorists have argued that pronunciation performance is always generated via analogies to words represented in the lexicon (mental dictionary), thus denying any important role for the assembled route.

However, there is a second, and more powerful, line of support for the role of an assembled route in English. This evidence is provided by studies of acquired dyslexics, who produce a double dissociation between the two routes. Specifically, one class of dyslexics, SURFACE DYSLEXICS, appear to have a selective breakdown in the lexical route but have an intact assembled route. These individuals are likely to regularize irregular words and exception words, e.g., they might pronounce *broad* such that it rhymes with *brode* (e.g., Marshall & Newcombe, 1980; McCarthy & Warrington, 1986; Shallice, Warrington, & McCarthy, 1983). A second class of acquired dyslexics, DEEP (phonological) DYSLEXICS, appear to have an intact lexical route but an impaired phonological route. These individuals can pronounce irregular words and other familiar words that have lexical representations; however, when presented a nonword that does not have a lexical representation, there is considerable breakdown in performance (Patterson, 1982; Shallice & Warrington, 1980). The argument here is that phonological dyslexics have a selective breakdown in the assembled route.

Although it would appear that the basic tenets of dual-route models are well established in the literature, an intriguing alternative single-route connectionist model has been developed by Seidenberg and McClelland (1989) that does an excellent job of handling some of the major findings that were originally viewed as strong support for the dual route model. This model could be viewed as a second generation of the original McClelland and Rumelhart (1981) model of letter recognition described above. One of the major differences between the two classes of models is that the later Seidenberg and McClelland model was specifically developed to account for lexical tasks such as word pronunciation and the lexical decision task, whereas the McClelland and Rumelhart model was developed in large part to account for letter recognition performance. A second major difference between the two models is that the McClelland and Rumelhart model involves localized representations for the major processing codes (i.e., features, letters, and words), whereas the Seidenberg and McClelland model involves distributed representations; that is, there is not a single representation that reflects the word *dog*. A third difference is that the McClelland and Rumelhart model assumes the existence of a specific architecture (i.e., sets of features, letters, and words along with the necessary connections), whereas the Seidenberg and McClelland model attempts to capture the development of the lexical processing system via the influence of a training regime. However, given these differences, both models account for performance by assuming a flow of activation across a set of relatively simple processing units and have been detailed sufficiently to allow for mathematical tractability. We now turn to a brief discussion of the Seidenberg and McClelland model.

As shown in Figure 3, the Seidenberg and McClelland model involves a set of input units that code the orthography of the stimulus and a set of output units that represent the phonology entailed in pronunciation. All the input units are connected to a set of hidden units (units whose only inputs and outputs are within the system being modeled, i.e., no direct contact to external systems, see McClelland & Rumelhart, 1986, p. 48), and all the hidden units are connected to a set of output units. The weights in the connections between the input and hidden units and the weights in the connections between the hidden units and phonological units do not involve any organized mapping before training begins. During training, the model is given an orthographic string, which produces some phonological output. The weights connecting the input and output strings are adjusted according to the back-propagation rule, such that the weights are adjusted to reduce the difference between the correct pronunciation and the model's output. During training, Seidenberg and McClelland presented the model with 2897 English monosyllabic words at a rate that is proportional to their natural frequency in English. The exciting result of this endeavor is that the model does a rather good job of producing the phonology that corresponds to regular words, high-frequency exception words, and even nonwords that were never presented. Although there is clearly some controversy regarding the degree to which the model actually captures aspects of the data (see e.g., Besner, 1990; Besner, Twilley, McCann, & Seergobin, 1990), the fact that it provides a quantitative account of aspects of simple pronunciation performance (without either explicit Venezky-type rules or even a lexicon) is quite intriguing and presents a powerful challenge to available word-recognition models.

One of the more important results of the Seidenberg and McClelland model is its ability to capture the frequency by regularity interaction. This finding was initially viewed as rather strong support for a dual-route model (cf. Andrews, 1982; Monsell, Patterson, Graham, Hughes, & Milroy, 1992; Paap & Noel, 1991; Seidenberg, Waters, Barnes, & Tanenhaus, 1984). The interaction is as follows: For high-frequency words, there is very little impact of the correspondence between orthography and phonology, whereas for low-frequency words there is a relatively large impact of such a correspondence. The dual-route

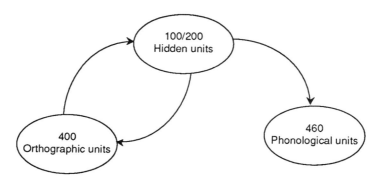

Fig. 3 Seidenberg and McClelland's (1989) implemented connectionist architecture. Copyright (1989) by the American Psychological Association. Reprinted by permission.

model accommodates this finding by assuming that for high-frequency words the lexical route is faster than the assembled route, and hence any inconsistent information from the assembled route does not arrive in time to compete with the pronunciation that is derived from the lexical route. For example, the incorrect assembled pronunciation for the high-frequency word *have* (such that it rhymes with *gave*) should not arrive in time to compete with the fast and correct lexical pronunciation. However, if one slows up the lexical route by presenting a low-frequency word, then one finds that the assembled output has time to interfere with the lexically mediated route, and hence response latency is slowed down. The important point for the dual route model is that the output of a low-frequency lexically mediated response can be inhibited by the availability of phonological information that is produced via the assembled route.

Although the dual route model would appear to provide a reasonable account for this interaction, this pattern also nicely falls from the Seidenberg and McClelland single route model. That is, the error scores (a metric that is mapped onto response latencies) for high-frequency regular words and exception words are quite comparable; however, for low-frequency words the error scores are worse for exception words than for regular words. Thus, one does not have to assume separate routes (or even a lexicon) to handle the frequency by regularity interaction, because this pattern naturally falls from the correspondences between the frequency of a particular spelling-to-sound correspondence even in a relatively opaque alphabetic system such as English. The interaction between frequency and regularity and the predictions from Seidenberg and McClelland's model are displayed in Figure 4.

Interestingly, the impact of the consistency of a given spelling-to-sound correspondence in English is also influenced by the characteristics of a given word's neighborhood. For example, Jared, McRae, and Seidenberg (1990) provide evidence that there are consistency effects in the pronunciation of regularly pronounced words (e.g., lint) primarily under conditions when the neighbors that have consistent spelling patterns (e.g., friends or mint) are higher in frequency than the neighbors that have inconsistent spelling patterns (e.g., enemies or pint). Such neighborhood frequency effects would appear to fall quite nicely from a connectionist model such as the Seidenberg and McClelland (1989) model. Alternatively, a rule-based model might suggest that the consistency of the neighbors defines the rules of translation from orthography to phonology. However, because of the difficulties noted above in specifying such rules, it is at the very least appealing that the Seidenberg and McClelland model is ideally suited to capture such neighborhood effects.

Although the Seidenberg and McClelland model does appear to provide an interesting alternative account to the dual-route model, there are still some important issues that need to be resolved. First, it is unclear how such a model might handle the fact that some acquired dyslexics appear to have only an intact assembled route while others appear to have only an intact lexical route (see Patterson, Seidenberg, & McClelland, 1989, for some discussion of this issue). Second, Monsell et al. (1992) have recently reported evidence that suggests that subjects can be biased by the presence of nonwords and exception words to rely on a more assembled route or a more lexical route. Third, there is intriguing evidence from Paap and Noel (1991) that provides evidence for differential attentional demands of the direct and assembled route, by indicating

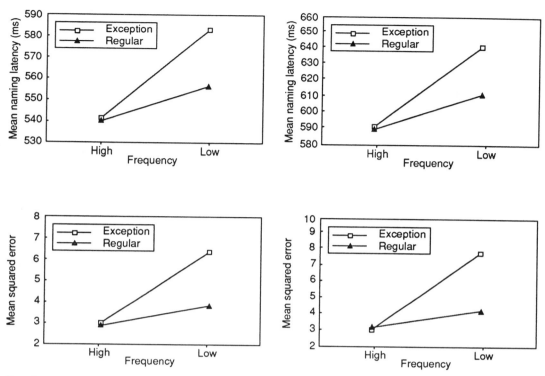

FIG. 4 Results and simulations of the (*left*) Seidenberg (1985) and (*right*) Seidenberg, Waters, Barnes, and Tanenhaus (1984, Experiment 3) studies: experimental results (*upper*) and simulations from the Seidenberg and McClelland (1989) model (*lower*). Copyright (1989) by the American Psychological Association. Reprinted by permission.

that a secondary attention-demanding task provides more interference with the assembled route than the direct route (also see Balota & Ferraro, 1993). Fourth, as described below, it appears that in some tasks, meaning-level representations can influence pronunciation and lexical decision performance. Thus, without some level of semantic input, it is unclear how an unembellished Seidenberg and McClelland model could account for such effects. Fifth, Besner (1990) and Besner, Twilley et al. (1990) have documented that the phonological error scores and the orthographic error scores do a rather poor job of simulating some characteristics of nonword performance. Of course, it is quite possible that future generations of the Seidenberg and McClelland type model (see, for example, Seidenberg & McClelland, 1990) will be able to handle these deficiencies. At this point, it seems most reasonable to acknowledge the accomplishments of this model and note the apparent problems with the current implementation. (The reader is also referred to Coltheart, Curtis, Atkins, & Haller, 1993, for a recent computational version of the dual route model.)

C. Types of Sublexical Stages of Analysis

At this point, it should be noted that I have yet to discuss specific types of sublexical but supraletter influences on word recognition. I have grouped together a set of effects under the "regularity" umbrella, even though there are a number of distinct classes of words that follow differing degrees of spelling-to-sound correspondences, e.g., words like *aisle* appear to have a unique spelling-to-sound correspondences, whereas, words like *gave* are pronounced consistently with the exception of a single high-frequency neighbor (*have*). I now turn to a brief discussion of three distinct levels of sublexical representation that have been at the center of this area of research: onsets and rhymes, morphology, and syllables.

1. Onsets and Rhymes

Treiman and her colleagues (e.g., Treiman & Chafetz, 1987; Treiman & Danis, 1988; Treiman & Zukowski, 1988) have argued that there is an intermediate level of representation in lexical processing between graphemes and syllables (also see Kay & Bishop, 1987; Patterson & Morton, 1985). They argue that syllables are not simply strings of phonemes, but there is a level of subsyllabic organization that is used in both speech production and recognition of visual strings. This subsyllabic distinction is between the onset and rhyme of a syllable. The onset of a syllable can be identified as the initial consonant or consonant cluster in a word. For example, /s/ is the ONSET for *sip*, /sl/ is the onset for *slip*, and /str/ is the onset for *strip*. The RHYME of a word involves the following vowel and any subsequent consonants. For example, in *sip, slip,* and *strip*, /ip/ would be the rhyme. Thus, syllables have a subsyllabic organization in that each syllable is composed of an onset and a rhyme.

Although our primary interest is in visual word processing, it is interesting to note that there has been evidence from a number of quite varied research domains that supports the distinction between onsets and rhymes in English. For example, there is evidence from the types of speech errors that speakers produce (MacKay, 1972), the distributional characteristics of phonemes within syllables (Selkirk, 1980), along with the types of errors that subjects produce in short-term memory tasks (Treiman & Danis, 1988).

In one of the studies addressing visual word recognition, Treiman and Chafetz (1987) presented strings like FL OST ANK TR to subjects with the task being to determine whether two of the strings in these four strings of letters could be combined to form a real word. In this case, one can see that FL and ANK can be combined to produce FLANK, with FL corresponding to the onset of the word *flank* and ANK corresponding to the rhyme. Now, consider performance on conditions where the strings again correspond to words but they are not broken at onsets and rhymes. For example, a subject might be presented FLA ST NK TRO. For these items, the correct answer is again FLANK, but now the FLA and NK do not correspond to onsets and rhymes. The results of the Treiman and Chafetz experiments indicated that anagram solutions were better when the breaks corresponded to onset-rhyme divisions compared to when the breaks did not. A similar pattern was found in a lexical decision task. In this study, the items were again presented such that there was either a break that matched the onset-rhyme division (e.g., CR//ISP, TH//ING) or a break that did not match the onset-rhyme division (e.g., CRI//SP and THI//NG). The results indicated that lexical decisions were reliably faster when the break matched the onset–rhyme division. Thus, Treiman and Chafetz argued that onset and rhyme units play a role in visual word recognition.

Interestingly, Patterson and Morton (1985) and Kay and Bishop (1987) argue for a functional role of a variable, WORD BODY, that clearly resembles the rhymes. The word body involves the vowel and the following consonant. For example, Kay and Bishop report that there is an effect of spelling-to-sound correspondence of the word body especially for low-frequency words. For example, in the word *spook*, the phonological correspondence to the *oo* is actually the most popular correspondence to this grapheme. However, the sound corresponding to the higher level word body *ook* is actually quite unpopular among the neighbors (e.g., *book, cook, hook*, etc.). Kay and Bishop provided evidence that in speeded word pronunciation, consistencies in higher level word bodies have more of an impact than consistency in lower level grapheme-to-phoneme correspondences, primarily for low-frequency words. Of course, it would be useful to determine whether this pattern would also fall from the Seidenberg and McClelland (1989) model.

2. Syllables

If the distinction between onsets and rhymes plays a functional role en route to word recognition, then one would also expect a functional role for the syllable. At this level it is quite surprising that there has been considerable disagreement regarding the role of the syllable in visual word recognition. For example, Spoehr and Smith (1973) argued for a central role of the syllable, whereas Jared and Seidenberg (1990) have recently questioned the role of the syllable as a sublexical unit. In fact, as Seidenberg (1987) points out, there is even some disagreement regarding where syllabic boundaries exist. For example, according to Howard's (1972) rules that emphasize intrasyllabic consonant strings surrounding a stressed vowel, *camel* would be parsed as (*cam*) + (*el*), whereas, according to Selkirk's (1980) more linguistically based view that emphasizes the maximal syllable onset principle, *camel* would be parsed (*ca*) + (*mel*). Obviously, before one can address the functional role of the syllable in visual word recognition, one must have some agreement on how to parse words into syllables. Fortunately, for the vast majority of words there is agreement on how words are parsed into syllables.

The question here of course is whether a word like *anvil* is parsed as (*an*) + (*vil*) en route to word recognition. It should again be emphasized here that the concern is not whether subjects have access to syllabic information, surely they must; that is, most subjects can accurately decompose most words into syllables. The more important question is whether this information is used in accessing the lexicon for visually presented words.

Prinzmetal, Treiman, and Rho (1986) reported an important set of experiments that investigated the impact of syllabic structure on early-level perceptual operations in word recognition. These researchers used a paradigm developed by Treisman and Schmidt (1982) in which feature integration errors are used to examine perceptual groupings. The notion is that if a set of strings (e.g., letters or digits) forms a perceptual group, then one should find migration of features (colors) toward that group. In the Prinzmetal et al. study, subjects were presented with words such as *anvil* and *vodka*. At the beginning of each trial, subjects were given a target letter with the task being to report the color of a target letter that would appear in the upcoming display. After the target letter was designated, subjects were presented a letter string with letters in different colors. The data of interest in such studies are the types of errors that subjects make as a function of syllabic structure. Consider the third letter position in the words *anvil* and *vodka*. In the word *anvil*, the third letter is part of the second syllable, whereas in the case of *vodka* the third letter is part of the first syllable. Now, if the syllable produces a perceptual grouping, then one might expect errors in reporting the colors such that the *d* in *vodka* might be more likely to be reported as the color of the *o*, compared to the *k*, whereas, the *v* in *anvil* might be more likely to be reported as the color of the *i*, compared to the *n*. This is precisely the pattern obtained in the Prinzmetal et al. study.

Seidenberg (1987) has questioned the conclusion that syllables are an access unit in visual word perception. He pointed out that there is a special level of orthographic redundancy at bigrams that breaks words into syllabic units. Specifically, Adams (1981) has noted that the letter patterns that often flank syllable patterns have relatively low bigram frequencies. In fact, the *nv* and *dk* are the lowest bigram frequencies in the words *anvil* and *vodka*. In general, if one considers relatively high frequency bisyllabic words, there appears to be a decrease in frequency of the bigrams that occur at syllabic boundaries. This bigram TROUGH may actually increase the likelihood of feature errors, due to the orthographic neighbors of the target instead of an actual subsyllabic parsing en route to word recognition.

In order to address this possibility, Seidenberg (1987, Experiment 3) looked at the probability of featural errors in the Prinzmetal et al. paradigm across words that have similar orthographic patterns and redundancy. Consider for example, the bisyllabic word *naive* and the monosyllabic word *waive*. If the syllable is an access unit that produces migration errors, then subjects should be more likely to misreport the color of the letter *i* as the color of the letter *v* than as the color of the letter *a* for *naive*, but this pattern should not occur for the monosyllabic word *waive*. Seidenberg found that similar feature migration errors were found for both bisyllabic words and monosyllabic words. This would suggest that the syllable was not used in access.

Interestingly, however, Rapp (1992) has recently reported an experiment that appears to question Seidenberg's conclusion regarding the influence of bigram troughs in the production of syllable effects. Rapp reported that illusory conjunctions followed syllabic constraints both for words that had a syllabic trough present (e.g., *anvil*) and words that do not have a trough present (e.g., *ignore*). Rapp argued from these data that merely the presence of a bigram trough is not sufficient to account for syllabic effects found in word recognition.

3. Morphemes

Another sublexical unit that has received considerable attention in the literature is the morpheme. One of the most compelling reasons that morphemes might play a functional role in word recognition is the generative nature of language. Rapp (1992) provides *chummily* as an interesting example. Although we may have never encountered the word *chummily*, we may assume that it means something like 'in a chummy way' or 'friendly' because it appears to have the morphological form *chummy* + *ly*. In fact, most linguistic models of lexical representation assume that there is some base form of representation and a set of rules that can be used to construct other forms of that item. The present question is whether a given form of a word such as *jumped* is parsed as (*JUMP*) + (*ED*) in route to word recognition. As in the case of syllables, we are not questioning whether morphemes are somehow represented in the processing system; the question is whether morphemic analyses play a role in processes tied to visual word recognition.

Much of the theoretical and empirical work regarding the role of the morpheme in visual word recognition was originally developed by Taft and Forster (1975, 1976; also see Taft, 1979a, 1979b, 1985, 1987). They argue that readers first decompose polymorphemic words into constituent morphemes. Readers then access lexical files that are listed under the root morpheme. For example, if the word *characteristic* were presented, the reader would first access the root word *character,* and once this root word was accessed, the subject would search through a list of polymorphemic words with the same root morpheme, e.g., *characteristic, uncharacteristic, characterized, characteristically, uncharacteristically,* and so on.

As noted above, there have been a number of studies reported in the literature that support the notion that there is a morphemic level of analysis in visual word recognition. For example, Taft (1979a, 1979b) found an effect of printed word frequency of the root morpheme (the sum of frequencies of all words with a given root) in lexical decision performance for items that were equated in surface frequencies (see, however, caveats by Bradley, 1980). This would appear to support the contention that root morphemes do play a special role in word recognition and it is not simply the frequency of the actual lexical string that is crucial.

Possibly, a more compelling finding in the literature deals with long-term morphemic priming effects (Stanners, Neiser, & Painton, 1979). In these studies, subjects are most often presented a sequence of lexical decision trials. At varying lags within the sequence, subjects might be presented two forms of a given word with the same root. The interesting comparison is the influence of an earlier presentation of a given root form on later lexical decisions to the actual root. For example, if either *jump* or *jumped* is presented earlier in a lexical decision task, what impact does this presentation have on later lexical decision performance on the root form *jump*? Stanners, Neiser, Hernon, and Hall (1979) found that both *jump* and *jumped* equally primed later lexical decisions to *jump*. Presumably, subjects had to access *jump* to recognize *jumped,* and hence there was as much long-term priming from *jumped* as for the actual stem itself. Interestingly, Lima (1987) has found that mere letter overlap does not produce such an effect. For example, she has reported that *arson* does not prime *son,* but *dishonest* does prime *honest.* Thus, it does not appear that mere letter overlap is producing this long-term priming effect (see review by Feldman & Andjelkovic, 1992, for a summary of evidence favoring nonorthographic accounts of morphemic priming effects.)

I have painted a relatively simple picture of morphemic analyses in word recognition. However, as Rayner and Pollatsek (1989) have pointed out, the influence of morphological processing in word recognition tasks (assuming there is an effect) is far from simple. For brevity, we simply list some of the findings here: First, suffixes that produce inflections of a given word but keep the grammatical class (e.g., *jump* vs. *jumped*) produce full long-term repetition priming in lexical decisions, whereas suffixes that produce derivations of a given form that belong to a different grammatical class produce reduced priming (e.g., *select* vs. *selective*) (Stanners, Neiser, Hernon, & Hall, 1979). Second, Stanners et al. found that there is reduced priming from verbs that have a less transparent relationship; for instance, there is reduced priming from *spoken* to *speak* compared to *jumped* to *jump*. Third, Bradley (1980) failed to provide evidence of root morpheme frequency or surface frequency effects for words that end in *-ION*. Thus, different types of morphemes apparently behave differently. Fourth, prefixed words (e.g., *rejuvenate*) produce faster lexical decision latencies (Taft, 1981) and shorter fixation durations in an on-line reading task (e.g., Lima, 1987), compared to words with prefix-like beginnings that are not actually prefixed stems (e.g., *repertoire*). If the parser first strips prefixes, then how would the parser know not to strip the prefix-like beginnings in nonprefixed stems? Fifth, it appears that morphological structure in nonwords (e.g., *walken* vs. *wilken*) is also accessed in the lexical decision task and produces interference in making nonword decisions (e.g., Caramazza, Laudanna, & Romani, 1988; Taft & Forster, 1976).

Seidenberg (1987) has also noted that there are often low-frequency bigram troughs at morphemic boundaries. He argues that prefixes are relatively common bigrams in the language, and hence the frequency of the bigram within a prefix is typically higher than the frequency of the bigram that straddles the prefix and the next morpheme. Hence, it is possible that at least some of the prefix-stripping effects that have been reported in the literature are due to the presence of a bigram trough at prefix boundaries. Again, one might expect such morphemic-like effects to naturally fall from a Seidenberg and McClelland type model, without a functional role for the morpheme directly represented.

Rapp (1992) addressed Seidenberg's concern about the presence of bigram troughs in producing some of the morphemic effects in word recognition research. She reported a lexical decision study in which the corresponding letters within a letter string were displayed in two colors. The colors of the letters either were consistent with morphological boundaries (e.g., *unTIE*) or inconsistent with morphological boundaries (e.g., *untIE*). Moreover, she compared items that had bigram troughs present with items that did not. The results indicated that words that included color differences at morphological boundaries produced reliably faster lexical decisions compared to words that did not and this effect was not modulated by the presence of a bigram trough. Thus, to the extent that Rapp's lexical decision task reflects more natural processes en route to word recognition in reading, the influence of morphological analyses do not appear to be simply due to the presence of a bigram trough that overlaps morphological boundaries. Of course, one might also ask whether there are other measures of orthographic redundancy that may account for the apparent influence of morphological analyses en route to word recognition.

D. Summary of Sublexical but Supraletter Organization

In the preceding sections, I have provided an abbreviated overview of some of the sublexical structures that researchers have argued are engaged in the journey from print to sound. There is still considerable debate regarding the nature of the impact of these variables. As I have tried to emphasize, one of the major issues is whether the influence of sublexical structures naturally falls from interactions amongst many lexical representations, as in Seidenberg and

McClelland's (1989) connectionist model, or whether these variables fall from direct parsing of words into these sublexical structures. Before turning to further discussion of this issue, it is important to complete our discussion of the empirical results that need to be accounted for by an adequate model of word recognition. It is in this light that we now turn to lexical-level variables.

IV. LEXICAL-LEVEL VARIABLES

By lexical-level variables, I simply refer to the influence of variables that have been quantified at the whole word level. For example, word frequency is a lexical variable. Specifically, a researcher can investigate the influence of the printed frequency of occurrence of a given word (e.g., *dog*) on word recognition task performance. Here, frequency is defined at the lexical level instead of the sublexical level.

A. Word Frequency

The frequency with which a word appears in print has a strong influence on word recognition tasks. Such effects have been observed in lexical decision performance (e.g., Forster & Chambers, 1973), pronunciation performance (e.g., Balota & Chumbley, 1984), perceptual identification performance (e.g., Broadbent, 1967), and on-line reading measures such as fixation duration and gaze duration measures (e.g., Inhoff & Rayner, 1986; Rayner & Duffy, 1986). This, of course, should not be surprising because printed word frequency should be related to the number of times one experiences a given word; and, experience with an operation should influence the ease of performing that operation.

The influence of word frequency in word recognition tasks has been accounted for by two rather broad classes of word recognition models (Forster, 1989). The ACTIVATION class of models is based in large part on Morton's (1969, 1970) classic logogen model and includes the more recent interactive activation and connectionist offspring, described above. For example, according to Morton's logogen model, frequency is coded via the resting level activations in word recognition devices (logogens). High-frequency words, because of the increased likelihood of experience, will have higher resting level activations than low-frequency words. Therefore, in order to surpass a word recognition threshold, the activation within such a logogen will need to be boosted by less stimulus information for high-frequency words than for low-frequency words. The second class of word recognition models is referred to as ORDERED SEARCH models (e.g., Forster, 1976, 1979; Rubenstein, Garfield, & Millikan, 1970). According to these models, the lexicon is serially searched with high-frequency words being searched before low-frequency words. For example, as shown in Figure 5, Forster (1976) has argued that the lexicon may be searched via several indexing systems: orthographic, phonological, or syntactic/semantic access bins. Each of these bins involves a frequency-ordered search, whereby high-frequency words are searched before low-frequency words, and once the target is located, the subject has immediate access to the word's master lexical representation. As one might expect, there are also hybrid models that include both activation and search characteristics, such as the Becker (1980), Paap et al. (1982), and Taft and Hambly (1986) models. For example, Becker suggests that

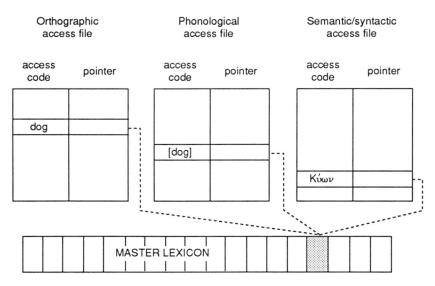

FIG. 5   Architecture of Forster's (1978) serial search model of word recognition.

activation processes define both sensorily and semantically defined search sets. These search sets are then compared to the target stimulus via a frequency-ordered search process.

An important question that has arisen recently regarding word frequency effects is the locus of the effect in the tasks used to build models of word recognition. All the above models attribute the influence of frequency to processes leading up to and including the magical moment of word recognition (see Balota, 1990). However, there is more recent evidence that suggests there are (a) decision components of the lexical decision task (Balota & Chumbley, 1984; Besner, Davelaar, Alcott, & Parry, 1984; Besner & McCann, 1987), (b) post-access components related to the generation and output of the phonological code in the pronunciation task (Andrews, 1989; Balota & Chumbley, 1985; Connine, Mullennix, Shernoff, & Yelen, 1990), and (c) sophisticated guessing aspects of the threshold identification task (Catlin, 1969, 1973) that are likely to exaggerate the influence of word frequency.

Consider, for example, the Balota and Chumbley (1984) model of the lexical decision task displayed in Figure 6. Balota and Chumbley have suggested that subjects will use any information that is available to discriminate words from nonwords in this task. Two pieces of information that are obvious discriminators between words and nonwords are the familiarity and meaningfulness (FM dimension) of the stimuli. Obviously, nonwords are less familiar and also less meaningful than words. However, both words and nonwords vary on these dimensions; in fact, the distributions may overlap (e.g., the nonword *chummingly* may be more familiar and meaningful than the low-frequency word *ortolidian*). Frequency effects in the lexical decision task may be exaggerated because low-frequency words are a bit more similar to the nonwords on the FM dimension than are high-frequency words. Hence, when there is insufficient information to make a fast "word" response, the subject is required to engage in an extra checking process (possibly checking the spelling of the word). This

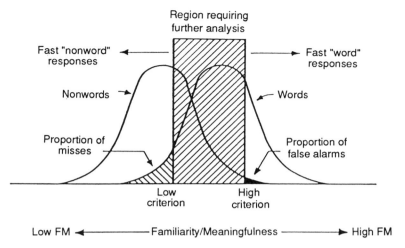

FIG. 6 Balota and Chumbley's (1984) two-stage model of the lexical decision task.

time-consuming extra checking process is more likely to occur for low-frequency words than for high-frequency words, thereby exaggerating any obtained influence of word frequency. (It is worth noting here that the two major implemented quantitative models of the lexical decision task, Ratcliff & McKoon, 1988, described below; and Seidenberg & McClelland, 1989, both make use of a familiarity dimension in modeling lexical decision performance.)

As noted, there has been considerable controversy in the literature regarding the locus of word-frequency effects in the tasks used to build word recognition models (e.g., see Balota & Chumbley, 1990; Monsell, Doyle, & Haggard, 1989; Savage, Bradley, & Forster, 1990). Of course, it is not surprising that some theorists have been reluctant to accept any concerns about the major tasks used to build models of word recognition. Moreover, some researchers have misrepresented the task analysis research as indicating that task analyzers were arguing that ALL frequency effects must be due to post-access processes. The primary intent of the task analysis work was to caution researchers that not all word-frequency effects can be unequivocally attributed to access processes in the tasks that are used to measure word recognition. Although a full discussion of this work is beyond the scope of the present review, it is sufficient to note here that there is little disagreement that word frequency influences some of the processes involved in word recognition, and most likely, this variable also influences other processes that are idiosyncratic to the tasks that are used to build models of word recognition. As exemplified throughout the word recognition literature, understanding the operations in the tasks used to build models of word recognition is a paramount first step in building adequate models.

B. Familiarity

A variable that is highly correlated with frequency is word familiarity. Some researchers have argued that the available printed word frequency norms by Kucera and Francis (1967) and Thorndyke and Lorge (1944) may not be the most sensitive estimates of the impact of frequency of occurrence on lexical representations. For example, printed word frequency counts do not take into consideration spoken word frequency. Thus, some researchers have turned to subjective rated familiarity norms to index the frequency with which a given lexical item has been processed (e.g., Boles, 1983; Connine et al., 1990; Gernsbacher, 1984; Nusbaum, Pisoni, & Davis, 1984). In fact, Nusbaum and Dedina (1985) and Connine et al. have provided evidence that one can find familiarity effects above and beyond frequency effects in the lexical decision and pronunciation tasks, respectively. Moreover, Connine et al. provided evidence that ease of production in a delayed pronunciation task (a task used to bypass many of the operations involved in lexical access) can be predicted by familiarity ratings when word-frequency measures no longer predict performance. Hence, Connine et al. suggest that subjective rated familiarity incorporates frequency in production in addition to frequency in print.

Just as in the case of printed word frequency, there is no question whether subjective rated familiarity provides a strong predictor in word recognition tasks. The more important issue (e.g., Balota, Ferraro, & Connor, 1991) is what sorts of information subjects use to make untimed subjective familiarity ratings. For example, it is possible that when subjects rate a word for familiarity they are not only rating the printed string for familiarity, but rather they may be rating the availability of a clear and vivid meaning for that word, or possibly even the extent to which an individual can identify a specific context for that word (Schwanenflugel, Harnishfeger, & Stowe, 1988). In fact, one finds quite strong correlations between familiarity and other more semantic variables such as meaningfulness, concreteness, and contextual availability (see Balota et al., 1991, for a review). The point here is simply that although there may be clear difficulties with word-frequency norms, it is also unlikely that subjective familiarity ratings will provide a pure measure of the extent to which an individual has been exposed to a given stimulus word.

C. Neighborhood Effects

Seidenberg and McClelland (1990) have suggested that average adult readers probably have 30,000 words in their vocabulary. Because these words are based on a limited number of 26 letters, there must be considerable overlap in spelling patterns across different words. One of the major tasks of an acceptable model of word recognition is to describe how the system selects the correct lexical representation among neighborhoods of highly related orthographic representations. Of course, it is possible that the number of similar spelling patterns may not influence lexical processing and that only a single representation must pass threshold for recognition to occur. However, as already mentioned, it appears that words are not recognized in isolation of other orthographically related representations.

Coltheart, Davelaar, Jonasson, and Besner (1977) introduced the N metric. N refers to the number of words that could be generated by changing only a single letter in each of the positions within a word. Although similar to phonological neighbors, discussed above, orthographic neighbors can obviously be different. For example, for the target word *hate, late* would be an orthographic and phonological neighbor, *hale* would be an orthographic neighbor, and *eight* would be a phonological neighbor.

There are two factors that need to be accommodated when discussing neighborhood effects. First, one needs to consider the influence of neighborhood size. That is, some words are embedded in relatively large orthographic neighborhoods, whereas other words are embedded in relatively small orthographic neighborhoods. Andrews (1989, 1992) has repeatedly observed an interesting effect of neighborhood size. Specifically, in both pronunciation and lexical decision performance, low-frequency words that are from large neighborhoods produce faster latencies than low-frequency words from small neighborhoods, whereas there is little or no influence of neighborhood size for high-frequency words. (This interaction is reminiscent of the influence of phonological regularity and word frequency discussed above.)

Second, one might also expect the frequency of the neighbors to play a role in word recognition tasks. In fact, Grainger (1990) and colleagues (Grainger, O'Regan, Jacobs, & Segui, 1989; Grainger & Segui, 1990) have argued that neighborhood frequency is more important than neighborhood size. They argue that performance will be worse whenever the target word has at least one orthographically similar word that is higher in frequency. Because the likelihood of a higher frequency neighbor should increase with the size of the neighborhood, the Grainger results appear to be at odds with the Andrews results. Andrews (1992) points to two issues that may help resolve the apparent discrepancy: First, she points out that the difference between the size of the small and large neighborhoods was smaller in Grainger's studies than in Andrews' studies. Moreover, Andrews points out that Grainger has only found this inhibitory effect in lexical decision, and hence it is possible that this pattern may reflect decision processes that have been tied to this task.

It would seem that both frequency of neighbors and size of neighborhoods should play a role in word recognition tasks. In this light, it is useful to mention the P. A. Luce and Pisoni (1989) neighborhood activation model, which they applied to auditory word recognition performance. This model takes into consideration target frequency, neighbor frequency, and neighborhood size via R. D. Luce's (1959) choice rule. Specifically, the probability of identifying a stimulus word is equal to the probability of the stimulus word divided by the probability of the word plus the combined probabilities of the neighbors. Of course, it is possible that the neighborhoods of the neighbors may play a role along with the degree of overlap of the neighbors. At this level, it would seem that models that attempt to capture the interaction across many lexical representations that are partially activated, as in the McClelland and Rumelhart (1981) model and, in an indirect fashion, in the Seidenberg and McClelland (1989) model, are ideally suited to accommodate such neighborhood effects. Finally, it should also be noted here that an interesting and important aspect of Luce and Pisoni's work is that such neighborhood frequency effects appear to modulate performance differently across lexical decision, pronunciation, and threshold identification. Again, we find the importance of task analyses in defining the influence of a variable in word recognition.

Before leaving this section, it should be noted that neighborhood size effects have taken on considerable currency in discriminating between the search models of word recognition (e.g., Becker, 1980; Forster, 1976, 1989; Taft & Forster, 1976) and the activation models of word recognition (e.g., McClelland & Rumelhart, 1981; Seidenberg & McClelland, 1989). Neighborhood size effects would appear to produce particular difficulties for serial search models. Specifically, the more items that need to be searched, the slower response latency should be. This is precisely opposite to the pattern reported by Andrews, who finds that larger neighborhoods produce faster response latencies, and only for low-frequency words. However, Seidenberg and McClelland (1989) have demonstrated that their model can nicely accommodate Andrews' effects of neighborhood size.

Although the Seidenberg and McClelland model can account for some influences of neighborhood density, there are still some limitations (see Andrews, 1992; Besner, Twilley et al., 1990a). For example, because frequency and neighborhood size are coded within the same network weights, it is unclear why neighborhood density would only have an effect for low-frequency words. Moreover, it is unclear why there are no neighborhood density effects for nonwords in the lexical decision task. Of course, there may be more to a word than the orthographic and phonological neighborhoods that apparently fall from the Seidenberg and McClelland model. It is in this light that we now turn to a discussion of the possibility that the MEANING of a word may play a role in word recognition.

V. SEMANTIC VARIABLES FOR ISOLATED WORDS

There have been a number of reports in the literature that indicate that semantic variables associated with lexical representations can modulate the ease of word recognition. This is an intriguing possibility because most models of word recognition would appear to indicate that the word must be recognized before the meaning of the word is determined. That is, the subject needs to recognize the string as the word *dog* before the subject accesses the meaning of the word *dog*. However, within an interactive activation model such as McClelland and Rumelhart's, one might envisage a higher level semantic representation above the word level that may accrue activation and provide top-down feedback in a cascadic fashion to influence word recognition performance (see Balota, 1990; Balota et al., 1991, for a further discussion of this issue).

Although there has been a considerable amount of work attempting to specify which semantic variables play a role in word recognition, much of this work has been open to alternative interpretations. Here we briefly review this work, emphasizing the major findings with respect to each of the major variables. Balota et al. (1991) have provided a more in-depth review of this literature.

A. Concreteness

If one could provide evidence that concrete words (those words which can be the object of a sense verb, e.g., *touch, see, hear*, etc.) were more easily recognized than abstract words, then this would provide some evidence of a semantic influence on word recognition performance. Although the concrete/abstract dimension has been the center of considerable research in word recognition (e.g., Bleasdale, 1987; Boles, 1983, 1989; Day, 1977; de Groot, 1989; James, 1975; Kroll & Merves, 1986; Paivio & O'Neill, 1970; Rubenstein et al., 1970; Winnick & Kressel, 1965), until recently, most of the results have been equivocal because of potentially confounding variables. For example, variables such as familiarity of the letter string were not measured in most of the studies. Because there appears to be a relatively strong correlation between familiarity and concreteness, this factor could be responsible for at least some of the observed effects (see Schwanenflugel et al., 1988).

An interesting and consistent finding that has occurred in the literature addressing concreteness effects is that there appears to be an interaction between concreteness and word frequency. Specifically, concrete words produce faster lexical decisions compared to abstract words, primarily for low-frequency words but not for high-frequency words (de Groot, 1989; James, 1975; Kroll & Merves, 1986). Although this finding appears to be relatively consistent in the word recognition literature, Kroll and Merves have argued that it is possible that this interaction may be more a reflection of postlexical decision processes that are tied to the lexical decision task rather than task-independent word recognition processes. Again, we find concerns about the dimensions of the tasks used to measure word recognition.

It is in this light that a study by Bleasdale (1987) is quite intriguing. Bleasdale was interested in the influence of semantic context on word recognition processes tied to abstract and concrete words. Because we are interested in the influence of concreteness on isolated word recognition, we will focus on results from Bleasdale's neutral context condition. In this condition, either abstract or concrete words were preceded by the word *blank*. There is no a priori reason to suspect that such neutral primes should differentially influence word identification processes for abstract and concrete words. (Although it is at least possible that *blank* may provide a better prime for concrete words than abstract words; consider *blank letter* vs. *blank love*.) Bleasdale found consistent evidence for an advantage of concrete words over abstract words in pronunciation performance. Moreover, the stimuli that Bleasdale used appeared to be well controlled on relevant variables that might be related to concreteness, such as rated subjective familiarity. Thus, the Bleasdale study provides some of the best evidence available to support an effect of concreteness on word recognition.

B. Meaningfulness

A second semantic variable that might play a role in word recognition is the MEANINGFULNESS of the stimulus. Of course, meaningfulness can be defined in many ways. For example, one might simply look up the number of meanings that are listed under a given word in the dictionary. Jastrzembski (1981) used this metric and found that words possessing many (>10) meanings produced faster lexical decisions than words possessing few (<4) meanings. However, Gernsbacher (1984) demonstrated that number of dictionary meanings of a given word does predict lexical decision time when familiarity is confounded with meaningfulness but does not predict lexical decision time when familiarity is controlled. Moreover, it is also unclear whether subjects actually have representations for all meanings. For example, the word *fudge* has 13 entries listed with it. Although possible, it seems unlikely the subjects have more than four or five distinct meanings of the word *fudge* available (see Millis & Button, 1989, for further discussion of different metrics of meaningfulness).

A second approach to meaningfulness has been to compare words that have multiple distinct meaning representations and words that appear to only have a single meaning representation. Consider the homograph *organ*; one meaning refers to 'musical instrument' and the second meaning refers to 'bodily system'. Rubenstein et al. (1970; also see Rubenstein, Lewis, & Rubenstein, 1971) found that, compared to nonhomographs, homographs produced faster lexical decisions. Unfortunately, Clark (1973) closely scrutinized the Rubenstein results and found that most of the effect was produced by a few idiosyncratic items, and hence when one conducts item analyses instead of the traditional subject analyses, the effect disappears. More recently, however, Kellas, Ferraro, and Simpson (1988) also found that homographs produced faster lexical decisions than nonhomographs. This effect was reliable both by subjects and by items (F. R. Ferraro, personal communication) and hence is not susceptible to the criticism leveled by Clark regarding the Rubenstein et al. study. Moreover, the stimuli appeared to be well equated on potentially important confounding factors such as familiarity. Finally, we (Balota and Ferraro) have recently replicated this same effect with the Kellas et al. stimuli in a pronunciation task. Thus, the effect does not appear to be task-specific.

In sum, it appears that the number of meanings available for a word does modulate performance on word recognition tasks. This of course would be expected if there were a top-down impact from a meaning-level representation to a word-level representation. It should also be noted, however, that—although the results are encouraging—because of its rather checkered past, more work clearly needs to be done to firmly establish an impact of meaningfulness above and beyond other variables in word recognition tasks.

C. Contextual Availability

Recently, Schwanenflugel et al. (1988; also see Schwanenflugel & Shoben, 1983) have provided evidence that a variable referred to as contextual availability can produce an influence on isolated word recognition in lexical decision performance above and beyond influences of correlated variables such as concreteness, familiarity, length, and so on. Contextual availability refers to how easily a subject is able to think of a particular context or circumstance in which a given word might occur. As examples, Schwanenflugel et al. present the words *baseball* and *emotion,* both of which would be rated relatively high in contextual availability, and the words *inversion* and *sloop,* both of which would be rated relatively low in contextual availability. The results of three lexical decision experiments indicated that contextual availability reliably predicted lexical decision performance above and beyond familiarity, word frequency, and word length.

Of course, just as in the case of familiarity, one might ask what sorts of information subjects use in making untimed contextual availability ratings. Are subjects somehow relying on the "wordness" of the stimuli, and wordness is the dimension that is actually predicting lexical decision performance? In this light, it would be quite useful to determine whether contextual availability might also predict pronunciation performance. However, until such data become available, the role of contextual availability in isolated lexical decision performance would appear to provide at least some converging evidence that meaning can play a role in a task used to measure isolated word recognition.

D. Other Semantic Variables That Produce Effects in Isolated Word Recognition Paradigms

Because of space limitations, I shall only briefly mention a few other findings that would appear to indicate that meaning can have an early impact in word recognition performance. First, there is evidence that concreteness of a word can influence the time taken to generate an associate from that word (e.g., de Groot, 1989). Because subjects must recognize a word en route to generating an associate, this effect might be due to word recognition processes. Second, and along these same lines, Chumbley and Balota (1984) have found that the time taken to generate associates from one group of subjects can be used as a predictor of lexical decision performance for the same set of words when presented in isolation to a second group of subjects, above and beyond other related variables such as frequency, length, and so on. Third, Whittlesea and Cantwell (1987) found that providing meaning for a nonword can produce a word superiority effect, and also a study by Forster (1985) found that providing meaning for a nonword can produce a masked form priming effect in the lexical decision task. Both the word superiority effect and the masked form priming effect would appear to tap relatively early lexical processes. Finally, there is evidence from masked semantic priming studies (e.g., Balota, 1983; Carr & Dagenbach, 1990; Dagenbach, Carr, & Wilhelmsen, 1989; Fowler, Wolford, Slade, & Tassinary, 1981; Hirshman & Durante, 1992; Marcel, 1983) suggesting that highly masked primes (that subjects apparently cannot consciously recognize) produce semantic priming effects, that is, facilitate the processing of related targets compared to unrelated targets (see, however, concerns raised by Holender, 1986, and the accompanying commentaries for a full discussion of the degree of conscious processing of the primes in these studies). At the very least, such threshold priming effects suggest that under presentation conditions that minimize conscious processing of the prime, meaning access can still occur.

E. Summary

The possibility that meaning-level representations play a role in isolated word recognition has relatively far reaching implications for current models of word recognition. Most of the available models emphasize the stages that subjects use in accessing the mental lexicon, with virtually no allowance for a top-down meaning-level influence. However, when reminded that the role orthographic patterns play in reading is to convey meaning and not simply to convey lexicality, then one might easily envisage an architecture that incorporates a relatively early influence of meaning. At this level, it should be no surprise that meaning-level representations may contribute to relatively early perceptual analyses and aid in constraining the percept, that is, recognition of the word.

VI. CONTEXT/PRIMING EFFECTS

Heretofore, I have primarily discussed the literature that deals with variables that influence isolated visual word recognition. Of course, readers typically encounter words in the context of other words. We now turn to a summary of the influences of contexts (hereafter referred to as primes) on word recognition processes. In these studies, two strings of letters are typically presented, and the researcher manipulates the relation between the two strings. For example, the strings may be orthographically related (*couch–touch*), phonologically related (*much–touch*), or semantically related (*feel–touch*). By manipulating the types of relationships between the primes and targets, one can obtain evidence regarding the architecture of the word recognition system. For a more detailed discussion of this literature, the reader is referred to Neely (1991) for single-word semantic priming studies and Stanovich and West (1983) for sentence context studies. In addition, the reader is referred to Simpson (this volume) for a review of the role of context in the processing of ambiguous words.

A. Orthographic Priming Effects

An interesting approach to identifying the access code in word recognition is the masked orthographic priming paradigm developed by Evett and Humphreys (1981; also see Humphreys, Besner, & Quinlan, 1988; Humphreys, Evett, Quinlan, & Besner, 1987). In this paradigm, subjects are briefly shown two strings of letters that are both preceded and followed by pattern masks. The two strings vary in terms of orthographic, phonological, or semantic relatedness. Here, we focus on the orthographic priming conditions. There are a number of interesting findings in the original Evett and Humphreys study: First, on most trials, subjects were unable to consciously identify the prime items, and hence any influence of the prime items presumably reflects early access processes. Second, subjects were better at identifying the second letter string when it shared letters with the first letter string even though these shared letters were presented in different case (i.e., there was priming from *lert* to LOST). Third, this effect occurred even when the prime items were nonwords.

There has been some controversy regarding the later finding of nonword orthographic priming. The theoretical controversy regarding the nonword orthographic priming effect concerns *where* in the processing system the orthographic priming effect takes place. If one only finds orthographic priming for words and not for nonwords, then this paradigm is most likely tapping lexical-level processes instead of sublexical orthographic processes. In fact, Forster (1987) and Forster and Davies (1984) failed to find orthographic priming effects from nonwords to target words in a lexical decision task. However, it is also possible that masked nonword primes in the lexical decision task bias the nonword response and hence produce some conflict with the word response on target word trials. In this light, it is noteworthy that Manso de Zuniga, Quinlan, and Humphreys (1987) and Sereno (1991) have reported masked orthographic priming effects in the pronunciation task. Hence, again the appearance of an effect of a variable appears to depend on the task used to measure that variable, and such a task dependency appears to have quite an important theoretical consequence.

It should also be noted here that there is considerable evidence that ortho-graphic codes can be accessed in the parafovea and can be used to facilitate later processing of visually presented words (e.g., Balota, Pollatsek, & Rayner, 1985; Balota & Rayner, 1983; Rayner, McConkie, & Ehrlich, 1978; Rayner, McConkie, & Zola, 1980; see Balota & Rayner, 1991, for a review). The work by Rayner et al. (1980) provides the clearest evidence for orthographic parafoveal priming. In this study, parafoveal letter strings were presented in a pronuncia-tion task. During the subject's saccade to the parafoveal target word, the first parafoveal string (e.g., *chovt*) was replaced by a different string (*chart*). Rayner et al. found that pronunciation latency was (a) facilitated if the preview string and the target string shared the first two or three letters, (b) not dependent on a match in case (upper or lower case) between the prime and target, and (c) uninfluenced by the lexicality of the parafoveal previews. (For further details of the work addressing eye movements, parafoveal processing, and reading, see Rayner and Sereno, this volume.)

In sum, there appears to be converging evidence from both foveal priming studies and parafoveal priming studies that orthographic codes that are not dependent on case-level information do facilitate word recognition performance. Hence, there is relatively strong evidence from this area for an abstract (case-independent) orthographic access code.

B. Phonological Priming Studies

As described above, there has been considerable debate concerning the role of phonological codes in word recognition. The extremes range from "all words must be recognized via a phonological (assembled) code" to the notion "all words are only accessed via an orthographic (addressed) code." Although there is some controversy regarding the role of a phonological code in visual word recognition, there is considerably less debate regarding the importance of phonological codes in reading text, wherein phonological codes produce repre-sentations that appear better suited for aspects of comprehension that place considerable demands on the working memory system (e.g., Baddeley, El-dridge, & Lewis, 1981; Besner, 1987; Slowiaczek & Clifton, 1980). The more narrow issue here is whether phonological codes are used in the word recogni-tion process. With this in mind, we now turn to the phonological priming literature.

Meyer, Schvaneveldt, and Ruddy (1974) reported one of the first studies of phonological priming effects. In the critical conditions of this study, subjects were presented with pairs of words that had (a) similar orthographic forms but different phonological forms (e.g., *couch–touch*), (b) similar orthographic and phonological forms (e.g., *bribe–tribe*), or (c) dissimilar orthographic and phono-logical forms (*chair–tribe*). Meyer et al. found that subjects were faster to make lexical decisions to orthographically and phonologically related pairs, compared to unrelated pairs, and slower to make lexical decisions to orthographically related but phonologically unrelated word pairs, compared to unrelated pairs. This pattern suggests a strong role of phonological information as an access code (also see Hillinger, 1980). However, H. G. Shulman, Hornak, and Sanders (1978) found that Meyer et al.'s results were only observed when the nonwords were pronounceable. When the nonwords were unpronounceable, Shulman et al. actually found facilitation for the orthographically related but phonologically unrelated pairs (e.g., *couch–touch*). Again, we find that the decision processes associated with the lexical decision task constrain one's interpretation of this finding. Tanenhaus, Flanigan, and Seidenberg (1980) provided evidence for orthographic and phonological activation in a Stroop paradigm wherein subjects were simply asked to name the color of the target word. Presumably because of competition between activated codes and the pronunciation response, subjects were actually slower to name the color of the target word when the primes and targets were orthographically and/or phonologically similar, compared to when they were unrelated.

Evett and Humphreys (1981) used the masked priming paradigm, described above, to investigate the viability of a phonological access code, under conditions wherein conscious processing was limited. They used conditions similar to the Meyer et al. study described above. The results of this study indicated that there was priming for pairs that were orthographically and phonologically related (e.g., *bribe–tribe*) compared to pairs that were orthographically related but phonologically unrelated (*break–freak*). Moreover, the effect occurred across case changes. In addition, in a similar masked priming paradigm, Humphreys, Evett, and Taylor (1982) found that identification accuracy was higher for targets (e.g., *chute*) that followed homophonic primes (e.g., *shoot*) compared to targets that followed graphemically related (e.g., *short*) or unrelated primes (*trail*). However, there was no facilitation from a nonword phonologically related prime (e.g., *smorl–SMALL*). Thus, the results from Humphreys et al. suggest that the phonological priming effect, as opposed to the orthographic priming effect discussed above, may be lexically mediated.

In an interesting variation of the masked phonological priming paradigm, Perfetti, Bell, and Delaney (1988) briefly presented target words (e.g., *made*) that were followed by nonword masks that were either phonologically related (e.g., *mayd*) or unrelated (*mard*) to the target word. The results indicated that under these conditions, subjects were more accurate at identifying the target word when it was masked by a phonologically related nonword compared to a phonologically unrelated nonword. Because these phonological effects occur quite strongly for nonwords, it would appear that, in contrast to the results of the Humphreys et al. study discussed above, these effects appear to be at a prelexical level.

It is also worth noting two studies by Van Orden (1987; Van Orden, Johnston, & Hale, 1988). These studies involved a semantic categorization task, in which subjects had to decide whether a given word was a member of a semantic category. The intriguing finding here is that subjects produced a considerably higher error rate for words that were homophones of an exemplar (e.g., *meet* for the category *food*), compared to an orthographically related control (e.g., *melt*). This finding would suggest a clear role of phonological information in accessing the semantics necessary for category verifications. Recently, Jared and Seidenberg (1991) have replicated and further specified the influence of phonology in this paradigm. Although there are a number of intriguing findings in the Jared and Seidenberg study, one of the major outcomes of this study is that the influence of phonology in the Van Orden paradigm primarily occurs for low-frequency words. This pattern appears to be consistent with the earlier observation of an interaction between frequency and spelling-to-sound regularity that was observed in word pronunciation performance.

Finally, it is also worth noting that just as in the case of orthographic priming, there is also recent evidence of phonological priming in the parafoveal priming paradigm described above. Specifically, Pollatsek, Lesch, Morris, and Rayner (1992) found that previews that were homophonic with targets (e.g., *site–cite*) facilitated performance (both in pronunciation latencies and fixation durations) compared to nonhomophonic previews that were controlled for orthographic similarity (e.g., *cake–sake*). Again, this pattern would appear to support a role for phonology as an access code.

C. Semantic Priming Effects

The SEMANTIC (associative) PRIMING paradigm is by far the most well researched area of priming. This enterprise began with a seminal study by Meyer and Schvaneveldt (1971). They found that subjects were faster to make lexical decisions to each word in a pair of words when the words were related (e.g., *cat–dog*) compared to when the words were unrelated (e.g., *cat–pen*). The prevailing Zeitgeist was ready to welcome such a finding for a number of reasons: First, the dependent measure was response latency, and response latency measures were becoming the mainstay of cognitive experiments. Second, the study nicely demonstrated top-down contextual influences (e.g., semantic relations) on what would appear to be bottom-up word recognition processes. This was a major emphasis in Neisser's (1967) *Cognitive Psychology* that had been published a few years earlier. Third, the effect was quite robust and easily replicated. Fourth, the semantic priming task appeared to be ideally suited to map out the architecture of meaning-level representations and the retrieval operations that act on such representations; both of these issues would at least appear to be critical to higher level linguistic performance.

There is little controversy that across the three major tasks used to build word recognition models (threshold identification, lexical decision, and pronunciation), words are better recognized when embedded in semantically related contexts compared to unrelated contexts. However, there are many questions that one might ask about this effect. For example, one might ask whether this benefit is truly semantic or simply involves associative co-occurrence across words within a language. Here, by a semantic relationship I am referring to words that share semantic features (E. E. Smith, Shoben, & Rips, 1974) and/ or entail subordinate or superordinate semantic category relations (e.g., Collins & Quillian, 1969). For example, *mouse* and *rat* are semantically related because both are members of the rodent category. However, *mouse* and *cheese* are primarily associatively related because these words do not share a simple semantic category relationship or involve much overlap in semantic features. Of course, teasing apart semantic influences from associative influences has been rather difficult because these relationships typically co-occur. In an attempt to address this issue, researchers have identified items that are of the same category (e.g., *glove–hat*) but do not entail a strong associative relation, e.g., are not produced in associative production norm studies in which subjects are asked to generate associates to a given word (e.g., Palermo & Jenkins, 1964). The results from three such studies (e.g., Lupker, 1984; Schreuder, Flores d'Arcais, & Glazenborg, 1984; Seidenberg, Waters, Sanders, & Langer, 1984) indicate that there is still some priming with such stimuli in both lexical decision and in pronunciation, although the pure semantic effects are somewhat smaller in pronunciation.

However, one must be somewhat cautious in accepting the conclusion that there are pure nonassociative semantic priming effects. This caution is warranted for the following reasons: First, and foremost, it is unclear whether the relatively small pure semantic priming effects might be due to some lingering associative level relationship for words that researchers have argued only have a semantic relationship (e.g., *glove–hat* are probably more likely to co-occur compared to the pair *glove–pen*). Second, as noted below, there is evidence that priming can occur across mediated pairs within the memory network. Thus, it is at least possible that some of the priming from *glove* to *hat* is due to *glove* priming *clothes* and *clothes* priming *hat*. Third, when one considers low category dominance pairs, words that are categorically related but may have little associative relationship, one finds that there is relatively little priming in pronunciation performance (Keefe & Neely, 1990; Lorch, Balota, & Stamm, 1986), however, in lexical decision performance, there appears to be equivalent priming for high and low category dominance pairs (e.g., Lorch et al., 1986; Neely, Keefe, & Ross, 1989). The difference between pronunciation and lexical decision performance is particularly noteworthy here. A number of researchers have suggested that at least part of the priming effect observed in the lexical decision task may be due to a type of postlexical checking processes. Subjects can use the relatedness between the prime and target to bias their "word" response because nonwords by definition are never semantically related to the primes. In fact, Neely et al. (1989) have found that the priming effect for low-dominance exemplars (words that are acceptable but are produced relatively infrequently in category-exemplar production norms, e.g., *bird–goose*) in the lexical decision task depends on the ratio of nonwords to words. Neely et al. argue that the nonword/word ratio should modulate the utility of the checking process in the lexical decision task. Also, the fact that the pronunciation task yields little priming for low dominance category exemplars may reflect a decreased reliance on such a checking process in the pronunciation task. Hence, these data also question the evidence for a pure semantic priming effect in access processes.

1. Mediated Priming Effects

At an intuitive level, the finding that subjects are better at recognizing words that are embedded in related contexts compared to unrelated contexts is no great surprise. (Of course, it is clearly not so intuitive what mechanisms are responsible for such effects.) However, the priming literature has also provided some very counterintuitive findings. Consider the two words *lion* and *stripes*. These two words do not have any obvious direct relation but do have an indirect relation through the word *tiger*. Such items have been referred to as mediated pairs, and the research addressing mediated priming effects has provided some interesting results. First, in a lexical decision task in which subjects only respond to the target string, there is little evidence for mediated priming (cf. Balota & Lorch, 1986; DeGroot, 1983; Den Heyer, Sullivan, & McPherson, 1987). However, if one changes the lexical decision task so that subjects either (a) make lexical decisions about the prime and target (McNamara & Altarriba, 1988) or (b) only make a response to word targets and not to nonword targets (Den Heyer et al., 1987), mediated priming does occur in the lexical decision task. Moreover, when one now turns to the pronunciation task, one does find mediated priming effects (Balota & Lorch, 1986). Researchers have again argued that checking processes tied to the lexical decision task can strongly control when mediated priming effects will be found in this task (e.g., Balota & Lorch, 1986; McNamara & Altarriba, 1988; Neely, 1991). The notion is that checking for a relationship between the prime and target will not yield a successful outcome for mediated prime–target pairs, because such pairs do not share any obvious relationship. Thus, a negative outcome from the checking process may override the mediated influence from the prime to the target.

2. Threshold Priming Effects

A second counterintuitive finding in this literature deals with the threshold semantic priming effects, noted earlier. In these experiments, researchers first determine each subject's threshold wherein he or she can no longer discriminate between the presence or absence of a stimulus. These thresholds are then used in a later semantic priming task, in which the prime is presented at this threshold and the target is presented in a lexical decision task. The intriguing finding here is that there is still evidence for semantic priming effects, under conditions in which subjects apparently can no longer make presence/absence decisions about the prime item (Balota, 1983; Carr & Dagenbach, 1990; Dagenbach et al., 1989; Fowler et al., 1981; Marcel 1983; Marcel & Patterson, 1978). There have also been similar findings reported in the pronunciation task (Carr, McCauley, Sperber, & Parmelee, 1982; Hines, Czerwinski, Sawyer, & Dwyer, 1986). Although, as noted, there is some concern regarding whether subjects are truly at an objective presence/absence threshold (see Cheesman & Merikle, 1984; Holender, 1986; Merikle, 1982), it is clear that primes presented under very degraded conditions still produce semantic priming effects. As in the mediated priming studies, these studies appear to indicate that conscious access to a prime–target relationship does not appear to be a necessary condition for semantic priming effects.

3. Backward Priming Effects

The third area that is somewhat counterintuitive in this area is backward priming. There are two types of backward priming effects. First, there is evidence (Balota, Boland, & Shields, 1989; Kiger & Glass, 1983) that indicates one can still find semantic priming (*dog–cat* versus *pen–cat*) even when the prime (*dog* or *pen*) is presented temporally after the target (*cat*). These results suggest that early on in target processing, subsequent related prime information/ activation can actually catch up to influence response latencies to the target. Such an effect would appear to most naturally fall from a cascadic framework in which partial activation is released from representations before such representations have reached threshold (see earlier discussion of the McClelland & Rumelhart, 1981, model).

A second type of backward priming effect is backward semantic priming. In backward semantic priming, prime–target pairs are presented that entail directional relations, e.g., *bell* is related to *boy* in the *bell–boy* direction, but not in the *boy–bell* direction. Koriat (1981) and Seidenberg, Waters, Sanders, and Langer (1984) have reported evidence of backward priming in the lexical decision task. However, when one turns to the pronunciation task, there is relatively little evidence of backward priming (Seidenberg, Waters, Sanders, & Langer, 1984), except under short stimulus onset asynchronies (SOAs, the temporal interval between the onset of the prime and the onset of the target) and auditorily presented primes (see Peterson & Simpson, 1989). The prevailing account for the difference between the backward priming effects in pronunciation and lexical decision is that the priming effects in the pronunciation task are more directional from the prime to the target, whereas in the lexical decision task subjects may check for a relationship between the target and the prime (see Neely, 1991). Thus, if the subject checks in a backward fashion from the target (*bell*) to the prime (*boy*), a relationship will be found to bias the word response in the lexical decision task.

D. Syntactic Priming

If associative/semantic context does indeed influence lexical processing, then it is quite possible that syntactically appropriate versus inappropriate contexts might also influence lexical processing. In fact, effects of syntactic context on word recognition might be quite informative. At one level, one might argue that associative pathways between syntactically appropriate words might be represented within the lexicon, simply due to associative co-occurrence of such pairs (cf. Ratcliff & McKoon, 1988). Likewise, one might argue that syntactic tags within lexical representations might produce priming to consistent syntactic representations. On the other hand, one might argue that syntactic representations are only engaged after word recognition, and hence one might not expect syntactic priming effects in word recognition tasks.

One of the first syntactic priming studies was reported by Goodman, McClelland, and Gibbs (1981). Goodman et al. found that subjects were faster to make lexical decisions to targets (e.g., *oven*) that followed syntactically appropriate primes (e.g., *my*) compared to syntactically inappropriate primes (e.g., *he*). Seidenberg, Waters, Sanders, and Langer (1984) replicated this pattern in a lexical decision task but only obtained marginal effects in the pronunciation task. As in the priming studies mentioned above, Seidenberg et al. argued that the syntactic priming effect in the lexical decision task was probably due to some postlexical processing of the relation between the prime and target. However, it would appear that the Seidenberg et al. arguments are not totally correct, because West and Stanovich (1986) obtained relatively large syntactic priming effects in both the pronunciation task and the lexical decision task.

More recently, Sereno (1991) noted that the past syntactic priming effects may have been due to attentional expectancies that subjects may have built up because of relatively long prime–target stimulus onset asynchronies used in these studies (see discussion below regarding long SOAs and attentional expectancies). If this were the case, then the previously observed syntactic priming effects may not have been due to influences at the lexical level. In order to test this possibility, Sereno relied on the three-word masking paradigm developed by Forster and Davies (1984). On each trial, subjects were first presented an unrelated forward masking word for 500 ms and then were briefly presented the prime word for 60 ms, which was followed by the target word presented until a response was made. Because the prime is both forward- and backward-masked, conscious processing, and hence backward checking, is presumably limited. Sereno used both a lexical decision task and a pronunciation task to insure that any observed priming effects could not be simply due to residual conscious processing of the prime and its influence on the backward checking process in the lexical decision task. The results indicated that there were no syntactic priming effects in the pronunciation task but there were reliable syntactic priming effects in the lexical decision task. Based on this pattern, Sereno argued that the observed syntactic priming effects in the lexical decision task are most likely due to post-lexical processes that are tied to that task.

Although the Sereno results are quite compelling, it is also worth noting a study by Samar and Berent (1986). In this study, Samar and Berent recorded evoked responses in a syntactic priming lexical decision task. The interesting finding in this study is that there was a reliable evoked response component peaking 140 ms after target presentation that discriminated between conditions in which words were presented in syntactically appropriate contexts (e.g., *the-job, we-bring*) compared to syntactically inappropriate contexts (e.g., *the-bring, we-job*). Although there are some aspects of this study that may diminish the strength of the arguments (e.g., relatively long 500 ms prime–target SOA, and the use of the lexical decision task), the relatively early peak in the evoked response would appear to support an early role for syntactic analyses (see Bentin, 1989, and Kutas and Van Petten, this volume, for further reviews of the evoked response literature.)

E. Prime Type by Factor Interactions

Of course, the importance of the semantic priming literature is not simply the demonstration that certain factors produce facilitation in the lexical decision task and pronunciation tasks; its importance is also due to the intriguing interactions that have been uncovered. Again, because of space limitations, we can only list some of the more important interactions: (a) semantic priming effects are larger for low-frequency words than for high-frequency words (Becker, 1979); (b) semantic priming effects are larger for degraded words compared to nondegraded words (Becker & Killion, 1977; Borowsky & Besner, 1991) (the interactive effects of semantic priming and degradation become even more intriguing when one considers that word frequency effects are typically additive with stimulus degradation; Becker & Killion, 1977; Borowsky & Besner, 1991; see Besner & Smith, 1992, for a recent attempt to accommodate the combined influences of frequency, degradation, and semantic context); (c) semantic priming effects are larger for poor readers than good readers (Stanovich, 1980); (d) semantic priming effects are larger for the lexical decision task than for the pronunciation task (e.g., Balota & Lorch, 1986); (e) semantic priming effects in pronunciation increase across prime–target SOAs equally for high-strength and low-strength prime–target pairs (Balota & Duchek, 1988; Lorch, 1982); (f) semantic priming effects are larger for lists that contain a high proportion of related to unrelated prime–target trials compared to lists that contain a relatively low proportion of related to unrelated prime–target trials, hereafter referred to as the PROPORTIONAL RELATEDNESS EFFECT (e.g., den Heyer,

Briand, & Dannenbring, 1983; Keefe & Neely, 1990; Neely et al., 1989); (g) the proportional relatedness effect is larger at long prime–target SOAs than at short prime–target SOAs (e.g., den Heyer et al., 1983); (h) the proportional relatedness effect does not occur for low-dominance prime–target exemplars in the pronunciation task but does occur for such items in the lexical decision task (Neely et al., 1989); (i) prime-induced expectancy effects are larger when the prime–target SOA is relatively long compared to when the prime–target SOA is short (Balota, Black, & Cheney, 1992; Burke, White, & Diaz, 1987; Favreau & Segalowitz, 1983; Neely, 1977); (j) facilitation of response latencies to targets in the lexical decision task following related primes compared to neutral primes (e.g., *xxxxx*) decreases across SOAs, whereas inhibition of unrelated contexts compared to neutral primes increases across SOAs (e.g., Favreau & Segalowitz, 1983; Neely, 1977).

F. Theoretical Accounts of Semantic Priming Effects

The importance of the semantic priming paradigm has not simply been restricted to models of word recognition, but has also extended to more general issues concerning representation and retrieval processes. I shall now briefly discuss some of the theoretical issues that have been nourished by this literature. I refer the reader to Neely (1991) for further discussion of these theoretical mechanisms.

1. Automatic Spreading Activation

The notion that semantic/lexical memory may be represented by nodes that reflect concepts and that such conceptual nodes are interconnected via associative/semantic pathways has been central to a number of developments in cognitive psychology (e.g., Anderson, 1976, 1983; Collins & Loftus, 1975; Posner & Snyder, 1975). As Anderson (1983) points out, the spreading activation metaphor has probably been most strongly supported by the semantic priming paradigm. According to the spreading activation framework, when a node in memory becomes activated via stimulus presentation or via internal direction of attention, activation spreads from that node along associative pathways to nearby nodes. Thus, the reason that subjects are faster to recognize *dog* when it follows *cat,* compared to when it follows *pen,* is that the underlying representations for these two words are connected via an associative/semantic pathway, and when *cat* is presented activation spreads from its underlying node to the node underlying *dog.* Thus, the representation for *dog* needs less stimulus information to surpass threshold.

Although there is a limited-capacity version of spreading activation theory (e.g., Anderson & Bower, 1973), by far most of the work in the priming literature has addressed the AUTOMATIC nature of the spreading activation mechanism. In one of the clearest expositions of this mechanism, Posner and Synder (1975) argued that the automatic spreading activation mechanism (a) is fast-acting, (b) is independent of subjects' conscious control, and (c) primarily produces facilitation for related targets and little inhibition for unrelated targets, compared to an appropriate neutral baseline condition (see Neely, 1977). Because of current controversies regarding the adequacy of a given neutral prime condition (see, e.g., Balota & Duchek, 1989; DeGroot, Thomassen, & Hudson, 1982;

Jonides & Mack, 1984; Neely, 1991), I focus primarily on Posner and Synder's first two characteristics.

There are a number of important semantic priming results that would appear to support Posner and Synder's automatic spreading activation mechanism. First, with respect to the notion that priming effects are independent of consciously controlled processing, the finding that one still obtains priming effects under conditions in which the primes are briefly presented and highly masked (e.g., Balota, 1983; Fowler et al., 1981; Marcel, 1983) would appear to provide strong support for this assumption. In addition, the finding that there are mediated priming effects at relatively short prime–target SOAs (e.g., from *lion* to *stripes*), when it is unlikely that subjects could generate an attentional expectancy for the mediated target, also supports the notion of an automatic spread of activation within a memory network. Finally, the findings that prime-expectancy instructions (Neely, 1977) and relatedness proportion manipulations have relatively little impact at short SOAs (den Heyer et al., 1983) support the notion that the automatic spreading activation mechanism is relatively fast acting (i.e., occurs at short SOAs) and is independent of subjects' conscious expectations.

Although there appears to be strong support for something akin to an automatic spreading activation mechanism, there are some caveats that need to be noted. One issue that has been relatively controversial is whether priming effects occur across unrelated words (e.g., facilitation from *lion* to *tiger* in *lion–chalk–tiger* compared to *frog–chalk–tiger*). It is unclear why an unrelated word would disrupt an automatic spreading activation mechanism. However, Gough, Alford, and Holley-Wilcox (1981), Masson (1991), and Ratcliff and McKoon (1988) have all reported failures to obtain priming across unrelated words. Interestingly, there are two recent studies by Joordens and Besner (1992) and McNamara (1992) that have obtained such priming effects. Of course, one might expect such priming effects to be relatively small because the unrelated word may have the effect of shifting attention away from the related prime, and this shift may override any pure spreading activation effect. In fact, Joordens and Besner note that there have been small but nonsignificant effects in the predicted direction in the earlier studies. A second potential problem with the automatic nature of spreading activaton is that semantic priming effects can be eliminated when subjects process the primes in a very shallow fashion, as when responding to whether a given letter is in the prime or an asterisk is beside the prime (e.g., Henik, Friedrich, & Kellog, 1983; M. C. Smith, 1979; M. C. Smith, Theodor, & Franklin, 1983). Unless the shallow processing task eliminates processing of the prime at the lexical level, one should expect automatic spreading activation and semantic priming effects under shallow processing conditions (see, Besner, Smith, & MacLeod, 1990, for further discussion of this issue). Finally, Balota et al. (1992) have recently provided evidence that prime-expectancy instructions (e.g., when subjects are instructed to expect exemplars from the *tree* category when presented the prime *metals*) can influence pronunciation performance even at very short prime–target SOAs. Thus, although there is some evidence in support of an automatic spreading activation mechanism involved in semantic priming tasks, it appears that we still do not fully understand the constraints under which this mechanism operates.

2. Attentional/Expectancy Effects

A second mechanism that presumably underlies semantic priming effects is a more attention-based expectancy factor (Balota, 1983; Becker, 1980; Favreau & Segalowitz, 1983; Neely, 1976, 1977). Here, when the prime is presented, subjects generate expectancies about potential candidate targets. When the expectancy is correct, facilitation occurs; however, when the expectancy is incorrect, inhibition occurs. This expectancy-based model of priming falls naturally from the work of Posner and Snyder (1975) and Neely (1977), wherein instructional manipulations and list context effects have larger influences at long SOAs (when expectancies have had time to be generated) than at short SOAs. Of course, at one level the impact of an attentional-based expectancy mechanism should not be surprising because it simply reflects the probability of correctly predicting the target word. The more intriguing work here is the specification of the parameters that modulate the expectancy effects, that is, the rate at which expectancies are generated across time, the duration at which the expectancy is maintained, and the characteristics of such an expectancy set (see Becker, 1980, 1985, for a detailed discussion of a semantic expectancy model).

3. Backward-Checking Accounts

As noted above, a number of researchers have argued that priming effects in the lexical decision task may reflect influences at a postlexical decision level (e.g., Balota & Lorch, 1986; DeGroot, 1984; Forster, 1979, 1981; Neely, 1976, 1977; Neely & Keefe, 1989; Seidenberg, Waters, Sanders, & Langer, 1984; Stanovich & West, 1983). Subjects can rely on finding a relationship between the prime and target to bias the "word" response in the lexical decision task, because nonwords are never related to the primes. This would have the effect of facilitating "word" decisions to related prime–target trials and possibly inhibiting "word" decisions to unrelated prime–target trials. As described above, there is considerable support for such a mechanism in the lexical decision task. For example, the finding that there is backward priming in the lexical decision task (e.g., priming from *boy* to *bell*) suggests that subjects can use the target to check in a backward direction (*bell* to *boy*) about any potential relationship to the prime item. Although the backward-checking mechanism would appear to be primarily a nuisance variable tied to the lexical decision task, one might argue that this checking process may reflect a tendency in natural language processing to integrate meanings across words (see Neely & Keefe, 1989, for a full discussion of the backward checking mechanism).

4. Ratcliff and McKoon's (1988) Compound Cue Model

Ratcliff and McKoon have developed a model that takes a quite different approach to priming effects in the lexical decision task. The model is based on a formal model of episodic recognition memory developed by Gillund and Shiffrin (1984). In Ratcliff and McKoon's model, items in short-term memory serve as a compound cue, with the more recently presented items having a larger influence on the output of the retrieval process. If the prime and target are associated, then this will provide a higher familiarity value than if the prime and target are not associated. Familiarity is then used to predict response latency via a random-walk decision process (Ratcliff, 1978) wherein high-familiar compound cues produce relatively fast "word" decisions and low-familiar compound cues (e.g., nonwords) produce relatively fast "nonword" decisions. Intermediate values of familiarity produce relatively slower and less accurate decisions. Hence, if familiarity is modulated by the degree to which primes and targets are either directly associated or share associates in memory, then one should find that related prime–target pairs will produce higher familiarity values and faster response latencies in the lexical decision task than unrelated prime–target pairs.

The compound cue model has a number of positive characteristics. First, the model is based on formal memory models. The quantitative aspect of this model is a clear strength over other theories of semantic priming. Second, as Ratcliff and McKoon point out, their model handles a number of important findings in the priming lexical decision literature that spreading activation or attentional expectancy mechanisms do not appear to handle. For example, the model nicely accounts for backward priming effects in the lexical decision task because the target *boy* and prime *bell* can serve as a compound cue that is directly related in memory and hence produces a high familiarity value. The model can also handle single-step mediated priming effects (from *lion* to *stripes* via *tiger*) but apparently cannot handle two-step mediated priming effects (e.g., *mane* to *stripes* via both *lion* and *tiger,* see McKoon & Ratcliff, 1992, and McNamara, 1992, for further discussion of mediated priming effects).

Although the compound cue model does provide an interesting alternative to prime-induced mechanisms, there are some limitations to this approach. For example, the model is primarily a model of the lexical decision task and hence does not account for the wealth of interesting priming data from the pronunciation task. The tripartite (spreading activation, attentional expectancies, and backward checking) framework accounts for both lexical decision and pronunciation results by assuming logogen-type word recognition devices that are also connected to a phonological output system used for pronunciation. Second, and more important, the distinction between the compound cue model and the spreading activation framework may be more apparent than real. In both frameworks, it is necessary to map the influence of relationships between words onto priming effects. Within the spreading activation framework, this mapping involves the preactivation of related concepts in memory, whereas within the compound cue model, this mapping is based on a rule that computes familiarity based on associations within long-term memory. At this level, the major distinction between the spreading activation framework and the compound cue model involves the mapping process.

G. Summary of Context/Priming Effects

The semantic priming literature has provided an extremely rich database for developing models of context effects, memory retrieval, and word recognition. Because of space limitations, I was unable to provide a review of other important models of semantic priming effects such as Becker's (1980) verification model, Norris' (1986) plausibility-checking model, Forster's (1981) bin model, and Masson's (1991) recent connectionist model. Each of these models provide intriguing alternative perspectives on semantic priming effects. However, at this point in theory development, I would agree with Neely (1991) that no single model of priming is available that readily accounts for the richness and diversity of this literature, and it would appear that multiple mechanisms will need to be postulated to account for the breadth of priming effects. At least at the present stage of development, it would appear that some variants of spreading activation, attentional prediction, and backward checking will need to be incorporated into a model to account for most of the observed semantic priming effects.

VII. CONCLUDING REMARKS

In the present chapter I have attempted to provide the reader with an overview of the major issues addressed in the word recognition literature. To conclude, I would like to address some of the major themes that have spanned a number of the sections.

First, in each of the sections, there has been evidence initially supporting a rather straightforward theoretical analysis, and then there have been reports by trouble-makers that constrain the strength of the theoretical inferences available from a given task. For example, even in the word superiority paradigm, there have been arguments that partial information from the target letter could, in conjunction with the word envelope, allow subjects to use a sophisticated guessing strategy to bias the correct choice (e.g., Krueger & Shapiro, 1979; Massaro, 1979). If this is the case, then the word superiority effect may not reflect top-down impacts in perception, but rather biases that occur at postperceptual levels, based on partial information. Similar concerns were raised about the threshold identification, lexical decision, and pronunciation tasks. Of course, task analyses can be frustrating for theoreticians. However, before inferences can be made regarding the underlying locus or loci of a given variable, one needs to be especially careful in developing tasks that faithfully reflect such processes. Clearly, the adequacy of any theory rests on the adequacy of the tasks used to build that theory.

A second consistent theme that has surfaced in this review is whether separable sublexical analyses are performed en route to word recognition, or the apparent influences of sublexical analyses are in large part merely a consequence of the activation and inhibition patterns across many lexical representations. Although some effects appear to be modeled quite well by interactive activation and parallel distributed processing systems, there have also been results that appear inconsistent with such systems. There are at least two likely outcomes to this area of work: First, more of the apparent sublexical effects may fall from these models when networks that are closer to the size of an adult's vocabulary are implemented (see Seidenberg & McClelland, 1990). Second, it may be necessary to implement sublexical processing modules within such connectionist models to incorporate these types of analyses. Ultimately, however, the potential for this level of explanatory power makes the connectionist modeling in word recognition very appealing.

A third theme in the present review is actually a type of statistical interaction that has been repeatedly observed. The vast majority of interactions in this literature are of the nature that Factor A has more of an effect at the level of Factor B that produces the slowest or least accurate performance. Consider, for example, word frequency. I have reviewed evidence indicating that compared to high-frequency words, low-frequency words produce larger effects of bigram frequency, phonological regularity, word-body strength, concreteness, semantic priming, task (lexical decision task vs. category verification vs. pronunciation), repetition priming, and neighborhood size, among others. There are at least two noteworthy aspects of these interactions. First, one may wish to argue that because of the development of automaticity, high-frequency words are recognized via routes that effectively bypass many sublexical stages of analyses. Hence, if one is interested in identifying many of the intriguing sublexical aspects of word recognition, one should primarily investigate the processing of low-frequency words. Alternatively, as Loftus (1978) has noted, on a simply statistical level, this particular type of interaction is one of the most difficult to interpret. In fact, it is possible that if one considered percentage of overall response latency change as a function of the levels for Factor A and B, many of these interactions would disappear. In this light, it may be the interactions that still remain after considering percentage change as the dependent measure that may be most informative regarding underlying mechanisms.

Finally, I should note that there are many issues that have not been reviewed simply because of space limitations. For example, I have not discussed word recognition performance in beginning readers and some of the lexical-level breakdowns that appear to occur in developmental dyslexia (see Seymour, 1986, for a review). Also, I decided to attempt to provide an overview of the well-established empirical findings at many different levels of the processing stream, at some cost to treatments of the diverse and rather elegant theoretical accounts of such findings. The emphasis on the empirical literature was in part due to the fact that alternative theoretical accounts at least in some cases appear to be equally plausible. As Anderson (1978) has pointed out, this can often be a striking limitation in cognitive theory development. We are still in search of the critical experiment in many cases to discriminate models. It is quite possible that we will be forced to await physiological evidence to help discriminate between some of these models. Although clearly still relatively early in its development, cognitive neuroscience has considerable potential to contribute to our understanding of the word recognition system.

In light of this chapter, I am hopeful that the reader agrees that at some level the word is to cognitive psychologists and linguists as the cell is to biologists. Both entail many substructures and interact with many higher level systems. The present overview of the word recognition literature may seem rather imposing, and sometimes it would appear that little progress is being made. However, I clearly do not feel that this is the case and believe that considerable progress has been made. At this level, the seductive simplicity of understanding lexical-level analyses surely is more apparent than real. As is often the case in a discipline, the more we know about a system, the more we realize what we need to know to understand that system.

ACKNOWLEDGMENTS

This work was, in part, supported by NIA grant 54297A. Thanks are extended to Sheila Black, Lisa Connor, Janet Duchek, Lisa Foley, Richard Ferraro, and especially Morton Gernsbacher for helpful comments on earlier drafts of this manuscript.

REFERENCES

Abrams, R. A., & Balota, D. A. (1991). Mental chronometry: Beyond reaction time. *Psychological Science, 2*, 153–157.

Adams, M. (1981). What good is orthographic redundancy? In H. Singer & O. J. L. Tzeng (Eds.), *Perception of print* (pp. 197–221). Hillsdale, NJ: Erlbaum.

Anderson, J. R. (1976). *Language, memory, and thought.* Hillsdale, NJ: Erlbaum.

Anderson, J. R. (1978). Arguments concerning representations for mental imagery. *Psychological Review, 85*, 249–277.

Anderson, J. R. (1983). A spreading activation theory of memory. *Journal of Verbal Learning and Verbal Behavior, 22*, 261–295.

Anderson, J. R., & Bower, G. H. (1973). *Human associative memory.* Washington, DC: Hemisphere Press.

Andrews, S. (1982). Phonological recoding: Is the regularity effect consistent? *Memory & Cognition, 10*, 565–575.

Andrews, S. (1989). Frequency and neighborhood size effects on lexical access: Activation or search? *Journal of Experimental Psychology: Learning, Memory, and Cognition, 15*, 802–814.

Andrews, S. (1992). Frequency and neighborhood effects on lexical access: Lexical similarity or othographic redundancy? *Journal of Experimental Psychology: Learning, Memory, and Cognition, 18*, 234–254.

Appelman, I. B., & Mayzner, M. S. (1981). The letter-frequency effect and the generality of familiarity effects on perception. *Perception & Psychophysics, 30*, 436–446.

Ashby, F. G. (1982). Deriving exact predictions from the cascade model. *Psychological Review, 89*, 599–607.

Baddeley, A. D., Eldridge, M., & Lewis, V. J. (1981). The role of subvocalization in reading. *Quarterly Journal of Experimental Psychology, 33A*, 439–454.

Balota, D. A. (1983). Automatic semantic activation and episodic memory encoding. *Journal of Verbal Learning and Verbal Behavior, 22*, 88–104.

Balota, D. A. (1990). The role of meaning in word recognition. In D. A. Balota, G. B. Flores d'Arcais, & K. Rayner (Eds.), *Comprehension processes in reading* (pp. 9–32). Hillsdale, NJ: Erlbaum.

Balota, D. A., Black, S. R., & Cheney, M. (1992). Automatic and attentional priming in young and older adults: Reevaluation of the two-process model. *Journal of Experimental Psychology: Human Perception and Performance, 18*, 485–502.

Balota, D. A., Boland, J. E., & Shields, L. (1989). Priming in pronunciation: Beyond pattern recognition and onset latency. *Journal of Memory and Language, 28*, 14–36.

Balota, D. A., & Chumbley, J. I. (1984). Are lexical decisions a good measure of lexical access? The role of word frequency in the neglected decision stage. *Journal of Experimental Psychology: Human Perception and Performance, 10*, 340–357.

Balota, D. A., & Chumbley, J. I. (1985). The locus of word-frequency effects in the pronunciation task: Lexical access and/or production? *Journal of Memory and Language, 24*, 89–106.

Balota, D. A., & Chumbley, J. I. (1990). Where are the effects of frequency in visual word recognition tasks? Right where we said they were! Comment on Monsell, Doyle, and Haggard (1989). *Journal of Experimental Psychology: General, 119*, 231–237.

Balota, D. A., & Duchek, J. M. (1988). Age-related differences in lexical access, spreading activation, and simple pronunciation. *Psychology and Aging, 3*, 84–93.

Balota, D. A., & Duchek, J. M. (1989). Spreading activation in episodic memory: Further evidence for age independence. *Quarterly Journal of Experimental Psychology, 41A*, 84–93.

Balota, D. A., Ferraro, F. R., & Connor, L. T. (1991). On the early influence of meaning in word recognition: A review of the literature. In P. J. Schwanenflugel (Ed.), *The psychology of word meanings* (pp. 187–218). Hillsdale, NJ: Erlbaum.

Balota, D. A. and Ferraro, F. R. (1993). A dissociation of frequency and regularity effects in pronunciation performance across young adults, older adults, and individuals with senile dementia of the Alzheimer type. *Journal of Memory and Language, 32*, 573–592.

Balota, D. A., & Lorch, R. F. (1986). Depth of automatic spreading activation: Mediated priming effects in pronunciation but not in lexical decision. *Journal of Experimental Psychology: Learning, Memory, and Cognition, 12*, 336–345.

Balota, D. A., Pollatsek, A., & Rayner, K. (1985). The interaction of contextual constraints and parafoveal visual information in reading. *Cognitive Psychology, 17,* 364–390.

Balota, D. A., & Rayner, K. (1983). Parafoveal visual information and semantic contextual constraints. *Journal of Experimental Psychology: Human Perception and Performance, 5,* 726–738.

Balota, D. A., & Rayner, K. (1991). Word recognition processes in foveal and parafoveal vision: The range of influence of lexical variables, In D. Besner & G. W. Humphreys (Eds.), *Basic processes in reading* (pp. 198–232). Hillsdale, NJ: Erlbaum.

Baron, J., & Thurston, I. (1973). An analysis of the word-superiority effect. *Cognitive Psychology, 4,* 207–228.

Becker, C. A. (1979). Semantic context and word frequency effects in visual word recognition. *Journal of Experimental Psychology: Human Perception and Performance, 5,* 252–259.

Becker, C. A. (1980). Semantic context effects in visual word recognition: An analysis of semantic strategies. *Memory & Cognition, 8,* 493–512.

Becker, C. A. (1985). What do we really know about semantic context effects during reading? In D. Besner, T. G. Waller, & E. M. MacKinnon (Eds.), *Reading research: Advances in theory and practice* (Vol. 5) (pp. 125–166). Toronto: Academic Press.

Becker, C. A., & Killion, T. H. (1977). Interaction of visual and cognitive effects in word recognition. *Journal of Experimental Psychology: Human Perception and Performance, 3,* 389–401.

Bentin, S. (1989). Electrophysiological studies of visual word perception, lexical organization, and semantic processing: A tutorial review. *Language and Speech, 32,* 205–220.

Besner, D. (1987). Phonology, lexical access in reading, and articulatory supression: A critical review. *Quarterly Journal of Experimental Psychology, 39A,* 467–478.

Besner, D. (1990). Does the reading system need a lexcon? In D. A. Balota, G. B. Flores d'Arcaise, & K. Rayner (Eds.), *Comprehension processes in reading* (pp. 73–99). Hillsdale, NJ: Erlbaum.

Besner, D., Davelaar, E., Alcott, D., & Parry, P. (1984). Basic processes in reading: Evidence from the FDM and the FBI. In L. Henderson (Ed.), *Orthographies and reading.* Hillsdale, NJ: Erlbaum.

Besner, D., & McCann, R. S. (1987). Word frequency and pattern distortion in visual word identification and production: An examination of four classes of models. In M. Coltheart (Ed.), *Attention and performance XII: The psychology of reading* (pp. 201–219). Hillsdale, NJ: Erlbaum.

Besner, D., & Smith, M. C. (1992). Models of visual word recognition: When obscuring the stimulus yields a clearer view. *Journal of Experimental Psychology: Learning, Memory, and Cognition, 18,* 468–482.

Besner, D., Smith, M. C., & MacLeod, C. M. (1990). Visual word recognition: A dissociation of lexical and semantic processing. *Journal of Experimental Psychology: Learning, Memory, and Cognition, 16,* 862–869.

Besner, D., Twilley, L., McCann, R. S., & Seergobin, K. (1990). On the association between connectionism and data: Are a few words necessary? *Psychological Review, 97,* 432–446.

Bjork, E. L., & Estes, W. K. (1973). Letter identification in relation to linguistic context and masking conditions. *Memory & Cognition, 1,* 217–223.

Bleasdale, F. A. (1987). Concreteness-dependent associative priming: Separate lexical organization for concrete and abstract words. *Journal of Experimental Psychology: Learning, Memory, & Cognition, 13,* 582–594.

Boles, D. B. (1983). Dissociated imageability, concreteness, and familiarity in lateralized word recognition. *Memory & Cognition, 11,* 511–519.

Boles, D. B. (1989). Word attributes and lateralization revisited: Implications for dual coding and discrete versus continuous processing. *Memory & Cognition, 17,* 106–114.

Borowsky, R., & Besner, D. (1991). Visual word recognition across orthographies: On the interaction between context and degradation. *Journal of Experimental Psychology: Learning, Memory, and Cognition, 17,* 272–276.

Bradley, D. (1980). Lexical representations of derivational relations. In M. Aronoff & M. Kean (Eds.), *Juncture* (pp. 37–55). Cambridge, MA: MIT Press.

Broadbent, D. E. (1967). Word-frequency effects and response bias. *Psychological Review, 74,* 1–15.

Broadbent, D. E., & Gregory, M. (1968). Visual perception of words differing in letter digram frequency. *Journal of Verbal Learning and Verbal Behavior, 7,* 569–571.

Burke, D. M., White, H., & Diaz, D. L. (1987). Semantic priming in young and older adults: Evidence for age constancy in automatic and attentional processes. *Journal of Experimental Psychology: Human Perception and Performance, 13*, 79–88.

Caramazza, A., Laudanna, A., & Romani, C. (1988). Lexical access and inflectional morphology. *Cognition, 28*, 297–332.

Carr, T. H., & Dagenbach, D. C. (1990). Semantic priming and repetition priming from masked words: Evidence for a center-surround attentional mechanism in perceptual recognition. *Journal of Experimental Psychology: Learning, Memory, & Cognition, 16*, 341–350.

Carr, T. H., Davidson, B. J., & Hawkins, H. L. (1978). Perceptual flexibility in word recognition: Strategies affect orthographic computation but not lexical access. *Journal of Experimental Psychology: Human Perception and Performance, 4*, 674–690.

Carr, T. H., McCauley, C., Sperber, R. D., & Parmelee, C. M. (1982). Words, pictures, and priming: On semantic activation, conscious identification, and the automaticity of information processing. *Journal of Experimental Psychology: Human Perception and Performance, 8*, 757–777.

Catlin, J. (1969). On the word frequency effect. *Psychological Review, 76*, 504–506.

Catlin, J. (1973). In defense of sophisticated guessing theory. *Psychological Review, 80*, 412–416.

Cattel, J. M. (1885). The intertia of the eye and brain. *Brain, 8*, 295–312.

Cattel, J. M. (1886). The time it takes to see and name objects. *Mind, 11*, 63–65.

Cheesman, J., & Merikle, P. M. (1984). Priming with and without awareness. *Perception & Psychophysics, 36*, 387–395.

Chumbley, J. I., & Balota, D. A. (1984). A word's meaning affects the decision in lexical decision. *Memory & Cognition, 12*, 590–606.

Clark, H. H. (1973). The language-as-fixed fallacy: A critique of language statistics in psychological research. *Journal of Verbal Learning and Verbal Behavior, 12*, 335–359.

Collins, A., & Loftus, E. (1975). A spreading activation theory of semantic processing. *Psychological Review, 82*, 407–428.

Collins, A., & Quillian, M. R. (1969). Retrieval time from semantic memory. *Journal of Verbal Learning and Verbal Behavior, 8*, 240–247.

Coltheart, M. (1978). Lexical access in simple reading tasks. In G. Underwood (Ed.), *Strategies of information processing* (pp. 151–216). London & New York: Academic Press.

Coltheart, M., Curtis, B., Atkins, P., & Haller, M. (1993). Models of reading aloud: Dual-route and parallel-distributed processing approaches. *Psychological Review, 100*, 589–608.

Coltheart, M., Davelaar, E., Jonasson, J., & Besner, D. (1977). Access to the internal lexicon. In S. Dornic (Ed.), *Attention and performance, VI* (pp. 535–555). Hillsdale, NJ: Erlbaum.

Connine, C., Mullennix, J., Shernoff, E., & Yelens, J. (1990). Word familiarity and frequency in visual and auditory word recognition. *Journal of Experimental Psychology: Learning, Memory, and Cognition, 16*, 1084–1096.

Craik, F. I. M., & Lockhart, R. S. (1972). Levels of processing: A framework for memory research. *Journal of Verbal Learning and Verbal Behavior, 11*, 671–684.

Dagenbach, D., Carr, T. H., & Wilhelmsen, A. (1989). Task-induced strategies and near-threshold priming: Conscious influences on unconscious perception. *Journal of Memory and Language, 28*, 412–443.

Day, J. (1977). Right-hemisphere language processing in normal right-handers. *Journal of Experimental Psychology: Human Perception and Performance, 3*, 518–528.

de Groot, A. M. B. (1983). The range of automatic spreading activation in word priming. *Journal of Verbal Learning and Verbal Behavior, 22*, 417–436.

de Groot, A. M. B. (1984). Primed lexical decision: Combined effects of the proportion of related prime-target pairs and the stimulus onset asynchrony of prime and target. *Quarterly Journal of Experimental Psychology, 36A*, 253–280.

de Groot, A. M. B. (1989). Representational aspects of word imageability and word frequency as assessed through word associations. *Journal of Experimental Psychology: Learning, Memory, and Cognition, 15*, 824–845.

de Groot, A. M. B., Thomassen, A., & Hudson, P. (1982). Associative facilitation of word recognition as measured from a neutral prime. *Memory & Cognition, 10*, 358–370.

den Heyer, K., Briand, K., & Dannenbring, G. (1983). Strategic factors in a lexical decision task: Evidence for automatic and attention-drive processes. *Memory & Cognition, 11*, 374–381.

den Heyer, K., Sullivan, A., & McPherson, C. (1987). *Mediated priming in a single-response lexical decision task.* Unpublished manuscript.

Erdmann, B., & Dodge, R. (1898). *Psychologische Untersuchungen über das Lesen.* Halle, Germany: M. Niemery.

Evett, L. J., & Humphreys, G. W. (1981). The use of abstract graphemic information in lexical access. *Quarterly Journal of Experimental Psychology, 33A,* 325–350.

Favreau, M., & Segalowitz, N. S. (1983). Automatic and controlled processes in first- and second-language reading of fluent bilinguals. *Memory & Cognition, 11,* 565–574.

Feldman, L. B., & Andjelkovic, D. (1992). Morphological analysis in word recognition. In R. Frost & L. Katz (Eds.), *Phonology, orthography, morphology, and meaning.* (pp. 343–360). New York: North Holland Elsevier Science Publishers.

Fodor, J. (1983). *The modularity of mind.* Cambridge, MA: MIT Press.

Forster, K. I. (1978). Accessing the mental lexicon. In R. J. Wales & E. C. T. Walker (eds.), *New approaches to language mechanisms* (pp. 257–287). Amsterdam: North-Holland.

Forster, K. I. (1979). Levels of processing and the structure of the language processor. In W. E. Cooper & E. Walker (Eds.), *Sentence processing: Psychological studies presented to Merrill Garrett* (pp. 27–85). Hillsdale, NJ: Erlbaum.

Forster, K. I. (1981). Priming and the effects of sentence and lexical context on naming time: Evidence for autonomous lexical processing. *Quarterly Journal of Experimental Psychology, 33A,* 465–495.

Forster, K. I. (1985). Lexical acquisition and the modular lexicon. *Language and Cognitive Processes, 1,* 87–108.

Forster, K. I. (1987). Form-priming with masked primes: The best match hypothesis. In M. Coltheart (Ed.), *Attention and performance XII: The psychology of reading* (pp. 127–146). Hove, England and Hillsdale, NJ: Erlbaum.

Forster, K. I. (1989). Basic issues in lexical processing. In W. Marslen-Wilson (Ed.), *Lexical representation and process* (pp. 75–107). Cambridge MA: MIT University Press.

Forster, K. I., & Chambers, S. M. (1973). Lexical access and naming time. *Journal of Verbal Learning and Verbal Behavior, 12,* 627–635.

Forster, K. I., & Davies, C. (1984). Repetition priming and frequency attenuation in lexical access. *Journal of Experimental Psychology: Learning, Memory, and Cognition, 10,* 680–689.

Fowler, C. A., Wolford, G., Slade, R., & Tassinary, L. (1981). Lexical access with and without awareness. *Journal of Experimental Psychology: General, 110,* 341–362.

Frost, R., Katz, L., & Bentin, S. (1987). Strategies for visual word recognition and orthographical depth: A multilingual comparison. *Journal of Experimental Psychology: Human Perception and Performance, 13,* 104–115.

Gernsbacher, M. A. (1984). Resolving 20 years of inconsistent interactions between lexical familiarity and orthography, concreteness, and polysemy. *Journal of Experimental Psychology: General, 113,* 256–280.

Gibson, E., Osser, H., Schiff, W., & Smith, J. (1963). An analysis of critical features of letters, tested by a confusion matrix. In *A basic research program on reading* (Cooperative Research Project No. 639). Washington, DC: U.S. Office of Education.

Gibson, J. J., & Gibson, E. (1955). Perceptual learning: Differentiation or enrichment? *Psychological Review, 62,* 32–41.

Gillund, G., & Shiffrin, R. M. (1984). A retrieval model for both recognition and recall. *Psychological Review, 91,* 1–67.

Glushko, R. J. (1979). The organization and activation of orthographic knowledge in reading aloud. *Journal of Experimental Psychology: Human Perception and Performance, 5,* 674–691.

Goodman, G., McClelland, K., & Gibbs, R. (1981). The role of syntactic context in word recognition. *Memory & Cognition, 9,* 580–586.

Gough, P. B., Alford, J. A., & Holley-Wilcox, P. (1981). Words and contexts. In O. L. Tzeng & H. Singer (Eds.), *Perception of print: Reading research in experimental psychology* (pp. 85–102). Hillsdale, NJ: Erlbaum.

Grainger, J. (1990). Word frequency and neighborhood frequency effects in lexical decision and naming. *Journal of Memory and Language, 29,* 228–244.

Grainger, J., O'Regan, J. K., Jacobs, A. M., & Segui, J. (1989). On the role of competing word units in visual word recognition. *Perception & Psychophysics, 45,* 189–195.

Grainger, J., & Segui, J. (1990). Neighborhood frequency effects in visual word recognition: A comparison of lexical decision and masked identification latencies. *Perception & Psychophysics, 47,* 191–198.

Haas, W. (1970). *Phonographic translation.* Manchester: Manchester University Press.

Hanna, P. R., Hanna, J. S., Hodges, R. E., & Rudorf, E. H. (1966). *Phoneme–grapheme correspondences as cues to spelling improvement*. Washington, DC: U.S. Department of Health, Education, and Welfare.

Healy, A. F., & Drewnowski, A. (1983). Investigating the boundaries of reading units: Letter detection in misspelled words. *Journal of Experimental Psychology: Human Perception and Performance, 9*, 413–426.

Henderson, L. (1982). *Orthography and word recognition in reading*. London: Academic Press.

Henik, A., Friedrich, F. J., & Kellogg, W. A. (1983). The dependence of semantic relatedness effects upon prime processing. *Memory & Cognition, 11*, 366–373.

Hillinger, M. L. (1980). Priming effects with phonemically similar words: The encoding-bias hypothesis reconsidered. *Memory & Cognition, 8*, 115–123.

Hines, D., Czerwinski, M., Sawyer, P. K., & Dwyer, M. (1986). Automatic semantic priming: Effect of category exemplar level and word association level. *Journal of Experimental Psychology: Human Perception and Performance, 12*, 370–379.

Hirshman, E., & Durante, R. (1992). Prime identification and semantic priming. *Journal of Experimental Psychology: Learning, Memory, & Cognition, 18*, 255–265.

Holender, D. (1986). Semantic activation without conscious identification in dichotic listening, parafoveal vision, and visual masking: A survey and appraisal. *Behavioral and Brain Sciences, 9*, 1–66.

Howard, I. (1972). *A directional theory of rule application in phonology*. Dissertation at Massachusetts Institute Technology.

Hubel, D. H., & Wiesel, T. N. (1962). Receptive fields, binocular interaction and functional architecture in the cat's visual cortex. *Journal of Physiology (London), 160*, 106–154.

Hubel, D. H., & Wiesel, T. N. (1968). Receptive fields and functional architecture of monkey striate cortex. *Journal of Physiology (London), 195*, 215–243.

Humphreys, G. W., Besner, D., & Quinlan, P. T. (1988). Event perception and the word repetition effect. *Journal of Experimental Psychology: General, 117*, 51–67.

Humphreys, G. W., & Evett, L. J. (1985). Are there independent lexical and nonlexical routes in word processing? An evaluation of the dual route theory of reading. *Brain and Behavioral Sciences, 8*, 689–740.

Humphreys, G. W., Evett, L. J., Quinlan, P. T., & Besner, D. (1987). Priming from identified and unidentified primes. In M. Coltheart (Ed.), *Attention and performance XII: The psychology of reading* (pp. 105–126). London: Erlbaum.

Humphreys, G. W., Evett, L. J., & Taylor, D. E. (1982). Automatic phonological priming in visual word recognition. *Memory & Cognition, 10*, 576–590.

Inhoff, A. W., & Rayner, K. (1986). Parafoveal word processing during eye fixations in reading; Effects of word frequency. *Perception & Psychophysics, 34*, 49–57.

James, C. T. (1975). The role of semantic information in lexical decisions. *Journal of Experimental Psychology: Human Perception and Performance, 1*, 130–136.

Jared, D., McRae, K., & Seidenberg, M. S. (1990). The basis of consistency effects in word naming. *Journal of Memory and Language, 29*, 687–715.

Jared, D., & Seidenberg, M. S. (1990). Naming multisyllabic words. *Journal of Experimental Psychology: Human Perception and Performance, 16*, 92–105.

Jared, D., & Seidenberg, M. S. (1991). Does word identification proceed from spelling to sound to meaning? *Journal of Experimental Psychology: General, 120*, 358–394.

Jastrzembski, J. E. (1981). Multiple meanings, number of related meanings, frequency of occurrence, and the lexicon. *Cognitive Psychology, 13*, 278–305.

Johnston, J. C., & McClelland, J. L. (1973). Visual factors in word perception. *Perception & Psychophysics, 14*, 365–370.

Jonides, J., & Mack, R. (1984). On the cost and benefit of cost and benefit. *Psychological Bulletin, 96*, 29–44.

Joordens, S., & Besner, D. (1992). Priming effects that span an intervening unrelated word: Implications for models of memory representation and retrieval. *Journal of Experimental Psychology: Learning, Memory, & Cognition, 18*, 483–491.

Juola, J. F., Leavitt, D. D., & Choe, C. S. (1974). Letter identification in word, nonword, and single letter displays. *Bulletin of the Psychonomic Society, 4*, 278–280.

Just, M. A., & Carpenter, P. A. (1980). A theory of reading: From eye fixations to comprehension. *Psychological Review, 87*, 329–354.

Kay, J., & Bishop, D. (1987). Anatomical differences between nose, palm, and foot, or the body in question: Further dissection of the processes of sub-lexical spelling–sound translation. In M. Coltheart (Ed.), *Attention and performance XII: The psychology of reading* (pp. 449–470). London: Erlbaum.

Kay, J., & Marcel, A. J. (1981). One process, not two, in reading aloud: Lexical analogies do the work of non-lexical rules. *Quarterly Journal of Experimental Psychology, 37A,* 39–81.

Keefe, D. E., & Neely, J. H. (1990). Semantic priming in the pronunciation task: The role of prospective prime-generated expectancies. *Memory & Cognition, 18,* 289–298.

Kellas, G., Ferraro, F. R., & Simpson, G. B. (1988). Lexical ambiguity and the timecourse of attentional allocation in word recognition. *Journal of Experimental Psychology: Human Perception and Performance, 14,* 601–609.

Kiger, J. I., & Glass, A. (1983). The facilitation of lexical decisions by a prime occurring after the target. *Memory & Cognition, 11,* 356–365.

Kinney, G. C., Marsetta, M., & Showman, D. J. (1966). *Studies in display symbol legibility. Part XII. The legibility of alphanumeric symbols for digitized television* (ESD-TR066-117). Bedford MA: The Mitre Corporation.

Koriat, A. (1981). Semantic facilitation in lexical decision as a function of prime–target association. *Memory & Cognition, 9,* 587–598.

Kroll, J. F., & Merves, J. S. (1986). Lexical access for concrete and abstract words. *Journal of Experimental Psychology: Learning, Memory, and Cognition, 12,* 92–107.

Krueger, L. E., & Shapiro, R. G. (1979). Letter detection with rapid serial visual presentation. Evidence against word superiority of feature extraction. *Journal of Experimental Psychology: Human Perception and Performance, 5,* 657–673.

Kucera, H., & Francis, W. (1967). *Computational analysis of present-day American English.* Providence, RI: Brown University Press.

LaBerge, D., & Samuels, S. J. (1974). Toward a theory of automatic information processing in reading. *Cognitive Psychology, 6,* 293–323.

Lima, S. D. (1987). Morphological analysis in sentence reading. *Journal of Memory and Language, 26,* 84–99.

Loftus, G. R. (1978). On interpretation of interactions. *Memory & Cognition, 6,* 312–319.

Lorch, R. F. (1982). Priming and search processes in semantic memory: A test of three models of spreading activation. *Journal of Verbal Learning and Verbal Behavior, 21,* 468–492.

Lorch, R. F., Balota, D. A., & Stamm, E. G. (1986). Locus of inhibition effects in the priming of lexical decision: Pre- or post-lexical access? *Memory & Cognition, 14,* 95–103.

Luce, P. A., & Pisoni, D. B. (1989). *Neighborhoods of words in the mental lexicon.* Unpublished manuscript.

Luce, R. D. (1959). *Individual choice behavior.* New York: Wiley.

Lupker, S. J. (1984). Semantic priming without association: A second look. *Journal of Verbal Learning and Verbal Behavior, 23,* 709–733.

MacKay, D. (1972). The structure of words and syllables: Evidence from words and speech. *Cognitive Psychology, 3,* 210–227.

Manelis, L. (1974). The effect of meaningfulness in tachistoscopic word perception. *Perception & Psychophysics, 16,* 182–192.

Manso de Zuniga, C. M., Humphreys, G. W., & Evett, L. J. (1991). Additive and interactive effects of repetition, degradation, and word frequency in the reading of handwriting. In D. Besner & G. Humphreys (Eds.), *Basic processes in reading visual word recognition* (pp. 10–33). Hillsdale, NJ: Erlbaum.

Manso de Zuniga, C. M., Quinlan, P. T., & Humphreys, G. W. (1987). *Task effects on priming under masked conditions.* Unpublished manuscript.

Marcel, A. J. (1980). Surface dyslexia and beginning reading: A revised hypothesis of pronunciation of print and its impairments. In M. Coltheart, K. Patterson, & J. C. Marshall (Eds.), *Deep dyslexia* (pp. 227–258). London: Routledge & Kegan Paul.

Marcel, A. J. (1983). Conscious and unconscious perception: Experiments on visual masking and word recognition. *Cognitive Psychology, 15,* 197–237.

Marcel, A. J., & Patterson, K. E. (1978). Word recognition and production: Reciprocity in clinical and normal studies. In J. Requin (Ed.), *Attention and performance VII* (pp. 209–226). Hillsdale, NJ: Erlbaum.

Marshall, J. C., & Newcombe, F. (1980). The conceptual status of deep dyslexia: An historical perspective. In M. Coltheart, K. Patterson, & J. C. Marshall (Eds.), *Deep dyslexia* (pp. 1–21). London: Routledge & Kegan Paul.

Massaro, D. M. (1979). Letter information and orthographic context in word perception. *Journal of Experimental Psychology: Human Perception and Performance, 5,* 595–609.

Massaro, D. M., Venezky, R. L., & Taylor, G. A. (1979). Orthographic regularity, positional frequency and visual processing of letter strings. *Journal of Experimental Psychology: General, 108,* 107–124.

Masson, M. E. J. (1991). A distributed memory model of context effects in word identification. In D. Besner & G. W. Humphreys (Eds.), *Basic processes in reading: Visual word recognition.* Hillsdale, NJ: Erlbaum.

Mayzner, M. S. & Tresselt, M. E. (1965). Tables of single-letter and digram frequency counts for various word-length and letter-position combinations. *Psychonomic Monograph Supplements, 1,* 13–32.

Mayzner, M. S., Tresselt, M. E., & Wolin, B. R. (1965a). Tables of pentagram frequency counts for various word-length and letter position combinations. *Psychonomic Monograph Supplements, 1,* 144–186.

Mayzner, M. S., Tresselt, M. E., & Wolin, B. R. (1965b). Tables of tetragram frequency counts for various word-length and letter-position combinations. *Psychonomic Monograph Supplements, 1,* 79–143.

Mayzner, M. S., Tresselt, M. E., & Wolin, B. R. (1965c). Tables of trigram frequency counts for various word-length and letter-position combinations. *Psychonomic Monograph Supplements, 1,* 33–78.

McCarthy, R., & Warrington, E. K. (1986). Phonological reading: Phenomena and paradoxes. *Cortex, 22,* 359–380.

McClelland, J. L. (1979). On the time relations of mental processes: An examination of systems of processes in cascade. *Psychological Review, 86,* 287–330.

McClelland, J. L., & Johnston, J. C. (1977). The role of familiar units in perception of words and nonwords. *Perception & Psychophysics, 22,* 249–261.

McClelland, J. L., & Rumelhart, D. E. (1981). An interactive activation model of context effects in letter perception: Part 1. An account of basic findings. *Psychological Review, 88,* 375–407.

McClelland, J. L., & Rumelhart, D. E. (Eds.). (1986). *Parallel distributed processing: Explorations in the microstructure of cognition* (Vol. 2). Cambridge, MA: MIT Press.

McGinnies, E., Comer, P. B., & Lacey, O. L. (1952). Visual-recognition thresholds as a function of word length and word frequency. *Journal of Experimental Psychology, 44,* 65–69.

McKoon, G., & Ratcliff, R. (1992). Spreading activation versus compound cue accounts of priming: Mediated priming revisited. *Journal of Experimental Psychology: Learning, Memory, & Cognition 18,* 1151–1172.

McNamara, T. P. (1992). Theories of priming: I. Associative distance and list context. *Journal of Experimental Psychology: Learning, Memory, and Cognition 18,* 1173–1190.

McNamara, T. P., & Altarriba, J. (1988). Depth of spreading activation revisited: Semantic mediated priming occurs in lexical decisions. *Journal of Memory and Language, 27,* 545–559.

Merikle, P. M. (1982). Unconscious perception revisited. *Perception & Psychophysics, 31,* 298–301.

Meyer, D. E., & Schvaneveldt, R. W. (1971). Facilitation in recognizing words: Evidence of a dependence upon retrieval operations. *Journal of Experimental Psychology, 90,* 227–234.

Meyer, D. E., Schvaneveldt, R. W., & Ruddy, M. G. (1974). Functions of graphemic and phonemic codes in visual word recognition. *Memory & Cognition, 2,* 309–321.

Millis, M. L., & Button, S. B. (1989). The effect of polysemy on lexical decision time: Now you see it, now you don't. *Memory & Cognition, 17,* 141–147.

Monsell, S., Doyle, M. C., & Haggard, P. N. (1989a). The effects of frequency on visual word recognition tasks: Where are they? *Journal of Experimental Psychology: General, 118,* 43–71.

Monsell, S., Patterson, K., Graham, A., Hughes, C. H., & Milroy, R. (1992). Lexical and sublexical translations of spelling to sound: Strategic anticipation of lexical status. *Journal of Experimental Psychology: Learning, Memory, and Cognition, 18,* 452–467.

Morton, J. (1969). The interaction of information in word recognition. *Psychological Review, 76,* 165–178.

Neely, J. H. (1976). Semantic priming and retrieval from lexical memory: Evidence for facilitatory and inhibitory processes. *Memory & Cognition, 4,* 648–654.

Neely, J. H. (1977). Semantic priming and retrieval from lexical memory: Roles of inhibitionless spreading activation and limited-capacity attention. *Journal of Experimental Psychology: General, 106,* 226–254.

Neely, J. H. (1991). Semantic priming effects in visual word recognition: A selective review of current findings and theories. In D. Besner & G. Humphreys (Eds.), *Basic processes in reading: Visual word recognition* (pp. 236–264). Hillsdale, NJ: Erlbaum.

Neely, J. H., & Keefe, D. E. (1989). Semantic context effects on visual word processing: A hybrid prospective/retrospective processing theory. In G. H. Bower (Ed.), *The psychology of learning and motivation: Advances in research and theory* (Vol. 24, pp. 207–248). San Diego, CA: Academic Press.

Neely, J. H., Keefe, D. E., & Ross, K. L. (1989). Semantic priming in the lexical decision task: Role of prospective prime-generated expectancies and retrospective semantic matching. *Journal of Experimental Psychology: Learning, Memory, and Cognition, 15,* 1003–1019.

Neisser, U. (1967). *Cognitive psychology.* New York: Appleton, Century, Crofts.

Noble (1952). An analysis of meaning. *Psychological Review, 59,* 421–430.

Norris, D. (1986). Word recognition: Context effects without priming. *Cognition, 22,* 93–136.

Nusbaum, H. C., & Dedina, M. (1985). *The effects of word frequency and subjective familiarity on visual lexical decisions.* Research on speech perception. (Progress Report No. 11). Bloomington: Indiana University.

Nusbaum, H. C., Pisoni, D. B., & Davis, C. K. (1984). *Sizing up the Hoosier mental lexicon: Measuring the familiarity of 20,000 words.* Research on speech perception. (Progress Report No. 10). Bloomington: Indiana University.

Osgood, C. E., Suci, G. J., & Tannenbaum, P. H. (1957). *The measurement of meaning.* Urbana: University of Illinois Press.

Paap, K. R., Newsome, S. L., McDonald, J. E., & Schvaneveldt, R. W. (1982). An activation–verification model for letter and word recognition: The word superiority effect. *Psychological Review, 89,* 573–594.

Paap, K. R., & Noel, R. W. (1991). Dual route models of print to sound: Still a good horse race. *Psychological Research, 53,* 13–24.

Paivio, A., & O'Neill, B. J. (1970). Visual recognition thresholds and dimensions of word meaning. *Perception & Psychophysics, 8,* 273–275.

Palermo, D. S., & Jenkins, J. J. (1964). *Word association norms: Grade school through college.* Minneapolis: University of Minnesota Press.

Patterson, K. E. (1982). The relation between reading and phonological coding: Further neuropsychological observations. In A. W. Ellis (Ed.), *Normality and pathology in cognitive functions* (pp. 77–111). San Diego, CA: Academic Press.

Patterson, K. E., & Morton, J. (1985). From orthography to phonology: An attempt at an old interpretation. In K. E. Patterson, J. C. Marshall, & M. Coltheart (Eds.), *Surface dyslexia* (pp. 335–359). Hillsdale, NJ: Erlbaum.

Patterson, K. E., Seidenberg, M., & McClelland, J. L. (1989). Connections and disconnections: Acquired dyslexia in a computational model of reading processes. In R. G. M. Morris (Ed.), *Parallel distributed processing: Implications for psychology and neurobiology* (pp. 131–181). Oxford: Oxford University Press.

Perfetti, C. A., Bell, L. C., & Delaney, S. M. (1988). Automatic (prelexical) phonetic activation in silent word reading: Evidence from backward masking. *Journal of Memory and Language, 27,* 59–70.

Petersen, S. E., Fox, P. T., Snyder, A. Z., & Raichle, M. E. (1990). Activation of extrastriate and frontal cortical areas by visual words and word-like stimuli. *Science, 249,* 1041–1044.

Peterson, R. R., & Simpson, G. B. (1989). The effect of backward priming on word recognition in single-word and sentence contexts. *Journal of Experimental Psychology: Learning, Memory, and Cognition, 15,* 1020–1032.

Pollatsek, A., Lesch, M., Morris, R. K., & Rayner, K. (1992). Phonological codes are used in integrating information across saccades in word identification and reading. *Journal of Experimental Psychology: Human Perception and Performance, 18,* 148–162.

Posner, M. I. (1986). *Chronometric explorations of mind.* Oxford: Oxford University Press.

Posner, M. I., & Snyder, C. R. R. (1975). Attention and cognitive control. In R. Solso (Ed.), *Information processing and cognition: The Loyola symposium* (pp. 55–85). Hillsdale, NJ: Erlbaum.

Prinzmetal, W., Treiman, R., & Rho, S. H. (1986). How to see a reading unit. *Journal of Memory and Language, 25,* 461–475.

Purcell, D. G., Stanovich, K. E., & Spector, A. (1978). Visual angle and the word superiority effect. *Memory & Cognition, 7,* 3–8.

Rapp, B. C. (1992). The nature of sublexical orthographic organization: The bigram trough hypothesis examined. *Journal of Memory and Language, 31,* 33–53.

Ratcliff, R. (1978). A theory of memory retrieval. *Psychological Review, 85,* 59–108.

Ratcliff, R., & McKoon, G. (1988). A retrieval theory of priming in memory. *Psychological Review, 95,* 385–408.

Rayner, K., & Duffy, S. A. (1986). Lexical complexity and fixation times in reading: Effects of word frequency, verb complexity, and lexical ambiguity. *Memory & Cognition, 14,* 191–201.

Rayner, K., McConkie, G. W., & Ehrlich, S. F. (1978). Eye movements and integration across fixations. *Journal of Experimental Psychology: Human Perception and Performance, 4,* 529–544.

Rayner, K., McConkie, G. W., & Zola, D. (1980). Integrating information across eye movements. *Cognitive Psychology, 12,* 206–226.

Rayner, K., & Pollatsek, A. (1989). *The psychology of reading.* Englewood Cliffs, NJ: Prentice-Hall.

Reicher, G. M. (1969). Perceptual recognition as a function of meaningfulness of stimulus material. *Journal of Experimental Psychology, 81,* 274–280.

Rice, G. A., & Robinson, D. O. (1975). The role of bigram frequency in perception of words and nonwords. *Memory & Cognition, 3,* 513–518.

Rubenstein, H., Garfield, L., & Millikan, J. A. (1970). Homographic entries in the internal lexicon. *Journal of Verbal Learning and Verbal Behavior, 9,* 487–494.

Rubenstein, H., Lewis, S. S., & Rubenstein, M. (1971). Homographic entries in the internal lexicon: Effects of systematicity and relative frequency of meanings. *Journal of Verbal Learning and Verbal Behavior, 10,* 57–62.

Rumelhart, D. E., & McClelland, J. L. (1982). An interactive activation model of context effects in letter perception: Part 2. The contextual enhancement effect and some tests and extensions of the model. *Psychological Review, 89,* 60–94.

Rumelhart, D. E., & McClelland, J. L. (Eds.). (1986). *Parallel distributed processing: Explorations in the microstructure of cognition* (Vol. 1). Cambridge, MA: MIT Press.

Samar, V. J., & Berent, G. P. (1986). The syntactic priming effect: Evoked response evidence for a prelexical locus. *Brain and Language, 28,* 250–272.

Savage, G. R., Bradley, D. C., & Forster, K. I. (1990). Word frequency and the pronunciation task: The contribution of articulatory fluency. *Language and Cognitive Processes, 5,* 203–226.

Schendel, J. D., & Shaw, P. (1976). A test of the generality of the word-context effect. *Perception & Psychophysics, 19,* 383–393.

Schreuder, R., Flores d'Arcais, G. B., & Glazenborg, G. (1984). Effects of perceptual and conceptual similarity in semantic priming. *Psychological Research, 45,* 339–354.

Schwanenflugel, P. J., Harnishfeger, K. K., & Stowe, R. W. (1988). Context availability and lexical decisions for abstract and concrete words. *Journal of Memory and Language, 27,* 499–520.

Schwanenflugel, P. J., & Shoben, E. J. (1983). Differential context effects in the comprehension of abstract and concrete verbal materials. *Journal of Experimental Psychology: Learning, Memory, and Cognition, 9,* 82–102.

Seidenberg, M. S. (1985). The time course of phonological code activation in two writing systems. *Cognition, 19,* 1–30.

Seidenberg, M. S. (1987). Sublexical structures in visual word recognition: Access units or orthographic redundancy? In M. Coltheart (Ed.), *Attention and performance XII: The psychology of reading* (pp. 245–263). Hillsdale, NJ: Erlbaum.

Seidenberg, M. S., & McClelland, J. L. (1989). A distributed developmental model of word recognition and naming. *Psychological Review, 96,* 523–568.

Seidenberg, M. S., & McClelland, J. L. (1990). More words but still no lexicon: Reply to Besner et al. (1990). *Psychological Review, 97,* 447–452.

Seidenberg, M. S., Waters, G. S., Barnes, M. A., & Tanenhaus, M. (1984). When does irregular spelling or pronunciation influence word recognition? *Journal of Verbal Learning and Verbal Behavior, 23,* 383–404.

Seidenberg, M. S., Waters, G. S. Sanders, M., & Langer, P. (1984). Pre- and post-lexical loci of contextual effects on word recognition. *Memory & Cognition, 12,* 315–328.

Selfridge, O. G. (1959). Pandemonium: A paradigm for learning. In *Proceedings of a symposium on the mechanisation of thought processes* (pp. 511–526). London: H. M. Stationery Office.

Selfridge, O. G., & Neisser, U. (1960). Pattern recognition by machine. *Scientific American, 203,* 60–68.

Selkirk, E. O. (1980). *On prosodic structure and its relation to syntactic structure.* Bloomington: Indiana University Linguistics Club.

Sereno, J. A. (1991). Graphemic, associative, and syntactic priming effects at a brief stimulus onset asynchrony in lexical decision and naming. *Journal of Experimental Psychology: Learning, Memory, and Cognition, 17,* 459–477.

Seymour, M. K. J. (1986). *Cognitive analysis of dyslexia.* London: Routledge & Kegan Paul.

Shallice, T., & Warrington, E. K. (1980). Single and multiple component central dyslexic syndromes. In M. Coltheart, K. Patterson, & J. C. Marshall (Eds.), *Deep dyslexia* (pp. 119–145). London: Routledge & Kegan Paul.

Shallice, T., Warrington, E. K., & McCarthy, R. (1983). Reading without semantics. *Quarterly Journal of Experimental Psychology, 35A,* 111–138.

Shulman, G. L. (1990). Relation attention to visual mechanisms. *Perception & Psychophysics, 47,* 199–203.

Shulman, H. G., Hornak, R., & Sanders, E. (1978). The effects of graphemic, phonetic, and semantic relationships on access to lexical structures. *Memory & Cognition, 6,* 115–123.

Slowiaczek, M. L., & Clifton, C. (1980). Subvocalization and reading for meaning. *Journal of Verbal Learning and Verbal Behavior, 19,* 573–582.

Smith, E. E., Shoben, E. J., & Rips, L. J. (1974). Structure and process in semantic memory: A featural model for semantic decisions. *Psychological Review, 81,* 214–241.

Smith, M. C. (1979). Contextual facilitation in a letter search task depends on how the prime is processed. *Journal of Experimental Psychology: Human Perception and Performance, 5,* 239–251.

Smith, M. C., Theodor, L., & Franklin, P. E. (1983). On the relationship between contextual facilitation and depth of processing. *Journal of Experimental Psychology: Learning, Memory, and Cognition, 9,* 697–712.

Spoehr, K. T., & Smith, E. E. (1973). The role of syllables in perceptual processing. *Cognitive Psychology, 5,* 71–89.

Spoehr, K. T., & Smith, E. E. (1975). The role of orthographic and phonotactic rules in perceiving letter patterns. *Journal of Experimental Psychology: Human Perception and Performance, 1,* 21–34.

Stanners, R. F., Neiser, J. J., Hernon, W. P., & Hall, R. (1979). Memory representation for morphologically related words. *Journal of Verbal Learning and Verbal Behavior, 18,* 399–412.

Stanners, R. F., Neiser, J. J., & Painton, S. (1979). Memory representation for prefixed words. *Journal of Verbal Learning and Verbal Behavior, 18,* 733–743.

Stanovich, K. E. (1980). Toward an interactive-compensatory model of individual differences in the development of reading fluency. *Reading Research Quarterly, 16,* 32–71.

Stanovich, K. E., & West, R. F. (1983). On priming by sentence context. *Journal of Experimental Psychology: General, 112,* 1–36.

Taft, M. (1979a). Lexical access via an orthographic code: The Basic Orthographic Syllabic Structure (BOSS). *Journal of Verbal Learning and Verbal Behavior, 18,* 21–39.

Taft, M. (1979b). Recognition of affixed words and the word frequency effect. *Memory & Cognition, 7,* 263–272.

Taft, M. (1981). Prefix stripping revisited. *Journal of Verbal Learning and Verbal Behavior, 20,* 284–297.

Taft, M. (1985). The decoding of words in lexical access: A review of the morphographic approach. In D. Besner, T. G. Waller, & G. E. MacKinnon (Eds.), *Reading research: Advances in theory and practice* (Vol. 5) (pp. 83–123). Orlando, FL: Academic Press.

Taft, M. (1987). Morphographic processing: The BOSS Re-emerges. In M. Coltheart (Ed.), *Attention and performance XII: The psychology of reading* (pp. 265–279). Hillsdale, NJ: Erlbaum.

Taft, M., & Forster, K. I. (1975). Lexical storage and retrieval of prefixed words. *Journal of Verbal Learning and Verbal Behavior, 14,* 638–647.

Taft, M., & Forster, K. I. (1976). Lexical storage and retrieval of polymorphemic and polysyllabic words. *Journal of Verbal Learning and Verbal Behavior, 15,* 607–620.

Taft, M., & Hambly, G. (1986). Exploring the cohort model of spoken word recognition. *Cognition, 22,* 259–282.

Tanenhaus, M. K., Flanigan, H. P., & Seidenberg, M. S. (1980). Orthographic and phonological activation in auditory visual word recognition. *Memory & Cognition, 8,* 513–520.

Thorndike, E. L., & Lorge, I. (1944). *The teacher's word book of 30,000 words.* New York: Columbia University, Teachers College Press.

Treiman, R., & Chafetz, J. (1987). Are there onset and rime-like units in printed words? In M. Coltheart (Ed.), *Attention and performance XII: The psychology of reading* (pp. 281–298) Hillsdale, NJ: Erlbaum.

Treiman, R., & Danis, C. (1988). Syllabification of intervocalic consonants. *Journal of Memory and Language, 27,* 87–104.

Treiman, R., & Zukowski, A. (1988). Units in reading and spelling. *Journal of Memory and Language, 27,* 466–477.

Treisman, A. M. (1986). Features and objects and visual processing. *Scientific American, 255,* 114–125.

Treisman, A. M., & Schmidt, H. (1982). Illusory conjunctions in the preception of objects. *Cognitive Psychology, 14,* 107–141.

Van Orden, G. C. (1987). A ROWS is a ROSE: Spelling, sound, and reading. *Memory & Cognition, 15,* 181–198.

Van Orden, G. C., Johnston, J. C., & Hale, B. L. (1988). Word identification in reading proceeds from spelling to sound to meaning. *Journal of Experimental Psychology: Learning, Memory, and Cognition, 14,* 371–386.

Venezky, R. L. (1970). *The structure of English orthography.* The Hague: Mouton.

West, R. F., & Stanovich, K. E. (1986). Robust effects of syntactic structure on visual word processing. *Memory & Cognition, 14,* 1040–112.

Wheeler, D. D. (1970). Processes in word recognition. *Cognitive Psychology, 1,* 59–85.

Whittlesea, B. W. A. & Cantwell, A. L. (1987). Enduring influence of the purpose of experiences: Encoding-retrieval interactions in word and pseudoword perception. *Memory & Cognition, 15,* 465–472.

Wijk, A. (1966). *Rules of pronunciation for the English language.* Oxford: Oxford University Press.

Winnick, W. A., & Kressel, K. (1965). Tachistoscopic recognition thresholds, paired-associate learning, and free recall as a function of abstractness–concreteness and word frequency. *Journal of Experimental Psychology, 70,* 163–168.

CHAPTER 10

CONTEXT AND THE PROCESSING OF AMBIGUOUS WORDS

GREG B. SIMPSON

I. INTRODUCTION

By the time that Fodor's *Modularity of Mind* was published in 1983, there was already a sizable literature concerned with the problem of lexical ambiguity (i.e., the retrieval of meanings of multiple-meaning words). The vast majority of these studies were concerned with a single question: To what extent do higher level semantic representations, such as those arising from the processing of a sentence, constrain the activity of a lower process (in this case, the identification of a word)? A decade ago, the area appeared to have matured to the point where an attempt at some closure seemed possible (Simpson, 1984). With the publication of Fodor's book, however, research in lexical ambiguity blossomed anew, as the question of interactions among comprehension subsystems assumed central status in cognitive science. In a box score approach, studies old and new were placed in the appropriate column. Those that found evidence that multiple meanings of an ambiguous word were activated in all contexts were interpreted as supporting the modularity position. Studies finding access only for the one meaning cued by the context were held to support the hypothesis that the various components of comprehension are highly interactive. The purpose of the present chapter is to provide an updated review of recent literature in ambiguity, some discussion of methodological issues, and a perspective on the future of the area. I will argue that the box score approach to the modularity debate has outlived its usefulness, and that researchers in this area need to move beyond this basic question to discuss issues concerning the nature of context and a person's interaction with it, and how these may affect processing.

In Section II of this chapter, I attempt to review some of the issues that were raised in the earlier discussion of the literature (Simpson, 1984) and to consider the bearing of recent research on those issues. The following section discusses the nature of context and suggests that further progress will be possible only by viewing context more comprehensively than has typically been the case, considering not only local sentence context but also the context of the experimental situation itself.

II. AN OVERVIEW OF LEXICAL AMBIGUITY PROCESSING

Previously, models of ambiguous word processing were subdivided into three broad theoretical classes (Simpson, 1984). Context-dependent (or selective access) models are those that claim that when an ambiguous word occurs in a context, only the single contextually appropriate meaning is activated in memory (Glucksberg, Kreuz, & Rho, 1986; Schvaneveldt, Meyer, & Becker, 1976; Simpson, 1981). Such a view is most compatible with an interactive conception of language comprehension (McClelland, 1987).

The remainder of the models hold that the initial activation of word meanings is not influenced by prior context. According to one version of this context-independent view (e.g., Hogaboam & Perfetti, 1975), the order of access to meanings is based on their relative frequencies. Whenever an ambiguous word is encountered, regardless of context, the most common meaning is retrieved. If this meaning is discovered to be inconsistent with the context, then it is discarded and a second meaning is retrieved. This process will continue until an acceptable match is found. In most cases, the result will be the same as under the context-dependent model. That is, because the context is most often consistent with the most frequent sense of the ambiguous word, an ordered access model predicts the processing of only one meaning on most occasions, but multiple meanings when the context is consistent with the less frequent (subordinate) meaning.

Finally, an exhaustive or multiple access model contends that all meanings are activated whenever an ambiguous word is encountered, and this activation proceeds without reference either to the context or meaning frequency (Conrad, 1974; Lucas, 1987; Onifer & Swinney, 1981; Swinney, 1979). The selection of the appropriate meaning (the one that matches the context) is a process that takes place only after all meanings have undergone initial processing. It is this model that generally has gained most acceptance and is the one that is compatible with a modular account of language comprehension processes. It is also easy to see now why the proposal of the lexicon as an autonomous module has led to such a proliferation of ambiguity research. The case of multiple-meaning words seems ideal for addressing the question of whether context can influence lexical access. If a meaning of a word can be shown to be activated despite being incompatible with its context, then this is taken as strong evidence that lexical processing proceeds without regard for sentence-level contextual factors.

It was also possible in the earlier review to divide the extant studies along methodological lines. The classes of methods used most frequently were identified as processing complexity tasks, ambiguity detection, and priming methods. Processing complexity tasks are those that infer the activation of one or more meanings based on a comparison of sentences containing homographs with unambiguous control sentences. Such methods include sentence verification, sentence completion, recall of rapidly presented (RSVP) sentences, phoneme monitoring (see Ferreira & Anes, this volume), and eye-movement techniques (see Rayner & Sereno, this volume). Generally, with these methods it is found that a sentence containing an ambiguous word leads to poorer performance. It is inferred that the performance decrement occurs because of extra processing caused by the necessity of selecting a single meaning of the ambiguity when more than one has been activated. Generally speaking, most of these methods have seen a decline in their use in recent years, owing principally to two criticisms. First, they are only indirect measures of meaning activation. That is, we may infer the activation of two meanings from the increased processing time, but the relative activation levels of each meaning cannot be discerned. Some recent views of ambiguity processing emphasize degrees of activation of different meanings, effectively striking a middle ground between pure context-dependent and exhaustive access models (e.g., Duffy, Morris, & Rayner, 1988; Neill, Hilliard, & Cooper, 1988). The processing complexity tasks usually are not suited to the testing of such models. A second criticism with respect to these methods is that they tend to be off-line tasks. As we have become very sensitive to the time course of lexical access processes, it has been seen as critical that we identify tasks that measure the processes up to the point of access, rather than later post-access processes. For most of the processing complexity tasks, it is not clear whether the effects that we see are traceable to initial meaning activation or to later selection processes that take place after multiple meanings of an ambiguity have been activated.

Recently, however, one task that relies on a processing complexity measure (eye movement) has been used to study ambiguity (Duffy et al., 1988; Rayner & Duffy, 1986; Rayner & Frazier, 1989; Rayner & Morris, 1991). In these studies, subjects read ambiguous words embedded in sentences that provide disambiguating information either prior to or following the ambiguity. Generally, these studies have found gaze duration on the ambiguous word to be affected by both the location of the disambiguating context and the type of homograph (balanced ambiguous words, whose meanings are relatively equal in terms of their frequency, and unbalanced ambiguities, for which one meaning is much more frequent).[1] When the disambiguating context follows the ambiguous word (i.e., when either meaning is still potentially appropriate), subjects look longer at balanced ambiguous words than at unambiguous control words, but unbalanced ambiguities do not show this difference. These data suggest that the processing load is increased for the balanced words as the subject processes both meanings of these homographs. For the unbalanced words, on the other hand, gaze duration is no longer than for unambiguous words, because the much more common meaning alone is retrieved immediately, with the result that these words function in the way that unambiguous (i.e., single-meaning) words do. When the critical context precedes the ambiguity, however, gaze duration on the homograph depends also on which meaning is biased by the context (Rayner & Frazier, 1989). For dominant-biased sentences, there is no difference in gaze duration for balanced and unbalanced homographs. However, for subordinate-

---

[1] Rayner and his colleauges (e.g., Rayner & Morris, 1991) use the terms "nonbiased" and "biased" for what are here called "balanced" and "unbalanced" homographs, respectively. The present terms were chosen to avoid confusion with the use of "bias" as a description of a contextual manipulation.

biased sentences, unbalanced ambiguous words now show longer gaze durations than do the balanced. In this case, it appears that the context has raised the activation level of the subordinate meaning to such a level as to make it compete with the dominant meaning for access. In other words, providing context biased toward the less common meaning effectively turns the unbalanced homograph into a balanced one. Rayner and his colleagues refer to this as REORDERED ACCESS.

These eye-movement studies do not seem to be as vulnerable to one of the criticisms often raised in objection to other processing complexity tasks, namely that they are off-line measures of processing. That is, because the eye movements are measured while the subject engages in normal reading, they are more clearly an unintrusive on-line assessment of processing. The second criticism of the processing complexity methods, that they only allow an inference about single versus multiple access, rather than permitting the separate indexing of activation levels, may still be relevant. On the other hand, by varying the type of homograph and the location of the biasing context, these studies appear to allow a stronger inference than do most of the tasks in the processing complexity family. That is, by showing that individual homographs can lead to greater or lesser load (i.e., longer or shorter gaze durations) depending on surrounding context, these studies come closer than other complexity measures to capturing directly the relative activation of different meanings. Perhaps the best advice would be to consider eye-movement measures in conjunction with the more popular priming methods (discussed below) that better index activation levels but are more intrusive (Rayner, 1991).

In the ambiguity detection method, the subject is presented with a sentence ending in a homograph and is asked to decide as rapidly as possible whether that word has another meaning (Forster & Bednall, 1976; Hogaboam & Perfetti, 1975; Neill et al., 1988). Hogaboam and Perfetti showed that subjects are faster to identify a word as ambiguous if its context is biased toward the less frequent meaning than if it is biased toward the more frequent, a result that has been replicated more recently in an experiment which better controlled subject strategies (Neill et al., 1988). The reason for this is that the more frequent meaning is assumed to be activated first in all contexts. If the person must search for a second meaning, this search will take longer the less frequent that meaning is. If the context biases the ambiguous word toward its subordinate meaning in the first place, however, the search for the other, more common, meaning will be very fast, as that meaning has already been activated by virtue of its frequency. Neill et al. argued for a model much like that of Rayner and his colleagues above: parallel access for all meanings, but access that is sensitive to the frequency of the meanings and to the context. In general, the criticisms of this task are similar to those raised regarding the processing complexity tasks. It is difficult to identify relative activation levels with the detection task, and the method's ability to capture on-line processes is not clear. However, the use of this method has been critical to our appreciation of the relative frequency of meanings, a factor largely ignored until the mid 1970s (Forster & Bednall, 1976; Hogaboam & Perfetti, 1975).

In the past decade, ambiguity studies have been dominated by priming tasks. In these methods, the subject hears or reads a sentence containing an ambiguous word. Upon the presentation of this ambiguous word, a target word is presented for a speeded response, usually naming or a lexical decision (see Haberlandt, this volume, for a more complete discussion of these tasks). The target is a word related to one of the homograph's meanings or is an unrelated control word. This technique has several characteristics to recommend it. First, it is generally believed to be more sensitive to on-line word recognition processes than the kinds of tasks discussed previously. Second, the method gives us a better idea of the degree of activation of different meanings than do the other families of tasks. Targets are usually words that are related to the same meaning of the ambiguity as that indicated by the context, related to another meaning, or unrelated. For example, a sentence such as *The church bought new pipes for the* **organ** might be followed by the targets MUSIC, HEART, or PAPER. By comparing the response times in these three conditions, we can estimate the degree of activation of each meaning relative to the unrelated control. Finally, priming methods are best suited to studying the time course of meaning activation, through manipulation of the time elapsing between the presentation of the homograph and the onset of the target. Because so much of the recent research has used the priming paradigm, it is appropriate that we devote some discussion to the results of these studies. Such a discussion is particularly important because it has often been the case that differences in results are attributed to one or more (often subtle) differences in methodology. The following discussion focuses on several of the variables that have been suggested as responsible for differences in results. It will be argued that in fact we are not able to account for the discrepancies in the literature by any straightforward classification of priming studies.

A. Priming by a Sentence Context

As discussed above, the priming procedure is implemented in several ways, varying according to the method of presentation of the context, the location of the ambiguity in the sentence, and the task performed on the target. The majority of the studies have used the cross-modal procedure, in which subjects hear a sentence and are presented with a visual target (Conrad, 1974; Glucksberg et al., 1986; Lucas, 1987; Oden & Spira, 1983; Onifer & Swinney, 1981; Seidenberg, Tanenhaus, Leiman, & Bienkowski, 1982; Simpson, 1981; Swinney, 1979; Tabossi, 1988; Tabossi, Colombo, & Job, 1987; Tanenhaus, Leiman, & Seidenberg, 1979). A much smaller number of studies have used visual presentation of the context as well as the target. Each sentence is presented at once (Simpson & Krueger, 1991) or word by word, using either an RSVP procedure in which each word replaces the previous one at the center of the screen (Kintsch & Mross, 1985; Till, Mross, & Kintsch, 1988), or an unfolding procedure in which each word appears to the right of the preceding word as it would in normal text (Paul, Kellas, Martin, & Clark, 1992). There is no a priori reason to think that these differences in the way that the context is presented should lead to a difference in results (specifically, that one method should favor context-dependent access while others favor multiple activation), and indeed, the results cannot be divided in this way. A number of the cross-modal studies have found priming for both meanings of the ambiguous word, regardless of context (Conrad, 1974; Lucas, 1987; Onifer & Swinney, 1981; Seidenberg et al., 1982; Swinney, 1979; Tanenhaus et al., 1979), while others have found selective access (Glucksberg et al., 1986; Oden & Spira, 1983; Simpson, 1981; Tabossi, 1988; Tabossi et al., 1987). Likewise, some of the studies using visual presentation support multiple access (Kintsch & Mross, 1985; Till et al., 1988), while the remainder find evidence for selective context effects (Paul et al., 1992; Simpson & Krueger, 1991).

Similarly, we cannot predict the results based on the target task. Word recognition tasks have come under close scrutiny in recent years, with particular emphasis on the lexical decision task. Because this task requires a binary decision, it has been likened to a signal-detection task (Balota, 1990; Seidenberg, Waters, Sanders, & Langer, 1984), and it has been suggested that a variable (such as context) that may appear to affect lexical access instead has its effects at a later post-access decision stage (but see Paul, Kellas, & Juola, 1992). The implication of this criticism is that the lexical decision task may be more likely to lead to results consistent with a context-dependent view, as it is more sensitive to postlexical processes, in this case the integration of a meaning with the context. Therefore, perhaps the naming task is preferable for examining initial activation processes. However, we again see several lexical decision experiments favoring a selective access account (Glucksberg et al., 1986; Simpson, 1981; Tabossi, 1988; Tabossi et al., 1987), and others not (Kintsch & Mross, 1985; Lucas, 1987; Onifer & Swinney, 1981; Swinney, 1979; Till et al., 1988). Likewise for naming, some studies support selective access (Simpson & Krueger, 1991) and others support a multiple access view (Seidenberg et al., 1982; Tanenhaus et al., 1979). Finally, a small number of studies have used the Stroop task, in which subjects are required to name the color of ink in which the target is printed. One such study found evidence for multiple access, showing color naming interference to be equal for targets related to either meaning (Conrad, 1974), while the two remaining studies showed selective effects of context (Oden & Spira, 1983; Paul et al., 1992). In summary, while it has occasionally been implied that the choice of experimental task may be critical in identifying the role of context, no straightforward division of results can be made according to task.

A third potential candidate for categorizing ambiguity studies is the location of the homograph within the context sentence. Many priming studies have used the homograph as the last word in the sentence (Conrad, 1974; Oden & Spira, 1983; Paul et al., 1992; Seidenberg et al., 1982; Simpson, 1981; Simpson & Krueger, 1991; Tanenhaus et al., 1979), while others place the homograph within the sentence, interrupting the subject's sentence comprehension to present the target (Blutner & Sommer, 1988; Kintsch & Mross, 1985; Lucas, 1987; Onifer & Swinney, 1981; Swinney, 1979; Tabossi, 1988; Tabossi et al., 1987; Till et al., 1988). On its face, this seems like a factor that could well have an impact on the pattern of activation that is found. One might argue, for example, that the sentence-final homograph allows sentence wrap-up processes peripheral to lexical access to influence the subject's target response. Seen in this light, the sentence-medial procedure would appear to be preferable. On the other hand, the competing demands of the two tasks (sentence comprehension and target response) would appear to be greater when one task is interrupted to perform the other. The hypothesis here might be that extra resource demands of the sentence-medial procedure could delay target recognition and allow more time for post-access processes to occur. In addition, it could be suggested that consistently interrupting the sentence to present another task leads, over the course of the experiment, to processing that is different from normal sentence comprehension. Depending on the outcome, hypotheses such as these could be used to bolster the case for either selective or multiple access. As it turns out, however, this candidate also cannot divide the studies in any simple way. Some experiments using sentence-final homographs have concluded that multiple meanings are initially activated (Conrad, 1974; Seidenberg et al., 1982; Tanenhaus et al., 1979), while others have argued for selective access of meaning (Oden & Spira, 1983; Paul et al., 1992; Simpson, 1981; Simpson & Krueger, 1991). Similarly, support can be found in the sentence-medial studies for multiple (Blutner & Sommer, 1988; Kintsch & Mross, 1985; Lucas, 1987; Onifer & Swinney, 1981; Swinney, 1979; Till et al., 1988) and for selective (Tabossi, 1988; Tabossi et al., 1987) access.

One factor that is clearly important for any discussion of lexical ambiguity (or indeed for any issue regarding on-line language comprehension processes) concerns the temporal relations between the context and the target. Since the first time-course studies were published (Swinney, 1979; Tanenhaus et al., 1979), it has become quite apparent that any explanation of ambiguity processes that does not include an account of changing activation patterns over time simply cannot hope to capture the complete picture of the processes relevant to the selection of a single appropriate meaning. It is easy to see why this should be the case: It is obvious that the outcome of the complete processing of an ambiguous word in context is awareness of a single meaning. The controversy concerns the timing of contextual effects. The context-dependent position is that the context acts immediately to restrict access to the appropriate meaning, while the context-independent view is that context is used only later, after all meanings are activated, to select the appropriate one. Swinney (1979) used a cross-modal procedure in which sentences containing ambiguous words were presented auditorily, and the homograph was followed by a target that was related to the contextually biased meaning or to the other meaning (or was unrelated). Targets were presented either immediately after the offset of the ambiguity or after a delay of three syllables. Lexical decisions to targets related to either meaning were facilitated relative to unrelated targets in the immediate condition, but only contextually appropriate targets were facilitated after the delay. Several studies have shown a similar pattern (Blutner & Sommer, 1988; Kintsch & Mross, 1985; Lucas, 1987; Onifer & Swinney, 1981; Seidenberg et al., 1982). These results led to a consensus that the initial activation of word meanings took place without input from contextual processes, which were used only in the post-access selection process. The results of studies that contradicted this conclusion (e.g., Simpson, 1981) could be faulted if any time had been allowed to elapse between the ambiguity and the target.

However, some more recent time-course studies (or studies using only an immediate presentation condition) have found patterns of results that are in conflict with this received view. Tabossi (1988; Tabossi et al., 1987) has found evidence that selective access may occur immediately if the context is sufficiently constraining. Her subjects performed lexical decisions immediately following the presentation of an ambiguous word in a cross-modal procedure. She found that sentences biased toward the dominant meaning led to the activation of that meaning only, provided that the context primed a salient feature of that meaning. For example, Tabossi et al. presented subjects with sentences such as *The violent hurricane did not damage the ships which were in the **port**, one of the best equipped along the coast.* This sentence highlights the salient feature of *port* that it is a safe haven for ships, and targets appropriate to that feature were primed. This result was extended in several ways by a recent series of studies by Paul, Kellas, Martin, and Clark (1992). These researchers used a Stroop task following sentences ending in ambiguous words and activating features appropriate to that word's dominant or subordinate meaning. Targets appropriate or inappropriate to the contextual meaning were presented 0, 300, or 600 ms following the sentences. Paul, Kellas, Martin, and Clark found slower color-naming times for the contextually appropriate targets than for the inappropriate (both for sentences biased toward the dominant meaning and for those biased toward the subordinate), even at the 0 ms interval.

In a study comparing priming and event-related potential (ERP) results (see Kutas & Van Petten, this volume), Van Petten and Kutas (1987) found that naming latencies to targets related to either meaning of a homograph showed priming relative to unrelated words, at stimulus onset asynchronies of 200 and 700 ms. These results, of course, are in line with the multiple access view. The ERP data, however, painted a different picture. The onset of the N400 response (i.e., the electrical potential that occurs around 400 ms after the onset of a stimulus and is associated with language processing) to the targets was earlier for contextually appropriate targets than for the inappropriate or unrelated targets. The authors concluded that the ERP results indicated a role for context in the initial processing of the homograph, and that the naming facilitation for the contextually inappropriate target was due to backward priming (in which the target reactivates the prime, and the two are processed in parallel; see Koriat, 1981; Peterson & Simpson, 1989).

Finally, Simpson and Krueger (1991) have recently extended the earlier research by Simpson (1981) to include a time course manipulation. Simpson used sentence-final homographs in a cross-modal experiment and found context-dependent meaning activation. In that study, however, an interval of 120 ms occurred between the offset of the ambiguous word and the presentation of the lexical decision target. A number of authors (e.g., McClelland, 1987; Onifer & Swinney, 1981) have pointed out that this may have been a long enough interval to compromise these results as an account of immediate activation processes. To test this possibility, Simpson and Krueger displayed sentences visually and presented targets 0, 300, or 700 ms following the subject's reading of the last word in the sentence (the homograph). At all three of these intervals, only the contextually appropriate targets were facilitated, for both the dominant- and subordinate-biased sentences. In sum, although there can hardly be any disputing the need for careful consideration of time-course issues, the existing studies still are not able to provide a coherent picture of the timing of access to different meanings of an ambiguity.

B. Summary

The above discussion, it must be admitted, does not paint a very encouraging picture, at least for the hope that ambiguity research may provide a definitive answer for questions of the autonomy of language comprehension processes.

Indeed, one might conclude at this point that the research examining the role of sentence context on lexical activation has run its course. All the models of ambiguity processing have found support from one or more studies, and, as the above discussion has attempted to make clear, there is no simple way of classifying studies methodologically in any way that sheds light on the discrepancies among results.

In an earlier review (Simpson, 1984), I tried to argue that the constellation of results at that time could best be explained by positing a system whereby all meanings are activated, but with the degree of activation being sensitive to influence by the relative frequencies of the meanings and by the context in which the ambiguous word occurs. There does not seem to be any compelling reason to change that position now. First, such a model has found converging support from research using methods quite different from priming, including ambiguity detection (Neill et al., 1988) and eye movements (Duffy et al., 1988; Rayner & Frazier, 1989). Second, it could also be argued that the confusing set of results among priming studies demands such a flexible view. It appears (in the absence of any other methodological basis for classifying the research) that some kinds of context are able to lead to the activation of a single meaning, while others do not constrain access. Such variable context effects across studies should not be surprising unless we become better able to provide an adequate account of what good context is, and what relevant information is contained in it. It is to a discussion of context, therefore, that we now turn.

III. ON THE NATURE OF SENTENCE CONTEXT

Discussions of context are, of course, frequent in the ambiguity literature, but there have been relatively few attempts to develop a principled account of context types. Simpson (1981) used three kinds of sentences in a cross-modal experiment: unbiased, weakly biased toward one meaning, and strongly biased toward a meaning. Classification of the sentences was determined by subject ratings. For example, for the homograph *bank,* the sentences were (1)–(5).

(1) *The men decided to wait by the bank.* (unbiased)
(2) *The fishermen decided to wait by the bank.* (weak bias-subordinate)
(3) *The businessmen decided to wait by the bank.* (weak bias-dominant)
(4) *I pulled the fish up onto the bank.* (strong, bias-subordinate)
(5) *I opened a checking account at the bank.* (strong bias-dominant)

Subjects did not find the rating task to be at all difficult, and their ratings did successfully predict the pattern of meaning activation in the lexical decision experiment: Unbiased sentences led to facilitation for the dominant meaning only; strongly biased sentences resulted in activation for the contextually appropriate meaning. Frequency and context both showed influences with weakly biased sentences: Those biased toward the dominant meaning facilitated that meaning only, but when frequency and context were in conflict (weakly biased toward the subordinate meaning), both meanings were activated. However, although there was a clear empirical distinction between strong and weak contexts, the qualitative differences among the contexts that led to that distinction are not easy to specify.

Seidenberg et al. (1982) proposed that the determining factor in whether a context sentence should constrain lexical access is whether it contains a strong lexical associate of one of the meanings of the homograph. For example, in the sentence *I opened a checking account at the **bank**,* it may be that the financial meaning of *bank* is primed not by the message-level representation of the sentence as a whole, but simply by the presence of words like *checking account*. Even worse, it could be that apparent priming would not require access of any meaning of *bank,* but simply that words like *checking account* directly prime a target such as *money*. As this kind of priming involves nothing more than word-level associations, the principle of an autonomous lexical processor is left intact. Although such direct priming has been shown in some cases (Burgess, Tanenhaus, & Seidenberg, 1989), it does not seem to be able to account for all the priming effects seen with sentences (O'Seaghdha, 1989; Simpson, Peterson, Casteel, & Burgess, 1989). In addition, it is difficult to distinguish the strong and weak contexts in Simpson (1981) based on the presence of lexical associates. Many of the sentences rated as strongly biased did not contain words that could serve as such associative primes (e.g., *While downtown I signed up for the **draft***), while many weakly biased sentences did contain such words (e.g., *The doctor found something wrong with the **organ***). Consequently, we are so far without a convincing candidate for distinguishing those contexts that will constrain meaning activation from those that will not.

The recent work of Tabossi (1988, 1989, 1991; Tabossi et al., 1987) has focused on the idea that context must activate certain kinds of information in order to restrict access to a single meaning. Specifically, a context sentence should be constrained such that it activates a salient feature of a single meaning (as discussed previously). A series of studies by Kellas and his colleagues (Kellas, Paul, Martin, & Simpson, 1991; Paul et al., 1992) has extended the arguments on the importance of feature activation for lexical access. These authors have attempted as well to expand on the concept of SALIENCE. They define the salience of a target in terms of the hypothesized overlap of semantic features of the target and the homograph in a certain context. They began by gathering normative associations to ambiguous words in biasing sentence contexts. Subjects generated as many aspects of the meaning of the homograph in that sentence context as they were able in one minute. This procedure is in contrast to the more common practice of using targets generated to homographs in isolation (e.g., as in the norms of Cramer, 1970, or of Nelson, McEvoy, Walling, & Wheeler, 1980). Targets can then be identified as relatively high or low on a continuum of salience relative to the meaning of the homograph in that context. For example, instead of generating a single associate to a word such as *plant* in isolation (the common method for association norms), subjects instead generated multiple responses to a sentence such as *The boy dropped the **plant**.* One frequently produced associate in this procedure was *leaves*, which is produced as well when *plant* is given in isolation (Cramer, 1970). However, another response that was produced to the above sentence (though by fewer subjects) was *spill*. This word would be very surprising as a response to the ambiguous word *plant* alone, but it can be seen as related to the word in the context of that sentence. In a Stroop experiment (Paul et al., 1992), both *leaves* and *spill* (high- and low-salient targets, respectively, for this sentence) showed slower color-naming times than targets related to the other meaning (*factory* and *people*), even at an immediate context-target interval. At longer intervals, only the highly salient target (*leaves*) still showed slowed responses. The same result was found for sentences biased toward the subordinate meaning. That is, immediately following the sentence *They closed that part of the* **plant,** both *factory* and *people* were activated, but after 500 ms, only *factory* still led to slowed color-naming.

These results suggest that context can activate substantially more information than simply the lexical associates of the homograph. The study also suggests again that intralexical priming is not the operative principle behind context effects, as these sentences do not seem particularly rich in the kind of lexical information that would be likely by itself to activate a meaning. In the example above, perhaps one could argue that the target *spill* is an associate of *dropped*. Therefore, perhaps *leaves* is primed by *plant* and *spill* by *dropped*. However, most of the sentences used in this study did not include associates of this kind. In addition, we would have to ask why the time course of priming between *plant* and *leaves* should differ from that of *dropped* and *spill*. Even if one argued that the former pair is more strongly associated than the latter, we would normally expect strength-of-association effects to differ at earlier points in the time course, rather than later. Instead, it appears as if context makes available certain kinds of information relevant to the semantic and pragmatic relations among words. For example, one would not expect to find color-naming interference for *spill* if the sentence had been *The boy dropped the* **television.** It seems, in other words, as if the information activated constitutes a range of features of an item that are relevant in context. We have not typically been able to discover these kinds of relations because of the common practice of selecting as targets only words that are generated to a homograph out of context. While this is a practice that is necessary for determining the relative dominance of a meaning, it may well miss a substantial amount of further information that will be activated under other circumstances.

It should be noted, however, that these results appear to be at odds with those obtained by Till et al. (1988). Subjects in Till et al. read sentences ending in homographs (sentence pairs were presented, and on the critical trial, the homograph was the last word in the first sentence). Following the homograph, a lexical decision target was presented. Targets were associates of the ambiguous word (from standard homograph norms), or they were inference words generated by subjects in a norming procedure. For instance, given the sentence *The old man sat with his head down and did not hear a word of the sermon during* **mass,** subjects generated *sleep* as an inference target (*church* was the appropriate associate target for this sentence, and *weight* was the inappropriate). Consistent with the multiple access view, both associates were primed following the sentence. The inference words are of particular interest here, as they appear to bear some similarity to the low-salient targets of Paul, Kellas, Martin, and Clark (1992) (i.e., in both cases, the targets appear to be words that are related to the sentence as a whole, rather than being associated with the ambiguous word in isolation). These inference words were primed at long intervals between the homograph and the target, but not at short ones, indicating that discourse (nonlexical) effects take more time to develop than do associative priming effects.

This time-course pattern found by Till et al. for inference targets appears to be quite different from that found by Paul, Kellas, Martin, and Clark (1992), whose subjects showed immediate activation even for low-salient targets related to one meaning of the homograph (e.g., *spill* following *The boy dropped the plant*), which, like the Till et al. stimuli, appear to be targets that would be inferred from the context rather than associated to the homograph. The discrepancy may be due to differences in the instructions to subjects in the respective norming procedures. Whereas the targets used by Paul et al. were words generated by subjects with the instructions to list features of the homograph as it is conceived in that sentence, those of Till et al. were words generated in response to instructions to read the sentence containing the honograph and write down a word that represented what they thought the sentence was about. These procedures clearly ask for different kinds of information. The instructions given by Paul, Kellas, Martin, and Clark (1992) were designed to tap a lexical representation of the homograph, albeit a lexical representation influenced by context. The inference targets used by Till et al., on the other hand, seem to come from something like a script level of comprehension. The fact that Paul, Kellas, Martin, and Clark (1992) showed priming for these targets earlier in the time course than did Till et al. may indicate that the Paul et al. targets were closer to the representation of the homograph itself in that context than were the targets used by Till et al.

This discrepancy in the research of Tabossi and Paul, Kellas, Martin, and Clark (1992) on the one hand, and Till et al. on the other, suggests that our approach to context must be undertaken very thoughtfully. It appears not to be enough to claim that a sentence context "biases one meaning" of an ambiguity. This kind of claim would imply that there are two possible outcomes of encountering an ambiguous word in context: Context makes available the information related to one meaning or to another. As indicated in the above example, however, it is hard to see how *spill* is related to any "meaning" of *plant*. The tendency in the past has been to consider the meanings of an ambiguous word as consisting of discrete sets of features, each set representing one of the meanings. The role of context is one of selecting among these feature sets. The results obtained by Paul, Kellas, Martin, and Clark (1992) challenge this view and suggest instead that the homograph and its context combine to activate a unique constellation of features that will overlap to varying degrees with features represented by the target.

Our difficulty in seeing this problem is due to our preoccupation (pointed out by Gerrig, 1986) with the PROCESS of comprehension, to the exclusion of an appreciation for the PRODUCTS of comprehension. Our focus on the processes involved in lexical access is understandable: They are central to the modularity/ interaction issue. Nevertheless, as Gerrig points out, any theory of processes must take into account the product of comprehension, as our conclusions about the nature of comprehension processes will be different under different conceptions about the nature of the information stored in the lexicon, and which of this information is made available upon the access of a word on a particular occasion. To take another example from Paul, Kellas, Martin, and Clark (1992) in order to appreciate that *business* is primed following *The woman bought the company,* all we need assume is that a spreading activation process has operated between the representations of *company* and *business*. We must conclude that very different kinds of processes are occurring, however, once we know that this sentence will prime *rich* as well. It also is not very helpful to claim that *rich* is facilitated by processes occurring after lexical access for *company* unless we know what information was made available on that access (i.e., what information is being acted on by the putative post-access processes).

Equally important, we may often not be certain that different experiments emphasize a common level of comprehension. This may in fact be an additional factor that underlies the discrepancy between Paul, Kellas, Martin, and Clark (1992) and Till et al. The sentence pairs in the latter study were much longer and more complex than the very simple sentences in Paul, Kellas, Martin, and Clark (1992). Till et al., therefore, may have been more likely to tap a script level of comprehension, which led to slower activation of a lexical target. The sentences used by Paul, Kellas, Martin, and Clark (1992), on the other hand, would have had less of a tendency to call on such higher level comprehension processes, making them more appropriate as contexts for a task performed on single lexical targets.

In fact, an unpublished study by Killion (1979) has demonstrated directly the effects that differences in sentence processing task can have on context effects in ambiguous word recognition. In a series of five experiments, Killion found selective access when subjects performed a sentence verification task on the context (deciding whether the sentence made sense according to their real-world knowledge) before responding to the target, and when they were instructed to "read and understand" the sentence. Roughly equal facilitation for each meaning was found under instructions simply to read the sentence. Finally, when the subjects were instructed to use the sentences as a prime (i.e., when they were told explicitly that the targets were often related to the sentences and that they should use the sentence to speed their word recognition response), or when they had to recall some of the sentences, both meanings were activated, but the facilitation for the contextually appropriate meaning was significantly greater than that for the inappropriate. Because all these experiments used the same materials, the differences must be attributed instead to differential processing of the context as a function of the sentence task. This set of experiments shows very plainly the critical relationship between the kinds of operations carried out during sentence processing and the output of lexical access. In this case, the scope of information activated during sentence comprehension is influenced by the processing task that is performed on the context, which, in turn, affects performance on the word recognition task.

The foregoing discussion is not meant to imply that heeding Gerrig's advice to consider the products of comprehension will suggest an ambiguity experiment that will resolve, once and for all, the modularity/interaction problem. It is still the case that a large number of well-designed and executed experiments have yielded discrepant results for reasons that have proven impossible to pinpoint. The point being made here is simply that we should not fail to consider the kinds of information that might be available as a result of processing a sentence. As Gerrig points out, only by such consideration will we be able to argue coherently about the comprehension processes that act on that information.

IV. CONCLUSIONS

The purpose of this chapter has been to discuss the progress that has been made in research in lexical ambiguity in the last decade. I have attempted to discuss progress on the theoretical front as well as to review the methodological issues that have plagued this area since its beginnings. Principal among these is the problem of identifying the earliest activation processes and their sensitivity to context. It appears that this concern has led to seemingly endless methodological refinements, but unfortunately the problem remains stubborn. It is not clear that any experiment will be able to resolve the issue unequivocally. Indeed, it is not clear that such resolution is necessary or even desirable. The range of results obtained in ambiguity studies suggests clearly that the extreme views of the lexicon as either fully autonomous or promiscuously interactive are not tenable. The fact that a number of studies have found strong evidence of multiple access, while another group has provided equally compelling evidence supporting a role of context, should suggest to us that the truth must almost surely lie somewhere in between and must be highly dependent on characteristics of the context and on characteristics of the tasks required of the subject.

In the earlier review (Simpson, 1984), it was argued that nearly all the priming studies showed a common pattern: Arguments of statistical reliability aside, virtually every study showed fastest responding to contextually appropriate targets, slower responding to inappropriate targets, and slowest responses to unrelated targets. In other words, there is consistent evidence that both meanings are facilitated relative to an unrelated control, but equally consistent evidence that the appropriate meaning is facilitated to a greater degree. Because all the meanings of an ambiguity map on to a common orthographic form, activation should accrue for all of them any time that form is encountered. However, it now seems clear also that we can hardly deny some role of context in constraining the degree of activation for a meaning. What is required is that we expand our overly narrow definition of context, which has traditionally encompassed only the meaning conveyed within a single sentence. We must realize that different sentence types (e.g., single proposition vs. script-inducing), different tasks, and even different procedures for constructing stimuli make important contributions to the context within which our subjects perform, and these may have profound effects on subjects' performance, and, by extension, our theories. Only by taking a broader view of context will we be able to direct our efforts more productively to understanding the nature of lexical ambiguity and its relation to other aspects of language comprehension, rather than focusing on it exclusively as a means to settle a single theoretical debate.

ACKNOWLEDGMENTS

I am grateful to Morton Gernsbacher, George Kellas, and Steve Paul for their comments on earlier drafts of the chapter.

REFERENCES

Balota, D. A. (1990). The role of meaning in word recognition. In D. A. Balota, G. B. Flores d'Arcais, & K. Rayner (Eds.), *Comprehension processes in reading* (pp. 9–32). Hillsdale, NJ: Erlbaum.

Blutner, R., & Sommer, R. (1988). Sentence processing and lexical access: The influence of the focus-identifying task. *Journal of Memory and Language, 27,* 359–367.

Burgess, C., Tanenhaus, M. K., & Seidenberg, M. S. (1989). Context and lexical access: Implications of nonword interference for lexical ambiguity resolution. *Journal of Experimental Psychology: Learning, Memory, and Cognition, 15,* 620–632.

Conrad, C. (1974). Context effects in sentence comprehension: A study of the subjective lexicon. *Memory & Cognition, 2,* 130–138.

Cramer, P. (1970). A study of homographs. In L. Postman & G. Keppel (Eds.), *Norms of word association* (pp. 361–382). New York: Academic Press.

Duffy, S. A., Morris, R. K., & Rayner, K. (1988). Lexical ambiguity and fixation times in reading. *Journal of Memory and Language, 27,* 429–446.

Fodor, J. A. (1983). *Modularity of mind.* Cambridge, MA: MIT Press.

Forster, K. I., & Bednall, E. S. (1976). Terminating and exhaustive search in lexical access. *Memory & Cognition, 4,* 53–61.

Gerrig, R. J. (1986). Process and products of lexical access. *Language and Cognitive Processes, 1,* 187–195.

Glucksberg, S., Kreuz, F. J., & Rho, S. H. (1986). Context can constrain lexical access: Implications for models of language comprehension. *Journal of Experimental Psychology: Learning, Memory, and Cognition, 12,* 323–335.

Hogaboam, T. W., & Perfetti, C. A. (1975). Lexical ambiguity and sentence comprehension. *Journal of Verbal Learning and Verbal Behavior, 14,* 265–274.

Kellas, G., Paul, S. T., Martin, M., & Simpson, G. B. (1991). Contextual feature activation and meaning access. In G. B. Simpson (Ed.), *Understanding word and sentence* (pp. 47–71). Amsterdam: North-Holland.

Killion, T. H. (1979). *Task effects in the processing of lexical ambiguity.* Unpublished manuscript, University of Dayton Research Institute, Dayton, OH.

Kintsch, W., & Mross, E. F. (1985). Context effects in word identification. *Journal of Memory and Language, 24,* 336–349.

Koriat, A. (1981). Semantic facilitation in lexical decision as a function of prime-target association. *Memory & Cognition, 9,* 587–598.

Lucas, M. M. (1987). Frequency effects on the processing of ambiguous words in sentence context. *Language and Speech, 30,* 25–46.

McClelland, J. L. (1987). The case for interactionism in language processing. In M. Coltheart (Ed.), *Attention and performance XII: The psychology of reading* (pp. 3–36). Hillsdale, NJ: Erlbaum.

Neill, W. T., Hilliard, D. V., & Cooper, E. (1988). The detection of lexical ambiguity: Evidence for context-sensitive parallel access. *Journal of Memory and Langauge, 27,* 279–287.

Nelson, D. L., McEvoy, C. L., Walling, J. R., & Wheeler, J. W., Jr. (1980). The University of South Florida homograph norms. *Behavior Research Methods and Instrumentation, 12,* 16–37.

Oden, G. C., & Spira, J. L. (1983). Influence of context on the activation and selection of ambiguous word senses. *Quarterly Journal of Experimental Psychology, 35A,* 51–64.

Onifer, W., & Swinney, D. A. (1981). Accessing lexical ambiguities during sentence comprehension: Effects of frequency of meaning and contextual bias. *Memory & Cognition, 15,* 225–236.

O'Seaghdha, P. G. (1989). The dependence of lexical relatedness effects on syntactic connectedness. *Journal of Experimental Psychology: Learning, Memory, and Cognition, 15,* 73–87.

Paul, S. T., Kellas, G., & Juola, J. F. (1992). Priming effects on lexical access and decision processes: A signal detection analysis. *Psychological Research, 54,* 202–211.

Paul, S. T., Kellas, G., Martin, M., & Clark, M. B. (1992). The influence of contextual features on the activation of ambiguous word meanings. *Journal of Experimental Psychology: Learning, Memory, and Cognition, 18,* 703–717.

Peterson, R. R., & Simpson, G. B. (1989). Effect of backward priming on word recognition in single-word and sentence contexts. *Journal of Experimental Psychology: Learning, Memory, and Cognition, 15,* 1020–1032.

Rayner, K. (1991, July). *Lexical ambiguity and eye fixations in reading.* Paper presented at the Sylvia Beach Language Comprehension Conference, Newport, OR.

Rayner, K., & Duffy, S. A. (1986). Lexical complexity and fixation times in reading: Effects of word frequency, verb complexity, and lexical ambiguity. *Memory & Cognition, 14,* 191–201.

Rayner, K., & Frazier, L. (1989). Selection mechanisms in reading lexically ambiguous words. *Journal of Experimental Psychology: Learning, Memory, and Cognition, 15,* 779–790.

Rayner, K., & Morris, R. K. (1991). Comprehension processes in reading ambiguous sentences: Reflections from eye movements. In G. B. Simpson (Ed.), *Understanding word and sentence* (pp. 175–198). Amsterdam: North-Holland.

Schvaneveldt, R. W., Meyer, D. E., & Becker, C. A. (1976). Lexical ambiguity, semantic context, and visual word recognition. *Journal of Experimental Psychology: Human Perception and Performance, 2,* 243–256.

Seidenberg, M. S., Tanenhaus, M. K., Leiman, J. M., & Bienkowski, M. (1982). Automatic access of the meanings of ambiguous words in context: Some limitations of knowledge-based processing. *Cognitive Psychology, 14,* 489–537.

Seidenberg, M. S., Waters, G. S., Sanders, M., & Langer, P. (1984). Pre- and postlexical loci of contextual effects on word recognition. *Memory & Cognition, 12,* 315–328.

Simpson, G. B. (1981). Meaning dominance and semantic context in the processing of lexical ambiguity. *Journal of Verbal Learning and Verbal Behavior, 20,* 120–136.

Simpson, G. B. (1984). Lexical ambiguity and its role in models of word recognition. *Psychological Bulletin, 96,* 316–340.

Simpson, G. B., & Krueger, M. A. (1991). Selective access of homograph meanings in sentence context. *Journal of Memory and Langauge, 30,* 627–643.

Simpson, G. B., Peterson, R. R., Casteel, M. A., & Burgess, C. (1989). Lexical and sentence context effects in word recognition. *Journal of Experimental Psychology: Learning, Memory, and Cognition, 15,* 88–97.

Swinney, D. A. (1979). Lexical access during sentence comprehension: (Re)consideration of context effects. *Journal of Verbal Learning and Verbal Behavior, 18,* 645–659.

Tabossi, P. (1988). Accessing lexical ambiguity in different types of sentential context. *Journal of Memory and Language, 27,* 324–340.

Tabossi, P. (1989). What's in a context? In D. S. Gorfein (Ed.), *Resolving semantic ambiguity* (pp. 25–39). New York: Springer-Verlag.

Tabossi, P. (1991). Understanding words in context. In G. B. Simpson (Ed.), *Understanding word and sentence* (pp. 1–22). Amsterdam: North-Holland.

Tabossi, P., Colombo, L., & Job, R. (1987). Accessing lexical ambiguity: Effects of context and dominance. *Psychological Research, 49,* 161–167.

Tanenhaus, M. K., Leiman, J. M., & Seidenberg, M. S. (1979). Evidence for multiple stages in the processing of ambiguous words in syntactic contexts. *Journal of Verbal Learning and Verbal Behavior, 18,* 427–440.

Till, R. E., Mross, E. F., & Kintsch, W. (1988). Time course of priming for associate and inference words in a discourse context. *Memory & Cognition, 16,* 283–298.

Van Petten, C., & Kutas, M. (1987). Ambiguous words in context: An event-related potential analysis of the time course of meaning activation. *Journal of Memory and Language, 26,* 188–208.

CHAPTER 11

SENTENCE PARSING

DON C. MITCHELL

I. PRELIMINARIES

Numerous problems have to be solved in the course of interpreting a sentence. First, the individual words have to be identified, making stored information available for higher level processes. Along with contextual information, punctuation, and intonation (where relevant), this raw material has to be used to decide what actions are being described or assertions expressed (instructions given, information sought), what roles identified people and objects play in these events, and how these people and objects relate to others outside the sentence and to one another. Where actions are qualified or objects assigned specific properties and characteristics, it is necessary to determine the appropriate connections or assignments, ensuring that the characteristics in question are not wrongly linked to entities appearing elsewhere in the sentence. The problems are made more complicated by the fact that all these decisions normally have to be made rapidly while the contents of the sentence are still unfolding.

Most psychologists tackling these issues borrow heavily from linguistics in formulating their research questions. Over the years they have drawn from a wide variety of conceptual systems, but historically the major influence has tended to come from successive phases of generative linguistic theory developed by Chomsky and his colleagues (e.g., Chomsky, 1965, 1981). At a very basic level, most, but not all, researchers have couched their work in terms of various linguistic metaphors of structure—the most obvious being the tree-diagrammatic representation of phrase structure rules. The tree diagram, normally referred to as a PHRASE MARKER, is capable of capturing some of the more prominent structural relationships such as links between objects and the properties assigned to them within the sentence. It can also be used to express major and subsidiary actions and can provide a good starting point for ascertaining the roles of different objects and people within the sentence. For psycholinguists working within this conceptual framework, the central problem in sentence processing is to determine how people convert a string of words into something like a tree diagram to represent the structure of the sentence. Of course, this approach does not have a complete monopoly of research in this area, but it is dominant enough to provide a useful entry point for the purpose of outlining important themes in current work on sentence processing.

As with many research issues, it has not proved easy to tackle the question directly. The main reason for this is that parsing operations are extremely rapid (Kieras, 1981) and their effects may be highly transitory. For this reason it has proved almost impossible to develop experimental measures that can convincingly be demonstrated to quantify the full range of parsing operations at the point in processing when they initially occur. In particular, with a very small number of exceptions, it has not yet proved feasible to tap into the basic structure-building procedures which presumably underlie the entire process. Using empirical techniques currently available, it is only very rarely that investigators have succeeded in uncovering incontrovertible evidence that one kind of structure takes measurably longer to assemble than another. Hence it has not proved very productive to try to start with such latency differences and to work back from them with the aim of drawing inferences about the parsing operations that might underpin them. Fortunately, it has turned out to be possible to use indirect procedures to obtain much of the information we need to tackle important issues in parsing. Many of these indirect methods exploit the fact that natural languages can be highly ambiguous. Readers or listeners are deliberately presented with ambiguous material and, on the basis of the way they handle the ambiguity, inferences can often be drawn about operations which are difficult to observe directly. It is for this reason that much of the empirical work on parsing hinges on the way people handle structurally ambiguous sentences.

In reviewing this work, I start by considering the kinds of tactics people adopt when they encounter regions of ambiguity. Do they concentrate on one reading or pursue two or more interpretations at the same time? Later I review the evidence on the rules and procedures people use to decide what to do first. It turns out that these have implications for many routine parsing operations. These issues are discussed at some length. Next, I briefly discuss how the string of words in an utterance might be used to recover possible underlying syntactic structures and how these candidate structures might be checked against the input to ensure that they conform to the detailed grammatical rules of the language. Finally, I end by considering the possible limitations of the approach to parsing work outlined here.

II. Strategies for Handling Ambiguity

Imagine that a reader or listener is part-way through interpreting a (partial) sentence like (1).

(1) *The cop informed the motorist . . .*

After processing the word "motorist" the reader might have constructed a parse tree something like (2).

(2)

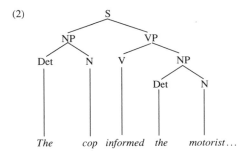

Suppose the sentence continues with an ambiguous string such as (3).

(3) *. . . that he had noticed . . .*

In these circumstances the reader might interpret (3) either as a complement structure or as a relative clause, each of which would result in a different kind of branching structure being added to the right-hand side of the tree.

If people really are constructing a parse tree as they work through the sentence, this raises the question about what happens with ambiguous strings like (3). In principle there are three different ways in which the structural analysis might be developed. First, the parser might assemble the structure for just one of the interpretations, effectively ignoring the other. Secondly, it might construct and store both analyses (or all of them if there are more than two). Thirdly, it might proceed with a partial analysis delaying making certain decisions until it is safe to do so. For example, in this case it might process the subordinate sentence within clause (3) without initially committing itself on the question of whether it should eventually be embedded within a relative clause or sentential complement.

In the literature each option has been given a variety of different names, and in each case there are also a number of different variations on the general proposal. The major versions of each strategy are outlined in the next few paragraphs.

A. Theoretical Proposals

1. Serial Processing

Numerous researchers have either proposed or just assumed that readers and listeners cope with structural ambiguity by initially pursuing just one analysis at the expense of the others. In some of the early work on sentence processing, this was the premise underlying several of the PERCEPTUAL STRATEGIES that Bever and his colleagues proposed to account for parsing processes (Bever, 1970; J. A. Fodor, Bever, & Garrett, 1974). It was entailed in some of the parsing PRINCIPLES put forward by Kimball (1973). It is also the conflict resolution mechanism employed in several artificial parsing systems such as augmented transition networks (ATNs) (e.g., Wanner, 1980; Woods, 1970). However, the strategy is probably most heavily emphasized in the work of Frazier and her colleagues (e.g., Frazier, 1978, 1987a; Frazier & Rayner, 1982), who have consistetly backed a model embodying the tactic of selecting a single reading of ambiguous structures. This model has been dubbed the GARDEN PATH model because one of the consequences of the strategy is that people can be misled or "led up the garden path" when the chosen interpretation turns out to be incompatible with material appearing later in the sentence.

It is possible to draw a number of relatively subtle distinctions among the various hypotheses proposing that the parser constructs just one structural analysis for an ambiguous string. At one extreme one can posit that the initial analysis proceeds exactly as if the material were completely unambiguous (e.g., without any record being filed that a choice has been made, and hence that an alternative analysis might be feasible). This might be called SERIAL ANALYSIS WITHOUT ANNOTATION. Alternatively, the existence of unexplored options might somehow be tagged or marked at the choice point, perhaps providing the basis for relatively efficient re-analysis procedures (cf. Frazier & Rayner, 1982). Following Frazier (1978, p. 4), this might be referred to as ANNOTATED SERIAL ANALYSIS. This kind of account presupposes that alternative structures are subjected to at least cursory analysis. In order to recognize the existence of alternative analyses and file this information in any annotated record, the parser would presumably have to assemble at least some portion of the competing structures and use this information to detect the fact that options exist. Turning to another facet of the model, the initial choice might be COMPLETELY DETERMINED by certain characteristics of the material, such as its syntactic structure (e.g., Frazier, 1978, 1987a), or else the selection might be made on a probabilistic basis with some variation in the analysis selected from one occasion to another or perhaps from individual to individual (PROBABILISTIC CHOICE) (cf. Frazier & Rayner, 1982, p. 201).

2. Parallel Processing

With parallel processing it is assumed that when the parser comes to a choice point, two or more structures are assembled concurrently. Thus, in (3), branches representing both the complement and the relative interpretation might be constructed at the same time (as in chart parsing: cf. Gazdar & Mellish, 1989, Chap. 6; see also Gorrell, 1987). As with the serial account, a variety of different versions of the parallel model have been proposed. In some cases it is assumed that there is no cost associated with constructing multiple representations (RESOURCE-FREE PARALLEL MODELS), while in others it is assumed that there is a processing load associated with concurrent analysis of this kind (RESOURCE-LIMITED PARALLEL MODELS). A second distinction concerns the degree to which there is particular emphasis on one or more analyses at the expense of others. On the one hand it is sometimes assumed that all analyses are treated equivalently (UNBIASED PARALLEL MODEL), while on the other it is suggested that there is an uneven commitment either in terms of the processing resources allocated to different analyses or to some other aspect of their development (WEIGHTED PARALLEL MODELS).

3. Minimal Commitment Models

The third class of models is one in which the parser neither commits itself to a single analysis nor carries out a comprehensive analysis of all the potential structures. Variants of this model have been called the MINIMAL COMMITMENT MODEL (Frazier & Rayner, 1982; Weinberg, 1991), the WAIT-AND-SEE MODEL

(Just & Carpenter, 1980), and the DELAY MODEL (Smith, Meier, & Foss, 1991), and it is a crucial characteristic of a form of parsing referred to as DE-TERMINISTIC PARSING (Marcus, 1980). The key feature of these models concerns the form of processing adopted in regions where the sentence is open to alternative interpretations. With the exception of Weinberg's model, which is considered below, the general proposal is that certain aspects of processing are temporarily suspended, reducing the treatment to an incomplete, low-level analysis. This new restricted form of scrutiny is maintained until the parser comes across information which resolves the original ambiguity. At this point the previously suspended operations are allowed to run and the analysis is brought up to date. Different models make varying assumptions about precisely which aspects of syntactic analysis are suspended. Several authors (e.g., Kennedy, Murray, Jennings, & Reid, 1989; Perfetti, 1990; Smith et al., 1991) have proposed that "small" linguistic units like noun phrases (NPs) and prepositional phrases (PPs) are assembled but that the processes that link them into higher structures and establish the dominance relations between them are put on hold. Perfetti (1990, p. 221) goes on to suggest that missing components of the analysis might eventually be filled in after being triggered not by syntactic processes, but by the degree to which different linguistic units (like simple and complex NPs) find referential support in the prior discourse context. In accounting for one particular form of ambiguity (PP-attachment), Smith et al. (1991) suggest a form of resolution based on the outcome of a low-level process in which PPs are tentatively matched up with the unfilled arguments of a recent verb. Slot–filler matching of this type is assumed to proceed without the benefit of prior attachment of the ambiguous structure to the full parsing tree. Other accounts propose more straightforwardly syntactic triggering mechanisms (e.g., Frazier & Rayner, 1987; Gorrell, 1991; Marcus, 1980). In yet other cases (e.g., Frazier & Rayner, 1982; Just & Carpenter, 1980), the details about the nature of the superficial processing and the mechanisms for triggering full analysis are not made fully explicit. In all variants of the model considered so far, the proposal is that full analysis is suspended at the beginning of the ambiguous region and reinstated once some crucial operation is applied to some aspect of the subsequent input. However, the model put forward by Weinberg (1991) represents a more radical departure. According to this account, the structures built during the first pass do not correspond to those in a conventional syntactic tree. Instead, they are statements specifying, for example, that certain linguistic entities dominate others. Roughly speaking, this corresponds to the dominating unit being higher up in the same branch of the syntactic tree as the subordinate unit, but for present purposes the crucial feature of the formalism is that it does not require the full details of the tree to be specified at all stages in the analysis. It allows the parser to remain uncommitted with respect to certain classes of syntactic criteria (for full details see Weinberg, 1991). Like the other models in this category, then, there is a sense in which structural analysis is partially suspended over certain regions of the sentence and subsequently brought up to date in a later phase of processing.

4. Hybrid Models

There are also models which propose that people use different strategies in differing circumstances. For example, Just and Carpenter (1992) have proposed that readers use parallel processing if they have the resources to do so but revert to using a serial strategy if they become overloaded. On this type of account, different readers could apply different strategies to precisely the same material.

B. Empirical Predictions

The models outlined above differ from one another in several important ways, but they all share one important feature. They are all proposals about short-lived processing commitments. They refer to decisions and tactics whose influence is restricted to no more than a few words or phrases. Not surprisingly, therefore, the data that have been used to discriminate between the models has largely revolved around on-line measures of sentence processing (for a comprehensive review of these methods see Rayner and Sereno, this volume, and Haberlandt, this volume). The models make differential predictions about the ease of processing parts of the sentence that are subject to alternative interpretations. They also differ in their projections about processing load at points where ambiguities are resolved.

1. Processing in the Ambiguous Region

Some of the models predict that there will be an extra processing load associated with material that is open to alternative interpretations. Others maintain that it will be processed in exactly the same way as unambiguous material, and yet others that the relative difficulties will be reversed. According to resource-limited versions of the parallel model, processing should be slowed by the need to develop and maintain multiple representations. A degree of slowing is also compatible with certain versions of the TAGGED SERIAL model (e.g., Frazier, 1978). In these models, tags of some (as yet unspecified) kind are set up when the parser encounters potential ambiguities, and these markers are used to guide reanalysis in the event that the initial analysis fails. If the maintenance of such tags imposes a processing load, then this could well cause the normal structure-building operations to proceed more slowly until the ambiguity is resolved, at which point the tags can be deleted. According to other versions of the serial model, there should be no difference at all between processing ambiguous and unambiguous material. On these accounts the parser simply selects its preferred reading and only abandons it if it results in some kind of inconsistency or anomaly. Prior to this, the material is simply analysed as if it were unambiguous, and hence all details of processing should be indistinguishable from that for truly unambiguous material. Resource-free parallel models also predict that ambiguity per se should not increase overall processing load, though in this case the reason is that multiple analyses impose no additional burden, not that they are left unexplored.

In contrast to these accounts, certain versions of the minimal commitment model predict that processing should be easier in regions of ambiguity. The reason for this is that full analysis is suspended, and this should presumably reduce the complexity of the remaining operations (cf. Smith et al., 1991).

2. Processing Load in the Ambiguous Region: The Evidence

The vast majority of studies reveal that ambiguous materials are no more difficult (and no less difficult) to process than appropriately matched unambiguous materials. This equivalence in processing time has been shown both in eye-tracking studies (e.g., Ferreira & Henderson, 1990, Experiment 1, first fixation data; Frazier & Rayner, 1982; Kennedy & Murray, 1984; Kennedy et al., 1989, Experiment 2) and in self-paced reading tasks (e.g., Cuetos & Mitchell, 1988; Ferreira & Henderson, 1990, Experiment 2; Holmes, Kennedy, & Murray, 1987; Kennedy & Murray, 1984; Kennedy et al., 1989, Experiment 1; Mitchell, Corley, & Garnham, 1992, Experiment 1).

In contrast to the preponderant findings, a small number of experiments have yielded results which appear to show ambiguity effects (e.g., Foss, 1970; MacDonald, Just, & Carpenter, 1992; Smith et al., 1991). However, in each case it turns out either that the effects are questionable or that they can be attributed to some phenomenon unrelated to ambiguity itself. In an early ambiguity study using sentences like *When I purchased the hat (for/with) my friend, the businessman seemed to be grateful,* Foss (1970) reported that processing load was more pronounced after structurally ambiguous segments than after unambiguous controls. However, trials with structural ambiguities of this kind were mixed with an equal number of lexically ambiguous materials, and the ambiguity effect reported in the critical condition was the combination of the two effects, and there was no indication whether the effect was reliable (or even in the same direction) for the syntactic ambiguities alone. Since the overall effects could, in principle, have been contributed exclusively by the lexical subset of the materials, it would be inappropriate to place much emphasis on this evidence. A second problem with this study was that processing load was measured AFTER the ambiguous segment, not WITHIN it. This means that performance could have been contaminated by operations occurring after the end of the ambiguous region. This last difficulty also makes it impossible to interpret the finding reported by Smith et al. (1991). These authors presented evidence purporting to show that ambiguous materials are processed more rapidly than unambiguous controls. However, the materials were structured in such a way that the controls were actually disambiguated at the point in the sentence where the effect showed up. As before, then, it is impossible to use these data to draw any conclusions about processing load within the ambiguous region itself.

Explaining the "deviant" findings in the third study is a little more difficult. In this study, MacDonald et al. (1992) reported that in some conditions certain readers spent more time reading ambiguous materials than comparable nonambiguous materials. The effect failed to show up with one of the three groups of subjects tested (low-capacity readers) and turned out to be statistically unreliable in two of the three experiments reported. Moreover, it was not discernible at all in the first of two segments of the ambiguous region. However, it did show up reliably in at least one condition in the study, producing a finding which is at odds with the overwhelming bulk of the remaining literature. The explanation of the anomaly may well lie in the detailed structure of the experiment. While the region in question was genuinely ambiguous in the trials on which performance was measured, over the experimental session as a whole the structural content of this region was strongly correlated with the way in which the sentence was later resolved. It is possible that certain subjects found they were able to exploit these regularities, adopting a strategy of disambiguating the sentences prematurely when they came across artificially generated resolution cues. If so, the results have little implication for the question of whether processing load is normally increased in ambiguous portions of sentences.

Overall, then, the evidence from processing load in the ambiguous region is most compatible with the models predicting that there should be no load differences in handling ambiguous and unambiguous materials. This includes all the untagged serial models and resource-free parallel models. The data are less obviously compatible with most of the other models. However, a word of caution is needed here: the failure to find differences in one direction or the other can easily be attributed to limitations in the precision of the experimental measures used to look for the effects. Bearing this in mind, it could be argued that these data fail to provide convincing evidence against other versions of the serial and parallel models or against the minimal commitment model.

3. Processing at the Beginning of the Disambiguating Region

The various models also make differential predictions about the processing load associated with material immediately after the end of the ambiguous region [e.g., in the vicinity of *to avoid* in (4)]. In a coherent sentence, this material must disambiguate in favor of one or other of the structural analyses permitted up to this point. The models differ with respect to the question of whether one continuation should be favored over another, and whether either or both of the alternatives should impose more of a processing load than comparable material presented in an unambiguous context.

(4) *The cop told the motorist that he had noticed to avoid overtaking the school bus.*

According to both tagged and untagged versions of the serial model, only one structural analysis (the preferred analysis) is pursued on the first pass through the ambiguous region. If the continuation is compatible with this reading, then all aspects of the analysis should proceed smoothly in the following region. Indeed, since the assumption is that alternative analyses are totally ignored, all computations should be identical to those for comparable material appearing in felicitous unambiguous contexts. In contrast to this trouble-free processing for certain types of structure, the model predicts that there should be very marked processing difficulties whenever the sentence continuation is not compatible with the preferred analysis. In these circumstances, the model stipulates that the existing structural interpretation has to be abandoned and replaced by a new configuration extending over both the ambiguous region and the material that follows. Reanalysis of this kind presumably takes time and effort, leading to the prediction that there should be an increase in processing load at the beginning of the disambiguation region (cf. Frazier, 1987a; Frazier & Rayner, 1982).

The nonprobabilistic version of the serial model is based on the assumption that readers and listeners uniformly select the same interpretation when faced with any particular ambiguity. The model therefore predicts that processing load immediately after the ambiguous region will be greater for nonpreferred than for preferred continuations, and that preferred continuations will be processed in exactly the same way as suitable controls. With probabilistic versions of the model, the situation is a little more complex. If the readings are chosen with equal probabilities, then the size of the reanalysis effect will depend primarily on the relative difficulty of replacing one structure with the other. If the processing load associated with replacing the first with the second is comparable with the reverse, then no processing differences are to be expected. However, since both entail reanalysis on a proportion of trials, both should show a greater processing load than that in a suitable unambiguous control condition. If one reading is selected with higher probability than another, then, for compatible continuations, the probability of incurring reanalysis costs will be reduced, and in these circumstances the processing load might well be lower than that for continuations that are consistent with the low-probability competitor. If the preferred structure is chosen with any probability less than one, then there should be a residual cost associated with reanalysis on the minority of trials when the "wrong" choice is made. Thus, in both conditions processing in the disambiguation region should be slower than that in a suitable unambiguous control.

Turning next to parallel models, it is difficult to see how unbiased versions of the model would predict any differential effects in the disambiguation region. If both (or all) of the potential structures are assembled without mutual interference (as in resource-free versions of the model), then somewhere among the alternatives under scrutiny there must always be a structure capable of providing a framework for any viable continuation. Of course, analyses that are not compatible with the actual continuation would have to be purged, and it could be argued that this process itself imposes a processing load. However, since there is no obvious reason why this load should vary as a function of the set of structures being deleted, this version of the model would not predict the occurrence of any differential continuation effects. Similarly, resource-limited versions of the model might be capable of accounting for increments in processing load in the disambiguation region, but, as before, these influences should not be selectively associated with one continuation rather than another. In contrast with this, there are circumstances in which differential effects might occur in either resource-free or resource-limited variants of the biased parallel model. For example, if there is a higher level of commitment to one reading than to others (represented, perhaps, by a higher level of activation in a neural network system), then it may take more processing effort to switch from the favored interpretation to a competitor than to make the change in the opposite direction. Differences of this kind could be reflected in latency variations in the disambiguation region.

Finally, the pattern of predictions for minimal commitment models depends on assumptions made about the detailed workings of the model. In minimal commitment models, certain parsing decisions are postponed during the first pass through some portion of the sentence, and any predictions about variations in processing AFTER this region depend on precisely what the model maintains is happening at this point. In many of the models (e.g., Kennedy et al., 1989; Perfetti, 1990; Smith et al., 1991), what happens is that some of the routine parsing operations are temporarily suspended and then reinstated. In others (e.g., Weinberg, 1991), none of the regular operations are suspended. Rather, the assumption is that the products of the standard operations do not constitute what in most other frameworks would be considered a full parse. For models in which routine analysis is partially suspended over the region of ambiguity, all predictions about processing load at the end of the region depend on whether the forms of analysis that remain operational are capable of detecting that the ambiguous region has ended. If they cannot do this, then clearly there is nothing that would enable the system to reactivate the operations that have been temporarily suspended, and so in models of this kind there should be no processing effects associated specifically with the transition beyond the end of the ambiguous region. If the disambiguating information can somehow be identified, then it might be used to resolve the ambiguity and trigger the reinstatement of all analyses required to bring processing up to date. In this second case, the task of dealing with the backlog of processing would presumably lead to increments in handling time in the region concerned (cf. Gorrell, 1987; Smith et al., 1991). Whether these effects would vary as a function of the type of continuation depends on the precise operations involved in the contrasting updating operations. If one analysis calls for a decidedly more intricate set of operations, then presumably the updating procedure should take longer. In this case readers or listeners should dwell on this region for longer than they would with alternative continuations. On the other hand, if the updating requirements are equivalent in the two different cases, then models of this kind predict no differential continuation effects.

Now, consider the class of minimal commitment models which is based not on suspending operations, but on building what in other frameworks would be regarded as incomplete structures (e.g., Weinberg, 1991). Here the predictions depend on whether the structures, such as they are, turn out to be compatible with the material in the disambiguation region. If they are, and the syntactic analysis of the sentence can be completed merely by adding a few new substructures, then the model predicts that there should be no marked processing load at this point. This is the prediction which is made for sentences like (5) (for details, see Weinberg, 1991).

(5) *Mary expected Fred to leave.*

On the other hand, if the disambiguating information turns out to be incompatible with the initial analysis, and the parser is therefore forced to withdraw some of the structures it proposed slightly earlier, the model then predicts that there will be boggle effects in the disambiguation region. In fact, for many ambiguous sentences the predictions are precisely the same as those made by the serial models considered earlier (see Weinberg, 1991).

Summarizing the analysis of minimal commitment models, then, most of the proposals either predict (or can easily be made to account for) a processing increment in the disambiguation region. In some cases an effect of this kind is expected irrespective of the nature of the continuation. In others the prediction varies from one continuation to another. To narrow down the options we need to turn to the empirical data again.

4. Processing Load in the Disambiguating Region: The Evidence

Numerous studies have shown that immediately following an ambiguous region, at least one continuation takes longer to process than the same material appearing in an unambiguous context. Crucially, this pattern of results has been reproduced with a variety of different types of ambiguity. For a start, disambiguation effects have been obtained when preposed adverbial clauses without commas as in (6) are compared with controls with commas (e.g., Adams, Clifton, & Mitchell, 1991; Mitchell, 1986; Mitchell & Holmes, 1985).

(6) *After the young Londoner had visited(,) his parents prepared to celebrate their anniversary.*

They also show up when reading time in the disambiguation region of reduced relatives [e.g., *turned out* in (7a)] is compared with the same material in sentences like (7b) using the unreduced form (e.g., Ferreira & Clifton, 1986; MacDonald et al., 1992).

(7) a. *The defendant examined by the lawyer turned out to be unreliable.*
    b. *The defendant that was examined by the lawyer turned out to be unreliable.*

Strong disambiguation effects occur when relative clauses are temporarily attached to what turns out to be the wrong head (or node in the phrase marker) (e.g., Carreiras, 1992; Cuetos & Mitchell, 1988; Mitchell & Cuetos, 1991; see also Section III,B,5 below) and when *that*-clauses in sentences starting like (2) above turn out to be relatives—rather than the initially preferred complement reading (e.g., Mitchell, Corley, & Garnham, 1992, Experiment I). Finally, there is some evidence that there is a penalty incurred when the complementizer (*that*) is excluded from sentences like *The historian read (that) the manuscript of his book had been lost* (e.g., Ferreira & Henderson, 1990, Experiment 1 and 2; Holmes, Stowe, & Cupples, 1989, but here only with their complement-biased subset of verbs; Mitchell & Holmes, 1985; Rayner & Frazier, 1987, but see Holmes, 1987; Holmes et al., 1987; Kennedy et al., 1989). Taken together, these findings provide strong support for the wide range of models that predict some kind of processing increment in the disambiguation region. To distinguish between the accounts, we have to turn to other phenomena.

Nonprobabilistic serial models predict that there should be no cost associated with the preferred, as opposed to the nonpreferred, continuation. Surprisingly, very few of the studies carried out to date have made any attempt to determine whether the supposedly preferred continuation is processed any more slowly than identical materials in unambiguous control sentences. Indeed, only two such studies come to mind, and unfortunately these yield inconsistent results. Mitchell and Cuetos (1991) found no sign of any penalty associated with the preferred continuation in a form of structural ambiguity to be considered in further detail below [see (15)]. In contrast, MacDonald et al. (1992), using sentences like (8a,b), showed that at least with one group of subjects (high-span readers) there was such an effect [i.e., the latter part of (8a) took longer to read than the control (8b), even though *warned about* is more likely to be interpreted as the main verb of the sentence than as a reduced relative].

(8) a. *The experienced soldiers warned about the dangers before the midnight raid.*
    b. *The experienced soldiers spoke about the dangers before the midnight raid.*

Clearly, more studies of this kind will have to be carried out before we can say with any confidence whether there are any costs associated with preferred continuations.

In sum, these data argue against unbiased versions of the parallel model but are generally compatible with the various forms of the biased model. The bulk of the evidence is compatible with the unconditional or nonprobabilistic version of the garden path model, the only exception being the suggestion that there may be processing costs associated with handling continuations consistent with the preferred, as well as the nonpreferred, interpretation of the ambiguous material. Results of this kind are difficult to explain if the preferred choice is selected unconditionally and the following material is treated as if it were unambiguous. Further tests will be required to establish whether this effect is reliable and whether processing increments show up in preferred continuations for other structures. In contrast to the support for the conventional version of the model, the data are entirely consistent with the probabilistic form of the garden path model. As indicated above, this variant of the model can account for different patterns of processing load by making different assumptions about the probability with which the parser chooses each of the alternative interpretations. This makes it somewhat more flexible than the traditional form of the model, which essentially requires that the probability values must be 1 and 0 for the preferred and unpreferred readings respectively.

Next, consider the minimal commitment model. For versions of the model in which selected parsing operations are suspended, the most obvious pattern of data would be one in which there is a processing cost associated with both (or all) of the potential continuations. The reason for this is that if full processing is resumed after a temporary suspension, then, irrespective of the nature of the continuation, there should be a backlog of analysis to complete. While it is obviously inappropriate to refer to "preferred" and "nonpreferred" continuations within this framework, this variant of the model clearly has no difficulty in accounting for the evidence that at least one of these causes problems. Unfortunately, as already indicated, the evidence in relation to the second continuation is far too patchy to form the basis for firm conclusions, and from this perspective the model remains essentially untested to date. However, there are data that bear more directly on the model. To orient the discussion of these data it is useful to reiterate one or two premises of the model. A core assumption is that the processing increments under consideration here represent the effects of activities geared to catching up with temporarily suspended operations. By hypothesis, these operations do not involve the reversal of decisions already made or the destruction of any links previously built. The processing increments are merely the result of rescheduling postponed calculations and analyses. However, problems arise when one tries to specify exactly which operations might be suspended from one type of ambiguity to another. The most obvious possibility is that the parser continues with all structure building that is compatible with both (or all) readings of the ambiguity, postponing just the links that are inconsistent with one or other interpretation. However, this proposal fails to account for the data. If high-level connections are left unmade, then the parser clearly has to postpone all decisions and consistency checks that are contingent on these connections. However, it is often low-level checks of this kind that provide the basis for disambiguating the sentence. If such operations are out of action when the crucial information arrives, then there is no way they could be used to recognize the "disambiguation information" in order to trigger an update.

As an illustration of this point, consider a sentence starting as in (9) (from Mitchell, 1987b).

(9) *Just as the guard shouted the . . .*

The NP after *shouted* can be incorporated into the parsing tree in (at least) two different ways. It can either be construed as the subject of the matrix clause as in (10a) or it can be taken as the direct object of the verb in the preposed clause as in (10b).

(10) a. *Just as the guard shouted the intruder escaped through the window.*
　　 b. *Just as the guard shouted the command an intruder escaped . . .*

Given the ambiguity at the determiner *the* following *shouted*, a minimal commitment parser should presumably avoid making either kind of attachment and choose instead to leave the NP completely detached until further information becomes available. At the same time, structure-dependent checks should be suspended so that, for instance, there should be no attempt to establish whether the NP in question conforms to the selection restrictions that the preceding verb might impose on its direct object. On these assumptions, disambiguating material like the noun *intruder* should be passed over unnoticed without triggering any kind of updating process or reanalysis. In fact, the evidence suggests that this is not what happens. The reading times for NPs violating the selection restrictions of one potential attachment are reliably longer than those for NPs which are compatible with both alternative linkages (cf. Mitchell, 1987b). These results suggest that the connections of this kind are made, tested, and then destroyed rather than being left unconstructed in the first place. Similar problems arise with other constructions, and to date no one has succeeded in showing how a parser that avoids building ambiguous structures can nevertheless proceed to carry out tests that are contingent on those structures. As long as this issue remains unresolved, demonstrations of this kind will continue to weaken the case for minimal commitment models that are based on the assumption that routine parsing operations are suspended in regions of ambiguity.

None of these problems would apply to the Weinberg parser. According to Weinberg's (1991) analysis, the assignment of thematic roles to phrases like *the intruder* in (10a) is not one of the forms of analysis that are set aside during the first pass. Consequently, the model has no difficulty in explaining the processing difficulties associated with such material. However, this version of the model encounters problems of a different kind. In particular, there are structures where it fails to predict processing difficulties that turn up quite reliably in on-line data. This applies particularly to sentences like (11) in which the analysis is assumed to proceed without the need to withdraw any structures.

(11) *The historian read the manuscript of his book had been lost.*

In fact, as mentioned above (for further detail see Section III,B,4), if sensitive measures are used, sentences of this kind do cause reliable boggle effects. This indicates that, at the very least, Weinberg's model will have to be refined before it is capable of accounting for all aspects of the data.

C. Overview of Ambiguity-Handling Models

Summarizing the evidence from on-line studies, then, the findings show overall that measures sampling processing load within the ambiguous region generally argue against tagged serial models and all kinds of resource-limited models, while the patterns of data in the disambiguation region are incompatible with unbiased parallel models. The limited data available are also inconsistent with existing formulations of the minimal commitment model. In contrast, all the experimental findings appear to be compatible with biased, resource-free versions of the parallel model and with most untagged versions of the serial model. There is a slight hint of evidence that probabilistic versions of the serial model may eventually turn out to be more viable than the more conventional nonprobabilistic statements which have dominated the literature up to now. Further studies will have to be carried out before we know whether the promise is likely to be fulfilled.

As this brief overview of the models shows, the most viable models of ambiguity-handling strategies all presuppose that the parser has a tendency to make structural commitments somewhat prematurely. These commitments may be complete (as in the nonprobabilistic serial models) or partial (as in the probabilistic serial and biased parallel models). In any event, there seems to be an unevenness of support for the various potential readings of any ambiguous structure, and this bias often appears to manifest itself well in advance of the appearance of any material that would licence a decision one way or the other. A complete account of parsing needs to specify the mechanisms that underlie this kind of choice. A variety of models are considered over the next few pages.

III. MECHANISMS OF INITIAL CHOICE

A. Theoretical Predictions

1. Strategies Based on Tree Structure Analyses

Of the potential candidates for initial choice mechanism, the strategies which are perhaps most widely discussed are those based on the idea that certain substructures of parsing trees may be built more readily than others. Individual strategies in this category have been proposed by numerous authors (e.g., Bever, 1970; J. D. Fodor & Frazier, 1980; Frazier, 1978,1987a; Frazier, Clifton, & Randall, 1983; Frazier & Fodor, 1978; Kimball, 1973; Wanner, 1980; and several others). The main characteristic shared by these proposals is that the parsing choices are held to be determined either by the form of parsing trees already assembled at the choice point or by the structure of extensions that could potentially be built beyond this position. Although there are several different proposals in this class, the most frequently cited are two strategies formulated by Frazier (1978). These are LATE CLOSURE and MINIMAL ATTACH-MENT (late closure: "When possible attach incoming material into the phrase or clause currently being parsed," Frazier, 1978, p. 33; minimal attachment: "Attach incoming material into the phrase marker being constructed using the fewest nodes consistent with the well-formedness rules of the language under analysis," Frazier, 1978, p. 24). While the application of these strategies depends on the precise theory of grammar underpinning the representation, the main point for present purposes is that on this type of account parsing choices are contingent on the properties of actual or potenial treelike representations. Roughly speaking, late closure ensures that new material is attached at the point in the tree where the parser is currently working, while minimal attachment depends on making reference to details of the existing structure before attaching new branches to the tree.

2. Lexical Frame-Driven Strategies

According to a second type of account, initial parsing choices are determined not so much by the structure of the parsing trees associated with different options, but by the properties of individual words in the sentence. One such model was put forward by Ford, Bresnan, and Kaplan (1982). According to this proposal, the stored information about a verb incorporates information about the different ways in which it can be used. The FRAME for each of these forms of usage specifies, among other things, the type of argument structure the verb form can enter into; for example, the word *positioned* can be incorporated into a structure in which the verb has both a direct object NP and a PP complement, as in (12).

(12) *The woman positioned the dress on the rack.*

For each verb a given form may be tagged as being more salient than the alternatives. The proposal is that the initial parsing decisions are dictated by the structural requirements of the most salient form. As soon as the verb is processed, the frame associated with the strongest form is activated and this is then used to assign structure to the ambiguous material. The crucial feature of this type of account, then, is that initial decisions are based on the use of word-specific structural information recovered from the lexicon.

3. Thematic Assignment Strategies

With frame-driven accounts it is assumed that parsing decisions are controlled relatively directly by detailed lexical information. Other theories bear a resemblance to these models in positing a role for specific lexical information but differ in placing the major burden of decision-making on other mechanisms, particularly operations associated with deriving semantic interpretations of sentences. For example, Pritchett (1988) and Tanenhaus, Carlson, and Trueswell (1989) have developed accounts of ambiguity resolution which highlight the effects of moment-to-moment difficulties in determining the thematic structure of sentences. Pritchett's (1988) theory is expressed within the framework of government and binding theory (Chomsky, 1981) and hinges on the proposition that every noun phrase in a sentence must eventually be associated with a specific thematic role (e.g., Agent, Patient, Goal, Proposition, etc.). For present purposes the crucial observation is that in the course of sentence processing there may be times at which a phrase might turn up in advance of the words which are responsible for assigning its role (e.g., in a sentence starting with an NP, like *The president will announce . . .*: here the NP gets its thematic role from the verb that follows). Equally, there may be occasions where role-assigners (like verbs) precede the noun phrase(s) on which they can legitimately discharge their roles (e.g., *John put . . . ,* where the verb is waiting for its two arguments to be filled). In either case Pritchett assumes that there is a certain cost associated with a state of incompleteness incurred in linking roles with NPs. To account for ambiguity resolution, he simply proposes that the parser selects the reading which imposes the lowest cost on the system. Refinements of the theory deal with the possibility that initial misparses might be followed by differential costs of re-analysis. However, as far as the initial choice is concerned, the suggestion is that the decision is based on local role assignments in the alternative readings (see Gibson, 1990, and Weinberg, 1991, for somewhat different developments of the theory). As Pritchett does, Tanenhaus, Carlson, and Trueswell (1989) place strong emphasis on the role of thematic structures in parsing. However, as is discussed below, these authors see thematic processes as linking operations which coordinate semantic and discourse information as well as lexical and syntactic structures. In either case, initial parsing choices are determined by what might be termed thematic operations rather than simply tree-based or lexical considerations.

4. Discourse-Driven Strategies

The next class of hypotheses is based on the assumption that initial choice depends not on lexical, syntactic, or thematic considerations but on the way the alternative readings fit in with the prior discourse context. This possibility has been promoted in a series of papers by Crain, Steedman, and Altmann (e.g., Altmann, 1988; Altmann & Steedman, 1988; Crain & Steedman, 1985; Steedman & Altmann, 1989). The theory applies most readily to materials in which a definite noun phrase is followed by a phrase or clause which could either function as a modifier or play some other structural role in the sentence, as in (4), (14a,b), and (20). According to the model, the choice between these alternatives is made on the basis of the degree to which the noun phrase fits in with the prior discourse context in either its modified or its unmodified form. If the context provides a unique antecedent for the unmodified form, then the ''nonmodifying'' interpretation is given to the ambiguous string. If the noun phrase requires modification before reference can be established, then the appropriate ''modifier'' reading is selected. In either case, the central consideration in selecting one interpretation rather than another is the degree to which the material fits in with the prior discourse context.

5. Exposure-Based Strategies

Another class of strategies rests on the assumption that preliminary decisions are made on the basis of past experience. These models start with the premise that there is a mechanism which enables readers and listeners to identify different types of ambiguity. From this, the parser gains access to accumulated actuarial information about the relative frequencies with which the relevant structures have been encountered in comparable circumstances in the past. The proposal, then, is simply that the parser selects the dominant form on each new encounter with the ambiguity in question (cf. Mitchell & Cuetos, 1991; Mitchell, Cuetos, & Corley, 1992; Tanenhaus & Juliano, 1992). To elaborate a little, the suggestion is that the choice is determined not by structural features of the ambiguity or by problems associated with completing structurally defined calculations, but by the statistical prevalance of comparable structures in the language under examination. The proposal is that the parser is linguistically tuned by exposure to the language and opts for the most common choice, doing this either systematically or on a probabilistic basis. Thus, it may be that with structures like, say, (2), the bulk of *that* continuations in normal usage turn out to be constituents of sentences in which the *that*-clause is assigned a complement rather than a relative structure. In that case the hypothesis is simply that the actuarially dominant complement reading will normally prevail in all new encounters with similarly structured sentences. The account put forward by Mitchell and Cuetos (1991) leans heavily on earlier analyses of strategies children develop to deal with (largely) unambiguous sentences in different languages (e.g., Bates & MacWhinney, 1987; the competition model of MacWhinney, 1987). This model offers a theoretical account of the process by which statistical/linguistic regularities might be learned. For present purposes, however, the main point is that the initial parsing decisions are made by strategies drawing on low-level actuarial information about prior language use.

6. General Processing Cost Strategies

In the theories outlined so far, there have been disagreements about the kinds of information the parser might use to make its initial choices. However, each account is apparently premised on the assumption that all parsing biases can be interpreted within a single unitary framework. In contrast to this, some authors (e.g., Just & Carpenter, 1992; McRoy & Hirst, 1990) have suggested that initial parsing choices may be subject to a multiplicity of influences. Following J. D. Fodor and Frazier's (1980) account of the prevalence of minimal attachment, McRoy and Hirst (1990) suggest that the preferred reading is simply the one that can be constructed most rapidly at the point in question (see also Frazier, 1987a). In a computational implementation of the model, this decision is made by a set of independent processing modules referred to as HYPOTHESIZERS. At choice points, devices representing individual readings set about computing the cost of this particular structure (i.e., a measure of how difficult it is to assemble). The structure with the lowest cost is then selected for further analysis. In this implementation the serial cost calculations are used largely to simplify the modeling task and are intended to stand for the timing characteristics of concurrent races in a fully parallel system. In contrast to the strictly structural decision rules considered above, the cost calculations here are assumed to be influenced by a wide range of factors, including preferences associated with specific words, discourse and semantic factors, and various kinds of priming. In its current form the model does not specify exactly how these factors are weighted, and the cost calculations are therefore relatively arbitrary. However, the model gives some idea of how a race-based parser might operate. In a second theory permitting multiple influences in parsing, Just and Carpenter (1992) have suggested that, in selecting one interpretation over another, a reader's use of certain kinds of information (such as discourse information) may depend on his or her individual capacity for comprehension. On any given occasion, high-capacity readers may have resources enabling them to take account of a broad range of potential constraints (perhaps including many of the alternatives considered above), while low-capacity readers are forced to restrict themselves to more immediate (i.e., syntactic) considerations. In extreme cases the individual's capacity may determine whether a choice needs to be made at all or whether the alternative readings can be pursued in parallel.

In summary, depending on the particular proposal, initial parsing choices may be determined by the relative complexity of the parsing tree, by structural preferences associated with particular words, by the prevalence of undischarged or unallocated thematic roles, by the relative acceptability of the different readings within a discourse context, or simply by the frequencies with which the different interpretations occur in general language usage. Or, as some authorities have suggested, the decision might be determined by any or all of these factors in various combinations. The next section summarizes the empirical evidence on the role of the various factors.

B. Empirical Evidence on Strategies Used for Selecting Interpretations

Before considering the mechanisms of initial parsing choice, it is necessary to introduce an important methodological problem; and this is that, with current experimental techniques, there is no way of guaranteeing that any experimental measure is tapping into the initial choice, rather than reflecting the effect of subsequent reanalysis. According to many accounts of parsing (e.g., Frazier, 1987a; Mitchell, 1987a, 1989; Rayner, Carlson, & Frazier, 1983), only a very small amount of time elapses between the first and second phases of processing. In focusing on the initial stages of analysis, it is essential to minimize the time interval between the point at which the parser starts to process an ambiguity and the point at which performance is probed. For studies in which this interval is allowed to become too long, initial processing is liable to be contaminated by revision effects of various kinds.

1. Tree Structure Strategies

There have been numerous studies that appear to show that initial parsing choices are influenced by factors that are readily described in tree structure terms. As predicted by Frazier's (1978, 1987a) late closure strategy, the reading time for material following the ambiguous noun phrases is consistently found to be greater in sentences that violate the strategy, like (13a), rather than conforming to it, as in (13b) (Ferreira & Henderson, 1991a; Frazier & Rayner, 1982; Kennedy & Murray, 1984; Mitchell, 1987a; Mitchell & Holmes, 1985).

(13) a. *As soon as he had phoned his wife started to prepare for the journey.*
     b. *As soon as he had phoned his wife she started to prepare for the journey.*

This pattern of reading times suggests that more reanalysis is needed when the ambiguous phrase (*his wife*) turns out to be the subject of the main clause than when it has to be configured as part of the preposed clause. This implies that the preliminary analysis must have favored the latter interpretation, exactly as expected on a decision rule which stipulates that new material be attached to the branch of the tree structure currently under analysis.

Work with other structures provides further support for the proposal that it is tree structural considerations which determine the interpretations initially assigned to ambiguous structures. Numerous studies have shown that the simplest form (in tree structural terms) is favored over more complex alternatives—as expected on Frazier's (1978, 1987a) minimal attachment strategy. This has been demonstrated with complement/relative clause ambiguities like (3) above (Mitchell, Corley, & Garnham, 1992). It has also been shown repeatedly with main clause/reduced relative ambiguities like (14a,b) (Britt, Perfetti, Garrod, & Rayner, 1992; Ferreira & Clifton, 1986; Rayner et al., 1983; Rayner, Garrod, & Perfetti, 1992).

(14) a. *The horse raced past the barn and fell.*
     b. *The horse raced past the barn fell.* (from Bever, 1970)

More controversially, it is claimed to apply to direct object/reduced complement ambiguities (Ferreira & Henderson, 1990; Frazier & Rayner, 1982; Rayner & Frazier, 1987) and to PP attachment ambiguities (Clifton & Ferreira, 1989; Clifton, Speer, & Abney, 1991; Ferreira & Clifton, 1986; Rayner et al., 1983, 1992). Unfortunately, both claims have been vigorously disputed in the literature. With ambiguities of the first kind, a number of studies have failed to find the advantage which minimal attachment predicts unreduced complements should show over reduced complements (e.g., Holmes, 1987; Holmes et al., 1987; Kennedy et al., 1989). The generality of the strategy has also been questioned by its apparent shortcomings in accounting for unexpected preferences in attaching prepositional phrases (as reported by Altmann & Steedman, 1988; Britt et al., 1992; Ford et al., 1982; Smith et al., 1991; Taraban & McClelland, 1988).

In the first case the disagreement revolves around the empirical facts, with one group of workers apparently finding support for the strategy and the other not. In the second, the crucial question is whether the putative structural biases in these experiments might have been swamped by operations brought into play after the phase of analysis under consideration. The role of potential distortions of this kind is considered in more detail in the sections on discourse and lexical strategies.

More immediately problematic for the view that initial parsing decisions are based (exclusively) on tree structural considerations is the finding that early parsing choices appear to be influenced by the presence or absence of punctuations, as in (6) above (Mitchell, 1987b; Mitchell & Holmes, 1985); by the way in which the sentence is segmented on the page or screen (Kennedy et al., 1989; Mitchell, 1987a); and, in the case of auditory presentation, by the prosodic pattern of the input (Beach, 1991; Marslen-Wilson, Tyler, Warren, Grenier, & Lee, 1992). This suggests that something other than a parsing tree must be consulted before a decision is made, and these findings therefore question the completeness of tree-driven accounts.

Another problem is that the tree-based rules apparently do not always apply in an equivalent manner across different languages. Using sentences like (15), Cuetos and Mitchell (1988; Mitchell & Cuetos, 1991; Mitchell, Cuetos, & Zagar, 1990) presented data indicating that while subjects reading English show a slight bias toward the relative clause attachment dictated by late closure, Spanish readers (reading Spanish translations of the sentences) showed clear evidence of the reverse effect (i.e., they preferred to attach the relative clause to *son* rather than *actress*) (also see Carreiras, 1992).

(15) *Someone shot the son of the actress who was on the balcony with her husband.*

Frazier (1990b) has interpreted the Spanish departure from late closure in terms of a discourse-based revision mechanism which is assumed to act very rapidly, reversing the preliminary tree-based choice (see also De Vincenzi & Job, 1993). However, this still fails to explain the fact that there are cross-linguistic differences in the way the biases operate and, moreover, Mitchell et al. (1990) and Mitchell and Cuetos (1991) point to several details of the data that question the overall account of the phenomenon. At the very least it seems that more details have to be added before a tree-driven model can be viewed as providing a full account of the data.

2. Lexical Frame Strategies

If the selection process is driven largely by reference to detailed information from the lexicon, then it should be possible to demonstrate that the initial bias varies when one lexical item is replaced by another. However, investigations of potential lexical effects of this kind are plagued by difficulties in drawing an empirical distinction between initial and revision (or filtering) effects. There are numerous studies demonstrating that lexical information influences parsing decisions at some point in the course of processing a sentence (Adams et al., 1991; Boland, Tanenhaus, Carlson, & Garnsey, 1989; Boland, Tanenhaus, & Garnsey, 1990; Clifton, Frazier, & Connine, 1984; Clifton et al., 1991; Ferreira & Henderson, 1990; Ford et al., 1982; Gorrell, 1991; Holmes, 1984; Holmes et al., 1989; Mitchell, 1987a; Mitchell & Holmes, 1985; Nicol & Osterhout, 1988; Tanenhaus, Boland, Garnsey, & Carlson, 1989). Some writers (e.g., Boland & Tanenhaus, 1991; Gorrell, 1991; Holmes et al., 1989; Tyler, 1989) prefer to interpret these as initial effects, and others as phenomena in which detailed lexical information is merely used to re-assess the viability of structures first generated on some other basis (i.e., as filtering effects; e.g., Clifton et al., 1991; Ferreira & Henderson, 1990; Frazier, 1987a, 1989; Mitchell, 1987a, 1989). Ultimately, the dispute comes down to a question of whether lexical information has an immediate effect on structural processing or whether its impact is delayed by a few hundred milliseconds. Unfortunately, in most cases current technologies do not equip us to answer the question, since there is often no way of telling whether an effect is an immediate one or whether it is introduced during a slightly delayed checking process. Rather than focusing on occasions when lexical influences do have an effect and arguing about precise timing details—most of which are beyond the resolution of current experimental techniques—Mitchell (1989) has suggested that it may be more productive to look at situations where lexical information apparently fails to have an "immediate" effect. In this vein, Mitchell (1987a) presented subject-paced reading data which suggest that readers may sometimes fail to use lexical information sufficiently rapidly to prevent attempts to assemble ungrammatical structures. The specific finding in this study was that, with displays ending just before the main verb, it takes longer to process material in which the first verb is strictly intransitive, like the first part of (16a), than to control displays in which the first verb is optionally transitive, such as *saluted* in (16b).

(16) a. *After the private had fainted the sergeant / decided to end the military drill.*
   b. *After the private had saluted the sergeant / decided to end the military drill.*

If the frame-related properties of verbs like *fainted* had been available for "immediate" use, then this would presumably have caused the following NP to be interpreted unambiguously as the subject of the matrix clause—an analysis which would be expected to run through without notable difficulty. The fact that the juxtaposition of intransitive verbs and noun phrases caused difficulties suggests that, far from having the analysis guided by lexical information, subjects were actually trying to interpret NPs like *sergeant* as the direct objects of intransitive verbs. This line of argument has been criticized on the basis that normal processing might be distorted by the artificial segmentation of the material on the screen (Boland & Tanenhaus, 1991; J. D. Fodor, 1988, 1989), and it has also been suggested that there might have been problems with the materials used in the original study (e.g., by Pritchett, 1991). However, Adams et al. (1991) have recently replicated Mitchell's (1987a) earlier findings using an eye-tracking task with a new set of materials in unsegmented displays. It therefore seems unlikely that the effect can be explained away as an experimental artifact. This being the case, the findings suggest that, contrary to the proposal that lexical information is "immediately" used to guide the structural analysis, there may be occasions on which frame information is initially ignored or overridden. This goes some way toward strengthening the case for filtering accounts of lexical effects and suggests that the initial choice must be made on the basis of factors other than lexically derived biases.

Like tree-driven accounts, lexical frame strategies would in any case have to be supplemented before they could handle the various punctuation and layout effects described above. While refinements of this kind may be feasible, it is difficult to see how they could offer any explanation for certain other bias effects. In particular, it is difficult to see how lexically derived biases could in any way be responsible for influencing the choice of head for ambiguously attached relative clauses, or for changes in these preferences across languages (cf. the Cuetos & Mitchell, 1988, findings mentioned above). Nor do they offer any explanation of the punctuation, prosody, and layout effects discussed in Section III,B,1.

3. Strategies Depending on Thematic Role Assignment

It seems likely that certain types of initial parsing preference can be adequately explained on the basis of decision rules organized around thematic operations (as in the account put forward by Pritchett, 1988). For example, Pritchett (1988) argues in sentences like (14), repeated here, the main clause interpretation (14a) predominates over the reduced relative reading (14b) because this interpretation results in fewer unassigned roles during the first pass through the sentence.

(14) a. *The horse raced past the barn and fell.*
   b. *The horse raced past the barn fell.*

Similar arguments account for the preference for the complement interpretation in sentences like (1)–(3) above. However, this type of account does not fare so well when it come to other forms of structural ambiguity. To handle certain ambiguities where the alternatives are apparently equivalent in thematic terms (e.g., forms involving closure effects), Gibson (1990) has argued that it is necessary to buttress the thematic account by adding new decision principles that have nothing at all to do with thematic processing. With his addition of a RECENCY PREFERENCE PRINCIPLE (late closure, in essence), he is able to handle Frazier and Rayner's (1982) classic findings with sentences like (13a,b) and certain other closure findings, such as the tendency to attach ambiguous adverbs in sentences like (17) to the preceding clause rather than the following structure (Mitchell & Holmes, 1985).

(17) *The girl who up to now had been cycling carefully crossed the road.*

However, like the tree diagram accounts, a recency principle of this kind would not be sufficient to equip even the elaborated form of the model to account for the apparent antirecency biases in Spanish discussed above (cf. Cuetos & Mitchell, 1988).

More damagingly for Pritchett's (1988) account of parsing preferences, it seems to make the wrong predictions for certain structures. Specifically, Pritchett (1988, p. 558) predicts that there should be no boggle effect when people encounter the second verb in reduced complement sentences like (18) (already discussed several times before).

(18) *The historian read the manuscript of his book had been lost.*

In fact, while there are disagreements about the precise interpretation of the phenomenon (as indicated above), on-line studies consistently show either that latencies in this region are longer than comparable parts of unreduced relatives (e.g., Ferreira & Henderson, 1990; Frazier & Rayner, 1982; Rayner & Frazier, 1987) or that they are longer than equivalent material in transitive control conditions (e.g., Holmes, 1987; Holmes et al., 1987; Kennedy et al., 1989). Neither pattern of results seems to be compatible with Pritchett's (1988) theory of parsing choice.

4. Discourse-Driven Strategies

The proposal here is that initial parsing biases are determined exclusively by the degree to which the competing readings generate interpretations which fit in with the prior discourse context. On first inspection, the account appears to receive support from the considerable body of evidence showing that discourse context is capable of influencing the outcome of the interpretive process (Altmann, 1988; Altmann & Steedman, 1988; Britt et al., 1992; Ferreira & Clifton, 1986, Experiment 3; Mitchell, Corley, & Garnham, 1992; Perfetti, 1990; Rayner et al., 1983; Trueswell & Tanenhaus, 1991). As with the lexical effect considered above, however, the crucial question is whether the prior material influences the initial bias or whether it plays its role in a slightly later phase of processing (e.g., filtering). The issue is currently subject to intense debate and is unlikely to be resolved in the near future (for recent discussion, see Britt et al., 1992; Clifton & Ferreira, 1989; Mitchell, Corley, & Garnham, 1992; Perfetti, 1990; Perfetti, Britt, Rayner, & Garrod, 1991; Rayner et al., 1992; Steedman &

Altmann, 1989; Taraban & McClelland, 1990). The outcome of the debate depends on demonstrating whether context exerts an effect at the very earliest stages of processing—before filtering and revision can reasonably have had a chance to influence the course of analysis. Formulated in this way, it is doubtful whether the issue could ever be resolved to everyone's satisfaction. If an experiment fails to show context effects, investigators favoring discourse-driven analysis are likely to attribute this either to weakness of the contexts employed or to insensitivities in the experimental task used to measure performance. If it succeeds in showing such an effect, researchers in the opposing camp will almost certainly argue that the sentence processing operations have been probed too late to avoid the contaminating effects of filtering processes. Both positions are relatively unassailable, questioning the utility of trying to adjudicate between them. However, in a parallel to the argument against frame-driven approaches given above, there does seem to be at least one way of undermining the proposal that discourse-based operations are the sole determinants of initial biases in sentence processing. This is by showing that the initial bias is in the opposite direction to one that should theoretically be favored by the context. The use of a weak context or an insensitive task could prevent an experiment from showing a positive context effect, but, given suitable precautions, flaws of this kind should never introduce a bias in the opposite direction. In a recent study of this kind using sentences like (19a,b), Mitchell, Corley, and Garnham (1992), presented evidence that people are initially biased in favor of the complement interpretation of the ambiguous *that*-clause, and that this preference is just as marked in relative-supporting contexts as it is in contexts that have been demonstrated to favor the complement reading.

(19) a. *The politician told the woman that he had been meeting . . .*
   b. *The politician told the woman that had been meeting . . .*
   c. *The politician and the woman that (he) had been meeting . . .*

The main evidence for the initial complement bias was the fact that in a subject-paced reading task the words *had been* took longer to read in the subject-relative version (19b) than in the object-relative (or complement) version of the sentence (19a). This indicates that immediately after reading the word *that*, people must have been expecting something other than the continuation that occurs in (19b). Since this effect disappeared when the prior context ruled out a complement interpretation of the *that he* clause, as in (19c), we inferred that the phenomenon must be bound up in some way with the availability of the complement reading when the word *that* is encountered. The most obvious interpretation is that on reading the word *that* in (19a) and (19b), readers were expecting a complement, and that they were garden-pathed in (19b) when the next two words could not be reconciled with this structure. In sentences in which *told* was replaced by *and*, as (19c), they were not expecting a complement, with the result that the boggle effect did not occur (see Mitchell, Corley, & Garnham, 1992, for further controls and a more detailed justification of this interpretation).

To test whether the initial complement bias was affected by context, we got people to read the test sentences in the framework of paragraphs designed to induce relative or complement readings of *that*-clauses. (The structure of these passages was based on the materials Altmann, 1988, had previously used for the same purpose.) The results showed that the faster reading of *had been* in (19a) than (19b) was evident in relative-supporting as well as complement-supporting contexts. In fact there was no difference in the magnitude of the effect in the two cases, suggesting that the initial complement bias is just as strong when the material appears in a relative-supporting context as in the complement-supporting context. In the relative case the initial bias was in the opposite direction to that ostensibly favored by the discourse material, so it seems clear that the preliminary syntactic choice must have been made by something other than a discourse-driven mechanism. Like most earlier context studies, this experiment showed that despite the absence of immediate effects, contextual information did appear to exert an influence on processing well before readers reach the end of the sentence. What the findings question, then, is not that there are contextual effects at some point in sentence processing. Rather, they challenge the suggestion that these effects exert their influence early enough to affect initial parsing choices.

Limitations of pure discourse-based accounts are also highlighted by several other studies cited above [e.g., those showing punctuation and layout effects; experiments showing attachment biases in sentences with preposed clauses like (13a,b)]. Taken together, these findings show that, like each of the earlier proposals, discourse strategies alone cannot account for all the early biases that show up in parsing processes.

5. Exposure-Based Strategies

Of the various accounts of the workings of the conflict resolution mechanism, perhaps the least fully investigated is the proposal that the readers' choices are determined by their past encounters with the ambiguous forms in question. Mitchell and Cuetos (1991) suggested that the cross-linguistic clause attachment differences discussed above might be best interpreted within this framework (see also Mitchell et al., 1990). The proposal was that people use prior actuarial information to make their preliminary decisions about (say) the attachment point of a relative clause following a phrase like *the son of the actress*. Specifically, the suggestion is that they opt for the outcome they have encountered most frequently in comparable circumstances in their past experience with the language. This conjecture has recently received support from several lines of evidence. First, as expected, preliminary corpus analyses confirm that in English sentences like (10), the majority of relative clauses are intended to be attached to the second NP (e.g., *actress*), while in Spanish the opposite bias seems to predominate (Mitchell, Cuetos, & Corley, 1992). Second, in the same paper we presented some developmental evidence that as Spanish children get older, their attachment biases progressively approach the high-attachment preferences shown by adults. This suggests that as they gain linguistic experience, they systematically adapt to the biases imposed by contact with the language. Third, we were able to use an intervention study to provide more direct support for the exposure hypothesis. In this experiment, groups of 7-year-old children, matched for initial bias, were required over a period of two weeks to read large numbers of stories deliberately written to contain sentences either with high-attachment bias for one group or low-attachment bias for another. When they were retested following this intervention, the results showed that their preferences had diverged significantly—in line with their exposure regimes.

These results provide preliminary support for the view that there is a relationship between people's biases about competing forms in ambiguous structures and the prevalence of these forms in their prior exposure to language. Of course, this falls a long way short of establishing that initial parsing choices are completely determined by statistical tuning mechanisms of this kind. As a first step in testing the generality of the hypothesis, it would be necessary to conduct corpus analyses to determine the relative incidence of competing interpretations for all the different ambiguous forms that have figured in the parsing literature. So far, this only seems to have been done for one kind of ambiguity other than attachment to phrases like *son of the actress,* namely, the heavily researched ambiguity of PP attachment in sentences like (20).

(20) *I saw the man with the telescope.*

In sentences of this form, PPs such as *with the telescope* can either be attached to the immediately preceding NP as a modifier or to the higher VP structure as an argument of the verb. In a corpus analysis of just under 900 sentences of this kind, Hindle and Rooth (1993) judged 64% to have been intended as noun attachments. Somewhat surprisingly, this bias is inconsistent with the VP bias which tends to show up in on-line studies (see Frazier, 1987a, for a review). However, a more detailed examination of the corpus data showed that there was marked variation in attachment bias depending on the particular words used in the sentence (e.g., the word sequence *send the soldiers into* resulted in VP attachment, while *give the soldiers with* might lead to NP attachment). It may therefore be that the mispredictions of the basic tuning hypothesis can be explained away in terms of lexical differences between materials used in on-line studies and sentences showing up in corpora. Whatever interpretation is given to these particular findings, it is clear that a full evaluation of exposure-based strategies must await the outcome of corpus analyses of dominance in a much wider range of ambiguous structures.

Taking stock of the various accounts of initial choice, it should be clear that all the options are still the subject of debate. In these circumstances it would be misleading to give the impression that any given account is generally favored over the others. However, the review of the evidence suggests that if there is a single mechanism for determining initial parsing choice, then the process is most likely to rest either on a tree-based calculation or on a measure of past exposure biases. Accounts grounded on thematic role assignments, lexical frame projections, and discourse-based calculations currently seem to be less successful and less complete in accounting for the data. With the exception of cross-linguistic data on relative clause attachment, tree-related computations provide a satisfactory account of all undisputed findings in the literature. Given a little elaboration to include a plausible tree-based account of relative clause attachment, this kind of proposal would remain a strong contender as an account of initial choice. At present the main competitors would be theories which account for early decisions on the basis of the relative frequencies with which comparable ambiguities have been resolved in different ways in the past. Since we currently have no clear evidence about the biases that people are likely to have been exposed to in their general use of language, we do not yet have the evidence needed to assess this type of account, and the proposal therefore remains highly speculative. However, the increasing availability of corpus analyses could well rectify this deficit over the next few years.

IV. ASSEMBLY AND CHECKING PROCESSES

Over the last few pages we have dwelt at length on the mechanisms used for selecting structures (or biasing analysis in favor of one structure rather than others in parallel accounts of parsing). However, up to now we have not considered how these privileged structures might be assembled and scrutinized as they are progressively elaborated to include more and more of the words in the sentence. And yet, descriptions of these operations must constitute a central part of any comprehensive model of parsing. Almost by definition, the assembly procedure must construct new linguistic representations, and clearly it must do this by drawing on whatever raw material is available while it is active. As highlighted by re-analysis effects, no construction process of this kind can be guaranteed to get the analysis right the first time. This suggests that there must be additional checking procedures to evaluate output or performance of the assembly process (cf. Mitchell, 1987a, 1987b, 1989). At present there is little consensus about how either assembly or checking procedures operate.

A. Assembly Processes

There have been various broad proposals as to how assembly procedures might function. They might use extremely general phrase structure rules to convert short, ordered strings of words into segments of parsing trees (or some formal equivalent of these forms) (e.g., Anderson, Kline, & Lewis, 1977; Frazier, 1989; Mitchell, 1987a, 1989). They might operate by recovering detailed, word-specific structural information from the lexicon and proceed to use this information to generate target structures (e.g., Ford et al., 1982). They might draw more on the thematic properties of words, delivering thematic rather than syntactic structures as their output (e.g., McClelland & Kawamoto, 1986; Tanenhaus, Boland et al., 1989; Tanenhaus, Garnsey, & Boland, 1990).

Whatever the form of the final description, it must unquestionably capture certain fundamental properties of sentence structure. For example, some sentences contain words that are obligatorily co-referential. Thus in (21), *herself* refers to *Julie* and not to *Christina* (or any other female person).

(21) *Christina asked Julie to tidy herself up.*

In its final form the parsing description must somehow represent such interrelationships between the words or phrases of sentences. Indeed, achieving this would only scratch the surface of the problem. Most linguistic theories postulate the existence of numerous, highly intricate interconnections between the individual components of this final description. Of these, the most extensively studied have been the links between NPs (or PPs) and various classes of structural entity postulated by theoretical linguists—or at least by those of some persuasions. In particular, much of the debate concerns connections with structures referred to as EMPTY CATEGORIES or TRACES (see J. D. Fodor, 1989, for a highly informative introduction). These are hypothetical linguistic objects rather like conventional pronouns, except that they have the distinctive property of being phonologically empty (i.e., not spoken or marked in ordinary language and consequently not represented in the writing system). For researchers working within theoretical frameworks making use of such empty categories, there are several technical problems the parser has to solve before it can succeed in assembling the initial structural representation of the sentence. It has to discover where the traces are located in the sentence (if, indeed, there are any traces). It then has to link (or co-index) each trace with an overt NP or PP (sometimes via a sequence of intermediate steps taking in one or more other traces). Thus, like the co-indexing of anaphors, the cross-linking of traces represents a crucial part of analyzing the structure of sentences. A comprehensive model of the assembly process would have to document how these and other kinds of structural relationships are discovered in the course of the parsing process.

B. Checking Processes

Structures assembled during the first pass through a sentence will often turn out to be incompatible either with material that arrives later or with information not taken into consideration during the assembly process. Checking processes are needed to ensure that any structure under scrutiny satisfies all the detailed linguistic constraints that have to be met in well-formed and felicitous sentences. Without making any attempt to provide an exhaustive list of such constraints, they must include basic syntactic conditions such as the requirements of number-matching between verbs and their subjects and number and gender agreement between adjectives, relative clauses, and their heads. For inflected languages they must also include appropriate case markings for noun phrases, and in agglutinative languages (e.g., Bantu languages) complex types of agreement based on noun class. For all languages the overall sentence structure has to be compatible with the argument structures associated with its constituent verbs. Noun phrases have to end up with one (and only one) thematic role, and the semantic properties of argument fillers have to be consistent with the requirements of the slots they fill. There are also numerous rules covering tense, hypothetical forms, the use of reflexives and other anaphoric devices, and a complex array of rules governing the interrelationships between traces and overt linguistic entities. To be completely acceptable, the hypothesized structure may even have to be compatible with material analyzed before the appearance of the sentence in question. For example, structures (like definite noun phrases) which have a referring function in the discourse context should be capable of being linked to suitable referential entities in the wider text representation.

It follows from all this that after the initial structural hypothesis has been formulated, there is still a great deal of detailed checking to be done to make sure the components of the structure conform to all the linguistic rules of the language in question. In many cases the rules apply specifically to the structures under examination, in which case it may be that the only sensible way of tackling the problem is to assemble the structure prior to checking whether the individual constituents fit together properly.

Not a great deal is known about how checking processes work. Rayner et al. (1983) and various of their colleagues (e.g., Ferreira & Clifton, 1986; Frazier, 1990a) have put forward a set of proposals covering some of the checking operations associated with the thematic properties of verbs. According to this account, a device referred to as the THEMATIC PROCESSOR provides a mechanism for comparing the thematic structure of the representation under examination with the set of relationships typically associated with the individual words the structure comprises. If the mismatch exceeds some criterion value, then the analysis can be blocked, eventually causing it to be replaced by another one. More recently, Mitchell (1989) outlined the basic features of a procedure which could, in principle, handle not only thematic relations, but many of the other constraints mentioned above as well. Under this scheme linguistic units of any type are represented by framelike representations derived from unification grammar (cf. Shieber, 1986), and checking processes are viewed merely as one phase of a standard structure-building operation in which higher level representations are synthesized from more basic units. Within the unification framework, success in satisfying the various syntactic, pragmatic, or even semantic constraints of the language basically serves as a precondition for successfully completing the synthesis or unification in question. Thus, consistency-checking operations can be seen as part of the process that allows new overarching structures to be assembled from simpler subunits. It is uncertain whether the routines implemented by computational linguists can be used effectively as a model of human constraint-checking, but at present very few competing formalisms seem rich enough to capture the full complexity of the process.

Irrespective of the way in which checking processes might be conceptualized, there are numerous questions that might be asked about these processes. First, do they operate without delay, and are the different kinds of test applied in a consistent order? When a test indicates that the current structural hypothesis is not acceptable, can the information derived from this test be used to guide the process of reanalysis, or does this process go ahead without referring to the nature of the failure? Can the substructures from a rejected analysis be kept so that they can be built into the new structure, speeding up the new assembly process, or does the new construction process have to start from scratch? Unfortunately, answers to these and other questions must await further research.

Whatever the answer to all these questions, a successful check will leave not only a complete parsing tree (or a unification structure for the entire sentence). The final representation will also be elaborated in various ways as a result of the tests just conducted. For example, all the appropriate thematic roles will have been assigned, so the representation will specify who did what to whom, and what instruments they used, and so on. Referring structures will also be co-indexed with representations in the discourse structure, paving the way for the processes used to incorporate the sentence into a wider textual structure, updating the text base, responding to questions and instructions, and so on.

In contrast, when the checks fail, the sentence will have to be reanalyzed—which itself is likely to be a process which is just as elaborate as all the initial structure-building operations considered up to now. Like the checking processes, this is an underresearched problem. After being given a high profile in some of the earlier work on parsing (e.g., by Frazier & Rayner, 1982), it has only recently been investigated in detail again (e.g., Ferreira and Henderson, 1991a, 1991b; Kennedy et al., 1989; Warner & Glass, 1987).

V. SUMMARY AND EVALUATION OF THE BROAD APPROACH ADOPTED HERE

There are a number of features of the foregoing account which might perhaps warrant a little further comment. The first concerns the apparent preoccupation with ambiguous material. Much of the work that has been reported here is based on what happens when people encounter ambiguous material. It may not be immediately obvious that this kind of emphasis has been sensible. Notwithstanding all the discussion above, there are times when material can only be structured in one way, and here the question of deciding between competing analyses does not arise. The more immediate question is how the (unique) structure is assembled and checked. Unfortunately, for reasons elaborated below, it has proven very difficult to obtain measurable effects with unambiguous structures, and with the possible exception of some work with center-embedded clauses (e.g., Hakes, Evans, & Brannon, 1976), virtually all the empirical work on parsing has revolved around structures that are at least temporarily ambiguous in one way or another. As it happens, this may not be a serious shortcoming. A number of the operations discussed above have to take place irrespective of whether the material is ambiguous. In such cases it may be immaterial whether the issues are investigated within the framework of ambiguous or unambiguous structures. The ambiguous materials merely serve to render relevant influences measurable. A reasonable analogy might be the use of bubble chambers in particle physics. While such environments might, just conceivably, distort the processes they are intended to measure, they are required to make the operations accessible to experimental investigation. The minimal distortion they might produce is best ignored. In the study of parsing we have little alternative to building on what we can measure, working on the preliminary assumption that our findings are representative of processes that operate more widely.

Another potential reservation about much of the current work on parsing concerns its heavy dependence on tree diagram constructs. A good part of the research rests on the notion that human parsing involves building something like linguists' tree diagrams. Not all investigators are satisfied that this is necessarily a sensible assumption to make, and some (e.g., MacWhinney, 1987; McClelland & Kawamoto, 1986; McClelland, St. John, & Taraban, 1989) have put considerable effort into developing models of sentence processing which avoid such representations entirely. Instead of constructing tree diagrams, the processor uses connectionist procedures to convert the sentence into either a preformed thematic grid (McClelland & Kawamoto, 1986) or into a more open-ended connectionist representation (St. John & McClelland, 1990). While systems of this kind represent an interesting departure and appear to capture some of the regularities underlying sentence processing, it is not clear whether they can be extended to handle all the linguistic constraints and relationships known to be important in comprehension. For example, current versions of the system do not deal with long distance dependencies or with the problems that occur when relative clauses can be attached to one of several potential heads. Moreover, if it proved possible to extend them to deal with all the relationships currently expressed within tree diagram frameworks, it is not clear that this would amount to anything more than developing connectionist equivalents of tree diagrams (cf. Pollack, 1991). The point is that while current models might be criticized for taking tree diagrams a little too literally, it seems likely that any sentence processing system operating with grammatical rules will have to incorporate broadly equivalent representations. Like most models, tree diagrams need not be considered as anything like a literal representation built "in the head." They merely provide part of a map to help us explore a relatively uncharted area of research territory.

A third, somewhat unexpected, characteristic of psycholinguistic work on parsing concerns its heavy emphasis on nonlinguistic issues. With the notable exception of the work on traces, much of the research has focused on questions such as whether syntactic representations are assembled serially or in parallel, and whether or not all structural details are incorporated during the first pass through the material. Similarly, a lot of effort has been put into determining whether different kinds of information are used in the course of the initial assembly of representations or during later structure-checking processes. The rather surprising feature of all these debates is that they play down linguistic issues. Instead of investigating how stored linguistic information might be used to assemble syntactic representations and check their internal consistency, psycholinguists have often chosen to concentrate on details such as the timing with which these operations are applied and with implications this might have for the architecture of the parsing system. Of course, these questions are not irrelevant to our understanding of parsing, but most investigators would probably agree that they do not get to the heart of the problem. What we need to know is how grammatical knowledge is brought to bear in assembling structures, running consistency checks, and so on. Over the past few years linguists and computational linguists have developed a number of theories which bear directly on these issues. However, these ideas often turn out to be difficult to exploit because the basic operations involve computational steps which are too subtle to track using current psycholinguistic techniques. Moreover, any attempt to refine these issues would almost certainly depend on a hierarchy of procedural assumptions of the kind currently still in hot dispute, yielding a highly insecure foundation for any program of investigation. It seems clear that future researchers will have to overcome these problems before substantial progress can be made on the more linguistic aspects of our understanding of human parsing.

Finally, it may be worth commenting on the fact that the work on parsing places excessive reliance on a single language (English) and, indeed, on an extremely limited number of structures within this language. Other than the fairly extensive cross-linguistic literature on thematic interpretation with conflicting linguistic cues, there has only been a limited amount of work on languages other than English. A selection of recent studies includes a certain amount of published work on Dutch (e.g., Flores d'Arcais, 1982, 1987; Frazier, 1987b; Frazier & Flores d'Arcais, 1989), Japanese (e.g., Mazuka, 1991; Mazuka & Lust, 1990), French (e.g., Holmes & O'Regan, 1981), Spanish (e.g., Carreiras, 1992; Cuetos & Mitchell, 1988), German (e.g., Bach, Brown, & Marslen-Wilson, 1986), Italian (e.g., Clifton & 1990; De Vincenzi & Job, 1993), and Hungarian (e.g., MacWhinney & Pleh, 1988). However, the volume of research comes nowhere near matching that devoted to English and, indeed, with the vast majority of the world's languages there has been no on-line parsing work at all. This paucity of research is regrettable, since language variation represents an extraordinarily rich natural experiment which could tell us a great deal about parsing processes in general. By overgeneralizing from the findings concerned with parsing procedures in English, it is possible that researchers are misconstruing the more general features of syntactic processing (cf. Cuetos & Mitchell, 1988; Mitchell & Cuetos, 1991; Mitchell et al., 1990).

VI. CONCLUSIONS AND FUTURE DIRECTIONS

The on-line research carried out over the last 20 years or so suggests that different factors may be involved in selecting structures to be built, in actually assembling those structures, in checking their compatibility with the detailed grammatical rules of the language, and in revising the structures when things go wrong. There is clear evidence that there are biases in the initial selection process, and a variety of models have been put forward to account for these effects. At the time of writing, the issue remains relatively open, but the most viable accounts appear to be those in which the decisions are made either by reference to tree-diagrammatic memory representations or to stored frequency-of-occurrence information derived from exposure to language. Numerous linguistic factors have been shown to influence the assembly and checking processes, but the different effects seem to be brought into play in a strictly regulated manner, with the evidence suggesting on balance that detailed lexical and discourse effects play little or no role in assembly, becoming prominent in the checking phase of processing. Little is known about the detailed workings of any of these processes. Theoretical generalizations would in any case be greatly limited by the fact that the bulk of the work revolves around a little more than a dozen structures in just one language. Future progress may depend in part on extending research of this kind to other languages—especially those that are most distantly related to English. Researchers would also benefit by importing a wider range of constructs from other relevant disciplines (e.g., computational linguistics), and it seems likely that the current upsurge in interest in statistical or corpus-based approaches to machine parsing will provide a strong stimulus for developing further exposure-based accounts of parsing.

ACKNOWLEDGMENTS

Portions of this work were supported by ESRC grant No. R0023-1596, by a grant from the Nuffield Foundation, by a small grant from the University of Exeter, and by two Acciones Integradas grants from the British Council and the Spanish Ministry of Education. Much of the writing was done in 1991 while I was visiting the Psychology Department at the University of Massachusetts, Amherst, as a Fulbright Scholar. I am grateful to everyone there for providing a stimulating and supportive working environment. I am also grateful to Fernando Cuetos and Martin Corley for suggestions and contributions arising during numerous discussions of the work presented here.

REFERENCES

Adams, B. C., Clifton, C., Jr., & Mitchell, D. C. (1991). *Lexical guidance in sentence parsing.* Poster presented at the meeting of the Psychonomics Society, San Francisco.

Altmann, G. T. M. (1988). Ambiguity, parsing strategies, and computational models. *Language and Cognitive Processes, 3,* 73–97.

Altmann, G. T. M., & Steedman, M. (1988). Interaction with context during human sentence processing. *Cognition, 30,* 191–238.

Anderson, J. R., Kline, P. J., & Lewis, C. H. (1977). A production system model of language processing. In M. A. Just & P. Carpenter (Eds.), *Cognitive processes in comprehension* (pp. 271–331). Hillsdale, NJ: Erlbaum.

Bach, E., Brown, C., & Marslen-Wilson, W. D. (1986). Crossed and nested dependencies in German and Dutch: A psycholinguistic study. *Language and Cognitive Processes, 1,* 249–262.

Bates, E., & MacWhinney, B. (1987). Competition, variation and language learning. In B. MacWhinney (Ed.), *Mechanisms of language acquisition* (pp. 157–193). Hillsdale, NJ: Erlbaum.

Beach, C. M. (1991). The interpretation of prosodic patterns at points of syntactic structure ambiguity: Evidence for cue trading relations. *Journal of Memory and Lanugage, 30,* 644–663.

Bever, T. G. (1970). The cognitive basis for linguistic structures. In J. R. Hayes (Ed.), *Cognition and the development of language* (pp. 279–360). New York: Wiley.

Boland, J. E., & Tanenhaus, M. K. (1991). The role of lexical representation in sentence processing. In G. B. Simpson (Ed.), *Understanding word and sentence* (pp. 331–366). North-Holland: Elsevier.

Boland, J. E., Tanenhaus, M. K., Carlson, G., & Garnsey, S. M. (1989). Lexical projection and the interaction of syntax and semantics in parsing. *Journal of Psycholinguistic Research, 18,* 563–576.

Boland, J. E., Tanenhaus, M. K., & Garnsey, S. M. (1990). Evidence for the immediate use of verb control information in sentence processing. *Journal of Memory and Langauge, 29,* 413–432.

Britt, M. A., Perfetti, C. A., Garrod, S., & Rayner, K. (1992). Parsing in discourse: Context effects and their limits. *Journal of Memory and Language, 31,* 293–314.

Carreiras, M. (1992). Estrategias de análisis sintáctico en el procesamiento de frases: Cierre temprano versus cierre tardío. *Cognitiva, 4,* 3–27.

Chomsky, N. (1965). *Aspects of the theory of syntax.* Cambridge, MA: MIT Press.

Chomsky, N. (1981). *Lectures on government and binding.* Dordrect: Foris.

Clifton, C., Jr., & De Vincenzi, M. (1990). Comprehending sentences with empty elements. In D. A. Balota, G. B. Flores d'Arcais, & K. Rayner (Eds.), *Comprehension processes in reading* (pp. 303–330). Hillsdale NJ: Erlbaum.

Clifton, C., Jr., & Ferreira, F. (1989). Ambiguity in context. *Language and Cognitive Processes, 4,* 77–103.

Clifton, C., Jr., Frazier, L., & Connine, C. (1984). Lexical expectations in sentence comprehension. *Journal of Verbal Learning and Verbal Behavior, 23,* 696–708.

Clifton, C., Jr., Speer, S., & Abney, S. P. (1991). Parsing arguments: Phrase structure and argument structure as determinants of initial parsing decisions. *Journal of Memory and Language, 30,* 251–271.

Crain, S., & Steedman, M. (1985). On not being led up the garden path: The use of context in the psychological syntax processor. In D. R. Dowty, L. Kartunnen, & A. M. Zwicky (Eds.), *Natural language parsing* (pp. 320–358). Cambridge: Cambridge University Press.

Cuetos, F., & Mitchell, D. C. (1988). Cross-linguistic differences in parsing: Restrictions on the use of the Late Closure strategy in Spanish. *Cognition, 30,* 73–105.

de Vincenzi, M., & Job, R. (1993). Some observations on the universality of the Late Closure strategy. *Journal of Psycholinguistic Research, 22,* 189–206.

Ferreira, F., & Clifton, C., Jr. (1986). The independence of syntactic processing. *Journal of Memory and Language, 25,* 348–368.

Ferreira, F., & Henderson, J. M. (1990). The use of verb information in syntactic parsing: Evidence from eye movements and word-by-word self-paced reading. *Journal of Experimental Psychology: Language, Memory and Cognition, 16,* 555–568.

Ferreira, F., & Henderson, J. M. (1991a). Recovery from misanalysis of garden-path sentences. *Journal of Memory and Language, 30,* 725–745.

Ferriera, F., & Henderson, J. M. (1991b). The use of verb subcategorization information in syntactic parsing. In G. B. Simpson (Ed.), *Understanding word and sentence* (pp. 305–330). North-Holland: Elsevier.

Flores d'Arcais, G. B. (1982). Automatic syntactic computation and use of semantic information during sentence comprehension. *Psychological Research, 44,* 231–242.

Flores d'Arcais, G. B. (1987). Syntactic processing during reading for comprehension. In M. Coltheart (Ed.), *Attention and performance XII: The psychology of reading* (pp. 619–633). Hillsdale, NJ: Erlbaum.

Fodor, J. A., Bever, T. G., & Garrett, M. F. (1974). *The psychology of language: An introduction to psycholinguistics and generative grammar.* New York: McGraw-Hill.

Fodor, J. D. (1988). On modularity in syntactic processing. *Journal of Psycholinguistic Research,* *17,* 125–168.

Fodor, J. D. (1989). Empty categories in sentence processing. *Language and Cognitive Processes,* *4,* 155–209.

Fodor, J. D., & Frazier, L. (1980). Is the human sentence processing mechanism an ATN? *Cognition,* *8,* 417–459.

Ford, M., Bresnan, J. W., & Kaplan, R. M. (1982). A competence based theory of syntactic closure. In J. W. Bresman (Ed.), *The mental representation of grammatical relations* (pp. 727–796). Cambridge, MA: MIT Press.

Foss, D. J. (1970). Some effects of ambiguity on sentence comprehension. *Journal of Verbal Learning and Verbal Behavior,* *9,* 699–706.

Frazier, L. (1978). *On comprehending sentences: Syntactic parsing strategies.* Unpublished doctoral dissertation, University of Connecticut, Storrs.

Frazier, L. (1987a). Sentence processing: A tutorial review. In M. Coltheart (Ed.), *Attention and performance XII: The psychology of reading* (pp. 601–681). Hillsdale, NJ: Erlbaum.

Frazier, L. (1987b). Syntactic processing: Evidence from Dutch. *Natural Language and Linguistic Theory,* *5,* 519–560.

Frazier, L. (1989). Against lexical generation of syntax. In. W. Marslen-Wilson (Ed.), *Lexical representation and process* (pp. 505–528). Cambridge, MA: MIT Press.

Frazier, L. (1990a). Exploring the architecture of the language system. In G. T. M. Altmann (Ed.), *Cognitive models of speech processing: Psycholinguistics and computational perspectives* (pp. 409–433). Cambridge, MA: MIT Press.

Frazier, L. (1990b). Parsing modifiers: Special purpose routines in the human sentence processing mechanism? In D. A. Balota, G. B. Flores d'Arcais, & K. Rayner (Eds.), *Comprehension processes in reading* (pp. 303–330). Hillsdale, NJ: Erlbaum.

Frazier, L., Clifton, C., Jr., & Randall, J. (1983). Filling gaps: Decision principles and structure in sentence comprehension. *Cognition,* *13,* 187–222.

Frazier, L., & Flores d'Arcais, G. B. (1989). Filler-driven parsing: A study of gap filling in Dutch. *Journal of Memory and Language,* *28,* 331–344.

Frazier, L., & Fodor, J. D. (1978). The sausage machine: A new two-stage parsing model. *Cognition,* *6,* 291–325.

Frazier, L., & Rayner, K. (1982). Making and correcting errors during sentence comprehension: Eye movements in the analysis of structurally ambiguous sentences. *Cognitive Psychology,* *14,* 178–210.

Gazdar, G., & Mellish, C. (1989). *Natural language processing in PROLOG: An introduction to computational linguistics.* Wokingham, U.K.: Addison-Wesley.

Gibson, E. (1990). Recency preference and garden path effects. In *Proceedings of the 12th Annual Conference of the Cognitive Science Society,* pp. 372–379.

Gorrell, P. G. (1987). *Studies of human sentence processing: Ranked parallel versus serial models.* Unpublished doctoral dissertation, University of Connecticut, Storrs.

Gorrell, P. G. (1991). *A note on the direct association hypothesis: A reply to Pickering and Barry (1991).* Unpublished manuscript, University of Maryland, College Park.

Hakes, D. T., Evans, J. S., & Brannon, L. L. (1976). Understanding sentences with relative clauses. *Memory & Cognition,* *4,* 283–296.

Hindle, D., & Rooth, M. (1993). Structural ambiguity and lexical relations. *Computational Linguistics,* *19,* 103–120.

Holmes, V. M. (1984). Parsing strategies and discourse context. *Journal of Psycholinguistic Research,* *13,* 237–257.

Holmes, V. M. (1987). Syntactic parsing; In search of the garden path. In M. Coltheart (Ed.), *Attention and performance XII: The psychology of reading* (pp. 587–599). Hillsdale, NJ: Erlbaum.

Holmes, V. M., Kennedy, A., & Murray, W. (1987). Syntactic structure and the garden path. *Quarterly Journal of Experimental Psychology,* *39A,* 277–294.

Holmes, V. M., & O'Regan, J. K. (1981). Eye fixation patterns during the reading of relative clause sentences. *Journal of Verbal Learning and Verbal Behavior,* *20,* 417–430.

Holmes, V. M., Stowe, L., & Cupples, L. (1989). Lexical expectations in parsing complement–verb sentences. *Journal of Memory and Language,* *28,* 668–689.

Just, M. A., & Carpenter, P. A. (1980). A theory of reading: From eye fixations to comprehension. *Psychological Review, 87,* 329–354.

Just, M. A., & Carpenter, P. A. (1992). A capacity theory of comprehension: Individual differences in working memory. *Psychological Review, 99,* 122–149.

Kennedy, A., & Murray, W. (1984). Inspection times for words in syntactically ambiguous sentences under three presentation conditions. *Journal of Experimental Psychology: Human Perception and Performance, 10,* 833–847.

Kennedy, A., Murray, W., Jennings, F., & Reid, C. (1989). Parsing complements: Comments on the generality of the principle of minimal attachment. *Language and Cognitive Processes, 4,* 51–76.

Kieras, D. E. (1981). Component processes in the comprehension of prose. *Journal of Verbal Learning and Verbal Behavior, 20,* 1–23.

Kimball, J. (1973). Seven principles of surface structure parsing in natural language. *Cognition, 2,* 15–47.

MacDonald, M. C., Just, M. A., & Carpenter, P. A. (1992). Working memory constraints on the processing of syntactic ambiguity. *Cognitive Psychology, 24,* 56–98.

MacWhinney, B. (1987). *Mechanisms of language acquisition.* Hillsdale, NJ: Erlbaum.

MacWhinney, B., & Pleh, C. (1988). The processing of restrictive relative clauses in Hungarian. *Cognition, 29,* 95–141.

Marcus, M. (1980). *A theory of syntactic recognition for natural language.* Cambridge, MA: MIT Press.

Marslen-Wilson, W. D., Tyler, L. K., Warren, P., Grenier, P., & Lee, C. S. (1992). Prosodic effects in minimal attachment. *Quarterly Journal of Experimental Psychology, 45A,* 73–87.

Mazuka, R. (1991). Processing of empty categories in Japanese. *Journal of Psycholinguistic Research, 20,* 215–232.

Mazuka, R., & Lust, B. (1990). On parameter setting and parsing: Predictions for cross-linguistic differences in adult and child processing. In L. Frazier & J. de Villiers (Eds.), *Language processing and language acquisition* (pp. 163–205). Netherlands: Kluwer Press.

McClelland, J. L., & Kawamoto, A. H. (1986). Mechanisms of sentence processing: Assigning roles to constituents. In J. L. McClelland, D. E. Rumelhart, & the PDP Research Group (Eds.), *Parallel distributed processing: Explorations in the microstructure of cognition* (Vol. 2) Cambridge, MA: Bradford Books.

McClelland, J. L., St. John, M., & Taraban, R. (1989). Sentence comprehension: A parallel distributed processing approach. *Language and Cognitive Processes, 4,* 287–335.

McRoy, S. W., & Hirst, G. (1990). Race-based parsing and syntactic disambiguation. *Cognitive Science, 14,* 313–353.

Mitchell, D. C. (1986). *On-line parsing of structurally ambiguous sentences: Evidence against the use of lookahead.* Unpublished manuscript, University of Exeter.

Mitchell, D. C. (1987a). Lexical guidance in human parsing: Locus and processing characteristics. In M. Coltheart (Ed.), *Attention and performance XII: The psychology of reading* (pp. 601–681). Hillsdale NJ: Erlbaum.

Mitchell, D. C. (1987). Reading and syntactic analysis. In J. Beech, & A. Colley (Eds.), *Cognitive approaches to reading* (pp. 87–112). Chichester: Wiley.

Mitchell, D. C. (1989). Verb guidance and lexical effects in ambiguity resolution. *Language and Cognitive Processes, 4,* 123–154.

Mitchell, D. C., Corley, M. B., & Garnham, A. (1992). Effects of context in human sentence parsing: Evidence against a discourse-based proposal mechanism. *Journal of Experimental Psychology: Language, Memory and Cognition, 18,* 69–88.

Mitchell, D. C., & Cuetos, F. (1991). The origins of parsing strategies. In C. Smith (Ed.), *Current issues in natural language processing* (pp. 1–12). Austin: University of Texas, Center for Cognitive Science.

Mitchell, D. C., Cuetos, F., & Corley, M. M. B. (1992). *Statistical versus linguistic determinants of parsing bias: Cross-linguistic evidence.* Paper presented at the 5th Annual CUNY Conference on Human Sentence Processing, CUNY, New York.

Mitchell, D. C., Cuetos, F., & Zagar, D. (1990). Reading in different languages: Is there a universal mechanism for parsing sentences? In D. A. Balota, G. B. Flores D'Arcais, & K. Rayner (Eds.), *Comprehension processes in reading* (pp. 285–302). Hillsdale, NJ: Erlbaum.

Mitchell, D. C., & Holmes, V. M. (1985). The role of specific information about the verb in parsing sentences with local structural ambiguity. *Journal of Memory and Language, 24,* 542–559.

Nicol, J., & Osterhout, L. (1988). *Reactivating antecedents of empty categories during parsing.* Unpublished manuscript, University of Arizona, Tucson.

Perfetti, C. A. (1990). The cooperative language processors: Semantic influences in an autonomous syntax. In D. A. Balota, G. B. Flores d'Arcais, & K. Rayner (Eds.), *Comprehension processes in reading* (pp. 205–230). Hillsdale, NJ: Erlbaum.

Perfetti, C. A., Britt, M. A., Rayner, K., & Garrod, S. (1991). Can a discourse model help a parser? In C. Smith (Ed.), *Current issues in natural language processing* (pp. 1–27). Austin: University of Texas, Center for Cognitive Science.

Pollack, J. B. (1991). Recursive distributed representations. *Artificial Intelligence, 46,* 77–105.

Pritchett, B. L. (1988). Garden path phenomena and the grammatical basis of language processing. *Language, 64,* 539–576.

Pritchett, B. L. (1991). Head position and parsing ambiguity. *Journal of Psycholinguistic Research, 20,* 251–270.

Rayner, K., Carlson, M., & Frazier, L. (1983). The interaction of syntax and semantics during sentence processing: Eye movements in the analysis of semantically biased sentences. *Journal of Verbal Learning and Verbal Behavior, 22,* 358–374.

Rayner, K., & Frazier, L. (1987). Parsing temporarily ambiguous complements. *Quarterly Journal of Experimental Psychology, 39A,* 657–673.

Rayner, K., Garrod, S., & Perfetti, C. A. (1992). Discourse influences during parsing are delayed. *Cognition, 45,* 109–139.

Shieber, S. M. (1986). *An introduction to unification-based approaches to grammar.* Stanford, CA: Center for the Study of Langauge and Information, Stanford University.

Smith, C. S., Meier, R. P., & Foss, D. J. (1991). Information and decision making in parsing. In C. Smith (Ed.), *Current issues in natural language processing* (pp. 1–43) Austin: University of Texas, Center for Cognitive Science.

Steedman, M., & Altmann, G. T. M. (1989). Ambiguity in context: A reply. *Language and Cognitive Processes, 4,* 105–122.

St. John, M. F., & McClelland, J. L. (1990). Learning and applying contextual constraints in sentence comprehension. *Artificial Intelligence, 46,* 217–257.

Tanenhaus, M. K., Boland, J. E., Garnsey, S. M., & Carlson, G. N. (1989). Lexical structure in parsing long-distance dependencies. *Journal of Psycholinguistic Research, 18,* 37–50.

Tanenhaus, M. K., Carlson, G., & Trueswell, J. C. (1989). The role of thematic structures in interpretations and parsing. *Language and Cognitive Processes, 4,* 211–234.

Tanenhaus, M. K., Garnsey, S. M., & Boland, J. (1990). Combinatory lexical information and language comprehension. In G. T. M. Altmann (Ed.), *Cognitive models of speech processing: Psycholinguistic and computational perspectives* (pp. 383–408). Cambridge, MA: MIT Press.

Tanenhaus, M. K., & Juliano, C. (1992). *What to do about 'that': Use of co-occurence information in parsing.* Paper presented at the 5th Annual CUNY Conference on Human Sentence Processing, CUNY, New York.

Taraban, R., & McClelland, J. L. (1988). Constituent attachment and thematic role assignment in sentence processing: Influences of content-based expectation. *Journal of Memory and Language, 27,* 597–632.

Taraban, R., & McClelland, J. L. (1990). Parsing and comprehension: A multiple constraint view. In D. A. Balota, G. B. Flores d'Arcais, & K. Rayner (Eds.), *Comprehension processes in reading* (pp. 231–263). Hillsdale, NJ: Erlbaum.

Trueswell, J. C., & Tanenhaus, M. K. (1991). Tense, temporal context and syntactic ambiguity. *Language and Cognitive Processes, 6,* 303–338.

Tyler, L. K. (1989). The role of lexical representations in language comprehension. In. W. Marslen-Wilson (Ed.), *Lexical representation and process* (pp. 439–462). Cambridge, MA: MIT Press.

Wanner, E. (1980). The ATN and the sausage machine: Which one is baloney? *Cognition, 8,* 209–225.

Warner, J., & Glass, A. L. (1987). Context and distance-to-disambiguation effects in ambiguity resolution: Evidence from grammaticality judgments of garden path sentences. *Journal of Memory and Language, 26,* 714–738.

Weinberg, A. (1991). *Minimal commitment: A parsing theory for the nineties.* Unpublished manuscript, University of Maryland, College Park.

Woods, W. A. (1970). Transition network grammars for natural language analysis. *Communications of the ACM, 13,* 591–606.

CHAPTER 12

FIGURATIVE THOUGHT AND FIGURATIVE LANGUAGE

RAYMOND W. GIBBS, JR.

I. INTRODUCTION

Real-life discourse contains many kinds of figurative language. Consider the following conversation between two parents (Bill and Pat) and their teenage son (Grant) from the documentary film series *The American Family*. The conversation takes place in the family's backyard by their swimming pool. It starts when Bill and Pat summon Grant over to discuss his lack of interest in summer work.

(1)	BILL:	*Come over here a little closer . . . I think*
(2)	GRANT:	*Well, I'd rather stay out of this*
(3)	BILL:	*You . . . want to stay out of swinging distance*
(4)	GRANT:	*Yeah, I don't want to hurt you.*
(5)	BILL:	*Well . . . I mean . . . I was talking with your mother, ya know, and I told her that you weren't interested in doing any more work, ya see . . . and I don't blame you . . . I think that's a very honest reaction, there's nothing wrong feeling, umm . . . it's a natural thing to do not wanting to work*
(6)	GRANT:	*No, ah . . . it's not that I don't want to work, it's just ah. . .*
(7)	PAT:	*What kind of work did you have in mind Grant? Watching the television, and listening to records*
(8)	GRANT:	*I don't need your help mom*
(9)	PAT:	*Playing the guitar, driving the car*
(10)	GRANT:	*Ah . . .*
(11)	PAT:	*Eating, sleeping*
(12)	BILL:	*No, ah, listen Grant, you are a very good boy, we're very proud of you*
(13)	GRANT:	*Yeah, I know you are*

(14) BILL: *No, we are . . . you don't give us any trouble ya know.*
(15) GRANT: *Well, you sure are giving me a hell of a lot.*
(16) BILL: *Well that's my job I think . . . if, ah, I don't, why nobody else will and that's what I'm here for you . . . is to kind of see that you get off to a good start . . . lucky you may be with the deal, that's my job is to see that you get to see how life's going to be.*
(17) GRANT: *Yeah.*
(18) BILL: *And, ah, if I don't then nobody else will . . . a lot of kids go around don't ever have that privilege of having a mean old man.*
(19) GRANT: *Yeah, sure is a privilege too.*

This conversation is not atypical of how many American families talk, particularly when parents converse with their teenage children. These participants employ figurative language, especially irony and sarcasm, to good effect not only to indirectly convey various communicative intentions, but also to assert their own figurative understanding of the topics under discussion. For example, Grant says in (4) that he doesn't want to hurt his father and means this literally, but intends in a jocular way to convey the pretense that he *could* hurt his father should they get into a physical fight. This utterance fulfills the need for father and son to defuse what must be mutually recognized as a potentially uncomfortable situation of the parents criticizing Grant for his unwillingness to work. Later, in (7), (9), and (11), Pat sarcastically echoes Grant's putative belief that watching television, listening to records, playing the guitar, and so on constitute meaningful work activities. Pat's sarcasm reflects her ironic understanding of Grant's claim that he wants to work while at the same time doing little other than watch TV, listen to records, play the guitar, and so on. Finally, in (19) Grant sarcastically comments on the privilege he feels in having *a mean old man* for a father.

What is remarkable about this conversation is that the participants (and we as audience) do not appear to experience any difficulty interpreting what was meant by any of these figurative utterances. In no sense were these figurative expressions conscious, calculated risks, but they seemed to easily fit in the natural flow of the conversation. The different figures of speech in this dialogue may not possess the same degree of poetic insight as seen in great works of literature, but the conversation exhibits many apt figurative phrases, each reflecting the participants' ability to think in ways that go beyond the literal.

Why do speakers use figurative language in their everyday discourse, and why do listeners often experience little difficulty in understanding nonliteral speech? Figurative language seems especially useful in informing others about one's own attitudes and beliefs in indirect ways. Speakers do not always want to make explicit what they think, and so say things in such a way that listeners must infer their true beliefs (Brown & Levinson, 1978). Such off-record speech acts include many instances of metaphor (e.g., *Harry is a real fish* meaning 'Harry is cold-blooded or slimy like a fish'), metonymy (e.g., *The ham sandwich is getting impatient for his check* meaning 'The customer who ordered the ham sandwich is getting impatient for his check'), irony (e.g., *John's a real genius* meaning 'John is not very smart'), understatement (e.g., *The house needs a touch of paint* meaning 'The house is in terrible need of paint'), rhetorical questions (e.g., *How should I know?* meaning 'I should not be held responsible for knowing such and such'), indirect speech acts (e.g., *It's cold in here* meaning 'Go close the window'), hyperbole (e.g., *I tried to call you a thousand times last night* meaning 'I tried to call you many times last night'), and tautologies (e.g., *Boys will be boys* meaning 'Boys will always act in an ill-mannered fashion'). Each type of figurative language provides speakers with the ability to deny what was meant by anything that his or her words say directly. Nonetheless, speakers mostly assume that the use of these figurative devices should be understood by listeners in the way they are intended because of the common ground between themselves and their listener(s).

There has been significant work in psycholinguistics and related disciplines in the past 15 years on how people interpret figurative language. This experimental evidence suggests that figurative speech does not require special cognitive processes to be understood, contrary to the widely held assumption in linguistics, philosophy, and literary theory that such language violates, or flouts, norms of cooperative conversation. The ease with which many figurative utterances are produced and comprehended is due in part to the context for linguistic understanding, or more specifically, common ground (i.e., the knowledge, beliefs, and attitudes that are recognized as being shared by speakers and listeners in any discourse situation). One of my aims in this chapter is to discuss some of the experimental evidence on how common ground provides the context for people's fluency with figurative speech.

Another aim here is to illustrate how our ability to conceptualize experience in figurative terms also motivates why people use and understand figurative speech so effortlessly. Metaphor, metonymy, irony, oxymora, and so on do not merely provide a way for us to talk about the way we think, reason, and imagine; these figures are also constitutive of our experience. Speakers cannot help but employ figurative discourse because they conceptualize much of their experience in figurative terms. Listeners find figurative speech easy to understand precisely because much of their thinking is constrained by figurative processes.

There is not an extensive body of psycholinguistic research investigating the connections between the figurative structure of cognition and the use of figurative language. But there is enough evidence from related cognitive disciplines to warrant serious consideration of the idea that how people speak and understand figurative language is very much dependent on figurative modes of thought. Even more interesting is the possibility that figurative thought motivates much of our use and understanding of what is normally considered to be literal speech. This chapter attempts to illustrate some of the emerging connections between figurative thought and everyday language.

II. THE UBIQUITY OF FIGURATIVE THOUGHT IN EVERYDAY LANGUAGE

How common is figurative language? Most language scholars presume that figurative language is relatively rare in comparison to literal speech because figurative speech is deviant and ornamental. This traditional view of figurative language follows from the belief that the mind has objectively determined concepts and categories and that there must be an unmediated or direct connection, of whatever kind, between the units of language and what they represent in the real world. Language directly represents objects or is an unmediated representation of facts. Semantics is taken as consisting in the relationship between symbols and the objective world independent of the minds of any beings. All true, semantic meanings are literal.

Despite the pervasiveness of this view in Western intellectual thought, there are good reasons to question the primacy of literal thought and language given the ubiquity of figurative schemes in both language and thought. Many scholars have commented on the ubiquity of figurative language, especially metaphor, in literature, poetry, and even scientific writing. But few empirical attempts have been made to approximate how frequently speakers and writers employ figurative language.

One historical analysis of the metaphors used in American English prose from 1675 to 1975 revealed significant metaphoric activity in each of the six 50 year periods considered (Smith, Pollio, & Pitts, 1981). Many human topics, such as rationality, emotions, the meanings of life and death, were enduring issues that writers discussed primarily in metaphorical terms. Another empirical study examined the figurative language found in transcripts of psychotherapeutic interviews, various essays, and the 1960 Kennedy–Nixon presidential debates (Pollio, Barlow, Fine, & Pollio, 1977). This simple frequency count revealed that people used 1.80 novel and 4.08 frozen metaphors per minute of discourse. If one assumes that people engage in conversation for as little as 2 hours per day, a person would utter 4.7 million novel and 21.4 million frozen metaphors over a 60 year life span. A different analysis of the metaphors produced in television debates and news commentary programs (e.g., the *MacNeil/Lehrer News Hour*) showed that speakers use one unique metaphor for every 25 words (Graesser, Long, & Mio, 1989). These, admittedly crude, analyses clearly demonstrate that figurative language is not the special privilege of a few gifted speakers but is ubiquitous throughout both written and spoken discourse.

A closer look at everyday language demonstrates that these empirical attempts to count instances of figurative language vastly underestimate the pervasiveness of figurative thinking in people's ordinary speech. Typical frequency counts of figurative language do not include analysis of literal speech that is motivated by figurative modes of thought. Even though we normally assume that literal meaning is distinct from figurative language, figurative modes of thinking are evident in many utterances that are mostly viewed as literal. Consider the following mundane expressions that people often use in talking about verbal arguments (G. Lakoff & Johnson, 1980).

Your claims are indefensible.
I've never won an argument with him.
I demolished his argument.
He attacked every weak point in my argument.
His criticisms were right on target.
He shot down all of my arguments.
If you use that strategy, he'll wipe you out.
You disagree, Okay, shoot!

At first glance, none of these expressions appear to be very figurative, at least in the same way that an utterance like *The sun is the eye of heaven* might be. Yet a closer look at these expressions reveals a systematic structuring whereby people think of arguments in terms of wars. We can actually win or lose arguments. We see the person we are arguing with as an opponent. We attack his positions and we defend our own. We plan and use strategies. We might find certain positions undefensible, requiring us to take new lines of attack. Each of these things do not simply reflect the way we *talk* about arguments, for we actually argue as if we were in a war. Though there is no physical conflict, there is a verbal battle, and the structure of an argument (e.g., attack, defense, counterattack, and so on) reflects our metaphorical conceptualization of arguing in terms of wars.

There are perhaps hundreds of conceptual metaphors, such as ARGUMENTS ARE WARS, that structure our everyday experience. Many literal expressions reflect metaphorical concepts, ones that are not merely not dead but very much alive and part of ordinary cognition. Consider the metaphorical concept TIME IS MONEY as seen in the following utterances (G. Lakoff & Johnson, 1980).

You're wasting time.
This gadget will save you hours.
You're running out of time.
How do you spend your time these days?
Do you have much time left?
The flat tire cost me an hour.
I've invested a lot of time in her.
I don't have enough time to spare for that.
He's living on borrowed time.
You don't spend your time profitably.

Here again we see how our understanding and experiencing of one kind of thing (e.g., time) in terms of another (e.g., money) gives rise to various linguistic expressions that seem quite literal despite their underlying metaphoricity. Each of the above expressions refers to specific metaphorical entailments of the TIME IS MONEY conceptual metaphor. Time like money can be spent, saved, wasted, borrowed, invested, budgeted, or squandered. Together these metaphorical entailments form a system of relationships that people find easy ways of talking about.

Some scholars believe that literal utterances such as those seen above are not really very metaphorical but contain different dead metaphors. For example, we talk about *legs* of tables and *arms* of chairs even though we do not actively view tables and chairs metaphorically in terms of human body parts. In the same way, we might refer to arguments as being *indefensible* or to time as being *wasted* or *borrowed* even though there are no longer active metaphors in our everyday conceptual system that motivate such language.

But there are plenty of basic conventional metaphors that are alive, certainly enough to show that what is conventional and fixed need not be dead (Gibbs, 1992c; G. Lakoff & Johnson, 1980; G. Lakoff & Turner, 1989). Theorists have not come to terms with the fact that much of what is often seen as literal language is motivated by figurative modes of thinking, because they hold the belief that all metaphors that are conventional must be dead and really not metaphors any longer. This position fails to distinguish between conventional metaphors, which are part of our everyday conceptual system (e.g., ARGUMENT IS WAR, TIME IS MONEY), and historical metaphors that have long since died out. The mistake derives from an assumption that things in our cognition that are most active and alive are those that are conscious. On the contrary, those that are most alive and most deeply entrenched, efficient, and powerful are those that are so automatic as to be unconscious and effortless (G. Lakoff & Johnson, 1980). Our understanding of arguments as wars or time as money is active and widespread, but these concepts are so deeply entrenched in our ordinary conceptual system that we tend to miss their metaphorical character. The unconscious part of conceptual metaphors provides the main reason why people fail to see the figurative nature of many literal expressions.

Recent work in cognitive linguistics and philosophy provides many good examples of how most of our basic concepts are understood metaphorically. One domain of experience that is clearly metaphorical is event structure (G. Lakoff, 1990). Various aspects of events, including states, changes, processes, actions, causes, and purposes, are understood metaphorically in terms of space, motion, and force. Consider some of the following groups of expressions that reflect different metaphorical understandings of events.

IMPEDIMENTS TO ACTIONS ARE IMPEDIMENTS TO MOTION
We hit a roadblock.
We are fighting an uphill battle.
We are in rough waters.
I've hit a brick wall.

AIDS TO ACTION ARE AIDS TO MOTION
It is smooth sailing from here on in.
It's all downhill from here.
There's nothing in our way.

GUIDED ACTION IS GUIDED MOTION
She guided him through it.
She walked him through it.
She led him through the rough parts.

INABILITY TO ACT IS INABILITY TO MOVE
I am tied up with work.
He is up to his neck in work.
I am drowning in work.
We are stuck on this problem.

A FORCE THAT LIMITS ACTION IS A FORCE THAT LIMITS MOTION
She held him back.
She is being pushed into a corner.
He is tied up at work.
He doesn't give me any slack.
He's up against the wall.

CAREFUL ACTION IS CAREFUL MOTION
I'm walking on eggshells.
He is treading on thin ice.
He is walking a fine line.

SPEED OF ACTION IS SPEED OF MOVEMENT
He flew through his work.
It is going swimmingly.
Things have slowed to a crawl.
She is going by leaps and bounds.

LACK OF PURPOSE IS LACK OF DIRECTION
He is just floating around.
He is drifting aimlessly.
He needs some direction.

Event structure metaphors provide an explanation for how all these expressions involving space, motion, and forces can be used to talk about states, actions, causes, and purposes. Again, we tend not to view expressions like these as metaphorical even though each utterance clearly reflects metaphorical concepts that are very much a part of our everyday conceptual system.

Even more metaphorical complexity is seen in other expressions referring to causation (G. Lakoff, 1990). Most generally, causation is metaphorically understood in terms of forces. But more specifically, caused actions are understood as forced motion, as seen in the following expressions.

CAUSES ARE FORCES
She pushed me into doing it.
They dragged me into doing it.
I am being pulled along by the current.
She leaned on him to do it.

There are two main kinds of forced motion: propulsion (e.g., sending, throwing, propelling, etc.), and the continuous application of force to produce motion (e.g., bringing and giving). Each type of forced motion has its own particular entailments. With propulsion, the application of force begins the motion, which continues afterward. With continuous application, motion continues only as long as the force is applied. These different entailments about force are mapped onto causation in the CAUSES ARE FORCES metaphor. And each case of force motivates different kinds of causative expressions.

Consider the statements *The home run brought the crowd to its feet* and *The home run sent the crowd into a frenzy.* At first, both sentences seem similar. But each involves different kinds of forced motion. In the first example, with *brought,* the effect of the cause goes on during the flight of the ball and then ceases. The crowd rises to its feet while the ball is in the air. In the second case, with *sent,* the crowd's frenzy begins after the home run. Thus, two special cases of force are mapped into two special cases of causation by the CAUSES ARE FORCES metaphor (G. Lakoff, 1990). This metaphor allows listeners to make sense of different causative expressions, none of which are particularly figurative.

One last example of a complex metaphorical structuring of experience can be seen in folk ideas about the nature of human communication. Much of our understanding and talk about human communication is done via the CONDUIT METAPHOR (Reddy, 1979). This conceptual metaphor has three main parts: (a) ideas or thoughts are objects, (b) words and sentences are containers for these objects, and (c) communication consists in finding the right word-container for your idea-object, sending this filled container along a conduit or through space to the listener, who must then take the idea-object out of the word-container. There are hundreds of expressions within the language that exhibit the influence of the conduit metaphor (Reddy, 1979). Here are some examples.

It's very hard to get that idea across in a hostile atmosphere.
Jane gives away all her best ideas.
Your real feelings are finally getting through to me.
Your concepts come across beautifully.
It's a very difficult idea to put into words.
A good poet packs his lines with beautiful feelings.
You cannot simply stuff ideas into sentences any old way.
The entire chapter is completely void of useful ideas.
To unseal the meaning in Wittgenstein's curious phrases is not easy.

The conduit metaphor pervades our common understanding of human communication. Moreover, many scholarly theories of language and meaning rest on aspects of the conduit metaphor. For example, the notion that words have meanings reflects the metaphorical idea that words are containers filled with different essences (e.g., senses). Comprehension is often characterized as "unpacking" or accessing the meanings of words in sentences. Metaphorical ideas about communication clearly influence theoretical explanations of language, meaning, and understanding.

This section provides just a few of the many illustrations showing how our figurative understanding of experience, especially in terms of metaphor, motivates not just special, figurative utterances, but *all* aspects of language. The hypothesis that permanent knowledge may be metaphorically structured makes it possible to explain what till now has been seen as unrelated literal expressions. Psycholinguists interested in figurative language mostly ignore the figurative motivation for much literal speech and focus instead on figures of speech that are easily identifiable as metaphor, irony, and so on. Yet the analysis of systematic literal expressions shows just how ubiquitous figurative thought is in our everyday lives. My primary thesis in this chapter is to demonstrate the different ways that figurative thought influences the way that people use and understand both everyday and literary language. Not suprisingly, most instances of figurative language directly reflect figurative modes of thought. But as this section clearly showed, much of what we often see as literal discourse is also motivated by figurative thought.

III. Does Figurative Language Violate Communicative Norms?

One reason why psycholinguists do not acknowledge the constraining influence of figurative thought on *all* aspects of language use is that they assume that the use of figurative language deliberately violates widely shared communication norms. This belief stems from the centuries-old assumption that literal language is a veridical reflection of thought and the external world, while figurative language distorts reality and only serves special rhetorical purposes. My claim thus far is that the analysis of literal language suggests the dominating presence of figurative modes of thinking. But let us look more closely at the idea that figurative language represents a distortion of normal thought and consequently must violate communicative norms.

The most influential contemporary ideas about figurative language understanding as violations of communicative norms come from Grice's (1975, 1978) theory of conversational inference. To illustrate this theory, consider the following exchange between two college students.

> JOE: *Are you going to the big dance tonight?*
> SUE: *Didn't you hear that Billy Smith will be there?*

How does Joe interpret Sue's response to his question? Although Sue's response is itself a question (a rhetorical one), it is considered an appropriate answer to Joe's original question. But in different circumstances it would convey different answers. For example, on the assumption that Sue likes Billy Smith, the implied answer will be yes, whereas on the assumption that she wants to avoid him, the implied answer will be no. The fact that the listener (Joe) presumably knows, for example, that Sue does not like Billy Smith, then Joe can easily deduce Sue's communicative intention that she will not be going to the dance.

Understanding that Sue's comment is meant as a particular answer to Joe's question requires that Joe go through a chain of reasoning regarding Sue's intentions, because her answer does not logically follow from his question. Grice (1975) called the intended message behind Sue's utterance an "implicature." He proposed that implicatures are a natural outcome of speakers' and listeners' cooperation in conversation because all speakers adhere to the "cooperative principle" (Grice, 1975). This states that speakers must "make your conversational contribution such as is required, at the stage at which it occurs, by the accepted purpose or direction of the talk exchange in which you are engaged" (p. 45). Thus, when Sue says what she does, Joe should take Sue's response as being cooperative and therefore as implicating something beyond what the response literally means.

How do speakers uphold the cooperative principle? Grice argued that speakers do this by adhering to four conversational maxims. These are:

Maxim of Quantity: Make your contribution as informative as is required, but not more so, for the current purposes of the exchange.

Maxim of Quality: Do not say what you believe to be false or that for which you lack adequate evidence.

Maxim of Relation: Say only what is relevant for the current purposes of the conversation.

Maxim of Manner: Be brief, but avoid ambiguity and obscurity of expression.

These maxims constitute what it means for a speaker to be cooperative. Part of the context for understanding verbal interaction is the shared assumption that speakers and listeners will each uphold the cooperative principle and its associated maxims. Listeners will use the cooperative principle to their advantage in determining what speakers intend because they assume that speakers will tailor their remarks to satisfy this principle.

Grice also noted that speakers do not always uphold these maxims. As long as the speaker generally adheres to the overall cooperative principle, he or she can flout any of these maxims to produce certain implicatures. That is, speakers can deliberately violate a maxim and specifically intend for listeners to recognize the deliberate violation. For example, Sue's response to Joe's question with another question can be seen as a deliberate violation of the convention that questions should be responded to with assertions and not another question. In this case Sue is obviously flouting the maxim of manner in order to implicate that she is not going to the dance that night. According to Grice's analysis, Joe would not consider Sue's response to be uncooperative. Instead, Joe would continue to assume that Sue's rhetorical response was cooperative and should seek an interpretation given what he assumes about Sue, and what he believes Sue assumes about him, in order to derive an acceptable and "authorized" interpretation.

This analysis of how listeners derive conversational implicatures has been applied to figurative language comprehension. Consider the teenage son Grant's sarcastic comment *Sure is a privilege too* at the end of the opening conversation. According to the Gricean view, listeners determine the conversational inferences (or "implicatures") of figurative utterances by first analyzing the literal meaning of these sentences. Second, the listener assesses the appropriateness and/or truthfulness of a literal meaning against the context of the utterance. Third, if the literal meaning is defective or inappropriate for the context, then and *only* then will listeners derive an alternative nonliteral meaning that makes the utterance consistent with the cooperative principle. Grice assumes, then, that figurative language requires additional cognitive effort to be understood, because such utterances violate one of the conversational maxims (usually Quantity and/or Quality). A similar rational analysis of figurative language interpretation proposes specific principles for listeners to calculate just how sentence and speaker meanings differ in metaphor, irony, indirect speech acts, and so on (Searle, 1975, 1979).

The *standard pragmatic view* that figurative language violates various communicative norms suggests three related claims about how figurative language is understood (Gibbs, 1984; Glucksberg & Keysar, 1990). The first claim is that understanding literal meaning is obligatory and is derived independent of, and prior to, what is meant. This hypothesis assumes that literal meaning is understood via semantic knowledge, while the implicated meaning of an utterance (i.e., its figurative interpretation) is determined via pragmatic knowledge. One difficulty with this hypothesis is that pragmatic knowledge may determine not only what is meant, but what is said literally as well. Imagine the following brief exchange:

KEN: *Are you hungry?*
DOUG: *I have had breakfast.*

Doug intends his utterance to conversationally implicate that he is not hungry because he has recently eaten breakfast. But what is the literal or **said** meaning of *I have had breakfast* that listeners presumably analyze independent of and prior to deriving the implicated meaning? Listeners would rarely claim that what a speaker literally said here was that he had had breakfast at least once before in his life. Instead, people assume that what is said has a far richer semantic content, referring to the idea that the speaker has recently, most likely that very day, eaten breakfast (Gibbs & Moise, 1992). This understanding of what an utterance literally says suggests the application of pragmatic knowledge very early on in the comprehension process.

Many commonly noted instances of conversational implicatures found in the philosophical and linguistic literature turn out not to be implicatures after all (Recanati, 1989). For instance, the said meaning of *John has three children* is traditionally assumed to be 'John has at least three children' even if what the speaker means to convey is that John has **only** three children. The conventional implicature that John has only three children is explained by application of the conversational maxims to the literally expressed proposition (Grice, 1975). But the 'only three children' reading of *John has three children* is pragmatically determined as part of what is said, and in fact, many speakers actually perceive this and other sentences in this way (Gibbs & Moise, 1992).

The significance of this discussion for figurative language interpretation is that pragmatic information is used not only in determining what is meant, but also in figuring out what is literally said (Carston, 1988; Recanati, 1989; Sperber & Wilson, 1986). Figurative language may be understood without undue difficulty since people need not first analyze the literal, pragmatic-free meaning of an utterance before determining its figurative, implicated interpretation. In fact, many reading-time experiments in psycholinguistics show that people do not always require additional mental effort to comprehend figurative utterances (e.g., Gibbs, 1984, 1989; Gibbs & Gerrig, 1989; Hoffman & Kemper, 1987). Listeners/readers often take no longer to understand the figurative interpretations of metaphor (e.g., *Billboards are warts on the landscape*), metonymy (e.g., *The ham sandwich left without paying*), sarcasm (e.g., *You are a fine friend*), idioms (e.g., *John popped the question to Mary*), proverbs (e.g., *The early bird catches the worm*), and indirect speech acts (e.g., *Would you mind lending me five dollars?*) than to understand equivalent literal expressions. The standard pragmatic view would, however, predict that people should take longer to comprehend figurative language than to process literal speech because figurative language violates conversational norms. Yet the experimental data overwhelmingly suggest that people can understand figurative utterances without having to first analyze and reject their said meanings when these nonliteral expressions are seen in realistic social contexts. Appropriate contextual information provides a pragmatic framework for people to understand figurative utterances without any recognition that these utterances violate conversational norms.

The second claim of the standard pragmatic view states that understanding figurative language requires that a defective literal meaning be found before seeking a nonliteral interpretation. But empirical results clearly demonstrate that people do not need to find a defective literal meaning before searching for a nonliteral meaning. For example, people apprehend the nonliteral meaning of simple comparison statements (e.g., *surgeons are butchers*) even when the literal meanings of these statements fit perfectly with context (Glucksberg, Gildea, & Bookin, 1982; Shinjo & Myers, 1987). Even without a defective literal meaning to trigger a search for an alternative figurative meaning, metaphor can be automatically interpreted.

The third claim of the standard pragmatic view suggests that additional inferences must be made to derive figurative meanings that are contextually appropriate. But again, the results of many reading-time and priming studies demonstrate that understanding figurative utterances does not necessarily require additional mental effort beyond that used to comprehend literal speech (Gibbs, 1986c; Gildea & Glucksberg, 1983; Inhoff, Duffy, & Carroll, 1984; Keyser, 1989; Ortony, Reynolds, Schallert, & Antos, 1978). Many kinds of metaphor, metonymy, irony, and indirect speech acts, even novel utterances, require the same kind of contextual information as do comparable literal expressions.

All these experimental findings from psycholinguistics are damaging to the general assumption that people understand figurative language as violations of conversational maxims. Similar psychological mechanisms appear to drive the understanding of both literal and figurative speech, at least insofar as very early cognitive processes are concerned. However, individuals may at a later point reflect on the products of figurative language understanding and make different judgments about these meanings or interpretations. Readers may, for example, slowly ponder the potential meanings of literary metaphors. Consider the opening lines of a famous poem by Archibald MacLeish titled ''Ars Poetica'' (1933, p. 122).

> A poem should be palpable and mute
> As a globed fruit,
>
> Dumb
> As old medallions to the thumb,
>
> Silent as the sleeve-worn stone
> Of casement ledges where the moss has grown—
>
> A poem should be wordless
> As the flight of birds.

MacLeish may have written these lines to express many ideas. He may have intended for us to understand his vision of poetry as part of nature, or how poetics conveys meaning by spatial language, or even how poems talk about themselves while presenting descriptions of the external world. We might reflect on each of these possibilities, for example, slowly considering the various ways in which poems can be wordless as the flight of birds. It is this experience of consciously elaborating on the meanings of figurative language that provides much of the basis for the assumption that such language requires extra work to be properly understood. But the indeterminacy of figurative meaning does not necessarily indicate that figurative language ordinarily violates communicative norms to speak clearly and truthfully, nor does it mean that readers or listeners are unable to create **some** interpretation for figurative expressions during the earliest moments of comprehension.

The following sections consider in more detail some of the ideas and experimental evidence on the role of figurative thought in people's intepretation of figurative language.

IV. METAPHOR

Most of the research in psycholinguistics on figurative language focuses on metaphor. These studies focus primarily on how the topic (the A term) and vehicle (the B term) in metaphorical expressions of the form A IS B (e.g., *Encyclopedias are goldmines*) or A IS LIKE B combine or interact during metaphor comprehension (see Cacciari and Glucksberg, this volume). Metaphor scholars generally assume that individual metaphors reflect novel mappings of knowledge from dissimilar domains of experience. But even isolated novel metaphors often reflect systematic metaphorical knowledge that motivates many figurative and literal expressions. Much poetic verse embellishes on more mundane, yet metaphorical, ways of thinking about common human experiences.

Consider one metaphorical concept that structures part of our experience in the mundane world: ANGER IS HEATED FLUID IN A CONTAINER. This conceptual metaphor is actually one of the limited number of ways that people in Western cultures conceive of anger. Our understanding of anger (the source domain) as heated fluid in a container (the target domain) gives rise to a number of interesting entailments. For example, when the intensity of anger increases, the fluid rises (e.g., *His pent-up anger welled up inside him*). We also know that intense heat produces steam and creates pressure on the container (e.g., *Bill is getting hot under the collar* and *Jim's just blowing off steam*). Intense anger produces pressure on the container (e.g., *He was bursting with anger*). When the pressure of the container becomes too high, the container explodes (e.g., *She blew up at me*). Each of these metaphorical entailments is a direct result of the conceptual mapping of anger onto our understanding of heated fluid in a container.

What poets primarily do is not create new conceptualizations of experience with each metaphorical statement, but talk about the entailments of ordinary metaphorical mappings in new ways. Consider this fragment from a poem titled "The Phenomenology of Anger" by Adrienne Rich (1973, p. 25).

> Fantasies of murder: not enough:
> to kill is to cut off from pain
> but the killer goes on hurting
>
> Not enough. When I dream of meeting
> the enemy, this is my dream:
>
> white acetylene
> ripples from my body
> effortlessly released
> perfectly trained
> on the true enemy
>
> raking his body down to the thread
> of existence
> burning away his lie
> leaving him in a new
> world; a changed
> man.

Rich specifies the heated fluid representing anger as acetylene that she can focus as a weapon upon the object of her emotion. Her verse is beautifully poetic yet makes use of the same figurative modes of thought that motivate common idioms such as *blow your stack, flip your lid,* or *hit the ceiling,* as well as conventional expressions about anger such as *His pent-up anger welled up inside him.* Rich's poem has great intuitive appeal for us precisely because she refers to, and elaborates on, a common metaphorical view of anger.

My argument is that our basic metaphorical conceptualizations of experience constrain how we think creatively and express our ideas in both everyday and poetic discourse. Many linguists, philosophers, literary theorists, and psychologists miss this important point because they fail to acknowledge the systematic, conceptual underpinnings of the vast number of linguistic expressions that are metaphorical and creative. What is frequently seen as a creative expression of some idea is often only a spectacular instantiation of specific metaphorical entailments that arise from a small set of conceptual metaphors shared by many individuals within a culture. Some of these entailments when expressed are products of highly divergent, flexible thinking. But the very existence of these entailments about concepts is motivated by underlying metaphorical schemes of thought that constrain, even define, the ways we think, reason, and imagine. Our understanding of many novel metaphorical expressions is based on common metaphorical knowledge that we use all the time to make sense of our everyday experience (Gibbs, 1992a). This possibility is ripe for future empirical study.

V. IDIOMS

Some of the best evidence for the metaphorical nature of everyday thought is found in the systematic analysis of idiomatic expressions. Consider the idiom phrases *spill the beans, button your lips,* and *lose your marbles.* Most scholarly examinations of idioms like these assume that such phrases are not figurative because they are dead or frozen metaphors. Speakers presumably make sense of idioms by learning arbitrary links between these phrases and their figurative meanings. People must learn these arbitrary links because idioms are noncompositional, since their meanings are not a function of the meanings of their individual parts (e.g., *spill the beans* = 'to reveal a secret', *button your lips* = 'to keep a secret', *lose your marbles* = 'to go crazy', and so on).

But do people have greater insight into the figurative meanings of idioms other than to realize that these phrases have conventional, nonliteral meanings? Even though idioms are not often seen as figurative, there has been substantial work on these phrases that takes issue with the long-standing belief in the dead metaphor view of idiomaticity. This work has shown that the individual words in many idioms systematically contribute to the overall figurative interpretations of these phrases, contrary to the noncompositional view of idioms (Fillmore, Kay, & O'Connor, 1988; Gibbs, 1990a; Gibbs & Nayak, 1989; G. Lakoff, 1987; Langacker, 1986; Nunberg, 1978). For example, speakers know that *spill the beans* is analyzable since *beans* refers to an idea or secret and *spilling* refers to the act of revealing the secret. Similarly, in the phrase *pop the question,* it is easy to discern that the noun *question* refers to a particular question (e.g., *Will you marry me?*) when the verb *pop* is used to refer to the act of uttering it. Speakers clearly recognize some relationship between the words in many idioms and their overall figurative interpretations.

There are interesting and important behavioral consequences of the idea that idioms are analyzable and not just giant lexical items. One series of studies showed that the semantic analyzability of an idiom affects people's intuitions about their syntactic productivity (Gibbs & Nayak, 1989). For instance, people find semantically analyzable or decomposable idioms more syntactically flexible than nondecomposable idioms. Thus, an analyzable phrase such as *John laid down the law* can be syntactically altered into *The law was laid down by John* without disrupting its figurative meaning. However, semantically nondecomposable idioms tend to be much more syntactically frozen (e.g., one cannot change *John kicked the bucket* into *The bucket was kicked by John* without disrupting its figurative meaning). Another series of studies indicated that semantic analyzability influences people's intuitions about the lexical flexibility of idioms (Gibbs, Nayak, Bolton, & Keppel, 1989). Thus, analyzable idioms can be lexically altered without significant disruption of their nonliteral meanings (e.g., *button your lips* to *fasten your lips*), but semantically nondecomposable phrases cannot (e.g., *kick the bucket* to *punt the bucket*). These data suggest that the syntactic versatility and lexical flexibility of idioms are not arbitrary phenomena, perhaps due to historical reasons, but can at least be partially explained in terms of an idiom's semantic analyzability.

The analyzability of idioms also plays an important role in their immediate, on-line, interpretations. Because the individual components in decomposable idioms (e.g., *lay down the law*) systematically contribute to the figurative meanings of these phrases, people process idioms in a compositional manner where the meanings of each component are accessed and combined according to the syntactical rules of the language. On the other hand, a strict compositional analysis of semantically nondecomposable idioms (e.g., *kick the bucket*) provides little information about the figurative meanings of these expressions. Reading-time studies showed that people took significantly less time to process decomposable or analyzable idioms than to read nondecomposable expressions (Gibbs, Nayak, & Cutting, 1989). These data suggest that people normally attempt to do some compositional analysis when understanding idiomatic phrases. This does not mean that people automatically compute the literal, context-free, interpretations of idioms (Gibbs, 1980, 1985). Rather, some compositional process attempts to assign some figurative meanings to the individual components in idioms during understanding. Children also experience greater difficulty learning the meanings of semantically nondecomposable idioms precisely because these phrases' nonliteral interpretations cannot be determined through analyses of their individual parts (Gibbs, 1987, 1991).

One reason why people see many idioms as being analyzable is because they tacitly recognize the metaphorical mapping of information between two conceptual domains that partially explains why these idioms mean what they do. For example, the idiom *John spilled the beans* maps our knowledge of someone tipping over a container of beans to a person revealing some previously hidden secret. English speakers understand *spill the beans* to mean 'reveal the secret' because there are underlying conceptual metaphors, such as THE MIND IS A CONTAINER and IDEAS ARE PHYSICAL ENTITIES, that structure their conceptions of minds, secrets, and disclosure (G. Lakoff & Johnson, 1980). The mapping of source domains such as containers and physical entities onto minds and ideas results in very specific entailments about the act of revealing a secret. Thus, the act of revealing a secret is usually seen as being caused by some internal pressure within the mind of the revealer, the action is thought to be done unintentionally, and the action is judged as being performed in a forceful manner (Gibbs & O'Brien, 1990).

One way of empirically uncovering speakers' tacit knowledge of the metaphorical basis for idioms is through a detailed examination of their mental images for idioms (Gibbs & O'Brien, 1990; G. Lakoff, 1987). Consider the idiom *spill the beans*. Try to form a mental image for this phrase and then ask yourself the following questions. Where are the beans before they are spilled? How big is the container? Are the beans cooked or uncooked? Is the spilling accidental or intentional? Where are the beans once they have been spilled? Are the beans in a nice, neat pile? Where are the beans supposed to be? After the beans are spilled, are they easy to retrieve?

One set of experiments examined people's mental images for groups of idioms with similar figurative meanings, such as idioms about revelation (e.g., *spill the beans, let the cat out of the bag, blow the lid off*), anger (e.g., *blow your stack, hit the ceiling, flip your lid*), insanity (e.g., *go off your rocker, lose your marbles, bounce off the walls*), secretiveness (e.g., *keep it under your hat, button your lips, keep in the dark*), and exerting control (e.g., *crack the whip, lay down the law, call the shots*) (Gibbs & O'Brien, 1990). Participants were asked to describe their mental images for these idioms and to answer questions about the causes, intentionality, and manners of action in their mental images for these phrases. People's descriptions of their mental images were remarkably consistent for different idioms with similar figurative meanings. These mental images were not simply representative of the idioms' figurative meanings, but captured more specific aspects of the kinesthetic events suggested by the idioms. For example, the anger idioms such as *flip your lid* and *hit the ceiling* all refer to the concept of 'getting angry', but participants specifically imagined for these phrases some force causing a container to release pressure in a violent manner. There is little in the surface forms of these different idioms to tightly constrain the images participants reported. After all, lids can be flipped and ceilings can be hit in a wide variety of ways, caused by many different circumstances. But participants' protocols revealed little variation in the general events that took place in their images for idioms with similar events that took place in their images for idioms with similar meanings.

Participants' responses to the questions about the causes and consequences of the actions described in their images were also highly consistent. When imagining anger idioms, for instance, people know that pressure (i.e., stress or frustration) causes the action, that one has little control over the pressure once it builds, its violent release is done unintentionally (e.g., the blowing of the stack), and that once the release has taken place (i.e., once the ceiling has been hit, the lid flipped, the stack blown), it is difficult to reverse the action. Each of these responses is based on people's folk conceptions of heated fluid or vapor building up and escaping from containers. Thus, people's metaphorical mapping of knowledge from a source domain (e.g., heated fluid in a container) onto target domains (e.g., the anger emotion) helps them conceptualize in more concrete terms what is understood about the target domain of anger. For example, our understanding that too much heated pressure can cause a sealed container to explode is mapped onto the target domain of anger such that we conceptualize the "explosion" of someone's anger as being performed unintentionally with force because of internal pressure. The metaphorical ways in which we partially conceptualize experiences, such as anger, actually provide part of the motivation for why people have consistent mental images, and specific knowledge about these images, for idioms with similar figurative meanings.

Psycholinguistic research also demonstrates that people's knowledge of the metaphorical links between different source and target domains provide the basis for the appropriate use and interpretation of idioms in particular discourse situations (Nayak & Gibbs, 1990). Participants in one study, for example, gave higher appropriateness ratings to *blew her stack* in a story that described the woman's anger as being like heat in a pressurized container (i.e., ANGER IS HEATED FLUID IN A CONTAINER), while *bit his head off* was seen as more appropriate in a story that described the woman's anger in terms of a ferocious animal (e.g., ANGER IS ANIMAL BEHAVIOR). Thus, readers' judgments about the appropriateness of an idiom in context were influenced by the coherence between the metaphorical information depicted in a discourse situation and the conceptual metaphor reflected in the lexical makeup of an idiom.

The fact that the nonliteral meanings of many idioms are motivated by preexisting metaphorical knowledge suggests that idioms should not be easy to paraphrase, in the same way that most metaphors resist paraphrase. Contrary to the dead metaphor view, which assumes that the meanings of idioms are arbitrary for speakers and can mostly be represented in short phrases or even single words (Palmer, 1981), idioms have rather complex interpretations. For example, phrases such as *spill the beans* cannot be simply paraphrased as meaning 'to reveal a secret' in the way that most idiom dictionaries do (cf. Boatner, Gates, & Makkai, 1975; Long & Summers, 1979). The mapping of source domains such as containers onto minds results in very specific entailments about the act of revealing a secret. Our knowledge about the behavior of containers under internal pressure partially structures our understanding about the revelation of secrets, such that the act of revealing a secret is usually seen as being caused by some internal pressure within the mind of the revealer, the action is thought to be done unintentionally because of the internal pressure that makes the container burst, and the action is judged as being performed in a forceful manner (Gibbs & O'Brien, 1990).

A recent series of experiments illustrated that people's understanding of idioms reflects the particular entailments of these phrases' underlying conceptual metaphors (Gibbs, 1992b). Participants' understanding of events corresponding to particular source domains in various conceptual metaphors (e.g., the source domain of heated fluid in a container for ANGER IS HEATED FLUID IN A CONTAINER) can be used to independently predict their interpretations of idioms. Thus, when people understand anger idioms, such as *blow your stack, flip your lid,* or *hit the ceiling,* they infer that the cause of the anger is internal pressure, that the expression of anger is unintentional, and that it is done in an abrupt, violent manner. These inferences are again predicatable from their independent understanding of the source domain of a fluid in a sealed container. On the other hand, people do not draw very specific inferences when comprehending literal paraphrases of idioms, such as *get very angry.* Such literal phrases are not motivated by the same set of conceptual metaphors as are specific idioms such as *blow your stack.* For this reason, people do not view the meanings of *blow your stack* and *get very angry* as equivalent despite their apparent similarity.

These data show how the metaphorical mappings between source and target domains in long-term memory preserve critical aspects of their source domains (i.e., their cognitive topology), mappings that directly influence people's understanding of idioms. Although not all idioms are motivated by independently existing conceptual metaphors, the psycholinguistic evidence strongly suggests that people make sense of many idioms because of their permanent metaphorical knowledge.

VI. Metonymy

Metonymy is a fundamental part of our conceptual system whereby people take one well understood or easily perceived aspect of something to represent or stand for the thing as a whole. Similar to metaphor, the conceptual basis of metonymy is easily seen in the similarity between various metonymic expressions. Consider the following statements.

Washington has started negotiating with Moscow.
The White House isn't saying anything.
Wall Street is in a panic.
The Kremlin agreed to support the boycott.
Hollywood is putting out terrible movies.
Paris has dropped hemlines this year.

These examples do not occur one by one, but reflect the general cognitive principle of metonymy where people use one well-understood aspect of something to stand for the thing as a whole or for some other aspect of it (G. Lakoff & Johnson, 1980). All the above expressions relate to the general principle by which a place may stand for an institution located at that place. Thus, a place like Wall Street stands for a particularly salient institution(s) located at that place, namely the stock exchanges and major banks.

Various metonymic models in our conceptual system underlie the use of many kinds of figurative and conventional expressions. Among these are the following.

OBJECT USED FOR USER
The sax has the flu today.
We need a better glove at third base.
The buses are on strike.

CONTROLLER FOR CONTROLLED
Nixon bombed Hanoi.
Ozawa gave a terrible concert last night.

THE PLACE FOR THE EVENT
Watergate changed our politics.
Let's not let Iraq become another Vietnam.

Our ability to conceptualize people, objects, and events in metonymic terms provides the basis for much of the way we reason and make inferences. Many conversational inferences about what speakers mean by what they say require metonymic reasoning. Consider the following exchange:

MARY: *How did you get to the airport?*
JOHN: *I waved down a taxi.*

John means to inform Mary that he got to the airport by hailing a taxi, having it stop and pick him up, and then having it take him to the airport. Successful interpretation of John's remark demands that the listener make this inference about what the speaker meant (i.e., a conversational implicature).

How does a listener infer that John actually got to the airport by taxi? Traveling from one place to another involves a series of actions where an individual finds some vehicle to take him to the desired location, gets into the vehicle, rides in it to the destination, arrives, and gets out. An idealized cognitive model of this series of events includes the following (G. Lakoff, 1987).

Precondition: You have (or have access to) the vehicle.
Embarcation: You get into the vehicle and start it up.
Center: You drive (row, fly, etc.) to your destination.
Finish: You park and get out.
End point: You are at your destination.

It is conventional to use one part of this idealized model to evoke the entire model. Thus, people can simply mention either the Precondition, Embarcation, or Center to stand for the entire series of events that make up the travel scenario. In the above brief exchange, John mentions a Precondition (i.e., getting access to a taxi by hailing one) to represent the entire travel scenario. Other possible responses that might work equally well specify other parts of the idealized model, such as:

I drove my car.   (Center)
I called my friend Bob.   (Precondition)
I hopped on a bus.   (Embarcation)
I stuck out my thumb.   (Precondition).

In each case above, people metonymically mention a subpart of the travel scenario to stand for the whole scenario. Listeners readily recognize that speakers intend for them to understand the entire scenario when one subpart of it is stated, because they share similar cognitive models. Such inferences about entire events based on the mention of a single part is evidence of metonymic thinking similar to that used in understanding metonymic expressions such as *Wall Street is in a panic.*

Psychological research provides good evidence that people reason metonymically when understanding language. Consider the following pairs of utterances (Gernsbacher, 1991).

a. *I need to call the garage (where my car was being serviced).*
b. *They said they'd have it ready by five o'clock.*
c. *I think I'll order a frozen margarita.*
d. *I just love them.*

In each of these examples, a plural pronoun occurs in the second sentence. But only singular noun phrases occur in the preceding sentences. Strictly speaking, these pronouns are illegal because of the prescription that a pronoun must agree with its antecedent in person, number, and case. However, a series of experimental studies demonstrated that people rate as more natural and read more quickly sentences with CONCEPTUAL ANAPHORS (e.g., the sentences with *They* and *them* in the above examples) than they do sentences with appropriate singular pronouns (e.g., sentences with the grammatically correct pronoun *it*) (Gernsbacher, 1991). Understanding conceptual anaphors requires our recognition that the singular entities mentioned (e.g., *the garage*) metonymically stand for some conceptual set (e.g., the people who work at the garage). Illegal plural pronouns are natural and easily understood precisely because of our pervasive ability to think metonymically about various people, places, events, and objects.

Many other studies show that people metonymically infer entire sequences of actions having only heard or read some salient subpart in a story. Consider the following simple tale.

John was hungry and went into a restaurant.
He ordered lobster from the waiter.
It took a long time to prepare.
Because of this he only put down a small tip when he left.

When people hear this brief episode, they presumably activate their knowledge of the activities normally associated with eating in a restaurant and use this information to fill in the gaps to make the story coherent. This type of knowledge, called **scripts** (Schank & Abelson, 1977), consists of well-learned scenarios describing structured situations in everyday life. To comprehend a message, such as the above passage, listeners must first decide what script is relevant and then how it is to be modified to fit the situation at hand.

A number of experiments show that people automatically infer appropriate script-related actions when these are not explicitly stated. For example, when listening to the above story, people infer *John ate the lobster,* and this inference becomes indistinguishable in their memories from the actual linguistic material they originally heard (Abbott, Black, & Smith, 1985; Bower, Black, & Turner, 1979; Gibbs & Tenney, 1980; Graesser, Woll, Kowalski, & Smith, 1980). Other studies suggests that prior activation of script-based knowledge provides readers with a highly available set of causal connections that can facilitate sentence-by-sentence intergration (Bower et al., 1979; Garrod & Sanford, 1985; Sanford & Garrod, 1981; Seifert, Robertson, & Black, 1985; Sharkey & Sharkey, 1987). Speakers (and writers) can assume that listeners will supply the necessary scriptlike inference needed to understand what is being said and so typically will leave implicit any information that listeners can supply themselves.

All the work on script-based language processing illustrates the importance of metonymic models in everyday thought. People's knowledge in long-term memory for coherent, mundane series of events can be metonymically referred to by the mere mention of one salient subpart of these events. We see that mention of the subpart metonymically stands for the whole event. This inference facilitates our being able to assume unstated propositions about what speakers and writers mean. For this reason, the extensive work on conversational implicature and knowledge-based parsing constitutes part of the evidence on the figurative nature of everyday thought and undersanding.

How do people ordinarily understand metonymic expressions? No studies have been conducted on people's comprehension of conventional metonymic expressions such as *Wall Street is in a panic.* As is the case with conventional expressions motivated by metaphor, conventional metonymies appear literal to us and we rarely notice the figurative nature of these utterances. But various studies have examined understanding of less conventional metonymic sentences such as *The ham sandwich is getting impatient for his check.* Metonymic expressions like this make little sense apart from some specific context (e.g., as when one waiter wants to inform another that his customer, who was served a ham sandwich, wants to receive the check). Metonymy serves in these instances as a kind of CONTEXTUAL EXPRESSION: words or phrases whose meanings depend on the context in which they are embedded (E. Clark & Clark, 1979; H. Clark, 1983; Gerrig, 1986). Psycholinguistic research demonstrates that readers can easily determine the appropriate referents for metonymic expressions in discourse (Gibbs, 1990b). Thus, readers can easily recognize that the word *tuxedo* in the statement *John fired the tuxedo because he kept dropping the tray* refers to a butler, despite the literal incongruity of this sentence. Understanding contextual expressions like this requires that a process of sense creation must operate to supplement ordinary sense selection. For instance, the contextually appropriate meaning of *tuxedo* cannot be selected from a short list of potential meanings in the lexicon because these potential senses are unlimited. Listeners must instead create a new meaning for a word that already has a conventional interpretation. Sense creation may occur only after the conventional meaning has been found to be in error, or sense creation and sense selection processes might operate simultaneously, perhaps in competition with each other in the determination of figurative meaning (Gerrig, 1989).

An experimental test of these alternative hypotheses had participants read short stories that established preempting meanings for old words (Gerrig, 1989). For example, people read stories ending with *The horse race is the most popular event*. In a conventional context, this final phrase referred to a standard race between horses, while in the innovative situation the final phrase referred to a unique situation where snails competed in a race that was the length of King Louis's horse. Readers took roughly the same time to comprehend this statement in both contexts. This overlap in reading times suggests that readers seem to be creating and selecting meanings for the phrase *the horse race* at the same time.

Context clearly facilitates people's interpretation of novel metonymies. But the context for comprehension specifically includes common ground information—the beliefs, knowledge, and attitude that are shared by both speakers and listeners. Consider the sentences *While I was taking his picture, Steve did a Napoleon for the camera* and *After Joe listened to the tape of the interview, he did a Nixon to a portion of it*. These utterances contain eponymous verbs (i.e., verbs created from proper nouns) that are metonymic in that each action stands for some specific act conventionally associated with an individual. Experimental research shows that people usually experience little problem interpreting these phrases, especially when they have specific knowledge of the person referred to by the eponymous verb phrase (e.g., the famous painting of Napoleon) (H. Clark & Gerrig, 1983). In other cases we often have greater difficulty understanding metonymic expressions because it is less clear which acts are most salient for an individual (e.g., *I met a girl at the coffee house who did an Elizabeth Taylor while I was talking to her*). The problem in these instances is that listeners do not recognize which piece of information, or in this instance which salient act of Elizabeth Taylor's, constitutes part of the common ground between themselves and the speaker (H. Clark & Gerrig, 1983). This makes it more difficult to understand exactly what a speaker meant by the eponymous phrase *did an Elizabeth Taylor*.

These studies demonstrate the significance of common ground information and metonymic reasoning in people's understanding of metonymic expressions. The next two sections on colloquial tautologies and indirect speech acts also provide evidence on how metonymic thought constrains people's use and understanding of nonliteral speech.

VII. COLLOQUIAL TAUTOLOGIES

Referring to a part by mention of the whole is a common aspect of metonymic expressions such as *The government stopped me for speeding last night* and The New York Times *is late for the senator's press conference.* Listeners usually experience little difficulty comprehending these kinds of metonymies. Another version of metonymy that has become quite colloquial for speakers is to refer to aspects of people, objects, and events through tautological statements. Consider the following brief exchange between two parents (Gibbs & McCarrell, 1990).

> MOTHER: *Did the children ever clean up their rooms?*
> FATHER: *Well, boys will be boys.*

The father's response to his wife's question is true by virtue of its logical form alone (as a nominal tautology) and, superficially, contributes no new information to the conversation. But the utterance *Boys will be boys* is readily interpretable, and most listeners would agree that the father intended to convey a particular meaning, something like 'Boys will be unruly and that it is often difficult to get them to do what you want'. Nominal tautologies are found with surprising frequency in everyday speech, literature (e.g., Gertrude Stein's famous line *A rose is a rose is a rose*), and advertising (e.g., *Motor oil is motor oil*).

The standard Gricean proposal suggests that the interpretation of nominal tautologies is context-dependent, with different meanings attached to the same tautology depending on the conversational context and the shared beliefs of the participants (Brown & Levinson, 1978; Fraser, 1988; Levinson, 1983). For the conversation described above, the father's remark *Boys will be boys* flouts the maxim of Quantity because the assertion of a tautology is not informative when taken literally. Yet it is clear that despite the apparent failure of cooperation, most listeners normally assume that the speaker is cooperative at some deeper level. We do this normally by inferring that the speaker is trying to remind us of some belief or attitude about boys, namely that boys can often misbehave. In another context, *Boys will be boys* might remind us of a different belief that boys are cute and adorable.

Critics of the Gricean view alternatively argue that there is a good deal of regularity in the interpretation of colloquial tautologies because these phrases are to some extent language-specific (Wierzbicka, 1987). Nominal tautologies such as *Boys will be boys* are simply not used in French, German, or Russian. English nominal tautologies can be distinguished in terms of their different syntactic patterns and their different nominal classifications (Wierzbicka, 1987). Tautologies of the syntactic form [N (abstract singular) is N (abstract singular)] (e.g., *War is war, Politics is politics,* and *Business is business*), convey a sober, mostly negative, attitude toward complex human activities that must be understood and tolerated. Tautologies of the form [N (plural) will be N (plural)] refer to some negative aspects of the topic but also convey an indulgent attitude toward this relatively unchangeable negative aspect (e.g., *Boys will be boys*). Phrases such as *Rapists will be rapists* or *Murderers will be murderers* seem less acceptable because it is unlikely that the speaker would wish to convey an attitude of indulgence toward the topic (i.e., rapists and murderers). In general, contrary to the pragmatic view, a semantic approach proposes that the specific syntactic form and lexical content of different nominal tautologies contribute significant semantic information to their interpretation and acceptability.

A third approach to colloquial tautologies is a hybrid theory that captures aspects of the previously described views. Within this framework, people's stereotypical attitudes toward the people, activities, or objects referred to by the noun phrases in nominal tautologies should play an important role in the use and acceptability of these colloquial expressions. We understand *Boys will be boys* as expressing a very different meaning than *Girls will be girls* does because of our different stereotypical attitudes about boys and girls. Interpreting colloquial tautologies requires a kind of metonymic reasoning, in that listeners must recognize how the mention of a whole refers to some salient part (e.g., how mention of boys refers to their unruly behavior). To the extent that speakers wish to remind listeners that they jointly share a negative stereotype about people, activities, or things, we can metonymically refer to the whole of these people or activities and let listeners infer which aspects are intended to be recognized.

The findings from one series of studies supports this view of how tautological sentences are interpreted (Gibbs & McCarrell, 1990). Tautologies with human role nouns (e.g., *Salesmen are salesmen, A teenager is a teenager*) and abstract nouns concerning human activities (e.g., *War is war, Promises are promises*) were the most interpretable and generally convey negative, sober attitudes. This was not the case for tautologies containing nouns referring to concrete objects (e.g., *Flowers are flowers, A bed is a bed*). Moreover, participants found modal tautologies with human role nouns (e.g., *Boys will be boys*) the easiest to interpret and modal phrases with concrete nouns (e.g., *Carrots will be carrots*) the most difficult to understand. Modal tautologies not only remind a listener of a preexisting stereotype, they also predicate its continued existence. This predication is informative only if it is possible for a change in the stereotypic behavior. The possibility of change is enhanced by the idea of 'volition' to which the modal verb *will* refers. While it is difficult to ascribe volitional behavior to concrete objects, salesmen and teenagers are more capable of change, so it makes more sense to refer to stereotypes associated with them by stating tautological expressions such as *Salesmen will be salesmen*. People may certainly have strong prototypical representations for some particular objects and events (Rosch & Mervis, 1975), but they do not have such detailed stereotypical attitudes toward concrete objects such as hats, beds, or carrots (Dahlgren, 1985).

These data on understanding colloquial tautologies suggest why speakers can easily remind listeners about their shared beliefs about certain people and human activities by stating simple redundant phrases, such as *Business is business* or *Mothers will be mothers*. Colloquial tautologies are convenient devices for evoking the shared stereotypical presuppositions among conversants without having to explicitly spell out those beliefs.

VIII. INDIRECT SPEECH ACTS

Metonymic reasoning, where people infer wholes from parts and parts from wholes, is also important in other acts of reference, where speakers make requests of listeners. Making requests requires that speakers specify enough information to enable someone to recognize which information or action is desired. But speakers also do not want to impose on their addressees and so usually formulate their requests indirectly.

There are a number of ways in which indirect speech acts can be made (H. Clark, 1979; H. Clark & Schunk, 1980; Gibbs, 1981, 1986c; Gibbs & Mueller, 1988). Each form specifies some part of the transaction of ''goods'' between speaker and listener, where the listener's task is to infer the entire sequence of actions that the speaker wishes the listener to engage in to comply with the request. Requesting someone to shut the door, for example, can be done by questioning the ability of the listener to perform the action (*Can you shut the door?*), questioning the listener's willingness to shut the door (*Will you shut the door?*), uttering a sentence concerning the speaker's wish or need (*I would like the door shut*), questioning whether the act of shutting the door would impose on the listener (*Would you mind shutting the door?*), making a statement about some relevant fact in the world (*It's cold in here*), or simply asking about what the listener thought about shutting the door (*How about shutting the door?*).

Making indirect speech acts provides addressees with options which enable them to either comply with requests or give some good reason why they can or will not do so without losing face (R. Lakoff, 1973). Most investigators view the above sentence forms as conventional ways of performing indirect directives, each of which is especially polite (Bach & Harnish, 1979; Ervin-Tripp, 1976; Morgan, 1978; Searle, 1975). That is, people use some sentence forms to make indirect speech acts and not others for arbitrary reasons, but tacitly agree to use only those particular forms as a matter of convention (see Lewis, 1969). For instance, it is just a convention of American English that speakers usually request the salt by stating *Can you pass the salt?* instead of using less preferred forms such as *I want the salt*.

However, the design and use of indirect speech acts is not based primarily on arbitrary linguistic conventions. Both conceptual and pragmatic knowledge are actively used in the production and interpretation of indirect speech acts. Speakers design their requests to specify the greatest potential obstacle for an addressee in complying with the request (Francik & Clark, 1985; Gibbs, 1986c). By mentioning salient obstacles, even ones that are more apparent than real, speakers assume that listeners can metonymically infer the entire sequence of actions that must occur for the transaction of goods to be completed. Such a strategy employs particular figurative knowledge to meet the pragmatic requirements of the discourse situation.

A good deal of experimental evidence supports the obstacle hypothesis.

Participants in three different sets of studies were quite accurate in formulating indirect speech acts that specified the obstacles present for potential addressees in different discourse situations (Francik & Clark, 1985; Gibbs, 1986c; Gibbs & Mueller, 1988). In one of these studies, for example, participants generated Possession utterances, like *Do you have change for a dollar?*, 68% of the time when they read stories where the main obstacle concerned the addressee's possession of the object desired by the speaker (Gibbs, 1986c). But people produced Possession requests only 8% of the time in contexts where the obstacle concerned the addressee's ability to fulfill the request, and participants never generated Possession utterances in situations where the addressee was unaware of the need for any action (i.e., State of the World obstacles). Similarly, people made requests using Permission sentences, like *May I see your lecture notes for a minute?*, 51% of the time in Permission contexts, but only 10% of the time in Possession scenarios. Speakers clearly seem sensitive to the obstacles present in many situations and formulated their requests accordingly. A second study demonstrated that participants correctly assessed the potential obstacles for the address 74% of the time when asked to design such requests in real life situations.

Specifying the potential obstacles for the addressee in making indirect requests also makes it easier for listeners to comprehend these speech acts. Participants in a reading-time experiment took significantly less time to read indirect requests that adequately specified the potential obstacle for an addressee than to understand indirect requests that did not adequately specify such obstacles (Gibbs, 1986c). People learn to associate specific obstacles for listeners in different social situations and know which sentence forms best fit these circumstances. Hearing indirect speech acts specified appropriately for the greatest potential obstacles at hand makes it easier for listeners to metonymically infer speakers' intended meanings.

These studies most generally emphasize how metonymic reasoning affects the pragmatics of making and understanding indirect speech acts. Although scholars claim that many indirect requests are understood via some sort of short-circuited process (Bach & Harnish, 1979; H. Clark, 1979; H. Clark & Schunk, 1980; Gibbs, 1979, 1981; Morgan, 1978; Munro, 1979; Searle, 1975), no one has specified what it is about some requests that makes them especially conventional. The results of these studies show how people prefer to highlight potential obstacles that stand in the way of listeners in completing the transaction of goods. The mere mention of these obstacles allows listeners to metonymically infer the unstated parts of the transaction of goods that constitutes request-sequences in conversation. The evidence on indirect speech acts is consistent with the claim that figurative thought facilitates people's use and understanding of nonliteral language.

IX. Irony/Sarcasm

The brief conversation presented at the beginning of this chapter provides some wonderful examples of irony and sarcasm. Consider again one section of this discourse where the mother, Pat, is criticizing her son for being uninterested in working.

(7) PAT: *What kind of work did you have in mind Grant? Watching the television, and listening to records*
(8) GRANT: *I don't need your help mom*
(9) PAT: *Playing the guitar, driving the car*
(10) GRANT: *Ah . . .*
(11) PAT: *Eating, sleeping*
(12) BILL: *No, ah, listen Grant, you are a very good boy, we're very proud of you*
(13) GRANT: *Yeah, I know you are*
(14) BILL: *No, we are . . . you don't give us any trouble ya know*
(15) GRANT: *Well, you sure are giving me a hell of a lot*

Pat conceives of Grant's situation as ironic because he claims to want to work but acts quite differently. Her sarcastic remarks convey both her frustration toward Grant and her understanding of the situation as ironic. We judge events as ironic in the way Pat did because of an awareness of the incongruity between expectation and reality even though, in some cases, other participants in the situation, such as Grant, appear to be blind to what is really happening. This awareness suggests that irony is not merely a matter of rhetoric or of language, but is a fundamental part of the figurative mind.

Literature abounds with wonderful examples of situations that scream out to us as ironic. To take just one example, the classic O. Henry story "The Gift of the Magi" describes a very poor pair of newlyweds who each wanted to give the other a special gift for Christmas, but neither had any money. The only thing of value the wife owned was her beautiful long hair, while the only valuable possession the husband had was a beautiful watch. The husband sold his watch to buy an ornate comb for his wife's hair, and the wife sold her hair to buy her husband a gold chain for his watch.

Many mundane situations in everyday life appear to us as ironic, and people use figurative language (e.g., irony, sarcasm, satire, parody) to express their ironical conceptualizations of these experiences. But traditional models of irony assume that these utterances are understood by taking the opposite of a sentence's literal meaning. Under this view, irony, similar to other instances of nonliteral speech, represents a violation of conversational norms rather than a more direct reflection of a figurative mode of thought. One immediate problem with the traditional view of irony is that in many cases the opposite of a sentence's literal meaning is unclear or does not come close to specifying a speaker's true ironic intent.

Consider Pat's extended statement in (7)–(11) about the kind of work Grant appears to want to do. The traditional view suggests that taken literally these utterances are grossly inappropriate, violating the maxim of Quality, so listeners are forced to assume the opposite of what they literally mean to make these utterances adhere to the cooperative principle. But the opposite of Pat's comments simply refers to Grant's belief that work is anything but watching TV, listening to records, playing the guitar, and so on. These interpretations do not capture the true ironic intention in Pat's utterances, namely, 'It is hypocritical of Grant to assert that he wants to work while doing nothing more than watching TV, playing the guitar, and so on'. The ironic meaning of Pat's extended statement arises not from assuming the opposite of what she literally said, but from recognizing the incongruity between what Grant says and what he does or believes. Recognition of the incongruity between what people say and what they do reflects the cognitive ability of people to think ironically. This ironic stance toward situations is not necessarily expressed in nonliteral language, since speakers may in some situations mean what they literally say but convey ironic meaning (Sperber & Wilson, 1981). For example, a driver can say to a passenger *I love people who signal,* when another car has just cut in front without signaling, and mean this sarcastically even though the statement reflects the speaker's true literal belief.

This examination of several instances of ironic talk demonstrates that our understanding of irony does not require that we recognize these utterances as violations of communicative norms. Psycholinguistic studies even show that people can readily interpret sarcastic expressions without any special intonation cues (Gibbs, 1986a, 1986b). It is clear that understanding irony does not necessarily require special cognitive processes beyond those used to comprehend literal speech. Again, these empirical findings from psycholinguistics are consistent with the idea that our understanding of figurative speech, such as irony and sarcasm, is facilitated by pervasive, figurative modes of thought. More recent research demonstrates that many utterances can be interpreted ironically even when speakers do not intend for us to understand them this way, simply because of the situation. Consider a situation in which a student who has just cheated on an exam sarcastically comments to a friend *I would never be involved in any cheating.* The speaker specifically intends for his audience to understand what is said as irony. But suppose that the speaker is a student who unwittingly helped another individual cheat during an exam and this student later commented that *I would never be involved in any cheating.* The speaker here does not intend for his utterance to be understood ironically, yet addressees and overhearers see the irony in what was actually said.

One study demonstrated that it is quite possible for people to understand a speaker's utterance as irony even though the speaker did not intend the utterance to be understood as such (Gibbs & O'Brien, 1991). This study even showed that people took much less time to read unintentionally ironic statements than to process intentionally ironic statements. It appears that people are sensitive to the presence of ironic situations, and actually find it easier to understand verbal statements that create those situations, even when the irony is not intended to be communicated, or even recognized, by the speaker.

The rejection of the standard pragmatic view of irony has prompted scholars to seek alternative explanations of irony and sarcasm. One idea that better captures irony understanding is the echoic mention theory (Jorgensen, Miller, & Sperber, 1984; Sperber & Wilson, 1981). According to this theory, ironic utterances are essentially about speakers' attitudes. Understanding irony is accomplished not when a nonliteral proposition replaces a literal one, but when a listener is reminded echoically of some familiar proposition (whose truth value is irrelevant), and of the speaker's attitude toward it. Consider the example of the mother who says to her son *I love children who keep their rooms clean* when her son has not, in fact, cleaned up his messy room. The irony here comes from the fact that the mother has echoed some previously mentioned statement or belief, or perhaps some unspoken agreement between herself and her son. That is, the son might have earlier offered to clean up his room, or it might just be his job to do so. When the mother says *I love children who keep their rooms clean,* she is, in a sense, quoting this previous statement or verbalizing a mutually shared belief that the son is supposed to keep his room clean.

Empirical research shows that people judge ironic utterances with explicit echoic mentions as being more ironic than statements that do not have such mentions (Gibbs, 1986b; Jorgensen et al., 1984). Thus, a statement such as *I love children who keep their rooms clean* is seen as more ironic in a context where there is some previous mention about the expectation that the son should keep his room clean than it is in a context that does not mention this belief or expectation. People also comprehend sarcasm based on explicit echos much faster than they do sarcastic expressions based on less explicit or nonexistent echos (Gibbs, 1986b).

Although ironic utterances accomplish their communicative intent by reminding listeners of some antecedent event, not all such reminders are echoic, nor do they all refer to actual or implied utterances (Kreuz & Glucksberg, 1989). For instance, when the mother says *I love children who keep their rooms clean,* she may simply be alluding to some mutually shared expectation between herself and her son that he is to keep his room clean. Similarly, the utterance *Another gorgeous day!* stated when it has been gray and raining for over two weeks need not echo anyone's utterance, thought, or opinion. It can simply allude to a generalized expectation or desire for good weather and, in doing so, expresses the speaker's disappointment at the actual weather.

The reminder theory of irony nicely explains why people rate positive statements, such as *A fine friend you are,* as being more sarcastic than negative statements, such as *You're a terrible friend* (Gibbs, 1986b; Kreuz & Glucksberg, 1989). Positive statements do not require explicit antecedents because these expressions implicitly allude to societal norms and expectations that are invariably positive (e.g., if you don't have anything nice to say, then don't say anything). But negative statements, such as *You're the worst friend someone can have!* said to a friend who has just done something very gracious, do not implicitly allude to these positive norms and require explicit antecedents if they are to be easily understood (Kreuz & Glucksberg, 1989). Echoic mention may really, then, be a special case of reminders that allude to prior occurrences or states of affairs.

A related explanation of irony claims that verbal irony involves pretense (H. Clark & Gerrig, 1984). Thus, when a mother says *I love children who keep their rooms clean,* she is pretending to be some unseen person who might actually believe that the mother's children actually keep their rooms clean. When listeners recognize this pretense, they should understand that the speaker is expressing in an ironic manner some derogatory attitude toward the idea expressed, the imaginary speaker, and the imaginary listener.

X. OXYMORA

One of the most visible figures of thought and speech that reflect our incongruous understanding of experience is oyxmora. Consider the following poem, titled "Defining Love," written in the 17th century by the Spanish poet Francisco de Quevedo (1986, p. 195).

> It's ice that burns, it is a frozen fire,
> it's a wound that hurts and is not felt,
> it's something well dreamt, an evil present,
> it's a brief retiring, that quickly tires.
>
> It's a carelessness that makes us care,
> a walk alone among the crowd,
> a loving only of being loved,
> a coward, with a brave man's name.
>
> It's a liberty locked up in prison,
> that last until the last convulsion;
> an illness which spreads if it's cured.
>
> This is young Cupid, this his abyss.
> Just see what friends he'll make with nothing,
> who's in all things against himself!

This poem describes the conflicting, contradictory thoughts and feelings that constitute love experiences. Poetry often expresses figurative impossibility where the contradictions of life are exposed through the figure of oxymora. Oxymora are traditionally defined as figures of speech that combine two seemingly contradictory elements. To take some examples from Shakespeare's *Romeo and Juliet*, consider the phrases *O heavy lightness! serious vanity!/ Mis-shapen chaos of well-seemings forms!/Feather of lead, bright smoke, cold fire, sick health!* (Act I, Scene I, lines 171–173)

Literally speaking, these statements seem nonsensical in that smoke isn't bright, fire isn't cold, and to be healthy isn't to be sick. Of course, we do have an ability to take contradictory, paradoxical stances toward people and events. This ability is more than just seeing alternative sides of some person or situation that cannot be grasped at the same time (in the way we see ambiguous figures). Rather, we seem able to conceptually grasp in a single instance two things that are apparently contradictory.

Oxymora, such as *bright smoke, lead feathers*, and *sick health*, do not simply represent figures of speech, but also reflect poetic schemes for conceptualizing human experience and the external world. Developments in the history of science have often been characterized as expressing oxymoronic thought. For instance, the transition from Ptolemy and Copernicus to Kepler implies a shift from thinking in terms of antithesis to thinking in terms of the oxymoron when celestial motion was seen as composed of both curves and straight lines (Hallyn, 1990). More generally, oxymora are frequently found in everyday speech, many of which are barely noticed as such, for example *intense apathy, internal exile, man child, loyal opposition, plastic glasses, guest host*, and so on. The ubiquity of these figures suggests some underlying ability to conceive of ideas, objects, and events in oxymoronic terms.

Why are some contradictory statements more meaningful than others? A distinction can be made between two types of oxymora (Shen, 1987). Direct oxymora consist of two terms that are antonyms, or two terms whose only difference consists of a change in the " $+/-$ " sign of their lowest, distinctive feature, all other features being identical (e.g., *a feminine man* and *living death*). Very few instances of oxymoron are direct. We rarely encounter statements that reflect complete opposite terms (e.g., *internal external, man woman, intense lazy*).

Indirect oxymora, on the other hand, consist of two terms that are not the direct antonyms of each other, but have one term that is the hyponym (or a specific example) of the first term's antonym. Consider the example *the silence whistles* (taken from the Hebrew poet Nathan Altherman's "Summer Night"). The antonym of *silence* is lexically realized by the word *sound,* whose semantic specification consists of the same features as for *silence* except that the " + " sign of the distinctive feature [silence] is replaced by the " − " sign. However, the second term of the oxymoron *the silence whistles* is not *sound,* but its hyponym *whistle,* which also shares the same feature list as *sound* with the additional feature of [+ sharpness]. Shakespeare's *bright smoke* has a second term *smoke* that is the hyponym of *dim,* which is the direct antonym of *bright.*

The vast majority of poetic oxymora such as those seen in de Quevedo's poem are indirect. One empirical analysis of the oxymora found in modern Israeli poetry found that a vast majority of the oxymora employed are indirect (Shen, 1987). Moreover, there are important differences in the acceptability of indirect oxymora, differences that can be explained through an analysis of the conceptual categories oxymoronic expressions designate. For instance, in the phrase *the silence whistles,* the superordinate category "sound" has several subordinate members that are specific types of sounds such as "cries," "whispers," "shouts," and "whistles." These different members of the category "sound" gives speakers a range of examples to choose from in forming new oxymora, specifically in selecting the actual hyponym for the second term of the phrase. This choice of hyponyms is constrained by the prototypical structure of the category. Members of a category differ in their degree of goodness, so hyponyms differ in their typicality with respect to their superordinate category.

Some oxymora have hyponyms of their first terms' antonyms that are prototypical examples of the superordinate category. For example, in the oxymoron *the silence cries,* the hyponym *cries* is a prototypical example of its superordinate category "sound." Shakespeare's *cold fire* has a second term that is a prototypical example of the category "hot," which is the first term's antonym. *The silence whistles* is a medium case of oxymoron because some instances of the category "sound" are better examples than *whistles,* such as *cry* and *shout,* while others are worse, such as *sigh. Sweet sorrow* has the hyponym *sorrow* that represents a medium example of the category "bitterness." Marked cases of oxymora include phrases in which the hyponym is a very bad exemplar of its superordinate category. In the phrase *the silence sighs* the hyponym *sighs* is a very bad example of the category "sound."

Preliminary research showed that a vast majority of indirect oxymora from Israeli poetry were medium cases (Shen, 1987). Psycholinguistic research shows that medium cases of indirect oxymora (e.g., *sacred dump*) are more difficult to process in isolation compared to either unmarked (e.g., *attractive wounds*) or marked (e.g., *apathetic passion*) cases (Gibbs & Kearney, 1994). Medium cases of oxymora require more complex processing because their hyponyms are medium examples of superordinate categories, with some terms being very good or typical examples of a category and other terms poor examples of a superordinate category.

These findings suggest that there are links between people's conceptual knowledge and their understanding of oxymora. People can easily interpret oxymoronic phrases because of our conceptual ability to understand incongruent events and experiences. The presence of irony and oxymora in the way we speak about our common experiences lends credence to the possibility that these figures provide part of the figurative foundation for everyday thought.

XI. CONCLUSION AND FUTURE DIRECTIONS

The psycholinguistic evidence clearly demonstrates that figurative utterances are not understood as apparent violations of conversational maxims. Understanding figurative discourse does not require that listeners replace a literal proposition with a nonliteral interpretation. People often find figurative discourse easy to interpret. I have argued that this is so because such language reflects pervasive figurative modes of thought. Speakers and listeners can usually assume that particular figurative conceptions of everyday experience provide part of the common ground for speaking and listening. We tend to see figurative concepts as literal because of the mistaken assumption that things in our cognition that are most alive and active are those that are conscious. But figurative ways of knowing are so deeply entrenched and automatic as to be unconscious and effortless. Systematic analyses of both everyday and literary language reveal many figurative modes of thinking, schemes that motivate how we speak and understand.

Part of the reason why figurative thought is not ordinarily seen as an important part of language use and understanding stems from the failure to distinguish between different levels at which cognition and language interact. Let me suggest four possible ways in which figurative thought might influence ordinary language use and understanding.

1. Figurative thought might play some role in changing the meanings of words and expressions over time, but does not motivate contemporary speakers' use and understanding of language.
2. Figurative thought might motivate the linguistic meanings that have currency within linguistic communities, or may have some role in an idealized speaker/hearer's understanding of language. But figurative thought does not actually play any part in an individual speaker's ability to make sense of or process language.
3. Figurative thought might motivate an individual speaker's use and understanding of why various words and expressions mean what they do, but does not play any role in people's ordinary on-line production or comprehension of everyday language.
4. Figurative thought might function automatically and interactively in people's on-line use and understanding of linguistic meaning.

Many cognitive scientists play fast and loose among these different possibilities when they claim that figurative cognition either does or does not play a role in language use and understanding. For example, the evidence from cognitive linguistics and psycholinguistics that supports possibilities (1), (2), and (3) does not necessarily indicate that possibility (4) is true. It is incorrect to suppose that figurative knowledge has an automatic, immediate role in people's on-line processing of language until the appropriate on-line experiments have been conducted. These experiments would hopefully employ methodologies similar to those used in studying on-line sentence processing. It is not clear, however, whether any of the available on-line methodologies used by psycholinguists (e.g., lexical decision, word naming, speeded recognition, gaze duration, reading times) can be adapted to study immediate processing of complex linguistic materials. Most experimental tasks encourage superficial processing of texts. Most on-line tasks can also be disruptive of inferences that listeners/readers draw in the normal course of language understanding. Finally, it is difficult to measure the extent to which people ordinarily access complex conceptual knowledge, such as different kinds of figurative thought, using on-line experimental tasks that focus on participants' speeded responses to single-word or short-phrase targets.

Beyond these methodological concerns, the question of when people use figurative thought in understanding everyday and literary language raises a deeper issue about what constitutes an act of understanding. Psycholinguistic research primarily focuses on very fast, unconscious mental processes that occur when people first read or hear language material [i.e., possibility (4) above]. Yet this emphasis only captures a small part of what it means to understand language. The extensive evidence discussed in this chapter certainly points to different levels of understanding, such as that associated with how people make sense of what linguistic expressions mean. People have conceptual knowledge, much of which is figuratively based, that allows them to understand why it just makes sense to talk, for instance, of arguments as wars, anger as heated fluid in a container, time as money, and love as journeys. It is not just an arbitrary fact of the language that English speakers, for example, talk about anger in terms of stacks being blown, ceilings being hit, or steam being released. Instead, people's bodily, real-world experiences help motivate such talk, and we use this knowledge to make sense of various linguistic expressions in the language [i.e., possibility (3) above]. We may not necessarily tap into this deeper conceptual knowledge each and every time we encounter language, especially if such language is highly conventional. But we clearly use such conceptual knowledge to make sense of why the language is the way it is. My argument is that psycholinguistic research needs to focus on these different aspects of what it means to understand language and not concentrate exclusively on those mental processes that operate in the first few hundred milliseconds of comprehension.

Another cautionary note is that psycholinguists must recognize that there may not be one theory that best accounts for how people understand figurative language. Previous attempts to explain figurative language understanding by specifying the ways sentence and speaker meaning differ in various kinds of nonliteral speech fail to capture how complex, figurative knowledge motivates such language in the first place. In many instances of figurative language, it is unclear whether the figurative meanings of utterances even vary from what these same expressions literally state. At the same time, it seems quite unlikely that there will be single, individual theories to explain understanding different types of figurative language (e.g., metaphor, idioms, irony, metonymy, and so on). Each kind of figurative thought, for example metaphor, gives rises to numerous types of linguistic expressions that may differ on a variety of lexical, syntactic, pragmatic, and conceptual dimensions. To argue that there may be a single theory of metaphor or idioms or irony vastly underestimates the true complexity of each kind of figurative language. Psycholinguistic theories of nonliteral speech understanding must be flexible and comprehensive to account for the diversity of figurative language.

Finally, one of my main messages in this chapter is that figurative thought underlies many instances of literal language in addition to motivating figurative speech. Future work must explore the extent to which people use figurative knowledge in making sense of and processing conventional expressions that for the most part seem quite literal. This work would be especially important because it could point the way to a better integration of ideas about sentence processing as studied by most psycholinguists with the growing body of research on figurative language understanding.

REFERENCES

Abbott, V., Black, J., & Smith, E. (1985). The representation of scripts in memory. *Journal of Memory and Language, 24,* 179–199.

Bach, K., & Harnish, R. (1979). *Linguistic communication and speech acts.* Cambridge, MA: MIT Press.

Boatner, M., Gates, J., & Makkai, A. (1975). *A dictionary of American idioms.* New York: Baron's Educational Series.

Bower, G., Black, J., & Turner, T. (1979). Scripts in memory for text. *Cognitive Psychology, 11,* 177–220.

Brown, P., & Levinson, S. (1978). Universals in language usage: Politeness phenomena. In E. Goody (Ed.), *Questions and politeness* (pp. 56–311). Cambridge: Cambridge University Press.

Carston, R. (1988). Implicature, explicature, and truth-theoretic semantics. In R. Kempson (Ed.), *Mental representation* (pp. 155–182). London: Cambridge University Press.

Clark, E., & Clark, H. (1979). When nouns surface as verbs. *Language, 55,* 797–811.

Clark, H. (1979). Responding to indirect speech acts. *Cognitive Psychology, 11,* 430–477.

Clark, H. (1983). Making sense of nonce sense. In G. B. Flores d'Arcais & R. Jarvella (Eds.), *The process of understanding language* (pp. 297–331). New York: Wiley.

Clark, H., & Gerrig, R. (1983). Understanding old words with new meaning. *Journal of Verbal Learning and Verbal Behavior, 22,* 591–608.

Clark, H., & Gerrig, R. (1984). On the pretense theory of irony. *Journal of Experimental Psychology: General, 113,* 121–126.

Clark, H., & Schunk, D. (1980). Polite responses to polite requests. *Cognition, 8,* 111–143.

Dahlgren, K. (1985). The cognitive structure of social categories. *Cognitive Science, 9,* 379–398.

de Quevedo, F. (1986). Defining love. In P. Higman (Trans.) *Love poems from Spain and Spanish America.* San Francisco: City Lights Books.

Ervin-Tripp, S. (1976). Is Sybil there? The structure of some American directives. *Language in Society, 4,* 25–66.

Fillmore, C., Kay, P., & O'Connor, M. (1988). Regularity and idiomaticity in grammatical constructions: The case of *let alone. Language, 64,* 501–538.

Francik, E., & Clark, H. (1985). How to make requests that overcome obstacles to compliance. *Journal of Memory and Language, 24,* 560–568.

Fraser, B. (1988). Motor oil is motor oil: An account of English nominal tautologies. *Journal of Pragmatics, 12,* 215–220.

Garrod, S., & Sanford, A. (1985). On the real-time character of interpretation during reading. *Language and Cognitive Processes, 1,* 43–61.

Gernsbacher, M. (1991). Comprehending conceptual anaphors. *Language and Cognitive Processes, 6,* 81–105.

Gerrig, R. (1986). Process models and pragmatics. In N. Sharkey (Ed.), *Advances in cognitive science* (Vol. 1, pp. 23–39). Chichester: Ellis Horwood.

Gerrig, R. (1989). The time course of sense creation. *Memory & Cognition, 17,* 194–207.

Gibbs, R. (1979). Contextual effects in understanding indirect requests. *Discourse Processes, 2,* 1–10.

Gibbs, R. (1980). Spilling the beans on understanding and memory for idioms. *Memory & Cognition, 8,* 449–456.

Gibbs, R. (1981). Your wish is my command: Convention and context in interpreting indirect requests. *Journal of Verbal Learning and Verbal Behavior, 20,* 431–444.

Gibbs, R. (1984). Literal meaning and psychological theory. *Cognitive Science, 8,* 275–304.

Gibbs, R. (1985). On the process of understanding idioms. *Journal of Psycholinguistic Research, 14,* 465–472.

Gibbs, R. (1986a). Comprehension and memory for nonliteral utterances: The problem of sarcastic indirect requests. *Acta Psychologica, 62,* 41–57.

Gibbs, R. (1986b). On the psycholinguistics of sarcasm. *Journal of Experimental Psychology: General, 115,* 1–13.

Gibbs, R. (1986c). What makes some indirect speech acts conventional? *Journal of Memory and Language, 25,* 181–196.

Gibbs, R. (1987). Linguistic factors in children's understanding of idioms. *Journal of Child Language, 14,* 569–586.

Gibbs, R. (1989). Understanding and literal meaning. *Cognitive Science, 13,* 243–251.

Gibbs, R. (1990a). Comprehending figurative referential descriptions. *Journal of Experimental Psychology: Learning, Memory, and Cognition, 16,* 56–66.

Gibbs, R. (1990b). Psycholinguistic studies on the conceptual basis of idiomaticity. *Cognitive Linguistics, 1,* 417–451.

Gibbs, R. (1991). Semantic analyzability in children's understanding of idioms. *Journal of Speech and Hearing Research, 34,* 613–620.

Gibbs, R. (1992a). Categorization and metaphor comprehension. *Psychological Review, 99,* 572–577.

Gibbs, R. (1992b). What do idioms really mean? *Journal of Memory and Language, 31,* 485–506.

Gibbs, R. (1992c). Why idioms are not dead metaphors. In C. Cacciari & P. Tabossi (Eds.), *On idioms* (pp. 57–78). Hillsdale NJ: Erlbaum.

Gibbs, R., & Gerrig, R. (1989). How context makes metaphor comprehension seem special. *Metaphor and Symbolic Activity, 3,* 145–158.

Gibbs, R., & Kearney, L. (1994). When parting is such sweet sorrow: Categories and understanding oxymoronic phrases. *Journal of Psycholinguistic Research, 23,* 75–89.

Gibbs, R., & McCarrell, N. (1990). Why boys will be boys and girls will be girls: Understanding colloquial tautologies. *Journal of Psycholinguistic Research, 19,* 125–145.

Gibbs, R., & Moise, J. (1992). *Distinguishing what is said from what is meant.* Manuscript in preparation.

Gibbs, R., & Mueller, R. (1988). Conversational sequences and preference for indirect speech acts. *Discourse Processes, 11,* 101–116.

Gibbs, R., & Nayak, N. (1989). Psycholinguistic studies on the syntactic behavior of idioms. *Cognitive Psychology, 21,* 100–138.

Gibbs, R., Nayak, N., Bolton, J., & Keppel, M. (1989). Speakers' assumptions about the lexical flexibility of idioms. *Memory & Cognition, 17,* 58–68.

Gibbs, R., Nayak, N., & Cutting, C. (1989). How to kick the bucket and not decompose: Analyzability and idiom processing. *Journal of Memory and Language, 28,* 576–593.

Gibbs, R., & O'Brien, J. (1990). Idioms and mental imagery: The metaphorical motivation for idiomatic meaning. *Cognition, 36,* 35–68.

Gibbs, R., & O'Brien, J. (1991). Psychological aspects of irony understanding. *Journal of Pragmatics, 16,* 523–530.

Gibbs, R., & Tenney, Y. (1980). The concept of scripts in understanding stories. *Journal of Psycholinguistic Research, 9,* 275–284.

Gildea, P., & Glucksberg, S. (1983). On understanding metaphor: The role of context. *Journal of Verbal Learning and Verbal Behavior, 22,* 577–590.

Glucksberg, S., Gildea, P., & Bookin, H. (1982). On understanding nonliteral speech: Can people ignore metaphors? *Journal of Verbal Learning and Verbal Behavior, 21,* 85–98.

Glucksberg, S., & Keysar, B. (1990). Understanding metaphorical comparisons: Beyond similarity. *Psychological Review, 97,* 3–18.

Graesser, A., Long, D., & Mio, J. (1989). What are the cognitive and conceptual components of humorous texts? *Poetics, 18,* 143–164.

Graesser, A., Woll, S., Kowalski, D., & Smith, D. (1980). Memory for typical and atypical actions in scripted activities. *Journal of Experimental Psychology: Human Learning and Memory, 6,* 503–515.

Grice, H. P. (1975). Logic and conversation. In P. Cole & J. Morgan (Eds.), *Syntax and semantics* (Vol. 3, pp. 41–58). New York: Academic Press.

Grice, H. P. (1978). Some further notes on logic and conversation. In P. Cole (Ed.), *Syntax and semantics* (Vol. 9, pp. 113–128). New York: Academic Press.

Hallyn, F. (1990). *The poetic structure of the world: Copernicus and Kepler.* New York: Zone Books.

Hoffman, R., & Kemper, S. (1987). What could reaction time studies be telling us about metaphor comprehension? *Metaphor and Symbolic Activity, 2,* 149–186.

Inhoff, A., Duffy, P., & Carroll, P. (1984). Contextual effects on metaphor comprehension in reading. *Memory & Cognition, 12,* 558–567.

Jorgensen, J., Miller, G., & Sperber, D. (1984). Test of the mention theory of irony. *Journal of Experimental Psychology: General, 113,* 112–120.

Keysar, B. (1989). On the functional equivalence of metaphoric and literal meanings. *Journal of Memory and Language, 28,* 375–385.

Kreuz, R., & Glucksberg, S. (1989). How to be sarcastic: The echoic reminder theory of verbal irony. *Journal of Experimental Psychology: General, 118,* 374–386.

Lakoff, G. (1987). *Women, fire, and dangerous things: What categories reveal about the mind.* Chicago: University of Chicago Press.

Lakoff, G. (1990). The invariance hypothesis: Is abstract reason based on image-schemas? *Cognitive Linguistics, 1,* 39–74.

Lakoff, G., & Johnson, M. (1980). *Metaphors we live by.* Chicago: University of Chicago Press.

Lakoff, G., & Turner, M. (1989). *No cool reason: The power of poetic metaphor.* Chicago: University of Chicago Press.

Lakoff, R. (1973). The logic of politeness: Or minding your p's and q's. In *Papers from the 9th Regional Meeting, Chicago Linguistic Society,* (pp. 292–305). Chicago: Chicago Linguistic Society.

Langacker, R. (1986). *Foundations of cognitive grammar* (Vol. 1). Stanford, CA: Stanford University Press.

Levinson, S. (1983). *Pragmatics.* Cambridge: Cambridge University Press.

Lewis, D. (1969). *Convention.* Cambridge, MA.: Harvard University Press.

Long, D., & Summers, M. (1979). *Longman dictionary of English idioms.* London: Longman.

MacLeish, A. (1933). *Poems 1924–1933.* Cambridge, MA: The Riverside Press.

Morgan, J. (1978). Two types of convention in indirect speech acts. In P. Cole & J. Morgan (Eds.), *Syntax and semantics* (Vol. 3, pp. 45–61). New York: Academic Press.

Munro, A. (1979). Indirect speech acts are not strictly conventional. *Linguistic Inquiry, 10,* 353–356.

Nayak, N., & Gibbs, R. (1990). Conceptual knowledge in the interpretation of idioms. *Journal of Experimental Psychology: General, 119,* 315–330.

Nunberg, G. (1978). *The pragmatics of reference.* Bloomington: Indiana University Linguistics Club.

Ortony, A., Reynolds, R., Schallert, D., & Antos, S. (1978). Interpreting metaphors and idioms: Some effects of context on comprehension. *Journal of Verbal Learning and Verbal Behavior, 17,* 465–477.

Palmer, F. (1981). *Semantics.* Cambridge: Cambridge University Press.

Pollio, H., Barlow, J., Fine, H., & Pollio, M. (1977). *Psychology and the poetics of growth: Figurative language in psychology, psychotherapy, and education.* Hillsdale, NJ: Erlbaum.

Recanati, F. (1989). The pragmatics of what is said. *Mind & Language, 4,* 295–329.

Reddy, M. (1979). The conduit metaphor. In A. Ortony (Ed.), *Metaphor and thought* (pp. 284–324). Cambridge: Cambridge University Press.

Rich, A. (1973). *Diving into the wreck.* New York: W. W. Norton & Company.

Rosch, E., & Mervis, C. (1975). Family resemblances. *Cognitive Psychology, 7,* 573–605.

Sanford, A., & Garrod, S. (1981). *Understanding written language.* Chichester: Wiley.

Schank, R., and Abelson, R. (1977). *Scripts, plans, goals and understanding: An inquiry into human knowledge structures.* Hillsdale, NJ: Erlbaum.

Searle, J. (1975). Indirect speech acts. In P. Cole & J. Morgan (Eds.), *Syntax and semantics* (Vol. 3, pp. 59–82). New York: Academic Press.

Searle, J. (1979). Metaphor. In A. Ortony (Ed.), *Metaphor and thought* (pp. 92–123). Cambridge: Cambridge University Press.

Seifert, C., Robertson, S., & Black, J. (1985). Types of inferences generated during reading. *Journal of Memory and Language, 24,* 405–422.

Sharkey, N., & Sharkey, A. (1987). What is the point of integration? The loci of knowledge-based facilitation in sentence processing. *Journal of Memory and Language, 26,* 255–276.

Shen, Y. (1987). On the structure and understanding of poetic oxymoron. *Poetics Today, 8,* 105–122.

Shinjo, M., & Myers, J. (1987). The role of context in metaphor comprehension. *Journal of Memory and Language, 26,* 226–241.

Smith, M., Pollio, H., & Pitts, M. (1981). Metaphor as intellectual history: Concepts and categories underlying figurative usage in American English from 1675–1975. *Linguistics, 19,* 911–935.

Sperber, D., & Wilson, D. (1981). Irony and the use-mention distinction. In P. Cole (Ed.), *Radical pragmatics* (pp. 295–318). New York: Academic Press.

Sperber, D. & Wilson, D. (1986). *Relevance: Cognition and communication.* Cambridge, MA: Harvard University Press.

Wierzbicka, A. (1987). Boys will be boys: "Radical semantics" vs. "radical pragmatics." *Language, 63,* 95–114.

CHAPTER 13

UNDERSTANDING FIGURATIVE LANGUAGE

CRISTINA CACCIARI AND SAM GLUCKSBERG

I. INTRODUCTION

Our aim in this chapter is to address some basic questions about figurative language in general, and about metaphor in particular. We examine what it is that makes a string of words a metaphor, how metaphors are understood, and how and why metaphors are used in discourse instead of "words proper" (Hobbes, 1962). We also consider the relationship between metaphor on the one hand and polysemy (i.e., multiple meanings) and lexical innovations on the other, with the purpose of elucidating some of the processes underlying sense extensions and sense creation.

Contemporary psycholinguistic research on figurative language essentially began in the 1970s. This surge of interest in the study of figurative language had been focused primarily on metaphor but has recently been extended to other forms of figurative expressions such as idioms, proverbs, and analogies (Glucksberg, 1991; Honeck & Hoffman, 1980). The predominant focus on metaphor is not surprising because metaphor has traditionally been considered the trope, that is, the figure of speech, par excellence. Indeed, Eco (1984), a prominent scholar in the theory of signs, notes that the term METAPHOR often serves as a general label for any and all rhetorical figures (cf. also Fernandez, 1991). Eco goes on to observe that "The chronicle of the discussion on metaphor is the chronicle of a series of variations on a few tautologies, perhaps on a single one: 'A metaphor is that artifice which permits one to speak metaphorically' " (Eco, 1984, p. 88). Since Aristotle, thousands of pages have been devoted to metaphor, "the most luminous and therefore the most necessary and frequent" of all the tropes (Vico, quoted in Eco, 1984). If we consider only the very recent literature, the sheer volume becomes overwhelming. Shibles (1971), for example, produced a bibliography of "recent" titles that contained almost 3,000 entries. In 1985, van Noppen and his colleagues listed 4,317 additional entries, all published after 1970, and van Noppen and Hols updated the 1985 list by adding 3,900 titles published between 1985 and 1990 (van Noppen, De Knop, & Jonden, 1985; van Noppen & Nols, 1990). Together, these three bibliographies contain more than 11,000 entries on metaphor and related topics from the literatures in philosophy, linguistics, semiotics, literary criticism, psychology, psychoanalogy, anthropology, religious studies, and, most recently, cognitive science.

This enormous surge of interest in figurative language can be attributed to several sources (cf. Hoffman & Honeck, 1980; Ortony, 1980). Perhaps the most important is the recognition that figurative language in general, and metaphor in particular, plays a central role not only in everyday discourse but also in reflecting (and perhaps shaping) how people think in a broad range of domains. As Quinn (1991) put it, metaphor instantiates the cultural models of the world we live in (cf. also Smith, Pollio, & Pitts, 1981). Figurative language is no longer perceived as merely an ornament added to everyday, straightforward literal language, but is instead viewed as a powerful communicative and conceptual tool. Because of the ubiquity of metaphoric use (see Gibbs, this volume) and the intense focus of research on metaphor, we concentrate our discussion of figurative language on metaphor.

II. METAPHOR

Traditionally, metaphor has been considered as a linguistic phenomenon, having to do primarily with stylistic matters. Recently, theorists have shifted from viewing metaphors as strictly linguistic entities to viewing metaphors in terms of conceptual processes (Glucksberg & Keysar, 1990; Lakoff, 1987; Lakoff & Johnson, 1980; Lakoff & Turner, 1989). Traditionally, the term metaphor is used to refer to various linguistic structures: ATTRIBUTIVE METAPHORS (i.e., metaphors of the form "A is a B," such as *Her faith is a house of cards*), RELATIONAL METAPHORS (i.e., of the form "A:B::C:D," often expressed in truncated form as in *George Bush considered Saddam Hussein the Hitler of the Middle East*), SINGLE WORD METAPHOR (i.e., a verb or an adjective used metaphorically, as in *The newsboy flew down the street on his new bike,* or, more subtly, as in Thorsten Veblen's turn of phrase, *The rich perform leisure*). More recently, the term metaphor has been used to refer also to conceptualization of states and objects that are considered to be metaphorical in nature (Lakoff, 1987; Lakoff & Johnson, 1980; Lakoff & Turner, 1989). This shift in the view of metaphor from a strictly linguistic entity to a more general conceptual representation has opened new directions for the study of metaphor. We first examine the traditional linguistic approach to metaphor and then turn to what we consider the conceptual approach to metaphor. To avoid confusion, in this chapter we use the term metaphor to refer to any linguistic expression that is intended and/or recognized as a metaphor by a speaker or listener (writer or reader). Following a convention introduced by Lakoff and his colleagues, we use the term METAPHOR in capital letters to refer to conceptual structures that may or may not be expressed linguistically.

A. Metaphors as Linguistic Entities

1. Recognizing a Metaphor

When we encounter an utterance, we are generally able to judge whether it is intended literally or not. The ease with which people deal with this distinction in everyday discourse belies the difficulty and complexity of the distinction as treated in the linguistic and psycholinguistic literature. To begin with, no universally accepted criteria for discriminating between literal and nonliteral expressions have yet been devised. Some writers (e.g., Cacciari, 1993; Dascal, 1987; Gibbs, 1984; Glucksberg, 1991; Lakoff, 1986) express serious doubt as to whether a sharp, principled distinction can (or should) be drawn between these two varieties of language use. The notion of levels of conventionalization of meanings and sentence uses might be more appropriate than a simple dichotomy between literal and nonliteral (Dascal, 1987).

Casting the issue as a continuum rather than one of a dichotomy corresponds to Rumelhart's claim (1979) that classifying an utterance as literal or nonliteral is no more analytic or important than classifying an utterance as formal or informal. Both kinds of judgments can reliably be made, but at the same time we are fully aware that an utterance may be more or less literal, or more or less formal. Even if we could clearly differentiate between literal and figurative utterances, it remains to be seen whether these two varieties of speech, even in their ideal forms, implicate difference processing mechanisms either for comprehension or for production.

Continuum or dichotomy, how do people identify metaphor? A number of alternative strategies have been proposed (Johnson, 1981). The traditional approach has listeners detecting some syntactic or semantic deviance within an utterance, which in turn motivates a listener to infer that a metaphor is intended. It soon became clear that literal and metaphorical expressions did not differ systematically with syntactic well-formedness, and so semantic clues to metaphoricity were proposed, namely, violation of selectional restrictions (Henle, 1958; Matthews, 1971). A selectional restriction is a constraint on semantic combination. Inanimate objects, for example, cannot think, and so it would be a violation to say that a chair believes in God. Whenever a listener (or reader) detects a semantic CLASH, as in such phrases as *The rich perform leisure,* a nonliteral intention should be inferred. The difficulty with this proposal is that it ". . . elevates a condition that [only] frequently holds (namely, semantic deviance) into a necessary condition of metaphor" (Johnson, 1981, p. 21). Moreover, one can often find contexts that would eliminate such semantic violations while preserving the possibility of both a literal and a metaphorical interpretation, as in *Your defense is an impregnable castle* (Levinson, 1983). This assertion can be understood in several alternative ways, some literal, some metaphorical, or even both simultaneously. Such WHOLE-SENTENCE META-PHORS are perfectly well formed syntactically and semantically, as in *The old rock has become brittle with age,* uttered in a conversation about a retired professor of rhetoric or a 12th-century monastery built of native stone. Such expressions require the context of the discourse to be identified as literal or metaphorical (Ortony, 1980).

As this last example makes clear, the form of the linguistic expression itself offers no reliable cues to metaphoricity. Would an alternative form of deviance provide such cues? One proposal is that a metaphor can be recognized whenever an expression is literally false with respect to an actual state of affairs in the world (Grice, 1975; Loewenberg, 1975; Searle, 1979). This proposal is at the core of the standard theory of metaphor (Glucksberg, 1991) but can be seriously questioned (Black, 1962; Cohen, 1976). The critical problem is that literal falsehood is not a necessary condition for metaphor and so cannot be a reliable cue for recognizing a nonliteral intent. Consider John Donne's line *No man is an island,* cited by Black (1979) in his critique of the standard theory of metaphor. This sentence is true both literally and figuratively, as are any number of more mundane expressions in everyday discourse, like *My husband is an animal* or *Tom's a real Marine!* The former sentence is true both literally and figuratively; the latter could be true literally, but even if not, it would be true figuratively (Keysar, 1989).

Examples such as these have led to an alternative proposal concerning the role of truth value for identifying metaphors. When people interpret utterances, a mental representation or mental model is constructed (Kintsch, 1974). Whenever there is a difference between "true in fact" and "true in the model," then a metaphor can be inferred (Miller, 1979). Of course, "not every statement that is literally incongruous or false is a metaphor . . . but it must be true in the model" (p. 212). Metaphor, according to Miller, presents an apperceptive problem:

> A metaphor that is literally false of the real world can still be added to our image and used to constrain our [mental] model, but it creates a tension between our conception of the real world and our conception of the world that the author had in mind. . . . If an author says that X is Y when we know in fact that X is not Y, we must imagine a world in which X is Y. This act of imagination is facilitated if, in the real world, X is like Y. (pp. 212–213)

In a similar vein, Ortony (1980) suggested that metaphors need not necessarily be literally false, merely contextually anomalous in their literal form but interpretable if taken nonliterally.

These proposals share the view that pragmatics, not linguistic analysis, should govern how metaphors are recognized and interpreted. If so, then literal truth value may be just a special case of a more general condition for recognizing metaphors. Grice (1975) proposed just such an argument. An utterance, he pointed out, can violate any one of several conversational maxims: the maxim of Quality (utterances should be truthful, to be sure), but also the maxims of Quantity (utterances should be informative), Manner (utterances should be clear and unambiguous), and Relation (they should be relevant). If any of these maxims appear to be violated, then a conversational implicature is signaled: Listeners should seek an interpretation that accounts for the apparent violation. Thus, when someone says that her husband is an animal, the maxims to be informative and relevant would be violated if only literal truth were intended. Therefore, a listener would infer some nonliteral message, such as her husband is crude, acts beastly toward her, and so on. This inference not only provides a substantive interpretation, but also "corrects" the conversational maxim violations. The speaker is no longer in violation of the maxims of informativeness and relevance. How listeners actually detect violations and make appropriate inferences, of course, remains to be investigated.

Irrespective of how people arrive at specific metaphor interpretations, it is clear that there are no necessary and sufficient conditions for an utterance to be a metaphor. As Black (1979) observed,

> The decisive reason for the choice of interpretation may be, as it often is, the patent falsity or incoherence of the literal reading—but it might equally be the banality of that reading's truth, its pointlessness, or its lack of congruence with the surrounding text and nonverbal setting. (p. 450)

We turn now from the issue of discriminating the literal and the nonliteral to the more specific (and perhaps more fruitful) questions of how metaphors have been defined and how the various definitions have led to alternative models of metaphor comprehension.

2. What Are Metaphors and How Are They Understood?

There are three main views of metaphor, each of which implicates a different model of metaphor comprehension. These are, in the most general terms, the COMPARISON VIEW, the INCOHERENCE VIEW, and the INTERACTION VIEW. We begin with the oldest and most traditional, the comparison view.

a. Metaphors as Comparisons.   The traditional and heretofore the most influential view of metaphors dates back to Aristotle. Metaphor is said to be a form of transfer of a name from one object to another, as in *Dew is a veil.* Figure 1 illustrates the structure of this simple metaphor. Adapting terminology introduced by Richards (1936), the TOPIC (originally termed the TENOR) of the metaphor is the concept 'dew', and the vehicle is 'veil'. The GROUND of the metaphor is the set of features that these two concepts share, indicated by the area of overlap in Figure 1. In some cases, the ground can be a superordinate category that subsumes both topic and vehicle, as in *the tooth of the mountain,* where mountain peak and tooth partake of the category 'sharpened form'. In other cases, it may be necessary to identify an underlying analogy in order to recover a metaphor's ground, as in Virginia Woolf's *She allowed life to waste like a tap left running* (cited in Gentner, Falkenhainer, & Skorstad, 1987).

Most generally, the comparison view of metaphor has generated a class of comprehension models that can be characterized as feature- or attribute-matching models. Matching models adopt the assumption that in attributive metaphors of the form "A is B," the A and B concepts are represented either as sets of features or as positions in an *n*-dimensional semantic space (cf. Johnson & Malgady, 1979; Marschark, Katz, & Paivio, 1983; Tourangeau & Sternberg, 1981). Regardless of the specific representational assumptions, matching models assume that metaphors are first transformed into comparison statements, and then the features or attributes of the vehicle are compared to, or mapped onto, the features of the topic. The two basic claims of this view—the transformation of the metaphor into an explicit comparison and the subsequent feature-mapping process—are each problematic, for different reasons. We examine the claim that metaphors are routinely transformed into explicit comparisons in a later section. In this section, we examine in detail some central issues involving the feature-matching process.

If the comparison view is correct, then metaphorical comparisons (i.e., similes) should be understood in exactly the same ways that literal comparisons are understood. Literal comparisons are in general more or less symmetrical. For example, the statement *copper is like tin* is not strikingly different than its inverse, *tin is like copper.* However, not all literal comparisons are perfectly symmetrical. As Tversky noted (1977), many comparisons are demonstrably asymmetrical. For example, Mexico is considered to be more similar to Spain than Spain to Mexico. The relevant generalization from this example is that people prefer to place the more salient concept (the more prototypical concept) in the predicate position and the less salient, or variant, concept in the subject or topic position. Thus, one would be more likely to say that a picture resembles

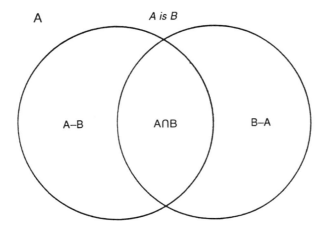

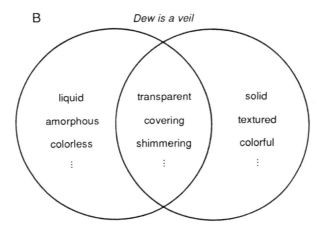

FIG. 1   (A) Venn diagram illustration of common and distinctive feature sets for the symbolic metaphor *A is B*. (B) Venn diagram illustration of the partition of open feature sets for the metaphoric example *Dew is a veil*. [Reproduced from Malgady & Johnson (1980), with permission.]

a person than the reverse. This asymmetry can be seen in several different behavioral measures, including judgments of degrees of similarity as well as preferences for one order over another.

One source for this asymmetry is the convention for marking given and new information (Clark & Haviland, 1977). Given information is normally placed in the subject (or topic) position of a statement, while new information is placed in the predicate. In Tversky's (1977) contrast model, asymmetries that may arise from the given–new convention (or for other reasons) are accounted for by differentially weighting the features that are not shared by subject and predicate concepts. Because the predicate as carrier of new information is considered to be more salient, its distinctive features are weighted more heavily than those of the subject. Thus, reversing a comparison statement results in a reduced degree of similarity, as well as a differential preference for the original order.

Ortony (1979) pointed out that metaphorical comparisons could not be accounted for by the contrast model because that model cannot account for the specific kind of asymmetry displayed by metaphors. For literal comparisons, reversing the order of subject and predicate does not render the statement unacceptable, nor does it lead to a different set of shared features. In contrast, for metaphorical comparisons either reversals are anomalous, or a new set of features emerges as the ground for the comparison. For example, reversing *Sermons are like sleeping pills* produces an anomalous statement, *Sleeping pills are like sermons*. When reversed metaphors do not result in anomalies, it is often because the particular topics and vehicles provide alternative grounds for interpretation. For example, the assertions *Billboards are like warts* and *Warts are like billboards* may be equally meaningful, but they imply different grounds: properties such as 'ugly' for the former, properties such as 'prominence' or 'attract attention' for the latter. In either case, each vehicle's stereotypical or salient properties are potentially relevant for and hence attributable to their respective topics.

In order to account for these latter two phenomena—reversed metaphors resulting in either anomalous statements or a different metaphor, that is, a new ground—Ortony (1979; see also Ortony, Vondruska, Foss, & Jones, 1985) elaborated Tversky's contrast model by introducing the concept of salience imbalance. In literal comparisons, the matching features of subject and predicate are equally high and salient, as in *Billboards are like placards*. By contrast, in metaphoric comparisons the matching features (the ground) of topic and vehicle are differentially salient: high in the vehicle, low in the topic. For example, the property 'puts people to sleep' is highly salient in the concept 'sleeping pills' but is relatively low-salient in the concept 'sermons'. Hence, *Sermons are like sleeping pills* would be an acceptable metaphoric comparison, but the reverse *Sleeping pills are like sermons* would not. *Sleeping pills are like sermons* would be considered anomalous because there is no highly salient property of sermons that can plausibly be attributed to sleeping pills. In this way, the salience imbalance notion can account for the unacceptability of reversed metaphors.

The salience imbalance hypothesis can also account for cases where a reversed metaphor produces new grounds for the comparison. In *Billboards are like warts*, a highly salient property of warts, such as ugliness, can plausibly be attributed to billboards. In *Warts are like billboards*, highly salient properties of billboards, such as prominence and ability to attract attention, can plausibly be attributed to warts. In both cases, the property that is highly salient in the vehicle is relevant to and potentially informative about the topic. Finally, the salience imbalance hypothesis accounts for literally anomalous comparisons, such as *Billboards are like pears*, by assuming that when matching properties are of low salience in both subject and predicate, then the statement is uninformative and hence anomalous.

The salience imbalance hypothesis, then, accounts for a number of important characteristics of both literal and metaphoric comparisons. First, it accounts for the extreme asymmetry of metaphoric comparisons by explaining how and why reversed metaphoric comparisons are either anomalous or are re-interpreted via new grounds for the comparisons. Second, it accounts for people's ability to judge that a comparison is metaphorical rather than literal. When the matching features of a comparison are highly salient in both subject and predicate, as in *Copper is like tin*, then it is judged to be literal. When the matching features of a comparison are high in the predicate but low in the subject, then that is taken as the defining characteristic of a metaphor, and the comparison is judged accordingly. Differential salience levels, then, is the property that discriminates metaphoric from literal comparisons.

Can literal comparisons themselves be characterized as involving a match of highly salient attributes? Recall that if a statement is informative, then it is acceptable; if not, it is anomalous. This assumption leads to an unanticipated paradoxical consequence. Feature salience is presumably a property of people's mental representations, not of the objects in the external world. If the matching properties of the subject and predicate of a literal comparison are highly salient for a listener, then the comparison provides no new information and so must be anomalous in context, just as tautologies such as *Dogs are animals* would be anomalous unless re-interpreted nonliterally (Glucksberg & Keysar, 1990). Comparison statements such as *Chaise longues are like sofas* can only be informative for a listener if he or she does not know much about chaise longues, and so can add a highly salient property of sofas to his or her mental representation of chaise longues. Until this property is added, the "matching" features of the comparison are significantly less salient (or, as we shall see below, entirely absent) in the listener's mental representation of the subject (*chaise longue*) and highly salient in the mental representation of the predicate (*sofa*). But this is precisely the cue that theoretically discriminates between literal and metaphorical comparisons. Unfortunately, this cannot be a valid cue to metaphoricity because all informative comparisons must involve attribution of highly salient properties of a predicate to a subject. Therefore we must seek some cue to metaphoricity other than salience imbalance. We return to this issue in our discussion of the interaction view.

The assumption of informativeness raises another important issue: Which features of a metaphor vehicle are attributed to the metaphor topic? In more general terms, how are the grounds for any comparisons determined? This would be less problematic if feature salience were context-independent and metaphor interpretation required only a stable hierarchy of concept features. But metaphor interpretation requires a large range of cultural conventions and mutually held beliefs. As Gibbs put it,

> Which properties of a metaphor are the salient ones depends precisely on what knowledge is shared by the speaker and the hearer on any given occasion. The properties of any given terms in a metaphor may be *ephemerally* rather than eternally salient. (1987, p. 40)

The notion that different features of a particular metaphor vehicle may be invoked depending on context is implicit in Tourangeau and Sternberg's (1981, 1982) critique of the shared features view of metaphoric comparisons. First, they note that shared features as embodied in shared category membership provide insufficient grounds for metaphor interpretation. In the example *The senator was a fox who could outwit the reporter every time*, the fact that both the senator and the fox belong to a common category (animals) is totally irrelevant as far as the figurative meaning is concerned. Second, in most cases we are concerned not with the defining characteristics of the vehicle, but instead with stereotypical and culturally bound attributes that we attach to an object, such as foxes being clever, and so on (see Black, 1962, 1979). Third, quite often the common category or feature shared by topic and vehicle can be shared only metaphorically. Tourangeau and Sternberg's (1982) example, *The headache wasn't severe and so was only a storm*, highlights that the meaning of *small* does not apply to headache and storm in the same way: "A storm occupies or fills physical space in a way that a headache does not" (p. 209). A strict overlap of features provides no mechanism for differential construals of word meanings, even within a single metaphor.

The matching process also provides no explicit mechanism for introducing new features or properties to the topic of metaphor (or the subject of any comparison, for that matter). The comparison view assumes some sort of preexisting link between topic and vehicle, the discovery of which will constitute the ground for comprehension. But this PRIOR ASSOCIATION assumption need not hold (Camac & Glucksberg, 1984; Marschark et al., 1983). For a listener, there need be no similarity whatever between a metaphor topic and vehicle prior to encountering the metaphor itself; the metaphor creates the similarity (cf. Lakoff & Johnson, 1980). When we first read John Donne's *No man is an island*, the idea that people cannot live isolated lives, and so are not similar to an island, was created, not simply retrieved from semantic memory. The dissimilarity of people and islands is the ground for this metaphor. When a metaphor's ground is a feature that is not shared, any matching process is, on the face of it, totally useless!

Similarly, when a new feature is introduced via a metaphor, feature-matching is again useless. As Ortony (1979) noted in his own critique of the salience imbalance hypothesis, we need to distinguish between ATTRIBUTE-PROMOTING and ATTRIBUTE-INTRODUCING. Attribute-promoting occurs when the ground of a metaphor increases the salience of a particular property of the metaphor topic, as in *Sermons are like sleeping pills* (assuming, of course, that 'sleep-inducing' is a stable but low-salient feature of our concept of sermons). Attribute-introducing occurs when the ground of a metaphor adds a property to the metaphor topic, as in *My uncle is a fountain of wisdom*. Presumably the listener knew nothing about the uncle in question, and the attribute 'wise' has been added to the listener's mental representation of 'my uncle'. In such attribute introduction cases, metaphor creates a similarity. Our example here is a trivial one. In science and other abstract knowledge domains, creating such similarities is tantamount to theory creations, as in Bohr's metaphor, *Atoms are like solar systems* (Gentner, 1983).

Finally, the feature-matching process may be too limited to capture the full range and impact of metaphor. Metaphors may "have more to do with the contingent, factual (real-world) attributes of the referents of the metaphorical focus than with the semantic features that can be claimed to express its meaning" (Levinson, 1983, p. 150).

In a related line of thought, Ortony (1979, 1980) argued that the communicative intention of the speaker of a metaphor is much more complicated than a simple property predication that would be equally well expressible by literal language. For instance, if a woman says *My husband is a teddy bear*, "her intention may be to predicate far more of him than can readily be achieved using single discrete literal predicates. She may want to convey a host of things about him: that he is warm, cuddly, lovable, harmless, soft, etc." (1980, pp. 77–78). It is precisely this "etc." that constitutes much of the force of metaphor and renders literal paraphrases so unsatisfactory or prolix. Ortony (1980) argues that when the woman describes her husband as a teddy bear, the metaphorical tension "arises as a result of the incompatibility of the humanness of her husband and the nonhumaness of the teddy bear" (p. 78). Tension elimination, according to the author, is achieved by ignoring the attributes of the vehicle that are perceived as being incompatible with the topic, so that

> the remaining salient attributes of the vehicle are attributed as a whole, that is an entire cognitive substructure is mapped onto the topic. By predicating the non conflicting attributes en masse, the articulation of discrete predicates is not required, nor even is a conscious recognition of them. (ibid.)

Interestingly, Ortony noted that this "holistic representation has characteristics that render metaphor representation much closer to perceptual representations than to a set of abstracted predicates articulated through the medium of language" (ibid.; for a related line of research, see Verbrugge, 1977, 1980).

In summary, a simple comparison view based on feature-matching processes seems insufficient to account for even the simplest of metaphor phenomena, including the problem of how people discriminate between literal and metaphorical comparisons. We turn now to an examination of the incoherence view, which holds that metaphors necessarily involve incoherence of some kind, and that such incoherence, coupled with other factors, can provide a valid cue for metaphoricity.

b. The Incoherence View.   There are at least two distinct versions of what we refer to as the incoherence view of metaphor, one drawn from generative semantics, the other from pragmatics and speech act theory. Both versions consider metaphors to be incongruous or otherwise defective statements, either semantically or pragmatically. According to the version derived from generative semantics, metaphors are anomalous. Metaphoric sentences cannot be understood in terms of their literal meanings because rules of syntax and semantic composition are violated (Chomsky, 1961; Katz, 1964; Kintsch, 1974). The rules that are violated are "corrected" during comprehension, when the literal interpretation of the sentence is replaced by a literal paraphrase of the metaphoric interpretation. The process by which this occurs has not been clearly specified, other than by the general proposition that this is accomplished via rules and inference procedures created by the semantic component of the language.

The second and more influential version of the incoherence view is based on speech act theory. On this view, metaphors are "defective" if taken literally. As Searle (1979) argued, upon hearing a sentence such as *Sam is a pig,* a listener would recognize that it cannot be literally true, and so if taken literally it is radically defective. "The defects which cue the hearer may be the obvious falsehood, semantic nonsense, violations of the rule of speech acts, or violations of conversational principles of communication" (p. 114). This suggests the following general strategy for detecting potential metaphors: "Where the utterance is defective if taken literally, look for an utterance meaning that differs from sentence meaning" (p. 114).

The comprehension process deriving from such an assumption would include the following steps.

1. Derive a literal interpretation of the sentence;
2. Assess the interpretability of that interpretation against the context of that sentence;
3. If that literal meaning cannot be interpreted, then and only then derive an alternative nonliteral interpretation.

This serial, three-stage comprehension model implies a principled distinction between literal and nonliteral sentence meanings. Literal meanings have unconditional priority, in that they are derived automatically and with relatively little effort. In contrast, nonliteral meanings are optional, which means that they can be ignored if, in a given context, the literal meaning makes sense. This implies that metaphor requires a highly specified context if its nonliteral meaning is to be inferred. Three basic psychological claims follow from this view: (a) literal language has unconditional priority; (b) metaphorical meanings require specific contexts to trigger a search for such meanings; (c) more contextual supports are required for nonliteral interpretations than for literal ones. Each of these claims can be seriously questioned, given the available empirical evidence.

With respect to the priority of literal meanings, it is not yet clear that people always and unconditionally process sentences sufficiently to derive a literal interpretation. Sentence processing may be truncated if, during such processing, an expression is recognized as, say, a familiar idiom (e.g., *He deserves a pat on the back*), or as a conventional indirect request (e.g., *Can you pass the salt*) (Cacciari & Tabossi, 1988, 1993; Gibbs, 1980). When nonliteral interpretation takes some time, of course, linguistic processing may well run its full course and produce a literal interpretation, as observed by Cacciari and Tabossi (1988), who used idioms that could not be recognized as such until the very end of the expression. In such cases, the only option available to a listener is to continue linguistic analysis until there is some reliable indicator to do otherwise. More generally, people should not truncate linguistic processing until it is certain that a literal interpretation can play no useful role. Because the literal meanings of many figurative expressions play a central role in the complete, final interpretations of utterances (cf. Cacciari & Glucksberg, 1990; Glucksberg, 1991), the optimal strategy would be to derive both the literal and the intended meanings of all utterances. For example, in the metaphoric expression *No man is an island,* the literal meaning of the string is a central component of the final, figurative interpretation—that people do not and cannot live in isolation from one another. Literal meanings therefore, are not abandoned or rejected in favor of an alternative, figurative interpretation, but instead are used to guide and constrain the inferential comprehension process (Glucksberg, 1991). Literal meanings, then, do not have automatic priority over nonliteral meanings. Nevertheless, they are generally computed and, when appropriate, integrated into the figurative interpretation.

If literal meanings do not have automatic priority, then it logically follows that figurative meanings are not necessarily optional—to be sought only if a literal meaning is defective, in Searle's (1979) terms. This logical conclusion has empirical support in a series of studies conducted by Glucksberg and his colleagues (Gildea & Glucksberg, 1983; Glucksberg, Gildea, & Bookin, 1982). Using a variant of the Stroop (1935) interference paradigm, these studies demonstrated that people apprehend the figurative meanings of sentences even when the literal meanings of those sentences are perfectly acceptable in context. In one of these studies (Glucksberg et al., 1982), college students were asked to verify the literal truth value of sentences such as *Some desks are junkyards* and *Some desks are roads*. Both of these sentences are literally false, but they are also acceptable in the context of a laboratory sentence verification task (responding *yes* if the sentence was true, and *no* if the sentence was false). Since both are acceptable, neither should trigger a search for alternative, nonliteral meanings. The desk–junkyard sentence, however, has some nonliteral "truth" value, while the desk–roads sentence does not. As we would expect if the nonliteral "truth" were to be apprehended, the former types of sentences took longer to judge as false than the latter, indicating that the people in this experiment automatically (i.e., non-optionally) apprehended metaphorical meanings even when literal meanings were sufficient for the task. More generally, Keysar (1989) showed that when either literal or metaphorical meanings are plausible in context, both are apprehended even when either one alone would suffice. The pattern of results from these studies strongly suggests that neither type of meaning has automatic priority in discourse.

These studies are also relevant to the issue of how context is used when literal or nonliteral meanings are intended. A supporting context was not required when a metaphorical meaning was clear and unambiguous, as in sentences such as *Some jobs are jails* (Gildea & Glucksberg, 1983). When a metaphorical meaning was ambiguous, as in sentences such as *Some marriages are iceboxes,* then context was required to make sense of the sentence, but that context was quite minimal. Merely providing the general topic of an interpretation, such as temperature, enabled people to quickly arrive at an interpretation, such as 'relationships can be emotionally cold'. This does not seem to be different either in the kind or degree of contextual support that is often required for comparably ambiguous literal expressions. As Gildea and Glucksberg (1983) concluded, "Ordinary, literal comprehension requires the same kinds of inference, decisions, and reliance on contextual information that metaphor comprehension does" (p. 589).

More generally, both the incoherence and comparison views of metaphor imply that metaphors are processed in ways that are more complex than those required for literally intended utterances. This would suggest that metaphors should take longer to understand than comparable literal expressions. This expectation has, in general, been disconfirmed—metaphors can be understood as quickly and as easily as literal expressions. Harris (1976), for example, found no differences in the time required to initiate paraphrases of metaphorical and comparable literal sentences. Ortony, Schallert, Reynolds, and Antos (1978) found no differences in reading times for sentences that could be interpreted either literally or metaphorically, provided there was a sufficient context for metaphorical or literal interpretation. When context was insufficient, then metaphorical sentences did take longer to read. Similarly, Inhoff, Lima, and Carroll (1984), as well as Shinjo and Myers (1987), found that attributive metaphors are read and understood as quickly as literal sentences when embedded in appropriate contexts. Some studies do find differences in the comprehensibility of metaphors and literal sentences. Gerrig and Healy (1983), for example, had subjects reading either metaphors or literal sentences preceded or followed by an informative context. They found longer reading times for metaphors with respect to literal sentences irrespective of the position of context (before or after the metaphor). This outcome, however, is the exception in the literature.

That metaphors are comprehended as quickly as literal sentences when context is adequate is consistent with the idea that identical processes are involved irrespective of language type. Even without special contexts, metaphorical meanings may be generated as quickly as literal ones. Connine and Blasko (1993) used a cross-modal priming technique (see also Ferreira and Anes, this volume) to assess the relative speed of activation of the literal and metaphorical meanings of words in simple metaphors such as *Indecision is a whirlpool*. While listening to such metaphors, subjects made lexical decisions either to literal associates of whirlpool such as 'water', metaphorical associates such as 'confusion', or to unrelated items such as 'allow'. Lexical decisions to either literal or metaphorical associates were faster than to unrelated words and did not differ from one another, even when the lexical decision targets were presented simultaneously with the end of the critical word, in this example *whirlpool*. These results indicate, once again, that literal and metaphorical meanings are accessed simultaneously, provided that both are relevant and apt. In this case, the semantics of *whirlpool* are central to the metaphorical use to which this word is put, namely, 'confusion'. Note that the whirlpool metaphor is not a frozen expression, and that it was rated as unfamiliar. When equally novel but non-apt metaphors were used, only literal meanings were activated, even when subjects were given ample time to generate a metaphorical interpretation. These results suggest that when a metaphor is interpretable, then its literal and figurative meanings are generated in parallel. Neither type of meaning seems to have processing priority over the other.

What information do people use to generate metaphorical meanings? Tourangeau and Rips (1991) investigated the basis for metaphor interpretation. A metaphor's meaning could be based on preexisting features of the topic and the vehicle, on salient features of the vehicle, or on relational features of the two terms. Using metaphors derived from poetry as well as more prosaic metaphors such as *The eagle is a lion among birds*, they found that interpretations were generally not based on preexisting features of a metaphor's components. Instead, metaphors were primarily interpreted in terms of emergent features, namely features that are not particularly characteristic of either the topic or the vehicle. For example, the metaphor ground of 'pleasantly surprising and pleasing' is not a salient feature of either the topic or the vehicle in William Carlos Williams' *Your knees are a southern breeze—or a gust of snow* (as cited in Tourangeau & Rips, 1991). The importance of emergent features, however, is not unique to metaphors. As Murphy (1988) and Medin and Shoben (1988) have shown, emergent features can also be important in understanding such literal constructions as *empty store*. The property of 'losing money' is not a salient characteristic of either *empty* or *store* but is a commonly reported property of the compound. Similarly, the properties attributed to the concept *blind lawyer,* such as 'courageous', are not usually attributed to either of the separate components *blind* or *lawyer* (Kunda, Miller, & Claire, 1990). It may well be that metaphor interpretation can be fruitfully considered a special case of conceptual combination. We return to this issue in our discussion of the interaction view and in the later treatment of sense creation.

c. The Interaction View. The third of the traditional theories of metaphor derives from the seminal work of Max Black (1962, 1979). As Johnson (1981) noted, Black's interaction view was a turning point in the literature on theories of metaphor. According to Black, in any metaphorical statement there are two distinct subjects: a primary one, the topic, and a secondary one, the vehicle. These two subjects must be seen as "systems of associated commonplaces" or as an "implicative complex." They are composed by whatever property, relation, or belief is commonly held to be true of an object even if it does not actually apply. Metaphors of the form "An A is a B" act by projecting on the primary subject (the A concept) a set of associated implications included in the system that is associated with the secondary term (the B concept). "The maker of a metaphorical statement selects, emphasizes, suppresses and organizes features of the primary subject by applying to it statements isomorphic with the members of the secondary subject's implicative complex" (Black, 1979, p. 28).

The interaction of the two subjects, or "inter-animation of words," as Richards (1936) expressed it, is the result of the following three operations:

> (a) The presence of the primary subject incites the hearer to select some of the secondary subject's properties; and (b) invites him to construct a parallel implication complex that can fit the primary subject; and (c) reciprocally induces parallel changes in the secondary subject. (p. 29)

Metaphor thus invites the listener to activity and not merely to a passive reception of the intended content: "I think of a metaphorical statement (even a weak one) as a verbal action essentially demanding uptake, a creative response from a competent reader" (p. 29).

One of Max Black's examples is the metaphor *Man is a wolf*. This sentence invites the listener to call up the commonplaces associated with wolves and to use them as a "filter" for restructuring his/her perception and categorization of another semantic system, that represented by men. The interaction is viewed by Black as a screening of one system of commonplaces by another that generates a new conceptual organization of, or a new perspective on, an object or event. In the case of *Man is a wolf*, the interaction simultaneously produces an anthropomorphic view of wolves and an animalization of men.

The interaction view has received scarce empirical attention, possibly because, as Tourangeau and Sternberg (1982) noted,

> Interaction theorists are mainly philosophers and critics, [so] it is not surprising that they don't make very concrete proposals about the processes necessary for interpreting metaphors or about how these processes might relate to the ordinary ones used in understanding literal language. (p. 213)

Nonetheless some recent psycholinguistic approaches to metaphor—notably Gentner's (1983) structure-mapping hypothesis, Verbrugge and McCarrell's (1977) resemblance hypothesis, and Tourangeau and Sternberg's (1981, 1982) domain interaction hypothesis—are reminiscent of Black's ideas.

Interestingly, Black's notion that metaphor operates via an interdomain connection is one of the crucial assumptions of recent approaches to polysemy and language change. For instance, Sweetser (1991) argues that metaphors operate between domains, and so pervasively that "speakers find an interdomain connection between knowledge and vision, for instance, or between time and space, to be as natural as the intra-domain connections between finger and hand or between man and woman'' (p. 19).

So far we have examined the views proposed by philosophers, linguists, and psychologists to explain the structure and the comprehension of metaphors. The comparison view, although still influential, has not led to a specific psychological model (with the important exception of Miller, 1979). In contrast, the incoherence view has provided the framework for processing models of metaphorical language. The interaction view has not been tested directly; nonetheless many of its suggestions have been developed in current psycholinguistic models of metaphor comprehension.

B. New Directions in Metaphor Theory: From Language to Categories

The new wave in metaphor theory is based on the argument that metaphor use and understanding involves not only linguistic or discourse processes, but also reasoning and inferential and conceptual processes. In particular, metaphor involves both the use of previously acquired categories and conceptual schema, and the creation of new categories and conceptual schema (Basso, 1976; Glucksberg & Keysar, 1990; Kennedy, 1990; Lakoff, 1987; Lakoff & Johnson, 1980; Lakoff & Turner, 1989). As Beck (1987) pointed out, ''metaphors force the mind to construct a high-order linkage between the entities referred to'' (p. 13); metaphors ''are like bridges'' (p. 11).

1. Metaphors as Class-Inclusion Assertions

Taken as implicit comparisons, metaphor reveals an intriguing paradox. Metaphors are often characterized as involving two unlike things compared, as in *My Luve is like a red, red rose* (Burns). Literal comparisons involve two like things, as in *Hornets are like bees*. Metaphorical comparisons, however, may be sensibly paraphrased as a class inclusion statement, as in *My love is a red, red rose*. Literal comparisons cannot be so paraphrased: *Hornets are bees* is not only patently false, it is uninterpretable. Why is it that two ''unlike'' things can be linked via a class inclusion statement while two ''like'' things cannot?

One resolution to this paradox is to treat metaphorical statements such as *My love is a red, red rose* or *My job is a jail* as true class inclusion assertions. In such constructions, the metaphor vehicle refers not to what would ordinarily be its taxonomic category, but instead to a category that now includes both the topic and the vehicle of the metaphor. The vehicle exemplifies or typifies that category, and the salient properties of that category are attributed to the metaphor topic. What category does *jail* in this context refer to? It refers to the category of things that are unpleasant, constraining, involuntary, difficult or impossible to get out of, and yes, even punishing. Members of this category could include jobs, marriages, schools, or any other entity that can be characterized as a metaphorical ''jail.''

This characterization of metaphors borrows Peirce's (1932) distinction between a word as an entity—a token—and a word as a name of a category—a type. The word *jail* as a metaphor vehicle refers to a type—that category of things which the literal jail typifies. The literal jail, in turn, refers to an actual token, the physical building that serves as a jail. The two tokens *job* and *jail* are, via the metaphor, assigned to the superordinate attributive category 'Jail', which does not have a name of its own.

This device of using the name of a prototypical category member to refer to a superordinate category that has not been lexicalized is analogous to one used by speakers of languages that, while having names for basic-level objects, do not have names for superordinate categories. One such language is American Sign Language (ASL). In ASL, basic-level objects have primary signs, comparable to single-word English names such as *chair, table, bed*. The superordinate category of 'furniture', however, has no sign of its own in ASL. Instead, ASL signers use basic object signs that are prototypical of that category, as in: HOUSE FIRE (+) LOSE ALL CHAIR-TABLE-BED ETC., BUT ONE LEFT, BED, which is interpretable as 'I lost all my furniture in the house fire but one thing was left: the bed' (Newport & Bellugi, 1978, p. 62).

Roger Brown (1958) captured the essence of this mechanism when he noted that

> when someone invents a new machine, or forms a concept, or buys a dog, or manufactures a soap powder his first thought is to name it. These names are almost never arbitrary creations produced by juggling the sounds of the language into a novel sequence. . . . The usual method of creating a new name is to use words or morphemes already in the language; either by expanding the semantic range of some word or by recombining morphemes. (p.139)

Brown's example is *the foot of the mountain*, where the word *foot* refers to two categories, a subordinate and superordinate category:

> Within this superordinate category, which we might name *the foundations or lower parts of things,* are two subordinate categories—the man's foot and the mountain's base. . . . Metaphor differs from other superordinate-subordinate relations in that the superordinate is not given a name of its own. Instead, the name of one subordinate is extended to the other. (p.140)

In a similar vein, Kennedy (1990) argued that when someone says *The camel is the ship of the desert,* it must be taken as a process of classification adopted

> in the face of a standard classification that the person is deliberately not using. . . . One important implication of this examination of metaphors as special-purpose classification is that the classification need not arise from the invention of a new higher order category, subsuming both vessels and camels. . . . Rather it is the camel that is changed from its standard category to a secondary one. (pp. 120–121)

On this line of argument, when someone says *My surgeon was a butcher,*

> She means just that, not that her surgeon was like a butcher. In using this expression, the speaker alludes to a prototypical or ideal exemplar of the category of bungling or harmful workers, and simultaneously uses that prototype's name to name that category. (Glucksberg & Keysar, 1993)

The use of ideal exemplars accomplishes the same attributive goals whether it refers to a preexisting category, as in highly familiar metaphors, or when a new attributive category is created. Perhaps the most common device for creating new attributive categories is to use the name of a highly salient event or person to refer to an entire class of events or persons that resemble the original. Doris Lessing, in her novel *The Golden Notebook,* describes the psychoanalyst who is treating the novel's major protagonists as

> Mother Sugar, otherwise Mrs. Marks, . . . as time passed, became a name for much more than a person, and indicated a whole way of looking at life—traditional, rooted, conservative, in spite of its scandalous familiarity with everything amoral. (1962, p. 26)

Here, as in metaphors in general, a complex concept, namely, 'traditional view of life while simultaneously dealing with amoral and scandalous goings on', has no conventional name, and so is given the name of an ideal exemplar of that category, Mother Sugar.

Viewing metaphor vehicles as typifying their intended attributive categories provides a principled explanation for why some metaphors seem apt and appropriate, while others that are equally comprehensible seem less apt. In our culture, platinum is as valuable as gold, yet gold is a far more typical member of the category of valuable things than is platinum. Thus to say that *Not all of Einstein's ideas were golden* seems far more apt than *Not all of Einstein's ideas were platinum.* These two assertions mean essentially the same thing and are easily understood, yet only the former seems apt. Similarly, if one wishes to characterize something as 'confining, stifling, etc.', s/he will most likely select the object or event that best typifies such situations (in our culture, jail). This may be one reason that metaphors can be considered WINDOWS (Beck, 1987) on our beliefs and on our cultural models (Holland & Quinn, 1987; Quinn, 1991; Sweetser, 1991).

A similar mechanism is apparent in one type of idiom. Idioms are word strings with conventionalized meanings. In many idioms, a prototypical instance of a person, event, or situation is used to describe new instances of such persons, events, or situations. When we say that some action is like *carrying coals to Newcastle,* we use the Newcastle exemplar as the prototypical instance of bringing something to someplace where there's already an overabundance of that something. Similarly, idioms such as *burn your bridges, killing two birds with one stone,* and *hiding ones head in the sand* all allude literally to prototypical actions that are used to describe new instances of those actions. Perhaps because their literal referents are relevant and appropriate to their idiomatic meanings, such idioms can be productive (Glucksberg, 1993). In a recent debate on the urgency of protecting New Jersey's beaches against the ravages of Atlantic storms, an irate legislator said, *We can no longer hide our heads in the sand because pretty soon there won't be any sand!*

The class inclusion model of metaphor is as yet untested except for some preliminary studies. In one such study, Cacciari (1990) asked Italian subjects to decide whether pairs of words belonged to the same category, e.g., *chair–table* (*sedia–tavolo*) would be a positive item, *doctor–drum* (*dottore–tamburo*) would not. Consistent with the view that metaphor topics and vehicles do belong to the same attributive category, subjects had difficulty rejecting apt metaphor pairs, such as *job–jail* (*lavoro–prigione*), where the correct answer would be a *no* response. Subjects took significantly more time to reject such pairs. Interestingly, pairs such as *job–penitentiary* (*lavoro–penitenziario*) were easy to reject, presumably because *penitentiary* is, for Italian subjects, a less typical member of the attributive category 'confining, stifling, etc., situations'. And in fact, *penitentiary* was rated as less typical than *jail* by Italian subjects. With appropriate materials, we expect the same results also for American subjects. At present, the class inclusion model is consistent with the known phenomena of metaphor comprehension and makes some testable predictions, such as the determinants of metaphor aptness and comprehensibility. Future research should provide more evidence on the adequacy of this model.

2. The Metaphorical Structure of Thought

Lakoff and his colleagues (Lakoff, 1987, 1990; Lakoff & Johnson, 1980; Lakoff & Turner, 1989) have proposed not only a model of metaphorical language, but rather a conception of human thought and reasoning that is intended as a fundamental reformulation of current linguistic and cognitive theory. The breadth of Lakoff's proposals concerning cognitive linguistics is beyond the scope of this chapter. Here we are only concerned with aspects of the proposal that have to do with the conceptual bases for metaphoric expressions.

The distinction between cognition and language is sharply drawn. According to Lakoff and Turner (1989), it is "a prerequisite to any discussion on metaphor that we make a distinction between basic conceptual metaphors, which are cognitive in nature, and particular linguistic expressions of these conceptual metaphors" (p. 50). Lakoff and Johnson are directly concerned only with the first level, conceptual metaphors. Particular linguistic expressions are treated only as byproducts of the conceptual level. Indeed, to identify a given word string as a metaphor is misleading because this would focus on the linguistic and idiosyncratic aspect of a metaphor instead of its conceptual nature. Linguistic expressions per se are not metaphors; only mappings of conceptual structures from one domain to another can qualify as being metaphorical. According to Lakoff and his colleagues, metaphor concerns thought and not language.

What sort of thought is metaphor? Part of the cognitive apparatus shared by the members of a given culture is a very large but finite set of basic conceptual metaphors that have the following characteristics (Lakoff & Turner, 1989, p. 51):

1. They are systematic, "in that there is a fixed correspondence between the structure of the domain to be understood (For instance 'death' in the conceptual metaphor DEATH IS DEPARTURE) and the structure of the domain in terms of which we are understanding it (departure)";
2. they are usually understood "in terms of common experience";
3. they are largely unconscious and "Their operation in cognition is mostly automatic";
4. they are widely conventionalized in language, namely, "There are a great number of words or idiomatic expressions in our language whose interpretation depends upon those conceptual metaphors." Novel expressions can also be understood in terms of these conventional correspondences.

According to this model, this set of structurally complex conceptual metaphors is organized at different levels. As biologists distinguish between genus and species, likewise Lakoff and Turner (1989) claim that there are two types of metaphors. The first type consists of "generic-level metaphors" that do not have fixed source and target domains and fixed lists of entities specified in the mapping. These metaphors (for instance EVENTS ARE ACTIONS) impose higher order constraints on what is an appropriate mapping or not. The second type consists of "specific-level" metaphors or "basic metaphors," and these, unlike the generic-level metaphors, are domain-specific. Some examples of generic-level and specific-level metaphors in people's (hypothetical) conceptualization of life and death are:

1. Generic-level metaphors: PURPOSES ARE DESTINATIONS, STATES ARE LOCATIONS, EVENTS ARE ACTIONS, etc.
2. Specific-level metaphors for the domains of life and death: LIFE IS A JOURNEY, DEATH IS DEPARTURE, PEOPLE ARE PLANTS, A LIFETIME IS A YEAR, A LIFETIME IS A DAY, DEATH IS REST, DEATH IS SLEEP, LIFE IS A PRECIOUS POSSESSION, LIFE IS A PLAY, etc. (cf. Lakoff & Turner, 1989, p. 52).

For example, DEATH IS DEPARTURE is a specific-level instantion of STATES ARE LOCATIONS. Consider the LIFE IS A JOURNEY metaphor. Conceptualizing life in this way consists of a mapping of the structures of JOURNEY onto that of LIFE. This mapping produces a reorganization of the conceptual domain that is the target of the metaphorical mapping, in this case, life. The reorganization (or the original organization when the concept is first acquired) reproduces the properties and relations typical of the source domain (e.g., journey). Each metaphorical mapping consists of the following operations (quotations from Lakoff & Turner, 1989, p. 63):

> "Slots in the source domain schema (e.g., journey) which get mapped onto slots in the target domain (e.g., life)"; some slots can exist independently of the metaphorical mapping, while others are instead created by it (e.g., the path slot).

> "Relations in the source domain which get mapped onto relations in the target domain"; for instance, the relationship between the traveler and his/her destination is mapped onto the life domain in terms of reaching a purpose.

> "Properties in the source domain which get mapped onto properties in the target domain"; for instance, the idea that the strength and weakness of the traveler modify the conduits of the travel gives rise to the idea of a person having strength and weakness in the conduit of life.

> "Knowledge in the source domain which gets mapped onto knowledge in the target domain" should allow mappings of inference pattern. For instance, the notion of entering into a dead end and the associated need for looking for another route is transformed into an existential dead end and the need for another course of action in one's life. The extent to which a source domain is mapped onto a target domain is regulated by the invariance hypothesis, which states that "All metaphorical mappings are partial. What is mapped preserves image-schematic structure, though not all image-schematic structure need be mapped. Furthermore, all forms of abstract inference, all details of image-mappings, and all generic-level structure arise via the invariance hypothesis." (Lakoff, 1990, p. 72)

Although conceptual metaphors are pervasive, Lakoff and his collaborators argue that this does not imply that everything is metaphorical. The contrast between literal and figurative rests on the idea of semantic autonomy: An expression or a concept in a language is semantically autonomous if it is meaningful completely in its own terms, namely, it does not derive any of its meanings from conceptual metaphors. Knowledge derived directly from bodily or perceptual experience constitutes the principal class of semantically autonomous concepts. Thus our conception of three-dimensional physical space is considered to be nonmetaphorical. Our knowledge of physical space, however, is used as the base domain for the target domain of time. To the extent that we conceive of time in terms of physical space, as in the notion that the future lies ahead of us, the past behind us, to that extent our conception of time is metaphorically based. Structural metaphors differ according to their level of abstractness, their degree of structural elaboration and complexity: there are ''image-schema mappings'' (such as LIFE IS A JOURNEY), ''image mappings,'' where an image is mapped instead of a concept (as in Breton's verse *My wife . . . whose waist is an hourglass*) and clusters of metaphors, one embedded into another, that give rise to complex metaphors.

There are serious problems with Lakoff's view. His ambitious proposals raise two empirical issues. First, are the conceptual structures that he hypothesizes actually in human semantic memory, that is, are they available? At one level, notions such as LIFE IS A JOURNEY (that we are mere travelers through an abstract domain of 'life') are intuitively coherent and, with a little reflection and thought, recognizable as a way to think and talk about life. At a more important level, are such conceptual mappings fixed and universal properties of the human conceptual system? Do all people have a systematic set of mappings from the base domain 'journey' to the target domain 'life'? Within a specific culture, if such a set of mappings is part of people's conceptual structure, are such mappings used during the course of producing or understanding metaphorical expressions? This last issue reflects the distinction between availability and accessibility (cf. Higgins, Rholes, & Jones, 1977). Availability refers to material that is stored in memory. Accessibility refers to whether that material is, in fact, activated and used in a particular context. A conceptual structure or analogy relevant to a given metaphorical expression may be available in semantic memory yet may not be accessed for either production or comprehension. An example is A LIFETIME IS A DAY, which may be interpreted in at least two ways. One interpretation that reflects the analogical mappings from the domain of 'days' to 'lifetimes' would be that

> birth corresponds to dawn, maturity to high noon, death to night, etc. If this interpretation is the one actually made in a given context, then the conceptual metaphor is both available and accessible. . . . It was indeed accessed. However, a listener or reader might interpret the lifetime–day metaphor as meaning that lifetimes are short, . . . they pass so quickly (Glucksberg, Keysar, & McGlone, 1992).

In this case, the dawn, noon, night analogies might have been available, but were not accessible. On more general grounds, Lakoff's proposals seem to leave little room for spontaneous novelty and creativity. In principle, all new metaphorical assertions are instantiations or elaborations of conceptual structures already existing in semantic memory. This is problematic because it is difficult to specify the preexisting conceptual structure that could underly the creation of the following expression, which appeared as a newspaper headline for a story about the 1992 flood in the city of Chicago: *City of Broad*

Shoulders Has Wet Feet. In order for this novel metaphoric expression to be generated, there must be a higher order conceptual metaphor that licenses thinking of cities as people. Once an entity such as a city can be conceptualized as a person, then just as a person can have wet feet, so can a city. But on this account, what cannot be conceptualized as a person? The only test of the limits of what can be conceptualized as a person are, ultimately, pragmatic. If an entity can be characterized as having any property or attribute of people (having skin, having hair, breathing, dying, eating, laughing, ad infinitum), then that entity can fill the slot "X is a Person." The invariance hypothesis will automatically filter out those attributes that are inappropriate, and so an appropriate conceptual mapping will always result. The problem with this account is that there are no principled constraints on what can or cannot be mapped onto what.

Another unsolved problem of the conceptual metaphor framework is how these conceptual structures are acquired initially. As Quinn (1991) convincingly argued,

> It would be a mistake to assume that given metaphors recur in talk about a domain [e.g., American metaphors about marriage] simply because the metaphors themselves have become "conventional"—in the term used by both Lakoff (1987, p. 380) and Johnson (1987, p. 106). [It may be more appropriate] to say that metaphors are reintroduced over and over again because they are satisfying instantiations of a 'conventional' or 'culturally shared' model, capturing multiple elements of that model (pp. 78–79).

The invention of a new metaphorical expression

> is constrained not by a necessity to stay within the entailments of particular conventional metaphors, as Johnson argues (1987, pp. 106–107), but by the necessity of finding metaphors that make sense in terms of the cultural model and do a particularly good job of this (p. 79).

For Quinn,

> Metaphor plays a comparatively minor role in constituting our understanding of our world, and that a relatively major role in constituting this understanding is played by cultural models of that world (..) the culturally shared framework on which varied individual understanding is elaborated. (pp. 91–92)

Quinn's critique of Lakoff's theory of metaphor concerns the development and nature of conceptual knowledge. We are more directly concerned with metaphorical expressions, and here Lakoff's views may be less relevant. Since Lakoff and his colleagues are expressly concerned with metaphoric thought, not with metaphoric expressions, their theory says little about such issues as why one expression is chosen over an apparently equivalent one. For example, why should people prefer *My job is a jail* to *My job is a traffic jam* when they want to characterize the stifling, confining, and unpleasant nature of their job? Even if, ultimately, Lakoff's views on the nature of conceptual structures were found to be correct, we would still need a model of metaphorical language in discourse. The mapping from conception to expression is, after all, direct and invariant over situations, cultures, or, for that matter, individual speakers.

3. Why Do People Use Metaphors?

The purposes served by metaphor as opposed to those served by literal language are many and various, yet the specific functions of metaphorical language have yet to be systematically studied. One reason for the lack of systematic study is the assumption that metaphorical expressions can, without loss, always be paraphrased literally. This assumption has been seriously questioned (Gibbs, 1987; Glucksberg & Keysar, 1990; Lakoff & Turner, 1989). A speaker's choice of a metaphorical over a literal expression is not simply a matter of style or preference; metaphor is not simply a fancy way to say something that could have been said literally (cf. Black, 1962, 1979). As Ortony noted, metaphor can perform three distinct functions particularly well: expressing the inexpressible, providing a compact form of expression for complex ideas, and providing for vividness of expression. Some notions are simply difficult to express literally, and so "Metaphors are a means of expressing things that are literally inexpressible in the language in question" (Ortony, 1980, pp. 77–78). For example, the vocabulary available in English for describing sensory experience such as auditory timbre is quite impoverished. Yet, by using terms metaphorically, as in such expressions as *a warm, richly textured organ chord*), we can express the (literally) inexpressible (cf. Beck, 1978; Marks, 1982; Marks & Bornstein, 1987). Metaphors are thus often used to describe something new by reference to something familiar, but the scope of metaphor extends beyond this general function. People use metaphors for "conceptualizing abstract concepts in terms of the apprehendable" (Glucksberg & Keysar, 1990, p. 15), as when spatial concepts and terms are extended to refer to temporal concepts and terms (Clark, 1973).

When alternative literal expressions are available in a language, they may be very prolix by comparison. Metaphors serve to predicate a complex of properties as a whole which often cannot be explicitly specified. When one interprets an expression such as *My job is a jail* as meaning that one's job is stifling, unrewarding, confining, etc., it is precisely the "etc." predication that constitutes both the emotive force and the ambiguity of metaphor. The specific function of metaphor can be seen in the difference between explicit metaphors that use the *is a* form and similes that use the *like* form. People may use the *is a* form "to alert a listener that a specific relation is intended, not a more general assertion of similarity" (Glucksberg & Keysar, 1990, p. 15), as in *That actor is a real Bela Lugosi* (Bela Lugosi was the actor who played the vampire in many of the Dracula movies in the 1930s and 1940s. His portrayal came to epitomize the eerie and sinister nature of vampires). Characterizing any actor as *a Bela Lugosi* places him in the category of those that are best exemplified by Bela Lugosi, so he "takes on all the properties of the type of actor, not of the actor Bela Lugosi himself" (p. 16). Saying that someone is merely *like* Bela Lugosi leaves unspecified exactly what properties are intended in the comparison. Metaphor are thus "used to communicate a complex, patterned set of properties in a shorthand that is understood by the members of a speech community who share relavant mutual knowledge" (p. 16).

The vividness thesis suggests that "there are phenomenological and psychological reasons for supposing that metaphors are more image-evoking and more vivid than even their best literal equivalents (if there is any)" (Ortony, 1980, p. 78). One of the domains where metaphor serves its best function (that of giving a detailed picture of our subjective experience) is that of internal states, in particular emotional states (cf. Ortony & Fainsilber, 1987).

In some cultures, metaphors are systematically used to describe persons.

In the Apache community in central Arizona, for example, metaphors of the form "An A is a B" constitute a distinct speech genre associated with adult men and women "who have gained a reputation for balanced thinking, critical acumen, and extensive cultural knowledge" (Basso, 1976, p. 99). The Western Apache call metaphors "wise words." The interpretation of these wise words relies on the following characteristics: Metaphors specify only one or more "behavioral attributes" that are "indicative of undesirable qualities possessed by the referents of the metaphor's constituents" (p. 104). Thus, if a Western Apache says *butterflies are girls,* what s/he intends is not "what they look like," but how they are alike on behavioral grounds: "Think about how they act the same," said one of Basso's Apache informants. The interpretation of the butterflies metaphor by Western Apache would be "they act mindlessly, just chasing around after each other, having a good time when they should be working, helping out with chores and younger children" (p. 194). A striking characteristic of the Apache wise words is that they invariably refer to negative attributes of people. Perhaps wise words are used in order to maintain standards of politeness; literal language can be far too explicit and more face-threatening than metaphorical language that can always leave an out. Wise words, unlike explicit attributions, can be ignored or misunderstood. In a similar vein, Levinson (1978, p. 92) argued that in metaphors "there is always a great range of interpretations (hence the evasion of the censor)," so in his example *Nixon is a fish,* "was it Nixon's slipperiness, scaliness, or swimming that I had in mind? I'm not saying."

Other, more general functions of metaphor have been suggested. Beck (1987; cf. Pollio & Smith, 1980) recently argued that metaphoric reasoning is "a key human skill" largely independent of what is usually considered as "intelligence" and thus ignored by many educational systems. The ability to reason by connecting different domains is certainly a key ability as far as analogical problem-solving and complex reasoning tasks are concerned, including scientific discovery (cf. Gentner, 1983; Hesse, 1953; Hoffman, 1983; Nersessian, in press). Metaphor has also been implicated in psychotherapeutic interactions (Billow, et al., 1987; Pollio, Barlow, Fine, & Pollio, 1977; Rothenberg, 1984) and in group problem-solving (Holskov Madsen, 1989). There is also some interest in the relative effectiveness of metaphor for persuasion purposes (Bosman & Hagendoorn, 1992). However, the specific functions of metaphor in these various settings have yet to be systematically studied.

III. SENSE EXTENSION AND SENSE CREATION

It is generally acknowledged that metaphorical language is, arguably, the most powerful source for meaning creation and sense (Lee, 1990; Lehrer, 1990; MacCormac, 1985; Nunberg, 1978, 1979). Words evolve additional meanings through metaphors. When such an evolution is consistent and stable enough within a speech community, a new lexical entry can be added to the list of possible meanings of a word, and lexicographers will then officially confirm a new sense by adding it to the dictionary. For example, the word *butcher,* in its 'clumsy, awkward, unskillful' sense has only recently been added to dictionaries of American English (as in *My surgeon was a butcher*). Metaphorical extension is one source of polysemy in a language, where a single word form can have a large number of related senses (Lehrer, 1990), namely where one "form that is intuitively 'one word' [can] have several normal uses" (Nunberg, 1979, p. 145). Perhaps an extreme case of polysemy of related senses is exhibited by the 26 different meanings of *line,* as described by Caramazza and Grober (1976). A more limited case is represented by using a word such as *newspaper* to refer equally appropriately to a publication and to its publisher (Nunberg, 1979). Presumably, at one time a word such as *newspaper* referred to the publication. At some later time, the sense of *newspaper* was extended to the person or company that published the paper. How does sense extension operate?

A. Sense Extension

The linguistic literature on polysemy has been focused on two issues: (a) the semantic relationship(s) among the multiple senses of a word, and (b) the rules or principles that govern sense extension. What principles determine whether and how senses may be extended from a given word? Nunberg (1978, 1979) proposed a number of "conceptually basic functions" for getting from one word sense (and use) to another. These include such functions as 'type of', 'source of', 'possessor of', and 'cause of' that can occur singly or recursively. Lehrer (1990; cf. Lehrer, 1974) investigated the plausibility of such a finite set of rules by examining a variety of lexical sets from different semantic fields (e.g., biological taxonomies, temperature descriptors, prepositions, perception verbs, etc.). Lehrer (1990) proposed a pragmatically oriented set of principles, such as the principle of conventionality: "One should use the conventional term to express a given meaning and one should not use a term with a conventional sense to mean something different—unless the speaker wishes to implicate something different" (p. 238). Other communicative principles include the avoidance of ambiguity, and principles of frequency and semantic generality. Lehrer concludes that polysemy in the lexicon may be predictable but that the principles are so vague that it is hard to know how to falsify or confirm them.

The general conclusion seems to be that to explain the generation of polysemous words, one must consider the ways in which function and rules interact with principles of different kinds, some internal to the lexicon, some external to it. For instance, principles of image schema transformation and metaphorical mappings from one semantic field to another are not dissimilar from those proposed by Lakoff and his colleagues for conceptual mappings from one domain to another. Whether in the service of conceptualization or sense extension, the metaphorical processes seem to be the same.

The cognitive semantic approach to polysemy (e.g., Sweetser, 1991) is based precisely on this kind of approach. More specifically, Sweetser and others make the explicit assumption that "linguistic categorization depends not just on our naming distinctions that exist in the world, but also on our metaphorical and metonymical structuring of our perceptions of the world" (Sweetser, 1991, p. 9). Words do not acquire new senses randomly, but according to a "cognitive structuring" that relates them in a motivated fashion. Even the study of the diachronic development of words can be informative, since "the historical order in which senses are added to polysemous words tells us something about the directional relationship between senses; it affects our understanding of cognitive structure to know that spatial vocabulary universally acquires temporal meanings rather than the reverse'' (p. 9).

If the claim that metaphor promotes linguistic change is correct, it might be interesting to trace the reverse process in polysemous meanings. One should be able to find that sense extension follows the same semantic constraints that operate on metaphors. Ullmann (1962; cf. Smith et al., 1981) suggested that the creation of a metaphor follows four universal laws: (a) the principle of anthropomorphization, according to which we use part of the human body to refer to abstract and concrete objects (e.g., *the heart of the matter*); (b) the use of concrete or experiential words to refer to abstract experience or objects (e.g., *to shed light on, bitter feelings*); (c) the use of animals, as in *muscle*, which derives from the Latin *musculus*, literally 'small mouse'; (d) synaesthetic metaphors where words referring to one sensory system are transferred to another one, as from taste to hearing (as in *sweet* sounds). As with most of the principles proposed so far, these four principles are intuitively plausible but perhaps too general and vague to permit rigorous empirical tests of their validity—or even of the conditions of their application.

B. Sense Creation

Suppose that someone tells you that his neighbor has a *vodka face* (Gerrig & Murphy, 1991; cf. also Lehnert, 1986). How can you compute the meaning of such a novel word compound, and what are the constraints (if any) that determine whether the pairing is acceptable or not? Consider another example, the utterance *Send him home with a couple of uniforms,* when the intended meaning is 'send him home with a couple of uniformed officers' (Gerrig, 1989). Clearly, people must use a finite set of interpretation procedures to deal with such innovative contextual expressions. The meanings of these expressions must be on the spot during a given discourse (Clark, 1983; Clark & Gerrig, 1983). How are such meanings created?

We will briefly examine some of the hypotheses proposed to deal with this question. Our aim is to show that sense creation is a general characteristic of language use, one that is not specific to either literal or figurative use. The sense creation comprehension problem includes all those cases where a listener encounters an expression that requires him/her to go beyond the lexical information and so use a much broader set of information sources including contextual and world knowledge, discourse principles, and so on. Complex concepts and contextual expressions are two such cases.

Complex concepts have received considerable attention in cognitive psychology recently (Gerrig, 1989; Gerrig & Murphy, 1991; Medin & Shoben, 1988; Murphy, 1988). A complex concept is one that is built out of more than one primitive concept and is not (yet) lexicalized. As Murphy noted, people often create novel noun–noun phrases in their conversation, and listeners seem to understand them with little or no difficulty. As Gerrig and Murphy (1991) put it, understanding such noun phrases as *dog smile* or *vodka face* is a matter of conceptual combination. Listeners must comprehend the components (head, e.g., *smile,* and modifier, e.g., *dog*) and combine them in a meaningful and plausible way, given the context. Murphy (1988) reviewed the main hypotheses on complex concept elaboration. The extensional model accounts for a complex concept's meaning in terms of the intersection of the sets corresponding to the two concepts involved. The concept specialization model assumes that these expressions have an asymmetric structure such that the second-named concept is the head and first-named modifies it. Concepts are represented as schemata, and the modifying concept acts by filling a slot in the head's concept's schema. So a very large database, namely one's world knowledge, must be accessed and will influence the processing of these expressions. The feature weighting model was proposed especially for adjective–noun concepts (e.g., *red table*) and assumes that people reweight the adjective's primary feature(s) in the noun concept as a function of the particular head noun. Murphy (1988) stressed that none of these models is able to fully account for a large range of expressions. According to Murphy, the empirical evidence available seems to favor some version of the concept specialization view (cf. Gerrig & Murphy, 1991). It has in fact been argued that novel noun–noun concepts can, in principle, have an infinite set of possible interpretations (Clark, 1983). Such sets can be narrowed down only in the context of a situated discourse. A discourse context might work "by highlighting the relevant relation between the modifier and the head noun, so that the listener knows which slot is likely to be specialized" (Murphy, 1988, p. 556). For instance, a phrase such as *apple juice seat* "makes no sense out of context but can be clear if one knows that it referred to the only seat at a table that had a glass of apple juice in front of it" (P. Downing, 1977, quoted in Murphy, 1988, p. 557). So a combination of perceptible situation, ostention, and memory for prior discourse, in addition to the words' meanings and more general world knowledge, is required in order to assign semantic interpretations and specific referential relations to these phrases.

Another problem for any theory of comprehension concerns contextually innovative expressions. These are expressions where a new meaning is assigned to a string of words instead of its conventional one (Clark, 1983; Clark & Gerrig, 1983; Gerrig, 1989). For instance, the conventional meaning of *foot race* is 'a race on foot', but if embedded in the specific context of a visit of Louis X to the town of Marni on the occasion of a snail race that can either be the length of King Louis's foot or the length of Louis's favorite horse, the string *foot race* acquires a different meaning, namely 'a race the length of King Louis's foot' (Gerrig, 1989). Gerrig contrasted two models of meaning creation. According to the first, "sense selection is always attempted first, so that sense creation requires error recovery" (p. 194). This view is analogous to the literal meaning priority hypothesis already proposed with respect to metaphor comprehension: Only when a literal reading fails should a figurative reading be attempted. An alternative hypothesis is that "sense selection and sense creation operate simultaneously, as concurrent processes. . . . The comprehender could construct the correct innovative reading at the same time s/he rejects the incorrect conventional meaning" (p. 195). Experimental evidence supports the concurrent processing strategy and not the error recovery one. Although the time course and the components of the process of meaning creation are far from being fully specified, Gerrig's has shown that people are reliably good at forming new interpretations of conventional expressions. Sense creation and sense selection coexist whenever people are required to use information about idiosyncratic situations (e.g., a race the length of a king's foot) in order to interpret a contextual expression whose meaning must be created and cannot simply be selected or retrieved from the mental lexicon. These results are analogous to those found for metaphor comprehension, where failure of a literal meaning is not a necessary triggering condition for seeking figurative meanings.

More generally, word comprehension may always involve a mixture of sense selection and sense creation. Listeners are quite sophisticated in handling word senses. "They consider the information the addressee shares with the speaker, evaluate the salience and coherence of potential interpretation against this common ground, and select or create interpretation as specific as this common ground allows—all with deceptive ease" (Clark & Gerrig, 1983, p. 607). There seem to be no principled plausible reasons to suppose that such a sophisticated process should differ depending on whether an interpretation requires either a literal or a figurative interpretation of word meanings (cf. Tannen, 1989). Our claim is that the general principles underlying the comprehension—the moment-by-moment process of creating meaning (Clark & Gerrig, 1983)—and the interpretation of a word—the product of that process—are applicable across the literal–figurative distinction.

IV. CONCLUSIONS

In this chapter we have examined the definitions of, and the processes of recognizing and understanding, metaphor. More particularly, we presented two main approaches to metaphor: one that treats metaphors as linguistic entities, and the more recent approach that treats metaphor as involving categorization and conceptual processes. We then speculated about why metaphors are used, both generally and in specific cultural settings such as the Western Apache, where metaphors are used for specific interpersonal functions. Finally, we considered sense extension and sense creation in order to argue for the strong and still controversial claim that the comprehension and interpretive processes people use to understand language in discourse are common to literal and figurative language use. Both types, if we wish to draw the distinction at all, require the application and integration of knowledge from linguistic and nonlinguistic domains.

REFERENCES

Basso, K. H. (1976). 'Wise words' of the Western Apache: Metaphor and semantic theory. In K. H. Basso (Ed.), *Meaning in anthropology* (pp. 93–121). Albuquerque: University of New Mexico Press.

Beck, B. (1978). The metaphor as a mediator between semantic and analogic modes of thought. *Current Anthropology, 19,* 83–94.

Beck, B. (1987). Metaphor, cognition and Artificial Intelligence. In R. S. Haskell (Ed.), *Cognition and symbolic structure: The psychology of metaphoric transformation* (pp. 9–30). Norwood, NJ: Ablex.

Billow, R. M., Rossman, J., Lewis, N., Goldman, D., Kraemer, S., & Ross, P. (1987). Metaphoric communication and miscommunication in schizophrenic and borderline states. In R. S. Haskell (Ed.), *Cognition and symbolic structure: The psychology of metaphoric transformation* (pp. 141–162). Norwood, NJ: Ablex.

Black, M. (1962). *Models and metaphors.* Ithaca, NY: Cornell University Press.

Black, M. (1979). More about metaphors. In A. Ortony (Ed.), *Metaphor and thought* (pp. 19–43). New York: Cambridge University Press.

Bosman, J., & Hagendoorn, L. (1992). Effects of literal and metaphorical persuasive messages. *Metaphor and Symbolic Activity, 6,* 271–292.

Brown, R. (1958). *Words and things.* Glencoe, IL: Free Press.

Cacciari, C. (1990). Effetto di interferenza e prototipicit nella comprensione della metafora. Paper presented at the Congresso Annuale della Divisione Ricera di Base, Bologna, Italy.

Cacciari, C. (1993). The place of idioms in a literal and metaphorical world. In C. Cacciari & P. Tabossi (Eds.), *Idioms: Processing, structure and interpretation* (pp. 27–55). Hillsdale, NJ: Erlbaum.

Cacciari, C., & Glucksberg, S. (1990). Understanding idiomatic expressions: The contribution of word meanings. In G. B. Simpson (Ed.), *Understanding word and sentence* (pp. 217–240). Amsterdam: Elsevier.

Cacciari, C., & Tabossi, P. (1988). The comprehension of idioms. *Journal of Memory and Language, 27,* 668–683.

Cacciari, C., & Tabossi, P. (Eds.). (1993). *Idioms: Processing, structure and interpretation.* Hillsdale, NJ: Erlbaum.

Camac, M. K., & Glucksberg, S. (1984). Metaphors do not use associations between concepts, they are used to create them. *Journal of Psycholinguistic Research, 13,* 443–455.

Caramazza, A., & Grober, E. (1976). Polysemy and the structure of the lexicon. In C. Rameh (Ed.), *Georgetown University round table on language and linguistics* (pp. 181–206). Washington, DC: Georgetown University Press.

Chomsky, N. (1961). Some methodological remarks on generative grammar. *Word, 17,* 219–239.

Clark, H. H. (1973). Space, time, semantics and the child. In T. E. Moore (Ed.), *Cognitive development and the acquisition of language* (pp. 27–64). New York: Academic Press.

Clark, H. H. (1983). Making sense of nonce sense. In G. B. Flores d'Arcais & R. J. Jarvella (Eds.), *The process of language understanding* (pp. 297–331). Chichester: Wiley.

Clark, H. H., & Gerrig, R. J. (1983). Understanding old words with new meanings. *Journal of Verbal Learning and Verbal Behavior, 22,* 591–608.

Clark, H. H., & Haviland, S. E. (1977). Comprehension and the given–new contract. In R. O. Freedle (Ed.), *Discourse production and comprehension* (pp. 1–40). Norwood, NJ: Ablex.

Cohen, T. (1976). Notes on metaphor. *Journal of Aesthetics and Art Criticism, 34*(3), 249–259.

Connine, C. M., & Blasko, D. G. (1993). Effects of familiarity and aptness in the processing of metaphor. *Journal of Experimental Psychology: Learning, Memory and Cognition, 19,* 295–308.

Dascal, M. (1987). Defending literal meaning. *Cognitive Science, 11,* 259–281.

Eco, U. (1984). *Semiotics and the philosophy of language.* Bloomington: Indiana University Press.

Fernandez, J. W. (Ed.). (1991). *Beyond metaphor: The theory of tropes in Anthropology.* Stanford, CA: Stanford University Press.

Gentner, D. (1983). Structure-mapping: A theoretical framework for analogy. *Cognitive Science, 7,* 155–170.

Gentner, D., Falkenhainer, B., & Skorstad, J. (1987). Metaphor: The good, the bad and the ugly. In Y. Wilks *TINLAP-3, Theoretical issues in natural language processing: position papers* (pp. 176–184). Las Cruces, NM: Computing Research Lab, New Mexico State University.

Gerrig, R. J. (1989). The time course of sense creation. *Memory & Cognition, 17,* 194–207.

Gerrig, R. J., & Healy, A. F. (1983). Dual processes in metaphor understanding: Comprehension and appreciation. *Journal of Experimental Psychology: Memory and Cognition, 9,* 667–675.

Gerrig, R. J., & Murphy, G. L. (1991). *Contextual influences on the comprehension of complex concepts.* Presented at the 32nd annual meeting of the Psychonomic Society, San Francisco.

Gibbs, R. (1980). Spilling the beans on understanding and memory for idioms in context; *Memory & Cognition, 8,* 149–156.

Gibbs, W. R. (1984). Literal meaning and psychological theory, *Cognitive Psychology, 8,* 191–219.

Gibbs, W. R. (1987). What does it mean to say that a metaphor has been understood? In R. S. Haskell (Ed.), *Cognition and symbolic structure: The psychology of metaphoric transformation* (pp. 31–48). Norwood, NJ: Ablex.

Gildea, P., & Glucksberg, S. (1983). On understanding metaphor: The role context. *Journal of Verbal Learning and Verbal Behavior, 22,* 577–590.

Glucksberg, S. (1991). Beyond literal meanings: The psychology of allusion. *Psychological Science, 2,* 146–152.

Glucksberg, S. (1993). Idiom meaning and allusional content. In C. Cacciari & P. Tabossi (Eds.), *Idioms: Processing, structure and interpretation* (pp. 3–26). Hillsdale, NJ: Erlbaum.

Glucksberg, S., Gildea, P., & Bookin, M. B. (1982). On understanding non-literal speech: Can people ignore metaphors? *Journal of Verbal Learning and Verbal Behavior, 21,* 85–98.

Glucksberg, S., & Keysar, B. (1990). Understanding metaphorical comparisons: Beyond similarity. *Psychological Review, 97,* 3–18.

Glucksberg, S., & Keysar, B. (1993). How metaphors work. In A. Ortony (Ed.), *Metaphor and thought* (2nd ed.) (pp. 401–424). Cambridge: Cambridge University Press.

Glucksberg, S., Keysar, B., & McGlone, M. S. (1992). Metaphor understanding and accessing conceptual schema: Reply to Gibbs. *Psychological Review, 99,* 578–581.

Grice, H. P. (1975). Logic and conversation. In P. Cole & J. Morgan (Eds.), *Syntax and semantics* (Vol. 3, pp. 41–58). New York: Academic Press.

Harris, R. (1976). Comprehension of metaphors: A test of the two stages processing model. *Bulletin of the Psychonomic Society, 8,* 312–314.

Henle, P. (1958). Metaphor. In P. Henle (Ed.). *Language, thought and culture* (pp. 173–195). Ann Arbor: University of Michigan Press.

Hesse, M. B. (1953). *Models and analogies in science.* Notre Dame, IN: University of Notre Dame Press.

Higgins, E. T., Rholes, W. S., & Jones, C. R. (1977). Category accessibility and impression formation. *Journal of Experimental Social Psychology, 13,* 141–154.

Hobbes, T. (1962). *Leviathan; or, The matter, forme and power of a commonwealth, ecclesiasticall and civil* (M. Oakeshott, Ed.). New York: Collier Books.

Hoffman, R. R. (1983). Recent research on metaphor. *RSSI, 3,* 35–62.

Hoffman, R. R., & Honeck, R. P. (1980). A peacock looks at its legs: Cognitive science and figurative language. In R. P. Honeck & R. R. Hoffman (Eds.), *Cognition and figurative language* (pp. 3–24). Hillsdale, NJ: Erlbaum.

Holland, D., & Quinn, N. (Eds.). (1987). *Cultural models in language and thought.* New York: Cambridge University Press.

Holskov Madsen, K. (1989). Breakthrough by breakdown: Metaphor and structured domains. In H. Klein & K. Kumar (Eds.), *Information system development for human progress in organizations.* Amsterdam: North-Holland.

Honeck, R. P. (1980). Historical notes on figurative language. In R. P. Honeck & R. R. Hoffman (Eds.), *Cognition and figurative language* (pp. 25–46). Hillsdale, NJ: Erlbaum.

Honeck, R. P., & Hoffman, R. R. (Eds.). (1980). *Cognition and figurative language.* Hillsdale, NJ: Erlbaum.

Inhoff, A. W., Lima, S. D., & Carroll, P. J. (1984). Contextual effects on metaphor comprehension in reading. *Memory & Cognition, 2,* 558–567.

Johnson, M. (1981). *Philosophical perspectives on metaphor.* Minneapolis: University of Minnesota Press.

Johnson, M., & Malgady, R. G. (1979). Some cognitive aspects of figurative language: Association and metaphor. *Journal of Psycholinguistic Research, 8,* 249–265.

Katz, J. (1964). Semi-sentences. In J. Fodor & J. Katz (Eds.), *The structure of language: Readings in the philosophy of language* (pp. 400–416). Englewood Cliffs, NJ: Prentice-Hall.

Kennedy, J. M. (1990). Metaphor—Its intellectual basis. *Metaphor and Symbolic Activity, 5,* 115–123.

Keysar, B. (1989). On the functional equivalence of literal and metaphorical interpretation in discourse. *Journal of Memory and Language, 28,* 375–385.

Kintsch, W. (1974). *The representation of meaning in memory.* Hillsdale, NJ: Erlbaum.

Kunda, Z., Miller, D. T., & Claire, T. (1990). Combining social concepts: The role of causal reasoning. *Cognitive Science, 14,* 551–557.

Lakoff, G. (1986). The meanings of literal. *Metaphor and Symbolic Activity, 1,* 291–296.

Lakoff, G. (1987). *Women, fire and dangerous things.* Chicago: University of Chicago Press.

Lakoff, G. (1990). The invariance hypothesis: Is abstract reason based on image-schema? *Cognitive Linguistics, 1,* 39–74.

Lakoff, G., & Johnson, M. (1980). *Metaphors we live by.* Chicago: University of Chicago Press.

Lakoff, G., & Turner, M. (1989). *More than cool reason: A field guide to poetic metaphor.* Chicago: University of Chicago Press.

Lee, C. J. (1990). Some hypotheses concerning the evolution of polysemous words. *Journal of Psycholinguistic Research, 19,* 211–219.

Lehrer, A. (1974). *Semantic fields and lexical structure*. Amsterdam: North-Holland.

Lehrer, A. (1990). Polysemy, conventionality, and the structure of the lexicon. *Cognitive Linguistics, 1*, 207–246.

Lehnert, W. G. (1986). The analysis of nominal compounds. *VS, 44/45*, 155–180.

Lessing, D. (1962). *The golden notebook*. London: Paladin Grafton.

Levinson, S. C. (1978). Commentary on B. Beck. The metaphor as a mediator between semantic and analogic modes of thought. *Current Anthropology, 19*, 92.

Levinson, S. C. (1983). *Pragmatics*. Cambridge: Cambridge University Press.

Loewenberg, I. (1975). Identifying metaphor. *Foundations of Language, 12*, 315–338.

Malgady, R. G., & Johnson, M. G. (1980). Measurement of figurative language: Semantic features model of comprehension and appreciation. In R. P. Honeck & R. R. Hoffman (Eds.), *Cognition and figurative language* (pp. 239–258). Hillsdale, NJ: Erlbaum.

Matthews, R. J. (1971). Concerning a 'linguistic theory' of metaphor. *Foundations of Language, 7*, 413–425.

MacCormac, E. R. (1985). *A cognitive theory of metaphor*. Cambridge, MA: MIT Press.

Marschark, M., Katz, A., & Paivio, A. (1983). Dimensions of metaphor. *Journal of Psycholinguistic Research, 12*, 17–40.

Marks, L. E. (1982). Bright sneezes and dark coughs, loud sunlight and soft moonlight. *Journal of Experimental Psychology: Human Perception and Performance, 8*(2), 177–193.

Marks, L. E., & Bornstein, M. H. (1987). Sensory similarities: Classes, characteristics and cognitive consequences. In R. S. Haskell (Ed.), *Cognition and symbolic structure: The psychology of metaphoric transformation* (pp. 49–65). Norwood, NJ: Ablex.

Medin, D., & Shoben, E. (1988). Context and structures in conceptual combination. *Cognitive Psychology, 20*, 158–190.

Miller, G. A. (1979). Images and models: Similes and metaphor. In A. Ortony (Ed.), *Metaphor and thought* (pp. 202–250). Cambridge: Cambridge University Press.

Murphy, G. (1988). Comprehending complex concepts. *Cognitive Science, 12*, 529–562.

Newport, E. L., & Bellugi, U. (1978). Linguistic expressions of category levels in a visual–gesture language. In E. Rosch & B. B. Lloyd (Eds.), *Cognition and categorization* (pp. 49–71). Hillsdale, NJ: Erlbaum.

Nersessian, N. (in press). How do scientists think? In R. Giere (Ed.), *Cognitive models of science*, (Minnesota Studies in the Philosophy of Science, Vol. 15). Minneapolis: University of Minnesota Press.

Nunberg, G. (1978). *The pragmatics of reference*. Bloomington: Indiana University Linguistic Club.

Nunberg, G. (1979). The non-uniqueness of semantic solutions: Polysemy. *Linguistics and Philosophy, 3*, 143–184.

Ortony, A. (1979). Beyond literal similarity. *Psychological Review, 86*, 161–180.

Ortony, A. (1980). Some psycholinguistic aspects of metaphor. In R. P. Honeck & R. R. Hoffman (Eds.), *Cognition and figurative language* (pp. 69–83). Hillsdale, NJ: Erlbaum.

Ortony, A., & Fainsilber, L. (1987). The role of metaphor in the descriptions of emotions. In Y. Wilks *TINLAP-3, Theoretical issues in natural language processing: positions papers* (pp. 181–184). Las Cruces, NM: Computing Research Lab, New Mexico State University.

Ortony, A., Schallert, D. L., Reynolds, R. E., & Antos, S. J. (1978). Interpreting metaphors and idioms: Some effects of context on comprehension. *Journal of Verbal Learning and Verbal Behavior, 17*, 465–477.

Ortony, A., Vondruska, R. J., Foss, M. A., & Jones, L. E. (1985). Salience, similes and the asymmetry of similarity. *Journal of Memory and Language, 24*, 569–594.

Peirce, C. S. (1932). *Collected papers*. Cambridge, MA: Harvard University Press.

Pollio, H. R., & Smith, M. K. (1980). Metaphoric competence and human problem solving. In R. P. Honeck & R. R. Hoffman (Eds.), *Cognition and figurative language* (pp. 365–392). Hillsdale, NJ: Erlbaum.

Pollio, H. R., Barlow, J. M., Fine, H. J., & Pollio, M. R. (1977). *Psychology and the poetics of growth: Figurative language in psychology*. Hillsdale, NJ: Erlbaum.

Quinn, N. (1991). The cultural basis of metaphor. In J. W. Fernandez (Ed.), *Beyond metaphor. The theory of tropes in anthropology* (pp. 56–93). Stanford, CA: Stanford University Press.

Richards, I. A. (1936). *The philosophy of rhetoric*. Oxford: Oxford University Press.

Rothenberg, A. (1984). Creativity and psychotherapy. *Psychoanalysis and Contemporary Thought, 7*, 233–268.

Rumelhart, D. E. (1979). Some problems with the notion of literal meaning. In A. Ortony (Ed.), *Metaphor and thought* (pp. 78–90). Cambridge: Cambridge University Press.

Searle, J. (1979). Metaphor. In A. Ortony (Ed.), *Metaphor and thought* (pp. 92–123). Cambridge: Cambridge University Press.

Shibles, W. A. (1971). *Metaphor: An annotated bibliography*. Whitewater, WI: Language Press.

Shinjo, M. & Myers, J. (1987). The role of context in metaphor comprehension. *Journal of Memory and Language, 26*, 226–241.

Smith, M. K., Pollio, H. R., & Pitts, M. K. (1981). Metaphor as intellectual history: Conceptual categories underlying figurative usage in American English from 1675–1975. *Linguistics, 19*, 911–935.

Stroop, J. R. (1935). Studies of interference in serial verbal reactions. *Journal of Experimental Psychology, 18*, 643–662.

Sweetser, E. (1991). *From etymology to pragmatics: Metaphorical and cultural aspects of semantic structure*. Cambridge: Cambridge University Press.

Tannen, D. (1989). *Talking voices: Repetition, dialogue and imagery in conversational discourse*. Cambridge: Cambridge University Press.

Tourangeau, R., & Rips, L. (1991). Interpreting and evaluating metaphor. *Journal of Memory and Language, 30*, 452–472.

Tourangeau, R., & Sternberg, R. (1981). Aptness in metaphor. *Cognitive Psychology, 13*, 27–55.

Tourangeau, R., & Sternberg, R. (1982) Understanding and appreciating metaphor. *Cognition, 9*, 27–55.

Tversky, A. (1977). Features of similarity. *Psychological Review, 85*, 327–352.

Ullmann, S. (1962). *Semantics: An introduction to the study of meaning*. Oxford: Basil Blackwell & Mott.

van Noppen, J. P., De Knop, S., & Jogen, R. (1985). *Metaphor: A bibliography of post-1970 publications*. Amsterdam: Benjamins.

van Noppen, J. P., & Hols, E. (1990). *Metaphor II: A classified bibliography of publications 1985 to 1990*. Amsterdam: Benjamins.

Verbrugge, R. R. (1977). Resemblances in language and perception. In R. Shaw & J. Bransford (Eds.), *Perceiving, acting and knowing: Toward an ecological psychology* (pp. 365–389). Hillsdale, NJ: Erlbaum.

Verbrugge, R. R. (1980). Transformations in knowing: A realistic view of metaphor. In R. P. Honeck & R. R. Hoffman (Eds.), *Cognition and figurative language* (pp. 87–125). Hillsdale, NJ: Erlbaum.

Verbrugge, R. R., & McCarrell, N. S. (1977). Metaphoric comprehension: studies in reminding and resembling. *Cognitive Psychology, 9*, 494–533.

CHAPTER 14

DISCOURSE INFERENCE PROCESSES

MURRAY SINGER

I. INTRODUCTION

Consider the following passage:

> Androclus, the slave of a Roman consul stationed in Africa, ran away from his brutal master and after days of weary wandering in the desert, took refuge in a secluded cave. One day to his horror, he found a huge lion at the entrance to the cave. He noticed, however, that the beast had a foot wound and was limping and moaning. Androclus, recovering from his initial fright, plucked up enough courage to examine the lion's paw, from which he prised out a large splinter (Gilbert, 1970).

This passage is drawn from an ordinary folktale and would present few problems to most readers. Yet, even cursory inspection reveals that, at every juncture, the reader is required to make inferences of different degrees of complexity. An inference is needed to determine that *wound* is an injury and not the past tense of wind (Simpson, this volume). Each instance of the pronoun *he* must be resolved to the correct referent (Sanford & Gerrod, this volume). One might infer that Androclus used either his fingers or a pointed instrument to remove the splinter. Syntactic and semantic cues promote causal inferences; Androclus ran away BECAUSE his master was brutal, and he reacted in horror BECAUSE lions are dangerous. There seems almost no limit to the number and variety of inferences that may be derived from this passage. The extent to which the opportunity to draw inferences pervades ordinary messages prompted Schank (1976, p. 168) to call inference the "core of the understanding process."

The present chapter is designed to examine the nature of discourse inference processes. If the examples provided here are any indication, however, such an endeavor would have to consider every element of comprehension. It is necessary, rather, to restrict the range of the present treatment.

The distinction among different levels of discourse comprehension is helpful in this regard. There is evidence that understanding results in representations of the surface form, linguistic structures, and propositional content of a message, and of the situation to which a message refers (Fletcher, this volume; van Dijk & Kintsch, 1983). The test base is an interconnected network of the idea units, or PROPOSITIONS, expressed in a message (Kintsch & van Dijk, 1978). The present chapter focuses predominantly on text base inferences and, to a lesser extent, on inferences involving the situation model. As a result, issues including word recognition and parsing, notwithstanding their inferential nature, lie generally beyond the scope of this chapter.

The chapter is organized as follows: Section II considers several definitions of discourse inference. Section III addresses the problem of the locus of inference. Sections IV and V examine two pivotal inference categories, namely, elaborative and bridging inferences. Section VI provides a more in-depth analysis of causal bridging inferences. Section VII identifies the discourse and reader characteristics that promote and guide inference processing. Certain methodological issues of inference processing research are considered in Section VIII. The conclusions appear in Section IX.

II. DEFINING DISCOURSE INFERENCE

In common terminology, IMPLICATION and INFERENCE refer to activities on the part of the speaker and the understander, respectively. This distinction is generally observed in the formal study of language processes. In addition, ideas which were not included in a message but which are captured by the internal representation of that message are called inferences. More formally, several definitions and criteria of discourse inference have been advanced. The following subsections examine some of them.

A. Definitions of Inference

One definition states that inferences must be realized as text base arguments and propositions that were not explicitly mentioned in a message (Singer & Ferreira, 1983). For example, *Julie soaked the bonfire, It went out,* may be propositionally analyzed as P1 (DOUSE, AGENT:JULIE, PATIENT:BONFIRE), P2 (GO-OUT, PATIENT:BONFIRE) (Kintsch, 1974). However, insofar as the understander may infer that Julie used water, and that soaking the bonfire caused it to go out, the resulting representation might include these implied ideas, as follows: P1 (DOUSE, AGENT:JULIE, PATIENT:BONFIRE, *INSTRUMENT:WATER*), P2 (GO-OUT, PATIENT:BONFIRE), *P3 (CAUSE, P1, P2)*.

A second definition asserts that "an inference represents encoded (nonexplicit) features of the meaning of a text" (McKoon & Ratcliff, 1989b, p. 335; see also Potts, Keenan, & Golding, 1988, pp. 404–405). According to this position, the instrument inference in the preceding bonfire example may consist of a subset of the features of water, such as +LIQUID (Smith, Shoben, & Rips, 1974). This definition also permits the weak representation of such features in the text base representation.

The "proposition" definition may constitute the more severe criterion of discourse inference. However, both definitions are consistent with different features of empirical evidence in this realm and will be invoked in the appropriate contexts.

B. Inference Encoding and Activation

One important inference distinction is that between the encoding of an implied idea and the transient activation of that idea that might accompany comprehension (Corbett & Dosher, 1978). Pertinent to this distinction is the finding that the words of a message activate their close associates, regardless of the relevance of those associates to the current context (Kintsch & Mross, 1985; Swinney, 1979). That is, the appearance of *bug* in a spying context activates the concept ANT. In spite of this, it seems infelicitous at best to suggest that the reader has drawn an inference about an insect. In this regard, it is conceivable that a word such as *nail* in a message may activate its close associate, HAMMER,[1] without HAMMER being permanently encoded in the message representation.

C. Logical and Pragmatic Inferences

The distinction between logical and pragmatic inferences was presented by Harris and Monaco (1978). Logical inferences are based on formal rules and, as a result, are 100% certain. For example, rules of arithmetic guarantee that *Julie had seven oranges and she gave five to Paul* logically implies that Julie wound up with two oranges. Pragmatic inferences, in contrast, are based on people's common knowledge; and, although they are often probable, they are not certain. In this regard, *The burglar was arrested* pragmatically implies that a police officer performed the arrest. That this inference is not obligatory is diagnosed by the acceptability of the conjoined *but not* sentence, *The burglar was arrested **but not** by a police officer* (Brewer, 1975; Harris & Monaco, 1978).

Although the logical–pragmatic distinction helped to impose order on familiar inference categories (e.g., Clark, 1977; Harris & Monaco, 1978; Rieger, 1975; Singer, 1988; Trabasso, 1981), its utility as a processing distinction is somewhat limited (Keenan, 1978). For example, the tempting hypothesis that logical inferences are more likely to accompany comprehension than are pragmatic inferences is untenable. Detecting all the logical implications of a message would result in an overwhelming inference explosion (Charniak, 1975; Rieger, 1975). Conversely, it is likely that certain pragmatic inferences accompany comprehension, due to their high probability and computational simplicity.

III. LOCUS OF INFERENCE: DO INFERENCES ACCOMPANY COMPREHENSION?

A central question concerning discourse inference has been whether certain inferences accompany comprehension, or whether they are drawn only at a later time, when the understander has time to ponder the message. This section briefly reviews the initial exploration of this question and identifies the contemporary inference research strategies that were derived from that investigation.

Many studies during the 1970s inspected people's inferences about semantic roles or CASES (Fillmore, 1968), such as the agent, patient, instrument, and location, and about semantic relations, such as cause and consequence. For

---

[1] The abstract concept or propositions underlying a word or phrase are presented in all capitals.

example, *the bear drank its fill from the lake* implies the patient, WATER; and *Mark jabbed the balloon with the pin* implies the consequence that it broke. In one study, people heard passages that included sentences such as *The man dropped the delicate glass pitcher on the floor* (Johnson, Bransford, & Solomon, 1973). Later, the subjects made recognition judgments about identical test sentences and about test sentences that expressed the implied consequences of the original, such as *The man **broke** the delicate glass pitcher on the floor.* Both the identical and consequence inference test sentences were recognized about 65% of the time. A similar result was detected for implied instrument inferences. Other test items that significantly changed the meaning of the passages were rarely recognized. Johnson et al. concluded that the false alarm responses to inference test sentences could be attributed to inference processes that operate during either comprehension or retrieval.

In an attempt to distinguish these two alternatives, I added a timed measure to the procedure and also instructed different groups either to recognize the test sentences or to judge their truth (Singer, 1979b). The rationale was that if an inference has accompanied comprehension, then judgment time should be similar for inference and identical test items. Like Johnson et al., I detected similar rates of positive responses to identical and inference items. However, judgments about inference items took 0.2–0.3 s longer than those about identical items. This suggested that the inferences in question had not reliably accompanied comprehension.

The same conclusion was suggested by parallel studies using the method of cued recall. Consistent with an inference-during-comprehension view, "implicit" recall cues, such as *scissors,* effectively reminded 5th grade students of antecedent sentences, such as *The athlete cut out an aritcle for his friend* (Paris & Lindauer, 1976). However, Corbett and Dosher (1978) found that *scissors* was an equally good recall cue for each of *The athlete cut out an article with **scissors** for his friend, The athlete cut out an article for his friend,* and *The athlete cut out an article with a **razor blade** for his friend* (emphasis added). Mentioning a razor blade should preclude an inference about scissors. Therefore, the effectiveness of the cue *scissors* for the razor blade sentence indicates that the subjects worked backward from the cue to an action suggested by the cue and hence to the correct sentence. Therefore, implicit cued recall cannot diagnose whether an inference has accompanied comprehension (see Section VIII; also Singer, 1978).

Corbett and Dosher's (1978) data also commented in a more positive manner on the locus of inference. They reported that when the recall of *The athlete cut out an article for his friend* was cued with the agent *athlete,* subjects intruded *scissors* in their recall only 1% of the time! This outcome discourages the conclusion that the highly probable case-filling elements under inspection were reliably inferred during comprehension.

These results indicated that even highly probable and simple pragmatic inferences are by no means guaranteed to accompany comprehension. This is in spite of the fact that the implied concepts may have received transient activation during encoding (Corbett & Dosher, 1978). Two general explanations of these results were offered. First, although the inferences under investigation were plausible elaborations (Corbett & Dosher, 1978) of their messages, they were not necessary: That is, comprehension could proceed without them. Second, drawing even a fraction of the elaborative inferences suggested by a message might readily overwhelm the limited resources available for comprehension (Charniak, 1975; Rieger, 1975; Singer, 1979a).

Other findings have confirmed that there are definite limits on the elaborative inference processing that accompanies comprehension (Dosher & Corbett, 1982; Lucas, Tanenhaus, & Carlson, 1990; McKoon & Ratcliff, 1986; Potts et al., 1988; Singer, 1976, 1980; Singer & Ferreira, 1983). However, there is accumulating evidence that some elaborations are reliably inferred. Evidence bearing on elaborative inferences in the text base and situation model of discourse are considered next.

IV. ELABORATIVE INFERENCES

A. Text Base Elaborations

1. The Role of Relevant Associates

As discussed earlier, the words of discourse automatically activate their close associates. In this regard, when *bug* is encountered in an espionage context, lexical decisions reveal the transient facilitation of both the relevant associate, SPY, and the irrelevant one, ANT (Swinney, 1979). It is possible that activated relevant associates form the building blocks of elaborative inferences (Kintsch, 1988).

Till, Mross, and Kintsch (1988; Kintsch & Mross, 1985) examined the activation of the semantic associates of discourse words and of nonassociates that expressed plausible implications of the discourse. The words of sentences such as (1) were displayed using a rapid serial visual presentation (RSVP; see Haberlandt, this volume), at 333 ms/word.

(1) *The townspeople were amazed to find that all the buildings had collapsed except the mint.*

Test words were presented for lexical decision at different stimulus onset asynchronies[2] (SOAs) relative to the onset of the final word, *mint*. The test words were relevant associates of *mint* (*money*), irrelevant associates (*candy*), and nonassociated but relevant inferences (*earthquake*). Lexical decision time reflected different activation profiles for the three categories. Irrelevant associates were facilitated, but this advantage lasted no more than 1/3 s. The facilitation of relevant associates was measurable for SOAs as small as 0.2 s, increased up to 0.5 s, and had not diminished by 1.5 s. Nonassociated inferences were facilitated as well, but only for SOAs longer than 1.0 s.

The enduring facilitation of relevant associates raises the possibility that they may provide the building blocks of inference. However, the results of Till et al. did not definitively establish the role of relevant associates in the construction of text base inferences. More positive evidence in this regard was provided using a priming technique (McKoon & Ratcliff, 1989b). Their subjects read pairs of passages and answered a series of questions after each pair. During

---

[2] Stimulus onset asychrony is the interval between the presentation of an earlier stimulus and that of a later, test stimulus.

the question phase, relevant associates (e.g., *money*) were facilitated both by prime words from the same text and by the neutral prime, *ready*. In contrast, nonassociated inference words (e.g., *earthquake*) were facilitated only by text primes. McKoon and Ratcliff concluded that associative elaborations are encoded in the text base, whereas their plausible inferences are at most weakly encoded.

A related hypothesis is that elaborative inferences concerning the implied semantic features (Bierwisch, 1970; Clark & Clark, 1977; Smith et al., 1974) of discourse words accompany comprehension. To test this hypothesis, McKoon and Ratcliff (1988) constructed passages such as (2).

(2) *The still life would require great accuracy. The painter searched many days to find the color most suited to use in the painting of the ripe tomato.*

The second sentence of (2) emphasizes the color of tomatoes. After reading a sequence of passages, subjects performed a primed verification task. Some test items were statements that either matched or mismatched the emphasized feature, such as *Tomatoes are red* and *Tomatoes are round*, respectively. When immediately preceded (and so primed) by a statement from its own passage, matching feature test items were answered faster than mismatching ones. McKoon and Ratcliff (1988) concluded that relevant semantic features are encoded in text representation.

2. Category Instantiation

Elaborative inferences that replace or INSTANTIATE general category terms with appropriate members have been studied extensively. For example, in *The red-breasted **bird** pecked the ground*, *bird* may be instantiated as ROBIN. To evaluate category instantiation, investigators have constructed category (*bird*) and specific (*robin*) versions of sentences such as (3).

(3) a. *Julie was convinced that spring was near when she saw a cute red-breasted bird in her yard.*
    b. *Julie was convinced that spring was near when she saw a cute red-breasted robin in her yard.*

Numerous methods have been used. First, investigators have measured the reading time of continuation sentences that anaphorically mention the specific term of (3a) and (3b). Reading time for a continuation such as *The robin pecked the ground* is about the same when it follows (3a) and (3b) (Garrod, O'Brien, Morris, & Rayner, 1990; McKoon & Ratcliff, 1989c, Experiment 2; O'Brien, Shank, Myers, & Rayner, 1988). This suggests that the readers' representation of (3a) and (3b) is similar.

Second, subjects' retrieval of and judgments about implied category members have been studied. Specific terms, such as *robin*, are even better recall cues for (3a) than are category names, such as *bird* (Anderson, Pichert et al., 1976). People need no more time to recognize a picture of a robin as an instance of bird after reading the general (3a) than the specific (3b) (Dubois & Denis, 1988). Likewise, people need less time to name the color (Stroop, 1935; see Section VIII) of implied category member words, such as *robin*, after the general category sentence (3a) than after a control sentence (Whitney, 1986).

Third, priming methods likewise support the instantiation hypothesis. In one study, subjects viewed general category sentences, such as (3a), and control sentences with similar wording (McKoon & Ratcliff, 1989c, Experiment 1). In a speeded recognition task, specific terms such as *robin* were immediately preceded either by words from the same text or by the neutral word *ready*. Both these primes facilitated the recognition of *robin* in the experimental condition relative to the control condition. McKoon and Ratcliff concluded that *bird* had been instantiated as ROBIN.

These converging results provide strong support for the instantiation hypothesis. Several other generalizations may be offered. First, the general category sentences that suggest typical category members, such as ROBIN, do not facilitate responses to atypical alternatives, such as TURKEY (Dubois & Denis, 1988; McKoon & Ratcliff, 1989c). Second, however, the atypical bird, TURKEY, may be instantiated by other sentences, such as *Julie was convinced that Thanksgiving was near when she saw a plump bird at the grocery* (Anderson, Pichert et al., 1976; Whitney, 1986). Third, those instantiation results that consisted of similar scores in the general and specific conditions may have appeared to rest on the null hypothesis. In most studies, however, the instantiation patterns were, in fact, part of significant interaction results that supported instantiation (e.g., Dubois & Denis, 1988; Garrod et al., 1990).

In conclusion, one explanation of these effects states that instantiation may produce the same representation as the one that results when the message directly mentions the category member (McKoon & Ratcliff, 1989c). In this regard, category member implication sometimes yields the same experimental result as explicitly stating it (Whitney, 1986) or instructing the subject to imagine the member (Dubois & Denis, 1988). A subtly different explanation is that discourse context may filter the features of a category in such a way that the representation of a category, such as *fruit*, is indistinguishable from that of its member, *orange* (Garrod et al., 1990; McKoon & Ratcliff, 1989c). This explanation is consistent with the observations that concept features, such as the color of tomatoes, may be integrated with a text representation (McKoon & Ratcliff, 1988).

B. Elaborative Inferences in Higher Level Representations

The construction of all discourse situation models, whether spatial (Perrig & Kintsch, 1985), conversational (Grice, 1975), or narrative (Malt, 1985; Morrow, Greenspan, & Bower, 1987), may be argued to constitute elaborative inference processing. This section considers a few instances of elaborative inferences about specific ideas in higher order discourse representations.

First, researchers have scrutinized the status of ideas posited to appear in the text macrostructure. The macrostructure is a hierarchical network of propositions that captures the main idea, or theme, of a discourse (Kintsch & van Dijk, 1978). The macropropositions are derived from the text microstructure by rules such as generalization and construction. For example, by the rule of construction, *Pete positioned the thumbtack on the chair* yields the macroproposition, PETE PLAYED A PRANK.

The inference, discussed earlier, that the collapse of the town's buildings refers to an earthquake is a macroconstruction. Lexical decisions about such inferences were facilitated at an SOA of 1 s relative to the onset of the last word of the implying sentence (Till et al., 1988). However, Till et al. acknowledged that this lengthy delay may have encouraged the subjects to adopt atypical inference strategies.

In another study, a priming technique was used to more clearly evaluate whether macroelaborations accompany comprehension (Guindon & Kintsch, 1984). Passages which permitted generalizations were constructed: for example, a passage about preparing for the decathlon concerned, but did not mention, the development of the body. In a primed recognition task, some test items, such as *body,* were related to the macroproposition. Contrasting distractor words were related to concepts that appeared only in micropropositions. For example, whereas the passage mentioned the development of the shoulders, hands, and chest, the word *feet* appeared as a distractor test item. The subjects had a difficult time rejecting the macroword test items: both correct rejection time and false alarms were higher for macrowords than microwords (Guindon & Kintsch, 1984, Experiment 2). This suggests that the macrowords had been encoded in the text representation. This pattern was observed whether or not the subjects wrote a summary statement before the recognition test. This latter outcome suggests that, unlike Till et al.'s (1988) result, this one cannot be attributed to task demands.

Elaborative inferences about narrative characters' goals have also been scrutinized. These inferences pertain to the understander's situation model of the causal interrelations among text ideas. Long, Golding, and Graesser (1992) proposed that, insofar as readers strive to explain discourse events (Magliano & Graesser, 1991; Schank, 1986; Trabasso, van den Broek, & Suh, 1989; van Dijk & Kintsch, 1983), they should draw elaborative inferences about characters' superordinate goals. For example, upon reading that a dragon kidnaps the princesses, one might infer that the dragon wants to ransom the daughters. In contrast, the explanation principle identifies no need to infer a goal subordinate to the kidnapping, such as that the dragon grabbed the daughters. Consistent with this hypothesis, Long et al. found that lexical decisions and naming responses were faster for superordinate than subordinate goal words that were derived from an on-line norming procedure.

It is noted that Long et al. (1992) did not apply the stricter criterion of comparing the status of implied superordinate goals with corresponding explicit text ideas. Their results are interpreted as providing preliminary support for their hypothesis.

V. Bridging Inferences

Recent research has thus shown that certain elaborative inferences accompany comprehension. However, previous findings of limited elaborative processing (e.g., Corbett & Dosher, 1978; Singer, 1979a, 1979b) lay the groundwork for two central, and interwoven, inference research strategies. The first strategy was to scrutinize bridging inferences (Clark, 1977; Haviland & Clark, 1974), which provide links among discourse ideas. Unlike elaborative inferences, bridging inferences are necessary for comprehension, because discourse coherence is disrupted if they are not drawn. For example, a complete understanding of *The tooth was pulled painlessly, The dentist used a new method* requires the bridging inference that the tooth was pulled by the dentist. A contrasting sequence, such as *The tooth was pulled painlessly, The patient liked the new method* certainly permits an elaborative inference about a dentist. However, coherence is not disrupted if the reader fails to draw this inference.

Bridging and elaborative inferences have also been called BACKWARD and FORWARD inferences, respectively: Bridging inferences require that the understander work backward from the current proposition to prior message ideas, whereas elaborative inferences are forward extrapolations (Clark, 1977; Just & Carpenter, 1978; Singer, 1980; Thorndyke, 1976).

The second strategy has been to identify those discourse and understander factors that promote and guide inference processes. The inference factor approach is examined in Section VII.

A. Coherence and Bridging

To comprehend a message, the understander must identify the relation between the current propositions and what has preceded. This has the crucial impact of preserving text coherence. The detection of text relations is addressed by the given–new strategy (Clark & Haviland, 1977). According to this analysis, the understander must first distinguish the given and new information conveyed by the current sentence. Second, a memory referent must be found for the given information. Third, the new sentence information may be integrated with the referent.

The given information of a sentence may or may not be coreferential with a word from earlier in the message. Furthermore, coreference may be either direct or indirect (Clark, 1977). In sequence (4a), for example, *beer* in the second sentence is coreferential with the first sentence. In sequences (4b)–(4d), in contrast, coreference of *beer* is established using a synonym, a category name, and a pronoun, respectively.

(4) a. *We got the beer out of the car. The beer was warm.*
   b. *We got the brew out of the car. The beer was warm.*
   c. *We got the beverage out of the car. The beer was warm.*
   d. *We got the beer out of the car. It was warm.*

In (4a)–(4d), the understander must resolve the anaphoric noun phrase of the second sentence, *the beer*. Anaphoric resolution is guided by a variety of complex factors (Garrod & Sanford, this volume). Furthermore, if enough text intervenes between an anaphoric phrase and its referent, the referent must be reinstated to working memory before reference may be detected (Haviland & Clark, 1974; Kintsch & van Dijk, 1978; Lesgold, Roth, & Curtis, 1979).

In instances such as (5), in contrast, the antecedent sentence includes no referent for the given element, *beer*.

(5) *We got the picnic supplies out of the car. The beer was warm.*

To understand (5), the reader must compute an idea that bridges the two sentences, such as that the picnic supplies included beer. Bridging is required when anaphoric resolution has failed (Haviland & Clark, 1974).

Some bridges require only the detection of a relation among discourse ideas. For example, to properly understand *The cat leapt up on the kitchen table, Fred picked up the cat and put it outside*, one must infer that the first event caused the second (Black & Bern, 1981). Other bridges entail the addition of new predicates or arguments to the text base (Duffy, Shinjo, & Myers, 1990; Singer & Ferreira, 1983; van den Broek, 1990a). For example, bridging the sentences of *The spy quickly threw his report in the fire, The ashes floated up the chimney,* requires the inference of a new proposition, such as THE REPORT BURNED TO ASHES.

B. Comparing Bridging and Elaborative Inferences

A central feature of the distinction between bridging and elaborative inferences is that only the former are necessary for coherence. This suggests that bridging inferences should be more likely to occur on line than corresponding elaborative inferences. To test this hypothesis, I examined inferences about concepts that filled the agent, patient, and instrument cases. Set (6) illustrates the agent materials.

(6) a. *The dentist pulled the tooth painlessly. The patient liked the new method.* (explicit)
    b. *The tooth was pulled painlessly. The dentist used a new method.* (bridging inference)
    c. *The tooth was pulled painlessly. The patient liked the new method.* (elaborative inference)

Sequence (6a) mentioned the dentist explicitly. In sequence (6b), coherence depends on the bridging inference that the dentist pulled the tooth. Sequence (6c) permits an elaborative inference about a dentist, but coherence does not depend on this inference. In the experiment, each sequence was followed by the test sentence, *A dentist pulled the tooth.* The results were consistent for agents, patients, and instruments: Correct verification times were approximately equal in the explicit and bridging conditions, but about 0.25 s slower in the elaborative conditions. These results supported the prediction that only bridging inferences reliably accompanied comprehension. The bridging sequence, (6b), had the confounding advantage of mentioning the dentist, but this alone cannot account for the virtually identical explicit and bridging verification times.

Parallel results have been obtained for inferences about the probable consequences of story events (Potts et al., 1988; Singer & Ferreira, 1983). This suggests that the coherence requirements underlying bridging inferences generalize across a considerable range of semantic relations (see also Hayes-Roth & Thorndyke, 1979; Just & Carpenter, 1978; Mandler & Murachver, 1985). This finding is inconsistent with the reasonable working hypothesis that certain semantic relations, such as the agent case and the causes and consequences of actions, might be so privileged as to result in reliable elaborative inferences when a probable element is available.

VI. CAUSAL BRIDGING INFERENCES

Bridging inferences that link text ideas by the relation of cause have been subjected to intense examination. This research has been spurred by the consensus that causal relations are fundamental to narratives, expository text, and many other types of discourse. Therefore, it is worthwhile to make causal bridges the focus of an inference "case study" (cf. McKoon & Ratcliff, 1990).

The study of causal bridging inferences encompasses both physical causes and motivational causes. In the latter regard, the perceived relationship between the sentences of *Laurie left early for the birthday party, She spent an hour shopping at the mall* is based on the reader's inference that Laurie was motivated to buy a birthday present. In general terms, causes, goals, and motives all enable particular outcome events and reactions (Schank & Abelson, 1977).

A. Representing Causal Networks

The study of causal bridging inferences is best understood against the backdrop of models of the representation and processing of discourse causal relations. A detailed treatment of the causal structure of narratives, in the form of a general transition network model, is shown in Figure 1 (Trabasso & van den Broek, 1985; Trabasso et al., 1989; van den Broek, 1990b). The model organizes the narrative categories of Setting, Event, Goal, Attempt, Outcome, and Reaction (Mandler & Johnson, 1977; Thorndyke, 1977) in terms of the relations of physical, motivational, and psychological causes, and enablements (Phi, M, Psi, and E, respectively). The arrows of Figure 1 indicate the causal means by which one category can enable another. For example, an Attempt can physically cause an Outcome, and a Goal can motivate another goal.

Potential causes of an outcome are evaluated using several criteria (Trabasso et al., 1989; van den Broek, 1990a). Consider the sequence, *Tom didn't see the banana peel, He fell down.* Not seeing the peel is a likely cause of Tom falling down if it is sufficient and especially "necessary in the circumstances" (Trabasso et al., 1989) for that outcome. Necessity in the circumstances means that if Tom had not failed to see the peel, he would not have fallen.

In addition, causes must be TEMPORALLY PRIOR to their outcomes and OPERATIVE at the time of the outcome. Needing to get a birthday present can motivate Laurie's shopping only if she needed it before the shopping trip, and if she had not acquired one before going shopping.

The causal network analysis is supported by the finding that adults' and childrens' recall and importance ratings of narrative ideas are higher (a) if they appear on the main causal chain of the representation rather than in a dead end (Omanson, 1982; Trabasso, Secco, & van den Broek, 1984; Trabasso &

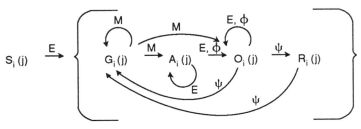

FIG. 1 General transition network model of discourse causal relations. [Source: Trabasso et al. (1989), Figure 1. Copyright 1989 by Ablex Publishing Corporation. Adapted by permission.]

Sperry, 1985); and (b) if they bear many connections to other ideas in the network (Graesser, Robertson, Lovelace, & Swinehart, 1980; Omanson, 1982; Trabasso et al., 1984; Trabasso & Sperry, 1985).

B. Causal Inference Processes

The structural model is complemented by processing analyses of the memory search and working memory "bookkeeping" of discourse comprehension. O'Brien (1987) proposed that if readers construct causal networks that include some distal connections, then an anaphoric phrase may reinstate an early discourse antecedent without reinstating intervening distractor antecedents. Consistent with this analysis, the emphasized anaphoric phrase of *Cathy's friend asked **what she had bought at the bakery*** reinstated its early antecedent, *pie*, without reinstating the recent text distractor antecedent, *doll* (which Cathy had later bought for her daughter) (O'Brien, 1987, Experiments 3 and 4; see also Corbett, 1984; O'Brien, Plewes, & Albrecht, 1990; van den Broek & Lorch, 1993). This analysis addresses the nature of search in a causal network. It may carry fruitful implications for how understanders search for the cause of a detected narrative outcome.

The understander's working memory may be managed in a fashion that promotes the causal analysis of text (Bloom, Fletcher, van den Broek, Reitz, & Shapiro, 1990; Fletcher & Bloom, 1988; Fletcher, Hummel, & Marsolek, 1990). According to Fletcher's CURRENT STATE STRATEGY, the most recent clause with causal antecedents but no consequences will be retained for further processing. Consider sequence (7).

(7) a. *Don was about to start all night duty at the hospital.*
    b. *He (checked/had checked) the list of patients.*

In the *checked* version of (7b), the circumstances of (7a) ENABLE Don to check the patient list (Schank & Abelson, 1977). Therefore, (7a) is said to have consequences. In the *had checked* version, in contrast, (7a) has no consequences, because checking the patient list has preceded the state of (7a). According to the current state strategy, the ideas of (7a) will be retained for further processing only for the *had checked* version.

The current state strategy raises the likelihood that causally related ideas will co-occur in working memory, a condition necessary for detecting their interrelation. At the same time, it states that, due to the limits of working memory capacity, understanders will detect only a subset of discourse causal relations. Evidence based on measures of word and sentence reading time, text recall, and time to recognize the verb of the crucial clause has supported this analysis (Bloom et al., 1990; Fletcher & Bloom, 1988; Fletcher et al., 1990).

C. Empirical Studies of Causal Bridging

Evidence that causal bridging inferences are drawn during comprehension converges from many sources. The following account examines relevant evidence derived from a variety of on-line and memory measures.

1. Reading Time

Degree of causal relatedness has been shown to affect bridging processes (Bloom et al., 1990; Keenan, Baillet, & Brown, 1984; Myers, Shinjo, & Duffy, 1987; Singer, Halldorson, Lear, & Andrusiak, 1992). In the Keenan and the Myers studies, norms were first collected to determine the relatedness between causes and their outcomes. For example (8), (9), and (10) illustrate sequences of high, moderate, and low relatedness, respectively (Myers et al., 1987).

(8) a. *Tony's friend suddenly pushed him into a pond.*
    b. *He walked home, soaking wet, to change his clothes.*
(9) a. *Tony met his friend near a pond in the park.*
    b. *He walked home, soaking wet, to change his clothes.*
(10) a. *Tony sat under a tree reading a good book.*
    b. *He walked home, soaking wet, to change his clothes.*

Other subjects then read these sequences. Reading time for the (b) outcomes increased systematically with decreasing causal relatedness. The reading time profile is interpreted to reflect the ease of drawing a bridging inference linking a text outcome to its cause.

2. Inference Judgment Time

The design of Singer [1980; see the *dentist* example, (6) above] was applied to bridging and elaborative inferences about the probable consequences of story actions (Singer & Ferreira, 1983). In the bridging inference condition, for example, sequences such as (11) were embedded in brief stories.

(11) *The spy quickly threw his report in the fire. The ashes floated up the chimney.*

After reading a story, the subjects then answered questions including ones that probed the bridging inferences, such as *Did the spy burn a report?* Answer time for the bridging questions was over 200 ms faster than for comparable elaborative inference questions, a difference similar in magnitude to that between the elaborative condition and the explicit condition. This outcome is consistent with the hypothesis that the bridging inferences linking outcome to cause accompanied comprehension.

To test the same hypothesis, Potts et al. (1988) presented their subjects with bridging sequences such as (11), and with comparable elaborative inference and explicit sequences. Across experimental conditions, Potts et al. controlled the appearance in the sequences of words semantically associated with the target inference. After reading a sequence, the subject viewed and had to name aloud a word representing the inference, such as *burn*. Naming time was similar in the explicit and bridging conditions, and slower in the elaborative condition (Potts et al., 1988, Experiments 3 and 4). It was concluded that the bridging inferences had accompanied comprehension. The naming task has been argued to preclude the possibility of evaluating the plausibility of the inference at retrieval time (Seidenberg, Waters, Sanders, & Langer, 1984).

3. Cued Recall

It was seen earlier that cued recall cannot definitively diagnose on-line inferences (Corbett & Dosher, 1978; Singer, 1978). With reference to causal bridging inferences, however, data from cued recall tasks converges with that yielded by other measures.

In one study, Black and Bern (1981) compared the bridging of the sentences in the causal (*bumping*) and temporal (*seeing*) versions of (12).

(12) a. *The boy lowered the flames and walked over to the refrigerator, bumping/seeing a bowl he had left on the table.*
   b. *Suddenly, it fell off the edge and broke.*

Memory tests revealed that the (a) and (b) versions of (12) mutually cued the recall of one another more effectively in the causal condition than the temporal condition. Likewise, the subjects exhibited superior free recall of causal sentences, both singly and in pairs. These results were interpreted to reveal the encoding of implied causal connections.

In the study of the impact of degree of causal relatedness on bridging processes, cued recall has complemented the reading time measure, discussed earlier. Sequence (13), considered earlier, illustrates moderate causal relatedness.

(13) a. *Tony met his friend near a pond in the park.*
   b. *He walked home, soaking wet, to change his clothes.*

In cued recall, the reader of (13) might later be asked how Tony got wet. This task has revealed a nonlinear relationship: cued recall performance is systematically higher for moderate relatedness than for high or low levels (Duffy et al., 1990; Keenan et al., 1984; Myers et al., 1987).

The latter nonlinear relationship would result if sentence pairs of moderate relatedness either are more likely to be bridged than high and low pairs, or are bridged by connections of special quality (Duffy et al., 1990). To distinguish these alternatives, Duffy et al. (1990) asked subjects either simply to read sentence pairs of varying causal relatedness, or to read the pairs and to write an elaboration connecting them. If the nonlinear relationship were due to differential likelihoods of bridging sentence pairs of different relatedness, then the elaboration task ought to eradicate the effect. That is exactly what the data revealed: The inverted-U shaped relation between cued recall and causal relatedness appeared only in the read-only condition. This suggests that sequences of high and low relatedness may be only "minimally" linked with reference to the relations of cause and time, respectively (Myers et al., 1987).

Two related observations about the minimal-linking conclusion are offered. The link between even highly related sentence pairs frequently depends on other mediating ideas or knowledge. For example, *Tony's friend suddenly pushed him into a pond, He walked home, soaking wet, to change his clothes* is mediated by the knowledge that ponds contain water and water is wet (Singer, Halldorson et al., 1992). Conversely, people are adept at rationalizing the connection between even remotely related ideas (Black & Bern, 1981; Bransford & Johnson, 1973). The nature of the minimal linking of discourse ideas will require further examination.

4. Validating Causal Bridges

Inference theorists agree that pragmatic bridging inferences are based on the understander's knowledge. I have tested this assumption in the framework of a VALIDATION MODEL of bridging inference. The analysis is as follows: Complete understanding of a sequence such as *Dorothy poured the bucket of water on the bonfire, The fire went out* requires the recognition that the first event caused the second. According to the validation model, the reader must know something that, when coupled with the fact that water was poured on the fire, accounts for it going out. It is as though the reader constructs a mental syllogism with a missing premise. For the present case, the syllogism is easily solved with a fact such as WATER EXTINGUISHES FIRE. The model asserts that understanding the bonfire sequence requires access to this knowledge.

The need to validate causal bridging inferences is exposed by the contrasting sequence, *Dorothy poured the bucket of water on the bonfire, The fire grew hotter*. This seems less agreeable than the former sequence, but we could notice this only with reference to pertinent knowledge.

In tests of the validation model, readers viewed either the causal sequence, (14a), or the control temporal sequence, (14b).

(14) a. *Dorothy poured the bucket of water on the fire. The fire went out.*
(causal)
b. *Dorothy placed the bucket of water by the fire. The fire went out.*
(temporal)

After either sequence, the subject answered question (14c), which probes the knowledge hypothesized to validate the causal bridge.

(14) c. *Does water extinguish fire?*

Consistent with the analysis, answer time for (14c) was faster in the causal than the temporal condition (Singer, Halldorson et al., 1992; Singer, Revlin, & Halldorson, 1990). This result obtains when the sequences are embedded in brief stories as well as for isolated sequences; and even when cause and outcome are reversed in their order of presentation, such as *The bonfire went out, Dorothy poured the bucket of water on it.* The effect is due neither to extra priming of the question by the words of the causal version of the antecedent, nor to extra compatibility of the question with the causal sequence: When the outcome, *The fire went out*, is deleted from the sequence, the effect disappears.

D. Bridging Near and Distal Causes

Evidence that causal bridging inferences accompany comprehension thus converges from numerous measures of inference processing. Several subtly different views of causal bridging have been derived from these findings. These views may be explained with reference to three hypotheses, ranging from the most to the least restrictive.

Hypothesis 1. Readers infer causal connections only between ideas that are nearby in a discourse.

Hypothesis 2. Readers infer causal connections based predominantly on nearby discourse ideas. However, in conditions of local causal incoherence, current ideas are bridged to others further back in the text. For example, the sequence *Carl took some butter out of the refrigerator, He went outside and picked some raspberries* lacks local causal coherence, because the first event does not cause the second. In this circumstance, the reader might link the second event to Carl's previously mentioned plan of baking a pie. This is achieved primarily by reinstating antecedent causes and motives to working memory.

Hypothesis 3. Readers infer causal connections based on nearby discourse ideas. Even in conditions of local coherence, however, certain distal causal connections are made. This can be achieved either by reinstating an antecedent cause to working memory, or by maintaining the cause in working memory until an outcome is detected.

Hypothesis 1 is ostensibly captured by the MINIMAL INFERENCE position (McKoon & Ratcliff, 1988). According to this view, causal bridging inferences serve primarily to link ideas close to one another in the text. The rationale of the minimal inference hypothesis is that inference processing is limited by a combination of the understander's resource limitations and passive nature (Den Uyl & van Oostendorp, 1980; McKoon & Ratcliff, 1988; van Dijk & Kintsch, 1983).

Upon closer examination, however, minimal inference seems more closely related to Hypothesis 2 than to Hypothesis 1. McKoon and Ratcliff (1988) proposed that readers may infer causal connections among nonadjacent ideas under the joint condition that (a) the text is locally causally incoherent, and (b) the reader adopts a special strategy. Indeed, reader strategies may promote global processing: for example, reading with the intention of summarizing enhances macroprocessing (Cirilo, 1981; Schmalhofer & Glavanov, 1986). However, it is debatable whether the construction of causal networks is a special strategy. In this regard, it seems almost as difficult to overlook the causal relationship between the sentences of *Tom stepped on the banana peel, He fell down* as to overlook the fact that *lamp* is an English word. In fact, it is failure to detect causal connections that probably requires special reading strategies, such as proofreading (Mayer & Cook, 1981). If the construction of causal networks is not a special comprehension strategy, minimal inference may be interpreted as an instantiation of Hypothesis 2.

The current state strategy of working memory regulation (Fletcher & Bloom, 1988) straddles the boundaries between Hypothesis 2 and Hypothesis 3. Consistent with Hypothesis 2, the current state strategy asserts that when no causal antecedent for the present clause is available, the reader reinstates one from long-term memory. The reinstated idea may be linked to the current text, resulting in a distal connection.

Other features of the current state strategy permit distal causal bridging even in the condition of local coherence. First, the fundamental rule of current state strategy states that the last causal chain idea with no discourse consequences will be maintained indefinitely in working memory. When this idea is eventually linked with a causal consequence, a distal connection will be discovered. For example, (15b) is not a consequence of (15a).

(15) a. *As Kate began to make a chocolate cake, her sister told her that the oven was broken.*
    b. *Her sister had tried to use the oven earlier but discovered that it would not heat up.*
    c. *From the parlor, Kate's mother heard voices in the kitchen.*

Therefore, (15a) is retained in working memory and causally linked to the nonadjacent (15c) (Fletcher et al., 1990). This is despite the fact that (15a) and (15b) are referentially coherent.

Likewise, the current state strategy holds that locally coherent clauses that satisfy goals purged from working memory prompt the reinstatement of those goals (Bloom et al., 1990). The goals and their outcomes may be distally bridged.

Explicitly congruent with Hypothesis 3 is the proposal that understanders seek explanations for discourse events and actions (Long et al., 1992; Magliano & Graesser, 1991; Schank, 1986; Trabasso et al., 1989; van den Broek & Lorch, 1993; van Dijk & Kintsch, 1983). The explanation principle might promote distal causal bridging under conditions of local coherence (Hypothesis 3) in one of two ways: First, current goals might be maintained in working memory until they are satisfied (Trabasso & Suh, 1993). Alternatively, if not maintained, current goals might be reinstated when the reader encounters attempts or outcomes related to the goal (Bloom et al., 1990; van den Broek & Lorch, 1993).

In summary, there is extensive evidence that causal bridging inferences accompany comprehension. Three views of causal bridging processing state that distal causal connections are generally not detected (Hypothesis 1), are detected only in conditions of local incoherence (Hypothesis 2), or are sometimes detected even in conditions of local coherence (Hypothesis 3). The following evidence, stemming from numerous inference measures, bears on these alternatives.

1. Reading Time

According to the current state strategy, even in the condition of local coherence, clauses that satisfy a purged goal prompt the reinstatment of that goal. In one story, for example, Danny, who was described as wanting a red bike, eventually earns enough money (Bloom et al., 1990). By the time the story states *He took his hard-earned money to the shop and bought the bike,* the goal of buying the bicycle had not been mentioned for many sentences. Bloom et al. proposed that the goal must therefore be reinstated from long-term memory. Consistent with this proposal, Bloom et al. found that reading time for such clauses was a systematic function of the distance between the clause and its goal in the causal network: In particular, the greater the distance, the longer the reading time.

2. Inference Judgment Time

If a goal no longer resident in working memory is reinstated by pertinent attempts and outcomes, judgment time measures ought to reveal goal facilitation after the reinstating idea. To test this hypothesis, researchers have created stories in which (a) a goal is established, (b) a goal attempt either succeeds or fails, and (c) a further story action ought to reinstate the goal, but only if it has not already been satisfied (Dopkins, Klin, & Myers, 1993; Trabasso & Suh, 1993). The stories are referentially coherent at the point of the reinstating story action. Set (16) shows the crucial sentences from a story of Trabasso and Suh.

(16) a. *Betty really wanted to give her mother a present.*
    b. *Betty bought her mother a purse.* (successful attempt)
    b′. *Betty found that everything was too expensive.* (failed attempt)
    c. *Betty decided to knit a sweater.*

In one study, recognition judgments about goal-related words, such as *present,* were made after the reinstating action, (16c) (Dopkins et al., 1993). Judgment time was faster when the prior goal attempt had failed than when it had succeeded. Likewise, the time needed to answer a goal question, such as *Did Betty want to give her mother a present?*, was faster in the failure than the success condition (Trabasso & Suh, 1993). This question was also facilitated by a later story action, such as *Betty folded the sweater carefully.*

A control condition of Dopkins et al. (1993), however, offered a noteworthy caveat. They reported that, if a reinstating action is coreferential with a distal story statement, reinstatement of the unsatisfied goal is averted. This is the only report to date of referential coherence superseding causal bridging.

3. Priming

If a story statement is integrated with its distal goals, then the goal should prime the statement in a subsequent test (McKoon & Ratcliff, 1980a, 1988). To test this hypothesis, van den Broek and Lorch (1993) constructed causally coherent stories in which outcomes satisfied goals that had been stated eight or more sentences earlier. In a subsequent test, the subject read a priming statement and then verified the crucial outcomes. Outcome verification was faster when it was primed by the distal goal than by the story title. Equally important, an action that immediately followed the goal, and so appeared on the causal chain between the goal and the outcome, did not prime the outcome (van den Broek & Lorch, 1993, Experiment 3).

4. Validating Distal Bridging Inferences

As discussed earlier, we have tested the hypothesis that causal bridging inferences must be validated with reference to world knowledge (Singer, Halldorson et al., 1992). In one experiment, this proposal was evaluated for inferences that bridge distal story statements. The subjects viewed motive or control sequences, illustrated by the (a) and (a′) versions of set (17) (Singer, 1993).

(17) a. *Laurie left early for the birthday party.* (motive)
      a′. *Laurie left the birthday party early.* (control)
      b. *She headed north on the freeway.*
      c. *She exited at Antelope Drive.*
      d. *She spent an hour shopping at the mall.*
      e. *Do people bring presents to birthday parties?*

Sentences (17b) and (17c) intervened between the motive, (17a) or (17a′), and attempt (17d). Therefore, the motive should have been purged from working memory by the time (17d) was encountered. The passage was causally coherent.

After reading, the subjects answered question (17e), posited to probe the knowledge needed to bridge (17a) and (17d). Answer time was faster in the motive than the control condition. This outcome suggests that narrative attempts are bridged to moderately distant goals.

5. Conclusions

There is general agreement that causal bridging inferences accompany comprehension, and that these bridges may link distal discourse ideas. However, a focus of controversy is whether distal causal connections are discovered in conditions of local coherence. The data examined here, stemming from numerous methods, converge on the conclusion that discovering distal causal connections does not require local incoherence.

Several other points about these studies are worth noting. First, it was mentioned earlier that bridging an outcome to a distal goal can result either from the maintenance of the goal in working memory throughout processing (Trabasso & Suh, 1993), or by reinstating the goal to working memory when the outcome is encountered. In a test of these alternatives, it was found that there is no judgment time advantage for the distal goal immediately prior to the appearance of its outcome (Dopkins et al., 1993). This result favors the reinstatement view, but additional tests of this hypothesis would be useful.

Second, a CONTEXT CHECKING (Forster, 1981; McKoon & Ratcliff, 1986) process might be argued to account for some of these results. According to this analysis, an understander may evaluate a test item by assessing its compatibility with the antecedent message, rather than by retrieving the test proposition from memory. In this event, relative advantages of inference test items may simply reflect greater compatibility with the antecedent, rather than diagnose the previous, on-line computation of an inference. Reconsider example (17). Suppose that the question *Do people bring presents to birthday parties?* is more compatible with the motive sequence, *Laurie left **early for the birthday party**, She spent an hour shopping at the mall,* than with the control sequence, *Laurie left **the birthday party early**, She spent an hour shopping at the mall.* Then, context checking might account for faster motive than control answer times.

However, inference investigators have refuted context checking in several ways. First, some have shown that their test items were not systematically more compatible with their inference antecedents than their control antecedents (Dopkins et al., 1993; van den Broek & Lorch, 1993; see also McKoon & Ratcliff, 1989a). Second, priming procedures, which diagnose encoded representations, have been used to provide converging evidence of on-line inference processing (Singer & Halldorson, 1993).

VII. FACTORS THAT AFFECT INFERENCE PROCESSES

As discussed earlier, findings of severe constraints on elaborative inference processing initiated two research strategies. The focus on bridging inferences was considered in the last section. This section examines some of the understander and discourse factors that constrain and guide inference processing, an approach that has been explicitly advocated in the literature (Goetz, 1979; Singer, 1988; Whitney & Waring, 1991).[3]

In the study of inference factors, the inference category under inspection and the on-line status of the inferences have not been addressed as rigorously as in other investigations. Where possible, these issues are considered here.

---

[3] Some content of Section VII is based on Singer (1988): Copyright 1988 by Academic Press, Inc.; adapted by permission; and Singer (1990): Copyright 1990 by Lawrence Erlbaum Associates, Inc.; adapted by permission.

A. Discourse Factors of Inference Processing

Researchers have examined the impact of coherence requirements, theme status, distance between related ideas, text affordances, and interestingness on inference processing. Coherence requirements were scrutinized in the section on bridging inferences. This section considers the other factors.

1. Theme and Inference

The INFERENCE THEME HYPOTHESIS states that inference processing focuses on the thematic ideas of a discourse. The rationale is that, in view of cognitive resource limitations, focusing on thematic ideas yields those inferences most useful to the understander.

To evaluate the inference theme hypothesis, investigators have compared people's judgments about the implications of thematic and peripheral discourse ideas. Discourse ideas have generally been identified as thematic or peripheral on the basis of their hierarchical level, causal connectivity, and causal chain membership in the discourse structure. To examine the impact of HIERARCHICAL LEVEL on inference processing, for example, Walker and Meyer (1980) presented readers with a text that included sentences (18a) and (18b).

(18) a. *The Spring Episode was the first revolution in Morinthia.*
     b. *All Morinthian revolutions were failures.*

Across different text versions, sentences (18a) and (18b) were either at high or low levels of the text base: that is, they were either thematic or peripheral. Later, the subjects judged the truth of implied facts, such as (19):

(19) *The Spring Episode was a failure.*

Consistent with the inference theme hypothesis, people were more accurate in their judgments of inferences derived from thematic than peripheral facts (see also Cirilo, 1981).

Second, the thematic status of discourse ideas has been manipulated in terms of their frequency of mention. Ideas that are mentioned frequently are likely to have high interconnectivity with other discourse propositions. Eamon (1978–1979) reported that people need less time to verify the true implications of ideas thematized by frequent reference than those of peripheral ideas. In addition, the frequent implication of concepts that are relatively unimportant in their scripts, such as having a cocktail during a restaurant meal, results in those concepts being incorrectly recognized as frequently as important script ideas (Walker & Yekovich, 1984).

Third, thematic status of text ideas has been manipulated by coupling them with important consequences or unimportant ones. For example, as a result of missing a plane, a character might either be late for a business meeting, or avoid death in a plane crash (Goetz, 1979). This manipulation likely places the crucial ideas either on or off the main CAUSAL CHAIN of the message. It has been found that people judge the implications of discourse ideas with important consequences more accurately than those without (Goetz, 1979). Likewise, sentence reading time is faster if there is an anaphoric reference to an important idea than to an unimportant one (Cirilo, 1981).

The theme inference hypothesis has been predominantly investigated with reference to elaborative inferences. For example, insofar as the sequence *The*

Spring Episode was the first revolution in Morinthia, All Morinthian revolutions were failures is referentially coherent, the deduction that the Spring Episode failed constitutes an elaboration. It is perhaps not surprising, therefore, that the on-line status of these thematic inferences is equivocal. For example, Walker and Meyer (1980) reported that true thematic inferences, such as *The Spring Episode was a failure*, were verified as quickly as comparable explicit statements. However, this was the case only when the two statements yielding the inference were adjacent to one another in the text. Similarly, Eamon's (1978–1979) subjects verified thematic implications faster than some explicit statements, but the implicit and explicit statements may not have been completely comparable.

In summary, there is evidence that the implications of thematic ideas are privileged in comparison to those of nonthematic ideas. Manipulations of thematic status likely influence the hierarchical level, connectivity, and causal chain membership of discourse ideas. All three of these structural indices probably increase the likelihood that thematic ideas will be retained in working memory longer than nonthematic ones (Fletcher & Bloom, 1988; Kintsch & van Dijk, 1978). This, in turn, increases the probability that they will become the focus of inference processing.

2. Distance

Proposed working memory limitations may require the rapid purging of most discourse ideas (Clark & Sengul, 1979; Jarvella, 1971; Kintsch & van Dijk, 1978). Therefore, the detection of coreference and of the construction of inferential bridges is likely to be inversely related to discourse distance.

In empirical studies, related sentences such as *The Spring Episode was the first revolution in Morinthia* and *All Morinthian revolutions were failures* have been presented in the same text, the near condition; or in two different texts, the far condition. The deductive implication *The Spring Episode was a failure* is verified more accurately (Hayes-Roth & Thorndyke, 1979), and incorrectly recognized more frequently (Walker & Meyer, 1980), in the near condition than the far condition. Walker and Meyer also found that correct judgment time was more than 2 s longer for the implications of far than near facts. The comprehension time for test sentences with near referents is less than that of test sentences with far referents (Cirilo, 1981; Ehrlich & Johnson-Laird, 1982). Finally, diagram accuracy indicates that it is easier to extract spatial information from descriptions in which crucial terms have near referents than far ones (Ehrlich & Johnson-Laird, 1982).

3. Discourse Affordances

The genre and form of a discourse may promote, or "afford," particular types of processing. For example, narratives, such as fairy tales, might prompt understanders to detect the interrelations among discourse ideas; whereas expository passages might favor the focus on individual ideas (Einstein, McDaniel, Owen, & Cote, 1990; McDaniel, Einstein, Dunay, & Cobb, 1986). Accordingly, Einstein et al. predicted that a comprehension "orienting task" would enhance text recall only if it encouraged processing not inherently afforded by the text. They compared relational processing tasks, such as reordering random text sentences, to individual item tasks, such as restoring letters that had been deleted from the texts. Consistent with the analysis, fairy tale recall was enhanced only by the individual item tasks; and expository text recall was enhanced only by the relational orienting tasks.

The impact of text affordances on the construction of situation models was examined by Perrig and Kintsch (1985). Their subjects read texts that described different locations in a fictitious town. The texts used either the format of a sequence of places along a driving route or map positions, such as north and south. These styles were posited to prompt the representation of linear and spatial situation models, respectively. A subsequent test confirmed that the subjects were more accurate in verifying new inference test statements written in the style consistent with the version of the text that they had read.

4. Interestingness

That interestingness will affect inference processing is a reasonable hypothesis but one that has not received much experimental testing. Several definitions of interestingness have been advanced. First, certain emotional topics such as power, sex, money, and death are inherently interesting (Schank, 1979). Second, to be most interesting, a discourse should present ideas that are of personal relevance but of only moderate familiarity to the reader (Kintsch, 1980; Schank, 1979). For example, an adult amateur astronomer might enjoy magazine articles on astronomy, but not a child's book on astronomy, nor a journal article on astrophysics. Third, atypical and unexpected events, such as a waiter spilling coffee on the customer, are interesting (Graesser, Gordon, & Sawyer, 1979; Nezworski, Stein, & Trabasso, 1982). The engaging quality of atypical events may be related to the fact that they have causal consequences.

B. Understander Factors of Inference Processing

Language understanders vary along many dimensions, including available cognitive resources, verbal ability, quality and quantity of knowledge, and comprehension goals. Insofar as inference processing depends on one's relevant knowledge and the ability to retrieve it, these factors are likely to significantly influence inference processing. The present section examines several understander characteristics which have been hypothesized to affect inference processing.

1. Processing Capacity

Working memory is proposed to serve as the workspace for mental computations and for the storage of currently active ideas (Baddeley, 1986; Baddeley & Hitch, 1974; Daneman & Carpenter, 1980; Just & Carpenter, 1992; Perfetti & Lesgold, 1977). Analyzing the word string of a spoken or written message places constant demands on working memory. In addition, insofar as comprehension entails the construction of several levels of representation, working memory will serve as the domain for coordinating the information passing among these representations (Carpenter & Just, 1989; Just & Carpenter, 1992; Whitney, Ritchie, & Clark, 1991).

The capacity constraints of working memory have clear implications for inference processing. First, greater capacity may facilitate the on-line computation of elaborative inferences that are not essential to coherence. Likewise, the higher the capacity of working memory, the more probable it is that the antecedent object of a bridging inference will have been retained in working memory.

The evaluation of these hypotheses has hinged centrally on the reading span task (Daneman & Carpenter, 1980), which reflects the trade-off between the computational and storage functions of working memory. In this task, the subject reads or hears sets of unrelated sentences and after each set attempts to recall the final word of each sentence. Reading span, the largest size set for which the subject usually answers correctly, correlates significantly with standardized verbal tests, such as the SAT; with factual question answering; and with pronoun resolution accuracy (Daneman & Carpenter, 1980). More traditional measures of immediate memory, such as word span, are not correlated with these comprehension scores.

Findings linking reading span and ELABORATIVE INFERENCE processing have been somewhat equivocal. In two studies, reading span correlated significantly with inference judgment accuracy for both simple (Masson & Miller, 1983) and complex discourse deductions (Dixon, Lefevre, & Twilley, 1988) but did not account for unique variance in the inference measures. This may be because the deductions were optional elaborations. Because elaborations of this sort are not reliably inferred by many readers, reading span cannot distinctively predict them.

Whitney et al. (1991) compared the inference profiles of low and high reading span subjects who produced talk-aloud protocols while they read complex passages. The high span subjects produced fewer specific elaborations of text ideas than did low span individuals. It is suggestive that this outcome is consistent with the observation that high span readers are less likely to commit themselves to one interpretation of an ambiguous word (Just & Carpenter, 1992). Caution is needed, however, because this difference was the only one that Whitney et al. detected across 12 comprehension and inference categories that they inspected.

A relationship between reading span and BRIDGING INFERENCE is suggested by Daneman and Carpenter's (1980) pronoun resolution findings. They showed that pronoun resolution accuracy increased systematically with reading span score and, within each level of reading span, decreased as the distance to the antecedent increased. Likewise, to draw a bridging inference, the understander must identify an antecedent idea to which the current proposition may be linked. Consistent with this analysis, we found that reading span was a significant predictor of people's accuracy in judging inference test statements that bridged nonadjacent message ideas (Singer, Andrusiak, Reisdorf, & Black, 1992).

2. Age

Insofar as activation resources have been proposed to diminish with age, the elderly may exhibit deficits in inference processing (Craik & Byrd, 1981; Craik & Simon, 1980; Just & Carpenter, 1992). The ability of young and elderly people to make simple and complex deductions was examined by Cohen (1979). The subjects listened to brief passages. For example, one passage stated that Mrs. Brown goes to the park on nice days, and also that it had rained for the past three days. An inference question asked, *Did Mrs. Brown go to the park yesterday?* (no). Young readers made more errors on inference questions than on explicit questions, but this difference was considerably larger in elderly

listeners. Likewise, Cohen's young subjects were better at detecting text anomalies than were elderly adults. This suggests that the young more effectively
discern the connection between related ideas in messages (see Hayes-Roth &
Thorndyke, 1979; Walker & Meyer, 1980).

Till and Walsh (1980) asked young and old adults to listen to a list of 16
sentences, including items such as *The student carefully positioned the thumbtack on the chair.* Afterward, each subject performed either a free recall test
or a cued recall test using implicational cues such as *prank* (cf. McKoon &
Ratcliff, 1986; Paris & Lindauer, 1976). The young listeners recalled more
sentences in cued recall than free recall, but the reverse was true for the old
listeners. This outcome indicated a deficit on the part of the elderly subjects to
detect implicit relationships between the cues and the corresponding sentences.

In a timed verification task, in contrast, young and old subjects were similarly slower in judging implicit test items than explicit ones (Belmore, 1981).
This similarity may have been due to the fact that sentence verification is closely
related to recognition, a memory task in which the elderly display little or no
deficit (e.g., Craik & Byrd, 1981). These findings underline the need to link
deficits of inference processing in the elderly to general proposals concerning
cognition and aging. For example, Craik and Byrd proposed that the elderly
have a smaller reservoir of cognitive resources to divide among all cognitive
tasks. Because only controlled processes (Schneider & Shiffrin, 1977) draw on
these resources, Craik and Byrd's proposal implies that the elderly should
exhibit deficits in controlled but not automatic inference processing. Inference
researchers will need to address hypotheses such as this.

3. Knowledge

It is a fundamental principle that many pragmatic discourse inferences are
derived from one's knowledge of the world. Therefore, the particular knowledge
of the understander is likely to affect inference processing. Consistent with
this analysis, Anderson, Reynolds, Schallert, and Goetz (1976) reported that
people's interpretations of ambiguous passages were influenced by their back-
grounds. One passage included sentences such as *What bothered Spike most
was being held, especially since the charge against him had been weak* and
The lock that held him was strong but he thought he could break it. Music
students saw a prison interpretation of the passage, but subjects who were
weightlifters understood it as referring to a wrestling match. In this respect,
the readers' knowledge influenced their inferential decisions about word sense.

Pertinent knowledge exerts its impact in highly specific ways. After listening
to a lengthy baseball passage, baseball experts were faster and more accurate
than novices in their judgment of implications relevant to the game, such as
whether a batter had struck out (Post, Greene, & Bruder, 1982; see also Spilich,
Vesonder, Chiesi, & Voss, 1979). However, baseball experts and novices did
not differ in their inferential judgments about "nongame" ideas, such as the
weather, nor even for arduous elaborations, such as how many hits a player
had.

One likely way in which the understander's knowledge guides inference
processing is by its influence on macroprocessing. Schemas relevant to the
type and content of a discourse guide the construction of the macrostructure
(Kintsch & van Dijk, 1978). For example, knowledge about baseball permits

the understander to distinguish between the relevant and irrelevant statements in the description of a game. The judgment of relevance determines whether a particular proposition will be selected for the macrostructure or deleted. In turn, the appearance of relevant propositions in the macrostructure is likely to affect the course of inference processes.

4. Orienting Tasks in Comprehension

People may attend to language messages with different implicit tasks, such as learning, solving a problem, summarizing, or simply enjoying. Some understander tasks may entail deeper processing than others, where deep processing involves the extraction of message meaning (Craik & Lockhart, 1972; cf. Morris, Bransford, & Franks, 1977). Craik and Lockhart proposed that deep processing results in stronger and longer lasting memory traces than shallow processing. A corollary is that inference processing might be curtailed in shallow tasks.

In one pertinent study, people read completely ambiguous passages (Schallert, 1976). In one passage, for example, crucial ideas, such as valuable pitchers cracking, could be interpreted as referring to either a baseball game or to work in a glass factory. Each reader was informed of one of these themes or the other, or was not given a theme. Furthermore, the subjects were instructed either to judge the degree of ambiguity of the passage (deep task) or to count the number of pronouns (shallow task). The subjects later incorrectly recognized implicational sentences related to their theme more often than those related to the other theme. However, this result was obtained only when the readers performed the deep task. In another study, one reader group performed a deep orienting task in examining sentences such as *The youngster watched the program*. They later recalled the sentences as well when provided with the implicit recall cue *television* as with the explicit cue *program* (Till & Walsh, 1980). In contrast, the implicit cues did not effectively prompt recall for shallow processors.

Rather than invoking the depth of processing principle, some investigators identified specific sets of goals that are associated with different reading orienting tasks (e.g., Cirilo, 1981; Walker & Meyer, 1980). They have predicted that these goals will guide the construction of quite different internal representations of text meaning and result in different patterns of inference processing.

In one study, one group was instructed simply to read passages at a normal pace, and a second group was instructed to reread the text if necessary so that they might learn the details of the passage (Walker & Meyer, 1980). The "learners" were more accurate than "readers" in verifying deductions such as *The Spring Episode was a failure,* examined earlier. The learners also produced these implications in a free recall task more often than did the readers.

One way in which orienting tasks may affect inference processing is by regulating the amount of macroprocessing. Summarizing, for example, may favor the derivation of macrogeneralizations and constructions (Brown & Day, 1983; Cirilo, 1981; Schmalhofer & Glavanov, 1986).

5. Conclusions

There are numerous discourse and understander variables that affect inference processing. Several footnotes to these analyses should be offered. First, inference factors almost certainly interact with one another in complex ways.

For example, theme status interacts with orienting task: People recognize thematic test sentences more than peripheral ones, but only when they have performed a reading task requiring deep processing (Schallert, 1976). Likewise, knowledge and theme interact: For example, high-knowledge readers outperform low-knowledge readers in their judgments about thematic (baseball) inference statements, but not for peripheral inferences (Post et al., 1982). Other interaction patterns of this sort were detected by Walker and Meyer (1980) and Cirilo (1981).

Second, the investigation of inference factors has, in general, not definitively determined whether the inferences were drawn on line. Some inference factor studies have predominantly relied on inference measures that do not identify the locus of inference, such as cued recall (Till & Walsh, 1980). Other studies have not compared people's judgments about inference test items with comparable explicit items (Post et al., 1982). However, the determination of whether the inferences under examination typically accompany comprehension may converge from other investigations.

Finally, further investigations of inference factors ought to highlight the inference category under examination. For example, working memory capacity may be less likely to influence elaborative inference processing than bridging inference, which is hindered if a crucial antecedent has been purged from working memory.

VIII. METHODS OF STUDYING INFERENCE PROCESSES

The evaluation of inference processes is inherently complicated and subtle. The number of techniques developed in this effort are numerous, but no more numerous than the critiques of these methods that have been offered. Nevertheless, researchers are in agreement on a number of issues. First, evidence that inferences of a certain category accompany comprehension ought to converge from on-line and memory measures of processing (e.g., Keenan, Potts, Golding, & Jennings, 1990; Magliano & Graesser, 1991). On-line and memory methods are considered below.

Second, it is ideal for the stimulus from which the crucial measure is derived to be identical in all experimental conditions. For example, to assess the impact of referential directness on bridging processes, Haviland and Clark (1974) manipulated the first sentences of (20a) and (20b) and measured the reading time of the identical second sentences.

(20) a. *We got some beer out of the car. The beer was warm.*
    b. *We got the picnic supplies out of the car. The beer was warm.*

In principle, sequences (21a) and (21b) permit the comparison of the same two conditions.

(21) a. *We got the picnic supplies out of the car. The picnic supplies were warm.*
    b. *We got the picnic supplies out of the car. The beer was warm.*

In this event, however, referential directness is confounded with many features of the contrasting second sentences. Statistical procedures, such as analysis of covariance, can remove the unwanted impact of extraneous variables. However, language materials are so complicated that it is hard to even identify all those variables.

Many issues of inference methodology are common to the broader domain of language processes, and are examined elsewhere in this Handbook (Kutas & Van Petten, this volume; Haberlandt, this volume). Furthermore, detailed critiques of inference methodology have been presented elsewhere (Keenan et al., 1990; Magliano & Graesser, 1991; McKoon & Ratcliff, 1990). This section briefly highlights the rationale and drawbacks of different inference methods.

A. Norms

A preliminary step to determining whether an inference reliably accompanies comprehension is to identify the inferences that the population considers valid. A researcher may wish to know whether people infer the probable consequences of actions, such as *Barbara jabbed the balloon with the pin.* In the norming procedure, subjects view stimuli of this sort and are asked to identify one or more outcomes. They generate replies such as *the balloon broke* and *there was a loud bang.* High frequency responses are then used as the test items in the experimental test.

A refinement of this procedure is to present complete texts during the norming procedure and to ask the subjects to provide information continuously or intermittently (Olson, Duffy, & Mack, 1984). The reader may be instructed to think aloud (e.g., Trabasso & Suh, in press). If the investigator is interested in a particular inference category, the reader may alternatively be asked to produce information that bears the relation of interest to the present sentence (Graesser, Robertson, & Anderson, 1981). The resulting norms provide a rich source of information about peoples' discourse inferences. However, because the subjects have been specifically instructed to generate inferences, their replies need not identify inferences that usually accompany comprehension. Rather, these responses specify an inference boundary: That is, if a certain inference does not frequently occur in the intentional norming procedure, it is unlikely to reliably accompany comprehension.

B. On-Line Inference Measures

On-line measures, collected while the understander comprehends a discourse, are used to reveal the processes and/or immediate products of comprehension. Reading time, the most frequently used on-line measure, is considered to have the potential to reflect the time that readers require to draw text inferences. Reading time may be collected for different text units, such as words, phrases, and sentences, and under different conditions of computer-controlled text display (Just, Carpenter, & Woolley, 1982). Consider set (22).

(22) a. *Mark's dog chased a squirrel near the picnic table. The squirrel climbed a tall oak tree.*
   b. *Mark's dog watched a squirrel near the picnic table. The squirrel climbed a tall oak tree.*

The first sentences of (22a) and (22b) are posited to be causally and temporally related to the identical second sentences, respectively (Singer, Halldorson et al., 1992). Faster reading time for *The squirrel climbed a tall oak tree* in

(22a) than (22b) would suggest that it takes less time to inferentially bridge causally than temporally related sentences.

Even when the target item is identical in all conditions, there are some shortcomings of reading time as an inference measure (McKoon & Ratcliff, 1980b). First, the inference condition may be confounded with variables such as the amount of repetition and the degree of semantic association between the targets and their different antecedents. Second, target reading time may be contaminated by the amount of processing that "spills over" from the antecedent to the target. Third, lengthy reading times may reflect difficulty of processing rather than the computation of an inference.

The monitoring of eye fixations provides on-line measures of the time and location of reading while permitting the reader to scan the text display more freely than in the reading time procedure (Just & Carpenter, 1980; Rayner, 1983). This technique permits an incisive examination of the processing time of text targets posited to require inference processing (e.g., Garrod et al., 1990). Eye fixations indicate whether the reader regressively searches the text for information to which the target must be inferentially linked (Just & Carpenter, 1978). The interpretation of eye fixation data is based on the assumptions that each word is fully processed as soon as it is fixated (Just & Carpenter, 1980) and that fixation is maintained on a word as long as the reader continues to process it (Ehrlich & Rayner, 1983).

C. Memory Measures

Memory tasks evaluate inference processing by examining the products of comprehension. One rationale of this approach is that if, according to a memory measure, an implied text idea has the same status as an explicit idea, then the idea was inferred during comprehension. However, this logic has some flaws. First, insofar as the memory representation may have changed between comprehension and test, the memory measure may reveal little about comprehension processes. Second, the memory measure may reflect retrieval rather than encoding processes. These issues are briefly explored with reference to retrieval and activation memory measures.

1. Retrieval Measures

Standard memory tests such as free recall, cued recall, and recognition have been used to assess inference processing. However, these measures may reflect retrieval processes as well as encoding processes. Reconsider a shortcoming of cued recall, examined earlier. Implicit cues, such as *scissors,* are effective prompts for antecedent sentences, such as *The athlete cut out an article for his friend* (Anderson, Pichert et al., 1976; Paris & Lindauer, 1976). However, Corbett and Dosher (1978) found that *scissors* was also an effective recall cue for *The athlete cut out an article with a **razor blade** for his friend.* This indicates that the effectiveness of implicit recall cues does not definitively diagnose an on-line inference. Rather, implicit cues may also permit people to work backward from the cue to an action suggested by the cue, and hence to the correct sentence.

Analogously, in recognition and recall, people may base their answers on the general knowledge pertinent to a message, rather than on the message representation (Bartlett, 1932). Furthermore, with increased delay between comprehension and test, the understander increasingly relies on relevant knowledge (Anderson & Pichert, 1978; Hasher & Griffin, 1978; Kintsch & van Dijk, 1978). In one study, people read a passage about Helen Keller that made no mention of her disabilities. In immediate testing, 5% of the subjects incorrectly recognized the test sentence *She was deaf, dumb, and blind* (Sulin & Dooling, 1974). One week later, in contrast, 50% of the subjects false-alarmed to this sentence!

Response time is frequently monitored in inference studies using retrieval tasks. The rationale is that if answer time is no greater in the inference test condition than the explicit condition, the inference must have been drawn during encoding. To avoid having to derive conclusions strictly from similar inference and explicit judgment times (and hence a failure to reject the null hypothesis), investigators frequently include contrasting noninference conditions in these designs (e.g., Singer, 1980).

Even timed retrieval measures, however, may reflect retrieval rather than encoding processes. For example, subjects may refrain from comparing an inference test item with the antecedent text and instead judge its plausibility with reference to pertinent knowledge. Indeed, even explicit items may be evaluated in this way (Reder, 1979, 1982). In this event, similar explicit and implicit answer times would reveal little about encoding inferences. To minimize the likelihood of subjects adopting the plausibility strategy, timed answering tasks should be administered at short delays and use distractor questions that are plausible in the context of the discourse (Reder, 1982).

2. Activation Measures

Numerous tasks have been used to determine whether a concept or an idea is active at different stages of comprehension. With reference to inference processes, the logic is that if facilitation is demonstrated for an implied concept, then it has been inferred. Typically, a subject reads a text and at some point is asked to make a judgment about a word. The judgment may be to recognize the word, to decide whether it constitutes an English word (a lexical decision), to name the color in which the word is presented (the Stroop task), or to name the word aloud.

Consider a Stroop (1935) task example. Stroop color naming of primed concepts is typically slowed (Warren, 1972). In one inference study, people needed no more time to name the color of the instrument *broom* in an appropriate context, *He swept the floor,* than in an inappropriate context, *He hit a home run* (Dosher & Corbett, 1982). Because color naming time was not slowed in the appropriate context, the authors concluded that people do not reliably infer probable instruments.

Activation measures are both widely used and controversial. They are convenient because they provide a timed measure about a single word. This yields answer times with smaller variability, and hence greater statistical power, than would result from a timed measure of phrases or sentences. Some of the features and controversies of the activation measures are next addressed.

1. Activation measures may reflect the transient activation of concepts during comprehension. As discussed earlier, the concept ANT is briefly facili-

tated when *bug* is encountered in the spying context (Kintsch & Mross, 1985; Swinney, 1979). Clearly, however, this facilitation does not signal the encoding of an inference about insects. By the same token, the transient activation of BROOM in the sweeping context does not guarantee an inference about the broom.

2. Activation measures may be embedded in a priming paradigm. That is, the test item that is the subject of recognition, lexical decision, or naming may be immediately preceded by a priming test word. The logic is that primes that facilitate their targets have been inferentially linked to the target during encoding (McKoon & Ratcliff, 1980a).

3. Activation measures can constitute either on-line or memory measures. For example, a primed lexical decision task that follows reading provides a memory measure (McKoon & Ratcliff, 1989c). In contrast, measuring lexical decisions after every sentence in a story is an intermittent on-line measure of activation (Long et al., 1992).

4. Some activation measures may index the retrieval process of context checking (Forster, 1981; Seidenberg & Tanenhaus, 1986), rather than encoding functions. Both word recognition and lexical decision reflect the postlexical access processes that contribute to the *yes* or *no* decisions that those tasks require. The degree of compatibility between the test word and the antecedent text may affect the *yes–no* decision. Relatively fast judgment times in the inference condition of an experiment may therefore reflect the compatibility between the test word and the antecedent message, rather than an inference that accompanied comprehension. Naming time, in contrast, does not reflect postlexical processing.

Notwithstanding these proposals, word recognition (McKoon & Ratcliff, 1989b) and lexical decision (Kintsch & Mross, 1985; Long et al., 1992) continue to be used as indices of inference processing. It has been argued, for example, that a fast recognition deadline precludes the possibility of postlexical processing (McKoon & Ratcliff, 1986). Potts et al. (1988) replied that deadline recognition decisions still reflect context checking and are based on that part of the processing that precedes the deadline.

5. Conversely, it has been countered that naming does not access text-level representations and therefore cannot be used to evaluate hypotheses about text base and situation representations (Lucas et al., 1990; McKoon & Ratcliff, 1989a). Consistent with this proposal, Lucas et al. found that lexical decisions suggested that an inferential *sweep–broom* link is formed upon reading (23a) and (23b), whereas naming did not.

(23) a. *There was a broom in the closet next to the kitchen.*
     b. *John swept the floor every week on Saturday.*

Other researchers, in contrast, have reported that lexical decisions and naming reflected comparable profiles concerning causal elaborative inferences (Long et al., 1992; Swinney & Osterhout, 1990). Thus, the exact status of these single word tasks remains controversial.

6. A final point of controversy is whether single word test items adequately capture a complex inference (Magliano & Graesser, 1991). For example, *dead* has been used to probe the consequence of an actress falling from the 14th

story (McKoon & Ratcliff, 1986), and *eat* has represented the superordinate goal inference that a dragon wanted to eat the princesses that it kidnapped (Long et al., 1992). Single words can be used to expose the propositional organization of texts (McKoon & Ratcliff, 1980a). However, using single words to probe complex inferences leaves open the possibility of confounding the encoding of the inference with the activation of the word concept. Ideally, to evaluate a complex proposition, subjects ought to be asked to evaluate a stimulus that expresses the whole proposition. Indeed, investigators have sometimes replaced single words with more complex stimuli, even in the context of priming paradigms (McKoon & Ratcliff, 1988).

D. Summary

The inherent complexity of the study of inference processes raises legitimate questions about virtually every method of studying this problem. It is important, however, that questions about the validity of any given method not be permitted to stymie the entire enterprise. To avoid the latter outcome, researchers have implicitly developed heuristics for studying inference processing: (1) Use on-line and retrieval methods in a converging fashion. (2) Collect norms to specify a population of inferences that people could, in theory, compute. (3) Construct the stimulus materials to control extraneous variables, such as the semantic association between the antecedent message and the target.

IX. CONCLUSIONS

There have been enormous strides in the study of discourse inference processes during the past 20 years. A capsule review of progress might state the following: Researchers initially assumed that highly probable elaborative inferences accompany comprehension. However, preliminary findings discouraged this conclusion. This outcome spawned two major trends in inference processing research. The first has been to study bridging inferences, which, by identifying connections among ideas, preserve text coherence. There is extensive evidence that bridging inferences accompany comprehension. The problem has been refined to ask precisely which bridges the understander can detect. The second trend has been to identify the message and understander characteristics that guide inference computation. Numerous factors in each category have been identified.

More incisive study has likewise indicated that some categories of elaborative inference are drawn during comprehension. Understanders have been shown to instantiate general category terms on line. It also appears that relevant semantic associates, semantic features of discourse concepts, and relevant generalizations and constructions of discourse are encoded during comprehension.

At the outset of this chapter, Schank's (1976) equation of inference and comprehension was invoked. Schank's quotation implies a central goal for inference research, namely that theories of inference processing merge with ostensibly more general theories of comprehension.

References

Anderson, R. C., & Pichert, J. W. (1978). Recall of previously unrecallable information following a shift in perspective. *Journal of Verbal Learning and Verbal Behavior, 17,* 1–12.

Anderson, R. C., Pichert, J. V., Goetz, E. T., Schallert, D. L., Stevens, K. V., & Trollip, S. R. (1976). Instantiation of general terms. *Journal of Verbal Learning and Verbal Behavior, 15,* 667–679.

Anderson, R. C., Reynolds, R. E., Schallert, D. L., & Goetz, E. T. (1976, July). *Frameworks for comprehending discourse* (Tech. Rep. No. 12). Urbana-Champaign: University of Illinois, Laboratory for Cognitive Studies in Education.

Baddeley, A. D. (1986). *Working memory* (Oxford Psychology Series, Vol. 11). Oxford; Oxford University Press (Clarendon).

Baddeley, A. D., & Hitch, G. (1974). Working memory. In G. H. Bower (Ed.), *The psychology of learning and motivation* (Vol. 8). New York: Academic Press.

Bartlett, F. C. (1932). *Remembering*. Cambridge: Cambridge University Press.

Belmore, S. M. (1981). Age-related changes in processing explicit and implicit language. *Journal of Gerontology, 36,* 316–322.

Bierwisch, M. (1970). Semantics, In J. Lyons (Ed.), *New horizons in linguistics* (pp. 166–184). Baltimore: Pelican Books.

Black, J. B., & Bern, H. (1981). Causal inference and memory for events in narratives. *Journal of Verbal Learning and Verbal Behavior, 20,* 267–275.

Bloom, C. P., Fletcher, C. R., van den Broek, P., Reitz, L., & Shapiro, B. P. (1990). An on-line assessment of causal reasoning during comprehension. *Memory & Cognition, 18,* 65–71.

Bransford, J. D., & Johnson, M. K. (1973). Considerations of some problems of comprehension. In W. Chase (Ed.), *Visual information processing*. New York: Academic Press.

Brewer, W. F. (1975). Memory for ideas: Synonym substitution. *Memory & Cognition, 3,* 458–464.

Brown, A. L., & Day, J. D. (1983). Macrorules for summarizing texts: The development of expertise. *Journal of Verbal Learning and Verbal Behavior, 22,* 1–14.

Carpenter, P. A., & Just, M. A. (1989). The role of working memory in language comprehension. In D. Klahr & K. Kotovsky (Eds.), *Complex informational processing: The impact of Herbert A. Simon*. Hillsdale, NJ: Erlbaum.

Charniak, E. (1975, June). Organization and inference in a frame-like system of common sense knowledge. In R. Schank & B. Nash-Webber (Eds.), *Theoretical issues in natural language processing. An interdisciplinary workshop*. Cambridge, MA: Massachusetts Institute of Technology.

Cirilo, R. K. (1981). Referential coherence and text structure in story comprehension. *Journal of Verbal Learning and Verbal Behavior, 20,* 358–367.

Clark, H. H. (1977). Inferences in comprehension. In D. LaBerge & S. J. Samuels (Eds.), *Perception and comprehension*. Hillsdale, NJ: Erlbaum.

Clark, H. H., & Clark, E. V. (1977). *Psychology and language*. New York: Harcourt Brace Jovanovich.

Clark, H. H., & Haviland, S. E. (1977). Comprehension and the given–new contract. In R. Freedle (Ed.), *Discourse production and comprehension*. Hillsdale, NJ: Erlbaum.

Clark, H. H., & Sengul, C. J. (1979). In search of referents for nouns and pronouns. *Memory & Cognition, 7,* 33–41.

Cohen, G. (1979). Language comprehension in old age. *Cognitive Psychology, 11,* 412–429.

Corbett, A. (1984). Prenominal adjectives and the disambiguation of anaphoric nouns. *Journal of Verbal Learning and Verbal Behavior, 23,* 683–695.

Corbett, A. T., & Dosher, B. A. (1978). Instrument inferences in sentence encoding. *Journal of Verbal Learning and Verbal Behavior, 17,* 479–492.

Craik, F. I. M., & Byrd, M. (1981). Aging and cognitive deficits: The role of attentional processes. In F. Craik & S. Trehub (Eds.), *Aging and cognitive processes*. New York: Plenum.

Craik, F. I. M., & Lockhart, R. S. (1972). Levels of processing: A framework for memory research. *Journal of Verbal Learning and Verbal Behavior, 11,* 671–684.

Craik, F. I. M., & Simon, E. (1980). Age differences in memory: The role of attention and depth of processing. In L. Poon, J. Fozard, L. Cermak, D. Arenberg, & W. Thompson (Eds.), *New directions in memory and aging*. Hillsdale, NJ: Erlbaum.

Daneman, M., & Carpenter, P. A. (1980). Individual differences in working memory and reading. *Journal of Verbal Learning and Verbal Behavior, 19,* 450–466.

Den Uyl, M., & van Oostendorp, H. (1980). The use of scripts in text comprehension. *Poetics, 9*, 275–294.

Dixon, P., LeFevre, J., & Twilley, L. C. (1988). Word knowledge and working memory as predictors of reading skill. *Journal of Educational Psychology, 80*, 465–472.

Dopkins, S., Klin, C., & Myers, J. (1993). Accessibility of information about goals during the processing of narrative texts. *Journal of Experimental Psychology; Learning, Memory, and Cognition, 19*, 70–80.

Dosher, B. A., & Corbett, A. T. (1982). Instrument inferences and verb schemata. *Journal of Verbal Learning and Verbal Behavior, 10*, 531–539.

Dubois, D., & Denis, M. (1988). Knowledge organization and instantiation of general terms in sentence comprehension. *Journal of Experimental Psychology: Learning, Memory and Cognition, 14*, 604–611.

Duffy, S. A., Shinjo, M., & Myers, J. L. (1990). The effect of encoding task on memory for sentence pairs varying in causal relatedness. *Journal of Verbal Learning and Verbal Behavior, 29*, 27–42.

Eamon, D. B. (1978–1979). Selection and recall of topical information in prose by better and poorer readers. *Reading Research Quarterly, 14*(2), 244–257.

Ehrlich, K., & Johnson-Laird, P. N. (1982). Spatial descriptions and referential continuity. *Journal of Verbal Learning and Verbal Behavior, 21*, 296–306.

Ehrlich, K., & Rayner, K. (1983). Pronoun assignment and semantic integration during reading: Eye movements and immediacy of processing. *Journal of Verbal Learning and Verbal Behavior, 22*, 75–87.

Einstein, G. O., McDaniel, M. A., Owen, P. D., & Cote, N. C. (1990). Encoding and recall of texts: The importance of material appropriate processing. *Journal of Memory and Language, 29*, 566–582.

Fillmore, C. J. (1968). The case for case. In E. Bach & R. T. Harms (Eds.), *Universals of linguistic theory* (pp. 1–88) New York: Holt, Rinehart & Winston.

Fletcher, C. R., & Bloom, C. P. (1988). Causal reasoning in the comprehension of simple narrative texts. *Journal of Memory and Language, 27*, 235–244.

Fletcher, C. R., Hummel, J. E., & Marsolek, C. J. (1990). Causality and the allocation of attention during comprehension. *Journal of Experimental Psychology; Learning, Memory, and Cognition, 16*, 233–240.

Forster, K. I. (1981). Priming and the effects of sentence and lexical contexts on naming time: Evidence for autonomous lexical processing. *Quarterly Journal of Experimental Psychology, 33A*, 465–495.

Garrod, S., O'Brien, E. J., Morris, R. K., & Rayner, K. (1990). Elaborative inferences as an active or passive process. *Journal of Experimental Psychology: Learning, Memory, and Cognition, 16*, 250–257.

Gilbert, J. (1970). *Myths and legends of ancient Rome.* London: Hamlyn.

Goetz, E. T. (1979). Inferring from text: Some factors influencing which inferences will be made. *Discourse Processes, 2*, 179–195.

Graesser, A. C., Gordon, G. E., & Sawyer, J. D. (1979). Recognition memory for typical and atypical actions in scripted activities: Tests of a script pointer and tag hypothesis. *Journal of Verbal Learning and Verbal Behavior, 18*, 319–332.

Graesser, A. C., Robertson, S. P., & Anderson, P. A. (1981). Incorporating inferences in narrative representations: A study of how and why. *Cognitive Psychology, 13*, 1–26.

Graesser, A. C., Robertson, S. P., Lovelace, E. R., & Swinehart, D. M. (1980). Answers to why-questions expose the organization of story plot and predict recall of actions. *Journal of Verbal Learning and Verbal Behavior, 19*, 110–119.

Grice, H. P. (1975). William James Lectures, Harvard University, 1967. Published in part as "Logic and conversation." In P. Cole & J. L. Morgan (Eds.), *Syntax and semantics* (Vol. 3, pp. 41–58). New York: Academic Press.

Guindon, R., & Kintsch, W. (1984). Priming macropropositions: Evidence for the primacy of macropropositions in the memory for text. *Journal of Verbal Learning and Verbal Behavior, 23*, 508–518.

Harris, R. J., & Monaco, G. E. (1978). The psychology of pragmatic implication: Information processing between the lines. *Journal of Experimental Psychology: General, 107*, 1–22.

Hasher, L., & Griffin, M. (1978). Reconstructive and reproductive processes in memory. *Journal of Experimental Psychology: Human Learning and Memory, 4*, 318–330.

Haviland, S. E., & Clark, H. H. (1974). What's new? Acquiring new information as a process in comprehension. *Journal of Verbal Learning and Verbal Behavior, 13*, 512–521.

Hayes-Roth, B., & Thorndyke, P. W. (1979). Integration of knowledge from text. *Journal of Verbal Learning and Verbal Behavior, 18*, 91–108.

Jarvella, R. J. (1971). Syntactic processing of connected speech. *Journal of Verbal Learning and Verbal Behavior, 10*, 409–416.

Johnson, M. K., Bransford, J. D., & Solomon, S. K. (1973). Memory for tacit implications of sentences. *Journal of Experimental Psychology, 98*, 203–205.

Just, M. A., & Carpenter, P. A. (1978). Inference processes during reading: Reflections from eye fixations. In J. W. Senders & R. A. Monty (Eds.), *Eye movements and the higher psychological functions.* Hillsdale, NJ: Erlbaum.

Just, M. A., & Carpenter, P. A. (1980). A theory of reading: From eye fixations to comprehension. *Psychological Review, 87*, 329–354.

Just, M. A., & Carpenter, P. A. (1992). A capacity theory of comprehension: Individual differences in working memory. *Psychological Review, 99*, 122–149.

Just, M. A., Carpenter, P. A., & Wooley, J. D. (1982). Paradigms and processes in reading comprehension. *Journal of Experimental Psychology: General, 111*, 228–238.

Keenan, J. (1978). Psychological issues concerning comprehension: Comments on ''Psychology of pragmatic implication. Information between the lines'' by Harris and Monaco. *Journal of Experimental Psychology: General, 107*, 23–27.

Keenan, J. M., Baillet, S. D., & Brown, P. (1984). The effects of causal cohesion on comprehension and memory. *Journal of Verbal Learning and Verbal Behavior, 23*, 115–126.

Keenan, J. M., Potts, G. R., Golding, J. M., & Jennings, T. M. (1990). Which elaborative inferences are drawn during reading? A question of methodologies. In D. A. Balota, G. Flores d'Arcais, & K. Rayner (Eds.), *Comprehension processes in reading.* Hillsdale, NJ: Erlbaum.

Kintsch, W. (1974). *The representation of meaning in memory.* Hillsdale, NJ: Erlbaum.

Kintsch, W. (1980). Learning from text, levels of comprehension, or: Why would anyone read a story anyway. *Poetics, 9*, 7–98.

Kintsch, W. (1988). The role of knowledge in discourse comprehension: A construction–integration model. *Psychological Review, 95*, 163–182.

Kintsch, W., & Mross, E. F. (1985). Context effects in word identification. *Journal of Memory and Language, 24*, 336–349.

Kintsch, W., & van Dijk, T. A. (1978). Toward a model of text comprehension and production. *Psychological Review, 85*, 363–394.

Lesgold, A. M., Roth, S. F., & Curtis, M. E. (1979). Foregrounding effects in discourse comprehension. *Journal of Verbal Learning and Verbal Behavior, 18*, 291–308.

Long, D. L., Golding, J. M., & Graesser, A. C. (1992). A test of the on-line status of goal-related inferences. *Journal of Memory and Learning, 31*, 634–647.

Lucas, M. M., Tanenhaus, M. K., & Carlson, G. N. (1990). Levels of representation in the interpretation of anaphoric reference and instrument inference. *Memory & Cognition, 18*, 611–631.

Magliano, J. P., & Graesser, A. C. (1991). A three-pronged method for studying inference generation in literary text. *Poetics, 20*, 193–232.

Malt, B. C. (1985). The role of discourse structure in understanding anaphora. *Journal of Memory and Language, 24*, 271–289.

Mandler, J. M., & Johnson, N. S. (1977). Remembrance of things parsed: Story structure and recall. *Cognitive Psychology, 9*, 111–151.

Mandler, J. M., & Murachver, T. (1985, November). *Script activation and lexical processing.* Presented at the annual meeting of the Psychonomic Society, Boston.

Masson, M. E. J., & Miller, J. A. (1983). Working memory and individual differences in comprehension and memory of text. *Journal of Educational Psychology, 75*, 314–318.

Mayer, R. E., & Cook, L. K. (1981). Effects of shadowing on prose comprehension. *Memory & Cognition, 9*, 101–109.

McDaniel, M. A., Einstein, G. O., Dunay, P. K., & Cobb, R. E. (1986). Encoding difficulty and memory: Toward a unifying theory. *Journal of Memory and Language, 25*, 645–656.

McKoon, G., & Ratcliff, R. (1980a). Priming in item recognition: The organization of propositions in memory for text. *Journal of Verbal Learning and Verbal Behavior, 19*, 369–386.

McKoon, G., & Ratcliff, R. (1980b). The comprehension processes and memory structures involved in anaphoric reference. *Journal of Verbal Learning and Verbal Behavior, 19*(6), 668–682.

McKoon, G., & Ratcliff, R. (1986). Inferences about predictable events. *Journal of Experimental Psychology: Learning, Memory, and Cognition, 12,* 82–91.

McKoon, G., & Ratcliff, R. (1988). Contextually relevant aspect of meaning. *Journal of Experimental Psychology: Learning, Memory, and Cognition, 14,* 331–343.

McKoon, G., & Ratcliff, R. (1989a). Assessing the occurrence of elaborative inference with recognition. *Journal of Memory and Language, 28,* 547–563.

McKoon, G., & Ratcliff, R. (1989b). Semantic associations and elaborative inference. *Journal of Experimental Psychology: Learning, Memory, and Cognition, 15,* 326–338.

McKoon, G., & Ratcliff, R. (1989c). Inferences about contextually defined categories. *Journal of Experimental Psychology: Learning, Memory, and Cognition, 15,* 1134–1146.

McKoon, G., & Ratcliff, R. (1990). Textual inferences: Models and measures. In D. A. Balota, G. Flores d'Arcais, & K. Rayner (Eds.), *Comprehension processes in reading.* Hillsdale, NJ: Erlbaum.

Morris, C. D., Bransford, J. D., & Franks, J. J. (1977). Levels of processing versus transfer appropriate training. *Journal of Verbal Learning and Verbal Behavior, 16,* 519–534.

Morrow, D. G., Greenspan, S. L., & Bower, G. H. (1987). Accessibility and situation models in narrative comprehension. *Journal of Memory and Language, 2,* 165–187.

Myers, J. L., Shinjo, M., & Duffy, S. A. (1987). Degree of causal relatedness and memory. *Journal of Verbal Learning and Verbal Behavior, 26,* 453–465.

Nezworski, T., Stein, N. L., & Trabasso, T. (1982). Story structure versus content in children's recall. *Journal of Verbal Learning and Verbal Behavior, 21,* 196–206.

O'Brien, E. J. (1987). Antecedent search processes and the structure of text. *Journal of Experimental Psychology: Learning, Memory, and Cognition, 13,* 278–290.

O'Brien, E. J., Plewes, P. S., & Albrecht, J. E. (1990). Antecedent retrieval processes. *Journal of Experimental Psychology: Learning, Memory, and Cognition, 16,* 241–249.

O'Brien, E. J., Shank, D. M., Myers, J. L., & Rayner, K. (1988). Elaborative inferences during reading: Do they occur on-line? *Journal of Experimental Psychology: Learning, Memory and Cognition, 14,* 410–420.

Olson, G. M., Duffy, S. A., & Mack, R. L. (1984). Thinking-out-loud as a method for studying real-time comprehension processes. In D. Kieras & M. Just (Eds.), *New methods in reading comprehension research.* Hillsdale, NJ: Erlbaum.

Omanson, R. C. (1982). The relation between centrality and story category variation. *Journal of Verbal Learning and Verbal Behavior, 21,* 326–337.

Paris, S. G., & Lindauer, B. K. (1976). The role of inference in children's comprehension and memory for sentences. *Cognitive Psychology, 8,* 217–227.

Perfetti, C. A., & Lesgold, A. M. (1977). Discourse comprehension and sources of individual differences. In M. Just & P. Carpenter (Eds.), *Cognitive processes in comprehension.* Hillsdale, NJ: Erlbaum.

Perrig, W., & Kintsch, W. (1985). Propositional and situational representations of text. *Journal of Memory and Language, 24,* 503–518.

Post, T. A., Greene, T., & Bruder, G. (1982, November). *"On-line" text processing in high- and low-knowledge individuals.* Presented at the annual meeting of the Psychonomic Society, Minneapolis.

Potts, G. R., Keenan, J. M., & Golding, J. M. (1988). Assessing the occurrence of elaborative inferences: Lexical decision versus naming. *Journal of Memory and Language, 27,* 399–415.

Rayner, K. (1983). The perceptual span and eye movement control during reading. In K. Rayner (Ed.), *Eye movements in reading: Perceptual and language processes.* New York: Academic Press.

Reder, L. M. (1979). The role of elaborations in memory for prose. *Cognitive Psychology, 11,* 221–234.

Reder, L. M. (1982). Plausibility judgments versus fact retrieval: Alternative strategies for sentence verification. *Psychological Review, 89,* 250–280.

Rieger, C. (1975, June). The commonsense algorithm as a basis for computer models of human memory, inference, belief, and contextual language comprehension. In R. Schank & B. Nash-Webber (Eds.), *Theoretical issues in natural language processing. An interdisciplinary workshop.* Cambridge, MA: Massachusetts Institute of Technology.

Schallert, D. L. (1976). Improving memory for prose: The relationship between depth of processing and context. *Journal of Verbal Learning and Verbal Behavior, 15,* 621–632.

Schank, R. C. (1976). The role of memory in language processing. In C. Cofer (Ed.), *The nature of human memory*. San Francisco: Freeman.

Schank, R. C. (1979). Interestingness: Controlling inferences. *Artificial Intelligence, 12*, 273–297.

Schank, R. C. (1986). *Explanation patterns: Understanding mechanically and creatively*. Hillsdale, NJ: Erlbaum.

Schank, R. C., & Abelson, R. (1977). *Scripts, plans, goals, and understanding*. Hillsdale, NJ: Erlbaum.

Schmalhofer, F., & Glavanov, D. (1986). Three components of understanding a programmer's manual: Verbatim, propositional, and situation representations. *Journal of Memory and Language, 25*, 279–294.

Schneider, W., & Shiffrin, R. M. (1977). Controlled and automatic human information processing: I. Detection, search, and attention. *Psychological Review, 84*, 1–66.

Seidenberg, M. S., & Tanenhaus, M. K. (1986). Modularity and lexical access. In I. Gopnik & M. Gopnik (Ed.), *From models to modules: Studies in cognitive science from the McGill workshops*, (pp. 135–157). Norwood, NJ: Ablex.

Seidenberg, M. S., Waters, G. S., Sanders, M., & Langer, P. (1984). Pre- and post-lexical loci of contextual effects on word recognition. *Memory & Cognition, 12*, 315–328.

Singer, M. (1976). Thematic structure and the integration of linguistic information. *Journal of Verbal Learning and Verbal Behavior, 15*, 549–558.

Singer, M. (1978). *The role of explicit and implicit recall cues*. Symposium presented at the meeting of the American Psychological Association, Toronto.

Singer, M. (1979a). Processes of inference in sentence encoding. *Memory & Cognition, 7*, 192–200.

Singer, M. (1979b). Temporal locus of inference in the comprehension of brief passages: Recognizing and verifying implications about instruments. *Perceptual and Motor Skills, 49*, 539–550.

Singer, M. (1980). The role of case-filling inferences in the coherence of brief passages. *Discourse Processes, 3*, 185–201.

Singer, M. (1988). Inferences in reading comprehension. In M. Daneman, G. MacKinnon, & T. Waller (Eds.), *Reading research: Advances in theory and practice* (Vol. 6, pp. 177–219). San Diego, CA: Academic Press.

Singer, M. (1990). *Psychology of language*. Hillsdale, NJ: Erlbaum.

Singer, M. (1993). *Constructing and validating motive bridging inferences*. University of Manitoba. Manuscript in preparation.

Singer, M., Andrusiak, P., Reisdorf, P., & Black, N. (1992). Individual differences in bridging inference processes. *Memory & Cognition, 20*, 539–548.

Singer, M., & Ferreira, F. (1983). Inferring consequences in story comprehension. *Journal of Verbal Learning and Verbal Behavior, 22*, 437–448.

Singer, M., & Halldorson, M. (1993). *Integrating inference-validating motive bridging inferences*. University of Manitoba. Manuscript under review.

Singer, M., Halldorson, M., Lear, J. C., & Andrusiak, P. (1992). Validation of causal bridging inferences *in discourse understanding. Journal of Memory and Language, 31*, 507–524.

Singer, M., Revlin, R., & Halldorson, M. (1990). Bridging-inferences and enthymeme. In A. Graesser & G. Bower (Eds.), *The psychology of learning and motivation* (Vol. 25, pp. 35–51). San Diego, CA: Academic Press.

Smith, E. E., Shoben, E. J., & Rips, L. J. (1974). Structure and process in semantic memory: A feature model of semantic decisions. *Psychological Review, 81*, 214–241.

Spilich, G. J., Vesonder, G. T., Chiesi, H. L., & Voss, J. F. (1979). Text processing of domain-related information for individuals with high and low domain knowledge. *Journal of Verbal Learning and Verbal Behavior, 18*, 275–290.

Stroop, J. R. (1935). Studies of interference in serial verbal reactions. *Journal of Experimental Psychology, 18*, 643–662.

Sulin, R. A., & Dooling, D. J. (1974). Intrusion of a thematic idea in retention of prose. *Journal of Experimental Psychology, 103*, 255–262.

Swinney, D. A. (1979). Lexical access during sentence comprehension: (Re)consideration of context effects. *Journal of Verbal Learning and Verbal Behavior, 18*, 545–569.

Swinney, D. A., & Osterhout, L. (1990). Inference generation during auditory language comprehension. In A. Graesser & G. Bower (Eds.), *Inferences and text comprehension*. San Diego, CA: Academic Press.

Thorndyke, P. W. (1976). The role of inferences in discourse comprehension. *Journal of Verbal Learning and Verbal Behavior, 15*, 437–446.

Thorndyke, P. W. (1977). Cognitive structures in comprehension and memory of narrative discourse. *Cognitive Psychology, 9,* 77–110.

Till, R. E., Mross, E. F., & Kintsch, W. (1988). Time course of priming for associate and inference words in a discourse context. *Memory & Cognition, 16,* 283–298.

Till, R. E., & Walsh, D. A. (1980). Encoding and retrieval factors in adult memory for implicational sentences. *Journal of Verbal Learning and Verbal Behavior, 19,* 1–16.

Trabasso, T. (1981). On the making of inferences during reading and their assessment. In J. T. Guthrie (Ed.), *Comprehension and teaching: Research reviews.* Newark, DE: International Reading Association.

Trabasso, T., Secco, T., & van den Broek, P. (1984). Causal cohesion and story coherence. In H. Mandl, N. Stein, & T. Trabasso (Eds.), *Learning and comprehension of text.* Hillsdale, NJ: Erlbaum.

Trabasso, T., & Sperry, L. L. (1985). Causal relatedness and importance of story events. *Journal of Memory and Language, 24,* 595–611.

Trabasso, T., & Suh, S. (1993). Understanding text: Achieving explanatory coherence through online inferences and mental operations in working memory. *Discourse Processes, 16,* 3–34.

Trabasso, T., & van den Broek, P. (1985). Causal thinking and the representation of narrative events. *Journal of Memory and Language, 24,* 612–630.

Trabasso, T., van den Broek, P., & Suh, S. (1989). Logical necessity and transitivity of causal relations in stories. *Discourse Processes, 12,* 1–25.

van den Broek, P. (1990a). The causal inference maker: Towards a process model of inference generation in text comprehension. In D. A. Balota, G. Flores d'Arcais, & K. Rayner (Eds.), *Comprehension processes in reading.* Hillsdale, NJ: Erlbaum.

van den Broek, P. (1990b). Causal inferences and the comprehension of narrative texts. In A. Graesser & G. Bower (Eds.), *The psychology of learning and motivation* (Vol. 25). New York: Academic Press.

van den Broek, P., & Lorch, R. F., Jr. (1993). Network representations of causal relations in memory for narrative texts: Evidence from primed recognition. *Discourse processes, 16,* 75–98.

van Dijk, T. A., & Kintsch, W. (1983). *Strategies of discourse comprehension.* New York: Academic Press.

Walker, C. H., & Meyer, B. J. F. (1980). Integrating different types of information in text. *Journal of Verbal Learning and Verbal Behavior, 19,* 263–275.

Walker, C. H., & Yekovich, F. R. (1984). Script based inferences: Effects of text and knowledge variables on recognition memory. *Journal of Verbal Learning and Verbal Behavior, 2,* 357–370.

Warren, R. E. (1972). Stimulus encoding and memory. *Journal of Experimental Psychology, 94,* 90–100.

Whitney, P. (1986). Processing category terms in context: Instantiations as inferences. *Memory & Cognition, 14,* 39–48.

Whitney, P., Ritchie, B. G., & Clark, M. B. (1991). Working-memory capacity and the use of elaborative inferences in text comprehension. *Discourse Processes, 14*(2), 133–146.

Whitney, P., & Waring, D. A. (1991). The role of knowledge in comprehension: A cognitive control perspective. In G. Simpson (Ed.), *Understanding word and sentence.* Amsterdam: Elsevier.

CHAPTER 15

QUESTION ASKING AND ANSWERING

ARTHUR C. GRAESSER, CATHY L. MCMAHEN,
AND BRENDA K. JOHNSON

I. INTRODUCTION

Two very frequent speech acts in conversation are questions and answers to questions. In fact, the question–answer adjacency pair is the most pervasive and systematic sequential pattern of speech acts in naturalistic conversation (Goffman, 1974; Schegloff & Sacks, 1973). When a speaker asks a question, there is an unbending obligation for the listener to answer or at least to acknowledge the question. Consequently, one easy way of controlling a conversation is to ask questions and thereby engage the listener to contribute actively (Dillon, 1982, 1988). Advertisers sometimes pose questions (without answers) in order to engage the public in active comprehension and to entice them to purchase their products (Frank, 1989).

This chapter reviews the research on question asking and answering in the fields of psychology and discourse processing. When appropriate, we identify theoretical contributions from fields outside psychology, such as linguistics, sociology, communications, education, and artificial intelligence. Our primary goal is to identify the psychological mechanisms that underlie question asking and answering in the context of text and conversation. An adequate theory would be able to explain what questions are asked and what answers are produced at particular points in connected discourse. This chapter focuses on the semantic, pragmatic, and conceptual content of questions and answers. It is beyond the scope of this chapter to analyze the syntactic and intonational patterns of questions and answers, even though these would be essential components in a complete theory of questioning (Bolinger, 1957; R. Brown, 1968; Crystal, 1969; Hudson, 1975; Wales & Taylor, 1987).

II. SYMBOLIC SCHEMES FOR ANALYZING QUESTIONS

Researchers in several fields have proposed schemes for classifying questions and schemes for decomposing questions into subconstituents. This section reviews the schemes that are most relevant to a psychological theory of questioning. These efforts are useful to the extent that they enhance the clarity, organization, and direction of psychological research.

A. Presupposition and Focus

Every question can be decomposed into PRESUPPOSED INFORMATION and the FOCAL INFORMATION being queried. For example, in the question *When did Frank drop out of college?* one presupposition is that Frank dropped out of college, whereas the focus addresses the time of that event. The presupposed information is in the common ground, that is, the mutual knowledge that the questioner believes is shared by the questioner and answerer (Clark & Marshall, 1981; Clark & Schaeffer, 1989; R. Kass & Finin, 1988). It is the GIVEN information from the perspective of the given–new contract in discourse processing theories (Clark & Haviland, 1977; Gernsbacher, 1990; Halliday, 1967; Needham, 1990). In a detailed and complete analysis, there would be several propositions presupposed in the example question, including: (a) Frank exists, (b) a particular college exists, (c) Frank went to the college, (d) Frank dropped out of the college, and (e) the questioner believes that both the questioner and answerer know a–e. In contrast to the presupposed information, the focus of the question draws the answerer's attention to the information that the questioner needs and hopes the answerer will supply. The answer includes new information that is outside the common ground, at least when genuine information-seeking questions are asked.

Some questions have incorrect or problematic presuppositions. Suppose, for example, that Frank never drank booze but the questioner asked *Did Frank stop drinking booze?* A cooperative answerer would correct the erroneous presupposition (e.g., *Frank never drank booze*) rather than merely answering the question *yes* or *no* (Kaplan, 1983). It is misleading to give a *yes* or *no* answer to this question even though this verification question technically invites a *yes* or *no* answer. A *yes* answer means that Frank once drank and subsequently stopped, whereas a *no* answer means that Frank continues to drink; for both of these answers, it is presupposed that Frank drank booze (Green, 1989; Grishman, 1986; Kempson, 1979). Cooperative answerers are expected to correct erroneous presuppositions rather than to supply a misleading *yes/no* answer. A crafty lawyer can trick a witness into accepting an erroneous presupposition by insisting that the witness supply a *yes* or *no* answer to this type of leading question (Loftus, 1975).

Listeners do not always carefully scrutinize the validity of the presuppositions of questions. A striking example of this is the Moses illusion (Erikson & Mattson, 1981; Reder & Cleeremans, 1990). When asked *How many animals of each kind did Moses take on the ark?* most people answer *two* in spite of the fact that they know that Noah rather than Moses took the animals on the ark. Listeners normally assume that the speaker is being cooperative and is presupposing only correct information (Grice, 1975), so the answerer does not expend much effort evaluating whether the presuppositions behind a question are true. In contrast, the answerer does notice incorrect information in the *focus* of a question, e.g., *Was it Moses who took two animals of each kind on the ark?* (Reder & Cleeremans, 1990).

B. Assumptions behind Information-Seeking Questions

Some questions are genuine information-seeking questions in the sense that the questioner is missing information and believes that the answerer can supply it. Van der Meij (1987) identified several assumptions that must be met before an utterance constitutes a genuine information-seeking question.

1. The questioner does not know the information asked for with the question.
2. The questioner believes that the presuppositions of the question are true.
3. The questioner believes that an answer exists.
4. The questioner wants to know the answer.
5. The questioner can assess whether a reply constitutes an answer.
6. The questioner believes the answerer knows the answer.
7. The questioner believes that the answerer will not give the answer in absence of the question.
8. The questioner believes that the answerer will supply the answer.
9. The questioner poses the question only if the benefits exceed the costs, for instance, the benefits of knowing the answer must exceed the costs of asking the question.

A question is not an information-seeking question to the extent that these assumptions are not met. For example, instead of being information-seeking questions, some interrogative utterances are indirect requests for the listener to do something on behalf of the speaker (Clark, 1979; Francik & Clark, 1985; Gibbs & Mueller, 1988; Gordon & Lakoff, 1971; Searle, 1969). When a speaker says *Could you pass the salt?* at a dinner conversation, the speaker wants the listener to perform an action rather than formulate a reply that addresses the listener's salt-passing abilities. This utterance fails to meet most of the nine assumptions listed above. Similarly, gripes (e.g., *Why don't you listen to me?*) are interrogative expressions that would fail to meet many of the assumptions of a genuine information-seeking question. It should be noted that speech acts are normally defined according to the assumptions shared by speech participants rather than by syntactic or semantic regularities (Allen, 1987; Bach & Harnish, 1979; Gibbs & Mueller, 1988; Hudson, 1975; Searle, 1969).

Given this theoretical context, there is the pressing issue of what constitutes a question. It is important to acknowledge that even an information-seeking "question," or what we call an INQUIRY, is not always expressed in an interrogative syntactic form, i.e., an utterance with a question mark(?).

(1) a. *What is your address?* (interrogative mood)
    b. *Tell me what your address is.* (imperative mood)
    c. *I need to know your address.* (declarative mood)

The utterances in (1) are inquiries, but only the first utterance is an interrogative expression. Moreover, it is not the case that all interrogative expressions are inquiries, as in (2).

(2) a. *What is your address?* (inquiry)
    b. *Could you pass the salt?* (request, directive)
    c. *Why don't you ever listen to me?* (gripe)

Therefore, there is hardly a direct mapping between the syntactic mood of an utterance and its pragmatic speech act category (Bach & Harnish, 1979; Hudson, 1975; Searle, 1969). For the purposes of this chapter, we define a question as either an inquiry, an interrogative expression, or both.

C. Categorization of Questions

Graesser, Person, and Huber (1992) developed an analytical scheme for classifying questions, which is presented in Table I. The question categories are defined primarily on the basis of the content of the information sought rather than on the question stems (i.e., *why, where, who,* etc.). Causal antecedent questions, for example, tap the previous events and enabling states that caused some event to occur. A causal antecedent question can be articulated linguistically with a variety of stems: Why did the event occur, How did the event occur, What caused the event to occur, What enabled the event to occur, and so on. Verification questions invite brief replies of *yes, no,* or *maybe*. Most of the question categories have an interrogative syntactic form. The two exceptions are the assertion and request/directive categories, which are inquiries expressed in a declarative or imperative mood.

The question categorization scheme proposed by Graesser, Person, and Huber (1992) is grounded both in theory and in empirical research. The theoretical foundations include models of question answering in artificial intelligence (Allen, 1987; Lehnert, 1978; Schank & Abelson, 1977; Souther, Acker, Lester, & Porter, 1989) and speech act classifications in discourse processing (D'Andrade & Wish, 1985). The classification scheme is empirically adequate in two senses. First, the scheme is exhaustive because it could accommodate thousands of questions that were asked in the context of tutoring and classroom interactions (Graesser, Person, & Huber, 1993). Second, the scheme is reliable because trained judges could classify the questions with a high degree of interjudge reliability.

The question categories vary in the length of the expected answers. Questions that invite short answers, such as verification questions and concept completion questions, place few demands on the answerer because a satisfactory answer is only a word or phrase. The answers to long-answer questions typically span several sentences. One way to induce a listener to talk is to ask a long-answer question, including causal antecedent, goal orientation, instrumental-procedural, and the others.

Some questions are hybrids of two or more question categories. Verification questions are frequently combined with another category. For example, the question *Did Frank drop out of school because of drinking?* is a hybrid between a verification question and a causal antecedent question. This hybrid question gives the option to the answerer as to whether to answer the short-answer verification question, the long-answer causal antecedent question, or both. The fact that there are hybrid questions should not be construed as a weakness in the classification scheme. Most adequate classification schemes in the social sciences are POLYTHETIC rather than MONOTHETIC (Stokal, 1974). Each observation can be assigned to one and only one category in a monothetic classification scheme, whereas an observation can be assigned to multiple categories in a polythetic classification.

TABLE I

Question Categories in Graesser, Person, and Huber (1993) Scheme

Question category	Abstract specification	Example
Short answer		
Verification	Is a fact true? Did an event occur?	*Is the answer five?*
Disjunctive	Is X or Y the case? Is X, Y, or Z the case?	*Is* gender *or* female *the variable?*
Concept completion	Who? What? What is the referent of a noun argument slot?	*Who ran this experiment?*
Feature specification	What qualitative attributes does entity X have?	*What are the properties of a bar graph?*
Quantification	What is the value of a quantitative variable? How many?	*How many degrees of freedom are on this variable?*
Long answer		
Definition	What does X mean?	*What is a* t *test?*
Example	What is an example label or instance of the category?	*What is an example of a factorial design?*
Comparison	How is X similar to Y? How is X different from Y?	*What is the difference between a* t *test and an F test?*
Interpretation	What concept or claim can be inferred from a static or active pattern of data?	*What is happening in this graph?*
Causal antecedent	What state or event causally led to an event or state?	*How did this experiment fail?*
Causal consequence	What are the consequences of an event or state?	*What happens when this level decreases?*
Goal orientation	What are the motives or goals behind an agent's action?	*Why did you put decision latency on the y-axis?*
Instrumental/procedural	What instrument or plan allows an agent to accomplish a goal?	*How do you present the stimulus on each trial?*
Enablement	What object or resource allows an agent to perform an action?	*What device allows you to measure stress?*
Expectational	Why did some expected event not occur?	*Why isn't there an interaction?*
Judgmental	What value does the answerer place on an idea or advice?	*Should I memorize the formula?*
Assertion	The speaker makes a statement indicating he lacks knowledge or does not understand an idea.	*I don't understand main effects.*
Request/directive	The speaker wants the listener to perform an action.	*Would you add those numbers together?*

D. Goals of Speech Participants

An adequate theory of questioning must keep track of the goals of the speech participants (Allen, 1983, 1987; Appelt, 1984; Bruce, 1982; Clark, 1979; Cohen, Perrault, & Allen, 1982; Francik & Clark, 1985; Graesser, Roberts, & Hackett-

Renner, 1990; Kaplan, 1983; R. Kass & Finin, 1988). Suppose a passenger rushes through an airport, approaches a flight attendant, and asks, *When does Northwest 422 leave?* A cooperative reply would give both time and location information (such as *1:33 at gate B21*) even though the literal question specifies only time information. The unsolicited location information is included in the answer because the answerer appropriately analyzed the goals of the questioner. The customer obviously was in a hurry and needed to make the flight on time; the customer had the goal of being at the correct gate in addition to the goal of being at the gate on time. In this example, the location information does not address the literal question but it does properly address the questioner's goals.

The Gricean maxims (Grice, 1975) can be viewed as goals for effective communication. The goals associated with the maxim of Quality are to be truthful and to avoid making claims that cannot be supported with evidence. The goals associated with the maxim of Manner are to avoid obscurity, to avoid ambiguity, to be brief, and to be orderly. Similarly, there are goals associated with the maxims of Quantity and Relation. Hovy (1988) has identified the goals that are associated with speech acts and the pragmatic components of conversation. The importance of tracking goals is compatible with the view that a theory of questioning is embedded in a more general theory of conversation and discourse context (Clark & Schaeffer, 1989; Cohen et al., 1982).

E. Question Generation Mechanisms

Graesser, Person, and Huber (1992, 1993) identified four clusters of mechanisms that generate questions in naturalistic conversation. Some of these mechanisms are familiar to researchers investigating question asking (A. Kass, 1992; Ram, 1990; Reisbeck, 1988; Schank, 1986) whereas others were discovered when Graesser, Person, and Huber (1992, 1993) analyzed transcripts of tutoring sessions and classroom interactions.

1. Questions That Address Knowledge Deficits

The speaker asks a question when he identifies a deficit in his knowledge base and wants to correct the deficit. These information-seeking questions occur in the following conditions:

1. The questioner encounters an obstacle in a plan or problem. For example, a passenger cannot find his gate so he asks a flight attendant, *Where is gate B45?*
2. A contradiction is detected. A person observes that a television is displaying a program when the set is not plugged into an electrical outlet, so the person holds the plug and asks, *How does this television work?*
3. An unusual or anomalous event is observed. A business person hears about a 110 point increase in the Dow Jones average and asks, *Why is there a sudden increase in the stock market?*
4. There is an obvious gap in the questioner's knowledge base. A child hears her parents use the rare word *aardvark* and asks *What does* aardvark *mean?*
5. The questioner needs to make a decision among a set of alternatives that are equally attractive. For example, a customer in a restaurant cannot decide

between the trout and the chicken dish, so he asks the waiter how each is prepared.

Graesser and McMahen (1993) reported that these conditions causally produce an increase in the number of questions that college students ask when they read stories and when they solve quantitative word problems. The students in that study were instructed to generate questions while they solved either the original versions of word problems or versions that were transformed to create knowledge deficits, for instance by deleting critical information to solve the problem, adding a contradiction, versus adding anomalous information. A subset of the students' questions directly referred to the transformations that produced knowledge deficits.

2. Questions That Monitor Common Ground

Some questions monitor the common ground between questioner and answerer. The speech participants need to establish, negotiate, and update their mutual knowledge in order to achieve successful communication (Clark & Marshall, 1981; Clark & Schaeffer, 1989). Questions are generated in order to inquire whether the listener knows anything about a topic (e.g., *Do you know about woodwind instruments?*), to verify that a belief is correct (*Isn't a flute a woodwind instrument?*), and to gauge how well the listener is understanding (*Do you follow?*). Tag questions are in this category (e.g., *A flute is a woodwind instrument, isn't it?*).

3. Questions That Coordinate Social Action

Some questions are needed for multiple agents to collaborate in group activities and for single agents to get other agents to do things. This cluster of question asking mechanisms includes the following five types of speech acts: indirect requests (e.g., *Would you do X?*), indirect advice (*Why don't you do X?*), permission (*Can I do X?*), offers (*Can I do X for you?*), and negotiations (*If I do X, will you do Y?*).

4. Questions That Control Conversation and Attention

Some questions are generated in order to impose control over the course of conversation and the attention of the speech participants. These include rhetorical questions, greetings, gripes, replies to summons, and questions that change the flow of conversation. The mechanisms in cluster 4 manage conversation, whereas those in cluster 3 manage the actions of agents.

A particular question might be inspired by multiple mechanisms of question generation. For example, when a hostess asks a timid guest the question *Did you read* The Prince of Tides? the question monitors common ground (cluster 2) and changes the flow of conversation (cluster 4).

III. QUESTION ANSWERING IN THE CONTEXT OF TEXT

This section reviews psychological research on question answering when adults answer questions in the context of narrative and expository text. The methods in these studies are quite simple. The subject first reads a text and later answers questions about the information in the text, as illustrated in Table II. The central theoretical challenge is to explain the answers to these questions and the time to generate these answers. The ANSWER DISTRIBUTION for a question is the set of particular answers to a question and the percentage of subjects who generate each answer (see Table II). An adequate theory would accurately discriminate between those answers that are in versus not in the answer distributions for particular questions. An ANSWER LATENCY is the amount of time it takes to generate a particular answer to a question. Answer latencies are typically collected on short-answer questions, namely the verification questions that invite a short answer (i.e., *yes, no, maybe, I don't know*). The processing components in a model are rigorously tested in experiments that collect answer latencies.

Psychological models of question answering have postulated numerous components or stages of question processing. The most frequently discussed processing components include syntactic parsing, transforming the question into a logical or canonical form, categorizing the question by assigning it to one of *n* categories (e.g., Table I), comparing representations or structures, executing an answering strategy, producing a response, and articulating an answer linguistically (Graesser, Lang, & Roberts, 1991; Graesser & Murachver, 1985; Norman & Rumelhart, 1975; Singer, 1984, 1985, 1986, 1990, 1991).

The time course of executing the processing components has received some attention. Some of these components are executed in parallel in a distributed, interactive fashion (Graesser, Lang, & Roberts, 1991; Robertson, Black, & Lehnert, 1985; Singer, 1991). In some cases, one component is initiated, if not completed, before another processing component begins (Graesser, Lang, & Roberts, 1991; Singer, 1985, 1990, 1991). The relative time course of some of

TABLE II
The Story of *The Czar and His Daughters* and Some Example
Question–Answer Protocols

The czar and his daughters

Once there was a czar who had three lovely daughters. One day the three daughters went walking in the woods. They were enjoying themselves so much that they forgot the time and stayed too long. A dragon kidnapped the three daughters. As they were being dragged off they cried for help. Three heroes heard their cries and set off to rescue the daughters. The heroes came and fought the dragon and rescued the maidens. Then the heroes returned the daughters to their palace. When the czar heard of the rescue, he rewarded the heroes.

Question–Answer protocols

Why did the heroes fight the dragon?
    in order to rescue the daughters (50% of answerers)
    in order to free the daughters from the dragon (13%)
    because the dragon kidnapped the daughters (38%)
    because the daughters were frightened (25%)
How did the heroes fight the dragon?
    The heroes went to the dragon (25%)
    The heroes used swords (63%)
    The heroes burned the dragon (13%)

the components is not entirely resolved. For example, investigators originally suspected that question parsing and question encoding preceded the selection and execution of an answering strategy (Singer, 1985, 1990; Woods, 1977). However, there is evidence that question answering strategies can sometimes begin execution during the process of encoding a question (Dyer, 1983; Robertson et al., 1985). Answerers might not feel confident they have understood the question until they have generated at least a portion of an answer to the question.

Current psychological models have benefited from the detailed models of question answering in artificial intelligence and computational linguistics (Allen, 1983, 1987; Dahlgren, 1988; Dyer, 1983; Kaplan, 1983; Lehnert, 1978; Lehnert, Dyer, Johnson, Young, & Hartley, 1983; McKeown, 1985; Souther et al., 1989; Woods, 1977). In most of these models, text and world knowledge are organized in the form of structured databases. Question answering strategies access these information sources and search through the structures systematically. Psychological studies were eventually conducted in order to test whether the formalisms and insights from these computational models are psychologically plausible.

In the remainder of this section we focus on one psychological model of question answering called QUEST (Graesser & Franklin, 1990; Graesser, Gordon, & Brainerd, 1992; Graesser & Hemphill, 1991; Graesser, Lang, & Roberts, 1991). At this point, QUEST is the only psychological model that handles a broad diversity of questions and that has been tested empirically with experimental methods (but also see Singer, 1985, 1990). QUEST was influenced by existing models of question answering in artificial intelligence and computational linguistics. There was also the benefit of a few psychological studies that analyzed question answering in the context of short stories (Goldman & Varnhagen, 1986; Graesser, 1981; Graesser & Clark, 1985; Graesser & Murachver, 1985; Graesser, Robertson, & Anderson, 1981; Stein & Glenn, 1979; Trabasso, van den Broek, & Lui, 1988), lengthy fairy tales (Graesser, Robertson, Lovelace, & Swinehart, 1980), scripts (Bower, Black, & Turner, 1979; Galambos & Black, 1985; Graesser, 1978), and expository text (Graesser, 1981).

A. Components of the QUEST Model of Question Answering

QUEST has four highly interactive components. First, during QUESTION CATEGORIZATION, QUEST translates the question into a logical form and assigns it to one of several question categories (see Table I). Second, QUEST identifies the INFORMATION SOURCES that are relevant to the question. Third, CONVERGENCE MECHANISMS compute the subset of proposition units (called STATEMENT NODES) in the information sources that serve as relevant answers to the question. These convergence mechanisms narrow the node space from hundreds of nodes in the information sources to a handful of good answers to a question. Fourth, PRAGMATIC FEATURES of the communicative interaction influence answer formulation, such as the goals and common ground of speech participants. It should be noted that QUEST was developed to account for the conceptual content of the answers rather than the parsing of the question syntactically and the process of articulating a reply linguistically.

An information source is a structured database that furnishes answers to a question. In order to illustrate the representation of an information source,

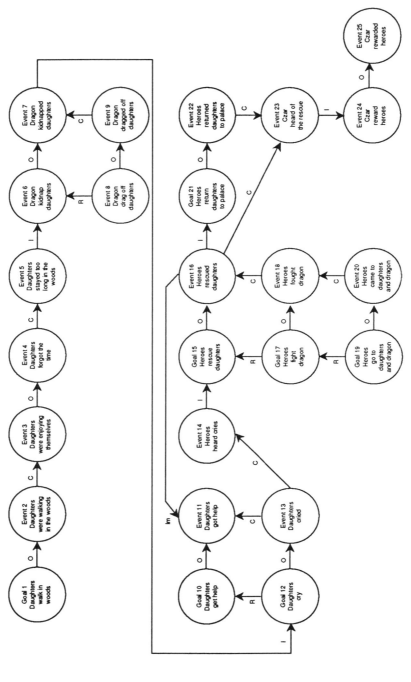

FIG. 1 An example conceptual graph structure that captures the plot in "The Czar and his Daughters." The statement nodes are in the circles. The arc categories are Consequence (C), Reason (R), Initiate (I), Outcome (O), and Implies (Im) (from Graesser, Lang, & Roberts, 1991). Copyright (1991) by the American Psychological Association. Reprinted with permission.

consider the story "The czar and his daughters" in Table II. The knowledge structure associated with the explicit text is presented in Figure 1. Each statement node is a proposition-like unit with node category (i.e., event, state, goal, style specification) and an identification number. The node categories are briefly defined below.

1. *State.* An ongoing characteristic which remains unchanged throughout the time frame under consideration, such as the story plot.
2. *Event.* A state change within the time frame.
3. *Goal.* An event, state, or style specification that an agent desires.
4. *Action.* A goal that is achieved after the agent executes a plan.
5. *Style Specification.* The speed, force, or qualitative manner in which an event unfolds.

The nodes are interrelated by different categories of DIRECTED ARCS. The SOURCE NODE is at the beginning of each directed arc and the END NODE is at the head. The complete representational system has nine arc categories: Consequence (C), Implies (Im), Reason (R), Manner (M), Outcome (O), Initiate (I), Set Membership, Property, and Referential Pointer. It is beyond the scope of this chapter to describe the composition rules and conceptual constraints of these nine categories in detail (see Graesser & Clark, 1985). It suffices to say that there are particular constraints that must be satisfied before two nodes can be linked by a particular arc category. For example, Reason arcs can relate goal nodes but not any other nodes categories; in contrast, Consequence arcs can never relate goal nodes. The source node of a Consequence arc must have existed or occurred in time prior to its end node, but both nodes can exist/occur simultaneously in the case of an Implies arc.

The representational system adopted by the QUEST model has properties that exist in a number of representational systems in the cognitive sciences. These include propositional theories (J. R. Anderson, 1983; Kintsch, 1974; Norman & Rumelhart, 1975), story grammars (Mandler, 1984; Stein & Glenn, 1979), causal chain theories (Black & Bower, 1980; Trabasso et al., 1988; Trabasso, van den Broek, & Suh, 1989), conceptual dependency theory (Lehnert, 1978; Schank & Abelson, 1977), rhetorical organization (Mann & Thompson, 1986; Meyer, 1985), and conceptual graphs (Sowa, 1983). These are the major theoretical systems for representing text at the semantic and conceptual levels.

Whenever a question is asked, QUEST computes an expression with three slots, as specified in (3).

(3) QUESTION (⟨Q-focus⟩, ⟨Q-category⟩, ⟨information sources⟩)

The question *Why did the heroes fight the dragon?* would be translated into expression (4).

(4) QUESTION (⟨heroes fight dragon⟩, ⟨goal orientation⟩, ⟨Figure 1 structure⟩)

The Q-focus corresponds to the focus of the question, in contrast to its presuppositions. The Q-category is one of the categories in Table I. The information sources are one or more knowledge structures that exist in long-term memory. Some information sources are EPISODIC knowledge structures that capture particular episodes that a person experienced or read about in the past. Other information sources are GENERIC structures that summarize the typical properties of the content it represents. For example, there are three generic knowledge structures that would be activated by the example question, one for each content word: HERO, FIGHTING, and DRAGON. QUEST assumes that long-term memory is a vast storehouse of these episodic and generic knowledge structures and that these structures furnish the content of the answers to questions.

A question may activate several information sources in working memory. For example, the question *Why did the heroes fight the dragon?* would probably activate the text structure (i.e., Fig. 1), generic structures triggered by the content words (HERO, FIGHTING, DRAGON), and a generic structure triggered by patterns of information (e.g., FAIRY TALE). Each information source is a structured database with dozens/hundreds of nodes, so there is a wealth of information available in working memory when a question is answered. Since many of these structures are generic and therefore quite familiar to the answerer, hundreds of these nodes are automatically activated to some degree. If there were five information sources and each source had 50 nodes activated automatically, then 250 nodes would be available in working memory. Clearly, most of these nodes would not be produced as an answer to the question. Instead, only a small subset of the 250 nodes (<10) are produced as answers when adults answer questions. The convergence mechanisms specify how QUEST begins with 250 nodes in the node space and narrows the space down to approximately 10 good answers.

Graesser and Clark (1985) identified those information sources that are particularly prolific when adults answer questions about episodes in short stories, such as the czar story in Table II. They analyzed a large range of questions that had the following stems: Why, How, When, Where, What enabled X to occur, What are the consequences of X, and What is the significance of X. Graesser and Clark reported that word-activated generic structures furnished about 72% of the answers and that pattern-activated generic structures produced a modest increment of 8% additional answers. The remaining 20% of the answers did not match any of the nodes in the generic knowledge structures; they were novel constructions formulated by interactions between the generic knowledge and the passage structure. The generic structures that are associated with the main verbs in questions were more prolific information sources than were the generic knowledge structures associated with nouns. This outcome was quite expected because (a) the passages were stories, (b) actions and events are central to narrative text, and (c) main verbs impose more constraints on actions and events than do nouns. Not surprisingly, the generic structures in working memory were substantially more prolific information sources than were those that had exited, but recently resided in working memory. Most of the answers (75%) came from generic structures rather than explicit text structures in the case of stories. In contrast, most answers came from the explicit textbase in the case of expository texts about scientific mechanisms (Graesser, 1981; Graesser & Hemphill, 1991).

B. Convergence Mechanisms in the QUEST Model

A key component of QUEST is the convergence mechanisms that narrow down the node space from dozens/hundreds of nodes to a handful of good answers to a question. This is accomplished by four subcomponents: (a) an intersecting node identifier, (b) structural distance, (c) an arc search procedure, and (d) constraint satisfaction.

1. Intersecting Nodes and Structural Distance

The intersecting node identifier isolates (or activates) those statement nodes from different information sources that intersect (i.e., match, overlap). The intersecting nodes have a higher likelihood of being produced as answers than do nonintersecting nodes (Golding, Graesser, & Millis, 1990; Graesser & Clark, 1985). For example, consider the following answers to the question *Why did the heroes fight the dragon?*.

(5) *In order to rescue the daughters.*
(6) *In order to free the daughters from the dragon.*
(7) *Because the daughters cried.*

Answer (5) has intersecting nodes from multiple knowledge structures: node 15 in the passage structure (see Fig. 1), the node "hero rescue victim" in the generic knowledge structure for HERO, and the node "agent X rescue Y" in the generic knowledge structure for FIGHTING. In contrast, answer (6) does not intersect any nodes in the passage structure and the generic knowledge structures triggered by the question. QUEST therefore predicts that answer (5) is better than answer (6).

The likelihood that a node is produced as an answer decreases exponentially as a function of its structural distance (i.e., number of arcs) from the nearest intersecting node (Graesser & Clark, 1985; Graesser & Hemphill, 1991; Graesser, Lang, & Roberts, 1991; Graesser & Murachver, 1985). Consider (5)–(7) in the context of the passage structure in Figure 1. Node 17 is queried with a *why*-question. Answer (5) matches node 15, whereas answer (7) matches node 13. Answer (5) is one arc from the queried node and answer (7) is three arcs away. Therefore, QUEST predicts that answer (5) is better than answer (7).

2. Arc Search Procedure

Each question category has a particular arc search procedure which restricts its search for answers to particular paths of nodes and relational arcs. Nodes on legal paths are substantially better answers than nodes on illegal paths (Golding et al., 1990; Graesser & Clark, 1985; Graesser & Hemphill, 1991; Graesser, Lang, & Roberts, 1991). When an information source is accessed, the arc search procedure is applied to each intersecting node in the information source (which is called an ENTRY NODE). For example, node 17 in Figure 1 is an entry node for the question *Why did the heroes fight the dragon?* because this node matches the Q-focus. Once an entry node is located in an information source, the arc search procedure executes a breadth-first search from the entry node by pursuing legal arcs that radiate from the entry node. There is a particular set of arc categories and arc directions that is legal for each question category. The legal paths for some of these question categories are specified below.

1. *Causal antecedent questions.* Legal nodes are on paths of backward Consequence|Implies|Outcome|Initiate arcs and forward Implies arc. Any sequence or combination of these arc categories would be legal as the arc search procedure radiates from the entry node.

2. *Causal consequence questions.* The inverse of causal antecedent questions.
3. *Goal orientation questions.* Legal nodes are on paths of (a) superordinate goals via paths of forward Reason and backward Manner arcs, (b) goal initiators via backward Initiate arcs, and (c) causal antecedents of the nodes in (b).
4. *Instrumental-procedural questions.* Legal nodes are on paths of (a) subordinate goals/actions via paths of backward Reason and forward Manner arcs and (b) goal initiators via backward initiate arcs.

For illustration, consider the question *Why did the heroes fight the dragon?* The entry node is node 17 in Figure 1, and the question category is goal orientation. The arc search procedure would produce the following legal answers to this question: nodes 1–9 and 12–15. The following nodes from Figure 1 are illegal: nodes 10, 11, 16, 19–25. Next consider the question *How did the heroes fight the dragon?* The entry node and knowledge structure are the same. This question is an instrumental-procedural question, so the legal answers include node 19, whereas the remaining nodes in Figure 1 are illegal. This example illustrates how the arc search procedure systematically samples nodes from the passage structure. The arc search procedure would be executed in the same way for each of the entry nodes in the generic knowledge structures.

3. Constraint Satisfaction

The semantic and conceptual content of the answer should not be incompatible with the content of the Q-focus. Constraint satisfaction discards those candidate nodes in the node space that are incompatible with the question focus. Stated differently, the question focus has semantic and conceptual constraints that are propagated among the nodes in the node space, ultimately pruning out the incompatible nodes. Nodes are incompatible if they directly contradict the question focus (e.g., *the heroes helped the dragon* contradicts the question focus of the heroes fighting the dragon) or if they are in a different time frame (e.g., the heroes were born). There is evidence that nodes which satisfy the constraints are better answers than nodes that violate the constraints (Graesser & Clark, 1985; Graesser, Lang, & Roberts, 1991).

4. Comparisons of Subcomponents of the Convergence Mechanism

There have been several tests of QUEST's convergence mechanism, as cited above. Each of these subcomponents has successfully predicted (a) the likelihood that adults produce particular answers to particular questions and (b) goodness of answer (GOA) judgments of particular question–answer pairs. Answer likelihoods are measured by asking a subject a particular question (such as *Why did the heroes fight the dragon?*) and observing the percentage of subjects who give a particular answer (e.g., 50% answered *in order to rescue the daughters*). When GOA judgments are collected, both the question and the answer are presented, and the subjects give a GOA decision by pressing either a GOOD ANSWER or a BAD ANSWER button. The convergence mechanisms have robustly predicted which nodes from the node space are good versus bad answers, as defined by these two measures. The convergence mechanisms have accounted for 40% to 75% of the variance of the scores, depending on the materials and the dependent measure. The arc search procedure has consistently been the most robust predictor of the answer likelihoods and the GOA decisions. Graesser, Roberts, and Hackett-Renner (1990) also reported that QUEST's arc search procedures can account for 82% of the answers produced in naturalistic contexts that have complex pragmatic constraints, such as telephone surveys, televised interviews, and business transactions.

It is possible to estimate convergence rates associated with the subcomponents of the convergence mechanism (Graesser, Gordon, & Brainerd, 1992). The arc search procedure cuts the node space to 10% of the original set of nodes when a random set of nodes in a generic knowledge structure is queried. Structural distance reduces it further to 4% of the original node space, and constraint satisfaction reduces it to 2%. Therefore, if the node space began with 250 nodes, then there would be five good answers that pass the arc search procedure, structural distance, and constraint satisfaction.

Graesser, Lang, and Roberts (1991) investigated how the above three subcomponents interacted when a GOA judgment is made. After reading a narrative text, subjects received question–answer pairs and decided as quickly as possible whether the answer was a good versus a bad answer to a question by pressing one of two buttons. Answer latencies were analyzed in addition to the likelihood that subjects decided the answer was good. These data could be explained by a particular processing model in which (a) the arc search and constraint satisfaction components were executed in parallel and prior to (b) the evaluation of structural distance; structural distance was evaluated only when there was a discrepancy in output between the arc search procedure component and the constraint satisfaction component. The subjects apparently used structural distance as a criterion for resolving conflicts between the arc search procedure and the constraint satisfaction components. The evaluation of structural distance was comparatively slow, and the answer latencies decreased as a function of structural distance. It should be noted that a spreading activation model (J. R. Anderson, 1983) would predict an increase (not a decrease) in GOA latencies as a function of structural distance. The structural distance evaluator involves a process of discriminating whether the answer node is close to the queried node in the text and whether the answer node occurred before or after the queried node in the story plot. Such discriminations are accomplished more quickly when the answer is more distant from the queried node, as would be the case in any comparative judgment task (Banks, 1977).

IV. QUESTION ASKING WHILE LEARNING

Questions have received a great deal of attention in education. An ideal learner perhaps is an active, curious, inquisitive student who troubleshoots his knowledge deficits and asks a large number of questions. It has been argued that learners should take a more active role in constructing, regulating, and monitoring their own learning and comprehension activities (Carroll, Mack, Lewis, Grischkowsky, & Robertson, 1985; Flavell, 1978; Papert, 1980). There is some evidence that good students actively monitor their comprehension failures (A. L. Brown, Bransford, Ferrara, & Campione, 1983; Chi, Bassok, Lewis, Reimann, & Glaser, 1989; Zimmerman, 1989).

Unfortunately, however, students do not naturally acquire the skills of identifying knowledge deficits and self-regulating their knowledge, so these skills need to be taught (Baker & Brown, 1980; Bransford, Arbitman-Smith, Stein, & Vye, 1985; A. L. Brown, 1988; Collins, 1985; Pressley, Goodchild, Fleet, Zajchowski, & Evans, 1989). It is well documented that students ask very few questions in classroom settings (Dillon, 1988; Good, Slavings, Harel, & Emerson, 1987; Kerry, 1987; van der Meij, 1988). Approximately 0.2 questions per student are asked during a typical hour in a classroom. There are several social barriers and costs to asking questions in a classroom, such as revealing one's ignorance and interrupting the teacher. In a tutoring environment, the question asking rate increases to approximately 10 student questions per hour (Graesser, Person, & Huber, 1993). Unfortunately, most student questions are shallow questions about definitions of terms and the facts that were explicitly mentioned in text, rather than deep questions that involve reasoning, inference, synthesis, and evaluation. Part of the problem is that 96% of the teacher questions in classrooms are shallow rather than deep questions, so students are not exposed to good role models (Kerry, 1987). In a tutoring environment, the rate of deep questions increases both for students and for tutors (Graesser, Person, & Huber, 1993). However, generally speaking, students need to be taught how to ask good questions.

On the optimistic side, there is evidence that training students in how to ask good questions leads to substantial improvements in the comprehension and acquisition of technical material (Davey & McBride, 1986; Gavelek & Raphael, 1985; King, 1989; Palinscar & Brown, 1984; Singer & Donlan, 1982). One way of doing this is to incorporate adjunct questions before, during, or after the reading material (R. C. Anderson & Biddle, 1975; Andre, 1987; Rickards, 1979; Rothkopf, 1965). Most of the research in this adjunct question paradigm has shown facilitation only for information relevant to the questions. Therefore, the insertion of adjunct questions into text may not lead to general improvements in deep comprehension. It appears that students need to receive extensive training on question asking skills before there will be persistent, widespread improvements in deep comprehension (Palinscar & Brown, 1984; Pressley et al., 1989).

Computers provide one promising avenue for training students how to spontaneously use effective question asking skills. In some recent systems, students can quickly ask questions by pointing to content elements on the computer screen and selecting a question from a menu of good questions (Graesser, Langston, & Lang, 1992; Schank, Fergeson, Birnbaum, Barger, & Greising, 1991; Sebrechts & Swartz, 1991). These menu-based question asking systems have some technical advantages over alternative query methods on computers (Lang, Graesser, Dumais, & Kilman, 1992; Tennant, 1987; Williams, 1984; Zloof, 1975). The student learns what questions are good by inspecting the menu of quality questions. Graesser, Langston, and Baggett (1993) reported that the number of student questions asked in their Point and Query computer system was 800 times the rate of student questions in a classroom environment and 15 times the rate in a tutoring environment. Additional research is needed, however, to assess whether the Point and Query system will permanently enhance curiosity, question asking, comprehension, and learning.

The questions that tutors ask in tutoring sessions have only recently been analyzed (Graesser, Person, & Huber, 1992, 1993; McArthur, Stasz, &

Zmuidzinas, 1990). There are some sophisticated ideal models of tutor questioning, such as the Socratic method (Stevens, Collins, & Goldin, 1982), the inquiry method (Collins, 1985, 1988), and the reciprocal training method (Palinscar & Brown, 1984). For example, in the Socratic method the tutor asks the student a series of carefully crafted questions so that the student actively discovers his major misconceptions during the course of answering the question. In the reciprocal training method, the tutor displays good question asking behavior, directs the student to model this behavior, provides qualitative feedback to the student, and eventually fades from the process as the student masters the skills of good question asking. Unfortunately, these sophisticated questioning methods are difficult for tutors to acquire and therefore virtually never occur in normal tutoring sessions. Instead, tutors normally grill students by asking them preformulated, scripted questions or questions triggered by obvious conceptual errors on the part of the student (McArthur et al., 1990).

When a tutor asks a student a difficult question, most of the student's answers are either partially correct, incoherent, vague, and error-ridden (Graesser, Huber, & Person, 1991). As a consequence, the tutor helps the student answer the question in the form of a collaborative process that takes several conversational turns. There is an average of 6 turns for *why*-questions and 10 turns for *how*-questions. Although the tutor originally asks a question, the tutor ends up supplying most of the correct information during the course of these turns. The process of answering a question in a tutoring session is therefore a collaborative process in which both speech participants construct an answer. Such collaborative processes have been emphasized in contemporary models of discourse and social interaction (Clark & Schaeffer, 1989; Fox, 1988; Resnick, Salmon, & Zeitz, 1991; Tannen, 1984).

In closing, the available research suggests that the questions posed by the typical student, teacher, and tutor are either infrequent or unsophisticated. Therefore, individuals need to be extensively trained in how to ask the right questions at the right time in a manner that is sensitive to the content of the world knowledge. One promising direction is to build computer interfaces and educational software around ideal question asking and answering. It is well documented that individuals dramatically improve their comprehension and acquisition of technical material to the extent that they acquire effective question asking and answering skills. Therefore, questions should continue to play a prominent role in education.

ACKNOWLEDGMENTS

This research was partially funded by grants awarded to the first author by the Office of Naval Research (N00014-88-K-0110 and N00014-90-J-1492).

REFERENCES

Allen, J. (1983). Recognizing intentions from natural language utterances. In M. Brady & R. C. Berwick (Eds.), *Computational models of discourse*. Cambridge, MA: MIT Press.
Allen, J. (1987). *Natural language understanding*. Menlo Park, CA: Benjamin/Cummings.
Anderson, J. R. (1983). *The architecture of cognition*. Cambridge, MA: Harvard University Press.

Anderson, R. C., & Biddle, W. B. (1975). On asking people questions about what they are reading. In G. Bower (Ed.), *The psychology of learning and motivation* (Vol. 9). New York: Academic Press.

Andre, T. (1987). Questions and learning from reading. *Questioning Exchange, 1*(1), 47–86.

Appelt, D. E. (1984). Planning English referring expressions. *Artificial Intelligence, 26*(1), 1–33.

Bach, K., & Harnish, R. M. (1979). *Linguistic communication and speech acts.* Cambridge, MA: MIT Press.

Baker, L., & Brown, A. L. (1980). Metacognitive skills in reading. In D. Pearson (Ed.), *Handbook of reading research.* New York: Plenum.

Banks, W. P. (1977). Encoding and processing of symbolic information in comparative judgment. In G. H. Bower (Ed.), *The psychology of learning and motivation* (Vol. 11, pp. 101–159). San Diego, CA: Academic Press.

Black, J. B., & Bower, G. H. (1980). Story understanding as problem-solving. *Poetics, 9,* 223–250.

Bolinger, D. L. (1957). *Interrogative structures of American English.* Tuscaloosa, AL: University of Alabama Press.

Bower, G. H. Black, J. B. & Turner, T. J. (1979). Scripts in memory for text. *Cognitive Psychology, 11,* 177–220.

Bransford, J. D., Arbitman-Smith, R., Stein, B. S., & Vye N. J. (1985). Analysis—improving thinking and learning skills: An analysis of three approaches. In S. F. Chipman, J. W. Segal, & R. Glaser (Eds.), *Thinking and learning skills* (Vol 1) (pp. 133–206). Hillsdale, NJ: Erlbaum.

Brown, A. L. (1988). Motivation to learn and understand: On taking charge of one's own learning. *Cognition and Instruction, 5*(4), 311–321.

Brown, A. L., Bransford, J. D., Ferrara, R. A., & Campione, J. C. (1983). Learning, remembering, and understanding. In J. H. Flavell & E. M. Markman (Eds.), *Handbook of child psychology* (4th ed., Vol. 3) (pp. 77–166). New York: Wiley.

Brown, R. (1968). The development of *Wh* questions in child speech. *Journal of Verbal Learning and Verbal Behavior, 7,* 279–290.

Bruce, B. C. (1982). Natural communication between person and computer. In W. G. Lehnert & M. H. Ringle (Eds.), *Strategies for natural language processing* (pp. 55–89). Hillsdale, NJ: Erlbaum.

Carroll, J. M., Mack, R. L., Lewis, C. H., Grischkowsky, N. L., & Robertson, S. R. (1985). Exploring a word-processor. *Human-Computer Interaction, 1,* 283–307.

Chi, M. Bassok, M., Lewis, M., Reiman, P., & Glaser, R. (1989). Self-explanations: How students study and use examples in learning to solve problems. *Cognitive Science, 13,* 145–182.

Clark, H. H. (1979). Responding to indirect speech acts. *Cognitive Psychology, 11,* 430–477.

Clark, H. H. & Haviland, S. E. (1977). Comprehension and the given–new contract. In R. O. Freedle (Ed.), *Discourse production and comprehension* (pp. 1–40). Norwood, NJ: Ablex.

Clark, H. H., & Marshall, C. R. (1981). Definite reference and mutual knowledge. In A. K. Joshi, B. Webber, & I. A. Sag (Eds.), *Elements of discourse understanding* (pp. 10–63). Cambridge: Cambridge University Press.

Clark, H. H., & Schaeffer, E. F. (1989). Contributing to discourse. *Cognitive Science, 13,* 259–294.

Cohen, P. R., Perrault, C. R., & Allen, J. F. (1982). Beyond question answering. In W. G. Lehnert & M. H. Ringle (Eds.), *Strategies of natural language comprehension* (pp. 237–248). Hillsdale, NJ: Erlbaum.

Collins, A. (1985). Teaching and reasoning skills. In S. F. Chipman, J. W. Segal, & R. Glaser (Eds.), *Thinking and learning skills* (Vol. 2) (pp. 579–586). Hillsdale, NJ: Erlbaum.

Collins, A. (1988). Different goals of inquiry teaching. *Questioning Exchange, 2,* 39–45.

Crystal, D. (1969). *Prosodic systems and intonation in English.* Cambridge: Cambridge University Press.

Dahlgren, K. (1988). *Naive semantics for natural language understanding.* Boston: Kluwer Academic Press.

D'Andrade, R. G., & Wish, M. (1985). Speech act theory in quantitative research on interpersonal behavior. *Discourse Processes, 8,* 229–259.

Davey, B., & McBride, S. (1986). Effects of question-generation training on reading comprehension. *Journal of Educational Psychology, 78,* 256–262.

Dillon, J. T. (1982). The multidisciplinary study of questioning. *Journal of Educational Psychology, 74,* 147–165.

Dillon, J. T. (1988). *Questioning and teaching: A manual of practice.* New York: Teachers College Press.

Dyer, M. G. (1983). *In-depth understanding: A computer model of integrated processing for narrative comprehension.* Cambridge, MA: MIT Press.

Erikson, T. A., & Mattson, M. E. (1981). From words to meaning: A semantic illusion. *Journal of Verbal Learning and Verbal Behavior, 20,* 540–552.

Flavell, J. H. (1978). Metacognitive development. In J. M. Scandura & C. J. Brainerd (Eds.), *Structural process theories of complex human behavior.* Leyden: Sijthoff.

Fox, B. (1988). *Cognitive and interactional aspects of correction in tutoring* (Tech. Rep. No. 88-2). Boulder: University of Colorado.

Francik, E. P., & Clark, H. H. (1985). How to make requests that overcome obstacles to compliance. *Journal of Memory and Language, 24,* 560–588.

Frank, J. (1989). On conversational involvement by mail: The use of questions in direct sales letters. *Text, 9,* 231–259.

Galambos, J. A., & Black, J. B. (1985). Using knowledge of activities to understand and answer questions. In A. C. Graesser & J. B. Black (Eds.), *The psychology of questions* (pp. 157–189). Hillsdale, NJ: Erlbaum.

Gavelek, J. R., & Raphael, T. E. (1985). Metacognition, instruction, and the role of questioning activities. In D. L. Forrest-Pressley, G. E. Mackinnin, & T. G. Waller (Eds.), *Metacognition, cognition, and human performance* (Vol. 2, pp. 103–136). Orlando, FL: Academic Press.

Gernsbacher, M. A. (1990). *Language comprehension as structure building.* Hillsdale, NJ: Erlbaum.

Gibbs, R. W., & Mueller, R. A. G. (1988). Conversational sequences and references for indirect speech acts. *Discourse Processes, 11,* 101–116.

Goffman, E. (1974). *Frame analysis.* Cambridge, MA: Harvard University Press.

Golding, J. M., Graesser, A. C., & Millis, K. K. (1990). What makes a good answer to a question?: Testing a psychological model of question answering in the context of narrative text. *Discourse Processes, 13,* 305–325.

Goldman, S. R., & Varnhagen, C. K. (1986). Memory for embedded and sequential structures. *Journal of Memory and Language, 25,* 401–418.

Good, T. L., Slavings, R. L., Harel, K. H., & Emerson, H. (1987). Student passivity: A study of question-asking in K–12 classrooms. *Sociology of Education, 60,* 181–199.

Gordon, P., & Lakoff, G. (1971). Conversational postulates. *Papers from the 7th regional meeting, Chicago Linguistics Society,* Vol. 7, pp. 63–84.

Graesser, A. C. (1978). How to catch a fish: The memory and representation of common procedures. *Discourse Processes, 1,* 72–89.

Graesser, A. C. (1981). *Prose comprehension beyond the word.* New York: Springer-Verlag.

Graesser, A. C., & Clark, L. F. (1985). *Structures and procedures of implicit knowledge.* Norwood, NJ: Ablex.

Graesser, A. C., & Franklin, S. P. (1990). QUEST: A cognitive model of question answering. *Discourse Processes, 13,* 279–303.

Graesser, A. C., Gordon, S. E., & Brainerd, L. E. (1992). QUEST: A model of question answering. *Computers and Mathematics with Applications, 23,* 733–745.

Graesser, A. C., & Hemphill, D. (1991). Question answering in the context of scientific mechanisms. *Journal of Memory and Language, 30,* 186–209.

Graesser, A. C., Huber, J. D., & Person N. K. (1991). *Question-asking in tutoring sessions.* Paper presented at the 32nd annual meeting of the Psychonomic Society, San Francisco.

Graesser, A. C., Lang, K. L., & Roberts, R. M. (1991). Question answering in the context of stories. *Journal of Experimental Psychology: General, 120,* 254–277.

Graesser, A. C., Langston, M. C., & Baggett, W. B. (1993). Exploring information about concepts by asking questions. In G. V. Nakamura, R. M. Taraban, & D. Medin (Eds.), *Categorization in humans and machines* (pp. 411–463). San Diego, CA: Academic Press.

Graesser, A. C., Langston, M. C., & Lang, K. L. (1992). Designing educational software around questioning. *Journal of Artificial Intelligence in Education, 3,* 235–241.

Graesser, A. C., & McMahen, C. L. (1993). Anomolous information triggers questions when adults solve problems and comprehend stories. *Journal of Educational Psychology, 85,* 136–151.

Graesser, A. C., & Murachver, T. (1985). Symbolic procedures of question answering. In A. C. Graesser & J. B. Black (Eds.), *The psychology of questions* (pp. 15–88). Hillsdale, NJ: Erlbaum.

Graesser, A. C., Person, N. K., & Huber, J. D. (1992). Mechanisms that generate questions. In T. E. Lauer, E. Peacock, & A. C. Graesser (Eds.), *Questions and information systems.* Hillsdale, NJ: Erlbaum.

Graesser, A. C., Person, N. K., & Huber, J. D. (1993). Question asking during tutoring and in the design of educational software. In M. Rabinowitz (Ed.), *Cognitive foundations of instruction* (pp. 149–172). Hillsdale, NJ: Erlbaum.

Graesser, A. C., Roberts, R. M., & Hackett-Renner, C. (1990). Question answering in the context of telephone surveys, business interactions, and interviews. *Discourse Processes, 13*, 327–348.

Graesser, A. C., Robertson, S. P., & Anderson, P. A. (1981). Incorporating inferences in narrative representations: A study of how and why. *Cognitive Psychology, 13*, 1–26.

Graesser, A. C., Robertson, S. P., Lovelace, E. R., & Swinehart, D. M. (1980). Answers to *why*-questions expose the organization of story plot and predict recall of actions. *Journal of Experimental Psychology: Human Learning and Memory, 6*, 503–515.

Green, G. M. (1989). *Pragmatics and natural language understanding*. Hillsdale, NJ: Erlbaum.

Grice, H. P. (1975). Logic and conversation. In P. Cole & J. L. Morgan (Eds.), *Syntax and semantics* (Vol. 3, pp. 41–58). New York: Academic Press.

Grishman, R. (1986). *Computational linguistics: An introduction*. Cambridge: Cambridge University Press.

Halliday, M. A. K. (1967). Transivity and theme. Part 2. *Journal of Linguistics, 3*, 199–244.

Hovy, E. H. (1988). *Generating natural language under pragmatic constraints*. Hillsdale, NJ: Erlbaum.

Hudson R. A. (1975). The meaning of questions. *Language, 51*, 1–31.

Kaplan, S. J. (1983). Cooperative response from a portable natural language system. In M. Brady & R. C. Berwick (Eds.), *Computation models of discourse* (pp. 167–208). Cambridge, MA: MIT Press.

Kass, A. (1992). Question-asking, artificial intelligence, and human creativity. In T. Lauer, E. Peacock, & A. C. Graesser (Eds.), *Questions and information systems* (pp. 303–360). Hillsdale, NJ: Erlbaum.

Kass, R., & Finin, T. (1988). Modeling the user in natural language systems. *Computational Linguistics, 14*, 5–22.

Kempson, R. M. (1979). *Semantic theory*. Cambridge: Cambridge University Press.

Kerry, T. (1987). Classroom questions in England. *Questioning Exchange, 1*(1), 32–33.

King, A. (1989). Effects of self-questioning training on college students' comprehension of lectures. *Contemporary Educational Psychology, 14*, 366–381.

Kintsch, W. (1974). *The representation of meaning in memory*. Hillsdale, NJ: Erlbaum.

Lang, K. L., Graesser, A. C., Dumais, S. T., & Kilman, D. (1992). Question asking in human-computer interfaces. In T. Lauer, E. Peacock, & A. C. Graesser (Eds.), *Questions and information systems* (pp. 131–165). Hillsdale, NJ: Erlbaum.

Lehnert, W. G. (1978). *The process of question answering*. Hillsdale, NJ: Erlbaum.

Lehnert, W. G., Dyer, M. G., Johnson, P. N., Young, C. J., & Hartley, S. (1983). Boris: An experiment in in-depth understanding of narratives. *Artificial Intelligence, 20*, 15–62.

Loftus, E. F. (1975). Leading questions and the eyewitness report. *Cognitive Psychology, 7*, 560–572.

Mandler, J. M. (1984). *Stories, scripts, and scenes*. Hillsdale, NJ: Erlbaum.

Mann, W. C., & Thompson, S. A. (1986). Relational propositions in discourse. *Discourse Processes, 9*, 57–90.

McArthur, D., Stasz, C., & Zmuidzinas, M. (1990). Tutoring techniques in algebra. *Cognition and Instruction, 7*(3), 197–244.

McKeown, K. R. (1985). Discourse strategies for generating natural-language text. *Artificial Intelligence, 27*, 1–41.

Meyer, B. J. (1985). Prose analysis: Purposes, procedures, and problems. In B. K. Britton & J. B. Black (Eds.), *Understanding expository test* (pp. 269–304). Hillsdale, NJ: Erlbaum.

Needham, W. P. (1990). Semantic structure, information structure, and intonation in discourse production. *Journal of Memory and Language, 29*, 455–468.

Norman, D. A., & Rumelhart, D. E. (1975). *Explorations in cognition*. San Francisco: Freeman.

Palinscar, A. S., & Brown, A. L. (1984). Reciprocal teaching of comprehension-fostering and comprehension monitoring activities. *Cognition and Instruction, 1*(2), 117–175.

Papert, S. (1980). *Mindstorms: Children, computers and powerful ideas*. New York: Basic Books.

Pressley, M., Goodchild, F., Fleet, J., Zajchowski, R., & Evans, E. (1989). The challenges of classroom strategy instruction. *Elementary School Journal, 89*, 301–342.

Ram, A. (1990). Knowledge goals: A theory of intelligence. In *Proceedings of the Cognitive Science Society* (pp. 206–214). Hillsdale, NJ: Erlbaum.

Reder, L. M., & Cleeremans, A. (1990). The role of partial matches in comprehension: The Moses illusion revisited. In A. C. Graesser & H. Bower (Eds.), *The psychology of learning and motivation: Inferences and text comprehension* (pp. 233–258). San Diego, CA: Academic Press.

Reisbeck, C. K. (1988). Are questions just function calls? *Questioning Exchange, 2*(1), 17–24.

Resnick, L., Salmon, M. H., & Zeitz, C. M. (1991). The structure of reasoning in conversation. In *Proceedings of the 13th Annual Conference of the Cognitive Science Society* (pp. 388–393). Hillsdale, NJ: Erlbaum.

Rickards, J. P. (1979). Adjunct post questions in text: A critical review of methods and processes. *Review of Educational Research, 49,* 181–196.

Robertson, S. P., Black, J. B., & Lehnert, W. G. (1985). Misleading question effects as evidence for integrated question understanding and memory search. In A. C. Graesser & J. B. Black (Eds.), *The psychology of questions* (pp. 191–218). Hillsdale, NJ: Erlbaum.

Rothkopf, E. (1965). Some theoretical and experimental approaches to problems in written instruction. In J. Krummboltz (Ed.), *Learning and the educational process.* Chicago: Rand McNally.

Schank, R. C. (1986). *Explanation patterns: Understanding mechanically and creatively.* Hillsdale, NJ: Erlbaum.

Schank, R. C., & Abelson, R. (1977). *Scripts, plans, goals, and understanding: An inquiry into human knowledge structures.* Hillsdale, NJ: Erlbaum.

Schank, R. C., Ferguson, W., Birnbaum, L., Barger, J., & Greising, M. (1991). ASK TOM: An experimental interface for video case libraries. In *Proceedings of the 13th Annual Conference for the Cognitive Science Society* (pp. 570–575). Hillsdale, NJ: Erlbaum.

Schegloff, E. A., & Sacks, H. (1973). Opening up closings. *Semiotica, 8,* 289–327.

Searle, J. R. (1969). *Speech acts.* London: Cambridge University Press.

Sebrechts, M. M., & Swartz, M. L. (1991). Question-asking as a tool for novice computer skill acquisition. In S. P. Robertson & G. M. Olson (Eds.), *Proceedings of the International Conference on Computer-Human Interaction* (pp. 293–297). Norwood, NJ: Ablex.

Singer, M. (1984). Toward a model of question answering: Yes-no questions. *Journal of Experimental Psychology: Learning, Memory, and Cognition, 18,* 285–297.

Singer, M. (1985). Mental processes of question answering. In A. C. Graesser & J. B. Black (Eds.), *The psychology of questions* (pp. 55–63). Hillsdale, NJ: Erlbaum.

Singer, M. (1986). Answering yes–no questions about causes: Question acts and question categories. *Memory & Cognition, 14,* 55–63.

Singer, M. (1990). Answering questions about discourse. *Discourse Processes, 13,* 261–277.

Singer, M. (1991). Independence of question-answering strategy and searched representation. *Memory & Cognition, 19,* 189–196.

Singer, M., & Donlan, D. (1982). Active comprehension: Problem solving schema with question generation for comprehension of complex short stories. *Reading Research Quarterly, 17,* 166–186.

Souther, A., Acker, L., Lester, J., & Porter, B. (1989). Using view types to generate explanations in intelligent tutoring systems. In *Proceedings of the 11th Annual Conference of the Cognitive Science Society* (pp. 123–130). Hilldale, NJ: Erlbaum.

Sowa, J. F. (1983). *Conceptual structures: Information processing in mind and machine.* Reading, MA: Addison-Wesley.

Stein, N. L., & Glenn, G. G. (1979). An analysis of story comprehension in elementary school children. In R. O. Freedle (Ed.), *New directions in discourse processing* (Vol. 2) (pp. 53–120). Norwood, NJ: Ablex.

Stevens, A., Collins, A., & Goldin, S. E. (1982). Misconceptions in students' understanding. In D. Sleeman & J. S. Brown (Eds.), *Intelligent tutoring systems* (pp. 13–24). New York: Academic Press.

Stokal, R. R. (1974). Classification. *Science, 185,* 115–123.

Tannen, D. (1984). *Coherence in spoken and written discourse.* Norwood, NJ: Ablex.

Tennant, H. R. (1987). Menu-based natural language. In S. C. Shapiro & D. Eckroth (Eds.), *Encyclopedia of artificial intelligence* (pp. 594–597). New York: Wiley.

Trabasso, T., van den Broek, P. W., & Lui, L. (1988). A model for generating questions that assess and promote comprehension. *Questioning Exchange, 2,* 25–38.

Trabasso, T., van den Broek, P. W., & Suh, S. Y. (1989). Logical necessity and transitivity of causal relations in stories. *Discourse Processes, 12,* 1–25.

van der Meij, H. (1987). Assumptions of information-seeking questions. *Questioning Exchange, 1*, 111–117.

van der Meij, H. (1988). Constraints on question asking in classrooms. *Journal of Educational Psychology, 80*, 401–405.

Wales, R., & Taylor, S. (1987). Intonation cues to questions and statements: How are they perceived? *Language and Speech, 30*, 199–211.

Williams, M. D. (1984). What makes RABBIT run? *International Journal of Man-Machine Studies, 21*, 333–352.

Woods, W. A. (1977). Lunar rocks in natural English: Explorations in natural language question answering. In A. Zampoli (Ed.), *Linguistic structures processing* (pp. 201–222). New York: Elsevier/North-Holland.

Zimmerman, B. J. (1989). A social cognitive view of self-regulated academic learning. *Journal of Educational Psychology, 81*(3), 329–339.

Zloof, M. M. (1975). Query by example. *Proceedings of the National Computer Conference, 44*, 431–438.

CHAPTER 16

COMPREHENSION AND MEMORY OF NARRATIVE TEXTS

INFERENCES AND COHERENCE

PAUL VAN DEN BROEK

> All happy families are alike but an unhappy family is unhappy after its own fashion. Everything had gone wrong in the Oblonsky household. The wife had found out about her husband's relationship with their former French governess and had announced that she could not go on living in the same house with him. This state of affairs had already continued for three days and was having a distressing effect on the couple themselves, on all the members of the family, and on the domestics. They all felt that there was no sense in their living together under the same roof and that any group of people who chanced to meet at a wayside inn would have more in common than they, the members of the Oblonsky family, and their servants. The wife did not leave her own room and the husband stayed away from the home all day. The children strayed all over the house, not knowing what to do with themselves. The English governess had quarrelled with the housekeeper and had written a note asking a friend to find her a new place. The head-cook had gone out at dinner-time the day before. The under-cook and the coachman had given notice. (Tolstoy, *Anna Karenin*, 1954, p. 1)

I. COMPREHENSION AND COHERENCE

Successful reading comprehension requires that the reader identify words, detect syntactical structures, and extract meaning from individual sentences. Yet an understanding of words and sentences in itself is not sufficient. A crucial component of successful comprehension is the identification of relations between the various parts of the text, as well as between the text and the reader's world knowledge. These relations tie together the events, facts, ideas, and so on that are described in the text. As a consequence, the text is perceived and represented in memory as a COHERENT structure, rather than as a disjointed assembly of individual pieces of information. This representation, in turn, forms the basis for later recall, retelling, and, in general, any task that requires access to information about the text in memory.

The construction of coherence is the result of INFERENTIAL PROCESSES that take place as the reader proceeds through the text. That is, the reader draws on his or her background knowledge to identify relations implied by the text, to activate information about events, facts, and themes that are not mentioned in the text, or to engage in both activities at the same time.

In the past twenty years great advances have been made in the understanding of both the nature of the memory representation of texts and the inferential processes during reading that lead to the construction of such representations. The representations can be described as networks of interconnected nodes, with each node referring to events that were described in the text or added by the reader. The generation of inferences has been found to be a complicated cognitive activity that consists of subprocesses, such as spread of activation and directed memory searches, each of which may take place automatically or only after other subprocesses have failed. The execution of these processes and the resulting representation depend on the reader's knowledge, attentional capacities, and purposes in reading, as well as on the information provided by the text and the demands imposed by the task.

The purpose of this chapter is to provide an overview of current research on the coherent representation of texts and the generation of inferences. In doing so, the chapter focuses on comprehension of narrative texts because most research has been done with those materials. It should be emphasized, however, that coherence, memory representations, and inferential processes are central to the reading of any type of text. Thus, the conclusions presented here in general can be expected to apply to the reading of nonnarrative types of text as well, although they likely will differ in the details.

The text that follows is divided into four sections. Section II focuses on the nature of the mental representation of texts. Section III reviews research on the inferential processes that take place as the reader proceeds through the text. Section IV integrates the findings reported in the two preceding sections by describing how transient inferential processes may lead to relatively stable mental representations. The final section briefly discusses individual and developmental differences in inferential processes.

II. THE STRUCTURE OF MENTAL REPRESENTATIONS OF TEXT

The retrieval of textual information from memory is far from random. Some events, facts, or states in a text systematically are recalled better than others; parts of a text tend to be recalled in a consistent and sensible order rather than in a haphazard sequence; readers show remarkable agreement in their intrusions in recall, that is, in information that is not mentioned in the text but added by the reader; and so on. Observations such as these suggest that the memory representation of a text resembles a coherent structure rather than an unorganized list (Bartlett, 1932).

The coherence of a representation results from the semantic relations that interconnect its elements. Many types of relations can connect the individual events, states, facts, and so on, that are described in a text. ANAPHORIC relations provide identity, by establishing that a person or object in one clause or sentence is identical to that in another clause. In the third sentence of Tolstoy's *Anna Karenin,* for example, the word *she* anaphorically refers to Oblonsky's wife rather than to the French governess or to some other, unmentioned woman. CAUSAL relations establish that the event described in one clause causes the event in a second clause. For example, in the same sentence in *Anna Karenin* most readers assume that Oblonsky's wife cannot continue to live in the house BECAUSE she found out about his affair, even though this is not stated explicitly in the text. Causal relations also may connect events in the text to antecedents that are not mentioned but that are plausible given the reader's world knowledge. For example, in *Anna Karenin* the reader may infer that Oblonsky's wife found out about the affair via rumors, by finding a note from the French governess, or some other way. Similarly, INSTRUMENT inferences activate the tools or methods that are used in events described in the text. In Tolstoy's story a reader may infer that the English governess used a pen, a pencil, or even a quill to write the note to her friend. As a final example of the kinds of relations that provide coherence to a text, THEMATIC or GLOBAL relations combine groups of clauses, thereby providing a theme to the text. In the above excerpt from *Anna Karenin,* all states and events come together under the theme of domestic turmoil.

These and other relations constitute the structure of the text. A considerable amount of psycholinguistic research has been devoted to exploring the role that this structure plays in the representation of the text in memory. Two issues are central in these investigations. First, which of these relations are incorporated in the mental representation? Second, what are the properties of this representation and how do these properties affect performance on tasks that require access to information from the text? Several types of relations have been considered.

A. Causal Relations

Causal relations are an important component of the structure of narrative texts. Narratives typically describe how events and actions cause changes in the states of objects and persons described in the text. Indeed, readers consider the presence of state changes to be a prerequisite for a text to be called a narrative (Stein, 1982). It is not surprising, therefore, that early investigators of comprehension suggested that causal relations also play an important role in the COMPREHENSION of narratives (Bartlett, 1932; Dewey, 1933/1963; Piaget, 1923/1959). These ideas remained dormant in psycholinguistics for nearly half a century, until theoretical and technological advances led to the development of explicit psychological theories of memory for texts. Although these theories varied in their emphases, they shared the assumption that causal relations are central components of the mental representation of a text (e.g., Mandler & Johnson, 1977; Nicholas & Trabasso, 1981; Rumelhart, 1975; Schank & Abelson, 1977; Stein & Glenn, 1979; Thorndyke, 1977; Trabasso, Secco, & van den Broek, 1984; van den Broek, 1990b; Warren, Nicholas, & Trabasso, 1979).

1. Causal Chains

One way of describing the causal structure of a narrative text is as a CAUSAL CHAIN of connected events, actions, and states that leads from the beginning of the text to its end (Black & Bower, 1980; Omanson, 1982; Schank & Abelson, 1977). Statements[1] that are on the causal chain maintain the causal flow of the text and therefore are important for the coherence of the story. As a result, they are hypothesized to take a prominent place in the memory representation of the text. Statements that are not part of the causal chain constitute DEAD ENDS. Dead end statements do not contribute to the coherence of the text and are peripheral to the flow of the story. As a result, they are hypothesized to be of minor importance to the representation of the text.

The psychological validity of the distinction between causal chain and dead end statements has been demonstrated in a number of empirical studies. The results in correlational studies indicate that statements that are on the causal chain through a story are recalled more frequently (Black & Bower, 1980; Trabasso et al., 1984; Trabasso & van den Broek, 1985), are included in summarization protocols more often (Trabasso & van den Broek, 1985), and are judged to be more important (Trabasso & van den Broek, 1985) than are statements that are dead ends. These results are confirmed in experimental tests, in which the causal chain status of statements was manipulated systematically: Identical statements are recalled more often when they are part of the causal chain than when they are dead ends (Omanson, 1982; Wolman, 1991; Wolman & van den Broek, 1993). Thus, statements on the causal chain consistently are found to be more important in the memory representation of a text than are dead end statements.

Causal chain theories have a number of limitations, however. First, in a causal chain each event has at most one antecedent and one consequent. As a result, many causal relations in a text are not captured. Consider the brief sample story in Table I. This story can be described a causal chain, with each event or state leading to the next (the statement *so that he had his afternoons free* exemplifies a dead end). In the causal chain of the sample story, the outcome, Brian's buying the CD player, is caused by his going to the store. Although going to the store certainly is a prerequisite for buying the CD player, this event hardly would seem to be the main cause for Brian's buying the CD player. The causal relation between these two statements is much weaker, for example, than that between his wanting a CD player and his buying the CD player. Indeed, his going to the store AND the fact that he wanted a CD player (and possibly even the fact that he owned $300) jointly caused his buying the player. Joint causality, where multiple antecedents together lead to a consequence, is not captured in a causal chain model of text structure. Likewise,

---

[1] Theorists differ with respect to the definition of what constitutes the basic unit of analysis in a text. Some analytic techniques decompose a text into propositions (e.g., Kintsch & van Dijk, 1978), others focus on clauses (e.g., Trabasso, van den Broek, & Suh, 1989), while yet others use sentences as the basic unit (e.g., Kintsch, 1988). Indeed, larger units, such as paragraphs or chapters, could be employed as well. The representational theories described in this chapter in principle can accommodate units at several levels of analysis. The generic terms STATEMENT and EVENT are used here to denote the events, states, actions, and so on that constitute the story unless specification of the unit of analysis as a proposition, clause, sentence, or otherwise is relevant to the point under discussion.

Table I
Sample Narrative

Story grammar category[a]	Statement number	Statement
S	1	One day, Brian was looking through the newspaper.
IE	2	He saw an ad for some fancy CD players.
IR	3	He really liked the way they looked.
G	4	Brian decided he wanted to buy one.
A	5	He called the store for the price of a nice model.
O	6	He did not have enough money.
G	7	He decided to work a paper route.
A	8	For months he got up early,
O	9	so that he had his afternoons free,
A	10	and delivered the newspapers.
O	11	He quickly earned the $300 that he needed.
A	12	On his first day off, he went to the store.
O	13	He bought the CD player that he had wanted for so long.
C	14	He was so happy that he immediately organized a party.

[a] Story grammar categories are labeled as follows: Setting (S), Initiating Event (IE), Internal Response (IR), Goal (G), Attempt (A), Outcome (O), Consequence (C).

causal chain models postulate that an event or action can have only one consequent.

A second limitation of the existing causal chain models is that the identification of causal relations is based on intuition rather than on an explicit definition or set of criteria. As a result, it frequently is unclear why a researcher considers one set of events to be causally related but another set to be unrelated. The arbitrariness in identifying causal relations makes interpretations of the findings between and even within studies difficult. Furthermore, the lack of criteria creates the erroneous impression that causality is a simple concept, with a causal relation either being present or absent. As philosophers (e.g., Hart & Honoré, 1985; Mackie, 1980) and psychologists (e.g., Cummins, Lubart, Alksnis, & Rist, 1991; Einhorn & Hogarth, 1986; Tversky & Kahneman, 1982; van den Broek, 1990b) have pointed out, many properties of the relation between two events contribute to the perception of causality, with some properties augmenting and others diminishing the strength of the relation. This suggests that causality is the result of an interaction of properties, with the relation between two events varying in causal strength along one or more dimensions. It should be noted that this problem, the absence of a definition of causality and the resulting use of intuition, is found not only in causal chain theories but in much of the literature on causal relations in text comprehension.

2. Causal Networks

The observation that statements may have multiple causes and/or consequences has led to the development of NETWORK models of the causal structure of a narrative text (Graesser, 1981; Graesser & Clark, 1985; Trabasso et al., 1984; Trabasso & van den Broek, 1985). According to network models, events in a story frequently are the result of a combination of causal antecedents rather than of one cause. Likewise, events often have multiple consequences. As a result, the causal structure of a text resembles a network rather than a causal chain.

As psychological models, network theories propose that the memory representation for a text most likely includes the causal relations between each event and those other events in the text that together led to its occurrence. In order to test the psychological validity of network models, investigators need to identify these relations. Because of the problems with reliance on intiuition that were noted above, investigators increasingly are using more formal and systematic methods for identifying the causal relations in a text. In one widely used method (cf. Trabasso et al., 1984, 1989; van den Broek, 1990b), for example, the researcher first identifies a set of potential causes for an event, consisting of those events that are TEMPORALLY PRIOR and OPERATIVE or active at the time that the event to be explained occurs.[2] Causal relations then are determined by identifying which of the candidate causes are NECESSARY AND SUFFICIENT IN THE CIRCUMSTANCES of the story for the event to occur. An event A is necessary in the circumstances for an event B if it is the case that if A had not happened then B would not have happened, given the circumstances of the story. An event A is sufficient in the circumstances if it is the case that if A occurs then B is likely to follow, given the context of the story (cf. Mackie, 1980; van den Broek, 1990b). The strength of the resulting relation is a function of the degree of necessity and sufficiency (van den Broek, 1990b). Finally, the identified causal connections are assembled into a causal network (Trabasso et al., 1989).

Whether one uses formal criteria, empirical methods (e.g., question answering; cf. Graesser & Clark, 1985), or intuition to identify relations, the purpose is to construct a causal network that describes the multiple causes and antecedents that an event may have. For natural texts the network structure can be

---

[2] With respect to operativity, an event may be temporally prior yet not operative. This can happen under at least three conditions. First, the candidate cause may have ceased to be operative. For example, consider (i).

(i)a. *The porcelain vase fell out of the window.*
  b. *Two weeks later the vase broke.*

Here, event (a) is temporally prior to event (b) but under normal circumstances it is not operative anymore by the time that event (b) takes place.

Second, the candidate cause may have taken place but not be operative yet. Consider (ii).

(ii)a. *Sheila dropped the check in the mailbox.*
  b. *Half an hour later she received a call from the bank.*

In this case, under normal circumstances the delay between sending a letter and its being received prevents (a) from causing (b).

Third, a candidate event is not operative because a more recent and/or specific statement contains the same information. This is illustrated in (iii).

(iii)a. *The boy was throwing the tennis ball against the wall of the house.*
  b. *Accidentally, he threw the ball at the bedroom window.*
  c. *With a loud sound the window broke in pieces.*

In this scenario, (b) contains the causally relevant information given in (a), but it is more recent and specific. As a result, (b) subsumes (a) and (a) ceases to be operative vis-à-vis the breaking of the window.

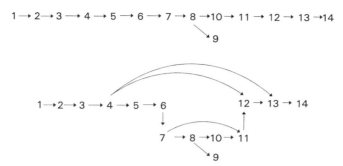

FIG. 1   Causal chain (*top*) and causal network (*bottom*) representations of the sample narrative.

quite extensive (cf. Trabasso & Sperry, 1985; van den Broek, Rohleder, & Narvaez, in press), but the application of the method can be illustrated by means of the artificial story in Table I. The causal network for the text is given in the bottom panel of Figure 1. For comparison, the causal chain model for the same text is given in the top panel. In these diagrams each node represents a main clause in the text, and each arc represents a causal relation.

In the network representation, some statements have several antecedents. For example, Brian's buying the CD player is motivated by his wanting a CD player and enabled by the facts that he has earned the money and that he went to the store. If any of these had not been the case, then in the context of this story the outcome would not have occurred. Likewise, some statements have several consequences. For example, the fact that Brian wants to buy a CD player causes him to call stores and to want money and eventually motivates him to go to the store and purchase the CD player.[3]

Networks such as these capture several causal properties of a narrative text. First, the network allows one to identify the causal chain that runs through the story. In this respect, the network model incorporates the causal chain model. Second, statements in a network representation vary in the number of their causal connections. Statements with a large number of connections have many causes and/or consequences and therefore play an important role in the structure of a text. Third, alternative causal chains may connect the beginning of a story to its end. For example, in the sample text the direct connection between the goal, Brian's wanting a CD player, and the outcome, Brian's buying one, indicates a possible causal chain that omits the details of Brian's working a paper route. Alternative causal chains may form a hierarchy, with the superordinate chains describing the events in the text at the most general and abstract level and subordinate levels providing increasingly more detail. In Figure 1, the hierarchical levels are indicated along the vertical dimension.

Each of these three properties of statements—being on or off the causal chain, number of connections, and hierarchical level—has been found to affect performance on measures of text comprehension.

---

[3] The relations that an event has to others may differ in their strengths. For example, as mentioned and as is discussed in more detail below, variations in necessity and sufficiency may result in causal relations of different strengths.

First, the role of the causal chain with respect to the coherence and memory representation of a text was discussed earlier. The causal chain connects the beginning of the narrative to its conclusion and thereby provides coherence to the text. Statements on this chain have been found to play a central role in the memory representation of the text. They are recalled more often, included in summaries more frequently, and judged to be more important than are statements that are not on the causal chain.

The most salient property of network models is that events may have multiple connections to other events in the text. The psychological validity of this property has been studied extensively. These studies fall into two categories. One category of studies focuses on the effects of multiple relations on the comprehension of statements, whereas the second category directly investigates the relations themselves.

The results of the first category of studies indicate that statements with many causal connections play a prominent role in the memory representation of a text. Highly connected statements are recalled more often than are statements with few causal connections (Fletcher & Bloom, 1988; Goldman & Varnhagen, 1986; Graesser & Clark, 1985; Trabasso et al., 1984; Trabasso & van den Broek, 1985; Wolman, 1991). This pattern has been observed both with experimentally constructed texts and with naturally occurring literary texts (van den Broek, Rohleder, & Narvaez, in press). Highly connected statements are also more likely to be included in summarization protocols than are less connected statements (Trabasso & van den Broek, 1985; van den Broek & Trabasso, 1986). Finally, statements with many connections are judged to be more important than statements with few connections (O'Brien & Myers, 1987; Trabasso & Sperry, 1985; Trabasso & van den Broek, 1985). These findings lead to the conclusion that a statement's importance in the memory representation of a text is strongly determined by its causal connections.

This conclusion is based on correlational analyses, thereby leaving open the possibility that the statements may have differed in respects other than the number of their connections. This possibility was eliminated in an experimental study in which the number of connections of statements was manipulated systematically while their content was held constant. Subjects were asked to judge the importance of the statements in the different versions. The results indicate that the perceived importance of a statement is a linear function of its number of connections: The more connections a statement has, the more important it is judged to be (van den Broek, 1988). Thus, correlational and experimental studies provide convergent evidence that causal connections affect the role of statements in the memory representation.

These findings demonstrate the importance of causal relations in the representation of texts. Note, however, that conclusions about the presence of RELATIONS in the representation are inferred from recall, summarization, etc., of STATEMENTS. The relations themselves are not directly probed. Thus, the results of these studies provide only indirect evidence that causal relations actually are incorporated in the memory representation of a text.

A second category of studies directly investigates the extent to which individual causal relations are stored in the memory representation of a text. The methods in these studies generally are based on the premise that activation of one member of a pair of events that are related in memory will result in increased activation of the other member. A hypothesized relation between two events can be tested by presenting subjects with one of the events and observing whether the other event is retrieved more quickly or more frequently than it is in a neutral condition. If an increase in availability of the second event is observed, then the hypothesized relation is supported; if availability is unchanged, then no evidence for the relation is obtained.

Evidence that the causal relations between pairs of statements are encoded in a memory representation comes from cued recall studies (Keenan, Baillet, & Brown, 1984; Myers & Duffy, 1990; Myers, Shinjo, & Duffy, 1987). In these studies, subjects read pairs of sentences that varied in the strength of their causal relation. Consider the pairs of statements (1)–(2) (from Myers & Duffy, 1990).

(1) a. *Jimmy's big brother beat him up.*
    b. *The next day he was covered with bruises.*
(2) a. *Jimmy went to his friend's house.*
    b. *The next day he was covered with bruises.*

Pair (1) describes two events which the authors (and, in a norming study, subjects) consider to be highly causally connected. Sentences in pair (2), in contrast, are only weakly connected. Sentence pairs with intermediate causal strengths were constructed as well. Subjects read a large set of sentence pairs such as these at their own pace. This was followed by a cued recall task, in which subjects were presented with one member of each sentence pair and were asked to generate the accompanying statement. The probability of correct recall for one statement was found to increase as the strength of its causal relation to the other statement increased (Keenan et al., 1984; Myers et al., 1987). The fact that the likelihood of recall was a function of the strength of the causal relation indicates that readers encode causal connections in their mental representation of statements. Subsequent analyses of the materials demonstrated that the perceived strengths of the relations between sentence pairs was a function of the necessity and sufficiency of each antecedent for the consequent (van den Broek, 1990a, 1990b), lending support to the use of those criteria to identify causal relations.

Converging evidence was obtained in a series of follow-up studies (Myers & Duffy, 1990). When subjects were explicitly instructed to construct a causal connection between the members of each pair, cued recall for the weakly related pairs increased to the same level as that for the strongly related pairs. This suggests that it was indeed the causal connection between the statements that forged the memory trace. Together these results support the notion that readers encode not only the individual events of pairs that they read, but also the causal relations that exist between them.

These conclusions, obtained on pairs of statements in isolation, have been replicated with respect to causal relations between events in stories. For example, correlational studies show that the speed with which readers retrieve from memory the referent to a person or object is a function of the causal structure of the text (O'Brien & Myers, 1987). On the one hand, the speed of reinstatement of the referent during reading was found to be correlated with the number of causal relations of the to-be-reinstated statement. On the other hand, speed of recall of the referent after reading was a function of the length of the causal chain from the beginning or the end of the story to the statement that contained the referent. Thus, the memory representation of a text resembles a network of causal relations.

The hypothesis that causal relations are incorporated in the memory representation of a text has been tested experimentally by means of a primed recognition paradigm (van den Broek & Lorch, 1993). Subjects read a series of texts and then performed a recognition task for statements from the texts. Subjects recognized a statement more quickly when it was preceded by a causally related statement than when it was preceded by a causally unrelated statement or by a general prompt. This was the case both when the causally related prime and target statements were adjacent in the surface structure of the text and when they were nonadjacent. These findings indicate, first, that the memory representation of a text includes the causal relations between its statements, and second, that the representation resembles a network rather than a chain.

The results obtained with question answering techniques provide convergent evidence for the presence of causal relations in the memory representation of a text. Statements given in answer to Why, How, and What-happened-next questions and the queried statements tend to be connected directly in a network representation of a text (Graesser & Clark, 1985; van den Broek & Thurlow, 1990).

Third, the hierarchical structure influences the memory representation of a text. Statements that are high in the hierarchical structure of a text tend to play an important role in the global structure of the text, contributing to its themes or MACROSTRUCTURE (cf. Kintsch & van Dijk, 1978; van Dijk & Kintsch, 1983). This role is reflected in the fact that statements high in the hierarchy are recalled more frequently than statements at lower levels in the hierarchy (Black & Bower, 1980; Goldman & Varnhagen, 1986; Johnson & Mandler, 1980; Mandler & Johnson, 1977). Similarly, high-level statements are more often included in summaries than low-level statements (van den Broek, Trabasso, & Thurlow, 1990). These findings suggest that statements at a high level in a story's hierarchical structure play a more prominent role in memory representation than do statements at lower levels.

Interestingly, the effects of hierarchical position differ across tasks. The probability that a statement will be recalled, for example, is affected both by hierarchical position and by causal chain status (Black & Bower, 1980). Its probability of being summarized, in contrast, is mostly determined by hierarchical position and only marginally by causal properties (van den Broek et al., 1990). For importance ratings the reverse has been observed: A statement's causal role strongly influences how important it is judged to be, whereas its position in a hierarchy per se only has a minor effect (van den Broek, 1988). Until more systematic investigations of task effects are performed, the observed differences should be interpreted with caution. One possibility is, however, that the memory representation of a text is accessed in different ways depending on the reader's task (cf. Graesser & Clark, 1985; van den Broek, 1988).

In sum, there is ample evidence that causal relations play an important role in the memory representation of a narrative. Individual statements in this representation may have multiple antecedents and consequences, if such relations are required for sufficient explanation of the events in the story.

As a result, the representation of the text can be described as a network of interconnected events. Two types of evidence attest to the psychological validity of such network representations. First, network properties of individual events, such as their causal chain status, hierarchical position, and number of causal relations to other statements in the text, have been found to influence their importance and memorability. Second, retrieval of information has been found to be a function of the relational properties of the text, such as whether a causal relation exists between the currently activated statement and the information to be retrieved and how great their distance is in the network.

In the above account, all causal relations have been considered to have the same properties. It is possible, however, to differentiate types of causal relations (Trabasso et al., 1989). PHYSICAL causality connects statements that describe changes in the physical states of objects or persons. For example, the statements *He accidentally pushed the vase off the table* and *The vase broke into a thousand pieces* are connected via physical causality. MOTIVATION describes the relations between a goal and its consequences. For example, Brian's goal of wanting to buy a CD player motivates the outcome of his buying the CD player. PSYCHOLOGICAL causation refers to the causal relations that have internal states such as emotions, plans, thoughts, and so on as their consequences. For example, Brian's liking the CD player psychologically causes Brian's goal of wanting one. Finally, ENABLEMENT describes the relation between an event and a precondition that is necessary but very weak in sufficiency for the consequence. For example, Brian's going to the store enables him to buy the CD player. The various types of relations may play different roles in the coherence of a text. They differ, for instance, in the extent to which they provide necessity and sufficiency in the circumstances of the story, and hence in their causal strength (van den Broek, 1990a). Physical causation tends to be strong in both respects, followed by motivation and physical causality in that order. Enablements usually provide some necessity but little or no sufficiency. Naive readers are sensitive to these differences: As necessity and sufficiency decline, so does the rated strength of the relation (Trabasso et al., 1984; van den Broek, 1990b). Thus, differences in causal strength affect the perception of the relations. The role of these differences in the memory representation itself has not yet been explored.

B. Anaphoric Relations

Anaphoric relations probably are the most prevalent type of relations in texts. These relations establish that an object or person in one sentence is identical to that in another sentence. Consider the sentences in (3).

(3) a. *Rachel and Rich were editing a book.*
    b. *She was having trouble thinking of worthy contributors.*

These two sentences are related by means of an ANAPHORIC REFERENCE, connecting the person identified by *she* in the second sentence with the person referred to by *Rachel* in the first sentence. Relations such as these form the backbone of the structure of a text.

Although the activation of anaphoric referents during reading has been investigated extensively (see Section III), there is relatively little research on the question whether the inferred anaphoric relations are incorporated in the memory representation of the text. The most detailed description of the referential structure of a text is provided by the leading edge model (Kintsch & van Dijk, 1978). According to this model, readers proceed through a text one sentence at a time, decomposing each sentence into its constituent propositions[4] and forging referential or anaphoric relations between these propositions and the propositions that were activated during the previous sentence cycle. Due to limitations in a reader's processing capacity, only some of the propositions in the prior cycle remain activated, and hence only a subset of all possible referential relations is identified. Propositions that are activated in many cycles, and hence are connected to many other propositions, have been found to be included more often in summarization (Kintsch & van Dijk, 1978) and in recall protocols (Miller & Kintsch, 1980) than propositions that are hypothesized to be retained in fewer cycles. Findings such as these suggest that the identified referential relations form part of the memory representation of the text.

As with causal relations, recall and summarization studies however provide only indirect evidence for the presence of relations in the representation itself. It is possible, for example, that the differences in retrieval probability reflect the number of cycles that propositions were activated rather than relations that were established during that activation. According to this interpretation, each cycle strengthens the memory tract for the propositions that are activated, resulting in higher retrieval rates for propositions that were activated in many cycles than for propositions that were processed in fewer cycles (Kintsch & van Dijk, 1978). In this view, there is no need to posit that the relations themselves are stored in the representation.

Few studies have investigated directly whether anaphoric relations are represented. One exception is a series of primed recognition studies, in which subjects read brief texts that contained multiple anaphoric relations (McKoon & Ratcliff, 1980). After reading a text, subjects received a list of target words and were asked to indicate as quickly as possible whether they had read each word. Each target word was preceded by another word that was either far from or close to the target word in the referential structure of the text. The speed with which subjects correctly recognized target words was found to depend on the referential distance between the prime and target words rather than on the surface distance. These results suggest that readers' representations indeed incorporate anaphoric relations.

In sum, the potential role that anaphoric relations may play in the memory representation of texts has received less attention than the role of causal relations. There is some evidence that such relations are indeed included in the

---

[4] According to this model, a proposition represents a piece of information that has a truth value, that is, that can be true or false. It includes a RELATIONAL CONCEPT and one or more ARGUMENTS. Thus, the sentence *The fierce dog chases the black cat* consists of three propositions:

  (i) *The dog chases the cat.*
  (ii) *The dog is fierce.*
  (iii) *The cat is black.*

In Kintsch and van Dijk's notation: (i) chase[dog,cat], (ii) is[dog,fierce], and (iii) is[cat,black].

memory representation, but convergent evidence is needed both to confirm these findings and to explore what properties of the resulting structure have psychological relevance.

C. Story Grammar Categories

Statements in a story not only vary with respect to their relations, they also differ systematically in the type of content that they convey. Following anthropological work on Russian and Inuit folktales (Colby, 1973; Propp, 1928), psychologists have categorized the different types of statements that occur in narrative texts in terms of their content. In addition, they have proposed grammatical rules that describe how statements with different types of content can legitimately be combined into a story (Mandler & Johnson, 1977; Rumelhart, 1975; Stein & Glenn, 1979; Thorndyke, 1977). These STORY GRAMMARS differ in details and use different labels to designate categories, but they show substantial overlap. In general, stories are described as consisting of SETTING information and one or more EPISODES. The setting statements provide the backdrop for the remainder of the story by describing characters, objects, temporal and geographical information, and so on. The episode describes the actions and events of the narrative itself. Each episode is organized around a goal and its outcome. The statements in an episode differ in their function. The INITIATING EVENT describes the occurrence of an event that sets the train of action in the story in motion. The initiating event results in an INTERNAL RESPONSE, describing the reaction of the protagonist, which in turn causes the implicit or explicit establishment of the protagonist's GOAL. The goal motivates one or more ATTEMPTS, which lead to the OUTCOME of the story. The outcome, finally, results in a REACTION, which describes the protagonist's reaction to the success or failure of the outcome. Most stories have multiple instantiations of each category, with the grammatical rules dictating their order. The left column in Table I provides the application of a story grammar analysis to the sample story.

Some categories are remembered better than others: Initiating events, outcomes, major settings, and, in some stories, goals tend to be recalled better than minor settings, internal responses, attempts, or reactions (Mandler & Johnson, 1977; Stein & Glenn, 1979; Trabasso et al., 1984). Readers also tend to recall the categories in the order suggested by story grammar theories. When presented with stories in which the goal information is displaced in various locations in the text, for example, subjects recall this information in the predicted location (Mandler, 1984; Nezworski, Stein, & Trabasso, 1982). Findings such as these support the distinctions among the categories as well as the combinatorial rules of the grammar.

Events and actions are organized in episodes, each of which revolves around a goal and its outcome (Haberlandt, Berian, & Sandson, 1980; Mandler & Johnson, 1977; Rumelhart, 1975; Stein, 1982; Thorndyke, 1977). In the story in Table I, for example, two episodes can be discerned, one involving the goal of wanting to work a paper route and the other concerning the goal of buying the CD player. The memory representation of texts reflects the episodic organization (Mandler, 1984). The conditional probability that a statement is recalled is higher when other statements of the same episode are recalled than when statements from other episodes are retrieved. When texts are scrambled, the episodic structure tends to be restored in recall (Mandler, 1984). Similarly, subjects draw inferences more easily within an episode than across episodic boundaries (Beeman & Gernsbacher, 1992; van den Broek, 1989).

Most stories consist of multiple episodes. These episodes can be interrelated in various ways (Goldman & Vernhagen, 1986; Johnson & Mandler, 1980). They may simply follow each other sequentially, or they may be embedded. Embedding occurs when the goals or outcomes of the episodes are interdependent. This results in a hierarchical structure, similar to those described in the causal network theory. The two episodes in the sample story are hierarchically connected, for example, because the episode concerning the paper route takes place in order to achieve the goal in the other episode, to buy the CD player. As was discussed above, events at higher levels in the hierarchy tend to play a more important role in the representation of the text than do events at lower levels (Black & Bower, 1980; Goldman & Vernhagen, 1986).

In sum, the statements in a story can be differentiated into distinct categories, each with its own function. Some of these categories, most notably initiating events, outcomes, and goals, tend to play a more prominent role in the representation of the text than others, such as attempts, internal responses, and consequences. Furthermore, statements are organized in episodes, each revolving around a goal. If episodes are interdependent, they may form a hierarchy, with the highest level being more central to the representation of the text than the lower levels.

D. The Representation of Texts: Summary and Discussion

The memory representation of a narrative is far from a random list of isolated statements. Instead, it is a coherent structure that incorporates the important relational and functional properties of statements in the text.

Central to the representation of narratives are the causal relations between events. By describing how one event leads to another, these relations provide coherence to the representation. Each event in a narrative may be caused by a combination of antecedents and may in turn give rise to several consequences. As a result, the relations between the events in a text form a causal network. Functional properties of causal networks exert a strong influence on how readers understand and remember a story. Events that are part of the causal chain that connects the beginning and the end of a story are more important in the representation of the text than are events not on this chain. Likewise, events that have many causal antecedents and consequences are accessed more easily and are deemed more important than are events that have few connections.

Other potential coherence-building relations may have similar effects on the representation of a text. There is some evidence, for example, that anaphoric relations are included as well. In general, however, the potential role that relations other than causal ones may play in the mental representation of texts has received little attention.

Content differences also influence the availability of events. Outcomes, initiating events, major settings, and sometimes goals are more prominent in the representation than are internal responses, attempts, and reactions. Statements in these categories are clustered in episodes, each of which revolves around an implicit or explicit goal. When episodes are interdependent, with one episode taking place in order to achieve the goal in the other episode, a hierarchical organization of causal chains results. Higher order episodes provide a more thematic description of the story than do lower order episodes and hence feature more centrally in the representation.

1. Dependencies Between Representational Dimensions

It is important to note that the various properties of text representations are interrelated. Anaphoric and causal relations, for example, often coincide (Kintsch, 1988; van den Broek, 1990a). In order to identify causal relations, the reader will frequently need to establish anaphoric relations, for instance to determine that the protagonist in two events is the same. Vice versa, a potential causal relation between two events may help the reader disambiguate an anaphor.

The overlap of anaphoric and causal relations makes it difficult to assess the relative contribution of each type of relation to the coherence of the mental representation. In one of the few studies in which a direct comparison of the two types of relations was made, causal structure was found to be a more powerful predictor of speed of recall or reinstatement than anaphoric properties (O'Brien & Myers, 1987). This finding, combined with the evidence that readers engage in extensive anaphoric inference generation during reading (see Section III), invites the speculation that the two types of relations exert their strongest influence at different moments in the reading and comprehension process. Anaphoric relations may play a central role during the initial construction of coherence, but subsequently may give rise, and be subsumed by, other types of relations, such as causal ones (Kintsch, 1988; Trabasso et al., 1989).

Similar interdependencies may exist between story grammars and relational properties of the text. For example, the finding that some categories are recalled better than others, and that they tend to be recalled in a systematic order, may be the result of the fact that categories tend to fulfill different functions. This possibility is suggested by the finding, described earlier, that the order in which goal information is recalled is determined by its function rather than its story grammar category (Nezworski et al., 1982). The causal function of statements, in particular, has been found to explain many observed category differences in recall. Statements in the categories that are recalled most frequently also are more often part of the causal chain and have more causal connections than statements in categories that are not well recalled (Trabasso et al., 1984). Varying a statement's causal properties changes its importance without altering its content or category (van den Broek, 1988). Thus, several category effects may find their origin in causal properties.

Causal connections and categories are related in yet another way. The different types of causal relations, namely, physical, motivational, psychological causality, and enablement, tend to involve certain categories but not others. For example, motivational relations usually connect a goal to attempts or, possibly, an outcome; psychological relations have internal responses, goals, or reactions as their consequences; and so on. Thus, the type of causal relation depends in part on the category of the related events.

A final example of the overlap between causal and categorical properties concerns the episodic structure of a text. An episode is defined as the set of events that are relevant to one goal, and thus by definition consists of a cluster of causally and/or referentially interrelated events. Similarly, the organization of multiple episodes is based on their interrelations. For example, the hierarchical structure of a text is the result of causal relations between the goals/outcomes of different episodes.

These examples illustrate that the various structural properties of a memory representation of a text may overlap. Causality, in particular, seems to play a role in many of the findings that have been observed. Yet not all observations can be reduced to causal factors. Although many differences in recall of categories can be explained by other properties, for example, others cannot. Some story grammar categories, in particular outcomes, are recalled better than one would expect on the basis of causal connectivity alone (Trabasso & van den Broek, 1985). Similarly, in tasks such as summarization, hierarchical effects remain even after the effects of causal factors have been removed. Thus, the various structural properties of a text make both common and unique contributions to the coherence of the memory representation. What exactly the relative contribution of each is and what circumstances affect this contribution remain open questions.

The possible dependencies and interactions between properties in the representation can be depicted graphically by including both the relational and functional properties of a text in the representation (Trabasso & van den Broek, 1985; Trabasso et al., 1989). Figure 2 shows a network that includes the causal and categorical properties of the sample story. Each event is labeled according to the category of its content. The subscripts for each event refer first to its position in the surface structure in the text, and second to its level in the hierarchical structure of the text. Several of the observed dependencies are illustrated: Some categories have more causal connections than others, hierarchical levels are defined by causal relations between episodes, and so on. In addition, one can identify various factors that have been found to influence memory for texts: causal relations, causal chains, hierarchical structure, content categories, and so on.

2. Task-Dependent Access to Memory Representation

The conclusions about the mental representation of texts are to a considerable extent dependent on the tasks that subjects perform. As the above review illustrates, various tasks have been employed to investigate the representation

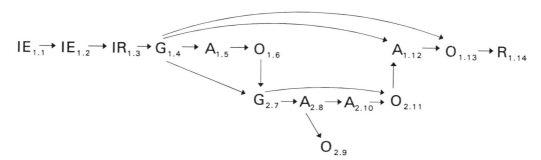

FIG. 2   Representation of causal, hierarchical, and story grammar properties of the sample narrative.

of texts in memory, including recall, summarization, importance ratings, questioning, recognition, lexical decision, and so on. The results obtained on these tasks agree to quite an extent, thus providing convergent evidence for the structure of the memory representation. Systematic differences in results have also been observed, however. For example, performance on recall tasks provides support for causal properties, such as causal chain and number of causal connections, for hierarchical structure, as well as for distinctions between categories. Summarization tasks show evidence for hierarchical structure and for story grammar categories, but much less so for local causal properties. In contrast, the results from importance judgment tasks indicate a strong effect of causal factors, but little of hierarchical position. During reading the speed of recall of a referent is a function of the length of the causal chain to that referent, but speed of recognition depends on its number of causal connections.

These differences suggest that a representation can be accessed in different ways, depending on the particular task. One can speculate, for example, that IMPORTANCE-RATING tasks explicitly ask subjects to assess the impact of one event on the remainder of the story and thereby provoke consideration of the event's causal connections (van den Broek, 1988). In a SUMMARIZATION task, the reader not only accesses a representation but also explicitly edits the retrieved information in order to achieve conciseness rather than completeness. As a result, the information that is included in summaries will tend to be that which is most thematic and abstract. Subjects are likely to select those categories from an episode that allow one to infer the omitted categories, usually goals and outcomes, and at the highest thematic level, high in the hierarchy (e.g., Goldman & Varnhagen, 1986). During RECALL, the representation of a text may be accessed in yet a different way. When asked to recall a story after reading is completed, a subject might access the representation at a random point and trace the causal path through the representation, activating the events that are encountered. The more paths that connect into a statement, the more likely it is that the entry point lies on a path to that event and hence the more likely it is that the event will be activated and recalled (e.g., Fletcher & Bloom, 1988; Graesser & Clark, 1985; Trabasso & van den Broek, 1985). A different situation arises when a subject is asked to recall an event during or immediately after reading. In this case, the entry point for retrieval is likely to be the most recently activated events (e.g., the last read statement). The likelihood of recall under these circumstances is a function of the length of the path from the recently activated events to the target (cf. O'Brien & Myers, 1987). In a RECOGNITION task, the subject receives the target information and has to verify whether it was part of the text or not. The speed with which subjects perform this task depends on the number of causal connections that the target statement has, suggesting that the recognition task elicits a parallel search for antecedents (O'Brien & Myers, 1987). These speculations about task differences are post hoc and have not been tested. They illustrate, however, the possibility that tasks differ in the way that they elicit access to the memory representation of the text. A systematic exploration of this possibility would not only allow the reconciliation of seemingly discrepant findings, but would result in a better understanding of the nature of the representation itself.

III. THE PROCESS OF COMPREHENSION

The memory representation of a text is the result of inferential processes that take place during reading. These inferential processes allow the reader to establish coherence as he or she proceeds through the text. In general, the more relations a reader detects, the more coherent the text representation is and the better comprehension will be. Limitations in the reader's information processing system restrict the generation of large numbers of inferences, however. Extensive inferential processes would overwhelm the attentional capacity of the reader or slow down reading to a snail's pace. Investigations of the inferential processes during reading are therefore usually based on the assumption that only a subset of all possible inferences is generated. The focus in these investigations is on two questions: Which of all possible inferences are made during reading, and what are the processes that are involved in the generation of inferences?

A. What Is an Inference?

Before discussing research on the inferential process, it is necessary to consider what researchers mean by *inference*. Although there is general agreement that the term *inference* refers to information that is activated during reading yet not explicitly stated in the text, there is disagreement about what type of activation qualifies as an inference.

One issue concerns the permanence of inferred information. On the one hand, activation can be TRANSIENT. Transient activation occurs when, during reading, information is activated for a brief period of time, sometimes less than a second (cf. Till, Mross, & Kintsch, 1988). After this period, activation dissipates without leaving a permanent trace. On the other hand, information can be activated and ENCODED in a permanent memory representation of the text (Sanford, 1990).

Researchers in text comprehension generally agree that activated information that is encoded in a relatively permanent representation constitutes an inference, but they differ in their position on transient activation. Regardless of whether one considers transient activation an inference or not, there are good reasons to include both transient activation and permanent encoding in theoretical accounts of inference generation.

First, transient activations and permanent encodings are not independent. On the one hand, transient activations provide important building blocks for the construction of a permanent encoding. Indeed, recent computational models of reading comprehension assign a central place to transient activations in their description of the construction of a more permanent representation (e.g., Golden & Rumelhart, 1993; Kintsch, 1988; N. E. Sharkey, 1990; A. J. C. Sharkey & Sharkey, 1992; St. John, 1992). On the other hand, transient activation itself frequently is influenced by the reinstatement of information that was encoded at previous points in the text. Thus, once the reader has formed a representation of one section of the text, he or she may access and reactivate parts of this representation when reading subsequent sections of the text. Second, the difference in the stability of transient activations and encoded information is one of degree only. As Bartlett (1932) demonstrated in his famous experiments on memory for the "War of the ghosts" story, encoded information is not as stable as it might seem. Thus, the memory representation of a narrative is likely to evolve even after transient activations have disappeared.

These considerations suggest that both transient activation and encoding are integral components of the reading process. Whether both should be called an inference may be a definitional issue rather than one with important theoretical implications (cf. Keenan, Potts, Golding, & Jennings, 1990; Lucas, Tanenhaus, & Carlson, 1990; Potts, Keenan, & Golding, 1988).

A second, similar issue is whether activations that are based on individual words rather than on sentences or phrases should be considered inferences. Although word-based activations usually are not considered to constitute inferences per se (cf. Singer, 1993; this volume), they may be powerful contributors to the generation of inferences (Kintsch, 1988; Sanford, 1990). As with transient activation, the activation of word-based associations therefore is included in many models of inference generation during reading.

A third issue is how strong or specific an activation needs to be in order to be called an inference. One possibility is that only activations that reach the same level of specificity and strength as concepts and events that are explicitly provided in the text constitute inferences. This position in effect dichotomizes activations into those that exceed and those that fall below a certain threshold, with only the former being inferences. Such a dichotomy is too simplistic in light of the fact that even concepts and events that are explicitly mentioned in the text are activated to different degrees and in light of current models of memory which emphasize that activations of concepts vary along a continuum (e.g., Just & Carpenter, 1992; Kintsch, 1988). Instead, inferential activity during reading is better conceptualized as the constant fluctuation of activations, with inferences sometimes being specific and strong and sometimes being vague and weak (cf. Dopkins, Klin, & Myers, 1993; Gernsbacher, 1990; van den Broek, Fletcher, & Risden, 1993). In this view, any change in activation of information that partially or completely derives from background knowledge or from memory for prior text constitutes an inference.

A final issue concerns the distinctions between READER-INDUCED and TASK-INDUCED inferences and, within the former, between AUTOMATIC and STRATEGIC inferences. Reader-induced inferences are generated spontaneously in the course of normal reading, whereas task-induced inferences are generated in response to the specific task in the experiment (recall, lexical decision, naming, questioning, etc.). Although task-induced inferences are interesting because they provide insight both into the differential availability of information from the text and into the cognitive processes that can operate on this information, they constitute a source of interference if a researcher is interested primarily in reader-induced processes. This is because it is difficult to separate reader- and task-induced inferences experimentally. Any task that requires subjects to respond opens the door, in principle, for task-induced processes such as context checking (Keenan, Golding, Potts, Jennings, & Aman, 1990). This issue is raised frequently with respect to tasks such as recall and questioning, in which subjects are invited to reflect. Recently, however, it has become clear that even tasks in which reflection is discouraged by requiring subjects to respond as quickly as possible may induce specific inferential processes (e.g., Keenan, Golding, et al., 1990; McKoon & Ratcliff, 1990). Procedures in which normal reading is not altered or interrupted, such as reading-time and eye-movement studies, are in principle free from task-induced inferences. Even in these tasks, though, specific instructions may confound spontaneous inferential activity. In addition, although these measurements indicate when the reader does something, they often do not provide information on what the reader does. In sum, it is difficult to identify which inferences are generated spontaneously. Therefore, conclusions on inferential processes must be based on convergent evidence from multiple tasks.

Reader-induced inferences themselves fall into two categories, AUTOMATIC and STRATEGIC inferences. Automatic inferences are beyond conscious control by the reader and therefore inevitable. In contrast, strategic inferences are the result of intentional efforts on the part of the reader and hence are not inevitable. This distinction also has proven to be difficult to translate into experimental procedures. Although it is tempting to assume that automatic processes are fast whereas strategic processes are slow, and thus to isolate the two types by measuring activation at different temporal delays, such an assumption may be false. In principle, it is possible that an inferential process is slow, yet automatic (Magliano, Baggett, Johnson, & Graesser, 1993; van den Broek, Fletcher, & Risden, 1993). Put differently, it is possible that certain inferences are inevitable and not under conscious control of the reader but take more time to be computed than other inferences. Thus, although it seems reasonable to assert that fast responses are more likely to be automatic than are slow responses, the reverse, that slow responses are not automatic, does not hold.

Thus, there is strong agreement that inferential processes during reading are central to the study of discourse comprehension, but researchers differ somewhat in their definitions of what exactly constitutes an inference. In addition, it is difficult to distinguish automatic, strategic, and task-induced inferences because each task has its strengths and weaknesses in separating these three. As a result, researchers prefer to use a variety of tasks in order to gather convergent evidence on inference generation during reading.

B. Anaphoric and Cataphoric Inferences

1. Anaphors

There is ample evidence that readers routinely establish coherence by resolving anaphoric references during reading. Reading-time measures indicate that readers slow down when they encounter an anaphor that needs to be resolved (Garrod & Sanford, 1990; Haviland & Clark, 1974). In addition, after reading a sentence with an unresolved anaphoric reference, the antecedent is more available than it is after a sentence that does not contain an anaphoric reference. Inappropriate referents are not available in either case (Corbett & Chang, 1983; Gernsbacher, 1989; McKoon & Ratcliff, 1980; O'Brien, Duffy, & Myers, 1986). Thus, when a reader encounters a statement that requires a search for an anaphoric antecedent, he or she slows down and reactivates the antecedent.

Recent psycholinguistic models have provided details on the mechanisms that are involved in the establishment of anaphoric coherence. The activation of an antecedent is the result of two component processes, enhancement of the antecedent and suppression of other concepts (Gernsbacher, 1989, 1990, 1991). According to Gernsbacher's (1990) structure building framework, the reading process is characterized by a constant shifting of activation of concepts. As the reader progresses through the text, the activation of some concepts is enhanced, while the activation of others is suppressed. Anaphors play an important role in this dynamic shifting of activation. By specifying the referent's identity, an anaphor enhances the activation of the referent; at the same time it suppresses activation of other, nonreferent concepts. Indeed, activation of the antecedent increases after the anaphor, whereas activation of other, nonreferent concepts decreases (Gernsbacher, 1989, 1991). An important implication of this model is that anaphors may differ in their effectiveness in modulating activation. The more specific the anaphor is with respect to the identity of its referent, the more quickly and effectively it enhances the antecedent and suppresses other concepts (Dell, McKoon, & Ratcliff, 1983; Gernsbacher, 1989, 1990; Gernsbacher & Faust, 1991a, 1991b).

When a proper antecedent is not available (i.e., is not among the currently activated concepts) when an anaphor is encountered, then a search of memory must be conducted. O'Brien and his colleagues (O'Brien, 1987; O'Brien & Albrecht, 1991; O'Brien, Plewes, & Albrecht, 1990) have proposed that this search takes place in a parallel backward fashion. According to their model, the anaphor initiates a spreading activation from the concepts presently active in memory to concepts mentioned earlier in the text. The spreading activation will continue simultaneously along all possible paths of associated concepts in the memory representation for the text until the anaphor is resolved. All concepts along the paths will be activated but only those that are consistent with the anaphoric phrase are activated beyond a threshold. In support of this account, O'Brien et al. (1990; O'Brien & Albrecht, 1991) demonstrated that antecedents that occur late in the text (i.e., close to the anaphor) are accessed more quickly than are antecedents that occur early in the text (i.e., far from the anaphor). The speed with which an antecedent was accessed also was found to be a function of the number of concepts to which it was associated: The more highly elaborated an antecedent was, the more quickly it was accessed. Thus, the efficiency with which an anaphoric resolution is obtained is a function of the length of the path connecting it to the anaphor and of the number of paths leading to it. In agreement with the model, potential but incorrect candidate antecedents were activated in the process of anaphoric resolution, provided that they occurred between the correct antecedent and the referent in the surface structure of the text.

The search for anaphoric resolution is not limited to memory for the text only. Candidate antecedents that are not explicitly mentioned but that are supported by the text are activated as well and can even terminate the search process (O'Brien & Albrecht, 1991). Control experiments have demonstrated that these elaborative antecedents are constructed at the time of retrieval, not during initial reading. This suggests that the anaphoric cue and the concepts from the text that are encountered during the search together constrain the activation of the reader's background knowledge enough to create a viable candidate antecedent.[5]

In sum, when an anaphor is encountered, coherence is maintained by the activation of an antecedent. In well-structured texts the antecedent is usually already part of the activated concepts, and enhancement and suppression take place. This leads to a further increase in the activation of the antecedent and a decrease in the activation of other, nonreferent concepts. When the antecedent is not among the concepts that already are activated, a backward parallel search takes place in which prior information from the text is checked against the anaphoric cue. Incorrect antecedents may be activated if they are in the path that leads to the correct antecedent. If a sufficient match is found between the anaphor and information in this backward search, enhancement and suppression take place on the candidate antecedents, and the search process stops. Although the search for a match often involves textual information only, background knowledge may be activated by the combination of anaphoric cue and retrieved textual information. In this case, an elaborative anaphoric inference is generated.

2. Cataphors

Whereas anaphoric inferences modulate the availability of previously mentioned concepts, cataphoric devices change the availability of concepts for the text that follows (Gernsbacher, 1990). Compare, for example, the two sentences in (4).

(4)   a. *I have **this** uncle.* . . .
       b. *I have **an** uncle.* . . .

Gernsbacher (1990) proposed that devices such as the indefinite article *this* signal that a concept is likely to be mentioned again. As a result, the identified concept should increase in availability. Indeed, concepts that were marked by cataphoric devices proved to be more strongly activated, more resistant to being suppressed, as well as more effective in suppressing other concepts (Gernsbacher & Jescheniak, 1993; Gernsbacher & Shroyer, 1989). Similar effects have been observed with respect to other devices, such as the order of mention (Gernsbacher, 1989; Morrow, 1985) and the foregrounding of a protagonist (Morrow, 1985; cf. O'Brien & Albrecht, 1991).

---

[5] This description of the process of anaphoric resolution as the propagation of constraints from multiple sources is consistent with recent models of memory retrieval. In Ratcliff's and McKoon's (1988) compound cue model of recognition, for example, the recognition cue combines with the memory traces for all potential targets to yield a set of compound cues. If a particular compound cue exceeds a threshold of activation, then successful recognition has occurred. Similarly, in Smolensky's (1986) harmony model, a particular stimulus recruits all knowledge in memory in parallel. When the constraints imposed by the stimulus and those that result from recruited knowledge resonate beyond a threshold, then comprehension has taken place.

C. Causal Inferences

A second type of inference that has received extensive attention from researchers is that of causal relations. Given the importance of causal structure for the
memory representation of narrative texts, one would expect that the generation
of causal relations is a major component of the inferential activities during
reading. As a reader focuses on a new statement, he or she may generate two
types of causal inferences. They may be BACKWARD, connecting the event to
its antecedents, or they may be FORWARD, anticipating future consequences
of the focal statement (note the correspondence between this distinction and
that between anaphors and cataphors).

1. Backward Causal Inferences

Backward causal connections provide coherence between the focal statement and antecedent statements. In principle, the reader can draw on three
sources for the identification of the causal antecedent(s) to a focal event. These
sources and the three resulting types of backward inferences are presented in
the top panel of Figure 3. First, as the reader proceeds to a new focal event,
information that was activated during processing of prior events may provide
the causal antecedent for the new event. In this case, a simple CONNECTING
inference establishes a connection between the two. Second, information from
the prior text that currently is not highly activated can be reactivated by the
reader in order to identify causal antecedents. That is, a REINSTATEMENT is
made to connect the focal event to prior text. Third, the reader can draw
on background knowledge in order to identify a plausible but unmentioned
antecedent to the focal event. In this case, the reader makes an ELABORATIVE
inference to provide an explanation for the focal event. In terms of classical
memory theories, these three sources correspond to short-term memory, long-
term episodic memory, and general semantic knowledge, respectively (cf.
Kintsch & van Dijk, 1978).

A CONNECTING INFERENCE is generated when the reader identifies a causal
relation between the focal event and information that has remained activated
after processing of the prior event. Thus, a connecting inference occurs when
a focal statement and one of its antecedents co-occur in short-term memory.
This is likely to happen, for example, when the focal event and the antecedent
are adjacent in the text. In this case, the antecedent is still activated when the
reader encounters the focal event, and hence a causal relation would be generated easily.

This hypothesis was tested by Keenan and Myers and their colleagues
(Keenan et al., 1984; Myers et al., 1987). These authors reasoned that if readers
indeed attempt to identify causal relations between adjacent sentences, then
the stronger a relation is, the more easily readers would identify it. Subjects
read sentence pairs that varied systematically in their causal strengths. In
addition to the recall data discussed in Section II, reading times for the second
sentence were recorded. The reading times showed the predicted patterns: the
stronger the causal relation, the more quickly subjects read the second statement. The possibility that the observed speed-up resulted because subjects,
for some reason, were paying less attention to the second sentences in the
highly connected pairs is ruled out by the results of the probe–recall task. As

Backward

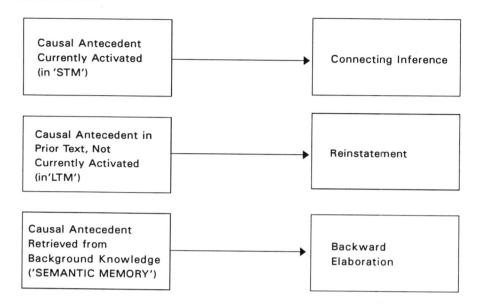

Forward

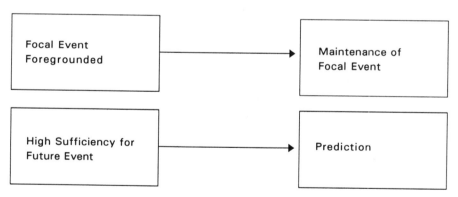

FIG. 3 Types of causal inferences during reading of narrative texts (based on van den Broek, 1990a).

described earlier, the results on this task indicate that a stronger memory connection was constructed for the high-causal than for the low-causal pairs. Thus, a strong causal relation resulted in both high reading speed and strong memory trace. Together, these findings indicate that people indeed infer connecting causal relations between adjacent sentences.

In stories, because they contain more than two sentences, information other than the immediately preceding statement still may be activated when the focal event is encountered. As a result, connecting inferences may involve nonadjacent events. At least two types of statements have been found to remain active over intervening statements and to be connected easily: statements that describe an as yet unexplained event, and statements that have causal antecedents but have not had consequences yet. Duffy (1986) showed that information that is unexplained, particularly when this involves the protagonist's goal, is often maintained as the reader proceeds through the text. Subjects judged the appropriateness of continuation sentences more quickly when they were connected to information that was left unexplained, and therefore was hypothesized to be activated, than when they were connected to events that had already been explained and hence deactivated. Likewise, statements that are explained but that have no consequences are maintained in memory. The results from reading time and recall studies indicate that events that lack a causal consequence remain activated in memory and are easily connected to their consequence (Bloom, Fletcher, van den Broek, Reitz, & Shapiro, 1990; Fletcher & Bloom, 1988). The availability of these events may even exceed that of events that were read more recently.

In sum, as the reader shifts attention to a new focal statement, some information from the preceding text will remain activated. Causal relations between the focal statement and events that still are activated or in short-term memory from previous cycles are identified easily via connecting inferences. Events that remain activated from previous cycles include events that were described in the immediately preceding statement, events from the preceding text that still are unexplained, and prior events that have not had consequences yet. The stronger the relation between the focal event and the activated information from the prior text, the more quickly the connecting inference will be generated.

The second type of backward inference, REINSTATEMENT, occurs when textual information that is no longer activated is reactivated (reinstated) in order to provide missing causal support. Empirical evidence suggests that causal reinstatements indeed occur during reading and that the resulting causal relations are generated and encoded in the memory representation of the text, provided that they are required for understanding the focal event. For example, presentation of the antecedent of a pair of statements that are hypothesized to be connected through a reinstatement increases the speed with which the consequent of the pair is recognized. The speed of recognition after priming by the supposedly reinstated antecedent is greater than that either after statements to which they are not related via reinstatements or after statements that were not part of the original text (van den Broek & Lorch, 1993). These findings indicate that causal connections that are generated via reinstatements are incorporated in the memory representation of the text.

Direct evidence that reinstatements are generated during reading is provided in a series of studies by Trabasso and Suh (1993). When asked to provide a verbal protocol of the reading processes, subjects frequently reinstated information from the prior text in order to explain current events. Furthermore, when interrupted during reading to perform a recognition task, subjects responded faster when the probe word referred to a statement that was hypothesized to be reinstated than to a probe word that did not refer to a reinstated event (Trabasso & Suh, 1993). Similar findings are reported by Dopkins et al. (1993). Thus, readers frequently reinstate information from the prior text in order to create causal connections to the focal event. In particular, they seem to do so when reinstatements are required in order to provide adequate causal justification for the focal event.

Little research has been conducted on the exact mechanism by which the reinstatement search takes place. The speed with which subjects respond when they are asked explicitly to reinstate information from their memory for a text suggests that reinstatements are located via a parallel backward search (O'Brien & Myers, 1987). Conclusions concerning the reinstatement search process await more extensive investigation, however.

The third type of backward inference, ELABORATIVE INFERENCES, is hypothesized to take place when the reader accesses background knowledge in order to connect two events. The background knowledge can provide either a missing intervening event, thus bridging two events described in a text, or a supporting event or fact that combines with the explicit antecedent to explain the focal event.

An unexpected pattern of results in the studies on cued recall and reading speed described earlier (Keenan et al., 1984; Myers et al., 1987) illustrates how elaborative inferences may affect comprehension and memory for textual information. As expected, in these studies high-causal event pairs were read more quickly and resulted in a stronger memory trace than low-causal pairs. Pairs of intermediate causal strength showed seemingly contradictory results, however. Their reading times were as predicted (between that of high- and low-causal pairs), but contrary to the predictions, their cued recall was better not only than that for low-causal pairs but also than that for high-causal pairs. In order to explain this pattern, Myers et al. (1987; Myers, 1990) suggested that readers may have generated elaborative inferences in an attempt to connect the two members of the intermediate- and low-causal pairs. For high-causal pairs, no elaborations were generated, because the events are so closely related that no further elaboration is necessary. For these pairs, a single strong connection was constructed. For the intermediate- and low-causal pairs, elaborative inferences are necessary in order to generate a causal connection. For the intermediate pairs, the elaborative activity likely was successful. As a result, the pair of statements was represented in memory as consisting of several highly interconnected nodes. For the low-causal pairs, either elaborative inferences were not attempted because readers considered the statements in the pair to be unrelated, or the obtained elaborations were unsuccessful in establishing a strong causal relation. The result was a weak mental representation of the sentence pairs. The highly interconnected memory representation for the intermediate pairs resulted in a memory trace that was stronger than that of either high- or low-causal pairs.

The hypothesis that variation in elaborative activity had caused the observed differences in probed recall was tested in a series of follow-up experiments, in which subjects were encouraged to generate an elaborative inference (Myers & Duffy, 1990). As predicted, the differences in cued recall probabilities between the sentence pairs of different causal strengths disappeared as a result of this manipulation. Thus, it was indeed elaborative inferential activity that caused different strengths in memory traces.

Direct evidence that readers activate background knowledge in order to explain events comes from research on sentence pairs in which information necessary for an explanation is missing. Consider (5) (from Singer, Halldorson, Lear & Andrusiak, 1992):

(5) a. *Dorothy poured water on the fire.*
     b. *The fire went out.*

A causal explanation of the second event, the fire going out, would require the reader to access background knowledge that provides a missing piece of information, namely that *Water extinguishes fire.*[6]

There is evidence that readers indeed access such background knowledge in order to understand the sentence pairs. When subjects are given questions about background knowledge as they are reading sentence pairs like the one presented in (5), they answer such questions more quickly when they immediately follow a sentence pair in which that information constituted a missing premise than in control situations in which the question and prior sentence pair were unrelated. In the example, the question would be, Does water extinguish fire? The speed-up in responses to questions like these after a sentence pair in which the information was a missing premise was found in a series of studies (Singer et al., 1992; Singer, Revlin, & Halldorson, 1990). Thus, it appears that readers activate world knowledge in order to provide causal explanations for events in texts.

In sum, various types of causal inferential processes may take place during reading. First, readers may make a CONNECTING inference by relating the focal statement to information that remains activated or in short-term memory after finishing the comprehension of the prior statements. Activated information may consist of the immediately preceding statement, events that have not yet had consequences, or events that are in need of further explanation. Second, readers may reactivate or REINSTATE information that was activated as part of comprehension of the previous text but is no longer in active memory. Third, the reader may draw on background knowledge in order to generate an ELABORATIVE inference, which adds information not contained in the text to the memory representation.

2. A Process Model of Backward Inferences: Establishing Sufficient Explanation

What determines which of these types of inferences will be generated? Under what circumstances will the reader be limited to causal antecedents that are already active in memory, generate an elaborative inference, or reinstate prior text? This issue is especially important because the limitations of the reader's information processing system prevent the construction of all of the large number of possible causal relations (Trabasso et al., 1989). It has been suggested that a distinction should be made between inferences that are required for coherence and those that are compatible but not necessary (Duffy, 1986; McKoon & Ratcliff, 1992; Noordman, Vonk, & Kempff, 1992; O'Brien, Shank, Myers, & Rayner, 1988; Potts et al., 1988; Singer & Ferreira, 1983; van den Broek, 1990a; Vonk & Noordman, 1990; Warren et al., 1979). In this view,

---

[6] Such sentence pairs resemble syllogisms with a missing premise, and following philosophical terminology are called ENTHYMEMES.

if causal relations are identified at all by the reader, then they are more likely to be those that are required than those that are not required.

Although the notion of required inferences is quite appealing, it is unclear what researchers mean by it. Frequently, the determination of inferences as required for adequate causal justification of a focal event is based on the researcher's intuitions about the experimental materials. The reliance on intuition prevents both replication and a systematic investigation of the circumstances in which the different types of inferences are generated.

One possibility is that *required* simply means that some causal relation to the prior text needs to be identified. From this perspective, the criterion *required* is satisfied if any causal relation can be established, regardless of the content or strength of that relation. With respect to the sample story in Table I, the only inference that would be required to integrate the statement *Brian bought the CD player* with the prior text is the statement *Brian went to the store*. There is no need to infer that Brian's wanting a CD player or his having earned money have anything to do with his buying the player. This definition is frequently adopted in models that posit that the reader constructs a causal chain through the story.

Although this definition of *required* provides a clear criterion, empirical findings suggest that inferences frequently extend beyond the identification of relations between adjacent events. In all the above-mentioned studies on elaborative inferences and reinstatements, for example, the focal event was connected directly to the immediately preceding statement. According to the proposed criterion, no inferences other than connecting ones would be required in these circumstances. Yet systematic elaborative and reinstatement activities were observed. Thus, this definition underestimates the number of inferences that readers make during normal reading.

The empirical findings can be explained by modifying the definition of what constitutes required inferences in terms of the content or quality of the inferred relations. According to this revised definition, required inferences are those that provide causally SUFFICIENT explanation for the focal event. A cause (or a set of causes) is sufficient for an event if, in the general circumstances of the narrative, the cause (or set of causes) by itself would likely result in the event. This definition emphasizes the bottom-up or content-driven aspects of reading: The extent to which an event is understood strongly influences the inferential process. As the reader proceeds through the text, he or she attempts to maintain sufficient explanation for the encountered events and will access activated information, background knowledge, and/or memory for prior text when needed to do so (van den Broek, 1990b).[7]

The notion that the reader attempts to establish sufficient explanation allows one to construct a hypothetical account of the inferential processes that will take place at each point in a text. As a reader begins processing a novel focal event, he or she attempts to connect the focal event to the events that are already in the focus of attention or short-term memory. This activated information is

---

[7] The use of the verb *attempt* should not be taken to mean that the inferential processes necessarily are strategic, that is, under conscious control of the reader. Indeed, during proficient and successful reading, these processes may be largely automatic, with more conscious efforts taking place only if the automatic processes do not provide adequate coherence.

likely to include the immediately preceding statement but, as mentioned above, it may include statements that still require explanation or that have not had consequences yet. If the activated information provides sufficient explanation, then a connecting inference is made and the inferential process stops, without having accessed background knowledge and without having reinstated information from the prior text. If no sufficiency is established, however, then the reader is likely to engage in further inferential activities, such as the reinstatement of prior events and the generation of elaborations. The resulting inferences will tend to provide sufficiency. Thus, sufficiency dictates when various types of inferences occur and what their content will be. Note the similarity between this account of causal inferential processes and that presented by researchers on anaphoric inferences, as described in the previous section.

The theoretical model accounts for the results in the previously mentioned studies. First, consider again the findings on cued recall and reading speed for sentence pairs that vary in the strength of their causal relations (Keenan et al., 1984; Myers et al., 1987). For the high-causal pairs, the first sentence provides sufficient explanation for the second sentence, and therefore a connecting inference is all that is required to establish a connection. Because such an inference depends only on information that is already in the focus of attention or short-term memory, it can be computed easily and quickly. For statement pairs that have intermediate or low causal strength, additional processing is required to establish sufficiency. Since no prior context is available, the reader has to draw on background knowledge and generate elaborative inferences. For the intermediate-strength pairs, the constraints provided by the two sentences are strong enough to yield elaborations that are successful in bridging the causal gap. As a result, the reading time for these pairs would increase relative to that for high-strength pairs, but the resulting memory trace would consist of multiple paths between the two sentences and the bridging elaborations and hence be very strong. In contrast, for the low-strength pairs the constraints are so weak that the computation of a bridging inference will take considerable time and effort and even then might fail to yield a clear and effective causal bridge. As a result, one would expect that reading of the low-strength pairs will be even slower and cued recall will be poorest. Thus, the observed patterns can readily be explained in terms of the notion that readers attempt to maintain sufficient explanation for the events they encounter during reading and that they generate elaborative inferences in order to do so.

An analysis of the elaborations that subjects produced in the Myers and Duffy (1990) study confirm this interpretation (van den Broek, Risden, & Husebye-Hartmann, in press). Across sentence pairs, the vast majority (87%) of the elaborations provided causal support for the second sentence. For pairs of intermediate causal strength, the combination of elaboration and the first sentence of the pair provided sufficient explanations. As a result, cued recall was very good. In contrast, for the low-strength pairs the elaborations improved the causal explanation provided by the first statement, but the combined strength of the explanation did not approach sufficiency. The failure to provide adequate explanation in the low-causal pairs resulted in the poor cued recall for these items. Interestingly, virtually all noncausal elaborations were generated in response to the high-strength pairs. Apparently, subjects found it very difficult to try to generate a bridging inference between a highly sufficient explanation and its consequence. This result is in agreement with the suggestion, made above and by Myers et al. (1987), that these pairs evoked no elaborative inferences. Together, these results support the hypothesis that the need for sufficient explanation drives the generation of connecting and elaborative inferences and that the extent to which the reader is able to establish sufficiency affects the strength of the memory trace.

Second, the model accounts for the results on elaborative inferences obtained by Singer et al. (1990; 1992). By definition, the missing premise in an enthymeme provides sufficiency that was lacking in the statement pair. According to the process model proposed above, an enthymeme therefore constitutes a situation in which the reader will activate information that provides sufficient explanation. The results confirm this prediction. In this context, it is interesting to note that Singer et al. (1992) demonstrated in several control experiments that background information was generated only when required to resolve an enthymeme. This supports the use of sufficiency as the basis for inferential activity.

Third, the model explains the findings on reinstatements described earlier. These findings indicate that information from prior text is reactivated when needed for the comprehension of a focal event (Dopkins et al., 1993) and that this reactivated information primes recognition of the focal event (van den Broek & Lorch, 1993). In both studies, the statements that were hypothesized to be reinstated contained information that was required in order to provide a sufficient explanation for the focal event. Thus, as predicted by the model, the need for sufficient explanation led to the reinstatement of information from the prior text.

Thus, the notion of sufficient explanation allows one to integrate and explain the results from prior studies on inference generation. Further evidence for the psychological validity of the model comes from direct experimental tests. The general strategy for these tests has been to systematically manipulate the extent to which various parts of the text provide sufficiency for a focal event. Consider the story fragment in (6), based on Thurlow (1991). The dots indicate intervening statements.

(6)   a. *Joanne was working late.*
       b. *It was raining hard.*
       c. *She left the office building.*
                        .
                        .
                        .
       d. *The wind blew open her folder.*
       e. *The papers got all wet.*

In this story, the event in (6d) is causally connected to the event in (6e). This connection does not provide sufficiency, however, because wind usually does not cause objects to become wet. In order to establish sufficient explanation, the reader needs to reinstate (6b).

Contrast this story with the version in (7).

(7)   a. *Joanne was working late.*
       b. *It was sunny outside.*

c. *She left the office building.*

.

.

.

d. *The wind blew open her folder.*
e. *The papers got all wet.*

In this version, the event in (7b) does not provide sufficiency for the event in (7e). Unlike in the first version, the prior text in the second version does not provide sufficient justification for the focal statement. Thus, in order to explain the event in (7e), readers will need to access background knowledge. They can do so, for example, by inferring that it was raining.

Finally, consider a third version, in (8).

(8) a. *Joanne was working late.*
     b. *It was raining hard.*
     c. *She left the office building.*

.

.

.

     d. *She dropped the papers in a puddle.*
     e. *The papers got all wet.*

In this version, the events in (8b) and (8e) can be connected. The event in (8d) now provides sufficient explanation for the event in (8e), however. Therefore, in this version a connecting inference between (8d) and (8e) suffices and no elaboration for reinstatement is required.

The present model makes specific predictions with respect to the processes that part (e) will evoke in each of these versions. In the first version, the readers are hypothesized to reinstate the event described in part (b). In the second version, sufficiency requires an additional inference as well, but here the inference needs to be generated from background knowledge. Hence, the model predicts an elaborative inference. In the third version, a connecting inference provides sufficient explanation.

If these predictions are correct, then systematic differences between the versions should be observed on various behavioral measures. First, reading times for the focal sentence (e) should be longer in the first and second versions than in the third version because of the additional processing required to establish sufficiency. Second, the concept 'rain' should be more activated following the focal sentence in version (6), where it is hypothesized to have been reinstated, than in the other versions. Third, when asked to explain why the papers got wet, subjects should provide both the immediate antecedent and the reinstated fact that it was raining in version (6), both the immediate antecedent and an elaboration that provides sufficiency in version (7), and only the immediately preceding statement in version (8).

The results of several recent studies provide evidence for these hypotheses. First, reading times increased when a reinstatement search or elaboration was posited to take place (van den Broek & Thurlow, 1990). Interestingly, the increase in reading time for the second version, in which an elaboration was required, was observed only when readers were instructed to make sure that they understood each statement before proceeding to the subsequent statement. When no such instruction was given, the slow-down was delayed until the next two statements. This finding resembles that reported by Duffy (1986). Apparently, subjects may buffer an unexplained event to see whether it will be explained later in the text. Second, answers to *why*-questions were as predicted. When the immediately preceding statement provided sufficiency for the focal event, it was given exclusively in answer to a *why*-question about the focal event. When a reinstatement was required as well, answers tended to include both the immediately preceding and the reinstated information. When an elaboration was required for sufficiency, subjects produced answers that contained both the immediately preceding event and an elaboration that provided sufficiency (van den Broek & Thurlow, 1990). Third, naming times for concepts that were hypothesized to have been reinstated (e.g., 'rain' in the example story) were shorter after the focal statement than before the focal statement. This pattern was observed only for those versions in which reinstatement of the concepts was required for sufficiency (Thurlow, 1991).

The results of lexical decision studies provide evidence that both reinstatements and elaborative inferences are generated in order to provide sufficient explanation for a focal statement during the reading of real stories as well (van den Broek, Rohleder, & Narvaez, in press). While reading short works of fiction, subjects occasionally were interrupted and asked to identify as quickly as possible whether a string of letters constituted a legitimate English word or not. Target words were selected to refer to events that were needed to provide sufficient explanation for statements in the text. Half the words referred to events that had taken place earlier in the text and needed to be reinstated; the other half referred to events that would constitute elaborations. Both types of target words were identified more quickly after they were needed to provide sufficient explanation for the focal statement than before the focal statement. They were also identified more quickly than after the focal statement in isolation. Thus, both reinstatements and elaborations occurred as predicted by the model. The fact that these findings were obtained with natural stories attests to the generalizability of the role of sufficiency.

In sum, backward causal inferences are generated routinely during reading. As the reader proceeds through the text, he or she attempts to maintain causal coherence and sufficient explanation by means of three types of inferences. Connecting inferences relate the event that is presently being read to events that are still highly activated from prior processing. These inferences are made with relatively little effort. Reinstatements reactivate memory for the prior text, and elaborative inferences draw on the reader's background knowledge to provide causal antecedents. Both are more effortful than connecting inferences.

3. Forward Causal Inferences

Forward inferences allow the reader to anticipate upcoming events. Possible forward inferences fall into two categories. First, the reader may use his or her knowledge of causality to make PREDICTIONS about future events.[8] Second, the

---

[8] As mentioned before, an inference need not involve the explicit and specific construction of a new concept or node. Thus, the phrase's prediction refers to the anticipation of any aspect of future events, ranging from a specific expectation that a particular event will take place to a vague sense that something will occur. Such anticipations may result from both automatic (e.g., spread of activation) and strategic processes.

reader may anticipate a causal role for the event that is currently being read and hence MAINTAIN activation of this event. These two types of forward inferences and the semantic principles that would dictate their occurrence are presented in the bottom panel of Figure 3.

Forward inferences are not required for maintaining coherence (Potts et al., 1988; van den Broek, 1990a; Vonk & Noordman, 1990). Therefore the generation of such inferences involves a trade-off: on the one hand, accurate prediction of an upcoming event will significantly aid in connecting that event to the text representation; on the other hand, erroneous predictions consume costly resources that could perhaps be spent better elsewhere (Noordman et al., 1992; Rayner & Pollatsek, 1989; cf. Vonk & Noordman, 1990).

The results of several empirical investigations suggest that the first type of forward inferences, predictive inferences, are not made reliably during reading. For example, it takes subjects considerably longer to answer questions about predictive inferences than about backward inferences (Singer & Ferreira, 1983). Likewise, concepts from backward inferences that are necessary for coherence are more quickly pronounced than words from predictive inferences, which are pronounced no more quickly than are control words (Magliano et al., 1993; Potts et al., 1988).

Although these findings demonstrate that it is more difficult to demonstrate the occurrence of predictive than backward inferences, they do not imply that predictive inferences are not made at all. There are several alternative reasons why one might find forward inferences to be made less reliably than backward inferences. First, if any predictive inferences are made, they are likely to be less constrained by the text than backward inferences. The reason for this is that backward inferences need to be compatible with the text in both their antecedents and consequences, whereas predictive inferences are constrained only by their antecedents. As a result, predictive inferences can be expected to be more variable in content and reliability than backward inferences. This poses a problem for the researcher because most experimental tasks (such as naming and lexical decision) require a high-speed response to a particular word. Such tasks are sensitive to exact or very close matches between inference and target word (Lucas et al., 1990; van den Broek, Fletcher, & Risden, 1993). Given the relatively large variability in possible predictive inferences, there is a serious risk that a predictive inference made by the reader does not exactly match the inference hypothesized by the researcher. Second, predictive inferences may be made when the prior text provides strong constraints but not when the prior text only provides weak support. In the cited studies, no attempt was made to assess how compellingly the prior text supported the accompanying target inference. This raises the possibility that data were combined across degrees of support. As a result, the variance would increase and the likelihood of statistical significance would be reduced. In sum, the variability in content as well as the variability in the probability of a forward inference and the ensuing null effects would lead to the erroneous conclusion that predictive inferences were not generated. In order to minimize these problems, researchers increasingly select texts and target words on the basis of norming studies rather than intuition.

The hypothesis that CONSTRAINTS play a major role in the generation of predictive inferences has been tested directly. One important source of constraints is the most recently processed event. If this event provides strong support for a particular inference, then the inference is likely to be computed. One important aspect of this support is the strength of the causal relation between the focal event and the potential inference (van den Broek, 1990a). Consider, for example, (9)–(10) (based on McKoon & Ratcliff, 1989).

(9)   a. *While shooting a film, the actress accidentally fell out the first floor window.*
      b. *While shooting a film, the actress accidentally fell out the 14th floor window.*

(10) Target inference: *The actress died.*

Sentence (9b) provides more causal sufficiency for the forward inference 'dead' than does (9a). If causal support influences the generation of predictive inferences, then a predictive inference is more likely following (9b) than (9a). The results in naming tasks confirm this expectation: information from the predictive inference (e.g., 'dead') was more available following a text that provides strong sufficiency for the inference than following a text that provides weak sufficiency (Murray, Klin, & Myers, 1993). Thus, causal constraints, in particular sufficiency, affect the generation of predictive inferences.

The amount of support for a possible predictive inference depends on other factors as well. For example, a reminder of earlier supporting information has been found to result in the generation of a predictive inference (McKoon & Ratcliff, 1986, 1989). Linguistic devices also may affect the likelihood of predictive inferences. For example, foregrounding of causally supporting information increases the probability of a forward inference (Whitney, Ritchie, & Crane, 1992).

The second type of forward inference involves the anticipation that a current event will play a causal role in subsequent parts of the text (van den Broek, 1990a; cf. cataphoric inferences, Gernsbacher, 1990). This type of forward inference concerns the maintenance of events that have already been mentioned in the text but are anticipated to become important for subsequent, as yet unmentioned events. Two forms of anticipation of future relevance already have been discussed above. Events that have not been explained yet are likely to be maintained in active memory, apparently because they are anticipated to be causally related to subsequent events (Duffy, 1986). Similarly, events that have a cause but no consequences yet are maintained, presumably because the reader anticipates their relevance for future events (Fletcher & Bloom, 1988; Fletcher, Hummel, & Marsolek, 1990). The possibility that other causal factors influence the maintenance of activation remains to be investigated.

In sum, two types of forward inference have been found to occur during reading. One type involves the prediction or expectation that a particular event will take place in subsequent text. A second type involves maintenance of activation for aspects of the current event because they are anticipated to become relevant later in the text. Although these inferences are generally more variable than backward inferences, they are generated if semantic and linguistic constraints are strong enough. With respect to predictive inferences, the degree of causal sufficiency of the focal event for the forward inference affects the generation of an inference. Maintenance of activation takes place when the current event is an unexplained yet salient event or when it has not had any consequences yet. Both types of forward inferences influence the pattern of activation that will be carried forward from a focal event and thereby are likely to affect the generation of subsequent backward inferences.

D. Instrument Inferences

A third type of inference concerns that of the instruments that are used in the actions in the text. Consider (11) (Corbett & Dosher, 1978).

(11) *The accountant dried his hands.*

When reading this sentence, a reader may infer that the accountant was using a towel to dry his hands.

The results of early investigations on instrument inferences indicate that such inferences are not generated during reading. Although instrument words (e.g., *towel*) successfully cue recall for sentences such as (11), they also do so for sentences in which an alternative instrument was mentioned explicitly (Corbett & Dosher, 1978). Thus, the appropriate instruments do not seem to be inferred preferentially. In addition, verification times for the instrument word consistently were found to take longer when the instrument was implied, as in (11), than when it was explicitly mentioned (Singer, 1979a, 1979b). These findings suggest that concepts associated with instrument inferences are not activated during reading.

Subsequent research however, indicates that instrument inferences are generated if the context constrains or implies the instrument. When the instrument is required for comprehension, for example, verification times for the instrument word have been found to be similar to those for explicitly mentioned words (Singer, 1980). For example, when reading sentence pairs such as *The worker drove the nail, The tool was too small for the task,* subjects activate the word *hammer* as much as when this instrument was mentioned explicitly. In addition, instruments that are either required for comprehension or highly associated to the text are effective cues in a probe recognition task (McKoon & Ratcliff, 1981). These results were obtained both immediately after reading and after a delay. Thus, the focal statement may influence the activation and the encoding of instrument inferences.

Context also affects the generation of instrument inferences. For example, an instrument is likely to be inferred when it has been mentioned explicitly in the preceding text (Lucas et al., 1990) or when the preceding context strongly biases toward a particular instrument (O'Brien et al., 1988).

Together these results indicate that instrument inferences are sometimes generated, particularly when they are required for adequate understanding or when the text strongly constrains or biases toward a particular instrument. In the latter case, both the focal sentence and the context contribute to the constraints. The stronger the constraints, the more likely and specific the instrument inference will be.

E. Thematic Inferences

Information in discourse is usually organized around themes. In *Anna Karenin,* for example, the introductory paragraph can be summarized under the theme of everything going wrong in the Oblonsky household. Recognition of the theme of a text is considered an important aspect of successful comprehension. Few studies have addressed the question of whether these inferences are generated in the course of regular reading. There is some indication that thematic inferences are generated for expository texts, but the evidence is not unequivocal (cf. Singer, this volume).

In narratives, themes usually revolve around goals (Mandler & Johnson, 1977; Stein, 1982). The results of recent studies suggest that thematic or superordinate goals are generated during the reading of narrative texts. For example, the naming speed for a word related to a superordinate goal has been found to be faster than for words related to a subordinate goal (Long & Golding, 1993). Interestingly, the superordinate goals in these studies usually provide sufficiency for the focal statement. As a result, it is not quite clear whether the superordinate goal is inferred because it represents a theme or because it is required in order to understand the focal statement.

Superordinate goals also tend to be maintained as the reader proceeds through the text. Naming and recognition speed for superordinate goal information has been found to remain high across extended text, unless the goal has been satisfied (Trabasso & Suh, 1993). The superordinate goal is replaced when a subordinate goal is encountered, only to be reactivated once the subordinate goal is resolved and pursuit of the superordinate goal resumes. This suggests that thematic goal information remains activated across intervening text. One possible reason for the maintenance of superordinate goal information is that such information is likely to have further consequences in the remainder of the text. As was discussed above, such information tends to be maintained in short-term memory (Fletcher & Bloom, 1988).

In sum, thematic inferences in narrative texts have received relatively little attention from researchers. There is some evidence, however, that thematic goal inferences are generated, possibly because of the causal role that they play in the text. Goal inferences include backward elaborative inferences as well as the maintenance of goal information over subsequent text.

F. Inferential Processes during Reading: Summary and Conclusions

It is clear that reading involves extensive inferential processes, ranging from automatic activations to strategic comprehension efforts. The most important types of inferences are those that provide coherence to the text by connecting the focal statements to prior events. In doing so, these inferences resolve anaphoric ambiguity and provide causally sufficient explanations for each focal statement. Thus, they are required for adequate comprehension. The results of a large number of studies indicate that coherence-building inferences are routinely made during reading. As each new statement is encountered, the identity of objects, protagonists, and so on is determined by means of anaphoric inferences to prior text or possibly to background knowledge. Similarly, backward causal inferences ensure that the events in focal statements are sufficiently explained by establishing causal relations to events that are still activated from previous comprehension cycles, by reactivating information from the prior text, or by accessing background knowledge.

A second group of inferences concerns expectations about the upcoming text. One type of expectation involves the anticipation that objects, persons, or events activated in the current comprehension cycle will be mentioned in upcoming discourse or will become causally relevant for events yet to be described. The first of these, future mention of objects, events, or persons that are activated currently, is anticipated by cataphoric inferences. Cataphoric inferences result from the linguistic and syntactic structure of the focal statement or from discourse conventions. The second type of anticipation concerns that of future causal relevance. This occurs when currently activated information is expected to play a causal role for events in upcoming text. This is particularly likely when the focal statement has not been explained adequately or has not had consequences yet. The anticipation of either future mention or future causal relevance leads to the maintenance of currently activated information.

A second type of expectation involves the anticipation of novel events. This occurs, for example, when the focal statement is sufficient cause for a particular consequence, given the circumstances of the story.

Experimental results suggest that forward inferences generally are less frequent and/or less specific than backward inferences. They are made, however, when the support for a particular inference is strong enough.

Other types of inferences have been found to occur during reading as well. For example, readers may infer the instruments with which actions are performed. Such inferences appear to be made reliably, however, only when the instruments are required for anaphoric or causal coherence or when they are highly associated with the particular actions described in the text. As a second example, themes for a story such as goals are inferred during reading and may be maintained over an extended portion of the text. Thematic inferences may be particularly likely if they are required for the establishment of causal coherence. Similar principles seem to apply to other types of inferences, not reviewed here. For example, although it is clear that readers can make spatial inferences (e.g., Morrow, Bower, & Greenspan, 1990), they may do so spontaneously only when the inference is required for the explanation of an event or strongly supported by the text (Zwaan & van Oostendorp, 1993; cf. Vonk & Noordman, 1990).

1. A General Process Model of Inference Generation

The findings on the occurrence of various kinds of inference show a consistent pattern. Inferences appear to occur under two types of circumstances. They are generated when they are required for comprehension, for instance to establish anaphoric reference or sufficient causal explanation; or when the contextual constraints heavily favor a specific inference, such as by association, causal sufficiency, linguistic cues, or a combination of these.

This suggests the existence of two inferential mechanisms (cf. Sanford, 1990). One mechanism is that of SPREAD OF ACTIVATION based on the constraints provided by the text. Various properties of a focal statement, such as associations, linguistic features, and being sufficient cause for other events, may trigger activation of other concepts. If this activation exceeds a threshold, then an inference is made. The stronger the constraints toward a particular inference are, the more likely it is that the activation will exceed the threshold (cf. Just & Carpenter, 1992).

The second mechanism concerns the ESTABLISHMENT OF COHERENCE in the text. Coherence-based inferences ensure that minimal levels of comprehension are maintained. For example, they establish sufficient causal explanation for the focal event and resolve referential ambiguities. In this sense, causal sufficiency and referential coherence are implicit criteria for comprehension held by the reader. Coherence-based inferences may involve the establishment of connections between information that is currently attended or in short-term memory, reinstatement searches, and retrieval of background knowledge, as well as highly strategic behaviors such as looking back through a text.

Association- and coherence-based inferences differ in several respects. First, they differ in the constraints on their content. Association-based inferences are constrained by patterns of activation: any event, object, or person that is sufficiently activated will be inferred, regardless of its function or the type of its relation to the focal statement. In contrast, coherence-based inferences are constrained primarily by their function of establishing coherence: If an inference is required in order to attain coherence, then it is likely to be made. Second, association-based inferences take place during reading of both texts and isolated sentences, whereas coherence-based inferences are unique to texts and rarely occur in response to isolated sentences.

Despite these differences, association-based and coherence-based inferential processes are neither mutually exclusive nor independent. On the one hand, inferences that are based on association may be all that is required for coherence. In this case, coherence-based inferences are identical to those based on association (Kintsch, 1988). On the other hand, coherence-based inferences that result from a backward search require a match in association between the focal statement and the information that is activated during the search. Thus, part of the generation of a coherence-based inference may be the establishment of an associative connection.

Together, the association-based and coherence-based inferential mechanisms give rise to the various types of inferences that were described in the previous section. Consider the inferential processes that take place as each focal statement is being read. These processes and the resulting inferences are summarized in Figure 4 (cf. van den Broek, Fletcher, & Risden, 1993). As a statement becomes focal, it triggers activation of its associations in the reader's background knowledge. If these activations, combined with residual activation from the previous comprehension cycle, exceed a threshold, then an inference is made. The resulting inferences may be forward, orthogonal, or backward relative to the temporal direction of the narrative. Forward inferences anticipate future events by means of cataphors, the anticipation of future relevance, or predictions of novel events. Orthogonal inferences embellish the focal statement by providing details or associations. Most important for comprehension, the combined patterns of activation may result in a connecting backward inference that integrates the focal event with the representation of the prior text. If the connecting inference provides referential and causal coherence, no further inferential processes are needed for comprehension, and the reader proceeds to the next statement.

A more complicated situation arises when simple associations do not provide adequate coherence. This occurs when they fail to establish anaphoric references or sufficient causal justification for the focal statement. When this happens, the lack of coherence evokes additional coherence-based processes. A search results, in which prior text is reactivated and/or background knowledge

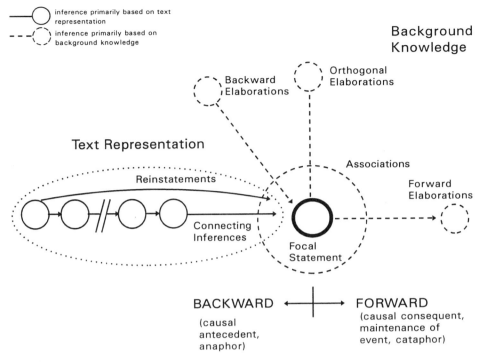

FIG. 4 A process model of inference generation during reading.

is accessed. The information that is activated during the search is matched against the focal statement. If the patterns of activation that result from the search and those that are based on the focal statement yield adequate anaphoric or causal relations, reinstatements or elaborative backward inferences are generated. Coherence is established, and the inferential process stops.

2. Properties of the Inferential Process

Several aspects of the inferential process are worth noting. First, the search-and-match process is likely to be resource-consuming regardless of whether it is intentional or automatic. As a result, differences in the time course of availability of information should be interpreted with great care. Although information that is activated immediately upon reading of the focal statement is likely the result of automatic processes, the reverse does not hold: A delay in availability does not imply an intentional activity but simply may reflect slow automatic processes.

Second, the inferential processes during reading depend on the presence on various constraints and resources. These constraints and resources determine both what inferential processes take place at a particular point during reading and what type of content the resulting inferences will contain. The constraints generally fall into two categories, semantic and procedural. These two types and their subtypes are described in Table II.

The information that is available to the reader provides semantic constraints and resources for the inferential process. There are three major sources of

TABLE II
Constraints and Resources in Inference Generation
during Reading

1. Semantic constraints and resources
    a. Text based constraints and resources
        Content
        Structure
    b. Background knowledge
        General knowledge
        Discourse-specific knowledge
    c. Reader's criteria for coherence
        Anaphora
        Causal sufficiency
        Reading goals/motivation
2. Procedural/computational constraints and resources
    a. Limitation in short-term memory/attentional resources
    b. Task demands
        Time limitations
        Criterial task

information. First, the text base both constrains and facilitates the generation of inferences. On the one hand, an inference must agree with the information provided in a text. On the other hand, the semantic and linguistic content and structure of the text base provides a starting point for the activation of information and thus helps in the construction of a coherent representation of the text. Second, a reader's background knowledge facilitates and limits the content of possible inferences. Background knowledge includes both general knowledge about events and knowledge that is specific to discourse. Differences in background knowledge will produce differences in the inferences that are generated. In extreme cases, the reader may lack adequate background knowledge and thus fail to make an inference, even under the most conducive circumstances. Third, the reader explicitly or implicitly employs criteria for coherence, such as anaphoric clarity and causal sufficiency. The criteria of coherence that a reader employs affect the inferential processes that will take place. The criteria are likely to vary as a function of inter- and intra-individual differences. Highly motivated readers, for example, are likely to employ more stringent criteria, whereas less motivated readers may be perfectly satisfied with looser criteria than those held by the modal reader described above.

The second type of constraints and resources concerns the availability of procedural and computational resources. Two factors affect these resources. First, the human information processing system is limited in the amount of information that can be processed simultaneously. If the inferential processes that are needed for the construction of a coherent representation do not exceed these limitations, then reading comprehension will be smooth and rapid. If the information that is activated presently does not provide coherence, however, then the reader must engage in additional processing if he or she is to comprehend the text. The additional processing may involve access to memory for prior text or activation of general background knowledge. Although the additional processes may establish coherence, they come at a cost. Reading slows down, and the resulting coherence still may be incomplete.

A second type of procedural/computational constraint results from the demands imposed by the task. On the one hand, some tasks may further deplete the already limited information processing capacity of the reader. For example, when the task requires the reader to proceed at a quick pace, then many of the processes required for comprehension cannot be executed. On the other hand, the nature of the task may determine the extent to which the reader will engage in inferential processes. For example, when the criterial task does not require comprehension, readers may well abstain from inferential processes. In contrast, when the task encourages the reader to proceed more slowly or prompts the reader to explore the text more deeply than during regular reading, then inferential activity beyond that which occurs spontaneously may result.

Together, the semantic and procedural constraints determine the inferential processes that take place during reading. The two types of constraints are likely to interact. For example, if information that is required for coherence is presented at widely separated locations in the text, then the procedural limitations of human information processing may interfere with the attempt to construct a coherent representation of the text. Thus, the need for coherence must be balanced against the limitations of the human information processing system. The cognitive demands of generating and maintaining all possible inferences would quickly overwhelm the attentional or short-term memory capacity of a reader (Rayner & Pollatsek, 1989; Singer, 1988; Warren et al., 1979).

A third aspect of the inferential process worth noting is that the above process model does not assume that the information in the text is provided in a chronologically and anaphorically/causally correct order.[9] As mentioned, readers may maintain information that they think will become relevant in subsequent text or that they anticipate will be explained further. Thus, readers may postpone completion of the inferential process and maintain information out of order. Conversely, after the inferential process has been completed, new information may confirm or modify the interpretation of previously read statements. Under these circumstances, reconstructive processes are likely to take place.

Fourth, the relation between coherence-based and association-based inferences can be conceptualized in various ways. One possibility is that the two mechanisms are fundamentally identical. Recent connectionist models of reading comprehension, for example, propose that coherence-based connections are part of the associative networks for events (Golden & Rumelhart, 1993; N. E. Sharkey, 1990; St. John, 1992). In this view, the reading of a focal statement evokes parallel distributed processing of associations which include or produce coherence-based inferences. As a result, coherence-based inferences are not different from association-based inferences, and the perception of special processes involved in the establishment of coherence is misguided. An alternative view holds that coherence-based and association-based inferences are structurally different. According to this view, coherence-based inferences are considered to be the result of a backward search that is separate from spread of activation. In this search, appropriate concepts will be enhanced in their activation, whereas inappropriate activations will be suppressed (cf. Gernsbacher, 1990). On the one hand, the backward search may take place only after the associative processes have not yielded adequate coherence (Kintsch, 1988).

---

[9] I thank Charles R. Fletcher for raising the issue of non-canonical ordering.

On the other hand, a directed search and spread of activation may begin simultaneously, with the backward search usually taking a longer amount of time than the spread of activation. These alternative views of the nature of the relation between association- and coherence-based inferences are currently the focus of extensive investigation.

IV. COMPREHENSION AND MEMORY FOR NARRATIVES: INFERENCES AND REPRESENTATIONS

The process of reading comprehension is a dynamic and cognitively complex activity, in which the reader attempts to construct a coherent representation of the text. The last 10 years have seen extensive research efforts to try to understand the details of the inferential processes during reading and of the structure of the mental representations. The reading process itself perhaps is best characterized as one of changing patterns of activation. As each new statement is encountered, activations fluctuate as a result of the association-based and coherence-based processes described above. As the statement is being comprehended, these activations settle into an increasingly stable pattern. When a subsequent statement is encountered, it creates its own pattern of activation that will interact with the developing pattern of the previous sentence. With each additional sentence, new activations are added and others extinguished until the end of the text is reached. The changes in activations depend on the semantic and procedural constraints on the reader. In this fashion, changes in activation occur as each sentence is comprehended. From this perspective, inferences should not be considered as all or none, that is, as being present or absent. Instead, concepts differ in the degree of their availability or in their ease of their being accessed (Just & Carpenter, 1992).

The transient fluctuations of activation that result from inferential processes during reading form the basis for a stable memory representation of the text. If comprehension is successful, then the mental representation resembles an interconnected network of events and facts. The various pieces of information in this network are connected through anaphoric, causal, as well as other types of relations. This network is accessed during any task which requires the retrieval of all or part of the information in the text. The way in which access takes place depends in part on the type of task that is being demanded of the reader. In general, however, the more interconnected the network is, the better comprehension and subsequent retrieval will be.

Any complete model of reading will need to describe how transient activations during reading eventually result in a relatively permanent memory representation, yet the nature of this transition has begun to be explored only recently. It is known, for example, that at various points during reading (e.g., at the end of a paragraph or of a text), the reading process slows down to allow for a settling of the activation pattern. It is unclear, however, by what mechanism this settling might result in stable encodings. Three possible models of the transition of transient activation to representation can be discerned. According to the CYCLE model, the strength of encoding of an event depends on the duration of its activation during reading. The longer an event is activated or the more often it is reactivated, the stronger its trace in the representation. Note that in this model the actual relations of the event are not encoded in the representation. Instead, an event is encoded in isolation, with the strength of encoding solely being a function of the length of time or frequency with which the event has been processed. A second model, the STRUCTURE model, posits that the relations that are identified during reading are actually encoded as part of the mental representation. According to this model, the memory representation is an interconnected structure rather than a arbitrary listing of events with various strengths. According to a third, HYBRID model, the representation of events includes their relations, but events also vary in their strength as a function of the frequency with which they have been processed during reading.

Transient activation and memory representation are related in the opposite direction as well. Transient activations during reading are frequently affected by a reinstatement of information from the developing mental representation of the text. Most models, for example, assume reinstatements based on searches of long-term memory for the text. Although it is clear that such reinstatements take place, the exact mechanisms are at present insufficiently understood.

In sum, considerable progress has been made in describing the inferential processes that take place during reading. Likewise, the structure of the mental representation that results from these processes is rather well understood. These two components of reading, the activations during reading and the mental representation, are related in a bidirectional fashion. On the one hand, transient activations eventually lead to the generation of a coherent mental representation. On the other hand, the transient activations themselves are influenced by the partial representations that have been constructed up to that point in the reading. Only recently have investigations started to explore the interrelation between on-line processing and off-line memory representation.

V. INDIVIDUAL DIFFERENCES IN READING COMPREHENSION

A final issue that needs to be discussed concerns individual differences. As our theoretical understanding of comprehension and memory for narratives has increased, it has become clear that there are substantial differences in discourse processing between individuals. Such differences have been noted between subjects at different ages as well as between subjects within the same age range. Many factors may contribute to these differences. Variations in the reading purpose, in the criteria for comprehension in background knowledge, in short-term attentional capacity, and so on are all likely to affect the extent to which the reader engages in inferential processes and consequently the properties of the resulting memory representation.

Perhaps most widely investigated are individual differences in the memory representation of a text. Developmental studies indicate that even children as young as four and a half years of age incorporate multiple causal relations in their memory representations of a narrative (Goldman & Varnhagen, 1986; Trabasso & Nickels, 1992; Trabasso, Stein, Rodkin, Munger, & Baughn, 1992; van den Broek, Lorch, & Thurlow, 1989). However, the density of the network increases with age. In particular, children become increasingly sensitive to relations that involve goals and also to interepisodic connections (Goldman & Varnhagen, 1986; van den Broek, 1989). Surprisingly, the memory representation of children with various degrees of intellectual capacity or familiarity with the language are remarkably similar: for example, children with mild mental retardation or learning disabilities have been found to be as sensitive to the causal properties of a text as children without disabilities (Wolman, 1991; Wolman & van den Broek, 1993). Similarly, readers of a second language are, if anything, more sensitive to causal connections and causal chains than are native speakers (Horiba, 1990). Within an age group, readers with extensive knowledge or familiarity of the information in the text construct richer and more interconnected networks than do people to whom the text conveys relatively novel information (Chi, 1988; Chiesi, Spilich, & Voss, 1979).

In recent years, considerable individual differences have been identified in the processes that take place during reading. One important source of individual differences consists of reader's READING SPAN, their ability to maintain textual information in short-term memory or attention. Readers that can maintain large amounts of textual information are able to process and encode information from different perspectives, whereas subjects who can maintain only moderate amounts of textual information selectively recall information from one perspective only (Lee-Sammons & Whitney, 1991). High reading span subjects construct fewer elaborations that unnecessarily narrow down their interpretation of the text than do low-span readers (Whitney, Ritchey, & Clark, 1991), but they also generate more elaborations that assist in the interpretation in an understanding of the text (Thurlow, 1991). Thus, high reading span readers more effectively generate elaborations that are useful but not overly restrictive of their interpretation of the text. Whereas high-skilled or high reading span readers expand or embellish their representation of the text in appropriate fashion, unskilled readers may engage in excessive inappropriate processing. Unskilled readers, for example, demonstrate less suppression of inappropriate references and interpretations of a focal statement than do skilled readers (Gernsbacher, 1990). These effects of reading skill on the comprehension of texts parallels finding on the comprehension of sentences: High reading span subjects tend to maintain multiple interpretations of ambiguous words, whereas low-span subjects have been found to restrict their interpretation prematurely (Just & Carpenter, 1992).

A second source of individual differences in inferential processes results from differences in the amount of knowledge that readers have about the textual information. Readers with high knowledge generate more elaborations than do readers with low knowledge (Kim, van Dusen, Freudenthal, & Williams, 1992). These elaborations improve the memory representation of the text, as demonstrated by the finding that sentences that prompted elaborations were recalled better than sentences that were not elaborated. Thus, readers with high reading spans or high knowledge keep more options open for interpretation and also provide more embellishments to the text. The result is a richer and stronger network representation.

These examples of individual differences in representation and in inferential processes illustrate that, although the general outline of the inferential processes and memory representation of narrative texts outlined above applies to readers of different skill levels and ages, individual variations do affect the properties of these processes. The exploration of such individual differences contributes greatly to our understanding of the dynamic and complex processes that take place in the comprehension of texts.

VI. CONCLUDING REMARKS

Recent research has greatly advanced our understanding of the reading process. The results of this research shed light on the extensive inferential processes that take place during reading as well as on the end result of these processes, the memory representation of the text. Inferential processes result from the spread of activation, as well as from an attempt to arrive at coherence in the text. As a result of these processes, the activation of concepts, facts, and events fluctuates as the reader proceeds through the text. Eventually, the fluctuating activation patterns settle into a relatively stable memory representation of the text. This memory representation resembles a network of events that are connected through semantic relations such as anaphoric reference and causal implication.

Many aspects of the comprehension processes are not yet fully understood. Examples are the mechanisms for the transition of fluctuating activations to stable representations and the precise impact of individual variations. The sheer fact that these questions can be posed and investigated, however, illustrates the enormous advances that have been made in the area of discourse processing in the past decades.

ACKNOWLEDGMENTS

I would like to thank Randy Fletcher, Morton Gernsbacher, Darcia Narvaez, and Kirsten Risden for their helpful comments on an earlier draft of this chapter. The writing of this chapter was supported by a single-quarter leave from the University of Minnesota and by grants from the Center for Research in Learning, Perception, and Cognition at the University of Minnesota, and the National Institute of Child Health and Human Development (HD-07151).

REFERENCES

Bartlett, F. C. (1932). *Remembering: A study in experimental and social psychology*. Cambridge: Cambridge University Press.

Beeman, M., & Gernsbacher, M. A. (1992). *Structure building and coherence inferencing during comprehension*. Unpublished manuscript. University of Oregon. Eugene, OR.

Black, J. B., & Bower, G. H. (1980). Story understanding as problem solving. *Poetics, 9*, 223–250.

Bloom, C. P., Fletcher, C. R., van den Broek, P., Reitz, L., & Shapiro, B. P. (1990). An on-line assessment of causal reasoning during text comprehension. *Memory & Cognition, 18*, 65–71.

Chi, M. T. H. (1988). Children's lack of access and knowledge reorganization: An example from the concept of animism. In F. E. Weinert & M. Perlmutter (Eds.), *Memory development: Universal changes and individual differences* (pp. 169–193). Hillsdale, NJ: Erlbaum.

Chiesi, H. L., Spilich, G. J., & Voss, J. F. (1979). Acquisition of domain-related information in relation to high and low domain knowledge. *Journal of Verbal Learning and Verbal Behavior, 18*, 257–274.

Colby, B. N. (1973). A partial grammar of Eskimo folktales. *American Anthropologist, 75*, 645–662.

Corbett, A. T., & Chang, F. R. (1983). Pronoun disambiguation: Accessing potential antecedents. *Memory & Cognition, 11*, 283–294.

Corbett, A. T., & Dosher, B. A. (1978). Instrument inferences in sentence encoding. *Journal of Verbal Learning and Verbal Behavior, 22,* 121–132.

Cummins, D. D., Lubart, T., Alksnis, O., & Rist, R. (1991). Conditional reasoning and causation. *Memory & Cognition, 19,* 274–282.

Dell, G. S., McKoon, G., & Ratcliff, R. (1983). The activation of antecedent information during the processing of anaphoric reference in reading. *Journal of Verbal Learning and Verbal Behavior, 22,* 121–132.

Dewey, J. (1933). *How we think, a reinstatement of the relation of reflective thinking to the education process.* Boston, New York: D. C. Heath and Company.

Dopkins, S., Klin, C., & Myers, J. L. (1993). The accessibility of information about goals during the processing of narrative texts. *Journal of Experimental Psychology: Learning, Memory and Cognition, 19,* 70–80.

Duffy, S. A. (1986). Role of expectations in sentence integration. *Journal of Experimental Psychology: Learning, Memory and Cognition, 12,* 208–219.

Einhorn, H. J., & Hogarth, R. M. (1986). Judging probable cause. *Psychological Bulletin, 99,* 3–19.

Fletcher, C. R., & Bloom, C. P. (1988). Causal reasoning in the comprehension of simple narrative texts. *Journal of Memory and Language, 27,* 235–244.

Fletcher, C. R., Hummel, J. E., & Marsolek, C. J. (1990). Causality and the allocation of attention during comprehension. *Journal of Experimental Psychology: Learning, Memory, and Cognition, 16,* 233–240.

Garrod, S., & Sanford, A. (1990). Referential processing in reading: Focusing on roles and individuals. In D. A. Balota, G. B. Flores d'Arcais, & K. Rayner (Eds.), *Comprehension processes in reading* (pp. 465–484). Hillsdale, NJ: Erlbaum.

Gernsbacher, M. A. (1989). Mechanisms that improve referential access. *Cognition, 32,* 99–156.

Gernsbacher, M. A. (1990). *Language comprehension as structure building.* Hillsdale, NJ: Erlbaum.

Gernsbacher, M. A. (1991). Cognitive processes and mechanisms in language comprehension: The structure building framework. In G. H. Bower (Ed.), *The psychology of learning and motivation* (Vol. 27, pp. 217–263). San Diego, CA: Academic Press.

Gernsbacher, M. A., & Faust, M. E. (1991a). The mechanism of suppression: A component of general comprehension skill. *Journal of Experimental Psychology: Learning, Memory, and Cognition, 17,* 245–262.

Gernsbacher, M. A., & Faust, M. (1991b). The role of suppression in sentence comprehension. In G. B. Simpson (Ed.), *Understanding word and sentence* (pp. 98–128). Amsterdam: North-Holland/Elsevier.

Gernsbacher, M. A., & Jescheniak, J. D. (1993). *Cataphoric devices in spoken discourse.* Manuscript submitted for publication.

Gernsbacher, M. A., & Shroyer, S. (1989). The cataphoric use of the indefinite *this* in spoken narratives. *Memory & Cognition, 17*(5), 536–540.

Golden, R. M., & Rumelhart, D. E. (1993). A parallel distributed processing model of story comprehension and recall. *Discourse Processes, 16,* 203–237.

Goldman, S. R., & Varnhagen, C. K. (1986). Memory for embedded and sequential story structures. *Journal of Memory and Language, 25,* 401–418.

Graesser, A. C. (1981). *Prose comprehension beyond the word.* New York & Berlin: Springer-Verlag.

Graesser, A. C., & Clark, L. F. (1985). *The structures and procedures of implicit knowledge.* Norwood, NJ: Ablex.

Haberlandt, K., Berian, C., & Sandson, J. (1980). The episode schema in story processing. *Journal of Verbal Learning and Verbal Behavior, 19,* 635–650.

Hart, M. L. A., & Honoré, A. M. (1985). *Causation in the law.* Oxford: Clarendon Press.

Haviland, S. E., & Clark, H. H. (1974). What's new? Acquiring new information as a process in comprehension. *Journal of Verbal Learning and Verbal Behavior, 13,* 512–521.

Horiba, Y. (1990). Narrative comprehension processes: A study of native and non-native readers of Japanese. *Modern Language Journal, 74,* 187–202.

Johnson, N. S., & Mandler, J. M. (1980). A tale of two structures: Underlying and surface forms in stories. *Poetics, 9,* 51–86.

Just, M. A., & Carpenter, P. A. (1992). A capacity theory of comprehension: Individual differences in working memory. *Psychological Review, 99*(1), 122–149.

Keenan, J. M., Baillet, S. D., & Brown, P. (1984). The effects of causal cohesion on comprehension and memory. *Journal of Verbal Learning and Verbal Behavior, 23*, 115–126.

Keenan, J. M., Golding, J. M., Potts, G. R., Jennings, T. M., & Aman, C. J. (1990). Methodological issues in evaluating the occurrence of inferences. In A. C. Graesser & G. H. Bower (Eds.), *The psychology of learning and motivation: Inferences and text comprehension* (Vol. 25, pp. 295–311). San Diego, CA: Academic Press.

Keenan, J. M., Potts, G. R., Golding, J. M., & Jennings, T. M. (1990). Which elaborative inferences are drawn during reading? A question of methodologies. In D. A. Balota, G. B. Flores d'Arcais, & K. Rayner (Eds.), *Comprehension processes in reading* (pp. 377–399). Hillsdale, NJ: Erlbaum.

Kim, S., van Dusen, L., Freudenthal, D., & Williams, D. (1992, January). *Understanding of elaborative processing in text comprehension: Text-provided elaboration versus self-generated elaboration.* Paper presented at the annual Winter Text Conference, Jackson Hole, WY.

Kintsch, W. (1988). The role of knowledge in discourse comprehension: A construction–integration model. *Psychological Review, 95*(2), 163–183.

Kintsch, W., & van Dijk, T. A. (1978). Toward a model of text comprehension and production. *Psychological Review, 85*, 363–394.

Lee-Sammons, W. H., & Whitney, P. (1991). Reading perspectives and memory for text: An individual differences analysis. *Journal of Experimental Psychology: Learning, Memory, and Cognition, 17*(6), 1074–1082.

Long, D. L., & Golding, J. M. (1993). Superordinate goal inferences: Are they automatically generated during comprehension? *Discourse Processes, 16*, 55–73.

Lucas, M. M., Tanenhaus, M. K., & Carlson, G. N. (1990). Levels of representation in the interpretation of anaphoric reference and instrument inference. *Memory & Cognition, 18*(6), 611–631.

Mackie, J. L. (1980). *The cement of the universe.* Oxford: Clarendon Press.

Magliano, J. P., Baggett, W. B., Johnson, B. K., & Graesser, A. C. (1993). The time course of generating causal antecedent and causal consequence inferences. *Discourse Processes, 16*, 35–53.

Mandler, J. M. (1984). *Stories, scripts, and scenes: Aspects of schema theory.* Hillsdale, NJ: Erlbaum.

Mandler, J. M., & Johnson, N. S. (1977). Remembrance of things parsed: Story structure and recall. *Cognitive Psychology, 9*, 111–151.

McKoon, G., & Ratcliff, R. (1980). Priming in item recognition: The organization of propositions in memory for text. *Journal of Verbal Learning and Verbal Behavior, 19*, 369–386.

McKoon, G., & Ratcliff, R. (1981). The comprehension process and memory structures involved in instrumental inference. *Journal of Verbal Learning and Verbal Behavior, 20*, 671–682.

McKoon, G., & Ratcliff, R. (1986). Inferences about predictable events. *Journal of Experimental Psychology: Learning, Memory, and Cognition, 12*, 82–91.

McKoon, G., & Ratcliff, R. (1989). Semantic associations and elaborative inferences. *Journal of Experimental Psychology: Learning, Memory and Cognition, 15*, 326–338.

McKoon, G., & Ratcliff, R. (1990). Textual inferences: Models and measures. In D. A. Balota, G. B. Flores d'Arcais, & K. Rayner (Eds.), *Comprehension processes in reading* (pp. 403–418). Hillsdale, NJ: Erlbaum.

McKoon, G., & Ratcliff, R. (1992). Inferences during reading. *Psychological Review, 99*, 440–466.

Miller, J. R., & Kintsch, W. (1980). Readability and recall of short prose passages: A theoretical analysis. *Journal of Experimental Psychology: Human Learning and Memory, 6*, 335–354.

Morrow, D. G. (1985). Prominent characters and events organize narrative understanding. *Journal of Memory and Language, 24*(3), 304–320.

Morrow, D. G., Bower, G. H., & Greenspan, S. L. (1990). Situation-based inferences during narrative comprehension. In A. C. Graesser & G. H. Bower (Eds.), *The psychology of learning and motivation: Inferences and text comprehension* (Vol. 25, pp. 123–135). San Diego, CA: Academic Press.

Murray, J. D., Klin, C. M., & Myers, J. L. (1993). Forward inferences in narrative text. *Journal of Memory and Language, 32*, 464–473.

Myers, J. L. (1990). Causal relatedness and text comprehension. In D. A. Balota, G. B. Flores d'Arcais, & K. Rayner (Eds.), *Comprehension processes in reading* (pp. 361–374). Hillsdale, NJ: Erlbaum.

Myers, J. L., & Duffy, S. A. (1990). Causal inferences and text memory. In A. C. Graesser & G. H. Bower (Eds.), *The psychology of learning and motivation: Inferences and text comprehension* (Vol. 25, pp. 159–173). San Diego, CA: Academic Press.

Myers, J. L., Shinjo, M., & Duffy, S. A. (1987). Degree of causal relatedness and memory. *Journal of Memory and Language, 26,* 453–465.

Nezworski, T., Stein, N. L., & Trabasso, T. (1982). Story structure versus content in children's recall. *Journal of Verbal Learning and Verbal Behavior, 21,* 196–206.

Nicholas, D. W., & Trabasso, T. (1981). Toward a taxonomy of inferences. In F. Wilkening & J. Becker (Eds.), *Information integration by children* (pp. 243–265). Hillsdale, NJ: Erlbaum.

Noordman, L. G., Vonk, W., & Kempff, H. J. (1992). Causal inferences during the reading of expository texts. *Journal of Memory and Language, 31*(5), 573–590.

O'Brien, E. J. (1987). Antecedent search processes and the structure of text. *Journal of Experimental Psychology: Learning, Memory, and Cognition, 13*(2), 278–290.

O'Brien, E. J., & Albrecht, J. E. (1991). The role of context in accessing antecedents in text. *Journal of Experimental Psychology: Learning, Memory, and Cognition, 17*(1), 94–102.

O'Brien, E. J., Duffy, S. A., & Myers, J. L. (1986). Anaphoric inference during reading. *Journal of Experimental Psychology: Learning, Memory, and Cognition, 12*(3), 346–352.

O'Brien, E. J., & Myers, J. L. (1987). The role of causal connections in the retrieval of text. *Memory & Cognition, 15,* 419–427.

O'Brien, E. J., Plewes, P. S., & Albrecht, J. E. (1990). Antecedent retrieval processes. *Journal of Experimental Psychology: Learning, Memory, and Cognition, 16*(2), 241–249.

O'Brien, E. J., Shank, D., Myers, J. L., & Rayner, K. (1988). Elaborative inferences during reading: Do they occur on-line? *Journal of Experimental Psychology: Learning, Memory, and Cognition, 14,* 410–420.

Omanson, R. C. (1982). The relation between centrality and story category variation. *Journal of Verbal Learning and Verbal Behavior, 21,* 326–337.

Piaget, J. (1959). *The language and thought of the child* (M. Gabain, Trans.). London: Routledge & Kegan Paul. (Original work published 1923).

Potts, G. R., Keenan, J. M., & Golding, J. M. (1988). Assessing the occurrence of elaborative inferences: Lexical decision versus naming. *Journal of Memory and Language, 27*(4), 399–415.

Propp, V. (1928). *Morphology of the folktale* (2nd ed.). Austin: University of Texas Press.

Ratcliff, R., & McKoon, G. (1988). A retrieval theory of priming. *Psychological Review, 21,* 139–155.

Rayner, K., & Pollatsek, A. (1989). *The psychology of reading.* Englewood Cliffs, NJ: Prentice-Hall.

Rumelhart, D. E. (1975). Notes on a schema for stories. In D. G. Bobrow & A. Collins (Eds.), *Representation and understanding: Studies in cognitive science.* New York: Academic Press.

Sanford, A. (1990). On the nature of text-driven inference. In D. A. Balota, G. B. Flores d'Arcais, & K. Rayner (Eds.), *Comprehension processes in reading* (pp. 515–533). Hillsdale, NJ: Erlbaum.

Schank, R. C., & Abelson, R. (1977). *Scripts, plans, and goals.* Hillsdale, NJ: Erlbaum.

Sharkey, A. J. C., & Sharkey, N. E. (1992). Weak contextual constraints in text and word priming. *Journal of Memory and Language, 31,* 543–572.

Sharkey, N. E. (1990). A connectionist model of text comprehension. In D. A. Balota, G. B. Flores d'Arcais, & K. Rayner (Eds.), *Comprehension processes in reading* (pp. 487–511). Hillsdale, NJ: Erlbaum.

Singer, M. (1979a). Processes of inference in sentence encoding. *Memory & Cognition, 7,* 192–200.

Singer, M. (1979b). Temporal locus of inference in the comprehension of brief passages: Recognizing and verifying implications about instruments. *Perceptual and Motor Skills, 49,* 539–550.

Singer, M. (1980). The role of case-filling inferences in the coherence of brief passages. *Discourse Processes, 3,* 185–201.

Singer, M. (1988). Inferences in reading comprehension. In M. Daneman, G. MacKinnon, & T. Waller (Eds.), *Reading research: Advances in theory and practice* (Vol. 6, pp. 177–219). New York: Academic Press.

Singer, M. (1993). Global inferences of text situations. *Discourse Processes, 16,* 161–168.

Singer, M., & Ferreira, F. (1983). Inferring consequences in story comprehension. *Journal of Verbal Learning and Verbal Behavior, 22,* 437–448.

Singer, M., Halldorson, M., Lear, J. C., & Andrusiak, P. (1992). Validation of causal bridging inferences in discourse understanding. *Journal of Memory and Language, 31,* 507–524.

Singer, M., Revlin, R., & Halldorson, M. (1990). Bridging inferences and enthymemes. In A. C. Graesser & G. H. Bower (Eds.), *The psychology of learning and motivation: Inferences and text comprehension* (Vol. 25, pp. 35–51). San Diego, CA: Academic Press.

Smolensky, P. (1986). Information processing in dynamical systems: Foundations of harmony theory. In D. E. Rumelhart & J. L. McClelland (Eds.), *Parallel distributed processing: Explorations in the microstructure of cognition* (pp. 194–281). London: MIT Press.

Stein, N. L. (1982). The definition of a story. *Journal of Pragmatics, 6,* 487–507.

Stein, N. L., & Glenn, C. G. (1979). An analysis of story comprehension in elementary school children. In R. O. Freedle (Ed.), *New directions in discourse processing* (Vol. 2, pp. 53–120). Hillsdale, NJ: Erlbaum.

St. John, M. F. (1992). The story gestalt: A model of knowledge intensive processes in text comprehension. *Cognitive Science, 16,* 271–306.

Stroop, J. R. (1935). Studies of interference in serial verbal reactions. *Journal of Experimental Psychology, 18,* 643–662.

Thorndyke, P. W. (1977). Cognitive structures in comprehension and memory of narrative discourse. *Cognitive Psychology, 9,* 77–110.

Thurlow, R. E. (1991). *The inference of causal antedents during the reading of narratives.* Unpublished doctoral dissertation, University of Minnesota, Minneapolis.

Till, R. E., Mross, E. F., & Kintsch, W. (1988). Time course of priming for associate and inference words in a discourse context. *Memory & Cognition, 16*(4), 283–298.

Tolstoy, L. N. (1954). *Anna Karenin* (R. Edmonds, Trans.). London: Penguin. (Original work published 1878).

Trabasso, T., & Nickels, M. (1992). The development of goal plans of action in the narration of a picture story. *Discourse Processes, 15,* 249–275.

Trabasso, T., Secco, T., & van den Broek, P. W. (1984). Causal cohesion and story coherence. In H. Mandl, N. L. Stein, & T. Trabasso (Eds.), *Learning and comprehension of text* (pp. 83–111). Hillsdale, NJ: Erlbaum.

Trabasso, T., & Sperry, L. (1985). Causal relatedness and importance of story events. *Journal of Memory and Language, 24,* 595–611.

Trabasso, T., Stein, N. L., Rodkin, P. C., Munger, M. P., & Baughn, C. R. (1992). Knowledge of goals and plans in the on-line narration of events. *Cognitive Development, 1,* 133–170.

Trabasso, T., & Suh, S. Y. (1993). Understanding text: Achieving explanatory coherence through on-line inferences and mental operations in working memory. *Discourse Processes, 16,* 3–34.

Trabasso, T., & van den Broek, P. W. (1985). Causal thinking and the representation of narrative events. *Journal of Memory and Language, 24,* 612–630.

Trabasso, T., van den Broek, P. W., & Suh, S. Y. (1989). Logical necessity and transitivity of causal relations in stories. *Discourse Processes, 12,* 1–25.

Tversky, A., & Kahneman, D. (1982). Causal schemas in judgments under uncertainty. In D. Kahneman, P. Slovic, & A. Tversky (Eds.), *Judgment under uncertainty: Heuristics and biases* (pp. 117–128). Cambridge: Cambridge University Press.

van den Broek, P. W. (1988). The effects of causal relations and hierarchical position on the importance of story statements. *Journal of Memory and Language, 27,* 1–22.

van den Broek, P. W. (1989). Causal reasoning and inference making in judging the importance of story statements. *Child Development, 60,* 286–297.

van den Broek, P. W. (1990a). The causal inference maker: Towards a process model of inference generation in text comprehension. In D. A. Balota, G. B. Flores d'Arcais, & K. Rayner (Eds.), *Comprehension processes in reading* (pp. 423–445). Hillsdale, NJ: Erlbaum.

van den Broek, P. W. (1990b). Causal inferences in the comprehension of narrative texts. In A. C. Graesser & G. H. Bower (Eds.), *The psychology of learning and motivation: Inferences and text comprehension* (Vol. 25, pp. 175–194). San Diego, CA: Academic Press.

van den Broek, P. W., Fletcher, C. R., & Risden, K. (1993). Investigations of inferential processes in reading: A theoretical and methodological integration. *Discourse Processes, 16,* 169–180.

van den Broek, P. W., & Lorch, R. F., Jr. (1993). Network representations of causal relations in memory for narrative texts: Evidence from primed recognition. *Discourse Processes, 16,* 175–198.

van den Broek, P. W., Lorch, E. P., & Thurlow, R. E. (1989). *Effects of causal structure, story-grammar categories, and episodic level on children's and adults' memory for television stories.* Paper presented at the biennial meeting of the Society of Research in Child Development, Kansas City, KS.

van den Broek, P. W., Risden, K., & Husebye-Hartmann, E. (in press). Comprehension of narrative events: Maintaining sufficient explanation. In R. F. Lorch, Jr. & E. O'Brien (Eds.), *Sources of coherence in text comprehension.* Hillsdale, NJ: Erlbaum.

van den Broek, P. W., Rohleder, L., & Narvaez, D. (in press). Causal inferences in the comprehension of literary texts. In R. J. Kreuz & M. S. McNealy (Eds.), *The empirical study of literature.* New York: Erlbaum.

van den Broek, P. W., & Thurlow, R. (1990). *Reinstatements and elaborative inferences during the reading of narratives.* Paper presented at the annual meeting of the Psychonomic Society, New Orleans, LA.

van den Broek, P. W., & Trabasso, T. (1986). Causal networks versus goal hierarchies in summarizing text. *Discourse Processes, 9,* 1–15.

van den Broek, P. W., Trabasso, T., & Thurlow, R. (1990). *The effects of story structure on children's and adults' ability to summarize stories.* Paper presented at the annual meeting of the American Educational Research Association, Boston.

van Dijk, T. A., & Kintsch, W. (1983). *Strategies of discourse comprehension.* New York: Academic Press.

Vonk, W., & Noordman, L. G. (1990). On the control of inferences in text understanding. In D. A. Balota, G. B. Flores d'Arcais, & K. Rayner (Eds.), *Comprehension processes in reading* (pp. 447–463). Hillsdale, NJ: Erlbaum.

Warren, W. H., Nicholas, D. W., & Trabasso, T. (1979). Event chain and inferences in understanding narrative. In R. O. Freedie (Ed.), *New directions in discourse processing* (pp. 23–52). Norwood, NJ: Ablex.

Whitney, P., Ritchie, B. G., & Clark, M. B. (1991). Working-memory capacity and the use of elaborative inferences in text comprehension. *Discourse Processes, 14,* 133–145.

Whitney, P., Ritchie, B. G., & Crane, R. S. (1992). The effect of foregrounding on readers' use of predictive inferences. *Memory & Cognition, 29,* 424–432.

Wolman, C. (1991). Sensitivity to causal cohesion in stories by children with mild mental retardation, children with learning disabilities, and children without disabilities. *Journal of Special Education, 25*(2), 135–154.

Wolman, C., & van den Broek, P. (1993). *Comprehension and memory for narrative texts by mentally retarded and learning disabled children.* Unpublished manuscript.

Zwaan, R. A., & van Oostendorp, H. (1993). Do readers construct spatial representations in naturalistic story comprehension? *Discourse Processes, 16,* 125–143.

CHAPTER 17

LEVELS OF REPRESENTATION IN MEMORY FOR DISCOURSE

CHARLES R. FLETCHER

I. INTRODUCTION

In their influential 1983 volume *Strategies of Discourse Comprehension,* van Dijk and Kintsch proposed that understanding a discourse results in three distinct (though interrelated) memory traces. The most superficial and short-lived of these represents the SURFACE FORM of the discourse—a syntactically, semantically, and pragmatically interpreted sequence of words. The meaning of the discourse per se is represented as an interconnected network of ideas called the PROPOSITIONAL TEXT BASE. The most enduring level of representation is referred to as the SITUATION MODEL. It is similar to the representation that would result from directly experiencing the situation that the discourse describes. Consider, for example, sentences (1)–(4).

(1) *The frog ate the bug.*
(2) *The bug was eaten by the frog.*
(3) *The frog had the bug for breakfast.*
(4) *The bug had the frog for breakfast.*

Each has a unique surface structure, the first two have the same propositional representation, and the first three describe the same situation. The first and last sentences differ at all three levels. These points are illustrated by Figure 1, which shows the surface, propositional, and situational representations of (1).

The goals of this chapter are to review the characteristics of each level of representation as well as the theoretical and empirical justification for distinguishing them. The empirical justification is based largely on two principles articulated by Singer (1990, pp. 52–53).

Principle 1. Sentence recognition should vary with the number of representations with which a test sentence is consistent.

Principle 2. It should be possible to identify [task,] understander and discourse factors that influence some of the levels but not others.

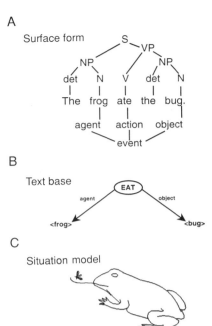

FIG. 1 An illustration of the (A) surface form, (B) text base, and (C) situation model for the sentence *The frog ate the bug.*

By Singer's first principle, subjects presented with (1) should have little or no trouble rejecting (4) in a recognition memory test because its representation is different at all three levels. Sentence (3) should be more difficult because it describes the same situation as (1). False positive responses should be fairly common for (2) because it deviates only at the surface level. Positive responses should be most likely when the test sentence matches all three levels of representation—that is, when (1) is repeated verbatim. Singer's second principle suggests that it should be possible to dissociate these effects by finding variables that have different effects on surface memory, memory for meaning, and memory for the situation.

II. SURFACE MEMORY

To understand a sentence we must parse a visual or auditory signal into individual words, identify the words, and recognize the semantic and syntactic relationships among them. Because memory increases as a function of depth and breadth of processing (Craik & Lockhart, 1972), all this attention to words and their relations to one another might be expected to produce long-lasting, accurate memory for the exact wording of sentences. Some classic experiments from the late 1960s and early 1970s suggest that this is not the case. In one study, Jarvella (1971) presented subjects with an extended description of the organized labor movement. The story was interrupted at irregular intervals, and subjects were asked to write down as much of the preceding discourse as they could recall verbatim. Two versions of the narrative were created, and three clauses immediately preceding each test point were varied to create two conditions, (5)–(6).

(5) *The confidence of Kofach was not unfounded. To stack the meeting for McDonald, the union had even brought in outsiders.*

(6) *Kofach had been persuaded by the international to stack the meeting for McDonald. The union had even brought in outsiders.*

The final two clauses were always physically identical (i.e., the same piece of audio tape), but in one condition, (5), the preceding discourse created a sentence boundary before the middle clause. In the other condition, (6), the sentence boundary followed the middle clause. As shown in Figure 2, this manipulation had a strong impact on the pattern of verbatim recall. When the next-to-last clause was part of the last sentence, subjects had no trouble remembering its exact form. When it was part of the preceding sentence, performance was substantially degraded. These and similar results (e.g., Bransford & Franks, 1971; Sachs, 1967) were taken as evidence that the surface form of a sentence is stored in short-term memory until its meaning is understood, then purged to make room for the next sentence. Any apparent long-term memory for surface structure was attributed to subjects' ability to reconstruct form from meaning.

A. Memory or Reproduction?

In the late 1970s, this interpretation was challenged when several experiments showed better-than-chance recognition memory for the surface form of naturally occurring discourse, at intervals ranging up to several days (e.g., Bates, Masling & Kintsch, 1978; Keenan, MacWhinney, & Mayhew, 1977; Kintsch & Bates, 1977). These results suggest that the representation of a sentence in long-term

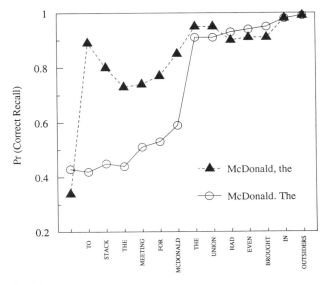

FIG. 2 Free recall as a function of word position and sentence structure (after Jarvella, 1971).

memory includes at least some surface information. Unfortunately, it is not obvious that chance is the appropriate baseline for reaching this conclusion. Consider, for example, a subject asked to decide which of these sentences occurred in a conversation:

(7) *Mary told me that she saw John at the basketball game.* (Target)
(8) *Mary told me that she saw him at the basketball game.* (Paraphrase)

This task appears to represent a straightforward application of Singer's first principle; if our subject chooses the target sentence (7) over a distractor (8) that differs only in its surface structure, he or she must have a stored representation of that surface structure. But if the subject's situation model includes the information that this was the first (or only) time John was mentioned in the conversation, he or she will correctly infer that (7) was the original sentence. After all, if John had not been mentioned before, he would not be referred to by a pronoun. The psycholinguistic literature offers a number of suggestions for dealing with this problem.

Several authors (Bates, Kintsch, Fletcher, & Giuliani, 1980; Fletcher, 1992; Stevenson, 1988) advocate using some type of control group in conjunction with an IN CONTEXT recognition test. On such a test, recognition items are embedded in the discourse, allowing control subjects access to all the propositional and situational information that might permit reconstruction of the correct surface forms. If the performance of these subjects falls short of that observed in subjects previously exposed to the discourse, this is taken as evidence for surface memory. Bates et al. (1980) recommend that in-context recognition tests be used in conjunction with REVERSED TEXT control groups. This procedure requires the creation of a discourse in which each recognition target is replaced by a meaning-preserving paraphrase, thus reversing the roles of recognition targets and distractors. If subjects presented with the original form of the text choose the original targets more often than those presented with the reversed form, this is taken as evidence of surface memory. The advantage of this procedure is its increased sensitivity to low levels of surface memory (Fletcher, 1992). Bates et al. (1980; replicated by Stevenson, 1988) used it to provide strong evidence of long-term memory for the surface form of sentences.

Indirect memory measures have also been used to demonstrate long-term memory for surface structure. In one study by Tardif and Craik (1989), subjects read several texts aloud, some in their original form and some in a paraphrased version. One week later the same subjects repeated the task, but on half the trials they were presented with the other version of the text. On the trials in which the subjects read the other version, their rereading times increased, leading the authors to conclude that surface information was still represented in memory after a one-week delay. Several experiments by Anderson (1974; Anderson & Paulson, 1977) found that subjects can judge the truth of a sentence more quickly when its surface form matches a sentence that was presented earlier. Again, this suggests long-term memory for surface form.

B. Some Factors That Influence Long-Term Memory for Surface Form

Several factors have been shown to influence long-term surface memory. One is distinctiveness. Kintsch and Bates (1977) tested surface memory for statements from classroom lectures. They found that performance was best for announcements, jokes, and asides—statements that stood outside the main thrust of the lectures. Surface memory for jokes may have also been influenced by something that Keenan et al. (1977) call INTERACTIVE CONTENT. Statements have interactive content if they tell us something about the relationship between the speaker and listener (i.e., Are they friends? Is there competition between them?). Keenan and her colleagues examined surface memory for two types of statements from an informal research meeting.

(9) *Do you always use CRT displays?* (Low interactive content)
(10) *Do you always put your foot in your mouth?* (High interactive content)

They found superior surface memory for statements that were high in interactive content. A third variable that influences surface memory is discourse context. Bates and her colleagues (1978, 1980) have shown that surface memory is better in contexts where speakers choose more marked, or explicit, referential constructions (e.g., full noun phrases rather than pronouns). Because marked forms are typically used in contexts where the referent is difficult to identify (Fletcher, 1984; Givón, 1983), it is tempting to conclude that this improvement in surface memory is caused by increased cognitive effort.

III. THE PROPOSITIONAL TEXT BASE

Memory for the meaning of sentences is more robust than memory for their form. It is also relatively unaffected by syntactic boundaries. In a classic demonstration of these points, Bransford and Franks (1971) presented subjects with a set of study sentences that included (11)–(14).

(11) *The ants ate the sweet jelly which was on the table.* (3 Propositions)
(12) *The ants in the kitchen ate the jelly.* (2 Propositions)
(13) *The ants in the kitchen ate the sweet jelly which was on the table.* (4 Propositions)
(14) *The jelly was sweet.* (1 Proposition)

These sentences, which describe a single event, were interspersed with sentences describing other events. Each event included four separate ideas or assertions that were recombined to form each sentence. Sentences 11 through 12 are created out of the ideas (15)–(18).

(15) (EAT AGENT:ANTS OBJECT:JELLY)
(16) (LOCATION:IN ANTS KITCHEN)
(17) (PROPERTY:SWEET JELLY)
(18) (LOCATION:ON JELLY TABLE)

A recognition memory test revealed that: (a) Subjects were completely unable to distinguish between old study sentences and new sentences that conveyed the same ideas. (b) They had no trouble rejecting test sentences that introduced new ideas. (c) The major determinant of recognition confidence was the number of old ideas contained in a test sentence [e.g., subjects were more confident that they had seen (13) than (12)].

However, these results beg the question, How is the meaning of a sentence represented in memory? During the early 1970s psychologists responded to this question by borrowing the notion of a PROPOSITION from philosophy and linguistics (see, e.g., Anderson & Bower, 1973; Kintsch, 1974; Norman & Rumelhart, 1975). Propositions are usually defined as the smallest units of meaning to which we can assign a truth value. They are also recognizable by their structure. Sometimes this structure is presented graphically, as in Figure 1b. The format used in (15)–(18) is also common. Each proposition includes a single predicate (such as EAT) and one or more arguments (such as ANTS and JELLY). The predicates are abstract representations of simple states, actions, or events. They are usually realized in the surface structure of sentences as verbs, adjectives, adverbs, or prepositions. Each predicate has one or more argument slots (such as AGENT and OBJECT) that must be filled before we can assess its truth value. These slots can be filled either by concepts (realized as nouns in surface structure) or by other propositions. The latter case is illustrated by (19).

(19) *Mary saw the ants eat the jelly.*

Here the proposition (EAT AGENT:ANTS OBJECT:JELLY) serves as an argument within the proposition (SEE AGENT:MARY OBJECT:(EAT AGENT:ANTS OBJECT:JELLY)). Several researchers, including Bovair and Kieras (1985) and Turner and Greene (1978), have developed procedures for determining the propositional structure of a discourse.

A. The Psychological Status of Propositions

The growing popularity of propositional theories in the 1970s was accompanied by vigorous attempts to determine the psychological status of propositions. Lesgold (1972) and Wanner (1975) both demonstrated that experimental subjects are more likely to recall a target word from a test sentence when they are given a retrieval cue from the same proposition than they are when the cue is taken from a different proposition. Kintsch and Glass (1974) found that subjects have a strong tendency to recall all of a proposition, or none or it. Kintsch and Keenan (1973) showed that (with the number of words held constant) sentences with few propositions are read more quickly than sentences with many propositions. Each of these findings is consistent with the assumption that meaning is stored in and retrieved from long-term memory in propositional units, but the most compelling evidence for the psychological reality of propositions comes from an ingenious priming experiment by Ratcliff and McKoon (1978). They presented subjects with a series of unrelated sentences like (20).

(20) *The mausoleum that enshrined the czar overlooked the square.*

This was followed by a probe recognition procedure. The results indicate that subjects are able to recognize that a target word (*square*) occurred in one of the study sentences in 671 ± 4 ms when the preceding test word is from a different sentence; in 571 ± 3 ms when the preceding word is from the same sentence but a different proposition (*czar*); and in 551 ± 3 ms when the preceding word is from the same proposition (*mausoleum*). The difference between the first two conditions indicates that probe words from the same sentence are psychologically closer together in memory than words from different sentences. More importantly, the 20 ms difference between the latter two conditions demonstrates that probe words from the same proposition are psychologically closer than probes from the same sentence but different propositions. It is important to note that these results obtain even when, as in (20), the probe words from different propositions are closer in the surface structure of the sentence than those from the same proposition.

B. The Organization of Propositions in the Text Base

The fundamental assumption shared by all models of discourse understanding is that the goal of the comprehension process is to create a COHERENT (i.e., richly interconnected) representation of meaning in memory. Attempts to understand the organization of propositions in the text base have focused on two variables: co-reference (or argument overlap) and co-occurrence in short-term memory (see, e.g., Fletcher & Bloom, 1988; Kintsch, 1974, 1988; Kintsch & van Dijk, 1978; van Dijk & Kintsch, 1983). Connections are assumed between all pairs of propositions in the textbase that share one or more arguments and co-occur in short-term memory during comprehension. As an example, after reading (11) the propositions (EAT AGENT:ANTS OBJECT:JELLY) and (LOCATION:ON JELLY TABLE) would be linked because they share the argument JELLY and their presence in the same sentence guarantees their co-occurrence in short-term memory.

The assumption that propositions must co-occur in short-term memory to be strongly linked in the propositional text base is consistent with contemporary theories of learning and memory (e.g., McClelland & Rumelhart, 1985; Raaijmakers & Shiffrin, 1981). Empirically, it has found support in research by Fletcher and Bloom (1988). They asked subjects to read and recall several short narratives. Their results reveal that the probability of recalling a proposition increases as the number of propositions in the text that it is related to increases, but only when it co-occurs with them in short-term memory. Similar results are reported by McKoon and Ratcliff (in press).

The claim that co-reference contributes to the coherence of a discourse is supported by the research of Fletcher, Chrysler, van den Broek, Deaton, and Bloom (in press). They presented subjects with study sentences consisting of two clauses conjoined by *and*.

(21) *The receptionist named the ship and the cow kicked over the stool.* (Co-occurrence only)
(22) *The receptionist named the cow and the cow kicked over the stool.* (Co-occurrence + co-reference)

In one condition, (21), the only relationship between clauses was their co-occurrence in the study sentence. In another condition, (22), the clauses shared a referent (e.g., *cow*). When subjects were presented with the first clause and asked to recall the second, their performance was significantly better in the latter condition (34 vs. 62% correct). Clearly, the availability of a shared argument increases strength of association between propositions in long-term memory.

Perhaps the strongest evidence for the role of co-reference in the organization of the text base comes from a priming study by McKoon and Ratcliff (1980). They presented subjects with simple stories (see Table I) followed by a probe recognition task. Probe words were recognized more quickly when

TABLE I
A Story from McKoon and Ratcliff (1980)

Story
   The crops drew insects.
   The insects troubled the farmer.
   The farmer surveyed the fields.
   The fields needed pesticides.
   The pesticides poisoned the crows.
   The crows fouled the countryside.

Propositions
   P1   (DRAW AGENT:CROPS OBJECT:INSECTS)
   P2   (TROUBLE AGENT:INSECTS OBJECT:FARMER)
   P3   (SURVEY AGENT:FARMER OBJECT:FIELD)
   P4   (NEED AGENT:FIELD OBJECT:PESTICIDES)
   P5   (POISON AGENT:PESTICIDES OBJECT:CROWS)
   P6   (FOUL AGENT:CROWS OBJECT:COUNTRYSIDE)

Referential connections
   P1–P2–P3–P4–P5–P6

they were preceded by another probe from the same story. More significantly, as the referential distance between the words increased, the facilitation decreased. Thus, a subject presented with the story in Table I would recognize *insects* more quickly if the preceding test word was *crows* rather than *countryside*.

Some authors, notably van Dijk (1980; van Dijk & Kintsch, 1983, Chap. 6), have argued that the propositional text base includes a hierarchical macrostructure created through the application of three macrorules.

1. *Deletion:* Delete each proposition which is neither a direct nor an indirect interpretation condition of a subsequent proposition. (This rule eliminates unimportant propositions.)
2. *Generalization:* A sequence of propositions may be replaced by a more general proposition denoting an immediate superset. [As an example, this rule would replace the sequence of propositions (LIKE AGENT:MARY OBJECT:SOFTBALL), (LIKE AGENT:MARY OBJECT:GYMNAS-TICS), and (LIKE AGENT:MARY OBJECT:BOWLING), with the single proposition (LIKE AGENT:MARY OBJECT:SPORTS).]
3. *Construction:* A sequence of propositions may be replaced by a single proposition that is entailed by the sequence. [This rule would replace the sequence (ENTER AGENT:FRED OBJECT:BUILDING), (ORDER AGENT:FRED OBJECT:HOTDOG), (EAT AGENT:FRED OBJECT:HOTDOG), and (PAY AGENT:FRED OBJECT:BILL) with the single proposition (VISIT AGENT:FRED OBJECT:RESTAURANT).]

These rules are applied to the propositions explicitly conveyed by the text (its microstructure) to produce a smaller set of summary propositions that form the first level of the macrostructure. The rules are then applied recursively to this (and succeeding) levels of the macrostructure to create the next level in the hierarchy. The process stops when the entire text base has been reduced to a single summary proposition. This claim is supported by experiments showing that propositions from the macrostructure of a text are recalled better than other otherwise similar micropropositions (e.g., Kintsch & van Dijk, 1978; Singer, 1982). In addition, Guindon and Kintsch (1984) found that macropropositions prime one another more strongly than comparable micropropositions.

IV. THE SITUATION MODEL

During the 1980s, comprehension researchers realized that the propositional text base has important limitations (see, e.g., Glenberg, Kruley, & Langston, this volume; Johnson-Laird, 1983; Mani & Johnson-Laird, 1982; van Dijk & Kintsch, 1983, pp. 338–344). If we assume that comprehension stops with the construction of a coherent propositional representation, a number of observations are difficult to explain. Among the more salient are:

1. *Individual Differences in Comprehension.* Two people can interpret the same discourse very differently yet still agree on what was said. As an example, the sentence *The mayor reminds me of Hillary Rodham Clinton* would be taken as a compliment by some listeners and as an insult by others. Yet it is unlikely that these two groups of listeners would develop different propositional representations of the sentence.
2. *Translation.* Research on both human and machine translation suggests that preserving a propositional representation is insufficient to guarantee a successful translation, especially when the source and target languages are associated with large cultural differences in shared knowledge and expectations (Hutchins, 1980).
3. *Reordering.* When experimental subjects are shown a story in which the order of events has been scrambled, they have no trouble reconstructing the canonical order despite the fact that it is not captured by the propositional text base (see, e.g., Bower, Black, & Turner, 1979).
4. *Cross-modality Integration.* Many tasks require that information from a discourse be combined with information from nonlinguistic sources (e.g., using a map in conjunction with written directions). Because the propositional text base represents only the linguistic information in the text, it seems too limited to support this type of integration (see, e.g., Glenberg & Langston, 1992; Morrow, Greenspan, & Bower, 1987).
5. *Updating.* People often read a text or engage in conversation to update their understanding of a familiar situation (e.g., reading the news or gossiping with a neighbor). Each new discourse modifies the participants' representation of the situation as a whole without necessarily changing their understanding of, or memory for, earlier texts and conversations.
6. *Learning.* If a student memorizes a computer programming text but still cannot write a novel program, something is amiss. The purpose of such a text is to convey a (productive or generative) mental model of a programming language; the words and propositions that convey that model are nothing more than a means to that end. As stated by van Dijk and Kintsch (1983, p. 342), "Learning from text is not usually learning a text."
7. *Perceptual and Sensory Qualities.* Some types of discourse leave the reader or listener with a clear sense of spatial and/or sensory properties that lie

beyond the propositional text base. A description of a sunset or of someone's refurnished living room are obvious examples (e.g., Gernsbacher, 1992; Paivio, 1986).

The response to these observations has been a large volume of research suggesting that readers (and listeners) use their prior knowledge in conjunction with the propositional content of a discourse to construct a mental representation of the situation that the discourse describes.

A. Spatial Models

Many discourses describe situations that could be represented as a network of propositions. This makes the task of distinguishing between the text base and the situation model fairly difficult. The most obvious exceptions to this generalization are descriptions of space. As a result, spatial descriptions have dominated research in this area. In one of the earliest experimental demonstrations of situation models, Mani and Johnson-Laird (1982) presented subjects with two types of text describing the spatial arrangement of four objects (see Table II). The texts in one group were completely determinate—consistent with just one arrangement of the objects. Texts in the other group were created by reversing two arguments in a manner that introduced a spatial ambiguity without altering the complexity of the propositional text base. These texts were each consistent with two distinct spatial layouts. Recognition memory was significantly better for the determinate descriptions. Mani and Johnson-Laird attribute this difference to subjects' inability to construct spatial models of the indeterminate descriptions.

TABLE II
Determinate and Indeterminate Spatial Descriptions
and Consistent Spatial Layouts (after Mani &
Johnson-Laird, 1982)

Determinate description
   The bookshelf is to the right of the chair.
   The chair is in front of the table.
   The bed is behind the table.

Spatial layout consistent with determinate description
     bed
     table
     chair   bookshelf

Indeterminate description
   The bookshelf is to the right of the chair.
   The chair is in front of the table.
   The bed is behind the chair.

Spatial layouts consistent with indeterminate description
   a. bed   b. table
     table   bed
     chair   bookshelf   chair   bookshelf

Morrow et al. (1987) have shown that spatial representations of a discourse have properties that are normally observed in spatial or visual images but not typically associated with propositional representations (see, e.g. Kosslyn, 1975). They asked subjects to memorize the layout of a hypothetical building, then presented them with narratives describing activities within that building. The narratives were interrupted occasionally by probe words identifying two objects. Subjects were asked to judge whether the objects were located in the same or different rooms. Reaction times increased as the distance between the protagonist's current location and the pair of objects increased. This suggests that readers use their knowledge of the building to keep track of the protagonist's location as they read.

Perrig and Kintsch (1985) were able to dissociate the propositional text base and the situation model by creating two texts describing a fictitious town. One text (the SURVEY text) was written from the perspective of an observer looking down on the town from above. It included statements such as *North of the highway just east of the river is a gas station.* The other text (the ROUTE text) presented the same information from the perspective of a driver passing through the town. It included sentences like *On your left just after you cross the river you see a gas station.* Subjects who read the survey text found it easier to draw a map of the town but more difficult to remember the text itself. Perrig and Kintsch argue that these differences arise because the survey text facilitates the construction of a spatial situation model, while the route text simplifies the task of constructing a coherent propositional text base (co-referential propositions occur closer together in the route text).

In light of these results, it is tempting to conclude that comprehension always results in the construction of a spatial situation model. A recent experiment by Zwaan and van Oostendorp (in press) addresses this possibility. They asked subjects to read part of a real, but edited, mystery novel describing the details of a murder scene, including the locations of the body and various clues. The text was modified to make the construction of a spatial model as easy as possible (e.g., all the locations were determinate). In spite of these modifications, subjects had difficulty verifying spatial inferences when they were asked to read the text normally. When instructions emphasized the construction of a spatial representation, performance improved, but at the cost of a considerable increase in reading time. These results led Zwaan and van Oostendorp to conclude that constructing, maintaining, and updating a spatial situation model is not a priority during normal comprehension of naturally occurring narratives.

B. Causal Models

It seems likely that different genres of discourse will lead to qualitatively different types of situation models. Some authors have suggested that causal models play a major role in the comprehension and recall of narrative texts (see, e.g., Black & Bower, 1980; Fletcher & Bloom, 1988; Graesser, 1981; Rumelhart, 1977; Schank, 1975; Trabasso & van den Broek, 1985; van den Broek, 1990, this volume). Most people feel that they understand an individual event in a narrative when they can identify its causes and enabling conditions, and that they understand the narrative as a whole when they can identify a causally connected chain of events that begins with its opening and ends with its final outcome. This intuition is supported by research showing that (a) events with many causal connections to other events in a narrative are recalled better and perceived as more important than events with few causal connections, and (b) events that lie along the causal chain connecting a narrative's opening to its outcome are recalled better and judged more important than causal dead ends (see, e.g., Black & Bower, 1980; Fletcher & Bloom, 1988; Goldman & Varnhagen, 1986; Trabasso & Sperry, 1985; Trabasso & van den Broek, 1985; van den Broek, 1988). It is also worth noting that scripts (Bower et al., 1979; Schank & Abelson, 1977) and story grammars (Rumelhart, 1977; Stein & Glenn, 1979), which have been implicated in the comprehension of highly stereotyped narratives, provide preexisting causal structures into which the elements of a text can be inserted.

Obviously, causal connections play a significant role in the mental representation of narratives. But are they represented in the situation model or the propositional text base? Several observations suggest that causal structure is more reasonably considered a property of the situation model. First, causal connections typically link *clusters* of propositions corresponding to states and events in some real or imagined world. Consider (23).

(23) *The 750 pound orange and black cat walked into the bedroom and the burglar left very quickly.*

This sentence includes six propositions that map into what most readers perceive as two causally related events, the entrance of the tiger and the exit of the burglar. Second, people readily perceive causal structure in their physical and social surroundings. Bauer and Mandler (1989) have shown that children between one and two years of age are more likely to reproduce a sequence of actions if those actions are causally related. Van den Broek, Lorch, and Thurlow (in press) found that both adults' and pre-school children's recall of television programs exhibit the same effects of causal connections and causal chain status observed in adults' recall of narratives. Third, while referential connections always improve memory for discourse, the impact of causal connections depends on the situation. Fletcher et al. (in press) compared co-referential conjoined sentences like (22), repeated here, with sentences that were both referentially and causally coherent, such as (24).

(22) *The receptionist named the cow and the cow kicked over the stool.*
(24) *The receptionist startled the cow and the cow kicked over the stool.*

They found that memory for causally coherent sentences (24) exceeds memory for co-referential sentences (22) only when (a) subjects are instructed to intentionally identify causal connections or (b) the sentences are embedded in a narrative. The impact of referential connections [i.e., (21) vs. (22)] was consistent across conditions.

Despite these observations, research by Fletcher and Bloom (1988; see also Bloom, Fletcher, van den Broek, Reitz, & Shapiro, 1990; Fletcher, Hummel, & Marsolek, 1990) has shown that the causal structure of a narrative influences the availability of propositions in short-term memory during the comprehension process and, thereby, the organization of propositions in the text base. This suggests that causal situation models are more tightly linked to the propositional text base than spatial situation models.

V. SIMULTANEOUS INVESTIGATIONS OF ALL THREE LEVELS

A. Recognition Memory

To date, all attempts to isolate the effects of surface memory, the propositional text base, and the situation model in a single experiment have used recognition memory as a criterion measure. The logic of this approach follows directly from Singer's first principle: If subjects are able to discriminate between target sentences from an earlier discourse and meaning-preserving paraphrases of those sentences, the difference is taken as a measure of surface memory. If performance improves when the distractors alter the meaning of the test sentences (but not the underlying situation), the improvement is taken as a measure of the text base's influence. Finally, if performance improves further when distractor sentences are inconsistent with the situation described by the discourse, this improvement is taken as a measure of the situation model's influence. The details of this procedure, and the potential pitfalls associated with it, are illustrated by a series of experiments reported in Fletcher and Chrysler (1990). Subjects read a series of texts that each describe a linear ordering among a set of five objects. An example is shown in Table III. They were then presented with one of three recognition memory tests: a surface test, a text base test, or a situation model test. In each case, subjects were required to choose which of two words had occurred in a test sentence (italicized in Table III).

(25) *George says that his wife was angry when she found out that the necklace cost more than the carpet/rug.* (Surface test)

(26) *George says that his wife was angry when she found out that the necklace cost more than the carpet/painting.* (Text base test)

(27) *George says that his wife was angry when she found out that the necklace cost more than the carpet/vase.* (Situation model test)

When the words were synonyms that had been used interchangeably in the test text, 71% of all responses were correct. When the distractor word altered a single proposition in the test sentence (but not the underlying order of the five objects), performance rose to 87% correct. When the distractor was inconsistent with the order described by the text, 98% of subjects' responses were correct. Fletcher and Chrysler (1990) argue that this pattern of results can be interpreted as evidence for the existence of three separate levels of representation if and only if (a) all three distractors differ from the surface form of the original

TABLE III
Example Text from Fletcher and Chrysler (1990)[a]

George likes to flaunt his wealth by purchasing rare art treasures. He has a Persian rug worth as much as my car and it's the cheapest thing he owns. Last week he bought a French oil painting for $12,000 and an Indian necklace for $13,500. *George says that his wife was angry when she found out that the necklace cost more than the carpet.* His most expensive "treasures" are a Ming vase and a Greek statue. The statue is the only thing he ever spent more than $50,000 for. It's hard to believe that the statue cost George five times what he paid for the beautiful Persian carpet.

[a] The test sentence is shown in italics.

sentence by the same amount; (b) the text base and situation model distractors differ from the propositional representation of the original sentence by the same amount; (c) subjects' ability to reject the surface form and text base distractors is not influenced by higher levels of representation (i.e., reconstructive inferences can be ruled out). A priori, the first two conditions appear to be met. All three distractors differ from the test sentence by a single word. Furthermore, the text base and situation model distractors differ from the test sentence by a single proposition. These observations are true for all of Fletcher and Chrysler's materials.

To test all three assumptions, Fletcher and Chrysler (1990) conducted a series of control experiments. First, they used a paired-associate learning paradigm to show that all three types of foils (e.g., *rug, painting,* and *vase*) are equally discriminable from their associated targets (*carpet*) at a surface/lexical level. This verifies the first assumption. Second, they were able to eliminate the difference between the text base and model tests by altering the texts so that both types of distractors were consistent with the situation model. This verifies the second assumption. Third, they used an in-context guessing procedure (see above) to show that subjects' ability to reject the surface and text base distractors is no better than chance when they have access to all the surface, text base, and situational information in the texts except that provided by the target words themselves. This verifies the third assumption. In light of these results, the data from Fletcher and Chrysler's original experiment provide strong support for all three levels of representation.

B. The Time Course of Retrieval from Long-Term Memory

Cognitive psychologists are well aware of the relationship between reaction time and performance accuracy. Experimental subjects can almost always respond more quickly if they are willing to make more errors. This relationship is usually viewed as an annoyance that complicates the interpretation of reaction-time data, but thoughtful researchers have long realized that it can be exploited (see, e.g., Pachella, 1974). Schmalhoffer and Glavanov (1986) used the trade-off between speed and accuracy to investigate the time course of retrieval from long-term memory of surface, propositional, and the situational information. They asked subjects to study a LISP programming manual, then tested their recognition memory using four types of probe sentences.

(28) *PSY100 is a legal atom that concludes with a number.* (Original)
(29) *PSY100 is a legal atom that which ends with a numeral.* (Paraphrased)
(30) *PSY100 is a legal atom which begins with a letter.* (Meaning changed)
(31) *PSY.100 is a legal atom that contains a dot.* (Correctness changed)

Subjects responded to each sentence by pressing a *yes* button if they believed it had occurred verbatim in the text, a *no* button if it had not. Response signals were used to solicit recognition responses 1, 3, 5, 7, 9, and 11 s after each test sentence was presented. For each of these intervals, Schmalhoffer and Glavanov computed the strength of subjects' surface, propositional, and situational representations as d' values (Green & Swets, 1966). The strength of the surface trace was computed by treating positive responses to the original sentences as hits and positive responses to paraphrases as false alarms. In calculating the

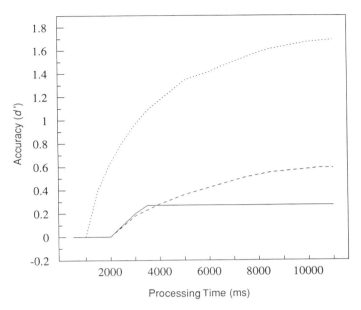

FIG. 3   The strength of the surface (*solid line*), propositional (*long-dashed line*), and situational (*short-dashed line*) representations as a function of processing time (after Schmalhofer & Glavanov, 1986).

strength of the propositional text base, positive responses to the paraphrases were considered hits while positive responses to sentences which changed meaning (but not correctness) were counted as false alarms. Finally, the strength of the situation model was computed by scoring positive responses to probes that changed meaning as hits and positive responses to those that changed correctness as false alarms. The results (see Fig. 3) reveal distinctly different speed–accuracy functions for the three levels of representation. The strength of the situation model rises quickly and reaches a relatively high asymptotic level, indicating a robust, easily searched representation. The strength of the propositional text base rises more slowly to a lower asymptote, while the surface trace rises quickly to the lowest asymptote of all. This demonstrates that the dynamics of retrieving the three types of representations from long-term memory are very different.

C. Decay Rate

Zimny (1987; also reported in Kintsch, Welsh, Schmalhoffer, & Zimny, 1990) has shown that surface, propositional, and situational representations have distinctively different decay functions. She presented subjects with brief narrative descriptions of highly stereotyped (i.e., scripted) activities such as going to a movie. After a delay ranging from 0 minutes to 4 days, each subject was asked to complete a recognition memory test that included (a) sentences taken verbatim from the stories, (b) paraphrases of story sentences, (c) sentences that were easily inferred from one of the stories, (d) new sentences that were consistent with the stereotyped activity described by one story, and (e) new sentences that were not consistent with the activities described in any of the stories. Positive responses to the inconsistent new sentences were treated as false alarms in calculating a d' score for each of the other sentence types. Then the difference in d' for the verbatim and paraphrase sentences was used to measure the strength of the surface representation, the difference between the paraphrases and the inferences to measure the strength of the propositional text base, and the difference between the inferences and the consistent new sentences to measure the strength of the situation model. The results, shown in Figure 4, again indicate strikingly different results for the three levels of representation. Surface memory was significant only when the recognition test immediately followed the stories. Memory for the propositional text base began quite high, decayed quickly, but always remained significantly better than zero. Memory for the situation also began quite high but showed no decay over the four-day interval.

VI. SUMMARY AND CONCLUSIONS

Van Dijk and Kintsch (1983) have claimed that comprehension results in separate mental representations of the form of a discourse, its meaning, and the situation that it refers to. This claim is supported by (a) theoretical arguments suggesting that each representation results from a distinct level of language processing; (b) memory experiments showing that shared levels of representation decrease subjects' ability to discriminate between sentences they have seen or heard and novel test sentences (Singer's principle 1); (c) experiments showing that the three levels of representation have different access times and different decay rates and are differentially influenced by sentence boundaries, co-reference, the determinacy of spatial descriptions, and a host of other variables (Singer's principle 2).

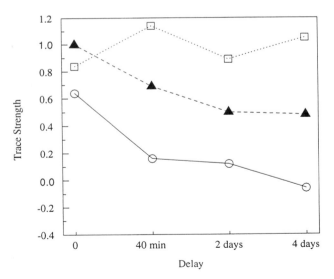

FIG. 4 The strength of the surface (*circles*), propositional (*triangles*), and situational (*squares*) representations as a function of the delay preceding a recognition memory test (after Kintsch et al., 1990).

The argument in favor of van Dijk and Kintsch's position is now so strong that its correctness is seldom—if ever—questioned. Despite this fact, a number of important questions remain unanswered. Among the more interesting are: (a) Do situation models always incorporate spatial and sensory qualities? (b) Are causal connections an important feature of the situation models associated with nonnarrative discourse? (c) Under what circumstances are the propositional text base and the situation model tightly linked (as with narratives), and under what circumstances are they relatively independent (as with spatial descriptions)? (d) Are macrostructures derived from and incorporated into the text base (the current assumption), or are they more properly considered a part of the situation model? (e) Do any surface features of a discourse have a direct impact on the construction of a situation model, or are all such influences mediated by the propositional text base? The current pace of discourse comprehension research suggests that answers to these and a great many other questions lie close at hand.

ACKNOWLEDGMENTS

I am grateful to Sue Chrysler, Morton Gernsbacher, and Paul van den Broek for their many helpful comments on an earlier draft of this chapter.

REFERENCES

Anderson, J. R. (1974). Verbatim and propositional representation of sentences in immediate and long-term memory. *Journal of Verbal Learning and Verbal Behavior, 13*, 149–162.

Anderson, J. R., & Bower, G. H. (1973). *Human associative memory*. Washington, DC: Winston.

Anderson, J. R., & Paulson, R. (1977). Representation and retention of verbal information. *Journal of Verbal Learning and Verbal Behavior, 16*, 439–451.

Bates, E., Kintsch, W., Fletcher, C. R., & Giuliani, V. (1980). The role of pronominalization and ellipsis in texts: Some memory experiments. *Journal of Experimental Psychology: Human Learning and Memory, 6*, 676–691.

Bates, E., Masling, M., & Kintsch, W. (1978). Recognition memory for aspects of dialogue. *Journal of Experimental Psychology: Human Learning and Memory, 4*, 187–197.

Bauer, P. J., & Mandler, J. M. (1989). One thing follows another: Effects of temporal structure on 1- to 2-year olds' recall of events. *Developmental Psychology, 25*, 197–206.

Black, J. B., & Bower, G. H. (1980). Story understanding as problem solving. *Poetics, 9*, 223–250.

Bloom, C. P., Fletcher, C. R., van den Broek, P., Reitz, L., & Shapiro, B. P. (1990). An online assessment of causal reasoning during comprehension. *Memory & Cognition, 18*, 65–71.

Bovair, S., & Kieras, D. E. (1985). A guide to propositional analysis for research on technical prose. In B. K. Britton & J. B. Black (Eds.), *Understanding expository text* (pp. 315–362). Hillsdale, NJ: Erlbaum.

Bower, G. H., Black, J. B., & Turner, T. J. (1979). Scripts in memory for text. *Cognitive Psychology, 11*, 177–220.

Bransford, J. D., & Franks, J. J. (1971). The abstraction of linguistic ideas. *Cognitive Psychology, 2*, 331–350.

Craik, F. I. M. & Lockhart, R. S. (1972). Levels of processing: A framework for memory research. *Journal of Verbal Learning and Verbal Behavior, 11*, 671–684.

Fletcher, C. R. (1984). Markedness and topic continuity in discourse processing. *Journal of Verbal Learning and Verbal Behavior, 23*, 487–493.

Fletcher, C. R. (1992). Assessing recognition memory for surface forms in discourse: A methodological note. *Journal of Experimental Psychology: Learning, Memory, and Cognition, 18*, 199–203.

Fletcher, C. R., & Bloom, C. P. (1988). Causal reasoning in the comprehension of simple narrative texts. *Journal of Memory and Language, 27,* 235–244.

Fletcher, C. R., & Chrysler, S. T. (1990). Surface forms, textbases and situation models: Recognition memory for three types of textual information. *Discourse Processes, 13,* 175–190.

Fletcher, C. R., Chrysler, S. T., van den Broek, P. W., Deaton, J. A., & Bloom, C. P. (in press). *The role of co-occurrence, co-reference, and causality in the coherence of conjoined sentences.* In R. F. Lorch, Jr. & E. J. O'Brien (Eds.), Sources of coherence in reading. Hillsdale, NJ: Erlbaum.

Fletcher, C. R., Hummel, J. E., & Marsolek, C. J. (1990). Causality and the allocation of attention during comprehension. *Journal of Experimental Psychology: Learning, Memory, and Cognition, 16,* 233–240.

Gernsbacher, M. A. (1992, May). *Readers' mental representations of fictional characters' emotional states.* Paper presented at the meeting of the International Association for the Empirical Study of Literature, Memphis, TN.

Givón T. (Ed.). (1983). *Topic continuity in discourse: A quantitative cross-language study.* Amsterdam: Benjamins.

Glenberg, A. M., & Langston, W. E. (1992). Comprehension of illustrated text: Pictures help to build mental models. *Journal of Memory and Language, 31,* 129–151.

Goldman, S. R., & Varnhagen, C. K. (1986). Memory for embedded and sequential story structures. *Journal of Memory and Language, 25,* 401–418.

Graesser, A. C. (1981). *Prose comprehension beyond the word.* New York: Springer-Verlag.

Green, D. M., & Swets, J. A. (1966). *Signal detection theory and psychophysics.* New York: Wiley.

Guindon, R., & Kintsch, W. (1984). Priming macropropositions: Evidence for the primacy of macropropositions in memory for text. *Journal of Verbal Learning and Verbal Behavior, 23,* 508–518.

Hutchins, E. (1980). *Culture and inference.* Cambridge, MA: Harvard University Press.

Jarvella, R. J. (1971). Syntactic processing of connected speech. *Journal of Verbal Learning and Verbal Behavior, 10,* 409–416.

Johnson-Laird, P. N. (1983). *Mental models.* Cambridge, MA: Harvard University Press.

Keenan, J. M., MacWhinney, B., & Mayhew, D. (1977). Pragmatics in memory: A study of natural conversation. *Journal of Verbal Learning and Verbal Behavior, 16,* 549–560.

Kintsch, W. (1974). *The representation of meaning in memory.* Hillsdale, NJ: Erlbaum.

Kintsch, W. (1988). The role of knowledge in discourse comprehension: A construction–integration model. *Psychological Review, 95,* 163–182.

Kintsch, W., & Bates, E. (1977). Recognition memory for statements from a classroom lecture. *Journal of Experimental Psychology: Human Learning and Memory, 3,* 150–159.

Kintsch, W., & Glass, G. (1974). Effects of propositional structure upon sentence recall. In W. Kintsch (Ed.), *The representation of meaning in memory* (pp. 140–151). Hillsdale, NJ: Erlbaum.

Kintsch, W., & Keenan, J. M. (1973). Reading rate and retention as a function of the number of propositions in the base structure of sentences. *Cognitive Psychology, 5,* 257–274.

Kintsch, W., & van Dijk, T. A. (1978). Toward a model of text comprehension and production. *Psychological Review, 85,* 363–394.

Kintsch, W., Welsch, D., Schmalhofer, F., & Zimny, S. (1990). Sentence recognition: A theoretical analysis. *Journal of Memory and Language, 29,* 133–159.

Kosslyn, S. M. (1975). Information representation in visual images. *Cognitive Psychology, 7,* 341–370.

Lesgold, A. M. (1972). Pronominalization: A device for unifying sentences in memory. *Journal of Verbal Learning and Verbal Behavior, 11,* 316–323.

Mani, K., & Johnson-Laird, P. N. (1982). The mental representation of spatial descriptions. *Memory & Cognition, 10,* 181–187.

McClelland, J. L., & Rumelhart, D. E. (1985). Distributed memory and the representation of general and specific information. *Journal of Experimental Psychology: General, 114,* 159–188.

McKoon, G., & Ratcliff, R. (1980). Priming in item recognition: The organization of propositions in memory for text. *Journal of Verbal Learning and Verbal Behavior, 19,* 369–386.

McKoon, G., & Ratcliff, R. (1992). Inference during reading. *Psychological Review, 99,* 440–466.

Morrow, D. G., Greenspan, S. L., & Bower, G. H. (1987). Accessibility and situation models in narrative comprehension. *Journal of Memory and Language, 26,* 165–187.

Norman, D. A., & Rumelhart, D. E. (1975). *Explorations in cognition*. San Francisco: Freeman.

Pachella, R. G. (1974). The interpretation of reaction time in information processing research. In B. Kantowitz (Ed.), *Human information processing* (pp. 41–82). Hillsdale, NJ: Erlbaum.

Paivio, A. (1986). *Mental representations: A dual coding approach*. New York: Oxford University Press.

Perrig, W., & Kintsch, W. (1985). Propositional and situational representations of text. *Journal of Memory and Language, 24*, 503–518.

Raaijmakers, J. G. W., & Shiffrin, R. M. (1981). Search of associative memory. *Psychological Review, 88*, 93–134.

Ratcliff, R., & McKoon, G. (1978). Priming in item recognition: Evidence for the propositional structure of sentences. *Journal of Verbal Learning and Verbal Behavior, 17*, 403–417.

Rumelhart, D. E. (1977). Understanding and summarizing brief stories. In D. LaBerge & S. J. Samuels (Eds.), *Basic processes in reading: Perception and comprehension* (pp. 265–304). Hillsdale, NJ: Erlbaum.

Sachs, J. S. (1967). Recognition memory for syntactic and semantic aspects of connected discourse. *Perception & Psychophysics, 2*, 437–442.

Schank, R. (1975). The structure of episodes in memory. In D. G. Bobrow & A. Collins (Eds.), *Representation and understanding: Studies in cognitive science* (pp. 237–272). New York: Academic Press.

Schank, R., & Abelson, R. (1977). *Scripts, plans, goals and understanding: An inquiry into human knowledge structures*. Hillsdale, NJ: Erlbaum.

Schmalhofer, F., & Glavanov, D. (1986). Three components of understanding a programmer's manual: Verbatim, propositional, and situational representations. *Journal of Memory and Language, 25*, 279–294.

Singer, M. (1982). Comparing memory for natural and laboratory reading. *Journal of Experimental Psychology: General, 111*, 331–347.

Singer, M. (1990). *Psychology of language: An introduction to sentence and discourse processing*. Hillsdale, NJ: Erlbaum.

Stein, N. L., & Glenn, C. G. (1979). An analysis of story comprehension in elementary school children. In R. O. Freedle (Ed.), *New directions in discourse processing* (Vol. 2, pp. 53–120). Hillsdale, NJ: Erlbaum.

Stevenson, R. J. (1988). Memory for referential statements in texts. *Journal of Experimental Psychology: Learning, Memory, and Cognition, 14*, 612–617.

Tardif, T., Craik, F. I. M. (1989). Reading a week later: Perceptual and conceptual factors. *Journal of Memory and Language, 28*, 107–125.

Trabasso, T., & Sperry, L. L. (1985). Causal relatedness and importance of story events. *Journal of Memory and Language, 24*, 595–611.

Trabasso, T., & van den Broek, P. (1985). Causal thinking and the representation of narrative events. *Journal of Memory and Language, 24*, 612–630.

Turner, A., & Greene, E. (1978). *Construction and use of a propositional text base. JSAS catalogue of selected documents in psychology* (Ms. No. 1713).

van den Broek, P. (1988). The effects of causal relations and hierarchical position on the importance of story statements. *Journal of Memory and Language, 27*, 1–22.

van den Broek, P. (1990). The causal inference maker: Towards a process model of inference generation in text comprehension. In D. A. Balota, G. B. Flores d'Arcais, & K. Rayner (Eds.), *Comprehension processes in reading* (pp. 423–445). Hillsdale, NJ: Erlbaum.

van den Broek, P., Lorch, E. P., & Thurlow, R. (in press). Children's and adults' memory for television stories: The role of causal factors, story grammar categories and hierarchical level. *Child Development*.

van Dijk, T. A. (1980). *Macrostructures: An interdisciplinary study of global structures in discourse, interaction, and cognition*. Hillsdale, NJ: Erlbaum.

van Dijk, T. A., & Kintsch, W. (1983). *Strategies of discourse comprehension*. New York: Academic Press.

Wanner, E. (1975). *On remembering, forgetting, and understanding sentences*. The Hague: Mouton.

Zimny, S. T. (1987). *Recognition memory for sentences from discourse*. Unpublished doctoral dissertation, University of Colorado, Boulder.

Zwaan, R. A., & van Oostendorp, U. (1993). Do readers construct spatial representations in naturalistic story comprehension? *Discourse Processes, 16*, 125–143.

ANALOGICAL PROCESSES IN COMPREHENSION

SIMULATION OF A MENTAL MODEL

ARTHUR M. GLENBERG, PETER KRULEY, AND WILLIAM E. LANGSTON

I. INTRODUCTION

We have several goals for this chapter, all related to the mental model construct. First, we use the construct to help flesh out several meanings of the term *comprehension*. Second, we briefly review some of the experimental data that demonstrate (to our satisfaction) that mental models are constructed while reading. Third, we describe a simulation model that derives propositions from text and uses those propositions to construct spatial mental models. We apply the simulation to two cases illustrating the on-line construction of mental models and how those models can be used to foster new learning. Fourth, we address several criticisms that have been leveled at the mental model account of comprehension. Finally, we briefly discuss the role of mental models in relation to other constructs such as schemata and causal chains.

II. WHAT DOES IT MEAN TO COMPREHEND?

Comprehension is a fuzzy term. We can talk about comprehending a word, a phrase, a sentence, or a discourse. We can talk about comprehending systems, like the economy. At the same time, people can have various levels of comprehension. A student can understand the mathematical operations that go into an equation, but not understand why the t statistic given by the equation is meaningful; another can understand why t is meaningful, but not understand why it is not meaningful when the assumptions of the test are violated; and the instructor can understand all of the above, and not understand what degrees of freedom are all about. How is it that we can comprehend in these ways?

How is it that we can be so certain that we understand at one level (why *t* is meaningful) when surely that understanding is deficient if we do not understand a fundamental component (degrees of freedom)? Is there anything that these forms of comprehension have in common? How can we, at times, be so wrong about what we comprehend (Glenberg, Sanocki, Epstein, & Morris, 1987)?

There is no action at a distance; causes have their effects through contact. Subatomic particles interact (at an apparent distance) by interchanging other particles (that have direct contact). Stars exert a gravitational attraction (at an apparent distance) by curving space-time to directly affect other bodies. Whether this is true of the physical world or just a construction of human intellect is pretty much irrelevant for the case we want to make. The important point is that our understanding depends on perceiving or postulating contact. The principle holds perhaps even more convincingly in the everyday world. The tree is held in place by the ground (acting on it directly). The flower grows because of the photons it captures; or in an earlier age, because of a life force contacting the seed directly. In the main, we understand by postulating contact. When we attempt to understand, the effort after meaning involves the perception or postulation of entities in contact.

Much like Gernsbacher, Varner, and Faust (1990), we believe that comprehension processes are not specific to language, but apply to our understanding of the physical and social worlds as well. In all these domains, comprehension involves building a structure of postulated contact between representations of entities. Thus, comprehension of a linguistic message requires that the linguistic elements be used to construct a set of (represented) entities in contact. In this way, the language producer induces in the comprehender a change in beliefs about the world, about the way entities in the world interact. The entities being operated on at any given time form a mental model.

Mental models have several characteristics (cf. Johnson-Laird, 1983). First, they consist of representations of entities (usually persons or objects). Because there is no action at a distance, the entities are potentially in contact with one another. That is, spatial relations among the entities are an important component of the mental model. Entities that are in contact can have a mutual influence. Mental models are labile. As entities contact one another, they alter their relations. Finally, mental models are limited. This is not a natural constraint on mental models; it is a characteristic of the human cognitive system. In brief, a mental model is a representation of the current understanding of a situation, whether that situation is described by the perceptual apparatus or whether that situation is described by a text.

Limitations forced on models by the cognitive system have several implications. First, models cannot be exact analogs of real situations. Instead, the entities in the models are more akin to pointers to collections of information in long-term store (LTS), as suggested by Sanford and Garrod (1981). Thus, when thinking about, say, an airplane, the model consists of an entity representing an airplane and depending on the context, some salient features such as wings. This entity points to or activates information about airplanes in LTS so that that information is available to control manipulation of the entity (how the airplane moves) in the model and reasoning about the entity.

Limitations on models also help us come to grips with the fuzzy nature of comprehension. We can (legitimately) state that we comprehend an event (or description of the event) whenever we can construct a model incorporating representations of some of the event's entities and relations among the entities. Our understanding of the event may be objectively faulty, if the wrong entities are included or if the wrong relations are included. Nonetheless, our impression is that we have comprehended, because we can construct a representation. Similarly, we can state that we comprehend a discourse when we are able to construct a model consisting of entities described in the discourse.

But, what are those entities doing in the model? Where did they come from? What are the characteristics of each entity? What supports those characteristics? To the extent that we can push the model, building submodels, and subsubmodels based on knowledge in LTS, our comprehension is more complete. Consider an example. I (AMG) think that I understand how an airplane works. The engine gets the plane going forward so that air flows over the wings. The wing is shaped so that the air flows more quickly over one of the surfaces (the bottom), creating a difference in air pressure that produces lift (represented in my model by arrows pointing upward under the wing). So far so good. But how does the engine work to get the plane going forward? Well, it burns a fuel . . . for every reaction there is an equal and opposite reaction . . . turbine blades whirl. But I don't know how to construct a model in which representations of these entities contact one another and interact. What are those turbine blades for? Thus, I understand how a plane flies at one level, the level for which I can construct a reasonably well connected model. The shallowness of my understanding is revealed as I try to construct explicit models for the entities in the original model. Given the eventual interconnectedness of all things, and the eventual limitations on our knowledge, comprehension can never be complete because it would require construction of models ad infinitum.

Limitations on models also help us to understand how we can so easily hold contradictory beliefs. I wouldn't be surprised to find out that my inchoate representation of an airplane's engine is incompatible with my notions of how lift is generated. Because these models and submodels are separately constructed and do not themselves interact, I never "notice" (Glenberg & Langston, 1992) the contradiction.

III. EVIDENCE THAT MENTAL MODELS ARE CONSTRUCTED DURING LANGUAGE COMPREHENSION

A. Textual versus Mental Model Accounts

Much of the work on language comprehension is consistent with mental model theory (for a review, see McNamara, Miller, & Bransford, in press). Thus demonstrations of limited capacity, effects of prior organized knowledge, and so on can be accommodated. The question we address here is what evidence uniquely (or at least differentially) supports the claim that mental models are built during language comprehension. The tack we take is simple, but powerful. Namely, as we will illustrate shortly, mental models are representations of situations or events or objects, not representations of a text per se. Thus, we can design materials in which the grammatical and propositional structure of the text is different from the spatial or logical structure of the situation. Then,

TABLE I
Example Text from Glenberg, Meyer, and Lindem (1987)

Setting Sentence:	John was preparing for a marathon in August.
Critical (associated):	After doing a few warm-up exercises, he put on his *sweatshirt* and went jogging.
Critical (dissociated):	After doing a few warm-up exercises, he took of his *sweatshirt* and went jogging.
Filler:	He jogged halfway around the lake without too much difficulty.
Filler:	Further along his route, however, John's muscles began to ache.

demonstrating that behavior is controlled by the structure of the situation rather than the structure of the text provides support for mental models.

As an example, consider the text in Table I, taken from Glenberg, Meyer, and Lindem (1987). Subjects read the text in one of two versions: using the associated sentence or the dissociated sentence. These two versions describe very different situations with different implications. In the associated condition, wherever John goes, the sweatshirt goes too. Thus, in the associated version, the situation at the end of the text has John and the sweatshirt spatially close, whereas in the dissociated version, John and his sweatshirt are separated. Contrast this with a textual representation based on propositions derived from the text.[1] In the associated condition, John and his sweatshirt are related in a proposition equivalent to (put on, John, sweatshirt). In the dissociated condition, John and his sweatshirt are also related by a proposition equivalent to (take off, John, sweatshirt). Note that the structural relation between John and sweatshirt is the same in both of the textual representations, in that John and sweatshirt occur in the same proposition.

To ascertain which of the structures (situational or textual) is controlling comprehension, Glenberg et al. (1987) used a probe recognition test for the word *sweatshirt*. The target word *sweatshirt* appeared after the critical sentence, one filler sentence, or two filler sentences, and the subjects' task was to respond *yes* as quickly as possible, if the target had appeared in the text. (Of course, sometimes the target was not in the text, and so the appropriate response was *no*.) Speed of responding was taken as a measure of activation or availability of the target concept.

Consider the predictions for speed of responding based on a representation of the situation (a mental model). Immediately after reading the critical sentence, the target is represented in the situation in both the associated and the dissociated cases. Thus, responding to the target (*sweatshirt*) should be fast whether the subject has read the associated or the dissociated version. After reading a filler sentence, the main actor, *John,* is activated by the pronominal reference. Will *sweatshirt* be activated? In the associated condition, *sweatshirt* and *John*

---

[1] We use the term TEXTUAL representation instead of PROPOSITIONAL representation for the following reason. A critical distinction between mental models and other forms of representation is what is represented—the situation described by the text, or the text itself. Some mental model theorists (e.g., Van Dijk & Kintsch, 1983) have used a propositional system to model representations of situations, whereas others propose that the situation should be represented analogically.

are both represented in the situation, whereas in the dissociated condition, only *John* should be represented. Thus, responding should be faster in the associated condition than in the dissociated condition. These predictions were confirmed, as demonstrated by the data reproduced in Figure 1.

According to the textual account, immediately after reading the critical sentence, responding to *sweatshirt* should be fast, because both propositions should be highly available. The textual account differs from the mental model account in its predictions for responding after the filler sentence. Because *John* and *sweatshirt* are equally closely related (by one proposition) in both the associated and dissociated conditions, responding should be equally fast (or slow). Obviously, this prediction is incorrect.

These results seem to provide strong support for the mental model account. Responding (and thus activation or availability of concepts) is controlled by the structure of the situation being described by the text, not by the (propositional) structure of the text. The implication is that the structure of the situation is being represented. Note that these results do not imply that a textual representation is

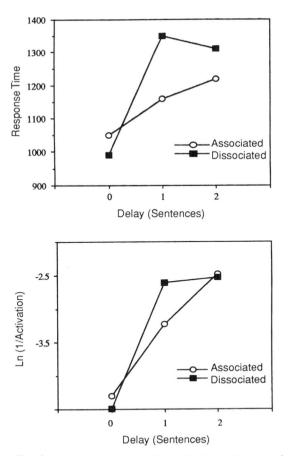

FIG. 1 The upper data are from Glenberg, Meyer, and Lindem (1987). The lower data are from the simulation of that experiment as described in the text.

not constructed, only that something in addition, a mental model, is also part of comprehension.

In fact, the results of Mani and Johnson-Laird (1982) imply that readers create both textual and situational representations. In their experiment, subjects read descriptions of spatial layouts (see Table II for examples). In the determinate condition, the description was consistent with just one layout. After reading these determinate descriptions, subjects were presented with four statements: one taken from the description that had just been read, one which was true of the spatial layout but not part of the description (either a paraphrase or a possible inference), and two distractors that were spatially inconsistent with the description. When asked to rank-order the statements according to how closely they resembled the original description, the subjects did not distinguish between sentences they had read and sentences that were true of the layout but which had not been read. Apparently, subjects had created a mental model of the layout, and they responded on the basis of it. In the indeterminate condition, the description was consistent with two layouts. In this case, subjects did distinguish between sentences they had read and other sentences that were true of the layout. Apparently, when subjects cannot form a consistent mental model, they tend to remember a textual representation. In addition, overall accuracy in distinguishing between statements that were true descriptions of the layout and statements that were false was best for the determinate descriptions, presumably because subjects needed to remember but a single model for the determinate descriptions.

Garnham (1981) provides a third illustration of behavior conforming to the structure of a situation rather than the structure of the text. Garnham's approach was to construct sentences that were equally confusable in terms of their surface representation, but either very confusable or not at all confusable in terms of the underlying situation being described in the sentences. Subjects were presented with sentences that differed from one another (essentially) by a single preposition. For instance, subjects might hear *The hostess bought a mink coat from the furrier* and *The hostess bought a mink coat in the furrier's*. Suppose that subjects are representing the situations described by the sentences. As these two sentences (are likely to) describe the same situation, they were expected to be confusable. Now consider two other sentences that also differ

TABLE II

Example Descriptions Corresponding to the Structure of Mani and Johnson-Laird (1982), Experiment 2

Determinate version (only one spatial layout is consistent with the description)
    The spoon is to the left of the glass.
    The fork is to the right of the glass.
    The knife is in front of the spoon.
    The dish is in front of the glass.
Indeterminate version (more than one spatial layout is consistent with the description)
    The spoon is to the left of the glass.
    The fork is to the right of the spoon.
    The knife is in front of the spoon.
    The dish is in front of the glass.

by a single preposition. *The hostess received a telegram from the furrier* and *The hostess received a telegram in the furrier's*. Because these sentences describe different situations, if the subjects are representing the situations, the latter two sentences should not be confusable.

Garnham's results supported these predictions. Sentences that differed only slightly in terms of surface representation were more confusable if they described the same situation than sentences that were equally similar in terms of surface representation but described different situations. Apparently, subjects were representing the situations, not just the sentences; that is, they were creating mental models. These results are very similar to those reported by Bransford, Barclay, and Franks (1972).

The conclusion that can be drawn from these and other experiments is that comprehension is an active process in which subjects form multiple levels of representation. One of these levels is almost surely closely tied to the text that subjects are seeing or hearing. However, subjects also form a more analogical representation of the underlying structure of the situation being described by the text. This additional representation, a mental model, could then be used to answer questions about the text, producing results like those described above.

B. When Are Mental Models Constructed?

Our daily intercourse with the world requires that the perceptual apparatus deliver veridical models of the world to guide our actions. The power of language as a communicative device derives from its ability to induce models in the comprehender that are approximations of the models based on perception. How we learn to use linguistic expressions to refer to model entities is a question we are not ready to tackle. Ours is more modest: When are mental models constructed from text?

Clearly, there are some basic requirements. The reader must be attending to the words and the grammatical relations. The reader must have basic knowledge of the meaning of the words. Furthermore, the reader must have knowledge of how to construct models in particular domains (and perhaps the motivation to do so). For example, when the text describes familiar objects in familiar situations, we can construct models that are closely analogous to spatial models created by the perceptual apparatus. Thus the domain knowledge is acquired from interactions with the environment and knowledge of spatial relation terms. Because of our familiarity with spatial relations, these sorts of models are easy to construct, and they appear to have characteristics similar to those based on models derived from perception (Bryant, Tversky, & Franklin, 1992). Note, however, that we are suggesting that it is the familiarity that is important, not that the text is necessarily spatial. A mental model can be constructed for any domain, but knowledge of several sorts seems to be required. First, knowledge about the characteristics of specific entities is required. Second, knowledge about the types of relations the entities can enter into is also needed. Third, on the assumption that mental models are constructed in a spatial medium, the reader must have knowledge of how to represent nonspatial entities and nonspatial relations in the spatial medium of the model.

It is this last type of knowledge that may be the most difficult for a novice in a domain. We think that lack of this type of knowledge underlies the usefulness of pictures, especially when reading in new domains, and it may underlie the extensive use of pictures in early readers. That is, the young reader has not yet developed the trick of using words to construct models, even in familiar domains. The pictures provide support for the models by concretely illustrating the entities and relations. Thus, the entities in the encoded picture serve as referents for the words in the text, and the encoded picture becomes a mental model.

This sort of reasoning underlay the experiments reported in Glenberg and Langston (1992). In these experiments, subjects were presented with texts that described simple four-step procedures. In each text, subjects were told that the middle two steps of the procedure were to be performed at the same time. A sample text ("Writing a Paper") is included in Table III.

For each text, there were at least two distinct representations that subjects could form. First, subjects could form a representation of the text itself. In this representation, step one would be first, followed by step two, which would be followed by step three, and so on. For the text presented in Table III, this representation might be something like the left half of Figure 2.

It was also possible for subjects to form a representation of the procedure described by the text. In this representation, step one would be first, followed by steps two and three, which would be represented as simultaneous, followed by step four. This representation might look something like the right half of Figure 2.

Note that in the representation of the text, certain pairs of steps are near to one another. For example, steps 1 and 2, *write a first draft* and *consider the structure,* are near in the text, whereas other pairs of steps, such as steps 1 and 3, *write a first draft* and *address the audience,* are relatively far from one another. However, in the representation of the procedure, both of these pairs of steps are near to one another. This distinction provided the basis for differential predictions from textual and mental model accounts.

The ordering task that subjects were asked to perform was designed to get at the representation of the procedure rather than the representation of the text. Subjects were presented names of two of the steps, and they were asked

TABLE III
Sample Text from Glenberg and Langston (1992)[a]

Writing a Paper

There are four steps to be taken when writing a paper. The first step is to *write a first draft.* To do this, you must follow an outline and disregard style.

The next two steps should be performed at the same time. One of these steps is to *consider the structure.* You must correct flaws in logic and gaps between main points.

The other step is to *address the audience.* You should explain novel terms adequately and support bold statements.

The final step is to *proof the paper* for grammar, punctuation, and style. It is a good idea to have someone else do this for you since you may not notice such surface details.

---

[a] Items in italics are the step names that were included in the pictures.

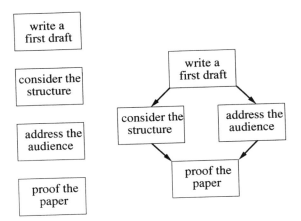

FIG. 2   On the left is a representation of the text in Table III (from Glenberg & Langston, 1992); on the right is a representation of the procedure described by the text.

to judge whether or not these two steps would be *performed* in the order in which they were presented at the test.

If subjects were reasoning from a mental model of the procedure, they should be equally facile at judging that far pairs (e.g., 1 and 3) are performed sequentially and that near pairs (1 and 2) are performed sequentially. In the mental model, there is no distinction between near and far pairs. However, if subjects are reasoning from a representation of the text, it should be easier to make judgments about near pairs whose members are described sequentially in the text than about far pairs whose members are described separately.

Note, however, that forming a spatial model of the procedure requires translating the temporal relation of precedence into a spatial relation such as *above*. To encourage the use of mental models, half the subjects were presented with simple, diagrammatic pictures which represented the order in which the steps in the procedure were to be performed. These pictures were similar to the right side of Figure 2. We reasoned that pictures would provide subjects with a framework for representing the procedure in a mental model.

Thus, the predictions were as follows. Subjects in the with-pictures condition should form a mental model of the procedure, leading to equally facile performance on near pairs and far pairs, because these pairs are equally near in the representation of the procedure. Subjects in the no-picture condition should have a more difficult time representing the procedure, and their responding should be based on the representation of the text. In this case, responding should be more accurate for near (in the text) pairs than far (in the text) pairs.

These predictions were supported by the results of Glenberg and Langston (1992). Subjects in the with-picture condition performed almost equally well on both near and far pairs, and subjects in the no-picture condition performed much better on near pairs than far pairs. These results support the hypothesis that pictures can facilitate the comprehension of texts by encouraging subjects to represent the information in the text in the form of a mental model.

IV. A MODEL MENTAL MODEL

The mental model account is complicated. We envision subjects reading, constructing, and maintaining a spatial mental model, updating the model, noticing relations, and so on. Can these tasks actually be coordinated within a limited capacity system? We built a simulation model to help us answer questions such as these. In outline, the simulation constructs propositions from (highly coded) words in sentences. These propositions are used to construct mental models and to direct the manipulation of the models. If a picture is available, it is used to guide the construction of the model. Once constructed, the model becomes a source of new information about the situation.

A. Nodes, Propositions, and the Mental Model

One component of the simulation's memory is the node. We use nodes to represent specific objects (or more generally, entities), as opposed to classes, and each object described by the text has a corresponding node. The node encodes a limited amount of information about the object including its count (singular or plural), animacy (animate or inanimate), gender (male, female, or neuter), and semantic class. Because the simulation does not have a permanent knowledge base, this information must be hand-coded into the "text" that the simulation processes.

Five types of propositions are derived from the text. (1) Word propositions encode verbatim the actual word(s) used to name an object. The proposition consists of the words used and a pointer to the node named by the words. (2) Language propositions encode some linguistic and semantic attributes such as whether the word is the grammatical subject and the given/new status, and they also include a pointer to the node. Although these propositions are necessary to the operation of the model, we have little to say about them in this chapter. (3) Description propositions encode unary attributes of objects such as size or color, and they also include a pointer to the node being described. (4) Existence propositions encode the fact that an object exists. (5) Finally, relational propositions encode relations among objects. The proposition includes a specification of the relation (e.g., *attached*) and pointers to the nodes taking part in the relation. One of the pointers is designated as the *focus* of the proposition. The focus node is typically the grammatical subject (determined from the language proposition).

Each of these types of propositions can be activated by various sources (described shortly). Because activation of propositions is continuous and graded, there is little distinction between information in working memory and information in long-term store. Propositions that are highly activated are easy to retrieve, whereas propositions that have little activation are difficult to retrieve. Propositions are never deleted from memory, however. Nodes are not directly activated. Instead, the activation (availability) of a node is given by the activation of all the propositions that point to that node. Thus, nodes, like propositions, are available to a graded degree.

We conceptualize the mental model as being constructed in a three-dimensional spatial medium corresponding to the visual/spatial sketchpad of working memory (Baddeley, 1990). The mental model is extremely limited in capacity because of limitations on activation. Entities in the model are pointers to nodes. Distance between pointers is representationally meaningful. That is, pointers that are closer together are more strongly related. The spatial dimensions ordinarily correspond to up/down, front/back, and left/right. However, when the simulation is assumed to have the requisite knowledge, the spatial dimensions may be used to represent other, text-relevant dimensions such as time, energy, mass, friendliness, and so on. The pointers (entities in the model) can be activated to various degrees, and when a pointer's activation falls below a threshold, it is removed from the model. Thus, unlike propositions and nodes, pointers in the mental model are temporary.

B. Processing in the Simulation

Processing is controlled by a working memory with multiple (but relatively fixed) capacities used for different tasks. The articulatory capacity is used to activate word and language propositions. The spatial capacity is used to read a word, examine a picture, and maintain pointers in the mental model. The general capacity can be deployed to support any of the activities already mentioned, and it is used to activate relation and description propositions. In addition, general capacity is used to support cognitive activities such as retrieving information and manipulating the pointers in the mental model.

Each activity (e.g., representing a pointer in the mental model, retrieving a proposition) requires a particular amount and type of capacity. However, the capacities are strictly limited and are quickly allocated. When available capacity is insufficient for an activity, capacity is recovered from memory using a proportionality algorithm. Each element in memory (mental model pointer or proposition) gives up a part of the capacity assigned to it proportional to the total amount of that capacity being used. This algorithm produces negatively accelerated forgetting (decrease in retrievability) and an extremely interactive system.

Retrieval is based on a resonance metaphor, much like the Minerva II model (Hintzman, 1986). The same retrieval process is used during comprehension (e.g., in retrieving antecedents for anaphors) and in memory tasks. In outline, retrieval works by assembling one or more propositions to use as retrieval cues. Next, activation is recovered proportional to the number of propositions used as cues. The cues are compared to all propositions in memory, and the activation of those propositions is increased in direct proportion to their current activation (recency), in direct proportion to their similarity to the cue (encoding specificity), and in inverse proportion to the number of propositions contacted by the cue (cue overload, or fan effects). The result of a retrieval operation is a redistribution of (the previously recovered) activation across the propositions and a consequent change in the availability of the nodes pointed to by the propositions.

Whenever a relation or existence proposition is constructed, the simulation treats the proposition as a direction to update the mental model. This updating involves several major steps. First, activation is recovered to drive the following steps. Then, appropriate pointers are inserted into the model, if they are not there already. Next, if the proposition describes a relation between pointers that is not extant in the model, the pointers are moved into that relation. If a picture of the situation is available, that picture is used to help construct the model. For example, the text might describe Object A as near to Object B. Given a picture, the mental model would be able to represent whether Object A is to the left or right of Object B.

Finally, the simulation learns from the mental model using a process we call NOTICING. After the mental model is manipulated, the simulation searches for all pointers within the NOTICING RADIUS of the pointer that was manipulated. If such a pointer is found, the simulation notices, that is, generates a proposition describing the relation between the manipulated pointer and the found pointer. These noticed propositions are supported by general capacity and stored in memory with pointers to the relevant object nodes. Prototypically, the noticed relation is spatial (e.g., *left of*), but the interpretation of the relation depends on the domain-relevant dimension assigned to the spatial dimension. By virtue of noticing, the simulation infers information that is not explicit in the text and learns from manipulation of its own mental model.

Reading a simple, one-proposition subject–verb–object sentence proceeds as follows. (Each step requires that a sufficient amount of capacity be available or be recovered. Discussion of this is suppressed for clarity.) First, the subject noun is read and represented verbatim using articulatory capacity. If the word is marked as "new," a new node is generated to represent the specific object. If the word is marked as "given," a search of memory is conducted for a possible referent; if none is found, a new node is generated. The search (using general capacity) uses the retrieval algorithm, and the cues consist of information available about the word (e.g., gender). When the verb is read, it is encoded as a relation of a proposition, and memory is searched (using the retrieval algorithm) for an appropriate initial argument (e.g., one that agrees in number with the verb). When the object noun is read, it is represented verbatim, and a node is retrieved or created for it. Then, the developing relation proposition is retrieved and completed.

When the completed proposition specifies a relation represented by one of the dimensions in the mental model, the proposition is treated as an instruction to update the model (using spatial capacity). First, however, if a picture is available, the picture is searched for the arguments of the proposition. If the arguments are found in the picture, then the spatial layout of the picture controls where the pointers to the objects are placed in the mental model.

Once the mental model has been updated, noticing occurs within the noticing radius of the pointer corresponding to the focus of the proposition. Any noticed relations are encoded propositionally and stored with the appropriate nodes.

Because the simulation respects work on memory, it can successfully simulate standard findings such as recency effects and long-term recency effects (Glenberg, Bradley, Kraus, & Renzaglia, 1983) due to changes in capacities devoted to various propositions, proactive interference and release from proactive interference due to cue overload (O. C. Watkins & Watkins, 1975), as well as some rather unusual new findings such as the revelation effect (M. J. Watkins & Peynircioglu, 1990). Also, the simulation has had success in simulating work on mental models (Glenberg, Meyer, & Lindem, 1987), effects of pictures on comprehension (Glenberg & Langston, 1992), map-learning (McNamara, Halpin, & Hardy, 1992), as well as retrieval of antecedents for anaphors (O'Brien, Plewes, & Albrecht, 1990).

C. Simulation and Data

To provide a sense[2] of how the simulation works, we describe in more detail how it deals with two phenomena, effects of mental models on foregrounding (Glenberg, Meyer, & Lindem, 1987) and learning of cognitive maps (McNamara et al., 1992). The simulation of Glenberg, Meyer, and Lindem (1987) illustrates how mental models are constructed from texts and how the model can influence comprehension processes. The simulation of the McNamara et al. results illustrates how pictorial information can be used to help construct mental models, and it illustrates the operation of the noticing process.

The point of the Glenberg, Meyer, and Lindem (1987) experiment was to demonstrate that the structure of the situation (as opposed to the structure of the text) plays an important role in foregrounding. When we say that a concept is foregrounded, we mean that the concept is readily available and thus easy to refer to, especially by a pronoun. To demonstrate that the structure of the situation influences foregrounding, Glenberg, Meyer, and Lindem (1987) showed that a critical object (e.g., *sweatshirt* in Table I) that is spatially associated with a main actor tends to remain foregrounded longer than a critical object that is spatially dissociated with the main actor. Figure 1 shows a comparison of the Glenberg, Meyer, and Lindem (1987) results and the results from the simulation. The dependent variable for the simulation is a transformation of the activation of the critical object node so that it can be more easily compared to reaction time.

The text used in the simulation is given in Table IV. It is a simplified version of the text in Table I. Figure 3 portrays the situation in the simulation's memory immediately after reading the associated sentence. We first describe how the simulation got into the state illustrated in Figure 3, and then we describe differences between the associated and dissociated conditions from that point on.

Upon starting a new sentence, the simulation captures enough activation to process a typical, simple sentence, namely the activation needed to encode a subject, an object, and a relation. The simulation then reads the word *John* hand-coded along a number of dimensions: number (singular), animacy (animate), gender (male), given–new (given–unless concepts are specifically

TABLE IV
Text Used in the Simulation of Glenberg, Meyer, and
Lindem (1987) Corresponding to the Associated and Filler
Sentences in Table I

Critical (associated):	John put on a white sweatshirt.
Filler:	John ran to the lake.
Filler:	John has muscles.

[2] What does it mean to "provide a sense?" In our judgment, the information we have given about the simulation is insufficient for you, the reader, to construct a coherent mental model of the simulation. Much like AMG's model of an airplane, your model of the simulation consists of submodels that do not yet connect, that do not yet constrain one another. By providing "a sense" we will give you more information that allows you to construct connected models to understand the simulation.

Mental Model

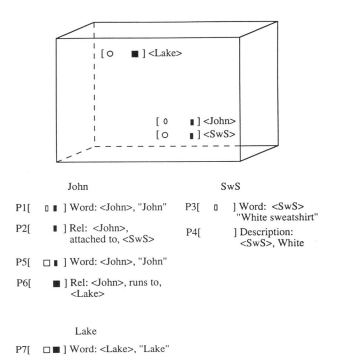

John   SwS

P1[▫ ▪] Word: <John>, "John"   P3[▫   ] Word: <SwS>
                                                        "White sweatshirt"
P2[▪] Rel: <John>,   P4[   ] Description:
              attached to, <SwS>   <SwS>, White

P5[▫ ▪] Word: <John>, "John"

P6[▪] Rel: <John>, runs to,
              <Lake>

                  Lake

P7[▫ ▪] Word: <Lake>, "Lake"

FIG. 3   Relevant aspects of the simulation after it has processed the associated sentence in Table
IV. The top portion illustrates the three-dimensional mental model. Symbols in angle brackets are
pointers to object nodes. The labels P1, P2, etc. refer to propositions derived from the text. The
widths of the symbols within the square brackets correspond to the amount of spatial (*ellipses*),
general (*filled rectangles*), and articulatory (*open rectangles*) capacity devoted to each proposition
and to each pointer in the mental model.

marked as new [e.g., by use of an indefinite article], they are treated as given),
and grammatical class (subject). In addition, a semantic code is assigned to
John that represents categorical information. These arbitrary semantic codes
provide a way of assigning entities either to the same or to different categories.
Because of the semantic code, the simulation does not confuse *John* with *Fido,*
which would otherwise be coded identically.

The simulation uses the coded information about '*John*' to search memory
for any nodes to which the word *John* may refer. Because this is the first word
of the text, none is found, and so a new node is created. The node includes
the information that 'John' is singular, animate, male, and the semantic code.
A proposition (P1, in Fig. 3) is formed that indicates that the word *John* was
used to refer to this node, and the first argument in the proposition is a pointer
to the node John (<John>). This proposition is supported with both articulatory
and general activation from the amount reserved at the beginning of the sentence.

The simulation then reads *puts on*. This is coded as the relation 'attached to', along with the information that a singular active subject is required for this relation. A relation proposition is created (P2), but at this time only the relation 'attached to' is specified. The arguments of the proposition must be either retrieved or read. The simulation uses the conditions singular and active to attempt to retrieve nodes that match the conditions specified by the coding of *puts on*. The node John will be found (if there has not been interfering activity such as a long phrase between the reading of *John* and *puts on*). The retrieval process boosts the activation of the word proposition (P1) and thereby the node corresponding to John. A pointer to the node becomes the focus of proposition P2, and this proposition is supported by general activation from that reserved at the beginning of the sentence. General activation is used, rather than articulatory activation, because the proposition does not correspond directly to anything that can be articulated in an articulatory loop. Note that the proposition is not yet completed, because what John is attached to has not yet been read. The incomplete proposition is given an extra boost of activation so that it is not inadvertently lost before the proposition can be completed.

The simulation then reads *a white sweatshirt. Sweatshirt* is coded as singular, new, inanimate, neuter, grammatical object, and given a semantic code. Because sweatshirt is coded as 'new' (based on the indefinite *a*), no search is conducted for a matching node. Instead, the Sws node is created. The fact that the words *white sweatshirt* were used to refer to the node is encoded by a word proposition, P3. In addition, descriptive information about this node, in particular that the object is white, is encoded by a description proposition (P4). Both these propositions are supported by the activation reserved at the beginning of the sentence.

Because *sweatshirt* was coded as a grammatical object, the simulation searches for an incomplete relation proposition and finds P2. A pointer to Sws is inserted into P2, and any extra activation used to keep P2 from being forgotten (before it was completed) is reduced.

After a relation proposition is completed, the simulation determines if that proposition has any implications for the situation (mental model) that is being represented. In this case, pointers to the John and Sws nodes are introduced into the mental model in close proximity. These pointers are supported by a combination of spatial and general activation.

Suppose that the test probe *sweatshirt* is presented at this time. Responding to this probe will be quick and accurate because the Sws node is highly activated. Note that this is the case in both the associated and the dissociated conditions (see below) because information about the sweatshirt has just been encoded in both cases.

Before the next sentence is attempted, the simulation again reserves activation. Because total activation in the system is limited, this reduces or SUPPRESSES information from the previous sentence. Upon reading the coded version of *John*, a search is initiated and the John node is found. A new proposition, encoding the fact that the specific word *John* was used again, is encoded (P5). This search process will have increased the activation of P1 (because the retrieval cue matches the proposition) and decreased the activation of other propositions, such as P3. The words *ran to* are encoded as the relation 'moves to', and the incomplete proposition (P6) is supported by extra activation, until it is completed.

Because *the lake* is coded as 'given' (based on the use of the definite article), a search for a compatible node is initiated. When none is found, a new node is created, and the proposition encoding the word *lake* is formed (P7). Because *lake* is coded as a grammatical object, the simulation attempts to retrieve an incomplete proposition (P6). When P6 is retrieved, a pointer to the lake node is added to it. All of this processing has greatly reduced the activation of propositions pointing to the Sws node.

At this point, some interesting processing occurs. With the completion of the proposition, the mental model is updated. A pointer to the lake node is entered into the mental model, and the simulation attempts to manipulate the mental model to be consistent with the recently encoded proposition, that John moves to the lake. In preparing to move the pointer representing John, the simulation notices that a pointer to Sws is very near to John. Should that pointer be moved too? The mental model does not represent (directly) the fact that John and Sws are attached, only that they are spatially close. The information that John is attached to his sweatshirt is given only in the propositions. Thus, the simulation attempts to retrieve information relating John and Sws by using as a retrieval cue a proposition consisting of a pointer to John, a pointer to Sws, and the relation 'attached to'. If a corresponding proposition can be retrieved, then both pointers in the model will be moved to the lake. In fact, the simulation is successful in retrieving P2, and both pointers are moved. These processes increase activation of the Sws node in several ways. First, activation of the Sws node is enhanced because retrieval of P2 increases the activation of P2 (and hence the activation of the Sws node). Second, manipulating the pointer to Sws in the mental model enhances the pointer's activation (and hence the activation of the Sws node). If the test probe *sweatshirt* is presented at this time, responding will be relatively quick. That is, retrieval of the Sws node will be facile because it is highly activated.

When the dissociated condition sentences are processed, the situation is exactly the same as in Figure 3, except that the relation in P2 is coded as 'next to' rather than 'attached to'. In this case, when the mental model is updated (after completing P6), the pointer to Sws is not moved, and it receives far less activation (because it is not manipulated in any way). Consequently, the Sws node is not highly activated, and responding to the probe is slower than in the associated condition.

Why did we elect not to represent in the mental model the fact that *John* and *sweatshirt* are attached (in the associated condition)? First, we envision the mental model as extremely limited in capacity because it utilizes the limited visual–spatial scratchpad of working memory. Second, John could enter into many different types of relations with many different types of objects, and it is not clear how to determine which ones should be represented in the mental model. In the current version, the rule is simple: only include in the mental model the relations being represented by the spatial dimensions; all other relations are represented propositionally in memory. Third, our procedure has a natural consequence. If an object is not integral to the following text, the pointer to the object's node will soon be dropped from the mental model, as illustrated next.

The second sentence after the critical associated sentence is *John has muscles*. On processing this sentence, the simulation adds a node for muscles and introduces a pointer to muscles into the mental model. Propositions are formed encoding that John and his muscles are attached. Because *sweatshirt* is not referred to again, its activation is extremely low, and responding to a probe will be slow (see Fig. 1). Furthermore, processing the mental model does not manipulate the pointer to Sws, its activation drops, and it is lost from the mental model (when its activation drops below a threshold, it is removed from the model). Thus, the model does not become cluttered with objects that could have been relevant but soon turn out to be of little interest. Figure 1 illustrates both the data from Glenberg, Meyer, and Lindem (1987) and the results from our simulation using the text in Table IV.

Our second demonstration of the simulation addresses two issues. The first is how pictures help comprehenders to construct mental models. The second is how mental models can produce new learning based on noticing (Glenberg & Langston, 1992). We use results presented in McNamara et al. (1992) to demonstrate these features of the simulation.

The McNamara et al. paper examines the contribution of spatial and temporal contiguity to the development of spatial relations. The subjects were to learn the locations of objects on a map, much like that illustrated in Figure 4. Object locations are represented by dots, and the names of the objects (in the figure, not the experiment) are given by letters of the alphabet. In the experiment, the objects occurred in two regions, as indicated by the heavy line down the middle of the figure. After learning, subjects received several types of tests. In the region test, subjects had to quickly decide to which region a named object belonged. In the recognition test, the subject simply decided if an object name occurred. Because we have not yet implemented regions into our simulation of mental models, we focus on the recognition test.

In the experiment, subjects had continuous access to a map giving the locations of the objects, but not the object names, much like the right side of Figure 4. The names of the objects were given one at a time, by presenting an object name next to its location. A critical variable was the order in which the names were presented. The left side of Figure 4 uses lower case letters to represent object names and Arabic numerals to represent order of presentation of the names. Note that the right side of the figure corresponds to what subjects

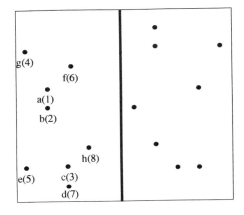

Fig. 4 The picture used to accompany the simulation of the McNamara et al. (1992) data. The left panel illustrates the object names (*letters*), the order in which the names were presented (*digits*), and their locations (*dots*). The right panel illustrates the map-like stimulus actually available to the subjects.

saw most of the time; subjects never saw anything corresponding to the left side of the figure.

Pairs of objects can be defined on the basis of whether the objects were temporally or spatially contiguous. Thus Objects a and b are both temporally and spatially contiguous, whereas Objects c and d are spatially contiguous, but not temporally contiguous. Objects e and f are temporally contiguous but spatially distant, whereas Objects g and h are temporally and spatially distant. These pairs were then used as primes and targets on the object–name recognition test. For example, a prime, the name of Object a, would be presented, and the subject would respond *yes*. Next, a target, the name of Object b, would be presented. The question of interest was how the spatial and temporal relations between the targets and the primes would affect speed of responding to the targets.

The response times to the targets (collapsed across the experiments reported by McNamara et al., 1992) are given in the upper part of Figure 5. Note the interaction: responding to a target name is facilitated by a prime that was spatially and temporally close during acquisition, but not when the relation was just spatial or just temporal. Data from the simulation are presented in the lower part of Figure 5.

To simulate these data, we used a picture that provided metric information about the locations. When an object was mentioned, the simulation consulted the picture, scaled the location in the picture to the dimensions of the mental model, and entered into the mental model a pointer representing the object. Thus, the location of the pointer in the mental model was controlled by its location in the picture.

Whenever the mental model is manipulated (e.g., by entering a new pointer), the simulation engages in noticing. (Noticing also occurred in the simulation of the Glenberg, Meyer, & Lindem, 1987, data, but discussion of it was suppressed for clarity.) The idea of noticing is to use the structure of the mental model to encode relations that are not given explicitly in the text. To notice, the simulation examines spatial locations within the noticing radius (a free parameter in the simulation) of a manipulated pointer. If another pointer is within that radius, the simulation encodes the relation between the two pointers and stores the proposition with pointers to the relevant nodes. Unlike other computational systems for generating inferences, this one is self-limited in three ways. First, noticing only occurs for objects represented in the limited capacity mental model. Second, noticing only occurs for objects within the noticing radius of manipulated pointers. Third, inferences are made only about the relations assigned (for the current text domain) to the spatial dimensions.

Consider how the simulation responds to the presentation of object names in the McNamara et al. experiment. When Object a is presented, a pointer is entered into the mental model, but there is nothing to notice. When a pointer to a node for Object b is entered into the mental model, the relation to Object a is noticed and stored. When the pointer to the node for Object c is entered into the model, no new relations are noticed, because the pointers to Objects a and b are outside the noticing radius of the pointer to Object c. The next (fourth) pointer entered into the model is the one to the node of Object g. With its entry, activation of the pointer to Object a is so low that it is dropped from the model. Similarly, by time the pointer to Object d is entered (seventh), the

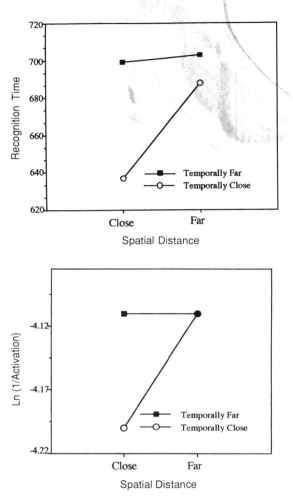

FIG. 5 The upper data are averages based on the experiments presented in McNamara et al. (1992). The lower data are from the simulation described in the text.

pointer for Object c has been dropped. Thus, although two objects may be spatially close in a picture, if their pointers are not concurrently resident in the mental model, no relation is noticed.

On the recognition test, responding to the name of an object requires retrieval of information about the object. That retrieval process activates various propositions, including propositions encoding noticed relations. For example, when the name of Object a (the prime) is presented, the proposition encoding its noticed relation to Object b is activated. This activated proposition partially activates the node for Object b (the target), producing facilitation when Object b is presented for recognition. On the other hand, responding to the name of Object c does not facilitate responding to the name of Object d, because no relation was noticed between these objects.

Thus our simulation of the McNamara et al. (1992) experiments demonstrates one way in which pictures can facilitate comprehension. In particular, a picture can provide metric information about objects to guide in the construction of mental models. Then the mental model can be used to notice (encode) new relations, thus learning more about the situation than is given by the text.

V. CRITICISM OF MENTAL MODEL THEORY

In this section we address (in varying amounts of detail) three criticisms of mental model theory. The first is that mental model theory is vague. Given the presentation of our simulation, there is no need to argue against the claim that vagueness is a necessary characteristic of mental models. A second criticism has been made in the area of thinking and reasoning. The argument is as follows. Mental models are by definition representations of specific situations, whereas reasoning uses rules and abstractions. Thus, mental models cannot play an important role in reasoning (Rips, 1986). Because this chapter focuses on comprehension, we will not concentrate on repelling this attack, but because reasoning-like processes play some role in comprehension, we discuss this criticism briefly. A third criticism is represented by the minimalist position that readers produce a minimum number of constructive inferences (McKoon & Ratcliff, 1992). Our major effort is directed toward this criticism.

A. The Role of Rules and Abstractions

How can a system grounded in specific entities and concrete instantiations come to grips with abstract systems of thought like mathematics? Our proposal is that under certain conditions, abstract rules can be used to replace concrete instantiations. Consider that $2 + 3 = 5$. Initial understanding requires that we be able to mentally construct a model with two entities, another with three entities, conjoin the two models, and note that the resulting model has five entities. After doing this when the entities are marbles, cars, and dots on a piece of paper, we may be able to induce the rule that $2 + 3 = 5$, or we may believe it when it is taught as a rule to be memorized. Once that rule is induced, it can replace the construction of specific models and be applied directly in the service of other models and rules. Now, when faced with adding 1002 and 1003, we need not envision very large sets, but need only call on this rule.

Application of rules can get us in comprehension trouble in several ways. First, the rules may be incorrect. That is, we may have induced a rule from too few instances, so in fact the rule has no generality even though we apply it generally. Second, the rule may have preconditions that are not met. Thus, $2 + 3 = 5$ does not hold for base 5. Similarly, the rule may have consequences that we do not appreciate, and so we do not incorporate those consequences into our models.

In his critique of mental model theory, Rips (1986) defended the notion of using abstract rules in thinking. In his view, propositional accounts are to be valued because they satisfy the formality constraint that underlies the computational approach to cognitive psychology; Rips also argued that the results of experiments advanced in support of mental models could be accommodated by propositional accounts. Clearly, there is nothing in mental model theory that denies the possibility of abstract rules. Rules are applied in particular contexts (e.g., mathematics) for which we have learned to trust the rules. In addition, it is hard to imagine how one could develop a model without incorporating abstract rules either implicitly or explicitly. AMG's airplane model depends on knowledge (rules) about air pressure, gravity, and so on. The point is that not all thinking should be modeled as forming deductions from abstract rules. Instead, rules are often used to derive and manipulate models of situations (Johnson-Laird, Byrne, & Tabossi, 1989).

Rips (1986) raised additional objections to the conception of mental models as simulations in which causal sequences of events are traced mentally in order to predict a final outcome. This is probably the closest sense of mental model to the approach we are outlining here, so we respond to these criticisms in some detail. The first problem cited by Rips arose in AI simulations which attempted to predict future states (e.g., the path of a bouncing ball) from qualitative information (e.g., approximate location or place); because of the fuzziness of the information, the simulation's performance was underdetermined and predictions were ambiguous. In our view, this problem challenges all accounts of human cognition, not just current mental models: human thinkers are plainly willing to make predictions in underdetermined situations, and Rips does not cite any propositional simulations that could successfully model these ambiguous situations. Also, it is not entirely relevant to the mental model studies under discussion here, which are characterized not by the use of inexact or qualitative information, but by the use of analogical representations and procedures. The one AI simulation cited by Rips achieved accurate prediction only by solving a system of equations applied to precise position information—a non-analogical approach; however, this fact does not rule out the possibility of efficient analogical processes achieving the same outcome.

An experiment by Gentner and Rips (Rips, 1986) was advanced as a further reason for questioning the status of mental models as simulations. Their college-age subjects attempted to predict the effect of increasing or decreasing one of five physical variables (air temperature, water temperature, air pressure, evaporation rate, and relative humidity) in a system consisting of a pan of water in a closed room. Specifically, the students were told the direction of change of one variable and asked to predict the change in a second variable. Substantial numbers of intransitivities were found in the obtained responses; for instance, 31% of their subjects said that water temperature changed evaporation rate and that evaporation rate changed air pressure but predicted no effect of changing water temperature on air pressure. Because a coherent mental model of the entire system should produce consistent responses, Rips contended that the existence of such intransitivities refuted the mental model approach and implied the use of (propositional) rules of thumb.

We disagree, believing that a critical difference between the Gentner and Rips experiment and other studies supporting mental models is the impossibility of representing the entire Gentner and Rips situation in a usable model in working memory. Consider that the most complex spatial layout used by Mani and Johnson-Laird (1982) can represented by the diagram of Figure 6. Here, lines connect objects that were explicitly described as being related (e.g., the spoon is the left of the glass), but, importantly, the other spatial relations that the subjects needed to know can all be seen in the diagram (e.g., the knife is to the left of the dish). In other words, all the responses called for in the

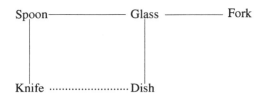

FIG. 6   A diagrammatic representation of a situation used by Mani and Johnson-Laird (1982). The layout of the objects in the diagram is consistent with the description heard by the subjects. Solid lines connect objects whose spatial relationship was explicitly described; the dotted line represents a possible inference.

experiment can be made using a single diagram of five elements (the lines are not necessary for responding). Similarly, Glenberg and Langston (1992) used flow charts containing four boxes to represent four-step procedures. In the Gentner and Rips study, using a set of five variables and disregarding order, there are ten relevant binary relations (e.g., increasing air temperature increases evaporation rate). Some of these relations are redundant in the sense that they can be inferred from other relations using the principle of transitivity, but even so, it seems unlikely that subjects were able to create complete usable mental models during the time allotted to the experiment. We can imagine representing the system spatially by a series of pulleys or a set of linked seesaws (à la Rube Goldberg), but we are unable to produce any representation that could be maintained in working memory in its entirety (at least in the absence of chunked relations based on long-term knowledge). Note that the intransitivities obtained by Gentner and Rips, which constitute failures to draw available inferences, are problematic for rule-based accounts as well: Why was it not possible to draw a deduction based on two available propositions? Evidently, whatever processes their subjects used when responding in the study were seriously hampered by memory capacity limitations or retrieval failures.

B. The Minimalist Position

Recently, McKoon and Ratcliff (1992) have defended a minimalist hypothesis which may be seen as contrary to mental model theory. According to the minimalist hypothesis, automatic inferences are drawn only under particular conditions, namely when the information is highly available or when the inference is necessary to maintain local coherence. Other inferences are not automatic, but under the control of specific reading strategies.

As McKoon and Ratcliff note, the minimalist hypothesis is more of a research strategy than a theory of comprehension. That is, the hypothesis guides the search for processes that are relatively independent of specific reading strategies; it does not deny the existence or relevance of those strategies. Thus the minimalist hypothesis may be viewed as a null hypothesis that should be tested in various situations.

We think that there is much in McKoon and Ratcliff's description of the minimalist hypothesis that accords well with mental model theory. For example, the mental model may be the source of highly available information in support of automatic inferences. Thus, Glenberg, Meyer, and Lindem (1987) demonstrated that a mental model may enhance the availability of entities used in anaphor resolution. Also, a mental model may support the activation of scriptal knowledge in support of some inferences (Sanford & Garrod, 1981). Finally, as McKoon and Ratcliff state, "More often than not, readers do have specific goals, especially when learning new information from texts, and so they often engage in strategic processing designed to achieve those goals." To the extent that a goal of reading is to learn new information, then constructing a mental model is a central activity.

There are two areas in which we disagree with McKoon and Ratcliff's analysis. The first is their description of mental model theory. They state, "The most important claim of many 'mental model' theories of text comprehension is that the mental representation of a text automatically depicts the events described by the text in a 'life-like' way," and later, "Readers automatically construct a full representation of the real-life situation described by a text." Unlike McKoon and Ratcliff, we do not attribute these claims to mental model theory. In particular, it is not inherent in mental model theory that models are constructed automatically, nor is it inherent that models be a "full representation of the real-life situation." We have already discussed the conditions under which mental models are constructed. For now, we note that it seems likely that construction of mental models is not automatic (in the sense of obligatory). Instead, construction of models probably requires highly available knowledge (e.g., when reading about simple social situations) or special strategies. In fact, Glenberg and Langston (1992) demonstrated that in comprehending some procedures, people appear to need pictures to help construct models.

To what extent is a mental model "lifelike" and "a full representation"? We have claimed that mental models are lifelike in the particular sense that there are some analogical correspondences between mental models and the situations they represent. Thus, a mental model that represents two people interacting may well have two separate entities to represent the two separate people (as opposed to a single, quantified proposition). In addition, mental models appear to represent spatial relations analogically (Bryant, Tversky, & Franklin, 1992; Glenberg, Meyer, & Lindem, 1987; Morrow, Greenspan & Bower, 1987). These relatively modest claims are a far cry, however, from the claim that "whatever information is in the real situation is also in the mental model."

Part of the confusion may be due to failure to make a distinction between inferences and information that is implicit in a representation. By their very nature, in a propositional representation, information either is encoded directly (each relation corresponding to a proposition) or must be derived through the application of rules of inference. On the other hand, the very nature of an analogical representation is that some information may be implicit in the representation. As an example, consider a description of four sticks, A, B, C, and D. The description states *B is taller than A, C is taller than B,* and *D is taller than C.* A propositional description of the text, allowing only minimal inferences for local coherence, would consist of four propositions corresponding to the four relations. Other information, such as the fact that D is taller than A, would have to be inferred using the knowledge that 'taller than' is a transitive relation. Furthermore, it would seem that at least two such inferences would have to be made (D is taller than B, because D is taller than C and C is taller than B; D is taller than A because D is taller than B and B is taller than A).

If height is represented analogically, however, then the information that D is taller than A does not require multiple application of rules of transitivity; it arises from a single comparison of the (analogical) representation of D to the (analogical) representation of A. Given such an analogical representation, a great variety of relations are readily available by application of simple comparison procedures. Thus mental models are full representations only in the sense that relations can be easily computed along any dimension represented analogically. Not all aspects of the mental model need be analogical, however, and certainly there is no claim that all possible components of the situation are represented in the model. Clearly, the burden is on the mental model theorist to specify exactly what information is represented analogically and how these comparison processes occur. We have tried to do just that in the description of our simulation.

In light of these distinctions, consider a prediction attributed by McKoon and Ratcliff to mental model theory. "A mental model for a text such as *the actress fell from the fourteenth story* should include the inference that she died. It would not be reasonable, from the mental model point of view, to leave her suspended in mid air." If, in fact, mental models were a complete representation of a real situation, then it might be reasonable to infer from the representation that the actress would die. However, it seems ludicrous to demand this of mental models. Given the brief segment of text, a mental model would include a representation corresponding to the actress and one corresponding to the fourteenth floor. If the model represents spatial relations analogically, then the actress would be (in the analogical representational medium) below the fourteenth floor. However, there is nothing in mental model theory to suggest that readers will necessarily fill in the rest of the details and have the actress plunge to her death. If the building is pyramidal in shape, she may crash the patio party being held on the thirteenth floor; if the building is an upscale apartment building, she may fall into a swimming pool. If she has been well equipped (perhaps by Ian Fleming's Q), she just may have a miniature parachute in her belt. Given these possibilities, it seems unlikely that a reader would attempt to fill in all the details before obtaining further information from the text. Note that all these potential outcomes are consistent with the mental model derived from the text, just as the fact that the actress is below the fourteenth floor is consistent with the mental model. Nonetheless, none of the outcomes need be inferred. Thus, McKoon, Ratcliff, and Seifert's (1989) data demonstrating that most people do not completely infer the actress's death is consistent with both the minimalist and mental model hypotheses.

If people do not automatically infer outcomes such as the death of the actress, why do they bother to construct mental models? Mental models allow the easy inference that the actress will die, if one is asked to infer what is likely to happen. Similarly, if the text continues with *She died instantly,* the mental model is useful in understanding how that could have come about.

Our second disagreement with McKoon and Ratcliff (1992) concerns Experiment 5 in their report. The experiment challenges the mental model interpretation of the results reported by Glenberg, Meyer, and Lindem (1987). On the mental model account, the target word (e.g., *sweatshirt* in Table 1) is highly activated in the associated condition because a representation of the target is attached to the foregrounded representation of the main actor. McKoon and Ratcliff propose that the target is highly activated because the associated construction confers salience on the proposition encoding the target. That is, by virtue of being associated with the main actor, John, the proposition encoding the target, sweatshirt, is treated as more important than if it had not been associated with the actor.

We believe that the salience account is subject to several weaknesses, which we address in turn. These weaknesses are that the account is vague, that some specifications of the account are consistent with mental model theory, and that both old data and new data indicate that the salience account of the Glenberg, Meyer, and Lindem (1987) data is wrong.

Perhaps the primary weakness of the salience account is that McKoon and Ratcliff do not specify the source of salience. How is it that one component of a text takes on added salience? One possibility is that it arises from different grammatical or propositional structures. That is, a particular construction (e.g., a cleft sentence) confers salience much as a grammatical construction can signal what is to be foregrounded. Whereas this may well be the case in general, it cannot account for the Glenberg, Meyer, and Lindem (1987) results, because the associated–dissociated variable preserves grammatical and propositional structure. Another possibility is that salience is conferred by the context. That is, the salience of a proposition, its importance in the discourse, depends on the situation in which the proposition is embedded. This interpretation, however, is virtually equivalent to the mental model account. In terms of our simulation, whether a pointer remains in the mental model (and is thereby foregrounded) depends on its role in the overall situation.

In any event, the salience account cannot be universal. In some situations, dissociating an actor with an object will make that object potentially more important (salient) than associating the two. For example, if an executive is carrying a briefcase full of money, it may be more important if he forgets the briefcase at the restaurant (thereby dissociating the briefcase from the executive) than if he takes the briefcase from the restaurant.

Several pieces of data are contrary to the salience account. First, consider data from Glenberg, Meyer, and Lindem (1987) illustrated in Figure 1. If the target has salience by virtue of being associated with the main actor, we might expect faster responding to the associated target than the dissociated target immediately after reading the critical sentence. As is evident from Figure 1, this is not the case. Nonetheless, one could argue that the very fast responding immediately after the criticial sentence reflects a floor effect, or is the result of recent access to a lexical representation of the target. Thus, in fairness to the salience account, these data may not be definitive.

McKoon and Ratcliff attempt to test the mental model and salience accounts by adding a second target (which we will refer to as the MR target) to the texts used by Glenberg, Meyer, and Lindem (1987). The MR target is described by McKoon and Ratcliff as a location for the Glenberg et al. target noun (which we will refer to as the GML target). For example, McKoon and Ratcliff modified the text in Table 1 so that the associated critical sentence was "After doing a few warm up exercises, he put on a sweatshirt *from the laundry and went jogging*. The modified dissociated sentence indicated *he put his sweatshirt in the laundry and went jogging*. In both cases, *laundry* is the MR target (see Table V).

According to McKoon and Ratcliff, the salience interpretation predicts fast responding to both the MR target and the GML target in the associated condition. The reasoning is that associating the GML target to the main actor confers salience on the proposition representing the relation between the GML and MR targets. Thus, the associated–dissociated variable should affect responding to both the GML target and the MR target.

TABLE V
Example Text from Glenberg and Mathew (1992)

	Laundry
Version A	John was preparing for a marathon in August. After doing a few warm-up exercises, he put on a sweatshirt from the laundry and went jogging.
Version B	John was preparing for a marathon in August. After doing a few warm-up exercises, he put his sweatshirt in the laundry and went jogging.
Which version?	A or B

The data reported in McKoon and Ratcliff are quite clear. The associated–dissociated variable had a large effect on responding to the GML target (verifying its occurrence in the text was faster in the associated condition by about 66 ms) and an equally large effect on responding to the MR target.

As it turns out, these data cannot be taken as evidence against the mental model account, because they are consistent with an interpretation of salience derived from our simulation. First, consider the situation described by the modified texts used in the McKoon and Ratcliff experiment. In the associated condition, the GML target and the main actor are attached and move away from the MR target. In the dissociated condition, the main actor and the GML target are separate, and the main actor moves away from both the GML target and the MR target. According to our mental model account, the GML target should be responded to more quickly in the associated case than in the dissociated case. The prediction is not so clear for the MR target. If responding is based solely on a mental model of the situation, then to the extent that the MR target is not represented in the mental model of either the associated or the dissociated condition, responding to the MR target should not be affected by the associated–dissociated variable. However, responding (deciding that a word occurred in the text) may be controlled by multiple levels of representation, such as a mental model representation and a textual representation. For example, entities in a mental model may activate propositions associated with the entities. In fact, we used this sort of mechanism in simulating the McNamara et al. (1992) findings. Thus, in the associated condition, when the GML target is in the mental model, it may activate the proposition encoding the fact that the GML target was encountered at the location of the MR target, and thus the MR target will also be activated. When the GML target is not in the mental model, the proposition relating the GML and MR targets will be less activated, and responding to both will be slower. If this reasoning is correct, responding to the MR target (and the GML target) should be affected by the associated–dissociated variable—the same prediction as that derived from the salience account.

Fortunately, we (Glenberg & Matthew, 1992) have data that directly test the McKoon and Ratcliff account that association with a main actor confers salience on both the GML and the MR targets. Subjects received pairs of two-sentence texts. One member of the pair consisted of the setting sentence and the modified associated sentence including both the GML and MR targets (see Table V). The other member of the pair consisted of the setting sentence and the modified dissociated sentence. One word (either the GML target or the MR target) was identified as a critical word for the pair of texts and was printed in boldface above the pair of texts. The subject's task was to judge whether the critical word was more important (salient) in the associated text or the dissociated text.

The major question was whether association with the main actor confers salience on the GML and the MR targets. First, however, it should be noted that subjects were very reliable in their judgments about the version in which the target was most salient. For each pair of texts, for half the subjects the associated member of the pair occurred first, and for the other half of the subjects the dissociated member of the pair appeared first. This counterbalancing precaution gave us a way to check on reliability. For each pair of texts we calculated four scores. For the GML target we obtained (1) the frequency with which the associated condition was chosen as conferring the greater salience when the associated condition was presented first, and (2) the frequency with which the associated condition was chosen as conferring the greater salience when the dissociated condition was presented first. We obtained the analogous scores for the MR target. If subjects are reliably judging salience, then the two GML scores should be significantly correlated, and the two MR scores should be correlated. On the other hand, if subjects cannot judge salience, or if their judgments are influenced by irrelevant variables such as order of presentation of the members of the pairs, then the correlations should be low. In fact, the correlation for the GML target, .71, and the correlation for the MR target. .59, were both significant beyond the .01 level.

Given that subjects can reliably judge salience, is that judgment affected by the associated–dissociated variable? Subjects judged the GML target to be more salient in the associated condition 58% of the time. This is reliably greater than chance (50% given the forced choice response), by both subjects [$t(23 = 3.29$] and texts [$t(22) = 3.34$]. However, subjects judged the MR target to be more salient in the associated condition only 40% of the time, which is significantly less than 50% by subjects [$t(23) = -4.41$] and by texts [$t(23) = 2.10$]. Thus, subjects found the MR target to be more salient in the dissociated condition than in the associated condition.

In summary, subjects can reliably judge salience. Also, salience is (weakly) related to the associated–dissociation variable for the GML word, but the relation is reversed for the MR word. Thus, contrary to the conclusion reached by McKoon and Ratcliff, it is unlikely that salience underlies the effect of the associated–dissociated variable on responding to the MR target.

VI. A MENTAL MODEL INTERPRETATION OF OTHER RESEARCH ON MEMORY FOR CONNECTED DISCOURSE

We have been focusing on the role of mental models in comprehension. We do not mean to imply, however, that other representational formalisms play little or no role. In fact, we think that mental models are but one (albeit important) actor in a complex play. Here we discuss the role of mental models in relation to long-term knowledge structures (e.g., scripts and frames) and causal chains.

A. Long-Term Knowledge and Mental Models

Our current simulation has little long-term knowledge (the exception being procedures for interpreting propositions as directions for updating the mental models), so we are forced to hand-code aspects of meaning such as animacy, gender, and so on. Also, the simulation does not represent anything corresponding to structured knowledge, such as the order of events at a birthday party, the components of a room, or the workings of an automobile. We do not claim that this type of knowledge is not needed for comprehension, only that we can simulate some aspects of comprehension without providing a serious treatment of knowledge structures. Nonetheless, we believe that mental models and long-term knowledge interact in important ways.

Some of the best evidence for the interaction of models and knowledge comes from Sanford and Garrod (1981). Consider the following text (taken from Sanford & Garrod, 1981).

Fred was being questioned (by a lawyer).
He had been accused of murder.
The lawyer was trying to prove his innocence.

Two variables of interest were the title of the text ("In Court" or "Telling a Lie") and whether or not the phrase in parentheses was presented. The dependent measure was time to read the third sentence containing the anaphoric phrase *The lawyer*. When the title is "In Court," Sanford and Garrod argue that long-term knowledge of courtroom procedure is activated, and that part of this knowledge is that lawyers do the questioning in court. Thus, processing the anaphor (the lawyer) should be relatively easy whether the antecedent is stated explicitly in the first sentence or not. In fact this is what they found: time to read the third sentence was fast and did not vary with explicit mention of the antecedent. On the other hand, when the title is "Telling a Lie," it is less likely that any activated long-term knowledge will include information about lawyers. Thus, processing the anaphor should be relatively difficult when the antecedent is not explicitly mentioned in the first sentence. Again, this is just what they found: reading was faster when the antecedent was explicitly mentioned in the first sentence compared to when it was not mentioned.

Long-term knowledge contributes to the maintenance of mental models in other ways, too. In our view, mental models are constructed in a spatial medium. To construct models for nonspatial domains, comprehenders must make some sort of assignment to the spatial dimensions. Thus, when reading about a temporal sequence, we use the left–right spatial dimension to represent temporal order (or the top–bottom dimension when dealing with flow charts). One component of long-term domain knowledge might be standard assignments of domain-relevant dimensions to spatial dimensions.

Another component of long-term knowledge needed for the control of mental models is information about the permissible transformations along a dimension. Thus (except in science fiction) the direction of causation along the temporal dimension is always one-way. Also, the temporal dimension is transitive, in that if Event A occurs before Event B and Event B occurs before Event C, then Event A must have occurred before Event C. In contrast, when representing social relations (e.g., degree of friendship), there is no guarantee of transitivity. Thus domain knowledge will constrain the types of manipulations permissible (or at least probable) in the model and the types of inferences that can (should) be drawn.

B. Causal Chains and Mental Models

One successful approach to story understanding is based on causal chain analysis (e.g., Trabasso & van den Broek, 1985). For each statement in a story, one determines its causes (considering the content of the story), and the various statements are linked together on the assumption of causal transitivity. In this type of analysis, two measures are important. The first is whether or not a statement is on the causal chain. That is, is the statement on a continuous path that can be constructed from causal relations emanating from setting statements to final, goal-attainment statements? The second measure is the causal connectivity of a statement, defined as the total number of causal antecedents and consequents of a particular statement. Trabasso and van den Broek (1985) demonstrated that these two measures accounted for a substantial proportion of variance in story recall, summarization, and judged importance of events within the story. Van den Broek and Trabasso (1986) examined the statements included in summaries of stories and compared predictions derived from the causal analysis approach and a hierarchical analysis of goals. Changes in the hierarchical level affected inclusion of a statement in a summary, but only when the change in hierarchical level was accompanied by a change in causal status of the statement.

Causal analyses are based on application (by the researcher) of a set of procedures (van den Broek & Trabasso, 1986). First, a context or set of circumstances is inferred. Next, subsequent statements are connected by causal inferences. These inferences make use of naive theories of physical and psychological causation. An event A is inferred to be the cause of B if (in the circumstances) if A had not occurred, B would not have occurred. Given this definition, many of the relations are perhaps better conceptualized as enablement (A enables or sets the conditions for B to occur) than causal. In any event, this reasoning process must be executed for all pairs of events, because a given event may have multiple causes or enablements.

Although causal analysis provides an impressive account of some aspects of the data, it cannot be a serious theory of the processes by which a causal structure is created by the comprehender. Because of time and capacity constraints, it is unlikely that a reader would compare each newly read statement with every other statement to determine its causal antecedents. Nonetheless, causal analysis is able to predict the data, and it corresponds to our intuitions that we do often apprehend the causes of events in narratives.

Mental model theory is a useful adjunct to causal analysis in several respects. First, mental models provide the substrate for the application of naive theories of causation. Constructing and manipulating a model in which the spatial dimensions are assigned to domain-relevant dimensions is a way of deriving predictions from theories and reasoning about the postulates of the theory (Johnson-Laird et al., 1989). Second, the mental model provides the context in which the reasoning progresses. Third, and perhaps most importantly, the mental model provides psychologically reasonable constraints on the reasoning process. Not all pairs of statements can be examined for causal connections. Which ones are examined? At least initially, those corresponding to elements in the model. Thus, each new text statement is interpreted as an instruction for updating the model. The new statement is likely to refer to elements in the model, and thus those elements enable the operations specified by the statements. To the extent that an element in the mental model is referred to often, it will remain in the model, it will enable many actions, and it will be perceived as central to the development of the story.

VII. CONCLUSIONS

Mental model accounts have been proposed as explanations of a cluster of experimental results that suggested the use of analogical mental operations. These accounts differ in their details and level of specificity, and we do not claim that the version of mental models we have presented is in complete agreement with any other theorist's; rather, we aimed to present our current thinking on the subject specifically enough to be useful to the theoretically minded reader. To summarize our view, mental models are spatially organized collections of representational elements that point to information in LTS. Mental models operate in the visual–spatial sketchpad of working memory and are analogical in the sense that the distance separating entities is meaningful for the processes that operate on the mental model. Our computer simulation of memory incorporates mental model operations, combined with a three-way division of resources and general capacity constraints in the form of a limited supply of activation. These features of our model give rise to performance resembling that obtained in various studies of memory, comprehension, and the role of pictures in comprehension.

Responding to criticisms highlights differences between competing accounts; consequently, central aspects of theories become more salient and more articulated. In response to the propositional view advanced by Rips (1986), we agree that propositional reasoning plays an important role in text comprehension and many other cognitive processes. However, we contend that the additional construct of the mental model provides the most useful explanation of results demonstrating that comprehenders' performance is influenced by the structure of the situation being described. This influence is observed not only for spatial descriptions, but also when subjects perform certain kinds of reasoning problems (Johnson-Laird et al., 1989). In a separate criticism, McKoon and Ratcliff (1992) argued for a minimalist approach, in which readers draw only those inferences necessary for immediate textual coherence. We have argued that their view cannot account for the results of Glenberg, Meyer, and Lindem (1987) and the follow-up Glenberg and Matthew (1992) study. Rather than taking an absolute minimalist or constructivist stance, we believe that the evidence is convincing that mental models are used in comprehension, but that their use is not automatic and depends on a number of factors. In particular, the comprehender must possess adequate domain knowledge to be able to represent the situation in terms of spatially arrayed basic elements and to operate appropriately on those elements when placed in the mental model.

The question of when mental models are employed is a matter of ongoing research. The success of our computer simulation suggests an exciting prospect: the use of mental models may be lawfully related to capacity limitations and structural properties of memory. That is, it may be possible to show that, under some circumstances, the combined use of mental models and propositional reasoning is more efficient than propositional reasoning alone for processing information. In other situations, mental models alone may support optimal cognition. The specification of the mechanisms that make this true, and of the circumstances that induce the use of mental models, is an appropriate goal for future investigations.

ACKNOWLEDGMENTS

Preparation of this chapter was funded in part by an Air Force Office of Scientific Research grant (89-0367) to Arthur Glenberg. The following students contributed substantially to the development of the simulation model discussed in the chapter: Kevin Cherkauer, Jeffrey Horvath, Matthew Koehler, and Sean Selitrennikoff.

REFERENCES

Baddeley, A. (1990). *Human memory*. Boston: Allyn & Bacon.

Bransford, J. D., Barclay, J. R., & Franks, J. J. (1972). Sentence memory: A constructive versus interpretive approach. *Cognitive Psychology, 3*, 193–209.

Bryant, D. J., Tversky, B., & Franklin, N. (1992). Internal and external spatial frameworks for representing described schemes. *Journal of Memory and Language, 31*, 74–98.

Garnham, A. (1981). Mental models as representations of text. *Memory & Cognition, 9*, 560–565.

Gernsbacher, M. A., Varner, K. R., & Faust, M. E. (1990). Investigating general comprehension skill. *Journal of Experimental Psychology: Learning, Memory, and Cognition, 16*, 430–445.

Glenberg, A. M., Bradley, M. M., Kraus, T. A., & Renzaglia, G. J. (1983). Studies of the long-term recency effect: Support for a contextually guided retrieval hypothesis. *Journal of Experimental Psychology: Learning, Memory, and Cognition, 9*, 231–255.

Glenberg, A. M., & Langston, W. E. (1992). Comprehension of illustrated text: Pictures help to build mental models. *Journal of Memory and Language, 31*, 129–151.

Glenberg, A. M., & Mathew S. (1992). When minimalism is not enough: Mental models in reading comprehension. *PSYCOLOQUY. 92.3.64. reading-inference*.

Glenberg, A. M., Meyer, M., & Lindem, K. (1987). Mental models contribute to foregrounding during text comprehension. *Journal of Memory and Language, 26*, 69–83.

Glenberg, A. M., Sanocki, T., Epstein, W., & Morris, C. (1987). Enhancing calibration of comprehension. *Journal of Experimental Psychology: General, 116*, 119–136.

Hintzman, D. L. (1986). "Schema abstraction" in a multiple-trace memory model. *Psychological Review, 93*, 411–428.

Johnson-Laird, P. N. (1983). *Mental models*. Cambridge, MA: Harvard University Press.

Johnson-Laird, P. N., Byrne, R. M. S., & Tabossi, P. (1989). Reasoning by model: The case of multiple quantification. *Psychological Review, 96*, 658–673.

Mani, K., & Johnson-Laird, P. N. (1982). The mental representation of spatial descriptions. *Memory & Cognition, 10*, 181–187.

McKoon, G., & Ratcliff, R. (1992). Inference during reading. *Psychological Review, 99*, 440–466.

McKoon, G., Ratcliff, R., & Seifert, C. (1989). Making the connection: Generalized structures in story understanding. *Journal of Memory and Language, 28*, 711–734.

McNamara, T. P., Halpin, J. A., & Hardy, J. K. (1992). Spatial and temporal contributions to the structure of spatial memory. *Journal of Experimental Psychology: Learning, Memory and Cognition, 18*, 555–564.

McNamara, T. P., Miller, D. C., & Bransford, J. D. (in press). Mental models and reading comprehension. In P. D. Pearson, R. Barr, M. Kamil, & P. Mosenthal (Eds.), *Handbook of reading research* (Vol. 2). New York: Longman.

Morrow, D. G., Greenspan, S. L., & Bower, G. H. (1987). Accessibility and situation models in narrative comprehension. *Journal of Memory and Language, 26,* 165–187.

O'Brien, E. J., Plewes, P. S., & Albrecht, J. E. (1990). Antecedent retrieval processes. *Journal of Experimental Psychology: Learning, Memory, and Cognition, 16,* 241–249.

Rips, L. J. (1986). Mental muddles. In M. Brand & R. M. Hornish (Eds.), *The representation of knowledge and beliefs.* Tucson: University of Arizona Press.

Sanford, A. J., & Garrod, S. C. (1981). *Understanding written language.* Chichester: Wiley.

Trabasso, T., & van den Broek, P. (1985). Causal thinking and the representation of narrative events. *Journal of Memory and Language, 24,* 612–630.

van den Broek, P., & Trabasso, T. (1986). Causal networks versus goal hierarchies in summarizing text. *Discourse Processes, 9,* 1–15.

van Dijk, T. A., & Kintsch, W. (1983). *Strategies of discourse comprehension.* New York: Academic Press.

Watkins, M. J., & Peynircioglu, Z. F. (1990). The revelation effect: When disguising test items induces recognition. *Journal of Experimental Psychology: Learning, Memory, and Cognition, 16,* 1012–1020.

Watkins, O. C., & Watkins, M. J. (1975). Build-up of proactive inhibition as a cue–overload effect. *Journal of Experimental Psychology: Human Learning and Memory, 1,* 442–452.

CHAPTER 19

UNDERSTANDING EXPOSITORY TEXT
BUILDING MENTAL STRUCTURES TO INDUCE INSIGHTS

BRUCE K. BRITTON

I. INTRODUCTION

The basic ideas of this chapter are simple. Expository texts are intended to build a structure in the readers' mind (Gernsbacher, 1990). For that structure to be the correct structure, that is, the one the author intends, the author must provide for two kinds of things in the text: (a) the instructions that the reader will need for building the structure, and (b) the building materials (i.e., concepts and propositions) that the reader needs as content elements for the intended structure. Some of these instructions and building materials have to be included in the text itself, while for others it may be sufficient for the text to refer the reader to his prior knowledge.

On the reader's side, he or she must (1) decode any instructions in the text that he needs to build the structure, and execute the instructions; (2) add any structure building instructions he needs that are not provided by the author; (3) use as building materials the concepts and propositions provided by the text; (4) retrieve any referred-to prior knowledge concepts and propositions, and use them in building the structure; and (5) add any building materials he needs that are not provided by the author. If the author has included what the reader needs, and the reader uses it correctly and completely, then the structure intended by the author will be created in the reader's mind.

The focus of this chapter is on the structure building instructions: both those that the author includes in the text, and those instructions that the reader must add because they have not been provided explicitly by the author. We focus on the instructions because they are important but have been relatively neglected.

To illustrate these ideas, we use a simple representation of the structure intended for the reader's mind, as a set of nodes and connecting links like that shown schematically in Figure 1. For now, consider each node to be something

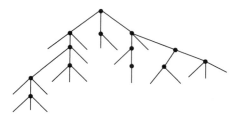

FIG. 1   Schematic node-link structures for representing mental structures produced by text.

about the size of a sentence. The sentences shown in Table I (from Christensen, 1967) can be arranged in a structure like that in Figure 1. The topmost node is *the essence of the religious spirit*. Subordinate to it are four effects of the religious spirit. This can be seen more clearly if we physically rearrange the paragraph on the page and number its sentences, as shown in Table II. Further clarification of the intended structure is provided by the diagram in Figure 2.

Considering each sentence as a node is a relatively coarse grain size, in that it leaves out some information that the author probably intended to be included in the mental structure; this information we see within each of the four effects, where the author has included some subordinate materials. We could unpack each sentence into a more complex set of nodes and links of its own and imagine a series of more detailed and complete versions of Figure 2. Or we could move in the opposite direction, toward generality, and consider each paragraph as a single node, or each section, chapter, and so on, and diagram those. This imagined series of diagrams, increasing in depth of detail in one direction and, in the other direction, decreasing in detail but increasing in generality, corresponds to a property of expository structures that turns out to be quite important: We can zoom in on any node to reveal its internal structure, or zoom out on any node-link structure to unitize the whole structure into a single node, which can then enter into relations with other nodes as a single unit. One of most striking phenomenological consequences of this is that the expositor, if he is a subject matter expert, can expand on his knowledge structures at almost any level of detail, from the 10 second version called for by an airline seatmate, to the 12 minute version for the professional convention, to the 50 minute class lecture, all the way up to the book length version. The

TABLE I
Thompson Text (From Christensen, 1967)

This is the essence of the religious spirit—the sense of power, beauty, greatness, truth infinitely beyond one's own reach, but infinitely to be aspired to. It invests men with pride in a purpose and with humility in accomplishment. It is the source of all true tolerance, for in its light all men see other men as they see themselves, as being capable of being more than they are, and yet falling short, inevitably, of what they can imagine human opportunities to be. It is the supporter of human dignity and pride and the dissolver of vanity. And it is the very creator of the scientific spirit; for without the aspiration to understand and control the miracle of life, no man would have sweated in a laboratory or tortured his brain in the exquisite search after truth.

Dorothy Thompson

TABLE II
Rearranged Thompson Text

---

1. This is the essence of the religious spirit—the sense of power, beauty, greatness, truth
    infinitely beyond one's own reach, but infinitely to be aspired to.
    2.1 It invests men with pride in a purpose and with humility in accomplishment.
    2.2 It is the source of all true tolerance, for in its light all men see other men as they see
         themselves, as being capable of being more than they are, and yet falling short,
         inevitably, of what they can imagine human opportunities to be.
    2.3 It is the supporter of human dignity and pride and the dissolver of vanity.
    2.4 And it is the very creator of the scientific spirit; for without the aspiration to
         understand and control the miracle of life, no man would have sweated in a laboratory
         or tortured his brain in the exquisite search after truth.
                                        Dorothy Thompson

---

reason these shifts of level of generality are so easy for the expositor, I shall argue, is because a grammar of exposition governs them. But more on that later.

To fill out the concept of these structures, Tables III and IV show another example of a text and its node-link structure. Here it is the multiple levels of increasing subordination that are evident, as contrasted with the single level of subordination in Table I.

Where are the "instructions" which are the focus of this chapter? In Table I, the top level of instructions is in the pronouns: It . . . It . . . It . . . It. Each of these pronouns, like all pronouns, issues an instruction to the reader to find the referent intended by the author; if he correctly carries out these instructions, then the intended structure can be established; otherwise it cannot. Another instruction is expressed by the parallelism in form of sentences 2.1–2.4 (Table II), which constitutes an instruction to the reader to take each of the sentences in the same way. Since no new theme is introduced in the subject position in any of sentences 2.1–2.4, the same 'it' is inferred to be the theme

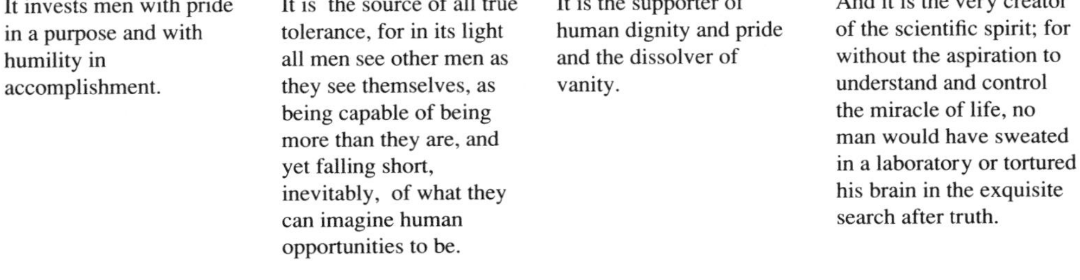

FIG. 2   Hypothetical mental structure for the text of Tables I and II.

TABLE III
Bronowski Text

The process of learning is essential to our lives. All higher animals seek it deliberately. They
are inquisitive and they experiment. An experiment is a sort of harmless trial run of some
action which we shall have to make in the real world; and this whether it is made in the
laboratory by scientists or by fox-cubs outside their earth. The scientist experiments and the
cub plays; both are learning to correct their errors of judgment in a setting in which errors
are not fatal. Perhaps this is what gives them both their air of happiness and freedom in these
activities (Bronowski, 1966, p. 111).

of all of them. The conjunction *and* in 2.4 is an additional but in this case
retrospective instruction with the same message; since it also instructs the
reader that it is at the end of the series, it may serve to put readers back on
the track who earlier misinterpreted the relations of these sentences. (Within
each sentence, conventional linguistic signals from standard sentence grammar
are syntactic instructions for constructing a mental structure for that sentence;
such sentence grammar instructions will not be considered further here, since
they are already reasonably well understood.)

It is important to notice that features of an expository text can serve as
structure building instructions, but detecting and correctly decoding the instructions is optional for the reader, and obeying the instructions once decoded is
also optional. This makes it possible that the instructions embedded in expository text may not be detected; and if detected, they may not be decoded
correctly; and if decoded correctly, they are unable to enforce obedience—the
reader is free to ignore them. This is partly because the instructions are often
expressed indirectly; but even if they were expressed directly, the reader would
have the option of ignoring them. The consequence is that the mental structures
that readers derive from a text often will be incomplete or incorrect, when
compared to the structure intended by the author.

It is possible easily to see the importance of detecting and decoding the
instructions in expository text by considering some possible revisions of any
text in which the instructions are progressively obscured. For example, we
could remove the parallelism of the text in Table I and leave out or change
some of the *its*, as shown in Table V. This obscures the instructions that the

TABLE IV
Bronowski Text Rearranged

1   The process of learning is essential to our lives.
 2   All higher animals seek it deliberately.
  3   They are inquisitive and they experiment.
   4   An experiment is a sort of harmless trial run of some action which we shall have
       to make in the real world; and this whether it is made in the laboratory by
       scientists or by fox-cubs outside their earth.
   5   The scientist experiments and the cub plays; both are learning to correct their
       errors of judgment in a setting in which errors are not fatal.
   6   Perhaps this is what gives them both their air of happiness and freedom in
       these activities.
                    (Bronowski, 1966, p. 111).

Table V
Edited Thompson Text

This is the essence of the religious spirit—the sense of power, beauty, greatness, truth infinitely
beyond one's own reach, but infinitely to be aspired to. Men are invested with pride in a
purpose and with humility in accomplishment. All tolerance has its source in it, for in its light
all men see other men as they see themselves, as being capable of being more than they are,
and yet falling short, inevitably, of what they can imagine human opportunities to be. Human
dignity and pride and the dissolving of vanity; all these are supported. And the very creator
of the scientific spirit is to be found there, for without the aspiration to understand and
control the miracle of life, no man would have sweated in a laboratory or tortured his brain in
the exquisite search after truth.

after Dorothy Thompson

---

reader needs to create a correct and complete representation. Under these circumstances the probability of constructing a complete and correct representation will decrease.

The generality of these notions over expository text can be seen by considering that between any sentence whatever and its successor there is some relation, that the relation may not only be subordinate as in Tables I and III, but also often has a specific character, nameable by a specific term, such as the four effects of Figure 2. The reader must either identify that relation and incorporate it correctly into his representation, or else not. Correct identification of the intended relation depends on the reader either using instructions provided by the author or inferring the intended relation on his own. Failure to identify the relation, or incorrect identification, will lead to an incomplete or incorrect representation of the text.

This applies not only to sentences, but also to larger units of the text. For example, between any paragraph and its successor, there is some relation—co-ordinate, subordinate, and/or specific—and that relation must either be correctly identified or not, depending on using the author's instructions or making inferences, with the outcome having consequences for the correctness and completeness of the reader's representation. It is the same for all units above paragraph size—sections, chapters, and so on—each unit has its main ideas, and the main ideas of each section are intended to be related to the main ideas of other sections, but the relation can either be constructed correctly by the reader or not.

To summarize, in an expository situation what we have is a structure of ideas and a set of sentences. The reader gets only the sentences, but what we want him to get is the structure of ideas. Whether he gets the right structure of ideas or not depends largely on what instructions the author has put in the sentences, and also on what the reader does with the instructions: If the author has put the instructions that the reader needs in the sentences, and the reader does what he is supposed to do with them, then he will get the intended structure of ideas. But if the author leaves out instructions that the reader needs, then the reader may get the wrong ideas, or an incomplete one, or none at all.

The upshot of this section of the chapter is that the reader of an expository text will often have difficulty following the author of an expository text, and most of the rest of this paper is an extended disquisition on the psycholinguistics of following the author: the linguistic features that affect the probability of following, the psychological processing activities that are involved, and the consequences for the reader's mental representation.

II. THE GRAMMAR OF EXPOSITION

The author of an expository text makes certain characteristic moves which push the discourse along. Considering these moves in the abstract, each move instructs the reader to treat the present section of the discourse differently than the section before the move, or else he will build an incomplete or incorrect representation. That is, if the author enlarges upon subtopic A, but then when he moves on to enlarge upon subtopic B, the reader continues to build his mental structure as if the author were still enlarging upon subtopic A, then the reader has failed to follow the author from A to B, and an incomplete or incorrect representation will result. In this case, materials that the author intended to be filed under subtopic B will instead have been incorrectly filed under subtopic A. Or if the author makes a summary statement of subtopic A, but the reader thinks that that statement is the beginning of subtopic B and builds his mental structure accordingly, then an incorrect representation will result, with the statement filed in subtopic B instead of subtopic A (Givón, 1992). Obviously, it is important that the moves that are made by the author are evident to the reader, so the reader can construct the intended mental representation.

A large part of the responsibility for making the author's moves evident is carried by a standard grammar of exposition, to be described in this section. I introduce this grammar for heuristic purposes—the same purposes for which syntactic grammars (Chomsky, 1957) and story grammars (Rumelhart, 1975) were introduced. Like those grammars, we currently make no claim to completeness, formal sufficiency, or full coverage for naturally occurring texts, but we issue a promissory note that the grammar of exposition will show heuristic value for understanding expository texts.

The grammar of exposition can be formulated as a set of rules that govern the form of most expositions. The rules are used (1) by the author to construct his exposition, and (2) by the reader to parse it. The grammar of exposition is signaled in the text in a way that is analogous to sentence and story grammars. That is, sentence and story grammars are often signaled by linguistic elements that provide instructions to the reader about the structure of the representation to be constructed for each sentence or for each story, respectively. In the same way, the grammar of exposition can be signaled by elements that provide instructions to the reader about the structure that relates expository sentences to each other, as well as the expository relations of larger units of the discourse: arguments, examples, paragraphs, sections, and so on. It is important to note that while the grammar of exposition can be represented at the surface level of the text by specific signals that provide clues that can be used to parse the exposition, nevertheless, just as with sentence and story grammars, the signals can often be absent, partial, ambiguous, or hard to identify, and their use depends importantly on the reader's implicit knowledge of the grammatical rules.

The basic expository move is to expand on the topic of the discourse, to enlarge on it, to expound, expose, develop, to dilate on and amplify it. This move occurs at all levels of an expository text, from the topmost level where the topic to be enlarged on is the overall subject of the text, as perhaps expressed in its title; to the middle levels, where the topic to be enlarged on is the subject of a subsection of the text, as expressed perhaps in a heading; down to the lowest level, where the topic to be enlarged on is the newly introduced part of the previous sentence.

We shall call this basic expository move EXPAND. [Upper case is used to designate moves of the expository grammar, and the imperative form of the verb is used as a reminder (1) that the grammar describes instructions that are issued by the author when he is writing the text, and (2) that the instructions issued by the author are calls upon the reader to carry out corresponding actions.]

Four other moves are required at the top level of the grammar: ENLARGE-ON, MOVE-ON, UNITIZE, and STOP. Of these, ENLARGE-ON is the most common, important, and complex. It is a move of essentially the same kind as EXPAND. (In fact the terms EXPAND and ENLARGE-ON could be interchanged without loss; here I reserve EXPAND for the topmost injunction of exposition, and assign ENLARGE-ON to serve for all the lower levels.)

MOVE-ON often follows ENLARGE-ON; it serves to stop the enlarging-on of any particular subtopic and signals a move to the next subtopic. The most obvious instructions to MOVE-ON are conventional phrases like *moving on to, our next topic is, turning to,* and so on. At the end of each sentence, MOVE-ON is usually signaled by the period; at the paragraph level by the end of the paragraph; at the section level by a new heading; and so on. Special purpose MOVE-ONs can be constructed to signal specific aspects of the move or its destination. Any form of MOVE-ON can be left unsignaled.

UNITIZE can also follow ENLARGE-ON; it reduces toward unity the contents of active memory, after it has been more or less filled up by the enlargement-on of the current topic. For example, UNITIZE can be implemented at the paragraph or section level by a statement of the form: "In summary, the x is caused by Y." UNITIZE can be signaled by any of a variety of linguistic and paralinguistic signals, or it can be unsignaled.

A UNITIZE operation of some type must occur at the end of each sizable discourse unit, simply because active memory cannot contain more than a very modest amount of information. So even at the sentence level, a UNITIZE operation is usually required because most sentences are long enough to more or less fully occupy active memory. Any UNITIZE operation can be guided by instructions from the author or implemented by the reader without instructions. In the extreme case, UNITIZE will operate by default, simply dropping the contents of active memory randomly until there is enough space to handle the next input discourse unit. An example of a more guided UNITIZE occurs when the reader selects the NEW information from the sentence (or paragraph, section, etc.) and drops the rest. Of course, since the author usually wants his reader to create a specific mental structure, he may take some pains to provide instructions to UNITIZE that adequately specify the unit(s) is to be carried over; if followed, these instructions will go a long way to ensure the construction of the intended structure.

Finally, STOP is the move which brings the discourse to an end. Table VI shows these top-level moves. Next we expand on each of them.

A. EXPAND

EXPAND, the basic expository move, is called for when the student does not understand something that the teacher wants him to understand. This triggers an EXPAND of the teacher's knowledge structure. We can imagine this as a process of unfolding, opening out, uncovering, displaying, setting forth, rendering accessible, exposing, spelling out, illustrating, elucidating, illuminating, giving details, and so on. The ultimate limits of EXPAND are either the primitives of the subject matter or the limits of the expositor's knowledge, but usually EXPAND is STOPPED before these limits are reached, either based on the expositor's judgement that he has reached a level adjacent to the student's level, or based on restrictions imposed from outside on the permissible length of the exposition. EXPAND is implemented by a series of ENLARGE-ONs, UNITIZEs, and MOVE-ONs, which may be nested.

B. ENLARGE-ON

Within the ENLARGE-ON operator there are several important parts, shown at the left of Table VI. Of these, the only obligatory part is the NEW information that is to be added by the learner to his existing mental structure. If this is missing, then ENLARGE-ON simply has not occurred: There has been a repetition of previously presented information, or a MOVE-ON, or another text has begun.

But ENLARGE-ON usually also contains some other elements that help the learner to build the mental structure that the author intended. Of these, the most common is the OLD information, which can be placed adjacent to the NEW information to instruct the learner about the location in his existing structure to which he is to attach the NEW information. A signal that specifies which OLD information is relevant at a particular point in a text can be very helpful to a learner who is attempting to build the mental structure that the

TABLE VI
Topmost Levels of Grammar of Exposition

ENLARGE-ON	EXPAND TOPIC		
	MOVE ON	UNITIZE	STOP
Connect OLD info to a node from previous structure	Reinstate earlier node—which one?	Introduce a new node	
Label link of OLD info to previous structure		Relate it to topic or earlier node or a node in working memory	
	ENLARGE-ON	ENLARGE-ON	
Obligatory: Add NEW info			
Label link of NEW info to OLD Node			
ENLARGE-ON UNITIZE	MOVE ON		

author intends; this is because if the learner's existing mental structure for the text has more than one element in it, a genuine question arises as to where the NEW information is to be placed among those existing elements. In such cases the presence of some element of OLD information that is mentioned adjacent to the NEW information can provide a clue as to the location at which to attach the NEW information in the previously existing structure: namely, the location of the mentioned OLD information. For example, if a text contains 26 elements A–Z, and the next sentence refers to a previously mentioned widget and a newly mentioned frammis, attaching it correctly to the structure would be easier with a sentence like *The M's widget is attached to the frammis* than with a sentence lacking any reference to any of the previous elements A–Z.

If the OLD information that is mentioned adjacent to the NEW is identical to an already existing part of the reader's structure, then correctly placing the NEW information will be easy. But often the reference to the OLD in the current section is to only part of the relevant existing structure, or is only in regard to some particular feature, aspect, or facet of it. For example, if X is a topic of the previous text, the next section might be concerned with "the learning of X" and express the NEW idea that it "causes Y." Here the facet of X that is being referred to is its "learning," and this specification must be incorporated in the reader's structure if all is to go well. That is, the reader is intended to know that reference is being made only to a PART-OF X, specifically the "learning" part. Generally, such things as PART-OF can be formulated as labels for links between the currently relevant OLD information and the previous structure. And finally there can be a label for the link between the OLD information and the NEW; such labels are very common within sentences and are commonly expressed there by a relational word like a verb, here the *causes* of *The learning of X causes Y.* When such links are intended between sentences, or between paragraphs, sections, chapters, and so on, the signals can be expressed in a variety of ways, but they are often left out.

So these optional elements of ENLARGE-ON include two kinds of labels: labels for the links between the OLD information and the previous structure, and labels for the links between the OLD and the NEW information. If the author has a specific type of link in mind, specifying the correct label for that link can be very useful to learners who are trying to construct the representation intended by the author; for in cases where the author has a specific link in mind, but does not specify his label, the learner will have to either try to figure out the correct link for himself, or not. If he does try to figure it out, he may succeed at the cost of some resources, or he may come up with the wrong label, leading to an incorrect representation, or he may fail to come up with any label, leading to an incomplete representation.

C. MOVE-ON

MOVE-ON is the mechanism by which the discourse moves to new topics and subtopics. The default form of MOVE-ON is MOVE-DOWN; it occurs when further ENLARGING-ON is intended. In this case, the new node is to be linked to the currently active node. MOVE-DOWN is typically unmarked.

Among the marked forms of MOVE-ON, the most common occurs with the introduction of a new node that is not related to the most recently active node but to a node that is immediately superordinate to it. Examples of this in marked form are in sentences 2.2, 2.3, and 2.4 of Table II. This form we can call MOVE-ACROSS. It can also be marked by phrases such as *Returning to take up the third of our four disjunctions*. But it should be noted that MOVE-ACROSS often goes unmarked by the author and so may be unnoticed by the reader, as might happen in the text of Table V.

Other commonly marked forms of MOVE-ON include: MOVE-UP, which occurs when making reference to nodes that are superordinate to ones superordinate to the last active one, such as *Harking back to our initial theme*; and MOVE-OUT, to nodes not previously mentioned in the discourse, usually either references to prior knowledge that is to be activated, or new information that must be introduced, such as *This brings in an issue not previously considered*. MOVE-ON instructions can quite elaborately specify their destination, as in *Now let us go beyond A, not in the direction of B, but in the direction of C, not toward greater C on the side of X, but to greater C on the side of Y*.

D. UNITIZE

The UNITIZE operator is very important in understanding expository text. It plays several roles. First, it is necessary for dealing with the limitations of active memory capacity, combined with the necessity to read on. At the end of each unit of the text (i.e., each sentence, each paragraph, each section, each chapter, etc.), only a certain amount of the information previously presented can be held in an activated state, and this amount is almost always very much smaller than the information that has been presented up to that point. So there arises the necessity of reducing the information in the direction of unity. The term UNITIZE is intended to indicate the movement toward unity. (I realize it could be easily interpreted to mean reduction all the way to unity, i.e., that only one thing is carried over in an activated state; but I do not intend that.) So the UNITIZE operator is inevitable as long as the learner keeps on reading. This is because the limitations of active memory cannot be dodged. UNITIZATION to deal with active memory limits can be guided by instructions from the author or not.

The second role for UNITIZE is even more important, because it largely determines the hierarchical structures of the reader's representation of the text. In this role, the UNITIZE operator is used to summarize a section of the text, to construct a macrostructural statement of it, to reduce an extended argument to a brief statement of its conclusion, to extract the point of a section of text, or to extract the point of the whole text. We can use the term CHUNKING (Miller, 1956) to refer to this aspect of the UNITIZE operation. In terms of the node-link representation, a zoom-out on a node-link structure is a UNITIZING operation. The operation of UNITIZE is, of course, under the exclusive control of the reader, like all the other operations, but it can be induced by instructions left by the author in the text. Sometimes these instructions can be fairly explicit, as in phrases like *In summary . . . , the point is . . . , the conclusion is,* and others, but most often they are implicit or absent.

We have briefly reviewed the grammar of exposition. Table VII provides some rewrite rules. We now move on to consider some general issues on the nature of the instructions that are used to build the mental structures and then provide some examples to illustrate the ideas.

TABLE VII
Pseudo-grammar of Exposition

EXPOSITION	⟶	TOPIC + EXPANSION
TOPIC	⟶	CONCEPT or PROPOSITION or NODE
NODE	⟶	CONCEPT or PROPOSITION or NODE
EXPANSION	⟶	ENLARGE-ON or MOVE-ON or UNITIZE or STOP
MOVE-ON	⟶	MOVE-DOWN (ENLARGE-ON) or MOVE-UP or MOVE-ACROSS (PAN)
ENLARGE-ON	⟶	Open subfile + insert link to old and name link to old and insert new and insert link to old and name link to old
UNITIZE	⟶	choose randomly or Apply leading edge strategy (Miller & Kintsch, 1980) or spread activation and choose most activated (Kintsch, 1988) or reduce (Turner, Britton, Andraessen, & McCutcheon, in press) or apply macrostructure operator (Kintsch & Van Dijk, 1978) or extract point (Colomb & Williams, 1987) or carry over conclusion or extract theme or insert in situation model

III. THE NATURE OF STRUCTURE BUILDING INSTRUCTIONS

The nature of the processing instructions embedded in expository text can best be understood by likening it to the linguistic notions of speech acts and indirect meaning, and the computational technique of object-oriented programming. The characteristic feature shared by all these notions is that they include both information and actions in the same unit. In the same way, almost any sentence of an expository text can contain both some of the information that the text is about, and also some instructions about what actions the reader should take with that information to insert it properly into his mental representation. This is similar to a speech act, like the judge saying *I sentence Mr. X to 5 years,* in that it contains not only the information that the criminal is sentenced to 5 years, but also constitutes an instruction that can make the serving of the sentence come true in the real world. Specifically, the utterance instructs agents of the judge to carry out certain actions that will implement the sentence. In the same way, an expository text that says *In summary, the point of this section is that x causes y* contains not only information about the relation of x to y, but also constitutes an injunction to the reader to carry out certain actions that, in this case, arrange the information that "x causes y" in a certain relation to other parts of the reader's representation. Of course the reader need not carry out these injunctions, any more than the agents of the judge need necessarily carry out his injunctions, but in both cases there may be undesirable consequences of the failure to do so.

The reader of expository text has an additional obstacle, in that the structure building injunctions of an expository text are most often indirect, rather than direct. Indirect linguistic expressions are ones like *Could you pass me the salt*; they can of course be answered in accordance only with their direct meaning—*Yes, I could pass you the salt*—but the socially skilled will more often answer them by carrying out the indirectly specified action, namely, passing the salt.

In expository texts, the author's instructions are very rarely expressed directly, along the lines of *Please add this idea to the previous idea by the relation caused-by*. Examples of nearly direct injunctions that occur in real texts are instructions to "imagine x" or "think back to section y," but these are not common. The most direct structure-building injunctions that occur commonly in expository texts are phrases that do not contain information about the topic of the text, but only information that can readily be interpreted as an instruction to do something with the accompanying text. The phrase *For example* can be interpreted as an injunction to link what follows to what preceded by the relation "example of." *In summary* and *the third point is* are other phrases of this type. But in many texts such phrases are quite rare; none such appear in Tables I and III, for example.

It will be evident from Tables II and IV and Figure 2 that another way the intended structure can be made quite clear is by various paralinguistic devices, such as the arrangement of text on the page, but these are only common within certain genres, such as instruction manuals. Also usable for this purpose, and much more common, are mixed linguistic-physical signals like punctuation, paragraph indentation, headings and their position, size, color, and so on. But purely linguistic structure building signals may appear to be relatively rare in much expository text. As it turns out though, this is largely an illusion. The illusion is caused partly by the fact that linguistic structure building signals often serve simultaneously as signals and as carriers of text information, with the two functions being difficult to separate and only the informational function being easily accessible to introspection. The illusion is also partly due to the fact that readers have developed procedural habits for dealing with implicit linguistic structure building instructions; these habits are so automatized that they do not normally appear in introspection.

To illustrate these ideas, an extended example of the operation of structure building instructions will be given. It illustrates the grammar of exposition, as well as several other types of explicit and implicit instructions.

A. An Example of Operation of Some Structure Building Instructions

One potent source of highly implicit structure building instructions is the overlap between units of the text. For example, whenever a later sentence contains a content word from an earlier sentence, the reader can use the overlap of the content words to build a structure that links the sentences. Such overlap is a conventional signal that instructs the reader that it is the overlapped node that is being enlarged on and that it is his responsibility to attach the incoming material to that node. For example, consider the title and first sentence of a text, given in (1)–(2).

(1) *The 1965 Air War in North Vietnam.*
(2) *By the beginning of 1965, American officials in both South Vietnam and the U.S. had begun to focus on North Vietnam as the source of the continuing war in South Vietnam.*

The terms *1965, North Vietnam,* and *war* in (2) overlap with the words in (1). Judging from these overlap clues alone, the apparent topic being ENLARGED-ON by (2) is either *1965, North Vietnam,* the *war,* or some combination of these. But how can the reader tell which of these it is? The overlap clues alone are not enough to decide in this case. But they do limit the possibilities. In such cases, the reader can either make a decision on some grounds other than overlap or else defer a decision and read on in the hope that the next sentence(s) will clarify what is being ENLARGED-ON.

We begin by assuming that he reads on. How will he use the information in the next sentence(s) to decide which node of (1) and (2) is being ENLARGED-ON? One way to understand this process is to consider the contributions of various possible next sentences. The next sentences which would most clarify the situation are ones which make clear retrospectively which node was being expanded on in (1) and (2). For example, if the next sentence were (3′a), it would appear that it was *1965* that was being expanded on in (2). If it were (3′b), then North Vietnam would be the subtopic being expanded. But the actual continuation was (3).

(3′) a. *Another thing that happened in the beginning of 1965 was that . . .*
     b. *North Vietnam intended . . .*
(3) *The South Vietnamese army was losing the ground war against North Vietnam.*

This makes it appear that the node being ENLARGED-ON by (3), and (it is retrospectively seen) by (2), is the node for "war," since this node appears as *Air War* in the title, *continuing war* in (2), and *ground war* in (3). (This text appears as the "Principled Revision" in Table VIII.)

Up to this point, we have considered only the overlap clue. We note that the role of overlap as a structure building instruction is difficult to separate introspectively from its role as content, because the same linguistic unit serves simultaneously as explicit informational content readily accessible to introspection, but also an implicit instruction to build a certain structure.

A second class of linguistic features that can play a role as structure building instructions is syntactic in character. For example, the syntactically most prominent word in the title is *war.* Its syntactic prominence comes from its role as the head of the noun phrase; its modification by *1965* and *Air*; and its locative specification by *in North Vietnam* serves to emphasize its status as head. As such, *war* might have been expected to be the topic of the text on syntactic grounds alone. In contrast, consider a title like

(1′) *Air War in the North: 1965*

Here the *1965* has a prominent position syntactically and might lead the reader to expect an ENLARGE-ON of 1965, leading to a likely choice of the first phrase of (2) as the to-be-expanded-on node, and increasing the likelihood of (3′a). (Note that we are here considering the implications of the syntax of

TABLE VIII
The First Two Paragraphs of the Principled Revision

The 1965 Air War in North Vietnam

By the beginning of 1965, American officials in both South Vietnam and the U.S. had begun to focus on North Vietnam as the source of the continuing war in South Vietnam. The South Vietnamese army was losing the ground war against North Vietnam and this caused frustrations among the American officials. The frustrations led to pressure to bomb North Vietnam. The idea of bombing North Vietnam found support among nearly all the American officials. However, the civilian and military officials had serious differences over both the objective and the methods of the bombing attacks.

Most of both civilian and military members of the Johnson Administration believed bombing attacks would accomplish several things. The bombing attacks would demonstrate clearly and forcefully the United States' resolve to halt communist North Vietnam's aggression and to support a free South Vietnam. At the same time, the bombing attacks would provide a boost for the South Vietnamese morale which was sagging because they were losing the war. The bombing attacks would also make North Vietnam pay an increasingly high price for supporting the war. Among the civilian officials, the motivation for the bombing attacks was psychological rather than military. For the civilian officials, the primary objective of the bombing was to break North Vietnam's willingness to support the war rather than its ability. Maxwell Taylor explained the civilian view: "The objective of our air campaign is to change the will of the enemy leadership."

---

a sentence for a later sentence, rather than within its own sentence, as in standard sentence grammar.)

A third class of features that plays a role as structure building instructions is the given–new structure (Haviland & Clark, 1974). Each sentence typically contains some given information, often repeated from the sentence before, and some new information which moves the discourse forward. Since in (2) the previously mentioned information includes *1965, North Vietnam,* and *war,* all mentioned in the title, the new information is probably in one or more of the rest: *By the beginning of, American officials in both South Vietnam and the U.S., had begun to focus on,* and *the source of the continuing war in South Vietnam.* According to the given–new contract, the discourse is moving forward in the direction of one or more of these new elements; but which one(s)?

An important clue is given by the fact that in the given–new structure, the canonical position of the to be ENLARGED-ON new information is typically nearer the end of its sentence than its beginning (the beginning usually being reserved for the given information). So on the basis of the typical given–new structure, the best guess for the to be ENLARGED-ON new information is information near the end of its sentence. So in (2) *war* is quite a likely choice since it occurs close to the end of its sentence. And indeed, the actual (3) confirms its correctness. This given–new rule was also followed in the next sentence (4) where *this* instructs the reader to search for a referent.

(4) *This caused frustrations among the American officials.*

Based on the given–new rule, the most likely location for the given information is the last phrase of (3), *losing the ground war against North Vietnam.* The new information would then be that the given *caused frustrations among the American officials.* And the canonical given–new rule is followed again in (5) and (6).

(5) *The frustrations led to pressure to bomb North Vietnam.*

(6) *The idea of bombing North Vietnam found support among nearly all
American officials.*

In (7), the reader will be asked to construct a mental structure that splits
the *American officials* of (6) into two categories: *civilian* and *military officials*.
The textual clue for this is implicitly given by the word *officials* as qualified by
its modifiers. Also the reader will be instructed to establish an adversative
relation between (7) and what appeared before. The clue for this is given
explicitly by the signal word *However.*

(7) *However, the civilian and military officials had serious differences over
the objective and the methods of the bombing attacks.*

This exemplifies another source of structure building instructions, namely signal
words and phrases that specify the nature of the intended links.

At this point, the first paragraph break occurs. Such breaks are typically
instructions to finish off one part of the representation and begin ENLARGING-
ON another node, often not the last node of the previous paragraph but one
superordinate to it. In (8) the to-be-enlarged-on node harks back not to (7), but
to the combined *American officials* of (6), as implicitly signalled by *both.*

(8) *Most of **both** civilian and military members of the Johnson
administration believed bombing attacks would accomplish several
things* (emphasis added).

Sentence (9) will follow the given–new rule by EXPANDING-ON the last
part of (8); i.e., it specifies one of the *several things* the *bombing attacks would
accomplish* of (8).

(9) *The bombing attacks would demonstrate clearly and forcefully the
United States' resolve to halt communist North Vietnam's aggression
and to support a free South Vietnam.*

In (10), another signal phrase *at the same time* will signal a MOVE-
ACROSS, that is, that this node is an ENLARGE-ON not of (9) but of (8),
that is, is another of the *several things*, rather than, as all the other nodes
except (8) so far have been, an ENLARGE-ON of an immediately preceding
node.

(10) *At the same time the bombing attacks would provide a boost for South
Vietnamese morale, which was sagging because they were losing
the war.*

Another such linguistic signal for MOVE-ACROSS appears as the *also* of (11).

(11) *The bombing attacks would also make North Vietnam pay an
increasingly high price for supporting the war.*

The structure of (8)–(11) is reminiscent of the sentences in Table II.

At this point, the second paragraph break occurs. For the next sentence
(12), the to-be-enlarged-on node is the *civilian* officials who were distinguished
from the *military* ones way back in (7).

(12) *Among the civilian officials, the motivation for the bombing attacks
was psychological rather than military.*

The rest of this text can be analyzed along the same lines, with five types of clues being used to help the reader follow the exposition: the grammar of exposition, overlap of content words, syntactic clues, the given–new structure, and explicit signal words and phrases. Based on these clues, the reader can mentally arrange these sentences into a tree structure like that shown in Figure 3.

B. A Contrasting Example of Structure Building Instructions

The text of sentences (1)–(12) was actually the principled revision of an original text: The first part of the original is shown in Table IX. This principled revision was intended to clarify the original text (Britton & Gulgoz, 1991). Here we consider the role of structure building instructions in reading the original text; by way of contrast this will throw further light on the nature of structure building instructions. The original text begins with (13) and (14).

(13) *Air War in the North, 1965*
(14) *By the fall of 1964, Americans in both Saigon and Washington had begun to focus on Hanoi as the source of the continuing problem in the South.*

There is no content word overlap between (13) and (14), so those clues are absent. Only if the reader goes beyond the words in these sentences can he create any overlap of ideas between (13) and (14). We are driven to consider this possibility shortly, because in the absence of any overlap of words or ideas, it is not clear how any of the clues we identified earlier might be used. That is, the implications of the syntax of (13) are unclear if none of its ideas overlap with (14); using the given–new strategy founders on the difficulty of finding any given in (14)—in fact, unless (14) is supplemented in some way, it could easily be entirely new and could even have come from a different text altogether; and explicit signal words are absent so far. It appears that the reader is reduced either to supplementing (14) to create some idea overlap with (13), or else reading on in the hope that the next sentence will clarify what node is being ENLARGED-ON.

We first consider the consequences of reading on. The next sentence is a complex sentence. Its first clause, (15a), provides no help in its original form, because it has no content word overlap with either (13) or (14). Nor is (15b) much use.

(15) a. . . . *frustration mounted over the inability of the ARVN to defeat the enemy in the field,*
     b. *pressure to strike directly at North Vietnam began to build.*

For although the adjective *North* overlaps with the noun *North* in (13), this is not much help unless the reader can supplement (13) to establish whether the referent is the same.

(15a) and (15b) are related by the preposed conjunction *As,* here meaning either 'coinciding in time' or 'causally related.' This also is no help in relating (13) or (14) to (15a) or (15b). So it appears that the reader is forced to either leave (13), (14), and (15) unconnected; to read on further in an attempt to connect them; or else to take the trouble to go beyond the words to create some overlap of ideas.

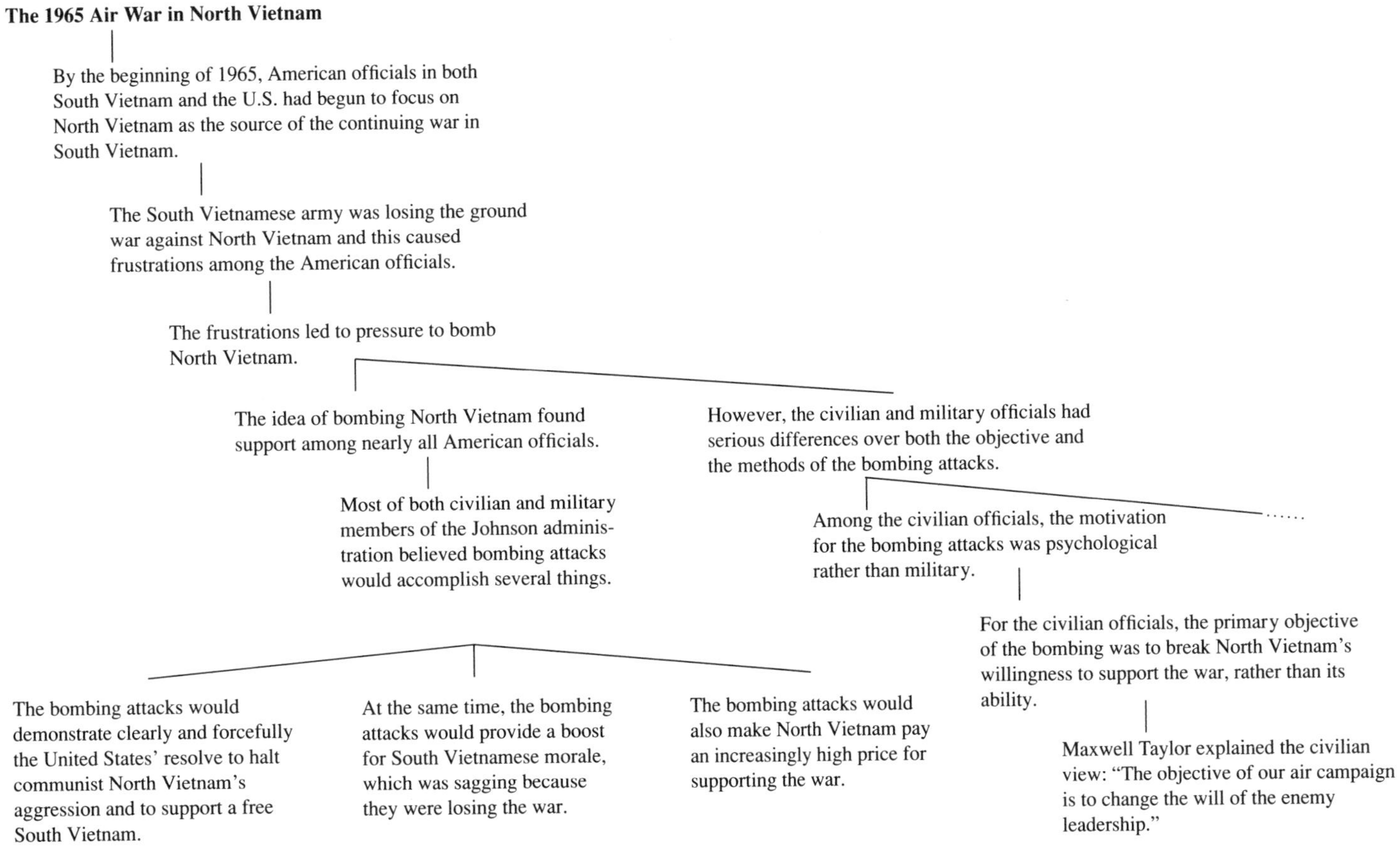

The 1965 Air War in North Vietnam

By the beginning of 1965, American officials in both South Vietnam and the U.S. had begun to focus on North Vietnam as the source of the continuing war in South Vietnam.

The South Vietnamese army was losing the ground war against North Vietnam and this caused frustrations among the American officials.

The frustrations led to pressure to bomb North Vietnam.

The idea of bombing North Vietnam found support among nearly all American officials.

Most of both civilian and military members of the Johnson administration believed bombing attacks would accomplish several things.

The bombing attacks would demonstrate clearly and forcefully the United States' resolve to halt communist North Vietnam's aggression and to support a free South Vietnam.

At the same time, the bombing attacks would provide a boost for South Vietnamese morale, which was sagging because they were losing the war.

However, the civilian and military officials had serious differences over both the objective and the methods of the bombing attacks.

Among the civilian officials, the motivation for the bombing attacks was psychological rather than military.

The bombing attacks would also make North Vietnam pay an increasingly high price for supporting the war.

For the civilian officials, the primary objective of the bombing was to break North Vietnam's willingness to support the war, rather than its ability.

Maxwell Taylor explained the civilian view: "The objective of our air campaign is to change the will of the enemy leadership."

FIG. 3 Hypothetical mental structures for the text in Table VIII.

TABLE IX
The First Two Paragraphs of the Original Version

Air War in the North, 1965

By the fall of 1964, Americans in both Saigon and Washington had begun to focus on Hanoi as the source of the continuing problem in the South. As frustration mounted over the inability of the ARVN to defeat the enemy in the field, pressure to strike directly at North Vietnam began to build. Although there was near unanimity among American officials over the aerial extension of the war into North Vietnam, serious differences arose over both the objective and the methods to be used.

Most members of the Johnson administration believed bombing attacks would accomplish several things. They would demonstrate clearly and forcefully the United States' resolve to halt communist aggression and to support a free Vietnam. At the same time, they would provide a boost for the sagging morale of the South Vietnamese. They would also make Hanoi pay an increasingly high price for supporting the Vietcong. Particularly among civilian advocates, the motivation for such a campaign was psychological rather than military, the primary objective not being Hanoi's capability but its willingness to support the war. "In a very real sense," explained Maxwell Taylor, "the objective of our air campaign is to change the will of the enemy leadership."

If the reader chooses to read on, (16) is also a compound sentence composed of (16a) and (16b), with an adversative relation signaled by the preposed conjunction *Although*.

(16) a. . . . *there was near unanimity among American officials over the aerial extension of the war into North Vietnam,*

   b. *serious differences arose over both the objective and the methods to be used.*

Because of its position, at first the reader might take *Although* as a signal to relate the whole of (16) adversatively to (15), but he might also consider its scope to be across the two parts of (16). With regard to the overlap clue, (16a) has *North Vietnam* in common with (15b), but (16b) does not overlap with any previous content words.

At this point, the first paragraph break occurs. This often signals that a new node is about to be expanded upon, but (17) does not have word overlap with any previous sentences, so without supplementing it, there are no clues to tell the reader which node to relate it to.

(17) *Most members of the Johnson Administration believed bombing attacks would accomplish several things.*

(18) *They would demonstrate clearly and forcefully the United States' resolve to halt Communist aggression and to support a free Vietnam.*

Sentence (18) also has no word overlap, but the pronoun *They* does issue an instruction to the reader to find the referent intended by the author from an earlier sentence. Since *they* almost always refers to a group of people, one natural candidate referent is the *members of the Johnson Administration,* and since this choice is roughly consistent with the content of (18), the reader may conclude that an appropriate link can be created with (17).

Reading on to (19), again, *they* instructs the reader to look for a referent, and *at the same time* serves as a signal of a coordinate structure in which (19) is to be related not to (18), but as an EXPAND-ON of (17).

(19) *At the same time, they would provide a boost for the sagging morale of the South Vietnamese.*

Similarly, for (20), the reader may or may not detect that the intended referent of *they* is actually not *members of the Johnson Administration* at all, but instead *bombing attacks,* because there are no clues for the correct assignment in the original text.

(20) *They would also make Hanoi pay an increasingly high price for supporting the Vietcong.*

Then the paragraph break occurs, followed by (21).

(21) *Particularly among civilian advocates, the motivation for such a campaign was psychological rather than military, the primary objective not being Hanoi's capability but its willingness to support the war.*

This has no overlap with (13)–(20), apart from the *Hanoi* of (14).

At this point the prospects for a well-connected structure are remote. The only evident word overlap is *North Vietnam* in (15b) and (16a) and of *Hanoi* in (14) and (20). This might lead the reader to think one of these is the topic being ENLARGED-ON.

But of course some readers will take the trouble to go beyond the words in the sentences to infer some of the ideas not explicitly represented, in the hope that adding the resulting ideas to their mental representation will lead to some overlap that will help them to link the sentences to each other. If they have the inclination to do so, along with sufficient time and the relevant prior knowledge, it is easy for readers with the necessary inference skills to do this. On the basis of general prior knowledge, one can go beyond *By the fall of 1964* in (14) to the idea that things which happen in the late part of one year often cause events in the next year. If in addition one has the relevant historical prior knowledge, he can go beyond *the North* in (13) to the idea of *North Vietnam*. If he has the relevant geographical prior knowledge, he can go beyond *Hanoi* in (14) to add the idea that Hanoi is the capitol of North Vietnam; and if he has prior knowledge about the relevant discourse structures, he can see that *Hanoi* is intended to stand for *North Vietnam*. The resulting mental representation might look something like (13')–(14'), with the ideas added by the reader in parentheses.

(13') *Air War in the North (Vietnam), 1965*
(14') *By the fall of 1964 (causing events in 1965) Americans in both Saigon and Washington had begun to focus on Hanoi (Capitol of North Vietnam) as the source of the continuing problem in the South.*

There is now idea overlap in the mental representations of (13') and (14'), which makes that clue available for use. Judging from the overlap alone, the apparent topic being ENLARGED-ON by (14) is either ''1965'' or ''North Vietnam.'' The reader could either decide between them on the basis of the syntax of (13), which might lead to choosing ''1965'' for the reasons specified at (1'), or could try to use the given–new strategy, which would lead to ''North Vietnam'' because it is (inferred) nearer the end of sentence (14). Or the reader could read on and try to use word overlap in (15) to retrospectively find out which node is being ENLARGED-ON. Unless something is added to it, (15a) is no help, but (15b) would probably lead to choosing "North Vietnam" because of idea overlap with (14). But since this leaves (15a) out of the representation, it is not wholly satisfactory.

In addition to looking for word overlap, the reader could try to go beyond the words of (15) to infer ideas not explicitly represented. Using the same kind of prior knowledge and inferencing abilities as for (13′) and (14′), (15a) might be represented as in (15a′).

(15) a′. *As (because) frustrations mounted over the inability of the ARVN (Army of the Republic of South Vietnam) to defeat the enemy (North Vietnam) in the field.*

If at this point the reader were to try to use the given–new structure, it might appear that the given information in (15a′) must be the only previously encountered idea, namely "North Vietnam" of (14′). But actually, the author appears to have intended that the previously mentioned idea should be "the continuing problem in the South" of (14′), which he refers to in (15a′) by the words *the inability of the ARVN to defeat the enemy in the field.* That is, the author appears to have intended for the reader to see that *the inability of the ARVN to defeat the enemy in the field* is *the continuing problem in the South.* Since this requires inferencing activities, enabled by certain domain-specific prior knowledge, only readers with such inferencing abilities, that prior knowledge, and the inclination can construct the intended structure.

At this point it is easy to see that the instructions included by the author in the original text may not be sufficient for many readers to create the mental structure he intended, as in Table V. And the same applies to the rest of the text, mutatis mutandis. This is shown empirically in Britton, Van Dusen, Glynn, and Hemphill (1990) and Britton and Gulgoz (1991).

IV. PSYCHOLINGUISTICS AND THE SOURCE OF THE PATHOLOGIES OF EXPOSITORY TEXT

If the reader detects the structure building instructions in the text, correctly infers any instructions left implicit by the author, recruits the prior knowledge that the author intends, and then carries out the instructions on the concepts and propositions provided by the text and prior knowledge, then he or she will end up with the mental structure that the text calls for.

But we know that readers of expository text often end up with incomplete or incorrect representations. Some of the reasons for this are primarily psycholinguistic in character, some have only secondary psycholinguistic involvement, and some are broader than psycholinguistics. We have just been considering some the pathologies of expository text that are primarily psycholinguistic. For example, if the code is obscured or largely missing, as in Table V or sentences (13)–(20), or if the reader has different actions attached to the code signals than the author is assuming, or if the reader is missing parts of the key to the author's code, then obviously the intended mental structure will be harder to build correctly. In terms of the grammar of exposition, the author may have failed to provide textual clues that the reader can use to infer when the text is ENLARGING-ON, when UNITIZING, and when MOVING-ON. In such cases the reader may think the author is making one move when the author has actually made a different one. Other possibilities are that the author fails to UNITIZE, or fails to provide clues to the specific label for the relation between a discourse unit and its predecessor, or provides ambiguous or misleading clues. But what is the explanation for the existence of these pathologies?

It appears that one underlying explanation for these widespread failures of expository text is certain illusions which are characteristic of the subject matter experts who write expository text. These illusions are caused by the nature of expert's knowledge structures. The authors of most expository texts are experts in the subject matter of their text. As such, they begin the task of writing an expository text with their own mental structure for the subject matter area. This structure, because they are experts, tends to be very well developed: large, densely interconnected, and highly structured. But it is also highly proceduralized and highly automatized; these characteristics tend to make the content of the expert's mental structure opaque even to the expert. Moreover, the expert no longer has easy access to the mental structure that he began with as a novice. For one thing, it has been forgotten from long disuse and concealed by later accretions. Those parts of the novice structure that were carried over to the expert structure are likely to be inextricably embedded in the rest of the expert structure, highly proceduralized, and automatic, and therefore opaque, while those parts that gave him trouble as a novice are likely to have been actively inhibited as part of the process of attaining expertise. The result is that the very thing that the author needs as evidence to tailor the text to the novices' most likely existing mental structure is likely to be unavailable.

So when the author reads over his own text, he is generally unable to read it with the mental structures characteristic of the novice, but instead must read it with his own knowledge structure. This gives him the illusion that the text is clear. This illusion arises from a fundamental illusion of human life: that others are like us. It is not that we believe that this is true; we know perfectly well it is not true. It is just that we have very little else to go on. Since we are stuck inside our own skin, we have an inevitable bias toward this illusion. I call it an "illusion" in strict analogy to perceptual illusions, in that perceptual illusions cause us to see things that are not present in the stimuli; in the same way, the subject matter expert sees things that are not there in his text. As with perceptual illusions, we know perfectly well that the things are not there, but that does not prevent us from seeing them.

The problem is that when the author reads over his own text, it is sufficient to redintegrate in the author's mind the structure he intends the reader to have. For example, when the author sees *Hanoi* he thinks immediately 'capital of North Vietnam'. But when the novice reads the text, he does not see the things that the expert sees (because they are not in the text), and so the novice is unable to follow the author.

This fundamental illusion gives the author a strong tendency to go too fast for the reader, making it difficult for the reader to follow him, and this is a source of some of the main pathologies to which expository text is subject. That is, since all the author has is his current mental structure, the natural tendency is to do what he normally does everyday as a practitioner of his special subject, which is to move quickly and freely about in his structure. But the author knows perfectly well that this will not teach the novice. Instead, the author must slow down his mental activities, "downshift" if you will, to explain things as he goes along. This is the source of the primary injunction of the grammar of exposition, which is to EXPAND the topic, to ENLARGE-ON the subtopics. So the author begins to move through the nodes, unpacking them and laying out their internal structure for the reader, ENLARGING-ON them until he MOVES-ON.

One important parameter of this process is the rate at which the author MOVES-ON. For present purposes this can be formulated as the rate at which the text develops new information. We can imagine a text which moves ahead in large jumps and contrast it with one which inches ahead in small steps. For example, an author explaining something to a professional colleague or giving a paper to a learned society will tend to move ahead in relatively large jumps, often leaving out links because he assumes the audience will make them without help. In contrast, in explaining the same thing to a naive undergraduate, many small steps will be needed, and the links between them must be specified in an explicit way. It is relatively rare for a speaker to be criticized for going too slowly and putting in too many links, but quite common for a speaker to be incomprehensible to certain parts of the audience because he is going too quickly, leaving out too many links. The important thing is to find a rate of development of new information at which the reader will be able to follow the exposition. Ideally, we want a rate of development that is optimal for the reader. But the natural tendency for the author will be to go at his normal, everyday rate, which is too fast for the reader.

We can reformulate in these terms the contrast between the original Vietnam text and the principled revision. This will help explain why the original text was written by its author in the form it was. In sentence (1), the author begins the original text by adding, to the notion of '1965' in the title, the notion of 'the fall of 1964'; by adding to the notion of 'the North' in the title, the notion of 'Hanoi'; and by adding to the notion of 'war' in the title, the notion of 'the continuing problem in the South'. For a subject matter expert, like the author, these additions cause no problems; when he reads the text the necessary mental operations to link these appropriately are not only run off quickly and free of error, but they also recruit his relevant prior knowledge of the topic across a broad front in what seems to him an effective, fluent, and graceful way.

In the next sentence, 'The inability of the ARVN to defeat the enemy in the field' is easily seen (by the author) to be 'the continuing problem in the South' of the first sentence, and indeed seems to serve well as a more explicit specification of the aspects of the general 'problem' that are most relevant to this text. And so on. For a person who is already knowledgeable about this subject matter, all these additions may appear to enrich appropriately the relevant concepts and context.

In the same way, in an elementary history text we might speak of George Washington as *Commander of the Continental army* in one place, as *the Father of his country* in another place, as *the first President* in another place, in order to enrich the student's concept of George Washington. And as long as the student performed the necessary mental operations of retrieving the referred-to concept and enriching it, the goal would be successfully achieved. But if instead the reader ended up thinking that three different people were the Commander, the Father, and the President, the text would have failed.

It is clear that an author who is expert in the subject matter of George Washington or the Vietnam War would think that a text that immediately started enriching concepts, like the original Vietnam text, was perfectly clear. It is perfectly clear to the author. That is, such a text is quite sufficient to redintegrate in the author's mind the structure he intends the reader to have. The problem is that it may not be sufficient to do so in the reader's mind.

For the same reasons, the author is likely to leave out the structure building instructions the reader may need to build the intended structure. As the author reads over the text, he does not find that any such instructions are needed for him to build the structure he intends.

I have said that an important parameter that determines the understandability of an expository text is the rate at which the author moves on. So if we slow down the rate of introduction of new ideas, the text should become more understandable. Examples from the principled revision will clarify what I mean. In the principled revision of the Vietnam text, the rate of introduction of new ideas is much slower than in the original text: in the first sentence the *1965* of the title remains *1965*; the *North Vietnam* of the title remains *North Vietnam*, instead of an attempt being made to enrich it by adding *Hanoi* to it; the *war* of the first sentence is carried over to the *war* of the second, instead of, as in the original, the *continuing problem in the South* being enriched by specifying it as *the ability of the ARVN to defeat the enemy in the field,* and so on. At the same time as the introduction of new ideas is slowed down, overlap clues are increased.

There are also some other sources for the pathologies of expository text. These will be considered only briefly because they are not primarily psycholinguistic. First, the mental structure intended by the author may not be one that produces the learning results that are intended. For example, some teachers of statistics may intend to produce in the reader's mind a deductive structure with axioms, postulates, theorems, and proofs, and this may be accomplished. But if the intention is for the learners to use their statistics knowledge to analyze data, then such a deductive structure may not be suitable because the deductive structure is not suited for that purpose. Stated generally, the problem is that the author has a theory of learning (more often implicit than explicit) that a certain kind of mental structure will lead to learning and performance of a certain kind, but that theory may be incorrect for some class of learning outcomes. Another example is Anderson's early theory (1990) that the way to create a structure that would lead to recall for word lists was to say the words loud and fast. In this case, the instructions to say the words loud and fast may have created a structure, but it did not have the desired characteristics.

Another problem arises because readers often do not engage in much cognitive activity while reading expository texts, sometimes because the texts are being read under compulsion, such as for required classes, or because they are only remotely related to the person's real goal, or for other reasons. This general deficit of mental activity may lead to a failure to detect the structure building instructions, carry them out, or recruit the called-for prior knowledge.

V. Inducing Insights by Exposition

The goal of most expository texts is to induce specific insights about the text's subject matter in the reader. An insight is a new understanding. It occurs when the reader sees a new relationship or set of relationships between mental entities (Lonergan, 1970). If we imagine the reader's mental structures before the insight as a network of nodes and links like that in Figure 1, then after the insight there is a new arrangement of these nodes and links. When such a rearrangement occurs, we are particularly willing to call it an insight when the rearrangement is in a subject matter area particularly important to us, or when the rearrangement has large implications for our existing mental structures. But insights actually come in many sizes, as will be seen.

We shall try to show that an insight is induced by an exposition when (a) the right mental structure has been built in the reader's mind, and then (b) a critical proposition occurs—here called the INSIGHT-PROPOSITION because it sets off the insight. The rest of this section is concerned with the insight-propositions and the characteristics of the mental structures required to set off the corresponding insights.

Here are some examples of possible insight-propositions, chosen to illustrate important aspects of such propositions.

Short-term memory exists.
Short-term memory has the property of limited capacity.
Germs cause disease.
Phlogiston causes fire.
The benzene molecule is shaped like a snake eating its tail.
Classical conditioning is explained by a connectionist model.
Working memory is the basis of general intelligence.
Expository text works by including instructions that the reader uses to build mental structures.

The first three of these are examples of old insights for most readers of this paper. That is, although they were not induced by recent expository text, for most readers of this paper they were probably new insights at one time and were induced by expositions at that time. The next four are included to make various distinctions between having an insight and assenting to its truth. The first of these is included as a historical example of an insight that once came with assent attached to it, but the assent was later withdrawn; nevertheless we can still have the insight corresponding to it. The next is an insight suitable for chemists, included to show that we are often willing to give assent that certain insights are true without fully understanding them. The next two are included to indicate that we can have considerable understanding of an insight-proposition without necessarily assenting to its truth. Finally, the last insight proposition could have been induced by the exposition of this paper.

Another point made by these examples is that an insight-proposition looks superficially like any other proposition, in that it is composed of a predicate and one or more arguments. But it differs from other propositions in that it is the occasion for new understandings to occur. How does the insight-proposition come to be the occasion for this new understanding to occur? The previous text can provide what is needed, if it is properly constructed. We will consider two related psycholinguistic techniques.

Both are techniques by which the terms that are to appear in the insight-proposition are enriched by the previous text. This can be done intentionally by the author. We can imagine the author conspiring to design the earlier parts of his text so that when the insight proposition is encountered later, he has caused the reader to construct a special-purpose meaning for each term in the insight-proposition—a meaning usually idiosyncratic to that particular text—such that those special-purpose terms, when juxtaposed with the predicate in the insight-proposition, interlock to cause the desired change in the reader's mental structures.

Both techniques arrange the previous text so that the words in the insight-proposition are given extra meaning, with the meaning having been packed into them by the preceding text (Britton, 1978, Study 6). The consequence is that when the author later uses the critical word in the insight-proposition, it makes the reader think of certain things, with those things being the ones the author needs the reader to think of for the desired rearrangement of mental structures to occur. The meaning created by the author is not just extra in the sense of quantitatively larger; it also has a particular shape, with that shape more or less carefully designed so that when the insight-proposition occurs, the shape of one of its arguments will interlock with the shape of its other argument(s) (when related by the predicate) to cause the desired rearrangement of the mental structure.

How can the shape of the word meanings of the insight-proposition cause the desired new arrangement of mental structures? For our first idea of shape, we will use a geometrical analogy. We can imagine a word's meaning as originally a simple, regular solid shape, like a sphere or cube, corresponding to its dictionary meaning before the text is read. Then as special meaning gets added to it by the text, the effect is to change that shape so that certain parts of it stick out, as it were, and it becomes a shape idiosyncratic to that word as developed in this particular text. Then we imagine the other argument of the insight-proposition as also being given a particular shape in the same sort of way.

If the two shapes fit together easily, like a lock and key, then when the insight-proposition occurs, the intended insight occurs; the event is analogous to a key unlocking a door, with the contents of the room thus revealed being the content of the insight.

For example, historically the *Germs cause disease* insight could not occur as long as disease was thought to be entirely due to divine punishment, because the shape of that concept of disease does not have a receptor site for the notion of a nondivine source. Similarly, the notion of germs had to be enriched by the idea of their reproduction, production of toxins, attacking of organs, and so on, before it could fit into the new concept of disease. At one time, exposition accomplished this shaping of the "disease" and "germ" arguments of the insight-proposition. Once the appropriate shaping had occurred, then the insight-proposition could link the mental structures having to do with diseases with those having to do with germs. This is the new arrangement of existing mental structures that constitutes the insight. All the things known about microorganisms could now become relevant to disease, and vice versa. Streaming over this link there now could be notions like "if we want to prevent disease, we should prevent germs"; "if we want to cure disease, we should kill germs"; and so on. Similarly, the insight-proposition that *Short-term memory has the property of limited capacity* allows the body of knowledge about short-term memory to get access to the body of knowledge about limited capacity, including knowledge from such areas as economics, computer science, introspection, and so on.

By what psycholinguistic techniques are special-purpose word meanings constructed in this way? For a schematic example, suppose we have a term A, later to appear in an insight-proposition, for which we want to create a meaning with a particular shape. The reader begins with the appropriate dictionary meaning. Three ways for the author to modify it are:

1. to carve off a particular part of its meaning by phrases like:
   We are concerned only with the effects of A,
   causes of A,
   learning of A,
   part B of A,
   emotional aspects of A,
   proofs of A,
   aspects of A related to B;
2. to add elements to A's meaning by phrases like:
   A cannot be considered apart from A',
   A must be considered with A',
   A inevitably leads to A',
   A is inseparable from A';
3. to rearrange aspects of A's meaning by phrases like:
   the most important aspects of A is A',
   the least important aspect of A is A',
   the A' aspect of A is more important than the A" aspect, but less important than A'''.

These three ways—adding to A's meaning, removing parts of it, and rearranging parts of it—may seem to exhaust the possible ways of changing the meaning. But it is important to note that these techniques can be applied in succession, and that they can be applied not only to the original meaning of A, but also successively to each successively transformed version of it. The result is that the meaning of a critical term can be changed out of all recognition from its original meaning. This is particularly obvious in political discourse, where a term can be successively wrapped in the flag, placed on a pedestal, associated with the Constitution, Abraham Lincoln, or other figures, given responsibility for various recent positive events, and so on, until its meaning is considerably enriched in a positive direction, or by similar techniques in the opposite direction. For example, take the idea of "abortion." By one side in the controversy, it is paired with term *right to choose,* thus associating it with rights to choose other things and so with the notion of freedom, and implicitly contrasted with its alternative, the *lack of the right to choose.* It is wrapped in the Constitution, linked to recent advances in women's rights, and so on. Its potential illegality (June 1992) is given inhibitory links with "coat hangers," "blood," "death of the mother," and so on. But the time this is done, it legitimizes insight-propositions with the concept of "abortion" that have only a limited class of forms.

By the other side, the negative of the term is paired with *the right to life*, thus associating it with the rights to life of those already born, and its opposite is paired with the *lack of the right to live*, or *death*. It is wrapped in the Constitution (as the Constitution was before the court decision at issue), linked to various positive aspects of that earlier era, and so on. The alternative is linked to the "murder of children," and so on.

At the end of this process, the meaning of the term *abortion* would be radically different for readers of the alternative texts. An insight-proposition that could form the conclusion of one text would be entirely inappropriate for the other text.

At the proposition level there is a related set of psycholinguistic techniques for building insights; it combines small insights into large ones. For insights occur in both small and large sizes, with the large ones commonly constructed out of small ones. The following example schematically illustrates a common technique for such construction.

For purposes of this section, we consider schematic propositions like *A has a specific Relationship* i *to B*, abbreviated A,R_i,B. If the reader understands such a proposition, she may have had an insight with certain characteristics: small or large, with broad implications or not, and so on.

If we then want to build up to a larger insight, with A,R_i,B as an element, one way to do this is to UNITIZE A,R_i,B into a single chunk and refer to it by some appropriate term in the next sentence. One class of terms commonly used at the between-sentence level to UNITIZE in this way is pronouns, like *this*. So we can write a sequence of propositions like (22)–(23), where by *This* is meant 'A,R_1,B'.

(22) A,R_1,B
(23) This, R_2,C

Here, (23) induces a (schematic) insight with three surface elements: *this*, R_2, and C. But since the pronoun *this* activates the compound A,R_1,B, the insight of (23) actually involves all of A, R_1, and B, as well as C and R_2. To induce a still larger insight, we can UNITIZE (23) by referring to it by *it* in (24).

(24) It, R_3,D

At this point, if all has gone well, we have in (24) a schematic textual representation of an insight including the relationship (R_3) of D to all of A, B, and C in their respective compound and hierarchical relationships R_1 and R_2. If this is the end of a section of the text, then we end up with this moderate-sized insight.

Suppose we then go on to another section of the text which describes the relationship of J, K, and L as in (25)–(27).

(25) J,R_4,K
(26) This (i.e., J,R_4,K), R_5,L
(27) That [i.e., (26)], R_6,M

We end up with another moderate sized idea (27), where *that* is a complex idea involving J,K, and L in their compound hierarchical relationships.

(27) That, R_6,M

It then becomes possible to say something like (28).

(28) (24) and (27), R_7,X

This includes all of (22)–(27)—A, B, C, D, J, K, L, M, and X, along with seven relationships all activated by a single proposition, namely (28). In this way large insights—much larger than a single proposition could express—can be built out of proposition-sized ones, if all goes well in the structure building process.

A useful way to imagine the consequences at this process is that each time it happens, the concept nodes involved acquire subnodes which have links to the concept node and to its other subnodes. Each time the concept occurs later in the text, its whole network has a chance of being activated, with the activation of each subnode being proportional to its weight, bias, and the activation, excitatory or inhibitory, it receives from other nodes. That is, the shape of the meaning of a concept in a text is the network it corresponds to, and the configuration of that network is determined by the text (as well as prior knowledge) and so depends on what subnodes have been created by the text, and on their connectivity and state of activity.

We now consider some psychological properties of insights constructed by these sorts of linguistic techniques. One thing that makes us willing to call something an insight is when the mental rearrangement that a proposition induces has implications for large parts of our existing mental structures. At this point the limited capacity of the human cognitive system may enter the picture; for example, it may not be possible to hold all the elements of (28) in mind at once. This is because the number of un-UNITIZED things one can hold in mind at once seems to be limited to about seven, and A, B, C, D, J, K, L, M, X, and R_{1-7}, if un-UNITIZED, are more than seven. So the insight produced by (28) cannot immediately involve all the elements and relations that went into it. However, there are several sets of circumstances in which the insight induced by (28) will quite quickly come to involve all the elements and relations that went into it. (This section is our consideration of the spread and "suddenness" property of some insights.) One such set of circumstances arises when the subrelations are highly automatized, so that the spread of activation among the elements and relations is very rapid, and so may be sudden or even appear instantaneous. Suppose, for example, one were talking to an experimental psychologist, and A, B, C, and D were about classical conditioning, and J, K, L, and M were about operant conditioning, and X was the notion of a connectionist model, and (28) was (29).

(29) *Classical conditioning and operant conditioning are explained by a connectionist model.*

The psychologist, if he has highly automatized links within his knowledges of classical conditioning, operant conditioning, and connectionist models, can quickly spread activation appropriately to all the subsidiary elements and relations of insight (29). The resulting changes in these subsidiary elements are not consequent logically on (29), but their meaning changes with its meaning. That is, (29) has implications for the notions of UCS, UCR, CS, CR, the operant response, reward, and so on, and for their relations.

Contrast this with a person who has not read the preceding text and who has no relevant knowledge; for him, (29) is not much more than (30).

(30) *P and Q are explained by X.*

It will be evident that for a person who has the relevant knowledge automatized, a much broader and deeper meaning will quickly develop. If it spreads broadly enough, that is, has large enough implications for other mental structures, or is personally important, it will be perceived as an insight. Whether it is perceived as sudden may depend on its speed of spread through the relevant mental structures.

Long-standing prior knowledge is not the only source of rapid spread of insights: A reader who had just finished automatizing the relevant relations by recent intense study might activate all of them just as quickly. Or a reader who had very recently read the previous parts of the text, or who had been recently reminded of them by some textual device, might fairly quickly spread activation to all the nodes in their relations.

An alternative route to activating all the material would be sustained reflection on (29), perhaps combined with thinking about relevant earlier sentences. This would give the experience not of suddenness, but rather of slow development. What is the mechanism by which the implications of an insight spread slowly through the related mental structures as a result of sustained reflection? One possible mechanism arises from the fact that within the knowledge domain of each argument of the insight-proposition there is a fixed number of nodes and a much smaller number of possible relationships. Candidate node-relation-node triples to which the insight can be applied can be generated exhaustively if the set of possibilities is small enough. Given the original insight and whatever subsidiary insights have been produced so far, these candidates can be matched against the existing set. Candidates (i.e., specific node-relation-node triples) that are contradictory to the original insight or its so far accepted subsidiaries can be rejected, others accepted.

For example, "classical conditioning" has the element of "reinforcement," and the learner may have already had the subsidiary insight to (29) that "reinforcement" in "classical conditioning" has a relationship to the "teaching input" in back-propagation "connectionist models." With this in mind, he can search the elements of "operant conditioning" for an argument corresponding to "reinforcement." If he finds "reward," then he can consider it might also have the same relationship to the "teaching input" as "reinforcement" did, thus producing the corresponding insight. If this exhaustive generation happens slowly, it may be akin to the psychoanalytic process of "working through." If it occurs quickly enough, a "Eureka experience" may result.

We can illustrate many of these ideas about insight with the archetypal example of insight in Western culture, which is the insight of Archimedes. This insight is famous for causing him to rush naked from his bath into the streets of Syracuse, shouting "Eureka!" ('I found it'). The elements there of suddenness, positive affect, and assent we put aside for now, to focus on how he came to "see the new relationship."

The story goes like this. One day Archimedes took a bath while thinking about his current scientific problem. Plutarch (c. 100/1932) tells us that while Archimedes was constantly thinking about his scientific problems, he very seldom took a bath; indeed, he used to

> forget his food and neglect his person, to the degree that when he was *occasionally carried by absolute violence to bathe* or have his body anointed, he used to trace geometrical figures in the ashes of the fire [used to heat the water] and diagrams in the oil on his body, being in a state of entire preoccupation, and in the truest sense, divine possession with his love and delight in science. (p. 378; emphasis and brackets added)

So it is not surprising that on the occasion in question, as he was lowered into the water of his brim-full tub, he should notice, for the first time in a long time, that the water was slopping over the side, and that the amount slopping over was more as more of Archimedes was lowered into the bath. In fact, he could imagine measuring exactly how much water slopped over.

Nor is it surprising that, at the same time, he should be preoccupied by his current scientific problem, which was the quantity of gold there was in his relative King Heiro's putatively pure gold crown. (The king was suspicious that some of his original ball of gold had been adulterated with silver by a thieving royal goldsmith; he had taken in advance the precaution of measuring the diameter of his original sphere of pure gold.) At the moment of his insight, Archimedes was experiencing that his own body had a very specific density, which determined the quantity of water that slopped over. Since he was preoccupied with the quantity of gold that was in the crown, this may have reminded him that gold, one of the densest metals, also has a very specific density. So that a ball of pure gold of the size that the king had given the goldsmith would, if lowered into Archimedes' tub, slop over a certain very specific quantity of water and no other; a ball adulterated with silver would slop over a lesser quantity. So juxtaposed in his mind at once were his problem—finding out the quantity of the king's measured ball of pure gold that was in the crown—and the solution—lowering the golden crown into a tub of water and seeing if it slopped over the same quantity of water as a gold ball of the same size the king had given the goldsmith. Hence the insight.

Could it be that Archimedes hated having his bath so much that, after being "carried by absolute violence" to it, he actually pretended to BE the crown (instead of himself) as he was lowered into the tub, saying to himself, "As the crown (I) is lowered into the tub, it displaces a certain quantity of water, if I am a pure gold crown. But if I am an adulterated crown I would displace a different quantity of water. Aha, I can find out if I am adulterated by lowering myself into the tub"?

How is this a rearrangement of Archimedes' mental structures? We can imagine that before his bath, various ideas were lying around in Archimedes' mind, in no particularly useful arrangement: the problem set him by King Heiro, the original ball of gold, a counterpart ball with exactly the same diameter, the actual finished crown, a hypothetical crown of pure gold, and a hypothetical crown with silver in it.

As he was lowered into his tub, he imagined measuring the quantity of water that slopped over. When this bath-related idea was juxtaposed with the crown-related ideas, he imagined lowering the finished crown into the tub, and measuring the quantity of water that slopped over. Then he imagined lowering a ball of pure gold the same size as the original, and measuring its slop-over. The two measurements would then be compared. If they were the same, then the crown was pure gold, otherwise not. (At this point we can generalize the notion of the insight-proposition to include, instead of a verbal formulation, an image.)

To put this in terms of the rearrangement of his mental structures, we can imagine that the various ideas that entered into the final insight were laying around in Archimedes' mind before the moment of insight, but in no particular arrangement in relation to his problem. But just before his insight, they were all juxtaposed in an activated state and fortuitously became arranged in a particular configuration, which was then recognized as the solution to the problem. All that remained was to ask the king for the loan of a ball of pure gold exactly as big as the one originally given the goldsmith and then see how much water slopped over for it, compared to the putatively pure gold crown.

In Archimedes' case, the juxtaposition of the critical elements needed for the insight occurred fortuitously. But in expository texts, we need not depend on fortuitous juxtapositions; instead, we can make special arrangements to induce the mental juxtaposition of the elements we want. These arrangements depend on the reader carrying out the instructions we give him; more precisely, on the author giving the reader instructions that he will carry out.

How are the author-provided instructions that are the topic of this chapter involved in the construction of insights by expository text? Within each sentence, the instructions at the level of sentence grammar construct the structure for that sentence, but, as everywhere in this chapter, we focus on the instructions that build the structures that relate different sentences to each other, and higher level structures.

We have already described the shaping of word meanings and the packing of subnetworks into the terms that are later to appear in the insight-proposition. The other author-provided instructions covered earlier in this paper play similar roles in constructing the mental networks later to be activated by the insight-proposition. The EXPAND, ENLARGE-ON, UNITIZE, and MOVE-ON expository moves serve respectively to open nodes for expansion, lay out a structure of nodes and links, chunk it, and move-on to the next nodes. For example, if the reader parses the author's expository grammar correctly, the topic of, say, "classical conditioning" can be opened at the beginning of a text section, a structure of nodes and links relating the UCS, UCR, CS, CR, and so on can be laid out, and then UNITIZED under the newly enriched term CLASSICAL CONDITIONING, and then "operant conditioning" can be opened and filled out in the same way, and so on. Doing this correctly also depends on following the other instructions in the text, for while the grammar of exposition can provide general guidance if its signals are present and interpreted correctly, other signal systems are often required as well. For example, to construct the proper between-sentence relations it may be necessary to use the overlap clues, the between-sentence syntactic rules, the given–new clues, and explicit signal words and phrases, as can be seen in examples (1)–(21), if the right subnodes are to be chunked into the right places.

In addition, the successful construction of insights in this way requires that the activation levels of the critical elements and their relations, along with appropriate subnodes and relations, be at values that will induce the intended spread of activation when the conspired-for juxtaposition occurs in the insight-proposition. These activation levels are partly determined by the text. For example, as you begin to read this sentence, certain previously mentioned ideas are highly active. These ideas we can imagine before the to-be-induced insight as lying around in your mind in no particularly helpful arrangement in relation to your problem(s). But it is these ideas that are most likely to be available for relating to the other ideas about to be presented. How did the active ideas get that way? The text may have activated them very recently, very strongly, or very frequently, or perhaps they were activated by some other ideas that recently were activated. Alternatively, they may have been emphasized linguistically, for instance by such phrases as *the most important thing in this chapter is* . . . ; this is equivalent to setting a positive bias on them. So the text can play a major role in setting the levels of excitatory activation of ideas by directly or indirectly controlling the strength, recency, and frequency of their activation. In addition, the text can cause ideas to be inhibited by such things as statements in the text that contain negative criticism of ideas or evidence against them, and ideas can be inhibited by virtue of their inhibitory links to ideas that have been activated. For a computational theory of this, we sketch a connectionist approach loosely following Kintsch (1988).

Abstractly, we can imagine that at any point in the reading of an expository text, the reader has a large network of nodes and links. Some are derived from the text, and some are from the reader's prior knowledge. Each node has an activation value. We can imagine the activation value of a node as corresponding to its "brightness"—highly active nodes are more lit up. Activation decays, so nodes not activated recently are less lit up than others. Each node is connected to other nodes. Some of the connections are excitatory and others are inhibitory.

Given a particular network with specific activation levels, we can imagine that the next sentence is about to be read. The consequences of that sentence for the mental representation are going to depend on what is in the sentence and on the state of the network that it is entering. For example, if the incoming sentence mentions the name of a node that is already present in the preexisting network, then that node will receive further activation as a result of its appearance in the current sentence. This activation will spread along excitatory and inhibitory links to directly related nodes and spread on from there to other nodes more tangentially related. Any new nodes mentioned for the first time in the current sentence will have to be added to the network; and their locations, activations, connections, and labels on connections can either be controlled by instructions in the text, by self-instructions, or by existing activations, or else be set at random. The network resulting after the current sentence's input will most likely be in a different state from before.

The effects of the sentence after that will again depend both on what is in that sentence and on the state of the network it is entering. It is obvious that to the extent that we can control the state of each successive network, and the content of each sentence, we can control the next network and ultimately the final network.

Certain final states of the network correspond to the insights we want to induce. For example, in Archimedes' case his final network had highly activated nodes for his problem, and these were excitatorially connected to the nodes for his solution, which in turn had just previously become excited by its similarity to the perceptual experience of watching the water slop over as he was lowered into his tub. If we wanted to produce Archimedes' insight by a text or by some other sequence of experiences, we would try to design the sequence of events to optimize the likelihood of producing the desired network. (The positive affect associated with his insight may have been due to the rapid reduction of uncertainty caused by it, as suggested by Tomkins, 1991.)

How do the instructions embedded in the text play a role in this computational process? The instructions tell the reader what nodes to place at which location in the structure, what biases to assign to them, what excitatory and inhibitory links to establish beween them and other nodes, and what weights to assign to each link. For example, the given part of an incoming sentence may tell the reader the location in the existing structure to go to, and then the new node can be placed there. If the new part is positively stated, then an excitatory link will be established; if it is said to be *very important*, the weight of that link can be set at a high value. If the new part is stated as a negative—for instance, *with regard to the given, it is not true that . . .*—then an inhibitory link can be established.

The grammar of exposition and the overlap clues can also play a role in adding to the network, for example by instructing the reader which nodes should be linked up. Signal phrases like *for example* can be used to create an instance subnode for the currently active concept and establish an excitatory link from it to the exemplar. And so on for all the categories of textual instructions covered earlier in this paper.

In general, the role of the text is like that of a subject matter expert instructing a technician to construct a connectionist network of a particular form. The reader is the technician. The subject matter expert has to provide the elements and issue instructions for how to construct them and what biases to establish, and the technician-reader has to be able to carry them out to construct a network. If all goes well, the reader will end up with the intended network, and it can then operate automatically. In particular, if the reader has constructed a copy of the network that supports the expert's expertise, then he should have the same expertise.

VI. CONCLUSIONS

Expository text is in code. The code tells the reader how to construct the mental structures that the author intends. But the code is not entirely under our control just yet. Authors and teachers are not using the code in a controlled way, and learners are not always using the same code as the authors. If the code were clearly specified in the text, and the readers followed it, then learning would be a matter of following directions to create the intended mental structures. But too often the code is not clearly specified in the text, so the readers must attempt problem-solving instead. Unfortunately, problem-solving often fails, and so comprehension fails too. Future psycholinguistic research on instructional expository text should be directed at bringing the code under the control of authors of instructional episodes, so that learners can use it to create the intended expertise.

ACKNOWLEDGMENTS

This research was supported in part by grants to Bruce K. Britton by the U.S. Air Force Office of Scientific Research, Air Force Human Resources Laboratory, Learning Abilities Measurement Project, Grant AFOSR-89-0515, the Office of Naval Research, Grant 442-8041–01, and the Educational Research Development Centers Program, PR award number 117A2007, administered by Office of Educational Research and Improvement, U.S. Office of Education.

REFERENCES

Anderson, J. R. (1990). *Cognitive psychology and its implications*. New York: Freeman.

Britton, B. K. (1978). Lexical ambiguity of words used in English text. *Behavioral Research Methods and Instrumentation, 10*, 1–7.

Britton, B. K., & Gulgoz, S. (1991). Using Kintsch's computational model to improve instructional text: Effects of repairing inference calls on recall and cognitive structures. *Journal of Educational Psychology, 83*, 329–345.

Britton, B. K., Van Dusen, L., Glynn, S. M., & Hemphill, D. (1990). The impact of inferences on instructional texts. In A. C. Graesser & G. H. Bower (Eds.), *The psychology of learning and motivation* (Vol. 25). San Diego, CA: Academic Press.

Bronowski, J. (1966). *The common sense of science*. Cambridge, MA: Harvard University Press.

Chomsky, N. (1957). *Syntactic structures*. The Hague: Mouton.

Christensen, F. (1967). *Notes toward a new rhetoric*. New York: Harper & Row.

Colomb, G. G., & Williams, J. M. (1987). *Discourse structures*. (Tech. Rep. No. 3). Chicago: University of Chicago, The Writing Programs.

Gernsbacher, M. A. (1990). *Language comprehension as structure building*. Hillsdale, NJ: Erlbaum.

Givón, T. (1992). *The grammar of referential coherence as mental processing instructions*. Unpublished manuscript.

Haviland, S. E., & Clark, H. H. (1974). What's new? Acquiring new information as a process of comprehension. *Journal of Verbal Learning and Verbal Behavior, 13*, 512–521.

Kintsch, W. (1988). The role of knowledge in discourse comprehension: A construction-integration model. *Psychological Review, 95*, 163–182.

Kintsch, W. & van Dijk, T. A. (1978). Toward a model of test comprehension and production. *Psychological Review, 85*, 363–394.

Lonergan, B. (1970). *Insight*. New York: Philosophical Library.

Miller, G. H. (1956). The magical number seven, plus or minus two: Some limits on our capacity for processing information. *Psychological Review, 63*, 81–97.

Miller, J. R. & Kintsch, W. (1980). Readability and recall of short prose passages: A theoretical analysis. *Journal of Experimental Psychology: Human Learning and Memory, 6*, 335–354.

Plutarch, (c.100/1932). *The lives of the noble Greeks and Romans*. (J. Dryden, Trans.) New York: Modern Library.

Rumelhart, D. E. (1975). Notes on a schema for stories. In D. G. Bobrow & A. M. Collins (Eds.), *Representation and understanding: Studies in cognitive science*. New York: Academic Press.

Tomkins, S. (1991). *Affect, imagery & consciousness*. New York: Springer.

Turner, A., Britton, B. K., Andraessen, P., & McCutcheon, D. (in press). A predication semantics model of text comprehension. In B. K. Britton & A. Graesser (Eds.), *Models of text comprehension*. Hillsdale, NJ: Erlbaum.

CHAPTER 20

RESOLVING SENTENCES IN A DISCOURSE CONTEXT

HOW DISCOURSE REPRESENTATION AFFECTS LANGUAGE UNDERSTANDING

SIMON C. GARROD AND ANTHONY J. SANFORD

I. INTRODUCTION

Over twenty years ago, Johnson-Laird (1974) described the fundamental problem of psycholinguistics as that of determining what happens when we understand sentences. Few today would disagree with this formulation. Yet for both historical and methodological reasons, the problem has usually been cast in terms of understanding isolated sentences without reference to the discourse context in which they almost invariably occur. This chapter attempts to redress the balance by considering what happens when we understand a sentence in relation to the discourse in which it occurs. As a point of departure, we take the view that sentence comprehension in this broader sense amounts to building a coherent interpretation of all the text encountered so far. This means that the process will have to evaluate the information presented in the current sentence in relation to some representation of the prior discourse which can then be updated and so form the setting for interpreting the next sentence, and so on. In other words, the central issue is one of how we resolve sentences against the current discourse representation.

The chapter begins with a discussion of the basic criteria for successful discourse comprehension, stated in terms of what it is to come up with a coherent and cohesive interpretation of a text as a whole. The outcome of this discussion is a characterization of sentence resolution as a process which anchors the interpretation of the sentence to the representation of the prior text.

HANDBOOK OF PSYCHOLINGUISTICS

II. CRITERIA FOR SENTENCE COMPREHENSION AT THE DISCOURSE LEVEL

Traditionally linguists have identified two characteristics that differentiate a text from just a collection of isolated sentences. The first is what they call cohesion, and the second, coherence (Brown & Yule, 1983; Halliday & Hasan, 1976; see also Sanford & Garrod, this volume).

Sentences are cohesive to the extent that they contain many expressions whose interpretation depends in some way on interpretations of prior expressions in the text and these co-interpretations serve to link the sentences together. One major source of cohesion comes from repeated reference or anaphora. For instance, the following pair of sentences cohere because the pronouns *she* and *it* in (2) take their interpretation from the noun phrases *Susan* and *some money* in (1).

(1) *Bill wanted to lend Susan$_1$ some money$_2$.*
(2) *She$_1$ was hard up and really needed it$_2$.*

Furthermore, the cohesive link contributes to the fact that sentences (1) and (2) constitute a piece of text. But cohesion is not all there is to bind sentences together into a text. For instance consider the following variant of sentences (1) and (2).

(1) *Bill wanted to lend Susan some money.*
(2′) *It is not nice to have close friends who are really hard up.*

Here there are no cohesive anaphoric links between the sentences, yet we still seem to have an acceptable text. What is important in this case is that the two sentences can be related into a coherent whole through inference. The reader will take it that the unpleasantness of having friends who are hard up is the reason why Bill wants to lend Susan some money, and by implication that Susan is Bill's friend. So a text's coherence comes from establishing the logical and psychological consistency between the events and states portrayed.

Cohesion and coherence are not independent. Even in texts such as (1)–(2′) there is a kind of cohesive bond set up, since it is assumed that "Susan" must be an instance of one of "Bill's close friends." In fact, it will often be the case that the interpretation of cohesion markers, such as pronouns, depends upon establishing coherence, and vice versa. For instance, consider the following further variant of sentences (1) and (2).

(1′) *Bill$_1$ wanted to lend his friend$_2$ some money.*
(2″) *He$_2$ was hard up and really needed it.*
(2‴) *However, he$_1$ was hard up and couldn't afford to.*

The same pronoun in almost identical clauses takes on different referential interpretations depending on the different coherence relations between the two sentences. At the same time, the form of coherence relation differs depending on the assignment of the pronoun. For instance, while his being hard up in (2″) is taken as a reason for Bill's wanting to lend money, his being hard up in (2‴) is taken as an obstacle to Bill's wanting to lend the money.

So collections of sentences become texts through the links that bind them together into a coherent structure. Some of the links are explicitly signaled through cohesion markers such as pronouns, whereas other links depend on establishing more abstract logical or psychological relationships between the events portrayed. Besides reference, there are many other sources of linkage. For instance, in narrative text there have to be temporal links which order the events in the story. In simple cases these are signaled with explicit temporal expressions, as in the following short passage.

Yesterday, Mary visited$_{(e1)}$ her grandmother. **Later,** *she stopped$_{(e2)}$ at a shop to buy some flowers.*

Here the events are explicitly ordered through the temporal cohesion device *later*. So event e_1 precedes event e_2. But again it is often the case that ordering comes from establishing a coherent chain of events. For instance, in the following variant the 'visiting' and the 'stopping at the shop' are interpreted as occurring in the opposite order.

Yesterday, Mary visited$_{(e2)}$ her grandmother. She stopped$_{(e1)}$ at a shop to buy some flowers. She then went and presented them to her as gift for her eightieth birthday.

So temporal cohesion, like referential cohesion, is often dependent on the coherence of the passage as a whole.

This brief discussion of what constitutes a text gives some clues about the kind of processes required in sentence resolution. The key processes will be those that anchor the interpretation of the sentence or its fragments to the prior discourse representation. Some of this anchoring will involve establishing referential links, some will involve establishing temporal links, while other anchoring processes will depend on the logical and psychological links between the events and states portrayed (i.e., in terms of their coherence).

In this chapter we attempt to give a characterization of how resolution is achieved on line as the sentence is actually being read. First, we need to establish what kinds of factors at the level of the sentence and of the prior discourse influence the ease of resolution. Here we mainly concentrate on factors surrounding the interpretation of sentences containing referential anaphors. This is partly because much more is known about them than about other cohesion devices, but also because they present a clear paradigm for the other cases.

There are many different forms of anaphor which vary in the degree to which they presuppose contextual interpretation, and their interpretation seems to be affected in a number of ways by the discourse context. The discussion is therefore organized around (a) what is known about how the form of the anaphor affects resolution, and (b) how this interacts with the structure and content of the prior discourse representation.

The second key issue which we address concerns the time course of resolution. From a processing point of view, the variety of decisions which have to be made in resolving a sentence raise a number of interesting questions. Much of what has been learned about interpreting isolated sentences leads to the conclusion that language processing is very efficiently organized in real time. On the whole, sentence interpretation appears to be both immediate and incremental. So one of the central questions to be asked about sentence resolution is what it would mean for it to be efficient in this way. This is discussed in Section V in relation to experimental evidence on immediacy.

III. Referential Factors in Resolution and the Nature of the Discourse Representation

A. Anaphoric Forms

Although we have considered anaphors in general as referential cohesion devices, they support a range of different functions. Ariel (1990) discusses how every known language contains a number of different anaphoric forms which vary in terms of their lexical specificity. In English they range from various forms of zero anaphora through unstressed and stressed pronouns, demonstratives, definite descriptions with and without modification, to proper names with and without modification. Each of these may be used anaphorically to pick up its interpretation from some other reference in the text. Some examples are shown in (3)–(6).

(3) *Jim bumped into Bill and φ fell over.*
(4) *Jim bumped into Bill and **he** fell over.*
(5) *Jim bumped into Bill and **the fool** fell over.*
(6) *Jim bumped into Bill and **Bill** fell over.*

Some linguists have argued that the different forms constitute a kind of referential hierarchy, with the lexically attenuated ones at the top and the fuller forms at the bottom (Silverstein, 1976). Position in the hierarchy is taken to predict a number of characteristics for the particular device, and these are summarized in Table I.

Apart from varying in degree of lexical specificity, the different forms also vary in terms of the degree to which their interpretation is governed by the surrounding text. For instance, the interpretation of zero anaphors is highly constrained by the syntactic context: whereas φ in (3) can only refer to Jim, as subject of the previous clause, the pronoun in (4) is ambiguous between Jim and Bill. A similar contrast can be made between pronouns and fuller definite descriptions; again the pronoun is more contextually constrained than the fuller form. Consider for instance the following short text.

(7) *Mary likes to go to Valentino's for lunch. She fancies **the waiter** there. For dinner she prefers Le Grand Bouffe, where the food is better but **the waiter**/*he is not nearly so handsome.*

Whereas the pronoun in this example has to take its meaning from the antecedent *waiter,* the fuller definite description does not. To this extent its interpretation is less constrained by the prior discourse context. The contrast is also reflected in the general distribution of the different devices in written text. Hence, whereas referential pronouns are hardly ever used without there being an explicit text antecedent, definite descriptions commonly occur without antecedents, as in the example above. In a recent large corpus study, Fraurud (1990) found that 60% of definite descriptions occurred as first mentions without any explicit discourse antecedents.

The final correlated feature of items in the hierarchy is their degree of referential rigidity. In general, the lower the item, the more referentially rigid it is. The same proper name in a text is likely to refer to the same individual throughout, whereas the same pronoun or zero anaphor is not. As we shall see

TABLE I
The Referential Hierarchy

Form	Position	Contextual presupposition	Referential role	Antecedent identification
Pronoun *he, it*	High	High	Referential maintenance	Low
Demonstrative NP *this man*				
Definite NP *the man*	Medium	Medium	Referential maintenance and establishment	Highish
Definite NP + modifier *the man in the hat*				
Proper name *John*	Low	Low	Referential establishment	High

below, pronominal reference tends to be relatively fluid and very dependent on shifts in the discourse focus. To a lesser degree the same can be said about definite descriptions which readily take on different referential interpretations depending on the local context in which they occur.

B. Factors Affecting the Overall Resolution Process

These differences in the function and semantics of the various types of anaphor raise questions about the uniformity of the interpretation process. Are all the different forms treated in exactly the same way, or is the interpretation sensitive to their different functions? One account which has been quite influential in the psychological literature is based on the idea that anaphors of whatever kind trigger the same kind of search procedure aimed at discovering the best matching textual antecedent (Haviland & Clark, 1974). In this account, what is important is simply the degree to which the anaphoric device uniquely identifies its discourse antecedent in that context. For the fuller forms, there is some evidence to support the view that the ease of matching anaphor to antecedent is certainly a factor in overall resolution.

Garrod and Sanford (1977) were able to show that the overall reading time of sentences containing definite anaphors was affected by the semantic relatedness between the antecedent description and the anaphor. When antecedent–anaphor descriptions were only weakly related (e.g., *a tank–the vehicle*), readers spent longer on the sentence containing the anaphor than when they were strongly related (e.g., *a bus–the vehicle*). In fact, the increased reading time matched closely the differences in verification time for the same items. However, it is unlikely that antecedent identifiability is the main factor in determining the ease of resolution for all anaphors. Two things would tend to go against it. First, if identifiability were that important, then we would expect that pronouns which are usually relatively nonspecific with respect to antecedent identifiability would tend to be much more difficult to interpret than they actually are. This is particularly true for plural pronouns, which can in principle admit a multitude of different interpretations by combining any number of possible antecedents. We shall see below that the pronoun used in the right circumstances leads to faster resolution of the sentence overall than a matching fuller description. The second problem arises in relation to the broader range of use of definite descriptions, particularly when they are used to introduce a new referent into the text.

One of the first studies that addressed the question of how anaphor–antecedent relations affected overall sentence resolution time was reported by Haviland and Clark (1974). They contrasted comprehension times for sentences like (10) when they followed either a sentence like (9), which introduced an explicit discourse antecedent for *the beer,* or a sentence like (8), which did not.

(8) *Mary unpacked some picnic supplies.*
(9) Mary unpacked some *beer.*
(10) *The **beer** was warm.*

In this situation, readers spent considerably longer on (10) when there was no explicit antecedent for the reference, i.e., following (8), than when there was one, i.e., following (9). This led Haviland and Clark (1974) to argue that definite descriptions such as *the beer* trigger a search for a matching textual antecedent; should the search fail, the reader then has to engage a special inference mechanism to create the missing antecedent and relate it to the prior discourse. The process of formulating a BRIDGING INFERENCE takes time, and that is why the reader takes longer to understand the sentence.

The trouble with this account is that the majority of definite descriptions do not have discourse antecedents to find; yet on the whole, comprehension seems to proceed perfectly well. In fact, Garrod and Sanford (1982, 1983) demonstrated that there were many situations where a definite reference could be used in the absence of an explicit discourse antecedent without producing any extra cost in terms of comprehension time. For instance, with the following set of materials, (13) takes no longer to read in the context of (12) than in the context of (11) (Garrod & Sanford, 1982; also see Cotter, 1984).

(11) *Keith took his **car** to London.*
(12) *Keith drove to London.*
(13) *The **car** kept overheating.*

Similar results obtain when a reference is made to a character who plays a well-established role in the situation portrayed by the current text. So, for instance, when reading about *the lawyer* in the context of a story about a court case, it makes no difference whether or not there is a matching antecedent reference (Garrod & Sanford, 1983).

The results from these studies suggest that there is more to resolution of reference than simply matching anaphors to antecedent mentions. In cases of situational anaphora as with (12)–(13), we must presume that the processing system is being directed as much by coherence mechanisms as by cohesion mechanisms. The only way of establishing a coherent link between (12) and (13) is to treat *the car* as fulfilling the role of *vehicle used to drive to London.* This is on the assumption that (13) is treated as what Hobbs (1979) calls an elaboration of (11). The fact that establishing the link takes no longer when it arises through a match between explicit antecedent and anaphor, as in (11)–(13), than when it arises through a direct mapping onto the situational role indicates the range of options for anchoring references to discourse representations. The fact that readers encounter problems with Haviland and Clark's (1974) materials but not with these has more to do with what kind of discourse representation is being set up in the two situations than with the priority of direct antecedent matching over bridging.

The ease of resolving sentences containing the fuller definite descriptions depends on how readily the reference can be mapped into the prior discourse representation. However, the representation seems to contain more than just a record of the prior referents. It also must contain information about the roles that new referents could play in the situation being portrayed. One way in which this might come about is through representations of the SCENARIO underlying the prior discourse which contain scenario-determined role slots into which new referents can be accommodated (see Garrod & Sanford, 1982, 1990, for a detailed discussion). To this extent definite descriptions anchor the sentence to the current discourse situation and so serve more than just a referential function. In effect they guide the process in establishing coherence relations between the current sentence and what has come before, through the assignment of referents to roles. With materials like those used by Haviland and Clark (1974), there is little in the relationship between the reference and the prior discourse representation to signal the coherence relation. Presumably beer is not normally considered to play a salient role in unpacking picnic supplies; hence the problem in resolving the sentence.

If the simple antecedent search account is not sufficient for fuller anaphors, how about pronouns? In contrast to the fuller descriptions, pronouns are not normally used in contexts where there is no explicitly mentioned referent onto which they can be mapped. So even though in a sense it may be obvious that Keith used a car to drive to London, sentences (12) and (14) do not make a felicitous text.

(12) *Keith drove to London yesterday.*
(14) *It kept breaking down.*

Although everything in the second sentence would point to it not being London which breaks down, the interpretation on the basis of this one matching antecedent seems to dominate [see Sanford, 1985; Sanford, Garrod, Lucas & Henderson, 1983, and compare the situation with the reference to *the waiter* in text (7)].

Pronouns therefore require an explicit antecedent reference from which to take their interpretation. The problem is that the pronoun itself only constrains its antecedent in terms of gender and number.[1] Consequently, there are usually many possible matching antecedents in the text. There seem to be two important additional constraints on pronoun resolution. The first relates to the FOCUS state of the antecedent, and the second to the degree to which the interpretation as a whole is coherent.

A number of people have argued that pronouns are in general only used to pick out referents which are currently in the focus of the reader's attention, and there are many accounts of how such referents are brought to attention.

---

[1] There are a number of additional syntactic constraints which may apply when the antecedent is in the same sentence, but here we are only concerned with resolution as it relates to cross-sentence anaphora.

In linguistics, Chafe (1976) refers to the process as antecedent FOREGROUNDING, which may admit to a number of distinct levels. In AI, Grosz and Sidner (e.g., Grosz, 1977; Grosz & Sidner, 1985) use the term FOCUSING and argue that it reflects the accessibility of antecedents as determined by the prior discourse structure. In a more psychological vein, we have argued for an account which assumes a limited capacity working memory partition called EXPLICIT FOCUS which contains a limited number of potential referents (Sanford & Garrod, 1981). Behind all these accounts is the recognition that at any time readers or listeners only attend to a restricted field of relevant antecedents, and it is against this background that pronouns are intepreted.

In all accounts of what we shall call FOCUSING, it is assumed that there will be a general preference for very recently mentioned referents to be in focus. However, what is more interesting is how some antecedents remain in focus over longer stretches of text whereas others do not. One way of establishing which potential antecedents remain focused in this way is to interrupt a text at any point and have readers write a plausible continuation sentence. The sentence can then be analyzed in terms of which antecedents are referred to in the continuation. Those mentioned most often should be the ones currently in mind and hence strongly represented in focus at that point. This offers an operational definition for focus which can then be used to test its consequences in terms of processing.

Using this definition, Sanford, Moar, and Garrod (1988) were able to evaluate some of the factors which may contribute to longer term focusing. With short narrative passages, it turned out that a key factor influencing the focus state of an antecedent was the form of the initial introduction of the character in question. In texts which contain more than one individual, the one introduced into a story by proper name seems to be strongly represented in focus throughout.

Sanford et al. (1988) were then able to establish how means of introduction affected reading time for sentences containing different anaphoric forms. The results confirm that the time to read the sentence containing unambiguous pronominal reference was markedly reduced when the pronoun referred to the named or focused character over a nonfocused one which could have been mentioned just as recently. However, in the case of the fuller anaphoric forms (i.e., either proper names or definite descriptions), there was no detectable influence of focus on sentence reading time. This differential effect is also confirmed in studies which examine the on-line nature of resolution, which we consider later in the chapter.

There are a number of other studies on pronoun resolution which are consistent with a general focusing account. Thus Hudson, Tanenhaus, and Dell (1986) manipulated reference to either the agent or patient of an antecedent sentence and showed a processing advantage for pronouns which referred to the agent. These antecedents they described as CENTERED, but since they were always also the subject of the prior sentence they would be classified as focused antecedents in the Sanford-Garrod terminology (see Purkiss's experiment cited in Sanford & Garrod, 1981). Thus one contrast in the Hudson et al. study involved the continuation sentences (16) or (17) following the antecedent (15).

(15) *Jack apologized profusely to Josh.*

(16) *He had been rude to Josh yesterday.*
(17) *He had been offended by Jack's comments.*

They observed that the reading time for the sentences where the pronoun referred to the centered or focused targets was faster than for those referring to the noncentered targets. They suggested that the *He* is initially interpreted as Jack in both cases but is subsequently reassigned on the basis of the plausibility of the sentence as a whole in cases such as (17). Subsequent experiments using a clause-by-clause presentation procedure confirmed this interpretation, since it was only when the disambiguation was toward the noncentered antecedent that the subsequent clause attracted longer reading time. Finally, their experiments also confirm the Sanford et al. (1988) finding that the reading time differences only occur when the reference is made with a pronoun. When they replaced the pronouns with matching proper names, no differences could be detected in the reading times.

This collection of studies is consistent with the accounts described above which would suggest that the rsolution of sentences containing pronouns should be sensitive to the focus state of the antecedent. Antecedents that are currently active in memory seem to be preferred over nonfocused antecedents, and this must in various ways reflect the structure of the prior discourse representation.

The second important constraint on the interpretation of pronouns relates more generally to the coherence of the sentence containing the pronoun. Thus in sentences like the following, readers spend less time identifying the antecedent to the pronoun when it is *he* than when it is *she,* even though both are technically unambiguous (Caramazza, Grober, Garvey, & Yates, 1977; also see Ehrlich, 1980):

(18) *Steven blamed Jane because she/he spilled the coffee.*

In other words, the overall coherence of the sentence can affect the pronoun–antecedent matching decision even when there is only one possible assignment on the basis of the syntax. A further demonstration of this where the pronoun assignment crosses the sentence boundary is reported by Stevenson and Vitkovitch (1986). They compared pronoun-antecedent assignment times for materials like the following:

(19) *Jane stood watching.*
      *Henry jumped across the ravine and **he** fell into the river.*
(20) *Jane stood watching.*
      *Henry jumped across the ravine and **he** picked up some money.*

In (19), the second clause of the second sentence is a highly plausible continuation of the first sentence. In (20), it is implausible. Stevenson and Vitkovitch (1986) demonstrated that the time to decide that *he* refers to Henry was longer in the second case than the first, even though the pronoun is completely unambiguous in terms of gender. Again this would suggest that even with explicit syntactic constraints, the coherence of the interpretation as whole enters into the assignment decision process.

However, it has to be said that explicit pronoun–antecedent assignment studies of this kind may not tell us very much about the precise time course of the resolution process. Though it may be tempting to think that the task will reflect the decision a reader makes immediately on encountering the pronoun, the overall decision times tend to be very long (e.g., around 3.7 s in the Stevenson and Vitkovitch, 1986 study), much longer than the normal time taken to read the clause. This would suggest that making the overt antecedent judgment may only be possible after reading the whole sentence, in which case it would reflect the overall resolution time as much as any initial mapping of pronoun to antecedent. Nevertheless, in relation to the overall resolution of sentences containing pronouns, there is a clear indication that the more general coherence of the text plays an important role.

To summarize the picture so far, it is clear that both the form of the anaphor and the nature of the discourse representation affect its role in resolving the sentence. The interpretation of sentences containing the fuller descriptions relies heavily on the extent to which the description identifies a clearly established role for its referent in the current text scenario, whereas the interpretation of sentences containing pronouns relies heavily on the degree to which the antecedent is in focus at the time of encountering the pronoun, as well as the more general coherence of the interpretation within the text at that point. The contrast between the processing of the different anaphoric forms is not particularly surprising, given that definite descriptions regularly occur in contexts where there is no explicit antecedent but pronouns do not. Similarly, in relation to the importance of focusing, pronouns, unlike the fuller descriptions, are referentially fluid to the extent that they can take on different referential interpretations even within the same sentence. This means that most pronouns could in principle match a multitude of different potential antecedents in any text of reasonable length, and the focusing constraint must serve to reduce the set of possible mappings. So, whereas the forms lower in the referential hierarchy seem to be adapted to introducing new referents or reintroducing old ones into a discourse, those at the top are adapted for maintaining reference to things currently in focus.

This difference in function may also have more general consequences for sentence resolution. Marslen-Wilson, Levy, and Tyler (1982) report a study which looked at the various factors leading speakers to refer to the same individual in different ways. The analysis was based on the distribution of referential forms in a comic book story that a subject had to retell. Each reference was classified according to its position in the kind of referential hierarchy discussed above, and the story was analyzed into a structure of events and episodes. They found that the degree of attenuation of the referential form was almost entirely predictable from the relationship in the story structure between the utterance containing the reference and the utterance containing its antecedent. If the reference was in a sentence which referred to the same event as the sentence containing the antecedent, then a zero or pronoun form was used. If it referred to a different event from the antecedent sentence but within the same story episode, a pronoun or even fuller form was used; whereas if the antecedent occurred in a sentence referring to a different episode, pronouns were only rarely used.

Marslen-Wilson et al.'s findings raise the possibility that the choice of referential device may itself signal the way in which the sentence is to be resolved. The more attenuated references seem to be associated with a close continuity of topic as well as maintenance of reference to focused antecedents, whereas the fuller forms seem to be associated with broaching a new topic and introducing or reintroducing referents. Recent studies reported by Vonk, Hustinx, and Simons (1992) confirm this signaling function of the different referential forms and point to differences in the rate of recovery of relevant antecedent information for sentences containing the different forms.

In looking at the role of the various referential devices afforded by the language and the possible influence of prior discourse representation in sentence resolution, we have concentrated only on global effects which relate to overall comprehension difficulty. However, the main thrust of this chapter is about the on-line processes that lead to resolution, and that is the issue to which we now turn.

IV. SENTENCE COMPREHENSION AS A PROCESS OF ON-LINE RESOLUTION

One of the first issues that arises in finding out what happens when we understand a sentence is the time course of the process, in other words, how the interpretation proceeds in relation to sampling the input. When you listen to a sentence, what you actually hear is a sequence of words encountered in a strict linear order. The same occurs during reading, since the eye moves from word to word in a predominantly left to right direction (Rayner & Pollatsek, 1989). There are a number of sound functional arguments for assuming that the interpretation process should match this linear sampling as closely as possible. First, to the extent that any word is left uninterpreted, it imposes a concurrent memory load on the system which could interfere with subsequent processing. Second, to the extent that the interpretation is delayed, this builds up a processing debt which will have to be redeemed later and so compete with the more basic sampling of the subsequent input.

Ideas such as these prompted Just and Carpenter (1980) to put forward what they call the immediacy hypothesis for reading. They proposed that every word encountered in the input should be processed to the deepest level possible before the eye moves on to the next word. There are really two aspects to immediacy: one relates to immediate recovery of information about the word, while the other relates to immediate integration of that information into the current interpretation of the sentence. Immediate recovery occurs at the deepest level if all the relevant information associated with the word is recovered as soon as it is encountered. For instance, all the possible meanings and syntactic forms of a word should be immediately available. On the other hand, immediate integration is more difficult to define, since it depends on the architecture of the processing system. In its most radical form, immediate integration presupposes an incremental processing system which continuously incorporates the current input into the interpretation being built up on the basis of the past input. So comprehension must proceed in a linear fashion, building up partial interpretations as it goes along.

Evidence for immediacy in the first sense of information recovery is easy to find in the literature on isolated sentence comprehension. For instance, there is solid evidence that all the alternative meanings of a word are recovered as soon as it is encountered (Frazier & Rayner, 1990; Swinney, 1979). Evidence for immediacy in the second sense of continuous incremental analysis also exists in relation to syntactic parsing, for instance, although the situation is somewhat more complicated.

Frazier and Rayner (1982) demonstrated that readers confronted with certain kinds of structural syntactic ambiguity would commit themselves in the first instance to one reading. Thus, having read a sentence up to the point given in (21), readers would treat it as though the prepositional phrase *on the cart* was attached to the verb *loaded* rather than to the noun phrase *the boxes*.

(21) *Sam loaded the boxes on the cart . . .*

They were able to demonstrate this by measuring the reader's eye movements with two versions of a sentence containing this ambiguous fragment.

(22) *Sam loaded the boxes on the cart **before lunch**.*
(23) *Sam loaded the boxes on the cart **onto the van**.*

When presented with (23), readers encountered difficulty at the point where the prepositional phrase attachment was disambiguated. They spent substantially longer fixating this region of the sentence and were much more likely to refixate the ambiguous fragment (21). Frazier and Rayner used this finding to argue that the syntactic parsing process was essentially incremental, so when points of ambiguity are encountered the reader will always adopt the reading which reflects the simplest structure, the one which involves minimal attachment.

From the present point of view, what is important about these findings is that they demonstrate a pressure toward immediate incremental analysis even at the risk of subsequent misunderstanding. At the same time they illustrate the main pitfall of doing it this way, which arises from the problem of early commitment. The system will either be forced to track multiple alternative analyses or may have to make an early and risky commitment to following one line of interpretation over the other. In fact, Frazier and Rayner (1987) found other cases of local syntactic ambiguity that do not trigger such immediate commitment.

For instance, when readers are given sentences such as (24) or (25), a different pattern of results emerges.

(24) *I know that the **desert trains** young people to be especially tough.*
(25) *I know that the **desert trains** are especially tough on young people.*

Here a potential syntactic ambiguity is present at the words *desert trains* which could either be treated as noun plus main verb of the sentence, as in (24), or as adjective plus noun, as in (25). These sentences were compared with the unambiguous controls (24′) and (25′).

(24′) *I know that **this** desert trains young people to be especially tough.*
(25′) *I know that **these** desert trains are especially tough on young people.*

Now if the processor was always interpreting incrementally, even at the expense of making an early commitment, then readers should take just as long or longer processing the ambiguous fragment *desert trains* in (24) and (25) than the disambiguated fragment in (24′) and (25′). In fact, quite the opposite pattern emerges. The readers spend more time fixating the words in the unambiguous case than the ambiguous one. However, they then spend less time on the remainder of the sentence. This is consistent with a mechanism that holds off interpretation of the ambiguous information and attempts to look ahead for disambiguators before committing itself to an immediate incremental analysis.

The important point about this literature on processing isolated sentences is that while immediacy in terms of recovery of information seems to be very much the rule, immediacy in terms of incremental processing and integration seems to be subject to a number of conditions which revolve around the whole question of making early syntactic or semantic commitments (see Frazier & Rayner, 1990, for a recent discussion).

If we assume that the sentence resolution process is inherent to sentence comprehension, then we would expect to find just such on-line principles driving it. The problem is to determine to what extent the processing decisions required in resolving the sentence can be thought of as analogous to the recovery processes and incremental interpretation processes underlying such things as syntactic parsing. Clearly, sentence resolution involves both information recovery and its integration into the interpretation of the sentence. Interpreting cohesion markers such as pronouns requires recovering contextual information onto which the pronoun can be mapped while establishing coherence relations requires integrating the interpretation of larger fragments of the sentence into the discourse representation as a whole. So a strong assumption of immediacy would be that the recovery process for cohesion markers be immediate and the coherence evaluation and integration be incremental.

We consider these two issues in turn. First, we consider evidence for immediacy in terms of recovery of the contextual information required to resolve a sentence, then we consider evidence for immediacy in terms of incrementality in sentence resolution.

A. Immediacy in Relation to Recovery of Contextual Information

A technique that has now been widely used to draw inferences about when information is recovered during reading involves what might be called CONTINGENT PRIMING. In the case of written material, the subject is presented with a text, usually word by word, and at a critical point some lexical judgment task is given. For example Dell, McKoon, and Ratcliff (1983) used the following text:

A burglar surveyed the garage set back from the street.
Several milk bottles were piled at the curb. The banker and her husband were on vacation.
The criminal/A cat slipped away from the street lamp.

At the critical point following either the anaphor *the criminal* or the non-anaphor *a cat*, they presented the test word *burglar* in a recognition task (i.e., Was the word in the prior text or not?). They found that recognition was primed immediately following *criminal* as compared to *cat*. They also obtained a similar enhancement for words drawn from the sentence in which the antecedent had occurred (e.g., *garage*) following the anaphor compared to the non-anaphor. This finding together with related findings from Gernsbacher (1989) suggests that the relevant antecedent information is recovered rapidly (at least within

250 ms) following exposure to the anaphor. Apart from the finding for the definite description anaphors such as *the criminal*, Gernsbacher (1989) has also demonstrated a similar pattern of results with proper name anaphors. In this case, she was able to show a reliable differential between positive priming for the antecedent and inhibition for a non-antecedent relative to a point just before the anaphor.

Therefore, it would seem that there is evidence for immediate recovery of contextual information, at least for anaphors low in the referential hierarchy. In the case of pronouns, the situation is somewhat more complicated. In a spoken cross-modal version of the contingent priming task, Shillcock (1982) demonstrated that there was enhanced recognition of the antecedent immediately following presentation of an unambiguous pronoun, and this was relative to a non-antecedent control. However, the only pre- versus post-presentation difference came out as a suppression of the non-antecedent control word. Gernsbacher (1989), on the other hand, did not find evidence for such a rapid priming difference in the case of unambiguous pronouns. The only clear difference in her study emerged at the end of the whole sentence containing the anaphor. So while there is clear indication that the fuller anaphors immediately recover antecedent information, with pronouns this does not seem always to be the case.

However, this apparent contradiction in the findings for the fuller anaphors versus pronouns may have something to do with the nature of the probes that are used. Cloitre and Bever (1988) report a number of experiments which suggest that noun anaphors only immediately activate surface information about their antecedents, whereas pronouns immediately activate deeper conceptual information. The experiments compared priming effects using a number of different tasks. In general, they found that tasks which tapped recovery of conceptual information about the antecedent, such as category decision, produced earlier effects following the pronoun than the noun anaphors; whereas the opposite was true for lexical decision, which taps surface information. At the same time, secondary effects associated with conceptual properties of the antecedent, such as concreteness, emerged in the immediate responses following the pronoun but not the noun anaphors. So one possibility is that the different referential devices are recovering different types of information from the prior discourse, with pronouns having a privileged status in terms of access to conceptual information about the antecedent. A recent set of experiments by Vonk et al. (1992) also tends to suggest that unambiguous pronouns may recover information related to the antecedent more rapidly than fuller anaphors.

So, in relation to the first criterion of immediacy—immediate information recovery—anaphoric processing gives some confirmation of Just and Carpenter's (1980) hypothesis, albeit with reservations about the degree of immediacy and the exact form of the information being recovered. However, it is perhaps worth pointing out that antecedent priming studies are not without their problems. In particular, presenting texts in a piecemeal, word-by-word fashion is a poor simulation of the normal reading process and may well interfere with the time course of the sentence resolution.

A less invasive procedure for establishing what is happening during reading is to track eye movements, and there have been a few studies which use this technique to look at recovery of contextual information. The first study we consider looked at the interpretation of unambiguous pronouns but with antecedents either close in the text or far removed. By measuring the amount of time the reader spent fixating the pronoun and subsequent regions of the sentence, Ehrlich and Rayner (1983) were able to demonstrate an antecedent distance effect. When the antecedent was distant, readers spent a reliably longer time fixating the region immediately after the pronoun and for a few words beyond it, as compared to the other condition. This result is consistent with the idea that the pronoun immediately triggers access to its antecedent, but recovery takes longer when the antecedent is distant and so presumably out of focus.[2] The result is broadly in line with the findings on the overall resolution of sentences containing pronouns (see above). However, it may also reflect subsequent integration processes which could be affected by encountering a reference to a character which is out of focus.

The second eye-tracking study that has some bearing on the time course of antecedent recovery looked at the interpretation of definite description anaphors. This study, reported by Garrod, O'Brien, Morris, and Rayner (1990) and based on an earlier study by O'Brien, Shank, Myers, and Rayner (1988), explored the effects of role restriction constraints on the time taken to interpret the anaphors. The basic rationale was similar in some ways to that in the Garrod and Sanford (1982) experiment described in Section III,A. Various contexts were constructed which could impose a potential restriction on the nature of an antecedent referent. An example set is shown in (26)–(29).

(26) *He **assaulted** her with his **weapon**.*
(27) *He **stabbed** her with his **weapon**.*
(28) *He **assaulted** her with his **knife**.*
(29) *He **stabbed** her with his **knife**.*

After a further intervening sentence, subjects were then presented with one of the target sentences in (30), and their eye movements were recorded.

(30) *He threw **the/a knife** into the bushes, took her money, and ran away.*

The basic question of interest was how the different types of contextual restriction on the antecedent *knife* might affect the subsequent fixation time for the reference to the knife in (30). In (28) and (29) the antecedent is explicitly introduced as *a knife*, whereas in (27) as opposed to (26) the verb implicitly restricts *the weapon* to be a knife. So one question that the study addressed was how these two forms of restriction might affect the amount of time the reader actually fixated on the subsequent anaphor *the knife*. The study also had a control condition to establish any general priming advantage that the context might give to the subsequent identification of the word *knife*, hence, the inclusion of the non-anaphoric matching NP *a knife* on half the trials. An example of one material in all its conditions is shown in Table II. The resulting fixation durations on the critical noun phrase are shown in Figure 1.

With the non-anaphoric controls, there was only a reading advantage when the antecedent exactly matched the lexical specification of the target noun. Contexts containing either (28) or (29) led to shorter reading times than contexts

---

[2] In general, if an antecedent has not been mentioned recently, it will be out of focus, unless it has been identified as a principal character in the narrative (see the earlier discussion).

TABLE II
Materials in Garrod, O'Brien, Morris, and Rayner (1990)

All the mugger wanted was to steal the woman's money. But when she screamed, he [stabbed] [assaulted] her with his (knife) (weapon) in an attempt to quieten her down. He looked to see if anyone had seen him. He threw {the} {a} *knife* into the bushes, took her money, and ran away.

Factors manipulated:
  1. Restricting versus nonrestricting context for the antecedent (i.e., *stabbed* vs. *assaulted*)
  2. Explicitly matching antecedent for the target noun knife (i.e., *knife* vs. *weapon*)
  3. Target in definite or indefinite NP (i.e., *a* vs. *the*)

---

containing either (26) or (27), but the implicit restriction from the verb had no effect whatsoever. However, with the anaphoric target sentences, fixation duration was equally reduced by either implicit restriction from the verb as in (27) or lexical specification on the antecedent as in (28) and (29). So the only case where there was a reliably longer reading time was when neither restriction applied, as in (26).

This experiment clearly demonstrates that an anaphor immediately recovers the contextual information in the antecedent. Although there was a lexical priming effect observed for the non-anaphoric control, there was no effect associated with the role restriction imposed by the verb or other part of the sentence. The role restriction effect observed in the anaphoric materials must therefore come from the establishment of the coherent link associated with resolving the definite description (see Section III,A).

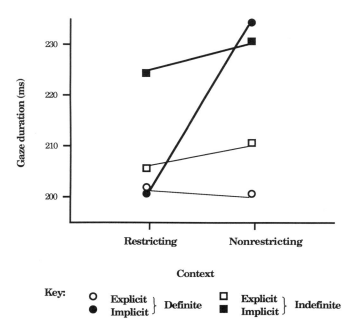

FIG. 1 Gaze durations on the target noun showing the effects of contextual restriction and explicitness of mention of the antecedent with definite reference (anaphoric) versus indefinite reference (non-anaphoric) repeats (from Garrod, O'Brien, Morris, & Rayner, 1990).

In conclusion, both the priming studies and a few eye-tracking experiments reported to date indicate that the recovery of contextually relevant information occurs at the time of encountering a fuller anaphor. In the case of pronouns, the evidence is not quite so clear-cut. The priming studies tend to suggest that the form of the antecedent is not so rapidly accessed with pronouns as with the fuller anaphors, but at the same time they tend to indicate that deeper conceptual information may be recovered more rapidly on occasion. However, the eye-tracking experiment by Ehrlich and Rayner (1983) would also indicate that immediacy may also be subject to focusing constraints on the antecedent in the case of pronouns. Below we consider the question of immediacy of integration of contextual information and in doing so find some support for this view.

B. Immediacy in Relation to Integration of Contextual Information

Establishing that some aspect of contextually relevant information has been recovered immediately following an anaphor does not license the stronger assumption that this information is immediately integrated into the sentence interpretation. This point is particularly important in relation to resolving sentences containing pronouns, where the overall coherence of interpretation seems to play such an important part.

One attempt to establish the immediacy of integration is reported in a study by Garrod and Sanford (1985) using a spelling error detection procedure. They presented materials of the form in (31) and measured the time readers took to detect the spelling error on the critical verb.

(31) *A dangerous incident in the pool*
Elizabeth was an inexperienced swimmer and wouldn't have gone in if the male lifeguard hadn't been standing by the pool. But as soon as she got out of her depth she started to panic and wave her hands about in a frenzy.
(a) *Within seconds Elizabeth senk (sank) into the pool.*
(b) *Within seconds Elizabeth jimped (jumped) into the pool.*
(c) *Within seconds the lifeguard senk into the pool.*
(d) *Within seconds the lifeguard jimped into the pool.*

The passages always introduced two characters described as being in different states. For instance, in this example the main character *Elizabeth* is described as out of her depth in the pool, while the subsidiary character *the lifeguard* is standing by the pool. The passages then continued with one of four critical sentences containing misspelled verbs depicting actions either consistent or inconsistent with what was known about each character in the story. Hence, given the current state of *Elizabeth*, it is consistent for her to *sink* at this point but not to *jump*, while the opposite is true for *the lifeguard*. Furthermore, the consistency or inconsistency is only apparent in relation to the whole anaphor–verb complex, in that it is not the jumping or sinking which is anomalous but the fact that Elizabeth should jump or the lifeguard sink.

The subjects read the materials one sentence at a time while monitoring for spelling errors. We reasoned that immediate and incremental resolution, if it occurred, should be reflected in increased latency for detection of the spelling error on the inconsistent verb. We found just such consistency effects in the case where the anaphors were proper names or definite descriptions, as in (31). However, when the full anaphors were replaced with unambiguous pronouns, a more complicated pattern of results emerged.

When the pronoun referred to the main character or thematic subject of the passage (e.g., *Elizabeth*, in this example), readers took longer to detect a misspelling on the inconsistent verb, but when it referred to the subsidiary character (e.g., *the lifeguard*), there was absolutely no evidence of such an effect. So these results suggested that the nature of any incremental resolution was dependent on both the linguistic form of the anaphors and the focus state of the discourse representation at that point.

Although these results are consistent with immediate integration and continuous incremental resolution of the sentence in relation to the discourse representation, the procedure suffers from the same kind of problems as the explicit antecedent assignment studies. In this situation, readers take a long time to detect spelling errors, and estimates of their reading rates indicate that they are only reading the material at about half the normal rate. Consequently, it is not clear to what extent the spelling error is being responded to as soon as the verb is encountered.

To overcome these inherent methodological limitations, Garrod, Freudenthal, and Boyle (1993) carried out an eye-tracking study based on the earlier Garrod and Sanford (1985) experiment. With the eye-tracking procedure it is possible to present the same kind of materials containing contextually consistent or inconsistent verbs and measure the point in the sentence when the reader first detects the inconsistency. We reasoned that this should appear as a first pass increase in fixation duration on either the verb itself or the immediate post-verb region of the sentence.

Apart from the full anaphor versus pronoun contrast, we also manipulated the degree to which the pronoun was disambiguated by gender and number. So there was a condition where the antecedents were gender-differentiated as in Garrod and Sanford (1985) and a matching condition where they were not (e.g., we changed *Elizabeth* to *Alexander*). The critical question is how early the inconsistency can be detected in the eye-movement record. An example set of materials for the various pronoun conditions is shown in (32).

(32) *A dangerous incident in the pool*

> **Elizabeth$_1$/Alexander$_2$** *was an inexperienced swimmer and wouldn't have gone in if **the male lifeguard$_3$** hadn't been standing by the pool. But as soon as she/he got out of her/his depth she/he started to panic and wave her/his hands about in a frenzy.*

> *Within seconds she$_1$ sank into the pool.* $+T+G+C$
> *Within seconds she$_1$ jumped into the pool.* $+T+G-C$

> *Within seconds he$_3$ sank into the pool.* $+T-G+C$
> *Within seconds he$_3$ jumped into the pool.* $+T-G-C$

> *Within seconds he$_2$ jumped into the pool.* $-T+G+C$
> *Within seconds he$_2$ sank into the pool.* $-T+G-C$

> *Note:* T = Theme, G = gender, C = consistency.

Considering first the results from the pronoun conditions, there is strong evidence for very early detection of inconsistency, but only in the case where the pronoun is gender-disambiguating and maintains reference to the focused thematic subject of the passage (conditions $+T+G+/-C$). The magnitudes of the consistency effects are shown in Figure 2A, represented as differences in fixation time between consistent and inconsistent verb condition in milliseconds per character. Turning to the pattern of results from the conditions with the fuller anaphors, a rather different pattern of results obtains. Here there is no evidence of an early detection of verb inconsistency (see Figure 2B).

However, in all anaphor conditions, there were marked effects of consistency appearing in the second pass fixations for the verb and subsequent regions. So while it is clear that all the readers ultimately detect the inconsistency, it seems that it is only in the case where the pronoun identifies the focused thematic subject of the passage that there is immediate integration of the relevant contextual information.

Taken together, these results suggest that the immediate resolution of the pronouns comes about through an interaction between the syntactic (gender) information in the pronoun and the focus state of the prior discourse representa-

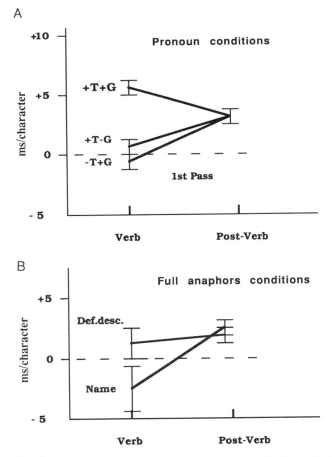

FIG. 2 First pass fixation durations (ms/character) for the critical verb and immediate post-verb regions, shown for the pronoun conditions (A) and the full anaphor conditions (B) of the Garrod et al. (1993) eye-tracking experiments.

tion. If it is the case both that an antecedent is focused and the pronoun uniquely identifies it through gender matching, then the system makes an early commitment to the full interpretation. When either of these conditions does not hold, then commitment is delayed until after the verb has been encountered. Presumably, this arrangement makes best use of a coherence-checking mechanism to fix the final interpretation of the pronoun.

The situation with the fuller anaphors is much more surprising. On the one hand, there is clear evidence from the antecedent priming literature discussed above that the fuller anaphors immediately recover some information about their antecedents, but on the other hand, this does not seem to lead to immediate commitment on the part of the processing system to this particular interpretation. One possible explanation for the apparent discrepancy comes from considering the degree to which the fuller forms presuppose that particular interpretation.

As we showed in (7) above, it is not always the case that a definite description has to take its meaning from a matching antecedent NP. This difference can be readily demonstrated with the materials used here where the target sentences containing the fuller descriptions would be perfectly acceptable without discourse antecedents. Thus, the amended version (33) of the example material is a well-formed text with the definite description but not with the associated pronoun.

(33) *Elizabeth wouldn't have gone in if her sister had not been standing by the pool. But as soon as she got out of her depth she started to panic and wave her hands about in a frenzy. Within seconds, the lifeguard/he jumped into the pool.*

In other words, the passage can be understood and is perfectly coherent even when the fuller description does not have a textually determined antecedent. This is clearly not the case with the pronoun version. So one possible consequence of the differences in contextual presupposition would be in terms of the requirements for immediate commitment to that contextual interpretation. For the more attenuated forms, activation of the relevant context is essential for any immediate semantic analysis; this is clearly not the case for the fuller forms.

The fact that it is possible to differentiate experimentally between immediate recovery and immediate integration motivates drawing a distinction between anaphor BONDING and anaphor RESOLUTION. As Sanford and Garrod (1989) suggest, anaphors may immediately set up bonds with potential antecedents without necessarily forcing a commitment to resolution at that stage. In processing terms, bonding amounts to locating where in the representation relevant information may be found, whereas resolution would involve commitment to one particular interpretation at that point in the process. Such a commitment would in effect pipe the relevation contextual information through to the processing system and so enable it to integrate subsequent information in the sentence directly into the discourse representation. In the same way that the syntactic processor may be loath to always make early commitments as in the Frazier and Rayner (1987) experiments, it seems that the sentence resolver may also be loath to make such immediate referential commitments except under rather special conditions.

V. SUMMARY AND CONCLUSIONS

At the outset of this chapter we promised to say something about what happens when a sentence is understood in relation to its discourse context. In fact, most of what has been discussed relates to just one way in which a sentence has to be contextually resolved, and that is in terms of its referential interpretation. First we summarize this discussion, and then we return to the more general issue of how resolution processes fit in with the interpretation of the sentence as a whole.

A. Resolving Referential Interpretations

The resolution process can be defined in terms of its goal of establishing a textually coherent interpretation that respects the cohesion constraints imposed by anaphors. Referential resolution can then be expressed as a process of anchoring the linguistic interpretation to the discourse representation. We argued that three main factors enter into the process: first, the nature of the active discourse representation onto which the interpretation can be referentially anchored; second, the form of the anaphor which instigates the anchoring; and finally, the coherence constraints arising from the logical and psychological relations which bind the resulting interpretation to the discourse context.

All these factors interact in the overall resolution of the sentence. First there are systematic differences in the way the system deals with the different forms of anaphor. We discussed them in relation to position on the referential hierarchy. Whereas processing the more attenuated forms at the top of the hierarchy is very sensitive to the focus state of the discourse representation, for those less attenuated forms lower on the hierarchy this does not seem to be the case. Thus, while pronouns tend to bond onto focused explicit antecedents in preference to nonfocused antecedents, this kind of focusing does not affect the processing of the fuller forms. However, fuller anaphors, in particular definite descriptions, are commonly used to introduce new referents into the discourse related to the representation only through situational roles. To this extent, interpreting the fuller forms usually involves establishing a coherent link between the reference and the discourse context, with or without antecedent co-reference. As a result, resolving sentences which contain such situational references is very much affected by whether or not the discourse representation already contains a role slot onto which the reference can be readily matched.

Finally, we addressed the more complex question of when these various processes occur in relation to the on-line analysis of sentences read in context. By analogy to the work on comprehension of isolated sentences, we drew a distinction between two aspects of immediacy in processing: first, immediate recovery of relevant information, and second, the immediate on-line integration of this information into the interpretation. In much the same way that syntactic parsing and lexical semantic access seem to be immediate in relation to information recovery, so is antecedent access immediate, at least for fuller anaphors and pronouns that bond onto focused antecedents. However, when it comes to on-line integration of the information, the picture is not so simple. To date, the limited evidence tends to indicate that the system is only prepared to adopt an early commitment to anaphoric resolution when a pronoun uniquely bonds to a focused antecedent. In any other case, whether with pronouns or fuller anaphors, there is evidence for delayed resolution of the sentence. In the case of the pronouns, it seems that the delay reflects a search for further constraints on anaphoric bonding arising from the rest of the sentence, whereas with the fuller forms this is less likely to be the case.

One possible explanation for delayed resolution in the case of the more explicit anaphors has been raised by Vonk et al. (1992) and relates to the different role of anaphors within the referential hierarchy. As we have seen above, devices high on the hierarchy tend to be used to maintain reference to strongly focused antecedents in sentences that maintain thematic continuity. Such sentences should anchor directly into the currently active discourse representation and so be amenable to incremental resolution. In contrast, references made with devices lower in the hierarchy tend to be used to introduce new referents or reintroduce old ones in sentences that do not maintain a strong continuity of theme. For instance, they commonly occur in sentences at the beginning of a new paragraph. It may be for this reason that the system is not prepared to make an early commitment to anchoring the sentence to the existing discourse representation but rather holds off resolution until all the relevant information has been evaluated. If this is the case, then different anaphoric devices may direct the processing of the sentence in rather different ways.

On the basis of these findings, a picture begins to emerge of the relationship between what we have been calling sentence resolution versus what is commonly called sentence comprehension.

B. Sentence Resolution as Part of On-line Sentence Interpretation

There is a tendency in the literature to describe the process of sentence comprehension as proceeding from analysis of form, through local meaning, to contextual integration in a stage-by-stage fashion. Thus, the initial processing is assumed to involve lexical and syntactic analysis, then semantic analysis, and only when this is complete is the sentence evaluated in relation to the discourse context. In terms of immediacy, it is therefore assumed that processes that are sensitive to the discourse context are more likely to be delayed.

The experiments which we have been discussing suggest that the picture is much more complicated than this. First, in relation to information recovery, there is every reason to believe that anaphors make contact with the overall discourse representation at the earliest point in processing. Many of the studies demonstrate contextual effects in the first pass fixation on the critical word (e.g., Garrod et al., 1990). So there is no evidence to support the view that contextual information is necessarily recovered any later than the semantic information about the word in question. However, when we consider the processes that build interpretations on the basis of incremental composition, there is some indication that syntactic analysis does have priority. Recent attempts to find cases where the context can override the garden path induced by syntactic structures, such as the prepositional phrase attachments described in Section IV, have proved largely unsuccessful. Thus, while there is some evidence that the early commitment to the structurally motivated reading may be alleviated in context (Britt, Perfetti, Garrod, & Rayner, 1992), in general contextual manipulations, such as focusing, only affect the early recovery from the syntactically motivated garden path (see Rayner, Garrod, & Perfetti, 1992). However, it turns out to be equally difficult to find cases where local semantic analysis can override these initial syntactic biases, and again the semantic effects only show up in relation to early recovery (e.g., Clifton, Speer, & Abney, 1991). Therefore, although it may be the case that certain kinds of syntactic processing dominate in the very earliest stages of comprehension, the influence of both local semantic analysis and more global resolution processes soon appears. In fact, the Garrod et al. (1993) finding described at the end of Section IV demonstrates the integration of contextual information at the earliest stage in reading, when there are strong grounds for early commitment.

The experimental work which we have reviewed here clearly demonstrates that contextual resolution is an essential component in the on-line interpretation of the sentence. This means not that it always proceeds immediately and incrementally, but rather that it is subject to exactly the same kind of on-line processing constraints that hold for other aspects of sentence comprehension, including syntactic analysis. Hence, the immediacy of sentence resolution at its deepest level will depend in each instance on the costs and benefits of making an early commitment to one type of contextual interpretation over another.

REFERENCES

Ariel, M. (1990). *Accessing noun-phrase antecedents*. London: Routledge.

Britt, M. A., Perfetti, C. A., Garrod, S., Rayner, K. (1992). Parsing in discourse: Context effects and their limits. *Journal of Memory and Language, 31,* 293–314.

Brown, G., & Yule, G. (1983). *Discourse analysis*. Cambridge: Cambridge University Press.

Caramazza, A., Grober, E. H., Garvey, C., & Yates, J. B. (1977). Comprehension of anaphoric pronouns. *Journal of Verbal Learning and Verbal Behavior, 16,* 601–609.

Chafe, W. (1976). Givenness, contrastiveness, definiteness, subjects, topics and point of view. In C. N. Li (Ed.) *Language comprehension and the acquisition of knowledge* (pp. 25–56). Washington, DC: Winston.

Clifton, C., Speer, S., & Abney, S. P. (1991). Parsing arguments: Phrase structure and argument structure as determinants of initial parsing decisions. *Journal of Memory and Language, 30,* 251–271.

Cloitre, M., & Bever, T. G. (1988). Linguistic anaphors, levels of representation and discourse. *Language and Cognitive Processes, 3,* 293–322.

Cotter, C. A. (1984). Inferring indirect objects in sentences: Some implications for the semantics of verbs. *Language and Speech, 27*(1), 25–45.

Dell, G. S., McKoon, G., & Ratcliff, R. (1983). The activation of antecedent information during the processing of anaphoric reference in reading. *Journal of Verbal Learning and Verbal Behavior, 22,* 121–132.

Ehrlich, K. (1980). Comprehension of pronouns. *Quarterly Journal of Experimental Psychology, 32,* 247–255.

Ehrlich, K., & Rayner, K. (1983). Pronoun assignment and semantic integration during reading: Eye-movements and immediacy of processing. *Journal of Verbal Learning and Verbal Behavior, 22,* 75–87.

Fraurud, K. (1990). Definiteness and the processing of NPs in natural discourse. *Journal of Semantics, 7,* 395–434.

Frazier, L., & Rayner, K. (1982). Making and correcting errors during sentence comprehension: Eye movements in the analysis of structurally ambiguous sentences. *Cognitive Psychology, 14,* 178–210.

Frazier, L., & Rayner, K. (1987). Resolution of syntactic category ambiguities: Eye movements in parsing lexically ambiguous sentences. *Journal of Memory and Language, 26,* 505–526.

Frazier, L., & Rayner, K. (1990). Taking on semantic commitments: Processing multiple meanings vs. multiple senses. *Journal of Memory and Language, 29,* 181–201.

Garrod, S., Freudenthal, D., & Boyle, E. (1993). The role of different types of anaphor in the on-line resolution of sentences in a discourse. *Journal of Memory and Language, 32,* 1–30.

Garrod, S., O'Brien, E. J., Morris, R. K., & Rayner, K. (1990). Elaborative inferencing as an active or passive process. *Journal of Experimental Psychology: Learning, Memory, and Cognition, 16*, 250–257.

Garrod, S. & Sanford, A. J. (1977). Interpreting anaphoric relations: The integration of semantic information while reading. *Journal of Verbal Learning and Verbal Behavior, 16*, 77–90.

Garrod, S., & Sanford, A. J. (1982). Bridging inferences in the extended domain of reference. In A. Baddeley & J. Long (Eds.), *Attention and performance. IX* (pp. 331–346). Hillsdale, NJ: Erlbaum.

Garrod, S., & Sanford, A. J. (1983). Topic dependent effects in language processing. In G. B. Flores d'Arcais & R. Jarvella (Eds.), *The process of language comprehension* (pp. 271–295). Chichester: Wiley.

Garrod, S., & Sanford, A. J. (1985). On the real-time character of interpretation during reading. *Language and Cognitive Processes, 1*, 43–61.

Garrod, S., & Sanford, A. J. (1990). Referential processing in reading: Focusing on roles and individuals. In D. A. Balota, G. B. Flores d'Arcais, & K. Rayner (Eds.), *Comprehension processes in reading* (pp. 465–486). Hillsdale, NJ: Erlbaum.

Gernsbacher, M. A. (1989). Mechanisms that improve referential access. *Cognition, 32*, 99–156.

Grosz, B. (1977). *The representation and use of focus in dialogue understanding* (Tech. Note No. 15). Menlo Park, CA: Artificial Intelligence Center, SRI International.

Grosz, B., & Sidner, C. (1985, August). Discourse structure and the proper treatment of interruptions. *International Journal of the Conference of Artificial Intelligence*, pp. 832–838.

Halliday, M. A. K., & Hasan, R. (1976). *Cohesion in English*. London: Longman.

Haviland, S. E. & Clark, H. H. (1974). What's new? Acquiring new information as a process in comprehension. *Journal of Verbal Learning and Verbal Behavior, 13*, 512–521.

Hobbs, J. R. (1979). Coherence and coreference. *Cognitive Science, 3*, 67–90.

Hudson, S. B., Tanenhaus, M. K., & Dell, G. S. (1986). *Proceedings of the Eighth Annual Conference of the Cognitive Science Society* (pp. 96–109). Hillsdale, N.J.: Erlbaum.

Johnson-Laird, P. N. (1974). Experimental psycholinguistics. *Annual Review of Psychology, 25*, 135–160.

Just, M. A., & Carpenter, P. A. (1980). A theory of reading: From eye-fixations to comprehension. *Psychological Review, 87*, 329–354.

Marslen-Wilson, W., Levy, E., & Tyler, L. K. (1982). Producing interpretable discourse: The establishment and maintenance of reference. In R. J. Jarvella & W. Klein (Eds.), *Speech, place and action* (pp. 339–378). Chichester: Wiley.

O'Brien, E. J., Shank, D. M., Myers, J. L., & Rayner, K. (1988). Elaborative inferences during reading: Do they occur on-line? *Journal of Experimental Psychology: Learning, Memory, and Cognition, 14*, 410–420.

Rayner, K., Garrod, S., & Perfetti, C. A. (1992). Discourse influences during parsing are delayed. *Cognition, 45*, 109–140.

Rayner, K., & Pollatsek, A. (1989). *The psychology of reading*. Englewood Cliffs, NJ: Prentice-Hall.

Sanford, A. J. (1985). Aspects of pronoun interpretation. In G. Rickheit & H. Strohner (Eds.), *Inferences in text processing* (pp. 183–205). North-Holland/Amsterdam: Elsevier.

Sanford, A. J., & Garrod, S. (1981). *Understanding written language: Explorations in comprehension beyond the sentence*. Chichester: Wiley.

Sanford, A. J., & Garrod, S. (1989). What, when and how: Questions of immediacy in anaphoric reference resolution. *Language and Cognitive Processes, 4*, 263–287.

Sanford, A. J., Garrod, S., Lucas, A., & Henderson, R. (1983). Pronouns without explicit antecedents. *Journal of Semantics, 2*, 303–318.

Sanford, A. J., Moar, K., & Garrod, S. (1988). Proper names as controllers of discourse focus. *Language and Speech, 31*, 43–56.

Shillcock, R. (1982). The on-line resolution of pronominal anaphora. *Language and Speech, 24*, 4.

Silverstein, M. (1976). Hierarchy of features and ergativity. In R. M. W. Dixon (Ed.), *Grammatical categories in Australian languages*. New Jersey: Humanities Press.

Stevenson, R. J. & Vitkovitch, M. (1986). The comprehension of anaphoric relations. *Language and Speech, 29*, 335–360.

Swinney, D. A. (1979). Lexical access during sentence comprehension: (Re) consideration of context effects. *Journal of Verbal Learning and Verbal Behavior, 18*, 545–567.

Vonk, W., Hustinx, L., & Simons, W. (1992). The use of referential expressions in structuring discourse. *Language and Cognitive Processes, 11*, 301–335.

CHAPTER 21

SELECTIVE PROCESSING IN TEXT UNDERSTANDING

ANTHONY J. SANFORD AND SIMON C. GARROD

I. INTRODUCTION

It is commonly assumed that the goal of reading a piece of text is to end up with a mental representation of that text. Texts which are unclear may give rise to poorly structured mental representations, while well-written texts, if read properly, will give rise to well-structured representations which are in some sense the result of the comprehension process. Whatever the details of such a process, the text should induce a coherent representation in the mind of the willing reader. Of course, the mental representation will not be a verbatim copy of the text itself unless special rote-learning procedures are adopted. Rather, subjects typically retain the gist of a text (Kintsch, 1974; Kintsch & van Dijk, 1978). The point is easily appreciated that one might read and remember the gist of a novel, but not generally retain it verbatim. In short, most of what is remembered is the product of comprehending the text rather than learning it.

The problem is bound up intrinsically with which inferences are drawn on the basis of a text. Since a text could support any number of inferences of varying degrees of plausibility, there must be some mechanism supporting the selection of some kinds of inference over others. The simplest idea is that only inferences necessary for the establishment of cohesion are drawn, but as we shall see, this criterion leaves room for interpretation, and there is evidence that elaborative inferences are made, and that inferences necessary for cohesion are not always drawn. In the next section, we show how selective processing may result from the differential status of characters in a discourse and conclude that some of the selectivity seems to be of a top-down nature. Finally, we turn to evidence from failures to detect anomalies in text as a source of evidence for both selective processing and incomplete processing in the service of text coherence. We conclude that some sort of criterion of satisfaction for coherence is implicated.

II. COHERENCE IN TEXT AND MIND

The term COHERENCE has been used in relation to texts and to the mental representation of texts. The idea of coherence in text is closely related to the notion of well-formedness. Thus Reinhart (1980) claims that it is coherence that distinguishes a text from a set of sentences which are unconnected. Brown and Yule (1983) call this the discourse-as-product view, since it is only about the text as an object in its own right. If a text is seen as an object, then it is clearly important that there are visible aspects of the text which represent the connections between sentences. These connectors are termed by Halliday and Hasan (1976; Halliday, 1982) COHESION DEVICES, because they hold the text together, giving it coherence. Halliday and Hasan distinguish five kinds of tie: conjunction (e.g., *and, but, because*), coreference, substitutions, ellipsis, and lexical cohesion.

The presence of surface markers of this type seems to be too weak a criterion for coherence in some instances: It does not rule out sets of sentences which we would not want to consider to be coherent in an everyday sense, such as (1).

(1) *I bought a Ford. The car in which President Wilson rode down the Champs-Elysee was black. Black English has been widely discussed. The discussions between the presidents ended last week. A week has seven days.* etc. etc.

The presence of coreference links (*Ford–The car, black–Black,* etc.) is not enough to specify what could reasonably be called a coherent text. (Enkvist, 1978, calls such examples PSEUDO-COHERENT, because they do hold together in any fashion.) Reinhart (1980) suggested that the following conditions are a better specification of what might make a text coherent. The discourse should be:

1. Connected. The sentences (clauses) of a text will be formally connected, in that each adjacent pair is either referentially linked, or linked by a semantic sentence connector.
2. Consistent. Each sentence has to be logically consistent with the previous sentence.
3. Relevant. Each sentence must be relevant to an underlying discourse topic and to the context of the utterance.

The first criterion of formal connection means that cohesion markers should be present. Again, it is possible to look for these in a text itself. The second is more problematic, for while it is possible to test for inconsistency (e.g., contradictions) in a text, it is not possible to test for consistency. Presumably, the second criterion is that each successive sentence is not inconsistent. Moving to relevance, it is not clear how relevance can be found in a text. Rather, it must be the product of inference and so makes Reinhart's definition partly dependent on a reader.

We have seen that surface cohesion markers are not sufficient for a text to be called coherent. Are they necessary, as Reinhart's formulation requires? The answer is no, because it is possible to have a text which we would want to call coherent, but which does not depend on the presence of any markers.

(2) *At dinner last night, John burnt his mouth.*
   The soup was too hot.

These utterances are connected only by way of an inference: The second sentence explains how John came to burn his mouth. Such constructions are commonplace in normal, easily comprehended writing.

Taking the perspective of a text linguist, Reinhart treats such examples as deviations from the ideal. She makes two points: first, that the more a text relies on inferential activity of this sort, and the less it is peppered with cohesion indicators, the less it conforms to the ideal text. The second point is more important. She views these kinds of inferences as unusual, requiring special procedures on the part of the reader to "impose coherence on the text." We find an analogous view being expressed in psychology, that such BRIDGING INFERENCES (Haviland & Clark, 1974) when they occur are time-consuming, and similar views are found in Kintsch and van Dijk (1978). To the extent that explicit cohesion markers are not found in a text, bridging inferences have to be made on this line of reasoning. Cohesion markers are typically thought of as being the controlling pointers which enable a coherent mental representation of a text to be constructed. Thus, for example, we find Graesser (1981) saying that coherence graphs are constructed on the basis of a simple coherence rule, connections are formed whenever two propositions share an argument.

A quite different view of coherence was put forward by Hobbs (1979). His view is that interpretability is to be equated with the coherence of a discourse. He views the processor (reader) as attempting to find coherence relations, which are mental relations, these relations being suggested by the text in hand but requiring complex inferences to be established. On Hobbs's view, coreference establishment can be a secondary phenomenon, following from a more general process of coherence establishment. Thus Hobbs says, "The sense in which a discourse is about some set of entities is . . . just the conscious trace of some deeper process of coherence" (1979, p. 68).

In the chapter by Garrod and Sanford (this volume), a discussion is given of the idea that reference resolution is really just part of a more general process of interpretation, and not prior to more general interpretation. This view is quite different from the ones discussed up to now which see coreference (argument repetition) as essentially prior to other sorts of interpretation; as Hobbs himself says, his claim turns the usual view of the role of coreference with respect to cohesion upside down. The fact that interpretation in general can precede reference resolution is a problem for any account that establishes reference first in order to build a propositional structure.

In summary, coherence does not seem to be a property of text; rather it is a property of the mental representation (interpretation) of a text. A text can yield a coherent mental representation even when it does not contain appropriate cohesion markers. From now on, we shall suppose that coherence occurs in the mind of the reader and is the establishment of a mental representation which consists of a connected set of ideas based on appropriately interpreted discourse. Both connectivity and appropriate interpretation are matters of degree, and we shall examine some influences on selective processes which underlie coherence, starting with the issue of inference control.

III. SELECTIVE INFERENCE IN THE SERVICE OF COHERENCE

It is clear that inferences are necessary for coherence on any account of text processing. But a text can lead to an infinite number of inferences, and it is therefore important to determine just which inferences are made during reading. By far the simplest approach to this question has been made within a framework that divides inferences into those which are necessary to support the construction of a coherent representation of the text in the mind of the reader (henceforth NECESSARY INFERENCES) and those which are not necessary, but which are mere elaborations (henceforth ELABORATIVE INFERENCES) (e.g., Just & Carpenter, 1987; Keenan, Potts, Golding & Jennings, 1990; O'Brien, Shank, Myers & Rayner, 1988; see also Vonk & Noordman, 1990, for a more elaborated set of distinctions). The essence of the distinction is illustrated by the materials in (3).

(3) *No longer able to control his anger, the husband threw the delicate porcelain vase against the wall. It cost him well over one hundred dollars to replace.*

In this case, the inference that *the vase broke* is a PLAUSIBLE INFERENCE and must be made in order to realize an important link between the first and the second sentence. The inference is therefore necessary. Note that the inference is not necessary in the logical sense; rather, it is necessary for coherence. This of course raises the question of what is coherence. For the moment, we note that in order to link the two sentences, an explanation for the second is required, and the most plausible explanation is that the vase broke. Also, note that this inference does not need to be drawn until the second sentence is encountered. Consider a second example.

(4) *No longer able to control his anger, the husband threw the delicate porcelain vase against the wall. He had been feeling angry for weeks, but had refused to seek help.*

Here, any inference that the vase broke would not be obviously useful for cohesion. Rather, the second sentence links to the previous one by providing an explanation and elaboration of it. If the inference that the vase broke had indeed been made, it would be merely ELABORATIVE. The contrast pair illustrates the distinction between forward and backward inferences. A FORWARD INFERENCE is one which is made before the text requires it in order to establish a cohesive link. It is therefore elaborative at the time it is made. A BACKWARD INFERENCE is one which is drawn to link a previous text fragment with a later one. This distinction has been used as the foundation of an account of which inferences will and will not be made during reading: Only inferences necessary for a coherent interpretation will be made, that is, necessary inferences. This has been called the deferred inference theory by Garnham (1985) and the minimalist position by McKoon and Ratcliff (1992). It depends on a specification of what is meant by a coherent representation, and this is a problem. But at its simplest, it does make the assumption that elaborative (forward) inferences will simply not be made.

Tests for elaborative inference-making have been carried out for several inference types, including highly predictable consequences of events. As Keenan, Potts, Golding, and Jenning (1990) observed in their very extensive review, the results obtained depend rather critically on the type of task or measurement instrument used to discover whether or not the inference was made. Setting observations such as these in a theoretically motivated frame, McKoon and Ratcliff (1990) suggest that inferences can be drawn over variable time scales, with varying degrees of specificity, and with varying degrees of strength. They argue this conclusion by examining converging evidence from different kinds of tasks. Although it makes the minimalist position fuzzy, McKoon and Ratcliff have shown that forward inferences are sometimes made but that they may be incomplete and late in becoming part of the memory representation of the text. For instance, in a number of studies, they presented sentence (5).

(5) *The director and the cameraman were ready to start shooting when suddenly the actress fell from the 14th floor.*

They used the test word *dead* in several tasks, such as lexical decision and recognition memory. When the decision made by the subject was at a short interval (such as speeded recognition or fast lexical decision), there was no evidence of priming of the test word by the context. When delays were introduced, there was evidence of priming (see McKoon & Ratcliff, 1990, for a discussion).

In their recent description of the minimalist position, McKoon and Ratcliff (1992) list a number of cases where they claim forward inferences have not been demonstrated. One example is filling in missing instruments. For example, given that *Mary stirred her coffee,* it might be supposed that the plausible instrument *spoon* might be entered into the memory representation of the discourse. Singer (1979) produced evidence that plausible instruments are not inferred. However, Garrod and Sanford (1982) tested for the presence of implied instruments in the representations of sentences, using a self-paced reading time paradigm. They found evidence compatible with a forward inference. Thus, it took no longer to read a sentence containing a reference to *car* after a sentence containing the verb *drive* than it did after one containing an explicit mention of *car.* Although these results seem to be at odds with the findings of Singer (1979), both sets of results are reliable, having been simultaneously replicated in a study by Cotter (1984). The difference appeared to be that in the Singer materials, the instruments were only strongly implied, whereas in the Garrod and Sanford set, they were more obviously necessary to the understanding of the verb. This provides at least some evidence for forward inferential activity. Garrod and Sanford (1983) carried out a similar study in which they introduced situations, such as *being in court.* Sentences containing subsequent references to entities prominent in these situations (such as *The lawyer*) were processed just as quickly when the individuals were implicit to the scene as they were if the individuals were explicitly mentioned in a preceding sentence. If the situation did not predict the presence of the entity, then there was a large difference in reading times for sentences mentioning individuals implicitly or explicitly.

McKoon and Ratcliff (1992) suggest that elaborative inferences may be made if the requisite background knowledge is easily accessed in memory and clearly claim that this is consistent with the spirit of the minimalist hypothesis. However, it is consistent with other hypotheses as well. For example, Sanford and Garrod (1981) suggested that a major property of the comprehension system is to relate linguistic input to background knowledge, if possible, and as soon as possible, and use the resultant representation to guide interpretation of subsequent input (terming this PRIMARY PROCESSING). The knowledge structures we called SCENARIOS, but they were meant to include knowledge structures ranging from the very simple and general to more detailed "situations." This is different from the minimalist position in philosophy, making the assumption that grounding incoming text in background knowledge is necessary to achieve a sense of understanding and to achieve coherence in many instances. For example, part of the argument is that it is often necessary to use a situation to give the correct interpretation to a linguistic structure in order to know what proposition is in fact being asserted. Further discussion of related approaches are discussed by Glenberg, Kruley, and Langston (this volume).

One problem is that once possible elaborative inferences are based on the availability or accessibility of general knowledge, the minimalist position and the primary processing accounts are not so easy to distinguish. The primary processing account assumes that a text is easy to read if it can be mapped onto familiar background knowledge structures and that the writer should try to make such mappings possible. It does not assume that all background knowledge representations will be equally rich or detailed (Sanford & Garrod, 1981, pp. 125–131). Furthermore, with the advent of connectionist realizations of schemata, it is easy to envisage how various aspects of a scenario may be differentially accessible at various points in processing, which is not unlike McKoon and Ratcliff's views on incomplete inferences. We are not saying that the two views are equivalent, only that it is not completely clear that experiments on which inferences are and are not made will necessarily rule one out.

It appears that elaborative inferences are sometimes made. What about necessary inferences? There is evidence that these are made in the cases of anaphora (Dell, McKoon & Ratcliff, 1983; Garrod, Freudenthal & Boyle, in press; Garrod & Sanford, 1977, 1985; Haviland & Clark, 1974; see also Garrod & Sanford, this volume, for complications) and for simple causal links (Keenan, Baillet, & Brown, 1984; Bloom, Fletcher, van den Broek, Reitz, & Shapiro, 1990). However, one problem with trying to show that "necessary" cohesion inferences are made is that the definition of *necessary* can all too easily become circular. A good illustration of the problem comes from the work of Vonk and Noordman (1990), on the processing of the conjunctions *because* and *but*. Vonk and Noordman considered sentences like (6).

(6) *Chlorine compounds are frequently used as propellants because they do not react with other substances.*

The necessary inference which follows from this, giving sense to the statement, is that *good propellants do not react with other substances.* This is a necessary condition for being a good propellant. Vonk and Noordman were interested in whether this inference, apparently necessary for intelligibility, would be drawn when (6) was read. A similar example is (7).

(7) *Because the wind was strong, they used Kevlar sails.*

Here the inference *Kevlar sails are good in wind* is necessary and would seem to be an important inference for intelligibility as well. Similar arguments can be made for statements using the contrastive conjunction *but*. For instance, (8) signals that *linguists do not know much about statistics.*

(8) *John is a linguist, but he knows a lot about statistics.*

Using a mixture of on-line reading time and question-answering time anaylses, Vonk and Noordman were able to show that when the text is about an unfamiliar topic, such inferences are not made during reading. If the inference is presented as a fact for verification after reading the text, subjects answer more quickly if the inference has been explicitly stated.

Vonk and Noordman's results indicate that even backward, necessary inferences that contribute to the cohesion of a text are not always made during reading. If the text is about a familiar topic, however, then inferences may be made on-line, as they found using the same methodology. Inferences may also be made if the reader has a specific technical purpose in reading the text, or if the inferences deal with familiar topics. Vonk and Noordman suggest that in normal reading, processing may be SHALLOW if the material is unfamiliar and the reader does not have a vested interest in the material. In the case of causal propositions, it appears to be the case that simply knowing that the two arguments of the predicate *because* have been given is enough to satisfy the processor of the coherence of that part of a text.

To summarize this section: Selective processes in coherence establishment may easily be defined as only those processes necessary for coherence. One problem with this formulation is that there is some evidence that forward inferences are made. Even those arguing for a minimalist position allow that elaborative inferences might be made if the relevant general knowledge is sufficiently accessible. Another problem with the formulation is that what is "necessary for coherence" needs to be determined: for example, Vonk and Noordman's demonstration of shallow processing when readers are confronted with causal connectives in a text about an unfamiliar topic. If familiarity of a topic means that knowledge about that topic is more readily accessed, then a case can be made for familiarity being a major variable in the richness of inferences. It may be that a high degree of coherence in mental structures (richly connected structure mapped onto a relevant background) is an ideal achieved only when reading familiar material, and that impoverished inferential activity leads to lower levels of coherence.

IV. Selectivity as a Function of Character in Narrative

Selective processes underlying cohesion are most marked in the case of character type in narratives. In narrative discourse, continuity is typically achieved through the connected actions and plans of main characters, with secondary characters playing only a minor role, and this may provide one basis for the selective control of inferential activity. Normally, the motivations of main characters are of interest, and their actions are seen as significant in contrast to the general actions of minor characters. We might therefore expect that inferential activity related to the establishment of connections would be especially prominent in relation to main characters. If a main character is going to be more prominent in a narrative, then one might expect that character and his actions to be more available to reference, particularly pronominal reference, which is associated with referential continuity (Karmiloff-Smith, 1980; Marslen-Wilson, Levy, & Tyler, 1982). Furthermore, there is evidence that the main character's perspective is used to describe other characters and parts of the narrative (Bates & MacWhinney, 1981). These considerations suggest that any definition of coherence in narrative text will be intrinsically bound up with coherence WITH RESPECT TO A POINT OF VIEW.

A number of studies have shown that references to main and subsidiary characters are processed in different ways. Anderson, Garrod, and Sanford (1983) explored the properties of characters which were classed as main or alternatively as scenario-dependent. Scenario-dependent characters are ones which owe their existence to a particular scenario. Thus an usherette is a character whose existence really depends upon a cinema. The term itself has meaning only because it specifies a role in cinema. In contrast, if Jane visits the cinema, her activities go beyond the bounds of the cinema; after all, she was not there before she visited. Using a self-paced reading paradigm, Anderson et al. showed that sentences containing pronominal anaphoric references to main characters were read more rapidly than sentences containing references to scenario-dependent characters. The original interpretation was that reference resolution was faster in the main-character case, but it may reflect a greater speed of attaching new information to the representation of the main character (see Garrod and Sanford, this volume, for a discussion of the distinction between finding a probable referent—bonding—and accessing information associated with that referent). Anderson et al. used stories which revolved around a particular scene (such as a visit to the cinema) and determined the maximum length of time such a visit could last. They showed that if reference was made to elapsed time which exceeded this maximum, then reading time for a sentence containing an anaphoric reference to the secondary character was longer than if the time elapsed was within the bounds of expectation for the scene. For example, if Mrs. Smith is at the hairdressers, then a reference to *ten hours later* should signal that Mrs. Smith has now left. If she has left, then the hairdresser is not relevant and so should become difficult to access. This is not true of *half an hour later*. The results are consistent with this. Importantly, references to the main character are not so affected. This is to be expected, since the main character does not depend on a particular setting for its relevance and significance. More recent work showing main character effects in scenes is to be found in Morrow, Greenspan, and Bower (1987).

Morrow (1985) examined the role of main character in both pronominal reference resolution and perceived perspective. He also pitted local text structure against a previously defined main character in order to investigate the effects of congruence and conflict. The main characters are typically in the foreground of narratives, and subsidiary characters in the background. Although the terms foreground and background are sometimes used to refer to discourse representations which are in the foreground or background of ATTENTION of the reader (Chafe, 1974; Sanford & Garrod, 1981), they are used by some people to refer to the structure of the discourse itself (Hopper, 1979; Labov, 1972). It is the latter interpretation that is used here, although it is assumed that text foreground influences attentional prominence. Text foreground is assumed to be marked in a number of ways. For instance, tense and aspect markers: Thus, foreground is indicated by simple past, while a background cue is the presence of stative and progressive verbs. So, for example, in introducing a setting, statives are typically used, rightly indicating the background status of the setting. In his experiments, Morrow defined a main character as a character who was introduced by being the topic of the first three sentences of his short vignettes and by using that character's perspective to describe other parts of the narrative. An example of his materials is shown in Table I.

The first part of the narrative introduces the main character (Paul) and the secondary character (Ben). In (A), Ben is introduced from Paul's perspective (*That noisy . . .*). (B) is a variant on (A) but makes the secondary character more active. In (C), however, the action (wondering) takes Ben's perspective. The sentence following these alternatives uses the phrase *his feet*. The question probes the interpretation. Thus with (A) and (B), the secondary character remains in the text background, while in (C) it moves to text foreground, creating a possible conflict. Morrow found that the likelihood of picking the main character as referent was high in (A) and (B), at 93% and 84% respectively, but low in (C), at 34%. So, if the secondary character is part of the text background, then the perception of states is ascribed to the main character. When there is conflict, this tendency is reduced; in his full series of experiments, Morrow showed that in conflict, readers used recency and the status of events to make a judgment but still did so from the perspective of the main character. In general, in the short run, characters do not change status given a minimal conflict.

Morrow's work raises the question of just what it is that might signal a character as the main one. A study by Sanford, Moar, and Garrod (1988) showed that the use of a proper name in contrast to a role description can be instrumental in affecting both likelihood of mention in continuation tasks and ease of reference resolution. This discovery was made as a result of attempting to see just what characteristics cause a character to be specified as a main character. In typical, short experimental narratives, main characters tend to be introduced before secondary characters; they tend to be introduced by proper names (*John, Mrs. Jones*) and not by role descriptions (*the ballerina, the waiter*). Also, when a particular scene is considered, main characters take the role of principal perspective-holder. Using simple two- or three-line narratives, Sanford et al. showed that the use of a proper name versus a role description, but not the order of mention, determined the likelihood of mentioning an individual in a continuation task. This can be sensed intuitively from the two examples in (9)–(12).

(9) *The priest waited by the church wall.*
(10) *Mary walked up to him.*

TABLE I
Narrative Used by Morrow (1985) in Experiment 1

Paul caught the flu and was feeling pretty awful. He told his eldest son Ben to keep the house quiet. He got up from bed to go to the bathroom, irritated by the noise. Traffic was rushing by the house. The kids were arguing in the den.
  (A) That noisy Ben was messing up the kitchen.
  (B) Noisy Ben was tramping around in the kitchen.
  (C) Ben was wondering when his father would feel better as he ate in the kitchen.
The floor felt cold on his feet.
Whose feet are referred to?

(11) *Father Brown waited by the church wall.*
(12) *The woman walked up to him.*

In the first pair, continuations more prominently mention Mary, while in the second, they mention Father Brown more often. Reading time results with sentences containing pronominal anaphors parallel the continuation results, in that sentences containing references to named characters are read more rapidly than those containing references to role-defined characters. Of course, none of this suggests that the name–role distinction is the only way of signaling main-characterhood. In many narratives, more than one character may have a proper name. However, it is still a powerful way to control focus (indexed through ease of reference resolution and likelihood of continuation). It is interesting to note that a narrative where the main character does not have a proper name is very unusual, yet the proper name need not provide any more information than gender. Proper names may be important processing markers. As Kripke (1972) observed, proper names are rigid designators, denoting the same individual in all possible worlds. This is not true for role descriptions. Thus it is possible for *John* to visit a restaurant, be served by *the waiter,* go to the cinema, visit another restaurant, and then be served by *the waiter.* No one would assume the waiter to be the same one, but John is the same character throughout (see Garrod and Sanford, this volume). Finally, it should be noted that Morrow's work used proper names for both main and secondary characters and relied on frequency of mention, perspective, and primacy in order to establish main characterhood. It is likely that his conflicting results would not have been so powerful if the secondary character had been given a role description.

The results from studies of reference resolution show one kind of selective influence in cohesion establishment. What of the broader claim that processing in general will be greater for main characters than for secondary ones? Sanford and Al-Ahmar (in Garrod & Sanford, 1988) observed that subjects tended to see setting information as more relevant to main characters than to secondary ones. Consider the following short text.

> *At the restaurant*
> *Juliet entered the restaurant.*
> *There was a table in the corner.*
> *The waiter took the order.*
> *Things seemed to go well that night.*

Sanford and Al-Ahmar observed that if subjects were then asked the question *Did things go well for Juliet that night?*, responses were typically affirmative. If, however, the same question was asked about the waiter, then the response pattern was typically much less clear. Indeed, some subjects pointed out that it is odd to ask such questions. In fact, if subjects are asked to respond quickly, in a self-paced reading time situation, then nearly 90% of the questions asked of the main character were responded to "yes," while only 50% respond "yes" to the secondary character. Intuitively, the question seems relevant to the main character, but not to the secondary one. Note that in order to interpret the sentence *Things seemed to go well that night* it has to be understood with respect to some person: It is a psychological predicate. One reason why the question might sound strange is if the sentence had been assigned to the view of the main character, so that it was directly associated with the main character in memory, and not with the secondary character.

In a follow-up study (Garrod & Sanford, 1988), a reading time investigation was carried out which sheds some light on what these patterns might mean. Typical material is shown in Table II.

The materials introduce main and secondary characters and have an optional atmosphere sentence. The critical target sentence can refer to either the main or the secondary character. Whichever is chosen on a particular trial, the previous sentence always reintroduces the same character so that the referent comes as no surprise on the target sentence presentation.

The results in Table III show quite clearly that reading time for the critical sentence is slowed dramatically in the ABSENCE of the *atmosphere* sentence in the case of the main character, but not in the case of the secondary character. This result can be interpreted as showing that the processor seeks explanations for the behavior of main characters. If that information is available, because it has already been presented, then it can be retrieved without difficulty. On the other hand, if it has not been presented, then there will be a delay while its availability is checked. This study does not really allow one to distinguish between the atmosphere information having been assimilated to a representation associated with the main character, as opposed to it merely being available in recent memory in an unconnected way. Either way, the findings for the secondary character show that the processor is not very much disrupted by the absence of information explaining the behavior of the secondary character. The results thus fit intuitions that the behavior of the main character needs causal explanation, not that of the secondary characters. Certainly, the actions of main characters are typically either explained or motivated directly in stories and narratives, whereas those of secondary characters are not. The present results suggest that this goes hand in hand with an automatic selective process which seeks the formation of richer structures around main characters.

In this section we examined some of the evidence for coherence of character-based narrative discourse being something which is conditional on character. Strong evidence can be found for selective effects in both reference resolution and point of view. Because of the close association of text foreground with main characters, it can be argued (but remains to be demonstrated) that all these effects are consistent with a system which is entirely driven by local discourse and not by any global representation of a "main character." Alternatively, it might be the case that the interpretation of local discourse depends

TABLE II
Sample Material from Garrod & Sanford (1988)

Lunch at the cafeteria
Alistair hung up his coat and picked a tray.
The waitress smiled as she poured the coffee.
The atmosphere was hot and sticky. (optional)
He took/She offered the cup. (character mention)
He/She mopped his/her brow. (target sentences)

Table III
Target Reading Times (ms)

	Main character	Secondary character
With *Atmosphere* Statement	1379	1430
Without *Atmosphere* Statement	1650	1463

on having a main character perspective. There is little evidence on this, other than the study by Garrod and Sanford reported above, in which when a main character carries out an action which is not explained, there is a delay in processing the sentence depicting that action. A similar delay is not observed for the secondary character. This suggests that the significance of the sentences for cohesion establishment is different in the two cases, and this cannot easily be explained without invoking preexisting structures to carry out the interpretation. It is clearly desirable to examine this point in more detail.

V. Partial Processing and Selectivity

Up to now we have considered selectivity as indexed by inferential activity and preferences in anaphor assignment. In each case, some evidence was found to suggest that information beyond that given in the propositions of the text was used in the service of coherence establishment. In this section we take up the argument that processing in support of coherence can be SHALLOW or DEEP and use the observations as further support for strong top-down influences on the manner in which current input is processed. The examples depend on failures to notice anomalies in a variety of materials, where the failure to notice can be attributed to only carrying out a partial analysis of the current input. Example (13), from Johnson-Laird (1981), is an example.

(13) *This book fills a much-needed gap.*

Readers do not always notice that this sentence asserts that it is the gap, not the book, which is needed. Obviously, the interpretation which they give is the one which makes pragmatic sense, yet to misunderstand the sentence requires that it be only partially analyzed (in this instance the mapping of syntax onto role structure). Partial analyses of this sort are especially interesting, since no one would deny that a fuller analysis is necessary to guarantee correct interpretation, and correct interpretation is necessary for the establishment of a veridical coherent representation. We believe that such phenomena are important indicators that the processor is attempting to match a linguistic description to something familiar—in this case, a reasonable view of the roles which gaps in the literature and books produced might normally play with respect to each other. In short, pragmatic mapping can override syntax. It is easy find other examples, such as *Ask not what you can do for your country; ask what your country can do for you* (Reder & Cleeremans, 1990), and *Can a man marry his widow's sister?* (Sanford, Barton, Moxey, & Paterson, in press). In both these cases, the problem seems to be that existing stereotyped knowledge of the situations seems to override sufficient processing detail to enable the anomaly to be detected.

What these examples seem to show is that processes necessary for true coherence can be incomplete, and that a sense of coherence is achieved on the basis of a good fit between some elements of the sentences concerned and stereotyped knowledge. This is consistent with the primary processing principle of mapping, discussed earlier. But is there any experimental evidence showing how these anomalies might actually arise? In fact, work on failures to detect anomalies in sentences has a long if patchy history, one of the earliest examples being due to Schlesinger (1968), who noted that subjects tended to interpret embedded sentences like (14) in a stereotypical way.

(14) *This is the hole that the rat which our cat whom the dog bit made caught.*

The stereotyped understanding depends upon what is well known about the behavior of dogs biting cats and cats catching rats. Yet a careful look at the syntax shows the sentence to be incongruous.

(15) *This is the hole (that the rat (which our cat (whom the dog bit) made) caught.*

In this case, pragmatics appears to override complete syntactic analysis in those subjects who get an incorrect, pragmatically plausible interpretation. Of course, the syntax in this example is near the boundary of what it is possible to process, and the point Schlesinger was making was that such sentence structures can be used if pragmatics supports them.

When the semantics of a sentence is sufficiently complex, an override of semantics by pragmatics can be obtained in an analogous fashion. Wason and Reich (1979) studies examples of type (16).

(16) *No head injury is too trivial to be ignored.*

The dominant interpretation of this example is *no matter how trivial a head injury is, it should not be ignored.* This sentence has the same form as (17).

(17) *No missile is too small to be banned.*

Here, the dominant interpretation is *however small a missile is, it should be banned.* But (16) and (17) have the same form, and (16) actually states that *however trivial a head injury, it should be ignored.* Wason and Reich showed that pragmatic plausibility overrides detailed semantic analysis with such materials. Along with the Schlesinger example, these data suggest that when the syntactic or semantic analysis of a sentence is sufficiently complex, pragmatics may override these analyses so that they remain incomplete.

Erickson and Mattson (1981) reported a striking example of partial processing, which they termed the MOSES ILLUSION. They asked subjects to answer question (18).

(18) *How many animals of each sort did Moses put on the Ark?*

Typically, a large number of subjects answer two, only to be surprised that it was not Moses but Noah who put the animals on the ark. Erickson and Mattson argued that failures to detect the anomaly resulted from the semantic relatedness between the terms *Moses* and *Noah*. So, in searching long-term memory for the answer to the question, a good match is obtained between the text term Moses and the term Noah in memory. If they are represented as features, for example, then they are similar in that they are both Old Testament figures. Erickson and Mattson claimed that the Moses illusion is an indicator of the incompleteness of normal language processing: They assume that the comprehension system will accept a term if it shows a high degree of fit with what is expected in that context, and that a full analysis of the meanings of expressions is not carried out (see also McClelland, St. John, & Taraban, 1989, for a discussion of how these effects are broadly compatible with an interactive account of sentence processing). Indeed, it would be unreasonable to suppose that a full set of attributes (features) associated with a given word is tested exhaustively against all of the attributes of the representation in memory, since in many cases the attribute list would be unbounded. In that case, the anomalous results are merely a way of indexing the incomplete analysis which occurs normally all the time. Certainly it is easy to produce similar effects with a host of other materials (e.g., Reder & Kusbit, 1991), so there is nothing significantly unique about the examples which we use here.

Subsequent research has confirmed that semantic overlap between the item presented and the true item influences detection rate. Van Oostendorp and Kok (1990) had subjects list attributes of persons referred to by proper names. When the overlap of attributes was high, subjects were more likely to miss a substituted term than when the overlap was low (see also van Oostendorp & de Mul, 1990). Reder and Kusbit (1991) carried out a much more extensive investigation in an attempt to narrow down the possible explanations for the Moses illusion. One possible basis is that subjects do in fact notice the illusion but do not report it because they assume that the error was made in good faith, in accordance with Grice's conversational maxims (Grice, 1975). Reder and Kusbit asked one group of subjects to detect anomalous items, explicitly, or to ignore distortions and answer questions as though they were perfectly formed. Subjects in the explicit detection situation still made errors, missing the anomalies, so Reder and Kusbit conclude that subjects were not just being "cooperative" in the normal case: The failures to detect were genuine. Furthermore, decision times were much longer in the explicit detection task, indicating that monitoring distortions is a difficult process.

A second possibility, according to Reder and Kusbit, is that the problem lies with the strength of the representation of the relevant knowledge in memory. Various training procedures, shown to enhance the memory trace of the relevant information, did not influence the size of the Moses illusion in the explicit detection task. Other data showed that reading times were faster for "distorted" target words (like *Moses*) than for undistorted examples (like *Noah*). Reder and Kusbit use such data to reject an account in which the critical items are poorly encoded as a basis for the illusion. They conclude that it is the process of matching the meanings of the memory representations with the properly encoded sentence which generates the failures to detect.

Bredart and Modolo (1988) showed that the likelihood of detecting an error depends on whether the critical name is part of the linguistic focus of the sentence. Earlier, Erickson and Mattson had contrasted the question form of the Moses item (18) with a statement form. With the statement form, subjects had to verify (19).

(19) *Moses put two of each kind of animal on the Ark.*

They found only weak evidence for increased detection rates with the declarative format. However, a stronger manipulation of focus was used by Bredart and Modolo (1988).

(20) *It was Moses who put two of each kind of animal on the Ark.*

In this case, the linguistic focus is certainly on Moses (the statement effectively being an answer to the question "Who put two of each . . ."). Detection rates were much higher with this format. Thus it appears that the significance which the anomalous item plays in the sentence in which it appears influences the extent to which a detailed semantic analysis of that item occurs.

The Moses illusion examples require a match of a statement to a piece of knowledge in memory and are thus directly pertinent to models of question-answering (e.g., Reder, 1982, 1987; Reder & Cleeremans, 1990). Other similar anomalies can be related to more general processes of cohesion establishment. Barton and Sanford (1993; Sanford et al., in press) studied the following example in some detail.

There was a tourist flight travelling from Vienna to Barcelona. On the last leg of the journey, it developed engine trouble. Over the Pyrenees, the pilot started to lose control. The plane eventually crashed right on the border. Wreckage was equally strewn in France and Spain. The authorities were trying to decide where to bury the survivors.

What is the solution to the problem?

Failures to notice that survivors are not buried are commonplace; subjects usually offer solutions like "They should be buried in their home countries" or "The survivors(!) should be buried where their relatives wish" (exclamation point added). When subjects are invited to rate the attributes of a typical air crash, dead victims are given an "almost-certain status." It is therefore reasonable to suppose that the failure to notice the term *survivors* is due to the fact that its analysis is swamped by an expectation of dead people. Because *survivors* is a word which fits with an air crash, it is accepted as a filler for the patient slot of the verb *to bury.*

Barton and Sanford attempted to use the ease of detecting this anomaly (and versions with related terms) to explore a number of potential constraints on the extent to which a role-filler is analyzed during comprehension. A group of subjects was invited to define the terms *survivor, injured, wounded,* and *maimed.* The responses indicate that *survivors* means 'remaining alive after some life-endangering event' (close to the dictionary definition). In contrast, 'being alive' is seldom explicitly mentioned as part of the definitions of the other words, although the subjects presuppose that the person referred to is alive, again consistent with the dictionary definition. Furthermore, when the subjects were asked whether each of the terms would be used when the referent person was alive, all subjects responded positively for all words.

With these results, it is possible to make the prediction that the term *survivors* would be detected more readily than the terms *injured, wounded,* and *maimed* (henceforth the INJURED terms) when they were substituted for the term *survivors.* Detection patterns confirmed this prediction. Thus, the more salient remaining alive is, the greater the chance of the mismatch being

detected. This is somewhat analogous to the observation that the more semantically related two nouns are in the Moses illusion, the lower the likelihood of
detection. Barton and Sanford also found that if the injured terms were preceded
by the qualifier *surviving,* then detection rates were as high as for the original
survivors case.

All this depends on the argument that it is the scenario (an air crash) which
imposes a high expectation of dead people, and that the stronger the mismatch
between the critical item and the representation of dead people, the more likely
it is to be detected. To test this, Barton and Sanford compared another scenario
which was about a bicycle accident. In rating the attributes of bicycle accidents,
dead victims was given a low value. In a detection experiment, detection rates
for the bicycle scenario averaged 80% in comparison to the lower 33% for the
air crash. Thus, scenario is an influence on detection rate, as was assumed.

Two results from this series of studies take us directly back to selectivity
on cohesion establishment. In the first, the item *surviving dead* was substituted
for *survivors.* This term is anomalous in its own right and should be seen as
nonsensical by any reader. However, it might be reasoned that the term *dead*
is a perfect fit to expectation. Now if a perfect fit satisfied local cohesion
requirements sufficiently well, the remaining information in the noun phrase
may be inhibited or perhaps left unanalyzed. In such a case, detection rate
should be low for *surviving dead.* On the other hand, if the meaning of *surviving
dead* is fully analyzed and then tested against the current representation, then
detection rate should be high for that item. Detection rate was very low, at 23%
(compared to 66% for *surviving injured, maimed,* and *wounded*). At debriefing,
nondetecting subjects had clearly failed to notice the illusion at all. Their written
explanations were still of the form "Bury them where their relatives wanted."
No subject assumed that *surviving dead* referred to anything bizarre like intact
corpses, for example.

This result is intriguing (and replicable; Barton & Sanford, 1993). It suggests
that if the fit of one component of a noun phrase to expectation is good enough,
then the rest of the noun phrase may not be analyzed. This idea clearly requires
further substantiation but is consistent with the sort of processes which must
underlie some of the examples described earlier showing pragmatic override
of syntactic and semantic analysis.

A final example of selectivity from the Barton and Sanford studies showed
that analysis of the term *survivors* is low if sufficient information for answering
the question is available in other parts of the discourse. A questionnaire was
produced with ten questions about attitudes toward social and cultural practices.
Each consisted of two sentences. The fifth item on the questionnaire is given
in (21).

(21) *Suppose there is an aircrash with many survivors.*
     Where should they be buried?

This format allows additional information to added to the first sentence. Three
types were used. The first was to extend information about the time of the
accident.

(22) *Suppose there is an air crash with many survivors, which happened last
     week.*

The second added information about the nature of the victims but did not say anything which might be usefully employed to decide where they should be buried.

(23) *Suppose there was an air crash with many survivors, most of whom were gravediggers.*

The final situation provided information which might be used to answer a question about where the victims should be buried (brackets indicate alternative endings).

(24) *Suppose there was an air crash with many survivors, most of whom were [Europeans] [of no fixed abode].*

Our prediction was that if information relevant to answering the question could easily be found, then it would lead to a reduced level of processing of the anomaly because a satisfactorily high level of coherence could be obtained without such processing. As predicted, detection rates for the basic version, and for those augmentations which do not supply information relevant to answering the question, give a high detection rate (averaging 76%); however, the average for the question-relevant augmentations was lower at 49%.

Our interpretation of the survivors problem data is as follows. First, the data show that in the presence of sufficient expectation of accident victims who are dead, the analysis afforded to items which should be consonant with that expectation receives relatively shallow processing. Another way to think of it is that these items exert little bottom-up impact because contextual inferences are so strong. The kind of mechanism we have in mind is that described by McClelland, Taraban, and St. John (1989). To the extent that those parts of the meaning of the critical items which are counter to expectation are accessed, the anomaly is detected. However, if part of the critical noun phrase is highly consonant with expectation (as is *dead* in the *surviving dead* case), then the *surviving* component makes no real impact at all. This observation suggests that global expectation prevents anomaly detection at the level of local semantics. It is difficult to reconcile this observation with an account of processing which requires local semantic coherence to be established before the phrase is integrated into a larger unit of meaning. It seems fair to speculate that at least some processes of semantic analysis are made in relation to global expectations (scenario-level coherence) at the same time as local coherence establishment is underway (phrase-level coherence) or even before it. Really, this amounts to another piece of data supporting an interactive account of text comprehension, and another piece of data which is consistent with the notion that some sort of mental scenario is developed whenever possible and is used predictively (and so selectively) in guiding cohesion-establishment.

Another kind of selectivity is suggested by the augmentation studies. If there is information available to enable the critical question to be answered, then detailed analysis of the term *survivors* does not take place. If it is not available, it does take place. This suggests that analysis is normally shallow and remains so if there is relevant information available, even though this information must be accessed through a pronominal anaphoric link between the term *survivors* and the pronoun *they*. This makes sense if it is supposed that the object slot of the verb *bury* is instantiated with the term *survivors* (in some undecomposed form), so that it can be addressed by a pronoun without its meaning being accessed. (An alternative, less tenable, perhaps, is that the object slot of the verb is simply marked as "satisfied" and is not instantiated at all. Oakhill, Garnham, and Vonk, 1989, discuss this possibility for certain situations where anaphoric references are tested for.) If information helpful to answering the question is not available, then a deeper analysis of the meanings of the components of the sentences takes place, and the anomaly may then be discovered. Of course, these conjectures about the time course of events await thorough empirical test.

Summarizing this section, there is a considerable amount of evidence for partial or incomplete processing during the interpretation of sentences. In general, the effects appear to result from pragmatic aspects of interpretation dominating lower level semantic processing. These effects offer some of the strongest evidence for the dominance of scenario-level information on interpretation and are good counterexamples to the claim that local semantic processing precedes more global interpretation. The survivors effect depends entirely on prior expectation based on what is normal in an air crash scenario. All in all, the results support the view that, wherever possible, information in long-term memory which can serve as an orienting scenario is retrieved and that other processes are then suppressed or otherwise ignored.

VI. SUMMARY AND CONCLUSIONS

Coherence is something in the mind of the reader, not in a text, although a text may make it easy or difficult for the reader to interpret. Because a text could, in theory, generate an effectively infinite number of inferences, the inferences made must be contained in some way. One means of containment is to make only those inferences which are necessary for the establishment of a coherent mental representation of a text. The most straightforward version of this idea is that only backward inferences are made. There are two problems with this account. First, while evidence suggests that relatively few forward inferences are made, there is evidence that some are, for example those supporting situational anaphora. The simple evaluation of which inferences have and have not been made is further complicated by the means of measurement, and the question of the accessibility of more complex representations, such as scenarios or mental models. Second, there are difficulties over specifying what is necessary for coherence. An illustration of this is Vonk and Noordman's work on the problem of the conjunction *because*.

A major influence on selective processing is character type in narratives structured around characters. There is substantial evidence for main characters being processed differently from secondary characters: They enter into the processing of reference in different ways from subsidiary characters, and narratives seem to be structured from the main character's or characters' perspective. These findings are consistent with the backward-inference-only theory if main character effects can be explained in terms of explicit aspects of the discourse (such as text foreground cues). However, it is more difficult to explain two other phenomena in this way. First, there is the way in which scenario-dependent characters drop in availability after the episodes on which they are dependent are signaled as over. This would seem to require that the characters are linked to a scenario representation which is actively involved in processing for coherence. Second, processing is disrupted if main characters carry out an action which is not predicted and has not been earlier explained, but secondary characters do not create such disruption. This difference cannot be explained in terms of purely bottom-up control of inferential activity, since the action is the same for both characters. Rather, the significance of an action must be being monitored from a main character perspective, which is of course an extralinguistic phenomenon.

The final material examined showed that processing at a local semantic level, where case assignment and other attachments take place, can be dominated by more global aspects of coherence establishment. In particular, if a text statement fits well with a piece of pre-established knowledge or can be understood easily on the basis of pragmatics, then that link seems to be made, even if there are details of a local nature which are inconsistent with that interpretation. It is suggested that such data are consistent with the view that significance establishment through text-to-knowledge mapping is achieved as early as possible, depending on the availability of suitable structures in memory. Taken together, our conclusions are that processing in the service of cohesion establishment is both selective and incomplete. We presume that the skilled writer can exploit these selective mechanisms, and that in normal discourse, aspects of the text which are central to the message will not be introduced in such a way as to yield minimal analysis.

REFERENCES

Anderson, A., Garrod, S. C., & Sanford, A. J. (1983). The accessibility of pronominal antecedents as a function of episode shifts in narrative discourse. *Quarterly Journal of Experimental Psychology, 35a,* 427–440.

Barton, S. B., & Sanford, A. J. (1993). A case-study of pragmatic anomaly detection: Relevance-driven cohesion patterns. *Memory and Cognition, 21,* 477–487.

Bates, E., & MacWhinney, B. (1981). A functionalist approach to the acquisition of grammar. In E. Ochs & B. Schiefflin (Eds.), *Developmental pragmatics* (pp. 167–211). New York: Academic Press.

Bloom, C. P., Fletcher, C. R., van den Broek, P., Reitz, L., & Shapiro, B. P. (1990). An online assessment of causal reasoning during comprehension. *Memory and Cognition, 18,* 65–71.

Bredart, S., & Modolo, K. (1988). Moses strikes again: Focalization effect on a semantic illusion. *Acta Psychologica, 67,* 135–144.

Brown, G., & Yule, G. (1983). *Discourse analysis.* Cambridge: Cambridge University Press.

Chafe, W. (1974). Language and consciousness. *Language, 50,* 111–133.

Cotter, C. A. (1984). Inferring indirect objects in sentences: Some implications for the semantics of verbs. *Language and Speech, 27,* 24–45.

Dell, G. S., McKoon G., & Ratcliff, R. (1983). The activation of antecedent information during the processing of anaphoric reference in reading. *Journal of Verbal Learning and Verbal Behavior, 22,* 121–132.

Enkvist, N. E. (1978). Coherence, psuedo-coherence, and non-coherence. In J.-O. Ostman (Ed.), *Report on text-linguistics: Cohesion and semantics* (pp. 109–128). Abo: Abo Academy Foundation Research Institute.

Erickson, T. A., & Mattson, M. E. (1981). From words to meaning: A semantic illusion. *Journal of Verbal Learning and Verbal Behavior, 20,* 540–552.

Garnham, A. (1985). *Psycholinguistics.* London: Methuen.

Garrod, S. C., & Sanford, A. J. (1977). Interpreting anaphoric relations: The integration of semantic information while reading. *Journal of Verbal Learning and Verbal Behavior, 16,* 77–90.

Garrod, S. C., & Sanford, A. J. (1982). Bridging inferences in the extended domain of reference.

In J. Long & A. Baddeley (Eds.), *Attention and performance IX* (pp. 331–346). Hillsdale, NJ: Erlbaum.

Garrod, S. C., & Sanford, A. J. (1983). Topic dependent effects in language processing. In G. B. Flores d'Arcais & R. Jarvella (Eds.), *The process of language understanding*. Chichester: Wiley.

Garrod, S. C., & Sanford, A. J. (1985). On the real-time character of interpretation during reading. *Language and Cognitive Processes, 1,* 43–61.

Garrod, S. C., & Sanford, A. J. (1988). Thematic subjecthood and cognitive constraints on discourse structure. *Journal of Pragmatics, 12,* 519–534.

Garrod, S. C., Freudenthal, D., and Boyle, E. (in press). The role of different types of anaphor in the on-line resolution of sentences in discourse. *Journal of Memory and Learning.*

Graesser, A. C. (1981). *Prose comprehension beyond the word.* New York: Springer.

Grice, L. P. (1975). Logic and conversation. In P. Cole & J. L. Morgan (Eds.), *Syntax and Semantics (Vol. 3), Speech Acts.* New York: Seminar Press.

Halliday, M. A. K. (1982). How is a text like a clause? In S. Allen (Ed.), *Text processing.* Stockholm: Almquist & Wiksell.

Halliday, M. A. K., & Hasan, R. (1976). *Cohesion in English.* London: Longman.

Haviland, S. E., and Clark, H. H. (1974). What's new? Acquiring information as a process in comprehension. *Journal of Verbal Learning and Verbal Behavior, 13,* 512–521.

Hobbs, J. R. (1979). Coherence and coreference. *Cognitive Science, 3,* 67–90.

Hopper, P. (1979). Aspect and foregrounding in discourse. In T. Givón (Ed.), *Syntax and semantics: Vol. 12. Discourse and syntax* (pp. 213–242). New York: Academic Press.

Johnson-Laird, P. N. (1981). Mental models of meaning. In A. Joshi, I. Sag, & B. Nash-Webber (Eds.), *Linguistic structure and discourse setting* (pp. 106–126). Cambridge: Cambridge University Press.

Just, M. A., and Carpenter, P. A. (1987). *The psychology of reading and language comprehension.* Boston and MA: Allyn and Bacon.

Keenan, J. M., Baillet, S. D., & Brown, P. (1984). The effects of causal cohesion on comprehension and memory. *Journal of Verbal Learning and Verbal Behavior, 23,* 115–126.

Keenan, J. M., Potts, G. R., Golding, J. M., & Jennings, T. M. (1990). Which elaborative inferences are drawn during reading? A question of methodologies. In D. A. Balota, G. B. Flores d'Arcais, & K. Rayner (Eds.), *Comprehension processes in reading* (pp. 377–402). Hillsdale, NJ: Erlbaum.

Karmiloff-Smith, A. (1980). Psychological processes underlying pronominalisation and non-pronominalisation in children's connected doscourse. In J. Kreiman & A. E. Ojeda (Eds.), *Papers in the parasession on pronouns and anaphora* (pp. 231–250). Chicago: Chicago Linguistic Society.

Kintsch, W. (1974). *The representation of meaning in memory.* Hillsdale, NJ: Erlbaum.

Kintsch, W., & van Dijk, T. A. (1978). Toward a model of text comprehension and production. *Psychological Review, 85,* 363–394.

Kripke, S. (1972). Naming and necessity. In D. Davidson & G. Harman (Eds.), *Semantics of natural language* (pp. 253–355). Dordrecht: Reidel.

Labov, W. (1972). *Language in the inner city.* Philadelphia, PA: University of Pennsylvania Press.

Marslen-Wilson, W., Levy, E., & Tyler, L. K. (1982). Producing interpretable discourse: The establishment and maintenance of reference. In R. J. Jarvella and W. Klein (Eds.), *Speech, place, and action* (pp. 339–378). Chichester: Wiley.

McClelland, J. L., St. John, M., & Taraban, R. (1989). Sentence comprehension: A parallel distributed processing approach. *Language and Cognitive Processes, 4,* 287–335.

McKoon, G., & Ratcliff, R. (1990). Textual inferences: Models and measures. In D. A. Balota, G. B. Flores d'Arcais, and K. Rayner (Eds.), *Comprehension processes in reading* (pp. 403–421). Hillsdale, NJ: Erlbaum.

McKoon, G. & Ratcliff, R. (1992). Inferences during reading. *Psychological Review, 99,* 440–466.

Morrow, D. G. (1985). Prominent characters and events organize narrative understanding. *Journal of Memory and Language, 24,* 304–319.

Morrow, D. G., Greenspan, S. L., & Bower, G. H. (1987). Accessibility and situation models in narrative comprehension. *Journal of Memory and Language, 26,* 165–187.

Oakhill, J., Garnham, A., & Vonk, W. (1989). The on-line construction of discourse models. *Language and Cognitive Processes, 4,* 263–286.

O'Brien, E. J., Shank, D. M., Myers, J. L., & Rayner, K. (1988). Elaborative inference during reading: Do they occur on-line? *Journal of Experimental Psychology: Learning, Memory and Cognition, 14,* 410–420.

Reder, L. M. (1982). Plausibility judgment vs. fact retrieval: Alternative strategies for sentence verification. *Psychological Review, 89,* 250–280.

Reder, L. M. (1987). Strategy selection in question answering. *Cognitive Psychology, 19,* 90–138.

Reder, L. M., & Cleeremans, A. (1990). The role of partial matches in comprehension: The Moses Illusion revisited. In A. Graesser & G. Bower (Eds.), *The psychology of learning and motivation, Vol 25.* (pp. 233–257). New York: Academic Press.

Reder, L. M. & Kusbit, G. W. (1991). Locus of the Moses Illusion: Imperfect encoding, retrieval, or match? *Journal of Memory and Language, 30,* 385–406.

Reinhart, T. (1980). Conditions of coherence. *Poetics Today, 1,* 161–180.

Sanford, A. J., & Garrod, S. C. (1981). *Understanding written language.* Chichester: Wiley.

Sanford, A. J., Moar, K. & Garrod, S. C. (1988). Proper names as controllers of discourse focus. *Language and Speech, 31,* 43–56.

Sanford, A. J., Barton, S. B., Moxey, L. M., & Paterson, K. B. (in press). Cohesion processes, coherence, and anomaly detection. In G. Rickheit & C. Habel (Eds.), Focus and coherence in text. Berlin: de Gruyter.

Schlesinger, I. M. (1968). *Sentence structure and the reading process.* The Hague: Mouton.

Singer, M. (1979). Processes of inference during sentence encoding. *Memory and Cognition, 7,* 192–200.

Van Oostendorp, H., & de Mul, S. (1990). Moses beats Adam: A semantic relatedness effect on a semantic illusion. *Acta Psychologica, 74,* 35–46.

Van Oostendorp, H., & Kok, I. (1990). Failing to notice errors in sentences. *Language and Cognitive Processes, 5,* 105–113.

Vonk, W., & Noordman, L. G. M. (1990). Control of inferences in text understanding. In D. A. Balota, G. B. Flores d'Arcais, & K. Rayner (Eds.), *Comprehension processes in reading* (pp. 447–464). Hillsdale, NJ: Erlbaum.

Wason, P., & Reich, S. S. (1979). A verbal illusion. *Quarterly Journal of Experimental Psychology, 31,* 591–597.

CHAPTER 22

THE PSYCHOLOGY OF DISCOURSE PROCESSING

WALTER KINTSCH

I. INTRODUCTION

This chapter is about discourse, but the rest of the title signals its focus and limitations: the focus is on processing, and the discussion is limited to the psychological aspects of discourse processing. A great deal of work on discourse has been done in other fields—linguistics, philosophy, formal semantics, computational linguistics, and artificial intelligence. The psychological work on discourse is a small but increasingly important component of that research. It is necessary, therefore, to sketch the role that psychological approaches play in this research area. I shall try to do this by discussing the issues that have been important in discourse research historically and by contrasting the psychological approach with typical examples of alternative approaches. But first some general perspectives on the study of discourse must be introduced.

II. ISSUES IN DISCOURSE ANALYSIS

A. Discourse as Object versus Discourse as Process

For many linguists, the data of linguistics are the well-formed sentences of a language. These are analyzed independent of the context in which they are produced and independent of the speakers or writers who produce them and the recipients (listeners, readers) for whom they are intended. Analogously, the objects of discourse studies are texts. That is, the analyst is concerned with the products of linguistic behavior, not with the behavior itself. An example of this kind of approach within linguistics would be the "text linguistics" of the 1970s (e.g., van Dijk, 1972), or the influential work on the "cohesion" of texts by Halliday and Hasan (1976), which conceives of cohesion as a relationship between two sentences. Much of the work in philosophy and formal semantics (Seuren, 1985) is also of this type, as is research in computational linguistics (e.g., Brady & Berwick, 1983) and natural language processing by computers (e.g., Allen, 1987).

In contrast, discourse processing may itself become an object of study. Within linguistics, this takes the form of asking how a recipient understands the producer's intended message on some concrete, specific occasion. The goal here is to try to describe not texts as static objects of analysis, but rather the way texts are used in the process of communication (Givón, 1979; Wittgenstein, 1953). In psychology, further considerations are added. How does language use depend on cognitive processing characteristics? What role do the limitations of short-term memory and attention play? What consequences do the properties of human memory retrieval have? How do people reproduce and reconstruct texts? Thus, the processing approach to texts is not quite the same within psychology and linguistics. Psychologists often work with written texts, neglecting the communicative situation in which comprehension processes are embedded. Linguists, on the other hand, focus on the latter, but usually do not take into account the constraints imposed by the human cognitive apparatus. In recent years, there have been signs that an effective rapprochement between these two approaches may be achievable: Linguists are beginning to take cognitive constraints seriously (Givón, 1989), and psychologists have become more attuned to the communicative function of language (Bates & MacWhinney, 1982).

B. Information Transaction versus Interaction in a Social Situation

Many students of language have embraced the simplifying assumption that language is primarily a matter of information transmission (e.g., W. Kintsch & van Dijk, 1978; Lyons, 1977). They focus on the intentional transmission of factual, propositional information. Thus, the texts studied in psychological experiments tend to be written materials—stories, essays, or chapters from textbooks—where the role of beliefs and feelings, or idiosyncratic goals are minimized. Psychologists study how such texts are comprehended, how they are remembered, how one learns from them, and so on. The focus on information transmission is not unreasonable, for without doubt information transmission is one of the major functions of language in our culture. However, it is not the only function.

Language is also a major means whereby people establish and maintain social interactions. In conversations as well as in many types of written texts, information transmission is often a secondary goal. The text is a tool for the formation of social relationships, for negotiation of social roles; its goal is to persuade or to entertain or to amuse (Labov, 1972; Sacks, Schegloff, & Jefferson, 1974). Indeed, much of our daily language use is concerned with social interaction and not with information transaction. By neglecting the interactional aspect of discourse, researchers run the risk of distorting their findings and conclusions. The interactional aspects of language are far too essential a feature to be excluded from investigation.

The psychological research on discourse reviewed below, including my own work, remains at this point mainly transactional, though there are some signs of a greater appreciation of the interactional perspective. In terms of the object versus process dimension, discourse research within psychology has been characterized by a shift in emphasis on the object produced in a discourse to how it is processed. In my own work, this shift took place between W.

Kintsch (1974), which was still product-oriented, and W. Kintsch and van Dijk (1978), which introduced a processing model for discourse comprehension.

C. The Role of Formal Theory in Discourse Analysis

Researchers in the area of discourse studies differ strongly on how formal they think theories should be. One can find anything, from the utmost rigor of formal semantic systems to an eschewal of any kind of theory in favor of a fuller description of the richness of language. In between are the computer systems used for natural language processing or simulation of human performance, which are formalisms, too, though not in the strict logical sense (e.g., they may not even be algorithmic but employ heuristic strategies).

Given the enormous complexity of language, how it varies and depends on the context in which it is used, its subtlety, the infinite shadings of meaning it can convey, it is questionable—and often is questioned—whether a formal description of language is at all possible. The position taken here is that it is at least worth trying. The business of science is formal description, and we would be foolish to give up without trying to employ the scientific method in such a significant domain as language and language behavior, just because at this point, we cannot handle many of its complexities.

Formalization is, however, a risky strategy that must be executed with great care. We must simplify and idealize, but it is all too easy to oversimplify, to create an idealization that neglects the essential features of language. The issues involved here have been recognized for as long as people have attempted to study language, and they remained unresolved. A brief look at the history of linguistic studies will at least clarify what the issues are.[1] From the very beginning, there has always been disagreement about just how much order there is in language that could be captured within a formal system. The followers of Aristotle opted for a research strategy that assumed that language was basically logical and that it could and should be interpreted with the methods of Aristotelian logic. Faced with the undeniable evidence of complexities that could not be handled by their logical apparatus, indeed, of seeming chaos, they retreated to a defensive position, claiming that language, when it first was adopted by our mythical ancestors as a system of conventions for the purpose of communication, was indeed pure and logical. Since then, however, it has become debased, as part of the general moral decline of the human race from ancestral purity to our present chaotic state. What we should study, however, is the pure, ideal language as it should be, not the messy reality. In contrast, the followers of Plato, among them the Stoic philosophers, maintained that language was not a rational convention, but a genuine product of nature, and hence messy and anomalous by its very essence.

The problem was, and is, that both points of view have their strong and weak points. The logicians offer us formal rigor but exclude all too much of the phenomenon they want to study. The anomalists are willing to deal with the real thing but are forced to substitute descriptions and taxonomic classification for explanatory analysis.

---

[1] A fuller discussion of these points is found in Seuren (1985), on which the present discussion is based.

Plato's philosophy, however, also provided a compromise solution to this dilemma: A distinction was made between the surface structure and the deep structure of language. The former was left to be rich and messy, whereas rule and order was to be found in the underlying deep structure. The task of linguistics then became to formulate the transformation rules that map deep structures into surface structures or generate one from the other. Even to this day, psychological approaches to discourse typically focus on the underlying semantic representation, rather than on the surface text directly. But before describing these approaches, the work on discourse in other disciplines needs to be sketched.

1. Formal Semantics

Formal semantics is the domain of the philosopher rather than the linguist or psychologist. Typically, it is concerned with the representation of the semantic deep structure of sentences or texts. (An exception is found in the work of Montague, 1974, where the sentences of the language themselves are assumed to be well-defined formal structures). Until recently, formal semantics employed idealizations of language that were so far removed from the reality of language use that they were of little general interest. Current approaches (e.g., Barwise & Perry, 1983; Seuren, 1985) attempt to overcome these limitations.

2. Linguistics

Most formal systems in linguistics are concerned with the sentence as the object of analysis (e.g., generative grammars). The formal, structural description of discourse began with the early "text grammars" (e.g., van Dijk, 1972). An example of an influential current linguistic discourse analysis is Grosz and Sidner (1986). Most of this work can be characterized as transactional in nature, that is, concerned with the use of language to convey information. Today, however, the interactional approach is also strong within linguistics, although it tends to be less formal. Brown and Yule (1983) provide an introduction to this research tradition with its emphasis on conversations, rather than texts.

3. Natural Language Processing by Computers

There appear to be two separate and antagonistic approaches to language processing by computers, one more linguistically, the other more psychologically oriented. The first approach takes its questions and problems from linguistics and puts them into a computational framework. Allen (1987) provides a good illustration of this work. Allen's textbook is divided into three parts, syntax, semantics, and pragmatics (which he paraphrases as "context and world knowledge"). The parsers he discusses are syntax-based and employ the technique of augmented transition networks, which are formalisms designed to account for the dependencies between language constituents (e.g., the grammatical agreement of subject and verb). The problems in semantics that are discussed include the assignment of case roles, scope of quantifiers, tense and aspect, and similar questions derived from the fields of linguistics and logic. Pragmatic issues concern inference techniques, logical and frame-based knowledge representations, and the representation of action. Finally, issues of discourse processing are taken up, such as a transition network for stories, or speech act theory in connection with question answering systems (see Graesser, McMahen, & Johnson, this volume).

The alternative approach is that of Schank (1972, 1982; Schank & Abelson, 1977) and his followers. Syntactic issues are minimized here and semantics has priority. Questions of knowledge representation in memory (scripts, memory organization packets), knowledge use, and inference are central. The focus is more on psychological issues (memory, reminding, understanding) than on the traditional problems of linguistics and logic. From the very beginning, this work has concentrated more on discourse (story understanding) than on the analysis of single, context-free sentences.

4. Interrelationships among Disciplines

The lines of influence go from philosophy (logic and formal semantics) to linguistics. Only recently has there been a strong backward influence from linguistics to semantics (e.g., Barwise & Perry, 1983). Natural language processing systems that are primarily syntax- and sentence-oriented are dominated by the issues and goals of linguistics. They have very little overlap with what for brevity is referred to here as the Schank school.

The psychological work on discourse analysis and discourse processing shows influences from both linguistics proper and the Schank school, whereas the overlap with formal semantic approaches as well as linguistic-based natural language processing research is minimal.

III. DISCOURSE ANALYSIS: PSYCHOLOGICAL APPROACHES

Although the historian will undoubtedly be able to point to relevant earlier work (especially Bühler, 1934), modern psychological research on discourse arose only in the early 1970s. This research was transactional (i.e., it focused on information transmission rather than the social aspects of discourse) and object-oriented. It was concerned with an analysis of texts, just as in linguistics, but with a different purpose. The purpose was to create a tool for psychological investigations, in particular, experiments on text memory and understanding.

With the ascendance of cognitive psychology in the 1960s, psychologists discovered meaning. Meaning seemed to be found just about everywhere—subjects even recalled random word lists in meaningful clusters! The problem of meaning could no longer be ignored. Thus, if one had to deal with meaning anyway, why not then turn to really meaningful materials—in other words, text. To study text recall (instead of word list recall), one needed a scoring scheme. Verbatim scoring was limited in its usefulness, and "idea units" were just too informal, subjective, and vague. Several researchers turned to linguistics to see whether it offered solutions to their problems. The results were a number of systems by means of which the semantic content and structure of a text could be represented in a way that was convenient and useful for psychological experimentation (e.g., Frederiksen, 1975; W. Kintsch, 1974) and educational studies (Meyer, 1975). At about the same time, Schank developed his representational system for his work on a natural language understanding program (Schank, 1972).

All these systems have much in common; they differ primarily in features that are related to the purposes their authors had in mind for their use. They are directly based on earlier work in linguistics (the case grammar of Fillmore,

1968; the propositional analyses of Bierwisch, 1969), which they adapt for their purposes.

The unit of analysis in these systems is the proposition.[2] A proposition consists of a relational term or predicate and one or more arguments. Arguments may be concepts (which, in turn, are introduced via existential propositions) or other propositions. The arguments of a proposition often need to be classified in terms of their semantic case roles. For example, consider the sentence *Mary gave John a book but he lost it*. It involves the concepts MARY, JOHN, and BOOK, and the following three propositions.

GIVE[agent: MARY, recipient: JOHN, object: BOOK]

LOSE[agent: JOHN, object: BOOK]

BUT[GIVE[MARY, JOHN, BOOK], LOSE[JOHN, BOOK]]

Propositions are constructed from a text on the basis of lexical information in long-term memory. For example, verb frames specify what sort of agents, recipients, and other cases a verb can take; frames for sentence connectives specify what sort of relation between sentences is implied by the connective; and so on. Clearly, such an analysis is quite rough (not even the tense of the sentence has been indicated), but frequently that is just what is needed for experimental purposes (and if it is not, another proposition (TENSE[GIVE[. . .], PAST] could be used).[3]

The propositions of a text are not listlike, but have a hierarchical structure. Superordinate propositions are at the top of the hierarchy, with several levels of subordination beneath. One way of constructing such a hierarchy is to place a topic proposition at the top of a (paragraph) hierarchy, and then subordinate to it all propositions that share a common argument with it. The next lower level in the hierarchy would be formed by those propositions that share an argument with the propositions at the current level, and so on (W. Kintsch, 1974). Other criteria have been used, by Meyer (1975) and Trabasso and van den Broek (1985), among others, which can be thought of as special-purpose refinements of the referential criteria described above.

For longer texts it is not sufficient to describe only the local structure of the text (microstructure), but the global structure or macrostructure must also be considered. The corresponding intuitive notion is that of the gist of a text. Macrostructures are hierarchical, subsuming the propositions of the microstructure under increasingly general macropropositions. The analysis of macrostructures is described in van Dijk (1980).

The differences among the various systems for propositional analysis are in part merely notational, reflecting the different purposes for which these systems were designed, and in part a matter of focus and depth of analysis. Thus, W. Kintsch (1974) uses the analysis sketched above which does not make many distinctions that are important in more fine-grained semantic analyses.

[2] The terminology and notation of W. Kintsch (1974) are used here because they are needed in the discussion of processing models below.

[3] Curiously, very few manuals have been published for teaching interested researchers how to propositionalize a text. The best sources available are Turner and Greene (1978) and Bovair and Kieras (1985).

Initially, its main use was for scoring recall protocols, and it was adapted to that purpose. Propositions were written in list form, in contrast to Norman and Rumelhart (1975), who preferred graphic representations, which are helpful for single sentences but difficult to handle for long texts. Frederiksen (1975) proposed a more detailed system, with finer distinctions, since he was mostly interested in the classification of different types of propositions and semantic relations. Meyer (1975, 1985) added something new: She was the first who concerned herself not only with the representation of the semantic structure of a text, but also its rhetorical form. This concern springs directly from her interest in educational applications, for rhetorical structure and signaling provide an important means to make texts more understandable and easier to recall. Schank's (1972) conceptual dependency notation was constructed to facilitate inferencing by computers. Hence, it employs a more abstract, canonical representation than some of the systems designed primarily for psychological purposes. For instance, instead of a predicate like GIVE above, Schank uses the more general term PTRANS (for physical transfer).

Indeed, herein may lie the only critical difference among all these systems: In most cases (Norman & Rumelhart, 1975; Schank, 1972), authors assumed a finite number of semantic primitives from which complex semantic concepts could be composed, much like chemical substances from the chemical elements. This assumption has obvious attractions and, furthermore, is fairly standard among the linguistic and philosophic predecessors of this work. Nevertheless, some authors, like W. Kintsch (1974), argued against the psychological reality of semantic primitives, and the question was for a while hotly debated. Although the experimental evidence eventually turned against semantic primitives (Fodor, Garrett, Walker, & Parks, 1980), it appears doubtful by now that this is an empirically decidable issue. Since one cannot test representation independent of process, findings critical of one kind of representational format can always be reinterpreted by making appropriate assumptions about processes.

The systems for discourse analysis that were developed in the 1970s led to a burst of activity in psychological research in discourse, resulting in a number of important and well-established findings.[4] For example, there is quite a bit of evidence—from cued and free recall studies, reading times, and priming studies, as summarized in van Dijk and Kintsch (1983)—for the psychological reality of propositions as a unit of meaning in processing text. Structural factors in text recall appear to be well understood: Propositions high in the text hierarchy are recalled better than propositions low in the hierarchy. This is a highly robust result and accounts for a good proportion of the variance in recall experiments with brief texts (Britton, Meyer, Hodge, & Glynn, 1980; W. Kintsch & Keenan, 1973; W. Kintsch, Kozminsky, Streby, McKoon, & Keenan, 1975; Manelis, 1980; Meyer, 1975, 1977; Yekovich & Thorndyke, 1981). The role of inferences in establishing and maintaining the coherence of a text (bridging inferences, Haviland & Clark, 1974) and in elaborating it (e.g., Mayer, 1980) has been extensively explored.

The role of the macrostructure in understanding and remembering longer texts has been documented by a number of authors (e.g., W. Kintsch 1977; W. Kintsch & Vipond, 1979). Others have studied the way texts signal discourse

---

[4] Van Dijk and Kintsch (1983, Chap. 2), provides a detailed review.

relevance through titles (e.g., Schwarz & Flammer, 1981), initial sentences (e.g., Thorndyke, 1977), summaries (e.g., W. Kintsch & Kozminsky, 1977), or frequency of mention (e.g., Perfetti & Goldman, 1974).

The rhetorical structure of text and its role in comprehension and recall has been documented by Meyer (1975, 1977) and W. Kintsch and Yarborough (1982), but most of the attention in this regard has focused on stories, leading to the development of "story grammars" (e.g., Mandler & Johnson, 1977). However, rhetorical structure is only one organizing principle for discourse; domain knowledge, organized in scripts or schemata, usually plays an even more important role (e.g., Black & Wilensky, 1979; Schank & Abelson, 1977).

Thus, the discourse analysis systems have proven quite fruitful, in that within a short period of time, many significant empirical results about various features of discourse were collected with their help. But these systems were in fact only a beginning: The interest of psychologists soon focused on the psychological processes themselves that are involved in discourse comprehension and memory.

IV. DISCOURSE PROCESSING MODELS

A. Current Approaches and Issues

What are the psychological processes that are involved when we speak or write (production), listen or read (comprehension)? Many psychological studies have concerned themselves with this problem in the past few years, although overwhelmingly with the comprehension rather than the production side. Most of these studies have focused on some select aspect of discourse processing, exploring it experimentally and explaining it theoretically. I can do no more here than mention a few of these studies, just to give the reader an impression of the kinds of problem that have been investigated. Kieras (1981) has studied the component processes in comprehension, such as parsing the text into syntactic and semantic units, memory activation, and topic identification. He has constructed a simulation model and used it to predict reading times for individual sentences in simple passages. Britton, Glynn, and Smith (1985) explored a model of how cognitive resources are allocated during reading of expository texts. They were particularly concerned with memory management during the reading of difficult texts. MacWhinney (1977) examined the way listeners (or readers) use the initial part of a discourse to construct a framework to which the remaining information can be appended. Questions of knowledge use in text comprehension have been studied, for instance, by Voss and Bisanz (1985). Other researchers have focused on the way textual information is used after it has been comprehended, for example, how consequences of events are inferred (Singer & Ferreira, 1983), or how questions are answered (Graesser, 1981).

Several general models of discourse processing have also been proposed in recent years. These models differ in their focus, their completeness, and their level of analysis but share many features in common. Truly systematic comparisons between alternative models have not been made yet, as theorists have been more interested in developing their own positions at this early stage, rather than testing them against alternatives.

Perfetti (1985) outlines a framework for discourse processing that concentrates on the role of the different verbal skills and abilities that are involved in reading comprehension. Just and Carpenter (1987) take their starting point from eye-movement data during reading but develop a very general and comprehensive processing model. Their READER model is formulated as a computer simulation and ranges from the level of word fixations to text-level processing. The structure building framework proposed by Gernsbacher (1990) assigns a major role to facilitatory and inhibitory mechanisms which control the formation of mental discourse representations. It constitutes an excellent integration of the psycholinguistic work at the sentence and discourse level. Finally, there is the processing model that I have been working on (W. Kintsch & van Dijk, 1978), which is examined in more detail below.

Perhaps the major issue that has emerged in this work in recent years concerns the need for a situational representation, in addition to the representation of the text itself. Johnson-Laird (1983) and van Dijk and Kintsch (1983) have made a strong argument that comprehension and memory for text do not depend only on the mental representation of the text and its structure that comprehenders construct, but also on their mental representation of the situation described by the text (the situation model as distinguished from the text model, or text base, in the terminology of van Dijk and Kintsch; the mental model of Johnson-Laird). In many cases the situation model and the text structure will be similar, but often they are structured quite differently, for example, when one reads a text that updates an old situation model, or where a well-structured knowledge domain conflicts with the text structure an author has chosen for rhetorical reasons.

Instead of superficially describing the many different approaches to discourse processing, I shall discuss here only a single approach but try to do that in more detail. Because I know it best, I choose the work from my own laboratory as the example to be discussed, in the hope that this discussion will allow the reader to form an informed opinion about discourse models in general, even though it slights the specific contributions of the other authors mentioned above.

B. The Construction–Integration Model

In this section, I describe a model of discourse comprehension in some detail and discuss the issues that arise in its empirical evaluation in order to provide some insights into the nature, promises, and problems of such modeling. As an example I use my own work on discourse comprehension in its latest version, the construction–integration model. The basic features of the model were developed in W. Kintsch and van Dijk (1978) and expanded in van Dijk and Kintsch (1983). The current version of the model was initially proposed by W. Kintsch (1988). W. Kintsch (1992a, 1992b) and W. Kintsch and Welsch (1991) contain fuller descriptions of the theory and its applications.

1. The Sequence of Cognitive States in Text Comprehension

Cognition can be characterized as a sequence of cognitive states. Newell and Simon (1972) claimed that these cognitive states are completely described by the contents of short-term memory. Of course, complex processes go into generating these contents, but only their end products are relevant for the characterization of cognition. Each cognitive state is the result of complex analyses that take place at different levels, from sensory to perceptual, linguistic, and conceptual levels. Various temporary buffers are needed in this processing for the storage of intermediate results, and what is processed is not merely input from the outside world, but also input from long-term memory, ranging from perceptual knowledge, lexical knowledge, to general world knowledge and beliefs. Important questions arise for the psychologist in the characterization of these processes. However, we shall not focus on these questions here, but instead on the sequence of cognitive states itself.

Just what counts as a cognitive state in text comprehension depends on the grain of the analyses that are to be undertaken. Mostly, sentences or phrases form the proper units of analysis, but for some purposes smaller units like single words are more appropriate (e.g., for the analysis of speed–accuracy trade-off functions in a sentence verification experiment, as in W. Kintsch, Welsch, Schmalhofer, & Zimny, 1990), or larger units such as paragraphs (as in the analysis of the macrostructure of the campaign speeches of presidential candidates by W. Kintsch & Vipond, 1979).

There are several largely synonymous ways to characterize a cognitive state: as the contents of short-term memory, as the focus of attention, or as the state of consciousness. The contents of short-term memory function as retrieval cues for items they are linked to in the long-term memory network. Thus, all information in long-term memory linked to retrieval cues in the focus of attention becomes directly available for further processing. Therefore, the effective size of working memory ("long-term working memory") is much larger than the limited capacity of short-term memory/focus of attention/consciousness (Ericsson & Kintsch, 1991).

Since a different text segment is being processed at each point in time, the mental representations of the text generated in different processing cycles may not be coherent. W. Kintsch and van Dijk (1978) have therefore assumed that a few elements generated in each cycle are carried over in a buffer into the next processing cycle, in the hope that they would serve as common bridging elements between the two structures. W. Kintsch (1988) has hypothesized that the most strongly activated element(s) in each processing cycle are the ones maintained in the short-term memory buffer. Various direct (e.g., Fletcher, 1981) and indirect (e.g., W. Kintsch & van Dijk, 1978; Miller & Kintsch, 1980) consequences of these assumptions have been investigated empirically.

2. Mental Representations of Texts

It is commonly acknowledged that the generation of cognitive representations involves many different kinds of processes, from the sensory to the perceptual, from the linguistic to the conceptual. It is important to realize, however, that the end product of these processes must also be characterized at different levels of representation. At a minimum, the surface (linguistic, or word) level must be distinguished from the propositional (conceptual or semantic) level and the situation model (Fletcher & Chrysler, 1990; van Dijk & Kintsch, 1983). However, this is not an exhaustive list, because for special texts (poetry, Kintsch, in press; word algebra problems, W. Kintsch & Greeno, 1985) additional levels of analysis become relevant. For poetry, such factors as rhyme and alliteration provide the significant constraint, while the mathematical structure of a problem co-determines the mental representation of word algebra problems. Furthermore, the surface, propositional, and situational representations are not always equally weighted. In many laboratory tests, the surface representation plays a very small role, so that it is often neglected in simulations.[5] The propositional representation of the meaning of a text—the text base—and the situation model that is constructed on the basis of the text are usually of greatest importance, both in laboratory tests and real life (e.g., W. Kintsch et al., 1990).

The procedures for generating a propositional representation from a text are not fully algorithmic, but hand coding frequently produces reliable results. The system used for this purpose is that of W. Kintsch (1974) discussed in Section III. The most detailed description of the use of that system within the present framework is given in W. Kintsch (1985).

The situation model (that is, the representation of the situation described by the text, rather than the text itself), on the other hand, is not necessarily represented propositionally. It might instead be a mental image, or it may be procedural (e.g., Perrig & Kintsch, 1985), abstract (in the sense of Johnson-Laird, 1983), or, of course, propositional (e.g., in the case of script-based texts, as in W. Kintsch et al., 1990).

The representational units constructed from a text (concepts, propositions, image elements, etc.) and their interrelations can be expressed in the form of a graph with nodes corresponding to the elements and links corresponding to the presence of a relation between the elements. Alternatively, the graph may be translated into the form of a matrix, the rows and columns of which correspond to the nodes of the graph and nonzero entries corresponding to the links between the nodes.

Different types of relations between nodes may exist and may be included in the network. The default rule is that nodes are related if they share a common element (e.g., two propositions share a common argument). For many purposes this argument-overlap rule suffices, but often a more detailed analysis is required. For instance, semantic and pragmatic relations among propositions are frequently indexed by a common argument, but not necessarily. Thus, *It rained today in Boulder. The streets are wet* is a coherent text but not indexed by argument overlap. On the other hand, argument overlap is sometimes merely incidental and does not indicate a significant semantic (or other) relation, as in *Peter smokes his pipe. Pipes are made of wood,* which is not a coherent text. Thus, links must be included in a network that are defined in other ways than merely via argument overlap when they play a significant role, such as causal relations in stories (W. Kintsch, 1992b; Trabasso & van den Broek, 1985).

The first step involved in the simulation of text comprehension is to construct a network of the representational units and their interrelations, as specified by the text. These construction processes need not be precise. For instance, it is not necessary at this point to select the right meaning of a homonym.

---

[5] How something is expressed plays a major role in what sort of text base or situation model is generated, of course, but the representation of that information as a component of the cognitive end state may not necessarily be relevant, except when verbatim memory is called for. For instance, an indefinite *this* used as an emphasizer may result in the creation of a very different memory representation of a text and therefore have great indirect effects, but whether the word *this* is remembered is usually irrelevant (W. Kintsch, 1992b).

Instead, constructions involving both meanings can be included in the net: for example, for *The bank collapsed,* two propositions may be formed, one for a financial institution, and one for a river bank. Similarly, parsing ambiguities can simply be considered in parallel. Thus, for *The linguists knew the solution of the problem was easy,* a reader likely constructs the proposition KNOW[LINGUISTS, SOLUTION] before reading the last two words of the sentence, which force a reinterpretation. The propositions KNOW[LINGUISTS, P], where P is the proposition EASY[SOLUTION], is now constructed and simply added to the network, without eliminating the earlier KNOW proposition. Such sloppy, imprecise construction processes, which do not take adequate account of the context, create networks which include irrelevant and even contradictory elements. To get rid of these contradictory and irrelevant elements is the function of a contextual integration process.

The integration process is conceptualized as a process of spreading activation in the network that continues until a stable state is reached. For this purpose the matrix representation must be used. An activity vector with initially equal activation values for all elements constructed is multiplied repeatedly (and renormalized) by the coherence matrix, until activity values stabilize. What happens normally as a result of these multiplications is that the strongly interconnected parts of the network are strengthened, while isolated parts become deactivated. In other words, things that belong together contextually become stronger, and things that do not, die off.

Thus, a coherent mental representation of the meaning of the text is achieved, in spite of the fact that only weak, sloppy construction rules were used that were applied with little regard for the context. Context in this model has its effect through the integration process; the construction processes that create the network that is later integrated operate in a simple, context-free manner. Schema theories, in contrast, assume that the schemata function as a control structure that ensures the context-sensitive operation of the construction rules in the first place. Thus, they do not need a subsequent integration process. However, the construction process itself becomes much more complex because context sensitivity is required.

3. Processing Cycles

Text processing is a sequential process. When a new sentence is comprehended, parts of the old network must also participate in the new integration process. The model assumes that the strongest proposition(s) from the previous sentence are always maintained in the focus of attention when a new sentence is processed, in order to preserve the coherence of the network. In other words, understanding always occurs in the context of the previous text, but because it is not possible to maintain in the focus of attention the whole previous text, only a portion of it that is likely to be important for the overall coherence of the text is maintained.

4. Knowledge Elaboration

The mental representation of a text contains not only information derived from the text, but also knowledge elaborations from the reader's long-term memory. In reading a text, we are often reminded of related things which are in some way relevant to the text. The question is how this relevance is maintained. Why are we not reminded of irrelevant, contextually inappropriate things? The answer proposed here is that we are indeed reminded of many irrelevant things, but that these irrelevant reminders become quickly deactivated in the integration process, before we can become conscious of them.

There are two possible explanations for the context sensitivity of knowledge elaborations. The traditional explanation is that there exist cognitive control structures such as schemata, frames, or scripts, which filter out inappropriate knowledge. Alternatively, according to the construction–integration model, one can conceive of knowledge activation as an uncontrolled, bottom-up process, determined only by the strength of the associations between items in long-term memory and the text. In this case, of course, many irrelevant and contradictory pieces of knowledge will be retrieved and included in the network that is being constructed. However, the integration process deactivates these again, because they do not satisfy the constraints imposed by the rest of the text.

The construction–integration model has testable empirical consequences. It predicts that strong associates that are contextually inappropriate are activated during comprehension but become quickly inhibited. Indeed, if immediately after the word *bridge* in the context of *river* either *water* or *play* is presented for a lexical decision, a priming effect will be observed for both. That is, response times to decide that *water* and *play* are English words will be reduced by about 30–40 ms, in comparison with neutral control words. If the lexical decision task is delayed for at least 350 ms after the presentation of *bridge,* a priming effect will be obtained only for *water,* not for the contextually inappropriate *play,* which has become inhibited by that time (e.g., Swinney, 1979; Till, Mross, & Kintsch, 1988). Readers are reminded of relevant knowledge, but not of irrelevant or contradictory knowledge, not because they filter out the latter, but because irrelevant items become inhibited when they do not fit into the constraints imposed by the network that comprises the mental representation of a text.

5. Macroprocesses

Understanding a text is not just a matter of understanding each phrase and sentence and linking them together in a coherent network. It also has global processing components. One global component has already been discussed: the construction of a model of the situation described by the text. The mental model of the text itself, however, also has a global structure—the macrostructure, as distinguished from the propositional microstructure. The macrostructure of a text consists of a hierarchy of propositions reflecting the rhetorical structure of the text. Frequently, this is correlated with the structure of the situation, but there are many rhetorical and pragmatic reasons why the global structure of a text may be different from the structure of the underlying domain.

Macrostructures are constructed strategically. That is, readers respond to certain cues in the text that tell them which portions of the text are likely to be important and weight those portions more heavily than unimportant parts of the text in their construction of the mental representation of the text. For instance, for some text types, the first sentence of a paragraph tends to be macrorelevant. If the author of the text has provided the comprehender with reliable and sufficient cues, and if the comprehender responds to these cues in the intended way, the macrostructure that will be constructed in comprehension will mirror the outline the author had in mind when generating the text. On the other hand, for example, if the comprehender has some idiosyncratic, special comprehension goals, the macrostructure generated may not correspond to the author's intention at all.

The construction of a macrostructure involves three types of operators to reduce information: deletion, generalization, and construction (van Dijk & Kintsch, 1983). All of these can be regarded as inference processes that reduce the amount of information in a text.

6. Inferences

In addition to macro-operators that reduce information, inferences that add information to a text play an important role in comprehension. Guthke (1991; see also W. Kintsch, 1993a) has proposed a twofold classification scheme for inferences that add information to a text. The first consideration is where the information comes from: whether it is retrived from long-term memory, or whether it is newly created by means of some generation procedure. Second, it is important whether the processes are automatic or controlled.

Automatic knowledge retrieval during comprehension is a locally determined, associative process whereby items in long-term memory that are strongly linked to the text are retrieved and become part of the text representation. However, since the retrieval is only locally guided, much of what is retrieved in this way is either irrelevant to the global text context, or even contradictory, and is rejected in the integration phase of comprehension.

Controlled retrieval from long-term memory occurs during comprehension in response to special task demands or in response to comprehension problems. For instance, if no contradiction-free situation model can be constructed, long-term memory may be searched systematically for information that might resolve the impasse.

Controlled generation of new information is what one typically thinks of as inferencing. It, too, occurs when impasses have to be resolved, or when the comprehender has special goals. It may occur during comprehension, but often texts are studied again or reviewed in memory to produce the necessary inferences. Just what the rules of inferencing are, and how they differ from the rules of logic, has been actively investigated, though not so much in the text comprehension literature as under the label of reasoning.

As is obvious from this brief discussion, "inferencing in comprehension" does not describe a unitary cognitive process. Instead, a number of quite different cognitive processes are involved in inferencing, which must be carefully distinguished (Graesser, 1993; Kintsch, 1993b).

7. Empirical Tests

In several experimental studies the construction–integration model was used to account for the results of experimental studies. These studies involve, on the one hand, rapid, basic cognitive processes, such as those occurring in word identification, on the order of 300–500 ms. On the other hand, complex processes spanning relatively long time periods have also been studied, as in the work on learning from texts and action planning.

Simulations of lexical processes have been described in W. Kintsch (1988) for the Till et al. (1988) data, and in W. Kintsch and Welsch (1991) for results reported by Gernsbacher, Hargreaves, and Beeman (1989) and McKoon and Ratcliff (1988).

Recognition of sentences from a text, as well as the speed–accuracy trade-off in sentence recognition, have been modeled by W. Kintsch et al. (1990).

Text recall and summarization have always been the main area of application for the theory. Several studies were based on the W. Kintsch and van Dijk (1978) model (e.g., Miller & Kintsch, 1980). W. Kintsch (1992b) uses the construction–integration model to investigate the role of semantic relations, domain knowledge, and syntactic cues in story recall and summarization. W. Kintsch (in press) is concerned with a type of poetic language—the factors that are important in the comprehension and reproduction of a simple nursery rhyme.

Otero and Kintsch (1992) analyze within the contruction–integration framework the conditions under which readers will fail to detect explicit contradictions in a text.

How readers comprehend and solve word problems in arithmetic has been simulated with the construction–integration theory by W. Kintsch (1988) and W. Kintsch and Lewis (in press). Nathan, Kintsch, and Young (1992) extend the theory to word algebra problems and develop a computer tutor based on the principles of the comprehension theory.

A simulation of what readers learn from reading a text is presented in E. Kintsch, McNamara, Songer, and Kintsch (1992). In these studies the readers' knowledge in a particular domain was evaluated before and after reading a relevant text, and the simulation of the text comprehension process is used to predict the observed changes in this knowledge structure.

A broad range of educational implications of the research on text processing conducted within the present framework, and in particular the construction–integration theory, are discussed in W. Kintsch et al. (1993).

Action planning, the generation of scripts for various kinds of action sequences where familiar components of actions have to be executed in the right order to achieve a goal given by some verbal instruction, was studied by Mannes and Kintsch (1991), and Doane, McNamara, Kintsch, Polson, and Clawson (1992).

Finally, the reader must be reminded that I have chosen here to focus exclusively on the work from a single laboratory for expository purposes only—not because there is a lack of noteworthy research from other laboratories. Other researchers have worked on the same problems discussed above, as well as on other problems not mentioned here. However, for the purposes of a handbook chapter it is perhaps better to describe one approach in enough detail rather than merely mentioning everything. I hope that the present chapter provides its readers with an understanding of the issues that are currently important in psychological research on discourse on the basis of the work described here, and thus enables them to further explore the rich literature in this area.

V. OUTLOOK

The study of language has a very long history in philosophy and linguistics. In contrast, the research described above is barely two decades old. Psychologists, of course, have built on the results achieved in other disciplines, as is quite apparent from the previous pages. But they have also provided a new element, a new concern with discourse processing, a focus on the constraints that the human cognitive apparatus imposes on that processing. I think this is an exciting and fruitful perspective. It is perhaps too early to expect our colleagues from other disciplines to appreciate this contribution—their attitude is rightly one of "show me." We need more research and more time to develop the psychological approach to discourse to a point where its achievements are recognized by all.

What this approach has to offer to other disciplines, even now, may be illustrated with the old controversy concerning where the meaning of a text is to be found: Is meaning inherent in the text, independent of anyone who reads that text? Is it what the author intended? Or is it a construction in the mind of the reader? Rosenblatt (1978) provides an excellent introduction to these issues in the context of literary texts. She points out that none of these extreme positions seems entirely satisfactory, and many philosophers, linguists, and students of literature have argued that meaning is something that is created during an act of comprehension, through the interaction between a text and a reader. The trouble with this position is its vagueness: Just what does this reader–text interaction consist of? The models of discourse processing that have been described here provide an answer to this question—not a complete one as yet, and not adequate for ambitious literary texts, but at least we have made a start. If we are successful, then discussions such as Rosenblatt's will, ten years from now, refer as much to psychological process models of comprehension as to literature from the older disciplines.

The study of discourse processing also has a role to play within the field of psychology itself. Here is an area where controlled experimental work is possible (though not easy), where formal models (computer simulations) can be used effectively—in other words, an area where serious scientific investigation is possible. But it is also a very complex area, an area of both theoretical and practical significance, with a certain face validity that laboratory studies in psychology involving simpler forms of behavior and more artificial tasks do not always have.

ACKNOWLEDGMENTS

The preparation of this chapter was supported by grant MH-15872 from the National Institute of Mental Health. I thank Eileen Kintsch for her editorial assistance.

REFERENCES

Allen, J. (1987). *Natural language understanding*. Menlo Park, CA: Benjamin/Cummings.
Barwise, J., & Perry, J. (1983). *Situations and attitudes*. Cambridge, MA: MIT Press.
Bates, E., & MacWhinney, B. (1982). Functionalist approaches to grammar. In E. Wanner & L.

Gleitman (Eds.) *Language acquisition: The state of the art* (pp. 173–218). New York: Academic Press.

Bierwisch, M. (1969). On certain problems of semantic representation. *Foundations of Language, 5,* 153–184.

Black, J. B., & Wilensky, R. (1979). An evaluation of story grammars. *Cognitive Science, 3,* 213–229.

Bovair, S., & Kieras, D. E. (1985). A guide to propositional analysis for research on technical prose. In B. K. Britton & J. B. Black (Eds.), *Understanding expository text* (pp. 315–362). Hillsdale, NJ: Erlbaum.

Brady, M., & Berwick, R. C. (1983). *Computational models of discourse.* Cambridge, MA: MIT Press.

Britton, B. K., Glynn, S. M., & Smith, J. W. (1985). Cognitive demands of processing expository text: A cognitive workbench model. In B. K. Britton & J. B. Black (Eds.), *Understanding expository text* (pp. 227–248). Hillsdale, NJ: Erlbaum.

Britton, B. K., Meyer, B. F. J., Hodge, M. H., & Glynn, S. (1980). Effect of the organization of text on memory: Test of retrieval and response criterion hypotheses. *Journal of Experimental Psychology: Human Learning and Memory, 6,* 620–629.

Brown, G., & Yule, G. (1983). *Discourse analysis.* Cambridge: Cambridge University Press.

Bühler, K. (1934). *Sprachtheorie.* Stuttgart: Fischer.

Doane, S. M., McNamara, D. S., Kintsch, W., Polson, P. G., & Clawson, D. (1992). Prompt comprehension in UNIX command production. *Memory & Cognition, 20,* 327–343.

Ericsson, A. K., & Kintsch, W. (1991). *Memory in comprehension and problem solving: A long-term working memory.* (Tech. Rep. No. ICS, pp. 91–13). Boulder, CO: University of Colorado.

Fillmore, C. J. (1968). The case for case. In E. Black & R. T. Harms (Eds.), *Universals of linguistic theory* (pp. 1–88). New York: Holt, Reinhart, & Winston.

Fletcher, C. R. (1981). Short-term memory processes in text comprehension. *Journal of Verbal Learning and Verbal Behavior, 20,* 264–274.

Fletcher, C. R., & Chrysler, S. T. (1990). Surface forms, textbases, and situation models: Recognition memory for three types of textual information. *Discourse Processes, 13,* 175–190.

Fodor, J. A., Garrett, M., Walker, E. C., & Parks, C. H. (1980). Against definition. *Cognition, 8,* 263–367.

Frederiksen, C. H. (1975). Representing logical and semantic structure acquired from discourse. *Cognitive Psychology, 7,* 371–458.

Gernsbacher, M. A. (1990). *Language comprehension as structure building.* Hillsdale, NJ: Erlbaum.

Gernsbacher, M. A., Hargreaves, D. J., & Beeman, M. (1989). Building and accessing clausal representations: The advantage of first mention versus the advantage of clause recency. *Journal of Memory and Language, 28,* 735–755.

Givón, T. (1979). *On understanding grammar.* New York: Academic Press.

Givón, T. (1989). *Mind, code and context: Essays in pragmatics.* Hillsdale, NJ: Erlbaum.

Graesser, A. C. (1981). *Prose comprehension beyond the word.* New York: Springer.

Graesser, A. C. (Ed.) (1993). Inference generation during text comprehension. [Special issue.] *Discourse Processes, 16,* 1–2.

Grosz, B. J., & Sidner, C. (1986). Attention, intention, and the structure of discourse. *Computational Linguistics, 12,* 12–54.

Guthke, T. (1991). *Psychologische Untersuchungen zu Inferenzen beim Satz- und Textverstehen.* Unpublished doctoral dissertation, Humboldt Universität, Berlin.

Halliday, M. A. K., & Hasan, R. (1976). *Cohesion in English.* London: Longman.

Haviland, S. E., & Clark, H. H. (1974). What's new? Acquiring new information as a process in comprehension. *Journal of Verbal Learning and Verbal Behavior, 13,* 512–521.

Johnson-Laird, P. N. (1983). *Mental models.* Cambridge, MA: Harvard University Press.

Just, M. A., & Carpenter, P. (1987). *The psychology of reading and language comprehension.* Boston: Allyn & Bacon.

Kieras, D. E. (1981). Component processes in the comprehension of simple prose. *Journal of Verbal Learning and Verbal Behavior, 20,* 1–20.

Kintsch, E., McNamara, D. S., Songer, N. B., & Kintsch, W. (1992). *Revising the coherence of science texts to improve comprehension and learning I: Traits of mammals.* (Tech. Rep. No. ICS, pp. 92–03). Boulder, CO: University of Colorado.

Kintsch, W. (1974). *The representation of meaning in memory.* Hillsdale, NJ: Erlbaum.

Kintsch, W. (1977). On comprehending stories. In M. S. Just & P. Carpenter (Eds.), *Cognitive processes in comprehension* (pp. 33–61). Hillsdale, NJ: Erlbaum.

Kintsch, W. (1985). Text processing: A psychological model. In T. A. van Dijk (Ed.), *Handbook of discourse analysis* (pp. 231–243). London: Academic Press.

Kintsch, W. (1988). The use of knowledge in discourse processing: A construction–integration model. *Psychological Review, 95,* 163–182.

Kintsch, W. (1992a). A cognitive architecture for comprehension. In H. L. Pick, P. van den Broek, & D. C. Knill (Eds.), *The study of cognition: Conceptual and methodological issues* (pp. 143–164). Washington, DC: American Psychological Association.

Kintsch, W. (1992b). How readers construct situation models for stories: The role of syntactic cues and causal inferences. In A. F. Healy, S. M. Kosslyn, & R. M. Shiffrin (Eds.), *From learning processes to cognitive processes: Essays in honor of William K. Estes* (pp. 261–278). Hillsdale, NJ: Erlbaum.

Kintsch, W. (1993). Information accretion and reduction in text processing: Inferences. *Discourse Processes, 16,* 193–202.

Kintsch, W. (in press). Kognitionspsychologische Modelle des Textverstehens: Literarische Texte. In K. Reusser & M. Reusser (Eds.), *Verstehen lernen—Verstehen lehren*. Bern: Hans Huber.

Kintsch, W., Britton, B. K., Fletcher, C. R., Kintsch, E., Mannes, S. M., & Nathan, M. J. (1993). A comprehension-based approach to learning and understanding. In D. L. Medin (Ed.), *The psychology of learning and motivation. Vol. 30.* (pp. 165–214). New York: Academic Press.

Kintsch, W., & Greeno, J. G. (1985). Understanding and solving word arithmetic problems. *Psychological Review, 92,* 109–129.

Kintsch, W., & Keenan, J. M. (1973). Reading rate and retention as a function of the number of propositions in the base structure of sentences. *Cognitive Psychology, 5,* 257–279.

Kintsch, W., & Kozminsky, E. (1977). Summarizing stories after reading and listening. *Journal of Educational Psychology, 69,* 491–499.

Kintsch, W., Kozminsky, E., Streby, W. J., McKoon, G., & Keenan, J. M. (1975). Comprehension and recall as a function of content variables. *Journal of Verbal Learning and Verbal Behavior, 14,* 196–214.

Kintsch, W., & Lewis, A. B. (1993). The time course of hypothesis formation in solving arithmetic word problems. In M. Denis & G. Sabah (Eds.), *Modèles et concepts pour la science cognitive: Hommage à Jean-François Le Ny* (pp. 11–23). Grenoble: Press Universitaires.

Kintsch, W., & van Dijk, T. A. (1978). Towards a model of text comprehension and production. *Psychological Review, 85,* 363–394.

Kintsch, W., & Vipond, D. (1979). Reading comprehension and readability in educational practice and psychological theory. In L. G. Nilsson (Ed.), *Perspectives of memory research* (pp. 325–366). Hillsdale, NJ: Erlbaum.

Kintsch, W., & Welsch, D. M. (1991). The construction–integration model: A framework for studying memory for text. In W. E. Hockley & S. Lewandowsky (Eds.), *Relating theory and data: Essays on human memory in honor of Bennett B. Murdock* (pp. 367–385). Hillsdale, NJ: Erlbaum.

Kintsch, W., Welsch, D., Schmalhofer, F., & Zimny, S. (1990). Sentence memory: A theoretical analysis. *Journal of Memory and Language, 29,* 133–159.

Kintsch, W., & Yarborough, J. J. (1982). Role of rhetorical structure in text comprehension. *Journal of Educational Psychology, 74,* 828–834.

Labov, W. (1972). *Sociolinguistic patterns*. Philadelphia: University of Pennsylvania Press.

Lyons, J. (1977). *Semantics*. Cambridge: Cambridge University Press.

MacWhinney, B. (1977). Starting points. *Language, 53,* 152–168.

Mandler, J. M., & Johnson, N. S. (1977). Remembrance of things parsed: Story structure and recall. *Cognitive Psychology, 9,* 111–151.

Manelis, L. (1980). Determinants of processing for propositional structures. *Memory & Cognition, 8,* 49–57.

Mannes, S. M., & Kintsch, W. (1991). Planning routine computing tasks: Understanding what to do. *Cognitive Science, 15,* 305–342.

Mayer, R. E. (1980). Elaboration techniques that increase the meaningfulness of technical text: An experimental test of the learning strategy hypothesis. *Journal of Educational Psychology, 72,* 770–784.

McKoon, G., & Ratcliff, R. (1988). Contextually relevant aspects of meaning. *Journal of Experimental Psychology: Learning, Memory, and Cognition, 14,* 331–343.

Meyer, B. J. F. (1975). *The organization of prose and its effect on memory*. Amsterdam: North-Holland.

Meyer, B. J. F. (1977). What is remembered from prose: A function of passage structure. In R. D. Freedle (Ed.), *Discourse production and comprehension: Advances in research and theory* (pp. 307–336). Norwood, NJ: Ablex.

Meyer, B. J. F. (1985). Prose analysis: Purposes, procedures, and problems. In B. K. Britton & J. B. Black (Eds.), *Understanding expository text* (pp. 11–64). Hillsdale, NJ: Erlbaum.

Miller, J. R., & Kintsch, W. (1980). Readability and recall for short passages: A theoretical analysis. *Journal of Experimental Psychology: Human Learning and Memory, 6*, 335–354.

Montague, R. (1974). *Formal philosophy*. New Haven, CT: Yale University Press.

Nathan, M. J., Kintsch, W., & Young, E. (1992). A theory of word algebra problem comprehension and its implications for the design of learning environments. *Cognition and Instruction, 9*, 329–389.

Newell, A., & Simon, H. A. (1972). *Human problem solving*. Englewood Cliffs, NJ: Prentice-Hall.

Norman, D. A., & Rumelhart, D. E. (1975). *Explorations in cognition*. San Francisco: Freeman.

Otero, J., & Kintsch, W. (1992). Failures to detect contradictions in text: What readers believe vs. what they read. *Psychological Science, 3*, 229–234.

Perfetti, C. A. (1985). *Reading ability*. New York: Oxford University Press.

Perfetti, C. A., & Goldman, S. R. (1974). Thematization of sentence retrieval. *Journal of Verbal Learning and Verbal Behavior, 13*, 70–79.

Perrig, W., & Kintsch, W. (1985). Propositional and situational representations of text. *Journal of Memory and Language, 24*, 503–518.

Rosenblatt, L. M. (1978). *The reader, the text, the poem*. Carbondale: Southern Illinois University Press.

Sacks, H., Schegloff, E. A., & Jefferson, G. (1974). A simplest systematic for the organization of turn-taking in conversation. *Language, 50*, 696–735.

Schank, R. C. (1972). Conceptual dependency: A theory of natural language understanding. *Cognitive Psychology, 3*, 552–631.

Schank, R. C. (1982). *Dynamic memory*. Cambridge: Cambridge University Press.

Schank, R. C., & Abelson, R. P. (1977). *Scripts, plans, goals, and understanding*. Hillsdale, NJ: Erlbaum.

Schwarz, M. N. K., & Flammer, A. (1981). Text structure and title—effects on comprehension and recall. *Journal of Verbal Learning and Verbal Behavior, 20*, 61–66.

Seuren, P. A. M. (1985). *Discourse semantics*. New York: Basil/Blackwell.

Singer, M., & Ferreira, F. (1983). Inferring consequences in story comprehension. *Journal of Verbal Learning and Verbal Behavior, 22*, 437–448.

Swinney, D. A. (1979). Lexical access during sentence comprehension: (Re)consideration of context effects. *Journal of Verbal Learning and Verbal Behavior, 18*, 523–534.

Thorndyke, P. W. (1977). Cognitive structures in comprehension and memory of narrative discourse. *Cognitive Psychology, 9*, 77–110.

Till, R. E., Mross, E. R., & Kintsch, W. (1988). Time course of priming for associate and inference words in a discourse context. *Memory & Cognition, 16*, 283–298.

Trabasso, T., & van den Broek, P. (1985). Causal thinking and the representation of narrative events. *Journal of Memory and Language, 24*, 612–630.

Turner, A., & Greene, E. (1978). *Construction and use of a propositional textbase*. JSAS: Catalogue of selected documents in psychology, (MS 1713).

van Dijk, T. A. (1972). *Some aspects of text grammars*. The Hague: Mouton.

van Dijk, T. A. (1980). *Macrostructures*. The Hague: Mouton.

van Dijk, T. A., & Kintsch, W. (1983). *Strategies of discourse comprehension*. New York: Academic Press.

Voss, J. F., & Bisanz, G. L. (1985). Knowledge and processing of narrative and expository texts. In B. K. Britton & J. B. Black (Eds.), *Understanding expository text* (pp. 173–198). Hillsdale, NJ: Erlbaum.

Wittgenstein, L. J. J. (1953). *Philosophical investigations*. Oxford: Basil/Blackwell.

Yekovich, F. R., & Thorndyke, P. W. (1981). An evaluation of alternative functional models of narrative schemata. *Journal of Verbal Learning and Verbal Behavior, 20*, 454–469

CHAPTER 23

RECENT CONTROVERSIES IN THE STUDY OF LANGUAGE ACQUISITION

PAUL BLOOM

I. INTRODUCTION

The question of how children acquire natural language has long occupied central stage within the sciences of the mind. In antiquity, philosophers such as Aristotle and Plato studied the case of a child learning a new word as a way to gain insights into both human psychology and the nature of word meaning. Word learning has been explored by more contemporary philosophers such as Quine and Fodor, who have used the logical structure of the acquisition problem to defend positions ranging from radical behaviorism to mad-dog nativism. Within linguistics, it has been argued that the main theoretical goal of this discipline should be to explain how children can come to possess knowledge of language through limited and impoverished experience (i.e., "Plato's problem"; see Chomsky, 1986).

As for cognitive psychology, every theoretical perspective has had the burden of explaining language acquisition. It could be argued that behaviorism's well-known failure in that domain (Brown & Hanlon, 1970; Chomsky, 1959) is why operant conditioning has been widely rejected as a theory of human learning. More recently, language development has served as the battleground for alternative perspectives such as connectionism and modularity.

As Pinker (1989a) notes, this focus on language acquisition should not be very surprising: Just as the emergence of natural language within the human species may be the most important aspect of our evolution, the acquisition of language is likely to be the most impressive intellectual accomplishment of individual humans. In fact, even if someone were uninterested in humans per se, they might still benefit from the study of children's acquisition of language—as children appear to be the only things (either living or nonliving) capable of performing this task. As such, computer scientists interested in language might study children for much the same reason that Leonardo da Vinci, who was interested in building a flying machine, chose to study birds.

There are radically different perspectives about the nature of the acquisition process. For some scholars, adult knowledge of language is presumed to be the product of general learning capacities and is acquired in much the same way that children learn how to ride a bicycle or to play chess (e.g., Anderson, 1983; Inhelder & Piaget, 1964). But one prominent alternative is that the human capacity for language is the product of a mental organ or faculty (Chomsky, 1980; Fodor, 1983), and thus there is no "learning" of language, just the growth of this faculty under certain environmental conditions, akin to the growth of arms or of the visual system.

All theorists agree, however, that there do exist differences between natural languages. In English, the name for dogs is *dogs*; in French, it is *chiens*; in English, adjectives precede nouns, in French, they follow them, and so on. Although these differences might well be superficial from a theoretical point of view, we need to explain how children come to speak the particular language that they are exposed to. In other words, we need a theory of language acquisition.

This chapter reviews a small subset of topics within the study of language acquisition, with special focus on areas where there has been both recent progress and continuing debate. Section II begins with a brief overview of the course of language development and the nature of adult input. Section III turns to the problem of how children learn the meanings of words, and Section IV concerns how they learn the syntactic categories that these words belong to. The following two sections focus on more specific issues in syntactic, semantic, and morphological development: Section V reviews a particular theory within the "principles and parameters" framework, and Section VI discusses how children might recover from morphological and semantic overgeneralizations. Section VII concludes.

II. A Brief Overview

A. The Course of Language Development

Language acquisition begins at birth, if not in the womb. Children who are only a few days old can discriminate their own language from another, presumably through sensitivity to language-specific properties of prosody (Mehler et al., 1988). Habituation studies show that infants start off being able to distinguish all phonemic contrasts made in natural language, but this ability fades over time, and by about 12 months of age, a child is capable only of distinguishing the speech sounds of the language that she is exposed to (see Gerken, this volume, for a review).

By about 7–10 months, children begin reduplicative babbling, producing sequences such as *babababa* or *dadadada*. At this age, deaf children will also start to babble—with their hands, producing sequences of sign language syllables that are fundamentally identical to the syllabic units found in vocal babbling (Petitto & Marentette, 1991). In general, there appear to be no significant differences between the acquisition of spoken and signed languages (Newport & Meier, 1985; Petitto, 1988; Petitto & Marentette, 1991), suggesting that the human capacity for language is geared to acquire abstract linguistic structure, and not specifically to acquire speech.

Children produce their first words—excluding *mama* and *dada*—by about 10 or 11 months (Nelson, 1973) and understand some words several months prior to this (e.g., Huttenlocher & Smiley, 1987). The most common class of words in children's early lexicons are names, either for specific individuals (*Mama*), objects (*car*), or substances (*water*); such words appear early for children of all languages and cultures (Gentner, 1982). Other early words include action verbs (*give*), adjectives (*big*), and certain hard-to-categorize expressions such as *hi* and *no!* Children's first words tend to refer to salient objects and actions in the child's environment; more abstract expressions, such as mental-state verbs, occur later.

By about 18 months, there is a "word spurt" or "naming explosion" in which there is a rapid increase in children's acquisition and use of words. At about the same time, children start to combine words into two-word phrases, such as *more cookie* and *big toy*. There is a strong correlation between the emergence of phrases and the onset of the word spurt (Bates, Bretherton, & Snyder, 1988; Nelson, 1973), supporting the view that there is some interdependence between word learning and syntactic development (see Section III,C).

The utterances that children produce at this stage are often called "telegraphic speech" (Brown & Bellugi, 1964), because they are very short, and because function words and morphemes (such as *the, and, of,* and *-ed*) are absent, giving children's sentences the minimalist flavor of telegrams or classified ads.

Even at this initial stage of grammatical competence, however, children command certain properties of the adult language. For one thing, word order errors are very rare (e.g., L. Bloom, 1970; P. Bloom, 1990b; Braine, 1963, 1976; Brown, 1973; Pinker, 1984). In fact, knowledge of word order appears to exist even prior to the onset of telegraphic speech. In one study, 17-month-olds were exposed to two videos, one where Big Bird was tickling Cookie Monster and the other where Cookie Monster was tickling Big Bird. They tended to look to the appropriate video when they heard *Big Bird is tickling Cookie Monster* versus *Cookie Monster is tickling Big Bird,* indicating a sensitivity to the semantic contrast between the sentences, something which would be impossible without some understanding of English word order (Hirsh-Pasek, Golinkoff, Fletcher, DeGaspe Beaubien, & Cauley, 1985). Children's obsession with word order extends even to languages where grammatical relations are encoded through case-markers. When acquiring such "free word order" languages, some children have been observed to initially use word order to express grammatical relations, and not utilize the word order freedom that an adult speaker would use (e.g., Newport & Meier, 1985, on ASL; see Pinker, 1984, for a review).

Two other properties of telegraphic speech are the frequent omission of subjects and other constituents (see Section V) and the absence of closed-class morphology (i.e., "function words" such as determiners, prepositions, prefixes, and suffixes). When closed-class morphemes do appear in child language, they emerge in a relatively fixed order; some morphemes, such as the present progressive (*-ing,* as in *walking*), show up earlier than others, such as the third-person regular (*-s,* as in *walks*) (Brown, 1973; de Villiers & de Villiers, 1973). Factors such as semantic complexity and phonological salience each partially determine the order of emergence of these morphemes, with frequency in adult speech less relevant (see de Villiers & de Villiers, 1985, for review). This suggests that these morphemes are absent in the first stages of word combinations because (a) they tend to be unstressed and hard for the child to perceive (and possibly to produce) and (b) children find it difficult to produce long strings of words and thus omit closed-class morphemes in their speech because they add little of essence to the meaning of sentences (e.g., P. Bloom, 1990a; Brown, 1973; de Villiers & de Villiers, 1985; Gerken, 1987; L. R. Gleitman & Wanner, 1982).[1]

Sometime before the age of about $2\frac{1}{2}$, the two-word stage ends. Children's utterances gradually increase in average length over a period of years, and function words become increasingly frequent in the contexts where they are grammatically required. More advanced syntactic devices begin to appear, such as yes–no questions (*Is there food over there?*), relative clauses (*The cookie that I ate*), and "control"-structures (*I asked him to leave*). Late-occurring errors include morphological overregularization (e.g., *goed* instead of *went*, *mans* instead of *men*), and usages of words in inappropriate semantic contexts (e.g., *I giggled the baby* instead of *I made the baby giggle*) (see Section VI). Children's vocabulary increases steadily after the word spurt; one often-cited estimate is that children acquire about nine new words a day from the age of 18 months to six years (Carey, 1978).

Finally, just as with the development of stereo vision in primates or the acquisition of song by birds (Marler, 1991), there is a critical period in language development for humans. If exposed to a language prior to the age of seven, children are capable of becoming totally fluent, but after this age, the prognosis becomes gradually worse. Studies of Chinese and Korean immigrants to the United States found that those who arrived after the age of seven never became totally competent in English, regardless of how long they were exposed to it (J. S. Johnson & Newport, 1989); a similar result has been found with people acquiring ASL as a first language (Newport, 1991).

As one would expect, there is no consensus about what all the above findings actually mean for a theory of language development. Some investigators see them as reflecting the growth of a genetically encoded language faculty. Alternatively, one might view children as learning language through use of more general cognitive and social capacities, and thus stages of development correspond to the sorts of intermediate levels of competence that one would find in the acquisition of any complex intellectual domain. A third view is that children acquire the grammar of their language at a very early age, and the patterns reflect the maturation of peripheral processing mechanisms and the

---

[1] One recent theory explains the lack of closed-class morphemes in telegraphic speech as the result of young children's inability to represent these morphemes as part of their linguistic repertoire (e.g., Guillfoyle & Noonan, 1989; Radford, 1990a, 1990b). It is proposed that children start off with grammars that can only encode open-class categories (nouns, verbs, adjectives) and then, perhaps through neural maturation, the capacity to have a full-fledged grammar emerges. One problem with this proposal is that this property of early child language is not universal. In languages where closed-class morphemes are stressed and syllabic, closed-class morphemes appear in children's speech prior to the age of two, at the point when children acquiring English are barely combining nouns and verbs (see Aksu-Koc & Slobin, 1985, on Turkish, and Pye, 1983, on Quicke Mayan). In addition, children acquiring English comprehend closed-class morphemes long before they are capable of producing them (e.g., Gerken, 1987), which undermines any grammatical theory of the "telegraphic" nature of children's early utterances.

development of nonlinguistic social and cognitive capacities. The extent to which these different perspectives are correct can only be resolved by looking at certain specific domains in detail.

B. Input to Language Development

Just as children may be specifically equipped to acquire language, adults seem to be inclined to make this task easier for them. Fernald (1992) reviews evidence suggesting that there exist universals in how human adults communicate with their offspring. Such communication tends to be slow, high-pitched speech with smooth, exaggerated intonation contours. While sometimes dubbed "motherese" (Newport, Gleitman, & Gleitman, 1977), this mode of communication tends to be used by both males and females when interacting with infants. Darwin (1877, cited by H. Gleitman, 1991) called it "the sweet music of the species" and infants resonate to it, preferring to listen to motherese than to the normal style of adult-to-adult speech (Fernald, 1985).

There may be several reasons why the inclination to use motherese has evolved. One speculation is that it helps establish a social bond between the caretaker and the offspring; across different languages and cultures, there appear to be universal speech patterns used to express praise, soothing, and disapproval—and infants respond to these prosodic and pitch differences in the appropriate manner (Fernald, 1992). But some of the benefits of motherese may be specifically linguistic. Grammatical phrase boundaries are often marked by changes in prosodic structure such as a pause or a change in pitch (Cooper & Paccia-Cooper, 1980), and thus exaggerated intonation might give infants clues as to how to parse adult utterances, which could help them to acquire the syntactic structure of their language (e.g., L. R. Gleitman & Wanner, 1982; Morgan, 1986). Supporting this, 7-to-10-month-olds prefer to listen to motherese where pauses (signaling the end of a sentence or phrase) coincide with a fall in pitch, suggesting that they expect a correspondence between the different prosodic cues to syntactic structure (Hirsh-Pasek, et al.).

Parental input appears to be optimal in other ways. Mothers' speech to children is virtually perfect from a grammatical standpoint (Newport et al., 1977), providing children with a reliable source of "positive evidence" (tokens of grammatical sentences) in the course of grammatical development. Some scholars have speculated that children also receive "negative evidence"—information as to which sentences are ungrammatical (Gold, 1967). Of course, adults do not explicitly announce to children that such-and-so is not a grammatical utterance. But they might react in some consistent way to children's ungrammatical sentences (by showing disapproval, for instance, or by responding with a non sequitur). If there are robust and universal correlations between children's ungrammatical sentences and adult behavior, and if children are sensitive to these correlations, then negative evidence might play some role in language development, particularly with regard to how children recover from error.

The first test of this hypothesis was carried out by Brown and Hanlon (1970), who found no correlation between the grammaticality of children's utterances and parental approval or disapproval. Nor was there a correlation between children's grammaticality and whether or not the parent responded with a non sequitur. As one might expect, parents are interested (and respond to) the content of what their children say, not to the structural properties of their sentences.

Several recent studies further explore this issue and have found that some parents respond differentially to children's errors; for instance, some repeat their children's ungrammatical sentences more often than they repeat grammatical sentences (Bohanon & Stanowicz, 1988; Demetras, Post, & Snow, 1986; Hirsh-Pasek, Treiman, & Schneiderman, 1984; Penner, 1987). As Grimshaw and Pinker (1989) point out, however, these effects are weak, apply only with younger children, and—most important of all—occur in only some of the parent–child dyads studied. But all children acquire language, and there is no evidence that those children with laissez-faire parents are fated to become linguistically retarded.

Note also that the sort of extensive parent–child interaction characteristic of middle class Western families may be the exception around the world; in other cultures, children acquire language in radically different contexts (e.g., Heath, 1983).[2] For these reasons, there is a growing consensus that negative evidence cannot play an essential role in the acquisition process (for discussion, see Bohanon, MacWhinney, & Snow, 1990; Gordon, 1990; Grimshaw & Pinker, 1989; Marcus, 1993; Morgan & Travis, 1989).

This is not to say, however, that children could learn language solely by hearing a string of sentences, without any supporting context. Following Macnamara (1972), most theories of language development assume that children have some access not only to tokens of the language but to some nonlinguistic encoding of the context. The need for some mapping between children's linguistic structure and their cognitive construal of the world is most obvious for theories of word learning but may also apply for the acquisition of syntax (e.g., P. Bloom, 1990b, 1994b; Macnamara, 1972, 1982, 1986; Pinker, 1979, 1984; Wexler & Cullicover, 1980).

III. THE ACQUISITION OF WORD MEANING

Perhaps the deepest mystery in the study of language acquisition is how children come to learn the meanings of words. Although there is considerable theoretical and empirical work on this topic, we have little understanding of how the process takes place. This might have to do with the nature of this problem; while syntax and phonology can be argued to be "closed" or "modular" systems, the

---

[2] One particularly interesting set of studies has focused on children who have created their own gestural communication system (HOME-SIGN) in the absence of exposure to a target language (see Goldin-Meadow & Mylander, 1990, for a review). To the extent that this system possesses the same syntactic and semantic properties of natural language, these studies suggest that, in the limit, input may actually be unnecessary for language development. Studies of creolization, which is the process through which a rudimentary communication system (a pidgin) gets transformed into a full-blown language (a creole), are also relevant in this regard (see Bickerton, 1984).

same cannot be true of word meaning. An adequate theory of how children learn the meanings of words such as *dogs* and *giving* requires some account of what it is to possess the corresponding concepts of DOGS and GIVING—which might in turn involve nothing less than a full-blown theory of human cognition (for different perspectives, see Carey, 1988; Jackendoff, 1986; Keil, 1989; Lakoff, 1987).

As a starting point, many investigators have construed the process of word learning as hypothesis formation and testing. The adult uses a new word, the child notes the context in which the word is used and formulates a hypothesis as to which concept the word corresponds to. Further instances where the word is used cause the child to strengthen, modify, or reject this initial hypothesis.

While this conception is implicit within much of psychology, philosophy, and linguistics, details differ: depending on one's theory of the child's conceptual resources, the initial hypothesis may be a single innate primitive concept (Fodor, 1981), or it can be some combination of innate primitive concepts, either as a set of necessary or sufficient conditions (e.g., Bruner, Oliver, & Greenfield, 1966; Inhelder & Piaget, 1964), or as a prototype or family resemblance structure (e.g., Rosch, 1973). Under some accounts, this initial hypothesis undergoes continued revision and modification (Bruner et al., 1966); alternatively, a single exposure might serve to trigger the requisite innate concept (Fodor, 1981; see also Carey, 1978, 1982, on "fast mapping").

Quine (1960) and Goodman (1983) discuss conceptual puzzles that arise from this perspective. From a logical standpoint, there is an infinity of possible hypotheses that are consistent with any exposure or set of exposures to a new word. Consider an adult pointing to Fido and saying to a child *Look at the dog*. Imagine that somehow the child is capable of determining what in the environment the word is intended to describe and that the relevant word is *dog*, not *look*, at, or *the*. There are countless possible meanings of this novel word. It could refer to the basic-level kind (dogs), a subordinate kind (poodle), a superordinate kind (animal), to the individual (Fido), to the color of the entity being pointed to (brown), to its shape (oblong), its size (large), a part of the entity (tail), and so on. There are also "crazy" hypotheses that are consistent with the word–scene pairing; the word *dog* could refer to the category including dogs and ex-presidents, or to dogs until the year 2000 and then cats.

More generally, the crazy hypothesis problem (or "the new riddle of induction"; Goodman, 1983) is that there is an infinity of inductive generalizations that are consistent with any finite set of instances. One solution is that there is an innate ordering on the hypotheses children make (Fodor, 1981). Children have evolved, for instance, to guess DOGS when exposed to a word that describes a dog, and this concept is ranked slightly ahead of the concept BROWN and far ahead of the concept DOG UNTIL THE YEAR 2000 AND THEN CATS. More generally, it has been argued that the logic of the word-learning problem requires that children possess special constraints on word meaning; these preclude certain classes of hypotheses from being considered in the first place and lead children to favor some hypotheses over others. In Section III,A some proposed constraints are discussed and supporting evidence is reviewed. Section III,B discusses some criticisms of these constraints, and Section III,C addresses the possible role of syntax in word learning.

A. Constraints on Word Meaning

One proposed constraint is called the WHOLE OBJECT ASSUMPTION, which is that "a novel label is likely to refer to the whole object and not to its parts, substance, or other properties." (Markman, 1990, p. 59). In several experiments, investigators have found that children ranging in age from two to five will initially categorize a word referring to a novel object as a name for that object and not as referring to a part of the object, a property of the object, or the stuff that the object is made of (e.g., Baldwin, 1989; Macnamara, 1982; Markman & Hutchinson, 1984; Markman & Wachtel, 1988; Soja, Carey, & Spelke, 1991; Taylor & Gelman, 1988).

Related to this is a second constraint, which is that "labels refer to objects of the same kind rather than to objects that are thematically related." (Markman, 1990, p. 59). Thematically related entities include those that fall into "spatial, causal, temporal, or other relations" such as a dog and its bone, a dog and the tree that it is under, a dog and the person who is petting it, and so on. One important aspect of this proposal is that it is intended to be special to word learning. In a task that does not involve language, children are highly sensitive to thematic relations (for instance, they will put a dog and a bone together when asked to sort objects into different piles) (Markman, 1981). Markman's hypothesis is that this "taxonomic assumption" forces children to override this bias and attend to taxonomies (such as the kind DOG) when faced with the task of inferring the meaning of a new word.

Markman and Hutchinson (1984) present a set of studies that directly test this hypothesis. In one experiment, 2- and 3-year-olds were randomly assigned to one of two conditions. In the No Word condition, they were shown a target picture (e.g., a dog) along with two other pictures, one of the same category (e.g., another dog) and one that was thematically related (e.g., a bone), and told *See this? Can you find another one?* In the Novel Word condition, children were shown the same pictures and told *See this dax. Can you find another dax?* Markman and Hutchinson found that children in the No Word condition tended to chose the thematic associate (the bone), while children in the Novel Word condition tended to choose the object that belongs to the same category as the target (the other dog). This suggests that the taxonomic assumption is special to word learning. Similar findings emerge from the work of Hutchinson (1984), and Backscheider and Markman (1990), all of who studied 18-to-24-month-olds.

These constraints are posited to explain the acquisition of words that refer to kinds of whole objects (e.g., *dog*), but the majority of lexical items acquired by children are not of this nature. Even 2-year-olds possess words that refer to specific individuals (*Fred*), substances (*water*), parts (*nose*), properties (*red*), actions (*give*), and so on. This motivates further constraints that determine how words can relate to one another within the lexicon; these can lead children to override the whole object and taxonomic constraints.

One such proposal is the MUTUAL EXCLUSIVITY ASSUMPTION (Markman & Wachtel, 1988), which is that each object can have only one label. This assumption does not hold for adults, as pairs of words such as *dog* and *pet* or *dog* and *Fido* are not mutually exclusive. But it could be argued that children are biased to assume that words have mutually exclusive reference and only give up this assumption when there is clear evidence to the contrary. The fact that children appear to have some difficulty with class inclusion relations (where categories exist at different levels of abstraction, such as *dog* and *animal*) has been taken as evidence that children are reluctant to abandon this assumption.

Further evidence from Markman and Wachtel (1988) illustrates the role that this assumption can play in language development. When children are given a novel word describing a novel object, they will interpret the word as referring to that object (following the taxonomic and whole object constraints), but when given a novel word describing an object that they already have a name for, they will move to other, less favored hypotheses, such as construing the novel word as a name for a part of the object or a name for the substance that the object is composed of. In a study by Golinkoff, Hirsh-Pasek, Lavallee, and Baduini (1985), children were shown two objects, one familiar and the other unfamiliar (for instance, a cup and a pair of tongs). When told (e.g.) *Point to the fendle,* they would tend to point to the unfamiliar object, suggesting that they assume that *fendle* could not mean 'cup', a result predicted by mutual exclusivity.

An alternative to mutual exclusivity is what Clark (1987) has called the PRINCIPLE OF CONTRAST. Following Bolinger (1977), she argues that there are no synonymous forms in natural language. In particular, every word differs in meaning from every other word, though in some cases (e.g., *couch* and *sofa*, *cup* and *mug*) the difference is very subtle. If children possess the principle of contrast, this could lead them to structure their lexicon so as to avoid interpreting new words as synonymous with existing forms.

Note that the principle of contrast is much weaker than mutual exclusivity. While it predicts that a child will construe a new word as having a different MEANING than a word that the child already possesses, the two words are free to overlap in REFERENCE. In particular, it is consistent with the principle of contrast that a child might construe a new word as having a dialectal or register difference from one that she already knows, or assume that it refers to a subordinate or superordinate. Thus the principle of contrast cannot, in itself, capture the findings of Golinkoff et al. (1985) and Markman and Wachtel (1988). I return to this principle in Section VI, as a proposed explanation for how children recover from certain sorts of morphological and semantic errors.

While constraints such as mutual exclusivity and the principle of contrast might explain why children sometimes abandon the taxonomic and whole object assumptions, they do not explain how children actually acquire names for parts, substances, or abstract entities, let alone how they learn the meanings of verbs, prepositions, determiners, and so on. But since the very same problems that occur for the acquisition of words like *dog* and *cup* also apply for words such as *water, giving,* and *on,* any theory of acquisition must address these words as well (P. Bloom, 1994a; Nelson, 1988).

One possibility is that the sorts of inferences children make will vary according to the ontological category of the entity that a word refers to. Soja et al. (1991, pp. 182–183) posit that the following two procedures apply in the process of word learning.

Procedure 1:
    Step 1: Test to see if the speaker could be talking about a solid object;
            if yes,
    Step 2: Conclude that the word refers to individual whole objects of the
            same type as the referent.

Procedure 2:
    Step 1: Test to see if the speaker could be talking about a nonsolid substance;
            if yes,
    Step 2: Conclude that the word refers to portions of substance of the same
            type as the referent.

Procedure 1 operates as a restricted version of the whole object and taxonomic assumptions, while Procedure 2 can account for the acquisition of substance names. One could also posit an additional Procedure 3 that tests whether the speaker is talking about an animate entity with its own distinctive characteristics and, if it does, causes the child to conclude that the word refers to that particular individual; such a procedure might account for the precocious acquisition of proper names (P. Bloom, 1990b).

B. Problems with Constraints

Some scholars, most notably Nelson (1988, 1990), have argued that the constraint approach is fundamentally misguided. One criticism was mentioned above; the same problems that arise for the acquisition of a word like *dog* also arise for words like *run* and *nap*, and most of the constraints currently proposed apply only to object names. The extensions proposed by Soja et al. (1991) partially deal with this problem, but they assume that children are somehow capable of determining what the speaker is talking about in the first place.

A second objection focuses on the claim that these constraints are present prior to word learning, perhaps as part of a special language acquisition device. Many investigators have suggested that children go through a stage (lasting for 6–12 months) where they use words in ways that violate proposed constraints. One-year-olds have been observed to apply words only in highly restricted contexts (e.g., Barrett, 1986; Lucariello & Nelson, 1986); for instance, only using *car* when watching cars move on the street from a certain location (L. Bloom, 1973). Children might also use words in "complexive" ways; for instance, a child might use the word *clock* to refer to clocks, to dials and timers, to bracelets, to objects that make buzzing noises, and so on, suggesting that the word refers not to a kind of object, but to "an associative complex of features" (Rescorla, 1980). Only when these usages largely disappear does the naming explosion begin. Nelson (1988) suggests that this is the point when the child "seems to have achieved the realization that words name categories of objects and events," which implies that the constraints are the result of early lexical development. If this were true, then they clearly cannot serve as an explanation for how children acquire their first words.

Finally, Nelson notes that the results found by Markman and other researchers suggest more of a bias than a constraint. Children do not always choose the taxonomic choice in Markman and Hutchinson's (1984) novel word task, for instance, but instead show only a statistical trend to do so. Along the same lines, Gathercole (1987, 1989) presents a host of counterexamples to the proposals of Clark and Markman from both the experimental literature and naturalistic observations (but see Clark, 1988, 1990). This suggests that children possess more of a bias than an absolute constraint, which once again is said to undermine the notion that the constraints are genetically hard wired and exist prior to word learning.

All these points have spawned considerable debate (Behrend, 1990; P. Bloom, 1994a; Kuczaj, 1990; Markman, 1989, 1990; Nelson, 1988, 1990), and some general points can be made. The argument that children must establish which entity the adult is describing in order to figure out which constraints to apply seems fundamentally correct. But it does not necessarily suggest a crucial flaw with the constraint framework, just a gap, and the issue is being pursued by scholars within this perspective (e.g., Baldwin, 1991; Macnamara, 1982, 1986). One framework for a solution involves exploring children's capacity to infer the intentions of adults, a project which links the problem of word learning to questions about children's innate "theory of mind"—their initial understanding of the beliefs and desires of others (e.g., Wellman, 1990).

The claim that there is a stage in which children do not understand words in the same way as adults is a matter of some debate. Some analyses suggest that children actually obey constraints on word meaning at the onset of lexical development (e.g., Backscheider & Markman, 1990; Huttenlocher and Smiley, 1987; Macnamara, 1982; Petitto, in press). But even if there are discontinuities, they might reflect neural maturation (as Nelson herself notes). If one accepts the possibility that constraints on word meaning are genetically encoded, then there is no reason to expect them to emerge at 12 months rather than 18 months. It is possible, then, that an early stage of non–adult-like word use is the result of children's attempt to acquire words before the appropriate neural constraints have kicked in; the fact that the naming explosion tends to occur at the same time as the onset of productive syntax may support this speculation (also see L. R. Gleitman, 1981).

Finally, there are many replies that the constraint theorist could offer to Nelson's observation concerning the seemingly probabilistic nature of the constraints and the known counterexamples in the literature. It is possible that "constraint" is a misnomer and that children actually possess "biases" to favor certain hypotheses over others. But this does not substantively change the theory; after all, biases can also be innate—consider, for instance, newborn infants' preference to track human faces (M. H. Johnson, Dziurawiec, Ellis, & Morton, 1991). Alternatively, children might possess absolute constraints, but given their well-known performance deficits and their problems coping with experimental situations, this knowledge may not be adequately reflected in their behavior.

Nelson's own position is that constraints on word meaning do not exist. She rejects the sort of hypothesis formation and testing model sketched out at the beginning of this section, arguing that "children, like adults, do not seek certainty of reference, but only communicability." She adopts aWittgensteinian (1953) alternative that conceptualizes understanding of language as the capacity to participate in a language game. As such, the development of language is better viewed as a social convergence process, where the adult and child work together to attain communicative success (Nelson, 1985; Vygotsky, 1962).

Nelson supports her perspective by citing several studies suggesting that mothers tailor their naming practices to the age and capacities of the child (e.g., Mervis, 1984), but these studies are not by themselves problematic for the notion of innate constraints. A constraint theorist might argue that regardless of how some mothers might aid children in the process of word learning, children are still faced with a logical infinity of candidate hypotheses—and psychologists have to develop a theory of the sorts of mental mechanisms that allow children to infer the correct hypothesis from the linguistic and nonlinguistic context that they are exposed to, that is, a theory of constraints. In other words, it is unclear how Nelson's alternative makes the induction problem discussed by Quine and Goodman go away. Note also that the most radical version of a Wittgensteinian account, one that attempts to describe the child's capacity in purely behavioral terms, without any appeal to mental processes or representations, is almost certainly not feasible as a theory of language learning (e.g., Chomsky, 1959; Macnamara, 1982).

Nevertheless, Nelson's own account is thoroughly mentalistic and could be viewed as staking out a middle ground between Plato and Wittgenstein. It is similar in certain regards to the "naive theory" proposals of Carey (1986, 1988) and Keil (1989), who suggest that children possess structured theories of certain conceptual domains (e.g., biology). New words are acquired as theoretical terms, characterized not in terms of combinations of features (i.e., definitions or prototypes) but through their interaction with other aspects of a larger conceptual structure. It has been argued that this alternative can explain developmental transitions in children's knowledge of terms such as *animal* and *alive* (Carey, 1986).

It is unclear at this point whether these perspectives can provide a plausible explanation of how children acquire simple basic-level expressions such as *cup* and *dog*. But the mere existence of such approaches suggests that there may be worthwhile alternatives to the straightforward "hypothesis-testing" theory of the acquisition and representation of word meaning. Theories that involve grammatical cues to meaning, discussed below, also illustrate further directions in how children acquire words.

C. Syntactic Cues to Word Meaning

In an important paper written over 35 years ago, Brown (1957) suggested that young children might "use the part-of-speech membership of a new word as a first clue to its meaning." To test this, he showed preschoolers a picture of a strange action done to a novel substance with a novel object. One group of children was told, *Do you know what it means to sib? In this picture, you can see sibbing* (verb syntax); another group was told, *Do you know what a sib is? In this picture, you can see a sib* (count noun syntax); and the third group was told, *Have you seen any sib? In this picture, you can see sib* (mass noun syntax). Then the children were shown three pictures, one that depicted the identical action, another that depicted the identical object, and a third that depicted the identical substance. They were asked to *show me another picture of sibbing* (or *another picture of a sib,* or *another picture of sib*). Brown found that children were sensitive to the syntax when inferring the meaning of the new word; they tended to construe the verb as referring to the action, the count noun as referring to the object, and the mass noun as referring to the substance.

Children's capacity to use syntax to infer meaning, a process sometimes called SYNTACTIC BOOTSTRAPPING (L. R. Gleitman, 1990), has been documented in several domains. Katz, Baker, and Macnamara (1974) found that even some 17-month-olds were capable of attending to the difference between count noun syntax (*This is a sib*) and noun phrase (NP) syntax (*This is sib*) when determining whether a novel word was a name for a kind of object or a proper name (see also Gelman & Taylor, 1984). When 3-year-olds acquire new words, nouns focus the child on basic-level kinds, while adjectives draw children's attention toward properties (Gelman & Markman, 1985; Taylor & Gelman, 1988; Waxman, 1990).

Brown's (1957) initial work on the count–mass contrast has been extended to younger children; 2- and 3-year-olds will tend to construe a novel count noun as referring to a kind of individual (such as a bounded physical object) and a novel mass noun as referring to a kind of non-individuated entity (P. Bloom, 1994a, 1994b; Landau, Jones, & Smith, 1988; Soja, 1992). This sensitivity extends even to words that refer to nonmaterial entities; 3-year-olds will construe a plural count noun that describes a series of sounds as referring to the individual sounds, and a mass noun describing the same series as referring to the undifferentiated noise (P. Bloom, 1994a).

The developmental relationship between these syntax–semantics mappings and the constraints on word learning discussed above is unclear. One possibility is that the shift to specific grammatical categories might arise through the course of development, as a fine tuning of more general constraints on word meaning (Landau et al., 1988; Markman, 1989). For instance, children might start off with the assumption that LABELS refer to whole objects of the same kind (Markman & Hutchinson, 1984), and only later restrict this inference to the syntactic category of COUNT NOUNS—and also alter the notion of "whole object" to include entities such as parts, collections, and nonmaterial entities, all of which are nameable by count nouns. Alternatively, constraints on word meaning in the sense discussed by Markman might not exist as psychological mechanisms. The syntax–semantics mappings could be innate, and there might never be a stage of development where children possess constraints on meaning that apply to all words in general (P. Bloom, 1994a; Macnamara, 1986).

In any case, shifting the focus from "labels" to specific parts of speech allows for an explanation of how children might acquire a broad class of words. When exposed to count noun syntax (e.g., *This is a sib*), they will be constrained to interpret the word as referring to a kind of individual, such as *dog* or *cup*; when exposed to mass noun syntax (e.g., *This is some sib*), they will interpret the word as having non-individuated reference, as with the words *water* and *sand*; and when exposed to NP syntax (e.g., *This is sib*), they will interpret the word as referring to a particular individual, as with *Fred* and *Mary*. Given that an understanding of these mappings exists very early in language development (e.g., Katz et al., 1974; Soja, 1992), they could play an important role in the acquisition of the meanings of nominals.

A distinct line of research concerns the acquisition of verbs, where there are intricate connections between syntactic structure and semantic or conceptual representations (L. R. Gleitman, 1990; Jackendoff, 1990; Pinker, 1989b; Talmy, 1985). Gleitman and her colleagues have carried out several studies suggesting that young children are capable of exploiting mappings from syntax to semantics in the course of verb acquisition (e.g., Hirsh-Pasek, Gleitman, Gleitman, Golinkoff, & Naigles, 1988; Landau & Gleitman, 1985; Naigles, 1990; see L. R. Gleitman, 1990, for a review).

In one study, 27-month-olds were shown two videos, one of a pair of puppets each performing the same action, the other of one puppet causing another to perform an action. Then the children heard an unknown verb in either the intransitive form (*Big Bird is gorping with Cookie Monster*) or the transitive form (*Big Bird is gorping Cookie Monster*). When given the intransitive form, children tended to look more at the scene where each puppet performed an action; when given the transitive form, children tended to look more at the scene where one puppet performed an action on another (Hirsh-Pasek et al., 1988).

In another study, Naigles (1990) showed 24-month-olds a video of a rabbit pushing a duck up and down, with both the duck and the rabbit making circles with one arm. As they watched the video, they were presented with a novel verb in either the intransitive form (*The rabbit and the duck are gorping*) or the transitive form (*The rabbit is gorping the duck*). Then they were shown two videos, one that had the rabbit and the duck making arm circles (but without any pushing), the other that had the rabbit pushing the duck (but without making arm circles), and told, *Where's gorping now? Find gorping!* When the children had been given the verb in the intransitive form, they tended to look more at the video that had the animals making arm circles; when given a verb in the transitive form, they tended to look more at the video that had one animal pushing the other. These studies suggest that children are sensitive to the syntactic contrast between intransitive and transitive syntax when inferring how many participants are involved in the act that the verb describes.

Criticisms could be raised about the scope of these results. For one thing, it is unclear whether children are actually using the grammatical information to infer aspects of verb meaning and store them in the lexicon, as opposed to merely using grammatical context to draw short-term inferences (Gathercole, 1986). For another, the syntax–semantics correspondences discussed by Gleitman and others may not be universal; if not, then they could not apply at the initial stages of word learning (Pinker, in press).

Finally, it should be stressed that these syntax-based approaches do not constitute a complete theory of word learning. At best, syntax can provide a clue to the broad semantic category that the novel word belongs to—whether it refers to a kind of individual (count noun), a property (adjective), an activity with one entity acting on another (transitive verb), and so on. But it cannot tell the child the precise meaning of the word, whether it refers to *cup* versus *dog* (both count nouns), to *good* versus *bad* (both adjectives), or *punch* versus *kick* (both transitive verbs) (P. Bloom, 1994a; Pinker, in press). Nevertheless, if very young children can use syntax to determine the general semantic category of a novel word, this source of information can significantly narrow down the possible meanings that it could have.

IV. THE EMERGENCE OF SYNTAX

The hypothesis that young children can learn aspects of word meaning through a sensitivity to grammatical structure assumes that they are able to parse adult utterances into categories such as noun and verb. More generally, linguistic theory explains adult understanding of language in terms of rules and principles that map over such syntactic categories. In English, for instance, adjectives precede nouns within the noun phrase; *the big dog* is acceptable, *the dog big* is not. To acquire English, children must not only learn the order of adjectives and nouns (which is not universal), they must categorize words such as *dog* and *idea* as nouns, and words such as *big* and *unpleasant* as adjectives.

Once children have acquired some of the rules of English and have categorized some words, this task of categorizing new words becomes relatively straightforward. For instance, given that we know that *the* is a determiner and *dog* is a noun, we can infer upon hearing *I saw the gorp dog* that *gorp* is probably an adjective (see Pinker, 1984, for an explicit algorithm of this process). But how do children initially determine the syntactic categories of novel words? Without some means of doing so, they cannot acquire and use properties of syntax.

Proposals can be distinguished in terms of how they characterize children's telegraphic speech. One class of theories—dubbed "discontinuous"—views children as gradually converging on grammatical competence through revision and extension of nongrammatical representations. Thus they assume that children's early word combinations are not governed by adult-like grammatical rules and principles (e.g., Bowerman, 1973, 1976; Braine, 1963, 1976; Macnamara, 1982; Maratsos, 1982, 1983; Schlesinger, 1971, 1988). Other accounts—dubbed "continuous"—propose that children possess knowledge of grammatical categories from the very onset of linguistic development. Such theories assume that the early word combinations of telegraphic speech are the result of rules and principles that order syntactic categories (L. Bloom, 1970; P. Bloom, 1990b; Brown & Bellugi, 1964; Menyuk, 1969; Miller & Ervin, 1964; Pinker, 1984; Valian, 1986).

A. Discontinuous Theories

One sort of discontinuous theory is that children initially categorize parts of speech according to their DISTRIBUTIONAL PROPERTIES, such as what words they go before, what words they go after, and their absolute position within an utterance. As a result of this analysis, children cluster words and phrases into categories that gradually come to correspond to noun and verb, count noun and mass noun (Karmiloff-Smith, 1979; Levy, 1988; Maratsos & Chalkley, 1981). Under the strongest version of this hypothesis, semantic properties of words—what they mean—are irrelevant.

This solution was known as a DISCOVERY PROCEDURE by linguists in the 1940s and is motivated by the widely perceived failure to find semantic correlates to syntactic categories. It is false, for instance, that all count nouns are names for objects (e.g., *problem*) or that all verbs name actions (e.g., *seem*). Further, some analyses of children's spontaneous speech suggest distributional categories; Braine (1963) characterized children's first word combinations in terms of a PIVOT GRAMMAR, analyzing two-word utterances as combinations of a small class of high-frequency words (pivots) that appear in fixed positions with a larger class of low-frequency words (open class words) that appear in different positions. Such an analysis is both nonsemantic and nonsyntactic; it is DISTRIBUTIONAL in the strongest sense. Finally, evidence that children might use prosody to carve up sentences into grammatically relevant units (Hirsh-Pasek et al.,

1987) introduces another source of evidence that a nonsemantic procedure could use.

Nevertheless, without some semantic information to limit the space of alternatives, a purely distributional analysis is unlikely to succeed (see Pinker, 1987, for a critical discussion). The number of correlations that an unconstrained analysis would have to sift through is enormous. For instance, in his analysis of the grammatical contrast between count nouns and mass nouns, Gordon (1982) has calculated that the child who tried to distinguish these two parts of speech through purely distributional differences would have to consider over eight billion possible contexts in order to converge on the distinction—and yet children command count/mass syntax by about the age of 2½ (P. Bloom, 1994a, 1994b; Gordon, 1982, 1985, 1988; Soja, 1992).

More generally, the pivot grammar analysis does not appear to describe the early word combinations of all children (Bowerman, 1973; Braine, 1976), and there is evidence that even 2-year-olds possess productive grammars, with categorization errors virtually nonexistent (P. Bloom, 1990b; Brown, 1973; Maratsos, 1982; Pinker, 1984; Valian, 1986). When one also takes into account the very precocious understanding of syntax–semantics mappings (see Section III,C), it seems that semantic information is likely to play some role in the assignment of new words to syntactic categories.

One motivation for distributional theories is that children can rapidly acquire semantically arbitrary distinctions, such as the gender contrast in a langauge like French (Karmiloff-Smith, 1979; Levy, 1988). Such a finding is important, but the mere fact that children can acquire these distinctions does not necessarily entail that they do so through the sort of distributional procedure discussed by Maratsos and Chalkley (1981). An alternative is that children might (for example) acquire gender contrasts within nouns and adjectives because they are disposed to search for these sorts of markings—not because they are analyzing all possible relations among words within adult utterances. Moreover, they might only be able to acquire these sorts of semantically arbitrary regularities after they have used some other procedure to infer which words are nouns and which are adjectives in the first place—in other words, this sort of categorization may be based on syntax, not on a distributional analysis.

In general, it is crucial to distinguish the capacity to syntactically categorize words based on their distributional properties from the capacity to draw inferences over syntactic structure. As noted above, someone who hears *I saw a glubble* can infer that *glubble* is a noun—because in English, *a* is a determiner and nouns follow determiners. But this sort of inference is based on an understanding of syntactic structure, which is precisely the knowledge that a learning procedure is supposed to yield. To put it another way, inference over syntactic structure provides a useful way to grammatically categorize new words, but it is not available to young children, who have not yet acquired the relevant syntactic knowledge. Inferences based on properties of words such as being the first word in a sentence, following the word *cat,* and so on, are available to very young children, but they are of dubious use in the course of language development, for the reasons noted above.[3]

---

[3] I am grateful to Steven Pinker for discussion of this issue.

A different discontinuous theory is that children start with rules ordering conceptual categories such as "object word" and "action word." At a later point in development these categories somehow get transformed into the appropriate syntactic ones. Schlesinger (1981, p. 230), for instance, suggests that "the child's earliest semantic categories are narrowly circumscribed and . . . he extends them gradually into the broader categories of the adult grammar through semantic assimilation." This analysis is motivated by "semantic" descriptions of children's telegraphic speech, where they possess rules that order these sorts of semantic categories, not categories such as noun and verb (Bowerman, 1973; Braine, 1976; Macnamara, 1982; Schlesinger, 1971, 1988).

One problem is that the idea of "semantic assimilation," that of a category becoming more abstract as a result of experience, is quite vague, and without some theory of how "object word" becomes "noun" such a theory runs the risk of begging the major theoretical question. Furthermore, although child language does have a semantically transparent flavor, with (for instance) a high proportion of nouns naming objects and a high proportion of verbs naming actions, even the youngest of children do use at least some nouns that do not describe objects and some verbs that do not describe actions. Similarly, as Maratsos (1982) has argued, children do not make the errors that one would expect if they were limited to the sorts of semantic categories posited by Schlesinger and Macnamara. For instance, nouns that seemingly name events (e.g., *nap*) are not miscategorized as verbs, even by very young children.

B. Continuous Theories

An alternative perspective is that children possess grammatical knowledge from the onset of language development, as part of an innate language faculty. As such, the problem for children is to hook up innate grammatical categories to the words that they are learning, and thus to "bootstrap" (Pinker, 1984) their way into the grammar of natural language. From this standpoint, the puzzle runs deep: Nouns, for instance, do not sound the same across all languages and do not always appear in the same position within sentences. One class of theories of how children syntactically categorize their first words involves universal mappings from cognition to syntax; children use these mappings (perhaps with the aid of prosodic or distributional information) to categorize their first words; principles of grammar can facilitate the categorization of further words and phrases.

One specific proposal has been dubbed SEMANTIC BOOTSTRAPPING (Grimshaw, 1981; Pinker, 1984, 1987); this is the hypothesis that children exploit one-way mappings from cognition to syntax (e.g., all names of objects are count nouns). These mappings are part of a special language acquisition device, not grammatical knowledge per se, and do not apply in the other direction (e.g., all count nouns are not names of objects). Thus children might learn that *dog* describes a solid object and infer that *dog* is a count noun. Once they have acquired the determiner *a,* they could learn from phrases such as *a dog* that count nouns follow *a,* and they could infer from a phrase such as *a problem* that *problem* is a count noun. In this way, these early categorizations, acquired through semantic bootstrapping, could allow children to acquire further count nouns for which the bootstrapping procedure does not apply.

An alternative proposal is that the syntax–semantics mappings that children use are actually part of knowledge of language and apply in both directions throughout the course of language development. For instance, adults and children are argued to possess mappings from the grammatical category "count noun" to the semantic category "kind of individual," where "individual" is defined in a sufficiently abstract way so as to include abstract entities such as "problem" and bounded periods of time such as "day" (see Bach, 1986; P. Bloom, 1994a, 1994b; Jackendoff, 1991; Langacker, 1987). This hypothesis gains support from experimental analyses of adult and children's acquisition of new words (P. Bloom, 1994b) and is consistent with both the capacity to infer syntactic structure from word meaning (semantic bootstrapping) and word meaning from syntactic structure (syntactic cues to word meaning).

Unlike syntactic cues to word meaning, however, there is little direct support for the claim that mappings from semantics to syntax (however described) enable children to syntactically categorize new words. This is largely because of methodological limitations; while there are many techniques (e.g., preferential looking) that can explore how children younger than two construe the meaning of a new word, it is as yet impossible to test how these children categorize the syntactic category that a word belongs to. As such, all the evidence for semantic cues to syntactic structure for children's early words is based on analyses of spontaneous speech data. In particular, these semantic approaches are supported by the strong isomorphism between syntax and semantics in telegraphic speech (Pinker, 1984). For instance, although some of children's count nouns do not refer to objects and some of their verbs do not refer to actions (thus showing that their categories are syntactic, not conceptual), their proportions of object count nouns and action verbs are higher than for adults, which is consistent with the view that children exploit semantic cues to categorize these first words.

The strongest argument for this sort of mapping theory is that, unlike the other alternatives discussed above, it offers an explicit account of how children can acquire syntactic structure. It is based on universals of language that are plausible (e.g., object names are categorized as nouns) and appears to offer an explicit and workable procedure which could allow children to successfully categorize at least some words. It remains to be seen whether more direct empirical confirmation will be found, or whether some sort of explicit alternative approach will emerge.

One final concern is the apparent contradiction between the claim that children use syntax to acquire word meaning and the claim that they use the meanings of words to acquire syntax. For instance, it has been argued both that children use their knowledge that the word *dog* refers to a kind of object to infer that *dog* is a count noun, and that they are using their knowledge that *dog* is a count noun to infer that *dog* refers to a kind of object. Clearly both of these proposals cannot be right, at least not for the same words.

From a logical standpoint, there are two possibilities: The first is that children use some sort of nonsemantic procedure to determine the syntactic structure of sentences and then use this syntactic information to initially acquire the meanings of some words (as proposed by L. R. Gleitman, 1990); the second is that children use some sort of nonsyntactic procedure to determine the meanings of words and then use this semantic information to determine the syntactic categories that the words belong to (as proposed by Pinker, 1984). Each possibility rests on a nontrivial assumption regarding the process of language development: The first assumes that it is possible to learn the syntactic category of a word without knowing what it means; the second assumes that it is possible to learn the meaning of a word without knowing its syntactic category.

There are no conclusive arguments in favor of either view, but certain considerations favor the second hypothesis, that children first learn the meanings of some words, determine their syntactic categorization, and only then use syntactic structure to infer the meanings of further words. For one thing, children appear to acquire the meanings of words prior to learning syntax (Meier & Newport, 1990). For another, as argued above, there does not as yet appear to be any alternative to semantics as a cue to syntactic structure; for instance, distributional evidence is probably not sufficient.

This suggests a hybrid view, in which children apply nonsyntactic procedures (e.g., the whole object and taxonomic constraints; Markman, 1990) to acquire the meanings of a small subset of words and use either semantic bootstrapping (Grimshaw, 1981; Pinker, 1984) or more general syntax–semantics mappings (P. Bloom, 1994a) to determine the grammatical categories that these words belong to. Once children develop some command of syntactic structure, syntactic information could facilitate the acquisition of the meanings of other words and might play an essential role in the acquisition of some aspects of verb semantics (L. R. Gleitman, 1990).

V. PARAMETER SETTING: THE CASE OF NULL SUBJECTS

One recent approach to the study of syntactic development is the "principles and parameters" theory (e.g., Chomsky, 1986; Hyams, 1986; Manzini & Wexler, 1987; Roeper & Williams, 1987). Its premise is that grammatical differences across languages are the result of limited variation on universal principles; this variation is captured in terms of PARAMETERS which are set by children through simple positive evidence. Acquiring the grammar of a language, then, is the process of determining the correct values for these linguistically defined parameters.

This differs from more orthodox theories of language development in that it assumes that the grammatical structure of natural language is almost entirely genetically encoded; the sole role of input is to select among the different alternatives that are biologically available. Thus the role of input for a parameter-setting theory is to "trigger" an innately encoded grammar; it does not serve as the basis for induction or analysis.

The most worked out case of parametric change in language development concerns the optionality of overt subjects. For some languages, such as English and French, tensed sentences must have overt subjects, as in *I go to the movies.* For others, such as Italian and Spanish, null subjects are possible, as in *vado al cinema* (literally, 'go to the movies'). Part of language acquisition involves a child's determining whether subjects are obligatory or optional in the language that she is exposed to.

This contrast is posited to result from different settings of a grammatical parameter; one effect of this difference is whether the language has the option of a phonologically empty subject or topic in a tensed sentence (Chomsky, 1981; Huang, 1984; Hyams, 1986; Rizzi, 1982). Although acquisition theorists standardly refer to this as the NULL SUBJECT PARAMETER, it should be stressed that under most acocunts the optionality of subjects is just one property of this parameter. For instance, it is sometimes maintained that the same setting that allows for the optionality of subjects also determines whether a language will have expletive subjects, which are subject NPs that have no meaningful content, such as *it* in *it is raining* (Hyams, 1986). As such, the parameter could just as well have been dubbed "the overt expletive parameter" (Kim, 1993).

Since the publication of Hyams (1986), the null subject parameter has been the focus of considerable study. One reason for this has to do with Hyams' proposal that the initial setting of this parameter is for subjects to be optional (as in Italian, but not English) and that children acquiring English go through a long period where they have not yet set their parameter to the appropriate setting. This proposal is discussed in Section V,A. More generally, studying how children acquire this property of grammar allows us to critically examine the predictions that parameter theories make about developmental change and the role of triggering data; some implications and extensions are reviewed in Section V,B.

A. Explanations for Subject Omission in Child English

One of the main characteristics of telegraphic speech is the occasional omission of words and phrases. In particular, it has long been noted that children acquiring English frequently produce sentences with missing subjects, such as *hug Mommy, play bed, writing book,* and *see running* (from Bowerman, 1973).

One class of explanations for these utterances posits that children know that subjects in English are obligatory but omit them due to performance factors. Put differently, although they might sometimes say *play bed* instead of *I play in bed,* they would agree that this sentence is ungrammatical. (Unfortunately, 2-year-olds are too young to make this sort of explicit judgment.) Candidate theories of the nature of the processing deficit have focused on children's difficulty in constructing long strings of morphemes (e.g., L. Bloom, 1970, 1991; P. Bloom, 1990a, 1993; Pinker, 1984) as well as their difficulty in producing certain phonological strings (Gerken, 1991).

Putting aside the question of subject omission, most scholars agree with Chomsky (1964) that children suffer from performance factors, more so than adults, and that these factors cause them to occasionally omit constituents. Two-year-olds not only omit subjects, they also omit objects, verbs, determiners, prepositions, and so on (e.g., L. Bloom, 1970; Bowerman, 1973; Braine, 1974, 1976; Feldman, Goldin-Meadow, & Gleitman, 1978; Pinker, 1984). There have been competence explanations proposed for some of these omissions, such as deletion rules in children's grammars or phrase structure rules with optional categories, but there is little doubt that at least some omissions occur for nongrammatical reasons (see Pinker, 1984, for discussion). For one thing, children will also omit elements when asked to imitate adult sentences (Brown & Fraser, 1963; Ervin, 1964; Gerken, 1991). For another, one needs to explain the general fact that young children's utterances are so short—it is hard to imagine some aspect of children's grammar that would restrict them to sentences that are an average of two words long.

Given the existence of performance limitations in child language, many scholars have argued that these can explain children's subjectless sentences. A similar explanation for older children's difficulty with certain properties of grammar has been extended by Crain (1991) and Grimshaw and Rosen (1990).

The alternative is that children possess a grammar that is in some sense different from that of adult English speakers. Under one theory, this grammatical account was of a grammar such as Italian ("pro-drop"; see Hyams, 1986); more recently, it has been proposed that these children possess a Chinese-like grammar ("topic-drop"; see Hyams & Wexler, 1993). As a result of either processing limitations or neural maturation of grammatical capacities, children go through a long period where they are insensitive to triggering data that would lead them to switch their null subject parameter to the English-like setting. There is a range of different theories as to the precise nature of the trigger and the reason why children are initially insensitive to it (Hyams, 1986, 1989; Hyams & Wexler, 1993; Lebeaux, 1987; Lillo-Martin, 1987; Pierce, 1987).

One argument in support of this parametric hypothesis is that subjects are omitted more frequently than objects (Hyams, 1986). In one analysis of three 2-year-olds (first studied by Brown, 1973, and stored on the CHILDES computer database; MacWhinney & Snow, 1985), subject NPs were omitted on average 55% of the time, while obligatory objects were omitted only an average of 9% of the time (P. Bloom, 1990a). This supports the claim that although some omissions (about 10%, say) are the result of processing problems, the preponderance of subject omissions is due to the fact that these children are encoding a null subject grammar.

There are other subject/object differences, however, that suggest an alternative explanation. The same study found that overt subjects are more likely to be pronouns than overt objects, and that among nonpronoun overt subjects and objects, subjects tend to be significantly shorter. While greater subject omission might be due to grammatical factors, the other two phenomena suggest that there is a subject/object asymmetry that is independent of grammar, which perhaps results from factors having to do with pragmatics and processing load, both which might lead to a greater deletion of subjects than objects (P. Bloom, 1990a, 1993; Pinker, 1984).

Another explanation for the subject/object difference emerges from the research of Gerken (1991). Using an imitation task, she found that children are far more likely to omit subjects than objects (as expected by the null subject account), but that they are also more likely to omit articles from subject NPs than from object NPs, and the identical pattern occurs in children's spontaneous speech. The omission of articles cannot be due to the missetting of a parameter and supports Gerken's claim that processing difficulties which specifically apply to metrical structure are the cause of subjectless sentences in child English.

A different argument advanced in support of the null subject theory is that at the point at which children stop omitting subjects, there is a multitude of other transitions in their grammars. The optionality of overt subjects is just one (quite salient) deductive consequence of the null subject parameter; others concern linguistic properties such as the presence or absence of expletives, modals (words like *must* and *will*), certain sorts of questions, and so on. These other effects can provide "triggers" that lead the child exposed to English to realize that her language actually has obligatory subjects. In particular, once children learn that English has expletives and modals, they should reset the parameter and stop omitting subjects (Hyams, 1986).

Hyams (1986) reviews data from different sources and suggests that is exactly what occurs: At the same point that children acquire expletives and modals, they stop omitting subjects. This conclusion, however, was based on published observations from a variety of sources; until recently there has been no careful statistical analysis of the relationship between subject omission and other aspects of child language. In the first large-scale analysis of this, Valian (1991) studied the speech of 21 children acquiring English and 5 children acquiring Italian, analyzing the frequency of omitted subjects and how it relates to factors such as the onset of expletive use, the onset of modal use, and inflectional morphology—all of which have been argued to serve as triggers for the end of the null subject period. She also looked at performance factors, such as the mean length of the child's utterance (MLU), the number of different types of verbs and direct objects that children used, and the average length of the VP.

Valian found that even prior to the age of two, Italian children were omitting subjects almost twice as often as the English children (see also Bates, 1976). There was no correlation between the proportion of omitted subjects and the grammatical factors that Valian looked at, but there were significant correlations between subject omissions and nongrammatical factors, such as age, MLU, and VP length (see L. Bloom, 1991, for a review of similar findings). This suggests that children who are exposed to Italian possess null subject grammars at an early age (and thus omit subjects very frequently). Children acquiring English know that subjects are obligatory but omit them due to processing factors; as their capacity to form long strings of words improves, the rate of omission decreases.

In sum, there is considerable evidence that even very young children acquiring English understand that subjects are obligatory. They omit far fewer subjects than children acquiring a language such as Italian, these omissions appear to be the result of performance considerations, and the gradual decline in subject omission is correlated with nongrammatical factors such as age. This is consistent with the proposal that the initial setting of the null subject parameter is that subjects are obligatory (as in English) and only when hearing sentences without subjects (as in Italian), will the child switch her parameter (P. Bloom, 1990b, 1993; Rizzi, 1982).

Nevertheless, the issue is hardly closed. The theory of null subjects is in flux, and it is conceivable that there exists some grammatical milestone (not explored by Valian) that coincides with a decrease in subject omission in children acquiring English. Further, there are puzzles that arise when one considers precisely how parameters can be set; these are discussed below.

B. Null Subjects and the Logic of Parameter Setting

The null subject parameter serves to illustrate the role of subset relations in language development (Berwick, 1982, 1985; Manzini & Wexler, 1987). The SUBSET PRINCIPLE—which applies to all facets of language development, not just parameter setting—can be summarized as follows: When there are grammatical options that produce languages that fall into subset–superset relations, the learner should always choose the grammar that generates the smaller language. For instance, if the only effect of the null subject parameter is the possible optionality of subjects, then the English setting would produce a proper subset of the Italian setting. Every sentence that one could produce with the English setting (e.g., *I go to the movies*) one could also produce with the Italian setting, but there are sentences that one could produce with the Italian setting and not with the English setting (e.g., *go to the movies*). In other words, a language which only allows overt subjects is a subset of a language with both overt subjects and null subjects.

To take another example from Pinker (1984, 1989a), a language which has fixed word order (only subject–verb–object, for instance) is a subset of a language with free word order (all orders of subject, verb, and object, for instance). The subset principle states that the initial hypothesis of the child should be that the target language has fixed word order, and this hypothesis should only be abandoned upon exposure to positive evidence. This is consistent with the data on children's acquisition of word order across different languages (see Section II,A).

What is the motivation for this principle? Assume that children obey the subset principle and choose the smaller language. If this is the language spoken by adults, no further grammatical development is needed; if not, then simple positive evidence suffices to cause grammatical change. For instance, if children start with an obligatory subject language, being exposed to a single sentence with a missing subject could cause them to shift their parameter to the larger (Italian-like) setting. Consider the consequences, however, if children violate the subset principle and start with the larger language. If a child's grammar allows both *I go to the movies* and *go to the movies,* and the adult language only allows for the first type of sentence, what could cause the child to switch her grammar?

If negative evidence existed, then parental feedback could lead children to "retract" their overgeneralizations and move to the smaller grammar, but in the absence of such evidence (see Section II,B), there is no obvious way for a child who has an overly large grammar to move to a smaller one. This motivates the subset principle.

In the case of the null subject parameter, then, the subset principle predicts that the child's initial hypothesis is that subjects are obligatory, as in English, and only through positive evidence will she move to the larger grammar where subjects are optional, as in Italian (e.g., P. Bloom, 1990a). However, Hyams' (1986) alternative, that children start off with the optional subject setting of the parameter, also does not violate the subset principle, since, under her analysis, the two settings of the parameter do not fall into a subset relationship. Instead, null subject languages and non-null subject languages overlap, so that each has properties that the other lacks. Italian, for instance, has sentences such as *go to the movies* which do not appear in languages like English, while English has sentences such as *It is raining* (with expletive *it*) that do not appear in languages such as Italian. Thus, with regard to the null subject parameter, English and Italian do not fall into a subset–superset relation; rather, they overlap, and the subset principle thus makes no prediction as to which should be the default setting.

It might be argued that there is something unrealistic about applying this principle to the actual course of development. Consider again the hypothetical child who starts with an optional subject grammar and assume, contrary to Hyams (1986), that such a grammar is a proper subset of an obligatory subject language such as English. A child with English-speaking parents might never be corrected (or get any special feedback) when she produces a sentence without a subject. But one could argue that a child would have to be quite dense to go for years without ever noticing that her parents are never omitting subjects. This cannot serve as proof that her parents are not speaking an Italian-like language—after all, Italian speakers could choose not to omit subjects—but it does serve as evidence. The notion that the nonappearance of a form over time could lead a child to conclude that this form is not grammatical in the target language has been dubbed INDIRECT NEGATIVE EVIDENCE (Chomsky, 1981). Note that this sort of evidence is more consistent with a hypothesis testing model of grammatical change (e.g., Valian, 1990) than with a parameter setting model, as it involves frequency-based induction, not triggering.

Valian (1990) raises some problems with the proposal that all children start off with obligatory subject grammars and only upon hearing sentences without subjects shift to an optional subject grammar. She notes that there are plenty of subjectless sentences in adult English; examples include imperatives (*Put that down!*), responses (Person A: *What are you doing?*; Person B: *Thinking*), some questions (*Want lunch now?*), and other cases that are not as easily classifiable (*Seems like rain, Wouldn't be prudent*). The existence of these sentences requires some theory of how children come to possess these subtle conditions on subject omission in a non-null subject language; how they acquire rules of ellipsis, for instance, and how they distinguish imperatives from nonimperatives. More to the point, somehow they have to filter out all these sentences when determining the parametric status of adult language. If children are not capable of realizing that *Want lunch now?* is an exceptional case, this should cause them to mistakenly reset the null subject parameter and assume that English allows for optional subjects in all tensed clauses.

Valian's own solution is to abandon a triggering analysis and instead adopt a hypothesis testing model, where children try out both parameter settings and determine which better captures the patterns in the target language. One alternative, however, is that the child has sufficient knowledge of the pragmatic circumstances under which subjects can be omitted in an obligatory subject language to filter out utterances such as *Want lunch now?* (Kim, 1993).

A related hypothesis is that children only focus on embedded clauses when setting parameters (Roeper, 1973; Roeper & Weissenborn, 1990). In the case of the null subject parameter this would largely solve the problem posed by Valian; in a language such as English, embedded sentences do not allow for deletions. One cannot say *I asked if want lunch now,* even though *want lunch now?* is marginally acceptable. Similarly *Seems like rain* is somewhat acceptable, and so is *I think that it seems like rain*—but not *I think seems like rain,* where the subject is omitted from the embedded clause. This proposal allows us to extend the proposal made by Rizzi (1982) and P. Bloom (1990a) as follows: The initial setting of the parameter is that subjects are obligatory, and only when exposed to embedded clauses without subjects (as in Italian, but not in English) will children switch to a null-subject grammar.

Other questions arise: Can children possess both settings of a parameter at the same time (Valian, 1990)? What is the role of parameter setting in second language acquisition (Flynn, 1987)? Is parameter setting consistent with gradual changes in children's knowledge (P. Bloom, 1993)? Subject omission in child language is a useful domain in which to explore the relationship between the idealizations of the grammatical theory of parameters and the actual process of language development.

VI. COGNITIVE ARCHITECTURE AND RECOVERY FROM ERROR: THE CASE OF VERBS

There are domains of language development (such as the acquisition of word order) where children are virtually error-free. These are frustrating from the standpoint of acquisition research; after all, we study children because they have not completed the acquisition process—to the extent that child language is perfect, one might just as well run experiments on adults. Errors, on the other hand, offer important insights. They might illustrate false or intermediate knowledge of the adult language and thus inform us about the manner in which children infer properties of language on the basis of the input they receive. In the case of subjectless sentences in the acquisition of English (discussed in Section V), errors such as *writing book* prompted hypotheses as to the nature of parametric change and the roles of competence and performance in the course of grammatical development.

For any systematic error, three descriptive questions arise: Why do children make this error, What is the time course of this error, and What makes them stop? While these questions have been addressed in the domains of word meaning and syntactic competence, they have received the most attention with regard to the overregularization of verbs. Sections VI,A and VI,B focus on the past tense morpheme, as this has been at the center of these debates, and Section VI,C briefly considers similar issues that arise in the study of verb semantics.

A. The Phenomenon of Overregularization

Most verbs in English form the past tense by adding the suffix -ed, as in *walk–walked, pass–passed, dance–danced, turn–turned,* and so on. These are called REGULAR verbs, and contrast with the approximately 180 IRREGULAR verbs where the past tense relates to the stem in some other way. Some irregular past tense forms differ entirely from their stems (*go–went*), others are identical (*hit–hit*), and others involve different sorts of vowel or consonant changes while preserving most of the phonological structure of the stem (*eat–ate, grow–grew, feel–felt*) (see Bybee & Slobin, 1982). Adults know the past tense forms of these irregular verbs (e.g., *went* is the past tense of *go*), and also know that the regular -ed suffix cannot apply to these verbs (e.g., *goed* is not an acceptable past tense of *go*).

The regular rule is productive; adults can use it to create past tense forms that they have never heard before. Upon hearing a new present tense verb such as *kermit*, an adult can use it in the past tense form, saying *I kermitted the file to my computer yesterday*. Berko (1958) found evidence for the same sort of productivity with young children. If she showed them a picture of a man doing an activity and told them, *Here is a man who likes to rick. Yesterday he did the same thing. Yesterday he . . .* , children will obediently say *ricked*. This finding refutes the naive claim that children acquiring language are limited to imitating the forms that they hear. In this task (and many others; see Marcus et al., 1992, for a review), children are quite capable of using a word that they had never been exposed to before.

Evidence for this productivity also appears in children's spontaneous speech (Ervin, 1964). Children will say things such as *I goed to the store* or *He breaked the glass*. The standard characterization of the time course of such errors is as a U-shaped curve, where the U is plotted as the percentage of correct performance over time. The left tail of the U is the earliest stage of morphological production, in which the child is performing perfectly, using both regulars (*walked*) and irregulars (*broke*) correctly. This is followed by a long period of overgeneralization (the sagging middle of the U) where children overregularize, producing forms such as *goed* and *breaked*. Finally, children stop overregularizing and return to adult-like competence (the right tail of the U).

One explanation for the initial two stages of the process is as follows: Children first acquire all the past tense forms through rote memory; they record that the past tense of *walk* is *walked* and the past tense of *break* is *broke*. At this early stage there is no psychological difference between the two classes of past tense verbs, neither is "regular" or "irregular." The onset of the second stage is when children determine that there is a productive rule at work (add the suffix *-ed* to form the past tense). Children start to overapply this rule, producing forms such as *breaked* and *goed*.

But what causes children to stop overregularizing and return to adult performance? One logical possibility is negative evidence—perhaps children receive some sort of punishment or feedback whenever they produce such forms and use this feedback to expunge these overregularizations from their lexicons. But negative evidence does not appear to exist (see Section II,B), and in particular, no investigator has found that children get differential feedback for their usage of verb morphology (Marcus, 1993).

The second logical possibility is that children and adults are "conservative"; unless they hear an adult use a form, they will reject it as ungrammatical. But this is demonstrably false. As the Berko (1958) study shows, children (and adults) are willing to use past tense forms that they have never heard before. Furthermore, if children are conservative, why do they overgeneralize in the first place?

Perhaps the most promising source of explanation has to do with some sort of "blocking" or "elsewhere" condition (Aronoff, 1976; Kiparsky, 1982; Pinker, 1984). Such a condition prohibits the application of a rule that would produce an item that already exists in the lexicon.[4] Thus the past tense form

---

[4] Why does blocking exist at all? One could imagine an alternative system where the presence of a rule precludes the use of a rote form, instead of vice versa. Thus *went* would be unacceptable because of the existence of *goed* and there would be no irregulars at all.

goed is blocked by *went*, and the plural form *mans* is blocked by *men*. The same sort of blocking can apply to the output of semantic rules; *gooder* sounds worse than *nicer* because *gooder* is blocked by the preexisting lexical form *better*, while nothing blocks *nicer*. Clark (1987) argues that this can be derived from the principles of contrast and conventionality (see Section III,A), but see Marcus et al. (1992) for a critical discussion of this.

Assuming that children possess such a principle, the solution may go as follows (e.g., Pinker, 1984): Children start off acquiring all past tense forms by rote, then induce the *-ed* rule. Overapplication of this rule leads to overregularization. But as irregular forms such as *broke* and *went* are reintroduced into the lexicon, they block the application of the past tense rule and the child stops overregularizing.

There are problems with this analysis, however (Gathercole, 1987; Marcus et al., 1992). First, why would a child overregularize in the first place? Given that she initially has the word *went* encoded as the past tense of *go*, one would expect blocking or contrast to keep her from using *goed*—but it does not. Second, the blocking theory predicts that there should be no period where the child uses both *goed* and *went* at the same time. But this is false; irregular past tenses and overregularizations coexist for years in children's lexicons (e.g., Cazden, 1968).

One defense of the blocking theory is that children might not know that *broke* is the past tense form of *break*. Thus children's productive use of *breaked* as a past tense of *break* would not violate contrast or blocking. Only once children come to realize that the adult form *broke* is synonymous with their rule-generated form *breaked* will they expunge *breaked* from their lexicon—and this process might take years (Clark, 1988, 1990).

This discussion of overregularization is based on certain premises—children possess a rule, they go through a stage where they believe that certain

---

One possibility (discussed in Pinker & Bloom, 1990) is that blocking has a functional explanation. For virtually any system with productive rules, there will be cases where it is unclear which rule to apply or how to apply it. For instance, many languages encode words that denote kinds of individuals as being count nouns (e.g., *a dog*), and words that denote kinds of portions as mass nouns (e.g., *muchwater*), and this rule can be productively applied by children and adults (P. Bloom, 1994a). But there are indeterminate cases, such as *peas*, where it is cognitively unclear whether to encode it as a kind of individual or a kind of portion. As a result, the categorization of such cases within a given language is arbitrary; in some languages, *pea* is a count noun; in others, it is a mass noun. Children must be equipped so that these arbitrary choices override their own biases in how to apply productive rules; even if a child acquiring English finds it more sensible to view *pea* as denoting a kind of portion (and would, in the absence of input, encode it as a mass noun), she must acquire it as a count noun, because this is how it is encoded in English, and she must speak the same language as the rest of the community. The clearest case of the need for arbitrary convention to override individual preference is in the case of names. There is no logical reason to describe dogs as *dogs* and not as *cats*, but given that this is how everyone else does it, children must be predisposed to acquire this arbitrary sound and to prefer it over their own inventions.

In general, some bias to favor rote over rule might evolve in any domain where there are (a) rules that generate novel forms; (b) instances where it is unclear how to apply these rules, and (c) the requirement of social conformity (i.e., everyone within a community must use the same form). If so, one might expect to find mechanisms similar to blocking in other cognitive structures that satisfy these criteria.

irregulars have -*ed* past tenses, and they need to recover from these errors. The theories discussed below challenge these assumptions and suggest radically different explanations for children's errors.

B. Alternative Conceptualizations

Since the earliest discussion of overregularization, the competence involved has been described as an implicit rule—add -*ed* to form the past tense—and children's errors are assumed to result from overapplication of this rule. One might think that this is the only type of explanation possible. But parallel distributed processing (PDP) or connectionist models provide an alternative to this sort of theory.

Under one connectionist analysis, the capacity to determine the past tense form of a verb stem is acquired through an associative network which can extract statistical regularities from the environment. Rumelhart and McClelland (1986) provide an explicit computer model that succeeds in capturing certain core properties of children's behavior—without positing any internalized rules, or any distinction between regular verbs and irregular verbs. The model works by being "trained" on correspondences between the phonological patterns of verb stems and phonological patterns of the past tense forms; these are represented by activation patterns of pools of units which are linked up in parallel to other units. After training is complete, the network will produce a string of output patterns corresponding to *walked* when presented with the input *walk* and patterns corresponding to *went* when presented with the input *go*. Further, the development of the model appears to capture the U-shaped curve; early in learning, the model performs correctly, then it overregularizes, then it returns to correct behavior. Rumelhart and McClelland (1986, p. 267) conclude "we have shown that a reasonable account of the acquisition of past tense can be provided without recourse to the notion of a 'rule' as anything more than a *description* of the language."

This model has been the subject of considerable critical discussion, most notably from Pinker and Prince (1988, 1991). Two criticisms are worth noting. First, Pinker and Prince argue that treating the morphological alteration as a mapping from different phonological forms is psychologically incorrect. They argue that a past tense rule applies to the verb stem (which is stored in the lexicon) and not to the sound of the verb. For instance, *ring* and *wring* have the same sound, but they are different stems and thus have different past tense forms: *rang* and *wrung*. Similarly, the past tense form of *go* is *went,* but if one coins a new stem with the same sound but derived from a name—for instance, a verb *Go* which means to play the Japanese game of Go against someone—it does not inherit the irregular morphology of its homophonic form. One would say *He Goed six opponents during last week's competition,* not *He went six opponents during the competition.* In general, verbs derived from other parts of speech are subject to the regular rule, regardless of their sound or meaning.

Pinker and Prince argue that the past tense rule is a universal default and applies to any form not lexically marked as having an irregular past tense. They further suggest that to capture this property of language in a PDP network would require explicitly wiring up such a model to encode rules; in other words, it would have to implement a symbolic system (for discussion, see Lachner &

Bever, 1988; MacWhinney & Leinbach, 1991; Marcus et al., 1992; Pinker, 1991).

A second criticism is that the Rumelhart and McClelland model only succeeds in capturing the U-shaped curve through unrealistic assumptions about the input. In particular, Rumelhart and McClelland started by first feeding their model a much higher proportion of irregular verbs than regular verbs and then following this with a set of verbs where the proportion of irregular verbs was much smaller. The motivation for this training procedure is that irregulars tend to be high-frequency, and thus one might expect them to be learned first by children. In an analysis of child speech, however, Pinker and Prince (1988) found that the ratio of irregular to regular verbs does not change at the period when children start to overregularize. Therefore the connectionist model would not adequately predict the outcome of the actual conditions of language development. More generally, Pinker and Prince argue that the onset of overregularization is not predicted by any properties of the input, but instead corresponds to the point at which children learn the regular rule of English (see also Marcus et al., 1992).

The import of these criticisms is a matter of some debate; some scholars have argued that the problems are special to the particular model advanced by Rumelhart and McClelland but that other implementations can account for them (e.g., MacWhinney & Leinbach, 1991; Plunkett & Marchman, 1991); others suggest that the problems are endemic to all models that lack a rule-based component (e.g., Lachner & Bever, 1988; Pinker & Prince, 1988, 1991).

Some recent results from Marcus et al. (1992) support a rule-based theory of children's overgeneralizations. Despite a longstanding interest in overgeneralization by acquisition theorists, some basic facts were unknown. In particular, Marcus et al. noted that there only existed crude estimates of how frequently children overregularize. Using the CHILDES database (MacWhinney & Snow, 1985), they analyzed the spontaneous speech of 83 children. Their main result was that overgeneralization errors were strikingly rare—the median rate of error was an error rate of 2.5%. They do find a U-shaped curve, however: children go through an extended period of correct usage before their first error, then errors start to occur, and later they decrease in adulthood.

The low rate of errors supports the following account (see also MacWhinney, 1978): regular past tenses are produced by a rule, whereas irregulars are stored in associative memory. When children and adults have an irregular form stored in memory, blocking stops the regular rule from applying, and thus forms such as *goed* and *runned* are unacceptable. Children overregularize because their memory trace for past tense forms is not strong enough to guarantee perfect retrieval, and when a child fails to retrieve an irregular such as *went*, the regular rule is applied, producing *goed*. This is supported by the fact that the more often parents use a given irregular verb—and thus the stronger the memory encoding by the child—the less likely a child is to overregularize this verb.

Under this view, overgeneralizations are speech errors, no different in kind from those occasionally made by adults. The only developmental transition that must be explained is how children acquire the -*ed* rule in the first place; Marcus et al. (1992) present some hypotheses, but there is as yet no definitive account.

The controversy over the cause of these errors will continue; the question of whether or not a past tense "rule" exists relates to the more general debate over the potential of PDP modeling as a theory of human cognition. But the existence of large-scale analyses of past tense errors and the use of computational models to test specific hypotheses have considerably sharpened this controversy. Unlike problems such as the acquisition of word meanings or the nature of parametric change, it might not be unreasonable to expect this very specific issue—Why do children overregularize and why do they stop?—to be resolved within some of our lifetimes.

C. Overregularization of Semantic Alternations

Not all the research into overgeneralization concerns morphological phenomena such as past tense marking. One of the most extensively studied areas in linguistics and language acquisition focuses on the different syntactic contexts in which verbs can appear. The examples below show the alternation between active and passive, the dative alternation, and the causative alternation; for a comprehensive review, see Pinker (1989b).

Passive:
Joan likes Mary. /
Mary is liked by Joan.
Joan stole the money. /
The money was stolen by Joan.

Dative:
Fred sent a package to Igor. /
Fred sent Igor a package.
Fred told a story to Igor. /
Fred told Igor a story.

Causative:
The glass broke. /
Bill broke the glass.
The baby burped. /
Bill burped the baby.

One intriguing property of these alternations is that not all verbs can participate in them. The examples below are cases where the alternation does not hold.

Passive:
Joan weighs 100 pounds. /
*100 pounds is weighed by Joan.

Dative:
Fred reported the story to the newspaper. /
*Fred reported the newspaper the story.

Causative:
The baby cried. /
*Bill cried the baby.

These exceptions pose a puzzle for theories of language acquisition, one first noted by Baker (1979). Consider the following three claims. First, children are PRODUCTIVE. For instance, even if they never heard *burped* in the causative form, they could say *Bill burped the baby*. Second, children receive NO NEGATIVE EVIDENCE. Thus if they produce a sentence such as *Bill cried the baby*, there exists no external input that could inform them of their error. Third, the exceptions are ARBITRARY. There is no reason why *burp* can appear in the causative form but *cry* cannot, or why *told* can appear in the dative form, while *reported* cannot.

At least one of these three claims must be false; if they were all true, there would be no way for children (or adults) to come to understand that sentences such as *Bill cried the baby* or *100 pounds was weighed by Joan* are ungrammatical. By virtue of being productive, children will produce such utterances, there would be no feedback informing them that these sentences are ill-formed (no negative evidence), and there would be no way for them to infer that these verbs should not appear in these contexts (arbitrariness). Given that we do reject sentences such as those above, this suggests that one of the three claims must be false.

Negative evidence does not exist, and since children do appear to be productive (see below), the only alternative is to reject the arbitrariness claim. Thus the reason why we accept some verbs in these alternations and reject others is because we possess criteria as to which verbs can appear in which syntactic context and can apply these criteria in a productive manner.

More generally, it is argued that the conditions on verb usage reflect the way the components of grammar interact with each other and with conceptual structure. For instance, the causative alternation is often argued to require DIRECT CAUSATION, and the reason why *burp* can participate in this alternation and *cried* cannot is that we construe burping a baby as being direct and causing a baby to cry as indirect. This condition on causative usage is itself derived from more basic syntax–semantics mappings, sometimes called LINKING RULES. Pinker (1989b) provides an extensive theory of the nature of linking rules and how they can resolve Baker's paradox; see Bowerman (1990) for a critical discussion, and Gropen, Pinker, Hollander, and Goldberg (1991) for a reply.

How do we know children can productively use verbs in different syntactic contexts? One source of evidence is experimental; when taught novel verbs, young children are capable of productively using them in different syntactic contexts. For instance, in one study, children were shown a pig doing a headstand and told *The pig is pilking*. They were then shown a bear causing a tiger to do an headstand and asked *What's the bear doing?* Children would often say *Pilking the tiger,* showing that they are capable of productively using novel verbs in the causative form. Similar studies have been done for other verb alternations, such as the passive and the dative. For all these, children are not only productive; they also appear to have some understanding of the semantic restrictions on which verbs can and cannot appear in these contexts (see Gropen et al., 1991; Gropen, Pinker, Hollander, Goldberg, & Wilson, 1989; Pinker, Lebeaux, & Frost, 1987; see Pinker, 1989b, for a review).

Furthermore, just as with past tense morphology, children appear to overgeneralize the semantic alternations. Bowerman (1982) gives examples of caus-

atives produced by her daughters from the ages of two to ten that are unacceptable for adults; these include:

You sad me [= *make me sad*]
Mommy, can you stay this open? [= *make it stay*]
I'm singing him [= *making him sing*]
Who deaded my kitty cat? [= *made dead*]
This one always sweaties me [= *makes me sweat*]
Don't giggle me [= *make me giggle*]

The existence of these errors is further evidence for productivity, but it
also motivates a theory of why children overextend these semantic rules and
what causes them to stop.

As with morphology, blocking or contrast is likely to play some role. For
instance, it is likely that the reason why *dead* cannot be causativized for adults
is because the existing English verb *kill* blocks the alternation. The child who
asked *Who deaded my kitty cat?* either might not know the verb *killed* or could
be failing to retrieve it from memory.

But this cannot be the whole explanation. There is no existing English verb
that means 'make giggle', yet *Don't giggle me* is still unacceptable for adults.
Thus the theories advanced by Clark (1987) and Marcus et al. (1992) cannot
apply. Why then would children produce such an utterance? It could be that
they have not yet completely acquired the relevant semantic restrictions on
the use of the causative (Bowerman, 1982; Mazurkewich & White, 1984). Alternatively, such errors might be due to children's different understanding of the
pragmatic conditions under which one could violate or stretch the semantic
rules (Pinker, 1989b). Given that these types of errors occur late in development,
the discovery of what makes them go away could enlighten us as to the very
final steps of grammatical development.

VII. CONCLUSION

The review above constitutes just a small sample of current research in language
acquisition. Other areas include (to choose almost at random) the role of spatial
cognition in the acquisition of nouns and prepositions (e.g., Landau & Jackendoff, 1993), children's understanding of conditions on pronoun interpretation
(e.g., Grimshaw & Rosen, 1990), and the infant's capacity to attend to the
relevant object or situation in the course of acquiring a new word (e.g., Baldwin,
1991)—not to mention all the research concerning the acquisition of phonology
or the development of pragmatic knowledge and discourse skills.

These areas are sufficiently diverse that few scholars are optimistic about
the prospects of coming up with "a theory of language acquisition." The type
of theory required for how children come to understand language-specific properties of *wh*-questions is likely to be quite different from the appropriate theory
of how they learn the meaning of *cup,* and both will differ from an account of
how children come to obey turn-taking conventions in conversation.

These different domains of study do share some important properties,
however, and these can explain why the study of language acquisition has
intrigued scholars from so many fields. For one thing, the acquisition of complex

linguistic structure on the basis of impoverished input poses puzzles of a theoretical depth rarely found in psychology, but at the same time these puzzles admit of direct empirical tests of the sort not usually applicable in linguistics and philosophy. More important, despite the often painfully specific character of acquisition problems (How do children learn that *goed* is not the past tense of *go*? How do they learn that *garments* is a count noun, but *clothing* is a mass noun?), there is the intuition that the study of these problems will provide insights into issues that concern all cognitive scientists: the nature of language and meaning, the mechanisms of developmental change, and the architecture of the mind.

ACKNOWLEDGMENTS

I thank Andrew Barss, Felice Bedford, Laura Conway, Morton Ann Gernsbacher, Gary Marcus, Steven Pinker, Nancy Soja, and Karen Wynn for very helpful comments on an earlier version of this paper.

REFERENCES

Aksu-Koc, A. A., & Slobin, D. I. (1985). The acquisition of Turkish. In D. I. Slobin (Ed.), *The crosslinguistic study of language acquisition: Vol. 1. The data*. Hillsdale, NJ: Erlbaum.

Anderson, J. R. (1983). *The architecture of cognition*. Cambridge, MA: Harvard University Press.

Aronoff, M. (1976). *Word formation in generative grammar*. Cambridge, MA: MIT Press.

Bach, E. (1986). The algebra of events. *Linguistics and Philosophy, 9*, 5–16.

Backscheider, A., & Markman, E. M. (1990). *Young children's use of taxonomic assumptions to constrain word meaning*. Unpublished manuscript, Stanford University, Stanford, CA.

Baker, C. L. (1979). Syntactic theory and the projection problem. *Linguistic Inquiry, 10*, 533–581.

Baldwin, D. A. (1989). Priorities in children's expectations about object label reference: Form over color. *Child Development, 60*, 1291–1306.

Baldwin, D. A. (1991). Infant contributions to the achievement of joint reference. *Child Development, 62*, 875–890.

Barrett, M. D. (1986). Early semantic representations and early word-usage. In S. A. Kuczaj, II & M. D. Barrett (Eds.), *The development of word meaning: Progress in cognitive development research*. New York: Springer-Verlag.

Bates, E. (1976). *Language and context*. New York: Academic Press.

Bates, E., Bretherton, I., & Snyder, L. (1988). *From first words to grammar: Individual differences and dissociable mechanisms*. Cambridge: Cambridge University Press.

Behrend, D. A. (1990). Constraints and development: A reply to Nelson (1988). *Cognitive Development, 5*, 313–330.

Berko, J. (1958). The child's learning of English morphology. *Word, 14*, 150–177.

Berwick, R. C. (1982). *Locality principles and the acquisition of syntactic knowledge*. Doctoral dissertation, Massachusetts Institute of Technology, Cambridge.

Berwick, R. C. (1985). *The acquisition of syntactic knowledge*. Cambridge, MA: MIT Press.

Bickerton, D. (1984). The language bioprogram hypothesis. *Behavioral and Brain Sciences, 7*, 173–212.

Bloom, L. (1970). *Language development: Form and function in emerging grammars*. Cambridge, MA: MIT Press.

Bloom, L. (1973). *One word at a time: The use of single word utterances before syntax*. The Hague: Mouton.

Bloom, L. (1991). *Language development from two to three*. Cambridge: Cambridge University Press.

Bloom, P. (1990a). Subjectless sentences in child language. *Linguistic Inquiry, 21*, 491–504.

Bloom, P. (1990b). Syntactic distinctions in child language. *Journal of Child Language, 17*, 343–355.

Bloom, P. (1993). Grammatical continuity in language development: The case of subjectless sentences. *Linguistic Inquiry, 24*, 721–734.

Bloom, P. (1994a). Possible names: The role of syntax-semantics mappings in the acquisition of nominals. *Lingua, 92*, 1–33.

Bloom, P. (1994b). Semantic competence as an explanation for some transitions in language development. In Y. Levy (Ed.), *Other children, other languages: Theoretical issues in language development*. Hillsdale, NJ: Erlbaum.

Bohanon, J. N., MacWhinney, B., & Snow, C. (1990). No negative evidence revisited: Beyond learnability or who has to prove what to whom. *Developmental Psychology, 26*, 221–226.

Bohanon, J. N., & Stanowicz, L. (1988). The issue of negative evidence: Adult responses to children's language errors. *Developmental Psychology, 24*, 684–689.

Bolinger, D. (1977). *Meaning and form*. London: Longman.

Bowerman, M. (1973). *Early syntactic development*. Cambridge: Cambridge University Press.

Bowerman, M. (1976). Semantic factors in the acquisition of rules for word use and sentence construction. In D. M. Morehead & A. E. Morehead (Eds.), *Normal and deficient child language*. Baltimore, MD: University Park Press.

Bowerman, M. (1982). Starting to talk worse: Clues to language acquisition from children's late speech errors. In S. Strauss (Ed.), *U-shaped behavioral growth*. New York: Academic Press.

Bowerman, M. (1990). Mapping thematic roles onto syntactic functions: Are children helped by innate "linking rules"? *Journal of Linguistics, 28*, 1253–1289.

Braine, M. D. S. (1963). On learning the grammatical order of words. *Psychological Review, 70*, 323–348.

Braine, M. D. S. (1974). Length constraints, reduction rules, and holophrastic phrases in children's word combinations. *Journal of Verbal Learning and Verbal Behavior, 13*, 448–456.

Braine, M. D. S. (1976). Children's first word combinations. *Monographs of the Society for Research in Child Development, 41*.

Brown, R. (1957). Linguistic determinism and the part of speech. *Journal of Abnormal and Social Psychology, 55*, 1–5.

Brown, R. (1973). *A first language: The early stages*. Cambridge, MA: Harvard University Press.

Brown, R., & Bellugi, U. (1964). Three processes in the child's acquisition of syntax. In Lenneberg, E. H. (Ed.), *New directions in the study of language*. Cambridge, MA: MIT Press.

Brown, R., & Fraser, C. (1963). The acquisition of syntax. In C. N. Cofer & B. Musgrave (Eds.), *Verbal behavior and learning: Problems and processes*. New York: McGraw-Hill.

Brown, R., & Hanlon, C. (1970). Derivational complexity and order of acquisition in child speech. In J. R. Hayes (Ed.), *Cognition and the development of language*. New York: Wiley.

Bruner, J. S., Oliver, R., & Greenfield, P. M. (Eds.). (1966). *Studies in cognitive growth*. New York: Wiley.

Bybee, J. L., & Slobin, D. I. (1982). Rules and schemes in the development and use of the English tense. *Language, 58*, 265–289.

Carey, S. (1978). The child as word learner. In M. Halle, J. Bresnan, & A. Miller (Eds.), *Linguistic theory and psychological reality* (pp. 264–293). Cambridge, MA: MIT Press.

Carey, S. (1982). Semantic development: The state of the art. In E. Wanner & L. R. Gleitman (Eds.), *Language acquisition: The state of the art*. New York: Cambridge University Press.

Carey, S. (1986). *Conceptual change in childhood*. Cambridge, MA: MIT Press.

Carey, S. (1988). Conceptual differences between children and adults. *Mind and Language, 3*, 167–181.

Cazden, C. B. (1968). The acquisition of noun and verb inflections. *Child Development, 39*, 433–448.

Chomsky, N. (1959). A review of B. F. Skinner's Verbal behavior. *Language, 35*, 26–58.

Chomsky, N. (1964). Formal discussion. *Monographs of the Society for Research in Child Development, 29*, 35–39.

Chomsky, N. (1980). *Rules and representations*. New York: Columbia University Press.

Chomsky, N. (1981). *Lectures on government and binding*. Dordrecht: Foris.

Chomsky, N. (1986). *Knowledge of language: Its nature, origin, and use*. New York: Praeger.

Clark, E. V. (1987). The principle of contrast: A constraint on language acquisition. In B. MacWhinney (Ed.), *Mechanisms of language acquisition*. Hillsdale, NJ: Erlbaum.

Clark, E. V. (1988). On the logic of contrast. *Journal of Child Language, 15*, 317–335.

Clark, E. V. (1990). On the pragmatics of contrast. *Journal of Child Language, 17*, 417–432.

Cooper, W. E., & Paccia-Cooper, J. (1980). Syntax and speech. Cambridge, MA: Harvard University Press.

Crain, S. (1991). Language acquisition in the absence of experience. Behavioral and Brain Sciences, 14, 597–650.

Darwin, C. H. (1877). A biographical sketch of a young child. Kosmos, 1, 367–376.

Demetras, M. J., Post, K. N., & Snow, C. E. (1986). Feedback to first language learning: The role of repetitions and clarification questions. Journal of Child Language, 13, 275–292.

de Villiers, J. G., & de Villiers, P. A. (1973). A cross-sectional study of the acquisition of grammatical morphemes in child speech. Journal of Psycholinguistic Research, 2, 267–278.

de Villiers, J. G., & de Villiers, P. A. (1985). The acquisition of English. In D. I. Slobin (Ed.), The crosslinguistic study of language acquisition: Vol. 1. The data. Hillsdale, NJ: Erlbaum.

Ervin, S. (1964). Imitation and structural change in children's language. In E. H. Lenneberg (Ed.), New directions in the study of language. Cambridge, MA: MIT Press.

Feldman, H., Goldin-Meadow, S., & Gleitman, L. R. (1978). Beyond Herodotus: The creation of language by linguistically deprived deaf children. In E. H. Lenneberg (Ed.), New directions in the study of language. Cambridge, MA: MIT Press.

Fernald, A. (1985). Four-month-old infants prefer to listen to motherese. Infant Behavior and Development, 8, 181–195.

Fernald, A. (1992). Human maternal vocalizations to infants as biologically relevant signals: An evolutionary perspective. In J. J. Barkow, L. Cosmides, & J. Tooby (Eds.), The adapted mind: Evolutionary psychology and the generation of culture. Oxford: Oxford University Press.

Flynn, S. (1987). A parameter setting model of L2 acquisition. Dordrecht: Reidel.

Fodor, J. A. (1981). The present status of the innateness controversy. In J. A. Fodor (Ed.) Representations. Cambridge, MA: MIT Press.

Fodor, J. A. (1983). Modularity of mind. Cambridge, MA: MIT Press.

Gathercole, V. C. (1986). Evaluating competing theories with child language data: The case of the count-mass distinction. Linguistics and Philosophy, 6, 151–190.

Gathercole, V. C. (1987). The contrastive hypothesis for the acquisition of word meaning: A reconsideration of the theory. Journal of Child Language, 14, 493–531.

Gathercole, V. C. (1989). Contrast: A semantic constraint? Journal of Child Language, 16, 685–702.

Gelman, S. A., & Markman, E. M. (1985). Implicit contrast in adjectives vs. nouns: Implications for word-learning in preschoolers. Journal of Child Language, 12, 125–143.

Gelman, S. A., & Taylor, M. (1984). How two-year-old children interpret proper and common names for unfamiliar objects. Child Development, 55, 1535–1540.

Gentner, D. (1982). Why nouns are learned before verbs: Linguistic relativity versus natural partitioning. In S. A. Kuczaj, II (Ed.), Language development: Vol. 2. Language, thought, and culture. Hillsdale, NJ: Erlbaum.

Gerken, L. A. (1987). Telegraphic speech does not imply telegraphic listening. Papers and Reports on Child Language Development, 26, 48–55.

Gerken, L. A. (1991). The metrical basis for children's subjectless sentences. Journal of Memory and Language, 30, 1–21.

Gleitman, H. (1991). Psychology. New York: Norton.

Gleitman, L. R. (1981). Maturational determinants of language growth. Cognition, 10, 103–114.

Gleitman, L. R. (1990). The structural sources of word meaning. Language Acquisition, 1, 3–55.

Gleitman, L. R., & Wanner, E. (1982). Language acquisition: The state of the state of art. In E. Wanner & L. Gleitman (Eds.), Language acquisition: The state of the art. New York: Cambridge University Press.

Gold, E. M. (1967). Language identification in the limit. Information and Control, 10, 447–474.

Goldin-Meadow, S., & Mylander, C. (1990). Beyond the input given: The child's role in the acquisition of language. Language, 66, 323–355.

Golinkoff, R. M., Hirsh-Pasek, K., Lavallee, A., & Baduini, C. (1985). What's in a word? The young child's predisposition to use lexical contrast. Paper presented at the Boston University Conference on Language Development, Boston.

Goodman, N. (1983). Fact, fiction, and forecast. Cambridge, MA: Harvard University Press.

Gordon, P. (1982). The acquisition of syntactic categories: The case of the count/mass distinction. Doctoral dissertation, Massachusetts Institute of Technology, Cambridge.

Gordon, P. (1985). Evaluating the semantic categories hypothesis: The case of the count/mass distinction. *Cognition, 20,* 209–242.

Gordon, P. (1988). Count/mass category acquisition: Distributional distinctions in children's speech. *Journal of Child Language, 15,* 109–128.

Gordon, P. (1990). Learnability and feedback: A commentary on Bohanon and Stanowicz. *Developmental Psychology, 26,* 217–220.

Grimshaw, J. (1981). Form, function, and the language acquisition device. In C. L. Baker & J. McCarthy (Eds.), *The logical problem of language acquisition.* Cambridge, MA: MIT Press.

Grimshaw, J., & Pinker, S. (1989). Positive and negative evidence in language acquisition. *Behavioral and Brain Sciences, 12,* 341.

Grimshaw, J., & Rosen, S. T. (1990). Knowledge and obedience: The developmental status of the binding theory. *Linguistic Inquiry, 21,* 187–222.

Gropen, J., Pinker, S., Hollander, M., & Goldberg, R. (1991). Affectedness and direct objects: The role of lexical semantics in the acquisition of verb argument structure. *Cognition, 41,* 153–195.

Gropen, J., Pinker, S., Hollander, M., Goldberg, R., & Wilson, R. (1989). The learnability and acquisition of the dative alternation in English. *Language, 65,* 203–257.

Guilfoyle, E., & Noonan, M. (1989). *Functional categories and language acquisition.* Unpublished manuscript, McGill University, Montreal, Canada.

Heath, S. B. (1983). *Ways with words.* Cambridge: Cambridge University Press.

Hirsh-Pasek, K., Gleitman, H., Gleitman, L. R., Golinkoff, R., & Naigles, L. (1988). *Syntactic bootstrapping: Evidence from comprehension.* Paper presented at the Boston University Conference on Language Development, Boston.

Hirsch-Pasek, K., Golinkoff, R., Fletcher, A., DeGaspe Beaubien, F., & Cauley, K. (1985). *In the beginning: One word speakers comprehend word order.* Paper presented at Boston University Conference on Language Development, Boston.

Hirsch-Pasek, K., Kemler Nelson, D. G., Jusczyk, P. W., Cassidy, K. V., Druss, B., & Kennedy, L. (1987). Clauses are perceptual units for prelinguistic infants. *Cognition, 26,* 269–286.

Hirsch-Pasek, K., Treiman, R., & Schneiderman, M. (1984). Brown and Hanlon revisited: Mother's sensitivity to ungrammatical forms. *Journal of Child Language, 11,* 81–88.

Huang, J. (1984). On the distribution and reference of empty pronouns. *Linguistic Inquiry, 15,* 531–547.

Hutchinson, J. E. (1984). *Constraints on children's implicit hypotheses about word meanings.* Unpublished doctoral dissertation, Stanford University, Stanford, CA.

Huttenlocher, J., & Smiley, P. (1987). Early word meanings: The case of object names. *Cognitive Psychology, 19,* 63–89.

Hyams, N. (1986). *Language acquisition and the theory of parameters.* Dordrecht: Reidel.

Hyams, N. (1989). The null subject parameter in language acquisition. In O. Jaeggli & K. Safir (Eds.), *The null subject parameter.* Dordrecht: Reidel.

Hyams, N., & Wexler, K. (1993). On the grammatical basis of null subjects in child language. *Linguistic Inquiry 24,* 421–459.

Inhelder, B., & Piaget, J. (1964). *The early growth of logic in the child.* New York: Norton.

Jackendoff, R. (1986). *Semantics and cognition.* Cambridge, MA: MIT Press.

Jackendoff, R. (1990). *Semantic structures.* Cambridge, MA: MIT Press.

Jackendoff, R. (1991). Parts and boundaries. *Cognition, 41,* 9–45.

Johnson, J. S., & Newport, E. L. (1989). Critical period effects in second language learning: The influence of maturational state on the acquisition of English as a second language. *Cognitive Psychology, 21,* 60–99.

Johnson, M. H., Dziurawiec, S., Ellis, H., & Morton, J. (1991). Newborns' preferential tracking of face-like stimuli and its subsequent decline. *Cognition, 40,* 1–19.

Karmiloff-Smith, A. (1979). *A functional approach to language acquisition.* New York: Cambridge University Press.

Katz, N., Baker, E., & Macnamara, J. (1974). What's in a name? A study of how children learn common and proper names. *Child Development, 45,* 469–473.

Keil, F. C. (1989). *Concepts, kinds, and cognitive development.* Cambridge, MA: MIT Press.

Kim, J. J. (1993). Null subjects: Comments on Valian (1990). *Cognition, 46,* 183–193.

Kiparsky, P. (1982). *Explanation in phonology.* Dordrecht: Foris.

Kuczaj, S. (1990). Constraining constraint theories. *Cognitive Development, 5,* 341–344.

Lachner, J., & Bever, T. (1988). The relation between linguistic structure and associationist theories of language learning: A constructive critique of some connectionist learning models. *Cognition, 28*, 195–247.

Lakoff, G. (1987). *Women, fire, and dangerous things: What categories reveal about the mind.* Chicago: University of Chicago Press.

Landau, B., & Gleitman, L. R. (1985). *Language and experience.* Cambridge, MA: Harvard University Press.

Landau, B., & Jackendoff, R. (1993). "What" and "where" in spatial language and spatial cognition. *Behavioral and Brain Sciences, 16*, 217–238.

Landau, B., Jones, S., & Smith, L. B. (1988). The importance of shape in early lexical learning. *Cognitive Development, 3*, 299–321.

Langacker, R. W. (1987). Nouns and verbs. *Language, 63*, 53–94.

Lebeaux, D. (1987). Comments on Hyams. In T. Roeper & E. Williams (Eds.), *Parameter-setting.* Dordrecht: Reidel.

Levy, Y. (1988). On the early learning of grammatical systems: Evidence from studies of the acquisition of gender and countability. *Journal of Child Language, 15*, 179–186.

Lillo-Martin, D. (1987). *Parameters in the acquisition of American Sign Language.* Paper presented at the Boston University Conference on Language Development, Boston.

Lucariello, J., & Nelson, K. (1986). Content effects on lexical specificity in maternal and child discourse. *Journal of Child Language, 13*, 507–522.

Macnamara, J. (1972). The cognitive basis of language learning in children. *Psychological Review, 79*, 1–13.

Macnamara, J. (1982). *Names for things: A study of human learning.* Cambridge, MA: MIT Press.

Macnamara, J. (1986). *A border dispute: The place of logic in psychology.* Cambridge, MA: MIT Press.

MacWhinney, B. (1978). The acquisition of morphophonology. *Monographs of the Society for Research in Child Development, 43.*

MacWhinney, B., & Leinbach, J. (1991). Implementations are not conceptualizations: Revising the verb learning model. *Cognition, 40*, 121–157.

MacWhinney, B., & Snow, C. E. (1985). The Child Language Data Exchange System. *Journal of Child Language, 12*, 271–296.

Manzini, R., & Wexler, K. (1987). Parameters, binding theory, and learnability. *Linguistic Inquiry, 18*, 413–444.

Maratsos, M. P. (1982). The child's construction of grammatical categories. In E. Wanner & L. R. Gleitman (Eds.), *Language acquisition: The state of the art.* Cambridge: Cambridge University Press.

Maratsos, M. P. (1983). Some current issues in the study of the acquisition of grammar. In P. Mussen (Ed.), *Carmichael's handbook of child psychology: Vol. 3. Cognitive development.* New York: Wiley.

Maratsos, M. P., & Chalkley, M. (1981). The internal language of children's syntax: The ontogenesis and representation of syntactic categories. In K. Nelson (Ed.), *Children's language* (Vol. 2). New York: Gardner Press.

Marcus, G. F. (1993). Negative evidence in language acquisition. *Cognition, 46*, 53–85.

Marcus, G. F., Pinker, S., Ullman, M., Hollander, M., Rosen, T. J., & Xu, F. (1992). Overgeneralization in language acquisition. *Monographs of the Society for Research in Child Development, 57*(4, Serial No. 228).

Markman, E. M. (1981). Two different principles of conceptual organization. In M. E. Lamb & A. L. Brown (Eds.), *Advances in developmental psychology.* Hillsdale, NJ: Erlbaum.

Markman, E. M. (1989). *Categorization and naming in children: Problems of induction.* Cambridge, MA: MIT Press.

Markman, E. M. (1990). Constraints children place on word meanings. *Cognitive Science, 14*, 57–77.

Markman, E. M., & Hutchinson, J. E. (1984). Children's sensitivity to constraints in word meaning: Taxonomic versus thematic relations. *Cognitive Psychology, 16*, 1–27.

Markman, E. M., & Wachtel, G. F. (1988). Children's use of mutual exclusivity to constrain the meaning of words. *Cognitive Psychology, 20*, 121–157.

Marler, P. (1991). The instinct to learn. In S. Carey & R. Gelman (Eds.), *The epigenesis of mind: Essays on biology and cognition.* Hillsdale, NJ: Erlbaum.

Mazurkewich, I., & White, L. (1984). The acquisition of the dative alternation: Unlearning overgeneralizations. *Cognition, 16,* 261–283.

Mehler, J., Jusczyk, P. W., Lambertz, G., Halsted, N., Bertoncini, J., & Amiel-Tison, C. (1988). A precursor of language acquisition in young infants. *Cognition, 29,* 143–178.

Meier, R. P., & Newport, E. L. (1990). Out of the hands of babes: On a possible sign advantage in language acquisition. *Language, 66,* 1–23.

Menyuk, P. (1969). *Sentences children use.* Cambridge, MA: MIT Press.

Mervis, C. B. (1984). Early lexical development: The contributions of mother and child. In C. Sophian (Ed.), *Origins of cognitive skills.* Hillsdale, NJ: Erlbaum.

Miller, W. R., & Ervin, S. M. (1964). The development of grammar in child language. *Monographs of the Society for Research in Child Development, 29,* 9–39.

Morgan, J. L. (1986). *From simple input to complex grammar.* Cambridge, MA: MIT Press.

Morgan, J. L., & Travis, L. L. (1989). Limits on negative information on language learning. *Journal of Child Language, 16,* 531–552.

Naigles, L. (1990). Children use syntax to learn verb meanings. *Journal of Child Language, 17,* 357–374.

Nelson, K. (1973). Structure and strategy in learning to talk. *Monographs of the Society for Research in Child Development, 38.*

Nelson, K. (1985). *Making sense: The acquisition of shared meaning.* Orlando, FL: Academic Press.

Nelson, K. (1988). Constraints on word meaning? *Cognitive Development, 3,* 221–246.

Nelson, K. (1990). Comment on Behrend's ''Constraints and development.'' *Cognitive Development, 5,* 331–339.

Newport, E. L. (1991). Contrasting concepts of the critical period for language. In S. Carey & R. Gelman (Eds.), *The epigenesis of mind: Essays on biology and cognition.* Hillsdale, NJ: Erlbaum.

Newport, E. L., Gleitman, H. R., & Gleitman, L. R. (1977). Mother I'd rather do it myself: Some effects and non-effects of maternal speech style. In C. E. Snow & C. A. Ferguson (Eds.), *Talking to children: Language input and acquisition.* Cambridge: Cambridge University Press.

Newport, E. L., & Meier, R. P. (1985). The acquisition of American Sign Language. In D. I. Slobin (Ed.), *The crosslinguistic study of language acquisition: Vol. 1. The data.* Hillsdale, NJ: Erlbaum.

Penner, S. (1987). Parental responses to grammatical and ungrammatical child utterances. *Child Development, 58,* 376–384.

Petitto, L. A. (1988). ''Language'' in the pre-linguistic child. In F. S. Kessel (Ed.), *The development of language and language researchers.* Hillsdale, NJ: Erlbaum.

Petitto, L. A. (in press). Modularity and constraints in early lexical acquisition: Evidence from children's early language and gesture. *Minnesota Symposium on Child Psychology, 25.*

Petitto, L. A., & Marentette, P. F. (1991). Babbling in the manual mode: Evidence for the ontogeny of language. *Science, 251,* 1493–1496.

Pierce, A. (1987). *Null subjects in the acquisition of French.* Paper presented at the Boston University Conference on Language Development, Boston.

Pinker, S. (1979). Formal models of language learning. *Cognition, 7,* 217–283.

Pinker, S. (1984). *Language learnability and language development.* Cambridge, MA: Harvard University Press.

Pinker, S. (1987). The bootstrapping problem in language acquisition. In B. MacWhinney (Ed.), *Mechanisms of language acquisition.* Hillsdale, NJ: Erlbaum.

Pinker, S. (1989a). Language acquisition. In D. N. Osherson & H. Lasnik (Eds.), *An invitation to cognitive science: Vol. 1. Language.* Cambridge, MA: MIT Press.

Pinker, S. (1989b). *Learnability and cognition.* Cambridge, MA: MIT Press.

Pinker, S. (1991). Rules of language. *Science, 253,* 530–535.

Pinker, S. (in press). How could a child use verb syntax to learn verb semantics? *Lingua.*

Pinker, S., & Bloom, P. (1990). Natural language and natural selection. *Behavioral and Brain Sciences, 13,* 707–784.

Pinker, S., Lebeaux, D. S., & Frost, L. A. (1987). Productivity and constraints in the acquisition of the passive. *Cognition, 26,* 195–267.

Pinker, S., & Prince, A. (1988). On language and connectionism: Analysis of a parallel distributed model of language acquisition. *Cognition, 28,* 73–193.

Pinker, S., & Prince, A. (1991). *Regular and irregular morphology and the psychological status of rules of grammar*. Proceedings of the 17th annual meeting of the Berkeley Linguistics Society Berkeley Linguistics Society, Berkeley, CA.

Plunkett, K., & Marchman, V. (1991). U-shaped learning and frequency effects in a multi-layered perceptron: Implications for child language acquisition. *Cognition, 38,* 43–102.

Pye, C. (1983). Mayan telegraphese: Intonational determinants of inflectional development in Quiche Mayan. *Language, 59,* 583–604.

Quine, W. V. O. (1960). *Word and object*. Cambridge, MA: MIT Press.

Radford, A. (1990a). *Syntactic theory and the acquisition of English syntax: The nature of early child grammars of English*. Oxford: Basil/Blackwell.

Radford, A. (1990b). The syntax of nominal arguments in early child English. *Language Acquisition, 3,* 195–223.

Rescorla, L. (1980). Overextension in early language development. *Journal of Child Language, 7,* 321–335.

Rizzi, L. (1982). *Issues in Italian syntax*. Dordrecht: Foris.

Roeper, T. (1973). Connecting children's language and the linguistic theory. In T. Moore (Ed.), *Cognitive development and the acquisition of language*. New York: Academic Press.

Roeper, T., & Weissenborn, J. (1990). How to make parameters work: Comments on Valian. In L. Frazier & J. de Villiers (Eds.), *Language processing and language acquisition*. Dordrecht: Kluwer.

Roeper, T., & Williams, E. (Eds.). (1987). *Parameter-setting*. Dordrecht: Reidel.

Rosch, E. (1973). Natural categories. *Cognitive Psychology, 4,* 328–350.

Rumelhart, D. E., & McClelland, J. L. (1986). On learning the past tenses of English verbs. In J. L. McClelland & D. E. Rumelhart (Eds.), *Parallel distributed processing: Explorations in the microstructure of cognition: Vol. 2. Psychological and biological models*. Cambridge, MA: MIT Press.

Schlesinger, I. M. (1971). Production of utterances and language acquisition. In D. I. Slobin (Ed.), *The ontogenesis of grammar*. New York: Academic Press.

Schlesinger, I. M. (1981). Semantic assimilation in the acquisition of relational categories. In W. Deutsch (Ed.), *The child's construction of language*. New York: Academic Press.

Schlesinger, I. M. (1988). The origin of relational categories. In Y. Levy, I. M. Schlesinger & M. D. S. Braine (Eds.), *Categories and processes in language acquisition*. Hillsdale, NJ: Erlbaum.

Soja, N. N. (1992). Inferences about the meanings of nouns: The relationship between perception and syntax. *Cognitive Development, 7,* 29–45.

Soja, N. N., Carey S., & Spelke, E. S. (1991). Ontological categories guide young children's inductions of word meaning: Object terms and substance terms. *Cognition, 38,* 179–211.

Talmy, L. (1985). Lexicalization patterns: Semantic structure in lexical forms. In T. Shopen (Ed.), *Language typology and syntactic description: Vol. 3. Grammatical categories and the lexicon*. New York: Cambridge University Press.

Taylor, M., & Gelman, S. (1988). Adjectives and nouns: Children's strategies for learning new words. *Child Development, 59,* 411–419.

Valian, V. (1986). Syntactic categories in the speech of young children. *Developmental Psychology, 22,* 562–579.

Valian, V. (1990). Null subjects: A problem for parameter-setting models of language acquisition. *Cognition, 35,* 105–122.

Valian, V. (1991). Syntactic subjects in the early speech of American and Italian children. *Cognition, 40,* 21–81.

Vygotsky, L. (1962). *Thought and language*. Cambridge, MA: MIT Press.

Waxman, S. (1990). Linguistic biases and the establishment of conceptual hierarchies: Evidence from preschool children. *Cognitive Development, 5,* 123–150.

Waxman, S., & Gelman, R. (1986). Preschoolers' use of superordinate relations in classifications and language. *Cognitive Development, 1,* 139–156.

Wellman, H. M. (1990). *The child's theory of mind*. Cambridge, MA: MIT Press.

Wexler, K., & Cullicover, P. (1980). *Formal principles of language acquisition*. Cambridge, MA: MIT Press.

Wittgenstein, L. (1953). *Philosophical investigations*. Oxford: Blackwell.

CHILD PHONOLOGY

PAST RESEARCH, PRESENT QUESTIONS, FUTURE DIRECTIONS

LouAnn Gerken

I. INTRODUCTION

Phonology is the study of the speech sound contrasts that are relevant to meaning in a particular language, and of the linguistic processes that apply to those sounds. For example, the observation that English speakers distinguish between the initial sounds of *vase* and *base,* while Spanish speakers do not, is part of the study of phonology. So is the observation that adding a plural marker to *cat* results in /kæts/, but adding a plural marker to *cad* results in /kædz/.[1] Phonology is also the study of stress patterns exhibited by the words of a particular language and of how information about sentence structure (syntax) is conveyed by a language's sound system. For example, the observation that most bisyllabic English words are stressed on the first syllable is part of phonology. So is the observation that English speakers tend to pause after the subject noun phrase *The big brown dog* in (1). The subfield of phonology that focuses on individual speech sounds or segments is SEGMENTAL PHONOLOGY, and the subfield that focuses on phenomena larger than a single segment (e.g., a syllable) is SUPRASEGMENTAL PHONOLOGY. In this chapter, I examine how infants and children come to discover the segmental and suprasegmental organization of their native language.

(1) *The big brown dog* (pause) *bit my neighbor.*

My goal in writing this chapter is not to provide an exhaustive review of the field of child phonology; it has grown far too large in the last 25 years for that. Rather, I outline research that relates to three theoretical issues that promise to challenge and motivate child phonologists in the coming years. The

---

[1] Following convention, I use slashes (/ /) to denote the phonological representation of an adult word form. I use square brackets ([ ]) to denote the phonetic representation of children's utterances.

first issue concerns the interaction of innate and experiential factors in language development. Two decades of research on infant speech perception have culminated in considerable information about the infant's initial capabilities and how these develop (e.g., Aslin, Pisoni, & Jusczyk, 1983; Eimas, Siqueland, Jusczyk, & Vigorrito, 1971; Jusczyk, 1992; Werker & Tees, 1984). More recently, work on infant babbling patterns has provided a fuller picture of how the infant's natural articulatory proclivities are influenced by the language environment (e.g., de Boysson-Bardies, Sagart, & Durand, 1984; Oller, 1980; Vihman, Macken, Miller, Simmons, & Miller, 1985). Phonology is the only linguistic domain in which we can examine development from birth onward; therefore, research on infant speech perception and babbling potentially provides a framework for viewing the joint effects of biology and environment on all of language acquisition.

A second theoretical issue to watch in the coming years concerns the relationship between consistent and variable phenomena, both within and across children. An example of a phenomenon that is consistent within a particular child might be producing *fis* each time the word *fish* is intended; whereas a variable phenomenon within a child would be producing *fish* this way only once or rarely. Some researchers have begun to treat variability within children as reflective of their phonological representations, rather than noise that should be ignored (e.g., Leonard, 1992; Menn & Matthei, 1992; Stemberger, 1992). In order to accommodate effects of within-child variability, these researchers are currently creating new models of language perception and production. These models promise to serve as catalysts for new theoretical and empirical developments. With regard to consistency versus variability across children, other researchers have begun to focus less on broad developmental generalizations and have begun instead to examine in fine detail on how various factors interact to create unique patterns of phonological development within each child (e.g., Ferguson & Farwell, 1975; Peters & Menn, 1991; Vihman et al., 1985). This new focus on variation among children offers a deeper understanding of the interplay between biology and experience.

The third theoretical issue that promises to guide future research concerns a growing body of data demonstrating that infants and children are highly sensitive to the suprasegmental characteristics of their language (e.g., stress, pausing, and fundamental frequency or average pitch; Fernald & Kuhl, 1987; Fernald & Mazzie, 1991; Gerken, 1992a, 1992b; Gerken & McIntosh, 1993; Gleitman, Gleitman, Landau, & Wanner, 1988; Gleitman & Wanner, 1982; Hirsh-Pasek, Kemler Nelson, Jusczyk, Wright Cassidy, & Druss, 1987; Jusczyk et al., 1992; Kemler Nelson, Hirsh-Pasek, Jusczyk, & Wright Cassidy, 1989; Mehler et al., 1988; Morgan, 1986; Morgan & Newport, 1981; Peters, 1983, 1985). Recent developments in the linguistic study of phonology have elucidated the relation between suprasegmental processes, on the one hand, and morphological (e.g., addition of past tense *-ed*) and syntactic processes, on the other (e.g., Hayes, 1989; Nespor & Vogel, 1986; Selkirk, 1984). These developments, in conjunction with infants' and children's sensitivity to suprasegmental processes, admit the tantalizing possibility that language learners could use suprasegmental patterns in the acquisition of morphology and syntax. If this is the case, the study of child phonology will come to occupy a central place in the study of language acquisition.

In order to best illustrate the importance of the three theoretical issues outlined above, the chapter is organized into two large sections and a third smaller one. The first large section deals with the acquisition of segmental phonology. For example, how do children exposed to English come to realize that *pig* is a different word from *big?* The theoretical issues that figure most heavily here are the interplay between innate and experiential factors in language acquisition and the treatment of phonological variability within an individual child. The second large section of the chapter deals with the acquisition of suprasegmental phonology and how it might serve as a basis for the acquisition of morphology and syntax. For example, could children use pausing patterns such as the one illustrated in (1) to infer that sentences are divided into subjects and predicates? The third, smaller section deals with individual differences in phonological acquisition.[2] For the most part, the chapter explores the development of phonology from infancy to approximately three years of age. Although substantial developments occur after this point, including the representation of allomorphy (e.g., /kæts/ vs /kædz/), word formation rules, and reading, the first three years of life provide an extremely rich empirical base from which to explore the theoretical considerations I have highlighted. (For discussion of some later developments, the reader can consult Braine, 1971; Derwing & Baker, 1979; Gordon, 1985, 1989; Moskowitz, 1973b; Walley, 1993.)

II. SEGMENTAL PHONOLOGY

Adult language users appear to have access to a representation of speech that can be described in terms of individual segments or phonemes corresponding roughly to the letters of the alphabet. This is attested most clearly by the fact that some inventive human created a writing system in which symbols stand for phonemes, and other humans can learn to read using this system (see Studdert-Kennedy, 1987). Alphabetic writing systems suggest that we have at least a metalinguistic ability to extract individual phonemes from our sound representation of words. Adult speakers and listeners also appear to have access to parts of phonemes or features. There are several possible featural analyses of the phonemes in a language (e.g., Chomsky & Halle, 1968). For the purpose at hand, I will use an analysis that categorizes speech sounds as consonants or vowels and further specifies three consonant features: the manner in which the airflow from the lungs is constricted and released to make the consonant (e.g., stop, nasal, fricative, affricate, liquid), the place in the mouth where the air is constricted (e.g., labial, dental, alveolar, palatal, velar), and whether the vocal cords vibrate as the consonant is produced (i.e., voiced, voiceless). A table listing the phonetic symbols for English consonants and vowels and the feature categorization of consonants appears in Section VI. One piece of evidence for a featural representation of speech sounds is that when speakers

---

[2] The reader should note that the presence of separate sections for segmental and suprasegmental phonology is not meant to imply that children separately acquire these two forms of linguistic knowledge. In fact, there is substantial evidence to the contrary (e.g., Ferguson & Farwell, 1975; Menyuk & Menn, 1979; Peters, 1983; Walley, 1993; Waterson, 1971). I have chosen this division only to better illustrate the distinct theoretical issues typically associated with the acquisition of segmental and suprasegmental phonology.

make slips of the tongue (e.g., saying *bick up the baby* instead of *pick . . .*), the incorrect segment frequently deviates by only a single feature from the intended one (Fromkin, 1971; MacKay, 1970; Nooteboom, 1967). Other evidence for features is that perceptual mistakes typically involve hearing a phoneme that differs by a single feature from the actual one (Blumstein, 1974; Cole, 1973; G. A. Miller & Nicely, 1955; Pisoni, 1975; Studdert-Kennedy & Shankweiler, 1970).

Section II explores how children develop an adult-like segmental representation of their language, focusing in particular on how children learn the phoneme contrasts required for accurate word perception and production. Section II,A examines infant speech perception abilities and considers the relation between these abilities and later phonological development. Section II,B examines infant babbling and its relation to infant perception and to the production of first words. Section II,C examines children's perception of early words and considers the role of perception and production in the development of phonological representations. Section II,D examines how young children's early word productions deviate from adult forms and from children's intended forms; it also evaluates three classes of theories that attempt to explain the relation between adult and child word forms. Finally, Section II,E summarizes the main findings in the development of segmental phonology and identifies some future research directions.

A. Precursors to Segmental Phonology in Infant Speech Perception

Research on infant speech perception began during the early 1970s, a time when Chomsky's (1965) strongly nativist approach to language acquisition was gaining a wider audience. Not surprisingly, a central goal of this research has been to determine the contribution of innate abilities to the development of phonology. One of the most notable discoveries about adult speech perception made during the 1950s and 1960s was that listeners appeared to perceive speech, but not other stimuli, in a categorical (i.e., noncontinuous) manner (Liberman, Cooper, Shankweiler, & Studdert-Kennedy, 1967). Therefore, much of the research on infant speech perception has focused on whether or not infants categorically perceive various speech contrasts, and if so, the implications of such perception for the nature of phonological development. Much of the current section mirrors this focus.

Before turning to the infant research, let me briefly illustrate the phenomenon of categorical speech perception in adults. In these experiments, adult listeners are presented with a continuum of synthetic (machine-made) speech stimuli. The stimuli all have a consonant-like burst of sound (what you might hear if you pop your lips to make a /p/ or a /b/) followed by a vowel-like steady state sound (what you might hear if you say *ahh*). The variable of interest is the temporal relation between the burst and the vowel, which is called VOICE ONSET TIME. English-speaking adults typically perceive all stimuli in which the vowel occurs 25 ms or more after the burst as the syllable /pa/ in which the consonant is voiceless, and all other stimuli as the syllable /ba/ in which the consonant is voiced (Lisker & Abramson, 1964). Further, English-speaking adults are unable to differentiate two stimuli from within a single phonemic category but are able to differentiate stimuli exhibiting an equivalent acoustic difference when these stimuli come from different categories (see Liberman et al., 1967, for further discussion).

In 1971, two laboratories discovered evidence of categorical speech perception in infants (Eimas et al., 1971; Moffit, 1971). The study by Eimas and his colleagues employed a synthetic speech continuum like the one described above, in which the steady state occurred either 20 ms before the burst (referred to as /ba/ −20), simultaneous with the burst (/ba/ 0), or 20, 40, 60 or 80 ms after the burst (/ba/ +20, /pa/ +40, /pa/ +60, /pa/ +80, respectively). One- and four-month-old infants were given a pacifier linked to a pressure transducer so that their sucking rate could be measured (Siqueland & deLucia, 1969). The infants were then presented with one of the stimuli until their sucking rate habituated, that is, decreased by a predetermined amount. Next, infants were presented with either the same stimulus, a different stimulus from within the same adult phoneme classification, or a different stimulus from a different adult phoneme classification. For example, an infant might be presented with /ba/ +20 during the habituation phase, and during the testing phase presented with either the same stimulus (/ba/ +20), a different stimulus from the same adult category (e.g., /ba/ 0), or a different stimulus from a different adult category (e.g., /pa/ +40). The measure of interest was whether infants dishabituated to the second stimulus, that is, whether their sucking rate increased significantly over the habituated sucking rate at the offset of the first stimulus. The results showed that infants dishabituated significantly only when the second stimulus represented a different phoneme for adult listeners. Thus, acoustic differences that are used by English-speaking adults to make the voiced/voiceless consonant distinction were treated as different by infants, while acoustic differences of equal size that are not linguistically relevant to adults were not treated as different by infants. The authors interpreted these results as evidence that the basis for phoneme perception is innate.

This study and the one by Moffit (1971) set off a volley of experiments testing infants' perceptions of a wide range of consonant and vowel discriminations. These studies demonstrated that, from early in life, English-learning infants are able to discriminate most English sound classes, including voicing of stop consonants (Eilers, Wilson, & Moore, 1979; Eimas et al., 1971; Lasky, Syrdal-Lasky, & Klein, 1975; Trehub & Rabinovich, 1972), place of articulation of stop consonants (Eimas, 1974; Jusczyk, 1977; Jusczyk & Thompson, 1978; C. Miller & Morse, 1976; J. Miller, Morse & Dorman, 1977; Moffit, 1971; Morse, 1972; Williams & Bush, 1978), vowels (Kuhl, 1980; Trehub, 1973), and liquids (Eimas, 1975; see Eilers, 1980, for a review). Discrimination of fricative consonants appears to be more difficult (Eilers & Minife, 1975; Eilers, Wilson, & Moore, 1977), suggesting some role for maturation or learning. Additional evidence of the importance of learning is related to the fact that different languages draw phonemic category boundaries at different places along an acoustic continuum. For example, adult Spanish-speakers perceive stimuli in which a steady state precedes or coincides with a burst as a voiced consonant (e.g., /ba/), but stimuli in which the steady state follows the burst as a voiceless consonant (e.g., /pa/). This pattern is shifted somewhat from the one we saw in adult English-speakers (Lisker & Abramson, 1964). However, research with 4-to-6-month-old Spanish-learning infants demonstrated that they are sensitive to the English boundary, not the Spanish one (Lasky et al., 1975; for a similar finding in Kikuyu, see Streeter, 1976). Such findings suggest that infant speech perception changes considerably with exposure to the target language (i.e., the language being learned); otherwise we cannot explain how Spanish-learning infants can become Spanish-speaking adults. One interpretation of the interaction between innate perceptual abilities and effects of the target language is that infants are born with the innate ability to perceive a wide range of phonetic contrasts. Through exposure to the target language, they can either maintain those contrasts that are relevant, modify phonetic categories that do not match those used in the target language, or ignore contrasts not used in the target language (for discussion, see Aslin & Pisoni, 1980; Best, 1994; Eimas, 1982).

However, other research has called into question this interpretation of the early infant speech perception data. One group of studies has demonstrated categorical perception for nonspeech stimuli (e.g., two short tones varying in their temporal relation to each other), suggesting that this mode of perception is not language-specific (Cutting & Rosner, 1974; Pisoni, 1977). Other research has demonstrated categorical perception of human speech in nonhuman mammals, casting further doubt on the linguistic basis of the phenomenon (Baru, 1975; Kuhl & Miller, 1975, 1978; Kuhl & Padden, 1983). Although some researchers continue to maintain that categorical perception in infants reflects innate language-specific processes (e.g., Best, 1984, 1994; Eimas, 1982; Eimas & Miller, in press), others have begun to rethink the relation between categorical perception and phonological development (e.g., Aslin & Pisoni, 1980; Aslin et al., 1983; Jusczyk, 1982, 1992; Walley, 1993). In particular, it is possible that, rather than reflecting language-specific perceptual abilities, categorical perception reflects regions of high sensitivity in the mammalian auditory system (Aslin & Pisoni, 1980; Aslin et al., 1983). Languages can take advantage of the auditory perception system by placing phoneme boundaries at auditory sensitivity peaks. English employs one of the highest sensitivity peaks as the boundary between voiced and voiceless consonants (e.g., /b/ and /p/, respectively), and this might be why both English-learning and Spanish-learning infants show sensitivity to the boundary used by English-speaking adults. However, languages can also place phoneme boundaries at lesser sensitivity peaks or employ a narrower or broader phoneme category than the one specified by the auditory system. As discussed above, adult Spanish-speakers employ a broader phonological category than adult English-speakers, resulting in some stimuli that are perceived by English-speakers as /ba/ but perceived by Spanish-speakers as /pa/ (Aslin & Pisoni, 1980). Thus, Spanish-learning infants must, through experience, broaden their innate perceptual category in order to make the same voiced/voiceless consonant distinctions made by Spanish-speaking adults.

Regardless of whether infant categorical perception abilities are language-specific or auditory in nature, it is clear that these abilities change through exposure to the target language. Therefore, infant speech perception research has begun to focus on the question of how infants and children learn which innate perceptual distinctions are relevant in the target language. To answer this question, researchers have examined infants' ability to discriminate sounds that are not linguistically relevant in the target language and what happens to these discrimination abilities with development (Aslin et al., 1983; Best, McRoberts, & Sithole, 1988; Eilers, Gavin, & Wilson, 1979; Lasky et al.,

1975; Streeter, 1976; Trehub, 1976; Werker, Gilbert, Humphrey, & Tees, 1981; Werker & Lalonde, 1988; Werker & Tees, 1984). Research using a categorical perception paradigm has demonstrated that very young infants are able to perceive most foreign language contrasts, and that these abilities are lost some time during the period between 6 and 12 months of age (Werker et al., 1981; Werker & Lalonde, 1988; Werker & Tees, 1984; but see Best et al., 1988, for a claim that certain perceptual abilities are not lost). The notion that 6-to-12-month-olds begin to focus on the sounds in the target language is further supported by data obtained from a preferential looking paradigm. Using this paradigm, in which infants hear a particular stimulus type as long as they look toward the appropriate loudspeaker, Jusczyk, Friederici, Wessels, Svenkerud, and Jusczyk (1993) found that 9-month-old, but not 6-month-old, English-learners were able to distinguish between English and Dutch word lists. Thus, by 9 months of age, infants appear to develop a representation of speech sounds that is specific to the target language. This is further confirmed by studies of infant babbling, which are presented in Section II,B.

How do infants represent the sounds in their native language and how does this representation develop? One possibility is that 6-to-12-month-olds begin to notice that particular acoustic strings co-occur with particular situations in the world (Jusczyk, 1982; Lewis, 1936; MacKain, 1982; Nakazima, 1970; Studdert-Kennedy, 1986). These sound/referent correspondences might be adult words, or they might be multiword utterances with a constant meaning (e.g., *Time-for-your-bath;* see Peters, 1977, 1983). Infants' early awareness of recurring referential utterances could cause them to attend to contrasts relevant in the target language and thereby ignore irrelevant contrasts (Jusczyk, 1986, 1992; Lindblom, 1986; Menyuk & Menn, 1979; Studdert-Kennedy, 1986). The nature of the representation underlying infants' growing attention to language-relevant contrasts is currently not well understood. The evidence that 6-to-12-month-olds have begun to represent speech in terms of discrete segments is currently sparse (Hillenbrand, 1983; Kuhl, 1980, 1985, 1986). This has prompted some researchers to hypothesize that holistic properities, such as prosodic structure and overall acoustic shape, provide a better characterization of early phonological representations (e.g., Ferguson & Farwell, 1975; Jusczyk, 1982, 1986; Menyuk & Menn, 1979; Studdert-Kennedy, 1986; Waterson, 1971). On the latter view, language learners develop an adult-like segmental representation only later, either because they need to recognize a growing number of similar-sounding words (Ferguson & Farwell, 1975; Jusczyk, 1982, 1986, 1992; Menyuk & Menn, 1979; Walley, 1993), or because a segmental representation is most conducive to efficient speech production (Lindblom, 1986; Studdert-Kennedy, 1986). These possibilities are discussed in more detail in Section II,C.

B. Precursors to Segmental Phonology in Babbling

Stark (1980) outlines five stages of infants' vocalizations before the onset of the first word. During the first three, and especially during the third, infants may accidently produce some sounds that resemble speech. However, only the fourth and fifth stages are referred to as ''babbling,'' and they are the focus of this section. BABBLING is a form of production in which elements are obviously repeated and in which the timing properties resemble those in speech

(Oller, 1986). Two major subtypes of babble have been identified: reduplicated babble and nonreduplicated or variegated babble (Oller, 1980). Recent research indicates that infants across a wide range of ages produce both types of babble (Mitchell & Kent, 1990; Oller, 1980; B. L. Smith, Brown-Sweeney, & Stoel-Gammon, 1989). Reduplicated babble is characterized by repetitions of a single consonant–vowel (CV) syllable (e.g., [bababa]), and infants appear to concentrate on a single CV type (e.g., [ba]) for a period of time and then concentrate on another (Gesell & Amatruda, 1941; Leopold, 1947; McCarthy, 1952; Nakazima, 1962; Oller, 1980; B. L. Smith & Oller, 1981; Stark, 1980). Variegated babble is characterized by strings of different syllables (e.g., [bamido]). In some forms of variegated babble, syllables are differentially stressed, and intonation contours are imposed on syllable strings, giving productions a sentence-like quality (de Boysson-Bardies, Sagard, & Bacri, 1981; Oller, 1980; Stark, 1980; Vihman & Miller, 1988).

Near the end of the first or beginning of the second year of life, children produce their first utterances that are clearly meaning-bearing. These can be either child renditions of adult words or protowords, the latter being idiosyncratic forms with semantic/referential status for the child (e.g., [di] used to draw adult's attention to an object; Ferguson & Farwell, 1975; also see Menn, 1976; Moskowitz, 1973a; Stoel-Gammon & Cooper, 1984; Velten, 1943). Recent research has focused on two related questions concerning the relation of babbling and early words or protowords. First, does the transition from babbling to speech reflect a continuous process, or are babbling and speech discrete developmental stages? Second, does perceptual input from the target language influence the babbling repertoire, or does babbling reflect the independent development of the production system (e.g., Lenneberg, 1967; Studdert-Kennedy, 1986)? The first question has its origins in early suggestions by Jakobson (1941/1968) that some children's transition from babbling to words is marked by a silent period. Jakobson further claimed that the sound repertoire used in babbling draws from all the world's languages, while the repertoire used in early words represents a subset of the phonemic contrasts used in the target language (also Section II,D). More detailed research has proven inconsistent with both claims. At the same time that children are still producing variegated babbling, they often begin to produce their first words or protowords (Ferguson, 1978; Leopold, 1953; Stoel-Gammon & Cooper, 1984; Vihman et al., 1985). In fact, early words can be embedded in strings of variegated babble (Landahl, 1982; Vihman et al., 1985; Vihman & Miller, 1988; also see Elbers & Ton, 1985). These observations contradict suggestions that babbling and speech are temporally distinct stages (Jakobson, 1941/1968). Further, babbling and speech appear to draw on the same repertoire of sounds (Cruttenden, 1970; Oller, Weiman, Doyle, & Ross, 1976; Stoel-Gammon & Cooper, 1984; Vihman et al., 1985). In a study by Vihman and her colleagues, the babbling and speech of 9-to-16-month-old infants were recorded and coded for four variables: place of articulation, manner of articulation, length of utterance in syllables, and syllable shape (e.g., CV). They found that variability between babbling and speech was significantly lower within individual infants than among infants for the first three measures. Perhaps more important, they found that those infants who regularly produced relatively rare sounds in babbling (e.g., velars such as [k] and liquids such as [l]) were the only infants who produced these sounds in their early words. This suggests that infants choose their first words based in part on the production repertoire they developed in babbling (Ferguson & Farwell, 1975; Schwartz & Leonard, 1982; also see Sections II,D and IV). Such findings are clearly at odds with the notion that babbling and speech are independent.

Other researchers have looked for effects of auditory input on infant babbling patterns. In contrast with early claims to the contrary (e.g., Lenneberg, 1967), deaf infants produce different babbling patterns than hearing infants, suggesting some role for perception in babbling (Kent, 1984; Oller, Eilers, Bull, & Carney, 1985). Researchers have also demonstrated differences among the babbling patterns of infants from different language communities (Atkinson, McWhinney, & Stoel, 1970; de Boysson-Bardies, Halle, Sagart, & Durand, 1989; de Boysson-Bardies et al., 1984; Oller & Eilers, 1982; Olney & Scholnick, 1976; Weir, 1966). De Boysson-Bardies and her colleagues (1989) examined the vowel productions of 10-month-old infants raised in homes where the ambient language was English, French, Cantonese, or Arabic. They found that acoustic characteristics of the vowels (frequency of the first two formants) exhibited more variability across linguistic communities than within linguistic communities. Further, they found that differences among the average vowel produced by adult speakers of the four languages were mirrored by the infants. For example, adults and infants from English-speaking communities produced vowels with the highest pitch, while adults and infants from Cantonese-speaking communities produced vowels with the lowest. These results clearly indicate that infant babbling is influenced by the phonological environment. Further research indicates that the time period during which babbling comes to resemble the target language approximates the period when infants lose the ability to make nonnative perceptual contrasts. In particular, research indicates that untrained adult listeners cannot discern differences based on target language in the babbling of 6-month-olds, while they can in 8-month-olds (de Boysson-Bardies et al., 1984). Recall from Section II,A that infants lose the ability to make nonnative perceptual contrasts during the end of their first year (e.g., Werker & Tees, 1984). Thus, infant perception and babbling studies present a coherent picture in which young language learners begin after about 6 months of age to focus on the sounds in the target language (see Jusczyk, 1992, for further discussion).

C. Children's Perception of Early Words

Recall from Section II,A that infants demonstrate amazing abilities to discriminate speech sounds. However, studies in which young children are asked to identify referents of newly taught or previously known words suggest that they cannot directly apply their perceptual expertise to this domain (Barton, 1976a, 1976b, 1980; Edwards, 1974; Eilers & Oller, 1976; Garnica, 1971; Shvachkin, 1973). In the earliest study examining young children's phoneme perception abilities, Shvachkin (1973) taught Russian-learning 10-to-24-month-olds nonsense words that referred to toys. Over a period of several months, each child learned several minimal word pairs (two words differing by only a single phoneme or feature, e.g., *vum* vs. *bum*). Phoneme discrimination was tested by asking children to find the toy associated with one member of a minimal pair. Shvachkin found that, by the end of the study, approximately half of all of the subjects (mean age 22 months) were able to make all of the discriminations tested. He also found that some contrasts were easier than others; for example, nearly all the children could discriminate word pairs that differed only in the vowel, or had initial consonants that differed in manner of articulation (e.g., /b/ vs. /v/). He claimed that discriminations were mastered in a relatively consistent order across children; however, a similar claim by Edwards (1974) has been questioned on statistical grounds (Barton, 1980). Shvachkin's nonsense word technique has been employed in two studies of English-learning children (Edwards, 1974; Garnica, 1971, 1973). Both demonstrated more frequent discrimination errors than Shvachkin, but both, like Shvachkin, found that some contrasts were easier than others. For example, Edwards found that all of her 20-to-47-month-olds could discriminate /p/ versus /b/, /ð/ versus /d/, and /g/ versus /k/, while only 50% were able to discriminate /s/ versus /z/ (see Barton, 1975, 1980 for further discussion).

Other studies have employed either familiar words or a combination of familiar and unfamiliar items. Eilers and Oller (1976) tested 22-to-26-month-olds on minimal pairs consisting of one familiar and one nonsense word (e.g., *fish* vs. *thish*) and found that children made on average about 36% discrimination errors. Like Shvachkin and Edwards, they also found that some contrasts were easier than others; all the children tested could distinguish /k/ versus /p/, while none could distinguish /f/ versus /θ/. Barton (1976b) tested 20-to-24-month-olds on two English minimal word pairs that they knew (*coat* vs. *goat* and *pear* vs. *bear*) and found that 80% of the children could discriminate at least one of the pairs. Barton (1976a) also found that 27-to-35-month-olds made only about 11% discrimination errors on a set of 20 minimal pairs involving words that they spontaneously produced. However, they made 42% errors on the same discriminations if one or both of the words in the minimal pair was one that they neither comprehended nor produced in a pretest. The most frequent error made by children who previously knew one of the words in a pair was to treat the unknown word as though it were the familiar one (Barton, 1976b). Unlike other investigators, Barton's subjects did not find some contrasts easier than others; however, this might be because their discrimination performance was nearly at ceiling for many pairs.

To summarize the results from these studies, it appears that children between the end of their first year and the beginning of their fifth year learn to distinguish among words that differ in only a single segment. Estimates about when children are able to make all of the linguistically relevant contrasts differ across studies. This is probably due in part to differences in the discrimination criteria employed (Barton, 1975, 1980) and to how well children in each study knew the words being tested. In any case, it seems clear that children are not able to directly apply the decontextualized perceptual abilities they demonstrated in infancy to associate a sound string and its referent; even children who previously knew both words in Barton's (1976a) study made 11% discrimination errors. Presumably, adults would not make any errors on this task. With regard to order of acquisition, most children were able to make contrasts involving differences in vowel, consonant manner, and voicing of stop consonants, while contrasts among fricative consonants appear to be later discriminated (Edwards, 1974; Eilers & Oller, 1976; Garnica, 1971; Shvachkin, 1973). The latter observation is consistent with studies of infant speech perception showing that contrasts involving fricatives are one of the few discriminations not made by infants (e.g., Eilers & Minifie, 1975). Another important generalization that can be made from these studies is that children are better able to discriminate pairs of words when both words in the pair were previously known. Discrimination errors occurred between 34.5 and 42% of the time when children did not previously know one or both words (Barton, 1976a; Garnica, 1971; Eilers & Oller, 1976), while the error rate dropped to only 11% when children spontaneously produced both words during the pretest (Barton, 1976a).

Why do children apparently regress in their speech perception abilities relative to the abilities they exhibited in infancy? One possibility is that the task used to test discrimination ability in children is more demanding than the task used with infants (Jusczyk, 1992; Locke, 1988). Recall that for infants to be credited with a particular speech contrast, they need only distinguish a new stimulus from an old one. In contrast, experiments with young children require them to match an acoustic string with its referent. Therefore, children's performance reflects not only their perceptual abilities, but also their ability to recall the referent of an auditory stimulus. The fact that children perform significantly better when both words of a minimal pair are well known suggests that the referential component of the task contributes to poor performance. One way to determine the contribution of the referential component is to compare children's discrimination performance on lexical access tasks like those described above and tasks in which the listener needs only to determine whether two stimuli are the same or different. Unfortunately, researchers have found it difficult to employ same/different tasks with children under the age of about three years (e.g., Graham & House, 1971; see Barton, 1980).

Another explanation that has been offered for children's apparent difficulty with word perception is that their goal is to recognize and produce whole words, not to learn phonemic contrasts per se (e.g., Chiat, 1979; Ferguson & Farwell, 1975; Fey & Gandour, 1982b; Jusczyk, 1992; Menyuk & Menn, 1979; Waterson, 1971). Therefore, children might represent early words in terms of holistic properties like prosodic structure and acoustic shape rather than in terms of individual segments (Ferguson & Farwell, 1975; Jusczyk, 1982, 1986; Macken, 1979; Menyuk & Menn, 1979; Studdert-Kennedy, 1986; Vihman & Velleman, 1989; Walley, 1993; Waterson, 1971). If this explanation is correct, what causes children to abandon a holistic representation in favor of a segmental one? One possibility is that the need to recognize an increasing number of acoustically similar items prompts a segmental reorganization of the lexicon (mental vocabulary). Because children's early lexicons are relatively small and contain few minimal pairs, they could recognize most words with a less detailed representation than the one employed by adults, who need to discriminate a much larger number of acoustically similar items (Charles-Luce & Luce, 1990; Jusczyk, 1985, 1992; Walley, 1993). As the lexicon becomes more dense (contains more minimal pairs), children are forced to adopt a segmental representation for more efficient word recognition (e.g., Jusczyk, 1985; 1992; Lindblom, 1992). Estimates about how dense the lexicon needs to be, and therefore at what age we should expect a segmental reorganization, range from when the first 50 words are acquired (e.g., Menyuk & Menn, 1979) to the early school years (Walley, 1993). Explicit modeling of word recognition in young children would be useful to determine what if any relation exists between lexical density and the ability to make perceptual contrasts.

A second potential motivation for children to abandon a holistic representation and adopt a segmental one is the need to consistently produce words, a task that requires the careful timing of a sequence of articulations and therefore entails a sequentially ordered representation of the sounds in a word (Lindblom, 1986; MacNeilage, 1980; Studdert-Kennedy, 1986; also see Vihman, 1993). Therefore, even though a holistic representation might allow reasonably accurate word recognition until the lexicon become quite dense, such a representation is not sufficient to allow consistent word production. The notion that speech production plays an important role in the development of adult-like segmental phonology is consistent with several aspects of the word perception studies. Barton (1976a, 1976b) found that children who spontaneously produced both words of a minimal pair in the pretest were best at discriminating these words in the actual experiment. Children who comprehended but did not produce both words in the pretest performed noticeably worse. Similarly, Shvachkin (1973) noted that some of his subjects were able to discriminate minimal pairs only if they were able to produce both words. Thus, it appears likely that the demands of speech production are at least partly responsible for the development of a segmental representation. Perhaps it is some combination of lexical density and production demands that triggers this development (Lindblom, 1986).

Alternatively, perception and production representations might develop independently (e.g., Elbert, Dinnsen, & Weismer, 1984; Locke, 1971; Macken & Ferguson, 1983; Menn, 1978, 1980, 1983; Spencer, 1986; Straight, 1980; Vihman, 1993; Zlatin & Koenigsknecht, 1976; see Section II,D). On this view, children's perception lexicon might remain relatively more holistic and less detailed for an extended period. In contrast, the production lexicon must be sequentially and segmentally specified at a much earlier point in time. One piece of evidence for distinct perception and production representations concerns the salience of initial consonants. Studies of 4-to-7-year-olds suggest that word-initial consonants are not so important in word recognition as they are to adults (Walley, 1987, 1988). This finding has been used to support the view that children employ nonsegmental word representations into their early school years (e.g., Walley, 1993). In contrast, word-initial consonants are a major determinant of whether children under the age of 2 years will attempt to produce particular words (Ferguson & Farwell, 1975; Shibamoto & Olmsted, 1978). The latter observation suggests that production representations may include at least partial information about individual segments or articulatory gestures (Vihman & Velleman, 1989). Such discrepancies between studies of perception versus production indicate that the relation between these two linguistic skills in the development of phonology (and language acquisition in general) is one that deserves further examination.

D. Children's Productions of Early Words

The starting point for much of child phonology is the simple observation that children's early words deviate from adult forms. For example, a child might consistently produce the adult word *fish* as *fis*. Although some child deviations might be due to misperception (see Section II,C), perceptual failure is not a complete explanation. This is illustrated by the so-called *fis* phenomenon (Berko & Brown, 1960; Dodd, 1975; Locke & Kutze, 1975; N. V. Smith, 1973). A child who produces *fish* as *fis* might nevertheless recognize that this form differs from the adult form, as indicated by a reaction to an adult producing the child form. Other evidence that children perceive contrasts that they apparently do not produce can be seen in children who maintain a production distinction between words, but do so in a way that is imperceptible to adults. For example, Macken and Barton (1980) demonstrated instrumentally that children between the ages of 18 and 30 months maintained a consistent voiced/voiceless stop contrast, but produced voice onset times for both within the adult voiced category (also see Braine, 1976; Fey & Gandour, 1982a, 1982b; Leopold, 1947). Perhaps many cases in which children apparently fail to produce a phonemic contrast are of this sort. The *fis* phenomenon and the nonstandard maintenance of contrasts do not necessarily imply that children have veridical representations of adult forms (e.g., Dinnsen, Elbert, & Wiesmer, 1980; Ingram, 1974; Macken, 1980; Menn, 1980; Vihman, 1982). However, these behaviors do suggest that children have access to word representations that are distinct from their produced forms. Therefore, any adequate theory of the systematic relation between child and adult forms must include a substantial production component.

As discussed in Section II,C concerning children's word perception, many researchers have suggested that children's earliest word representations are holistic (Ferguson & Farwell, 1975; Menyuk & Menn, 1979; Waterson, 1971). On this view, early deviations from an adult model are best described not in terms of individual segments, but rather in terms of the articulatory gestures required for the whole word (e.g., Lindblom, 1986; Lindblom, MacNeilage, & Studdert-Kennedy, 1983; MacNeilage, 1980; Studdert-Kennedy, 1986), or suprasegmental characteristics such as rhythm or fundamental frequency (e.g., Macken, 1979; Peters, 1977, 1983; Waterson, 1971). For example, Ferguson and Farwell (1975) noted ten attempts by a young child to say the word *pen*. Although none of the attempts resembled the adult form in terms of segmental characteristics, most exhibited the proper articulatory gestures required to produce the adult form. The problem was that these gestures were improperly sequenced; for example, the lip closure needed for /p/ occurred later in the sequence than it should have (see Studdert-Kennedy, 1986, for further discussion). Macken (1979) noted that her Spanish-learning subject assimilated new words into old rhythmically defined word shapes. For example, the child produced *cuchara* 'spoon' as [čana] and *Fernando* (a name) as [mano] for some time. But upon observing the prosodic similarity between these words, she began to produce both words with the same initial segment [č]. In a similar vein, Peters (1977, 1983) notes that many children's early utterances exhibit unclear or variable segments but consistent intonation contours.

As children learn more words, they appear to develop more detailed word representations, reflected by the fact that their deviations from an adult model can be described in terms of individual segments. At this point, their deviations become more obviously systematic. For example, a child who says *fish* as *fis* is also likely to say *dish* as *dis*. In Sections II,D,1 and II,D,2, respectively, I illustrate several types of systematic relations between child and adult forms and outline three classes of theories designed to explain some or all of these relations. In Section II,D,3, I discuss children's slips of the tongue, a form of data that is only recently being employed to study the nature of young children's productions. Slips are one-time-only productions that deviate from the child's normal, and presumably intended, form of the utterance in question. Children's slips appear to share several properties with their consistent deviations, as well as with adult slips (Gerken, in press; Jaeger, 1992; Stemberger, 1989; Wijnen, 1990), and I discuss the implications of these similarities, as well as some differences, for theories of phonological development.

1. The Relation between Child and Adult Word Forms

Most of children's early word productions can be characterized as simplifications of adult forms.[3] This is probably because young children have considerably less neuromotor control over their articulation than do adults (e.g., Kent, 1981; Locke, 1980; MacNeilage, 1980; Netsell, 1981; B. L. Smith, 1988). Some of the simplifications exhibited by children's word forms can be described in terms of a change in one or more phonemes of the adult form. I discuss five of these: substitution, deletion, cluster reduction, metathesis, and assimilation. (More thorough discussions of these simplifications and others can be found in Ingram, 1974; Menn, 1978; and N. V. Smith, 1973).

(2) a. *fish* → *fis*   substitution
   b. *fish* → *ish*   deletion
   c. *sky*   → *sy*   cluster reduction
   d. *snow* → *nos*   metathesis
   e. *dog*   → *dod*   assimilation
   f. *duck* → *guck*   assimilation

In SUBSTITUTION, the child produces a different segment than one in the adult form. In (2a), the child has produced an [s] where an /š/ exists in the adult form. There is typically featural overlap between the substituted sound and the segment it replaces; in this example, /s/ and /š/ are both voiceless fricatives differing only in the place of articulation from palatal in *fish* to alveolar in *fis*. In DELETION, the child fails to produce a segment that is in the adult form, as in (2b). In CLUSTER REDUCTION, the child reduces the number of segments in a consonant cluster relative to the adult form, often by deleting of one of the consonants, as in (2c). In METATHESIS, the child produces the segments that occur in the adult form, but in a different order, as in (2d). In ASSIMILATION, the child replaces a phoneme or feature from one part of a word with a phoneme or feature from another part, as in (2e) and (2f). In (2e), the word-final /g/ is replaced by word-initial /d/, while in (2f), the alveolar place of articulation of /d/ is replaced by the velar place of articulation from the word-final /g/ (the voicing feature from /d/ is retained, resulting in /g/ instead of /k/). Note that assimilation can either be perseveratory, in which earlier phonemes or features replace later ones (2e), or anticipatory, in which phonemes or features from later in the word replace earlier ones (2f).

---

[3] Not all of children's deviations from adult word forms reflect simplifications. Some appear to be designed to preserve distinctions at the expense of simplicity. For an example, see Fey and Gandour (1982a).

Other relations between child and adult word forms are more complex and cannot be described in terms of mere simplifications. One of these is CHAIN SHIFTS. For example, a child might produce *truck* as *duck* but also produce *duck* as *guck* (Macken, 1980; Menn, 1978; N. V. Smith, 1973; Stemberger, 1992). Thus, the child assimilates the place of articulation of word-final /k/ to produce word-initial [g] in *duck guck* but produces an unassimilated form in connection with another lexical item *truck*. Children also appear to engage in AVOIDANCE of words containing particular segments that the child is presumably unable to accurately produce (Ferguson & Farwell, 1975; Schwartz & Leonard, 1982). For example, a child who is unable to produce word-initial /d/ might avoid producing words like *dog* and *duck,* even though s/he can comprehend these words (Schwartz, 1988). IDIOMS are child word forms that are not subject to the same sound changes as similar forms. For example, Hildegard Leopold correctly produced *pretty* at a time when she reduced other consonant clusters (Leopold, 1939, cited in Moskowitz, 1973a). Another example of an idiom can be seen in a child who continued to produce *took* as *gook,* even after other similar words no longer were subjected to such assimilation processes (Macken, 1980; N.V. Smith, 1973). If an idiom exhibits a relatively mature form and then takes on a less mature form that is more consistent with other similar words, it becomes a REGRESSION. For example, if the idiom *pretty* subsequently underwent cluster reduction (e.g., [pIti]), it would be classified as a regression.

2. Theories of Children's Consistent Deviations from an Adult Model

Theories of children's phonological productions can be classified into three major types. One class of theories holds that universal perceptual and/or articulatory constraints prevent the child from producing adult phonemic contrasts (Donegan & Stampe, 1979; Jakobson, 1941/1968; Stampe, 1969). A second class holds that children employ rules to change their perceived form into one that they can produce (Ingram, 1974; Kiparsky & Menn, 1977; Menn, 1978, 1980; N. V. Smith, 1973). A third, more recent class of connectionist approaches holds that child deviations from an adult model are natural accidents of the speech production system (Gerken, in press; Leonard, 1992; Menn & Matthei, 1992; Stemberger, 1992). In the remainder of this section, I outline these three types of theories and discuss how they handle relations between adult and child word forms.

The first class of theories is represented by Jakobson (1941/1968) and Stampe (1969; Donegan & Stampe, 1979). Jakobson, a linguist, proposed the earliest modern account of children's systematic deviations from adult word forms and in doing so brought child phonology into the purview of linguistic theory (see Menn, 1980, for discussion). He characterized children's task as learning to produce the phonemic contrasts relevant to their language. On Jakobson's view, a child who produces *fis* for *fish* has not yet mastered the contrast between palatal fricatives consonants (e.g., /š/) and alveolar fricatives (e.g., /s/). Jakobson proposed that the order in which contrasts were learned mirrored the frequency with which particular contrasts occurred in languages of the world. For example, all languages distinguish between consonants and vowels, and therefore, on Jakobson's account, children should acquire this contrast first. In contrast, few languages distinguish oral and nasal vowels (e.g., French *beau* vs. *bon,* respectively), and this is consistent with the observation that children who are learning such languages acquire this contrast relatively late. A somewhat different account of the relation between child and adult word forms is offered by Stampe (1969; Donegan & Stampe, 1979). On this view, every child is born with the same set of phonological "processes," which are merely constraints on what is easy to perceive and to articulate. In each language, speakers "suppress" some of these natural processes (i.e., overcome some of the constraints) in order to allow for a range of phonological contrasts wider than allowed for under the original constraints. Children must therefore learn to suppress the same processes (i.e., overcome the same constraints) as the adults in their linguistic community.

Both Jakobson's and Stampe's theories provide an account of relations between child and adult forms based on substitutions of one segment for another. Within these frameworks, substitutions reflect cases in which the child has not learned to contrast a particular pair of phonetic features. However, these theories do not account so easily for other types of simplifications. For example, a production of *gog* for *dog* could be described as a substitution of velar /g/ for alveolar /d/, perhaps suggesting that the child has not yet acquired that contrast. However, this explanation misses the generalization across many of children's word forms that one segment in a word can influence other segments. Donegan and Stampe (1979, p. 136) attempt to account for anticipatory assimilation on the grounds that it results from the organization of the nervous system and is therefore universal. Although anticipatory assimilations are more common than perseveratory assimilations, the existence of the latter would seem problematic for the universal hypothesis. A more serious challenge to both Jakobson and Stampe is posed by chain shifts such as the *truck–duck–guck* example given above. In this example, the child produces a particular contrast (i.e., between /d/ and /g/), but does so in connection with a word for which adults make a different contrast. Similar issues arise with regard to metatheses, idioms, and regressions. In a metathesis, the child makes relevant contrasts, but not in the correct word positions. Idioms and regressions are cases in which the child exhibits a contrast in one word or at one time but does not apply the contrast across words or across time. Avoidance presents another problem for theories focusing on contrasts. A child who avoids words containing a particular phoneme exhibits an implicit ability to contrast those sounds they can produce with those they cannot. In sum, theories that view children's deviations from an adult model as failures to preserve phonemic contrasts cannot account for the range of relations that exist between adult and child word forms.

In another class of theories, children's deviations arise from the application of phonological rules to the child's perceived representation of a word. On some accounts, the rules are universal and innate, and the simplifying nature of many of children's deviations arises from conspiracies among sets of rules (Kisseberth, 1970; N. V. Smith, 1973, 1978). On other accounts, individual sets of rules are created by each child in response to output constraints which limit the number of producible word forms (Ingram, 1974; Kiparsky & Menn, 1977; Macken & Ferguson, 1983; Menn, 1978, 1980, 1983). Output constraints are most easily illustrated with regard to children's phonological simplifications, such as those in (2a–f) (see Menn, 1978). Absolute position constraints allow certain consonants to be produced in only certain word positions. For example, children might be able to produce only voiced consonants in word-initial positions, and this can result in substitutions such as *toe* → *doe*. Absolute position constraints are also implicated in some cases of metathesis. For example, *snow* → *nos* might arise if the child has a position constraint such that nasal consonants must precede oral consonants in an utterance. Consonant harmony constraints prevent the child from producing in a single utterance two consonants that differ greatly in their featural composition. This can result in the child developing a rule in which the features from one consonant are assimilated to those of another, as in *duck* → *guck*. Alternatively, the child can delete one of the consonants, as in *fish* → *ish*. Children also appear to exhibit consonant sequence constraints, such that a sequence of two consonants cannot be produced; such a constraint might be responsible for consonant cluster reduction.

On the view that children's early productions reflect output constraints, children can either use rules to change the perceived form of a word into one they can produce (as in simplifications), or they can avoid difficult words altogether (for a discussion of individual differences in the use of avoidance versus simplification strategies, see Section IV). Thus, unlike the theories outlined earlier, rule-based theories incorporating output constraints can account for avoidance patterns. Rule-based theories can also account for chain shifts, which are thought to reflect the ordered application of rules (Ingram, 1974; Menn, 1978; but see Macken, 1980, for an alternative account). Although idioms and regressions are not automatically explained by rule-based accounts, Menn (1978, 1983) has attempted to deal with these apparent exceptions to rule application by proposing that children have separate perception and production lexicons that are linked via a common semantic representation (also see Dinnsen & Elbert, 1984; Ferguson, Peitzer, & Weeks, 1973; Ingram, 1974; Spencer, 1986; Straight, 1980). On the two-lexicon hypothesis, the child applies phonological rules once to the perceived form of words and stores the result in the output lexicon. Although the output lexicon is occasionally updated to make it consistent with the current rule system, this process takes time. Thus, idioms represent cases in which a word retains its old form until it is subjected to new rules during the updating process, which can result in regressions. In sum, the rule-based approach to children's early productions in conjunction with the two-lexicon hypothesis is able to account for the range of relations between child and adult word forms outlined in Section II,D,1.

However, rule-based approaches exhibit several unsatisfying characteristics; two of these are related specifically to the two-lexicon hypothesis. First, children often engage in long periods of alternation between two or more forms for a single adult word (e.g., Leonard, 1992; Menn & Matthei, 1992; Priestly, 1977). What is the nature of this variability if production forms are stored in a separate output lexicon? Another problem concerns observations that some children consistently produce two-word utterances in which the word-initial consonants influence each other (Donahue, 1986; Macken, 1979; Matthei, 1989; Scollon, 1976; Stemberger, 1988). For example, Donahue (1986) noted that her child chose word combinations in which word-initial consonants shared their place of articulation (e.g., *big bird,* mommy's baby). She also noted that as assimilation of velar place of articulation became frequent in single words (e.g., *doggy* → *goggy*), her child applied the same process to multiword utterances (e.g., *two duckies* → *ku guckies*). Thus, it appears that the same output constraints that apply to single words also apply to multiword utterances. On the two-lexicon hypothesis, the child creates rules to handle output constraints, applies these rules to individual words, and stores the results in an output lexicon. Presumably, phrases are created by combining entries from the output lexicon. However, phrase-based errors such as those observed by Donahue suggest that output constraints operate after words from the lexicon have been combined. A more general problem with rule-based accounts is that children's consistent deviations share many properties with their one-time-only slips of the tonuge and with adult slips of the tongue (Gerken, in press; Jaeger, 1992; Locke, 1980; Stemberger, 1989; Vihman, 1981; see Section II,D,3). Slips of the tongue probably do not reflect the speaker's temporary use of rules to change the intended form into one that is easier to produce; rather, they reflect processes inherent to speech planning and production. Therefore, it might be possible to account for both consistent deviations and slips without reference to rules (Gerken, in press; Stemberger, 1992).

Recently, several connectionist models have been developed to account for adult production errors or slips of the tongue (e.g., Dell, 1986; MacKay, 1987; Stemberger, 1985), and these models are currently being explored by child phonologists (Leonard, 1992; Menn & Matthei, 1992; Stemberger, 1992). Because connectionist models are probabalistic in nature, they can easily account for the variability in children's productions. They also have the potential to account for systematicity in deviations across words, because activation spreads across the lexicon, causing phonologically similar items to behave similarly. Finally, connectionist models have the potential to deal with the observation that some phonemic contrasts appear to be inherently easier for most children; this can result if initial activation states on some phoneme and feature nodes are set higher than on others. At this time, no one has yet developed a connectionist model of children's deviations, and therefore this endeavor must be viewed with caution. However, connectionist approaches to children's early productions will clearly influence how we think about phonological development in the coming years.

3. Children's Slips of the Tongue

Children begin to make sound-based slips of the tongue very early in their speaking careers. Jaeger (1992) observed the earliest slip in her corpus when one of her children was 16 months old. Examples of three child slips appear in (3a–c). These slips exhibit many of the properties of adult slips; I discuss these in detail below. However, the most important aspect to note about child sound-based slips is that the units involved are segments. The existence of child slips such as those in (3a–c) strongly suggests that young children have access to a production representation of words that is based on phonological segments or sequences of articulatory gestures (a possibility that has yet to be explored). The fact that children show evidence of such a detailed production representation at a time when their word perception abilities have been described as relatively holistic is consistent with the view that perception and production representations develop separately.

(3) a. *dissess the dog* (intended: *kisses the dog*)
    b. *brushin' his teesh* (intended: *teeth*)
    c. *Hi, Fritty Pace* (intended: *pretty face*)

Children's slips share several characteristics with their consistent deviations (discussed in Section II,D,1) and adult slips (Gerken, in press; Jaeger, 1992; Stemberger, 1989). All three can be categorized as either noncontextual errors, in which the intruding segment does not come from the utterance, or contextual errors, in which the intruding segment originates in the utterance. An example of a noncontextual consistent deviation is substitution (2a), and an example of a contextual deviation is assimilation (2e–f). Contextual deviations and slips can be further categorized as anticipations (3a), perseverations (3b), or exchanges (3c). In child deviations, child slips, and adult slips, the involved segments tend to share one or (usually) more phonetic features (Fromkin, 1971; Jaeger, 1992; Locke, 1980, 1983; MacKay, 1970; Nooteboom, 1967; Stemberger, 1989; Wijnen, 1990), typically manner and/or voicing (Jaeger, 1992; Locke, 1983; Stemberger, 1989; Van den Broecke & Goldstein, 1980). Children's between-word assimilations, children's slips, and adults' slips tend to involve word-initial consonants (Dell, 1986; Donahue, 1986; Fromkin, 1971; Gerken, in press; Jaeger, 1992; Matthei, 1989; Nooteboom, 1969; Stemberger, 1989; Wijnen, 1990). Child deviations and adult slips result in more anticipations than either perseverations or exchanges (Donahue, 1986; Locke, 1980, 1983; Matthei, 1989; Nooteboom, 1969; Vihman, 1978). This pattern also appears in three out of four corpora of slips made by children under 30 months (Gerken, in press; Jaeger, 1992; Wijnen, 1990; but see Stemberger, 1989). These similarities among children's deviations, slips, and adult slips suggest that a common mechanism is responsible for all three (Gerken, in press; Stemberger, 1992; also see Locke, 1980). There are also potential differences between children's deviations and slips, on the one hand, and adult slips on the other. For example, adults, but not children, make more frequent slips that result in a real word than a nonword (lexical bias effect; Baars, Motley, & MacKay, 1975; Dell & Reich, 1980; Stemberger, 1989). Another difference is that adult slips more frequently involve segments from words sharing phonemes than not sharing phonemes (repeated phoneme effect; Dell, 1984; Stemberger, 1989). This effect has not been discovered in either child deviations or slips, despite the fact that Stemberger (1989) explicitly searched for it in the latter. Such differences potentially provide clues about the development of speech planning and production and suggest directions for future research.

E. Summary of the Development of Segmental Phonology

As the reader can see from the size of each of the preceding sections, the study of segmental phonology in infants and young children is somewhat uneven. In infants, techniques for studying perception are much better established than those for studying production. In contrast, techniques for studying phoneme perception in very young children are extremely limited, while production data abound. Hopefully, the coming years will allow us to fill in some of the gaps and thereby provide a more complete picture of how children come to perceive and produce the relevant speech sounds of their language. But, despite our current uneven state of knowledge, we have learned a great deal in the past 25 years. First, we know that infants are born with astonishing abilities to perceive contrasts among speech sounds. Second, we know that some time during the second half of their first year, infants begin to focus specifically on the sounds of their language community. This is demonstrated by the fact that, during this period, the ability to make nonnative contrasts drops out, infants start to prefer their native language over a foreign language, and babbling begins to take on the characteristics of the speech community. We also know that young children have some difficulty discriminating minimal word pairs, especially when the words are not well known to them. The word familiarity effect probably indicates that many studies using relatively unfamiliar items have underestimated children's word perception abilities. However, further research is needed to determine the extent of children's word discrimination abilities and whether these abilities depend on lexical density and/or on whether the child can access production representations of the words in question. Finally, we currently have a great deal of data on children's early word productions and on the relation between child and adult word forms.

Future research on the acquisition of segmental phonology will continue to address at least two important questions. First, what is the nature of infants' and children's representation of speech? Is it based on individual segments? Or, is it based on more holistic stimulus properties, and if so, what are these? This question is part of a more general question: Can innate perception and production abilities interact with the linguistic environment in such a way as to result in new forms of mental representation? Or are adult forms of phonological representation nonderivable and therefore innately given to the child? The other important theoretical question that will guide future research concerns the relation of systematicity and variability in children's productions and the relation between early consistent deviations and later slips of the tongue. Perhaps connectionist models offer a framework for viewing both of these relations. Or perhaps probabalistic systems, such as connectionism, must be combined with active rule or strategy creation in order to adequately account for the range of child production data (see Macken, 1987, for a discussion of the need for both deterministic and probabilistic representations). In any case, the future promises exciting gains in our understanding of the development of segmental phonology.

III. Suprasegmental Phonology

Suprasegmental phonology is the study of sound properties of languages that apply to units larger than a single segment (e.g., syllables). Suprasegmental processes include word stress patterns, sentence level stress, pausing, and intonation. Studies of the development of suprasegmental phonology typically differ in their focus from studies of segmental phonology. As we saw in Section II, the latter have focused on how learners might acquire the adult phonological system by examining how infants and children come to perceive and produce the phonemic contrasts of their language. Although some developmental studies of suprasegmental phonology have considered how children might acquire adult rules for word stress (e.g., Allen, 1983; Dresher & Kay, 1990; Hochberg, 1988), most have focused on how learners might use the suprasegmental structure of their language to cue the locations of syntactically relevant units in the speech stream, including words, phrases, and clauses (Gleitman et al., 1988; Gleitman & Wanner, 1982; Hirsh-Pasek et al., 1987; Jusczyk et al., 1992; Kemler Nelson et al., 1989; Morgan, 1986; Morgan, Meier, & Newport, 1987; Morgan & Newport,

1981; Peters, 1983, 1985). It is primarily the latter aspect of suprasegmental phonology that I examine in Section III. Section III,A examines the nature of suprasegmental information in child-directed speech.[4] Section III,B examines the learner's perceptual sensitivity to these cues. Section III,C examines the suprasegmental properties of babbling and early single and multiword productions. And Section III,D provides a summary of our current understanding of the role of suprasegmental phonology in syntax acquisition and suggests future research directions.

A. Suprasegmental Characteristics of Input to Infants and Children

The world's languages exhibit canonical patterns of strong and weak syllables in a word. For example, most Turkish words end in a strongly stressed syllable (e.g., Poser, 1984), while the vast majority of English words begin with a strongly stressed syllable (Cutler & Carter, 1987). Gleitman and Wanner (1982) have suggested that stressed syllables are more perceptually salient than others and that young children initially break into the speech stream by identifying meaningful units with these syllables. Data on input to infants and children suggest that stress and rhythmic characteristics of child-directed speech are exaggerated in comparison with adult-directed speech. Moerk (1972) noted that most, if not all, cultures have rhythmically regular songs, rhymes, games, and language routines that are directed at language-learning children. These might serve to draw children's attention to word stress patterns typical of the language. Garnica (1977) found that mothers of 2-year-olds speak to their children with heavy stress on both the verb and the object noun in short imperatives, whereas they emphasize only the object noun in adult-directed speech. Similarly, Fernald and Mazzie (1991) demonstrated that adults use exaggerated stress to highlight new or important words when speaking to young children.

Languages also exhibit suprasegmental cues to phrases and clauses. It has long been noted that suprasegmental processes such as pausing, large changes in fundamental frequency, and vowel lengthening all tend to coincide with syntactic boundaries (e.g., W. Cooper, 1975; W. Cooper & Paccia-Cooper, 1980; Crystal, 1969; Gee & Grosjean, 1983; Klatt, 1975; Lehiste, 1970; Martin, 1970; Streeter, 1978; but see below). Suprasegmental processes tend to be especially reliable cues to syntax in the slow, careful speech that is characteristic of parents' speech to children (W. Cooper & Paccia-Cooper, 1980; Ferguson, 1964, Morgan, 1986; Newport, Gleitman, & Gleitman, 1977; Sachs, Brown, & Salerno, 1976). And like stress and rhythmic information, supresegmental cues to phrases and clauses are exaggerated in speech to infants and children in comparison with adult-directed speech (e.g., Ferguson, 1964; Fernald & Simon, 1984; Fernald et al., 1989; Garnica, 1977; Morgan, 1986). Across several languages, researchers have observed that child-directed speech exhibits a higher average pitch and wider pitch range than adult-directed speech (Blount & Padgug, 1976; Ferguson, 1964; Kelkar, 1964; Remick, 1976; Ruke-Dravina, 1976; Sachs et al., 1976). These observations have been confirmed by instrumental

---

[4] I use the term CHILD-DIRECTED SPEECH to refer to all speech with exaggerated suprasegmental characteristics. However, the reader should note that subtle differences in these characteristics might be employed for learners of different ages (e.g., Stern et al., 1983).

measures of fundamental frequency (Fernald, 1984; Fernald & Simon, 1984; Fernald et al., 1989; Garnica, 1973, 1977; Grieser & Kuhl, 1988; Menn & Boyce, 1982; M. Papousek, Papousek, & Symmes, 1994; M. Papousek, Papousek, & Haekel, 1987; Shute & Whedall, 1989; Stern, Spieker, Barnett, & MacKain, 1983; Warren-Leubecker & Bohannon, 1984). In addition, Broen (1972) and Bernstein-Ratner (1986) have shown that child-directed speech contains longer pauses and exaggerated segment lengthening at syntactic boundaries compared with adult-directed speech.

It appears that most, if not all, cultures exhibit exaggerated suprasegmental characteristics in child-directed speech (but see Heath, 1983; Ratner & Pye, 1984; Schieffelin, 1979; also see Fernald et al., 1989). Why do speakers of many languages across many cultures produce similar suprasegmental charcteristics in their speech to infants and young children? One possibility is that speakers consciously use exaggerated suprasegmental cues to teach language to young learners. This notion is challenged by the observation that people tend to speak to their pets with the same short, repetitive utterances exhibited by child-directed speech (Hirsh-Pasek & Treiman, 1982). Another possibility is that high pitch and wide pitch excursions are used to get and hold the attention of infants and young children (e.g., Garnica, 1977; Sachs, 1977; see Section III,B). A third possibility is that speakers use exaggerated suprasegmental processes to impart positive emotions to infants and children (Lewis, 1936; H. Papousek & Papousek, 1981; Stern, 1985). Yet another possibility is that speakers do not consciously use exaggerated suprasegmentals for any particular function. Rather, this form of speech might be a part of our biological makeup that is triggered when addressing dependent organisms (Sachs, 1977), or it might be a learned aspect of particular cultures (Ferguson, 1964). It is also possible that some combination of these explanations is correct. Clearly, one important goal for future research is to determine the universality of the child-directed register and to also determine how it interacts with culture-specific beliefs about language development (e.g., Fernald et al., 1989).

Regardless of the reason that speakers produce special suprasegmental characteristics in child-directed speech, it is important to note that these characteristics are ultimately governed by the grammar. That is, a speaker might employ high pitch and wide pitch excursions to hold the infant's attention, but these changes in fundamental frequency are expressed as exaggerations of normal prosody and therefore tend to occur at syntactic boundaries. Thus, suprasegmental phonology represents a domain in which purely linguistic processes might interface with attentional and affective processes, with the possible result that language acquisition is made easier for the learner. Because suprasegmental processes are governed by the grammar, we also need to consider the place of suprasegmental phonology within linguistic theory in general. As discussed above, suprasegmental processes such as pausing and segment lengthening tend to occur at syntactic boundaries, and early accounts held that suprasegmental phonology directly reflected syntactic structure (e.g., Chomsky & Halle, 1968). However, there are also cases in which suprasegmental processes do not appear to mirror syntactic structure. For example, in sentences like (4a), speakers tend to pause between the main syntactic constituents: the subject noun phrase and the verb phrase. However, in sentences containing pronoun subjects like (4b), speakers tend to pause between the verb and object noun phrase (Gee & Grosjean, 1983; see also Section III,C). Although the latter are also syntactic constituents, they are not the most syntactically crucial.

(4) a. *The man* (pause) *chased the dog.*
    b. *He chased* (pause) *the dog.*

In recent theories, such mismatches between syntax and phonology have been used to support the existence of an intervening grammatical component: "prosodic phonology" (e.g., Gee & Grosjean, 1983; Hayes, 1989; Nespor & Vogel, 1982, 1986; Selkirk, 1981, 1984, 1986; also see chapters in Inkelas & Zec, 1990). On this view, syntactic structures influence the creation of hierarchically arranged prosodic structures, which are composed of prosodic categories such as clitic group, phonological phrase, and intonational phrase. And it is these prosodic structures that govern suprasegmental phonological processes. This new look at the phonology/syntax interface suggests that the exaggerated suprasegmental cues exhibited by child-directed speech might not directly provide information to infants and children about syntactic structure, but rather about prosodic structure. Indeed, several studies have shown that when prosodically defined units are different from syntactic units, children are better able to identify the prosodic untis (Ferreira & Morrison, in press; Gerken, 1992b; Read & Schreiber, 1982). Further research is needed to determine the extent of phonology/syntax mismatches in child-directed speech and how young children might derive syntactic structure from prosodic structure (see Gerken, 1992b, for further discussion).

B. Infants' and Children's Perception of Suprasegmental Information

A growing body of research indicates that young language learners are highly sensitive to suprasegmental information in the speech stream. Leopold (1939), in one of the earliest observations of the role of prosody in language acquisition, noted that his daughter was able to identify the association between the utterance *tick-tock* and a clock only if he produced it with a particular intonation contour (also see Fernald, 1989; Lewis, 1936). More recent studies have examined three main effects of prosody on infant speech perception. First, several studies have demonstrated that infants prefer to listen to child-directed speech over adult-directed speech (R. P. Cooper & Aslin, 1990; Fernald, 1985; Fernald & Kuhl, 1987; Mehler, Bertoncini, Barriere, & Jassik-Gerschenfeld, 1978; Werker & McLeod, 1989). Fernald (1985) demonstrated that this preference is not specifically for the speech of the infant's own mother, and Fernald and Kuhl (1987) demonstrated that the basis of the preference is the high pitch and wide pitch range exhibited by child-directed speech. A second line of research has demonstrated that infants are sensitive to the suprasegmental characteristics of their native language. Mehler and his colleagues demonstrated that newborns prefer speech in their mother's language over speech in a foreign language, even when both samples are low pass filtered to leave intact only suprasegmental cues (Mehler et al., 1988). American infants as young as 6 months are able to distinguish between English and Norwegian word lists that have been low pass filtered (Jusczyk, Friederici, Wessels, Svenkerud, & Jusczyk, 1993). American infants as young as 9 months prefer to listen to words with a strong–weak pattern rather than a weak–strong pattern (Jusczyk, Cutler, & Redanz, 1993).

Recall that strong–weak is the predominant stress pattern of English (e.g., Cutler, 1990; Cutler & Carter, 1987). A third line of research suggests that infants are sensitive to acoustic cues to syntactic boundaries. In a series of studies, infants were presented with spoken passages in which pauses were inserted into syntactic boundaries (as marked by other cues such as lengthening and falling intonation) or into nonboundary positions. Infants as young as 6 months attended longer when pauses coincided with clause boundaries (Hirsh-Pasek et al., 1987; Kemler Nelson et al., 1989), and infants as young as 9 months attended longer when pauses coincided with major phrase boundaries (Jusczyk et al., 1992).

Why do infants prefer child-directed speech? Are they able to use the exaggerated suprasegmental characteristics of this register to identify suprasegmental properties of the target language and syntactically relevant units? Or, do they simply prefer child-directed speech because it is more interesting or emotionally satisfying? Although the data addressing this question are scant, they suggest that child-directed speech is useful in the task of language learning. In the studies described above in which pauses were inserted at syntactic boundaries or in nonboundary positions, two types of speech samples were used: adult-directed and child-directed (Jusczyk et al., 1992; Kemler Nelson et al., 1989). The researchers found that, for both types of speech, infants listened longer when pauses coincided with syntactic boundaries. However, they also found that the boundary effect was heightened for child-directed speech. In a similar vein, Gerken and McIntosh (1993) have found that children who only produce one word at a time are better able to comprehend a target word in computer-synthesized sentences produced with high pitch and wide pitch excursions than in sentences produced with more subdued fundamental frequency characteristics.[5] Although the current body of data is suggestive, further research is needed to determine more specifically how language learners might benefit from child-directed speech, and whether this register is necessary for the normal acquisition of language.

C. Suprasegmental Properties of Early Productions

Studies of infants' and children's productions also confirm their sensitivity to suprasegmental information. De Boysson-Bardies and her colleagues (1984) have demonstrated that infants as young as 8 months exhibit in their babbling the canonical suprasegmental patterns of their native language. Other researchers have found that English and French infants produced different proportions of rising versus falling intonation contours, reflecting differences in the predominant intonation contours found in the target language (Whalen, Levitt, & Wang, 1991). Recall from Section II,D that Peters (1983) identified a subset of children who tend to produce prosodically defined linguistic units instead of individual words. Branigan (1979) has demonstrated that children before the age of 2 years

---

[5] It is interesting to note that exaggerated suprasegmental cues improved children's performance primarily for sentences with grammatically correct function morphemes (e.g., *Find the dog for me*), not for sentences with ungrammatical function morphemes (e.g., *Find was dog for me*). We are currently attempting to determine whether it is suprasegmental cues per se that caused this difference, or whether some other characteristic about the synthesized voices (e.g., vocal tract length) might aid children in detecting segmental characteristics of function morphemes.

impose falling intonation on their two-word utterances, even when the two words are separated by several hundred milliseconds. Other research suggests that children organize their intended utterances into prosodic structures that are similar to those proposed in recent linguistic theories of prosodic phonology (Gerken, 1992b). For example, children appear to group the subject noun phrase and the verb phrase in distinct phonological phrases when the subject is a proper or common noun, whereas they group the subject and verb into a single phonological phrase in sentences with pronoun subjects. As discussed in Section III,A, this arrangement of phonological phrases is consistent with current linguistic theory and with data on adult pausing (Gee & Grosjean, 1983; Nespor & Vogel, 1986).

Young children also appear to be sensitive to rhythmic properties of their language. Recall from Section II,D that Macken (1979) observed a child who treated words as similar based partially on the pattern of strong and weak syllables they contained. Elbers (1985) noted that her 2-year-old son's attempts to recall a new word frequently resulted in the production of words with the same number of syllables and stress pattern as the intended item. In children's productions of multisyllabic words, they are more likely to omit weak syllables than strong ones (e.g., Blasdell & Jensen, 1970; DuPreez, 1974; Ingram, 1974; N. V. Smith, 1973). Many researchers have taken children's weak syllable omissions to reflect perceptual biases (e.g., Chiat, 1979; Echols & Newport, 1992; Gleitman & Wanner, 1982; Klein, 1978). However, children omit weak syllables from some stress patterns more frequently than others, a fact that might be taken as evidence against the perceptual position (Gerken, 1992b; Wijnen, Krikhaar, & den Os, in press). For example, children more frequently omit weak syllables from word-initial than from word-final positions (Allen & Hawkins, 1980; Echols & Newport, 1992; Gerken, 1992b; Ingram, 1974; Klein, 1978; Vihman, 1980). This is illustrated by the fact that children are more likely to omit the weak syllable from *giRAFFE* than from *MONkey* (Ingram, 1974). Gerken (1991) has proposed that this pattern of weak syllable omissions reflects a metrical production template for a strong syllable followed by an optional weak syllable (also see Gerken, 1992b; Wijnen, Krikhaar, & den Os, in press). Children might form such a template in response to the canonical strong–weak stress pattern of English words (e.g., Cutler, 1990; Cutler & Carter, 1987). Thus, weak syllable omissions might reflect children's sensitivity to the stress pattern of their particular language rather than universal perceptual biases. Or perhaps certain metrical patterns are intrinsically easier to produce than others. These questions must be answered by future research.

Recent studies suggest that many characteristics of children's early multiword utterances that have previously been attributed to morphological or syntactic development can be explained in terms of children's sensitivity to the suprasegmental patterns of their language. For example, English-speaking children typically omit function morphemes, such as articles and verb inflections. Some researchers have suggested that these omissions reflect an early linguistic organization that is based on words with concrete referents (e.g., Bates, 1976; Bowerman, 1973; Schlesinger, 1971). Alternatively, it is possible that children's omissions reflect a perception or production bias for strong syllables. The latter view is supported by children learning Quiché Mayan, who preserve strongly stressed verb affixes to the exclusion of less strongly stressed verb stems (Pye, 1983). Similarly, Gerken (in press) has demonstrated that mean length of utterance (MLU; a measure of young children's morphological development) correlates highly with their weak omissions from multisyllabic words. This suggests that children's omissions of weakly stressed function morphemes is related to more general phonological production processes involved in weak syllable omission. Gerken (1987a, 1987b; Gerken, Landau, & Remez, 1990) has also demonstrated that children's omission of syllabic function morphemes, such as the article *the* and the verb inflection *-es,* can be explained in terms of the strong–weak metrical production template described above with regard to multisyllabic words. The metrical template also accounts well for English-speaking children's subjectless sentences, another phenomenon that had previously been given a syntactic explanation (Gerken, 1990a, 1990b, 1990c, 1991; Hyams, 1986; see also Bloom, this volume).

D. Summary of the Development of Suprasegmental Phonology

Studies on child-directed speech strongly suggest that this register contains rich and reliable suprasegmental cues to linguistic structure. Studies on infants' and children's sensitivity to the suprasegmental patterns of their language suggest that they can potentially use these cues in acquisition. Several areas for future study remain. First, we need to determine the universality of child-directed speech. If some form of this register is universal, then it might be part of the speaker's biological makeup, or it might be a response to universal attentional or emotional characteristics of infants and children. A related question concerns the importance of child-directed speech for language learning. If the register is universal, then it might prove necessary for normal language acquisition. Alternatively, if the register is not universal, we need to compare the course of language acquisition in those cultures where it is employed and where it is not. A third promising research domain concerns the relation between suprasegmental phonology and syntax in language acquisition. Current theories of prosodic phonology hold that suprasegmental processes are not governed directly by syntax, but rather reflect prosodic structures. A few studies with young children suggest that they are sensitive to these structures (Ferreira & Morrison, in press; Gerken, 1992b; Read & Schreiber, 1982). Future research must determine whether infants and children ever represent prosodic structures to the exclusion of syntactic structures and how prosodic structures might be used to derive syntactic structures (see Gerken, 1992b, for further discussion).

IV. Individual Differences in the Acquisition of Phonology

The majority of research presented in the previous sections is directed at finding consistent patterns of phonological perception or production across learners. The goal of finding universal language acquisition patterns across children and across languages partially reflects the view that this process is innately determined (e.g., Chomsky, 1965, 1981). However, there is also a growing interest in variability among children, and several researchers are beginning to focus on individual differences in language acquisition (e.g., Bretherton, McNew, Snyder, & Bates, 1983; Ferguson, 1979; Nelson, 1973; Peters, 1977, 1983; Peters & Menn, 1991; Vihman, 1986, 1993; Vihman & Greenlee, 1987). Initially, the existence of variability among children was taken to suggest that language development does not represent the unfolding of a biological program, as previously proposed (e.g., Lenneberg, 1967), but rather that children actively discover the structure of their language (e.g., Kiparsky & Menn, 1977; Macken & Ferguson, 1983). However, it must be noted that the study of individual differences does not necessarily represent a wholesale rejection of nativist approaches to language acquisition. Rather, variation in language learning style can provide us with detailed information about the range of innate abilities and about the processes by which innate and experiential factors interact to result in normal development. Studies of individual differences can also help us to understand the processes behind abnormal patterns of language acquisition (e.g., see Leonard, 1992).

Researchers have noted at least two dimensions along which children vary in their phonological acquisition patterns. One dimension is whether the child's earliest productions are segmentally detailed or whether they are better described as maintaining the suprasegmental pattern of the ambient language at the expense of segmental accuracy (e.g., Bretherton et al., 1983; Menn, 1978; Peters, 1977, 1983; also see Nelson, 1973). Another, possibly related, dimension along which children differ is whether they avoid words that they cannot accurately produce, resulting in relatively accurate renditions of the words they do produce, or whether they attempt many words, resulting in substantial deviations from the adult form (e.g., Ferguson, 1979; Leopold, 1947; Macken, 1978). Several explanations have been offered for the existence of individual differences in early phonological development. One is that variability in individual children's perception and production systems leads to differences in the aspects of language that they find most salient or easiest to produce (e.g., Studdert-Kennedy, 1986). Another potential source of variability stems from differences in personality. For example, children who avoid words that they cannot accurately produce might be more conservative than children who do not use avoidance strategies (e.g., Leopold, 1947; Macken, 1979; see Zelnicker & Jeffrey, 1976, for a potentially related difference in cognitive style). A third source of variability is the chance discovery of certain production routines and perceptual contrasts in infancy (e.g., Vihman et al., 1985). For example, if an infant accidently stumbles across liquids during babbling, then s/he might produce a higher proportion of liquids than other children in both babbling and early words (Vihman et al., 1985). Finally, individual differences in phonological acquisition patterns might reflect differences in the types of input children receive. Although at least two studies have failed to find input effects (Leonard, Newhoff, & Mesalam, 1980; Vihman, 1993), it is too early to rule out such influences on individual differences.

Do individual differences in early phonological development have consequences for later development? Several studies have found similar production patterns in babbling and early words, suggesting some degree of continuity (Stoel-Gammon & Cooper, 1984; Vihman, 1986; Vihman & Greenlee, 1987; Vihman et al., 1985). However, the extremity of differences among children appears to subside over development, suggesting that the influence of the target language has a powerful normalizing effect (de Boysson-Bardies & Vihman, 1991; Vihman, 1986, 1993). Therefore, it is not surprising that one study that looked for continuity in acquisition patterns between the ages of 1 and 3 years discovered somewhat equivocal results (Vihman, 1986; Vihman & Greenlee, 1987). A further difficulty with comparing individual children's early patterns of language development with their later patterns is that particular language learning styles might appear in different guises over development. For example, a child who avoids certain words at age 18 months might show a form of morphological or syntactic conservatism at a later age (see Peters & Menn, 1991). Thus, it is difficult to know where to look for continuity. Nonetheless, the longitudinal study of individual differences in language learning promises to influence our understanding of phonological development, and perhaps language development in general.

V. Conclusion

In this chapter, I have reviewed some of the main areas of research in child phonology. This research addresses at least three important theoretical issues. The first is the relation between innate and experiential factors in language acquisition. Because we can begin to examine phonological development from birth, child phonology provides the most complete model currently available for understanding infants' initial capacities and how these change with exposure to the target language. One focus for future research is when and how children develop a phoneme-based representation of language and the relative importance of word recognition and production in this development. The second theoretical issue addressed by research in child phonology concerns variation in phonological forms found within a single child and across children. Psychological theories have long struggled with the problem of variability versus consistency in human behavior, and child phonology provides an excellent testing ground for solutions to this problem. The longitudinal study of individual differences also provides a microanalysis of how innate predispositions are affected by experience. The third theoretical issue concerns children's use of suprasegmental cues in the acquisition of syntax. Future research must determine whether exaggerated suprasegmental cues in adult input are necessary for the normal acquisition of language and whether it is possible for children to derive syntactic representations from prosodic ones. All three of these issues are important for our general understanding of human language. The fact that child phonology provides a rich empirical base for addressing them promises the field a central place in the future of psycholinguistics.

VI. Appendix: English Consonants and Vowels

(1) Phonetic symbols and feature analysis for English consonants

| | Place | | | | |
Manner	Labial	Interdental	Alveolar	Palatal	Velar
Stops					
Voiced	b *big*		d *die*		g *goat*
Voiceless	p *pig*		t *tie*		k *coat*

Manner	Place				
	Labial	Interdental	Alveolar	Palatal	Velar
Nasals	m *milk*		n *nose*		ɔ *sing*
Fricative					
Voiced	v *vine*	ð *this*	z *zip*	ž *azure*	
Voiceless	f *fine*	θ *thin*	s *sip*	š *sure*	
Affricates					
Voiced				ǰ *edge*	
Voiceless				č *etch*	
Liquids/	w *walk*		l *lash*		h *hide*
Semivowels			r *rash*		

(2) Phonetic symbols for English vowels

i	*beet*			u	*boot*
I	*bit*	ʌ	*but*	ʊ	*book*
e	*bait*			o	*boat*
ɛ	*bet*	ə	*about*	ɔ	*bought*
æ	*bat*	a	*box*		

ACKNOWLEDGMENTS

I thank Morton Gernsbacher, Ann Peters, and Marilyn Vihman for helpful comments and suggestions on a previous draft.

REFERENCES

Allen, G. (1983). Linguistic experience modifies lexical stress perception. *Journal of Child Language, 10*, 535–549.

Allen, G., & Hawkins, S. (1980). Phonological rhythm: Definition and development. In G. H. Yeni-Komshian, J. F. Kavanagh, & G. A. Ferguson (Eds.), *Child phonology* (Vol. 1, pp. 227–256). New York: Academic Press.

Aslin, R., & Pisoni, D. (1980). Some developmental processes in speech perception. In G. H. Yeni-Komshian, J. F. Kavanagh, & G. A. Ferguson (Eds.), *Child phonology* (Vol. 2, pp. 67–96). New York: Academic Press.

Aslin, R., Pisoni, D., & Jusczyk, P. (1983). Auditory development and speech perception in infancy. In M. Haith & J. Campos (Eds.), *Handbook of child psychology: Infant development* (pp. 573–687). New York: Wiley.

Atkinson, K. B., McWhinney, B., & Stoel, C. (1970). An experiment in the recognition of babbling. *Papers and Reports on Child Language Research, 1*, 71–76.

Baars, B. J., Motley, M. T., & MacKay, D. G. (1975). Output editing for lexical status from artificially elicited slips of the tongue. *Journal of Verbal Learning and Verbal Behavior, 14*, 382–391.

Barton, D. (1975). Statistical significance in phonemic perception experiments. *Journal of Child Language, 2*, 297–298.

Barton, D. (1976a). Phonemic discrimination and the knowledge of words in children under three years. *Papers and Reports on Child Language Development, 11*, 61–68.

Barton, D. (1976b). *The role of perception in the acquisition of phonology*. Doctoral dissertation, Indiana University Linguistics Club, London.

Barton, D. (1980). Phonemic perception in children. In G. H. Yeni-Komshian, J. F. Kavanagh, & G. A. Ferguson (Eds.), *Child phonology* (Vol. 2, pp. 97–116). New York: Academic Press.

Baru, A. V. (1975). Discrimination of synthesized vowels [a] and [i] with varying parameters (fundamental frequency, intensity, duration and number of formants) in dog. In G. Fant & M. A. A. Tatham (Eds.), *Auditory analysis and perception of speech* (pp. 91–101). New York: Academic Press.

Bates, E. (1976). *Language and context*. New York: Academic Press.

Berko, J., & Brown, R. (1960). Psycholinguistic research methods. In P. H. Mussen (Ed.), *Handbook of research methods in child development*. (pp. 517–557). New York: Wiley.

Bernstein-Ratner, N. (1986). Durational cues which mark clause boundaries in mother–child speech. *Journal of Phonetics, 14,* 303–309.

Best, C. T. (1984). Discovering messages in the medium: Speech perception and the prelinguistic infant. In H. E. Fitzgerald, B. M. Lester, & M. W. Yogman (Eds.), *Theory and research in behavioral pediatrics* (pp. 97–105). New York: Plenum.

Best, C. T. (1994). The emergence of native-language phonological influences in infants: A perceptual assimilation model. In H. C. Nusbaum & J. C. Goodman (Eds.), *The transition from speech sounds to spoken words* (pp. 167–224). Cambridge, MA: MIT Press.

Best, C. T., McRoberts, G. W., & Sithole, N. M. (1988). Examination of the perceptual reorganization for contrasts: Zulu click discrimination by English-speaking adults and infants. *Journal of Experimental Psychology: Human Perception and Performance, 14,* 245–360.

Blasdell, R., & Jensen, P. (1970). Stress and word position as determinants of imitation in first-language learners. *Journal of Speech and Hearing Research, 13,* 193–202.

Blount, B. G., & Padgug, E. J. (1976). Prosodic, paralinguistic, and interactional features in parent–child speech: English and Spanish. *Journal of Child Language, 4,* 67–86.

Blumstein, S. (1974). The use and theoretical implications of the dichotic technique for investigating distinctive features. *Brain and Language, 1,* 337–350.

Bowerman, M. (1973). *Early syntactic development: A cross-linguistic study with special reference to Finnish*. Cambridge: Cambridge University Press.

Braine, M. D. S. (1971). The acquisition of language by infant and child. In C. E. Reed (Ed.), *The learning of language*. New York: Appleton-Century-Crofts.

Braine, M. D. S. (1976). Review of *The acquisition of phonology* by N. V. Smith. *Language, 52,* 489–498.

Branigan, G. (1979). Some reasons why successive single word utterances are not. *Journal of Child Language, 6,* 411–421.

Bretherton, I., McNew, S., Snyder, L., & Bates, E. (1983). Individual differences at 20 months: Analytic and holistic strategies in language acquisition. *Journal of Child Language, 10,* 293–320.

Broen, P. (1972). The verbal environment of the language learning child. *ASHA Monograph, 17.*

Charles-Luce, J., & Luce, P. A. (1990). Similarity neighborhoods of words in young children's lexicons. *Journal of Child Language, 17,* 205–215.

Chiat, S. (1979). The role of the word in phonological development. *Linguistics, 17,* 591–610.

Chomsky, N. (1965). *Aspects of the theory of syntax*. Cambridge, MA: MIT Press.

Chomsky, N. (1981). *Lectures on government and binding*. Dordrecht: Foris.

Chomsky, N., & Halle, M. (1968). *The sound pattern of English*. New York: Harper & Row.

Cole, R. A. (1973). Listening for mispronunciations: A measure of what we hear during speech. *Perception & Psychophysics, 11,* 153–156.

Cooper, R. P., & Aslin, R. N. (1990). Preference for infant-directed speech in the first month after birth. *Child Development, 61,* 1584–1595.

Cooper, W. (1975). *Syntactic control of speech timing*. Unpublished doctoral dissertation, Massachusetts Institute of Technology, Cambridge.

Cooper, W., & Paccia-Cooper, J. (1980). *Syntax and speech*. Cambridge, MA: Harvard University Press.

Cruttenden, A. (1970). A phonetic study of babbling. *British Journal of Disorders of Communication, 5,* 110–117.

Crystal, D. (1969). *Prosodic systems and intonation in English*. London: Cambridge University Press.

Cutler, A. (1990). Exploiting prosodic probabilities in speech segmentation. In G. T. M. Altmann (Ed.), *Computational and psychological approaches to language processes* (pp. 105–120). Cambridge, MA: MIT Press.

Cutler, A., & Carter, D. M. (1987). The predominance of strong initial syllables in the English vocabulary. *Computer Speech and Language, 2,* 133–142.

Cutting, J. E., & Rosner, B. S. (1974). Categories and boundaries in speech and music. *Perception & Psychophysics, 16*, 564–570.

de Boysson-Bardies, B., Halle, P., Sagart, L., & Durand, C. (1989). A crosslinguistic investigation of vowel formants in babbling. *Journal of Child Language, 16*, 1–17.

de Boysson-Bardies, B., Sagard, L., & Bacri, N. (1981). Phonetic analysis of late babbling: A case study of a French child. *Journal of Child Language, 8*, 511–524.

de Boysson-Bardies, B., Sagart, L., & Durand, C. (1984). Discernable differences in the babbling of infants according to target language. *Journal of Child Language, 11*, 1–15.

de Boysson-Bardies, B., & Vihman, M. M. (1991). Adaptation to language: Evidence from babbling and first words in four languages. *Language, 67*, 297–319.

Dell, G. S. (1984). Representation of serial order in speech: Evidence from the repeated phoneme effect in speech errors. *Journal of Experimental Psychology: Learning, Memory, and Cognition, 10*, 222–233.

Dell, G. S. (1986). A spreading activation model of retrieval in sentence production. *Psychological Review, 93*, 283–321.

Dell, G. S., & Reich, P. A. (1980). Toward a unified theory of slips of the tongue. *LACUS Forum, 3*, 448–455.

Derwing, B. L., & Baker, W. J. (1979). Recent research on the acquisition of English morphology. In P. Fletcher & M. Garman (Eds.), *Studies in language acquisition* (pp. 209–223). Cambridge: Cambridge University Press.

Dinnsen, D. A., & Elbert, M. (1984). On the relationship between phonology and learning. In M. Elbert, D. A. Dinnsen, & G. Weismer (Eds.), *Phonological theory and the misarticulating child* Rockville, MD: American Speech-Language-Hearing Association.

Dinnsen, D. A., Elbert, M., & Wiesmer, G. (1980). Some typological properties of functional misarticuting systems. In W. O. Dressler (Ed.), *Phonologica 1980* (pp. 83–88). Innsbruck: Innsbrucker Beitrage Zur Sprachenwissenschaft.

Dodd, B. (1975). Children's understanding of their own phonological forms. *Quarterly Journal of Experimental Psychology, 27*, 165–172.

Donahue, M. (1986). Phonological constraints on the emergence of two word utterances. *Journal of Child Language, 13*, 209–218.

Donegan, P., & Stampe, D. (1979). The study of natural phonology. In D. A. Dinnsen (Ed.), *Current approaches to phonological theory* (pp. 126–173). Bloomington: Indiana University Press.

Dresher, E., & Kaye, D. (1990). A computational model for metrical phonology. *Cognition, 34*, 137–195.

Du Preez, P. (1974). Units of information in the acquisition of language. *Language and Speech, 17*, 369–376.

Echols, C. H., & Newport, E. L. (1992). The role of stress and position in determining first words. *Language Acquisition, 2*, 189–220.

Edwards, M. L. (1974). Perception and production in child phonology: The testing of four hypotheses. *Journal of Child Language, 1*, 205–219.

Eilers, R. E. (1980). Infant speech perception: History and mystery. In G. H. Yeni-Komshian, J. F. Kavanagh, & G. A. Ferguson (Eds.), *Child phonology* (Vol. 2, pp. 23–39). New York: Academic Press.

Eilers, R. E., & Minife, F. D. (1975). Fricative discrimination in early infancy. *Journal of Speech and Hearing Research, 18*, 158–167.

Eilers, R. E., & Oller, D. (1976). The role of speech discrimination in developmental sound substitutions. *Journal of Child Language, 3*, 319–330.

Eilers, R. E., Gavin, W., & Wilson, W. R. (1979). Linguistic experience and phonemic perception in infancy: A cross-linguistic study. *Child Development, 50*, 14–18.

Eilers, R. E., Wilson, W. R., & Moore, J. M. (1977). Developmental changes in speech discrimination in infants. *Journal of Speech and Hearing Research, 20*, 766–780.

Eilers, R. E., Wilson, W. R., & Moore, J. M. (1979). Speech discrimination in the language-innocent and the language-wise: A study in the perception of voice-onset time. *Journal of Child Language, 6*, 1–18.

Eimas, P. (1974). Auditory and linguistic processing of cues for place of articulation by infants. *Perception & Psychophysics, 16*, 513–521.

Eimas, P. (1975). Auditory and phonetic coding of the cues of speech: Discrimination of the [r–l] distinction by young infants. *Perception & Psychophyisics, 18*, 341–347.

Eimas, P. (1982). Speech perception: A view of the initial state and perceptual mechanisms. In J. Mehler, E. C. T. Walker, & M. Garrett (Eds.), *Perspectives on mental representation* (pp. 339–360). Hillsdale, NJ: Erlbaum.

Eimas, P., & Miller, J. D. (in press). A constraint on the discrimination of speech by infants. *Language and Speech*.

Eimas, P., Siqueland, E., Jusczyk, P., & Vigorrito, K. (1971). Speech perception in infants. *Science, 171,* 303–306.

Elbers, L. (1985). A tip-of-the-tongue experience at age two? *Journal of Child Language, 12,* 353–365.

Elbers, L., & Ton, J. (1985). Play pen monologues: The interplay of words and babbles in the first words period. *Journal of Child Language, 12,* 551–567.

Elbert, M., Dinnsen, D. A., & Weismer, G. (1984). Introduction. In M. Elbert, D. A. Dinnsen, & G. Weismer (Eds.), *Phonological theory and the misarticulating child.* Rockville, MD: American Speech–Language–Hearing Association.

Ferguson, C. A. (1964). Baby talk in six languages. *American Anthropologist, 66,* 103–114.

Ferguson, C. A. (1978). Learning to pronounce. In F. D. Minife & L. L. Lloyd (Eds.), *Communicative and cognitive abilities.* Baltimore, MD: University Park Press.

Ferguson, C. A. (1979). Phonology as an individual access system: some data from language acquisition. In C. J. Fillmore, D. Kempler, & W. S.-Y. Wang (Eds.), *Individual differences in language ability and languge behavior* (pp. 181–201). New York: Academic Press.

Ferguson, C. A., & Farwell, C. B. (1975). Words and sounds in early acquisition. *Language, 51,* 419–439.

Ferguson, C. A., Peitzer, D. B., & Weeks, T. E. (1973). Model-and-replica phonological grammar of a child's first words. *Lingua, 31,* 35–65.

Fernald, A. (1984). The perceptual and affective salience of mothers' speech to infants. In L. Feagans, C. Garvey, & R. Golinkoff (Eds.), *The origins and growth of communication* (pp. 5–29). Norwood, NJ: Ablex.

Fernald, A. (1985). Four-month-old infants prefer to listen to motherese. *Infant Behavior and Development, 8,* 181–195.

Fernald, A. (1989). Intonation and communicative intent in mothers' speech to infants: Is the melody the message? *Child Development, 60,* 1497–1510.

Fernald, A., & Kuhl, P. K. (1987). Acoustic determinants of infant preference for motherese speech. *Infant Behavior and Development, 10,* 279–293.

Fernald, A., & Mazzie, C. (1991). Prosody and focus in speech to infants and adults. *Developmental Psychology,* 209–221.

Fernald, A., & Simon, T. (1984). Expanded intonation contours in mother's speech to newborns. *Developmental Psychology, 20,* 104–114.

Fernald, A., Taeschner, T., Dunn, J., Papousek, M., de Boysson-Bardies, B., & Fukui, I. (1989). A cross-language study of prosodic modifications in mothers' and fathers' speech to preverbal infants. *Journal of Child Language, 16,* 477–501.

Ferreira, F., & Morrison, F. (in press). Children's knowledge of syntactic constituents: Effects of ages and schooling. *Developmental Psychology*.

Fey, M. E., & Gandour, J. (1982a). Rule discovery in phonological acquisition. *Journal of Child Language, 9,* 71–81.

Fey, M. E., & Gandour, J. (1982b). The pig dialogue: Phonological systems in transition. *Journal of Child Language, 9,* 517–519.

Fromkin, V. A. (1971). The nonanomalous nature of anomalous utterances. *Language, 47,* 27–52.

Garnica, O. (1971). The development of perception of phonemic differences in initial consonants by English-speaking children: A pilot study. *Papers and Reports on Child Language Development, 3,* 1–29.

Garnica, O. (1973). The development of phonemic perception. In T. E. Moore (Ed.), *Cognitive development and the acquisition of language* (pp. 214–222). New York: Academic Press.

Garnica, O. (1977). Some prosodic and paralinguistic features of speech to young children. In C. E. Snow & C. A. Ferguson (Eds.), *Talking to children* (pp. 63–88). Cambridge: Cambridge University Press.

Gee, J., & Grosjean, F. (1983). Performance structures: A psycholinguistic and linguistic appraisal. *Cognitive Psychology, 15,* 411–458.

Gerken, L. A. (1987a). *Function morphemes in young children's speech perception and production.* Unpublished doctoral dissertation, Columbia University, New York.

Gerken, L. A. (1987b). Telegraphic speaking does not imply telegraphic listening. *Papers and Reports on Child Language Development, 26,* 48–55.

Gerken, L. A. (1990a). Do adults and children have different feet? *Chicago Linguistic Society, 26,* 19–27.

Gerken, L. A. (1990b). A metrical account of subjectless sentences. *North East Linguistics Society, 20,* 121–134.

Gerken, L. A. (1990c). Performance constraints in early child language: The case of subjectless sentences. *Papers and Reports on Child Language Development, 29,* 54–61.

Gerken, L. A. (1991). The metrical basis for children's subjectless sentences. *Journal of Memory and Language, 30,* 431–451.

Gerken, L. A. (1992a). *Sentential processes in early child language: Evidence from the perception and production of function morphemes* (Cognitive Science Tech. Rep.). Buffalo, NY: SUNY.

Gerken, L. A. (1992b). *Young children's representation of prosodic phonology: Evidence from English-speakers' weak syllable omissions* (Cognitive Science Tech. Rep.). Buffalo, NY: SUNY.

Gerken, L. A. (in press). A slip of the tongue approach to language development. In J. Charles-Luce, P. Luce, & J. R. Sawusch (Eds.), *Spoken language: perception, production and development.* Norwood, NJ: Ablex.

Gerken, L. A., Landau, B., & Remez, R. E. (1990). Function morphemes in young children's speech perception and production. *Developmental Psychology, 27,* 204–216.

Gerken, L. A., & McIntosh, B. J. (1993). The interplay of function morphemes and prosody in early language. *Developmental Psychology, 29,* 448–457.

Gesell, A., & Amatruda, C. S. (1941). *Developmental diagnosis.* New York: Hoeber.

Gleitman, L., Gleitman, H., Landau, B., & Wanner, E. (1988). Where learning begins: Initial representations for language learning. In F. Newmeyer (Ed.), *The Cambridge linguistic survey, Vol. III, Language: Psychological and Biological Aspects* (pp. 150–193). New York: Cambridge University Press.

Gleitman, L., & Wanner, E. (1982). The state of the state of the art. In E. Wanner & L. Gleitman (Eds.), *Language acquisition: The state of the art* (pp. 3–48). Cambridge: Cambridge University Press.

Gordon, P. (1985). Level-ordering in lexical development. *Cognition, 21,* 73–93.

Gordon, P. (1989). Levels of affixation in the acquisition of English morphology. *Journal of Memory and Language, 28,* 519–530.

Graham, L. W., & House, A. S. (1971). Phonological oppositions in children: A perceptual study. *Journal of the Acoustical Society of America, 49,* 559–566.

Grieser, D. L., & Kuhl, P. K. (1988). Maternal speech to infants in tonal language: Support for universal prosodic features in motherese. *Developmental Psychology, 24,* 14–20.

Hayes, B. (1989). The prosodic hierarchy in meter. In P. Kiparsky & G. Youmans (Eds.), *Phonetics and phonology: Rhythm and meter.* San Diego, CA: Academic Press.

Heath, S. B. (1983). *Ways with words.* Cambridge: Cambridge University Press.

Hillenbrand, J. (1983). Perceptual organization of speech sounds by infants. *Journal of Speech and Hearing Research, 26,* 268–282.

Hirsh-Pasek, K., Kemler Nelson, D. G., Jusczyk, P. W., Wright Cassidy, K., & Druss, B. (1987). Clauses are perceptual units for prelinguistic infants. *Cognition, 26,* 269–286.

Hirsh-Pasek, K., & Treiman, R. (1982). Doggerel: Motherese in a new context. *Journal of Child Language, 9,* 229–237.

Hochberg, J. G. (1988). First steps in the acquisition of Spanish stress. *Journal of Child Language, 15,* 273–292.

Hyams, N. (1986). *Language acquisition and the theory of parameters.* Dordrecht: Reidel.

Ingram, D. (1974). Phonological rules in young children. *Journal of Child Language, 1,* 49–64.

Inkelas, S., & Zec, D. (1990). *The phonology–syntax connection.* Chicago: Chicago University Press.

Jaeger, J. (1992). Not by the chair of my hinny hin hin: Some general properties of speech errors in young children. *Journal of Child Language, 19,* 335–366.

Jakobson, R. (1968). *Kindersprache, Aphasie und allgemeine Lautgetze* (Child language, aphasia and phonological universals) (A. R. Keiler, Trans.). The Hague: Mouton. (Original work published 1941)

Jusczyk, P. W. (1977). Perception of syllable-final stop consonants by two-month-old infants. *Perception & Psychophysics, 21,* 450–454.

Jusczyk, P. W. (1982). Auditory versus phonetic coding of speech signals during infancy. In J. Mehler, E. C. T. Walker, & M. Garrett (Eds.), *Perspectives on mental representation* (pp. 361–387). Hillsdale, NJ: Erlbaum.

Jusczyk, P. W. (1985). On characterizing the development of speech perception. In J. Mehler & R. Fox (Eds.), *Neonate cognition: Beyond the blooming buzzing confusion* (pp. 199–229). Hillsdale, NJ: Earlbaum.

Jusczyk, P. W. (1986). Toward a model of the development of speech perception. In J. S. Perkell & D. H. Klatt (Eds.), *Invariance and variability in speech processes.* Hillsdale, NJ: Erlbaum.

Jusczyk, P. W. (1992). Developing phonological categories from the speech signal. In C. A. Ferguson, L. Menn, & C. Stoel-Gammon (Eds.), *Phonological development: Models, research, implications* (pp. 17–64). Parkton, MD: York Press.

Jusczyk, P. W., Cutler, A., & Redanz, L. (1993). Infants' sensitivity to predominant word stress patterns in English. *Child Development, 64*, 675–687.

Jusczyk, P. W., Hirsh-Pasek, K., Kemler Nelson, D., Kennedy, L., Woodward, A., & Piwoz, J. (1992). Perception of acoustic correlates of major phrasal units by young infants. *Cognitive Psychology, 29*, 252–293.

Jusczyk, P. W., & Thompson, E. (1978). Perception of a phonetic contrast in multisyllabic utterances by 2-month-old infants. *Perception & Psychophysics, 23*, 105–109.

Jusczyk, P. W., Friederici, A. D., Wessels, J., Svenkerud, V. Y., & Jusczyk, A. M. (1993). Infants' sensitivity to segmental and prosodic characteristics of words in their native language. *Journal of Memory & Language, 32*, 402–420.

Kelkar, A. (1964). Marathi baby talk. *Word, 20*, 40–54.

Kemler Nelson, D., Hirsh-Pasek, K., Jusczyk, P. W., & Wright Cassidy, K. (1989). How prosodic cues in motherese might assist language learning. *Journal of Child Language, 16*, 53–68.

Kent, R. D. (1981). Articulatory–acoustic perspectives on speech development. In R. E. Stark (Ed.), *Language behavior in infancy and early childhood* (pp. 127–136). New York: Elsevier.

Kent, R. D. (1984). *Keynote address.* Annual Child Phonology Conference, Purdue University, West Lafayette, IN.

Kiparsky, P., & Menn, L. (1977). On the acquisition of phonology. In J. MacNamara (Ed.), *Language learning and thought* (pp. 47–78). New York: Academic Press.

Kisseberth, C. W. (1970). The functional unity of phonological rules. *Linguistic Inquiry, 1*, 291–306.

Klatt, D. (1975). Vowel lengthening is syntactically determined in connected discourse. *Journal of Phonetics, 3*, 129–140.

Klein, H. B. (1978). *The relationship between perceptual strategies and production strategies in learning the phonology of early lexical items.* Unpublished doctoral dissertation, Columbia University, New York.

Kuhl, P. (1980). Perceptual constancy for speech sound categories in early infancy. In G. H. Yeni-Komshian, J. F. Kavanagh, & G. A. Ferguson (Eds.), *Child Phonology* (Vol. 2, pp. 41–66). New York: Academic Press.

Kuhl, P. (1985). Categorization of speech by infants. In J. Mehler & R. Fox (Eds.), *Neonate cognition: Beyond the blooming buzzing confusion* (pp. 231–262). Hillsdale, NJ: Erlbaum.

Kuhl, P. (1986). Reflections on infants' perception and representation of speech. In J. S. Perkell & D. H. Klatt (Eds.), *Invariance and variability in speech processes* (pp. 19–30). Hillsdale, NJ: Erlbaum.

Kuhl, P., & Miller, J. D. (1975). Speech perception in the chinchilla: Voiced–voiceless distinction in alveolar plosive consonants. *Science, 190*, 69–72.

Kuhl, P., & Miller, J. D. (1978). Speech perception in the chinchilla: Identification functions for synthetic VOT stimuli. *Journal of the Acoustical Society of America, 63*, 905–917.

Kuhl, P., & Padden, D. (1983). Enhanced discriminability at the phonetic boundaries for the place feature in macaques. *Journal of the Acoustical Society of America, 73*, 1003–1010.

Landahl, K. L. (1982). *The onset of structured discourse: A developmental study of the acquisition of language.* Unpublished doctoral dissertation, Brown University, Providence, RI.

Lasky, R. E., Syrdal-Lasky, A., & Klein, R. E. (1975). VOT discriminations by four- to six-and-a-half month old infants from Spanish environments. *Journal of Experimental Child Psychology, 20*, 213–255.

Lehiste, I. (1970). *Suprasegmentals.* Cambridge, MA: MIT Press.

Lenneberg, E. H. (1967). *Biological foundations of language.* New York: Wiley.

Leonard, L. B. (1992). Children with phonological disorders. In C. A. Ferguson, L. Menn, &

C. Stoel-Gammon (Eds.), *Phonological development: Models, research, implications* (pp. 495–507). Parkton, MD: York Press.

Leonard, L. B., Newhoff, M., & Mesalam, L. (1980). Individual differences in early child phonology. *Applied Psycholinguistics, 1,* 7–30.

Leopold, W. F. (1939). *Speech development in a bilingual child: A linguist's record: Vol. 1. Vocabulary growth in the first two years.* Evanston, IL: Northwestern University Press.

Leopold, W. F. (1947). *Speech development in a bilingual child: A linguist's record: Vol. 2. Sound learning in the first two years.* Evanston, IL: Northwestern University Press.

Leopold, W. F. (1953). Patterning in children's language. *Language Learning, 5,* 1–14.

Lewis, M. M. (1936). *Infant speech: A study of the beginnings of language.* New York: Harcourt Brace.

Liberman, A. M., Cooper, F. S., Shankweiler, D. P., & Studdert-Kennedy, M. (1967). Perception of the speech code. *Psychological Review, 74,* 431–461.

Lindblom, B. (1986). On the origin and purpose of discreteness and invariance in sound patterns. In J. S. Perkell & D. H. Klatt (Eds.), *Invariance and variability in speech processes* (pp. 493–510). Hillsdale, NJ: Erlbaum.

Lindblom, B. (1992). Phonological units as adaptive emergents of development. In C. A. Ferguson, L. Menn, & C. Stoel-Gammon (Eds.), *Phonological development: Models, research, implications* (pp. 131–163). Parkton, MD: York Press.

Lindblom, B., MacNeilage, P. F., & Studdert-Kennedy, M. G. (1983). Self organizing processes and the explanation of phonological universals. In B. Butterworth, B. Comrie, & O. Dahl (Eds.), *Explanation of linguistic universals* (pp. 181–203). The Hague: Mouton.

Lisker, L., & Abramson, K. (1964). A cross-language study of voicing in initial stops: Acoustic measurements. *Word, 20,* 384–422.

Locke, J. L. (1971). Phoneme perception in two- and three-year-old children. *Perceptual and Motor Skills, 32,* 215–217.

Locke, J. L. (1980). The prediction of child speech errors: Implications for a theory of acquisition. In G. Yeni-Komshian, J. Kavanaugh, & C. Ferguson (Eds.), *Child phonology* (Vol. 1, pp. 193–210). New York: Academic Press.

Locke, J. L. (1983). *Phonological acquisition and change.* New York: Academic Press.

Locke, J. L. (1988). The sound shape of early lexical representations. In M. D. Smith & J. L. Locke (Eds.), *The emergent lexicon: The child's development of a linguistic vocabulary* (pp. 3–22). San Diego, CA: Academic Press.

Locke, J. L., & Kutze, K. J. (1975). Memory for speech and speech for memory. *Journal of Speech and Hearing Research, 18,* 176–191.

MacKain, C. (1982). Assessing the role of experience in infant speech discrimination. *Journal of Child Language, 9,* 527–542.

MacKay, D. G. (1970). Spoonerisms: The structure of errors in the serial order of speech. *Neuropsychologia, 8,* 323–350.

MacKay, D. G. (1987). Constraints on theories of sequencing and timing in language perception and production. In A. Allport, D. MacKay, W. Prinz, & E. Scheerer (Eds.), *Language perception and production* (pp. 407–429). London: Academic Press.

Macken, M. A. (1978). Permitted complexity in phonological development: One child's acquisition of Spanish consonants. *Lingua, 44,* 219–253.

Macken, M. A. (1979). Developmental reorganization in phonology: A hierarchy of basic units of acquisition. *Lingua, 49,* 11–49.

Macken, M. A. (1980). The child's lexical representation: The "puzzle–puddle–pickle" evidence. *Journal of Linguistics, 16,* 1–19.

Macken, M. A. (1987). Learning and constraints on phonological acquisition. In B. MacWhinney (Ed.), *Mechanisms of language acquisition* (pp. 367–397). Hillsdale, NJ: Erlbaum.

Macken, M. A., & Barton, D. (1980). A longitudinal study of the acquisition of stop consonants. *Journal of Child Language, 7,* 41–74.

Macken, M. A., & Ferguson, C. A. (1983). Cognitive aspects of phonological development: Model, evidence, and issues. In K. E. Nelson (Ed.), *Children's language* (Vol. 4, pp. 255–282). Hillsdale: NJ: Erlbaum.

MacNeilage, D. (1980). Distinctive properties of speech control. In G. E. Stelmach & J. Requin (Eds.), *Tutorials in motor behavior.* Amsterdam: Elsevier.

Martin, J. G. (1970). Toward an analysis of subjective phrase structure. *Psychological Bulletin,* *74,* 153–166.

Matthei, E. H. (1989). Crossing boundaries: More phonological evidence for phonological constraints on early multi-word utterances. *Journal of Child Language, 16,* 41–54.

McCarthy, D. (1952). Organismic interpretation of infant vocalizations. *Child Development, 23,* 273–280.

Mehler, J., Bertoncini, J., Barriere, M., & Jassik-Gerschenfeld, D. (1978). Infant perception of mother's voice. *Perception, 7,* 491–497.

Mehler, J., Jusczyk, P. W., Lambertz, G., Halsted, N., Bertoncini, J., & Amiel-Tison, C. (1988). A precursor of language acquisition in young infants. *Cognition, 29,* 143–178.

Menn, L. (1976). *Pattern, control and contrast in beginning speech.* Unpublished doctoral dissertation, University of Illinois, Urbana.

Menn, L. (1978). Phonological units in beginning speech. In A. Bell & J. B. Hooper (Eds.), *Syllables and segments.* Amsterdam: North-Holland.

Menn, L. (1980). Phonological theory and child phonology. In G. H. Yeni-Komshian, J. F. Kavanagh, & G. A. Ferguson (Eds.), *Child phonology* (Vol. 1, pp. 23–41). New York: Academic Press.

Menn, L. (1983). Development of articulatory, phonetic, and phonological capabilities. In B. Butterworth (Ed.), *Language production* (Vol. 2, pp. 3–50). London: Academic Press.

Menn, L., & Boyce, S. (1982). Fundamental frequency and discourse structure. *Language and Speech, 25,* 341–383.

Menn, L., & Matthei, E. (1992). The "two-lexicon" account of child phonology: Looking back, looking ahead. In C. A. Ferguson, L. Menn, & C. Stoel-Gammon (Eds.), *Phonological development: Models, research, implications* (pp. 211–247). Parkton, MD: York Press.

Menyuk, P., & Menn, L. (1979). Early strategies for the perception and production of words and sounds. In P. Fletcher & M. Garman (Eds.), *Studies in language acquisition* (pp. 49–70). Cambridge: Cambridge University Press.

Miller, C., & Morse, P. (1976). The heart of categorical speech discrimination in infants. *Journal of Speech and Hearing Research, 19,* 578–589.

Miller, G. A., & Nicely, P. E. (1955). An analysis of perceptual confusions among some English consonants. *Journal of the Acoustical Society of America, 27,* 338–352.

Miller, J., Morse, P., & Dorman, M. (1977). Cardiac indices of infant speech perception: Orienting and burst discrimination. *Quarterly Journal of Experimental Psychology, 29,* 533–545.

Mitchell, P. R., & Kent, R. D. (1990). Phonetic variation in multisyllable babbling. *Journal of Child Language, 17,* 247–265.

Moerk, E. (1972). Principles of interaction in language learning. *Merrill-Palmer Quarterly, 18,* 229–257.

Moffit, A. R. (1971). Consonant cue perception by twenty- to twenty-four-week-old infants. *Child Development, 42,* 717–731.

Morgan, J. L. (1986). *From simple input to complex grammar.* Cambridge, MA: MIT Press.

Morgan, J. L., Meier, R. P., & Newport, E. L. (1987). Structural packaging in the input to language learning. *Cognitive Psychology, 22,* 498–550.

Morgan, J. L., & Newport, E. (1981). The role of constituent structure in the induction of an artificial language. *Journal of Verbal Learning and Verbal Behavior, 20,* 67–85.

Morse, P. A. (1972). The discrimination of speech and non-speech stimuli in early infancy. *Journal of Experimental Child Psychology, 14,* 477–492.

Moskowitz, B. A. (1973a). The acquisition of phonology and syntax. In K. K. J. Hintikka, J. M. E. Moravsik, & P. Suppes (Eds.), *Approaches to natural language* (pp. 48–84). Dordrecht: Reidel.

Moskowitz, B. A. (1973b). On the status of the vowel shift in English. In T. E. Moore (Ed.), *Cognitive development and the acquisition of language* (pp. 223–260). New York: Academic Press.

Nakazima, S. A. (1962). A comparative study of the speech developments of Japanese and American English childhood. *Studia Phonologica, 2,* 27–46.

Nakazima, S. A. (1970). A comparative study of the speech developments of Japanese and American English childhood. *Studia Phonologica, 5,* 20–42.

Nelson, K. (1973). Structure and strategy in learning to talk. *Monographs of the Society for Research in Child Development, 38.*

Nespor, M., & Vogel, I. (1982). Prosodic domains in external sandhi rules. In H. van der Hulst & N. Smith (Eds.), *The structure of phonological representations* (Vol. 1, pp. 225–255). Dordrecht: Foris.

Nespor, M., & Vogel, I. (1986). *Prosodic phonology*. Dordrecht: Foris.

Netsell, R. (1981). The acquisition of speech motor control: A perspective with directions for research. In R. E. Stark (Ed.), *Language behavior in infancy and early childhood* (pp. 127–156). New York: Elsevier.

Newport, E., Gleitman, H. & Gleitman, L. (1977). Mother, I'd rather do it myself. In C. Snow & C. Ferguson (Eds.), *Talking to children* (pp. 109–147). Cambridge: Cambridge University Press.

Nooteboom, S. G. (1967). Some regularities in phonemic speech errors. *Annual Progress Report, Institute for Perception Research IPO, 2,* 65–70.

Nooteboom, S. G. (1969). The tongue slips into patterns. In A. G. Sciarone, A. S. van Essen, & A. N. Van Reed (Ed.) *Leyden Studies in Linguistics and Phonetics* (pp. 114–132). The Hague: Mouton.

Oller, D. K. (1980). The emergence of the sounds of speech in infancy. In G. H. Yeni-Komshian, J. F. Kavanagh, & G. A. Ferguson (Eds.), *Child phonology* (Vol. 1, pp. 93–112). New York: Academic Press.

Oller, D. K. (1986). Metaphonology and infant vocalizations. In B. Lindblom & R. Zetterson (Eds.), *Precursors of early speech* (pp. 21–35). New York: Stockton.

Oller, D. K., & Eilers, R. E. (1982). Similarity of babbling in Spanish- and English-learning babies. *Journal of Child Language, 9,* 565–577.

Oller, D. K., Eilers, R. E., Bull, D. H., & Carney, A. E. (1985). Prespeech vocalizations of a deaf infant: A comparison with normal metaphonological development. *Journal of Speech and Hearing Research, 28,* 47–63.

Oller, D. K., Weiman, L. A., Doyle, W. J., & Ross, C. (1976). Infant babbling and speech. *Journal of Child Language, 3,* 1–11.

Olney, R. L., & Scholnick, E. K. (1976). Adult judgements of age and linguistic differences in infant vocalization. *Journal of Child Language, 3,* 145–156.

Papousek, H., & Papousek, M. (1981). Musical elements in infant's vocalization: Their significance for communication, cognition, and creativity. In L. P. Lipsitt (Ed.), *Advances in infancy research* (pp. 163–224). Norwood, NJ: Ablex.

Papousek, M., Papousek, H. & Symmes, D. (1994). Melodic units in maternal speech in tonal and non-tonal languages: Evidence of a universal parental support for linguistic communication. *Infant Behavior and Development, 14,* 415–440.

Papousek, M., Papousek, H., & Haekel, M. (1987). Didactic adjustments in fathers' and mothers' speech to their three-month-old infants. *Journal of Psycholinguistic Research, 6,* 49–56.

Peters, A. (1977). Language learning strategies. *Language, 53,* 560–573.

Peters, A. (1983). *The units of language acquisition*. Cambridge: Cambridge University Press.

Peters, A. (1985). Language segmentation: Operating principles for the perception and analysis of language. In D. I. Slobin (Ed.), *The crosslinguistic study of language acquisition: Vol. 2. Theoretical issues* (pp. 1029–1067). Hillsdale, NJ: Erlbaum.

Peters, A., & Menn, L. (1991). *The microstructure of morphological development: Variation across children and across languages* (Cognitive Science Tech. Rep.). Boulder: University of Colorado.

Pisoni, D. B. (1975). Dichotic listening and processing phonetic features. In F. Restle, R. M. Shiffrin, N. J. Castellan, H. R. Lindman, & D. B. Pisoni (Eds.), *Cognitive theory* (Vol. 1, pp. 79–102). Hillsdale, NJ: Erlbaum.

Pisoni, D. B. (1977). Identification and discrimination of the relative onset of two component tones: Implications for the perception of voicing in consonants. *Journal of the Acoustical Society of America, 61,* 1352–1361.

Poser, W. (1984). *The phonetics and phonology of tone and intonation in Japanese*. Doctoral dissertation, Massachusetts Institute of Technology, Cambridge.

Priestly, T. M. S. (1977). One idiosyncratic strategy in the acquisition of phonology. *Journal of Child Language, 4,* 45–66.

Pye, C. (1983). Mayan telegraphese. *Language, 59,* 583–604.

Ratner, N. B., & Pye, C. (1984). Higher pitch in BT is not universal: acoustic evidence from Quiche Mayan. *Journal of Child Language, 11,* 515–522.

Read C. & Schreiber P. (1982). Why short subjects are hard to find. In E. Wanner & L. Gleitman (Eds.), *Language acquisition: The state of the art* (pp. 78–101). Cambridge: Cambridge University Press.

Remick, H. (1976). Maternal speech to children during language acquisition. In W. von Raffler-Engel & Y. Lebrun (Eds.), *Baby talk and infant speech*. Lisse, Netherlands: Swets & Zeitler.

Ruke-Dravina, V. (1976). Gibt es Universalien in der Ammensprache? *Salzberger Beitrage zur Linguistik, 2,* 3–16.

Sachs, J. (1977). The adaptive significance of linguistic input to prelinguistic infants. In C. E. Snow & C. A. Ferguson (Eds.), *Talking to children* (pp. 51–61). Cambridge: Cambridge University Press.

Sachs, J., Brown, R., & Salerno, R. A. (1976). Adults' speech to children. In W. von Raffler-Engel & Y. Lebrun (Eds.), *Baby talk and infant speech*. Lisse, Netherlands: Swets & Zeitler.

Schieffelin, B. B. (1979). Getting it together: An ethnographic approach to the study of the development of communicative competence. In E. Ochs & B. B. Schieffelin (Eds.), *Developmental pragmatics*. New York: Academic Press.

Schlesinger, I. M. (1971). Production of utterances in language acquisition. In D. I. Slobin (Ed.), *The ontongenesis of grammar* (pp. 63–101). New York: Academic Press.

Schwartz, R. G. (1988). Phonological factors in early lexical acquisition. In M. D. Smith & J. L. Locke (Eds.), *The emergent lexicon: The child's development of a linguistic vocabulary* (pp. 185–202). San Diego, CA: Academic Press.

Schwartz, R. G., & Leonard, L. B. (1982). Do children pick and choose? An examination of phonological selection and avoidance in early lexical acquisition. *Journal of Child Language, 9,* 319–336.

Scollon, R. (1976). *Conversations with a one year old*. Honolulu: University of Hawaii Press.

Selkirk, E. (1981). On the nature of phonological representation. In T. Myers, J. Laver, & J. Anderson (Eds.), *The cognitive representation of speech* (pp. 379–388). Amsterdam: North-Holland.

Selkirk, E. (1984). *Phonology and syntax*. Cambridge, MA: MIT Press.

Selkirk, E. (1986). On derived domains in sentence phonology. *Phonology Yearbook, 3,* 371–405.

Shibamoto, J. S., & Olmsted, D. L. (1978). Lexical and syllabic patterns in phonological acquisition. *Journal of Child Language, 5,* 417–457.

Shute, B., & Wheldall, K. (1989). Pitch alternations in British motherese: Some preliminary acoustic data. *Journal of Child Language, 16,* 503–512.

Shvachkin, N. Kh. (1973). The development of phonemic perception in early childhood. In C. A. Ferguson & D. I. Slobin (Eds.), *Studies of child language development* (pp. 92–127). New York: Holt, Rinehart & Winston.

Siqueland, E. R., & deLucia, C. A. (1969). Visual reinforcement of non-nutritive sucking in human infants. *Science, 165,* 1144.

Smith, B. L. (1988). The emergent lexicon from a phonetic perspective. In M. D. Smith & J. L. Locke (Eds.), *The emergent lexicon: The child's development of a linguistic vocabulary* (pp. 75–106). San Diego, CA: Academic Press.

Smith, B. L., Brown-Sweeney, S., & Stoel-Gammon, C. (1989). A quantitative analysis of reduplicated and variegated babbling. *First Language, 9,* 175–190.

Smith, B. L., & Oller, D. K. (1981). A comparative study of premeaningful vocalizations produced by normally developing and Down's syndrome infants. *Journal of Speech and Hearing Disorders, 46,* 46–51.

Smith, N. V. (1973). *The acquisition of phonology*. Cambridge: Cambridge University Press.

Smith, N. V. (1978). *Lexical representation and the acquisition of phonology* (Forum Lecture). Urbana, IL: Linguistic Society of America Summer Institute.

Spencer, A. (1986). Toward a theory of phonological development. *Lingua, 68,* 3–38.

Stampe, D. (1969). The acquisition of phonetic representation. *Chicago Linguistic Society, 5,* 443–454.

Stark, R. E. (1980). Stages of speech development in the first year of life. In G. H. Yeni-Komshian, J. F. Kavanagh, & G. A. Ferguson (Eds.), *Child phonology* (Vol. 1, pp. 73–92). New York: Academic Press.

Stemberger, J. P. (1985). An interactive activation model of language production. In A. W. Ellis (Ed.), *Progress in the psychology of language* (Vol. 1, pp. 143–186). London: Erlbaum.

Stemberger, J. P. (1988). Between-word processes in child phonology. *Journal of Child Language, 15,* 39–61.

Stemberger, J. P. (1989). Speech errors in early child language production. *Journal of Memory and Language, 28,* 164–188.

Stemberger, J. P. (1992). A connectionist view of child phonology: Phonological processing without phonolological processes. In C. A. Ferguson, L. Menn, & C. Stoel-Gammon (Eds.), *Phonological development: Models, research, implications* (pp. 165–189). Parkton, MD: York Press.

Stern, D. N. (1985). *The interpersonal world of the infant.* New York: Basic Books.

Stern, D. N., Spieker, S., Barnett, R. K., & MacKain, K. (1983). The prosody of maternal speech: Infant age and context related changes. *Journal of Child Language, 10,* 1–15.

Stoel-Gammon, C., & Cooper, J. A. (1984). Patterns of early lexical development. *Journal of Child Language, 11,* 247–271.

Straight, H. S. (1980). Auditory versus articulatory phonological processes and their development in children. In G. H. Yeni-Komshian, J. F. Kavanagh, & G. A. Ferguson (Eds.), *Child phonology* (Vol. 1, pp. 43–72). New York: Academic Press.

Streeter, L. (1976). Language perception in 2-month-old infants shows effects of both innate mechanisms and experience. *Nature (London) 259,* 39–41.

Streeter, L. (1978). Acoustic determinants of phrase boundary perception. *Journal of the Acoustical Society of America, 64,* 1582–1592.

Studdert-Kennedy, M. (1986). Sources of variability in early speech development. In J. S. Perkell & D. H. Klatt (Eds.), *Invariance and variability in speech processes.* Hillsdale, NJ: Erlbaum.

Studdert-Kennedy, M. (1987). The phoneme as a perceptuomotor structure. In A. Allport, D. MacKay, W. Prinz, & E. Scheerer (Eds.), *Language perception and production* (pp. 58–76). London: Academic Press.

Studdert-Kennedy, M., & Shankweiler, D. P. (1970). Hemispheric specialization for speech perception. *Journal of the Acoustical Society of America, 48,* 579–594.

Trehub, S. E. (1973). Infants' sensitivity to vowel and tonal contrasts. *Developmental Psychology, 9,* 91–96.

Trehub, S. E. (1976). The discrimination of foreign speech contrasts by infants and adults. *Child Development, 47,* 466–472.

Trehub, S. E., & Rabinovitch, M. S. (1972). Auditory–linguistic sensitivity in early infancy. *Developmental Psychology, 6,* 74–77.

Van den Broecke, M. P. R., & Goldstein, L. (1980). Consonant features in speech errors. In V. A. Fromkin (Ed.), *Errors in linguistic performance: Slips of the tongue, ear, pen and hand* (pp. 47–65). New York: Academic Press.

Velten, H. (1943). The growth of phonemic and lexical patterns in infant language. *Language, 19,* 281–292.

Vihman, M. M. (1978). Consonant harmony: Its scope and function in child language. In J. H. Greenberg (Ed.), *Universals of human language: Vol. 2. phonology* (pp. 281–334). Stanford, CA: Stanford University Press.

Vihman, M. M. (1980). Sound change and child language. *Current Issues in Linguistic Theory, 14,* 304–320.

Vihman, M. M. (1981). Phonology and the development of the lexicon: Evidence from children's errors. *Journal of Child Language, 8,* 239–264.

Vihman, M. M. (1982). A note on children's lexical representations. *Journal of Child Language, 9,* 249–253.

Vihman, M. M. (1986). Individual differences in babbling and early speech: Predicting to age three. In B. Lindblom & R. Zetterson (Eds.), *Precursors of early speech* (pp. 95–109). New York: Stockton.

Vihman, M. M. (1993). Manuscript submitted for publication. Variable paths to word production.

Vihman, M. M., & Greenlee, M. (1987). Individual differences in phonological development: Ages one and three. *Journal of Speech and Hearing Research, 30,* 503–521.

Vihman, M. M., Macken, M. A., Miller, R., Simmons, H., & Miller, J. (1985). From babbling to speech: A reassessment of the continuity issue. *Language, 61,* 397–446.

Vihman, M. M., & Miller, R. (1988). Words and babble on the threshold of language acquisition. In M. D. Smith & J. L. Locke (Eds.), *The emergent lexicon: The child's development of a linguistic vocabulary* (pp. 151–183). San Diego, CA: Academic Press.

Vihman, M. M., & Velleman, S. L. (1989). Phonological reorganization: A case study. *Language and Speech, 32,* 149–170.

Walley, A. C. (1987). Young children's detections of word-initial and -final mispronunciations in constrained and unconstrained contexts. *Cognitive Development, 2*, 145–167.

Walley, A. C. (1988). Spoken word recognition by young children and adults. *Cognitive Development, 3*, 137–165.

Walley, A. C. (1993). The role of vocabulary growth in children's spoken word recognition and segmentation ability. *Psychological Review, 13*, 286–350.

Warren-Leubecker, A., & Bohannon, J. N. (1984). Intonation patterns in child-directed speech: Mother–father differences. *Child Development, 55*, 1379–1385.

Waterson, N. (1971). Child phonology: A prosodic view. *Journal of Linguistics, 7*, 179–211.

Weir, R. (1966). *Language in the crib*. The Hague: Mouton.

Werker, J. F., Gilbert, J. H. V., Humphrey, K., & Tees, R. C. (1981). Developmental aspects of cross-language speech perception. *Child Development, 52*, 349–355.

Werker, J. F., & Lalonde, C. E. (1988). Cross-language speech perception: Initial capabilities and developmental change. *Developmental Psychology, 24*, 672–683.

Werker, J. F., & McLeod, P. J. (1989). Infant preference for both male and female infant-directed talk: A developmental study of attentional and affective responses. *Canadian Journal of Psychology, 43*, 230–246.

Werker, J. F., & Tees, R. C. (1984). Cross-language speech perception: Evidence for perceptual reorganization during the first year of life. *Infant Behavior and Development, 7*, 49–63.

Whalen, D. H., Levitt, A. G., & Wang, Q. (1991). Intonational differences between the reduplicative babbling of French- and English-learning infants. *Journal of Child Language, 18*, 501–516.

Wijnen, F. (1990). *The development of language production mechanisms*. Doctoral dissertation, Catholic University of Nijmegen.

Wijnen, F., & Krikhaar, E. & den Os, E. (in press). The (non)realization of unstressed elements in children's utterances: A rhythmic constraint? *Journal of Child Language*.

Williams, L., & Bush, M. (1978). The discrimination by young infants of voiced stop contrasts with and without release bursts. *Journal of the Acoustical Society of America, 63*, 1223–1225.

Zelnicker, T., & Jeffrey, W. E. (1976). Reflective and impulsive children: Strategies of information processing underlying differences in problem solving. *Society for Research in Child Development Monographs, 168*.

Zlatin, M. A., & Koenigsknecht, R. A. (1976). Development of the voicing contrast: A comparison of voice onset time in stop perception and production. *Journal of Speech and Hearing Research, 19*, 93–111.

CHAPTER 25

INDIVIDUAL DIFFERENCES IN CHILDREN'S TEXT COMPREHENSION

JANE OAKHILL

I. INTRODUCTION

There is now a very large literature on children who have reading problems. However, the majority of this work has focused on children who have a problem with words—dyslexics, for example. Relatively little research has addressed the issue of children who are good at word recognition but who, nevertheless, have difficulty in understanding and remembering text. Indeed, because of the way reading is often assessed—listening to children read aloud, tests of single-word recognition—problems in understanding text may go unnoticed. Because understanding written material is an important component of almost all aspects of learning in school, difficulties in this area can have pervasive effects. It is, therefore, crucial that teachers can identify children who have such difficulties and know how to help them overcome them.

Obviously, reading depends on far more than the ability to decipher words and understand sentences, though, of course, word recognition skills and an adequate vocabulary are essential aspects of the skill. In order to understand a text adequately, the meanings of the individual sentences and paragraphs must be INTEGRATED and the main ideas of the text identified, so that the GIST MEANING can be derived. I start, therefore, with a very brief outline of some of the main skills that are thought important for comprehension (for a more detailed account, see Oakhill & Garnham, 1988, Chap. 2).

In most cases, INFERENTIAL SKILLS will be needed to go beyond what is stated explicitly in a text—authors need to leave some of the links implicit; otherwise any text would be extremely long and tedious. Even apparently simple texts can only be understood by making inferences that are, in processing terms, fairly complex. Consider, for example, the following children's story (Charniak, 1972).

Jane was invited to Jack's birthday party.
She wondered if he would like a kite.

She went to her room and shook her piggy bank.
It made no sound.

This story can only be understood against a background of knowledge about birthday parties, the convention of taking presents to them, the need for money to buy presents, and so on. A reader from a culture where these assumptions were not made would find this story virtually impossible to understand. For example, the full implication of the lack of sound in the last sentence is far from explicit in the text, however obvious it might be to skilled readers.

Second, readers need to DERIVE THE STRUCTURE of the text. For stories, this can mean that they must identify the main character(s) and their motives, follow the plot of the story, and extract the main theme. In the case of expository text, they will need to identify the main topic, extract the important information, follow any arguments in the text, and extract the gist meaning.

Third, readers will need to MONITOR their own comprehension. They need to keep track of whether their understanding is adequate or not, and to know how to deal with any difficulties. Children in particular may not realize that they have not fully understood a portion of text and may not know what to do about their lack of understanding even if they do realize.

In this chapter, I first survey the main theoretical stances on comprehension problems and present some of our own work, in particular, that relating to the skill areas outlined above. I then turn to ways in which comprehension difficulties might be remediated.

II. THEORIES OF INDIVIDUAL DIFFERENCES IN COMPREHENSION SKILL

Research on individual differences in comprehension has focused on three main theoretical areas. The first posits that comprehension problems arise because of difficulties at the level of single words. The second proposes that some children have difficulties in the syntactic and semantic analysis of sentences. The third, to which most of the experimental work presented later is addressed, argues that poor comprehenders have difficulty with the higher order comprehension skills outlined above: making inferences from text, integrating the ideas in it, selecting the main theme, and monitoring their own comprehension. I discuss each of these hypotheses in a little more detail below.

A. Word Level Explanations

At first sight, it might seem paradoxical to propose that comprehension problems are, after all, single-word reading problems. However, such a proposal probably provides a good characterization of the comprehension difficulties of at least some children. Obviously, such difficulties might arise because of vocabulary problems—readers will not be able fully to understand a text if they do not know the meanings of the individual words in it. However, a more subtle deficit at this level has been proposed. Perfetti's verbal efficiency or "bottleneck" hypothesis argues that the speed and automaticity of word decoding (i.e., the ability to access the meaning and pronunciation of a word from the mental lexicon) should have a central role in explanations of comprehension failure, and that individual differences in comprehension ability can be related to differences in these processes. On his view, decoding accuracy is not sufficient. The verbal efficiency hypothesis assumes that the various skills involved in reading are in competition for limited processing resources, so that the less efficient one process, the fewer other processes can be executed at the same time. Thus, the efficiency of word-level processes is a potential source of individual differences in comprehension skill. There are many sources of evidence to support the idea that, in general, slow and inefficient decoders are poor comprehenders (see Perfetti, 1985, for a review). Perfetti and Hogaboam (1975b), for example, found large differences in the time taken to name single words between skilled and less skilled comprehenders (3rd and 5th grades). Although the groups were not matched for decoding skills, the results could not be explained simply by differences in word recognition accuracy, since the skilled readers had significantly shorter naming times even for very common words, almost all of which were identified correctly by both groups of subjects.

However, although there is a tendency for fast decoding and good comprehension to go together, there is no evidence for a direct causal link between the two. The existence of rapid decoders who are poor comprehenders, and vice versa, demonstrates that deficiences in decoding speed and automaticity cannot provide a complete account of comprehension problems. Cromer (1970) for instance, was able to identify two groups of college students who differed in comprehension ability even though they were matched for vocabulary, IQ, and word recognition skills, including speed of decoding. Our own work (see Oakhill, 1981; Yuill & Oakhill, 1991, for details) has also failed to find differences in speed or automaticity of single-word decoding in children who differ in comprehension skill. Furthermore, if decoding speed were causally related to comprehension, then one would expect that training in rapid decoding would result in an improvement in comprehension. However, many studies have shown that this is not generally the case (Fleischer, Jenkins, & Pany, 1979; Perfetti & Hogaboam, 1975a; Yuill & Oakhill, 1988a). Fleischer et al., for instance, trained 4th and 5th grade poor readers to recognize words as rapidly as a control group of good readers. This single-word training, and subsequent training in rapid phrase decoding, increased decoding speed for single words but did not improve comprehension, even though the passages in the comprehension test were comprised solely of the trained words. Such results suggest that although rapid decoding is necessary for comprehension, it is not sufficient. Perfetti and Lesgold (1979) acknowledge this fact and suggest that rapid decoding may be the result of extensive reading practice, rather than being causally implicated in reading. However, a study by Lesgold, Resnick, and Hammond (1985) argues against this idea. They showed that, whereas there was a clear relation between early word recognition efficiency and later comprehension skill, the converse relation did not hold—early comprehension skill was not associated with later word recognition efficiency. These data suggest that word recognition skills facilitate the acquisition of comprehension skills, but not vice versa. Perhaps fast and automatic decoding has only an indirect effect on comprehension—allowing it to develop, rather than influencing it directly.

In summary, there is probably no direct link between fast decoding and good comprehension. It may be precisely because decoding is such a basic part of reading that children who read more decode faster. Furthermore, speed and automaticity of decoding are closely associated with a large vocabulary and accurate decoding. Once these two factors are taken into account, fast decoding is not such a reliable indicator of good comprehension.

B. Sentence Level Explanations

Another possibility is that poor comprehenders have difficulties at the level of sentences, failing to understand certain syntactic constructions. The idea that poor comprehenders fail to make use of syntactic constraints in text has been explored extensively by Cromer and his colleagues (e.g., Cromer, 1970; Oakan, Wiener, & Cromer, 1971; Steiner, Wiener, & Cromer, 1971). They argued that poor comprehenders tend to read word by word, rather than processing the text in meaningful units. Cromer (1970) identified two groups of poor comprehenders. One group, who had poor vocabulary and decoding skills as well as poor comprehension, he termed the DEFICIT group. The other group—the DIFFERENCE group—had comprehension difficulties even though their vocabulary and decoding skills were commensurate with those of good comprehenders of the same age.[1] Thus, poor comprehenders in the difference group had a specific comprehension problem. In this respect, these subjects were very similar to the less skilled comprehenders in our own experiments (Oakhill, 1981; Yuill & Oakhill, 1991).

In Cromer's (1970) experiment, the subjects were presented with texts in one of four modes: (1) as whole sentences, (2) as sentences segmented into meaningful phrases (e.g., *the cow jumped/ over the moon*), (3) as sentences fragmented into phrases (e.g., *the cow/ jumped over the/ moon*), and (4) as single words. After each text, the subjects were asked a series of questions about the text, and their pattern of errors varied according to the text presentation condition. The pattern of results suggested that the difference group normally reads word by word, so they are not affected by the disruptive conditions. Chunking the sentences into meaningful units aids their comprehension. Subjects in the deficit group, on the other hand, were not helped by division of the sentences into meaningful phrases. Their problem did not arise simply from inefficient text organization. The finding that the good comprehenders were not helped when the text was chunked into meaningful phrases, but were disrupted in the fragmented phrase and single-word modes, suggests that they normally

---

[1] It should be noted that Cromer's work has been criticized extensively by Calfee, Arnold, and Drum (1976), who doubt the existence of people who can decode fluently but not understand what they read. They argue that three basic flaws in Cromer's work undermine the conclusions that can be drawn.

1. The difference poor readers (those who have adequate vocabulary but poor comprehension scores) are an atypical group and, because of the phenomenon of regression toward the mean, one would expect that, if they were retested, their comprehension would improve or their vocabulary scores decline. In fact, on a subsequent test, the scores of a substantial number of the difference readers and their controls switched, providing fuel for Calfee et al.'s worries.
2. Although Cromer's experimental findings did support the idea that the difference poor readers perform differently from their controls, his statistical analyses are questionable.
3. The poor readers took longer than good readers to decode single words, bringing into question whether they were really fluent readers.

organize text into phraselike units. Unlike poor comprehenders, they use sentence structure to aid their comprehension.

These results suggest that poor comprehenders tend to read word by word and do not use the sentence and text structure to guide them. This reading style is similar to the listlike style that Clay and Imlach (1971) describe poor comprehenders as using. Other measures, such as eye–voice span, cloze procedures, and assessments using geometrically transformed texts (e.g., texts in which the letters are presented upside down or back to front) have also shown that unskilled readers are less sensitive to syntactic cues than skilled readers, and that these differences persist even when IQ and decoding skills are taken account of (see Gibson & Levin, 1975; Willows & Ryan, 1981).

C. Text Level Explanations

I have already discussed the very important role of integration and inference in text comprehension. Many studies, including many of my own, indicate that skilled and less skilled comprehenders differ in the extent to which they integrate information in a text and in their use of inferences (for a review, see Yuill & Oakhill, 1991). Before going on to describe some of this work, a brief description of the rationale behind the experiments, and the method for selecting subjects, is appropriate.

The method we have used to investigate the particular problems of poor comprehenders has been to compare groups of good and poor comprehenders who are matched in other important ways. All the children who were subjects in the studies of my own that I describe here were selected from classes of 7–8-year-olds, using a British reading test, the *Neale Analysis of Reading Ability* (Neale, 1966), and the *Gates–MacGinitie Vocabulary Test* (Gates & MacGinitie, 1965). The Neale test provides measures of both children's ability to read words aloud in context and their comprehension of short passages. In all the studies reported, the performance of a group of good comprehenders was compared with that of a less skilled group on measures thought to be important to comprehension skill. The groups of skilled and less skilled comprehenders were selected so that they were matched on ability to read words aloud (Neale accuracy score) and on skill at understanding the meaning of isolated printed words (Gates–MacGinitie score), but they differed in their ability to answer questions about short texts (Neale comprehension score). The matching on accuracy scores was based on the regressed scores of the two groups, as this procedure takes into account the possibility that the two skill groups were derived from populations that differ in word recognition ability. If this were so, then the groups might be found to differ in accuracy scores when retested, because of regression toward the mean scores of the populations from which they were derived (McNemar, 1962; see also n. 1). The characteristics of typical groups of subjects used in my own experiments are shown in Table I.

Preliminary studies failed to show any differences between skilled and less skilled comprehenders' decoding speed, accuracy, or automaticity (see Yuill & Oakhill, 1991, Chap. 3, for details). It is unlikely, then, that the observed comprehension differences arose because of problems at the single-word level. A further possibility, outlined above, that poor comprehenders have difficulties at the sentence level and fail to understand certain syntactic constructions, was

TABLE I
Characteristics of Skilled and Less
Skilled Comprehenders

	Less skilled	Skilled
Age (yr)		
Chronological	7.9	7.9
Accuracy	8.4	8.4
Comprehension	7.3	9.1
Gates–MacGinitie score[a]	38.0	38.3

[a] Maximum = 48.0.

assessed by administering Bishop's *Test for reception of grammar* (Bishop, 1982). This test assesses children's understanding of a very wide range of sentence constructions, but again no overall differences were found between groups. In addition, no differences have been found between good and poor comprehenders on standard tests of short-term memory (Oakhill, 1981; Oakhill, Yuill, & Parkin, 1986), nor in their ability to recall the exact wording of sentences and short texts (Oakhill, 1982). So, the poor comprehenders' problem cannot, it seems, be attributed to any straightforward decoding or memory problems, although there are aspects of memory which do differentiate between the groups. Although they do not differ in traditional short-term memory tasks, as discussed later, they do differ in tasks that measure working memory capacity (i.e., tasks that require simultaneous storage and processing). The remainder of our studies fall naturally into five categories and are discussed under five subheadings below.

1. Inference and Integration

Many studies indicate that skilled and less skilled comprehenders differ in the extent to which they integrate information from different parts of a text and make inferences. For example, Garnham, Oakhill, and Johnson-Laird (1982) showed that less skilled comprehenders have difficulty taking advantage of the cohesive links in a text. We presented skilled and less skilled comprehenders with short stories that varied in cohesiveness. One set of stories described a normal sequence of events. The other two types were derived by scrambling the normal stories, thereby destroying the plausibility of the sequence. In the RANDOM versions, the sentences were simply reordered. In these cases, there was neither a plausible sequence of events nor cohesive links between the sentences. In the REVISED RANDOM versions, on the other hand, the cohesive links (but not the plausibility) was restored, for example by replacing uninterpretable pronouns with full noun phrases. Both the skilled and the less skilled comprehenders found the randomized stories difficult to remember. However, only the skilled group were helped by the restoration of referential continuity—they recalled more of the revised than of the random stories, whereas the less skilled group were equally poor with both types.

Although many results show that skilled comprehenders make more inferences from text (e.g., Oakhill, 1982, 1984; Oakhill et al., 1986), to some extent the ability to make inferences is dependent on memory for text. Many measures of comprehension, including the Neale test, impose memory demands: The children are not permitted to look back to the text in order to answer the comprehension questions. Therefore, one must ask: If poor comprehenders make fewer inferences than good comprehenders, is it because they have poorer inferential abilities, or is it because they cannot remember the information on which the inferences are based?

I have investigated this issue by conducting a relatively naturalistic study of the relation between memory and comprehension in good and poor comprehenders (Oakhill, 1984). The children's ability to answer questions both from memory and when they could refer back to the text was investigated. Some of the questions could be answered from information that was explicit in the text; others required an inference to go beyond the information explicitly stated. For instance, in one story, there is mention of the fact that a boy *pedaled* to school but no specific mention of a bicycle. When asked how the boy traveled to school, readers would have to infer from the reference to pedaling, and other subtle information in the story, that he traveled by bike. The results showed that, as expected, the good comprehenders did better on the questions overall. Both groups made fewer errors when the passage was available, and the literal questions were, in general, easier. However, the different patterns of data in the two availability conditions are of particular interest: The skilled comprehenders were better able than were the less skilled comprehenders to answer both types of question from memory. When the passages were made available, however, the less skilled comprehenders remained poor at answering the questions that required an inference, but their performance on literal questions was commensurate with that of the skilled group. Thus, the poorer question-answering ability of the less skilled group cannot be explained simply in terms of poor memory. The less skilled comprehenders were poor at answering inferentially based questions even when the text was made available to them (35.4% errors compared with 9.9% for the skilled group in this condition).

It could be argued that the poor comprehenders failed to answer inferential questions because they lacked the relevant background knowledge. However, this seems a highly implausible explanation given the sort of knowledge that was required. Other possible explanations are that the less skilled comprehenders did not realize that inferential processing was necessary or relevant to understanding the passages, or that they had difficulty in accessing the relevant knowledge and integrating it with the information in the text because of processing limitations. Further studies, to be discussed later, suggest that both these latter types of explanation might apply to some extent.

A second study looked at the children's ability to make inferences that do not depend on the incorporation of general knowledge. All the relevant information was provided in the texts. In this experiment, skilled and less skilled comprehenders listened to and tried to remember a series of short (three-sentence) "stories." After hearing the stories, they were given a recognition memory test, in which they were asked whether or not sentences had occurred in the stories (for details, see Oakhill, 1982; Oakhill et al., 1986). For each story, there were four sentences in the test: two had actually occurred in the story, one was a valid inference from the story, and the fourth was an invalid inference (i.e., it did not follow from the story, or it was inconsistent with it). Studies of skilled adult readers (e.g., Bransford, Barclay, & Franks, 1972; Bransford & Franks, 1971) have shown that they tend to integrate separate sentences from a text to extract the overall meaning, and that they find it hard to recall the exact wording. The prediction in this experiment was that, if good comprehenders are more likely to integrate information from different parts of a text as they understand it, then they should be more likely in the recognition test to accept the valid inference items as sentences they had actually heard in the story. This is what we found. Although both groups of subjects made more errors on the valid inference foils than on the invalid inference foils, the difference in errors between the valid and invalid inferences was much larger for the good comprehenders. They actually made more errors on the valid inference foils than did the poor comprehenders, which is exactly the pattern that would be predicted if the good comprehenders were making a more active attempt to integrate the ideas in the texts. There was no significant difference between the groups in their acceptance rate for the original sentences (ones they had actually heard in the stories). From these data we concluded that, although there were no straightforward differences between the groups in ability to remember sentences from stories they had just heard, the good comprehenders had better memory for the meaning of the text, as shown in their greater tendency to say that they had heard the valid inference foils, all of which contained information that could be inferred from the stories. That such difficulties occur even for aurally presented materials demonstrates that the less skilled comprehenders' problem cannot be accounted for in terms of word decoding difficulties because it is not even specific to reading.

A further experiment was concerned with a different type of inferential processing: INSTANTIATION. Anderson and his colleagues (Anderson & Ortony, 1975; Anderson et al., 1976) have argued that adults tend to give a word a more specific interpretation in context than in isolation (i.e., they instantiate a particular meaning for the word as a function of the context in which it occurs). In Anderson's experiments with adults, the subjects were presented with sentences such as:

The fish attacked the swimmer.

This sentence contains a general noun (*fish*) in a context that biases the reader toward interpreting the noun in a particular way (in this case, as some sort of aggressive/dangerous fish). In a subsequent cued-recall test for such sentences, Anderson et al. found that a specific noun (in this case, *shark*) was a better recall cue than was the noun that actually appeared in the sentence (*fish*). This evidence suggests that adult subjects derive more specific representations of the entities in the sentences which depend on the specific context. They instantiate a particular type of fish. Using a similar task, I showed that children, too, make such instantiations, but that good comprehenders are much more likely to do so than are poor ones (see Oakhill, 1983).

Related work by Merrill, Sperber, and McCauley (1981) supports the conclusion that less able readers do not readily select the contextually most appropriate meaning for a word. Merrill et al. asked fifth graders to read a series of sentences in which certain attributes of a key word were emphasized. For instance, in *The boy sat near the fire,* some attributes of *fire,* such as *warmth,* are more immediately brought to mind than others (e.g., *smoke*). Immediately after reading each sentence, the children had to name the color of the ink in which one of the attribute words was printed. It is a well-known finding that the meaning of a word, and how salient that meaning is, can increase the time to name the color in which it is presented. In these sentence contexts, good comprehenders showed interference for words that were related to the attribute emphasized by the context (*warmth*) but not for words related to unemphasized attributes (*smoke*). Poor comprehenders, however, showed interference for both types of words. In addition to sentence contexts, the experimenters also used word contexts. In these contexts, both groups of subjects showed equal increases in interference when the word whose color was to be named followed a semantically related word (e.g., *cat–fur* or *cat–claw*) compared with the condition where it followed an unrelated word (e.g., *man–fur*). The investigators argue that these findings point to differences in the way good and poor comprehenders encode sentences. Good comprehenders derive a contextually appropriate encoding almost immediately, but poor comprehenders appear to derive a more general, though presumably less useful, encoding in which more of the word's attributes are available to them.

Taken together, these studies demonstrate that skilled comprehenders more readily integrate the ideas in a text, making inferences where necessary to elaborate on single-word meanings and to help them derive the overall meaning. The poor comprehenders have trouble in making a variety of different types of inferences, even when the text is read to them and even when there is no memory load.

2. Anaphoric Links

An important factor in guiding skilled text integration is the use of anaphoric links in text, such as verb phrase ellipsis (e.g., *John likes cycling to work. Bill does, too*) and pronouns. In one study (Oakhill & Yuill, 1986), we found that poor comprehenders had difficulty in supplying an appropriate pronoun (*he* or *she*) in simple sentences, such as:

Sally gave her shoes to Ben because . . . needed them.

In cases where the link between the first and second clauses was slightly less straightforward, the poor comprehenders had even greater difficulty. In sentences such as the following they made almost twice as many errors as the good comprehenders:

Steven gave his umbrella to Penny because . . . wanted to keep dry.

In further experiment (Yuill & Oakhill, 1988b), we used a more naturalistic text (a short story) and explored children's use of a wider range of cohesive ties. We classified the cohesive ties in the story according to Halliday and Hasan's (1976) categories: reference, ellipsis, substitution, and lexical ties. The subjects read the story through once (with help from the experimenter if necessary) so that they could get the gist of the whole. They were then given a fresh copy of the story to look at, with the expressions of interest underlined. We assessed the children's understanding of the cohesive ties in two ways. First, they were asked what the words of interest "pointed back to" or "stood for," and then, if they could not respond to these probes, they were asked a more direct question. For instance, if the text were *Bill went fishing.* **He** *carried* *his rod to the bus stop,* the child would be asked, *Who carried his rod to the bus stop?* The results from this experiment were very straightforward: There were significant differences between the groups for all types of cohesive ties, on both tasks. Even when asked the direct questions, the less skilled comprehenders were correct overall only 72% of the time, compared with 90% for the good comprehenders. Thus, the less skilled comprehenders made numerous errors, even when they were asked direct questions, and even though the text was constantly available for them to refer to. It is hardly surprising that such children have text comprehension difficulties if they cannot understand even quite straightforward cohesive devices.

3. Understanding the Main Point and Structure of a Story

The integration of information in a text depends on several skills. I have already mentioned the importance of inferences, but readers also need to appreciate the main ideas in a text—what it is about—and to understand how it is structured. A number of studies have shown that young children find it difficult to make explicit judgments about what is important in a story, and that this ability develops slowly during the early school years (see Oakhill & Garnham, 1988, Chap. 5). There has been little research to explore good and poor comprehenders' ability to understand the hierarchical structure of text, or what is important in it.

In some of our own research (see Yuill & Oakhill, 1991, Chap. 7), we have asked groups of good and poor comprehenders to recount stories prompted by picture sequences. One general finding from these studies was that the poor comprehenders seemed to have a less integrated idea of the stories as a whole—they tended to give picture-by-picture accounts, as though they were describing a series of unrelated events rather than constructing an integrated sequence of statements. In their stories, too, the main point was often unclear. In order to measure their understanding of the picture sequences on which their stories were based, we asked them to decide, *What was the most important thing about the story—the point of it?* The children were given four statements to choose from for each story: one was the main point (as judged by adults), one was a major event in the story, one described the setting of the story, and one was an incorrect main point (that would indicate a misunderstanding of the story). The data showed that the good comprehenders were clearly better able to understand the main point of these picture sequences. We looked at the data in two different ways. First, the good comprehenders were above chance at selecting the main point in all stories, whereas the less skilled comprehenders performed above chance level for only 3 out of 6 stories. Second, the skilled comprehenders picked out the main point 79% of the time, whereas the less skilled comprehenders succeeded only 46% of the time.

These data are interesting from another point of view. They indicate that not only do the poor comprehenders have trouble in listening comprehension tasks, but that their comprehension difficulties are really very broad—they extend even to the understanding of picture sequences. These children do not have any general communication difficulties but, it seems, do have problems in these decontextualised comprehension tasks, which are so common in school learning and assessment situations.

4. Metacognition and Comprehension Skill

As we saw earlier, the ability to monitor comprehension during reading is important, and studies of young children have shown that they often fail to realize that they have not adequately understood a text. Good comprehenders seem to have a better awareness of what comprehension is and when it has occurred (Golinkoff, 1975–1976), and there is evidence that poor comprehenders' problems arise partly because they fail to monitor their own comprehension, or at least because they make less use of monitoring strategies.

Garner (1980) has shown that poor comprehenders tend to be less aware of their own lack of understanding. She asked 7th and 8th grade good and poor comprehenders to read passages that contained obvious inconsistencies. The children had to decide how easy each section of the passages was to understand, and explain why any difficult passages were hard. Garner found that good comprehenders reliably classified the inconsistent passages as harder to understand than the consistent ones, and their comments showed that they understood the source of the problems. By contrast, the poor comprehenders did not discriminate between the consistent and inconsistent sections and, even when they reported a lack of understanding, they did not pick out the inconsistent sections as a source of problems. They explained their difficulties with comments such as "The words were longer" or "I didn't like that part as well." Garner points out that poor monitoring ability may be either a cause or a consequence of poor comprehension: Poor comprehenders might expect most texts to make little sense, because they always find understanding difficult!

Another study by Garner (1981) investigated the monitoring skills of 5th and 6th grade poor comprehenders, all of whom had average or above-average word recognition skills. The results showed that they rated an inconsistent passage as easy to understand as a consistent one, but that they rated a passage containing polysyllabic modifiers whose meaning they did not know as being less comprehensible because it contained "tough words" or "long words." Garner characterizes the poor comprehenders as being more concerned with individual words than the text as a whole.

Further research by Garner and Kraus (1981–1982) showed that almost all of a group of 7th grade good comprehenders detected inconsistencies in a text, but that none of the poor comprehenders reported them. They also gave the children a questionnaire about reading which provides further evidence that poor comprehenders do not integrate the information from different parts of a text (and, therefore, do not detect inconsistencies) because their attention is directed to other parts of the text. The responses to the questionnaire were revealing: Although none of the poor comprehenders had decoding problems, most of them mentioned the importance of word decoding in reading (a response that was never made by the good comprehenders), and few mentioned understanding or extraction of meaning. For instance, when asked what makes something difficult to read, good comprehenders gave responses such as "not being familiar with the main ideas," "badly written stuff where the ideas are hard to get," whereas the poor comprehenders stressed the word level: "small print," "long words." These results reinforce the idea that, even when they are not poor decoders, poor comprehenders put the emphasis on accurate decoding rather than attending to the meaning of the text.

Work by Paris and Myers (1981) has come to similar conclusions. They gave 4th grade children passages to read that contained difficult or anomalous information and used three indices of comprehension monitoring: spontaneous self-corrections during oral reading, underlining of incomprehensible words and phrases, and study behavior (asking questions or using a dictionary). The poor readers showed less evidence of comprehension monitoring on all three measures. In addition, a measure included to assess the children's perception of the effectiveness of a number of reading strategies showed that the poor readers were less aware than good ones of which strategies could be detrimental to understanding. Again, they seemed to focus on word decoding, rather than comprehension goals. For example, they rated the strategy "saying every word over and over" as very helpful.

Our own work, too, has indicated that good and poor comprehenders differ in their views about reading (Yuill & Oakhill, 1991). We interviewed children to elicit information about their views on reading and, in particular, their beliefs concerning comprehension. When asked what makes someone a good reader, both groups stressed speed and accuracy. However, "not knowing words" was a particularly important indicator of poor reading for the less skilled children: There was a significant difference between the groups in the number of times this attribute was mentioned. Interestingly, there was no evidence that the less skilled comprehenders experienced reading as a difficult or unpleasant activity. They rated their enjoyment of reading as slightly higher than did the good comprehenders, and also rated themselves as better readers. Somewhat worryingly, their teachers often concurred with their own judgments of their reading ability! These interview data support the intuition that many of the poor comprehenders were not concerned about their comprehension failures, and viewed reading primarily in terms of decoding.

In one experiment, we explored children's comprehension monitoring more objectively by exploring their ability to detect anomalies (see Yuill, Oakhill, & Parkin, 1989). The children were presented with stories containing obvious anomalies, and we also explored the influence of working memory load on their ability to resolve the anomalies. The children were read short stories describing an adult's apparently inconsistent response to a child's action. In the stories of interest, information that resolved the apparent inconsistency was included somewhere in the story. For example, in one story a mother is pleased with her son when he refuses to share candy with his little brother. The resolving information in this story is that the brother is on a diet. (There were other control conditions: consistent stories, and ones where the anomaly was not resolved, but these are not the focus of interest.)

We manipulated the memory demands of using the resolving information by varying the distance between the apparent anomaly and the resolving information, and we also included the resolving information either before or after the anomaly. We expected that resolving information that followed the anomaly would be more difficult to use because it would require retrospective resolution (i.e., the anomaly could not be resolved when it was first encountered). After each story, the children were asked if the adult should have acted as he or she did, and if so, why (they would only get this question correct if they had used the resolving information). They were also asked two further questions, one to check that they had remembered important information from the story, and another to make sure that they agreed with the implicit rule on which the inconsistency was based (i.e., that it is good to share candy, for the story above). Almost all the children answered the memory and implicit rule questions correctly. But their ability to detect the anomalies showed a striking pattern of results: When the inconsistency and its resolution were in adjacent sentences, the skilled and less skilled comprehenders were correct about 70% of the time. However, when the two pieces of information were separated by two sentences, the performance of the good comprehenders was not affected, whereas that of the poor group dropped to only 17% correct. These data provide convincing evidence that the less skilled comprehenders understood the task and, indeed, were perfectly able to answer the questions when the two pieces of information could be integrated readily. However, when this integration was made more difficult by imposing a memory load, their performance deteriorated markedly. As predicted, both groups tended to find it harder to use resolving information when it followed rather than preceded the anomaly, but the before/after difference was slightly but not significantly larger for the less skilled comprehenders (22% vs. 5%).

5. Working Memory in Text Comprehension

Although the above studies document some of the specific difficulties of poor comprehenders, they do not explain why the less skilled comprehenders should have difficulty with text integration, inferences, and comprehension monitoring. One obvious possibility is that they have poor working memories. Many recent accounts of reading emphasize the importance of various aspects of memory. Short-term memory is needed for the temporary storage and integration of information, long-term memory for more permanent storage and as a source of relevant background knowledge, for instance, for inference making. Both, therefore, will play an important part in comprehension, but it is short-term and working memory that is the focus of this section.

Studies of the relation between short-term memory and comprehension skill are equivocal. In general, children with reading problems are found to have smaller short-term memories than normal readers, as measured by the standard digit span technique (Torgeson, 1978–1979). However, Perfetti has failed to find such differences in similar tasks (Perfetti & Goldman, 1976; Perfetti & Lesgold, 1979). One reason for these discrepant findings may be that the children in the different studies had different reading problems. Few studies have addressed the issue of whether children with a specific comprehension problem, as opposed to some more general reading problem, have deficient short-term memories. Some work of our own has clarified this issue (see Oakhill et al., 1986). Several studies have shown that where good and poor readers do differ on memory span tasks, these differences are due primarily to differences in the efficiency of phonological coding in working memory (see Stanovich, 1986; Wagner & Torgeson, 1987). Phonological recoding is important in comprehension because phonological codes are more durable than visual codes for storing early parts of a sentence to combine them with what comes later. To investigate whether skilled and less skilled comprehenders who are matched in decoding skills differ in their use of phonological coding, we ran an experiment (Oakhill et al., 1986) using a technique developed by Hitch and Halliday (1983). The children in our experiment were asked to remember short lists of one-, two-, and three-syllable spoken words. Both skilled and less skilled comprehenders recalled more short than long words, but there were no differences between the groups. The children were also asked to remember series of pictures corresponding to the words in the lists. Sensitivity to word length in this condition would indicate that the children were coding the picture names in a phonological form. Again, there was a main effect of length of the picture names, but no differences between the groups. Both groups showed evidence of verbal recoding of the picture names. These results support the idea that there is no general difference in capacity between skilled and less skilled comprehenders.

However, the tasks we have discussed so far are primarily tests of storage capacity. Oakhill et al. (1988) suggested that good and poor comprehenders might differ on a task that makes heavier demands on working memory—a task that requires simultaneous storage and processing. Recent research with adults has shown that working memory is related to comprehension skill (see Daneman, 1987, for a review). Working memory is a limited-capacity system for the simultaneous storage and processing of information, and Daneman and Carpenter (1980, 1983) have shown that various aspects of skilled comprehension (remembering facts, detecting inconsistencies, resolving pronouns) are related to a verbal test of working memory. In their test, the subjects were required to read and understand a series of sentences (processing requirement) while simultaneously trying to remember the final word in each (storage requirement). Because Daneman and Carpenter's reading span test requires reading and understanding sentences, we felt that the skilled comprehenders may be at an advantage in performing it. We therefore developed an analogous task using numerical materials. The children were presented with lists of numbers to read aloud (processing requirement) and had to remember the final digit of each number group (storage requirement). The memory load was varied by increasing the number of final digits to be recalled: 2, 3, or 4. So, for example, in the two-digit case, the child might read the numbers 7–4–2 and 1–0–9 and then recall 2 and 9. We found that, although there was no difference between the groups in the easiest (two-digit recall) version, there were differences in the three- and four-digit versions of the task. We have replicated this finding with two further groups of skilled and less skilled comprehenders. So, one suggestion to explain the poor comprehenders' difficulties in making inferences and integrating text is that they cannot hold sufficient information in working memory.

If poor comprehenders have deficient working memories, then it is hardly surprising that they have difficulties integrating information from different parts of a text and making inferences. Indeed, the idea of a working memory deficit fits in nicely with our study of anomaly detection, above, in which we showed that it was only when the apparent inconsistency and the resolving information were separated that the less skilled comprehenders had any difficulty.

D. Individual Differences: Conclusions

The general impression from this series of experiments is that the less skilled comprehenders' problem cannot be attributed to any straightforward memory deficit. The poor comprehenders' verbatim recall of text is no worse than that of the skilled group, but they have difficulty in integrating the ideas in texts and in remembering the gist of the whole. They also have difficulty monitoring their own comprehension. The experiments on working memory suggest that the lack of such processing skills may be related to the less skilled comprehenders' poorer working memory capacity. However, before coming to any general conclusions, other studies, in which attempts have been made to improve the comprehension of the less skilled group, should be considered. These studies suggest that a working memory explanation probably cannot provide a complete account of the less skilled comprehenders' problems.

III. IMPROVING READING COMPREHENSION

There are three main ways in which comprehension and learning from text can be improved, only one of which I will consider in any detail here. First, there are various additions or changes that can be made to a text to improve its comprehensibility and memorability. Such additions and changes are made FOR readers and require no active effort on their part. Additions might include pictures, titles, and summary statements; other changes are usually aimed at improving the organization and coherence of the text. Second, readers can engage in various activities either during or after reading the text, for example: underlining, note-taking, and summary writing. Such activities are usually referred to as study aids. Although such aids are generally thought of as a means by which students learn from text, research has also shown that they can be used to improve comprehension (for a summary, see Oakhill & Garham, 1988). The third set of aids to comprehension is processing strategies that children can be taught to apply as they are reading—ways to think about the text, about whether it relates to what they know, and about whether their understanding is adequate. Such strategies are designed primarily to improve comprehension rather than to aid learning. They differ from the first two types of aid in that they rely entirely on what goes on in the reader's head, rather than on external aids to understanding and learning. Most remediation studies have trained children in the use of this third type of aid because poor comprehenders can most usefully be helped by giving them procedures that they can apply to any text.

If a skill that poor comprehenders lack is causally related to their comprehension problems, training in that skill may improve their comprehension. The outcome from a training study comparing good and poor comprehenders that most strongly suggests a causal role for the trained skill is when training brings poor comprehenders up to the level of good comprehenders, but the good comprehenders do not benefit from the training program (presumably because they already possess the skill being trained). Below, I consider some research efforts that have attempted to improve comprehension skill.

A. Training in Rapid Decoding

Many people regard decoding speed and automaticity as a crucial factor in reading comprehension (see Perfetti, 1985, for a review). However, attempts to improve comprehension by training in rapid decoding have generally failed (e.g., Fleisher et al., 1979). Such results suggest that rapid decoding, although necessary for efficient comprehension, may be only one of a number of skills required, and that training may have no direct effect on comprehension.

B. Background Knowledge, Inferences, and Question Generation

Less skilled comprehenders can make inferences and use their background knowledge to interpret a text (Oakhill, 1982, 1983), so it seems reasonable to suppose that they might make more use of such skills if they were more aware of the value of doing so. Such children might not fully appreciate that they ought to use relevant knowledge and experience to interpret a text. One way of encouraging poorer comprehenders to make information explicit would be to train them in the selection of pictures or summary statements that integrate the information in a text. Another way might be for teachers to discuss stories with children and to encourage them to make predictions and inferences by asking appropriate questions. Such techniques might also impress on children the legitimacy of making inferences and using background knowledge to help their understanding.

Such methods have been shown to be successful in improving comprehension. Au (1977, cited by Wittrock, 1981) found that children's reading comprehension was improved considerably by a one-year training program that emphasized the construction of meaning from text. The children verbalized their experiences as they read stories and were encouraged to relate what was happening in the stories to their background knowledge and to make inferences from the text.

Hansen (1981) attempted to train children in awareness of how their prior knowledge could be used in story comprehension. All her subjects (7-year-olds) were average or above-average readers. There were three groups: The first (control) group read a series of texts that was followed by a mixture of about one inferential to five literal questions; the second group received *only* questions requiring an inference; the third (strategy) group was encouraged to integrate information in a text with prior knowledge. With this third group, a weaving metaphor was used to suggest how prior knowledge and information from the text should be put together, and the children were encouraged to predict what might happen in the text, using their own relevant prior knowledge. Both the latter two groups were better able to answer comprehension questions in a subsequent test than were the control group, with strategy training tending to be more effective. However, the results held only for the passages used in training and did not transfer to new stories, though there was some improvement on a standardized reading test. These results emphasize the need for children to be taught when to apply newly acquired skills.

Such training might prove to be particularly helpful to children with comprehension difficulties. Hansen and Pearson (1983) used a training program, with 9-year-old good and poor comprehenders, that combined Hansen's strategy training with inferential question techniques. The training helped the poor comprehenders both in understanding the original passages and new ones, but there was no training effect for the good readers. These findings suggest that encouraging poor comprehenders can be effective in improving their comprehension, but that better readers make inferences spontaneously.

Yuill and Joscelyne (1988, Experiment 2) provided further support for this conclusion. They instructed 7-to-8-year-old good and poor comprehenders in how to make inferences from specific words in texts. In the stories they used, the locations and main consequences were not explicitly stated, and had to be inferred. For example, one story was about a boy reading a schoolbook in the bath. He got soap in his eye and dropped the book. However, the main consequence—that the book fell into the water and got wet—was not explicitly stated, but could be inferred from particular words in the text. Similarly, the location of the story could be worked out from the use of certain words in the text—the room was *steamy*, the boy was lying down, and there was mention of *soap* and a *towel*. Once it has been inferred that the boy was reading in the bath, the clues to the main consequence—the splash and the boy's exclamation of horror—suggest that he dropped the book in the water. This inference is further supported by the information that the boy was worried about what he would tell his teacher, and that he planned to buy a new book. The children were trained to use "cue words" in the story to infer the missing information. The results showed that the trained poor comprehenders, but not the good comprehenders, were better at answering comprehension questions than control subjects who were given no training.

Other studies have explored the efficacy of asking children to generate their own questions about texts as a means of improving comprehension. Some studies of self-generated questions have failed to show effects (see Tierney & Cunningham, 1984, for a review). However, as Tierney and Cunningham point out, few such studies have given the children training or practice in question generation and, in other cases, the training procedures have often severely limited the types of question that can be asked. As Weaver and Shonkoff (1978) argue, if only factual questions are generated, children may need to think very little about what they are reading and may miss the major points of a text. What is needed, they suggest, is a mixture of questions, requiring responses at various levels—literal, inferential, interpretive, evaluative, and so on. Indeed, Andre and Anderson (1978–1979) showed that high-school children who were explicitly instructed in how to formulate questions and use them in their learning generated a higher proportion of good comprehension questions, and their comprehension scores on a subsequent test were slightly (though not significantly) higher than those of children who were simply told to generate their own questions as they read a text (though both question generation groups did better than a group who just reread the texts). The lower ability subjects benefited most from the training. Training in question generation has also proven to be effective with much younger children. Cohen (1983) showed that training in question generation, combined with instruction in how to apply such skills to reading short stories, improved the comprehension of 3rd grade children (8-year-olds).

The results of the studies reviewed above show that relatively simple procedures can increase constructive processing of text and enhance reading comprehension. Obviously, to benefit from the use of such procedures, children must possess the relevant prior knowledge to draw inferences and to elaborate on what is explicit in a text. However, readers may possess the relevant background knowledge but, nevertheless, fail to access and use it in comprehension. Strategies for organizing and retrieving information might also need to be taught.

C. Training in Metacognitive Skills

Our own interviews with poor comprehenders suggest that when they are not specifically instructed about what they should get out of a text, they are not usually aware of their comprehension problems. For example, as we saw above, they are less likely than skilled comprehenders to notice anomalies in a text. The ability to decide whether or not a text has been adequately understood is a crucial step toward becoming an independent reader. Young children are often not aware that their understanding is inadequate, and they are poor at detecting omissions and inconsistencies (Markman, 1977).

Reis and Spekman (1983) showed that 11- and 12-year-old poor comprehenders were considerably better at detecting reader-based inconsistencies (i.e., those that violate what the reader knows about the world) than they were at detecting text-based inconsistencies (conflicting information in the text). Although even those children who were very poor at detecting inconsistencies could be trained to do so, such training only improved their ability to detect reader-based, and not text-based, inconsistencies. Reis and Spekman suggest that even poor comprehenders evaluate their comprehension to some extent but tend to use different standards to those used by better readers—they are able to monitor how a text relates to their own knowledge about the world, but not whether it is internally consistent.

Brown, Palincsar, and Armbruster (1984) combined training in question generation, summarization, clarification, and prediction in a program specifically designed to enhance the comprehension skills of 12-year-olds with comprehension difficulties. (Although the ability to generate and answer questions is not, in itself, a metacognitive skill, question generation can be used as part of a metacognitive training program if children are taught to make up questions that help them assess whether they have understood the text.) The children were also informed about why and how the activities were important. Their ability to ask effective questions and to produce good summaries improved dramatically during the training period, but it again emerged that fairly extensive training may be necessary before children can incorporate such skills into their repertoire and can use them effectively. The children also showed reliable and lasting improvements on various measures of comprehension, including standardized reading tests. Similar studies by Paris and his associates have also shown that training in metacognitive awareness can improve both reading strategies and comprehension. For instance, Paris, Cross, and Lipson (1984) gave 3rd and 5th graders training in a rich variety of comprehension strategies, including understanding the purpose of the text, attending to main ideas, monitoring comprehension, and drawing inferences. They found that the children given such training performed better on cloze comprehension and error detection tasks, though not on standardized comprehension tests.

Another comprehension aid that could be used to encourage comprehension monitoring is mental imagery. For instance, Bales (1984) showed that below-average 4th and 5th grade readers could benefit from mental imagery instructions. The children were told to *make pictures in your head to help you determine if there is anything not clear or not easy to understand*. Compared with a control group who were told to *do whatever you can to help you determine if there is anything not clear or not easy to understand*, the imagery group were able to detect more of the inconsistencies in a text. These findings suggest that imagery can be used as a monitoring strategy, and that poor readers can use it. The relevance of imagery in improving comprehension more generally is discussed in the next section.

Collins and Smith (1982) have suggested a specific three-stage program of training in comprehension monitoring and predictive skills. In the first stage, MODELING, the teacher takes the lead, reading stories and commenting on what is entailed in understanding them. For example, the teacher generates hypotheses about the text, points out sources of difficulty and how to overcome them, and comments on ways of gaining insight into the text. During this stage, the teacher gradually encourages the children to take an active part in these activities, in preparation for the next stage, STUDENT PARTICIPATION. During this stage, the teacher shifts the responsibility for generating hypotheses, and for detecting and remedying comprehension failures, to the children. In the final stage, READING SILENTLY, the children are expected to use the skills they have learned in independent reading. Collins and Smith suggest that children can be encouraged to use these skills by giving them texts with problems to spot, or texts with questions that encourage them to predict what will happen next.

The above review includes studies of poor readers generally, as well as average readers, but the results are difficult to generalize to populations of poor comprehenders such as those I have studied, who have a specific comprehension (not a word recognition) problem. One study of ours attempted to improve the inferential skills of the less skilled group by giving them a series of short training sessions (Yuill & Oakhill, 1988a).

As we saw in the above review, several studies have found that encouraging children to make inferences can be effective in improving comprehension (though most of these studies have looked at the effects of training on poor readers generally, rather than children who have a specific comprehension deficit). Several of the experiments described above showed that less skilled comprehenders are poor at making inferences, even when the text is available to them. An effective training program for such children should, therefore, encourage children to make inferences as they read. However, inference training in itself may not be enough. There is some evidence that poor comprehenders do not always understand when it is appropriate to use their everyday knowledge in interpreting a text and thus may make unwarranted and inappropriate inferences. In the present study, training in question generation was combined with instruction in making inferences, to sensitize the children to the types of inference they should make, as well as to help them in the techniques for drawing inferences. We also aimed to encourage and guide the children in going beyond the information given in the passages, by including a type of "macrocloze" task, in which they read stories with sentences omitted and tried to guess what information was missing. In general, the aim of the procedures was to encourage the children to take a more active part in their comprehension—to encourage both appropriate inferential processing and comprehension monitoring.

The inference training procedure included fairly explicit training in activities to help comprehension. However, it may be possible for children to develop appropriate inference skills without such explicit instruction. To assess this possibility, we included a control comparison condition in which the subjects were given intensive practice in standard comprehension exercises—that is, simply answering comprehension questions about the texts.

An alternative account of poor comprehension—discussed briefly at the beginning of this chapter—is the decoding bottleneck hypothesis (e.g., Perfetti, 1977). This hypothesis proposes that if readers do not recognize words sufficiently quickly and automatically, the processing required for word recognition will place an additional burden on short-term memory and will consequently reduce the resources available for comprehension processes. Although several sources of evidence have indicated that inefficient decoding is not causally implicated in poor reading comprehension, in order to rule out such an explanation of poor comprehension in the present subjects, a comparison training group who were given practice in rapid decoding was included in the study. This group also served as a control for various features of the two treatment conditions that could contribute indirectly to any improvements in performance, namely individual attention, familiarity with the experimenter, and reading practice. The group trained in rapid decoding had practice reading the same texts as the other groups, and practice in rapid decoding of word lists from them.

We assessed the effects of three types of training (inference skills, comprehension exercises, and rapid decoding) on separate groups of good and poor comprehenders. The children were selected as described previously, using the Neale and Gates–MacGinitie tests. The children within each comprehension skill group were allocated to the three different conditions so that the subjects in each treatment group were adequately matched on the measures of interest.

The INFERENCE-TRAINED GROUPS engaged in three types of activity:

1. Lexical inference (all sessions). This activity was introduced with sentences such as *Sleepy Tom was late for school again.* Each child had to pick one of the words and to say what information it gave about the sentence. For example, we know that *Tom* is a male person and, combined with the word *school,* that he is probably a pupil, since his first name is given. *Sleepy* suggests that he overslept, perhaps because he stayed up late the previous night, and suggests why he was *late. Again* suggests that he has often been late before, perhaps because he habitually stays up late. The children then applied such analyses to short, abstract, stories such as the following:

> *Billy was crying. His whole day was spoilt. All his work had been broken by the wave. His mother came to stop him crying. But she accidentally stepped on the only tower that was left. Billy cried even more. "Never mind," said his mother, "We can always build another one tomorrow." Billy stopped crying and went home for his tea.*

For example, they could use the word *wave* as a clue that the story setting is a beach. The children were then encouraged to link together single lexical inferences, for example by using the location inferred from *wave* to guess that the *tower* was a sand castle.

2. Question generation (four occasions). After discussing question-words (*who, where, why,* etc.) and being given examples of how questions can be derived from a text, the children were invited to generate their own questions from single sentences, then from stories. For example, the children generated

questions such as *Who was crying?* and *Where was Billy?* for the story given above. Each child took turns at being "the teacher," and the other children answered the questions put to them.

3. Prediction (one occasion). The children read texts in which sentences had been obscured, and tried to guess what each hidden sentence was, based on clues from surrounding sentences. The hidden sentence was then revealed, and the predictions checked.

The COMPREHENSION EXERCISE GROUPS were told about the importance of reading for comprehension and, after sharing between them the reading of a given text, they were asked comprehension questions by the experimenter. The experimenter did not give detailed feedback about responses, but did correct obviously wrong answers. In addition, the children often discussed the answers and corrected one another. The questions were designed to be similar to those in the sorts of comprehension exercises for slightly older children commonly found in school and comprised a mix of inferential and literal questions. For example, the questions for the "Beach" story given above were as follows: (a) *Where was Billy?* (b) *Why was Billy crying?* (c) *What had the wave broken?* (d) *Why did his mother go to him?* (e) *Why did Billy cry even more?*

The children in the RAPID DECODING GROUPS were first told of the importance of rapid word recognition. Each session then followed a similar pattern. First, the children were shown a list of words taken from that session's text, and the experimenter read the list through. Each child practiced reading the list as quickly and accurately as possible. Then the children took turns at reading the specified text. Finally, each child read the word list again, and the experimenter recorded the time taken, using a stopwatch. In the subsequent session, the children reread the previous word list, and their time was recorded. The word lists comprised about 20% of the words of each text and included those that were the most difficult to recognize.

Each of the three groups received seven training sessions (in small groups) of about 30 minutes each, over a period of $3\frac{1}{2}$ weeks, and the same ten narrative texts were used in all three conditions for both skill groups. After the training had been completed, the children's comprehension was assessed again using a different (parallel) version of the Neale test. The results of this assessment showed that the less skilled comprehenders benefited from inference training more than did the skilled group. Furthermore, the less skilled comprehenders given inference training improved significantly more than those in the decoding control group (though not significantly more than those in the comprehension exercises control group). There were no differences between the groups in reading speed or accuracy at the end of the training period. It is also interesting to note that the skilled comprehenders were not, in general, superior to the less skilled group in speed of decoding—in fact, they tended to be slower.

These results show that, for less skilled comprehenders, inference training was both more beneficial than was decoding practice and was more helpful to them than it was to the skilled comprehenders. The less skilled comprehenders given inference training improved slightly, but not significantly, more than those given comprehension exercises. The effect of inference training was very marked for the less skilled comprehenders, with an average increase in Neale comprehension age of over 17 months within a period of two months. This result is particularly impressive given that few training studies have demonstrated improvements on standardized tests—most have reassessed performance only on the particular skills trained.

The absence of a significant difference between inference training and comprehension exercises suggests that both contained some extra element that the decoding training lacked, such as the discussion of stories, and that both promoted comprehension processes normally lacking in less skilled comprehenders. We had not expected the comprehension exercises to be so successful in improving comprehension, but the effects may have been due to the fact that children in the exercise group often corrected one another and discussed their answers. These incidental activities may have increased their awareness of their own comprehension. In addition, as the passages used were rather obscure and left a good deal of information to be inferred, they may have encouraged the children to do more inferential processing and reflecting on their comprehension processes than would the sorts of passages standardly used in such activities. Thus, the inference training might have been effective not because the children adopted wholesale the strategies they had been taught, but because they developed a greater degree of awareness of their own comprehension. Such awareness might be fostered either by training such as that given, or by intensive small-group practice in comprehension exercises.

D. Imagery

In the preceding section, I mentioned the use of imagery in improving comprehension monitoring. But imagery might also improve comprehension more generally—it may have its effects by maintaining attention, or by promoting deeper semantic processing of the text. Imagery instruction has proved successful with children. For instance, Pressley (1976) taught 8-year-olds to generate images for sections of stories as they read them. Compared to children who only read the stories, those who produced images were better able to answer questions about them. However, the ability to use imagery instructions improves with age, and it is not until about 8 that children can learn to use self-generated images to improve their comprehension of stories. Guttman, Levin, and Pressley (1977) found that the reading comprehension of 3rd graders, but not kindergartners, could be improved by imagery instructions, or by partial pictures. Those children given partial pictures were told to use them to help to construct an image of what they could not see. In contrast, the same study showed that children from kindergarten, 1st, and 3rd grades all recalled more information when the stories were accompanied by complete pictures—the amount of improvement was similar at all three ages. However, as with many of the other comprehension aids I have discussed, imagery instructions do not automatically enhance comprehension, even for children older than 9 (see Levin, 1981, for a review). Levin argues that one reason for the discrepant findings is that not all types of image are equally helpful, and that different types of material may call for different types of image.

We explored whether children's comprehension might be improved by giving them training in imagery strategies (Oakhill & Patel, 1991). We also addressed the issue of whether imagery is particularly suitable for aiding memory for some sorts of information by asking the children three different types of questions. The first type, which we termed FACTUAL, tapped memory for facts that were explicit in the text. The second main type of question, INFERENTIAL, asked about information that could only be inferred from the story, and the third type, DESCRIPTIVE, asked about details that would be particularly likely to come to the reader's attention if an effective image had been formed.

Peters, Levin, McGivern, and Pressley (1985) suggest that different forms of imagery instruction might be suitable for different passages and identified two distinct types of imagery which they termed REPRESENTATIONAL and TRANSFORMATIONAL. Representational imagery is the fairly direct translation of the text into an image. In transformational imagery, however, as the name suggests, some aspects of the text are transformed so that the image does not correspond directly to the text but is used as a sort of mnemonic. Peters et al. argued that this form of imagery might be useful for recalling difficult-to-remember things, such as names and numerical data, which are more prevalent in nonnarrative passages and which do not necessarily lend themselves to representation in an imageable form. An example from Peters et al.'s study provides an illustration of how transformational imagery might be used. Their subjects (8-year-olds) had to remember what each person was famous for, given sentences such as:

Larry Taylor was famous for inventing a house on a turntable.

They were instructed to transform the names into more imageable forms (in this case, a tailor) and to integrate this image with an image of the rest of the sentence. The results confirmed the authors' predictions: Transformational imagery substantially improved subjects' recall of difficult-to-remember factual information (e.g., names), but was not critical for information that could be more directly coded into an image. Representational imagery, by contrast, did not significantly facilitate memory for the difficult information. In our experiment, we incorporated training in both sorts of imagery technique, in order to optimize the effectiveness of imagery training.

Some work has investigated the effects of imagery training on poor comprehenders specifically and has shown that they seem to derive special benefit from visual imagery instructions. Levin (1973) tested two groups of 4th grade poor comprehenders—those with decoding and vocabulary problems, and those with adequate decoding and vocabulary skills. The subjects given imagery instructions were told to try to *think of a picture in their mind* as they read each sentence. Such instructions improved comprehension (compared with simply reading the story) for the second, but not for the first, group of poor readers. Indeed, the second group (those with adequate decoding skills) performed as well as good comprehenders when they were given imagery instructions. We also investigated the effects of imagery instructions on good and poor comprehenders but explored in more detail whether imagery might facilitate recall of different types of information, by asking the subjects different types of questions about the passages, as outlined above.

The children were given the same tests as in the first training study (above) except that, in order to provide a rapid assessment of their comprehension, the Neale test was adapted as a group test of listening comprehension (previous work by Oakhill, e.g., 1982, 1983, has shown that children who have a reading comprehension problem also have difficulty with listening comprehension). The good and poor comprehenders (whose mean age was 9.7) were subdivided into two matched groups, one of which was given training in imagery. Nine stories were written using suitable vocabulary, so that all participants would be able to read them without difficulty.

The imagery training took place in small groups (of 4 or 5 children) over three sessions, on different days. The children were told that they would be learning to "think in pictures" as they read stories, to help them to answer questions about them. We used nine stories altogether: four for training, and five in the test session. For each story, the three types of question described above (inference, descriptive, and factual) were asked. In the first training session the children read one of the stories, and the experimenter then produced two drawings: one was a cartoonlike sequence of four pictures which represented the sequence of events in the story, and the other was a single picture, depicting the main event in the story. The children were shown how each of the pictures related to the story and were encouraged to use these "pictures in their minds" to help them answer questions about the stories. For a second story in this session, the children were not shown pictures but were encouraged to formulate their own mental images. They discussed their pictures and received feedback and suggestions.

In the second training session, both representational and transformational drawings were presented, and their uses were explained. The children were then told that they should try to form three different types of image as they read through a new story: a cartoon sequence with four frames to represent the sequence of events in the story, an image of the main event, and a transformational image to help them remember specific details. In the final training session the children were not shown any drawings. The imagery procedure was reiterated, the children read and answered questions about a new story, and a final discussion of their mental pictures took place, as in the first two sessions.

The children who did not receive imagery training saw the same stories, also in three sessions. They read the stories and answered the questions, and their answers were then discussed with them. The children in this condition spent as long with the experimenter as those in the imagery training groups. In the test phase, the groups who had received the imagery training were reminded to form mental images as they read the stories and to use their pictures to help them to answer the questions. The children in the control condition were told to read the stories very carefully and to answer the questions in as much detail as possible.

We found that good comprehenders answered more questions correctly than poor ones, and that the children given imagery training performed better than those in the control group. The prediction that the poor, but not the good, comprehenders would benefit from imagery training was tested by comparing the effects of training for the two groups. As predicted, the poor comprehenders given imagery training showed a marked improvement in memory for the passages: They performed significantly better on the test questions than did the control group of poor comprehenders. There was no such difference in the case of the good comprehenders. Imagery training did not have a differential effect for the different types of questions.

The results show that imagery training was especially effective for those children who do not possess adequate comprehension skills, but that it had a general effect on their performance and did not differentially affect the retention of information of different types. Poor comprehenders may show a particular benefit from imagery training because it enables them, or forces them, to integrate information in the text in a way that they would not normally do. The finding that the comprehension of the good group did not improve with imagery training does not necessarily mean that they already use imagery and hence do not benefit from training in its use. It may be that they have some other equally efficient strategy for remembering information from text, and that training in imagery provides them with no additional advantage.

One way in which training in imagery strategies may help poor comprehenders is by giving them a strategy to help them overcome some of the limiting factors on their comprehension skills. For instance, the ability to use imagery strategies may give poor comprehenders a way of helping to circumvent their memory limitations by enabling them to use a different, and perhaps more economical, means of representing information in the text.

E. Remediation Studies: Conclusions

Although I have by no means provided an exhaustive survey of the many different learning aids and strategies, I hope that the above review will provide some idea of ways in which children's comprehension might be improved. There is obviously no "best" aid or strategy that can be recommended, and the effects of training are often crucially dependent on the type and length of the training given. An important consideration in educational settings is that some methods may be more practicable than others.

I would like to end this section with two notes of caution. First, most methods for improving comprehension assume that poor readers will benefit from being taught strategies that skilled ones use naturally. However, the fact that poor readers have failed to acquire these skills might indicate that, at least in some cases, they are unable to do so. A study by Brown and Smiley (1978) illustrates this problem. They showed that children who learned best from text were those who spontaneously took notes or underlined, but less proficient learners did not benefit from the suggestion that they should use these strategies. So, it cannot be assumed that poor comprehenders will automatically become good ones if they are taught the skills that good comprehenders possess.

Second, instruction in skills such as comprehension monitoring should be restricted to children who have reached the stage where they are reading to learn. The introduction of such training to children who have not yet mastered decoding may be counterproductive because they may not have enough processing capacity to do both aspects of reading together. Therefore, it seems sensible to wait until decoding is reasonably proficient before introducing training in comprehension strategies. This does not mean that children should not learn from the outset that comprehension is the purpose of reading. The claim is simply that training in conscious comprehension strategies should not be introduced too early.

IV. CONCLUSIONS

The picture that emerges of less skilled comprehenders is of children who are poor at making inferences and connecting up ideas in a text not only when they read, but also when they are read to. Working memory may play a part in such skills—our own studies showed that less skilled comprehenders had deficient working memories when compared with a skilled group. However, it seems unlikely that all their difficulties could be explained in terms of working memory, because the final study showed that inference skills could be trained. Presumably, however, such training did not affect the children's working memory capacity. One possibility is that the training procedures provided the less skilled comprehenders with strategies that helped them to circumvent their working memory deficiencies.

Acknowledgments

Many of the experiments reported here were the result of a long-standing collaboration with Nicola Yuill, whose contribution is gratefully acknowledged. The experiments were supported by a Social Science Research Council (UK) postgraduate award, and subsequently by an Economic and Social Research Council (UK) project grant (COO232053).

References

Anderson, R. C., & Ortony, A. (1975). On putting apples into bottles—A problem of polysemy. *Cognitive Psychology, 7,* 167–180.

Anderson, R. C., Pichert, W., Goetz, F. T., Shallert, D., Stevens, K. V., & Trollip, S. R. (1976). Instantiation of general terms. *Journal of Verbal Learning and Verbal Behavior, 15,* 667–679.

Andre, M. E. D. A. and Anderson, T. H. (1978–1979). The development and evaluation of a self-questioning study technique. *Reading Research Quarterly, 14,* 605–623.

Bales, R. E. J. (1984). *Induced mental imagery and the comprehension monitoring of poor readers.* Unpublished doctoral dissertation, University of Maryland, College Park.

Bishop, D. V. M. (1982). *Test for reception of grammar.* London: Medical Research Council.

Bransford, J. D., Barclay, J. R., & Franks, J. J. (1972). Sentence memory: A constructive versus interpretive approach. *Cognitive Psychology, 3,* 193–209.

Bransford, J. D., & Franks, J. J. (1971). The abstraction of linguistic ideas. *Cognitive Psychology, 2,* 331–350.

Brown, A. L., Palincsar, A. S., & Armbruster, B. B. (1984). Instructing comprehension-fostering activities in interactive learning situations. In H. Mandl, N. L. Stein, & T. Trabasso (Eds.), *Learning and comprehension of text.* Hillsdale, NJ: Erlbaum.

Brown, A. L., & Smiley, S. S. (1978). The development of strategies for studying prose passages. *Child Development, 49,* 1076–1088.

Calfee, R. C., Arnold, R., & Drum, P. A. (1976). A review of *The psychology of reading* by E. Gibson and H. Levin. *Proceedings of the National Academy of Education, 3,* 1–80.

Charniak, E. (1972). *Toward a model of children's story comprehension.* Unpublished doctoral dissertation and Technical Report AI-TR-266. Massachusetts Institute of Technology, Boston.

Clay, M. M., & Imlach, R. H. (1971). Juncture, pitch and stress as reading behavior variables. *Journal of Verbal Learning and Verbal Behavior, 10,* 133–139.

Cohen, R. (1983). Self-generated questions as an aid to reading comprehension. *The Reading Teacher, 36,* 770–775.

Collins, A., & Smith, E. E. (1982). Teaching the process of reading comprehension. In D. K. Detterman & R. J. Sternberg (Eds.), *How and how much can intelligence be increased?* Norwood, NJ: Ablex.

Cromer, W. (1970). The difference model: A new explanation for some reading difficulties. *Journal of Educational Psychology, 61,* 471–483.

Daneman, M. (1987). Reading and working memory. In J. R. Beech & A. M. Colley (Eds.), *Cognitive approaches to reading* (pp. 57–86). Chichester: Wiley.

Daneman, M., & Carpenter, P. A. (1980). Individual differences in working memory and reading. *Journal of Verbal Learning and Verbal Behavior, 19,* 450–466.

Daneman, M., & Carpenter, P. A. (1983). Individual differences in integrating information between and within sentences. *Journal of Experimental Psychology: Learning, Memory and Cognition, 9*, 561–584.

Fleisher, L. S., Jenkins, J. R., & Pany, D. (1979). Effects on poor readers' comprehension of training in rapid decoding. *Reading Research Quarterly, 15*, 30–48.

Garner, R. (1980). Monitoring of understanding: An investigation of good and poor readers' awareness of induced miscomprehension of text. *Journal of Reading Behavior, 12*, 55–63.

Garner, R. (1981). Monitoring of passage inconsistency among poor comprehenders: A preliminary test of the 'piecemeal processing' explanation. *Journal of Educational Research, 74*, 159–162.

Garner, R., & Kraus, C. (1981–1982). Good and poor comprehender differences in knowing and regulating reading behaviors. *Educational Research Quarterly, 6*, 5–12.

Garnham, A., Oakhill, J. V., & Johnson-Laird, P. N. (1982). Referential continuity and the coherence of discourse. *Cognition, 11*, 29–46.

Gates, A. I., & MacGinitie, W. H. (1965). *Gates–MacGinitie reading tests.* New York: Columbia University Teachers' College Press.

Gibson, E. J., & Levin, H. (1975). *The psychology of reading.* London: MIT Press.

Golinkoff, R. M. (1975–1976). A comparison of reading comprehension processes in good and poor comprehenders. *Reading Research Quarterly, 11*, 623–659.

Guttman, J., Levin, J. R., & Pressley, M. (1977). Pictures, partial pictures, and young children's oral prose learning. *Journal of Educational Psychology, 69*, 473–480.

Halliday, M., & Hasan, R. (1976). *Cohesion in English.* London: Longman.

Hansen, J. (1981). The effects of inference training and practice on young children's reading comprehension. *Reading Research Quarterly, 16*, 391–417.

Hansen, J., & Pearson, P. D. (1983). An instructional study: Improving the inferential comprehension of good and poor fourth-grade readers. *Journal of Educational Psychology, 75*, 821–829.

Hitch, G. J., & Halliday, M. S. (1983). Working memory in children. *Philosophical Transactions of the Royal Society of London, Series B, 302*, 325–340.

Lesgold, A., Resnick, L. B., & Hammond, K. (1985). Learning to read: A longitudinal study of word skill development in two curricula. In G. E. MacKinnon & T. G. Waller (Eds.), *Reading research: Advances in theory and practice* (Vol. 4). Orlando, FL: Academic Press.

Levin, J. R. (1973). Inducing comprehension in poor readers. *Journal of Educational Psychology, 1*, 19–24.

Levin, J. R. (1981). On functions of pictures in prose. In F. J. Pirozzolo & M. C. Wittrock (Eds.), *Neuropsychological and cognitive processes in reading.* London: Academic Press.

Markman, E. M. (1977). Realizing that you don't understand: A preliminary investigation. *Child Development, 48*, 986–992.

McNemar, Q. (1962). *Psychological statistics* (3rd ed.). New York: Wiley.

Merrill, E. C., Sperber, R. D., & McCauley, C. (1981). Differences in semantic encoding as a function of reading comprehension skill. *Memory & Cognition, 9*, 618–624.

Neale, M. D. (1966). *The Neale analysis of reading ability* (2nd ed.). London: Macmillan Education.

Oakan, R., Wiener, M., & Cromer, W. (1971). Identification, organization and reading comprehension in good and poor readers. *Journal of Educational Psychology, 62*, 71–78.

Oakhill, J. V. (1981). *Children's reading comprehension.* Unpublished doctoral thesis, University of Sussex.

Oakhill, J. V. (1982). Constructive processes in skilled and less-skilled comprehenders. *British Journal of Psychology, 73*, 13–20.

Oakhill, J. V. (1983). Instantiation in skilled and less-skilled comprehenders. *Quarterly Journal of Experimental Psychology, 35A*, 441–450.

Oakhill, J. V. (1984). Inferential and memory skills in children's comprehension of stories. *British Journal of Educational Psychology, 54*, 31–39.

Oakhill, J. V., & Garnham, A. (1988). *Becoming a skilled reader.* Oxford: Basil/Blackwell.

Oakhill, J. V., & Patel, S. (1991). Can imagery training help children who have comprehension problems? *Journal of Research in Reading, 14*, 106–115.

Oakhill, J. V., & Yuill, N. M. (1986). Pronoun resolution in skilled and less-skilled comprehenders: Effects of memory load and inferential complexity. *Language and Speech, 29*, 25–37.

Oakhill, J. V., Yuill, N. M., & Parkin, A. J. (1986). On the nature of the difference between skilled and less-skilled comprehenders. *Journal of Research in Reading, 9*, 80–91.

Oakhill, J. V., Yuill, N. M., & Parkin, A. J. (1988). Memory and inference in skilled and less-skilled comprehenders. In M. M. Gruneberg, P. E. Morris, & R. N. Sykes (Eds.), *Practical aspects of memory* (Vol. 2). Chichester: Wiley.

Paris, S. G., Cross, D. R., & Lipson, M. Y. (1984). Informed strategies for learning: An instructional program to improve children's reading awareness and comprehension. *Journal of Educational Psychology, 76,* 1239–1252.

Paris, S. G., & Myers, M. (1981). Comprehension monitoring, memory and study strategies of good and poor readers. *Journal of Reading Behavior, 13,* 5–22.

Perfetti, C. A. (1977). Language comprehension and fast decoding: Some psycholinguistic prerequisites for skilled reading comprehension. In J. Guthrie (Ed.), *Cognition. Curriculum and comprehension.* Newark, DE: IRA.

Perfetti, C. A. (1985). *Reading ability.* Oxford: Oxford University Press.

Perfetti, C. A., & Goldman, S. R. (1976). Discourse memory and reading comprehension skill. *Journal of Verbal Learning and Verbal Behavior, 15,* 33–42.

Perfetti, C. A., & Hogaboam, T. (1975a, November). *The effects of word experience on decoding speeds of skilled and unskilled readers.* Paper presented at the Psychonomics Society, Denver, CO.

Perfetti, C. A., & Hogaboam, T. (1975b). Relationship between single word decoding and reading comprehension skill. *Journal of Educational Psychology, 67,* 461–469.

Perfetti, C. A., & Lesgold, A. M. (1979). Coding and comprehension in skilled reading and implications for reading instruction. In L. B. Resnick & P. Weaver (Eds.), *Theory and practice of early reading* (Vol. 1). Hillsdale, NJ: Erlbaum.

Peters, E. E., Levin, J. R., McGivern, J. E., & Pressley, M. (1985). Further comparison of representational and transformational prose-learning imagery. *Journal of Educational Psychology, 2,* 129–136.

Pressley, G. M. (1976). Mental imagery helps eight-year-olds remember what they read. *Journal of Educational Psychology, 24,* 53–59.

Reis, R., & Spekman, N. (1983). The detection of reader-based versus text-based inconsistencies and the effects of direct training of comprehension monitoring among upper-grade poor comprehenders. *Journal of Reading Behavior, 15,* 49–60.

Stanovich, K. E. (1986). Cognitive processes and reading problems of learning-disabled children: Evaluating the assumption of specificity. In J. Torgesen & B. Wong (Eds.), *Psychological and educational perspectives on learning disabilities.* Orlando, FL: Academic Press.

Steiner, R., Wiener, M., & Cromer, W. (1971). Comprehension training and identification for poor and good readers. *Journal of Educational Psychology, 62,* 506–513.

Tierney, R. J., & Cunningham, J. W. (1984). Research on teaching reading comprehension. In P. D. Pearson (Ed.), *Handbook of reading research.* New York: Longman.

Torgeson, J. K. (1978–1979). Performance of reading disabled children on serial memory tasks: A selective review of recent research. *Reading Research Quarterly, 14,* 57–87.

Wagner, R., & Torgeson, J. K. (1987). The nature of phonological processing and its causal role in the acquisition of reading skills. *Psychological Bulletin, 101,* 192–212.

Weaver, P., & Shonkoff, F. (1978). *Research within reach: A research-guided response to concerns of reading educators.* St. Louis, MO: Cemrel Inc.

Willows, D. M., & Ryan, E. B. (1981). Differential utilization of syntactic and semantic information by skilled and less skilled readers in the intermediate grades. *Journal of Educational Psychology, 73,* 607–615.

Wittrock, M. C. (1981). Reading comprehension. In F. J. Pirozzolo & M. C. Wittrock (Eds.), *Neuropsychological and cognitive processes in reading.* New York: Academic Press.

Yuill, N. M., & Joscelyne, T. (1988). Effects of organisational cues and strategies on good and poor comprehenders' story understanding. *Journal of Educational Psychology, 80,* 152–158.

Yuill, N. M., & Oakhill, J. V. (1988a). Effects of inference awareness training on poor reading comprehension. *Applied Cognitive Psychology, 2,* 33–45.

Yuill, N. M., & Oakhill, J. V. (1988b). Understanding of anaphoric relations in skilled and less skilled comprehenders. *British Journal of Psychology, 79,* 173–186.

Yuill, N. M., & Oakhill, J. V. (1991). *Children's problems in text comprehension: An experimental investigation.* Cambridge: Cambridge University Press.

Yuill, N. M., Oakhill, J. V., & Parkin, A. J. (1989). Working memory, comprehension ability and the resolution of text anomaly. *British Journal of Psychology, 80,* 351–361.

CHAPTER 26

PSYCHOLINGUISTICS AND READING ABILITY

CHARLES A. PERFETTI

I. INTRODUCTION

Individuals differ widely in their language abilities, as in virtually everything else. Differences are manifest not only in primary language abilities and disabilities, but also in secondary language processes, specifically reading and writing. Because a narrow focus allows a deeper analysis, the question I address in this chapter is the following: What are the fundamental sources of individual differences in reading? This seemingly narrow focus actually yields a very broad range of issues general to language processes.

Individual differences can be understood only by connecting them to assumptions about basic processes. The chapter includes, accordingly, substantial attention to how reading works and what learning to read is about, addressing individual differences in the context of basic reading and language processes. The first section describes a framework that places learning to read in the context of language. The second section addresses reading failure and dyslexia. The third section discusses individual differences in ordinary reading, with a focus on comprehension. A final section selectively discusses theories of individual differences.

Although the chapter covers a number of issues, it is by no means intended to be a comprehensive review. In addition to being selective, it is argumentative in part. I argue that reading is primarily a language process and that problems in learning to read arise primarily from linguistic processing problems. I also suggest that, while individual differences in comprehension exist in a wide variety of higher order abilities, basic language "reflexes" account for substantial sources of those differences that are truly reading differences rather than general intellectual differences.

II. LANGUAGE BY EAR AND BY EYE

To discuss reading ability as part of a handbook of psycholinguistics is to reflect a central assumption not shared by all researchers who have considered reading ability. This assumption is that reading is essentially a psycholinguistic process. It is, of course, not only a psycholinguistic process, since it prominently includes visual perception. At least some subtypes of specific reading disability or dyslexia have traditionally been seen as reflecting a deficit in visual processing. Although serious doubts have been raised about visual processing deficits (Stanovich, 1986; Vellutino, 1979), the possibility of such deficits continues to remain open, given recent research (Martin & Lovegrove, 1987, 1988). Whatever the eventual decision on this question, it is fair to claim that the prominence of language processes in reading and reading failure justifies a focus on language, with visual processes only in the background. Reading processes are initiated by visual contact with print, but the defining events, lexical and comprehension processes, are essentially linguistic and cognitive processes.

Whether reading is a process exactly equivalent to spoken language processing is another matter. It is perfectly consistent to assert that reading consists primarily of language processes, while holding open the possibility that these processes are somewhat different when language is spoken compared with when it is written. On the face of it, there are some interesting differences between language by ear and language by eye. Perfetti (1985) suggests seven differences derived from two more basic features of print and speech: (1) the physical design of the signal, and (2) the social design of the message.

A. Physical Design

The visual–spatial design of print contrasts with the temporal–auditory design of speech, producing three or four important differences between speech and print processing: (1) the importance of prosodic and paralinguistic features in speech and their absence in print; (2) the reduced memory demands of written texts relative to spoken ones; and (3) the marking of word boundaries in most writing systems, compared with the lack of clear physical boundaries in much spoken language. A fourth difference partially deriving from this physical design feature is the relative naturalness of speech and the highly conventionalized nature of reading, a factor of dramatic importance to learning how to read and to failures of learning.

Each of these differences implies that some processing demands will be unique in reading. The absence of markers for discourse structure, such as the contrast between given and new information marked by stress and intonation in spoken language (Chafe, 1976, 1982), means that syntactic cues must carry a bigger load in marking discourse structure in reading. The reader must rely primarily on linguistic devices, such as determiners, coreference, subordination, to guide the building of discourse structure.

Then there is the matter of syntax itself, which allows multiple parses on a word-by-word basis. Speech cues, stress and timing, have the potential for helping listeners choose the correct parse, although clear evidence for this is scarce. Reading clearly produces plenty of temporary garden paths as readers make word-by-word decisions about structural assignments, as attested by the large literature on garden paths during reading (Ferreira & Clifton, 1986; Frazier & Rayner, 1982; Mitchell, 1987; Perfetti, 1990).

B. Social Design

The social design of the message is a matter of the social context of messages. The contrast between the socially interactive and pragmatically functional context of speech and the individualistic one-way character of reading has potentially profound consequences. For example, the content of what is spoken is negotiated between participants, whereas the content of what is read is fixed by a writer in advance. This is no mere matter of content, but is mainly about the dynamic context of the message. Whereas spoken language is often a contextually driven process in which shared knowledge and shared reference frames inform the interpretation of messages, written texts are often decontextualized, requiring a process in which the reader focuses on propositional meaning of text. What David Olson referred to as AUTONOMOUS TEXTS (Olson, 1977) require an orientation toward intrinsic text meanings—propositional meanings—with less influence from the nonpropositional, situational meanings that are part of conversations.

Such message differences are not intrinsic to the contrast between spoken and written language, but are associated with typical pragmatic and paralinguistic characteristics. Speech registers, for example, are less formal on average than are written text registers. Written texts tend toward more nominalizations (Chafe, 1982) and more subordinate clauses (O'Donnell, 1974). But spoken language can take on these characteristics as well, and when it does, as in the case of academic lectures and speeches, speech and reading are more similar in message context. The perceived similarity of spoken language and written language may even increase with increasing literacy and education, and processing differences diminish (Perfetti, 1987). "Hyperliterates," on this account, may process spoken language as they do written language.

C. What Is Learning to Read?

These differences between spoken and written language are potentially important for learning to read and individual differences. Assumptions about the relationship between the two forms of language expression often seem to be at the base of disagreements about what learning to read is about. If print is something like "speech writ down," then reading is a matter of decoding print into language and then using language processes. The assumption is that these lanaguage processes are sufficient to be useful in reading. But if the language processes used in reading are very different from those used in speech, then this assumption would appear to be unwarranted.

1. The Knowledge Approach

Some reading researchers have argued that learners need to be provided with the knowledge that substitutes for what is missing in the transition from spoken to written classroom language (Anderson & Pearson, 1984). Such researchers tend to de-emphasize the importance of print decoding and emphasize instead higher order knowledge-driven processes in comprehension (Anderson

& Pearson, 1984; Spiro, 1980). Higher level knowledge strutures are clearly important in comprehension, as has been well demonstrated (Barlett, 1932; Bransford & Johnson, 1973; Anderson, Spiro, & Anderson, 1978). The knowledge approach to reading emphasizes the need to provide the reader with knowledge required by a text.

2. The Linguistic Approach

The alternative perspective is provided by the assumption that the main task in reading is to learn to decode print. Knowing one's language and knowing how to decode provide the basic ability to read with comprehension to the same level afforded by basic language competence. Indeed, among adults, for whom decoding abilities have achieved individual asymptotic levels, very high correlations are observed between spoken and written comprehension (Gernsbacher, Varner, & Faust, 1990; Palmer, MacLeod, Hunt, & Davidson, 1985; Sticht, 1977). Gernsbacher et al. (1990), for example, report correlations of .92 between written and spoken comprehension among their sample of college students.

A clear articulation of the connection between spoken and written language comprehension is provided by Gough and colleagues in the assumption that "Reading Comprehension = Decoding × Language Comprehension" (Gough & Tunmer, 1986; Gough & Walsh, 1991; Hoover & Gough, 1990). When they learn to decode, children will comprehend what they read as well as they comprehend what they hear. This view, which might be termed the LINGUISTIC PERSPECTIVE, also has been persuasively articulated by the Haskins Laboratory researchers and their students (Liberman & Shankweiler, 1979, 1991; Liberman & Liberman, 1990). This perspective rests on the central assumption that speech is natural, while reading is conventional, and the concomitant assumption that the naturalness of speech derives from its special biological status. The latter assumption is that speech is encoded by specialized mechanisms that allow the encoding of continuous and unreliable acoustic information into discrete linguistic segments (A. M. Liberman, 1982; Liberman, Cooper, Shankweiler, & Studdert-Kennedy, 1967). It is useful to note, however, that the central claim of the linguistic approach, that reading is a matter of learning the code that associates print with speech, does not require any strong assumptions about the nature of speech processing. It merely requires that learning to read is learning a code that maps print to speech.

3. Acquired Modularity

One version of the linguistic approach emphasizes not only the basic acquisition of the code, but the acquisition of a high degree of attention-free or automatic use of the code (LaBerge & Samuels, 1974; Perfetti, 1985; Perfetti & Lesgold, 1977, 1979). The verbal efficiency theory (Perfetti & Lesgold, 1977; Perfetti, 1985) claims that automated decoding processes are required to allow reading comprehension to attain the same high level as listening comprehension. One interpretation of this claim is that lexical processes in reading become modular, such that one can speak of the ACQUIRED MODULARITY of lexical processes as well as syntactic processes in reading (Perfetti, 1989; Stanovich, 1990). Immediate access to the lexicon, for the skilled reader, becomes encapsulated, rapidly occurring and relatively unaffected by nonlexical information. An alternative expression of this idea, free of the extra implications of modularity, is that there are reading REFLEXES, which develop to high levels of automaticity.

These two alternative perspectives, the knowledge-based and the linguistic approaches to reading, can be seen as complementary rather than antagonistic, provided the two central facts are established: (1) Learning to read is centrally the acquisition of how a conventional written system maps onto a learner's natural spoken language. (2) Written texts make demands that are not identical to those made by speech. To appreciate the differences between spoken and written text is not to abandon the centrality of decoding as the paramount achievement in reading. The knowledge approach is clearly inadequate to deal with the central linguistic basis of reading. To appreciate the dependence of reading on the mapping of print to speech, however, is not to claim that this mapping is all there is to gaining proficiency in reading.

I turn to a discussion of what it means to learn to read and to fail in learning to read.

III. LEARNING TO READ

Despite some significant differences between print and speech, the central fact for the acquisition of reading competence is that a learner must learn a writing system, specifically how the writing system encodes his or her language. Whatever else one intends by the term READING SKILL, the ability to map print to speech, DECODING, is the fundamental achievement of learning to read.

Writing systems differ just as languages do. However, while a case can be made that the child biologically knows the principles of language design prior to acquiring spoken language (Pinker, 1984), there is no parallel case to make for writing systems. Writing systems are the result of human invention, altered, refined, and reinvented. They vary, even after centuries of convergent development, in how they work. To learn to read English, Italian, Hungarian, and Korean is to learn an alphabetic writing system, in which graphic units associate with phonemes; to learn to read Chinese is to learn a logographic system, in which graphic units associate primarily with morphemes; to learn to read Japanese kana is to learn a syllabary system, in which graphic units correspond to syllables; to learn to read Arabic, Hebrew, and Persian is to learn a modified alphabetic system in which consonants are more reliably represented than are vowels. There appears to be nothing in the child's native language endowment to provide constraints for the learning of his writing system. Whether the child will learn an alphabetic or logographic system, or no system at all, is a matter of cultural and national traditions. It is interesting that even the mere possibility of writing systems is not part of the natural language endowment. The design of languages may be universal; the design of writing systems, definitely not.

A. The Alphabetic Principle

Reading in an alphabetic orthography requires the discovery of the alphabetic principle: A written symbol corresponds to a phoneme, a meaningless speech segment. As widely noted, the Phoenician–Greek invention of the alphabet, and hence the "discovery" ("invention" might be better) of the alphabetic principle, appears to have been a unique cultural achievement, one that followed far behind the adaptation of visual forms to symbols for objects and meanings (Gelb, 1952). It should not be surprising then, as Gleitman and Rozin (1977) noted, that learners might have some trouble in replicating this discovery.

Discovery is not the only form of learning, fortunately, so the idea of reading instruction is that children can learn to read by being taught, directly or indirectly, the alphabetic principle. A discussion of how reading is taught would be beyond the scope of this chapter (see Adams, 1990). One component of the instruction problem is quite relevant, however, and that is the fact that there are obstacles to learning the alphabetic principle.

B. Phonological Awareness

A major obstacle is that young children are likely to have only dim awareness of the phonological structure of their language. Because phonemes are abstractions over highly variable acoustic events, detecting their status as discreet speech segments that exist outside ordinary word perception is a problem. This abstractness may be a special problem for stop consonants, which both lack acoustic duration and vary greatly in their acoustic properties depending on their vowel environments. The child learning to read an alphabetic writing system needs to discover the alphabetic principle but may lack at least half of what is needed. Letters must be associated with phonemes, but the child may not have adequate representation of phonemes.

Moreover, the child is provided with no advance knowledge about how a writing system might map phonological or even acoustic properties of the language. Rozin, Bressman, and Taft (1974), for example, found that many preschool children could not perform their *mow–motorcycle* test, which asked children which of two printed words corresponded to each of two spoken words, *mow* and *motorcycle*. Successful performance on this task requires not awareness of phonemes, but merely the idea that acoustic length might correspond to visual length or number of letters. Lundberg and Torneus (1978) reported in Sweden, where reading instruction does not begin until 8, even 6-year-old children performed inconsistently on the *mow–motorcycle* test. The difficulty children have with such a test is consistent with the claim, made in the preceding section, that there is no preliterate knowledge concerning writing systems. There is perhaps not even advanced knowledge that the writing system will map acoustic features of the language.

Phonemic awareness, or explicit reflective knowledge (Perfetti, 1991), is even more problematic. Liberman, Shankweiler, Fischer, and Carter (1974) demonstrated this problem. Among children who were trained to tap once with a stick for each sound in a short word, only a handful of kindergarten (age 5) and no preschool (age 4) children could perform this task successfully. A number of other studies confirmed the general inability of many preliterate children to demonstrate awareness of phonemes in various tasks and began to show a relationship between phonemic awareness and learning to read (Fox & Routh, 1976; Lundberg, Olofsson, & Wall, 1980; Stanovich, Cunningham, & Cramer, 1984; Tunmer, Herriman, & Neesdale, 1988). The literature demonstrating the details of this relationship has become substantial. [See Rieben & Perfetti (1991) and Brady & Shankweiler, (1991) for collections of research.]

The question raised by the correlation between phonemic awareness and learning to read is whether the relationship is causal. The evidence of training studies (Bradley & Bryant, 1983; Treiman & Baron, 1983; Vellutino & Scanlon, 1991) gives some support to the causality conclusion, as do longitudinal studies using cross-lag correlations (Mann, 1991; Perfetti, Beck, Bell, & Hughes, 1987). It seems correct to conclude that reflective knowledge or awareness functionally mediates learning how to read in an alphabetic writing system.

There are two additional aspects to this awareness issue. First, it is possible that there are different dimensions of phonological ability measured in different tasks of awareness (Perfetti et al., 1987; Wagner, Balthazor, Hurley, Morgan, Rashotte, Shaner, Simmons, & Stage, 1987) even if there is a unitary core of phonological ability (Stanovich, Cunningham, & Cramer, 1984). Second, it is clear that the relationship between phonemic awareness and learning to read is not one-directional, but reciprocal. It is possible that these two facts are linked. In a longitudinal study using cross-lag correlations, Perfetti, Beck, Bell, and Hughes (1987) found that a simple ability to synthesize phonemes into syllables predicted progress in first grade reading, whereas an ability to delete the initial or final phonemes from syllables did not; instead, the deletion performance, a more analytic ability, was initially predicted by progress in learning to read, and later, in turn, predicted further progress in reading. Such results strongly suggest that for the more analytic phonemic abilities there is a reciprocal relationship, in which phonemic ability first is promoted through literacy acquisition and then enables further gains in literacy. Some prerequisite phonemic knowledge, however, functions immediately to facilitate the acquisition of reading.

The other side of the phonemic awareness–reading relationship has also received support from studies of adult illiterates (Morais, Cary, Alegria, & Bertelson, 1979; Morais, Bertelson, Cary, & Alegria, 1986). These studies find that adult illiterates are very weak in tasks requiring analysis of phonemic structure, although they do much better at syllable-level and rhyming tasks. Such results suggest the limited level of phonological awareness that can be developed outside literacy contexts. Indeed, although there are many opportunities for oral language use to promote rhyming and syllabic ability, there is little outside of literacy contexts that can serve to draw attention to the existence of phonemes. This fact does not negate the functional role of knowledge of phonemes in learning to read. It simply reflects the complexity of the reading task and the invisibility of phonemic structures. The relationship between phonemic awareness and learning to read is a reciprocally interactive one.

C. Nonalphabetic Writing Systems

Logographic writing systems present an important comparison with alphabetic systems. Chinese children learn to read characters that, despite potential cues to pronunciation in complex characters, are largely related by meaning, not phonology. (For a fuller discussion of the composition of Chinese characters and the implications for reading see Perfetti, Zhang, & Berent, 1992.) By one estimate, children are expected to master the reading and writing of 3500 characters during the 6 years of elementary school (Leong, 1973). Whereas learning to read an alphabetic system allows a productive (rule-based) process in principle, the logographic system requires this learning to be largely associative. If phonemic awareness depends on alphabetic literacy, readers of Chinese should show little awareness of phonemes.

There is an alphabetic system as well for Chinese readers, the PINYIN system. (Pinyin comprises alphabetic symbols that aid in the pronunciation of characters.) Read, Zhang, Nie, and Ding (1986) tested two groups of adults in a phoneme analysis task, one who had learned the traditional logographic system, and one who had, in addition, learned pinyin. Only the pinyin group performed the phonemic analysis task successfully. The group who had learned only characters performed comparably to a group of illiterates.

A more complex picture appears to hold for learners of Japanese, who learn to read the kanji system (Chinese characters) and the kana system, based on syllables. Mann (1986) found that first grade students performed poorly on phonemic awareness, but that fourth grade students performed well. Phonemic awareness thus is slowed but does emerge: This eventual emergence may be aided by the fact that although kana is a syllabary, some individual phonemes are, in effect, represented by virtue of being syllables (e.g., the 5 vowels and final /n/). Furthermore, children learn kana from texts that display a vowel syllable and full syllables containing that vowel on the same line. As Alegria & Moarias (1991) suggest, such a system might allow the child some progress, although with some labor, in noticing the segmental structure of Japanese.

The overall picture has become reasonably clear, considering evidence from different writing systems. Phonemic awareness is very limited as a spontaneous human ability, yet it is important in learning to read. In an alphabetic system, learning to read promotes awareness of phonemes and, in turn, depends on the emergence of this awareness. In a logographic system, reading does not promote phonemic awareness.

D. Theories of Learning to Read

Theories of reading acquisition have not been developed to the level of detail that theories of skilled reading have. Much of the earliest research was largely atheoretical, and the theories that have been developed have tended to informally portray broad stages of development (Chall, 1983; Marsh, Friedman, Welch, & Desberg, 1981).

If reading acquisition is viewed as primarily the development of a print-addressable lexicon, or the development of identification and decoding ability, then the form that theories must take is considerably sharpened. A central question then becomes the REPRESENTATION problem (Perfetti, 1991, 1992). What is the form of the learning reader's representation of words, and how does the representation system change with learning? Two closely related theories have addressed this problem in terms of reading stages, differing mainly on the transition between stages. A third theory describes representational change without sharply defined stages.

Gough and colleagues (Gough & Hillinger, 1980; Gough & Juel, 1991; Gough & Walsh, 1991) have described an essentially two-stage account of reading, one in which the child uses any information possible in attempting to discriminate one word from another, as he builds up a visually accessible lexicon, absent any decoding knowledge. Gough and Juel (1991) refer to this first stage as SELECTIVE ASSOCIATION, an idiosyncratic association between some part of a printed work and the name of the word. Under the right circumstances, including an increase in phonological awareness and an intention to encode all rather than just some of the letters of the word, the child can move into the CIPHER stage of true reading.

An alternative model of what pushes the child through the acquisition process comes from Ehri (1980, 1991; Ehri & Wilce, 1985). On Ehri's account, children do not begin at a visual-only stage as they do in Gough's account. Right from the beginning they use the names of the sounds of the letters as cues to word identification. Although letter names do not represent the phonemes of the word they appear in, they have enough phonetic overlap to be useful, as when a child uses the names of the letters *J* and *L* to remember the sound of the word *jail*. Learning the alphabet, not necessarily the alphabetic principle, is the key that moves a child into the first stage of reading, resulting in a stage that Ehri (1991) calls PHONETIC CUE READING. The acquisition process is the establishment of word representations that have both phonological and orthographic components.

A third theoretical description focuses directly on the acquisition of word representations (Perfetti, 1991, 1992) without postulating stages. Learning to read is the acquisition of increasing numbers of orthographically addressable words (quantity acquisition) and the alteration of individual representations along quality dimensions. The two quality dimensions are SPECIFICITY, an increase in the number of position-correct specific letters in a representation, and REDUNDANCY, the increasing establishment of redundant phonemic representations. The redundancy concept rests on the assumption that word names (pronunciations) are part of the child's earliest representations and that phonemes are added in connection with individual letters with learning. Important in establishing these sublexical connections is first phonemic awareness and then increasing context-sensitive decoding knowledge. Thus, the phonological representations become redundant, existing both at the lexical level and the phonemic level. Together, increasing specificity and redundancy allow high-quality word representations that can be reliably activated by orthographic input. As individual words become fully specified and redundant, they move from the functional lexicon, which allows reading, to the autonomous lexicon, which allows resource-cheap reading.

These theories represent a shared attention to the development of word representations as what needs to be explained, and at least the first two demonstrate clear links with experiments on learning how to read. The next question is the extent to which individual differences, specifically reading failures, are connected to the components that comprise word representations, especially phonology.

IV. Reading Failure and Dyslexia

The importance of phonology for learning to read certainly implies it has a role in understanding failures to learn to read, or failures to progress adequately in reading. And the research indeed very strongly indicates that children who are not good at reading show problems in phonological processing. Indeed, one of the most interesting developments has been evidence that there is an inheritable phonological processing deficit that associates with reading failure in children (Olson, Wise, Conners, & Rack, 1990; Pennington, 1990).

It is probably useful to make a distinction concerning phonological abilities. The preceding section focused on phonemic awareness, or explicit reflective knowledge. A second kind of phonological knowledge is the implicit knowledge required in ordinary speech processing and in at least some reading. These two categories of phonemic knowledge can be referred to as REFLECTIVE and REFLEXIVE respectively. It is not always clear what kind of phonological deficit is implicated in reading problems. It is possible that both reflective and reflexive knowledge derive from some core phonological processing mechanism, and there is evidence for a unitary phonological ability in the intercorrelations of various phonological tasks (Stanovich et al., 1984). Many children, on the other hand, will have intact phonological abilities in the sense they can process spoken words and have problems only when the demands of analysis and reflection are added. As a general point, someone who has serious problems in identifying spoken words is someone who surely has a language disability. With the possible, but controversial, exception of certain acquired language disorders, anyone who has a language disability will also have a reading disability.

The vast literature on developmental dyslexia cannot be easily summarized, nor shall I attempt to do so. Instead, I will focus selectively on the psycholinguistic factors that affect children who fail to learn to read or lag behind their peers in reading achievement. The typical developmental dyslexia definition is exclusionary: two or more years behind in reading achievement in the absence of clear social and neurological factors. Some components of reading failure may apply only to carefully, clearly defined disability, but others appear to apply to a less selective definition of low reading skill.

A. Phonological and Working Memory Deficits

The evidence leads to a fairly clear conclusion, namely, that reading disability is associated with problems in phonological processing; including both explicit awareness and the routine use of phonological information in processing language. One of the most important facts concerns working memory. Young, less skilled readers (a designation I use to increase generality and to accommodate the fact that the definitions of reading groups are variable) have poorer memory for words they have just read in a text (Goldman, Hogaboam, Bell, & Perfetti, 1980) and also for words they have just heard in a text (Perfetti & Goldman, 1976). Importantly, memory differences between skilled and less skilled readers are found in discourse even when they are not found in memory for digits (Perfetti & Goldman, 1976). Although memory differences are sometimes found in digit span and sometimes not, memory differences for just-read and just-heard sentences are remarkably consistent. This implies that a working memory rather than a storage memory is the relevant factor, an assumption that appears to have been verified by the memory span work of Daneman and Carpenter (1980) with adults. It is the association of reading and speech processing that gives the clue that, whatever the exact source of the difference, there is something about language processing across modalities that is at issue.

It is possible that this something is the phonological processing system. This system, or at least a subsystem of it dedicated to working memory functioning, holds verbal material for brief periods of time. Such storage is required by sentence comprehension, parsing, and integrating processes. This system has to have access to the names of words, that is, their pronunciations, not merely their meanings. Phonologically indexed names serve the function of REFERENCE SECURING, allowing a reader to represent words as full linguistic objects and to reaccess them as needed (Perfetti & McCutchen, 1982).

Evidence that less skilled readers have less effective phonological memories has come from two sources. In one, the data show memory differences between skilled and less skilled readers for language tasks in the absence of such differences in nonlanguage tasks (Katz, Shankweiler, & Liberman, 1981; Liberman, Mann, Shankweiler, & Werfelman, 1982). In the other, the data tend to show that memory confusions based on phonological similarity, specifically rhyming, are characteristic of skilled readers, but not less skilled readers, for letter names, words, and sentences (Liberman, Shankweiler, Liberman, Fowler, & Fischer, 1977; Bryne & Shea, 1979; Mann, Liberman, & Shankweiler, 1980). The rhyme difference is sometimes not found (Perfetti, 1985), and sometimes found for younger but not for older children (Olson, Davidson, Kliegl, & Davies, 1984). Confusions among rhyming words are influenceable by strategies, and some skilled readers may have better strategies for dealing with this task, to reduce confusions.

Whether the phonological processing deficit extends beyond memory for speech to the perception of speech is less clear. Although some studies suggest that less skilled readers do poorly at perceiving speech in noise but have no trouble with environmental sounds (Brady, Shankweiler, & Mann, 1983), other studies cast doubt on this conclusion (Snowling, Stackhouse, & Rack, 1986; Pennington, Van Orden, Smith, Green, & Haith, 1990). (Differences in the conclusions partly result from methodological issues that I discuss below.) It is also possible that severe dyslexics have even more severe problems, with at least one study suggesting that dyslexics fail to show categorical perception of phonemes (Godfrey, Syrdal-Lasky, Millay, & Knox, 1981).

B. Phonological and Lexical Deficits

For a child, the central defining characteristic of failing to read is the inability to read words. One expects, by definition, young reading-disabled children not to read words well. The phonological system is heavily implicated in this deficit.

Pseudoword naming provides one of the clearest cases of involvement of the phonological system with orthography. To pronounce a nonword such as *brait,* the reader must convert an orthographic input into a phonological output, a test of true decoding, even if performed by analogy along the lines proposed by Glushko (1981), or along a distributed PDP network (McClelland, 1986; Seidenberg & McClelland, 1989). A basic result is that naming time differences between words and pseudowords are greater for less skilled than for skilled readers (Hogaboam & Perfetti, 1978). Reading a pseudoword is often something quite beyond the reach of a disabled reader. Data from a search task (described in Perfetti, 1985) in which subjects searched for a target in a display of same-type items provides an estimate of the processing costs for pseudowords among garden-variety less skilled readers. When subjects searched for a bigram among a set of bigrams, the slope relating search time to number of targets was only slightly greater for less skilled readers than skilled readers (30 ms). For words, the corresponding difference was about 100 ms, while for pseudowords, the corresponding slope difference was 140 ms, indicating that less skilled readers were paying a processing price for pseudowords that was predicted neither by their processing time for letters nor even by their processing times for words.

Results from other studies support this conclusion, even when reading-matched designs rather than age-matched designs are used (Olson, 1985; Olson, Wise, Conners, & Rack, 1990; Siegel & Ryan, 1988; Snowling, 1980; Stanovich, 1988). Although some studies have not found this additional pseudoword difference (Bruck, 1988; Vellutino & Scanlon, 1987), sampling and methodological explanations might account for most of the discrepancies (Olson, et al., 1990). The weight of the evidence suggests that some process connected with pseudoword reading is especially problematic for disabled readers over a fairly wide age range.

It is not completely clear how this problem should be more specifically described. The mechanism may be the quality of phonological representations, given the considerable data demonstrating phonological memory and even perception differences. On the other hand, the faulty mechanism may be one of decoding, a problem with mapping phonological structures to orthographic ones. One way to conceptualize the problem is to suppose that phonological representations are unreliable for disabled readers, whether spoken or written. Decoding adds stress to the phonological system, requiring structural analysis of orthographic patterns plus phonological translation.

It is, in addition, not clear whether a single deficit or more than one is involved. The data suggest a working memory factor, apparently phonological; a decoding factor, also phonological; and, for more severely disabled readers, even a speech perception factor. It is possible that there is a single factor having to do with the coding of phonological information, one that affects memory as well as word identification, although there seems to be no clear evidence on this possibility. There is evidence showing a naming deficit in disabled readers, one not confined to pseudowords or even words, but quite general across digits and pictures, implicating a general phonological retrieval deficit (Wolf, 1986, 1991). This general naming deficit is not characteristic of low-skill readers in general, since at least some show naming deficits only for words and pseudowords (Perfetti, Finger, & Hogaboam, 1978).

C. Evidence for a Heritable Phonological Ability

Reading disability has long been supposed to have a familial component, and this supposition has been supported by studies showing that the within-family disability rate far exceeds the outside-family disability rate (DeFries & Decker, 1982). More direct evidence that such patterns reflect genetic influences rather than environmental comes from a longitudinal study of monozygotic (MZ) and same-sex dizygotic (DZ) twins reported by Olson, Wise, Conners, and Rack (1990; see also Pennington, 1989). While MZ twins have identical genes, DZ twins share genes only to the same extent as ordinary siblings (50%). Olson et al. studied 64 pairs of MZ twins and 53 pairs of DZ twins in which one twin had been diagnosed as reading-disabled on the basis of a word recognition test. A twin of a MZ disabled reader was more likely to be below average in word reading than the twin of a DZ disabled reader, consistent with the hypothesis that word reading disability is heritable.

More intriguing, however, are the results obtained for two tests assumed to reflect different components of word identification. One, phonological coding, was the time to read aloud pseudowords (both one- and two-syllable); the second, considered a measure of "orthographic coding," was the time to decide which of two homophonic letter strings was a real word, as between *rain, rane*. The idea is that pseudoword reading reflects primarily phonological coding processes, whereas the word decision task requires knowledge about spelling patterns, independent of phonology. (Olson et al. acknowledge that phonological processes cannot be ruled out in reading words, but that the decision task requires reference to orthographic knowledge.) The key result is the heritability estimates, based on the correlations between general word recognition and each of the two component tasks. The correlation between phonological coding (pseudoword naming) and word recognition was significantly heritable (.93), whereas the correlation between orthographic coding and word recognition was not heritable (zero). To put it another way, for MZ twins one can predict the word recognition of the second twin by knowing the pseudoword reading of the disabled twin; knowing the orthographic score of the disabled twin does not allow prediction of the word recognition of the second twin.

The interpretation of these results seems statistically straightforward, if a bit elusive in specific mechanism. Knowing that *rain* (but not *rane*) is a word is a matter of learning—a result of environment rather than heredity; to pronounce *framble* (one of Olson et al.'s pseudowords) is a matter of phonological coding that has a genetic component. A learner acquires skill in reading words, in part, by reading specific words, and this is what the orthographic test largely reflects. Phonological skill in reading, which is arguably a general ability beyond knowledge of specific words, has a large genetic component. It is not directly inheritable, Olson et al. suggest, but a reflection of segmentation ability (phonemic awareness), which is heritable. As a practical matter, one cannot infer from such results that there is little point to training phonological skills in disabled readers. On the contrary, as Olson et al. argue, it is exactly what must be done, since a genetic factor has made the spontaneous acquisition of phonological skill less likely.

V. Methodological Issues

Research on individual differences faces methodological problems that cannot be ignored entirely, although a full treatment of them is beyond the goals of this chapter. The most important issue has been the design of research comparing skilled and less skilled readers, or skilled readers and dyslexics. Much of the research has compared two groups of readers at the same age, one group average or better on some standard measure and one below average on the measure. (Another issue is how far below average the less skilled group has to be.) This simple contrastive design yields differences that are difficult to interpret. If the less skilled group is found to be below average on some reading-related task, say pseudoword identification or letter recognition, this fact may reflect their deficiency in what the task is assumed to measure, say phonological coding; but it might merely be an accompaniment of their lower level of skill.

Reading experience, typically higher for a skilled group than a less skilled group, may lead to observed differences in tasks that tap components of reading.

This of course is merely the usual inferential dilemma of correlations; but it is compounded in disability research to the extent that it frustrates the testing of specific hypotheses about characteristics of specific reading disability, for example, that it involves phonological deficits. By contrast, if a comparison is between two groups, a younger normal group and an older disabled group, matched on a reading level, finding a difference on some task may have a more constrained interpretation. If, for example, the younger normal group outperforms the older disabled group in pseudoword decoding, despite their equivalence in word reading level, then one might conclude that the disabled reader has achieved his limited (relative to age expectations) reading level by qualitatively different means, with a phonological deficit in this hypothetical case.

Criticisms of the age-match design and advocacy for reading-match design (Backman, Mamen, & Ferguson, 1984; Bryant & Bradley, 1985; Bryant & Goswami, 1986) have led to an increase in the use of the reading-match design. It is quite possible that conclusions reached with reading level–match designs will converge with those of age-match designs; on the other hand, there is some disagreement even among results exclusively from reading-match designs. (Olson et al., 1990, provides an analysis of contradictory pseudoword data within reading-match designs, and Stanovich, 1988, provides a more general discussion of inconsistent conclusions.) There are arguments in favor of the age-match design as well (Shankweiler, Crain, Brady, & Macaruso, 1992). Shankweiler et al. argue that when theoretical considerations motivate specific hypotheses, and when the results of studies converge, then the age-match design is providing useful data to constrain causal hypotheses about reading disability. It is easy to agree with such a claim. The clear lesson, however, is that both types of design, easily incorporated into a single double-match design, will do more to provide such constraint than either design by itself.

It is worth noting that research on individual differences in adult reading has managed to ignore this dilemma, although the logic of group comparisons applies to all ages. The easy out is that adult subjects, usually taken from college, do not provide reading level match at different ages. It is not likely that anyone wants to assume that a less skilled college senior is appropriately matched with a more skilled college freshman. Still, one can imagine adult comparisons of less skilled noncollege students with younger, more skilled high school students.

A related methodological issue is the definition of reading disability. There are stringent definitions of reading problems in some cases and less stringent definitions in others, both in terms of degree and exclusivity. There is some importance in defining low reading ability to exclude general low intellectual functioning; otherwise one is not studying reading but intelligence. The fact that intellectual functions, including reading, are intercorrelated is a nuisance, and not all research is successful at separating them. There is good reason to try, however, if one accepts the possibility of language-specific or reading-specific problems, although controlling for IQ creates its own problems (Stanovich, 1986, 1988).

The research on adults has largely evaded the implication of this problem, just as it has the reading level–design issue. One of the obstacles to a unified theory of individual differences is the fact that adult research has compared poorly defined subgroups. On the other hand, in at least some adult studies that have been concerned with whether there is a difference between garden-variety less able readers and those defined by analogy with specific disability criteria, the differences have been less than dramatic (Bell & Perfetti, in press).

VI. BEYOND BEGINNING READING

Individual differences exist also among older children and adults who have had some success in learning to read. Such differences appear both in higher level processes, that is, comprehension, and in word identification. Indeed, word identification problems continue to be found even among college readers (Bruck, 1990; Cunningham, Stanovich, & Wilson 1990; Bell & Perfetti, in press). Because lexical sources of adult comprehension problems cannot be ruled out, it is worthwhile to understand how lexical processes work in skilled reading.

Getting the story of lexical processing right is important for practical matters as well. Critics of decoding instruction sometimes buttress their arguments by claiming that skilled word identification is strictly a (nonphonological) visual process (e.g., Smith, 1985) or that it is primarily a context-driven process (Goodman, 1970). Both of these dubious claims are challenged in this section.

A. Word Reading and Context

Reading texts—reading for meaning—is the goal toward which word reading skills are directed. This truism has led to instructional proscriptions against teaching decoding, an educational philosophy sloganized by Goodman and Smith as a "psycholinguistic guessing game" (Goodman, 1967, 1970; Smith, 1973). The idea is that because words are read in context, the learner has multiple cues available to identify words, or, more in the spirit of the psycholinguistic game, to figure out the meanings. There is nothing very "psycholinguistic" about the process Goodman had in mind. It is mainly a matter of using context to glean meanings, and while "graphonic" and "syntactic" cues were also suggested, they appear to be secondary to the "semantic" cuing system, which included everything in the context and the reader's nonlinguistic knowledge. This approach contradicts the assumption that the orthography and its mapping to phonology is privileged evidence in identifying a word.

A different role for context is implied by word identification models, modular models, and even most interactive ones. Words are identified through sublexical processes that rely on orthographic and phonological components that, either serially or in some degree of interaction, lead to access of a word in memory. The role of context is to verify word identification and select contextually relevant meanings. Nearly all models of word identification, no matter how different they are in critical detail, are consistent with the claim that the hallmark of a skilled reader is context-free word identification (Perfetti, 1989). Contrary to the Goodman–Smith claim, on this assumption, skilled readers' use of context is limited by their basic fluent abilities in identifying words. It is less skilled readers who use contexts to identify words, simply because their context-free word identification skills are not up to the task of reading.

This context issue appears to have been empirically settled in two ways. First, context effects in word identification were long ago well documented for adults (Morton, 1964; Schuberth & Eimas, 1977; Stanovich, 1983; Tulving & Gold, 1963) and for children (Perfetti, Goldman, & Hogaboam, 1979; West & Stanovich, 1978). Setting aside some issues about the exact locus of context effects in identification, and the related problem that different methods (lexical decision vs. naming vs. eye movements) vary in the size of context effects, the general conclusion is that some part of the process of identifying a word is facilitated by context. It appears likely that at least some of the effect of context is on lexical access itself, although this may be small relative to post-access effects. The lexical access part of the effect might be limited to words previewed in the parafovea, where letters are visually degraded, leaving foveal access to be largely context-free, a suggestion made by Rayner and Pollatsek (1989). Even if the locus of context facilitation is relatively late in the series of component processes, that is, at the stage of verification (Mitchell & Green, 1978), this has practical significance for reading words in texts. While readers do not "verify" words in actual reading, as they might prior to naming a word in an experiment, they must engage in some integrative and interpretive processes as part of "post-access."

The second answer to the context issue is that skilled readers do not make greater use of context than less skilled readers. Any differences in context use as a function of skill go in the opposite direction, favoring less skilled readers. In one study, Perfetti, Finger, and Hogaboam (1978) varied the predictability of words by manipulating the size of the set from which they were drawn. The names of the four seasons are a small set, whereas the names of the 12 months is a larger, but still closed set, one to which new members cannot be added. The set of proper first names, by contrast, is both large and open. Perfetti et al. (1978) found that skilled third graders were barely affected by set size, but that less skilled readers were considerably affected, naming words from a large open set especially slowly. Perfetti et al. reported a parallel result for digit naming, with less skilled readers more affected by the size of the set from which the digits could be drawn than were the skilled readers. These results suggest that less skilled readers are more, not less, dependent on the predictability of the word in context. Theoretically, the concept of an activated memory node is central. The skilled reader is capable of retrieving a word from an inactive memory. This is what it means to have context-free word identification skill. The less skilled reader is more dependent on having a word to be retrieved already active.

Many studies have directly addressed skill and age differences in the size of discourse and sentence context effects on word identification (Perfetti, Goldman, & Hogaboam, 1979; Perfetti & Roth, 1981; Schwantes, 1981; Simpson, Lorsbach, & Whitehouse, 1983; Stanovich, West, & Feeman, 1981; West & Stanovich, 1978). In none of these studies has a greater context effect been found for skilled readers. On the contrary, less skilled readers showed more context facilitation in times to name words than did skilled readers in any study that reported a difference. To be clear, the conclusion is not that skilled readers do not use context. Perfetti et al. (1979) found that the same skilled readers who were relatively little affected by context in the time to name words were very much better than less skilled readers in predicting what word would appear next in a discourse. The skill reflected in this difference is one that aids post-identification processes, those that select the appropriate meaning of a word and integrate it into a message representation.

The interpretation of context facilitation effects in identification does depend on baseline identification rates. Perfetti and Roth (1981) found that when words were visually degraded so as to slow down word identification time for skilled readers, they showed context facilitation effects identical to those shown by less skilled readers on undegraded words. Thus simply slowing down a reader's word identification rate increases the facilitation of context. This is not merely a statistical artifact, although statistical issues do emerge in this area (especially the fact that means and variances tend to be correlated in naming times, producing nonhomogeneity of variance across skill groups). It reflects the theoretical relationship between a rapidly executing process and the ability of some outside source of information to affect it.

Under ordinary circumstances, skilled word identification has modular characteristics: It occurs rapidly by a process that operates exclusively on specialized data structures, orthographic strings, and their connections to lexical and phonological representations. Discourse context provides the wrong kind of data for such a process, because words are not highly predictable in ordinary context. In discourse, the message level (to use Forster's, 1979, description) is not a matter of representing words, but messages. The difference between a fully predictable word, as in *Jack and Jill went up the *hill**, and one only probabilistically predictable, as in *In my garden, I planted *carrots** (or *tomatoes? basil? roses? basil?*) is devastating to a mechanism that operates on word prediction. It is negligible, however, to a system in which one level operates on orthographic structures to identify words and another level operates on words (and other things) to construct messages. It is to be expected, then, that skilled reading will get by well without context and will not be fooled by unpredictability. Perfetti and Roth (1981) report that skilled readers' naming times for words that are anomalous in a given context—that is, not just unpredictable, but counterpredicted (e.g., *Mary reached into her purse and pulled out a *carrot**)—were hardly affected relative to low predictability contexts. Less skilled readers, however, were dramatically affected, in the way one might expect for a process that was slow and unreliable enough to allow specific word predictions to be generated and then disconfirmed.

B. Phonology in Skilled Lexical Processes

1. Classical Versus PDP Approaches

The central debate in lexical processes, and cognition generally, has become one of symbolic "classical" approaches versus subsymbolic parallel distributed processing (PDP) approaches. For lexical access, the question has become whether there are two routes to a lexical entry, as proposed by dual route theory (Coltheart, 1978; Besner, 1990; Paap & Noel, 1991), or whether there is a single activation system, in which identification of words is an emergent property of parallel activation networks (Seidenberg & McClelland, 1989; Van Orden, Pennington, & Stone, 1990). The dual route theories claim that readers contact lexical entries along two routes, one that "assembles" phonology from grapheme–phoneme correspondences and then looks up the phonological output, and another that directly contacts a lexical entry based on the orthographic input. One route is phonological recoding and the other route is direct access, with the faster of the two routes determining access in any given case (Besner, 1990).

PDP models contrast with dual route theories in their mechanism, since they postulate parallel activation along networks of distributed sublexical information. Words are not recognized sometimes with phonology and sometimes not, but merely ''identified'' as an automatic consequence of patterns of phonological and graphic input features. But the real bone of contention is the disappearance of the lexicon under PDP models (Besner, 1990; Seidenberg & McClelland, 1990). Lexicon or no lexicon, that is the question.

Psycholinguistics, by its ancestry, is sympathetic to the classical position. The debate between classical and connectionist models affects the explanatory status of mental concepts, not just ''lexicon,'' but also ''grammar,'' ''inference,'' and ''belief,'' among other cherished concepts. An important and apparently overlooked point, however, is that one can adopt a ''classical'' position on the existence of a lexicon without accepting the assumption of two routes to the lexicon (see Perfetti, Zhang, & Berent, 1992). A lexicon is needed for reasons other than lexical access—parsing, for example—so it cannot really disappear in any profound sense. Moreover, the association of PDP models with single activation mechanisms and classical models with dual route mechanisms is an accidental correlation, not a necessary one.

The alternative to consider is that phonological activation is a routine and essentially automatic part of word identification in an alphabetic writing system. The evidence that seemed to favor a direct visual route is less decisive than it once appeared. Evidence strongly in support of phonological activation in English has come from backward masking (Perfetti, Bell, & Delaney, 1988; Perfetti & Bell, 1991) and priming studies (Perfetti & Bell, 1991) and from homophonic interference in category decisions (Van Orden, 1987; Van Orden, Johnston, & Hale, 1988). In the masking data, for example, a briefly presented word (*rate*) is better identified when it is backward masked by a pseudoword that shares all its phonemes (RAIT) relative to a mask that shares the same number of letters but fewer of the phonemes (RALT). Parallel effects are found when the mask precedes (primes) the target word, except that phonological primes require about 40 ms to gain their advantage over orthographic primes, compared with around 30 ms for orthographic primes to gain their advantage over control primes, implying a time course of orthographic–phonological activation. Similar phonological priming effects in reading French are reported by Ferrand and Grainger (1992), and similar masking and priming effects are reported for Serbo-Croatian by Lukatela and Turvey (1990a, 1990b).

The conclusion is not that the case for automatic phonological activation has been proved, because some data appear to count against an automatic interpretation of both the masking results (Brysbaert, Praet, & d'Ydewalle, 1990) and the Van Orden category results (Jared & Seidenberg, 1991). However, the results summarized above, along with results from other paradigms (Frost, 1991), certainly keep open the possibility of automatic phonological activation. As to the question of lexicon versus no lexicon, it is not an issue. A model that posits a lexicon with an interactive network of words, letters, and phonemes will handle automatic phonological activation rather well. Such a model was implied by the model of Rumelhart and McClelland (1981) in the pre–PDP days of interactive models. It provides a framework for phonological activation principles to operate within a classical architecture, a lexicon with restricted outside access and fully interactive inside access (Perfetti, 1992).

There are important writing system comparisons on this point. Shallow orthographies such as Serbo-Croatian and Italian might encourage more phonological processing than relative deep orthographies such as English, or a deeper-still orthography such as Hebrew (Frost, Katz, & Bentin, 1987). Chinese, as a logographic system, does not involve phonology prior to lexical access, but evidence suggests that phonological activation accompanies the identification of a character (Lam, Perfetti, & Bell, 1991; Perfetti & Zhang, 1991). Perfetti et al. (1992) suggest a universal phonological principle, namely that phonological activation occurs as rapidly as allowed by the writing system.

2. Implications for Individual Differences

The conclusions concerning phonological processing can be fairly conservative and still have some rather strong implications for individual differences. It appears that phonological information is either routine and automatic or at least fairly common (under dual route assumptions). Either state of affairs is sufficient to counter claims that skilled reading is a visual-only process, or the equivalent claim by Smith (1985, p. 103) that skilled readers of English "recognize words in the same way that fluent Chinese readers [do]."

There is another way, however, in which getting the details right might matter for individual differences. A lot of disability diagnosis and research has assumed that disabled readers might have a deficit in a "phonological route," leaving only a direct or "visual" route or vice versa (e.g., Boder, 1973). Such approaches are subject to criticism (Vellutino, 1979), even if the dual route theory is correct. The more general problem is whether there might be two kinds of word reading, one primarily orthographic and one primarily phonological.

Stanovich and West (1989) have identified the possible independence of two different processing abilities, one primarily orthographic and one phonological. They found that a measure of reading experience, the author recognition test, was a strong predictor of word processing ability, even after accounting for phonological processing skill. Factor analysis of a number of tasks chosen to represent phonological and orthographic processes revealed a highly coherent structure with an orthographic factor and phonological factor each having some unique factor-loading from experimental tasks. The index of reading experience loaded on both factors, but especially on the orthographic factor, which included tasks that require LEXICAL knowledge, that is, knowledge of spellings, such as the time to select which of two homophonic letter strings was a real word, as in *rume–room*. The phonological factor included decision times to select which of two letter strings was homophonic to a real word, *kake–dake,* and the times to name pseudowords. Stanovich and West (1989) suggest that experience in reading leads to lexical knowledge that goes well beyond decoding. Practice builds specific lexical knowledge, as also suggested by the growth in lexical specificity (Perfetti, 1992), discussed in a previous section. These data also make a clear link with the Olson et al. longitudinal study of dyslexia. An orthographic factor is not heritable, but dependent on print experience.

Whether separable orthographic and phonological components map onto dual route processing is another matter. There is certainly a resemblance between claiming that there is an orthographic route to the lexicon and claiming that there is an orthographic component to reading. But they are not the same. Experience with print strengthens word representations by increasing the quality of lexical representations, making spellings more reliable and more quickly accessed. Whether phonological processes continue to be involved for such representations is what the phonological debate has been about. And that debate remains undecided.

C. Text-Level Processes

Comprehension is a matter of building a mental representation of a text message, something that requires lexical processes, syntactic processes, and inference processes all in some degree of interaction with nonlinguistic knowledge. As in the case of phonology and lexical access, the story about individual differences in the higher level processes depends on the theoretical account of comprehension. This section presents one such account, focusing on the issues that make a difference for individual differences.

A descriptively coherent view of comprehension comprises an interactive model with constraints on interactions. It continues to be plausible to view the linguistic components, but not the knowledge components, as autonomous as proposed by Forster (1979), and as modular in the sense of Fodor (1983). A reader, as well as a listener, accesses words and parses sentences, rapidly and without undue influence from higher level knowledge. However, the construction of message representations is the result of interactions between local semantic representations (propositions) and knowledge that the comprehender has about a number of relevant things, some obtained from the discourse, some from outside the discourse. In processing terms, there appear to be some constraints on how rapidly knowledge outside the local linguistic representation can be made useful. The existence or perhaps the strength of these constraints is what divides models into modular and interactive models respectively.

1. Lexical Meaning

The evidence for autonomous meaning processing at the word level has appeared relatively strong. For words that have more than one meaning, activation for multiple meanings occurs immediately with selection of the contextually appropriate one delayed by a few milliseconds of processing time (Swinney, 1979; Tanenhaus, Lieman, & Seidenberg, 1979; Kintsch & Mross, 1985). The mechanism by which an inappropriate meaning becomes less activated appears to be one of suppression rather than decay (Gernsbacher & Faust, 1990).

Empirical challenges to the conclusion favoring an autonomous process of meaning activation exist, with some studies showing that dominant meanings can be selected more quickly by context than secondary meanings (Duffy, Morris, & Rayner, 1988; Simpson, 1981; Simpson & Kruger, 1991; Tabossi, 1988). Such challenges are not inconsistent with a modular view of meaning selection, if a lexical entry is assumed to have ordered information concerning its meanings (Hogaboam & Perfetti, 1975). The picture might not be as simple as it seemed at first, but a conservative statement is that the ability of a favorable discourse to suppress in advance the unneeded meanings of a word is quite limited. A word's dominant meaning is activated regardless of context, especially if the difference between the frequencies of the dominant and subordinate meaning is large.

2. Syntactic Processing

The process by which the constituents of a sentence are established and interconnected, parsing, remains a strong candidate for a modular process (see Mitchell, this volume). Research on garden path phenomena is largely consistent with a limited role of discourse context in overriding garden paths (Rayner, Carlson, & Frazier, 1983; Ferreira & Clifton, 1986; Mitchell, Corley, & Garnham, 1992). The story is likely to be complicated by the fact that some discourse influences for processing some syntactic structures do occur. Clear evidence for such influence is that readers' parsing preferences for post-nominal Prepositional Phrase attachment, as in *The girl hit the boy with the boomerang,* can be overridden by discourse context under some conditions (Britt, Perfetti, Garrod, & Rayner, 1992). Britt (in press) has recently shown that such override effects are enabled by the argument structure of the verb in combination with favorable referential discourse conditions (Crain & Steedman, 1985).

One way to view the pattern of results as a whole in this area is that override effects, as tested by stringent on-line measures, are not readily obtained, and they are obtained more readily for some syntactic structures than others (Britt et al., 1992; Perfetti, 1990). To be able to identify precisely the conditions of override is part of developing the boundaries on which parts of syntactic processing is autonomous and which are not (Perfetti, 1990).

3. Discourse Level Processes

Comprehension is, or at least includes, the construction of mental representations of worlds described by texts, variously referred to as situation models (van Dijk & Kintsch, 1983), mental models (Johnson-Laird, 1983), and (unfortunately) text models (Perfetti, 1985). This level of comprehension, in the framework of partially autonomous processors, is distinct from a propositionally defined semantic representation (a text representation) that is essentially linguistic (Kintsch, 1988; van Dijk & Kintsch, 1983). In an autonomous framework, the lexically specified output of a parser, along with coreferential information ("argument overlap"), is the input to a propositional level of text representation. A model of the situation, a full mental model, is a combination of the text representation with knowledge-driven inferences provided by the comprehender.

Work on the discourse level of representation has had a course typically independent from the traditional syntactic/semantic concerns of psycholinguistics. It naturally begins, for example, where syntax leaves off. [Examples of text comprehension theories with no role for sentence level representations include Kintsch (1974); Graesser (1981); Rumelhart (1975); Schank & Abelson (1977); Trabasso and van den Broek (1985); among many others.] Of course, it has long been clear that syntactic categories, semantic roles, and discourse functions are interrelated in some systematic ways (Chafe, 1976; Givón, 1986; Perfetti & Goldman, 1974; Tomlin, 1983; Yekovich, Walker, & Blackman, 1979). And syntactic influences on discourse-level understanding have been an occasional focus of systematic comprehension research (Sanford & Garrod, 1981; Gernsbacher, 1990; Kintsch, in press).

For example, Gernsbacher has shown that a comprehender's text representation is affected by cataphoric markers in discourse. When a storyteller introduces, for example, an egg into the story by saying *She found **this** egg,* the egg is more likely to be referred to in the remainder of the discourse than if the egg is introduced with *She found **an** egg* (Gernsbacher & Shroyer, 1989). Concepts introduced by cataphoric markers, spoken stress as well as the indefinite *this,* are also more activated in the subjects' text representations (Gernsbacher & Jescheniak, 1993).

If the distinction between text-based linguistic representations and situation-based mental models is a real one, then the distinction, in processing terms, depends on knowledge-driven inferences. The first is semantically shallow, containing meaning representations generated with minimal inferencing machinery, perhaps only those inferences that are controlled by text anaphora. The second is semantically deep, containing situation-specific meanings, rich in inferences that cannot be systematically driven by linguistic structures. Although one view maintains that only the second, the mental model, is psychologically real (Johnson-Laird, 1983), the inference-poor, linguistically rich text level is a logical product of assuming that sentence meanings are part of what a comprehender constructs (Perfetti, 1989). This level can also be demonstrated independent of the situation level in certain circumstances (Perrig & Kintsch, 1985).

With or without an intermediate propositional level of representation, inferences are central, because they produce the deepest level of discourse understanding. The issue has been, When do what kinds of inferences occur? Readers do appear to generate those inferences that maintain referential coherence when the inference is textually required (Corbett & Dosher, 1978; Dell, McKoon, & Ratcliff, 1983; Haviland & Clark, 1974; Just & Carpenter, 1978). Inferences that maintain causal coherence may also be made when needed (Keenan, Baillet, & Brown, 1984), although evidence is less strong on exactly when such inferences occur. On the other hand, for a whole range of elaborative inferences—those that a comprehender might be expected to make in establishing a situation model but are not required by mere linguistic coherence—the evidence is equivocal. Most evidence does not support the assumption of early on-line elaborative inferences (Corbett & Dosher, 1978; McKoon & Ratcliff, 1986, 1989; Singer, 1979; Singer & Ferreira, 1983), while some evidence suggests early inferences under restricted conditions (O'Brien, Shank, Myers, & Rayner, 1988). McKoon and Ratcliff (1989) suggest that inferences are encoded to different degrees of explicitness, with some, for instance those that involve prediction of events, encoded only vaguely. Such less encoded inferences are readily made specific when required but are not specifically computed as part of comprehension. A related possibility is that elaborated inferences are not typically made as part of the text representation but can be observed in the situation model when readers are encouraged to attend to meaning (Fincher-Kiefer, 1993). It is also possible that inferences required to maintain causal coherence among story elements are more likely to be made than other kinds of elaborative inferences (Trabasso & Suh, 1993).

A full review of these issues is beyond the goal of this chapter, and they are reviewed elsewhere in this volume (Fletcher, this volume; Glenberg, Kruley, & Langston, this volume). The main point in the present context is that comprehenders achieve multiple levels of text representation, at least one that is heavily linguistic and at least one that is heavily driven by nonlinguistic knowledge. The processing question concerns how the comprehender moves from one level to another. The evidence, uneven though it is, suggests limited construction of richer models, consistent with a comprehension architecture that allows more passive automatic processes at the lower levels, and more active and less automatic processes at the inferential level. Implicit is the claim that the inferential processes are potentially more resource-demanding than the lower level processes. Because there is some cost to making them, they are not always made.

4. Implications for Individual Differences

The general framework outlined in the above sections identifies four general levels of representation that must be integrated during normal comprehension. It assumes that, as an approximation, lexical and syntactic processes have autonomous characteristics, with some limited influences from other levels of information. However, real comprehension requires the third and fourth levels, using linguistic input in interaction with individual knowledge to produce a situation model. To claim that comprehension is a completely interactive process, without constraint on information exchange, is possible but neither fruitful for individual differences nor consistent with the bulk of the evidence. Within a system with some hierarchical components showing some autonomy, one can hypothesize individual differences to be in specific components.

Individual differences can occur in lexical processing, syntactic processing, and inference-making. We should not expect simple isolated problems, however, because processing mechanisms operate on all levels within a limited resource system. Instead we should observe interactive problems in which comprehension differences are widespread across various tasks, traceable to specific component processes only through careful research logic. We should also expect clear evidence, isolating only one or another component, to be very rare.

The following sections summarize some of the very limited evidence that bears on the localization of individual differences in comprehension. In each case, the question is whether some component process difference is found to associate with independently assessed reading comprehension skill, either for adults or children.

5. Individual Differences in Processing Lexical Meaning

The selection of meaning in contexts is largely assumed to be a two-stage process: (1) a general activation stage in which a lexical entry is accessed and its associated meanings nonselectively activated, and (2), a few milliseconds (100–400 ms) later, a selection stage in which the meaning appropriate for context is selected, or gains further activation, and meanings inappropriate for context are suppressed. (See section VI,C,1.) Skilled and less skilled readers may differ in these meaning selection processes. Merrill, Sperber, and McCauley (1981) had fifth grade children read sentences in which some attributes connected with a key word were emphasized over others. In *The girl fought the cat,* for example, the verb appears to make *claw* more emphasized than *fur.* In a variation on the Stroop task, subjects named the color of a key word (*fur* or *claw*) presented one second after reading the sentence. Interference is expected based on the activation of meanings of words whose color must be named (Conrad, 1974). Relative to control words, skilled readers showed slower naming times only for emphasized attributes, such as *claw* but not *fur,* whereas less skilled readers were slower for both kinds of attributes.

The implication is that skilled readers are locked more quickly into a contextually relevant meaning, within at least 1 s, compared with less skilled readers, for whom both relevant and less relevant meanings are still activated. A relevant mechanism for failing to lock in an appropriate meaning might be a CODE ASYNCHRONY in lexical access (Perfetti, 1985) or a SUPPRESSION process (Gernsbacher, 1990). Note, however, that in the Merrill et al. study "relevant" meanings are really attributes that are the result of elaborative inferences, not distinct meanings. It is possible that skilled readers were generating such inferences more than less skilled readers, although the general lack of evidence of on-line elaborative inferences casts doubt on this interpretation. Finally, it is also possible that such results reflect not an already accomplished meaning selection (or inference), but a process prompted by the presentation of the test word itself.

Further evidence from Gernsbacher, Varner, and Faust (1990) has sharpened the picture somewhat. College students classified by comprehension skill were given a word-fit task: At the end of a short sentence, subjects decided whether a visually presented target word fit the meaning of a sentence. Gernsbacher et al. (1990) found that when the final word of the sentence was ambiguous, such as *spade,* there was a skill difference in the time to reject a target word related to the contextually inappropriate meaning of the ambiguous related word. For example, in the sentence *He dug with the spade,* the target word *ace* should be rejected as a fit to the meaning of the sentence; however, because *ace* is related to another meaning of *spade,* it should have some initial activation. Indeed, both skilled and less skilled comprehenders showed long reaction times (RTs) to reject *ace* (relative to control sentences) when it appeared 100 ms after the sentence. When *ace* appeared 850 ms after the sentence, however, only less skilled readers showed long RTs to reject it.

In a related study reported in Gernsbacher and Faust (1990; also Gernsbacher, 1990), less skilled comprehenders showed more facilitation from biasing context in meaning-fit decisions, that is, cases in which the target word fits the meaning of the sentence, as *garden* would in *He dug with the spade.* The comparison condition is the more neutral *He picked up the spade,* which fails to select an appropriate sense of *spade* but allows *garden* to fit. The difference in acceptance times between these two conditions was greater for less skilled comprehenders than for skilled comprehenders. As Gernsbacher (1990) argues, this pattern of results suggests not a problem with the use of context, since less skilled readers show more context facilitation, but a problem with suppression. Less skilled comprehenders are less able to suppress irrelevant meanings.

Part of this picture is consistent with the conclusions reached on context use by Perfetti and Roth (1981; Perfetti, 1985) and Stanovich (1980, 1981). Less skilled comprehenders are good users of context. The rest of the story diverges a bit. Whereas the research on word identification (Perfetti et al., 1978; West & Stanovich, 1978) suggested that less skilled readers have ineffective word identification processes, which enable them to use context even more than skilled comprehenders, Gernsbacher's work on meaning selection suggests a specific additional problem, one of processing the results of word identification.

The less skilled reader is seen as having multiple meanings hang around for too long, unable to use context to suppress unwanted meanings despite skill in context use.

One would not want to conclude that additional mechanisms are necessary to account for comprehension differences if just one (word identification) or two (word identification plus capacity limitations) will do. Gernsbacher (1990), however, buttresses the argument for a suppression deficit with data showing that less skilled readers are slower to reject irrelevant homophones (Gernsbacher & Faust, 1991). After reading a sentence ending with a homophone, such as *He had lots of patients* (homophone: *patience*), subjects performed the meaning-fit task. The key case is time to reject a word related to the homophonic meaning of the final word of the sentence, *calm* in this case, relative to the rejection time following a nonhomophonic control condition. Both skilled and less skilled comprehenders were slower at rejecting *calm* 100 ms after the final word of the sentence; after 1000 ms, only less skilled comprehenders were slower.

Gernsbacher and Faust (1991) demonstrate a parallel difference in a visual scene task, one in which subjects must decide whether an object named by a word had appeared in a just-viewed visual display. In the critical condition, the display comprised objects that might be together in a typical scene, such as farm objects or kitchen objects, and the following target word named an object that had not appeared in the display. The time to correctly reject a word, such as *tractor,* was longer when it was potentially part of the set of displayed objects (farm objects) than when it was not (kitchen objects) for both skilled and less skilled comprehenders 50 ms following the offset of the display. After 1000 ms, however, only less skilled comprehenders were affected. Along with some additional data from tasks involving pictures and words (Gernsbacher & Faust, 1991), these results seem to support a highly general suppression deficit in less skilled comprehenders (Gernsbacher & Faust, 1991; Gernsbacher, 1990). Because data from pictures produce the same pattern as data from sentences, the deficit is claimed to be a general cognitive one, not a language-specific one.

If these conclusions are correct, then the question of individual differences becomes again one of careful definition. Disability research requires some attention to specific problems, that is, reading problems in the absence of general intellectual differences. Additional individual differences, those in comprehension generally, are questions of general cognitive functioning, that is, intelligence. One might expect that such general differences reflect not only or perhaps not even problems primarily in language modules, but in cognitive control mechanisms.

6. Individual Differences in Processing Syntax

The issue for syntax is not whether there are individual differences that arise in processing syntactic tasks, but what to make of such differences. Dyslexic children and even garden-variety less skilled readers across a wide age range show problems handling various aspects of English morphology and syntax (Fletcher, Satz, & Scholes, 1981; Mann, Shankweiler, & Smith, 1984; Vogel, 1975). The question is whether such problems arise from some deficit in processing syntax or from some other source that infects performance on syntactic tasks.

It is in the historic disposition of psycholinguistics to assume that linguistic structures are universally available through the language faculty. However, it is clear that with syntax, as with anything else, practice helps. The competence to understand a center embedding or an object relative, to take two structures known to cause problems, can be better manifested when someone has opportunities to practice this competence. Furthermore, some syntactic structures are more typical of written language than spoken language. The opportunity for practice, therefore, is limited by the ability to read. This continuing development of reading skill as a result of initial success at reading—and the parallel increasing failure as a result of initial failure—is undoubtedly a major contributor to individual differences in reading. Stanovich (1986) discusses this rich-get-richer aspect of reading skill, borrowing from Merton (1968) and Walberg and Tsai (1983) the biblical metaphor: "For unto every one that hath shall be given, and he shall have abundance: but from him that hath not shall be taken away even that which he hath" (Matthew 25:29).

Seeing syntactic problems as Matthew effects places them intermediate to the two hypotheses that have been developed in this area. On one account, syntactic problems, where they are observed, reflect a lag in the development of linguistic structures (Byrne, 1981; Fletcher et al., 1981; Stein, Cairns, & Zurif, 1984). Such an account, at first glance, seems consistent with the fact that syntactic deficits are observed in spoken language, not just written language. However, an alternative to a structural deficit was proposed by Perfetti and Lesgold (1977), who argued that the basic causes of less skilled comprehension were localized in working memory limitations. Problems in discourse comprehension, on this view, arise neither from intrinsic syntactic problems nor from higher level discourse structure problems, but from processing bottlenecks partly, but not wholly, arising from lexical processing inefficiency.

Although clear evidence favoring either a structural deficit or a processing limitation hypothesis is not easily obtained, there are hints that the processing deficit hypothesis may be closer to correct. Crain and Shankweiler (1988; also Crain, Shankweiler, Macaruso, & Bar-Shalom, 1990) have argued that, on the structural deficit hypothesis, one should expect differential problems in syntax. That is, the structures that cause problems for less skilled readers should not be just those that cause some problems for skilled readers. Instead, using data of Mann, Shankweiler, and Smith (1984), they demonstrate a single pattern of error on subject- and object-relative clauses for both skilled and less skilled third grade readers. Less skilled readers had more trouble with relative clauses, but the sameness of skilled and less skilled error patterns counts against a structural deficit explanation.

Further evidence against a structural deficit account, and in favor of a processing deficit account, comes from Crain et al. (1990). They found that problems in processing temporal clauses (*Push NP₁ before/after you push NP₂*) increased as assumed processing load increased, either by making the NP more complex (not affecting the clause structure) or by not satisfying certain presuppositions associated with normal use of these clauses. Crain et al. (1990) also report garden path data that they argue are inconsistent with a structural deficit hypothesis, again relying on identical error patterns across groups of skilled and less skilled readers in support of this conclusion.

It is interesting that syntactic errors in Broca's aphasia, usually assumed to reflect a basic loss of syntactic ability, might also be reinterpreted as a processing deficit using this pattern-of-errors logic (Shankweiler, Crain, Gorrell, & Tuller, 1989). Since acquired language disorders are beyond the scope of this chapter, the point is simply to note how far one might go in connecting language problems to processing limitations rather than structural deficits. True dyslexics, garden-variety less skilled readers, and perhaps some acquired language disorders as well reflect not a loss of grammatical knowledge or a structural deficit, but a processing limitation arising from the demands of syntactic processes for limited resources.

The processing limitation account of individual differences has received its most extensive theoretical development by Just and Carpenter (1992), following a large body of literature showing working memory differences between skilled and less skilled comprehenders. Especially relevant for syntax are data on garden path effects reported by King and Just (1991). High-span readers (high in working memory for language) did not show garden path effects for reduced relative sentences previously shown, by Ferreira and Clifton (1986), to produce such effects. Low span (less working memory capacity for language) did show such effects. Moreover, the data seem to suggest that skilled readers are carrying forward both readings of a sentence throughout its structurally ambiguous region. Such evidence is entirely consistent with the idea that syntactic differences among individuals are driven by processing resource differences rather than structural differences. They go well beyond that, however, in challenging the assumption that parsing procedures reflect universal principles rather than resource-sensitive strategies. The first point is clear, but it will take a while to settle the claims surrounding this second point.

The Matthew effect and the processing limitation hypothesis are complementary in the account they provide to syntactic processing problems. The one emphasizes the need for success in reading so as to allow successful practice with more complex aspects of the task, and the other emphasizes the limitations that processing mechanisms have to work with. The point of convergence is that success in reading at the lexical and phonological levels will improve the opportunities for becoming more skilled in handling those syntactic structures that require more capacity. The right kind of practice, in effect, increases functional capacity.

7. Individual Differences in Discourse Level Processing

A key point about syntactic processing applies also to individual differences at the discourse level. It is a question not of whether they exist, but whence they arise. To say that individuals differ in comprehension is to say that they differ in the comprehension of discourse. All standard tests of comprehension require readers to answer questions about texts. As in the case of syntax, there are three possibilities, with the processing limitations hypothesis and the Matthew effect combining to account for increasing problems with discourse arising from inadequate opportunities to practice comprehension.

The third possibility is discourse structure deficits, although this possibility has not attracted a great deal of attention. Specific problems in knowing the structures of narratives or, more plausibly, specific expository structures may arise. Indeed, the only way to learn about how texts are organized is to read a lot of them, so not observing individual differences in knowledge of text structures would be surprising.

Because discourse processing depends on so many processes in the construction of a mental model of the content of a text, these three possibilities are by no means exhaustive. For example, one can imagine individual differences in integrating sentences by establishing coreference, and indeed such differences are found (Frederiksen, 1981). Or one might suppose that readers differ in the monitoring of their text comprehension, and indeed they appear to do so (Ryan, 1982). Or one can suppose that individual differences in knowledge produce individual differences in comprehension, and these differences too are found (Anderson, Reynolds, Shallert, & Goetz, 1977; Spilich, Vesonder, Chiesi, & Voss, 1979). Low-knowledge readers, however, can compensate for low knowledge with reading skill, at least to a limited extend (Adams & Perfetti, 1993; Perfetti, 1989). Besides, such differences are patently uninteresting to a theory of individual differences in general language comprehension, assuming such a general skill exists apart from individual knowledge. (For a defense of their existence see Perfetti, 1989.)

The question, given a proliferation of possibilities, becomes whether there is anything more principled than a list in the search for individual differences in discourse level processes. The major possibility concerns inferences. Inferences are essential to constructing mental models, and it is quite likely that some of the differences observed in individual comprehension arise from who makes inferences when under what conditions. The trick is going to be to discover whether such differences are systematic enduring characteristics of individuals, as lexical abilities and working memory are, or whether they are essentially haphazard, reduced to knowledge differences, which vary with content domains and particular interactions with texts, some of which fail to trigger inferences for some individuals.

Comprehension as the building of mental models (Johnson-Laird, 1983) provides a useful theoretical framework for this question. On the way to constructing a coherent mental model, a reader must make inferences. Skilled readers do construct better mental models (by definition), and it might be their inference ability that is responsible for this. Evidence on children's comprehension from Oakhill (1982) and Garnham, Oakhill, and Johnson-Laird (1982), along with other research summarized in Oakhill and Garnham (1988), is suggestive in this regard.

Oakhill (1982) found differences between 6- and 7-year-old children in a spoken language task, such that skilled readers made more semantically congruent false alarms in a recognition memory test following a brief passage that encourages inferences. Consider this example: *The car crashed into the bus. The bus was near the crossroads. The car skidded on the ice.* One might expect the mental model to include both the car and the bus in relation to the crossroad, so that subjects might false-alarm to a sentence that represents this fact, such as *The car was near the crossroads.* On the other hand, the mental model should not include anything about a skidding bus, so a model-incongruent foil such as *The bus skidded on the ice* should not produce false alarms. Oakhill (1982) found that the model-congruent foils generally produced more false alarms than the incongruent ones, and that this difference was more pronounced for skilled readers than less skilled readers. Skilled readers, however, also made (nonsignificantly) fewer recognition errors on actually occurring sentences, so perhaps their basic representation of the text was better also. Such data are consistent both with a lower level processing difference—more accurate propositional representation—and with an inferential difference. Furthermore, the pattern of error differences is the same for the two reader groups suggesting a quantitative difference rather than a difference in kind; that is, less skilled readers made inferences as well.

The Garnham et al. (1982) study manipulated discourse structure directly by comparing performance on a short four-sentence story appearing normally and with two kinds of scrambling. One kind simply scrambled the four sentences, disrupting both the event structure and the referential coherence, whereas the other scrambled the order in the same way but retained referential coherence by having proper names precede rather than follow pronouns that referred to them. For example, the fully scrambled version was as follows: *She had just won it and was hurrying home to show her sister. Suddenly the wind caught it and carried it into a tree. Jenny was holding tightly to the string of her beautiful new balloon. She cried and cried. The balloon hit a branch and burst.* The referential modification simply substituted *Jenny* for *she* and *beautiful new balloon* for *it* in the first sentence, deleting *beautiful new* in the third sentence, and substituting *it* for *The balloon* in the final sentence.

In both kinds of scrambling, the mental model is difficult to construct but the referential coherence allows the reader to make some mental rearrangements—inferences—on the sentences to make a mental model. Garnham et al. found that only skilled readers were able to take advantage of the referentially coherent text, a fact that both Garnham et al. and Johnson-Laird attribute to their ability to make inferences. Although this is the most straightforward analysis of the data, there was also a nonsignificant difference in the fully scrambled version as well. The most interesting form of the inference account requires no differences in lower level processes, such that inferences provide the only explanation for the pattern of results. Moreover, the processing limitation explanation always looms as a possibility, unless it is ruled out by showing that two groups are the same in a measure of capacity. Making inferences on poorly constructed texts is especially resource-demanding. Finally, scrambled texts require problem-solving in a way that normal texts do not. Skilled readers are probably better problem-solvers than less skilled readers, but such differences again push the analysis of reading skill toward the analysis of intelligence.

There are other hints at inference making differences related to reading skill, for example in the extent to which inferences about superordinate goals are made during story reading (Long & Golding, 1993). My reading of the inference story is that we should expect individual differences in inferencing, just as in other processes. If so, two tricky questions follow. (1) Are such inference differences characteristic of individuals, that is, true individual differences, or characteristic of specific reader–text events? (2) Assuming they are true individual characteristics, what causes them? If two individuals have the same knowledge, what causes the relevant knowledge to be triggered for one but not the other?

Everyone, including the most skilled reader, must sometimes fail to make an appropriate inference. But are there individuals who, despite adequate knowledge and sufficient reading skill, fail systematically to draw inferences? Probably. But there are probably many more whose inference problems, to the extent they are systematic, are derivative of inadequate reading experiences, victims of the Matthew effect.

VII. THEORIES OF INDIVIDUAL DIFFERENCES

There are many ideas about qualitative differences in processing within the dyslexia field, which has been dominated by assumptions of distinct deficit types, especially phonetically based and visually based deficits (e.g., Boder, 1973). Theories with broader aims in explaining individual differences in reading have attended to basic cognitive mechanisms, such as lexical processes, memory, and comprehension. Few of these are developed in enough detail to be more than theoretical frameworks, however. This section briefly summarizes a few of them that make contact with the issues discussed in this chapter.

A. The Interactive–Compensatory Model

A model directly tied to individual differences in context use is the interactive–compensatory model of Stanovich (1980; Stanovich et al., 1981). Less skilled readers have less effective decoding skills, but, because word identification is viewed as an interactive process, they can compensate for this weakness by making more use of context. Such a model captures the facts of skill differences in context facilitation. It also predicts that as a child gains skill in reading, context facilitation will diminish, a prediction confirmed by Stanovich et al. (1981) in a longitudinal study of second grade readers.

B. Verbal Efficiency Theory

The verbal efficiency theory (Perfetti & Lesgold, 1979; Perfetti, 1985, 1988) is directed at comprehension as well as word identification. It assumes that word identification processes for skilled readers are relatively automatized through learning and practice. It further assumes that this relative automatization plays a role in comprehension by allowing resources to be devoted to certain comprehension processes rather than to word identification. Less skilled readers have problems in comprehension partly because their ineffective word identification processes require resources that are thereby less available for comprehension. This model predicts that some differences observed in higher level comprehension processes, such as inference making, arise from lexical sources. Skill differences in context facilitation are accounted for by assuming that the contribution of an outside source of information, namely context, is limited by the speed with which a relatively automatic process operates. The theory assumes not that speed of processing defines automaticity, but rather that it reflects it. What allow word identification to be relatively resource-free are fully specified and redundant lexical representations (Perfetti, 1992) that, with practice, trigger word identification. Less skilled readers have variable low-quality lexical representations, as evidenced by poorer spelling knowledge and phonological knowledge. Support for this model has remained mostly correlational, with correlations between measures of comprehension and lexical processes consistently showing a strong relationship (Perfetti, 1985; Stanovich, 1988), even for adults (Bell & Perfetti, in press; Cunningham et al., 1990). Walczyk (1993) found that the relationship between decoding speed and comprehension is enhanced when readers are forced to read at a fast pace. More direct evidence linking gains in lexical processing to gains in comprehension is lacking.

C. The Capacity Model

Another model that emphasizes the role that limited processing resources plays in comprehension is the capacity limitation model of Just and Carpenter (1992), who have extended the initial observations of Daneman and Carpenter (1980) into a comprehensive model of individual differences. Daneman and Carpenter (1980) reported that adult subjects' performance in text comprehension was well predicted by their memory span, measured by their ability to remember final words from lists of sentences. In its fuller development, the model accounts for a wide array of individual differences, including individual differences in syntactic processing, to individual differences in working memory capacity. It shares with verbal efficiency theory an emphasis on resource limitations in comprehension. It has been developed and supported, however, in much more detail. Since this model is treated by (Carpenter, Miyake, and Just, this volume), it will not be discussed further here.

D. The Phonological Capacity Model

A variant of a capacity model is described by Crain and Shankweiler (1988; Shankweiler & Crain, 1986). In the Shankweiler–Crain model, working memory regulates information flow from a phonological buffer. Less skilled readers, as their core problem, have deficits in the processing of phonological information, which creates a bottleneck in the flow of information to higher levels in the processing system. Thus, comprehension as well as lexical processes are adversely affected by this capacity limitation.

E. The PCVD Model

The phonological core variable difference (PCVD) model (Stanovich, 1988), unlike the models described above, which are frameworks for process models, is a strictly descriptive, statistical model. The PCVD model is an attempt to integrate the observations made on garden-variety low-skill readers and dyslexics. The disabilities area has traditionally attempted to describe specific, discrete subtypes of reading problems, sharply distinguishing low reading skill as a reading-specific disorder from low reading skill as a more general learning problem linked to IQ. Stanovich's model responds to some of the methodological issues that plague both the definition of dyslexia and the research designs that are used to study reading problems.

The basic suggestion is that reading skill is distributed as a continuum, contrary to the claim that there is a statistically identifiable bump at the lower end of the continuum corresponding to a specific reading disability, as concluded by Rutter and Yule (1975) on the basis of a large sample study. Others have suggested a continuity rather than a discontinuity view of reading failure (Perfetti, 1985), and some have argued that the Rutter and Yule conclusions were based on statistical artifact (Rodgers, 1983; Share, McGee, McKenzie, Williams, & Silva, 1987). Stanovich's proposal accommodates the continuity view while holding to a concept of specific reading disability. Stanovich endorses Ellis's (1985) metaphor of specific reading disability as analogous to obesity rather than measles. Dyslexia, like obesity, is a real and dangerous condition but, unlike measles, one for which definitive lines can be drawn only arbitrarily. Stanovich's suggestion is to view both reading ability and the bivariate distribution of IQ/reading ability as continuous. This means there is also a continuum between the "pure dyslexic" (IQ high relative to reading) and the garden-variety poor reader (lower and more typical IQ). The central processing deficit of both dyslexics and garden-variety poor readers (the distinction blurs at the boundary because of the continuum) is phonological, affecting their decoding ability. The garden-variety poor reader has a phonological deficit, although perhaps in a less severe form, but, in addition, has a variety of cognitive deficits as well.

Although this is a descriptive model rather than a process model, it is important in organizing the kinds of processing deficits observed in children and in addressing the difficult issues of definition. Furthermore, it suggests a useful perspective on how to view individual differences at high levels of skill (e.g., college students), where there is little reason to expect a pronounced phonological deficit. Such differences should be more noticeable in a range of cognitive processes, rather than specifically reading processes.

F. The Structure Building Theory

A theory that integrates individual differences into a model of comprehension is the structure building framework (SBF) of Gernsbacher (1990). Comprehension in the SBF is a process of laying foundation for comprehension in response to initial text segments, mapping subsequent information onto this foundation, and shifting from a current foundation to begin a new one when the text suggests doing so (when a text segment is incoherent with the currently active structure). Two specific mechanisms occur as part of structure building: enhancement—the increase in activation given to contextually relevant information—and suppression, the inhibition of contextually irrelevant information.

Individual differences in the SBF occur in many aspects of structure building: Less skilled comprehenders are less effective in laying foundations and mapping new information onto these foundations. Two problems in structure building are especially targeted within SBF: (1) Less skilled comprehenders shift too often from a current structure to a new structure—too much shifting, or not enough mapping—a mechanism that explains their poorer memory for recently comprehended information. (2) Less skilled comprehenders have ineffective suppression mechanisms, explaining why they are less able to reject an inappropriate meaning of an ambiguous words, among other things. Gernsbacher (1990) summarizes evidence with adult subjects that is very consistent with this description.

The SBF has two particularly interesting properties in the context of individual differences. For one, it is detailed enough to make specific predictions about exactly where individual differences will show up in some tasks. It predicts some nonobvious differences, something not true of most individual difference theories. For example, the prediction that less skilled comprehenders show the effects of a contextually inappropriate word meaning 1000 ms after reading the word is nonobvious on less detailed accounts of comprehension that emphasize memory limitations or lexical bottlenecks.

A second interesting feature of the SBF is its generality. It is not a theory of language comprehension specifically but of comprehension generally. It encompasses, for example, individual differences in processing pictures as well as both spoken and written language. In support of this generality are data showing parallel suppression problems in picture tasks for less skilled comprehenders, and high intercorrelations among comprehension measures of stories presented as written texts, spoken texts, and pictures.

VIII. AN ANALYSIS OF THEORETICAL PROGRESS

A. Recent Models

The theoretical advances in understanding individual differences can be appreciated by noticing the increasing precision of recent models, including computational components (Just & Carpenter, 1992) but especially including mechanistically grounded explanations. Individual differences can be observed in very specific processing events during reading and linked to an individual cognitive capacity (Just & Carpenter, 1992). And they can be inferred within the logic of information processing experiments and linked to individual cognitive processes (Gernsbacher, 1990). Both represent an advance over earlier theories, such as verbal efficiency theory, which, although it made strong processing assumptions, has been supported mainly through correlations.

There remain some questions, however, about how to explain individual differences. The main problem verbal efficiency theory addressed was the connection between two kinds of low-level processing factors and higher level comprehension. Its central claim is that observed differences in higher level comprehension were often (not exclusively) the result of lower level processing bottlenecks arising at the lexical level and the working memory level. It claims there are three central facts that constrain a theory of individual differences: (1) the pervasiveness of lexical processing differences between skilled and less skilled comprehenders, (2) the only slightly less pervasive working memory differences between skilled and less skilled comprehenders, and (3) the equally pervasive correlation between low skill in reading and low skill in spoken language processes. Other differences, including some at higher levels that might be independent of lower levels, are to be expected on this account. They are empirically less pervasive, however, and when found are often reported without adequate control over differences in lower level processes. Thus, the three facts described above are privileged in constraining theories of individual differences.

What is the state of affairs in addressing these facts theoretically? A major problem, which has often been ignored, is whether there is one mechanism or two that is responsible for poor reading comprehension. Do low-skill readers have some defective mechanism that produces ineffective lexical processes and a second defective mechanism that produces lower functional memory capacities? Or is there a single mechanism that is responsible for the two most pervasive facts associated with less skilled reading? A lexical problem can easily produce a derived working memory problem as well. And, although it is less obvious, working memory capacity problems might produce an observed lexical problem, given certain assumptions about how working memory handles linguistic input. Working memory limitations might, for example, limit the growth of vocabulary (Gathercole & Baddeley, 1989). Possible answers to this question of one or two mechanisms were spelled out in Perfetti (1985, pp. 113–119), and they interact with the third constraining fact: It is difficult to see how a single lexically based explanation, at least one that involves decoding, can explain differences in spoken language comprehension.

Existing theories of individual differences, including the capacity limitation hypothesis, leave some question about how the three central facts will be handled. The move that is tempting to make is to assume that there are indeed two problems, one associated with lexical processes and one associated with working memory limitations. Many children have both problems. But adult samples, especially those drawn from college populations, are self-selected for skill at lexical processing. Their problems are primarily in working memory. Adult studies on the memory hypothesis have typically not assessed lexical processes, however, and lexical differences are linked to comprehension and reading speed differences among the college populations that are the subjects of these studies (Jackson & McClelland, 1979; Palmer et al., 1985; Cunningham et al., 1990). In addition, some studies have found decoding differences that cannot be reduced to either more elementary processes (letter processing) or to memory processes (Hammond, 1987). The capacity explanation can handle lexical processing failures only by assuming that capacity limitations restrict the amount of lexical processing. This is plausible, but it still leaves a bridge to build: How does it explain problems with processes that are patently lexical and sublexical, such as the problems even low-skill adults have with reading pseudowords?

One alternative for a single mechanism, presented in Perfetti (1985), is that the quality of linguistic coding is the central mechanism at issue, a deceptively complex process that depends on orthographic knowledge, phonological knowledge, and semantic information associated with lexical entries. The claim is that the hallmark of skilled reading is an INACTIVE memory system that is capable of responding to a linguistic symbol, in any modality, with a rapid retrieval of the codes that are part of that symbol's memory location (Perfetti, 1985, p. 118). This possibility is consistent with the three central constraining facts of comprehension differences and allows a single-mechanism explanation rather than a double-mechanism explanation. It explains memory differences not by assuming some capacity limitation, but by assuming that the processes that hold linguistic inputs in high states of activation (working memory) are something like re-instantiations of the processes that activate the memories in the first place. These processes include linguistic coding, the multiple activations of a phonological–semantic representation.

A fair summary is that the precise source of lexical and working memory differences remains somewhat unclear. One should probably continue to ask what it is that tasks of working memory and time to name words and pseudowords have in common, such that there might be a single mechanism.

How about other mechanisms, such as the suppression deficit identified by Gernsbacher (1990)? This may represent an additional mechanism, or a better specification of a lexical processing difficulty that explains memory differences. There is a family resemblance among the conclusions reached by Gernsbacher (1990), Carpenter and Just (1988; Just & Carpenter, 1992), and Perfetti (1985) concerning individual differences in comprehension. All focus on the efficiency of cognitive mechanisms, that is, the functioning of processes within some imposed limitations. The suppression mechanism, in such a context, can be described as a process that serves efficient use of limited capacity by controlling the semantic computations that would otherwise explode. The reader must suppress an unwanted meaning of a word quickly to continue to build a representation quickly within a limited capacity system. The failure of such a mechanism results in a processor that is cluttered with irrelevant information. Thus, suppression might be an explanation of observed differences in both working memory and comprehension. Certainly, the fit seems more natural this way than the other way around (i.e., capacity differences explain suppression differences?). There is, nevertheless, no compelling reason yet to think that suppression can replace capacity by explaining it.

What about its relation to lexical processes? First, in Gernsbacher's studies, differences in baseline level lexical processing were generally found both when subjects were college students (Gernsbacher et al., 1990) and when they were air force recruits (Gernsbacher & Faust, 1991). For example, it is not merely that less skilled comprehenders were slower at rejecting the inappropriate meaning of ambiguous words; they were also slower at rejecting the inappropriate meaning of an unambiguous word (Gernsbacher et al., 1990, Experiment 4). Thus, consistent with many other studies, these adult subjects showed less effective lexical processing, sentence comprehension, or both. The effects attributed to suppression are additional relative effects, namely a less pronounced IMPROVEMENT in low comprehenders' RTs to inappropriate meaning after 1000 ms, compared with skilled readers. Such patterns are consistent with differences of degree, rather than differences of kind. And because they build on initial differences in simple sentence verification, they are consistent with differences in lexical process or in related comprehension processes.

Another example shows more clearly the potential for a lexical explanation. Gernsbacher and Faust (1991, Experiment 1) showed differences in rejecting the inappropriate meaning of a homophone. (See section, VI,C5 for an example.) Subjects in this task must reject the word *calm* as being unrelated to a sentence they had just read about *patients*. Because there is a homophone *patience* which might activate *calm* and interfere with decisions, all subjects have slow RTs at an immediate delay, but only less skilled subjects show an effect after 1000 ms. Again, however, less skilled subjects have considerably slower RTs throughout the conditions of the experiment, consistent with the assumption that other lexically based processing problems are present. And problems with homophones are exactly what one would expect on a lexical processing account, at least one that claims that less skilled readers are characterized by unreliable, low-quality word REPRESENTATIONS (Perfetti, 1991, 1992). If some subjects' representation of the word spelled *patients* is unstable, there will be a low-quality encoding that may last for a while. A test of this possibility is to give subjects the word *patients* or the word *patience* just after reading and at later intervals. A lexical representation account predicts difficulty for less skilled subjects that is independent of the meaning of a carrier sentence.

The advantages of the suppression mechanism are its explicit link to comprehension empirically and its specific predictions. Along with other elements of the SBF, it provides a coherent account of how comprehension fails, although many issues remain open, especially the extent to which the critical processes are under strategic control or are automatic (Gernsbacher, 1990). There is no reason to expect those processes that the theory links causally to comprehension failure will reduce to the processes of lexical representation or word identification. On the other hand, there is no reason to diminish our suspicion that a major problem for many if not most less skilled comprehenders lies in just these factors.

B. General Cognition and Language

One final point needs emphasis. Some of the apparent variability in theoretical accounts of individual differences depends on the relationship among reading-specific, language-specific, and cognitive-general components of comprehension. It is quite clear that comprehension requires a massive dose of general cognitive processing. Applying knowledge, making inferences, and solving problems are all patently nonlanguage tasks and are well served by general cognitive machinery. High correlations among higher level comprehension tasks should be expected. This does not mean, however, that there are not some language-particular processes lying at the heart of the story about individual differences. The critical role played by phonological processes in learning to read shows that the development of skill in reading is controlled by a kind of knowledge that is specific to language, even if it has analogies elsewhere in cognition. It is quite likely that among adults, especially college students, problems traceable to phonological processes have largely disappeared through selection. Their problems ought to be different in kind, dependent on a greater number of processes, many of which are fully general. Individual differences in such processes are usually thought of as intellectual functioning or intelligence differences, rather than language differences.

The question of whether language-specific processes continue to matter at this general level depends on what is meant by "continue to matter." The final product of comprehension is the result of fully interactive language and general cognitive processes. One can notice how much common variance there is in the products of comprehension, for instance $r = .92$ between comprehension of written and spoken stories in Gernsbacher et al. (1990). And one can note that moving away from language decreases the correlation in comprehension: Gernsbacher et al. (1990) report a correlation of .72 between spoken stories and picture stories. This leaves some noncommon variance, about 50%, between picture and language comprehension. Some processes are presumably more heavily involved in picture comprehension (problem solving, inference making). Other processes are more important in language comprehension (lexical and syntactic processes). Some are highly general and seen in both, such as application of conceptual and schematic knowledge.

Thus, there is room for a lot of things to go wrong when comprehension fails. When it is language comprehension, one should expect both language and general cognitive factors to be candidates. What is interesting is that relatively few of these can be plausibly singled out as critical. One can simplify things by pointing to a few components that, on theoretical grounds, have a wide impact on other processes that use their output.

IX. CONCLUSION

Individual differences in reading are to be expected in all components of the reading process, from lexical levels to higher level comprehension processes. It is important to distinguish higher levels of reading skill from learning to read, however. Learning to read, because of differences in the contexts of spoken and written language and, centrally, because of its dependence on phonological knowledge, is a decoding problem. Failures in learning to read are predominantly failures in some component of phonological processing. Although other sources of dyslexia are possible, phonological processing, which might be a heritable trait, plays a large role. The major accomplishment in learning to read is learning to decode, and the major failure in not learning to read is not learning to decode.

For higher level comprehension processes, the focus changes slightly. If comprehension is an interplay of modular and interactive processes, any observed problem in comprehension can arise from multiple sources in different mixes. Individual differences in inference making, comprehension monitoring, and so on are likely, but whether they are primary individual difference characteristics or derivative problems remains to be seen. Primary lexical and functional capacity problems also limit comprehension, as predicted by the verbal efficiency and capacity limitation theories. The fact that skill begets practice and practice begets further skill plays a role in maintaining skill differences and may partly explain or at least interact with capacity differences observed in adults. Comprehension differences can arise from such processes of structure building and shifting as well. It remains to be seen whether such processing differences represent additional processes that can go wrong, or are manifestations of lexical and capacity problems.

There are two major theoretical challenges for individual difference research. One is to untangle general cognitive functioning from language processing, because the theoretical stories for general cognitive processing and language processing will only partly, even if substantially, overlap. It is likely that the more global the comprehension task, the more one will observe mixtures of language and general cognitive processes. The second challenge, a related one, is to discover a principled set of processing explanations for individual differences, as opposed to a list of all processes that occur during reading. Every new hypothesized difference brings a cost to parsimony. This is what makes understanding individual differences perhaps the ultimate challenge in language and cognition generally.

REFERENCES

Adams, B. C., & Perfetti, C. A. (1993). A trading relationship between reading ability and domain knowledge in children's text comprehension. Manuscript submitted for publication.

Adams, M. J. (1990). *Beginning to read: Thinking and learning about print*. Cambridge, MA: MIT Press.

Anderson, R. C., & Pearson, P. D. (1984). A schema-thematic view of basic processes in reading comprehension. In P. D. Pearson, R. Barr, M. L. Kamil, & P. Mosenthal (Eds.), *Handbook of reading research* (pp. 255–291). New York: Longman.

Anderson, R. C., Reynolds, R. E., Schallert, D. L., & Goetz, E. T. (1977). Frameworks for comprehending discourse. *American Educational Research Journal, 14*, 367–381.

Anderson, R. C., Spiro, R. J., & Anderson, M. C. (1978). Schemata as scaffolding for the representation of information in connected discourse. *American Educational Research Journal, 15*, 433–440.

Alegria, J., & Morais, J. (1991). Segmental analysis and reading acquisition. In L. Rieben, & C. A. Perfetti (Eds.), *Learning to read: Basic research and its implications* (pp. 135–148). Hillsdale, NJ: Erlbaum.

Backman, J. E., Mamen, M., & Ferguson, H. B. (1984). Reading level design: Conceptual and methodological issues in reading research. *Psychological Bulletin, 96*, 560–568.

Barlett, F. C. (1932). *Remembering: A study in experimental and social psychology*. Cambridge: Cambridge University Press.

Bell, L., & Perfetti, C. A. (in press). Reading disability and low reading skill: Some adult comparisons. *Journal of Educational Psychology*.

Besner, D. (1990). Does the reading system need a lexicon? In D. Balota, G. B. Flores d'Arcais, & K. Rayner (Eds.), *Comprehension processes in reading* (pp. 73–99). Hillsdale, NJ: Erlbaum.

Boder, E. (1973). Developmental dyslexia: A diagnostic approach based on three atypical reading–spelling patterns. *Development Medicine and Child Neurology, 15*, 663–687.

Bradley, L., & Bryant, P. E. (1983). Categorizing sounds and learning to read—a causal connection. *Nature (London), 301*, 419–421.

Brady, S. A., & Shankweiler, D. (Eds.) (1991). *Phonological processes in literacy: A tribute to Isabelle Y. Liberman*. Hillsdale, NJ: Erlbaum.

Brady, S., Shankweiler, D., & Mann, V. (1983). Speech perception and memory coding in relation to reading ability. *Journal of Experimental Child Psychology, 35*, 345–367.

Bransford, J. D., & Johnson, M. K. (1973). Considerations of some problems of comprehension. In W. G. Chase (Ed.), *Visual information processing*. New York: Academic Press.

Britt, M. A. (in press). The interaction of referential ambiguity and argument structure in parsing prepositional phrases. *Journal of Memory and Language*.

Britt, M. A., Perfetti, C. A., Garrod, S., & Rayner, K. (1992). Parsing in discourse: Context effects and their limits. *Journal of Memory and Language, 31*, 293–314.

Bruck, M. (1988). The word recognition and spelling of dyslexic children. *Reading Research Quarterly, 23*, 51–69.

Bruck, M. (1990). Word-recognition skills of adults with childhood diagnosis of dyslexia. *Developmental Psychology, 26*, 439–454.

Bryant, P. E., & Bradley, L. (1985). *Children's reading problems*. Oxford, England: Blackwell.

Bryant, P. E., & Goswami, U. (1986). Strengths and weaknesses of the reading level design: A comment on Backman, Mamen, and Ferguson. *Psychological Bulletin, 100*, 101–103.

Bryant, P. E., & Goswami, U. (1987). Phonological awareness and learning to read. In J. R. Beech & A. M. Colley (Eds.), Cognitive approaches to reading (pp. 213–243). New York: Wiley.

Brysbaert, M., Praet, C., & d'Ydewalle, G. (1990). *Phonological recoding in reading isolated words: A secondary and optional channel* (Tech. Rep. No. 110). Leuven: University of Leuven (Belgium), Department of Psychology.

Byrne, B. (1981). Deficient syntactic control in poor readers: Is a weak phonetic memory code responsible? *Applied Psycholinguistics, 2*, 201–212.

Byrne, B., & Shea, P. (1979). Semantic and phonetic memory codes in beginning readers. *Memory & Cognition, 7*, 333–338.

Carpenter, P. A., & Just, M. A. (1988). The role of working memory in language comprehension. In D. Klahr & D. Kotovsky (Eds.), *Complex information processing: The impact of Herbert A. Simon* (pp. 31–68). Hillsdale, NJ: Erlbaum.

Chafe, W. L. (1976). Givenness, contrastiveness, definiteness, subjects, topics, and points of view. In C. N. Li (Ed.), *Subject and topic* (pp. 25–56). New York: Academic Press.

Chafe, W. L. (1982). Integration and involvement in speaking, writing, and oral literature. In D. Tannen (Ed.), *Spoken and written language: Exploring orality and literacy, Vol IX* (pp. 35–53). Norwood, NJ: Ablex.

Chall, J. S. (1983). *Learning to read: The great debate*. Updated ed. New York: McGraw-Hill.

Coltheart, M. (1978). Lexical access in simple reading tasks. In G. Underwood (Ed.), *Strategies of information processing* (pp. 151–216). New York: Academic Press.

Conrad, C. (1974). Context effects in sentence comprehension: A study of the subjective lexicon. *Memory & Cognition, 2*, 130–138.

Corbett, A. T., & Dosher, B. A. (1978). Instrument inferences in sentence encoding. *Journal of Verbal Learning and Verbal Behavior, 17*, 479–491.

Crain, S., & Shankweiler, D. (1988). Syntactic complexity and reading acquisition. In A. Davison & G. M. Green (Eds.), *Linguistic complexity and text comprehension: Readabiltiy issues reconsidered* (pp. 167–192). Hillsdale, NJ: Erlbaum.

Crain, S., Shankweiler, D., Macaruso, P., & Bar-Shalom, E. (1990). Working memory and comprehension of spoken sentences: Investigations of children with reading disorder. In G. Vallar & T. Shallice (Eds.), *Neuropsychological impairments of short-term memory* (pp. 477–508). Cambridge: Cambridge University Press.

Crain, S., & Steedman, M. (1985). On not being led up the garden path: The use of context by the psychological syntax processor. In D. R. Dowty, L. Karttunen, & A. M. Zwicky (Eds.), *Natural language parsing: Psychological, computational, and theoretical perspectives* (pp. 320–358). Cambridge: Cambridge University Press.

Cunningham, A. E., Stanovich, K. E., & Wilson, M. R. (1990). Cognitive variation in adult students differing in reading abiltiy. In T. H. Carr & B. A. Levy (Eds.), *Reading and its development: Component skills approaches* (pp. 129–159). New York: Academic Press.

Daneman, M., & Carpenter, P. A. (1980). Individual differences in working memory and reading. *Journal of Verbal Learning and Verbal Behavior, 19*, 450–466.

DeFries, J. C., & Decker, S. N. (1982). Genetic aspects of reading disability: A family study. In R. N. Malatesha & P. G. Arron (Eds.), *Reading Disorders: Varieties and treatments* (pp. 255–279). New York: Academic Press.

Dell, G. S., McKoon, G., & Ratcliff, R. (1983). The activation of antecedent information during the processing of anaphoric reference in reading. *Journal of Verbal Learning and Verbal Behavior, 22*, 121–132.

Duffy, S. A., Morris, R. K., & Rayner, K. (1988). Lexical ambiguity and fixation times in reading. *Journal of Memory and Language, 27*, 429–446.

Ehri, L. C. (1980). The development of orthographic images. In U. Frith (Ed.), *Cognitive processes in spelling*. London: Academic Press.

Ehri, L. C. (1991). Learning to read and spell words. In L. Rieben & C. A. Perfetti (Eds.), *Learning to read: Basic research and its implications* (pp. 57–73). Hillsdale, NJ: Erlbaum.

Ehri, L. C., & Wilce, L. S. (1985). Movement into reading: Is the first stage of printed word learning visual or phonetic? *Reading Research Quarterly, 20*, 163–179.

Ellis, A. W. (1985). The cognitive neuropsychology of development (and acquired) dyslexia: A critical survey. *Cognitive Neuropsychology, 2*, 169–205.

Ferrand, L., & Grainger, J. (1992). Phonology and orthography in visual word recognition: Evidence from masked nonword priming. *Quarterly Journal of Experimental Psychology, 45A*, 353–372.

Ferreira, F., & Clifton, C., Jr. (1986). The independence of syntactic processing. *Journal of Memory and Language, 25*, 348–368.

Fincher-Kiefer, R. (1993). The role of predictive inferences in situation model construction. *Discourse Processes, 16*, 99–124.

Fletcher, J. M., Satz, P., & Scholes, R. J. (1981). Developmental changes in the linguistic performance correlates of reading achievement. *Brain and Language, 13*, 78–90.

Fodor, J. A. (1983). *Modularity of mind: An essay in faculty psychology*. Cambridge, MA: MIT Press.

Forster, K. I. (1979). Levels of processing and the structure of the language processor. In W. E. Cooper & E. C. T. Walker (Eds.), *Sentence processing: Psycholinguistic studies presented to Merrill Garrett* (pp. 27–85). Hillsdale, NJ: Erlbaum.

Fox, B., & Routh, D. K. (1976). Phonemic analysis and synthesis as word-attack skills. *Journal of Educational Psychology, 68*, 70–74.

Frazier, L., & Rayner, K. (1982). Making and correcting errors during sentence comprehension: Eye movements in the analysis of structurally ambiguous sentences. *Cognitive Psychology, 14,* 178–210.

Frederiksen, J. R. (1981). Sources of process interactions in reading. In A. M. Lesgold & C. A. Perfetti (Eds.), *Interactive processes in reading* (pp. 361–386). Hillsdale, NJ: Erlbaum.

Frost, R. (1991). Phonetic recoding of phonologically ambiguous printed words. Paper presented at the 32nd annual meeting of the Psychonomic Society, San Francisco.

Frost, R., Katz, L., & Bentin, S. (1987). Strategies for visual word recognition and orthographical depth: A multilingual comparison. *Journal of Experimental Psychology: Human Perception and Performance, 13,* 104–115.

Garnham, A., Oakhill, J., & Johnson-Laird, P. N. (1982). Referential continuity and the coherence of discourse. *Cognition, 11,* 29–46.

Gathercole, S. E., & Baddeley, A. D. (1989). Evaluation of the role of phonological STM in the development of vocabulary in children: A longitudinal study. *Journal of Memory and Language, 28,* 200–213.

Gelb, I. J. (1952). *A study of writing.* Chicago: University of Chicago Press.

Gernsbacher, M. A. (1990). *Language comprehension as structure building.* Hillsdale, NJ: Erlbaum.

Gernsbacher, M. A., & Faust, M. E. (1990). The role of suppression in sentence comprehension. In G. B. Simpson (Ed.), *Understanding word and sentence* (pp. 97–128). Amsterdam: North-Holland.

Gernsbacher, M. A., & Faust, M. E. (1991). The mechanism of suppression: A component of general comprehension skill. *Journal of Experimental Psychology: Learning, Memory, and Cognition, 17,* 245–262.

Gernsbacher, M. A., & Jescheniak, J. D. (1993). Cataphoric devices in spoken discourse. Manuscript submitted for publication.

Gernsbacher, M. A., & Shroyer, S. (1989). The cataphoric use of the indefinite *this* in spoken narratives. *Memory & Cognition, 17,* 536–540.

Gernsbacher, M. A., Varner, K. R., & Faust, M. E. (1990). Investigating differences in general comprehension skill. *Journal of Experimental Psychology: Learning, Memory, and Cognition, 16,* 430–445.

Givón, T. (1986). *The pragmatics of word order: Predictability, importance, and attention.* Amsterdam: Benjamins.

Gleitman, L. R., & Rozin, P. (1977). The structure and acquisition of reading. I: Relations between orthographies and the structure of language. In A. S. Reber & D. L. Scarborough (Eds.), *Toward a psychology of reading: The proceedings of the CUNY conference.* New York: Wiley.

Glushko, R. J. (1981). Principles for pronouncing print: The psychology of phonography. In A. M. Lesgold & C. A. Perfetti (Eds.), *Interactive processes in reading* (pp. 61–84). Hillsdale, NJ: Erlbaum.

Godfrey, J. J., Syrdal-Lasky, A. K., Millay, K. K., & Knox, C. M. (1981). Performance of dyslexic children on speech perception tests. *Journal of Experimental Child Pyschology, 32,* 401–424.

Goldman, S. R., Hogaboam, T. W., Bell, L. C., & Perfetti, C. A. (1980). Short-term retention of discourse during reading. *Journal of Educational Psychology, 72,* 647–655.

Goodman, K. S. (1967). Reading: A psycholinguistic guessing game. *Journal of the Reading Specialist, 6,* 126–135.

Goodman, K. S. (1970). Reading: A psycholinguistic guessing game. In H. Singer & R. B. Ruddell (Eds.), *Theoretical models and processes of reading.* Newark, DE: International Reading Association.

Gough, P. B., & Hillinger, M. L. (1980). Learning to read: An unnatural act. *Bulletin of the Orton Society, 20,* 179–196.

Gough, P. B., & Juel, C. (1991). The first stages of word recognition. In L. Rieben & C. A. Perfetti (Eds.), *Learning to read: Basic research and its implication* (pp. 47–56). Hillsdale, NJ: Erlbaum.

Gough, P. B., & Tunmer, W. E. (1986). Decoding, reading, and reading disability. *Remedial and Special Education, 7,* 6–10.

Gough, P. B., & Walsh, M. A. (1991). Chinese, Phoenicians, and the orthographic cipher of English. In S. A. Brady & D. P. Shankweiler (Eds.), *Phonological processes in literacy: A tribute to Isabelle Y. Liberman* (pp. 199–209). Hillsdale, NJ: Erlbaum.

Graesser, A. C. (1981). *Prose comprehension beyond the word.* New York: Springer-Verlag.

Hammond, K. (1987). Verbal efficiency: An explanation. Unpublished doctoral dissertation, University of Pittsburgh, Pittsburgh, PA.

Haviland, S. E., & Clark, H. H. (1974). What's new? Acquiring new information as a process in comprehension. *Journal of Verbal Learning and Verbal Behavior, 13,* 512–521.

Hogaboam, T. W., & Perfetti, C. A. (1975). Lexical ambiguity and sentence comprehesion. *Journal of Verbal Learning and Verbal Behavior, 14,* 265–274.

Hogaboam, T. W., & Perfetti, C. A. (1978). Reading skill and the role of verbal experience in decoding. *Journal of Educational Psychology, 70,* 717–729.

Hoover, W. A., & Gough, P. B. (1990). The simple view of reading. *Reading and Writing, 2,* 127–160.

Jackson, M. D., & McClelland, J. L. (1979). Processing determinants of reading speed. *Journal of Experimental Psychology: General, 108,* 151–181.

Jared, D., & Seidenberg, M. (1991). The role of phonology in the activation of meaning. Paper presented at the 32nd annual meeting of the Psychonomic Society, San Francisco.

Johnson-Laird, P. N. (1983). *Mental models.* Cambridge, MA: Harvard University Press.

Just, M. A., & Carpenter, P. A. (1978). Inference processes during reading: Reflections from eye fixations. In J. W. Senders, D. F. Fisker, & R. A. Monty (Eds.), *Eye movements and the higher psychological functions.* Hillsdale, NJ: Erlbaum.

Just, M. A., & Carpenter, P. A. (1992). A capacity theory of comprehension: Individual differences in working memory. *Psychological Review, 99,* 122–149.

Katz, R. B., Shankweiler, D., & Liberman, I. Y. (1981). Memory for item order and phonetic recoding in the beginning reader. *Journal of Experimental Child Psychology, 32,* 474–484.

Keenan, J. M., Baillet, S. D., & Brown, P. (1984). The effects of causal cohesion on comprehension and memory. *Journal of Verbal Learning and Verbal Behavior, 23,* 115–126.

King, J., & Just, M. A. (1991). Individual differences in syntactic processing. *Journal of Memory and Language, 30,* 580–602.

Kintsch, W. (1974). *The representation of meaning in memory.* Hillsdale, NJ: Erlbaum.

Kintsch, W. (1988). The role of knowledge in discourse processing: A construction-integration model. *Psychological Review, 95,* 163–182.

Kintsch, W. (in press). How readers construct situation models for stories: The role of syntactic cues and causal inferences. In A. F. Healy, S. Kosslyn, & R. M. Shiffrin (Eds.), *Essays in honor of William K. Estes.* Hillsdale, NJ: Erlbaum.

Kintsch, W., & Mross, F. (1985). Context effects in word identification. *Journal of Memory and Language, 24,* 336–339.

Lam, A., Perfetti, C. A., & Bell, L. (1991). Automatic phonetic transfer in bidialectal reading. *Journal of Applied Psycholinguistics, 12,* 299–311.

LaBerge, D., & Samuels, S. (1974). Toward a theory of automatic information processing in reading. *Cognitive Psychology, 6,* 293–323.

Leong, C. K. (1973). Reading in Chinese with reference to reading practices in Hong Kong. In J. Downing (Ed.), *Comparative reading: Cross-national studies of behavior and processes in reading and writing.* New York: Macmillan.

Liberman, A. M. (1982). On finding that speech is special. *American Psychologist, 37,* 148–167.

Liberman, A. M., Cooper, F. S., Shankweiler, D., & Studdert-Kennedy, M. (1967). Perception of the speech code. *Psychological Review, 74,* 431–461.

Liberman, I. Y., & Liberman, A. M. (1990). Whole language vs. code emphasis: Underlying assumptions and their implications for reading instruction. *Annals of Dyslexia, 40,* 51–76.

Liberman, I. Y., Mann, V. A., Shankweiler, D., & Werfelman, M. (1982). Children's memory for recurring linguistic and nonlinguistic material in relation to reading ability. *Cortex, 18,* 367–375.

Liberman, I. Y., & Shankweiler, D. (1979). Speech, the alphabet, and teaching to read. In L. B. Resnick & P. A. Weaver (Eds.), *Theory and practice of early reading, Vol. 2* (pp. 109–132). Hillsdale, NJ: Erlbaum.

Liberman, I. Y., & Shankweiler, D. (1991). Phonolgy and beginning reading: A tutorial. In L. Rieben & C. A. Perfetti (Eds.), *Learning to read: Basic research and its implications* (pp. 3–17). Hillsdale, NJ: Erlbaum.

Liberman, I. Y., Shankweiler, D., Fischer, F. W., & Carter, B. (1974). Explicit syllable and phoneme segmentation in the young child. *Journal of Experimental Child Psychology, 18,* 201–212.

Liberman, I. Y., Shankweiler, D., Liberman, A. M., Fowler, C. A., & Fischer, F. W. (1977).

Phonetic segmentation and recoding in the beginning reader. In A. S. Reber & D. L. Scarborough (Eds.), *Toward a Psychology of Reading: The Proceedings of the CUNY Conference* (pp. 207–225). Hillsdale, NJ: Erlbaum.

Long, D. L., & Golding, J. M. (1993). Superordinate goal inferences: Are they automatically encoded during comprehension? *Discourse Processes, 16,* 55–73.

Lukatela, G., & Turvey, M. T. (1990a). Automatic and pre-lexical computation of phonology in visual word identification. *European Journal of Cognitive Psychology, 2,* 325–344.

Lukatela, G., & Turvey, M. T. (1990b). Phonemic similarity effects and prelexical phonology. *Memory & Cognition, 18,* 128–152.

Lundberg, I., Olofsson, A., & Wall, S. (1980). Reading and spelling skills in the first school years predicted from phonemic awareness skills in kindergarten. *Scandinavian Journal of Psychology, 21,* 159–173.

Lundberg, I., & Torneus, M. (1978). Nonreaders' awareness of the basic relationship between spoken and written words. *Journal of Experimental Child Psychology, 25,* 404–412.

Mann, V. A. (1986). Phonological awareness: The role of reading experience. *Cognition, 21,* 65–92.

Mann, V. A. (1991). Phonological abilities: Effective predictors of future reading ability. In L. Rieben & C. A. Perfetti (Eds.), *Learning to read: Basic research and its implications* (pp. 121–133). Hillsdale, NJ: Erlbaum.

Mann, V. A., Liberman, I. Y., & Shankweiler, D. (1980). Children's memory for sentences and word strings in relation to reading ability. *Memory & Cognition, 8,* 329–335.

Mann, V. A., Shankweiler, D., & Smith, S. T. (1984). The association between comprehension of spoken sentences and early reading ability: The role of phonetic representation. *Journal of Child Language, 11,* 627–643.

Marsh, G., Friedman, M., Welch, V., & Desberg, P. (1981). A cognitive-developmental theory of reading acquisition. In G. E. MacKinnon & T. G. Waller (Eds.), *Reading research: Advances in theory and practice, Vol 3.* New York: Academic Press.

Martin, F., & Lovegrove, W. (1987). Flicker contrast sensitivity in normal and specifically disabled readers. *Perception, 16,* 215–221.

Martin, F., & Lovegrove, W. J. (1988). Uniform-field flicker masking in control and specifically-disabled readers. *Perception, 17,* 203–214.

McClelland, J. L. (1986). The programmable model of reading: Psychological and biological models. In D. E. Rumelhart & J. L. McClelland (Eds.), *Parallel distributed processing: Explorations in the microstructure of cognition, Vol. 2* (pp. 170–215). Cambridge, MA: MIT Press.

McKoon, G., & Ratcliff, R. (1986). Inferences about predictable events. *Journal of Experimental Psychology: Learning, Memory, and Cognition, 12,* 82–91.

McKoon, G., & Ratcliff, R. (1989). Assessing the occurrence of elabortive inference with recognition: Compatibility checking vs compound cue theory. *Journal of Memory and Language, 28,* 547–563.

Merrill, E. C., Sperber, R. D., & McCauley, C. (1981). Differences in semantic encoding as a function of reading comprehension skill. *Memory & Cognition, 9,* 618–624.

Merton, R. (1968). The Matthew effect in science. *Science, 56–63.*

Mitchell, D. C. (1987). Lexical guidance in human parsing: Locus and processing characteristics. In M. Coltheart (Ed.), *Attention and performance XII: The psychology of reading* (pp. 601–618). Hillsdale, NJ: Erlbaum.

Mitchell, D. C., Corley, M. M. B., & Garnham, A. (1992). Effects of context in human sentence parsing: Evidence against a discourse-based proposal mechanism. *Journal of Experimental Psychology, 18,* 69–88.

Mitchell, D. C., & Green, D. W. (1978). The effects of context and content on immediate processing in reading. *Quarterly Journal of Experimental Psychology, 30,* 609–636.

Morais, J., Bertelson, P., Cary, L., & Alegria, J. (1986). Literacy training and speech segmentation. *Cognition, 24,* 45–64.

Morais, J., Cary, L., Alegria, J., & Bertelson, P. (1979). Does awareness of speech as a sequence of phones arise spontaneously? *Cognition, 7,* 323–331.

Morton, J. (1964). The effects on context on the visual duration threshold for words. *British Journal of Psychology, 85,* 165–180.

Oakhill, J. (1982). Constructive processes in skilled and less skilled comprehenders' memory for sentences. *British Journal of Psychology, 73,* 13–20.

Oakhill, J., & Garnham, A. (1988). *Becoming a skilled reader*. New York: Basil Blackwell.

O'Brien, E. J., Shank, D. M., Myers, J. L., & Rayner, K. (1988). Elaborative inferences during reading: Do they occur on-line? *Journal of Experimental Psychology: Learning, Memory,and Cognition, 14*, 410–420.

O'Donnell, R. C. (1974). Syntactic differences between speech and writing. *American Speech, 49*, 102–110.

Olson, D. R. (1977). From utterance to text: The bias of language in speech and writing. *Harvard Educational Review, 47*, 257–281.

Olson, R. K. (1985). Disabled reading processes and cognitive profiles. In D. Gray & J. Kavanagh (Eds.), *Biobehavioral measures of dyslexia* (pp. 215–244). Parkton, MD: York Press.

Olson, R. K., Davidson, B. J., Kliegl, R., & Davies, S. (1984). Development of phonological memory in disabled and normal readers. *Journal of Experimental Child Psychology, 37*, 187–206.

Olson, R., Wise, B., Conners, F., & Rack, J. (1990). Organization, heritability, and remediation of component word recognition skills in disabled readers. In T. H. Carr & B. A. Levy (Eds.), *Reading and its development: Component skills approaches* (pp. 261–322). New York: Academic Press.

Paap, K. R., & Noel, R. W. (1991). Dual-route models of print and sound: Still a good horse race. *Psychological Research, 53*, 13–24.

Palmer, J., MacLeod, C. M., Hunt, E., & Davidson, J. E. (1985). Information processing correlates of reading. *Journal of Memory and Language, 24*, 59–88.

Pennington, B. F. (1989, November). Development of phonological processing in dyslexia. Paper presented at the annual meeting of the Orton Dyslexia Society, Dallas, TX.

Pennington, B. F. (1990). Annotation: The genetics of dyslexia. *Journal of Child Psychology and Psychiatry, 31*, 193–201.

Pennington, B. F., Van Orden, G. C., Smith, S. D., Green, P. A. & Haith, M. M. (1990). Phonological processing skills and deficits in adult dyslexics. *Child Development, 61*, 1753–1778.

Perfetti, C. A. (1985). *Reading ability*. New York: Oxford University Press.

Perfetti, C. A. (1987). Language, speech, and print: Some asymmetries in the acquisition of literacy. In R. Horowitz and S. J. Samuels (Eds.), *Comprehending oral and written language* (pp. 355–369). New York: Academic Press.

Perfetti, C. A. (1988). Verbal efficiency in reading ability. In G. E. MacKinnon, T. G. Waller, & M. Daneman (Eds.), *Reading research: Advances in theory and practice, Vol. 6* (pp. 109–143). New York: Academic Press.

Perfetti, C. A. (1989). There are generalized abilities and one of them is reading. In L. B. Resnick (Ed.), *Knowing, learning and instruction: Essays in honor of Robert Glaser* (pp. 307–335). Hillsdale, NJ: Erlbaum.

Perfetti, C. A. (1990). The cooperative language processors: Semantic influences in an autonomous syntax. In D. A. Balota, G. B. Flores d'Arcais, & K. Rayner (Eds.), *Comprehension processes in reading* (pp. 205–230). Hillsdale, NJ: Erlbaum.

Perfetti, C. A. (1991). Representations and awareness in the acquisition of reading competence. In L. Rieben & C. A. Perfetti (Eds.), *Learning to read: Basic research and its implications* (pp. 33–44). Hillsdale, NJ: Erlbaum.

Perfetti, C. A. (1992). The representation problem in reading acquisition. In P. B. Gough, L. C. Ehri, & R. Treiman (Eds.), *Reading acquisition* (pp. 145–174). Hillsdale, NJ: Erlbaum.

Perfetti, C. A., Beck, I., Bell, L., & Hughes, C. (1987). Phonemic knowledge and learning to read are reciprocal: A longitudinal study of first grade children. *Merrill-Palmer Quarterly, 33*, 283–319.

Perfetti, C. A., & Bell, L. (1991). Phonemic activation during the first 40 ms of word identification: Evidence from backward masking and masked priming. *Journal of Memory and Language, 30*, 473–485.

Perfetti, C. A., Bell, L., & Delaney, S. (1988). Automatic phonetic activation in silent word reading: Evidence from backward masking. *Journal of Memory and Language, 27*, 59–70.

Perfetti, C. A., Finger, E., & Hogaboam, T. (1978). Sources of vocalization latency differences between skilled and less skilled young readers. *Journal of Educational Psychology, 70*, 730–739.

Perfetti, C. A., & Goldman, S. R. (1974). Thematization and sentence retrieval. *Journal of Verbal Learning and Verbal Behavior, 13*, 70–79.

Perfetti, C. A., & Goldman, S. R. (1976). Discourse memory and reading comprehension skill. *Journal of Verbal Learning and Verbal Behavior, 14,* 33–42.

Perfetti, C. A., Goldman, S. R., & Hogaboam, T. W. (1979). Reading skill and the identification of words in discourse context. *Memory & Cognition, 7,* 273–282.

Perfetti, C. A., & Lesgold, A. M. (1977). Discourse comprehension and sources of individual differences. In P. A. Carpenter & M. A. Just (Eds.), *Cognitive processes in comprehension* (pp. 141–183). Hillsdale, NJ: Erlbaum.

Perfetti, C. A., & Lesgold, A. M. (1979). Coding and comprehension in skilled reading and implications for reading instruction. In L. B. Resnick & P. A. Weaver (Eds.), *Theory and practice in early reading, Vol. 1* (pp. 57–84). Hillsdale, NJ: Erlbaum.

Perfetti, C. A., & McCutchen, D. (1982). Speech processes in reading. In N. Lass (Ed.), *Speech and language: Advances in basic research and practice* (pp. 237–269). New York: Academic Press.

Perfetti, C. A., & Roth, S. F. (1981). Some of the interactive processes in reading and their role in reading skill. In A. M. Lesgold & C. A. Perfetti (Eds.), *Interactive processes in reading* (pp. 269–297). Hillsdale, NJ: Erlbaum.

Perfetti, C. A., & Zhang, S. (1991). Phonological processes in reading Chinese words. *Journal of Experimental Psychology: Learning, Memory, and Cognition, 17,* 633–643.

Perfetti, C. A., Zhang, S., & Berent, I. (1992). Reading in English and Chinese: Evidence for a "universal" phonological principle. In R. Frost & L. Katz (Eds.), *Orthography, phonology, morphology, and meaning* (pp. 227–248). Amsterdam: North-Holland.

Perrig, W., & Kintsch, W. (1985). Propositional and situational representations of text. *Journal of Memory and Language, 24,* 503–518.

Pinker, S. (1984). *Language learnability and language development.* Cambridge, MA: Harvard University Press.

Rayner, K., Carlson, M., & Frazier, L. (1983). The interaction of syntax and semantics during sentence processing: Eye movements in the analysis of semantically biased sentences. *Journal of Verbal Learning and Verbal Behavior, 22,* 358–374.

Rayner, K., & Pollatsek, A. (1989). *The psychology of reading.* Englewood Cliffs, NJ: Prentice Hall.

Read, C., Zhang, Y., Nie, H., & Ding, B. (1986). The ability to manipulate speech sounds depends on knowing alphabetic reading. *Cognition, 24,* 31–44.

Rieben, L., & Perfetti, C. A. (Eds.). (1991). *Learning to read: Basic research and its implications.* Hillsdale, NJ: Erlbaum.

Rodgers, B. (1983). The identification and prevalence of specific reading retardation. *British Journal of Educational Psychology, 53,* 369–373.

Rozin, P., Bressman, B., & Taft, M. (1974). Do children understand the basic relationship between speech and writing? The Mow–Motorcycle test. *Journal of Reading Behavior, 6,* 327–334.

Rumelhart, D. E. (1975). Notes on a schema for stories. In D. Bobrow & A. Colling (Eds.), *Representation and understanding: Studies in cognitive science.* New York: Academic Press.

Rumelhart, D. E., McClelland, J. L. (1981). Interactive processing through spreading activation. In A. M. Lesgold & C. A. Perfetti (Eds.), *Interactive processes in reading* (pp. 37–60). Hillsdale, NJ: Erlbaum.

Rutter, M., & Yule, W. (1975). The concept of specific reading retardation. *Journal of Child Psychology and Psychiatry, 16,* 189–197.

Ryan, E. B. (1982). Identifying and remediating failures in reading comprehension: Toward an instructional approach for poor comprehenders. In G. E. MacKinnon & T. G. Waller (Eds.), *Advances in reading research, Vol. 3.* New York: Academic Press.

Sanford, A. J., & Garrod, S. C. (1981). *Understanding written language: Explorations of comprehension beyond the sentence.* New York: Wiley.

Schank, R. C., & Abelson, R. P. (1977). Scripts, plans and knowledge. *Proceedings of the Fourth International Joint Conference on Artificial Intelligence.* Tbilisi, Georgia.

Schuberth, R. E., & Eimas, P. D. (1977). Effects of context on the classification of words and nonwords. *Journal of Experimental Psychology: Human Perception and Performance, 3,* 27–36.

Schwantes, F. M. (1981). Locus of the context effect in children's word recognition. *Child Development, 52,* 895–903.

Seidenberg, M. S., & McClelland, J. L. (1989). A distributed, developmental model of word recognition and naming. *Psychological Review, 96,* 523–568.

Seidenberg, M. S., & McClelland, J. L. (1990). More words but still no lexicon: Reply to Besner et al. (1990). *Psychological Review, 97*(3), 447–452.

Shankweiler, D., & Crain, S. (1986). Language mechanisms and reading disorder: A modular approach. *Cognition, 24,* 139–168.

Shankweiler, D., Crain, S., Brady, S., & Macaruso, P. (1992). Identifying the causes of reading disability. In P. B. Gough, L. C. Ehri, & R. Treiman (Eds.), *Reading acquisition* (pp. 275–305). Hillsdale, NJ: Erlbaum.

Shankweiler, D., Crain, S., Gorrell, P., & Tuller, B. (1989). Reception of language in Broca's Aphasia. *Language and Cognitive Processes, 4,* 1–33.

Share, D. L., McGee, R., McKenzie, D., Williams, S., & Silva, P. A. (1987). Further evidence relating to the distinction between specific reading retardation and general reading backwardness. *British Journal of Developmental Psychology, 5,* 35–44.

Siegel, L. S., & Ryan, E. B. (1988). Development of grammatical-sensitivity, phonological, and short-term memory skills in normally achieving and learning disabled children. *Developmental Psychology, 24,* 28–37.

Simpson, G. B. (1981). Meaning dominance and semantic context in the processing of lexical ambiguity. *Journal of Verbal Learning and Verbal Behavior, 20,* 120–136.

Simpson, G. B. & Krueger, M. A. (1991). Selective access of homograph meanings in sentence context. *Memory & Language, 32,* 96–115.

Simpson, G., Lorsbach, T., & Whitehouse, D. (1983). Encoding contextual components of word recognition in good and poor readers. *Journal of Experimental Child Psychology, 35,* 161–171.

Singer, M. (1979). Processes of inference during sentence encoding. *Memory & Cognition, 7,* 192–200.

Singer, M., & Ferreira, F. (1983). Inferring consequences in story comprehension. *Journal of Verbal Learning and Verbal Behavior, 22,* 437–448.

Smith, F. (1973). *Psycholinguistics and reading.* New York: Holt Rinehart, & Winston.

Smith, F. (1983). *Psycholinguistics and reading.* New York: Holt, Rinehart, and Winston.

Smith, F. (1985). *Reading without nonsense* (Second edition). New York: Teachers College Press.

Snowling, M. (1980). The development of grapheme–phoneme correspondence in normal and dyslexic readers. *Journal of Experimental Child Psychology, 29,* 294–305.

Snowling, M., Stackhouse, J., & Rack, J. (1986). Phonological dyslexia and dysgraphia—a developmental analysis. *Cognitive Neuropsychology, 3,* 309–339.

Spilich, G. J., Vesonder, G. T., Chiesi, H. L., & Voss, J. F. (1979). Text processing of domain-related information for individuals with high and low domain knowledge. *Journal of Verbal Learning and Verbal Behavior, 18,* 275–290.

Spiro, R. J. (1980). Constructive processes in prose comprehension and recall. In R. J. Spiro, B. C. Bruce, & W. F. Brewer (Eds.), *Theoretical issues in reading comprehension: Perspectives from Cognitive Psychology, Linguistics, Artificial Intelligence, and Education* (pp. 245–278). Hillsdale, NJ: Erlbaum.

Stanovich, K. E. (1980). Toward an interactive–compensatory model of individual differences in the development of reading fluency. *Reading Research Quarterly, 16,* 32–71.

Stanovich, K. E. (1981). Attentional and automatic context effects in reading. In A. M. Lesgold & C. A. Perfetti (Eds.), *Interactive processes in reading* (pp. 241–267). Hillsdale, NJ: Erlbaum.

Stanovich, K. E. (1983). Psychological, neurological, and educational research in dyslexia. *Contemporary Psychology, 28,* 25–26.

Stanovich, K. E. (1986). Matthew effects in reading: Some consequences of individual differences in the acquisition of literacy. *Reading Research Quarterly, 21,* 360–407.

Stanovich, K. E. (1988). Explaining the differences between the dyslexic and the garden-variety poor reader: The phonological-core variable-difference model. *Journal of Learning Disabilities, 21,* 590–604.

Stanovich, K. E. (1990). Concepts in developmental theories of reading skill: Cognitive resources, automaticity, and modularity. *Developmental Review, 10,* 72–100.

Stanovich, K. E., Cunningham, A. E., & Cramer, B. (1984). Assessing phonological awareness in kindergarten children: Issues of task comparability. *Journal of Experimental Child Psychology, 38,* 175–190.

Stanovich, K. E., & West, R. F. (1989). Exposure to print and orthographic processing. *Reading Research Quarterly, 24,* 402–433.

Stanovich, K. E., West, R. F., & Feeman, D. J. (1981). A longitudinal study of sentence context effects in second-grade children: Tests of an interactive–compensatory model. *Journal of Experimental Child Psychology, 32*, 185–199.

Stein, C. L., Cairns, J. S., & Zurif, E. B. (1984). Sentence comprehension limitations related to syntactic deficits in reading-disabled children. *Applied Psycholinguistics, 5*, 305–322.

Sticht, T. G. (1977). Comprehending reading at work. In M. A. Just & P. A. Carpenter (Eds.), *Cognitive processes in comprehension* (pp. 221–246). Hillsdale, NJ: Erlbaum.

Swinney, D. A. (1979). Lexical access during sentence comprehension: (Re)consideration of context effects. *Journal of Verbal Learning and Verbal Behavior, 18*, 645–659.

Tabossi, P. (1988). Accessing lexical ambiguity in different types of sentential contexts. *Journal of Memory and Language, 27*, 324–340.

Tanenhaus, M. K., Lieman, J. M., & Seidenberg, M. T. (1979). Evidence for stages in the processing of ambiguous words in syntactic contexts. *Journal of Verbal Learning and Verbal Behavior, 18*, 427–440.

Tomlin, R. S. (1983). On the interaction of syntactic subject, thematic information, and agent in English. *Journal of Pragmatics, 7*, 411–432.

Trabasso, T., & Suh, S. (1993). Understanding text: Achieving explanatory coherence through online inferences and mental operations in working memory. *Discourse Processes, 16*, 3–34.

Trabasso, T., & van den Broek, P. (1985). Causal thinking and the representation of narrative events. *Journal of Memory and Language, 24*, 612–630.

Treiman, R., & Baron, J. (1983). Phonemic-analysis training helps children benefit from spelling-sound rules. *Memory & Cognition, 11*, 382–389.

Tulving, E., & Gold, C. (1963). Stimulus information and contextual information on determinants of tachistoscopic recognition of words. *Journal of Experimental Psychology, 66*, 319–327.

Tunmer, W. E., Herriman, M. L., & Neesdale, A. R. (1988). Metalinguistic abilities and beginning reading. *Reading Research Quarterly, 23*, 134–158.

van Dijk, T. A., & Kintsch, W. (1983). *Strategies of discourse comprehension*. New York: Academic Press.

Van Orden, G. C. (1987). A ROWS is a ROSE: Spelling, sound, and reading. *Memory & Cognition, 15*, 181–198.

Van Orden, G. C., Johnston, J. C., & Hale, B. L. (1988). Word identification in reading proceeds from spelling to sound to meaning. *Journal of Experimental Psychology: Learning, Memory, and Cognition, 14*, 371–385.

Van Orden, G. C., Pennington, B., & Stone, G. (1990). Word identification in reading and the promise of subsymbolic psycholinguistics. *Psychological Review, 97*, 488–522.

Vellutino, F. R. (1979). *Dyslexia: Theory and research*. Cambridge, MA: MIT Press.

Vellutino, F. R., & Scanlon, D. M. (1987). Phonological coding, phonological awareness, and reading abiltiy: Evidence from a longitudinal and experimental study. *Merrill-Palmer Quarterly, 33*, 321–363.

Vellutino, F. R., & Scanlon, D. M. (1991). The effects of instructional bias on word identification. In L. Rieben & C. A. Perfetti (Eds.), *Learning to read: Basic research and its implications* (pp. 189–203). Hillsdale, NJ: Erlbaum.

Vogel, S. A. (1975). *Syntactic abilities in normal and dyslexic children*. Baltimore: University Park Press.

Wagner, R. K., Balthazor, M., Hurley, S., Morgan, S., Rashotte, C., Shaner, R., Simmons, K., & Stage, S. (1987). The nature of prereaders phonological processing abilities. *Cognitive Development, 2*, 355–373.

Walberg, H. J., & Tsai, S. L. (1983). Matthew effects in education. *American Educational Research Journal, 20*, 359–373.

Walczyk, J. J. (1993). Are general resource notions still viable in reading research. *Journal of Educational Psychology, 85*, 127–135.

West, R. F., & Stanovich, K. E. (1978). Automatic contextual facilitation in readers of three ages. *Child Development, 49*, 717–727.

Wolf, M. (1986). Rapid alternating stimulus naming in the development dyslexias. *Brain and Language, 27*, 360–379.

Wolf, M. (1991). Naming speed and reading: The contribution of the neurosciences. *Reading Research Quarterly, 26*, 123–141.

Yekovich, F. R., Walker, C. H., & Blackman, H. S. (1979). The role of presupposed and focal information in integrating sentences. *Journal of Verbal Learning and Verbal Behavior, 18*, 535–548.

CHAPTER 27

LANGUAGE DEFICITS IN "SPECIFIC" READING DISABILITY

RICHARD K. OLSON

I. INTRODUCTION

Traditional definitions of specific reading disability or dyslexia include children with severe reading problems, who are typically below the 10th percentile in spite of normal-range IQ, sensory acuity, and educational opportunity. The reading deficits of dyslexic children place serious constraints on their educational progress. Therefore, the National Institutes of Health have recognized dyslexia as a major public health problem and currently support several large research programs to explore the etiology and remediation of dyslexia. One of these programs is the Colorado Reading Project, which has conducted twin studies of the genetic and environmental etiology of dyslexia and associated deficits (DeFries, Olson, Pennington, & Smith, 1991).

The popular media view of dyslexia holds that it is primarily caused by a disorder in visual perception. For example, abnormal eye movements have been suggested as a causal factor in dyslexia. Although individual differences in reading eye movements such as the proportion of regressive fixations and average length of forward movements appear to be influenced by genetic factors (Berry & Olson, 1991), we have found no evidence for a higher incidence of eye-movement disorders in our dyslexic subjects (Olson & Forsberg, 1993; Olson, Kliegl, & Davidson, 1983). Other differences in dyslexics' visual processing have recently been reported (cf. Livingstone, Rosen, Drislane, & Galaburda, 1991; Lovegrove, Martin, & Slaghuis, 1986), but the existence and possible causal role of visual deficits in dyslexia remains controversial. It is clear that many visual skills are not significantly different between dyslexic and normal groups (Vellutino, 1979).

Most researchers have rejected the visual deficit hypothesis in favor of a deficit in language processes as the primary cause of dyslexia (Catts, 1989; Olson, Kliegl, Davidson, & Foltz, 1985; Stanovich, 1986a; Vellutino, 1979). Stanovich reviewed a large number of studies on dyslexics' language skills, ranging from low-level perceptual processes to higher level comprehension processes. Dyslexic children have been reported to be inferior to same-age normal readers in their perceptual discrimination of phonemes, phonological awareness measured by tasks requiring the isolation and manipulation of phonemes within words, speed and accuracy in lexical access for picture names, verbal short-term and working memory, syntactic awareness, and semantic processing in tasks such as listening comprehension. Tunmer, Herriman, and Nesdale (1988) have proposed that dyslexic children suffer from a broad-ranging deficit in "metalinguistic ability," defined as the ability to reflect on and manipulate the structural features of spoken language.

The traditional concept of specificity for deficits in reading in "specific" reading disability or dyslexia appears to be challenged by the broad range of language deficits cited above. However, in most studies the primary criterion for specificity of reading deficits in dyslexic children has been a normal-range IQ, typically above 90, so significant mean differences in IQ often exist between dyslexic and normal groups. Even in studies where dyslexic and normal groups have been carefully matched on a comprehensive IQ test such as the Wechsler Intelligence Scale for Children (WISC) (Wechsler, 1974), the dyslexics' scores on the verbal subtests are usually lower than their scores on the visual–perceptual subtests. Of course, reduced print exposure associated with poor reading skills may constrain the development of vocabulary and general knowledge assessed in the Wechsler verbal tests.

A critical question to be addressed in this chapter is the causal relations between the various language deficits and dyslexia. Although the range of language deficits is impressive, their importance in the etiology of dyslexia is not clear. As suggested above for verbal IQ, many of the reported language deficits could be primarily a consequence rather than a cause of reading problems. Stanovich (1986b) has argued that many dyslexic children suffer from a reverse "Matthew effect," wherein early reading problems constrain the development of language skills that are normally developed through reading and reciprocally support further development in reading. For example, advances in oral vocabulary and syntactic knowledge may depend on exposure to the less frequent words and complex syntax found in more advanced text. Dyslexic readers have less exposure to advanced text and thus fall farther behind their normal peers in both reading and language skills.

On the other hand, there may be some specific language deficits that directly constrain the initial development of basic reading skills in dyslexic children. One approach to the question of causal direction has been to assess prereaders' language skills before those skills have had a chance to interact with the development of reading skills. Some of these studies have observed the correlations between language and later reading skills. Others have trained prereaders' language skills and observed the effect on later reading development. I briefly review the major results of these important studies at the end of the chapter.

Nearly all studies of dyslexic children measure reading and language skills after there has been ample opportunity for the skills to interact in development. This raises obvious problems for disentangling the dominant direction of causal influences. The approach that a number of researchers have used is to compare the profiles of component reading and language skills in younger normal and older dyslexic groups that have been carefully matched on a measure of reading skill (the "reading level match" comparison). A causal role in dyslexia is suggested for those component skills that are significantly worse in the dyslexic group compared to younger normal children at the same reading level (Bryant & Goswami, 1986). The basic rationale for this conclusion is that if reading development is responsible for the development of a language skill, older dyslexic subjects should be at least as strong in that language skill when compared to younger normal subjects at the same reading level. Results from reading level match studies reviewed in the following section suggest a primary causal role for dyslexics' deficits in specific phonological reading and language processes. This hypothesis is also supported by studies showing a relation between preschoolers' phonological skills and later reading development in the early grades.

A second focus of the chapter is on the genetic and environmental etiology of dyslexics' deficits in component reading and language skills. Studies of identical and fraternal twins in the Colorado Reading Project have revealed that genes and environment play an approximately equal role in the dyslexic group's difficulty in reading isolated words, but deficits in the phonological decoding component of word recognition and related language skills are uniquely heritable (Olson, Gillis, Rack, DeFries, & Fulker, 1991; Olson, Wise, Conners, Rack, & Fulker, 1989). The chapter concludes with a discussion of implications for general models of dyslexia and approaches to remediation.

II. Reading Level Match Comparisons of Component Reading and Language Skills

Researchers and educators have often remarked on the difficulty most poor readers seem to have in reading isolated words and particularly in "sounding out" or phonologically decoding unfamiliar words and pronounceable nonwords such as *tegwop* (Calfee, Lindamood, & Lindamood, 1973; Perfetti & Hogaboam, 1975). As a result, the processes involved in printed word recognition and related language skills have become a primary focus of research on dyslexia.

The emphasis on word recognition and related language skills does not deny the importance of reading comprehension, which of course is the ultimate goal of reading, and dyslexics certainly have problems in this area. But reading comprehension is independently influenced by two separable skills, word recognition and listening comprehension (Conners & Olson, 1990; Gough & Tunmer, 1986; Tunmer & Hoover, 1992). The path models in Figure 1 from Conners and Olson illustrate the independent contributions of word recognition and listening comprehension to performance on the reading comprehension section of the Peabody Individual Achievement Test (PIAT) (Dunn & Markwardt, 1970). The path coefficients on the straight lines indicate the independent variance in reading comprehension accounted for by a predictor variable after controlling for variance in the other predictor variable. The values on the curved lines are simple correlations between the predictor variables. The upper path model is for 86 older dyslexic children (mean age = 15.6 years). The lower model is for 86 younger normal children (mean age = 10.4 years) who were matched to the dyslexics on level of word recognition. In both samples there were significant independent contributions from word recognition and listening comprehension

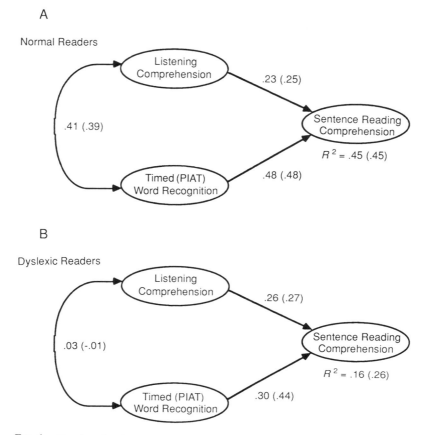

to PIAT reading comprehension, and the independence was significantly greater in the dyslexic sample when the correlations on the curved lines were compared.

Conners and Olson (1990) extended their path models to discover variables that contributed independent variance to listening comprehension and other variables that contributed to word recognition. The dyslexic subjects' verbal IQ scores on the WISC contributed significant independent variance to listening comprehension but not to word recognition. This result is consistent with the dyslexic group's profile for raw score verbal knowledge on the WISC (not age-scaled IQ), listening comprehension, and reading comprehension. Although all three of these variables were significantly lower in the dyslexic group when compared to a same-age normal group, the dyslexics' scores were significantly higher than in the younger normal group matched on word recognition. Apparently the older dyslexics were able to use their superior verbal knowledge and listening comprehension to also achieve superior reading comprehension, in spite of their more serious deficits in printed word recognition.

An extension of the above path model for word recognition revealed independent contributions from subjects' performance on a measure of orthographic coding and a measure of phonological decoding. The orthographic coding task required subjects to select the word from word–pseudohomophone pairs (e.g., *rane–rain; salmon–sammon*) as quickly as possible. Note that both letter strings in each pair would sound the same if sounded out, but only one letter string had the correct orthographic pattern for a word. Simply sounding out the letter strings would not be sufficient for subjects to make a correct choice. The phonological decoding task required subjects to read pronounceable nonwords aloud as quickly as possible (e.g., *ter, calch, tegwop*). For both the orthographic and phonological decoding tasks, subjects' final scores were based on the combined z scores for percent correct and median latency for correct responses.

The dyslexic group was significantly worse on both the orthographic and phonological decoding tasks compared to a same-age normal group, but a differential pattern emerged when the dyslexics were compared to younger normal readers at the same level of word recognition. The dyslexics were slightly but significantly ($+.36$ sd) better in orthographic coding, primarily due to their faster response latency in this task. However, the dyslexics were substantially ($-.78$ sd) worse in the phonological decoding task due to their deficits in both accuracy and speed (Olson et al., 1989).

Reading level match deficits in dyslexics' nonword reading have been reported in a number of other studies, but a minority of studies have reported no deficits. The studies with null results were often interpreted to mean that dyslexic children simply suffered from a general developmental lag in all component reading processes. However, Rack, Snowling, and Olson (1992) carefully compared the studies that reported a phonological deficit with those that did not (see also Olson, Wise, Conners, & Rack, 1990). It was apparent that some studies had sample sizes that were too small or reading deficits that were not severe enough to detect a phonological deficit. Other studies appeared not to have correctly matched the dyslexic and normal groups due to problems with regression to the mean from selecting groups on extreme scores in unreliable measures of word recognition. Additional factors such as the difficulty of nonword stimuli may have caused differences between studies. The bottom line was that when phonological decoding was appropriately measured and the groups were correctly matched on word recognition, the dyslexic groups' phonological decoding deficits were substantial.

Olson et al. (1990) and Rack et al. (1992) noted that dyslexic children who have a phonological decoding deficit must somehow compensate for this deficit to reach their relatively higher level of word recognition. Orthographic coding seems an unlikely candidate for a compensatory skill because the dyslexics' slight advantage was only in speed of responding, and their level of accuracy in the orthographic task was consistent with their level of word recognition. As an alternative explanation, we proposed that because the dyslexic subjects were much older, they may have had greater exposure to print than the younger normal readers. If this hypothesis is correct, the dyslexics' greater print exposure may have compensated for their deficits in phonological decoding, allowing word recognition and orthographic coding to advance in spite of their phonological deficit. A second possibility for compensation is suggested by Conners and Olson's (1990) finding that their older dyslexic group had a significantly better oral vocabulary as measured by the WISC. Dyslexic subjects may be able to read orally familiar words with less dependence on phonological decoding processes, compared to younger reading-matched normal subjects who do not have those words in their oral vocabulary.

Olson et al. (1990) concluded that there is strong evidence for a phonological decoding deficit in most dyslexic readers that constrains their development of printed word recognition. However, phonological decoding is a component of *reading* skill. Are deficits in phonological processes specific to reading, or are there more general phonological deficits in language processes that contribute to dyslexics' deficits in phonological decoding? Conners and Olson (1990) extended their path model to find variables that contributed independent variance to phonological decoding. Subjects' performance on a phoneme awareness task accounted for substantial independent variance in phonological decoding within both the dyslexic and normal groups. The phoneme awareness task required subjects to isolate the initial phoneme of each spoken target word, place the phoneme at the end of the word, add the sound *ay*, and pronounce the result. For example *pig* would be pronounced *igpay* (this task is much like the children's game Pig Latin). Other studies with younger subjects and different measures of phoneme awareness have also shown its strong relation to phonological decoding (cf. Bowey, Cain, & Ryan, in press; Juel, Griffith, & Gough, 1986; Tunmer & Nesdale, 1985).

The strong correlations found between phoneme awareness and phonological decoding are consistent with the results of several reading level match studies. In the study by Conners and Olson (1990; see also Olson et al., 1989), the dyslexics' phoneme awareness (Pig Latin) was .55 sd below that of the younger normal readers. Manis, Szeszulski, Holt, and Graves (1990) reported similar deficits in a phoneme deletion task and in a nonword reading task. Bowey et al. (in press) found deficits in 4th grade dyslexics' nonword reading and in their ability to recognize the odd word among three spoken words that did not share the same medial or final phoneme (e.g., *tan* **tip** *tag*). Similar results were reported earlier by Bradley and Bryant (1978). Rohl and Tunmer (1988) employed a spelling level match comparison for dyslexic and normal groups to test Ehri's (1986) hypothesis that spelling is the critical skill that constrains dyslexic readers' performance in phoneme awareness and decoding. Nevertheless, Rohl and Tunmer's dyslexic readers still showed significant deficits in phoneme awareness and in the spelling of nonwords, compared to spelling age–matched controls (see also Bruck & Treiman, 1990). A few studies have reported no deficits in both phonological decoding and phoneme awareness, but these studies appear to have problems in subject selection and matching of the groups on reading level (reviewed by Rack et al., 1992).

The implied causal role for phoneme awareness deficits in dyslexia must be reconciled with evidence that the development of phoneme awareness is linked to reading experience. Studies of adult illiterates who were later trained to read indicate a strong reciprocal influence on the development of phoneme awareness (Morais, Bertelson, Cary, & Alegria, 1986). However, the studies reviewed above suggest that most dyslexics do not benefit from this reciprocal influence as much as normal readers (also see Bruck, 1992). Therefore, Olson et al. (1990) proposed that dyslexics' deficits in the interactive development of phoneme awareness during reading constrains their development of phonological decoding.

Unfortunately, there are problems with the attribution of causal influence from deficits in reading level match comparisons. For example, Goswami and Bryant (1989) suggested that the inappropriate use of contextually based guessing strategies for word recognition that are sometimes promoted by teachers could be a primary cause of phonological deficits and subsequent reading failure. Two issues are raised by this hypothesis. One is the third-factor explanation: Both phonological awareness and phonological decoding are deficient but there is some other factor, such as contextually based guessing, that causes both deficits. The second issue concerns the biological versus environmental origin of deficits. On the environmental side, Ehri (1989) has argued that poor teaching of letter–sound knowledge may produce phonological processing deficits and dyslexic reading behavior. In support of Ehri's position, several studies have demonstrated that code-based teaching leads to better phonological skills than teaching that only emphasizes contextually based guessing of words (Evans & Carr, 1985; Johnston & Thompson, 1989; Seymour & Elder, 1986; Tunmer & Nesdale, 1985), although it should be added that most children taught by contextually based methods do not turn out to be dyslexic. In contrast to Ehri's environmental orientation, Liberman, Shankweiler, and Liberman (1989) suggested that biologically based constitutional weaknesses in phonological structures may be the cause of dyslexic reading. Of course, both these hypotheses could be correct with the balance of environmental and biological influence varying across individuals. In the next section we assess the balance of biological (genetic) and environmental influence on dyslexics' group deficits. The question of a third-factor influence on phonological decoding and awareness is raised again at the end of the chapter.

Before turning to the genetic evidence, we need to consider some basic language skills in dyslexics that are deficient in age match comparisons but not in reading level match comparisons. Conners and Olson's (1990) subjects were also tested on a second measure of phonological awareness wherein subjects generated all the words they could think of in one minute that rhymed with a target word. The dyslexics' performance on the rhyming task was worse than the age match controls but nearly equal to the reading-matched controls. Rhyming has often been included among tasks purported to measure phonological awareness. However, rhyming tasks have been shown to be less difficult than tasks requiring the isolation of individual phonemes (phoneme awareness) because rhyming seems to be based on a larger and more natural linguistic unit (Goswami & Bryant, 1990; Treiman, 1991). Preschoolers and illiterate adults can perform rhyming tasks but usually have great difficulty with phoneme awareness tasks.

In addition to the phonological awareness measures discussed above, phonological memory has also been viewed as important in reading development. Wagner and Torgesen (1987) noted the role of memory in phoneme blending tasks wherein isolated phonemes of a word are presented in sequence and the child is asked to remember and blend the phonemes to form the target word. Shankweiler and Crain (1986) have emphasized the memory demands inherent in tasks requiring complex syntactic processing. Many studies have noted differences between age-matched dyslexic and normal groups in a variety of verbal memory tasks, but the performance of reading level–matched groups tends to be similar. For example, Conners and Olson's (1990) reading-matched groups were not significantly different on a measure of verbatim sentence memory or on the WISC digit span test. Likewise, Bowey et al. (in press) found no deficits in 4th grade poor readers' digit span, although like Conners and Olson's dyslexic subjects, they were lower in phoneme awareness compared to reading-matched controls.

Tunmer and Hoover (1993) noted the absence of a memory deficit in reading level match studies to support the idea that a child's achievement in reading is the primary influence on the development of verbal memory. Tunmer and Hoover cited additional evidence for this hypothesis, including a lack of prediction from prereaders' verbal memory to later reading (Bradley & Bryant, 1985), and Ellis's (1990) cross-lag comparisons of LISREL path coefficients for memory to later reading and reading to later memory. The influence from reading to later memory was clearly the stronger path between 5 and 6 years of age. Recent genetic analyses by Wadsworth, DeFries, Fulker, Olson, and Pennington (1993) also supported a causal influence from reading to memory, although a third factor influencing both reading and memory could not be ruled out. A review of the literature by Pennington, Van Orden, Kirson, and Haith (1991) supported the third factor view.

Naming speed and accuracy for pictured objects is another general category of phonological processing that has shown consistent deficits in age match comparisons of dyslexic and normal readers. Katz (1986) found that young dyslexic children's naming errors indicated the deficient retrieval of phonological representations, as they were able to recognize the correct names. Wolf (1984) reported that naming speed in kindergarten predicted later reading ability, and Olson et al. (1985) found slower naming of common pictures in older dyslexic subjects compared to age-matched controls. The naming task that seems to best differentiate dyslexic from normal children is the rapid sequential naming of colors, numbers, letters, and objects (Denkla & Rudel, 1976). Bowers and Swanson (1991) found that rapid naming accounts for significant independent variance in phonological decoding, beyond that accounted for by measures of phonological awareness. This result has been replicated in the Colorado Reading Project. However, our most recent unpublished reading level match comparisons in a new sample revealed that the older dyslexic subjects were significantly faster than the younger normal readers. The dyslexics in this new sample were again equal to the controls on memory span and rhyming, and significantly worse on phonological decoding and phoneme awareness.

The absence of reading level match deficits in rhyming, memory, and naming tasks does not prove that there is a primarily reciprocal influence on these skills from reading development (Bryant & Goswami, 1986). The dyslexic children are much older and may have compensatory knowledge and experience that improves their performance up to or above the levels of the younger matched normal readers. In memory, the older dyslexics might have learned better rehearsal strategies that could compensate for a weak phonological memory base. In rhyming, the dyslexics might benefit from their greater oral vocabulary. In rapid naming, the dyslexics' greater experience with the symbols and developmental increases in general processing speed could have pulled them above the younger reading-matched controls. Thus, the fact that memory, rhyming, and naming speed are inferior in dyslexics compared to age-matched normals still allows the possibility of their associated causal role in dyslexia. Behavioral genetic analyses reviewed in the following section lend some support to this hypothesis.

In summary, reading level match comparisons have shown that most dyslexic children have greater problems in reading isolated words than in reading comprehension, and the phonological decoding component of printed word recognition is uniquely deficient. Correlated deficits have also been observed in language tasks that require the isolation and manipulation of individual phonemes in spoken words. The unique deficits in phonological decoding and phoneme awareness suggest that they may play an important causal role in the etiology of dyslexia. The primarily biological basis for these deficits is clarified in the following section.

III. BEHAVIORAL GENETIC STUDIES OF READING AND LANGUAGE DEFICITS

In the Colorado Reading Project we have compared the similarities of identical and fraternal twin pairs to provide estimates of genetic and shared-environment influence on reading and language deficits. Identical twins develop from the same sperm and egg (monozygotic, MZ) and thus share all their genes. Fraternal twins are derived from two different sperm–egg combinations (dizygotic, DZ), just as ordinary siblings, and they share half their segregating genes on average. The behavioral genetic interpretation of data from MZ and DZ twins is based on several important assumptions, including additive influence from any relevant genes, no assortative mating, and an equal degree of shared environment for MZ and DZ pairs (Plomin, DeFries, & McClearn, 1990). If these assumptions are not violated to a significant degree, comparing MZ and DZ within-pair differences provides estimates for the proportions of genetic and shared-environment influence on average twin resemblance.

Our dyslexic and normal comparison groups included 3rd to 12th grade MZ and same-sex DZ twins ascertained from 27 Colorado school districts. The twins were invited to participate in laboratory testing if either member of a pair's school records (teacher reports, remedial classes, and/or test scores) showed evidence of a reading problem. To provide a normal-range comparison group, a smaller sample of twins with no record of reading problems was also tested in the laboratory, although some of these twins turned out to have significant deficits and were therefore included in the disabled group. In addition to the reading and language measures described in the previous section for the reading level comparisons (word recognition, phonological and orthographic coding, memory span, naming speed, phonological awareness), the twins were given the full Wechsler (1974) IQ test, and parent questionnaire data were collected on the twins' medical, social, and educational background. Twins were excluded from the analyses if they had both verbal and performance IQ scores below 90, evidence of neural damage such as seizures, or obvious sensory, social, emotional, or educational conditions such as poor school attendance that might cause reading problems.

Twin studies of the full range of individual differences across the population usually compare the correlations for MZ and DZ pairs. However, a more appropriate and powerful statistical approach can be used to assess the group heritability for selected characteristics, such as dyslexia, which are deviant from the normal population (DeFries & Fulker, 1985). In this approach, an affected twin (the PROBAND) is identified based on a severity criterion for deviation from the mean of the normal population. (In the analyses described here, probands included those individuals who were at least 1.5 sd below the mean of the control group.) Genetic and shared-environment influence was then assessed by comparing the MZ and DZ cotwins' regression toward the control group mean.

Suppose that the average proband deficit for both MZ and DZ twins is 2 sd below the population mean for a particular measure. If there is no test error and individual differences in performance on that measure are completely heritable, the MZ cotwins should show no regression to the population mean because they share identical genes. DZ cotwins should regress halfway (1 sd) to the population mean because they share half their segregating genes, on average. If there is no heritability for a particular measure, MZ and DZ cotwins would show equal or no regression to the population mean. Differential cotwin regression between these two extreme examples would indicate an intermediate level of heritability.

Twin data are also informative about the degree to which shared environment is important for individual differences. If both MZ and DZ cotwins showed no regression to the population mean, this would indicate that shared environment accounted entirely for individual differences across the twin pairs. In the more likely case in which MZ cotwins regress somewhat to the mean due to test error and nonshared environment, and DZ cotwins regress more, but somewhat less than halfway to the mean, the combined influence of shared environment and genetic factors is indicated for the probands' group deficit.

We have only an approximate estimate of the population mean and standard deviation based on our control sample, which was normally distributed but did not include some of the most extreme deficits in reading. This would tend to give a slight underestimation of deficit heritabilities in our analyses. However, any general bias of this sort, or biases due to minor violations of other assumptions of the twin method, should not influence the important contrasts in heritabilities for different skills that are emphasized in this chapter.

The regression procedure used in the present analyses was developed by DeFries and Fulker (1985). Their procedure yields estimates and standard errors for the proportion of genetic influence on the probands' group deficit (h_g^2) and the proportion of shared-environment influence (c_g^2). The difference between the sum of these estimates and 1.0 indicates the proportion of twin differences due to nonshared environment and/or test error.

We begin with the results for the previously discussed measures of single-word recognition, phonological decoding (oral nonword reading), and orthographic coding (*rane* vs. *rain*). The present heritability estimates are based on the current sample that has increased in size since our previous reports (Olson et al., 1989, 1990, 1991).

Estimates and standard errors for heritability (h_g^2) and shared environment (c_g^2) along with the proband and cotwin means for MZ and DZ pairs are presented in Table I. For word recognition, it can be seen that the heritability and shared environment estimates are .47 and .48, respectively leaving a small proportion (.05) of individual differences associated with test error and nonshared environment.

The strong influence of shared environment on deficits in word recognition may seem surprising in view of our exclusion of poor readers with obvious environmental deficits such as poor school attendance or low socioeconomic

Table I

Genetic (h_g^2) and Shared Environment (c_g^2) Influence on Group Deficits in Disabled Readers' Word Recognition and Component Coding Skills[a]

	MZ		DZ		Influence[c]	
Task[b]	Proband	Cotwin	Proband	Cotwin	h_g^2 (SE)	c_g^2 (SE)
Word recognition (MZ = 183, DZ = 129)	−2.65	−2.52	−2.62	−1.89	.47 (.09)*	.48 (.11)*
Orthographic (MZ = 132, DZ = 92)	−2.77	−2.71	−2.71	−1.56	.56 (.13)*	.29 (.13)*
Phonological (MZ = 151, DZ = 105)	−2.63	−2.28	−2.62	−1.50	.59 (.12)*	.27 (.12)*

[a] Probands were selected independently for each measure to be at least 1.5 sd below the normal group mean.
[b] The numbers of MZ and DZ pairs for each measure are presented in parentheses.
[c] h_g^2 = 2CMZ/PMZ − CDZ/PDZ; c_g^2 = 2CDZ/PDZ − CMZ/PMZ; * = $p < .01$ for estimates significantly greater than 0.

level. In fact, few twins were excluded on these criteria, although we avoided testing twins in one Colorado school district that was very low in average socioeconomic level and educational achievement. Apparently there was still a wide range of environment for reading development in the twins' homes and schools. It should be noted that the relative balance of genetic and shared environment influence on probands' group deficits depends on both the strength of genetic factors and the range of twin pair environmental differences. If we broadened the environmental range in the sample, estimates of heritabililily would be lower and shared environment would be higher.

To begin exploring the basis of shared-environment influences, we have employed measures of print exposure developed by Cunningham and Stanovich (1991) that are based on the recognition of age-appropriate book titles. The sample for these measures is still quite small, but there is significant shared-environment covariance between the group, deficits in word recognition, and print exposure.

For the group deficits in orthographic and phonological coding, genetic factors appeared to be relatively more influential than shared environment (see Table I). These results seem to differ from the nearly equal genetic and shared-environment influence on the group deficit in word recognition, although the standard errors for the present estimates are too large to yield statistically significant contrasts. If the present pattern of results is maintained and the contrasts become significant as we continue our testing of twins, they will indicate that deficits in phonological and orthographic coding both have uniquely strong influences from genetic factors.

Why might genetic effects be stronger for deficits in orthographic and phonological coding than for word recognition? Successful performance in the orthographic coding task requires the precise representation of specific spelling patterns for words. Accurate and rapid phonological decoding of nonwords requires the precise representation and efficient access of grapheme–phoneme correspondences. Simple word recognition, on the other hand, may often be successful in spite of weak phonological and orthographic codes. It may be that more environmentally influenced variables such as print exposure and oral vocabulary play a larger role in dyslexics' recognition of printed words.

Within the dyslexic twin sample, word recognition is correlated with phonological coding ($r = .80$) and with orthographic coding ($r = .60$). Bivariate genetic analyses allow us to estimate the degree to which the phenotypic correlations between word recognition and the two coding skills is due to shared genetic influence (Olson, Forsberg, & Wise, in press). The bivariate genetic covariance with word recognition was assessed by selecting probands to be low on word recognition and comparing the MZ and DZ cotwins' regression on phonological coding or orthographic coding. The resulting estimates for the common genetic influence on the phenotypic correlations (for the group deficits) were 58% (.14 SE) for word recognition and phonological decoding and 69% (.29 SE) for word recognition and orthographic coding. Thus, the majority of genetic influence on the probands' group deficit in word recognition was in common with genetic influence on deficits in both the phonological and orthographic coding tasks. A third bivariate analysis for probands' deficits in phonological coding and cotwins orthographic coding (phenotypic $r = .50$) indicated a common genetic influence for the correlated variance of 66% (.22 SE).

These results indicate a strong and largely overlapping genetic etiology for dyslexics' deficits in word recognition, phonological coding, and orthographic coding. However, these are *reading* tasks. There may be more basic cognitive deficits with significant genetic etiology that are ultimately responsible for the genetic influences on dyslexics' reading deficits. We hypothesized that weaknesses in basic phonological *language* skills, particularly phoneme awareness, might be the source of genetic influence on dyslexics' deficits in reading (Olson et al., 1989). The reading-level-match deficit in phoneme awareness discussed earlier and its high correlation with phonological decoding make this particular language skill a likely candidate.

The first line in Table II includes estimates of h_g^2 and c_g^2 for phoneme awareness (Pig Latin). Data from a second measure of phoneme awareness recently added to the test battery, phoneme deletion (*say* prot *without the* er *sound*: *pot*) are included on the second line of Table II. The simple bivariate r between the two phoneme awareness measures was .74 (see Table III). The group deficits on both measures showed significant heritability, with a smaller but significant amount of shared-environment influence.

Bivariate genetic analyses based on probands' deficits in the reading tasks and cotwins' regression to the mean on the phoneme awareness (Pig Latin) task were performed to estimate shared genetic influences on the phenotypic correlations. The resulting estimates for the common genetic proportions of the phenotypic correlations with phoneme awareness were 75% (.26 SE) for word recognition, 78% (.27 SE) for phonological coding, and 85% (.39 SE) for orthographic coding. Thus, substantial proportions of dyslexics' group deficits in phonological awareness, phonological coding, orthographic coding, and word recognition are caused by the same genetic factors.

The results were quite different for rhyme generation, with no significant heritability or genetic covariation with phonological decoding, but significant and relatively substantial shared-environment effects. (This result is different from the Olson et al., 1989, study with a smaller sample, which yielded evidence

TABLE II
Genetic (h_g^2) and Shared Environment (c_g^2) Influence on Group Deficits in Language Skills[a]

	MZ		DZ		Influence[c]	
Task[b]	Proband	Cotwin	Proband	Cotwin	h_g^2 (SE)	c_g^2 (SE)
Pig Latin	−2.80	−2.27	−2.58	−1.42	.50 (.15)*	.30 (.15)*
(MZ = 101, DZ = 82)						
Phoneme deletion	−2.74	−2.26	−3.26	−1.86	.51 (.25)*	.31 (.25)
(MZ = 51, DZ = 27)						
Rhyme generation	−2.23	−1.68	−2.18	−1.35	.27 (.19)	.49 (.19)*
(MZ = 77, DZ = 43)						
Rapid naming	−2.15	−1.54	−2.11	−1.14	.35 (.16)*	.36 (.15)*
(MZ = 77, DZ = 51)						
Digit span	−1.90	−1.06	−1.97	−0.59	.51 (.18)*	.04 (.16)
(MZ = 76, DZ = 50)						
Verbal IQ	−2.19	−1.90	−2.24	−1.45	.44 (.11)*	.42 (.12)*
(MZ = 110, DZ = 83)						
Perceptual IQ	−2.14	−1.81	−2.07	−1.11	.61 (.14)*	.23 (.14)
(MZ = 79, DZ = 54)						

[a] Proband scores were at least 1.5 sd below the normal mean.
[b] The numbers of twin pairs for each measure are in parentheses.
[c] * = $p < .05$ for significance of estimates from 0.

for genetic influence.) The type of phonological awareness measured in rhyme generation may be quite different from the awareness of individual phonemes (Treiman, 1991). Children only need to discover the overlap among the relatively larger rime units (the vowel and following consonants) across different words in their lexicon. Rime units may be much more assessable and depend on a more global level of phonological awareness than tasks that require the isolation and manipulation of individual phonemes.

Rhyme generation's lack of significant heritability or genetic covariance with phonological decoding may seem to contradict the longitudinal data of Bryant, MacLean, Bradley, and Crossland (1990). They showed significant correlations between 3-year-olds' knowledge of nursery rhymes, later phonolog-

TABLE III
Correlations between Phonological Decoding and Language Skills for Dyslexic Probands and Cotwins[a]

	Pig Latin	Phoneme deletion	Rhyme generation	Rapid naming	Digit span	Verbal IQ
Phonological decoding	.60	.70	.54	.47	.25	.35
Pig Latin		.74	.55	.26	.28	.34
Phoneme deletion			.63	.37	.31	.43
Rhyme generation				.25	.37	.40
Rapid naming					.24	.09*
Digit span						.19

[a] * = $p > .05$. All other correlations $p < .01$, with at least 300 subjects for each r.

ical awareness, and still later reading development. It is possible that for these young preschoolers, rhyme sensitivity is closer to the leading edge of their development in phonological awareness and thus predicts later phoneme awareness, but rhyme generation may measure something different in older children and adults. The phenotypic correlation between rhyme generation and the Pig Latin measure of phoneme awareness within our dyslexic twin sample was significant (see Table III). However, bivariate genetic analyses indicated that the relation between deficits in the two measures was due to shared environment rather than genetic factors.

The remaining oral language measures presented in Table II include rapid naming of numbers and letters (Denkla & Rudel, 1976), forward digit span from the WISC, and a measure of verbal IQ based on a composite of the information, similarities, vocabulary, and comprehension subtests of the WISC. Deficits in all three of these measures were significantly heritable, with significant shared environment for rapid naming and verbal IQ. Most important, significant bivariate genetic covariance was found between probands' deficits in phonological decoding and cotwins' deficits in rapid naming ($h_g^2 = .59$) and in digit span ($h_g^2 = .61$), but genetic covariance with verbal IQ ($h_g^2 = .34$) was not significantly greater than zero.

Wadsworth et al. (1993) recently analyzed the genetic correlation between measures of reading and memory for individual differences in the normal range. The reading measure was based on LISREL estimates of common variance for the PIAT word recognition, spelling, and reading comprehension tests. The memory measure was of common variance in digit span, memory for sentences, and memory for words. The heritability estimates for reading ($h^2 = .89$) and memory ($h^2 = .93$) were quite high, and in contrast to estimates for deficits in reading (word recognition), there was no significant influence of shared environment. However, similar to the previous high estimates for genetic covariance between probands' deficits in memory (digit span) and cotwins reading (phonological decoding or word recognition), 80% of the phenotypic correlation ($r = .39$) between individual differences in memory and reading was due to genetic factors. Further analyses are in progress with other reading and language measures to assess their heritabilities and genetic correlations.

The last variable in Table II is a composite of the WISC block design, picture completion, object assembly, and picture arrangement. Deficits in this measure were significantly heritable, but the genetic covariance with phonological decoding and word recognition was not significant (Forsberg and Olson, 1992). This result indicates that only deficits in the verbal measures (excluding rhyme and verbal IQ) were both heritable and genetically linked to deficits in phonological decoding and word recognition.

A limitation of our behavioral genetic analyses is that we are only able to assess the heritability of group deficits. The degree and specific type of genetic as well as shared-environment influence could vary widely across individuals. Genetic linkage analyses within several different families containing dyslexic probands have suggested heterogeneity in the apparent mode of genetic transmission (Smith, Kimberling, & Pennington, 1991). (The genetic linkage procedure relates reading deficits to specific loci on the chromosomes.) This result raises the possibility of different genetic pathways through different language deficits.

Behavioral genetic analyses cannot identify specific genes, but they can be used to assess differences in the level of heritability for different subgroups defined by relevant variables (DeFries et al., 1991). In our most recent analyses (Olson, unpublished data), subjects who had the most severe deficits in each of the language skills tended to have the highest heritabilities for their deficits in phonological decoding. This approach will be more informative as our sample size increases.

In summary, the results from the language tasks, with the exception of rhyme and verbal IQ, showed both significant heritability and common genetic influence with deficits in phonological decoding. The phoneme awareness tasks showed the most robust genetic effects and highest correlations with phonological decoding. However, the hypothesized causal genetic pathway from deficits in phoneme awareness to deficits in phonological decoding is not proven. A direct genetic influence on the phonological decoding of print could indirectly influence the development of phoneme awareness, naming, memory, and verbal IQ. Alternatively, there may be a general phonological processing deficit, independent of reading, that has a direct influence on phonological decoding and language skills. This phonological *g* model and a more general metalinguistic model of dyslexia are compared in the next section.

IV. GENERAL MODELS OF DYSLEXIA AND IMPLICATIONS FOR REMEDIATION

There is little disagreement that phonological decoding and language deficits are present in most dyslexics. However, there are fundamentally different views on how to account for these deficits. Tunmer and Hoover (1993) used the term PHONOLOGICAL *g* MODEL to characterize Stanovich's (1988) hypothesis that a general deficit in phonological processing is the basis for dyslexics' reading and language deficits (see also Snowling, 1987). Wagner, Torgesen, Laughon, Simmons, and Rashotte (1993) described *g* as the "quality of phonological representations" that accounts for individual differences and shared variance in their young subjects' word decoding, phoneme awareness, memory, and naming speed. These authors seem to be referring to the quality of a basic perceptual representation when they state that "a gross analogy would be comparing one's acquisition of Morse code by studying clear versus noisy tapes."

An early perceptual deficit in the representation of phonemes might constrain the development of a broad range of phonological processes. Two studies of dyslexics' categorical perception of phonemes that differed slightly in second formant transition (e.g., *da ga*) have shown deficits compared to age-matched normal readers (Godfrey, Syrdal-Lasky, Millay, & Knox, 1981; Reed, 1989). Morais (1991) suggested from this evidence that early problems in phoneme perception, perhaps associated with early otitis media (ear infection), may be a primary cause of phonological deficits in dyslexics. However, Bishop and Edmundson (1986) found that otitis media was not a major factor in the etiology of developmental language disorders. In the Colorado Reading Project, early ear infection ascertained from parent reports appeared to have significant genetic influence, but the frequency of these reports was not significantly different for the normal and dyslexic twin groups. In the early stages of the Colorado Reading

Project, we used the same stimuli and procedures employed in the categorical perception study by Godfrey et al. (1981). Our age-matched dyslexic and normal groups were significantly different on the phoneme discrimination tasks due to the very large sample size, but phoneme discrimination was a very poor predictor of phonological decoding and word recognition when compared to the other language measures.

Shankweiler and Crain (1986) defined their phonological *g* model of dyslexia as a deficiency in the ability to generate, maintain, and operate on phonological representations in working memory. Tunmer and Hoover (1993) criticized the model's emphasis on memory by citing evidence that the causal direction is primarily from reading development to verbal memory (discussed in Section II). However, Tunmer and Hoover's main reason for rejecting this and other versions of the phonological *g* model is that there are nonphonological linguistic and general cognitive skills in prereaders that strongly predict later individual differences in phonological awareness and decoding.

Tunmer and Hoover reviewed a number of studies of beginning readers' syntactic skills (grammatical judgment, oral cloze, correction of word order violations, morpheme deletions) that showed substantial correlations with measures of phonological awareness and decoding. For example, Willows and Ryan (1986) reported that measures of syntactic awareness in beginning readers were related to their reading achievement even when vocabulary and general cognitive ability were controlled. Moreover, syntactic awareness has been found to be more highly correlated with phonological decoding or word recognition than with reading comprehension (Bowey & Patel, 1988; Siegel & Ryan, 1988), and Stanovich, Cunningham, and Feeman (1984) found that phonological decoding correlated more highly with a measure of syntactic awareness (oral cloze) than with a measure of phonological awareness! In a study of differences between older dyslexic and younger normal groups matched on reading, Tunmer, Nesdale, and Wright (1987) found a significant deficit in syntactic awareness (oral cloze and word order correction) for the dyslexic group. This result adds an apparently nonphonological deficit to the reading level match deficits in dyslexics' phoneme awareness and phonological decoding. Longitudinal studies of prereaders provide further evidence for a causal link between early syntactic development and later reading ability (Scarborough, 1990; Tunmer, 1989).

Both phonological awareness and syntactic awareness accounted for substantial and approximately equal amounts of independent variance in beginning readers' phonological decoding (Tunmer et al., 1988). Tunmer et al. argued that the unique additional variance associated with syntactic awareness comes from its contribution to beginning readers' ability to use context, in association with their limited decoding skills, to identify unfamiliar words. Better prediction and correct decoding of words in reading is assumed to make further contributions to phonological decoding, beyond those associated only with phonological awareness. An alternative interpretation of this independent variance will be considered after discussing the Tunmer et al. explanation of the common variance for syntactic and phonological awareness.

Tunmer et al. (1988) proposed a cognitive-developmental model to account for the common variance in phonological awareness, phonological decoding, and syntactic awareness. They argued that all these skills require a "metalinguistic ability," defined as "the ability to reflect on and manipulate the structural features of spoken language." Metalinguistic development is further linked to Piagetian concepts about general developmental changes in children's ability to analytically reflect on and control their intellectual processes in a variety of tasks (Flavell, 1985). This bold departure from the phonological g model was backed up by data showing that prereaders' ability to analytically "decenter" in tests of nonphonological concrete operations was strongly predictive of their ability to develop phonological awareness, phonological decoding, and syntactic awareness during early reading instruction. This is an important result, because some types of syntactic processing may be directly influenced by the quality of phonological representation and/or phonological memory (Kelly, 1992; Shankweiler & Crain, 1986).

The cognitive-developmental model, with its claim for basic cognitive differences, seems to leave little room for the notion of specificity in dyslexia. However, it is possible that the broad group of poor readers contains individuals that have different etiologies for their problems in phonological awareness and decoding. Recall that phonological awareness and syntactic awareness made independent contributions to phonological decoding (Tunmer et al., 1988). This result could arise through the different influences of these two skills within subjects, as Tunmer et al. suggested, or it could arise from different influences across subjects. Some subjects might have common problems in phonological awareness, decoding, and syntax due to broad metalinguistic and metacognitive deficits, while others might have more specific deficits in phonological processes. Certainly the correlations for syntactic abilities or concrete operations with phonological awareness are less than perfect.

Stanovich (1988) has expressed a related idea in his contrasting of more common, garden variety poor readers who have broad cognitive deficits, perhaps often including phonological processes, with dyslexic poor readers having more specific problems in phonological processes. Stanovich has proposed that listening comprehension might be a good way to distinguish garden variety and dyslexic readers. Tunmer's (1989) own data provide some support for this approach. He found that syntactic awareness was related to later listening comprehension, but phonological awareness was not!

A better understanding of the phonological and general cognitive contributions to different individuals' reading deficits may depend on more complete behavioral profiles. Measures of syntactic awareness and cognitive control processes have recently been added to the test battery in the Colorado Reading Project. We hope to distinguish subjects in our sample with specific phonological problems from those with additional metalinguistic and metacognitive problems. We had initially assumed that the Wechsler IQ test would tap these skills, but evidence from Tunmer and others indicates that the verbal knowledge reflected in IQ tests may be largely independent of metalinguistic and metacognitive skills that are important for reading development. When our sample size for the new measures is sufficient, we will be able to assess individual differences in the genetic and behavioral pathways to deficits in phonological processes in reading and language.

The genetic and environmental etiology of the dyslexias has been the primary focus of this chapter. However, much of what we have learned about the role of phonological deficits in dyslexia has had a direct influence on approaches to remediation. The high heritability we found for deficits in phonological decoding should not discourage attempts to remediate these deficits. The behavior-genetic results only suggest that some extraordinary environmental intervention may be needed to improve dyslexics' phonological processes in reading and language.

The training of prereaders' phonological awareness, prior to reading instruction, has resulted in modest but statistically significant advantages in later reading development (Lundberg, Frost, & Peterson, 1988). Wise and Olson (1991) noted in their review of training studies that combining phonological awareness training with reading instruction seems to be the most effective approach to facilitate reading development in both normal and dyslexic children. However, dyslexics may need much more intense and specialized instruction to reach functional levels of phonological awareness and decoding. The articulatory awareness training program developed by Lindamood and Lindamood (1979) has been shown to be quite effective in improving severe dyslexics' phonological awareness and decoding (Alexander, Andersen, Heilman, Voeller, & Torgesen, 1991). Talking computers have also been shown to be effective tools for the remediation of decoding deficits (Barron et al., 1992; Olson & Wise, 1992; Wise et al., 1989).

For most dyslexics, the remediation of deficits in word decoding removes the major constraint on their reading comprehension. But for other poor readers, particularly those with relatively low IQ, reading comprehension and listening comprehension may lag behind their advances in decoding skills. There may also be deficits in poor readers' ability to understand picture stories (Gernsbacher, Varner, & Faust, 1990). Such general comprehension deficits may be due partly to constraints on the development of verbal knowledge associated with reduced print exposure. More basic problems in comprehension may be associated with the type of metalinguistic and metacognitive deficits referred to in the cognitive-developmental model of Tunmer et al. (1988). Carefully guided instruction and modeling of basic comprehension processes (metacognitive skills) has been shown to significantly improve the reading comprehension of poor readers whose decoding skills are adequate (Palinscar & Brown, 1984).

In conclusion, it is clear that the majority of dyslexic children have highly heritable deficits in phonological decoding that constrain their development of printed word recognition and reading comprehension. Correlated deficits have been found in measures of phoneme awareness that seem to develop from the same genes. Nevertheless, it is clear that intensive remedial programs can be very effective when they are jointly directed toward dyslexics' deficits in phonological decoding of printed words and phoneme awareness in speech.

ACKNOWLEDGMENTS

This work was supported in part by program project and center grants from the NICHD (HD-11681 and HD-27802), and RO1 HD-22223. The contributions of staff members of the many Colorado school districts that participate in our research, and of the twins and their families, are gratefully acknowledged. Co-investigators on the Colorado Reading Project are John DeFries, David Fulker, Richard Olson, Bruce Pennington, and Shelly Smith. Fran Conners, Helen Forsberg, John Rack, and Barbara Wise made invaluable contributions to the research on component reading and language processes. Many thanks to Morton Gernsbacher, Judy Bowey, and Maggie Bruck for helpful comments on the manuscript.

REFERENCES

Alexander, A. W., Andersen, H. G., Heilman, P. C., Voeller, K. K. S., & Torgesen, J. K. (1991). Phonological awareness training and remediation of analytic decoding deficits in a group of severe dyslexics. *Annals of Dyslexia, 41,* 193–206.

Barron, R. W., Golden, J. O., Seldon, D. M., Tait, C. F., Marmurek, H. H. C., & Haines, L. P. (1992). Teaching prereading skills with a talking computer: Letter–sound knowledge and print feedback facilitate nonreaders' phonological awareness training. *Reading and Writing: An Interdisciplinary Journal, 4,* 179–204.

Berry, C., & Olson, R. K. (1991). Heritability of eye movements in normal and reading-disabled individuals. *Behavior Genetics, 21*(6), 560–561.

Bishop, D. V. M., & Edmundson, A. (1986). Is otitis media a major cause of specific developmental language disorders? *British Journal of Disorders of Communication, 21,* 321–338.

Bowers, P. G., & Swanson, L. B. (1991). Naming speed deficits in reading disability: Multiple measures of a singular process. *Journal of Experimental Child Psychology, 51,* 195–219.

Bowey, J. A., Cain, M. T., & Ryan, S. M. (in press). A reading-level design study of phonological skills underlying fourth-grade children's word reading difficulties. *Child Development.*

Bowey, J. A., & Patel, R. K. (1988). Metalinguistic ability and early reading achievement. *Applied Psycholinguistics, 9,* 367–383.

Bradley, L., & Bryant, P. (1978). Difficulties in auditory organization as a possible cause of reading backwardness. *Nature (London), 271,* 746–747.

Bradley, L., & Bryant, P. (1985). *Rhyme and reason in reading and spelling.* Ann Arbor: University of Michigan Press.

Bruck, M. (1992). Persistence of dyslexics' phonological awareness deficits. *Developmental Psychology, 28,* 874–886.

Bruck, M., & Treiman, R. (1990). Phonological awareness and spelling in normal children and dyslexics: The case of initial consonant clusters. *Journal of Experimental Child Psychology, 50,* 156–178.

Bryant, P. E., & Goswami, U. C. (1986). Strengths and weaknesses of the reading level design: A comment on Backman, Mamen, and Ferguson. *Psychological Bulletin, 100,* 101–103.

Bryant, P. E., MacLean, M., Bradley, L. & Crossland, J. (1990). Rhyme and alliteration, phoneme detection, and learning to read. *Developmental Psychology, 26,* 429–438.

Calfee, R. C., Lindamood, P., & Lindamood, C. (1973). Acoustic-phonetic skills and reading: Kindergarten through twelfth grade. *Journal of Educational Psychology, 64,* 293–298.

Catts, H. (1989). Defining dyslexia as a developmental language disorder. *Annals of Dyslexia, 39,* 50–64.

Conners, F., & Olson, R. K. (1990). Reading comprehension in dyslexic and normal readers: A component-skills analysis. In D. A. Balota, G. B. Flores d'Arcais, & K. Rayner (Eds.), *Comprehension processes in reading* (pp. 557–579). Hillsdale, NJ: Erlbaum.

Cunningham, A. E., & Stanovich, K. E. (1991). Tracking the unique effects of print exposure in children: Associations with vocabulary, general knowledge, and spelling. *Journal of Educational Psychology, 83,* 264–274.

DeFries, J. C., & Fulker, D. W. (1985). Multiple regression analysis of twin data. *Behavior Genetics, 15,* 467–473.

DeFries, J. C., Olson, R. K., Pennington, B. F., & Smith, S. D. (1991). Colorado reading project: An update. In D. Duane & D. Gray (Eds.), *The reading brain: The biological basis of dyslexia* (pp. 53–87). Parkton, MD: York Press.

Denkla, M. B., & Rudel, R. G. (1976). Naming of pictured objects by dyslexic and other learning disabled children. *Brain and Language, 39,* 1–15.

Dunn, L. M., & Markwardt, F. C. (1970). *Examiner's manual: Peabody Individual Achievement Test.* Circle Pines, MN: American Guidance Service.

Ehri, L. (1986). Sources of difficulty in learning to spell and read. In M. Wolraich & D. Routh (Eds.), *Advances in developmental and behavioral pediatrics* (pp. 121–195). Greenwich, CT: JAI Press.

Ehri, L. (1989). The development of spelling knowledge and its role in reading acquisition and reading disability. *Journal of Learning Disabilities, 22,* 356–365.

Ellis, N. (1990). Reading, phonological skills and short-term memory: Interactive tributaries of development. *Journal of Research in Reading, 13,* 107–122.

Evans, M., & Carr, T. (1985). Cognitive abilities, conditions of learning and the early development of reading skill. *Reading Research Quarterly, 20,* 327–350.

Flavell, J. (1985). *Cognitive development.* Englewood Cliffs, NJ: Prentice-Hall.

Forsberg, H., & Olson, R. K. (1992). Heritable deficits in phonological awareness, rapid naming, and short-term memory skills are linked to disabled readers' heritable deficits in phonological decoding. *Behavior Genetics, 22,* 722.

Gernsbacher, M. A., Varner, K. R., & Faust, M. E. (1990). Investigating differences in general comprehension skill. *Journal of Experimental Psychology: Learning, Memory, and Cognition, 16,* 430–445.

Godfrey, J. J., Syrdal-Lasky, A. K., Millay, K. K., & Knox, C. M. (1981). Performance of dyslexic children on speech perception tests. *Journal of Experimental Child Psychology, 32,* 401–424.

Goswami, U., & Bryant, P. (1989). The interpretation of studies using the reading level design. *Journal of Reading Behavior, 21,* 413–424.

Goswami, U., & Bryant, P. E. (1990). *Phonological skills and learning to read.* Hillsdale, NJ: Erlbaum.

Gough, P. B., & Tunmer, W. E. (1986). Decoding, reading, and reading disability. *Remedial and Special Education, 7,* 6–10.

Johnston, R. S., & Thompson, G. B. (1989). Is dependence on phonological information in children's reading a product of instructional approach? *Journal of Experimental Child Psychology, 48,* 131–145.

Juel, C., Griffith, P., & Gough, P. (1986). Acquisition of literacy: A longitudinal study of children in first and second grade. *Journal of Educational Psychology, 78,* 243–255.

Katz, R. (1986). Phonological deficiencies in children with reading disability: Evidence from an object naming task. *Cognition, 22,* 225–257.

Kelly, M. H. (1992). Using sound to solve syntactic problems: The role of phonology in grammatical category assignments. *Psychological Review, 99,* 349–364.

Liberman, I., Shankweiler, D., & Liberman, A. (1989). The alphabetic principle and learning to read. In D. Shankweiler & I. Liberman (Eds.), *Phonology and reading disability: Solving the reading puzzle* (pp. 1–33). Ann Arbor: University of Michigan Press.

Lindamood, C. H., & Lindamood, P. C. (1979). *Lindamood auditory conceptualization test.* Hingham, MA: Teaching Resources Corporation.

Livingstone, M. S., Rosen, G. D., Drislane, F. W., & Galaburda, A. M. (1991). Physiological and anatomical evidence for a magnocellular deficit in developmental dyslexia. *Proceedings of the National Academy of Sciences of the U.S.A., 88,* 7943–7947.

Lovegrove, W., Martin, F., & Slaghuis, W. (1986). A theoretical and experimental case for a visual deficit in specific reading disability. *Cognitive Neuropsychology, 3,* 225–267.

Lundberg, I., Frost, J., & Peterson, O. (1988). Effects of an extensive program for stimulating phonological awareness in preschool children. *Reading Research Quarterly, 23,* 263–284.

Manis, F. R., Szeszulski, P. A., Holt, L. K., & Graves, K. (1990). Variation in component word recognition and spelling skills among dyslexic children and normal readers. In T. Carr & B. A. Levy (Eds.), *Reading and its development: Component skills approaches* (pp. 207–259). San Diego, CA: Academic Press.

Morais, J. (1991). Phonological awareness: A bridge between language and literacy. In D. Sawyer & B. Fox (Eds.), *Phonological awareness in reading: The evolution of current perspectives* (pp. 31–71). New York: Springer-Verlag.

Morais, J., Bertelson, P., Cary, L., & Alegria, J. (1986). Literacy training and speech segmentation. *Cognition, 24,* 45–64.

Olson, R. K., & Forsberg, H. (1993). Disabled and normal readers' eye movements in reading and non-reading tasks. In D. M. Willows, R. S. Kruk, & E. Corcos (Eds.), *Visual processes in reading and reading disabilities* (pp. 377–392). Hillsdale, NJ: Erlbaum.

Olson, R. K., Forsberg, H., & Wise, B. (in press). Genes, environment, and the development of orthographic skills. In V. W. Berninger (Ed.), *The varieties of orthographic knowledge I: Theoretical and developmental issues.* Dordrecht, The Netherlands: Kluwer Academic Publishers.

Olson, R. K., Gillis, J. J., Rack, J. P., DeFries, J. C., & Fulker, D. W. (1991). Confirmatory factor analysis of word recognition and process measures in the Colorado Reading Project. *Reading and Writing: An Interdisciplinary Journal, 3,* 235–248.

Olson, R. K., Kliegl, R., & Davidson, B. J. (1983). Dyslexic and normal readers' eye movements. *Journal of Experimental Psychology: Human Perception and Performance, 9,* 816–825.

Olson, R. K., Kliegl, R., Davidson, B. J., & Foltz, G. (1985). Individual and developmental differences in reading disability. In G. E. MacKinnon & T. G. Waller (Eds.), *Reading research: Advances in theory and practice* (Vol. 4, pp. 1–64). Orlando, FL: Academic Press.

Olson, R. K., & Wise, B. W. (1992). Reading on the computer with orthographic and speech feedback: An overview of the Colorado Remedial Reading Project. *Reading and Writing: An Interdisciplinary Journal, 4*, 107–144.

Olson, R. K., Wise, B., Conners, F., & Rack, J. (1990). Organization, heritability, and remediation of component word recognition and language skills in disabled readers. In T. H. Carr & B. A. Levy (Eds.), *Reading and its development: Component skills approaches* (pp. 261–322). San Diego, CA: Academic Press.

Olson, R. K., Wise, B., Conners, F., Rack, J., & Fulker, D. (1989). Specific deficits in component reading and language skills: Genetic and environmental influences. *Journal of Learning Disabilities, 22*, 339–348.

Palinscar, A. S., & Brown, A. L. (1984). Reciprocal teaching of comprehension-fostering and comprehension-monitoring activities. *Cognition and Instruction, 1*, 117–175.

Pennington, B. F., Van Orden, G., Kirson, D., & Haith, M. (1991). What is the causal relation between verbal STM problems and dyslexia? In S. Brady & D. Shankweiler (Eds.), *Phonological processes in literacy*. Hillsdale, NJ: Erlbaum.

Perfetti, C., & Hogaboam, T. (1975). The relationship between single word decoding and reading comprehension skill. *Journal of Educational Psychology, 67*, 461–469.

Plomin, R., DeFries, J. C., & McClearn, G. E. (1990). *Behavior genetics: A primer*. San Francisco: Freeman.

Rack, J. P., Snowling, M. J., & Olson, R. K. (1992). The nonword reading deficit in developmental dyslexia: A review. *Reading Research Quarterly, 27*(1), 28–53.

Reed, M. A. (1989). Speech perception and the discrimination of brief auditory cues in reading disabled children. *Journal of Experimental Child Psychology, 48*, 270–292.

Rohl, M., & Tunmer, W. (1988). Phonemic segmentation skill and spelling acquisition. *Applied Psycholinguistics, 9*, 335–350.

Scarborough, H. S. (1990). Very early language deficits in dyslexic children. *Child Development, 61*, 1728–1743.

Seymour, P., & Elder, L. (1986). Beginning reading without phonology. *Cognitive Neuropsychology, 3*, 1–36.

Shankweiler, D., & Crain, S. (1986). Language mechanisms and reading disorder: A modular approach. *Cognition, 24*, 139–168.

Siegel, L. S., & Ryan, E. B. (1988). Development of grammatical sensitivity, phonological, and short-term memory skills in normally achieving and learning disabled children. *Developmental Psychology, 24*, 28–37.

Smith, S. D., Kimberling, W. J., & Pennington, B. F. (1991). Screening for multiple genes influencing dyslexia. *Reading and Writing: An Interdisciplinary Journal, 3*, 285–298.

Snowling, M. (1987). *Dyslexia: A cognitive developmental perspective*. Oxford: Basil/Blackwell.

Stanovich, K. E. (1986a). Cognitive processes and the reading problems of learning disabled children: Evaluating the assumption of specificity. In J. K. Torgesen & B. Y. L. Wong (Eds.), *Psychological and educational perspectives on learning disabilities*. Orlando, FL: Academic Press.

Stanovich, K. E. (1986b). Matthew effects in reading: Some consequences of individual differences in the acquisition of literacy. *Reading Research Quarterly, 21*, 360–407.

Stanovich, K. E. (1988). Explaining the difference between the dyslexic and garden-variety poor readers: The phonological-core variable-difference model. *Journal of Learning Disabilities, 21*, 590–604.

Stanovich, K. E., Cunningham, A. E., & Feeman, D. J. (1984). Intelligence, cognitive skills, and early reading progress. *Reading Research Quarterly, 19*, 278–303.

Treiman, R. (1991). Phonological awareness and its roles in learning to read and spell. In E. J. Sawyer & B. J. Fox (Eds.), *Phonological awareness in reading: The evolution of current perspectives*. New York: Springer-Verlag.

Tunmer, W. E. (1989). The role of language-related factors in reading disability. In D. Shankweiler & I. Liberman (Eds.), *Phonology and reading disability: Solving the reading puzzle* (pp. 91–131). Ann Arbor: University of Michigan Press.

Tunmer, W. E., Herriman, M. L., & Nesdale, A. R. (1988). Metalinguistic abilities and beginning reading. *Reading Research Quarterly, 23*, 134–158.

Tunmer, W. E., & Hoover, W. (1992). Cognitive and linguistic factors in learning to read. In P. Gough, L. Ehri, & R. Treiman (Eds.), *Reading acquisition* (pp. 175–214). Hillsdale, NJ: Erlbaum.

Tunmer, W. E., & Hoover, W. (1993). Components of variance models of language-related factors in reading disability: A conceptual overview. In R. M. Joshi & C. K. Leong (Eds.), *Reading disabilities: Diagnosis and component processes* (pp. 135–174). Dordrecht: Kluwer Academic Publ.

Tunmer, W. E., & Nesdale, A. R. (1985). Phonemic segmentation skill and beginning reading. *Journal of Educational Psychology, 77*, 417–427.

Tunmer, W. E., Nesdale, A. R., & Wright, A. D. (1987). Syntactic awareness and reading acquisition. *British Journal of Developmental Psychology, 5*, 25–34.

Vellutino, F. R. (1979). *Dyslexia: Theory and research.* Cambridge, MA: MIT Press.

Wadsworth, S. J., DeFries, J. D., Fulker, D. W., Olson, R. K., & Pennington, B. F. (1993). Reading performance and verbal short-term memory: A twin study of reciprocal causation. Submitted for publication.

Wagner, R. K., & Torgesen, J. K. (1987). The nature of phonological processing and its casual role in the acquisition of reading skills. *Psychological Bulletin, 101*(2), 192–212.

Wagner, R. K., Torgesen, J. K., Laughon, P., Simmons, K., & Rashotte, C. A. (1993). The development of young readers' phonological processing abilities. *Journal of Educational Psychology, 85*, 1–20.

Wechsler, D. (1974). *Examiner's manual: Wechsler Intelligence Scale for Children—Revised.* New York: The Psychological Corporation.

Willows, D., & Ryan, E. (1986). The development of grammatical sensitivity and its relationship to early reading achievement. *Reading Research Quarterly, 21*, 253–266.

Wise, B. W., & Olson, R. K. (1991). Remediating reading disabilities. In J. E. Obrzut & G. W. Hynd (Eds.), *Neuropsychological foundations of learning disabilities: Issues, methods, and practice* (pp. 631–658). San Diego, CA: Academic Press.

Wise, B. W., Olson, R. R., Anstett, M., Andrews, L., Terjak, M., Schneider, V., & Kostuch, J. (1989). Implementing a long-term computerized remedial reading program with synthetic speech feedback: Hardware, software, and real-world issues. *Behavior Research Methods, Instruments, & Computers, 21*, 173–180.

Wolf, M. (1984). Naming, reading, and the dyslexias: A longitudinal overview. *Annals of Dyslexia, 34*, 87–115.

CHAPTER 28

LEARNING A LANGUAGE LATE: SECOND LANGUAGE ACQUISITION IN ADULTS

KERRY KILBORN

I. INTRODUCTION

Most native speakers have a firm intuitive feeling for what constitutes fluency in their language. This is apparent to us as listeners when we perceive even the slightest shade of foreign accent in another's speech. Likewise, as speakers we are able to adjust our own speech downward to compensate for a nonnative listener's lack of fluency. In an effort to operationalize this clear intuition, numerous studies of second language (L2) acquisition from both applied and theoretical perspectives have employed a variety of methods in order to map out the stages and styles of L2 acquisition. An underlying assumption in virtually all studies has been that the end of the acquisition continuum is, in principle, "native-like fluency" (Hyltenstam, 1992).

At the same time, it is widely believed that adults cannot learn a second language to the same degree that children learn their first language (Krashen, 1978, 1982; Lenneberg, 1967; Lenneberg & Lenneberg, 1975; Scovel, 1969). That is, the level of fluency, however defined, which can be attained by an adult L2 speaker will never be equal to that of an adult L1 speaker. There is certainly some truth in this; in the vast majority of speakers, L2 performance differs in some obvious ways from L1 performance (e.g., perhaps most prominently in the area of phonology; see Flege & Hillenbrand, 1984; Flege, 1988). Many factors may contribute to the apparent inability of adults in this domain. Of these factors, the three which have received the most attention by researchers are (a) neuropsychological factors (e.g., the issue of plasticity, or variants on the notion of a "critical period" for native-like language acquisition; Lenneberg, 1967; Krashen, 1973; Krashen, 1975; Snow & Hoefnagel-Hohle, 1978; Albert & Obler, 1978; Colombo, 1982; Vaid, 1983, 1986; Johnson & Newport, 1989); (b) affective factors (e.g., adult–child or individual differences in the level of motivation brought into the acquisition process; Gardner & Lambert, 1972; Gardner, 1980); and (c) cognitive factors (e.g., an adult L2 learner may apply metalinguistic strategies which are not part of an L1 speaker's repertoire to solve some communication problem; these may eventually be incorporated into the L2 user's language processing system, leading to qualitative differences in the process of language acquisition, and hence differences in the final form of the target language; Krashen, 1982; Kilborn & Ito, 1989; MacWhinney, 1992; McDonald & Heilenman, 1992).

Despite much work, and notwithstanding our clear intuitions, a definition of fluency has proven elusive. One reason for this is that the performance characteristics which define fluency at any given point during acquisition may be, like bilingualism itself, a matter of degree. In this chapter we consider a psycholinguistic framework for the study of language use, the COMPETITION MODEL (Bates & MacWhinney, 1989), which until recently has not been associated with L2 acquisition. As we shall see, the competition model has features which make it especially well suited to deal with cross-linguistic variation in language processing between individuals who speak different languages, as well as within individuals who speak more than one language. We present a competition-style study of language processing in adults of varying fluency levels and discuss what the results can contribute to a performance definition of fluency in L2. First, it will be useful to review several proposals regarding the development of fluency in a second language. Historically, L2 acquisition has been addressed within the domains of theoretical and applied linguistics, with some limited treatment in experimental psycholinguistics. These often disparate fields, while sharing many common interests, seldom share the same biases and assumptions about what it means to be fluent in a language.

II. COMPETENCE VERSUS PERFORMANCE: L2 LEARNING UNDER REAL-WORLD CONSTRAINTS

The volume of applied work has far outstripped psycholinguistic approaches to L2 acquisition. While applied workers are well aware of performance problems, the most important models of L2 acquisition to date have depended on a competence-based linguistic theory. By this we mean that their theoretical underpinnings tend to characterize the language system in terms of the presence or absence of rules. Performance models, on the other hand, tend to emphasize mechanisms which map more or less directly onto actual behavior; because the inherent variability in language performance does not easily lend itself to explanation in terms of rules, these approaches have sought to account for such behavior in other ways (e.g., differential weighting of input cues, a concept shared by the competition model and various distributed or connectionist models of information processing). We return to the issues of performance and rules in L2 acquisition shortly. First, we briefly review several competence based L2 acquisition theories.

III. COMPETENCE-BASED THEORIES OF L2 ACQUISITION

A. The Role of Rules

Formal linguistics has long provided child language researchers with at least some of the theoretical tools necessary to ply their trade. Despite having to deal with frequent shifts in linguistic theory, L1 researchers have borrowed heavily from formal linguistics to describe the state of the language systems they observe. Not surprisingly, the descriptions are typically in terms of rules, which are defined for the present purposes as a statement of the conditions that require, in discrete and categorical terms, the presence or absence of a given linguistic form. As we shall see, a formal description of language acquisition may be possible in terms of rules, but rules may be a less useful construct in building a performance model that accounts for the developmental aspects as well as the steady-state features of first and second language acquisition.

Like the majority of models of L1 acquisition, most models of L2 acquisition also emphasize the role of rules in some form. Some models have incorporated theoretical linguistic constructs more or less directly. For example, L2 acquisition has served as a testing ground for the generality of universal grammar (Flynn, 1984; Adjemian & Liceras, 1984) and of government and binding (White, 1980). Other approaches to L2 acquisition have been somewhat more neutral regarding specific linguistic theories but nevertheless share with the more dogmatic approaches the view that a language is acquired (i.e., fluency is achieved) when the rules of the target language are internalized. Two of the most influential models of this type are the interlanguage hypothesis and the monitor theory.

B. The Interlanguage Hypothesis

One such model in which rules play a central role, the INTERLANGUAGE HYPOTHESIS (IL) (Selinker, 1972), has been and continues to be influential in both theoretical and applied linguistic areas. According to IL, a second language learner has at any given point in the acquisition process an interim-stage grammar. This interim, or interlanguage, grammar changes in response to incoming data, so that with continued exposure to sufficient and appropriate input, the interlanguage grammar, by a series of successive approximations, moves closer and closer to the standard grammar of the target language. The interlanguage grammar is described in terms of its component rules (which may be derived from the target language, transferred from the native language, or "invented" by the learner). At any one point in time, however, the L2 speaker's interlanguage grammar is relatively static. One of the advantages to this characterization of L2 acquisition is that it helps to account for the fact that many L2 learners seem to stop making much progress after some point (which varies from learner to learner) and never move beyond the final interlanguage grammar they acquire. In Selinker's terms, the interlanguage FOSSILIZES. We return to the issues raised in the interlanguage literature in the discussion section, where we point out several ways in which a probabilistic model of language processing can account in a somewhat different way for much of the same data.

C. The Monitor Theory

One approach which has emphasized different types of learning processes to achieve fluency is Krashen's MONITOR THEORY (Krashen, 1982). Although there are many other aspects to the theory, a critical part is the distinction between ACQUISITION and LEARNING, two separate processes which jointly contribute to developing competence in a second language (these terms are capitalized when they are used in the specialized sense of Krashen's theory). Acquisition, as defined by Krashen, is "similar, if not identical, to the way children develop ability in their first language" (Krashen, 1982, p. 10). Acquisition is characterized by a lack of conscious awareness of rule use in performance; it is responsible for the ability to "know" or "feel" that a sentence is grammatical or ungrammatical, without explicit reference to the rules of grammar.

The second process, which coexists with but is independent of Acquisition, is Learning. According to Krashen, Learning is responsible for the explicit knowledge of grammatical rules, an ability to state them, the conscious "knowing about" a language. The role of Learning is to edit, or monitor, the form of an utterance based on the explicit knowledge base at the speaker's disposal. The utility of the monitor, while somewhat restricted by constraints on real-time performance and on the amount of rule-based knowledge available to the L2 learner, is to provide items that have not yet been acquired. Ultimately, however, an adult's competence in a second language derives mainly from the unconscious internalization of rules; indeed, Krashen states that Acquisition "is responsible for our fluency" in a second language (Krashen, 1982, p. 15).

In a review of the monitor theory, McLaughlin (1978) takes issue with the Acquisition/Learning distinction, and the data cited in its support, that is at the heart of Krashen's theory. McLaughlin points out that "it is impossible to know whether subjects are actually operating on the basis of 'rule' or 'feel'" (McLaughlin, 1978, p. 317). Subjects may be able to state a rule on demand that they do not employ "consciously" under normal processing demands; conversely, subjects may claim to use a "feel" as the basis for a judgment because they are unsure how to express a rule they do use. In short, the distinction between Acquisition and Learning, both in theory and in practice, appears to be unclear and may be difficult to substantiate. As such, it does not provide an adequate account of the L2 acquisition (in the non-Krashen sense) process.

IV. PERFORMANCE-BASED APPROACHES TO L2 ACQUISITION

The notion of a rule may be too rigid to adequately capture a process as complex and dynamic as language acquisition. Rule-based models have two major shortcomings. First, they tend to be "all-or-nothing": either a rule is present or it is not. We are often faced with the problem of how to talk about having "some but not all" of a language, but it is decidedly unsatisfactory from a formal theoretical perspective to frame the issue as learning or losing "part" of a rule. A second language learner may use or comprehend a passive in the appropriate discourse context only about half the time, or usually but not always apply a vowel harmony rule correctly. But what position could half a passive, or 75% of a vowel harmony rule, hold in a learner's L2 grammar?

Second, rule-based models derive from theoretical accounts of single linguistic systems, considered one at a time. This is desirable from a linguistic point of view, but it may not account in a natural way for the real-time processing considerations that constrain actual language use, for a learner's incomplete L2 grammar, or for the possibility of interference and transfer between linguistic systems. If we choose to characterize the expanding language system of a second language learner in terms of rules, we risk over-emphasizing the aspects of language (and language-specific) performance which easily fit the rules we have adopted, and missing other, potentially crucial aspects of the acquisition process which do not conform to our rule system. In light of recent cross-linguistic findings, this is clearly the case with both aphasia and L1 acquisition, but it is perhaps most obvious in L2 acquisition (Bates & MacWhinney, 1981; Menn & Obler, 1990; Kilborn & Ito, 1989; Kilborn, 1991). For this reason, we will discuss the L2 learner in terms of a PARTIAL LANGUAGE SYSTEM, as compared with the complete L1 system in the same individual, or in native speakers of the target language. Unless language acquisition follows the lines of linguistic rules absolutely, we may be forced to reconsider the usefulness of formal linguistic rules in describing such cases; when behavior deviates from the rules, our explanations become necessarily ad hoc.

While more mainstream theoretical linguistic accounts hold much promise for the descriptive study of L2 acquisition, it has become apparent that the role of rules may prove elusive in accounting for actual language acquisition and use. As a result, several alternative approaches have been suggested. In most cases, the new models cite the need to bring any theory of L2 acquisition in line with more general considerations drawn from theories of learning and cognition. In this regard, one theme that has been articulated in several models has been the notion that the general principles that govern the development of proficiency in virtually any behavior also apply to language learning. Carroll (1981), Tarone (1982), and McLaughlin (1978), among others, separately raise the issue of the role of automatic versus controlled processes as it applies to second language acquisition. The notion of automatic versus controlled processing has been investigated by a number of researchers (Posner & Snyder, 1975; Schneider & Shiffrin, 1977; Shiffrin & Schneider, 1977). In general, automatic processes are said to focus attention and generate responses without conscious effort. Controlled processes, in contrast, require deliberate, conscious effort and generally take longer to carry out than automatic ones. Controlled processes can, through repeated exposure and practice, gradually become automatic. Thus, controlled and automatic processes need not be viewed as opposites; instead, they range on a continuum, from completely controlled at one extreme to completely automatic at the other.

Carroll (1981), noting the relevance of the automatic versus controlled distinction for L2 acquisition, argues that the same features which define automatic processes may account for the range of performance parameters observed during the progression from novice to advanced L2 speaker. Automatic and controlled processes are viewed here as well as endpoints on a performance continuum. The learner begins by making a conscious choice on the basis of knowledge about what would be an appropriate response in a certain situation. A response is reinforced or strengthened by success in achieving a communicative goal, and altered or refined when it does not produce the desired result. This process results in the response becoming "increasingly automatized, in the sense that it does not require the degree of conscious choice and attention that it does at first initiation" (Carroll, 1981, p. 465).

Tarone (1982) has related the automatic/controlled distinction to work on the variable role of attention in shaping the particular IL style. According to Tarone, styles range on a continuum from superordinate, in which attention is paid to the form of the language, to the vernacular, in which attention is directed at content and not at form. Tarone associates the superordinate style with controlled processing and the vernacular style with automatic processing.

The previous work contrasts with experimental psycholinguistic approaches as well as some applied approaches to L2, which have focused on aspects of language processing and acquisition which do not necessarily speak to issues in theoretical linguistics. These aspects include lexical processes in bilinguals (e.g., one lexicon or two? central or separate conceptual stores?), perceptual processes (e.g., can an L2 learner realign voice onset time boundaries?), neuropsychological processes (e.g., is there differential hemispheric involvement across languages?), and sentence and discourse processing features in L2 (e.g., does the L2 speaker use the same information sources, and to the same degree, as L1 speakers in integrating input; under what conditions does interference, or transfer, from L1 inhibit, or facilitate, native-like performance in L2?). While the parameters of L2 use under restricted conditions take center stage here, there is often little or no attempt to relate findings to a more general model of language performance.

Although there are some clear advantages to rule-based approaches to these issues, there is an inherent trade-off: such proposals have overall coherence and an important descriptive role, but they do not correspond to the facts of variability in natural languages and lack explanatory power. Previous psycholinguistic approaches account for aspects of variability in a piecemeal fashion but lack overall coherence. The solution: We must look for a comprehensive performance model that can subsume a wide range of performance facts.

The studies described below are squarely in the performance tradition: We are working here with a model that is designed to test performance parameters of language use, in contrast with competence-oriented models. At the same time, we are trying to move the study of first and second language performance into a more unified psycholinguistic framework. To this end, we have adapted the competition model to the study of second language learning. The competition model is a general model of sentence processing (in both comprehension and production) which has been applied to the study of first language learning, cross-linguistic differences in adult sentence processing, and language breakdown in aphasia. For our purposes, the model makes specific, testable claims about second language development (Bates & MacWhinney, 1981, 1989; MacWhinney, 1992) and language transfer (McDonald & Heilenman, 1992; Liu, Bates, & Li, 1992). In addition, a number of studies have implemented tasks drawn from the competition model which provide a measure of language processing as it takes place in real time. Below we discuss several representative studies of second language learning and language transfer assessed experimentally within the competition model framework. First, however, we turn to an overview of the model.

V. THE COMPETITION MODEL

In contrast with (by now) more traditional accounts of language acquisition, the competition model grew out of a research program on first language learning in which importance was attached not only to the linguistic forms that are acquired, but also to the cognitive constraints that govern learning and using forms for communication in any natural language (Bates & MacWhinney, 1982, 1989; MacWhinney, 1987b). The competition model derives from a consideration of the functional aspects of mapping linguistic forms to underlying meaning. Since this is a performance model, which attempts to describe real-world language behavior, the resolution of form–function relations during processing must take place in real time. The model adheres to functionalist tenets in that form–function mappings are made as directly as possible. However, the strong functionalist position which posits one form to one function is rejected in favor of a multiplicity of form–function mappings: Natural languages rarely make use of one-to-one mappings; rather, a single form can map onto many functions, and a single function can map onto several forms (see also Cooreman & Kilborn, 1991). The probabilistic feature of the competition model leads to the treatment of statistical tendencies and obligatory rules as quantitatively rather than qualitatively different. This is important because relations between surface forms and functions can be described in terms of strength or degree of interaction. Particular instances within the system of many-to-many form–function mappings in a given language are assigned weights in this model. This is done according to the statistical distributions of certain constructions, e.g., how often and how reliably a given form is used to perform a given function. The sources of information a listener uses to decide which function is meant to be expressed by a given form are referred to as CUES. The usefulness of a particular cue is determined by a combination of factors, including how reliable a cue is (i.e., whether it always maps the same forms to the same functions), and how often the cue is available (e.g., animacy may be heavily depended on when an animate–inanimate distinction is present, as in *The boy broke the window,* but not in *The ball broke the window*).

In a cross-linguistic study of sentence interpretation, MacWhinney, Bates, and Kliegl (1984) presented native speakers of English, German, and Italian with simple transitive sentences in their native language in which the contrasts of word order, noun–verb agreement, animacy, and contrastive stress were varied systematically (case markers are perhaps the single most important cue to thematic roles in German; this factor was held neutral here in order to allow more direct comparison with English and Italian, which do not make similar case distinctions). Subjects were asked to decide for each sentence which noun was the actor, or grammatical subject. The results showed that Americans relied strongly on word order, interpreting NVN strings as SVO, NNV as OSV, and VNN as VOS. Agreement, animacy, and stress also reached significance in English, but these effects accounted for only a minute portion of the variance overall. These findings replicate earlier studies with English speakers reported in Bates, McNew, MacWhinney, Devescovi, and Smith (1982). In contrast with English, German speakers tended to rely much more on animacy and agreement contrasts; word order played little or no role in the sentence interpretation strategies of the German subjects. The results in general support the predictions of the competition model, derived from language-specific cue validity and cue reliability considerations.

A. Across Language, within Subjects: Language Processing in Bilinguals

Viewed from a bilingual perspective, the competition model approach has a number of implications when we compare sentence processing within individuals who speak two languages. As we noted earlier, L1 strategies may strongly interfere or interact with appropriate L2 strategies. The competition model allows a test of at least four hypotheses of bilingual sentence processing (see also Kilborn, 1987; Kilborn & Ito, 1989; MacWhinney, 1992; Liu, Bates, & Li, 1992).

1. *Differentiation.* Strategies appropriate for the second language (L2) are acquired and applied exclusively in the context of L2 (i.e., the bilingual behaves essentially as a monolingual in each language).
2. *Forward transfer.* Strategies appropriate for the first language (L1) are applied, perhaps inappropriately, to the second language (L2).
3. *Backward transfer.* L2 strategies that have been learned and applied to L2 come to supplant L1 strategies.
4. *Amalgamation.* New strategies may be adopted in the course of L2 learning and become assimilated into one amalgamated set that is applied to processing in both languages.

These are not mutually exclusive; each of these possibilities might be true at some point in the process of acquiring a second language. Furthermore, these different hypotheses point out that a single level progression from beginner to fluent bilingual is only one of several possible courses for L2 acquisition to follow. If L2 learning turns out to be more or less unidimensional, it would be rather convenient for the model we have adopted here. If, on the other hand, there are many routes to fluency, any model will have to be considerably more complex than the competition model in its current form, whether rules are incorporated in some form or not. In any case, the competition model provides a formalism for describing what it means to be "between languages"; rule-based models, which derive most of their explanatory power not from real-time processing considerations but from language-specific theoretical linguistic accounts, have a harder time accommodating such facts.

The implications of the competition model for bilingualism have been tested now in a number of studies. In the first application of the competition model paradigm to bilingual sentence processing, Bates and MacWhinney (1981) found that all but one of the native Italian and German speakers who performed a sentence interpretation task in English relied on cues appropriate to their native language (i.e., agreement in Italian, and animacy and agreement in German). One German subject adopted English-appropriate strategies for English.

Following this lead, other researchers have applied the competition model to studies of bilingual speakers of a wide variety of languages, including various combinations of English, Chinese, French, Dutch, German, Japanese, Tagolog, Spanish, Serbo-Croatian, and Hindi (Miao, 1981; Wulfeck, Juarez, Bates, & Kilborn, 1986; MacWhinney, 1987a; Gass, 1987; Harrington, 1987; Kilborn & Cooreman, 1987; McDonald, 1987; Kilborn & Ito, 1989; MacWhinney, 1992; Vaid & Pandit, 1991). Most studies have reported support for forward transfer and, to a lesser extent, amalgamation of strategies. Kilborn (1989) showed that forward transfer from German as L1 to English as L2 was reflected not only in the distribution of cue weightings, but also in the temporal pattern of on-line sentence processing. Backward transfer—difficulty in maintaining L1 processing strategies—was first reported for Chinese–English bilinguals first exposed to L2 either before age 4 or between 12 and 16 years (Liu, Bates & Li, 1992).

In addition to exploring the forms of transfer, a few studies have investigated the competition model's prediction of the gradual emergence of conventions or rules, via a continuous increase in the strength or DETERMINING FORCE (MacWhinney, Bates, & Kliegl, 1984) of statistical form–function assignments. The implication for L2 acquisition is a strong one: The application of cues in form–function mapping in L2 ought to approach distributionally predicted levels as fluency in L2 increases. McDonald and Heilenman (1992) carried out a cross-sectional study of the development of proficiency in French under formal teaching by native English speakers. They found that learners first dropped their English word order strategy in favor of a French-appropriate word order strategy, later elaborating this by the addition of an appropriate verb agreement strategy. A similar pattern of development was reported for Japanese learners of English and American learners of Japanese (Kilborn & Ito, 1989). We turn now to a detailed study of sentence processing in which a competition model paradigm is applied to investigate patterns of transfer and the development of proficiency in a second language.

B. Implications of the Competition Model for German–English Bilinguals

The bilingual subjects in the current study are native speakers of German whose second language is English. The competition model allows some specific predictions about language processing in each language and about the potential for transfer of processing strategies from one language to the other. Before presenting the findings from the current experiment, a brief survey of some structural characteristics of English vis-à-vis German will suggest a source for the language differences to be reported here.

Viewed from a cross-linguistic perspective, the competition model approach to language processing has a number of implications when we compare German and English. On the surface, German and English, which are diachronically related Germanic languages, have many features in common. The two languages share many cognates, both locate articles and other modifiers prenominally, and the canonical word order for simple, active declarative sentences is Subject–Verb–Object (SVO). However, some important differences exist between German and English, differences which, depending on what kind of model we choose to explain processing behavior, could lead to quite different predictions about how the two languages are processed. One such difference is the richer morphological system in German, which, in contrast to English, provides a broadly available and regular set of markings, mainly on verbs and articles, for tense, number agreement, and case. Another such difference involves word order. In English, the unmarked word order in both main and subordinate clauses is SVO. In German, SVO applies to main clauses, but subordinate clauses receive SOV (Koster, 1975). There is not general agreement as to which order is more basic in German (Bierwisch, 1963; Bach, 1968; Ross, 1970).

If language processing is an essentially rule-based behavior, reflecting the same type of rules linguists use to describe the range of forms and their usage in a language, then we would not expect to find a difference between German and English on SVO forms, which map onto the same functions in each language. However, the competition model predicts that processing in a particular language will be shaped by the distribution of form–function mappings in that language. In other words, sentence interpretation strategies do not reflect the application of rules per se; rather, an incoming sentence form activates all the potential interpretations which are, to a greater or lesser degree, compatible with the input. The greater the degree of compatibility, the more a particular form is activated, and eventually only one interpretation wins. If the presence of partially overlapping structures (e.g., SOV and SVO word orders in German) in a language can impinge on sentence interpretation, then we ought to find that German, which allows much more word order variation than English, differs from English on this dimension. Specifically, German listeners should "trust" word order configurations as cues to meaning less than their English counterparts do. At the same time, German listeners may also place more "trust" in verb morphology, a source of information that is considerably more reliable than verb morphology in English.

VI. General Methodological Considerations

The experiment presented here investigates the contribution of three primary cues, or information sources—word order, animacy, and verb agreement—to the process of sentence comprehension. The task is to select the actor in sentences which contain various COALITIONS and COMPETITIONS among a set of cues to sentence meaning. Thus, the subject must decide in the face of sometimes conflicting information which cues to actively attend to and which to relegate to less importance. The nonnative subjects performed each task twice: once in L2 and once in L1. This provides an important within-subject comparison, allowing each subject to serve as his or her own control across languages.

A. Subjects

1. German–English Bilingual Subjects

Fifteen native speakers of German were assigned to two groups, an Advanced L2 group ($N = 7$) and a Novice L2 group ($N = 8$), according to performance on a battery of fluency measures. A language proficiency questionnaire was used in conjunction with an interview to determine the fluency level of each bilingual subject in English. The written questionnaire permitted the subject to give a self rating of L2 proficiency, a measure that has been found to correlate highly with objective tests (Fishman & Cooper, 1969; Kilborn, 1987; Liu, Bates, and Li, 1992). Each L2 subject performed each of the experimental tasks in English and in German. Subjects were randomly assigned to language order groups (independent of fluency), so that half performed the task in English first, and half in German.

2. Monolingual English Subjects

One group of 20 monolingual English speakers performed the same English language components of the tasks as the bilingual subjects. As native speakers of English, performance on the sentence interpretation task by this group ought to be near optimum levels, and will thus provide a baseline for cross-group comparisons. This group represents the standard for the development of skill in language processing tasks.

B. Design/Materials

Subjects listened to sentences consisting of two nouns and one verb. The task was simply to choose the actor in each case ("who did it"). The independent factors varied along the following dimensions.

1. *Word order* (NVN, NNV, VNN)
2. *Animacy* (both nouns animate; first animate/second inanimate; first inanimate/second animate; both inanimate)
3. *Verb agreement morphology* (morphological marking favors the first noun only; the second noun only; both; or neither)
4. *Group* (monolingual English; bilingual German–English; *language* is treated as a separate factor within the bilingual group)

Five sets of stimuli were constructed around five different verbs, which were combined to form short sentences with two different animate nouns and two different inanimate nouns within each set. Each sentence consisted of exactly two article–noun units plus a verb. The verbs were always in the third person singular. When a noun was also singular, it agreed in number with the verb; when a noun was plural, it violated the agreement constraint. All possible combinations of two nouns and one verb were presented, resulting in 48 (3 word orders × 4 Agreement × 4 Animacy) sentences per set, for a total of 240 sentences.

A matching set of German stimuli was also constructed in the same manner for use in the second language condition with the L2 speakers. The German material was matched to the English set in terms of word frequency and length; however, translation equivalents were not used in order to avoid spurious effects of translation during performance of the task. We should also note that the nouns selected in German were restricted to the feminine gender. This renders the case marking cue ambiguous, since feminine nouns receive the identical definite article form *die* in both nominative and accusative cases. The same form is also used for nominative and accusative plurals. Thus, articles in German provided neither case nor number information. However, it is unlikely that this will produce "unnatural" effects, since the same situation occurs regularly in normal usage of German.[1] Sample sentences are provided in Table I.

C. Procedure

Subjects were instructed in the language of the current test to listen carefully to each sentence and to decide as quickly as possible which of the two nouns was the actor or grammatical subject in that sentence (the order of the words "actor" and "grammatical subject" were counterbalanced across subjects in order to offset any potential bias that one form of instruction may have induced). Subjects responded by saying out loud the name of the noun chosen as the actor or grammatical subject. For example, if the sentence *The trees the boy kicks* is presented, the subject may simply say *The boy*. Each subject received a total of 240 digitally recorded sentences. No two sentences were ever repeated; however, within each set of 240 sentences, there were exactly 5 repetitions of each sentence type (i.e., there were 5 sentences of the type NNV, FirstNounAgrees, IA, but the sentence *The tree the boys kicks* appeared only once).

It is important to note that there are no right or wrong answers in this paradigm, so that "percent correct" is meaningless. The scoring procedure developed in other studies of this type (Bates & MacWhinney, 1989), has been adopted here. In this procedure, a score of 1 is assigned when a subject chooses the first noun of a sequence and 0 when the second noun is chosen. The values for all the tokens of each different sentence type are averaged, and the average is used as raw data for statistical analysis. These scores have been converted to "percent first noun choice" in the report below. A score near 100% means that the first noun is nearly always chosen as the grammatical subject, a score near 0% means that the second noun is nearly always chosen, and a score near 50% means approximately equal choice of first and second nouns in a particular sentence type, or random performance.

The data are presented in two parts. We begin in Part 1 by looking at sentence interpretation strategies in English according to the factor Group (English monolinguals compared with German–English bilinguals), and within the bilingual group alone, according to the factor Language [German (L1) compared with English (L2)]. In Part 2, we present the results of a further analysis within the bilingual group in which subjects were assigned to either Advanced or Novice subgroups according to scores on an independent fluency rating scale.

---

[1] Varying the word order, agreement, and animacy conditions results in some combinations which are to a lesser or greater degree marked or ungrammatical. For example, sentences in which verb agreement favors neither noun (i.e., both nouns are plural and the verb is singular, as in *The teachers kicks the baskets*) are ungrammatical regardless of word order or animacy. This situation is not entirely unnatural. Jordans (1986) has documented an extensive range of case errors in written (e.g., newspapers) as well as spoken German. These by no means render an utterance uninterpretable and underscore the need for natural language processing to be flexible and tolerant of "noise" in the signal, whether in the medium or form of the message. For a more extensive response to the issue of ungrammaticality, see Bates & MacWhinney (1989).

TABLE I
Sample Sentences in Interpretation Task

Sentence	Word order	Animacy favors	Verb agreement favors
The waitress pushes the cowboys.	NVN	both nouns	first noun
The telephones pushes the cowboy.	NVN	second noun	second noun
Kisses the table the apple.	VNN	neither	both nouns
The baskets the teacher kicks.	NNV	second noun	second noun
Die Frau greift die Lampe.	NVN	first noun	both nouns
Greift die Decke die Lampen.	VNN	neither	first noun
Die Katzen reibt die Brille.	NVN	first noun	second noun
Die Tassen die Omas schiebt.	NNV	second noun	neither

D. Results: Part 1

We present the results according to the main factors Word Order, Verb Agreement, and Animacy. In each case we focus on a single cue, collapsing across other cues. We begin by presenting the findings from monolingual English speakers together with those from the German subjects in both English (L2) and German (L1). This allows us to compare the effects of each cue to sentence meaning directly between groups and, within the bilingual group, between languages. The effects discussed below have been analyzed statistically, but in the interest of brevity the statistical results are omitted. For a more detailed consideration of these analyses, see Kilborn (1987, 1989).

1. Word Order

Beginning with the Word Order factor, observe in Figure 1 that monolingual English speakers choose the first noun in NVN strings—that is, they make an SVO interpretation—more than 90% of the time. This is consistent with findings from a multitude of sentence processing experiments of this type carried out in English. Also consistent with previous findings is the strong preference by native English speakers for the second noun in noncanonical NNV and VNN strings.

Turning to the German group, a different pattern emerges in their native German. First noun choice in NVN strings is 61%, dropping to about 53% and 48% for NNV and VNN strings, respectively. It is immediately apparent that, while some preference for the first noun in NVN sentences is expressed, the overall effect of word order in German as L1 is quite ameliorated compared with the same cue in English as L1.

The same figure shows the results for the word order cue in English as a second language. A mild first noun preference emerges in NVN sentences, where an SVO interpretation is made 70% of the time. This is intermediate between German and the pattern observed in English monolinguals, perhaps indicating that these second language learners have begun to move away from essentially neglecting word order as a cue to thematic role toward some reliance on word order. In noncanonical strings, the choice rate in English VNN strings is unchanged from that in German, while in NNV sentences there is again movement in the direction of English monolinguals. Overall, the pattern of

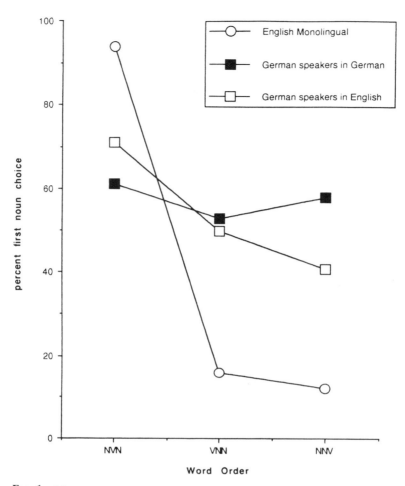

FIG. 1 Means of percent first noun choice on the Word Order factor for English monolinguals in English, and for German–English bilinguals in English and in German.

noun choice data indicates that German subjects make little or no use of word order as a cue to sentence meaning in German. In English, however, there is evidence that the bilingual subjects as a group have developed some sensitivity to the importance of the word order cue, as observed in the significant shift toward the pattern of performance of monolingual English speakers.

2. Verb Agreement

Figure 2 illustrates the effect of verb agreement morphology. Monolingual English speakers make almost no use of this cue to sentence meaning, showing only a marginal difference in choice rate between the two conditions in which a clear distinction was available (46% when agreement favors only the first noun versus 36% when the morphological cue favors only the second noun). As we saw above, monolingual English speakers make strong, consistent use

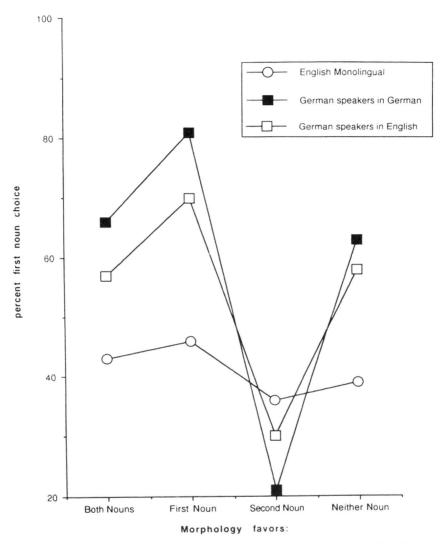

FIG. 2   Means of percent first noun choice on the Verb Agreement factor for English monolinguals in English, and for German–English bilinguals in English and in German.

of word order. In competition with verb agreement, the word order cue is the clear winner.

In stark contrast, German speakers in German choose the noun which agrees in its morphological marking with the verb about 80% of the time, regardless of order. Thus, in the sentences *The dogs bites the waiter* or *The waiter the dogs bites,* German speakers in German are likely to select *The waiter* as actor, favoring the agreement cue; English speakers, relying heavily on order information, are much more likely to choose *The dogs.* This is a clear language difference in processing, based on the relative validity of morphological cues as opposed to word order cues in German and English. In competition model terms, morphological information is more heavily weighted than order information in German.

Turning to the performance of native Germans in English, we see that the verb agreement cue plays a similar processing role in L2 as in L1. The noun which agrees in number with the verb in English is chosen as the actor 70% of the time, regardless of order. In light of the findings in German, this is an instance of forward transfer of L1 strategies into L2 processing.

3. Animacy

The effect of the animacy cue is illustrated in Figure 3. As with verb agreement, monolingual English speakers made essentially no use of semantic cues. A marginal difference is observed between the conditions where a distinction obtains (45% choice in A–I, 37% in I–A).

Looking again at the German speakers in German, we see that animacy is clearly an important cue to sentence interpretation. Where both an animate and an inanimate noun were present, the animate was chosen in more than two-thirds of all cases.

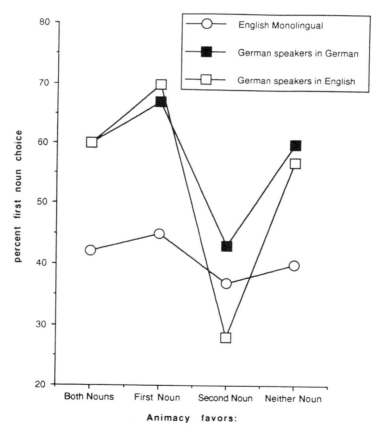

FIG. 3 Means of percent first noun choice on the Animacy factor for English monolinguals in English, and for German–English bilinguals and in German.

The same pattern is observed in the performance of the German speakers in English. Animacy proved to be as strong a cue in L2 as in L1, determining choice in the large majority of cases where a distinction was available. This is another instance of transfer of an L1 strategy into L2 processing.

In the introduction, we outlined four hypotheses suggested by the competition model for bilingual sentence processing. Very briefly, these are: (a) first language (L1) strategies may be applied to both languages; (b) a second set of strategies is acquired and applied exclusively in the context of L2 (i.e., the bilingual behaves essentially as a monolingual in each language; (c) L2 strategies are not only applied to L2 but may even supplant L1 strategies; and (d) new strategies may be adopted in the course of L2 learning and become assimilated into one amalgamated set that is applied to processing both languages.

The data presented here provide clear evidence of transfer of L1 strategies into L2 processing. We have seen that native speakers of English depend heavily on word order cues in sentence processing, almost to the exclusion of other potential cues. In contrast, German speakers make extensive use of agreement and animacy cues in their native language, and virtually none of word order. With regard to sentence processing in English by native German speakers, the current study provides rather strong support for hypothesis (a) Verb agreement and animacy cues—the strongest cues in German—were the consistent winners in English as a second language. It appears from this that L1 cues—agreement and animacy in German—have been transferred directly into English sentence processing. In other words, the same strategies that German speakers apply in German carried over into their second language. The competition model handles this direct transfer without problem: The L2 speaker continues to rely on cue weights assigned to various form–function mappings in L1.

We also found that, in addition to agreement and animacy cues, L2 subjects made some use of word order cues in English. At first we may assume that hypothesis (b) has received some support as well—L2 strategies are acquired and used only in the context of L2. However, if L2 strategies are adopted straightforwardly, then the cue weight assigned to word order ought to reflect the form–function mapping of the word order cue in English. To a degree this was true. First noun choice rate was highest overall in NVN sentences, though still substantially lower than in English as L1. However, the characteristic second noun strategy in English did not appear in L2 speakers; actor assignment fell into a random range in VNN and NNV sentences. However, when the results in English do diverge from those in German, it is in the direction predicted by monolingual English findings. This kind of transfer is also handled easily by the competition model. The partial use of word order in English by L2 speakers may be evidence of a system in transition: The L2 learners may realize that word order must be assigned a different cue weight in English to make up for an impoverished morphological system.

In summary, we found that native speakers of German applied cue weightings that are appropriate in German to processing in English as L2. The most parsimonious explanation is that German processing strategies, in which verb agreement and animacy are the dominant cues, transfer more or less directly to L2. We also found evidence that these L2 speakers exhibit some sensitivity to the dominant cue in English, namely word order. However, the word order cue, while shifting in the direction predicted by monolingual English speakers, maintains an in-between status in the L2 grammar of these subjects, both in terms of the degree of reliance among different word order patterns, and also its relative weight vis-à-vis other cues.

Below we return to what it means to be between languages when we consider how changes in sentence processing strategies may provide a diagnostic for the development of fluency in L2.

E. Achieving Fluency

So-called "balanced" bilinguals have been the focus of much research aimed at uncovering the cognitive factors associated with second language acquisition. Segalowitz and his colleagues (Favreau & Segalowitz, 1982, 1983; Segalowitz, 1986) have suggested the use of the term BALANCED to imply that the bilingual is equally proficient in both languages in all domains of language use. However, as Segalowitz has pointed out, this construct may not be particularly useful in practice, since the truly balanced bilingual may be nearly nonexistent. In a series of studies involving FLUENT BILINGUALS (this term emphasizes that equivalent levels of proficiency are apparent only under normal communication conditions), Segalowitz has shown that in certain language-related tasks (e.g., speeded reading, retrieval from semantic memory), L2 performance falls behind L1. The performance differences in this case were attributed to between-language differences in the level of automatic processing.

If balanced bilingualism is seldom, if ever, attained, then we are forced to consider bilingualism to be a matter of degree, for both the beginning second language learner as well as the most fluent bilingual. This makes it all the more imperative that we arrive at a performance-based definition of fluency. In the following section we explore one approach to this question by examining the performance of our bilingual subjects in the previous experiment in terms of the range of L2 proficiency levels represented.

In the following analysis, the German–English bilingual subjects were assigned to an Advanced or a Novice group on the basis of scores on a standardized language questionnaire (Kilborn, 1987; Liu, Bates, & Li, 1992). The relevant parts of the questionnaire included two objective measures of language exposure, (a) number of years of formal English training (German school curriculum is fairly uniform in this regard), and (b) number of years of informal exposure to English (i.e., extended residence in an English-speaking country); and one subjective measure consisting of self-ratings on a 7 point fluency scale of spoken and written comprehension and production in English. These scores were totaled for each subject, giving a single, unweighted score which served as an operationally defined fluency index. A median split divided subjects into two groups: The Novice group consisted of subjects with the eight lowest overall scores, while the Advanced group consisted of subjects receiving the seven highest scores. This group factor was then used as a blocking variable in a between-subjects analysis of the data from the comprehension task.

F. Results: Part 2

As in Part 1, the results in this section are presented according to the main factors of Word Order, Verb Agreement, and Animacy. All the results reported are from the same sentence interpretation task, reanalyzed with Fluency (Advanced vs. Novice) used as a between-subjects factor. The figures below include the results from the English monolingual group for comparison.

1. Word Order

Figure 4 shows a significant Group by Word Order interaction: the Advanced group made more consistent use of word order as a cue to sentence meaning in English than Novices. In NVN, the canonical word order in English, and in NNV the Advanced group leans in the direction of monolingual English speakers. The weak first noun preference in VNN, also observed in German, persists in English.[2]

The effect of the word order cue in the Novice group is, by contrast, nearly flat, showing a weak first noun preference across the board. In Part 1, we suggested that the partial adoption of word order as a cue to sentence meaning in English was evidence for an emerging sensitivity to this type of structural information in L2. We now see that most of this effect is due to performance by the most fluent L2 speakers.

2. Verb Agreement

The Group by Verb Agreement interaction is shown in Figure 5. The use of verb agreement as a cue to sentence meaning in English was much more pronounced in the Novice than in the Advanced group. When a clear morphological distinction was available—i.e., when only the first or the second noun agreed in number with the verb—Novice bilinguals used this information more than 90% of the time. This is an instance of forward transfer: The Novice group is transferring a strategy used in German to sentence processing in English as L2.

Advanced bilinguals, in contrast with the Novice group in English, do not rely heavily on morphological cues in English. While the greatest difference in first noun choice is still between the maximally distinct conditions, that difference is less than 20 percentage points. Their performance closely resembles that of the monolingual English speakers. While some differences from the English monolinguals still persist that could be traced to forward transfer, the Advanced group appears to be approaching differentiation in their application of language-specific processing strategies in their two languages.

3. Animacy

There was also a significant Group by Animacy interaction, shown in Figure 6. The Novice group made consistent use of animacy cues in English, choosing the animate noun in animate–inanimate or inanimate–animate pairings more

---

[2] With regard to English VNN sentences, however, very little movement in the direction of English monolinguals was observed across groups. A structural characteristic of German provides a hint for why this difference should be so prominent. In particular, one frequent word order variant in German is VSO for question forms (e.g., *Trifft der Junge den Ball?* 'Kicks the boy the ball?'). The relative strength of the German question form VSO may win in competition with other potential interpretations, including English VOS. In English, VSO is not a possible interpretation. (However, the English translation 'Did the boy kick the ball?' offers a partial VSO structure via the mechanism by auxiliary-fronting, as in (V-*did*) S–V–O. Despite this, these data suggest that the main verb plays the most important role in the development of word order strategies.)

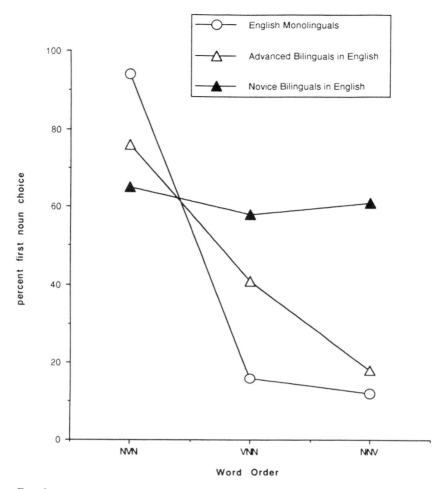

FIG. 4   Means of percent first noun choice on the Word Order factof for English monolinguals in English, and for Advanced and Novice German–English bilinguals in English.

than 80% of the time. As with the Verb Agreement cue, performance by the Novice group on the Animacy cue parallels their own performance in German. Novice bilinguals are continuing to rely consistently and in approximately the same measure on the same cues to processing in English as L2 as they do in their native German.

In comparison, the Advanced group did not depend on Animacy to nearly the same extent in English as did the Novice bilinguals. Here again, performance by the Advanced bilingual subjects in L2 closely paralleled that of the English monolinguals. This is additional evidence that the constellation of cue weights applied to sentence comprehension in L1 has been more or less successfully suspended in favor of new weightings appropriate to L2.

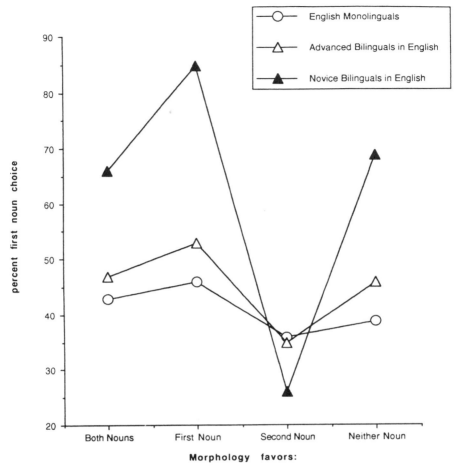

FIG. 5   Means of percent first noun choice on the Verb Agreement factor for English monolinguals in English, and for Advanced and Novice German–English bilinguals in English.

G. Summary

Taken together, these results indicate that cues which were found to play a much more central role in German for all these subjects, namely, verb agreement and animacy, reliably carry over into English for the Novice bilinguals. Conversely, the Advanced bilinguals were found to make much less use of cues appropriate to German processing, relying instead on word order as a cue to meaning in English. However, their use of word order differs somewhat from the way monolinguals use the same cue. First noun choice rate in NVN sentences, while higher than in Novice bilinguals, did not quite reach the same level found in monolinguals. And the characteristic second noun strategy, while emerging quite nicely on NNV strings, was not observed on VNN orders. We suggested above that this may be accounted for by the relative strength of the

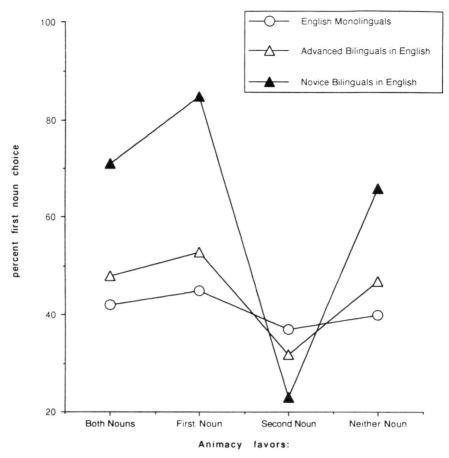

FIG. 6 Means of percent first noun choice on the Animacy factor for English monolinguals in English, and for Advanced and Novice German–English bilinguals in English.

question form VSO in German. This was, incidentally, the reason several subjects gave for their responses on VNN trials when asked after the testing session was finished.

VII. DISCUSSION

Grosjean and Soares (1986) outlined the issue of language interaction and the role of a language switch mechanism in explaining how bilinguals are able to process mixed language input with no apparent decrement in performance. Grosjean proposed that the two language systems are simultaneously active in a bilingual speech mode, and their various components interact to allow smooth integration. By contrast, this interaction is held to a minimum in a monolingual speech mode; the bilingual does his best to turn off the nonrelevant language, presumably via some language switch or monitor mechanism (Macnamara and Kushnir, 1971). As stated by Grosjean, "the question of interest is how the language processing of bilinguals in the monolingual speech mode differs from that of monolinguals given this residual activation of the other language" (1986, p. 146). The research reported here deals with processing in L1 and L2 in a monolingual mode.

We have presented data which suggest what may constitute that "residual activation of the other language" and what its consequences may be for language processing in general. We have shown that a psycholinguistic approach to second language acquisition can provide insight into the sort of language transfer alluded to in Grosjean's question, and more generally, into some performance aspects of the process of becoming fluent.

While the data thus far are generally supportive of the competition model, several challenges do arise. One is persistence: Bates and MacWhinney (1981) report that one native German with many years of exposure to English still interpreted English sentences on the basis of form–function mappings appropriate to German. An essentially cue-driven system ought to take advantage of the often vast differences across languages, allowing the L2 learner to eventually tune his processing system to the language at hand.

A second problem for the competition model is the issue of individual differences. Vaid and Pandit (1991), Wulfeck et al. (1986), Kilborn and Cooreman (1987), and Harrington (1987) all report consistent subgroup differentiation within their bilingual subjects: It appears that when alternative processing strategies are open to subjects, they may simply choose one of several possibilities and stay with that one. The repeated finding of similar subgroup differentiation in the context of even typologically different languages suggests that this effect is not accidental or due to language-specific factors. Moreover, it sounds a cautionary note by indicating that individual differences may be an important factor in any language processing study, and especially in within-subject comparisons of bilingual language use. Liu, Bates, and Li (1992) investigated a broad range of factors that could contribute to differing transfer effects within a cross section of subjects of varying fluency levels. They documented different forms of transfer and related these to the age at which learners were first exposed to a second language. They found that novice bilinguals (both Chinese–English and English–Chinese), defined in much the same way as in the present chapter, displayed forward transfer. Advanced bilinguals who first learned English between 6 and 10 years displayed differentiation; and backward transfer was found in Chinese exposed to English before 4 years of age.

A third problem for the competition model has to do with the notion of transfer from L1 to L2. While the transfer phenomena observed here and in Liu, Bates, and Li (1992) are accounted for in a straightforward way, other findings provide a challenge. Kilborn and Ito (1989), in a study involving native English speakers learning Japanese, report that transfer of another, less obvious kind may influence L2 processing. The canonical word order in Japanese is SOV. The competition model predicts that if an English-based word order strategy invades Japanese, it ought to result in OSV interpretations of NNV strings, as in English. However, contrary to the competition model notion of transfer, native English speakers interpreted NNV strings in Japanese as SOV at a much higher level than native Japanese, whereas native Japanese speakers did not show a preference based on word order, relying instead on animacy. Simple transfer of a particular word order bias cannot account for this finding. What transfer may consist of in this case is the top-down application of a global word order strategy from L1, producing an almost rule-like effect: Rather than a language-specific SVO bias, what invades is a higher level strategic bias to pay attention to word order as a cue to sentence meaning.

One goal of this research was to map out differences between novice and advanced L2 speakers. The ability to decode and integrate different sources of linguistic information was identified as a potentially rich domain in which to explore the development of fluency. For example, it was suggested earlier that some types of information may present more problems to the novice than others, resulting in differential rates of acquisition of various components. We now know that, while this is generally true, it is more accurate to say that the interplay of different information sources as they come on line is one crucial variable in second language performance. We know from the comprehension experiment presented here that the balance between L1 and L2 cue weightings applied to processing in L2 shifts gradually in the direction of L1 norms with exposure. The findings reported by Liu, Bates, and Li (1992) suggest that the ways in which the balance shifts are linked in complicated ways to age of first exposure.

VIII. L1 AND L2: A DIFFERENCE IN KIND?

The "balanced" bilingual, rare though he or she may be, is assumed to have achieved "native-like fluency." Rigorously controlled experimental approaches to language learning can contribute to a better understanding of what it means to have "part" of a language, and to achieve fluency. But since we have little more than our clear intuitions—and a modicum of research—to help us define fluency, we are left with a question. One of the fundamental issues in second language acquisition research is whether the paths taken by the learner during the course of L1 vis-à-vis L2 acquisition are different, or in important ways the same. A growing body of cross-linguistic research has shown that different languages are characterized by different processing strategies. The research presented and cited extensively here suggests that, in individuals who speak more than one language, processing strategies in L2 differ from monolingual strategies as a function of the individual's level of fluency. As we pointed out earlier, such differences may have a multitude of causes; we have explored one of these factors here, namely the presence and persistence of a well-established processing bias, begun when cue settings were first established in L1. It is possible that vastly different mechanisms are at work in L1 versus L2 acquisition. However, the competition model suggests another possibility. L1 and L2 acquisition may differ not so much in terms of their underlying properties as they do in the emphasis placed on the imperativeness of making complete and unambiguous form–function assignments. The strength, and later persistence, of L1 cues may derive from principles of OPTIMALITY, which demand that the L1 learner establish the best, most complete form–function assignments possible, regardless of cognitive cost. L2 acquisition, on the other hand, is more likely to reflect principles of ECONOMY, since the L2 learner is primarily motivated to learn to communicate efficiently and quickly, even if it means failing to achieve native-like performance on some parameters.

IX. MULTILINGUALISM AND THE RESEARCH ENTERPRISE

The vast majority of research on language learning and use—whether from the point of view of psycholinguistics, linguistics, or most of the many allied fields of inquiry—is not concerned with the special case of the multilingual. The implicit rationale tends to be along the lines: Let's address the clean, easy to study case of a monolingual speaker of X (typically an English-speaking college sophomore, or an 18-month-old whose utterances are clear enough for easy transcription), and once we have built a comprehensive model of monolingual language competence and performance, we will be in a better position to extend our model to multilinguals (or other languages). This sounds reasonable, but is probably wrong. Quite apart from the questionable wisdom of building a theoretical edifice on the strength of data gleaned overwhelmingly from anglophone second-year university students, there is an inherent scientific risk in assuming that monolingualism is the norm.

The multilingual individual is not such a special case at all. As it happens, the majority of the world's population is born into a multilingual community. Most of us who are not confronted with other languages at birth encounter them at some point. Nevertheless, it is the relatively small minority of monolinguals, typically English speakers, on whom theories of language acquisition and performance are based. It would seem prudent from a scientific point of view to accept some of the complications that inevitably enter when languages come into contact in favor of creating greater theoretical scope and ecological validity for our research enterprise. There are benefits to be gained from recognizing that multilingualism is a common, if not (yet) universal feature of human behavior. A theory that accounts for processing facts in one language but fails when confronted with data from other languages must be revised or rejected. The same applies to a theory tailored to monolinguals that does not generalize freely to multilinguals. Paying attention to the cross-linguistic validity of our theory of acquisition or processing, or whatever, can buy us better, more robust theories.

To this end, what is needed most at this time is closer cooperation between three related fields that have essential elements to offer to the psycholinguistic study of multilingualism. One such field is the rather disparate conglomerate called functional linguistics, and especially the branch which deals with typology—the comparative study of different languages—in order to provide a stable and broad database on fundamental structural differences and similarities among languages (Comrie, 1981, 1987; Givón, 1984, 1989; Ferguson, 1991). Second, we need input from specialists in sociolinguistics, in order to develop a keener awareness of the social and affective factors that interact with cognitive and linguistic factors to define the complex fabric that individuals face when cultures and languages mix (Hakuta, Ferdman, and Diaz, 1987). Finally, we must continue the search for the neuropsychological substrates of language learning and use, in order to build a clearer picture of how the brain deals with linguistic information, including how two or more languages are represented simultaneously (Vaid & Pandit, 1991; Vaid, 1986; Albert & Obler, 1980). Achieving fluency by any definition undoubtedly will involve complex interactions at all these levels; ultimately, a satisfactory definition of fluency must take each into account.

REFERENCES

Adjemian, C., & Liceras, J. (1984). Accounting for adult acquisition of relative clauses: Universal grammar, L1, and structuring the intake. In F. R. Eckman, L. H. Bell, & D. Nelson (Eds.), *Universals of second language acquisition* (pp. 101–118). Rowley, MA: Newbury House.

Albert, M., & Obler, L. (1978). *The Bilingual Brain*. New York: Academic Press.

Bach, E. (1968). Nouns and noun phrases. In E. Bach & R. Harms (Eds.), *Universals in linguistic theory*. New York: Holt, Rinehart, and Winston.

Bates, E., & MacWhinney, B. (1981). Second language acquisition from a functionalist perspective: Pragmatic, semantic and perceptual strategies. In H. Winitz (Ed.), *Annals of the New York Academy of Sciences conference on native and foreign language acquisition*. New York: New York Academy of Sciences.

Bates, E., & MacWhinney, B. (1982). Functionalist approaches to grammar. In E. Wanner & L. Gleitman (Eds.), *Language acquisition: The state of the art*. New York: Cambridge University Press.

Bates, E., & MacWhinney, B. (1989). Functionalism and the competition model. In B. MacWhinney & E. Bates (Eds.), *The crosslinguistic study of sentence processing*. New York: Cambridge University Press.

Bates, E., McNew, S., MacWhinney, B., Devescovi, A., & Smith, S. (1982). Functional constraints on sentence processing: A cross-linguistic study. *Cognition, 11*, 245–299.

Bierwisch, M. (1963). *Grammatik des deutschen Verbs*. Berlin: Studia Grammatica II.

Carroll, J. B. (1981). Conscious and automatic processes in language learning. *The Canadian Modern Language Review, 37*(3), 462–474.

Colombo, J. (1982). The critical period concept: Research, methodology, and theoretical issues. *Psychological Bulletin, 91*(2), 260–275.

Comrie, B. (1981). *Language universals and linguistics typology*. Oxford: Blackwell.

Comrie, B. (Ed.). (1987). *The world's major languages*. London: Croom Helm.

Cooreman, A., & Kilborn, K. (1991). Functionalist linguistics: Discourse structure and language processing in second language acquisition. In T. Huebner & C. A. Ferguson (Eds.), *Crosscurrents in second language acquisition and linguistic theories*. Amsterdam: John Benjamins.

Favreau, M., & Segalowitz, N. (1982). Second language reading in fluent bilinguals. *Applied Psycholinguistics, 3*, 329–341.

Favreau, M., & Segalowitz, N. (1983). Automatic and controlled processes in the first- and second-language reading of fluent bilinguals. *Memory and Cognition, 11*, 565–574.

Ferguson, C. A. (1991). Currents between second language acquisition and linguistic theory. In T. Huebner & C. A. Ferguson (Eds.), *Crosscurrents in second language acquisition and linguistic theories* (pp. 425–435). Amsterdam: John Benjamins.

Fishman, J., & Cooper, R. (1969). Alternative measures of bilingualism. *Journal of Verbal Learning and Verbal Behavior, 8*, 276–282.

Flege, J. E. (1988). The production and perception of foreign languages. In H. Winitz (Ed.), *Human communication and its disorders* (pp. 224–401). Norword, NJ: Ablex.

Flege, J. E., & Hillenbrand, J. (1984). Limits on phonetic accuracy in foreign language speech production. *Journal of the Acoustical Society of America, 76*, 708–721.

Flynn, S. (1984). A universal in L2 acquisition based on a PBD typology. In F. R. Beckman, L. H. Bell, & D. Nelson (Eds.), *Universals in second language acquisition* (pp. 75–87). Rowley, MA: Newbury House.

Gardner, R. (1980). On the validity of affective variables in second language acquisition: Conceptual, contextual and statistical consideration. *Language Learning, 30*, 255–270.

Gardner, R., & Lambert, W. (1972). *Attitudes and motivation in second-language learning*. Rowley, MA: Newbury House.

Gass, S. (1987). Sentence interpretation in L2 learning. *Applied Psycholinguistics, 8*, 329–350.

Givón, T. (1984). *Syntax: A functional–typological introduction. Vol. 1*. Amsterdam: J. Benjamins.

Givón, T. (1989). *Mind, Code and Context: Essays in Pragmatics*. Hillsdale, NJ: Lawrence Erlbaum.

Grosjean, F., & Soares, C. (1986). Processing mixed language: Some preliminary findings. In J. Vaid (Ed.), *Language processing in bilinguals: Psycholinguistic and neuropsychological perspectives*. Hillsdale, NJ: Lawrence Erlbaum.

Hakuta, K., Ferdman, B. M., & Diaz, R. M. (1987). Bilingualism and cognitive development: Three perspectives. In S. E. Rosenberg (Ed.), *Advances in applied psycholinguistics*. New York: Cambridge University Press.

Harrington, M. (1987). Processing transfer: Language-specific strategies as a source of interlanguage variation. *Applied Psycholinguistics, 8*, 351–378.

Hyltenstam, K. (1992). Non-native features of near-native speakers: On the ultimate attainment of childhood L2 learners. In R. J. Harris (Ed.), *Cognitive processing in bilinguals*. Amsterdam: North-Holland.

Johnson, J., & Newport, E. (1989). Critical period effects in second language learning: The influence of maturational state on the acquisition of English as a second language. *Cognitive Psychology, 21*, 60–99.

Jordans, P. (1986). Production rules in interlanguage: Evidence from case errors in L2 German. In E. Kellerman and M. Sharwood-Smith (Eds.), *Crosslinguistic Influences in Second Language Aquisition* (pp. 91–109). New York: Pergamon Press.

Kilborn, K. (1987). Sentence processing in a second language: Seeking a performance definition of fluency. Unpublished doctorate dissertation. University of California at San Diego.

Kilborn, K. (1989). Sentence processing in a second language: The timing of transfer. *Language and Speech, 32*(I), 1–23.

Kilborn, K. (1991). Selective impairment of grammatical morphology due to induced stress in normal listeners: Implications for aphasia. *Brain and Language, 41*(2), 275–288.

Kilborn, K., & Cooreman, A. (1987). Sentence interpretation strategies in adult Dutch-English bilinguals. *Applied Psycholinguistics, 8*, 415–431.

Kilborn, K., & Ito, T. (1989). Sentence processing strategies in adult bilinguals. In B. MacWhinney & E. Bates (Eds.), *The crosslinguistic study of sentence processing*. New York: Cambridge University Press.

Koster, J. (1975). Dutch as an SOV language. *Linguistic Analysis, 1*, 111–136.

Krashen, S. (1978). Individual variation in the use of the Monitor. In W. Ritchie (Ed.), *Principles of second language learning*. Academic Press: New York, NY.

Krashen, S. (1982). *Principles and practice in second language acquisition*. New York: Pergamon Press.

Krashen, S. D. (1973). Lateralization, language learning, and the critical period: Some new evidence. *Language Learning, 23*(1), 63–74.

Krashen, S. D. (1975). The development of cerebral dominance and language learning: More new evidence. In D. Dato (Ed.), *Developmental psycholinguistics: Theory and applications*. Washington: Georgetown University.

Lenneberg, E. H., & Lenneberg, E. (1975). *Foundations of language development: A multidisciplinary approach*. New York: Academic Press.

Lenneberg, E. H. (1967). *Biological foundations of language*. New York: Wiley.

Liu, H., Bates, E., & Li, P. (1992). Sentence interpretation in bilingual speakers of English and Chinese. *Applied Psycholinguistics, 13*, 451–484.

Macnamara, J., & Kushnir, S. (1971). Linguistic independence of bilinguals: The input switch. *Journal of Verbal Learning and Verbal Behavior, 10*, 480–487.

MacWhinney, B. (1987a). Applying the competition model to bilingualism. *Applied Psycholinguistics, 8*, 315–327.

MacWhinney, B. (1987b). Cues, competition, and learning. In J. Miller (Ed.), *Wisconsin papers on language development*. Madison, Wisconsin: Univeristy of Wisconsin.

MacWhinney, B. (1992). Competition and transfer in second language learning. In R. J. Harris (Ed.), *Cognitive processing in bilinguals* (pp. 371–390). Amsterdam: North-Holland.

MacWhinney, B., Bates, E., & Kliegl, R. (1984). Cue validity and sentence interpretation in English, German, and Italian. *Journal of Verbal Learning and Verbal Behavior, 23*, 127–150.

McDonald, J. (1987). Sentence interpretation in bilingual speakers of English and Dutch. *Applied Psycholinguistics, 8*, 379–415.

McDonald, J. L., & Heilenman, L. K. (1992). Changes in sentence processing as second language proficiency increases. In R. J. Harris (Ed.), *Cognitive processing in bilinguals*, (pp. 325–336). Amsterdam: North-Holland.

McLaughlin, B. (1978). The monitor model: Some methodological considerations. *Language Learning, 28*, 309–332.

Menn, L., & Obler, L. K. (Eds.). (1990). *Agrammatic Aphasia: A cross-language narrative sourcebook*. Amsterdam: John Benjamins.

Miao, X. (1981). Word order and semantic strategies in Chinese sentence comprehension. *International Journal of Psycholinguistics, 8*, 23–33.

Posner, M. I., & Snyder, C. R. R. (1975). Facilitation and inhibition in the processing of signals. In P. M. A. Rabbitt & S. Dornic (Eds.), *Attention and Performance V*. London: Academic Press.

Ross, J. R. (1970). Gapping and the order of constituents. In M. Bierwisch & M. Heidolph (Eds.), *Progress in Linguistics* (pp. 249–259). The Hague: Mouton.

Schneider, W., & Shiffrin, R. (1977). Automatic and controlled information processing in vision. In D. Laberge & S. Samuels (Eds.), *Basic processes in reading: Perception and comprehension*. Hillsdale, NJ: Lawrence Erlbaum Association.

Scovel, T. (1969). Foreign accents, language acquisition and cerebral dominance. *Language, 19*, 245–253.

Segalowitz, N. (1986). Skilled reading in the second language. In J. Vaid (Ed.), *Language processing in bilinguals: Psycholinguistic and neuropsychological perspectives*. (pp. 3–19). Hillsdale, NJ: Lawrence Erlbaum.

Selinker, L. (1972). Interlanguage. *International Review of Applied Linguistics, 10*, 209–231.

Shiffrin, R. M., & Schneider, W. (1977). Controlled and automatic human information processing: II. Perceptual learning, automatic attending and a general theory. *Psychological Review, 84*, 127–190.

Snow, C., & Hoefnagel-Hohle, M. (1978). Age differences in second language acquisition. In E. M. Hatch (Ed.), *Second language acquisition: A book of readings*. Rowley, MA: Newbury Publishers.

Tarone, E. E. (1982). Systematicity and attention in interlanguage. *Language Learning, 32*(1), 69–84.

Vaid, J. (1983). Bilingualism and brain lateralization. In S. Segalowitz (Ed.), *Language functions and brain organization*. (pp. 315–339). New York: Academic Press.

Vaid, J. (Ed.). (1986). *Language processing in bilinguals: Psycholinguistic and neuropsychological perspectives*. Hillsdale, NJ: Lawrence Erlbaum.

Vaid, J., & Pandit, R. (1991). Sentence interpretation in normal and aphasic Hindi speakers. *Brain and Language, 41*(2), 250–274.

White, L. (1980). *Grammatical theory and language acquisition*. Bloomington, IN: Indiana University Linguistics Club.

Wulfeck, B. B., Juarez, L., Bates, E., & Kilborn, K. (1986). Sentence interpretation strategies in healthy and aphasic bilingual adults. In J. Vaid (Ed.), *Language processing in bilinguals: Psycholinguistics and neurological perspectives*. Hillsdale, NJ: Lawrence Erlbaum.

CHAPTER 29

LANGUAGE PRODUCTION

GRAMMATICAL ENCODING

KATHRYN BOCK AND WILLEM LEVELT

I. INTRODUCTION

The processes of language production can be divided into those that create the skeleton of an utterance and those that flesh the skeleton out. In this chapter we are concerned chiefly with the former, a set of processes which we term GRAMMATICAL ENCODING (Levelt, 1989). Grammatical encoding comprises both the selection of appropriate lexical concepts (entries in the speaker's vocabulary) and the assembly of a syntactic framework. It contrasts with PHONOLOGICAL ENCODING, which comprises the assembly of sound forms and the generation of intonation. The product of these processes is not speech itself, but a specification of an utterance that is adequate for controlling the processes of articulation or speech production.

The components of grammatical encoding are no more accessible to conscious experience than the corresponding components of comprehension. Just as in comprehension, we typically become aware only of disruptions. But unlike disruptions of comprehension, many disruptions of production are public events: A speaker who intends to say *meals on wheels* and instead says *wheels on meals* usually knows that something has gone wrong, as does anyone within earshot. Because of their ready availability, speech errors are a rich source of clues to how language production works (Cutler, 1988).

Deciphering these clues has been the focus of several pioneering studies (Dell & Reich, 1981; Fromkin, 1971; Garrett, 1975; Meringer & Meyer, 1895/1978). The details of the analyses diverge in important ways (some of which we touch on later), but there is reasonable agreement on the broad outline of production processes that is sketched in Figure 1. This outline roughly follows proposals by Garrett (1980, 1982, 1988) and, although it is motivated primarily by analyses of speech errors, it is intended to provide an account of normal production. The bridge from errors to normal production is built largely on the existence of strong constraints on the forms of speech errors, which are taken to point to relatively immutable components of the production process.

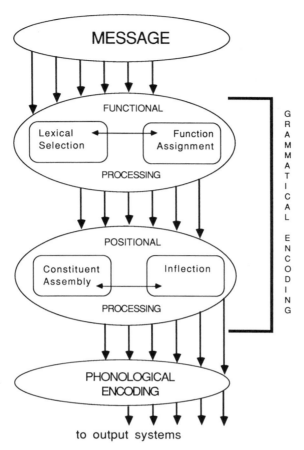

FIG. 1   An overview of language production processes.

We use the model in Figure 1 to organize and introduce the main topics of this chapter. It shows four levels of processing, the message level, the functional level, the positional level, and the phonological level. The message captures features of the speaker's intended meaning and provides the raw material for the processes of grammatical encoding. These processes are grouped into two sets, functional and positional. The primary subcomponents of functional processing are lexical selection (which involves the identification of lexical concepts that are suitable for conveying the speaker's meaning) and function assignment (which involves the assignment of grammatical roles or syntactic functions). Positional processing involves the creation of an ordered set of word slots (constituent assembly) and morphological slots (inflection). Finally, phonological encoding involves spelling out the phonological structure of the utterance, in terms of both the phonological segments of word forms and the prosody of larger units.

The processes of grammatical encoding can be more concretely specified by going through the steps involved in generating a simple utterance and constructing errors that might arise at each step. We number these steps for expository convenience, but the numbers are not intended to denote a strict ordering of implementation. As the target utterance we use *She was handing him some broccoli.* The message behind this utterance presumably includes notions about a past progressive event in which a female action-agent transfers by hand a nonspecific object from a certain class of vegetables to a male action-recipient.

The first step, lexical selection, involves identifying the lexical concepts and LEMMAS suitable for conveying the message. Lemmas carry the grammatical information associated with individual lexical concepts, such as their form class (noun, verb, etc.). For conveying the broccoli message, appropriate lemmas include masculine and feminine pronominal indices, a noun (*broccoli*), and a verb (*hand*) that relates the elements or ARGUMENTS of events involving an agent, a recipient, and a theme.[1] A common type of speech error that appears to reflect a problem of lexical selection is a SEMANTIC SUBSTITUTION, which would occur if our hypothetical speaker said *She was handing him some cauliflower.* These substitutions preserve general features of the meaning of the intended word (Hotopf, 1980) and are nearly always members of the same grammatical form class (noun, verb, adjective, adverb, or preposition). In Stemberger's error corpus (1985), 99.7% of all lexical substitutions represented the same form class as the target.

The second step is function assignment. This involves assigning syntactic relations or grammatical functions (e.g., subject–nominative, object–dative). During the formulation of *She was handing him some broccoli,* the feminine pronoun lemma should be linked to the nominative (subject) function, the masculine to what we will call the dative function,[2] the argument represented by *broccoli* to the accusative function, and *hand* to the main verb function. Errors of function assignment arise when elements are assigned to the wrong functions. For example, if the feminine and masculine pronoun lemmas were linked to the dative and nominative functions respectively, the resulting utterance would most likely be *He was handing her some broccoli.* These EXCHANGE errors, like other types of exchanges, involve constituents of the same type (both are noun phrases). They are not simple exchanges of word forms, as our example illustrates: The error is not *Him was handing she some broccoli.*

The next two steps constitute positional processing, so called because it fixes the order of the elements in an utterance. As this implies, the order may not be imposed during functional processing. One indication comes from a contrast in scope between the features of different types of errors (Garrett, 1980). Exchanges of whole words occurred within the same phrases only 19% of the time in Garrett's corpus (1980), implying that adjacency is not a strong conditioning factor. In contrast, when sounds are exchanged (as in *sot holdering iron*), they originated in the same phrase 87% of the time.

We consider constituent assembly first. This is the creation of a control hierarchy for phrasal constituents that manages the order of word production

---

[1] In event-role terminology, the theme is the object in the event that undergoes movement. This sense of theme should not be confused with the unrelated sense of discourse theme.

[2] The dative is roughly the same as the traditional indirect object.

and captures dependencies among syntactic functions. For *She was handing him some broccoli,* the hierarchy can be depicted in this way:

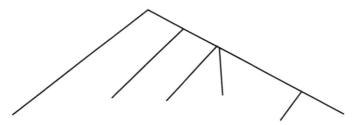

The basic features of such hierarchies are largely predictable from the types of syntactic functions that have to be represented and from the syntactic features of the selected lemmas.

The last of the grammatical encoding processes, inflection, involves the generation of fine-grained details at the lowest levels of this structure. In English, many of these details involve elements that carry information about number, tense, and aspect but are bound to other words. So, the expression of the progressive feature on the verb *handing* requires elaboration of one node of the tree, as shown below:

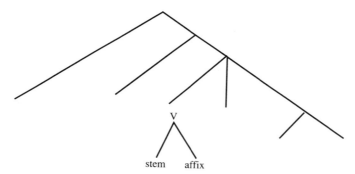

The generation of these details is in no strict sense distinguishable from the rest of constituent assembly, but we discuss it separately in order to showcase a debate over whether the elements dominated by the "twigs" of the structural tree behave uniquely.

One type of error that is identified with inflection is known as STRANDING. Stranding is illustrated in the utterance of a speaker who intended to say *You ended up ordering some fish dish* and instead said *You ordered up ending some fish dish* (Garrett, in press). In such errors, the bound suffixes (*-ed, -ing*) show up in their proper locations in the utterance but affixed to the wrong words, arguing that the inflections are positioned separately from their word stems. Another type of error that may arise during inflection is called a SHIFT (Garrett, 1975) and consists of the mislocation of an affix. Such an error could lead to the utterance of *She was hand himming some broccoli* by our hypothetical speaker. The elements involved in such errors are much more likely to be involved in errors than the final syllables of word stems, such as the *-id* in *morbid* (Stemberger, 1985), implying that strandings and shifts are not simple mislocations of syllables but mislocations of pieces of grammatical structure.

With all this done, it still remains necessary to spell out the phonological content of the utterance. That is the province of phonological encoding, which we will not treat here (see Gerken, this volume).

In the remainder of this chapter, we fill out the picture of grammatical encoding by critically examining each of its hypothesized subcomponents and marshalling evidence about them from different sources, including computer modeling and experimental research on production. The experimental work serves at least three essential purposes. First, it serves to test hypotheses derived from error observations under better controlled circumstances, making it possible to rule out alternative explanations of production processes. Second, it permits examination of features of language production that errors cannot illuminate, if only because those features are seldom or never involved in errors. Even the most familiar types of speech error are surprisingly rare events (Deese, 1984; Garnham, Shillcock, Brown, Mill, & Cutler, 1982; Heeschen, in press). And finally, experimental work makes it possible to explore whether the features of production that are postulated on the basis of error analyses hold equally under the circumstances that lead to normal, error-free production. Errors, by definition, reflect unusual circumstances that cannot straightforwardly be taken to represent the norm. So, any hypothesis that attributes a certain property to the production system in order to account for a particular sort of error is vulnerable to the objection that the property is in fact aberrant.[3]

At the outset, we adopt a very strong position about the nature of these processing systems. It is that each one is influenced only by information represented at the level directly above it. For example, we assume that the processes of lexical selection and function assignment are under the control of information in the message and are unaffected by the sounds or phonological features of words. This is neither a majority view nor an obviously correct one, and there are compelling reasons to subject it to careful scrutiny (Dell, 1986; Stemberger, 1985). However, it is an assumption that is a testable and (perhaps all too easily) disconfirmable, so that its flaws can be readily corrected as further evidence about these processes accumulates.

We also assume that language production is incremental (Kempen & Hoenkamp, 1987; Levelt, 1989), so that variations in the order in which information is delivered from one component to the next can readily affect the order in which elements appear in speech (Bock, 1982). When higher level processing components drive lower level ones, incremental production implies that the higher levels need not complete their work on an utterance before the next level begins. This is illustrated in Figure 1 in terms of hypothetical temporal connections between the processing levels. The implementation of incrementality requires the formulation, at every level, of piecemeal units relevant to the form and content of the developing utterance, so our review touches on the information partitionings within each processing component.

---

[3] It is for this reason that the most persuasive hypotheses that emerge from error analyses are based on what stays right in an utterance when something else goes wrong.

II. LEXICAL SELECTION

In fluent speech we normally produce two to three words per second (Maclay & Osgood, 1959), but there are occasional bursts (ANACRUSES) of up to seven words per second (Deese, 1984). Even at these rates, we retrieve the appropriate items from our mental lexicons. This is a surprising skill, given that we know tens of thousands of words (Oldfield, 1963) and that errors of lexical selection are rare: estimates of selection-error rates per thousand words of speech range from 0.25 (Deese, 1984) through 0.41 (Garnham et al., 1982) up to 2.3 (Shallice & Butterworth, 1977).

Empirical research in lexical selection relies on three sources of evidence. First, though selection errors are rare, they have been carefully collected and analyzed. Second, word finding can be particularly troublesome in aphasic patients; the ways in which they err can reveal processes of retrieval that are deeply hidden in normal speech. Third, lexical selection has increasingly come to be studied experimentally. The experiments often involve picture naming, with naming latencies measured under various conditions. In the following we address only the first and last sources of evidence (for studies in aphasia, see Garrett, 1992 and chapters in this volume by Caplan and by Zurif and Swinney) in terms of a theoretical framework developed by Levelt (1989; Levelt et al., 1991a) and Roelofs (1992). That framework is presented first.

A. A Network Model of Lexical Access

Our mental store of words and basic information about them is called the mental lexicon. It is obviously not the case that all possible words of our language are stored somewhere in our minds, because there is an infinity of possible words. Take the numerals. They form an infinite set and a corresponding infinite set of words, including compounds such as *twenty-three thousand two hundred seventy-nine*. This is unlikely to be an entry in the mental lexicon. Rather, such words are constructed when needed. Languages differ greatly in the use their speakers make of this ability: Speakers of Turkish, for instance, produce new words in almost every sentence (cf. Hankamer, 1989), whereas speakers of English rarely do so. When we talk about lexical access here, we sidestep this productive lexical encoding to focus on the retrieval of stored words from the mental lexicon.

Our knowledge of words involves three types of information. First, we know a word's meaning. We know that a sheep is a kind of domestic animal, that it has a wool pelt, that it produces milk, etc. These are all properties of our concept SHEEP.

Second, a word has syntactic properties. The word *sheep* is a noun. In French *mouton* is also a noun, but in addition it has male syntactic gender, in contrast to *chèvre* 'goat', which has female gender. A word's syntactic properties can be fairly complex. Verbs, in particular, are specified for the optional or obligatory arguments they command. For example, the verb *hit* typically takes a subject and a direct object (i.e., it is a transitive verb), and because this is something that a speaker knows about the verb *hit*, it is part of the mental lexicon. This type of information is called the verb's SUBCATEGORIZA-TION FRAME. The verb *hand*, from our earlier example, has two subcategorization frames. The first one, the prepositional frame, includes a direct object position and an oblique (prepositional) object position (as in *She was handing some broccoli to him*), and the second one, the double object frame, maps the dative to the direct object position and the accusative to a so-called second object position (as in *She was handing him some broccoli*). The word as a syntactic entity is technically called a LEMMA.

Lemmas contrast with LEXEMES, which capture the word's form properties. These constitute its morphological and phonological shape. The word *sheep* is monomorphemic and consists of three phonological segments, /ʃ/, /i/, and /p/. The word *handing* consists of two morphemes, a stem and a suffix, and six phonological segments, /h/, /æ/, /n/, /d/, /ɨ/, and /ŋ/.

In the network model, these different types of information correspond to nodes within three levels of representation, the conceptual level, the lemma level, and the lexeme level. A part of this lexical network is shown in Figure 2. It depicts some of the knowledge we have about the words *sheep* and *goat*.

At the conceptual level, the nodes represent concepts. They are linked by labeled arcs that represent the nature of relationships. Since a sheep is an animal, this is represented by an ISA connection between the nodes SHEEP

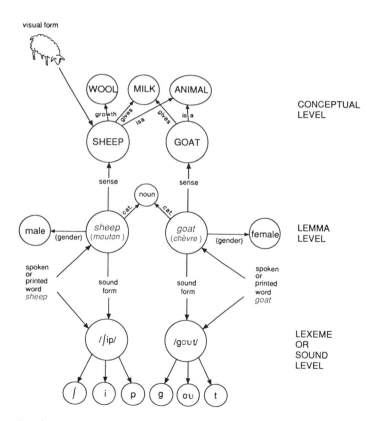

FIG. 2 A part of the lexical network. Note that the arrows represent types of connections within the network, not the flow of information during production or comprehension.

and ANIMAL. A word's meaning as a whole is represented by such a network of relations (as introduced by Collins & Loftus, 1975, and Collins & Quillian, 1969), although individual lexical concepts themselves are represented by unitary nodes. In this respect, the model departs from a compositional representation of word meaning. We will not go into this perennial issue in lexical representation (for further discussion, see Bierwisch & Schreuder, 1992; Fodor, Garrett, Walker, & Parkes, 1980; Levelt, 1989; McNamara & Miller, 1989).

Some conceptual nodes have direct connections to nodes at the second, lemma level. This subset of conceptual nodes represents lexical concepts. Not all concepts are lexical: DEAD TREE is a perfectly well formed concept, but one without a lexical concept. Yet English has a lexical concept for *dead body* (CORPSE).

The nodes at the lemma level represent syntactic properties. The lemma *sheep* has a category link to the noun node; in French the lemma *mouton* has a gender link to the male node, and so on. At the lexeme level, the network represents the word's form properties. The lexeme node /ʃip/ thus has labeled links to its constituent phonological segments, /ʃ/, /i/, /p/.

Lexical access in this model is represented by activation spreading from the conceptual level to the lemma level to the lexeme level (note that Fig. 2 does not depict the activation trajectories; the arrows in the figure characterize permanent relationships rather than processing dynamics). We will not consider how a speaker first conceives of the notions to be expressed (see Levelt, 1989, and for a very different view, Dennett, 1991), but beyond that, the first requirement for lexical selection in normal speech is the existence of an active lexical concept. A concept node can become activated in myriad ways. One simple procedure to induce this is to present a picture for naming. In an experiment, a subject can be given a picture (e.g., one of a sheep, as shown in Fig. 2) and asked to name it as fast as possible. The assumption is that the picture activates the concept.

An active lexical concept spreads its activation to all connected concept nodes. So if the SHEEP node is active, the GOAT node will receive some activation as well (either directly, or via mediating nodes such as ANIMAL or MILK). In addition, activation will spread from the lexical concept node to the corresponding lemma node. In this framework, lexical selection is selection of the appropriate lemma node. So, if SHEEP is the active lexical concept, the lemma *sheep* should be retrieved. It would be an error of selection if *goat* were retrieved. There is nonetheless a small chance for such a mishap, because some activation spreads from SHEEP to GOAT and from there to the lemma *goat*.

In Roelofs' (1992) implementation of this model, the probability that any given lemma will be selected during a specified time interval is the ratio of its activation to the total activation of all lemmas in an experimental set (i.e., the Luce ratio; Luce, 1959). This makes it possible to predict the time course of lexical selection under various experimental conditions (see below). Some of those conditions are designed to directly activate lemma nodes through the presentation of spoken or written words (see Fig. 2), creating competitors for other lemmas activated from the conceptual level.

The model as it is depicted deals only with lemmas for lexical concepts.

But not all words in fluent speech correspond to lexical concepts. In *listen to the radio, to* does not represent a concept. Rather, the lemma for the transitive verb *listen* requires the preposition *to,* so the lemma *to* must be activated via an indirect route at the lemma level. We refer to this as INDIRECT ELECTION.

The major joint in the model is between the lemma and lexeme levels of representation. Between lexical concepts and lemmas, there are systematic relations. So, a verb's meaning is regularly related to its subcategorization frame (Fisher, Gleitman, & Gleitman, 1991; Keenan, 1976). But between lemmas and lexemes, the relation is highly arbitrary (de Saussure, 1916/1955). There is no systematic reason why a SHEEP should be called *sheep* (or *mouton*). Still, there are some statistical relations between the syntactic and phonological properties of words (Kelly, 1992). Nouns, for instance, tend to contain more syllables than verbs; they also contain front vowels more often than verbs (Sereno & Jongman, 1990). Kelly (1992) argues that language learners and users may sometimes rely on such statistical relations in parsing and speech production.

The most dramatic reflection of the rift between the lemma and lexeme levels is the so-called tip-of-the-tongue (TOT) phenomenon. It was described by William James in 1890 in one of the most frequently quoted passages in cognitive psychology:

> Suppose we try to recall a forgotten name. The state of our consciousness is peculiar. There is a gap therein: but no mere gap. It is a gap that is intensely active. A sort of wraith of the name is in it, beckoning us in a given direction, making us at moments tingle with the sense of our closeness, and then letting us sink back without the longed-for term. If wrong names are proposed to us, this singularly definite gap acts immediately so as to negate them. They do not fit into its mould. And the gap of one word does not feel like the gap of another, all empty of content as both might seem necessarily to be when described as gaps. . . . The rhythm of a lost word may be there without a sound to clothe it; or the evanescent sense of something which is the initial vowel or consonant may mock us fitfully, without growing more distinct (1890/1950, pp. 251–252).

The TOT phenomenon was later discussed by Woodworth (1938) and systematically studied for the first time by R. Brown and McNeill (1966). R. Brown and McNeill presented the definitions of infrequent words such as *sextant* and asked subjects to produce the defined word. Whenever subjects entered a tip-of-the-tongue state, they reported whatever came to mind about the target word. In many cases the subjects knew the initial consonant or vowel, the number of syllables, and the stress pattern. Related words might come to mind that shared these properties (such as *secant* for *sextant*). These findings have been confirmed and elaborated in many subsequent studies (see A. S. Brown, 1991, and Levelt, 1989, for comprehensive reviews). Most of these studies deal with TOT states in normal speakers, but there are also clinical conditions that persistently arouse TOT states. These are called anomias (see Butterworth, 1992, and Garrett, 1992, for further discussion).

In terms of the network model, the TOT phenomenon is a failure to access the lexeme from the lemma. The speaker knows the meaning to be expressed (i.e., the concept) and the word's syntax (that it is a plural noun, a transitive verb or whatever; i.e., the lemma). Only the word form is blocked. Some aspects of the form may surface, revealing something about the process of phonological encoding (see Levelt, 1989, and Gerken, this volume, for reviews). Because TOTs appear to arise subsequent to lemma activation, they are not problems of lexical selection, but of lexeme activation.

B. Errors of Lexical Selection

There are three major types of lexical selection errors, called substitutions, blends, and exchanges. In all three cases a nontarget lemma is activated and an incorrect word form is produced. But there are different ways in which this derailing activation can come about. Consider examples (1)–(6) of substitutions.

(1) . . . *carrying a bag of cherries. I mean grapes* (Stemberger, 1985)
(2) *He's a high–low grader* (Fromkin, 1973)
(3) *Get out of the clark* [intended: *car*] (Harley, 1984)
(4) *A branch falling on the tree* [intended: *roof*] (Fromkin, 1973)
(5) *He's the kind of soldier a man . . . wants to emanate* [intended: *emulate*] (Bock, 1987)
(6) *I urgently request you to release the hostages unarmed–unharmed* (Fromkin, 1973)

One potential cause of a substitution error is that an alternative lexical concept is activated along with the target. In (1) the speaker intended to express the notion GRAPE, but CHERRY was activated at the same time. This may result from activation spreading at the conceptual level. Because GRAPE and CHERRY are semantically related (both are small round fruits), there is some linkage between them in the conceptual network. If both lexical concepts then activate their lemmas, there is a chance for the unintended one (*cherry*) to be accidentally selected (given a probabilistic selection rule like that of Roelofs, 1992).

Example (2) also involves a semantic relation: *high* and *low* are antonyms. Antonyms and other semantic oppositions in fact form the most frequent type of word substitution. Their causation may be similar to the above case, but there is an additional feature. *High* and *low* are strong associates (stronger than *grape* and *cherry*). It is not clear where word association should be represented in a network model such as the one in Figure 2. It may be a special form of conceptual relation, but it might also involve direct lemma-to-lemma connections.

Example (3) has a different etiology. The speaker intended to say *Get out of the car* to someone but at that moment glanced up at a storefront with the word *Clark's* printed on it. Then *clark* intruded, creating an environmental contamination (Garrett, 1980). There was no conceptual spreading of activation from CAR to CLARK. Rather, the printed word *Clark* seems to have activated the corresponding lemma.

Example (4) has a still different cause. It appears that *branch* may have activated its associate *tree,* allowing the lemma *tree* to be selected instead of the target lemma *roof.* Again it is unclear whether activation spread at the conceptual level (from BRANCH to TREE), at the lemma level (from *roof* to *tree*), or both. Was the speaker really thinking of a tree when the error occurred? We will never know.

Example (5), in which the target word was replaced by a sound-related word, is due neither to conceptual- nor to lemma-level priming. In fact, it is not strictly an error of lexical selection under our present definition because, in terms of the model, the error need not have involved the activation of a nontarget lemma (i.e., the lemma *emanate*). Fay and Cutler (1977) called this type of error a malapropism and argued that such errors arise during lexeme processing. At that level the lexicon is organized in terms of form, not meaning. And indeed, malapropisms show no systematic meaning relation to the corresponding targets (Garrett, 1980), as testified by such cases as *sympathy* for *symphony, bodies* for *bottles,* and *garlic* for *gargle.* Revealingly, there is a strong similarity to the "wrong names" that occur during TOT states, which also seem to arise during lexeme processing.

The final example, (6), is a mixed error: The error *unarmed* and the target *unharmed* have both a semantic and a phonological connection. Mixed errors such as *dictionary* for *directory* and *oyster* for *lobster* are controversial. In their corpus of naturally observed errors, Dell and Reich (1981) found that the probability of a mixed error was higher than would be predicted if semantic and phonological errors have independent sources. They concluded that phonological similarity increases the probability of a semantic substitution. This conclusion has been supported in other research (Harley, 1984; Martin, Weisberg, & Saffran, 1989; Stemberger, 1983; but see del Viso, Igoa, & García-Albea, 1991).

In a network model such as the one developed by Dell (1986) or the one depicted in Figure 2, this can be handled by postulating feedback from the lexeme to higher levles, crossing the lexeme/lemma rift (rather than the purely top-down flow that we have thus far assumed). However, that move may be unnecessary. First, there is experimental evidence from error-free speech (Levelt et al., 1991a) that is inconsistent with this option. We return to this below. Second, mixed errors may be predominantly environmental contaminations, as suggested by Garrett (in press). If so, it may be that their origin is special, not the consequence of general feedback between lexemes and lemmas. Third, the overrepresentation of mixed errors could result from a mechanism of self-monitoring. According to Levelt (1989), self-monitoring can begin as soon as there is a phonetic plan for the word, and so before articulation is initiated. If *unarmed* is internally but erroneously planned, a cohort of sound-related words will be activated in the speaker's comprehension system, among them *unharmed.* Its meaning can be activated via this phonological route, and in addition via a semantic route, allowing the activated notion UNARMED to prime the related notion UNHARMED even further. Since that is the intended meaning, the monitor may pass the (erroneous) item.

Let us now turn to a second type of lexical selection error, blends (7)–(8).

(7) *The competition is a little stougher* [*stiffer/tougher*] (Fromkin, 1973)
(8) *The sky is shining* [*The sky is blue/The sun is shining*] (Harley, 1984)

Most blends are of type (7), the fusion of two words that are near-synonyms in the context of conversation. Whereas substitutions reveal a predilection for antonyms and close associates, blends of antonyms are exceptional (Hotopf, 1980; Levelt, 1989). Instead, it is quasi-identity of meaning that characterizes the blending components. The source of blends may therefore be earlier than substitutions.

This makes blends something of a puzzle (Garrett, 1980). Their antecedents are early, but the errors themselves—the phonological merging of two word forms—are late. The merging is phonologically systematic, respecting the sylla-ble constituency of both components (MacKay, 1972; Wells, 1951). It is possible that this late merging is the result of the parallel encoding of two different utterances (Butterworth, 1982; Garrett, 1980; Harley, 1984) triggered by the speaker's conceptual indecision. This possibility is reinforced by the existence of sentence blends such as (8), which likewise appear to result from the parallel encoding of two related notions.

The third type of selection error includes exchanges such as (9)–(12).

(9) *Seymour sliced the knife with a salami* (Fromkin, 1973)
(10) *I got into this guy with a discussion* (Garrett, 1980)
(11) *a hole full of floors* (Fromkin, 1973)
(12) *threw the window through the clock* (Fromkin, 1973)

In (9), *knife* slipped into the noun slot in the direct object noun phrase in place of *salami* (perhaps because it was at that moment more activated). So far, this is simply a sort of word subsitution. But then, because *knife* was no longer available for the next noun slot, *salami* was inserted in its stead to create a second error. Because insertion in the wrong syntactic slot is possible only if the syntactic category of the word is the same, word exchanges usually occur between words of the same form class (over 80% of the time; Garrett, 1980; Stemberger, 1985).

In (9), the exchange involved words, not whole phrases. A whole-phrase exchange would have yielded *Seymour sliced a knife with the salami,* in which the articles accompany their respective nouns. Phrase exchanges do occur, however, as example (10) shows. Here the phrases *this guy* and *a discussion* were exchanged. The existence of such exchanges complicates the picture, because it can be difficult to tell a word exchange from a phrase exchange. A clear case is shown in example (11) which, like (9), is a word exchange. The target was *a floor full of holes,* and when the nouns *floor* and *hole* exchanged, *hole* left its inflectional marking behind. This is characteristic of unambiguous word exchanges: they strand other parts of their phrases, including adjectives and closed-class[4] elements (see Berg, 1987, for further discussion). However, when all the phrasal elements that accompany the exchanging words are the same, as they are in (12), it is impossible to tell whether the exchange is lexical or phrasal.

Such ambiguities are problematic because the exchange straddles the boundary between lexical and syntactic processing. Genuine phrase exchanges may have a different etiology than genuine word exchanges, one more similar to the one sketched for pronoun exchanges in the introduction. Some support for this conjecture comes from an informal survey of the word exchanges in Fromkin's (1973) Appendix, which showed that unambiguous word exchanges (e.g., *takes plant in the place*) are more likely to exhibit sound similarities and less likely to exhibit meaning similarities than exchanges which could be phrase exchanges (e.g., *used the door to open the key*).

[4] The members of the closed class include function words and inflectional morphemes.

C. Experimental Studies of Lexical Selection

There is a long tradition of experimental research in lexical selection that falls under the heading of "object naming" and dates back to Cattell (1885). Cattell found that subjects were slower in naming pictures than in reading words. This result finds a natural explanation in the network model of Figure 2. Written words have direct access to lemmas, whereas picture information has to be relayed via concepts.

Cattell's result has been extensively studied. One of its offshoots is research on interference between words and pictures, as embodied in what is now known as the picture interference paradigm (Lupker, 1979; see Glaser, 1992, for an excellent review of this literature since Cattell). This is a double stimulation paradigm. The primary stimulus is a picture, which the subject is instructed to name as fast as possible. The secondary stimulus is a printed or spoken distractor word, which the subject is instructed to ignore. Subjects are rarely completely successful in carrying out this latter instruction, however: The picture-naming latencies are normally affected by the presence of the distractor.

There are usually two variables in such an experiment. The first is the relation between the distractor and target word (the picture's name). When the picture is one of a sheep, the distractor may be a superordinate (*animal*), the identical word (*sheep*), a subordinate (*ram*), a cohyponym (*goat*), a sound-related word (*sheet*), or an unrelated word (*house*). The second variable is the stimulus onset asynchrony or SOA. This is the interval between picture onset and distractor onset. If it is negative, the distractor precedes the picture onset; if it is positive, the distractor follows the picture onset.

A classic picture-interference study is Glaser and Düngelhoff's (1984). In one of their experiments they used an SOA range from −400 to +400 ms in steps of 100 ms. A printed distractor word was either semantically related to the target (a cohyponym) or unrelated (there was also an identity condition which we ignore here). All distractors were names of pictures in the response set. The REAL line plotted in Figure 3 shows the difference between the related and unrelated conditions in naming latencies over the whole range of SOAs.

Clearly, the naming response was sometimes delayed when semantically related distractors were presented, compared to when the distractors were unrelated to the target word. This is called SEMANTIC INHIBITION, and it can be understood in terms of the network model (see Fig. 2). When the picture depicts a sheep, activation spreads to the concept SHEEP, and thence to the lemma *sheep*. An unrelated distractor word such as *house* directly activates the corresponding lemma *house*. Because there are now two active lemmas, and both are possible responses in the experiment (i.e., *house* is sometimes a target), the probability of selecting *sheep* at any one moment is smaller than if there were no distractor (because the Luce ratio is smaller). If a related distractor is presented (e.g., *goat*), the delay should be even greater. This is because activation from the concept SHEEP spreads to the concept GOAT and down to the lemma *goat*. The latter will therefore be more activated than *house* is in the unrelated condition. The results of Roelofs' (1992) simulation of Glaser and Düngelhoff's experiment is shown in Figure 3 as the SIM line. The fit is statistically perfect. Roelofs' own experiments produced further support for this model.

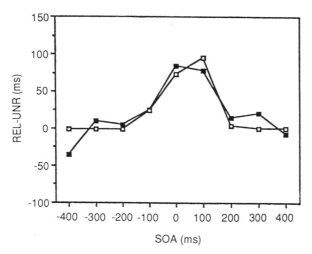

Fig. 3 Picture naming in the picture-word interference paradigm at nine stimulus-onset asychro-nies (SOAs). The REAL data (*filled squares*) are from Glaser and Düngelhoff (1984); the SIM data (*open squares*) are a simulation reported by Roelofs (1992). In the related (REL) condition the interfering probe word was semantically related to the picture target, and in the unrelated (UNR) condition it was not.

In a very similar study, but with spoken distractor words, Schriefers, Meyer, and Levelt (1990) found a comparable semantic inhibition effect. In addition, they showed that semantic inhibition disappeared when the subject's task was not picture naming but picture recognition. In the recognition task, the subject was first shown the pictures (as in the picture naming experiment). Then the pictures were presented among a set of new ones. The subject's task was to push a *yes* button when the picture was an old one and the *no* button when it was new. The pictures and distractors were the same ones used in the naming experiment, but now there was no trace of semantic inhibition. This implies that the effect is lexical, not conceptual. Because semantic inhibition cannot be merely a word form effect, this finding points to the involvement of lemma representations even in picture naming, when the subject is not constructing sentences. A similar disappearance of semantic inhibition in a recognition task was observed by Levelt et al. (1991a).

Schriefers (1990) was also able to separate conceptually and lexically in-duced latency effects in an experimental setting. The subjects viewed two geometrical shapes of different sizes (e.g., a large and a small triangle), one of which was marked by a cross. The task was to say *bigger* when the marked shape was the bigger one and *smaller* when it was the smaller one of the two. When both shapes were rather large the *bigger* response was facilitated, and when both were rather small the *smaller* response was facilitated. Schriefers argued that this congruency effect is of conceptual, nonlexical origin, because it was also found when the response was nonverbal (made by push buttons), when no lexical access was required. The situation was quite different for another effect, the markedness effect: *Bigger* responses were usually faster than *smaller* responses (and similarly for other marked versus unmarked adjectives; see Bierwisch, 1969, for an analysis of this distinction), but this markedness difference disappeared when subjects responded nonverbally. On the basis of these and other findings, Schriefers suggested that markedness is a property of adjective lemmas.

Earlier we argued that the major rift in lexical access is between the lemma and the lexeme levels of processing. In their picture naming study, Schriefers et al. (1990; see above) used not only semantic distractor words, but also phonological ones in the picture–word interference task. The semantic distractors caused inhibition at an SOA of − 150 ms (i.e., the onset of the spoken word preceded the picture by 150 ms). Phonological distractors (e.g., *sheet* when the picture was one of a sheep) produced a facilitatory effect at SOAs of 0 and + 150 ms (in agreement with findings by Meyer, 1990, 1991). But there was no trace of phonological facilitation at the SOA of − 150 ms. The implication is that phonological encoding strictly follows lexical selection.

The two-stage theory that is suggested by this result was reconfirmed by Levelt et al. (1991a). A different type of dual stimulation task was used but, as in the previous experiments, the subjects' main task was picture naming. On about one third of the trials, a spoken probe (a word or nonword) was presented at one of three SOAs. The subjects' secondary task was lexical decision: They pushed a *yes* button when the probe was a word and a *no* button when it was a nonword. The dependent variable was the latency of this response. Among the probes were semantically related ones (e.g., *goat* when the picture was one of a sheep) and phonologically related ones (e.g., *sheet*). Assuming that the processes of lexical selection affected latencies for semantic probes and that lexeme encoding affected latencies for phonological probes, Levelt et al. were able to examine whether the data fit their two-stage model better than a connectionist network model which allows for feedback from the lexeme to the lemma level (Dell, 1986). That turned out to be true (see Dell & O'Seaghdha, 1991, 1992; Levelt, 1992, and Levelt et al., 1991b, for detailed discussion of these controversial issues). Further findings from this research indicated that a lemma spreads activation to its lexeme only after it has become selected; lemmas that are merely active do not spread activation to the lexeme level. This contradicts predictions from both connectionist (Dell, 1986; MacKay, 1987) and cascade-type models (Humphreys, Riddoch, & Quinlan, 1988).

The conclusion was that the lexical access system for production has a highly modular organization. Lexical selection strictly precedes and is unaffected by phonological encoding. And that makes good sense. Lexical selection and phonological encoding are dramatically different: Lexical selection involves a semantically driven search through a huge lexicon, whereas phonological encoding involves the creation of a pronounceable phonetic pattern for each individual word. Interactions between such processes pose the threat of mutual disruption, yet lexical access is remarkably fast and accurate. Modularity may be nature's protection against error.

A final question about lexical selection concerns word frequency. Frequency seems to have reliable effects on production, as reflected in picture naming times. Oldfield and Wingfield (1965; also see Lachman, Shaffer, & Hennrikus, 1974) found a high correlation between the latency to name a pictured object and the frequency of the object's name in the language. So, the average speech onset latency was 640 ms for high-frequency *basket,* compared to 1080 ms for low-frequency *syringe.* What is the locus of this effect in the network model? Is it the concept, the lemma, the lexeme, or all three? It could even be a very late phenomenon, having to do with the initiation of articulation. Wingfield (1968) excluded the first alternative by measuring recognition latencies for the pictures—a conceptual process—and found no effect of frequency. Going from picture to concept therefore does not create the frequency effect; lexical access is apparently essential.

At the other extreme, articulatory initiation, the chief evidence for a word frequency effect comes from Balota and Chumbley (1985). They asked subjects to read a word, but to utter it only after a *go* signal which appeared at SOAs ranging from 150 to 1400 ms. Under these conditions one probably measures articulatory initiation rather than selection or phonological encoding, but there was a frequency effect of 26 ms averaged across SOAs in two experiments (for further discussion, see Balota & Chumbley, 1990; Monsell, 1990; Monsell, Doyle, & Haggard, 1989). Clearly this is not the full word frequency effect, as measured by Oldfield and Wingfield. And perhaps it is not a word frequency effect at all, but a syllable frequency effect. Levelt and Wheeldon (in press) found that word and syllable frequency contribute independently and additively to production onset latencies. It may be, then, that most or all of the "real" word frequency effect has its origin somewhere between conception and articulation.

How, then, to distinguish between the lemma and lexeme levels as sources of word frequency effects? Jescheniak & Levelt (in press) assessed the contribution of lemmas with a gender decision task using Dutch words which, like French words, come in one of two grammatical genders. In this task, Dutch-speaking subjects saw pictures and indicated the gender of the word that named the depicted object. They did this by pressing one of two buttons, thereby judging the gender of the target noun without actually uttering it. In another task they simply named the pictures. Each picture appeared three times under both task conditions, and in both there was an initial frequency effect. But in the gender decision task the frequency effect dissipated, disappearing entirely on the third trial. In naming, however, the frequency effect remained undiminished over trials. From these and other experiments, Jescheniak & Levelt concluded that the persistent frequency effect is a lexeme effect. The ephemeral effect of frequency on gender judgment may have its origin in the connection between the lemma and gender nodes (see Fig. 2) and is perhaps only a recency effect. After a lemma's gender is accessed, that information may be readily available for reuse.

In conclusion, the lexeme may be the primary locus of the frequency effect. This conclusion is consistent with findings on prelexical hesitations in spontaneous speech (Butterworth, 1980; Garrett, 1975; Levelt, 1983).

III. FUNCTION ASSIGNMENT

As message elements are mapped onto concepts and lemmas, they must also be assigned to syntactic functions. The primary problem of function assignment is to specify which elements will serve as the subject of the incipient utterance and which, if any, will serve as objects of various kinds. It is obviously necessary to separate this problem from lexical selection, since the same words may serve different functions in different sentences (e.g., *Girls like boys* versus *Boys like girls*) and even in the same sentence (e.g., *People need people*). It is also useful to treat this problem as one of grammatical encoding rather than one of message formulation, because very similar messages may be expressed in ways that differ only in the assignments of grammatical functions (e.g., *She was handing him some broccoli* vs. *She was handing some broccoli to him*). But just as the selection of lemmas is heavily influenced by the content of a message, so is the process of function assignment.

Function assignment should also be separated from constituent ordering for reasons that can be difficult to appreciate for speakers of English. English observes a relatively rigid ordering of the constituents that play different roles, but in languages with more flexible constituent orders, constituents can appear in different positions serving the same grammatical functions (often signaled by differences in case). Even in English, there are deviations from canonical word order which point to a function assignment process that is different from the ordering process. For example, a speaker can emphasize an object by "fronting" it, as in *Him I can't stand,* and if, as in this example, the fronted constituent is a pronoun (the only type of English element that reliably marks grammatical function), it will retain its objective case.

The problems that have to be addressed by a theory of function assignment have to do with the nature of the functions that are assigned, the kinds of information that control the assignment, the nature of the elements that the functions are assigned to, and the organization of the processes that carry out these operations. The first three of these problems are matters of intense debate in linguistics, and the last, more obviously the province of psycholinguistic research, has received little systematic attention. We briefly examine the first two and the last one in turn, from the perspective of the kinds of psycholinguistic data that have been brought to bear on them (the third problem remains unaddressed in the psycholinguistic literature). Again, the data come from experiments on normal speech and from observations of speech errors. However, because speech errors that are unambiguously attributable to syntactic problems are woefully scarce (Fay, 1980; Garrett, 1975; Stemberger, 1983, 1985), we rely heavily on experimental data.

A. What Functions Are Assigned?

The most familiar candidate functions are those known as the SUBJECT and DIRECT OBJECT (and, less familiarly, INDIRECT and OBLIQUE objects). The familiarity of these labels disguises enormous linguistic problems of specification and definition that we cannot begin to address (for discussion, see Bresnan, 1982; Marantz, 1984; Perlmutter, 1982; Williams, 1981), but we assume that an adequate account of grammatical functions will highlight something close to the traditional set, and that they are marked morphologically in case languages and structurally in configurational languages (such as English). To simplify the discussion, we use traditional case terminology to refer to the grammatical functions that are assigned (e.g., nominative, accusative, dative, genitive), and traditional grammatical relations terminology (subject, direct object, etc.) to refer to where the elements that are assigned these functions actually appear in English sentences (since most of the work that we consider is on English).[5] So, in English, the element that is assigned the nominative function appears in subject position.

This apparently innocuous statement disguises a substantive theoretical claim about the process of function assignment. The claim is that, within grammatical encoding, there is no level of processing at which the element that serves as the subject of the sentence plays a role that can be realized as a different grammatical relation. On this argument, there is no point at which (for example) the direct object of an active sentence (e.g., *the bone* in *A dog carried the bone*) has the same representation as the subject of its passive paraphrase (e.g., *The bone was carried by a dog*).

This claim runs counter to a traditional conception of deep structure in psycholinguistics (see Foss & Hakes, 1978, for a review), according to which "underlying" objects may be realized as subjects. The problem with this conception is that there is no evidence that function assignments normally undergo changes during grammatical encoding, and some evidence that they do not (Bock, Loebell, & Morey, 1992; Tannenbaum & Williams, 1968). Because relation changing operations (such as transformations) are likely to introduce considerable processing complexity (see Bresnan & Kaplan, 1984, for discussion), it is more parsimonious to assume that the relations are assigned just once and maintained throughout the grammatical encoding process.

This does not deny the existence of a level at which—to return to the example above—there is some uniform representation of the bone in *A dog carried the bone* and *The bone was carried by a dog*. However, we would prefer to locate this uniformity within nonlinguistic cognition (cf. Bransford, Barclay, & Franks, 1972), either in the conception of the event itself or in the components of the message. The referent of the phrase *the bone* may play the same part in a mental model of the event, regardless of how the event is described.

Likewise, the rejection of relation changing operations does not mean that there can be no underlying grammatical representation for utterances. It implies only that there is a one-to-one correspondence between the underlying and surface roles. In our minimalist conception, the underlying roles are the ones assigned during functional processing and the surface roles are the ones assigned during positional processing. Figure 4 sketches this arrangement.

Phrase exchanges (e.g., *I went to the mechanical mouse for an economy five and dime* instead of *I went to the economy five and dime for a mechanical mouse*; Garrett, 1980) represent a type of error that may arise from missteps of function assignment. They have two properties which point to something other than a simple misordering of words. The first, noted briefly in the introduction, is restricted to errors in which the inverted phrases are made up of pronouns (e.g., *you must be too tight for them* instead of *they must be too tight for you*; Stemberger, 1982), because only pronouns exhibit their function assignments. The distinctive feature of pronoun errors is that the pronouns bear the appropriate case for the position in which they erroneously appear, rather than

---

[5] Since nonconfigurational languages lack strict isomorphisms between functions and positions, it is important to remember that the relations here refer to positions only in English sentence structure.

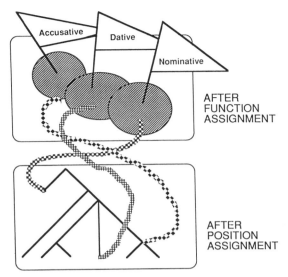

FIG. 4 The relationship between grammatical functions (after function assignment) and grammatical relations (after position assignment).

the case for the position in which they should have appeared. According to Stemberger (1982), this is the norm for such errors in English, and Berg (1987) reports a similar trend for German.

The second property of phrase exchange errors that appears to favor function assignment as the source of the problem is that the verbs in the error-bearing utterances tend to agree with the subject that is actually produced rather than with the subject that was intended (e.g., *that's supposed to hang onto you* instead of *you're supposed to hang onto that* and *most cities are true of that* instead of *that's true of most cities*; Stemberger, 1982). Stemberger (1985) reports that this occurred in 6 of the 7 relevant errors in his corpus. It suggests that the element that appears in subject position in the error also bears the role of subject during the formulation of the agreeing verb, compatible with the hypothesis that a function assignment error is the source of the exchange. The element's appearance in an incorrect position is only a secondary consequence of a deeper malfunction.

Experimental evidence consistent with the separation between functional and positional assignments comes from Bock et al. (1992). They used a sentence structure priming paradigm in which speakers first produced a priming sentence in one of two different syntactic structures and then saw a conceptually unrelated event which they described with a single sentence. The event was designed to be describable in either of the two primed structures (see Bock, 1990, for a more complete description of the paradigm). The results revealed separate, independent effects of the primed structure itself and of the conceptual features of the elements that served different grammatical functions. In the present scheme, these separate effects may be traced to positional and functional processing, respectively.

B. What Information Controls Functional Assignments?

Most discussions of the controllers of function assignments have focused on subject assignments (e.g., Bates & MacWhinney, 1982; Bock, 1982), although object assignments are receiving increasing attention (e.g., Bock & Warren, 1985; Gropen, Pinker, Hollander, & Goldberg, 1991; Gropen, Pinker, Hollander, Goldberg, & Wilson, 1989). The sets of controllers that dominate these discussions are (a) thematic or EVENT roles coupled with the primitive conceptual features that may help to individuate these roles and (b) discourse or ATTENTIONAL roles. We assume that these kinds of information are represented in the message, and that their effects on the process of function assignment are in part mediated by the structural and semantic conventions of the speaker's language, importantly including the subcategorization conventions or argument structures of lemmas represented in the lexicon.

1. Event Roles

The sets of event roles proposed in the literature vary widely, with little agreement about appropriate criteria for individuating them. Most of the sets include something corresponding to an agent (the instigator of an event), a patient or theme (a person or object that is affected, moved, or located), a recipient or goal (a beneficiary or moved-to location), an experiencer or instrument (the vehicle of an event or action), as well as other roles such as time and source.

There is a seductive and well-known correspondence between event roles and grammatical relations. Agents are often subjects, patients are often direct objects, and recipients are often indirect objects. However, there are both systematic and idiosyncratic violations of these correspondences: Agents sometimes appear as the oblique (*by*) objects of passive verbs and patients, recipients sometimes serve as subjects of certain active verbs (e.g., *undergo, receive*), and the same participants standing in roughly the same conceptual relationship sometimes appear in different grammatical relations (e.g., *Many people fear snakes; Snakes frighten many people*). Because the mapping between event roles and functional roles seems to be heavily influenced by the specific requirements of different verbs and verb forms (Grimshaw, 1990), one of the most important factors in the control of functional role assignment is the choice of the verb during lexical selection. This has so far received little attention in production research (but see Jarvella & Sinnott, 1972; Gropen et al., 1989, 1991).

The difficulty of specifying a uniform set of event roles has led to various linguistic proposals for reducing them to more primitive meaning relations (Bierwisch, 1986; Jackendoff, 1987). An array of psycholinguistic evidence suggests that these relations are in some way bound up with such substantive notions as animacy (see Bock et al., 1992, for review) and concreteness (Bock & Warren, 1985; Clark & Begun, 1971; C. T. James, Thompson, & Baldwin, 1973). In general, this work suggests that the more animate or concrete the participant in an event, the more likely it is to appear in the subject relation in an utterance.

The simplest interpretation of many of these results is that animate or concrete elements are more likely to appear early in a string of words. However, there is evidence that implicates functional role assignment rather than serial positioning in these effects. It comes from experiments in which the effects of animacy and concreteness on word order in conjunctions (where the role assignments are the same but the positions of the words differ; e.g., *the farmer and the refrigerator* vs. *the refrigerator and the farmer*) were contrasted with their effects on the order of constituents in sentences (where the roles as well as the positions differ; e.g., *The farmer bought the refrigerator* vs. *The refrigerator was bought by the farmer*). The results show that the simple word ordering impact of these factors is weak to nonexistent, whereas the ordering variations that follow from changes in grammatical role assignment are robust (Bock & Warren, 1985; McDonald, Bock, & Kelly, 1993).

2. Attentional Roles

Event roles and attentional roles are intimately related, insofar as different event roles naturally vary in attentional values. For example, Osgood (1980) emphasized the natural perceptual prominence of agents that derives from their movements, and studies of visual attention have confirmed such a tendency in young children (Robertson & Suci, 1980). Still, relative attentional values may vary with changes in the relative prominence of participants, with corresponding consequences for functional role assignments.

This is a natural expectation that has surprisingly weak confirmation in studies of event or scene descriptions (Bates & Devescovi, 1989; Flores d'Arcais, 1987; Osgood, 1971; Sridhar, 1989). The general finding from such studies is that when the elements' event roles and animacy (for example) are equated, variations in the prominence of elements within events have only weak effects on function assignments.

A much more powerful influence is found when prominence is manipulated by discourse or conversational means. Perhaps the most potent device is a question. Imagine that a person observes a scene in which a girl chases a boy and then is asked *What was going on with the girl?* or *What was going on with the boy?* Many studies have shown that in these or similar circumstances, the questioned entity tends to be assigned the subject role in the answer (Bates & Devescovi, 1989; Bock, 1977; Carroll, 1958). Pictures of individual event participants or single words referring to them, presented as cues for the description of previously or subsequently apprehended events, seem to have similar effects (Bock, 1986a; Bock & Irwin, 1980; Flores d'Arcais, 1975; Perfetti & Goldman, 1975; Prentice, 1967; Turner & Rommetveit, 1968).

It is a short step to the information structure of sentences in discourse. By information structure, we mean the distribution of given (or topical) and new information (Clark & Haviland, 1977; Halliday, 1970). The linguistic marking of given information differs from that of new information in a variety of ways, including prosody (Cutler & Isard, 1980; Fowler & Housum, 1987; Needham, 1990; but see Eefting, 1991) and positioning within sentences (MacWhinney & Bates, 1978; Smith, 1971). Linked to given information's general tendency to appear early in sentences is its affinity for the subject relation (Tomlin, 1986).

It seems likely that the sentence-level effects of topicalization are attributable to forces similar to those responsible for the effects of concreteness of individual entities. Both may be regarded as increasing the definiteness or relative mental prominence of participants in the events that sentences describe.

Bock and Warren (1985) termed this mental prominence CONCEPTUAL ACCESSI-
BILITY.

Although grammatical functions could in principle be assigned in any order
or even all at once, there are reasons to suspect that, at least in English, there
is a preference for combinations of elements that permit the nominative function
to be assigned first. Elements that are accessible (in the senses described above)
tend to appear as subjects more often than as objects (see Bock, 1987, for
review), particularly when accessibility arises from the message or the meaning
rather than from factors that primarily affect the word form (such as frequency or
phonological simplicity; see Bock, 1986a; Levelt & Maassen, 1981; McDonald et
al., 1993; Streim & Chapman, 1987). This tendency finds a reflection in
proposals about hierarchies of grammatical functions or relations (Keenan &
Comrie, 1977), in which subjects dominate all other functions. From a processing standpoint, the advantage of such an arrangement is clear: Things that
present themselves more prominently or more readily are given a function that
allows them to lead in the utterance itself.

C. What Is the Nature and Organization of the Processes That Carry Out Function Assignments?

Woven into the preceding discussion was a claim about the organization of
function assignment that we now consider explicitly. It is that verbs somehow
control function assignment.

A verb's specification of its normally expressed arguments may serve to
organize function assignment around a unit that is roughly equivalent to the
clause. A simple one-clause sentence such as *She was handing him some
broccoli* consists of a single main verb and its arguments. The verb *hand*
requires three arguments, an agent, a recipient, and a theme. During functional
processing, the element corresponding to the agent should be assigned the
nominative function, the one corresponding to the recipient should be assigned
the dative function, and the one corresponding to the theme should be assigned
the accusative function. The realization of these as the subject, first object (the
object that immediately follows the verb), and second object creates a full or
simple clause.

One of the implications of this view of the organization of production was
examined by Bock and Cutting (1992). Their method involved the elicitation
of a type of verb agreement error called an ATTRACTION ERROR. Such errors
occur when the head of the subject noun phrase is separated from the verb, as
are *generalization* and *are* in the observed error *The only generalization I would
dare to make about our customers are that they're pierced*. Bock and Cutting's
speakers were asked to convert complex subject phrases into full sentences by
completing them. The phrases contained a head noun (e.g., *The claim*) followed
either by a phrase postmodifier of the head (as in *The claim about the newborn
baby . . .*) or a clause postmodifier of the head (as in *The claim that wolves
had raised the baby . . .*). Although these subject phrases differed in structural
complexity, they were equated in length (in terms of numbers of syllables).
The critical fragments ended in a plural noun (*babies*) intended to elicit verb
agreement errors in the completions (cf. Bock & Miller, 1991). The question
was whether the clause postmodifier would promote or retard this tendency
relative to the phrase postmodifier.

A simple sequential view of production suggests that the clause imposes a processing load analogous to the problems created by clauses in comprehension (Caplan, 1972; Jarvella, 1971), predicting an increase in errors after clauses. Alternatively, if production is hierarchically organized, guided by the requirements of verbs, the prediction is that clause postmodifiers will actually reduce the number of errors. Consider a fragment completion along the lines of *The claim that wolves had raised the babies was rejected*. Here, agreement in the outer clause (e.g., *The claim was rejected*) may be partially protected from the material in the inner clause (*wolves had raised the babies*). Because the error-eliciting word *babies* occurs within a different clause (bound to a different verb) in *The claim that wolves had raised the babies was rejected* than in *The claim about the newborn babies was rejected,* the agreement operation may be protected from the irrelevant plural. The results from three experiments supported the "protection" hypothesis: Errors were more likely to occur after phrase than after clause postmodifiers. This points to clauses as important organizing forces in functional processing.

The centrality of the verb to this organization becomes even clearer when the straightforward equation between verbs and clauses breaks down. Not all clauses are full, simple ones, and these divergences offer a better glimpse of the role that the verb may play.

Ford and Holmes (1978; also see Ford, 1982; and Holmes, 1988) examined such cases in a study in which subjects spoke extemporaneously on a prescribed topic while at the same time monitoring for a randomly presented auditory tone. The reaction times to the tones were then analyzed as a function of their location in the subject's speech stream. The critical locations were the beginnings and ends of functional verb units that did and did not straightforwardly correspond to the beginnings and ends of simple clauses. For example, *I began the book* is a simple clause with only one functional verb unit, whereas *I began working a lot harder* contains two functional verb units, one for the finite (tensed) verb *began* and a second for the nonfinite verb *working*. The results revealed a reliable increase in tone detection latencies at the ends of functional verb units, regardless of whether those units corresponded to simple clauses.

Other results consistent with verb-centered control of function assignment comes from evidence about the minimum scope of advance preparation in production (Lindsley, 1975), which seems to require at least some planning of the verb. Evidence about the maximum scope comes primarily from contextual speech errors, errors in which the source seems to be interference from another element of the intended utterance. The wide majority of such errors originate from material in the same clause (Garrett, 1980). However, word exchange errors originate in adjoining clauses 20% of the time, leading Garrett (1980) to the suggestion that no more than two clauses may be planned at once. Holmes (1988) discusses whether such two-clause errors typically involve verbs that take clausal arguments (and so require the formulation of two clauses at once), but the question remains open.

Finally, there is an intriguing (but inconclusive) asymmetry between verbs and the other major grammatical categories (nouns, adjectives, and adverbs) in their susceptibility to semantic substitution. Hotopf (1980) reported error data from both English and German which suggests that the tendency for verbs to undergo semantic substitution is vastly lower, both in actual incidence and as a percentage of opportunities. This resistance to substitution could stem from the centrality of the verb to higher level production processes. But it could also be because the lexical organization of verbs is different from that of nouns (Huttenlocher & Lui, 1979) or because the nature of meaning relationships among verbs makes the diagnosis of a substitution more difficult (Gentner & France, 1988).

D. Summary of Functional Processing

Functional processing, as we have described it, yields an activated set of lemmas and a set of syntactic functions, linked together via the argument structures of the lemmas (notably that of the verb). This is illustrated in Figure 5. Beyond this, there must be a specification of individual elements, such as the indefiniteness of the "broccoli" argument indicated by *some*, the past progressive nature of the action, and the singularity of the verb. We show some of these specifications as annotations on the argument structure in Figure 5 but postpone their discussion until we get to the topic of inflection below.

IV. Constituent Assembly

The partial functional structure in Figure 5 consists of temporary (and therefore labile) linkages among stored elements and carries no intrinsic order. To convert this into an utterance, something has to impose a sequence on the elements. There is a great deal of evidence that in order to do this, speakers follow

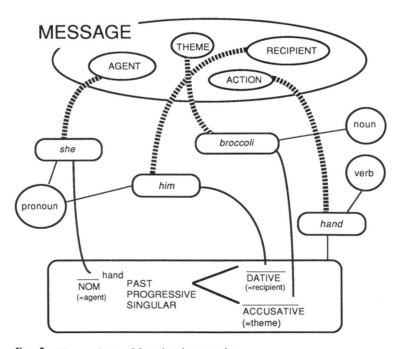

Fig. 5   The products of functional processing.

something like the scheme specified in a hierarchical constituent structure. The evidence comes from formal analysis, from pauses in speech, and from errors in sentence recall.

Formal linguistic analysis provides the traditional arguments for hierarchical structure. Without such a notion it is difficult to explain structural ambiguity (as found in the alternative readings of *The old [men and women] were left behind in the village* vs. *The [old men] and [women] were left behind in the village*), or sentence segmentation (why a sentence such as *The girl that kissed the boy blushed* is not understood to assert that a boy blushed, despite the fact that it contains the sequence *the boy blushed*), or verb agreement (verbs agree not with what immediately precedes them, in a positional sense, but with a particular constituent structure category, roughly, the highest noun phrase in the same clause; compare *The boy who watched the clowns **was** amused* and *The boys who watched the clown **were** amused*).

Data from language performance indicate that such structures somehow characterize the products of speech production processes. Normal prosodic patterns (Cooper, Paccia, & Lapointe, 1978; Grosjean, Grosjean, & Lane, 1979) and hesitations (Boomer, 1965; Butterworth, 1980; Butterworth & Beattie, 1978; Maclay & Osgood, 1959; see Garrett, 1982, for review) have been argued to reflect structures that are larger than individual words but smaller than full clauses. Although pause patterns are multiply determined, reflecting forces other than syntactic structure (Gee & Grosjean, 1983; Levelt, 1989; Selkirk, 1984), they appear to be heavily influenced by phrase structure. Likewise, the products of sentence recall (which are also products of language production) indicate that speakers organize sentences in terms of phrasal constituents (Johnson, 1965, 1966a, 1966b).

Such things help to establish that speakers create utterances that have hierarchically organized phrase groupings, or frames. However, they say nothing about the information that is encoded or elaborated in frames or about the processes that create them. The next two sections review those questions.

A. What's in a Frame?

The structure of a sentence could in principle reflect the structure of any of several different sorts of information, including event role information, syntactic function information, and prosodic information. Since phrase structure often confounds these possibilities, it is difficult to disentangle them by observation alone. Bock and Loebell (1990) employed an experimental approach to this issue that relies on a tendency among speakers to use the same form repeatedly, sometimes with different words (Bock, 1986b; Levelt & Kelter, 1982; Schenkein, 1980; Tannen, 1987; Weiner & Labov, 1983). Bock and Loebell examined whether the form repetition tendency changed when the repeated structures represented different event roles or different prosodic patterns. They found no effects of these variations, although the form repetition tendency itself was clearly in evidence. Together with the findings of Bock et al. (1992), the appearance is that the structure is formed under the control of information that is not readily interpretable as conceptual, semantic, or prosodic.

The obvious alternative candidates are the syntactic functions and the grammatical categories of the lemmas that realize them. For example, subjects are typically configured in one way within a sentence structure and direct objects in another. Nouns occur as the heads of noun phrases, verbs as the heads of verb phrases, prepositions as the heads of prepositional phrases, and so on. So, given the nominative function and a noun lemma to fill it, adequate information is available to create or retrieve the rudiments of a subject noun phrase in the proper position in an utterance frame.

B. The Processes of Constitutent Assembly

An influential theory of phrase structure elaboration was proposed by Yngve (1960). According to the model, production processes generate a phrase structure tree from top to bottom and left to right, so the first part of the sentence to be elaborated is the leftmost daughter. As the processor traverses this branch, it stores information about commitments to rightward branches that have yet to be elaborated. For example, to produce the simple structure shown below (which would be appropriate for an uninflected version of a sentence such as *Our dog chases squirrels*),

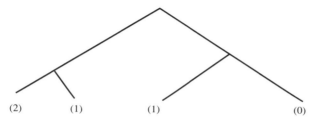

(2)   (1)   (1)   (0)

the generator starts at the top, where a commitment must be made to one rightward elaboration (the verb phrase) and proceeds leftward past the first node (the noun phrase), where it incurs another commitment to a rightward elaboration (the head noun) and terminates at the determiner branch. The number of commitments at this point, two, is shown in parentheses. The generator then returns to elaborate the noun phrase by creating the noun branch. Finally, it returns to the top and proceeds to elaborate the verb phrase.

Yngve's theory makes a very concrete prediction about the effects of branching on the difficulty of producing a sentence. Since commitments to right branches are stored while the generator elaborates other branches to the left, the cost of storage may appear as an impairment to fluency, perhaps as a slowing of speech rate or as an increase in the probability of error. The number of such commitments grows as a function of the depth in the tree of the left branches, with a corresponding increase in the storage cost. Storage cost is typically assessed by counting the number of left branches dominating each terminal element (word) of the sentence (which yields the number of right-branching commitments) and dividing by the total number of words (which yields a measure of mean depth). For the structure above, the mean depth is 1.0.

This model has been examined by a number of investigators, including Johnson (1966a, 1966b), Martin and Roberts (1966, 1967; Martin, Roberts, & Collins, 1968), and Perfetti (1969a, 1969b; Perfetti & Goodman, 1971). Little consistent support has been found for the detailed predictions of the depth hypothesis (see Fodor, Bever, & Garrett, 1974, Chaps. 5 and 6, and Frazier,

1985, for review and further discussion), perhaps because mean depth is insufficiently sensitive to structure assembly. The measure is a global one, whereas disruptions of surface syntactic elaboration may be local. Likewise, most tests of the depth hypothesis have employed methods (such as sentence recall) that are not suited to the detection of a speaker's transient encoding problems.

Some support for a broader implication of Yngve's model came from experiments by Forster (1966, 1967, 1968a, 1968b). Forster looked at the ease and speed of completing sentences that had words deleted at the beginning or end. He found that it was more difficult to create the beginnings of sentences, as would be expected if the existence of rightward commitments burdens the generation of sentences. Evidence that this was not exclusively the result of practice in generating sentences from left to right came from comparisons of sentence completion performance across languages that differed in the degree to which their sentences characteristically branch to the left.

Still, there is something highly artificial about the task that Forster employed, although it is an artificiality that is built into Yngve's model. Speakers may rarely know exactly how their sentences will end before they begin them, but depth calculations cannot be made precisely unless they do. So, while Forster's experiments generally supported the original theory, they involved a task that diverges from ordinary production in just the way that the theory does, making it unclear whether the results can be generalized to normal formulation processes.

A related form of support for Yngve's theory comes from the tendency for "heavier" or more complex constituents to appear later in sentences, which reduces their depth. Thus, the sentence *The clerk showed the woman a book with a picture on its cover of Nancy Reagan glaring at Raisa Gorbachev* sounds much more natural than *The clerk showed a book with a picture on its cover of Nancy Reagan glaring at Raisa Gorbachev to the woman.* There is no comparable disparity between the formally similar sentences *The clerk showed the woman a book* and *The clerk showed a book to the woman.* A related phenomenon occurs in language acquisition, where subject-elaborated noun phrases have been found to appear later in the course of development than object-elaborated noun phrases (Pinker, 1984). However, as Frazier (1985) pointed out, these facts are compatible with any approach which predicts that complex constituents tend to appear at points of low complexity within a sentence.

A computational model that avoids the pitfalls of Yngve's approach has been proposed by de Smedt (1990; also see Kempen & Hoenkamp, 1987; Lapointe & Dell, 1989). What distinguishes the model is that it permits incremental production. It does this by building pieces of phrase structure as the lemmas and function assignments that demand particular phrasal fragments become available, and fitting the fragments together according to constraints on possible unifications (see Kay, 1985, for a discussion of unification procedures). The phrase structure is thereby assembled in a piecemeal and heuristic fashion under the control of lemmas and their functions, rather than by means of an algorithm that generates a tree into which words must be inserted. The predictions of the model seem most likely to concern problems that might arise during unification attempts among incompatible fragments, but these predictions remain to be worked out and tested.

V. INFLECTION

In order to examine a heated controversy in the production literature, we consider under the heading of inflection not only inflection proper, but also the formulation of the function words that are often associated with grammatical phrases of different types (e.g., determiners for noun phrases, auxilliaries for verb phrases, and prepositions for prepositional phrases). Function words and inflectional affixes (together with derivational affixes,[6] which we will largely ignore) constitute the elements of the CLOSED CLASS, so called because its inventory (both in the language and in the vocabulary of individual adult speakers) undergoes change much more slowly than the inventory of the open class (nouns, verbs, adjectives, and adverbs).

One source of the controversy is a relatively undisputed fact about speech errors: The elements of the closed class are less likely to be involved than elements of the open class. So, the words in blends, in semantic and phonological substitutions, and in exchanges tend to be members of the open class. Even sound errors, which are much more likely to be indiscriminate about syntactic classifications than word errors, seem to be constrained by open and closed class membership, occurring principally within open class words in spontaneous speech.

At issue is how to account for this regularity. Open and closed class words differ in many other ways, and these differences suggest alternative accounts for their behavior. So, open class words by and large occur less frequently than closed class words, they are learned later in language acquisition, they are longer, and they are more likely to bear stress. Such factors, alone or together, could create a predisposition to error that has nothing to do with word class per se.

In the following sections, we present two alternative accounts of how the elements of the closed class receive their places within a sentence structure. Along with these accounts we consider some of the other evidence that has been brought to bear on the issue.

A. Inflections as Frame Features

Beyond the general features of the behavior of closed class elements in errors, Garrett (1982) has called on another disparity between them and open class elements in arguing that the closed class is a special word class or separate vocabulary. Among some aphasics, the closed class is disproportionately absent from speech (Saffran, Schwartz, & Marin, 1980), despite the general rule that high-frequency words are more likely to be preserved in aphasic speech. Garrett has also presented an analysis of normal speech errors which suggests that they are more likely to occur among open class words even when frequency is controlled (Garrett, 1990).

---

[6] The distinction between derivational and inflectional affixes is based in part upon whether they change the grammatical category of the word to which they apply. By this criterion, the plural affix for nouns and number, tense, and aspect affixes for verbs are inflectional, whereas derivational affixes change verbs into nouns (e.g., *-tion,* as in *creation*), nouns into verbs (e.g., *-ate,* as in *pulsate*), nouns into adjectives (e.g., *-ly,* as in *princely*), and so on. However, not all derivational affixes change form class (e.g., *un-, mis-*).

To account for such evidence, Garrett (1982) argued that the elements of the closed class are intrinsic features of the grammatical frame. Unlike open class words, which have to be linked to the frame in some fashion (e.g., by being assigned a grammatical function or a position), the closed class elements in an important sense are the frame, serving to define as well as mark the functions and grammatical features (e.g., definite, plural, past tense, and so on) of the open class words.

For this to happen, we might imagine that during functional assignment, each function is tagged with additional specifications appropriate to its realization. For example, if the subject is specified as definite and plural, the frame generated for the subject noun phrase should include, in addition to a branch for the head noun itself, a definite determiner branch and a branch for the plural inflection, along the lines of

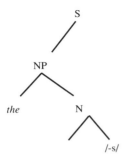

Since the additional branches are nothing more than the corresponding closed class elements themselves, they may be directly encoded after a few minor morphophonological adjustments.

B. A Mixed Model

The challenges to the frame view come from at least two directions. One focuses on an alternative explanation for the disparate behaviors of open and closed class elements in speech errors, seeking to attribute them to the differences in frequency of the class members. These differences are enormous: In the CELEX database (which includes almost 18 million words of English text; Burnage, 1990), the 70 most frequent English words are function words (though some of them, like *can*, have content usages) and range from 60,958 occurrences per million (*the*) to 1,798 per million (*now*); the first unambiguously open class word (*time*) has a frequency of 1,791 per million. Examinations of the relationship between word frequency and error proclivity have shown that infrequent forms are more likely to participate in errors than frequent forms (Dell, 1990; Stemberger & MacWhinney, 1986), consistent with a frequency hypothesis.

A second challenge is directed at the claim that closed class words define the frame. To test this, Bock (1989) examined whether structural repetition (the tendency to repeat similar phrase structures across successive sentences) is dependent on identity of closed class elements. She found equally strong structural repetition when the closed class members of sentences were different or the same, suggesting that the phrasal configurations of sentences are controlled by forces that are not fully equatable with their closed class elements.

To accommodate such challenges to Garrett's view of the inflection process, Lapointe and Dell (1989) offered a modified account that distinguishes between the free standing elements of the closed class (such as determiners and auxilliaries) and inflectional affixes (such as the plural and past tense). In their model, only the affixes are given directly in the frame. The freestanding function words have to be inserted by an additional operation, so that the frame for the noun phrase shown above would appear as something closer to the following.

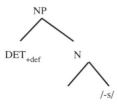

The motivation for this treatment was an analysis by Lapointe (1985) of simplification errors in the speech of English- and Italian-speaking aphasics. Within the errors, Lapointe noted a difference in the behavior of freestanding function words and affixes. Whereas function words tended to be omitted, affixes tended to be replaced with other affixes, suggesting that affixes are in some sense more intrinsic to the frame than function words.

The model's treatment of function words nonetheless distinguishes them from content words as well as from affixes. They differ from content words in the mechanism by which their phonological or morphosyntactic representation is linked to the frame, prior to phonological encoding, maintaining something of the spirit of the separate class view.[7] Specifically, the assumption is that for each designated function word slot there is only one filler, so that there is no competition among candidates. However, during phonological encoding, function and content words undergo the same operations, suggesting that, other things equal, open and closed class words should be equally prone to sound errors. This prediction received support from experimental studies of error elicitation reported by Dell (1990).

C. The Generation of Bound Inflections

Spontaneous speech errors strongly suggest that bound inflected forms are accessed separately from stem forms during generation. Most of the evidence for this comes from stranding errors such as the one cited in the introduction (*You ordered up ending some fish dish*; Garrett, in press). Stemberger (1985) found that inflectional affixes were stranded in 88.9% of the errors in which it was possible in his corpus. Both the frame model and the mixed model imply that stranding is a consequence of normal frame generation coupled with some failure of lexical access, and not a frame generation problem, in agreement with Stemberger (1985). The question to be addressed here, then, is how the hierarchical framework comes to have the appropriate configuration to control the appearance of the bound elements of the closed class.

---

[7] However, this separate class does not constitute a separately stored vocabulary, but a class of words whose use is heavily constrained by syntactic features.

For many elements of the closed class, including the freestanding ones, the notion of indirect election can be called on to explain how such elements become part of the frame. As discussed in the section on lexical selection, certain lemmas carry specifications about the closed class elements that can or must accompany them. These specifications may be represented in a way that can be directly incorporated into a structural frame, so that the choice of a lemma that carries such information guarantees the compilation of the element into the developing utterance. For example, if the plural form of *goat* (*goats*) is selected, the lemma should mandate the construction of a noun phrase in which the stem of the head noun is affixed with the plural /-s/. However, if the choice were the plural form of *sheep* (*sheep*), no affix would be called for.

A related but more difficult question has to do with the circumstances that lead to the selection of lemmas that require closed class elements. In some cases these selections may be under direct control of message elements, as when a verb is specified for past tense. But in others the connection to message features can be less straightforward, as when there are syntactic dependencies among inflectional features. So, why do speakers say *She **was** handing him some broccoli* rather than *She **were** handing him some broccoli?* In such dependent relationships, two (or more) constituents of a sentence reflect a value of some feature that triggers an inflectional variation. These constituents need not be adjacent: In subject–verb agreement, for example, agreement can cross an indeterminate amount of intervening material. What is necessary is that the agreeing constituents stand in appropriate structural or syntactic-functional relationships (so in English, agreement operates between the head of the subject noun phrase and the finite verb).

Indirect evidence about the workings of the agreement operation in production comes from studies of errors of attraction. As noted above, attraction errors have the property that the number of the verb agrees with the number of some (usually plural) constituent of the sentence other than the head noun phrase. Assuming that such errors are constrained by the factors that control normal agreement (an assumption that obviously may be wrong), Bock and Miller (1991) and Bock and Eberhard (1993) explored how various number characteristics affect the incidence of attraction errors in speech. These characteristics included the "multipleness" of the referent of the subject (as it might be represented in the message; cf. Pollard & Sag, 1988), the semantic multipleness versus grammatical plurality of the attracting noun phrase, the regularity of plural marking, and spurious surface features of plurality (plural-like pronunciation, as in the word *rose*). The only factor that reliably created attraction errors was grammatical plurality (i.e., subcategorized plurality) of the attracting noun. Because grammatical plurality is a property of lemmas rather than of nonlinguistic concepts or messages, lemmas may be the principal source of number agreement features in English utterances.

The obvious place to state this dependency in the general architecture we have set out is within functional processing, since it is there that the relevant relationships are represented. In functional processing terms, the creation of the dependency requires that the finite (tense and number carrying) verb and the noun lemma linked to the nominative function have the same number. For this to happen, the verb must inherit the subject's number feature, or the subject must inherit the verb's number feature, or both must inherit the same value of a feature that is stated elsewhere (one possible locus is in the message, on a linguistic argument persuasively developed by Pollard & Sag, 1988). The distribution of attraction errors, both in spontaneous and elicited speech, points toward the first of these alternatives.

Linked to the question of the origins of the frame features that control the appearance of inflections is a current controversy over the representation of regularly and irregularly inflected forms in the lexicon (Kim, Pinker, Prince, & Prasada, 1991; Pinker, 1991; Rumelhart & McClelland, 1987). One position in this debate is that regular and irregular forms are represented in the same way,[8] so that there is no explicit sense in which inflected regular forms consist of a stem and an affix. As Stemberger (1985) observed, this position is challenged by the evidence that inflected forms in complete utterances tend to be created—or to fall apart—in a piecemeal way, along morphological rather than phonological lines. Such evidence adds weight to the alternative, a rule-based origin for the production of inflected forms in connected speech.

VI. CONCLUSION

By way of summary, Figure 6 sketches the products of each set of grammatical encoding processes that we have discussed, taking the (by now hackneyed) example *She was handing him some broccoli* as the target utterance. Functional processing serves to integrate a set of lexical specifications with a set of syntactic functions, which in turn guide the creation of a framework for the positioning of words. This framework controls positional processing, the output of which is an ordered set of word forms and their inflections.

We have reviewed several types of evidence in developing this picture, among them the constraints that have been observed on errors in spontaneous and elicited speech. In closing we should point out one notable absence from this discussion. Missing is Freud's (1917/1976) account of errors such as the parliamentarian's *Gentlemen, I take notice that a full quorum of members is present and herewith declare the sitting closed.* Because Freud's account has become part of the fabric of popular culture, it is important to consider its bearing on an explanation of how people talk. The main drawback of Freud's analysis, as Freud himself acknowledged, is that few speech errors have discernible psychodynamic content. Yet most speech errors, whether or not they carry clues to a speaker's unconscious impulses, display an impressively regular set of linguistic restrictions (note that the parliamentarian's slip is a thoroughly ordinary semantic substitution). It follows that errors of speech may carry fewer clues to the mysteries of unconscious motivation than to the mundane and relatively mechanical underpinnings of speech.

Unfortunately, the clues about these underpinnings are sometimes ambiguous or conflicting and are always open to alternative interpretations. For such

---

[8] In a certain sense, they may not be represented at all as lemmas or lexical forms (Seidenberg & McClelland, 1989).

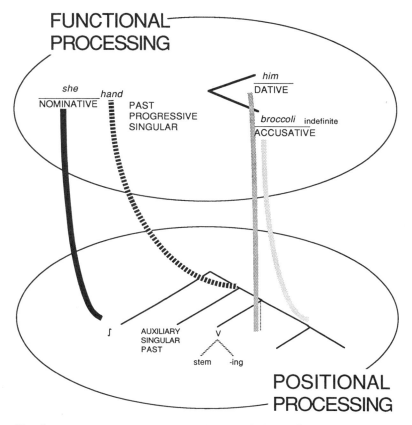

FIG. 6 An illustration of the events of grammatical encoding.

reasons, computational and experimental approaches have assumed increasing importance in the study of language production. Computational models like those of Dell (1986; Dell, Juliano, & Govindjee, 1993), de Smedt (1990), Kempen and Hoenkamp (1987), and Roelofs (1992) offer concrete proposals about the organization of processing and, in the best cases, generate specific predictions about the consequences of the mechanisms they embody. Because the overt characteristics of language production are readily observable and quantifiable, the predictions made by these models are amenable to testing across a wide array of data. For such reasons, the computational approach to production offers great promise.

Systematic, controlled empirical testing is a necessary complement to computational models, and here too, there have been promising developments. As the present review suggests, there is now an array of experimental methods that strategically target the underlying dynamics of production, most of them relying on techniques (like interference and priming) that transiently sideswipe or enhance specific subcomponents of formulation between messages and articulation. These developments are nonetheless fairly new and narrowly spread over the range of issues in production, in part because of the challenge of manipulating the language production process without disrupting the fundamental features of the underlying communicative intention.[9] Critical observations are therefore sparse at many points, making the research we have reviewed little more than a preliminary step toward the understanding of grammatical encoding.

ACKNOWLEDGMENTS

During the preparation of this chapter, Kathryn Bock was supported in part by a fellowship from the Max Planck Society and by grants from the Fulbright Program and the National Science Foundation (BNS 90-09611).

REFERENCES

Balota, D. A., & Chumbley, J. I. (1985). The locus of word-frequency effects in the pronunciation task: Lexical access and/or production? *Journal of Memory and Language, 24,* 89–106.

Balota, D. A., & Chumbley, J. I. (1990). Where are the effects of frequency in visual word recognition tasks? Right where we said they were! Comment on Monsell et al. (1989). *Journal of Experimental Psychology: General, 119,* 231–237.

Bates, E., & Devescovi, A. (1989). Crosslinguistic studies of sentence production. In B. MacWhinney & E. Bates (Eds.), *The crosslinguistic study of sentence processing* (pp. 225–253). Cambridge: Cambridge University Press.

Bates, E., & MacWhinney, B. (1982). Functionalist approaches to grammar. In E. Wanner & L. R. Gleitman (Eds.), *Language acquisition: The state of the art* (pp. 173–218). Cambridge: Cambridge University Press.

Berg, T. (1987). The case against accommodation: Evidence from German speech error data. *Journal of Memory and Language, 26,* 277–299.

Bierwisch, M. (1969). On certain problems of semantic representations. *Foundations of Language, 5,* 153–184.

Bierwisch, M. (1986). On the nature of semantic form in natural language. In F. Klix & H. Hagendorf (Eds.), *Human memory and cognitive capabilities: Mechanisms and performances* (Part B, pp. 765–784). Amsterdam: North-Holland.

Bierwisch, M., & Schreuder, R. (1992). From concepts to lexical items. *Cognition, 42,* 23–60.

Bock, J. K. (1977). The effect of a pragmatic presupposition on syntactic structure in question answering. *Journal of Verbal Learning and Verbal Behavior, 16,* 723–734.

Bock, J. K. (1982). Toward a cognitive psychology of syntax: Information processing contributions to sentence formulation. *Psychological Review, 89,* 1–47.

Bock, J. K. (1986a). Meaning, sound, and syntax: Lexical priming in sentence production. *Journal of Experimental Psychology: Learning, Memory, and Cognition, 12,* 575–586.

Bock, J. K. (1986b). Syntactic persistence in language production. *Cognitive Psychology, 18,* 355–387.

Bock, J. K. (1987). Coordinating words and syntax in speech plans. In A. Ellis (Ed.), *Progress in the psychology of language* (pp. 337–390). London: Erlbaum.

Bock, J. K. (1989). Closed-class immanence in sentence production. *Cognition, 31,* 163–186.

Bock, J. K. (1990). Structure in language: Creating form in talk. *American Psychologist, 45,* 1221–1236.

Bock, J. K., & Cutting, J. C. (1992). Regulating mental energy: Performance units in language production. *Journal of Memory and Language, 31,* 99–127.

[9] The assumption that this is possible is itself a point of controversy (Butterworth & Hadar, 1989; McNeill, 1985, 1987, 1989).

Bock, J. K., & Eberhard, K. M. (1993). Meaning, sound, and syntax in English number agreement. *Language and Cognitive Processes, 8,* 57–99.

Bock, J. K., & Irwin, D. E. (1980). Syntactic effects of information availability in sentence production. *Journal of Verbal Learning and Verbal Behavior, 19,* 467–484.

Bock, J. K., & Loebell, H. (1990). Framing sentences. *Cognition, 35,* 1–39.

Bock, J. K., Loebell, H., & Morey, R. (1992). From conceptual roles to structural relations: Bridging the syntactic cleft. *Psychological Review, 99,* 150–171.

Bock, J. K., & Miller, C. A. (1991). Broken agreement. *Cognitive Psychology, 23,* 45–93.

Bock, J. K., & Warren, R. K. (1985). Conceptual accessibility and syntactic structure in sentence formulation. *Cognition, 21,* 47–67.

Boomer, D. S. (1965). Hesitation and grammatical encoding. *Language and Speech, 8,* 148–158.

Bransford, J. D., Barclay, J. R., & Franks, J. J. (1972). Sentence memory: A constructive versus interpretive approach. *Cognitive Psychology, 3,* 193–209.

Bresnan, J. (Ed.). (1982). *The mental representation of grammatical relations.* Cambridge, MA: MIT Press.

Bresnan, J., & Kaplan, R. M. (1984). Grammars as mental representations of language. In W. Kintsch, J. R. Miller, & P. G. Polson (Eds.), *Method and tactics in cognitive science* (pp. 103–135). Hillsdale, NJ: Erlbaum.

Brown, A. S. (1991). A review of the tip-of-the-tongue experience. *Psychological Bulletin, 109,* 204–223.

Brown, R., & McNeill, D. (1966). The "tip of the tongue" phenomenon. *Journal of Verbal Learning and Verbal Behavior, 5,* 325–337.

Burnage, A. G. (1990). *Celex: A guide for users.* Nijmegen, The Netherlands: University of Nijmegen.

Butterworth, B. (1980). Evidence from pauses in speech. In B. Butterworth (Ed.), *Language production* (Vol. 1, pp. 155–176). London: Academic Press.

Butterworth, B. (1982). Speech errors: Old data in search of new theories. In A. Cutler (Ed.), *Slips of the tongue and language production* (pp. 73–108). Berlin: Mouton.

Butterworth, B. (1992). Disorders of phonological encoding. *Cognition, 42,* 261–286.

Butterworth, B. L., & Beattie, G. W. (1978). Gesture and silence as indicators of planning in speech. In R. N. Campbell, & P. T. Smith (Eds.), *Recent advances in the psychology of language: Formal and experimental approaches.* New York: Plenum.

Butterworth, B., & Hadar, U. (1989). Gesture, speech, and computational stages: A reply to McNeill. *Psychological Review, 96,* 168–174.

Caplan, D. (1972). Clause boundaries and recognition latencies for words in sentences. *Perception & Psychophysics, 12,* 73–76.

Carroll, J. B. (1958). Process and content in psycholinguistics. In *Current trends in the description and analysis of behavior* (pp. 175–200). Pittsburgh: University of Pittsburgh Press.

Cattell, J. M. (1885). Über die Zeit der Erkennung und Benennung von Schriftzeichen, Bildern und Farben [The time to recognize and name letters, pictures, and colors]. *Philosophische Studien, 2,* 635–650.

Clark, H. H., & Begun, J. S. (1971). The semantics of sentence subjects. *Language and Speech, 14,* 34–46.

Clark, H. H., & Haviland, S. E. (1977). Comprehension and the given–new contract. In R. O. Freedle (Ed.), *Discourse production and comprehension* (pp. 1–40). Norwood, NJ: Ablex.

Collins, A. M., & Loftus, E. F. (1975). A spreading–activation theory of semantic processing. *Psychological Review, 82,* 407–428.

Collins, A. M., & Quillian, M. R. (1969). Retrieval time from semantic memory. *Journal of Verbal Learning and Verbal Behavior, 8,* 240–247.

Cooper, W. E., Paccia, J. M., & Lapointe, S. G. (1978). Hierarchical coding in speech timing. *Cognitive Psychology, 10,* 154–177.

Cutler, A. (1988). The perfect speech error. In L. M. Hyman & C. S. Li (Eds.), *Language, speech and mind: Studies in honour of Victoria A. Fromkin* (pp. 209–223). London: Routledge.

Cutler, A., & Isard, S. D. (1980). The production of prosody. In B. Butterworth (Ed.), *Language production* (Vol. 1, pp. 245–269). London: Academic Press.

Deese, J. (1984). *Thought into speech: The psychology of a language.* Englewood Cliffs, NJ: Prentice-Hall.

Dell, G. S. (1986). A spreading–activation theory of retrieval in sentence production. *Psychological Review, 93,* 283–321.

Dell, G. S. (1990). Effects of frequency and vocabulary type on phonological speech errors. *Language and Cognitive Processes, 5,* 313–349.

Dell, G. S., Juliano, C., & Govindjee, A. (1993). Structure and content in language production: A theory of frame constraints in phonological speech errors. *Cognitive Science, 17,* 149–195.

Dell, G. S., & O'Seaghdha, P. G. (1991). Mediated and convergent lexical priming in language production: A comment on Levelt et al. (1991). *Psychological Review, 98,* 604–614.

Dell, G. S., & O'Seaghdha, P. G. (1992). Stages of lexical access in language production. *Cognition, 42,* 287–314.

Dell, G. S., & Reich, P. A. (1981). Stages in sentence production: An analysis of speech error data. *Journal of Verbal Learning and Verbal Behavior, 20,* 611–629.

del Viso, S., Igoa, J. M., & García-Albea, J. E. (1991). On the autonomy of phonological encoding: Evidence from slips of the tongue in Spanish. *Journal of Psycholinguistic Research, 20,* 161–185.

Dennett, D. (1991). *Consciousness explained.* Boston: Little, Brown.

de Saussure, F. (1955). *Cours de linguistique générale.* [Course in general linguistics]. (5th ed.). Paris: Payot (Original work published in 1916).

de Smedt, K. J. M. J. (1990). *Incremental sentence generation.* Doctoral dissertation, Katholieke Universiteit Nijmegen, Nijmegen, The Netherlands.

Eefting, W. (1991). The effect of "information value" and "accentuation" on the duration of Dutch words, syllables, and segments. *Journal of the Acoustical Society of America, 89,* 412–424.

Fay, D. (1980). Transformational errors. In V. A. Fromkin (Ed.), *Errors in linguistic performance: Slips of the tongue, ear, pen, and hand* (pp. 111–122). New York: Academic Press.

Fay, D., & Cutler, A. (1977). Malapropisms and the structure of the mental lexicon. *Linguistic Inquiry, 8,* 505–520.

Fisher, C., Gleitman, H., & Gleitman, L. R. (1991). On the semantic content of subcategorization frames. *Cognitive Psychology, 23,* 1–62.

Flores d'Arcais, G. B. (1975). Some perceptual determinants of sentence construction. In G. B. Flores d'Arcais (Ed.), *Studies in perception: Festschrift for Fabio Metelli* (pp. 344–373). Milan, Italy: Martello-Giunti.

Flores d'Arcais, G. B. (1987). Perceptual factors and word order in event descriptions. In G. Kempen (Ed.), *Natural language generation* (pp. 441–451). Dordrecht: Martinus Nijhoff.

Fodor, J. A., Bever, T. G., & Garrett, M. F. (1974). *The psychology of language.* New York: McGraw-Hill.

Fodor, J. A., Garrett, M. F., Walker, E. C. T., & Parkes, C. H. (1980). Against definitions. *Cognition, 8,* 263–367.

Ford, M. (1982). Sentence planning units: Implications for the speaker's representation of meaningful relations underlying sentences. In J. Bresnan (Ed.), *The mental representation of grammatical relations* (pp. 797–827). Cambridge, MA: MIT Press.

Ford, M., & Holmes, V. M. (1978). Planning units and syntax in sentence production. *Cognition, 6,* 35–53.

Forster, K. I. (1966). Left-to-right processes in the construction of sentences. *Journal of Verbal Learning and Verbal Behavior, 5,* 285–291.

Forster, K. I. (1967). Sentence completion latencies as a function of constituent structure. *Journal of Verbal Learning and Verbal Behavior, 6,* 878–883.

Forster, K. I. (1968a). The effect of removal of length constraint on sentence completion times. *Journal of Verbal Learning and Verbal Behavior, 7,* 253–254.

Forster, K. I. (1968b). Sentence completion in left- and right-branching languages. *Journal of Verbal Learning and Verbal Behavior, 7,* 296–299.

Foss, D. J., & Hakes, D. T. (1978). *Psycholinguistics: An introduction to the psychology of language.* Englewood Cliffs, NJ: Prentice-Hall.

Fowler, C. A., & Housum, J. (1987). Talkers' signaling of "new" and "old" words in speech and listeners' perception and use of the distinction. *Journal of Memory and Language, 26,* 489–504.

Frazier, L. (1985). Syntactic complexity. In D. R. Dowty, L. Karttunen, & A. M. Zwicky (Eds.), *Natural language parsing: Psychological, computational, and theoretical perspectives* (pp. 129–189). Cambridge: Cambridge University Press.

Freud, S. (1976). Introductory lectures on psychoanalysis. In J. Strachey (Ed.), *The complete psychological works* (Vol. 15). New York: Norton. (Original work published 1917).

Fromkin, V. A. (1971). The non-anomalous nature of anomalous utterances. *Language, 47,* 27–52.

Fromkin, V. A. (Ed.). (1973). *Speech errors as linguistic evidence.* The Hague: Mouton.

Garnham, A., Shillcock, R. C., Brown, G. D. A., Mill, A. I. D., & Cutler, A. (1982). Slips of the tongue in the London–Lund corpus of spontaneous conversation. In A. Cutler (Ed.), *Slips of the tongue and language production* (pp. 251–263). Berlin: Mouton.

Garrett, M. F. (1975). The analysis of sentence production. In G. H. Bower (Ed.), *The psychology of learning and motivation* (pp. 133–177). New York: Academic Press.

Garrett, M. F. (1980). Levels of processing in sentence production. In B. Butterworth (Ed.), *Language production* (Vol. 1, pp. 177–220). London: Academic Press.

Garrett, M. F. (1982). Production of speech: Observations from normal and pathological language use. In A. Ellis (Ed.), *Normality and pathology in cognitive functions* (pp. 19–76). London: Academic Press.

Garrett, M. F. (1988). Processes in language production. In F. J. Newmeyer (Ed.), *Linguistics: The Cambridge survey: III. Language: Psychological and biological aspects* (pp. 69–96). Cambridge: Cambridge University Press.

Garrett, M. F. (1990, March). *Processing vocabularies in language production.* Paper presented at the CUNY Conference on Human Sentence Processing, New York.

Garrett, M. (1992). Disorders of lexical selection. *Cognition, 42,* 143–180.

Garrett, M. F. (in press). Errors and their relevance for models of language production. In G. Blanken, J. Dittman, H. Grim, J. Marshall, & C. Wallesch (Eds.), *Linguistic disorders and pathologies.* Berlin: de Gruyter.

Gee, J. P., & Grosjean, F. (1983). Performance structures: A psycholinguistic and linguistic appraisal. *Cognitive Psychology, 15,* 411–458.

Gentner, D., & France, I. M. (1988). The verb mutability effect: Studies of the combinatorial semantics of nouns and verbs. In S. I. Small, G. W. Cottrell, & M. K. Tanenhaus (Eds.), *Lexical ambiguity resolution* (pp. 343–382). San Mateo, CA: Morgan Kaufman.

Glaser, W. R. (1992). Picture naming. *Cognition, 42,* 61–105.

Glaser, W. R., & Düngelhoff, F.-J. (1984). The time course of picture–word interference. *Journal of Experimental Psychology: Human Perception and Performance, 10,* 640–654.

Grimshaw, J. (1990). *Argument structure.* Cambridge, MA: MIT Press.

Gropen, J., Pinker, S., Hollander, M., & Goldberg, R. (1991). Syntax and semantics in the acquisition of locative verbs. *Journal of Child Language, 18,* 115–151.

Gropen, J., Pinker, S., Hollander, M., Goldberg, R., & Wilson, R. (1989). The learnability and acquisition of the dative alternation in English. *Language, 65,* 203–257.

Grosjean, F., Grosjean, L., & Lane, H. (1979). The patterns of silence: Performance structures in sentence production. *Cognitive Psychology, 11,* 58–81.

Halliday, M. A. K. (1970). Language structure and language function. In J. Lyons (Ed.), *New horizons in linguistics* (pp. 140–165). Baltimore, MD: Penguin.

Hankamer, J. (1989). Morphological parsing and the lexicon. In W. Marslen-Wilson (Ed.), *Lexical representation and process* (pp. 392–408). Cambridge, MA: MIT Press.

Harley, T. A. (1984). A critique of top-down independent levels models of speech production: Evidence from non–plan-internal speech errors. *Cognitive Science, 8,* 191–219.

Heeschen, C. (in press). Morphosyntactic characteristics of spoken language. In G. Blanken, J. Dittman, H. Grim, J. Marshall, & C. Wallesch (Eds.), *Linguistic disorders and pathologies.* Berlin: de Gruyter.

Holmes, V. M. (1988). Hesitations and sentence planning. *Language and Cognitive Processes, 3,* 323–361.

Hotopf, W. H. N. (1980). Semantic similarity as a factor in whole-word slips of the tongue. In V. A. Fromkin (Ed.), *Errors in linguistic performance: Slips of the tongue, ear, pen, and hand* (pp. 97–109). New York: Academic Press.

Humphreys, G. W., Riddoch, M. J., & Quinlan, P. T. (1988). Cascade processes in picture identification. *Cognitive Neuropsychology, 5,* 67–103.

Huttenlocher, J., & Lui, F. (1979). The semantic organization of some simple nouns and verbs. *Journal of Verbal Learning and Verbal Behavior, 18,* 141–162.

Jackendoff, R. (1987). The status of thematic relations in linguistic theory. *Linguistic Inquiry, 18,* 369–411.

James, C. T., Thompson, J. G., & Baldwin, J. M. (1973). The reconstructive process in sentence memory. *Journal of Verbal Learning and Verbal Behavior, 12,* 51–63.

James, W. (1950). *The principles of psychology* (Vol. 1). New York: Dover. (Original work published 1890).

Jarvella, R. J. (1971). Syntactic processing of connected speech. *Journal of Verbal Learning and Verbal Behavior, 10,* 409–416.

Jarvella, R. J., & Sinnott, J. (1972). Contextual constraints on noun distributions to some English verbs by children and adults. *Journal of Verbal Learning and Verbal Behavior, 11,* 47–53.

Jescheniak, J. D., & Levelt, W. J. M. (in press). Word frequency effects in speech production: Retrieval of syntactic information and of phonological form. *Journal of Experimental Psychology: Learning, Memory, and Cognition.*

Johnson, N. F. (1965). The psychological reality of phrase-structure rules. *Journal of Verbal Learning and Verbal Behavior, 4,* 469–475.

Johnson, N. F. (1966a). The influence of associations between elements of structured verbal responses. *Journal of Verbal Learning and Verbal Behavior, 5,* 369–374.

Johnson, N. F. (1966b). On the relationship between sentence structure and the latency in generating the sentence. *Journal of Verbal Learning and Verbal Behavior, 5,* 375–380.

Kay, M. (1985). Parsing in functional unification grammar. In D. R. Dowty, L. Karttunen, & A. M. Zwicky (Eds.), *Natural language parsing: Psychological, computation, and theoretical perspectives* (pp. 251–278). Cambridge: Cambridge University Press.

Keenan, E. L. (1976). Towards a universal definition of "subject." In C. N. Li (Ed.), *Subject and topic* (pp. 303–333). New York: Academic Press.

Keenan, E. L., & Comrie, B. (1977). Noun phrase accessibility and universal grammar. *Linguistic Inquiry, 8,* 63–99.

Kelly, M. H. (1992). Using sound to solve syntactic problems: The role of phonology in grammatical category assignments. *Psychological Review, 99,* 349–364.

Kempen, G., & Hoenkamp, E. (1987). An incremental procedural grammar for sentence formulation. *Cognitive Science, 11,* 201–258.

Kim, J. J., Pinker, S., Prince, A., & Prasada, S. (1991). Why no mere mortal has ever flown out to center field. *Cognitive Science, 15,* 173–218.

Lachman, R., Shaffer, J. P., & Hennrikus, D. (1974). Language and cognition: Effects of stimulus codability, name-word frequency, and age of acquisition on lexical reaction time. *Journal of Verbal Learning and Verbal Behavior, 13,* 613–625.

Lapointe, S. G. (1985). A theory of verb form use in the speech of agrammatic aphasics. *Brain and Language, 24,* 100–155.

Lapointe, S. G., & Dell, G. S. (1989). A synthesis of some recent work in sentence production. In G. N. Carlson & M. K. Tanenhaus (Eds.), *Linguistic structure in language processing* (pp. 107–156). Dordrecht: Kluwer.

Levelt, W. J. M. (1983). Monitoring and self-repair in speech. *Cognition, 14,* 41–104.

Levelt, W. J. M. (1989). *Speaking: From intention to articulation.* Cambridge, MA: MIT Press.

Levelt, W. J. M. (1992). Accessing words in speech production: Stages, processes and representations. *Cognition, 42,* 1–22.

Levelt, W. J. M., & Kelter, S. (1982). Surface form and memory in question answering. *Cognitive Psychology, 14,* 78–106.

Levelt, W. J. M., & Maassen, B. (1981). Lexical search and order of mention in sentence production. In W. Klein & W. Levelt (Eds.), *Crossing the boundaries in linguistics* (pp. 221–252). Dordrecht: Reidel.

Levelt, W. J. M., Schriefers, H., Vorberg, D., Meyer, A. S., Pechmann, T., & Havinga, J. (1991a). The time course of lexical access in speech production: A study of picture naming. *Psychological Review, 98,* 122–142.

Levelt, W. J. M., Schriefers, H., Vorberg, D., Meyer, A. S., Pechmann, T., & Havinga, J. (1991b). Normal and deviant lexical processing: Reply to Dell and O'Seaghdha (1991). *Psychological Review, 98,* 615–618.

Levelt, W. J. M., & Wheeldon, L. (in press). Do speakers have access to a mental syllabary? *Cognition.*

Lindsley, J. R. (1975). Producing simple utterances: How far ahead do we plan? *Cognitive Psychology, 7,* 1–19.

Luce, R. D. (1959). *Individual choice behavior.* New York: Wiley.

Lupker, S. J. (1979). The semantic nature of response competition in the picture–word interference task. *Memory & Cognition, 7,* 485–495.

MacKay, D. G. (1972). The structure of words and syllables: Evidence from errors in speech. *Cognitive Psychology, 3,* 210–227.

MacKay, D. G. (1987). *The organization of perception and action: A theory for language and other cognitive skills.* New York: Springer-Verlag.

Maclay, H., & Osgood, C. E. (1959). Hesitation phenomena in spontaneous English speech. *Word, 15,* 19–44.

MacWhinney, B., & Bates, E. (1978). Sentential devices for conveying givenness and newness: A cross-cultural developmental study. *Journal of Verbal Learning and Verbal Behavior, 17,* 539–558.

Marantz, A. (1984). *On the nature of grammatical relations.* Cambridge, MA: MIT Press.

Martin, E., & Roberts, K. H. (1966). Grammatical factors in sentence retention. *Journal of Verbal Learning and Verbal Behavior, 5,* 211–218.

Martin, E., & Roberts, K. H. (1967). Sentence length and sentence retention in the free learning situation. *Psychonomic Science, 8,* 535.

Martin, E., Roberts, K. H., & Collins, A. M. (1968). Short-term memory for sentences. *Journal of Verbal Learning and Verbal Behavior, 7,* 560–566.

Martin, N., Weisberg, R. W., & Saffran, E. M. (1989). Variables influencing the occurrence of naming errors: Implications for models of lexical retrieval. *Journal of Memory and Language, 28,* 462–485.

McDonald, J. L., Bock, J. K., & Kelly, M. H. (1993). Word and world order: Semantic, phonological, and metrical determinants of serial position. *Cognitive Psychology, 25,* 188–230.

McNamara, T. P., & Miller, D. L. (1989). Attributes of theories of meaning. *Psychological Bulletin, 106,* 355–376.

McNeill, D. (1985). So you think gestures are nonverbal? *Psychological Review, 92,* 350–371.

McNeill, D. (1987). *Psycholinguistics: A new approach.* New York: Harper & Row.

McNeill, D. (1989). A straight path—to where? Reply to Butterworth and Hadar. *Psychological Review, 96,* 175–179.

Meringer, R., & Meyer, K. (1978). *Versprechen und Verlesen.* Amsterdam: Benjamins. (Original work published 1895)

Meyer, A. S. (1990). The time course of phonological encoding in language production: The encoding of successive syllables of a word. *Journal of Memory and Language, 29,* 524–545.

Meyer, A. S. (1991). The time course of phonological encoding in language production: Phonological encoding inside a syllable. *Journal of Memory and Language, 30,* 69–89.

Monsell, S. (1990). Frequency effects in lexical tasks: Reply to Balota and Chumbley. *Journal of Experimental Psychology: General, 119,* 335–339.

Monsell, S., Doyle, M. C., & Haggard, P. N. (1989). Effects of frequency on visual word recognition tasks: Where are they? *Journal of Experimental Psychology: General, 118,* 43–71.

Needham, W. P. (1990). Semantic structure, information structure, and intonation in discourse production. *Journal of Memory and Language, 29,* 455–468.

Oldfield, R. C. (1963). Individual vocabulary and semantic currency: A preliminary study. *British Journal of Social and Clinical Psychology, 2,* 122–130.

Oldfield, R. C., & Wingfield, A. (1965). Response latencies in naming objects. *Quarterly Journal of Experimental Psychology, 17,* 273–281.

Osgood, C. E. (1971). Where do sentences come from? In D. D. Steinberg & L. A. Jakobovits (Eds.), *Semantics: An interdisciplinary reader in philosophy, linguistics and psychology* (pp. 497–529). Cambridge: Cambridge University Press.

Osgood, C. E. (1980). *Lectures on language performance.* New York: Springer-Verlag.

Perfetti, C. A. (1969a). Sentence retention and the depth hypothesis. *Journal of Verbal Learning and Verbal Behavior, 8,* 101–104.

Perfetti, C. A. (1969b). Lexical density and phrase structure depth as variables in sentence retention. *Journal of Verbal Learning and Verbal Behavior, 8,* 719–724.

Perfetti, C. A., & Goldman, S. R. (1975). Discourse functions of thematization and topicalization. *Journal of Psycholinguistic Research, 4,* 257–271.

Perfetti, C. A., & Goodman, D. (1971). Memory for sentences and noun phrases of extreme depth. *Quarterly Journal of Experimental Psychology, 23,* 22–23.

Perlmutter, D. M. (1982). Syntactic representation, syntactic levels, and the notion of subject. In P. Jacobson & G. K. Pullum (Eds.), *The nature of syntactic representation* (pp. 283–340). Dordrecht: Reidel.

Pinker, S. (1984). *Language learnability and language development.* Cambridge, MA: Harvard University Press.

Pinker, S. (1991). Rules of language. *Science, 253,* 530–535.

Pollard, C., & Sag, I. A. (1988). An information-based theory of agreement. In D. Brentari, G. Larson, & L. MacLeod (Eds.), *Papers from the 24th annual regional meeting of the Chicago Linguistic Society: Part Two. Parasession on agreement in grammatical theory* (pp. 236–257). Chicago: Chicago Linguistic Society.

Prentice, J. L. (1967). Effects of cuing actor vs. cuing object on word order in sentence production. *Psychonomic Science, 8,* 163–164.

Robertson, S. S., & Suci, G. J. (1980). Event perception by children in the early stages of language production. *Child Development, 51,* 89–96.

Roelofs, A. (1992). A spreading activation theory of lemma retrieval in speaking. *Cognition, 42,* 107–142.

Rumelhart, D. E., & McClelland, J. L. (1987). Learning the past tenses of English verbs: Implicit rules or parallel distributed processing? In B. MacWhinney (Ed.), *Mechanisms of language acquisition* (pp. 195–248). Hillsdale, NJ: Erlbaum.

Saffran, E. M., Schwartz, M. F., & Marin, O. S. M. (1980). Evidence from aphasia: Isolating the components of a production model. In B. Butterworth (Ed.), *Language production* (Vol. 1, pp. 221–241). London: Academic Press.

Schenkein, J. (1980). A taxonomy for repeating action sequences in natural conversation. In B. Butterworth (Ed.), *Language production* (Vol. 1, pp. 21–47). London: Academic Press.

Schriefers, H. (1990). Lexical and conceptual factors in the naming of relations. *Cognitive Psychology, 22,* 111–142.

Schriefers, H., Meyer, A. S., & Levelt, W. J. M. (1990). Exploring the time course of lexical access in language production: Picture–word interference studies. *Journal of Memory and Language, 29,* 86–102.

Seidenberg, M. S., & McClelland, J. L. (1989). A distributed, developmental model of word recognition and naming. *Psychological Review, 96,* 523–568.

Selkirk, E. O. (1984). *Phonology and syntax.* Cambridge, MA: MIT Press.

Sereno, J. A., & Jongman, A. (1990). Phonological and form class relations in the lexicon. *Journal of Psycholinguistic Research, 19,* 387–404.

Shallice, T., & Butterworth, B. (1977). Short-term memory impairment and spontaneous speech. *Neuropsychologia, 15,* 729–735.

Smith, C. (1971). Sentences in discourse. *Journal of Linguistics, 7,* 213–235.

Sridhar, S. N. (1989). Cognitive structures in language production: A crosslinguistic study. In B. MacWhinney & E. Bates (Eds.), *The cross-linguistic study of sentence processing.* (pp. 209–224). Cambridge: Cambridge University Press.

Stemberger, J. P. (1982). Syntactic errors in speech. *Journal of Psycholinguistic Research, 11,* 313–345.

Stemberger, J. P. (1983). *Speech errors and theoretical phonology: A review.* Bloomington: Indiana University Linguistics Club.

Stemberger, J. P. (1985). An interactive activation model of language production. In A. Ellis (Ed.), *Progress in the psychology of language* (pp. 143–186). London: Erlbaum.

Stemberger, J. P., & MacWhinney, B. (1986). Frequency and the lexical storage of regularly inflected forms. *Memory & Cognition, 14,* 17–26.

Streim, N., & Chapman, R. S. (1987). The effects of discourse support on the organization and production of children's utterances. *Applied Psycholinguistics, 8,* 55–66.

Tannen, D. (1987). Repetition in conversation: Toward a poetics of talk. *Language, 63,* 574–605.

Tannenbaum, P. H., & Williams, F. (1968). Generation of active and passive sentences as a function of subject or object focus. *Journal of Verbal Learning and Verbal Behavior, 7,* 246–250.

Tomlin, R. S. (1986). *Basic word order: Functional principles.* London: Croom Helm.

Turner, E. A., & Rommetveit, R. (1968). Focus of attention in recall of active and passive sentences. *Journal of Verbal Learning and Verbal Behavior, 7,* 543–548.

Weiner, E. J., & Labov, W. (1983). Constraints on the agentless passive. *Journal of Linguistics, 19,* 29–58.

Wells, R. (1951). Predicting slips of the tongue. *Yale Scientific Magazine, 26,* 9–30.

Williams, E. (1981). Argument structure and morphology. *Linguistic Review, 1,* 81–114.

Wingfield, A. (1968). Effects of frequency on identification and naming of objects. *American Journal of Psychology, 81,* 226–234.

Woodworth, R. S. (1938). *Experimental psychology.* New York: Holt.

Yngve, V. H. (1960). A model and an hypothesis for language structure. *Proceedings of the American Philosophical Society, 104,* 444–466.

CHAPTER 30

DISCOURSE IN PRODUCTION

HERBERT H. CLARK

I. INTRODUCTION

Discourse is language use in the large. It is more than the use of sounds, words, or sentences. It is extended activities that are carried out by means of language. Originally, discourse was synonymous with conversation—the word *discourse* comes from Latin *discursus* "conversation." Nowadays, it also includes stories, novels, newspaper articles, speeches, lectures—any extended but circumscribed piece of language use created for a coherent purpose. In common parlance, the term discourse is reserved for the ongoing activity. But that activity comes packaged in bounded units, each with a clear entry and exit. So we will want to speak not merely of DISCOURSE as an activity but of DISCOURSES as discrete units of that activity. This chapter is about the production of discourses.

Many discourses are spontaneous, produced without detailed planning beforehand. These include everyday conversations and extemporaneous narratives. Other discourses are the carefully crafted products of unhurried writing, rewriting, and editing. These include novels, newspaper articles, letters, plays, prepared lectures, and radio news reports. The processes of creating these two types of discourse are quite different. In this chapter, I confine myself to extemporaneous discourses, for it is there that we see the processes of production in their most telling form.

A. Two Views of Discourse

What, then, is a discourse? It can be viewed as a product, as an object that gets produced by people speaking. This is a position that has evolved largely among linguists and philosophers. It can also be viewed as a process, what the people speaking actually do, a position that has been developed mostly by sociologists and anthropologists. These two views are different in what they imply about language use in discourse.

The first view, in its simplest form, is that a discourse is a text or sequence of sentences that is coherent by virtue of its internal linguistic structure (Halliday & Hasan, 1976; van Dijk, 1972, 1977). Let me call this the TEXT VIEW of discourse. Here, for example, is a minimal discourse.

My sister hurt herself yesterday. She stepped on a rake.

What makes this a discourse is that the two sentences could form a coherent segment of a conversation or novel. A discourse, then, is a linguistic unit larger than a sentence and having one or more potential uses. It is analogous to a sentence rather than an utterance: It is a linguistic type that is divorced from any particular speaker, addressee, or circumstances in which it is actually used. This view evolved from the study of sentence grammars, so the goal is ordinarily to specify the linguistic properties that make discourses coherent and able to serve the purposes they serve.

The second view is that a discourse is a joint activity carried out by an ensemble of two or more people trying to accomplish things together (Atkinson & Heritage, 1984; Button & Lee, 1987; Goffman, 1971, 1981; C. Goodwin, 1981; Sacks, Schegloff, & Jefferson, 1974). Let me call this the JOINT ACTIVITY VIEW of discourse. The idea is that conversations, stories, and other discourses are not created by speakers acting autonomously. Rather, they are the emergent products of an ensemble of people working together. Even stories told by single narrators are the outcome of such a process (Sacks, 1974). According to these arguments, we cannot understand what a discourse is as a product without understanding how it was created by means of this process.

B. Product or Process?

The joint activity view has many advantages over the text view, at least for the study of spontaneous discourse. Consider the coherence of a discourse. According to the text view, this is a property of the text as a linguistic unit. Just as we can examine the internal structure of a sentence and decide whether or not it is grammatical, we can examine the internal structure of a discourse and decide whether or not it is coherent. But this is simply wrong. As we will discover, the coherence of a discourse, whether it is a conversation or a monologue, emerges from what the participants are trying to accomplish as they produce the utterances they do (Morgan & Sellner, 1980; Sacks et al., 1974). We should not look for linguistic properties that distinguish possible from impossible discourses, for there are none.

It is also wrong to view discourses as purely linguistic objects—texts are purely linguistic objects—for discourses include much more than the sentences uttered. They also encompass: gestures with the hands and face (Bavelas, 1990; Bavelas, Black, Chovil, Lemery, & Mullett, 1988; Bavelas, Black, Lemery, & Mullett, 1986; Bavelas, Chovil, Lawrie, & Wade, 1993; Chovil, 1991; C. Goodwin, 1981; M. H. Goodwin & Goodwin, 1986; Kendon, 1980, 1987; McNeill, 1985, 1992; McNeill & Levy, 1982; Schegloff, 1984); tone of voice representing anger, surprise, and amazement; nonsyntactic expressions such as *oh, yes, well,* and *okay*; metacommunicative comments such as *uh, um, like,* and *y'know*; and a wide range of pauses, repairs, interruptions, and overlapping speech that would not be considered part of a text (see later). These features are ubiquitous in spontaneous discourses yet are excluded on principle from the text view of discourse—and most other product views as well. In contrast, they fall directly out of the joint activity view. Their presence in discourse is a mystery until we view discourse as a joint activity.

The text view has come down to us primarily as an account of written discourses—stories, essays, novels, descriptions, and contrived examples like the woman stepping on the rake. But the fundamental form of discourse—indeed the only universal, spontaneous form—is face-to-face conversation, and that is a very different beast indeed. A written discourse is to a face-to-face conversation as a stuffed grizzly bear is to a live one. We may learn a great deal from inspecting the lifeless remains in the corner of a museum. But to understand the real thing, we must seek it out in its natural habitat and study how it actually lives.

In this chapter, I view discourse primarily as a joint activity. My reasons are practical as well as theoretical, for most research on spontaneous production comes from investigators with this view.

II. DISCOURSE AS A JOINT ACTIVITY

People do not talk just to hear themselves speak. They talk with others to get things done. Think about conversations you initiate with others. You talk with a department store clerk to buy some shoes. You call up your sister to get a lost address. You discuss with your spouse what groceries to shop for. You tell a colleague a joke to amuse her. What you and your partner do each time is carry out one or more joint tasks, joint enterprises, or what I will call JOINT PROJECTS: you buy shoes from the clerk; you get an address from your sister; you and your spouse decide what groceries to buy; and you amuse your colleague with a joke. These are not descriptions of texts or acts of speaking. They are descriptions of projects you achieve jointly with your partner by means of your talk. Discourses are ordinarily, perhaps always, initiated and carried out to complete such projects. The participants do not always finish the projects they start—for a variety of reasons—yet that is what they ordinarily try to do. One of the fundamental issues of discourse, then, is this: How is a discourse created by people initiating and carrying out joint projects?

To begin, let us consider a telephone conversation from a large corpus of British conversations (Svartvik & Quirk, 1980). In this transcription, a comma indicates the end of a tone unit, spaced dash and spaced period indicate long and short pauses respectively, colons indicate stretched vowels, and adjacent pairs of phrases in asterisks (e.g., *seminar* and *yes*) indicate overlapping speech (8.3d.230).[1]

---

[1] Unless otherwise noted, the other spontaneous examples in this chapter come from the Svartvik-Quirk corpus as well. Each is marked by text number (e.g., 8.3d) and beginning line (e.g., 230).

1. A. (rings)
2. B. *Benjamin Holloway,*
3. A. *this is Professor Dwight's secretary, from Polymania College,*
4. B. *ooh yes, –*
5. A. *uh:m . about the: lexicology *seminar,**
6. B. **yes**
7. A. *actually Professor Dwight says in fact they've only got two more m . uh:m sessions to go, because I didn't realize it it . finishes at Easter,*
8. B. *I see, yes, *uh:um**
9. A. **so* it . wouldn't really be .*
10. B. *much point, . *no,**
11. A. **no,* .* (laughs)
12. B. *OK right, thanks very much,*
13. A. *OK . *bye,**
14. B. **bye,**

This is a brief but complete discourse between Alice, Professor Dwight's secretary, and Benjamin, Professor Dwight's student. Alice initiated the call to complete one major joint project—to give Benjamin a message from Professor Dwight—and they succeeded. Unremarkable as this conversation is, it illustrates four elements of all joint activities—personnel, accumulation of common ground, action sequences, and grounding.

A. Personnel

If a discourse is a joint activity, it needs personnel—at least two participants—and every discourse has them. The conversation here has two—Alice and Benjamin. Their PARTICIPATION ROLES, as I will call them, change from one action to the next. When Alice says *about the lexicology seminar* she is the speaker and he the addressee, yet when he says *yes* overlapping with *seminar,* he is the speaker and she the addressee. Participation roles are roles in particular joint actions.

Participation roles proliferate when there are more than two people (Clark & Carlson, 1982a; Clark & Schaefer, 1987b, 1992; Goffman, 1976). The first contrast is between PARTICIPANTS ("ratified participants," Goffman called them) and nonparticipants, or OVERHEARERS. The participants mutually believe they are engaged in the speaker's joint action at the moment, whereas overhearers do not. Participants divide into speakers, addressees, and SIDE PARTICIPANTS. The addressees are "those ratified participants who are addressed, that is, oriented to by the speaker in a manner to suggest that his words are particularly for them, and that some answer is therefore anticipated from them, more so than from the other ratified participants" (Goffman, 1976, p. 260). The other participants are side participants. Overhearers divide into two types. BYSTANDERS have access to what the speakers are saying, and their presence is fully recognized. EAVESDROPPERS have access to what the speakers are saying, but their presence is not fully recognized. Professor Dwight, for example, might eavesdrop on another line. These participation roles apply as much to written as to spoken discourses, but there they are nearly invisible, and they are ignored in most analyses. We might picture participation roles in a set of concentric regions like this:

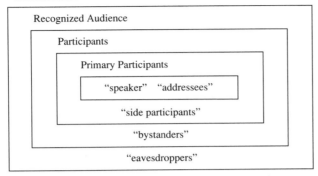

Total Audience

Recognized Audience

Participants

Primary Participants

"speaker" "addressees"

"side participants"

"bystanders"

"eavesdroppers"

The participants in a discourse also have what I will call PERSONAL ROLES. Alice and Benjamin are, first of all, individuals with their own identities, beliefs, feelings, and desires. In this task, Alice and Benjamin also have professional identities. She is Professor Dwight's secretary, and he is Professor Dwight's student, and they are talking to each other in these roles. Notice that she identifies herself, not as "Alice Jones," but as "Professor Dwight's secretary, from Polymania College." In other calls she might identify herself as "Alice" or "Miss Jones." Personal roles also apply to written discourse, but are ignored in most analyses.

B. Accumulating Common Ground

The participants in a joint activity can succeed only by coordinating on their individual actions. This is so whether they are paddling a canoe, performing in a musical ensemble, playing tennis, shaking hands, waltzing, or conversing on the telephone. Failures of coordination regularly lead to breakdowns in the joint activity. But two people can only coordinate by making rather strong assumptions about each other. What are these assumptions, and how do they change in a discourse?

1. Common Ground

Two people take for granted, or presuppose, that they share certain knowledge, beliefs, and assumptions—and they each presuppose that they both presuppose this. The totality of these presuppositions is their COMMON GROUND (Stalnaker, 1978). It is the sum of their mutual knowledge, mutual beliefs, and mutual assumptions (Clark & Carlson, 1982b; Clark & Marshall, 1981; Lewis, 1969; Schiffer, 1972). Two people's common ground can be divided into two main parts. Their COMMUNAL common ground represents all the knowledge, beliefs, and assumptions they take to be universally held in the communities to which they mutually believe they belong. Their PERSONAL common ground, in contrast, represents all the mutual knowledge, beliefs, and assumptions they have inferred from personal experience with each other (Clark, 1993; Clark & Marshall, 1981).

Alice and Benjamin belong to a diverse set of cultural groups, systems, or networks that I will call cultural communities. Alice, for example, might view herself as a member of these communities: the British, the English, London residents, members of Polymania College, classical musicians, the Catholic church, and Arsenal soccer fans. Within each community, there are facts, beliefs, and assumptions that every member believes that almost everyone in that community takes for granted. She might assume all Londoners know where Piccadilly Circus, Regent's Park, and Soho are, what the Bakerloo Line, Madam Tussaud's, and the Tate are, and so on. So, once she and Benjamin reach the mutual belief that they are both Londoners, she can assume that all this information is part of their common ground. And that goes for universal information in all communities they establish comembership in (see Fussell & Krauss, 1989, 1991, 1992; Jameson, 1990; Krauss and Fussell, 1991). It is no accident that strangers often begin conversations by establishing the communities they belong to (*I'm from California—where are **you** from? I'm a psychologist—what do **you** do?*), for these can instantly create vast areas of common ground.

Alice and Benjamin's personal common ground is based instead on openly shared experiences. Some of these experiences are PERCEPTUAL. Once Alice and Benjamin have viewed or heard something together—for instance, they jointly saw a glass fall off a table or heard a telephone ring—they can assume that event is part of their common ground. Other joint experiences are CONVERSATIONAL. When Alice said to Benjamin *This is Professor Dwight's secretary, from Polymania College* and they established he had understood her, they could assume this information was also part of their common ground. Acts of communication are successful only when they add as intended to the participants' common ground.

2. Adding to Common Ground

Common ground is important to a discourse because it is the background, the context, for everything the participants jointly do and say in it (Clark & Carlson, 1981; Clark & Haviland, 1977; Gazdar, 1979; Lewis, 1969; Stalnaker, 1978). To see how, consider another joint activity, a chess game.

When two people meet to play chess, they each assume an initial common ground for the game. As communal common ground, they might presuppose the rules for chess, proper chess etiquette, each other's rankings, and other such information. As personal common ground—perhaps they have played each other before—they might assume mutual knowledge of each other's strategies, weaknesses, appearance, personal habits, and more. All this forms the initial context for the game. Once the game starts, the two of them add to their common ground with every move they make. White's first move adds to the initial common ground, creating a new common ground. Black's next move adds to the newly created common ground. And so on. Each move is taken with respect to the current common ground. For good chess players, this consists of more than the current state of the board. It represents the history of that game—how the board got that way. It includes their previous strategies, blunders, revealed weaknesses, and so on. The point is this: Common ground accumulates with every move, and each new move is taken, and interpreted, against the current common ground.

So it goes in discourse. When Alice and Benjamin opened their conversation, they too began with an initial common ground. Benjamin's first move, *Benjamin Holloway,* relied on a British convention for answering telephones by giving one's name, and Alice relied on the same common ground in interpreting that as his name. Next, when Alice said *This is Professor Dwight's secretary, from Polymania College,* she assumed as part of their common ground that Benjamin was acquainted with Professor Dwight from Polymania College. She would not have made this assumption of just anyone. She made it of the person who answered only after they established the mutual belief that he was Benjamin Holloway.

So every public move in a discourse is taken and interpreted against the current common ground of the participants. Their current common ground, however, has two parts. The DISCOURSE RECORD includes all the common ground they take to have accumulated in the discourse proper and what they have publicly accomplished in it. The rest is OFF THE RECORD. So what the participants do in a discourse is viewed both against the accumulating discourse record and against off-record common ground.

C. Action Sequences

The participants in a discourse work to complete overarching joint projects. These generally divide into smaller joint projects performed in sequence. Alice and Benjamin's conversation, for example, consists of three broad actions in sequence.

    I. A and B open the conversation (lines 1–4)
  II. A and B exchange information (lines 5–12)
III. A and B close the conversation (lines 13–14)

Each of these actions divides into further actions in sequence. Action I, for example, consists of these three actions.

Ia. A and B open the telephone channel (lines 1–2)
Ib. B identifies himself to A (line 2)
Ic. A identifies herself to B (lines 3–4)

Actions II and III divide in similar ways. All these actions are JOINT actions—A and B doing something together. Not only is the entire conversation a joint activity, but so are its parts.

Why are two actions taken in sequence? The commonest reason is that the second action is CONDITIONAL on the completion of the first. The second action must come second if common ground is to accumulate in an orderly way. This accounts for much of the sequencing in Alice and Benjamin's conversation. The two of them cannot exchange information until they have opened the conversation; they cannot close the conversation until they have opened it and carried out their main joint project—exchanging the information. And the same goes for many subactions. So these sequences are determined not by what Alice and Benjamin are trying to say, but by what they are jointly trying to do.

The most basic device for sequencing in conversation is the ADJACENCY

PAIR (Schegloff & Sacks, 1973). The prototype is the question–answer pair, as in this actual example (4.1.75):

A. *well has she brought you all your things then?*
B. *yes*

Adjacency pairs have two parts, a first pair part and a second pair part. The two parts belong to different types, here question and answer, and are produced by different speakers. The crucial property is CONDITIONAL RELEVANCE: Once A has produced the first pair part of one type (a question), it is conditionally relevant for B to produce a second pair part of the right type (an answer). Notice how the two parts must be in this order. B cannot know what type of response is appropriate until A has completed her utterance, revealing it to be a question that expects an answer of a certain type (*yes* or *no*). Adjacency pairs are inherently a sequencing device.

Adjacency pairs are really MINIMUM JOINT PROJECTS. What A is doing in asking B a question is PROJECTING a task for the two of them to complete—the exchange of information specified in her question. If he is willing and able, he will answer the question, not only taking up the proposed project, but completing it. That makes adjacency pairs ideal building blocks for dialogues. Many dialogues consist almost entirely of adjacency pairs. Alice and Benjamin's conversation is replete with them.

Adjacency pair	Example
Part 1. Summons	A. (rings)
Part 2. Response	B. *Benjamin Holloway*
Part 1. Assertion	A. *this is Professor Dwight's secretary, from Polymania College*
Part 2. Assent	B. *ooh yes –*
Part 1. Assertion	A. *uhm . about the lexicology *seminar**
	B. **yes**
	A. *actually Professor Dwight says in fact they've only got two more m . uhm sessions to go, because I didn't realize it it . finishes at Easter*
Part 2. Assent	B. *I see, yes*
Part 1. Assertion	A. *so it . wouldn't really be .*
	B. *much point,*
Part 2. Assent	B. *. no*
Part 1. Thanks	B. *thanks very much*
Part 2. Response	A. *OK .*
Part 1. Good-bye	A. **bye**
Part 2. Good-bye	B. **bye**

The pattern here suggests that overarching joint projects, like Alice and Benjamin's exchange of information, are accomplished through a sequence of minimum joint projects, and they are. But how? That is a question we will return to later.

D. Contributions

When Alice says she is Professor Dwight's secretary from Polymania College, it looks as if she is acting on her own. But she isn't. She is not making an assertion to just anyone. She is making it to Benjamin. To succeed, she must get Benjamin to attend to, identify, and understand her utterance precisely as she is issuing it. That alone requires joint actions.

Alice and Benjamin, however, must satisfy an even more stringent requirement. Recall that for a discourse to be orderly, the participants must keep track of their accumulating common ground. Now for Alice's assertion to get added to her and Benjamin's common ground, she and Benjamin must satisfy a GROUNDING CRITERION: They must reach the mutual belief that he has understood what she meant to a degree sufficient for current purposes (Clark & Schaefer, 1989; Clark & Wilkes-Gibbs, 1986). The process of reaching this criterion is called GROUNDING. During their conversation, Alice and Benjamin must ground each utterance. What emerges from the grounding of an utterance is what has been called a CONTRIBUTION.

Contributions normally have two phases: a PRESENTATION PHASE and an ACCEPTANCE PHASE. In the presentation phase, speakers present an utterance for their addresses to understand, and in the presentation phase, the addressees give the speakers evidence they have understood well enough for current purposes. Consider Amanda's attempt in 1 to ask her husband a question (5.9.518):

1. Amanda. *were you there when they erected the new signs?*–
2. Bertrand. *th–which new *signs**
3. Amanda. **litt*le notice boards, indicating where you had to go for everything*
4. Bertrand. *no,–that must have been in the year after me, you graduated*

In 1, Amanda presents the utterance *Were you there when they erected the new signs?* This is the presentation phase of her question. The problem is that Bertrand does not understand her reference to *the new signs*. So in 2, he initiates the acceptance phase by giving Amanda evidence that he understands everything except *the new signs*, which she therefore clarifies in 3. So only in 4 does he complete the acceptance phase. He does that by going on to the second pair part of the adjacency pair initiated by Amanda's question. With the answer *no* he implies that he has understood her question well enough to answer it—well enough for current purposes.

Addressees are expected to provide speakers not only with negative evidence when they haven't understood something, but with positive evidence when they believe they have.[2] Positive evidence has two common forms.

The first is the RELEVANT NEXT CONTRIBUTION. Let us return to three lines from Alice and Benjamin's conversation.

---

[2] Notice that addressees provide this evidence, but overhearers do not, and that should put overhearers at a disadvantage in understanding what speakers mean. Overhearers, in fact, understand less accurately than addressees (Schober & Clark, 1989).

2. B. *Benjamin Holloway*
3. A. *this is Professor Dwight's secretary, from Polymania College*
4. B. *ooh yes –*

In 2 Benjamin presents his name in order to identify himself. In the very next utterance Alice presents an utterance in order to identify herself as well. In doing this she provides two types of positive evidence that she has understood Benjamin's utterance. First, she passes up the opportunity to initiate a repair of his utterance ("Who?" "Bejamin who?"). And, second, she initiates a contribution that is the appropriate next contribution given her understanding of his utterance. Both signals imply she believes she has understood him well enough for current purposes. Benjamin in turn uses the same technique to imply that he has understood Alice's introduction: he goes on with *oh yes* to complete the adjacency pair she initiated.

The second common form of positive evidence is what has been called BACK CHANNEL RESPONSES (Yngve, 1970). Take these two lines from Alice and Benjamin's conversation.

5. A. *uh:m . about the: lexicology *seminar**
6. B. **yes**

In 5 Alice presents the first phrase of her message from Professor Dwight, and Benjamin accepts it as having been understood with a simple acknowledgement *yes*. With this response, he is claiming to have understood Alice's utterance so far and is telling her in effect "Go on." Acknowledgments like these are often called CONTINUERS (Schegloff, 1982). Note that Benjamin's *yes* is timed to overlap with the end of Alice's presentation. This is typical of acklowledgments. By making the *yes* overlap, he shows he is leaving the floor to Alice. Other acknowledgments include *uh huh, yeah*, and, in British English, *m*. In face-to-face conversation, they also include head nods, smiles, raised eyebrows, and frowns (Chovil, 1991).

Contributions can take an unlimited variety of forms, for utterances can be presented and accepted in an unlimited number of ways. One curious but common form of contribution is the COLLABORATIVE COMPLETION (Lerner, 1987; Wilkes-Gibbs, 1986). Consider three lines from Alice and Benjamin's conversation.

9. A. *so it . wouldn't really be .*
10. B. *much point, . *no**
11. A. **no* .* (laughs)

In 9 Alice presents the beginning of a sentence (*so it wouldn't really be*) and pauses briefly as if she were searching for the right words to complete it delicately. Benjamin, perhaps to save her embarrassment, presents a possible completion *much point*. It gives Alice explicit evidence that he believes he has understood her entire assertion. Indeed, he immediately accepts the entire assertion, including his completion, by assenting to it with *no*. She in turn accepts both with an echoed *no* and a laugh.

So far, then, we have surveyed four elements of a discourse viewed as a joint activity. (a) Personnel: Every joint activity has participants as distinguished from nonparticipants—bystanders and eavesdroppers. The participants have personal roles both as individuals and as professional or societal agents.

(b) Common ground: At the beginning of a discourse, the participants assume an initial common ground, which they infer on the basis of shared cultural groups and prior joint experiences. Then, with each new public move, they add to that common ground. They produce and interpret each new utterance against their current common ground. (c) Joint actions: People participate in a discourse to carry out broad joint projects. They typically accomplish these projects through smaller joint projects completed in sequence. The minimal joint project is the adjacency pair, as in a question and answer. (d) Contributions: Minimal joint projects are themselves accomplished through contributions. One person presents an utterance, and all the participants ground it before preceeding on.

III. CREATING CONVERSATIONS

Conversations are not designed in the large. They emerge bit by bit as two or more people use language to try to accomplish certain things together. When people agree to a conversation initiated by another person, they generally do not know why the other person initiated it. They do not know what projects the other had in mind or whether they will agree to take them up if proposed. When Benjamin answered the telephone, he had no idea who was calling or why. That emerged only as he and Alice proceeded turn by turn. You can answer a telephone call not knowing it is a crank caller, but once you discover it is, you can refuse to proceed and terminate the conversation. You can refuse to continue any joint action in conversation.

Conversations, then, are LOCALLY MANAGED (Sacks et al., 1974). The actions people take in conversation are ordinarily parts of joint actions, and these must be agreed to moment by moment. Conversations emerge only as a result of this process. But if conversations are locally managed, how do the participants accomplish their global projects? This question has a surprising answer. It requires us to consider how turns are created and how larger units emerge as a result.

A. Turns

Conversations appear to proceed turn by turn—one person talking at a time. What are these turns, and where do they come from? Perhaps the most influential answer was offered by Sacks et al. (1974). In conversation, they argued, the participants speak in units that are potential turns—so-called TURN-CONSTRUCTIONAL UNITS. These range in size from a single word (e.g., Alice's *OK*) to clauses filled with many embedded clauses (e.g., Alices's *uh:m . about the: lexicology seminar actually Professor Dwight says in fact they've only got two more m . uh:m sessions to go, because I didn't realize it it . finishes at Easter*). The end of each turn-constructional unit is a TRANSITION-RELEVANCE PLACE—a point at which there may be a change in turns. The participants then follow a set of turn-allocation rules, to quote Sacks et al.:

(1) For any turn, at the initial transition-relevance place of an initial turn-constructional unit:
(a) If the turn-so-far is so constructed as to involve the use of a "current speaker selects next" technique, then the party so selected has the right and

is obliged to take next turn to speak; no others have such rights or obligations, and transfer occurs at that place.

(b) If the turn-so-far is so constructed as not to involve the use of a "current speaker selects next" technique, then self-selection for next speakership may, but need not, be instituted; first starter acquires rights to a turn, and transfer occurs at that place.

(c) If the turn-so-far is so constructed as not to involve the use of a "current speaker selects next" technique, then current speaker may, but need not continue, unless another self-selects.

(2) If, at the initial transition-relevance place of an initial turn-constructional unit, neither 1a nor 1b has operated, and, following the provision of 1c, current speaker has continued, then the rule-set a–c reapplies at next transition-relevance place, and recursively at each next transition-relevance place, until transfer is effected. (p. 704).

The result of these rules is an orderly sequence of turns.

As formidable as these rules look, they are quite straightforward. Suppose the current speaker is A in a conversation with B and C. If A produces the first part of an adjacency pair addressed to B (e.g., she asks B *well has she brought you all your things then?*), then A is using a "current speaker selects next" technique and selects B as the next speaker. From that moment on, B has the right and is obliged to take the next turn. The expectable thing for B to do, of course, is produce an appropriate second pair part (e.g., the answer *yes*). If, instead, A completes her turn without producing a first pair part, then the next turn goes to the person who speaks up first—B or C. If neither of them speaks, then she is free to extend her turn with another turn-constructional unit. And so on. These rules, Sacks et al. argued, account for many features of spontaneous conversation. They allow for the number of participants to vary, for what they say to vary, for turn size to vary, for turn order to vary, for conversation length to vary, and for many other such features.

In this model, turn-taking is governed by competition for the floor. The current speaker, say A, has the floor until the end of the current turn-constructional unit. At that point, unless A has addressed B or C with the first part of an adjacency pair (rule 1a), the floor goes to whoever speaks up first, A, B, or C (by rules 1b and 1c). If one of them wants to speak up first, they should try to PREDICT the end of A's turn, not merely REACT to it—as in an alternative model of turn-taking proposed by Duncan (1972, 1973). If they do, Sacks et al. argued, next speakers ought to time their next turn to begin at the end of the current turn with a minimum of gap, and they do. In one study, 34% of all speaker switches took less than 0.2 s from the end of one speaker's speech to the beginning of the next speaker's speech (Beattie & Barnard, 1979). That would be impossible if the next speakers were merely reacting to the end of the current turn. The next speaker should also occasionally mispredict the end of the current turn, and this happens too. In this example, B overlaps slightly with A, perhaps because A stretched the vowel in *size* (Sacks et al., 1974, p. 707).

A. *sixty two feet is pretty good si:*ze**
B. **oh*:: boy*

In the next example, Caller overlapped with Desk because she apparently did not foresee that Desk would add the vocative *Ma'am* to the end of the current turn-constructional unit (Sacks et al., ibid.).

> Desk. *It is a stretcher patient *Ma'am**
> Caller. **it's-* uh yes he is.*

This example also shows that Caller repaired the problem caused by the overlap and restarted her turn from the beginning. The Sacks et al. model accounts for precision timing in other phenomena as well.

The turn allocation rules, however, fail to account for a number of strategies that are common in conversation. Here are just a few.

1. Acknowledgments. Many acknowledgments, such as Benjamin's *yes* in line 6 of his telephone conversation with Alice, are timed to overlap with the ends of the units they acknowledge (see also C. Goodwin, 1986). The overlap is systematic and deliberate, which flies in the face of rules 1a–1c. Traditionally, these are therefore not considered turns. But if they are not, what are they, and how are they to be accounted for?
2. Collaborative completions. Recall that Alice's utterance in line 9, *so it . wouldn't really be . ,* got completed by Benjamin in line 10, *much point*. Here, Benjamin deliberately began speaking in the middle of a turn-constructional unit, contrary to rules 1a and 1b.
3. Recycled turn beginnings. Often, next speakers deliberately start their turns before the previous turn is complete in order to signal they want the next turn, as in this example (Schegloff, 1987, pp. 80–81).

> A: *Yeah my mother asked me. I says I dunno. I haven't heard from her. I didn't know what days you had *classes or anything.**
> B: **Yeah an I didn' know* **I didn't know** when you were home or–I was gonna.*

Not only does B start his turn early, but once A's turn is finished, he recycles the beginning of the turn in the clear (as highlighted) to make sure A has attended to it and heard it properly.

4. Invited interruptions. Current speakers sometimes invite addressees to interrupt as soon as they understand, whether or not it is at the end of a turn-constructional unit. Here is an example (Jefferson, 1973, p. 59).

> A. *I heard you were at the beach yesterday. What's her name, oh you know, the tall redhead that lives across the street from Larry? The one who drove him to work the day his car *was– **
> B. **Oh Gina!**
> A. *Yeah Gina. She said she saw you at the beach yesterday.*

B interrupted A mid-utterance, and with A's consent and encouragement. A and B's collaborative strategy here goes counter to rules 1a–1c.

5. Strategic interruptions. Other times, next speakers interrupt current speakers mid-turn for other reasons they consider legitimate. Here is an example (1.9.83).

> A: *and as long as I'm in my own – little nit and nobody's telling me what to do*
> B: *yes*

A: *there doesn't really seem *anything**
B: **but how* long do you think it'll take them to finish?*

When B interrupts A with *but how long . . .* , he does so because he believes his question is more pressing at that moment than what A was saying. A may well agree. This too goes counter to rules 1a–1c.

6. Nonlinguistic actions. In face-to-face conversation, speakers use a variety of nonlinguistic signals that defy analysis into turns. Suppose you were talking to Calvin to confirm a story you had heard about him: *So you were at the theater? and Susan walked in and sat down beside you? and she didn't say anything?* Calvin could answer the first two parts by nodding animatedly over your questions and the third part by shaking his head. His gestures are equivalent to the second pair parts of adjacency pairs, to answering *yes, yes,* and *no* after each phrase. The problem is that they are not turns because they are entirely overlapping (see Brennan, 1990). This goes counter to the turn allocation rules, too.

B. Emergence of Turns

An alternative view of turns is that they are an emergent phenomenon (Brennan, 1990). Turns—when they do occur—have three main properties: (a) they consist of turn constructional units, (b) they are ordered, and (c) they are nonoverlapping. These properties, one can argue, derive from more basic properties of contributions and minimal joint projects.

Consider the requirement of nonoverlapping speech. To make a contribution, A must get B to attend to, identify, and understand the utterance she is presenting. If the utterance has any complexity, she cannot achieve this if her presentation overlaps with B's utterance. People cannot successfully attend to two complex tasks at once. So in several earlier examples, speakers repeated speech that had overlapped, as when Caller said **it's – * uh yes he is* and when B said **Yeah an I didn' know* I didn't know when . . .* Yet, when a presentation is simple enough, it can overlap and still be attended to and understood. This is standard with acknowledgments (*yes* and *uh huh*), head nods, and smiles. And as Alice and Benjamin's conversation illustrates, it is also common on the telephone to overlap the exchange of *bye*'s (see Clark & French, 1981).

Consider turn order. For two utterances not to overlap, they must be produced in one or the other order. What determines the order? Rule 1a is simply a statement of how adjacency pairs work. If A produces a first pair part of an adjacency pair, it is conditionally relevant for B immediately to produce a second pair part. That selects B as the next speaker. The order is required because B cannot usually know what the second part should be until A has completed the first part. Sometimes, however, B is able to perform the second part overlapping the first, as by nodding, and then rule 1a does not apply. Rules 1b and 1c arise when two presentations cannot be attended to, identified, understood, or taken up when they overlap, and when the participants still have joint projects to pursue.

Finally, consider turn constructional units. What constitutes such a unit is not specified within the rules of turn-taking per se. They are units of the contributions speakers are trying to make and of the joint projects they are trying to initiate or complete. They too are jointly determined. They will generally be phrases, clauses, or sentences, but they need not be, as in collaborative completions, invited interruptions, and other cases.

In short, the participants in a conversation will take turns when they have to in order to be understood or to know what to contribute. But they can often succeed with speech that overlaps and turn constructional units that are incomplete. In conversation, people's goal is not to follow certain rules of language. It is to succeed in the joint projects they undertake. Their local concern is not to create turns, but to complete their contributions and joint projects.

C. Pre-sequences

Whatever the status of turns, conversations are still managed locally and interactionally. The participants proceed contribution by contribution and by initiating and completing adjacency pairs or minimum joint projects. The puzzle is how they complete larger projects. How did Alice manage to give Benjamin the information she wanted to give him? Part of the solution lies in the use of special initiators to project the larger tasks. These special initiators are called PRE-SEQUENCES (Schegloff, 1980).

The idea is neatly illustrated with PRE-QUESTIONS. Consider this fragment of a British conversation (7.1d.1320).

> Ann. *oh there's one thing I wanted to ask you*
> Betty. *mhm–*
> Ann. *in the village, they've got some of those . i– you're going to get to know, . what it is, but it doesn't matter really*
> Betty. *mhm*
> Ann. *u:m . those rings, that are buckles – –*
> Betty. *that are buckles*
> Ann. *yes, tha– they they're flat,*
> Betty. *mhm*
> Ann. *and you wrap them round,*
> Betty. *oh yes I know*
> Ann. *and, . you know, . *they're* a little belt .*
> Betty. **m* m*
> Ann. *would you like one .*
> Betty. *oh I'd love one Ann –*

The first turn *oh there's one thing I wanted to ask you* is a pre-question. With it Ann asks Betty in effect whether she could ask her a question, and with *mhm*, Betty assents. But does Ann then ask the question? No. She launches into a series of preliminaries to the question—a description of a belt of interest—and asks her question *would you like one* only after that. What is going on here?

Pre-questions are devices for making conversational room to provide preliminaries to questions. As Schegloff put it, they are preliminaries to preliminaries. Ann presents her pre-question as a way of getting Betty to allow her to prepare Betty for the question proper. If she had been able to ask the question straight off, she wouldn't have needed the pre-question. So the pre-question and its response constitute a device for Ann and Betty to agree to turn the floor over to Betty for as much space as she needs to get to the question. It projects a larger, encompassing joint task that consists of three parts: (a) a pre-question plus a response, (b) preliminaries to a question and answer, and (c) the question and answer.

A similar device is the PRE-ANNOUNCEMENT and its response, as illustrated here (4.1.790).

> Kate. **well d'you know what they got**
> Luke. **what –**
> Kate. *they didn't get replies from . from most people, – hardly any replies at all – –* [continues]

With *well d'you know what they got?* Kate lets Luke know she has some potential news, and she projects two alternatives. If he already knows *what they got,* he can say "yes" or display the news, and they can go on from there. If he doesn't, he can say "no" and then she will tell him. He takes the second alternative and, instead of saying "no," he takes up her projected task directly and asks *What?* So Kate's pre-announcement is designed to get him to ask her for her news. With it she gets his agreement for her to take as much conversational room as she needs to tell the news.

Pre-sequences come in a variety of forms, serving a variety of purposes. They are used in making room for preliminaries to questions, for conditions to requests, for entire conversations, for stories, for taking leave, and for many other purposes. Here are just a few common pre-sequences.

Type of Pre-sequence	Example
Pre-question	A. *oh there's one thing I wanted to ask you*
Response	B. *mhm*
Pre-announcement	A. *well d'you know what they got*
Response	B. *what –*
Pre-invitation	A. *Are you doing anything tonight?*
Response	B. *No.*
Pre-request	A. *Do you have hot chocolate*
Response	B. *Yes, we do.*
Summons	A. *Hey, Molly*
Response	B. *Yes?*
Summons by telephone	A. (rings telephone)
Response	B. *Benjamin Holloway*
Pre-closing statement	A. *Well okay*
Response	B. *Okay*
Pre-narrative	A. *I acquired an absolutely magnificent sewing machine, by foul means, did I tell you about that?*
Response	B. *no*

Pre-sequences, then, create local adjacency pairs that project more extended joint tasks. They initiate the larger joint projects by establishing agreements by the participants to let them proceed. Pre-sequences are an ingenious solution to the problem of how to achieve global aims by local means.

D. Opening a Conversation

How do people create a conversation from nothing? When A (a woman) wants to talk to B (a man), she cannot proceed on her own. She must get B to join her in the activity that will turn out to be their conversation. To create a conversation, then, A and B must coordinate three things: (a) their ENTRY into that joint activity, (b) the BODY of that activity, and (c) their EXIT from it. Pre-sequences come in handy in all three phases. Let us look first at the entry.

People do not take deliberate actions without a reason, and that holds for conversations as well. When A initiates a conversation, she does so because she wants to accomplish something with B—give him a message, get information from him, invite him to a party. So in opening a conversation with B, she meets these requirements.

A1. A is willing and able to enter a conversation now.
A2. A is willing and able to enter a conversation now with B.
A3. A is willing and able to enter a conversation now with B to accomplish joint project P.

Note that 1 is presupposed by 2, and 2 by 3, so 1 can be satisfied without 2 or 3, and 2 without 3. Now when Alice calls Benjamin, she can be sure she meets A1–A3, but she can hardly be sure Benjamin meets B1–B3.

B1. B is willing and able to enter a conversation now.
B2. B is willing and able to enter a conversation now with A.
B3. B is willing and able to enter a conversation now with A to accomplish joint project P.

Maybe he cannot talk now (he is in the shower); maybe he does not want to talk to her (he is mad at her); maybe he cannot take up her proposed project (he has never heard of Professor Dwight's seminar).

A must therefore engineer B's entry into the conversation in steps. To establish A1 and B1, she rings B's telephone. She is willing and able to talk now, and if B is too, he will answer, knowing that whoever is calling is projecting a potential conversation, perhaps with him. The result is an adjacency pair, a summons and a response (Schegloff, 1968, 1979).

1. A. (rings B's telephone)
2. B. *Benjamin Holloway*

A's move shows her willingness to talk, and B's response shows his. This, of course, is a pre-sequence that projects a potential conversation between A and B.

To establish A2 and B2, A and B must be willing and able to proceed once they mutually know who they are talking to. Alice and Benjamin achieve that mutual knowledge in these turns.

    2. B. *Benjamin Holloway*
    3. A. *this is Professor Dwight's secretary, from Polymania College*
    4. B. *ooh yes* –

Benjamin's opening response identifies him to the caller, and Alice's next turn identifies her to him. His identification is grounded by her going on, and hers is grounded by his assent *ooh yes*. His assent plus pause is also an invitation for her to proceed. So by line 4, A and B have established not only A1 and B1, but A2 and B2. Note that in establishing mutual knowledge of their identity, A and B also establish a vast network of personal and communal common ground, which is essential to everything else they do in the conversation. No wonder they establish their identities as early as possible.

    Next, to establish A3 and B3, one of them, A or B, must propose the first main joint project the two of them are to carry out. Which one is to do this? Ordinarily, it is A. She would not have initiated the call without a reason—without a broad joint project in mind. Here is what Alice does.

    5. A. *uh:m . about the: lexicology *seminar**
    6. B. **yes**

With 5 she introduces the first topic, and with 6, Benjamin acknowledges it and shows a willingness to consider it further. With these moves, they have embarked on the body of the conversation, carrying out the main official business of the call.

    Opening a telephone conversation, therefore, ordinarily meets requirements A1 through B3 in four steps.

Step 1. Common channel. A and B establish a common channel.
Step 2. Shared identity. A and B establish mutual knowledge of their identities, personal or professional.
Step 3. Joint willingness. A and B establish a joint willingness to talk to each other.
Step 4. First topic. A and B establish a commitment to consider a first joint project.

These steps are sometimes more elaborate, or problematic, than Alice and Benjamin's opening suggests. Here are two variations.

    People often answer the telephone with a simple "hello," and that can greatly complicate steps 2 and 3 (Schegloff, 1968, 1979). Consider this example (Schegloff, 1986, p. 115).

    B: (rings)
    C: *Hello::,*
    B: *H'llo, Clara?*
    C: *Yeh,*
    B: *Hi. Bernie.*
    C: Hi *Bernie.*
    B: *How're you.*
    C: *I'm awright, how're you.*
    B: *Okay:?*
    C: *Good.*
    B: *Laura there?* [first topic]

How do Clara and Bernie establish mutual knowledge of their identities? Bernie initially is forced to identify Clara from the voice sample in *Hello* and from the fact that she was a potential answerer of the telephone. They jointly establish her identity when Bernie guesses *H'llo, Clara?* and she confirms it with *yeh*. But who is he? All Clara has to go on is the voice sample in *H'llo, Clara?* and the fact that he guessed who she is. She does not seem to know (at least, she gives Bernie no evidence), and they cannot go on until she does. So Bernie says *Hi*, giving Clara another voice sample. Bernie's *Hi* seems entirely superfluous given he has already said "hello," but it is not superfluous as evidence of his identity. Clara still gives no evidence of recognition, so Bernie is finally forced to identify himself, *Bernie*. She returns with an enthusiastic *Hi Bernie*. This too would seem superfluous given she has already said "Hello," but it is used also to show her newfound recognition. In openings like these, then, people do not identify themselves until they have to. They give their partners the chance to recognize them first, and that gives their partners a feeling of personal achievement.[3]

In calls to "directory enquiries," the British counterpart to North American "information," the operator's first turn is nonstandard, and this can also lead to complications (Clark & Schaefer, 1987a). Here is a typical opening.

> Customer: (rings)
> Operator: *Directory Enquiries, for which town please?*
> Customer: *In Cambridge.*
> Operator: *What's the name of the people?*

In her very first turn, the operator not only identifies herself (*Directory Enquiries*) but also introduces the first topic (*for which town please?*), presupposing she knows why the customer is calling. This is odd, of course, because it is ordinarily the callers who expect to introduce the first topic. Indeed, some customers got confused, as in this call.

> Customer: (rings)
> Operator: *Directory Enquiries, for which town please?*
> Customer: *Could you give me the phone number of um: Mrs. um: Smithson?*
> Operator: *Yes, which town is this at please?*
> Customer: *Huddleston.*
> Operator: *Yes. And the name again?*
> Customer: *Mrs. Smithson.*

In this call the customer introduced the first topic *Could you give me . . .* as if he had not even heard *For which town please?*

---

[3] In the Netherlands (and presumably elsewhere), the two participants normally identify themselves immediately, as in these translations (Houtkoop-Steenstra, 1986).

> Caller: (rings)
> Answerer: *With Mies Habots.*
> Caller: *Hi, with Anneke de Groot.*

With Mies Habots is short for 'You are speaking with Mies Habots.'

Opening a conversation, then, is subject to many constraints. The main ones come from what the participants need to do to enter any joint activity. On the telephone, there are added constraints from conventions for answering the telephone, but even these appear to have evolved to satisfy the primary requirements for entry into joint activities.

E. Closing a Conversation

Closing a conversation is shaped by other requirements. A and B's main problem is that they have to leave the conversation together. If A left unilaterally, B might be offended, because he would think he was still in a conversation with A when he was not. To leave together, A and B must satisfy three requirements.

1. A and B mutually believe they have completed the last topic.
2. A and B mutually believe they are prepared to exit.
3. A and B mutually believe they are exiting now.

As in the opening, A and B satisfy these requirements in steps. Let us consider closing a telephone conversation (Schegloff & Sacks, 1973).

The first task is to agree that the last topic is complete. A may be ready to close a conversation when B is not, because he has another topic to bring up, or vice versa, so reaching that agreement is tricky. The characteristic solution, according to Schegloff and Sacks, is for one person, say A, to offer a PRE-CLOSING STATEMENT, like *yeah* or *okay*, to signal a readiness to close the conversation. If B has another topic to bring up, he can do it in response. If he does not, he can accept the statement with *yeah* or *okay*, and that opens up the closing section. So a pre-closing statement and its response constitute a pre-sequence: They project the closing of the conversation.

As illustration, consider the end of a conversation between a mother and a daughter, June and Daphie (7.3h.1012).

1. June. *yes*
2. Daphie. *thanks very much*
3. June. **OK?**
4. Daphie. **right,** **I'll see you this**
5. June. **because* there how did you did you beat him?*
6. Daphie. *no, he beat me, four one* (. laughs)
7. June. *four one .*
8. Daphie. *yes, . I was doing quite well in one game, and then then I l– I lost*
9. June. *oh, how disgusting*
10. Daphie. *yes .*
11. June. **OK, . *right***
12. Daphie. **right**
13. June. *see you tonight*
14. Daphie. *right, bye*
15. June. *bye love*
16. Both. (hang up telephones)

In 1 and 2, June and Daphie complete one topic (an exchange of information not shown here), and this is potentially the last topic. In 3, June seems to offer a pre-closing statement (*OK?*), and in 4, Daphie treats it as one when she accepts it (*right*) and begins the closing section (*I'll see you this evening*). Instead, June raises another topic—Daphie's squash game—and that takes precedence. Once this topic has run its course (5–10), June offers a second pre-closing statement (*OK . right*) which Daphie accepts (*right*), and the two of them enter the closing section proper (13–16).

Once the last topic is closed, the participants still have to prepare for their exit. If they are acquaintances, they may want to reassure each other that the upcoming break does not imply anything wrong with their relationship. The break is not permanent. They will resume contact in the future (Goffman, 1971). Here are five minor projects people often accomplish in taking leave, and in this order (Albert & Kessler, 1976, 1978).

1. Summarize the content of the conversation just completed.
2. Justify ending contact at this time.
3. Express pleasure about each other.
4. Indicate continuity of their relationship by planning for future contact either specifically or vaguely ("see you tonight").
5. Wish each other well ("bye").

The last two actions often get conventionalized as farewells. Action 4 is expressed in such phrases as *see you, auf Wiedersehen, tot ziens, au revoir*, and *hasta la vista*, and 5 in *good-bye, good evening, guten Abend, goede dag, bon soir, adieu, bon voyage, buenas noches, adios*, and *shalom*. With these actions, the participants reach the mutual belief that they are prepared to exit the conversation.

The final problem is to break contact together. On the telephone, that means hanging up the receivers. Now, if A hangs up before B, that may offend B because it ends the joint activity unilaterally. So A and B try to time their breaks to be simultaneous. They work up to saying "bye" together, at which moment they begin replacing their receivers. If they do this just right, neither of them hears the click of the other's receiver.

F. Making Room for Narratives

When A is talking to B, she cannot launch into a narrative on her own. She must get B to agree to dispense with their turn-by-turn talk for the moment and give her room to complete the narrative. The basic requirement is this.

NARRATIVE REQUIREMENT: The participants in a conversation mutually believe that they want A to tell a particular narrative now.

A and B must therefore agree that: (a) they both want A to tell the narrative; (b) they want this narrative in particular; and (c) they want it told now. How do they manage this?

Narratives can be introduced by either the prospective narrator or the prospective audience. The simplest method is for a member of the prospective audience to request a particular story now, as here (1.3.215).

Barbara. *how did you get on at your interview, . do tell us*
Annabel. *. oh – – God, what an experience, – – I don't know where to start, you know, it was just such a nightmare – –* [proceeds to give a 30 minute narrative]

Barbara proposes a particular joint project—that Annabel tell them now how she got on at her interview—and, in the second part of the adjacency pair, Annabel takes up the proposed project with a 30 minute narrative. But what if Barbara does not know Annabel has a particular story she wishes to tell now? Then Annabel must arrange for Barbara to want her to tell it now, as she actually does here (1.3.96).

> Annabel. *I acquired an absolutely magnificent sewing machine, by foul means, did I tell you?*
> Barbara. *no*
> Annabel. *well when I was . doing freelance advertising* – [proceeds to give a 5 minute narrative]

In the initial adjacency pair, Annabel alludes to a story and asks Barbara if she has told it to her, and Barbara replies *no*. The two of them clearly take the adjacency pair to be more than a question and answer. They treat it as a PRE-NARRATIVE that licenses Annabel to tell her story, for she immediately launches into a 5 minute story.

How do pre-narratives work? The question was taken up in detail by Sacks (1974) for jokes. The cardinal rule for jokes, Sacks noted, is this: Don't tell people a joke they have already heard. So prospective joke tellers must check whether their audience has heard the joke they want to tell. They may do this by giving a brief précis of it, "Did you hear the joke about the President and his dog?" They must also check for the other requirements—does the audience want to hear the joke, and if so, now? What holds for jokes largely holds for any type of narrative, as illustrated by Annabel in her pre-narrative. She first gave a précis of her story, *I acquired an absolutely magnificent sewing machine, by foul means*—a blatant advertisement for the story—and then checked whether Barbara had heard it before, *did I tell you?* Only when Barbara said *no* did Annabel take them to be jointly committed to her telling the narrative now.

Where, then, do conversations come from? The evidence I have summarized suggests they are created by people trying to accomplish extended joint projects piece by piece. Conversations are a joint activity, so the participants have to establish agreement among themselves at each moment on what they are doing. That requires local management, and so the participants in a conversation appear to proceed turn by turn. On closer look, however, these turns are an emergent phenomenon. They arise as the participants try to contribute to the conversation, grounding what they say, and as they try to complete joint projects. To construct more extended joint projects, the participants often exploit such pre-sequences as pre-questions, pre-opening summons, pre-closing statements, and pre-narratives. They use local means to accomplish global aims.

IV. Creating Narratives

Narratives seem different from conversations, because they seem to be produced by individuals speaking on their own. Once Annabel is asked *how did you get on at your interview, . do tell us,* she appears to hold forth by herself until she is finished. But appearances belie reality. Narratives rely just as heavily on coordination among the participants as conversations do. It is simply that the coordination is hidden from view.

What needs to be coordinated? When Annabel tells about her job interview, she is engaged in a joint project: She is trying to get her addressees to experience vicariously selected parts of what she experienced at her interview, and that requires their joint commitment to a coordinated action. Her original experience was at turns hilarious, exasperating, disappointing, and nerve-racking, and she wants her addressees to understand how. At the center of such a joint project is a SITUATIONAL MODEL, a mental representation or model of the situation being described (e.g., Johnson-Laird, 1983; Miller, 1979; van Dijk & Kintsch, 1983). Annabel and her addressees jointly expect the addressees to create such a model of her job interview as she describes it and thereby to experience selected aspects of the situation as she herself experienced it.

What does it take to coordinate on situational models? Unfortunately, too little is known about what they are, what they contain, how they work. Yet a model of an individual situation S probably represents or presupposes at least these elements (Morrow & Clark, 1988).

1. An observer O, ordinarily the narrator, with a particular viewpoint on S

2. The spatial and temporal frame of reference determined by O's viewpoint

3. Individual objects, states, events, and processes located with respect to O's frame of reference

4. O's focus of attention within the frame of reference

5. O's experience of changes in the objects, states, events, and processes as S unfolds in time

6. Changes in O's viewpoint and focus of attention within the frame of reference

It is not easy for narrators and addressees to coordinate on these elements. How they manage relies in part on the way the narrators formulate their narratives. Let us see how.

A. Intonation Units

One of the most conspicuous features of spontaneous narratives is that they emerge in bursts of words about one clause long. Consider an excerpt from one of the "pear stories," narratives that Chafe (1980) and his colleagues recorded by asking people to describe what happened in a short film about pear-pickers. In this transcription, pauses are represented in seconds by the numbers in parentheses, slight breaks in tempo by double periods, and stretched vowels by dashes (Chafe, 1980, p. 28).

a. *(1.15) A—nd (.1) then a boy comes by,*
b. *(.1) on a bicycle,*
c. *the man is in the tree,*
d. *(.9) and the boy gets off the bicycle,*
e. *and . . looks at the man,*
f. *and then (.9) uh looks at the bushels,*
g. *and he . . starts to just take a few,*
h. *and then he decides to take the whole bushel.*

Each line represents a relatively clear unit of production. These units have been called tone groups (Halliday, 1967), tone units (Crystal, 1969; Crystal & Davy, 1975; Svartvik & Quirk, 1980), intonation groups (Cruttenden, 1986), intonation units (Chafe, 1992), information blocks (Grimes, 1975), idea units (Chafe, 1979, 1980), and lines (Gee, 1986). For convenience I will adopt the term INTONATION UNIT.

Intonation units, as the name implies, are defined by their intonation or prosody, roughly as follows.

1. Intonation. Each intonation unit is identified with a single prosodic contour that ends with a terminal contour.

Prosodic contours and terminal contours are not defined by any single property. According to Chafe (1992), an intonation unit may have one or more of these features: (a) pauses preceding and following the intonation unit; (b) acceleration at the beginning and deceleration at the end of the unit, often finishing with a lengthened word; (c) a decline in pitch level; (d) a falling pitch contour at the end; and (e) creaky voice at the end. In the pear stories, for example, 88% of the intonation units were preceded by pauses, which averaged about 1 s in length. In contrast, creaky voice appears to be found much less often.

Although intonation units are defined by prosody, they tend to have properties 2–6 as well (Chafe, 1979, 1980, 1992; Gee, 1986).

2. Focal accent. Each intonation unit tends to have a single focal accent—a point of highest perceived pitch or loudness—ordinarily at or near the end of the unit (see also Halliday, 1967).
3. Finite clauses. Intonation units tend to be single finite clauses, that is, clauses with finite verbs (verbs with tense). When they are not finite clauses, they are at least constituents, usually smaller than finite clauses. In the pear excerpt, five of the eight intonation units (a, c, d, g, and h) are finite clauses. Two more (e and f) are predicates with a single finite verb. The remaining intonation unit (b) is a prepositional phrase.
4. Entry problems. In narratives and other discourses where planning takes time, intonation units are sometimes interrupted at or near their beginnings with hesitations, repeats, or repairs. In the pear excerpt, there were pauses before three of the eight intonation units (a, b, and d). There were slight breaks in tempo after the first or second word of four intonation units (a, e, f, and g). And the first word was stretched in intonation unit a.
5. Length. The intonation units in Chafe's pear stories were six words long on average and lasted two seconds. They varied in length, of course, but less so than other units—like sentences. This appears typical for spontaneous narratives.
6. And. In narratives, intonation units often begin with and (then), but, or so. Five of the eight intonation units in the pear excerpt begin with and, three of these with and then. In Chafe's pear stories, about 40% of the intonation units began with and. This property is not surprising. Intonation units tend to be finite clauses, and in narratives, successive events tend to be described with finite clauses conjoined with and, and then, or so. This is a point we will return to.

These six properties suggest that intonation units are a basic unit of planning. To get intonation (Property 1) right, speakers need to plan the entire intonation unit in some detail. They need to plan its length to know how high a pitch to start on and when to decelerate. They need to plan whether or not it is a question to know which terminal contour to use. They need to plan what is new information to know where to place the focal accent (Property 2). Indeed, finite clauses and other constituents of about six words (Properties 3 and 5) are just the units, according to research on slips of the tongue, that speakers ordinarily formulate at one time (see Bock & Levelt, this volume). Finally, the entry problems (Property 4) suggest that in creating difficult narratives speakers take more time before each intonation unit to plan it and are often still formulating parts of it as they begin to produce it (see also Boomer, 1965; Ford, 1982; Ford & Holmes, 1978).

Intonation units are more than just units of linguistic formulation. They represent the way narrators think about what they are describing. Narrators appear to attend to one part or aspect of their situational models at a time and to express what they are attending to in a single intonation unit (Chafe, 1979, 1980). That would explain why intonation units tend to be single clauses. It would also explain why they each express "one new idea," a single increment of new information, in a constituent containing the focal accent, and why the rest of the intonation unit expresses given information (Chafe, 1992; Gee, 1986; Halliday, 1967). It is for these reasons that intonation units are sometimes called information blocks or idea units.

Idea units like these should be ideal for listeners trying to build their own situational models. With each new intonation unit, listeners are led to focus on a particular part of their evolving model and construct one new addition to it. In the pear excerpt, they build on it by first introducing a boy coming by, then putting him on a bicycle, then returning their attention to the man in the tree (mentioned earlier), then returning to the boy to create him getting off the bicycle, and so on. When narrators produce intonation units in an orderly way, listeners are able to form a smooth, piece by piece construction of the situational model they were intended to build.

Despite their appearance, intonation units are also shaped by the audience. Note first that intonation units are also the building blocks of conversations. Most turns consist of an integral number of intonation units, often just one, and these are the units that get grounded. The intonation units in narratives are no different. The audience takes active part in shaping them—accepting them as having been understood or forcing them to be reformulated or extended—by producing or withholding nods, smiles, and "uh huh"'s (Bavelas et al., 1993; Chovil, 1991; C. Goodwin, 1981). In turns 30 words or longer in the Svartvik-Quirk corpus of British conversations, there was an explicit acknowledgment like "yeah" or "m" every 15 words (at the median), and they occurred at or near the ends of intonation units (Oreström, 1983). But what goes unrecorded on audiotape and in almost all transcripts are the many smiles and nods of acknowledgment. These should be especially prevalent in narratives because verbal acknowledgments get suppressed when there are two or more addressees and when narrators tell jokes or fictional stories. And in narratives, the audience can always interrupt to clear up mishearings or misunderstandings, and they often do (Polanyi, 1989; Sacks, 1974). Indeed, many narratives are created bit by bit through prompts from an audience, or by two narrators telling a story to a third person as a sort of duet (Falk, 1979; Polanyi, 1989; Tannen, 1984).

Narrators, then, appear to treat intonation units as presentation phases of assertive contributions to a discourse. They look for their audience to accept these presentations by nodding, smiling, saying "yeah" or "uh huh," showing continued interest, or acknowledging with some other signal. Narratives are just a special type of conversation. Like other conversations, they proceed contribution by contribution, each of which is completed through the joint actions of speaker and addressees. It is just that in narratives the turns are longer, and the methods of grounding are less obvious.

B. Sentences and Sections

Narrators create at least three units that are larger than the intonational unit. One is the SENTENCE (Chafe, 1979, 1980; cf. Gee's, 1986, STANZAS). In the pear excerpt, the sentence ends with a period, which marks an intonation that is heard as teminating a sentence. Most sentences consist of a series of intonation units (an average of four in Chafe's pear stories), but unlike intonation units, they vary enormously in length. Just as intonation units appear to describe a single focus of attention, sentences appear to describe a single center of interest (Chafe, 1980).

Sentences in turn combine to form larger units called NARRATIVE SECTIONS (Gee, 1986), which correspond roughly to paragraphs in written narratives (Chafe, 1979). Like intonation units, sections are defined in part by their prosody, as reflected in these two properties.

1. Constituency. Sections consist of intonation units.
2. Termination. Sections tend to end with a falling-pitch glide.

Yet sections appear to be created to deal with a single topic and perspective, as reflected in the next three properties (Gee, 1986).

3. Topic. Sections have a single large topic or theme.
4. Perspective. Sections reflect a single place, time, and set of characters.
5. Parallelism. The sentences of a section, and their intonation units, tend to fall into parallel structures or patterns.

It is as if narrators create sections as they focus their attention on successive pieces of a single scene, and when they change scenes, they terminate one section and start another.

Sections are yet another basic planning unit in narratives. The most striking evidence is the added hesitancy and indecision that narrators display at their entry.

6. Entry problems. Sections tend to begin with increased hesitations, repeats, and repairs, and with intonation units smaller than a finite clause.

In the following excerpt from another pear story, the narrator begins a new section in the third line, as judged by others reading a transcript with the problems edited out (Chafe, 1980, p. 44).

> (.45) And . . as he's holding onto the handlebars
> he t takes off with them.
> (1.1) Um—(.7) then (.4) uh—(2.1) a . . girl on a bicycle,

(1.15) *comes riding towards him,*
. . in the opposite direction.

It took this narrator 6.25 s (the highlighted stretch of speech) to get from the end of the previous section to *a girl on a bicycle,* the first solid phrase of the next section. These planning difficulties are typical as narrators enter new sections that change the topic and require new perspectives (Chafe, 1979, 1980; Gee, 1986; Gee & Grosjean, 1984). New sections, one might say, begin at discontinuities in the experience being simulated.

The largest unit is the narrative as a whole, which consists of one or more sections. These units exhibit the usual entry problems for a section, but in exaggerated form, as in this start of a pear story (Chafe, 1979, p. 167).

(4.25) *Um . . it starts out . . there's a (3.3) well,*
(1.45) *the— landscape is like uh— a f— (2.35) sort of peasant landscape but it isn't really farmland,*
it's like an orchard.
(.6) *it's a small orchard,*
(.65) *and— uh— (.55) it's green.*

As Chafe noted, this narrator had trouble deciding what to focus on first. She began with the first event (*it starts out*), switched to the first character (*there's a*), then fell back to the physical setting, which would be needed for her audience to build the proper situational model. She even had trouble deciding how to describe the setting—a farm but not really a farm, like an orchard, but a small one, a green one. She worked hard to start her addressees off on the right model.

C. Perspective

When you tell a 5-year-old, say Tommy, the story of Little Red Riding Hood, you want him to create a situational model of what happens to Hood on her way to her grandmother's house. You want him to view what happens from particular perspectives. In the first scenes, you might have him follow Hood as she puts bread and wine in a basket, sets out for grandmother's house, and meets a wolf. Later, you might have him follow the wolf as it goes to grandmother's house, locks her up, and takes her place. You must get Tommy to take first one perspective and then another.

Perspective is a complex notion with many subtypes. (1) SPATIAL PERSPEC-TIVE is the physical point of view an observer takes on an object. You would choose between "The wolf went into Grandmother's house" and "The wolf came into Grandmother's house" depending on whether you wanted Tommy to view the scene from outside or inside Grandmother's house. (2) TEMPORAL PERSPECTIVE is the view an observer takes on events in time. You would choose "The wolf was lying in Grandmother's bed" or "The wolf lay in Grandmother's bed" or even "The wolf is lying in Grandmother's bed" depending on how you wanted Tommy to conceive of the event at the moment. (3) FIGURE–GROUND is the observer's implicit focus of attention—what is taken to be figure and ground. You would choose between "There were beautiful flowers along the path" and "The path went through beautiful flowers" depending on which you wanted Tommy to focus on—the flowers or the path. (4) CONCEPTUAL PERSPECTIVE is one's conceptual stance toward something—for example, whether you would refer to the wolf as "a wolf" or as "a polite stranger." All these subtypes of perspective, and others, are essential to coordinating on the construction of situational models (see, e.g., Schober, 1990, 1993).

One type of perspective that is special to narratives is FOREGROUND and BACKGROUND. The idea is that narrators divide what they say into two structures (Grimes, 1975; Hopper, 1979; Hopper & Thompson, 1980; Labov, 1972; Polanyi, 1989; Polanyi-Bowditch, 1976). They treat one set of events, which Labov called the NARRATIVE EVENTS, as the foundation of the narrative. These are the FOREGROUND of the narrative. Everything else is BACKGROUND.[4] In the pear excerpt, these are the narrative events.

> a. (1.15) *A—nd (.1) then a boy comes by,*
> d. *(.9) and the boy gets off the bicycle,*
> e. *and . . looks at the man,*
> f. *and then (.9) uh looks at the bushels,*
> g. *and he . . starts to just take a few,*
> h. *and then he decides to take the whole bushel.*

Narrative events establish the temporal basis of the narrative, so they are described in strict chronological order (except at the beginnings of flashbacks and flashforwards). In this excerpt, they are introduced by *and* or *and then*, which mark chronological order even more explicitly. The background is used, in contrast, to comment on, situate, or otherwise evaluate the narrative events, as in these intonational units from the pear excerpt.

> b. *(.1) on a bicycle,*
> c. *the man is in the tree,*

These two elements situate the boy's coming by and the man in the tree, two pieces of information needed for the foreground.

Narrators distinguish foreground from background by their choice of construction. If they want to specify moments in time, they must describe elements that resemble clock ticks. They should choose PUNCTUAL events like coming by, getting off, looking, starting, and deciding, because these can be ordered chronologically. They should not choose durative or nonpunctual elements like being on a bicycle or in a tree or knowing or not finding something, which cannot be ordered chronologically. Indeed, as foreground narrators prefer events of the following types (Hopper & Thompson, 1980): (1) goal directed events; (2) punctual events (e.g., *hit* vs. *sleep,* or *take* vs. *have*); (3) volitional events (*look at* vs. *see*); (4) affirmative events (*find* vs. *not find*); and (5) real events in which an agent acts on a patient. Narrators have additional methods of marking such events as foregrounded. The common way in English is to express them in independent clauses (not subordinate clauses) and in the simple past or historical present tense (not in the progressive). Some languages, like French, reserve a special narrative past for these clauses.

---

[4] The terms FOREGROUND and BACKGROUND are not the most felicitous terms, since the foreground is often not as important to the narrative as the background. To add confusion, the foreground is sometimes called the backbone of the narrative; other times, it is called the skeleton (Labov, 1972).

Narrators therefore divide intonation units into foreground and background in order to coordinate with their audience on the construction of situational models. The audience keeps track of the main story line events by identifying the foreground of the narrative—the narrative clauses—and they elaborate, situate, and modify these events by identifying the background. If the narrators have done their job right—and most do—the audience should find it easy to identify which intonation units are which.

Narrators can get their audience to create an even more vivid situational model, as Schiffrin (1981) argued, by expressing the foreground not in the past tense but in the NARRATIVE PRESENT. Consider this narrative excerpt from a woman describing being trapped in a stalled car (Schiffrin, 1981, p. 48).

> *We just pulled into this lot*
> *it was just in this lot*
> **and all of a sudden the buzzer sounds**
> **and all these guys hh come hh out**
> *and we didn't know what t' do*
> *cause we were stuck.*
> *so we asked some guy*
> *t' come over an' HELP us.*
> **So he opens the car**
> **and everyone gets out except me and my girlfriend.**
> *We were in front*
> *we just didn't feel like getting out.*
> **And all of a sudden all these sparks start t' fly.**

Most of the time the narrator expresses herself in the past tense. And yet, for certain intonation clauses (highlighted), she switches to the historical present. She does this, according to Schiffrin, as "a way of making a past event sound as if it were occurring at the moment of speaking—a way of making it more vivid" (p. 57). This way the narrator helps us represent the experience in a situational model as if it were happening right now.

Narrators choose their utterances, then, to get their audience to represent a situation from just the right perspective. That perspective helps the audience create the imaginary experience as the narrators are themselves creating it, with its sights, sounds, emotions, and actions.

D. Narrative Organization

Narratives come with an organization. This has been shown in literary and linguistic analyses of both written and spontaneous narratives. But where does the organization come from? Surely spontaneous narrators do not begin with a total plan, or outline, and then fill it in with the details. They seem rather to begin with certain goals, and what they say is determined by the moment-by-moment constraints they try to satisfy en route to those goals. The organization of narratives is not pre-planned. It emerges. Here we will examine only a few features that shape its emergence.

We have seen that narrators, to be effective, must enable their addressees to initiate, build on, and complete their mental representation of the situation being described. They must satisfy at least these two related requirements.

Connectedness. With each new intonation unit, narrators must enable their audience to add the intended increment to the situational model at just the right point.

With-respect-to-ness. Narrators must enable their audience to create each new element in a situation model with respect to other elements in the model.

As simple as these requirements look, they help shape the emergent organization of narratives. To see how, let us consider two types of narratives: narratives of personal experience, and narrative descriptions.

1. Narratives of Personal Experience

Spontaneous narratives of personal experience, according to a study by Labov (1972; cf. Polanyi, 1989), tend to divide into six parts.

1. Abstract (a brief summary of the whole story). An example is Annabel's *I acquired an absolutely magnificent sewing machine, by foul means.*

2. Orientation (a stage setting about the who, when, what, and where of the story). In some narratives, the orientation appears as an identifiable sentence or section, as from this teenager's story: *It was on Sunday and we didn't have nothin' to do after I—after we came from church. Then we ain't had nothing to do.* In other narratives, it is incorporated in the first intonation units of the complicating action, as in the highlighted pieces of Annabel's continuation.

> well **when I was . doing freelance advertising –**
> **the advertising agency**
> **that I . sometimes did some work for .**
> rang me

3. Complicating action (what happened). Annabel continues with narrative clauses (highlighted) that raise the point to be resolved in her narrative.

> **and said um – we've got a client**
> who wants um – – a leaflet designed .
> to go to s– uh instructions how to use a sewing machine
> **and I said I haven't used a sewing machine for years–**
> **and uh he said well . go along and talk to them**
> **and I went along and tal–**
> and I was quite honest about it
> **I said you know I . I haven't used one for years**

She then continues with a series of intonation units describing what happened.

4. Evaluation ("the point of the narrative, its raison d'être: why it was told, what the narrator is getting at," Labov, 1972, p. 266). The evaluation is often not a separate section, but is expressed in background clauses set in among the complicating actions and the resolution. In Annabel's complicating action, the evaluation is expressed in the intonation units that are not highlighted—*who wants um – – a leaflet designed, . to go to s– uh instructions how to use a sewing machine* and *and I was quite honest about it.*

5. Result or resolution (how the complicating action got resolved). Annabel eventually completes her story by returning to her original point, how she *acquired an absolutely magnificent sewing machine, by foul means,* and adding a twist about her ignorance of sewing machines.

so I've got this fabulous machine
which I – in fact and in order to use it
I have to read my instruction booklet
cos it's so complicated

6. Coda (a signal that the narrative is finished). In Annabel's narrative, the resolution itself signals the end of the narrative.[5] In other narratives, there is a separate signal of completion, such as "And that's what happened." Codas "bring the narrator and the listener back to the point at which they entered the narrative" (Labov, 1972, p. 365).

These six divisions reflect, in part, narrators' attempts to satisfy the requirements of connectedness and with-respect-to-ness.

Before Annabel introduces her story, she and Barbara have a situational model of their here-and-now. To get Barbara into the story-world, she introduces it with respect to their here-and-now by means of the abstract. With *I acquired* she makes the story-world an actual world in her own past, and with *sewing machine* she introduces the central element of the story.

Before Annabel can describe any events in the story-world, she must situate it more precisely and populate it with the needed players and props. She does this in her orientation. With *when I was doing freelance advertising,* she specifies the past time more precisely, and with *the advertising agency that I sometimes did some work for,* she introduces the main protagonist. In effect, she and Barbara zoom in on a closer perspective of the story-world.

In the complicating action and evaluation, Annabel takes Barbara through the episode itself. She establishes its time course by the chronological order of her narrative clauses. She satisfies the requirement of with-respect-to-ness by relating the first event (*the advertising agency . . . rang*) to the background time (*when I was doing freelance advertising*), and then the second event to the first, and so on. With each new section, there is a new orientation, which gets related to the previous orientation. And so it goes. The complicating action cannot be resolved, of course, until it has been completed, so the resolution necessarily comes after the complicating action.

Once Annabel has led Barbara through the entire episode, the two of them must zoom out to view it as a whole and return to the situational model of the here-and-now. Annabel accomplishes this by describing her current situation (*I've got this fabulous machine,* etc.). Other narrators do it with codas ("And that's what happened").

Narrators are really guides. Starting from the here-and-now, they show you the story-world as a whole (with the abstract). Then they zoom in on that world, orient you to its features, and guide you from one narrative event to the next until you reach the resolving event. Then they zoom back out to the here-and-now. The six divisions emerge as they try to connect each new element to elements already in the model. The point is even clearer in narrative descriptions.

---

[5] In jokes, too, the resolution—the punch line—signals the end of the joke. It would be superfluous to add "And that's it."

2. Narrative Descriptions

In a study by Linde and Labov (1975), about a hundred New Yorkers were asked *Could you tell me the layout of your apartment?* Despite the many ways they could have described their apartments, most of them guided their interrogator on an imaginary tour, as in this example (p. 927).

> *You walked in the front door.*
> *There was a narrow hallway.*
> *To the left, the first door you came to was a tiny bedroom.*
> *Then there was a kitchen,*
> *and then bathroom,*
> *and then the main room was in the back, living room, I guess.*

Each tour was systematic. (a) It began at the front door. (b) When visitors came to a one-room branch, they looked into it but didn't enter. (c) When they came to a branch with rooms beyond the first room, they always entered. And (d) when they reached the end of a branch, and there were other branches to traverse, they jumped back instantaneously to the fork point where the other branches originated. Because of guidelines a, b, and c, the visitors saw every room, and because of guideline d, they didn't view a cul-de-sac twice, once going in and a second time going out. When people were asked, in other studies, to describe a single room, they took a similar tack (Ehrich & Koster, 1983; Ullmer-Ehrich, 1982). They generally led their addressees on gaze tours of each room.

With these apartment tours, the New Yorkers were about as explicit as they could be about creating situational models. They often made their addressees the tourist, the person from whose point of view the tour was being experienced, by having them do the walking (*you keep walking straight ahead* or *now if you turn right*) or the viewing (*you would find* or *you see a window*). These tactics satisfy the requirement of connectedness. With guideline a, the tourists tie the apartment-world to the front door, the single most prominent point they can relate to the here-and-now. And with guidelines b, c, and d, they relate everything back to the front door.

Recall that, with the requirement of with-respect-to-ness, narrators place things in their model with their choice of figure and ground. The main point in describing an apartment or a room is to say what is where. In the apartment tours, narrators located a path with respect to the front door and then located objects with respect to that path, as in *And on your left, you would find the master bedroom* or *In the corner stands a cabinet*. It was typical to mention the ground first (*your left* and *the cabinet*) and the figure second (*the master bedroom* and *a cabinet*) (Ehrich & Koster, 1983; Linde & Labov, 1975).

People's choices of figure and ground, however, are tightly constrained by their conception of with-respect-to-ness between objects. Consider an analysis of room descriptions by Shanon (1984). The contents of a room, he found, fit this hierarchy.

1. the room proper
2. parts of the room: the walls, floor, and ceiling
3. windows, doors
4. major pieces of furniture

5. objects with a definite place of their own
6. objects without a definite place of their own

At the top of the hierarchy are the permanent, highly predictable contents that can be taken as common ground, as part of people's general schema or frame for a room. At the bottom are the optional, movable, more particular objects that cannot be taken as common ground. This hierarchy was directly reflected in people's room descriptions. Objects not yet mentioned were more likely to be introduced with definite descriptions (like *the floor*) the higher they were in the hierarchy (cf. Brewer & Treyens, 1981). Conversely, objects not yet mentioned were more likely to be introduced in subordinate clauses (like *curtain* in *a closet that has a curtain across it*) the lower they were in the hierarchy. The same phenomena are manifest in apartment descriptions. Major but not minor rooms may be introduced with definite articles; and major rooms may be introduced as subjects of clauses, but minor rooms only in complements (Linde & Labov, 1975).

What this hierarchy reflects, really, is people's perspective on the room's contents: what they see with respect to what. In Shanon's study, objects at level 4 were virtually always described with respect to those at level 4 or above, and analogously at each other level. A chair was described as in front of a window; the window was not described as behind the chair. The hierarchy accounted for 97% of such descriptions. Presumably, these reflect the narrators' focus of attention in their situational models. The chair was represented with respect to the window, and not vice versa. Narrators try to get their audience to add objects that cannot be taken for granted with respect to those that can.

Narratives, then, emerge as people try to get others to build a model of a narrative-world. Narrators try to satisfy many constraints as they go along. Because people have a limited focus of attention, narrators and their audiences proceed one intonation unit at a time, grounding each one as they go along. Because people need to build situation models that are connected, narrators get their audiences to add each new element with respect to what they already have. They try to maintain consistent perspectives and to signal changes in perspective. It is these constraints that organize narrations into intonation units, sentences, sections, and whole narratives.

Narrating is a skill. Some people are good at it, and others not. It takes children years to learn how to tell a decent story, and some never get very good at it. You may know people who are fluent, articulate, and attentive to their audience and yet still unable to tell an effective story. What makes storytellers good, in the end, is their ability to draw us into their story world, to make us see and feel what is happening, to get us to join them in building a vivid situational model of that world. So far, we have only a glimpse of how storytellers do this.

V. CONCLUSION

This, then, has been a selective tour through the production of spontaneous discourse. We have looked particularly closely at two features of the landscape. The first is the social nature of discourse. Discourse is an activity carried out by two or more participants working jointly, and that requires coordination at all levels of planning and execution. One result is that discourses are managed locally. Their global organization is only an emergent outcome of that process. The second feature is the purposive nature of discourse. People engage in a discourse not merely to use language, but to accomplish things. They want to buy shoes or get a lost address or arrange for a dinner party or trade gossip or teach a child improper fractions. Language is simply a tool for achieving these aims. Discourses are joint activities of people trying to accomplish goals beyond language, and the course they take is governed by the purpose and partnership of the participants.

REFERENCES

Albert, S., & Kessler, S. (1976). Processes for ending social encounters: The conceptual archeology of a temporal place. *Journal of Theory of Social Behavior, 6,* 147–170.

Albert, S., & Kessler, S. (1978). Ending social encounters. *Journal of Experimental Social Psychology, 14,* 541–553.

Atkinson, J. M., & Heritage, J. (1984). *Structures of social action: Studies in conversational analysis.* Cambridge: Cambridge University Press.

Bavelas, J. B. (1990). Nonverbal and social aspects of discourse in face-to-face interaction. *Text, 10,* 5–8.

Bavelas, J. B., Black, A., Chovil, N., Lemery, C. R., & Mullett, J. (1988). Form and function in motor mimicry: Topographic evidence that the primary function is communicative. *Human Communication Research, 14,* 275–299.

Bavelas, J. B., Black, A., Lemery, C. R., & Mullett, J. (1986). "I *show* how you feel": Motor mimicry as a communicative act. *Journal of Personality and Social Psychology, 50,* 322–329.

Bavelas, J. B., Chovil, N., Lawrie, D. A., & Wade, A. (1993). Interactive gestures. *Discourse Processes, 15,* 469–489.

Beattie, G. W., & Barnard, P. J. (1979). The temporal structure of natural telephone conversations (directory enquiry calls). *Linguistics, 17,* 213–229.

Boomer, D. S. (1965). Hesitation and grammatical encoding. *Language and Speech, 8,* 148–158.

Brennan, S. E. (1990). *Seeking and providing evidence for mutual understanding.* Unpublished doctoral dissertation, Stanford University, Stanford, CA.

Brewer, W. F., & Treyens, J. C. (1981). Role of schemata in memory for places. *Cognitive Psychology, 13,* 207–230.

Button, G., & Lee, J. R. E. (1987). *Talk and social organization.* Philadelphia: Multilingual Matters.

Chafe, W. (1979). The flow of thought and the flow of language. In T. Givón (Ed.), *Syntax and semantics 12: Discourse and syntax* (pp. 159–181). New York: Academic Press.

Chafe, W. (1980). The deployment of consciousness in the production of a narrative. In W. Chafe (Ed.), *The pear stories.* Norwood, NJ: Ablex.

Chafe, W. (1992, August). *Intonation units and prominences in English natural discourse.* Proceedings of the University of Pennsylvania Prosodic Workshop, Philadelphia.

Chovil, N. (1991). Discourse-oriented facial displays in conversation. *Language and Social Interaction, 25,* 163–194.

Clark, H. H. (1993). Communities, commonalities, and communication. In J. Gumperz & S. Levinson (Eds.), *Rethinking linguistic relativity.* Cambridge: Cambridge University Press.

Clark, H. H., & Carlson, T. B. (1981). Context for comprehension. In J. Long & A. D. Baddeley (Eds.), *Attention and performance IX* (pp. 313–330). Hillsdale, NJ: Erlbaum.

Clark, H. H., & Carlson, T. B. (1982a). Hearers and speech acts. *Language, 58,* 332–373.

Clark, H. H., & Carlson, T. B. (1982b). Speech acts and hearers' beliefs. In N. V. Smith (Ed.), *Mutual knowledge.* London: Academic Press.

Clark, H. H., & French, J. W. (1981). Telephone goodbyes. *Language in Society, 10,* 1–19.

Clark, H. H., & Haviland, S. E. (1977). Comprehension and the given–new contract. In R. O. Freedle (Ed.), *Discourse production and comprehension* (pp. 1–40). Hillsdale, NJ: Erlbaum.

Clark, H. H., & Marshall, C. R. (1981). Definite reference and mutual knowledge. In A. K. Joshi, B. Webber, & I. A. Sag (Eds.), *Elements of discourse understanding*. Cambridge: Cambridge University Press.

Clark, H. H., & Schaefer, E. F. (1987a). Collaborating on contributions to conversation. *Language and Cognitive Processes, 2,* 19–41.

Clark, H. H., & Schaefer, E. F. (1987b). Concealing one's meaning from overhearers. *Journal of Memory and Language, 26,* 209–225.

Clark, H. H., & Schaefer, E. F. (1989). Contributing to discourse. *Cognitive Science, 13,* 259–294.

Clark, H. H., & Schaefer, E. F. (1992). Dealing with overhearers. In H. H. Clark (Ed.), *Arenas of language use*. Chicago: University of Chicago Press.

Clark, H. H., & Wilkes-Gibbs, D. (1986). Referring as a collaborative process. *Cognition, 22,* 1–39.

Cruttenden, A. (1986). *Intonation*. Cambridge: Cambridge University Press.

Crystal, D. (1969). *Prosodic systems and intonation in English*. Cambridge: Cambridge University Press.

Crystal, D., & Davy, D. (1975). *Advanced English conversation*. London: Longman.

Duncan, S. (1972). Some signals and rules for taking speaking turns in conversation. *Journal of Personal and Social Psychology, 23,* 283–292.

Duncan, S. (1973). Toward a grammar for dyadic conversation. *Semiotica, 9,* 29–47.

Ehrich, V., & Koster, C. (1983). Discourse organization and sentence form: The structure of room descriptions in Dutch. *Discourse Processes, 6,* 169–195.

Falk, J. (1979). *The conversational duet*. Unpublished doctoral dissertation, Princeton University, Princeton, NJ.

Ford, M. (1982). Sentence planning units: Implications for the speaker's representation of meaningful relations underlying sentences. In J. Bresnan (Ed.), *The mental representation of grammatical relations*. Cambridge, MA: MIT Press.

Ford, M., & Holmes, V. M. (1978). Planning units in sentence production. *Cognition, 6,* 35–53.

Fussell, S. R., & Krauss, R. M. (1989). The effects of intended audience on message production and comprehension: References in a common ground framework. *Journal of Experimental Social Psychology, 25,* 203–219.

Fussell, S. R., & Krauss, R. M. (1991). Accuracy and bias in estimates of others' knowledge. *European Journal of Social Psychology, 21,* 445–454.

Fussell, S. R., & Krauss, R. M. (1992). Coordination of knowledge in communication: Effects of speakers' assumptions about what others know. *Journal of Personality and Social Psychology, 62,* 378–391.

Gazdar, G. (1979). *Pragmatics: Implicature, presupposition, and logical form*. New York: Academic Press.

Gee, J. P. (1986). Units in the production of narrative discourse. *Discourse Processes, 9,* 391–422.

Gee, J. P., & Grosjean, F. (1984). Empirical evidence for narrative structure. *Cognitive Science, 8,* 59–85.

Goffman, E. (1971). *Relations in public*. New York: Basic Books.

Goffman, E. (1976). Replies and responses. *Language in Society, 5,* 257–313.

Goffman, E. (1981). *Forms of talk*. Philadelphia: University of Pennsylvania Press.

Goodwin, C. (1981). *Conversational organization: Interaction between speakers and hearers*. New York: Academic Press.

Goodwin, C. (1986). Between and within: Alternative and sequential treatments of continuers and assessments. *Human Studies, 9,* 205–217.

Goodwin, M. H., & Goodwin, C. (1986). Gesture and coparticipation in the activity of searching for a word. *Semiotica, 68,* 51–75.

Grimes, J. E. (1975). *The thread of discourse*. The Hague: Mouton.

Halliday, M. A. K. (1967). Notes on transitivity and theme in English. Part 2. *Journal of Linguistics, 3,* 199–244.

Halliday, M. A. K., & Hasan, R. (1976). *Cohesion in English*. London: Longman.

Hopper, P. J. (1979). Aspect and foregrounding in discourse. In T. Givón (Ed.), *Syntax and semantics 12: Discourse and syntax* (pp. 213–241). New York: Academic Press.

Hopper, P. J., & Thompson, S. (1980). Transitivity in grammar and discourse. *Language, 56,* 251–299.

Houtkoop-Steenstra, H. (1986). *Opening sequences in Dutch telephone conversation* (Report No. 101, Tilburg Papers in Language and Literature). Tilburg, The Netherlands: Tilburg University.

Jameson, A. D. (1990). *Knowing what others know.* Unpublished doctoral dissertation, University of Amsterdam.

Jefferson, G. (1973). A case of precision timing in ordinary conversation: Overlapped tag-positioned address terms in closing sequences. *Semiotica, 9,* 47–96.

Johnson-Laird, P. N. (1983). *Mental models: Towards a cognitive science of language, inference, and consciousness.* Cambridge, MA: Harvard University Press.

Kendon, A. (1980). Gesticulation and speech: Two aspects of the process of utterance. In M. R. Key (Ed.), *Nonverbal communication and language* (pp. 207–227). The Hague: Mouton.

Kendon, A. (1987). On gesture: Its complementary relationship with speech. In A. W. Siegman & S. Felstein (Eds.), *Nonverbal behavior and nonverbal communication* (2nd ed., pp. 65–97). Hillsdale, NJ: Erlbaum

Krauss, R. M., & Fussell, S. R. (1991). Constructing shared communicative environments. In L. B. Resnick, J. M. Levine, & S. D. Teasley (Eds.), *Perspectives on socially shared cognition.* Washington, DC: APA Books.

Labov, W. (1972). The transformation of experience in narrative syntax. In W. Labov (Ed.), *Language in the inner city.* Philadelphia: University of Pennsylvania Press.

Lerner, G. H. (1987). *Collaborative turn sequences: Sentence construction and social action.* Unpublished doctoral dissertation, University of California, Irvine.

Lewis, D. (1969). *Convention.* Cambridge, MA: Harvard.

Linde, C., & Labov, W. (1975). Spatial networks as a site for the study of language and thought. *Language, 51,* 924–939.

McNeill, D. (1985) So you think gestures are nonverbal? *Psychological Review, 92,* 350–371.

McNeill, D. (1992). *Hand and mind.* Chicago: University of Chicago Press.

McNeill, D., & Levy, E. (1982). Conceptual representations in language activity and gesture. In R. J. Jarvella & W. Klein (Eds.), *Speech, place and action: Studies in deixis and related topics.* Chichester: Wiley.

Miller, G. A. (1979). Images and models, similes and metaphors. In A. Ortony (Ed.), *Metaphor and thought.* Cambridge: Cambridge University Press.

Morgan, J. L., & Sellner, M. B. (1980). Discourse and linguistic theory. In R. J. Spiro, B. C. Bruce, & W. F. Brewer (Eds.), *Theoretical issues in reading comprehension: Perspectives from cognitive psychology, linguistics, artificial intelligence, and education* (pp. 165–200). Hillsdale, NJ: Erlbaum.

Morrow, D. G., & Clark, H. H. (1988). Interpreting words in spatial descriptions. *Language and Cognitive Processes, 3,* 275–292.

Oreström, B. (1983). *Turn-taking in English conversation.* Lund, Sweden: Gleerup.

Polanyi, L. (1989). *Telling the American story.* Cambridge, MA: MIT Press.

Polanyi-Bowditch, L. (1976). Why the whats are when: Mutually contextualized realms of narrative. In K. Whistler et al. (Eds.), *Proceedings of the second annual meeting of the Berkeley Linguistics Society* (pp. 59–78). Berkeley, CA: Berkeley Linguistics Society.

Sacks, H. (1974). An analysis in the course of a joke's telling in conversation. In R. Bauman & J. Scherzer (Eds.), *Explorations in the ethnography of speaking* (pp. 337–353). Cambridge: Cambridge University Press.

Sacks, H., Schegloff, E. A., & Jefferson, G. (1974). A simplest systematics for the organization of turn-taking in conversation. *Language, 50,* 696–735.

Schegloff, E. A. (1968). Sequencing in conversational openings. *American Anthropologist, 70,* 1075–1095.

Schegloff, E. A. (1979). Identification and recognition in telephone conversation openings. In G. Psathas (Ed.), *Everyday language: Studies in ethnomethodology.* New York: Irvington.

Schegloff, E. A. (1980). Preliminaries to preliminaries: "Can I ask you a question?" *Sociological Inquiry, 50,* 104–152.

Schegloff, E. A. (1982). Discourse as an interactional achievement: Some uses of 'uh huh' and other things that come between sentences. In D. Tannen (Ed.), *Analyzing discourse: Text and talk. 32nd Georgetown University Roundtable on Languages and Linguistics 1981* (pp. 71–93). Washington, DC: Georgetown University Press.

Schegloff, E. A. (1984). On some gestures' relation to talk. In J. M. Atkinson & J. Heritage (Eds.), *Structures of social action: Studies in conversational analysis.* Cambridge: Cambridge University Press.

Schegloff, E. A. (1986). The routine as achievement. *Human Studies, 9*, 111–151.

Schegloff, E. A. (1987). Recycled turn beginnings: A precise repair mechanism in conversation's turn-taking organization. In G. Button & J. R. E. Lee (Eds.), *Talk and social organization*. Philadelphia: Multilingual Matters.

Schegloff, E. A., & Sacks, H. (1973). Opening up closings. *Semiotica, 8*, 289–327.

Schiffer, S. R. (1972). *Meaning*. Oxford: Blackwell.

Schiffrin, D. (1981). Tense variation in narrative. *Language, 57*, 45–62.

Schober, M. F. (1990). *Spatial perspective in language use*. Unpublished doctoral dissertation, Stanford University, Stanford, CA.

Schober, M. F. (1993). Spatial perspective-taking in conversation. *Cognition, 4*, 1–24.

Schober, M. F., & Clark, H. H. (1989). Understanding by addressees and overhearers. *Cognitive Psychology, 21*, 211–232.

Shanon, B. (1984). Room descriptions. *Discourse Processes, 7*, 225–255.

Stalnaker, R. C. (1978). Assertion. In P. Cole (Ed.), *Syntax and semantics 9: Pragmatics* (pp. 315–332). New York: Academic Press.

Svartvik, J., & Quirk, R. (1980). *A corpus of English conversation*. Lund, Sweden: Gleerup.

Tannen, D. (1984). *Conversational style: Analyzing talk among friends*. Norwood, NJ: Ablex.

Ullmer-Ehrich, V. (1982). The structure of living space descriptions. In R. J. Jarvella & W. Klein (Eds.), *Speech, place, and action*. New York: Wiley.

van Dijk, T. A. (1972). *Some aspects of text grammars*. The Hague: Mouton.

van Dijk, T. A. (1977). *Text and context*. London: Longman.

van Dijk, T. A., & Kintsch, W. (1983). *Strategies of discourse comprehension*. New York: Academic Press.

Wilkes-Gibbs, D. (1986). *Collaborative processes of language use in conversation*. Unpublished doctoral dissertation, Stanford University, Stanford, CA.

Yngve, V. H. (1970). *On getting a word in edgewise*. Papers from the Sixth regional meeting of the Chicago Linguistics Society, Chicago, pp. 567–578.

CHAPTER 31

LANGUAGE AND THE BRAIN

DAVID CAPLAN

I. INTRODUCTION

Language is a distinctly human ability that is vital to the cognitive and communicative abilities that underlie the success of humans both as individuals and as a species. The neural basis for language is thus of considerable biological interest. This chapter discusses the gross functional neuroanatomy of language. It reviews and interprets data derived from psycholinguistic studies of acquired language deficits, new neuroimaging techniques, and new uses of experimental methods, such as electrocorticography, that bear on this topic. The model that emerges from these studies differs in some important ways from the most widely accepted models of the gross functional neuroanatomy of language that exist today (Geschwind, 1970, 1979; Benson, 1979).

This chapter is organized as follows. First, I present a brief overview of the language processing system, as it emerges from contemporary studies in linguistics, psycholinguistics, and computer science. Following a brief description of basic methods of studying language–brain relationships, I review the role of cortical structures in language. In this section, I focus on the evidence for the localized versus the distributed nature of the neural substrate for language functions and I introduce the issue of individual variation in language localization. I then briefly discuss the role of subcortical structures in language and the nature of hemispheric specialization for language. In Section VII, I consider the determinants of the neural organization for language, and in Section VIII, I conclude with a discussion of the nature of language impairments and other clinical issues.

II. THE LANGUAGE PROCESSING SYSTEM

The human language processing system is described in detail in the various chapters of this book. I here present a capsule overview of its essential features, as an introduction to the issues to be discussed.

Human language can be viewed as a code that links a set of linguistic forms to a number of aspects of meaning. These forms are activated in the usual tasks of language use—speaking, auditory comprehension, reading, and writing.[1] There is wide agreement among linguists, psychologists, and computer scientists that these different forms are activated by different COMPONENTS of a LANGUAGE PROCESSING SYSTEM (Fodor, 1983; Shallice, 1988). Components of the cognitive processing system are devices that accept as input a certain type of representation (either linguistic or nonverbal) and operate on these inputs to activate another type of representation. For a component of the cognitive system to be part of the language processing system, at least one of these representations must be part of the language code. For instance, a component of the language processing system might accept as input the semantic representation (meaning) activated by the presentation of a picture and produce as output a representation of the sound pattern of the word that corresponds to that meaning. A component of the cognitive system that took as input a representation of contours and surfaces produced by early visual processes and produced as output a representation of the form of a visually presented object (Marr, 1982) would not be part of the language processing system. Components of the language processing system can be conceived of as either algorithmic operations [often simulated in a computer with basic von Neumann characteristics (Pylyshyn, 1984)] or as stochastic processes [increasingly simulated in so-called "connectionist," "parallel distributed processing," or "neurally realistic" computer models (McClelland & Rumelhart, 1986a)].

The operations of the language processing system are both obligatory and largely unconscious. The obligatory nature of language processing can be appreciated intuitively by considering that we are generally unable to inhibit the performance of many language processing tasks once the system is engaged by an appropriate, attended input. For instance, we must perceive a spoken word as a word, not just as a nonlinguistic percept (Marslen-Wilson, 1973). The unconscious nature of most of language processing can be appreciated by considering that when we listen to a lecture, converse with an interlocutor, read a novel, or engage in some other language processing task, we usually have the subjective impression that we are extracting another person's meaning and producing linguistic forms appropriate to our intentions without paying attention

---

[1] The auditory–oral and written modalities of language use differ in ways that may be relevant to their neurobiological basis. The ability to use language in auditory–oral tasks (speaking and auditory comprehension) develops in all neurologically normal humans exposed to a normal linguistic environment during the first five to ten years of life (Slobin, 1985). Not all spoken languages have written forms, and mastery of written language processing requires special instruction. Individuals in whom auditory–oral language does not develop do not acquire written languages (Furth, 1966) [though congenitally deaf subjects acquire natural sign language under normal conditions of exposure (Poizner et al., 1989)]. There is no evidence for the existence of written forms of languages over 10,000 years ago, while spoken language presumably existed well before this period (Lieberman, 1984). For these reasons, auditory–oral language has the characteristics of a functional ability that evolved relatively early in the human species, while written language has many of the characteristics of an acquired skill that builds on auditory–oral language processing (as well as on other cognitive capacities). These differences may correlate with quite different neural organization for auditory–oral and written language functions. In this chapter, I am primarily concerned with the neural basis of auditory–oral language functions, though some examples of breakdown of written language processing are presented where they are relevant to particular neurolinguistic models.

to the details of the sounds of words, sentence structure, and so on. In general, cognitive processes that are automatic and unconscious are thought to require relatively little allocation of mental resources (Shiffrin & Schneider, 1977). However, many experimental results indicate that language processing requires the allocation of attention and/or processing resources (Wanner & Maratsos, 1978). The efficiency of each of the components of the language processing system has been conceived of as being a function of the resources available to that component, up to the maximum level of resource utilization of which the component is capable (Shallice, 1988). Components of the system are remarkably efficient. For instance, it has been estimated on the basis of many different psycholinguistic experimental techniques that spoken words are usually recognized less than 125 ms after their onset [i.e., while they are still being uttered; (Marslen-Wilson, 1973)]. Similarly, normal word production in speech requires searching through a mental word production "dictionary" of over 20,000 items, but still goes on at the rate of about 3 words per second with an error rate of about 1 word mis-selected per million and another 1 word mispronounced per million (Levelt, 1989). The efficiency of the language processing system as a whole requires this level of efficiency of each of its components but also is achieved because of the massively parallel computational architecture of the system, which leads to many components of the system being simultaneously active.

Components of the language processing system are hierarchically organized. For instance, all aspects of language processing devoted to activating a word's sound pattern from its meaning may be considered to be a single component of the system, and this component contains a large number of different subcomponents [e.g., activating the individual sounds of a word, activating the syllabic structure of a word, activating the stress pattern of a word, etc. (Levelt, 1989)]. In turn, each of these subcomponents consists of a number of operations [e.g., activating consonants and vowels, adjusting stress contours to accommodate the effects of word formation processes, etc. (Levelt, 1989)].

At least three types of language representations are clearly identified in the language processing system: the LEXICAL LEVEL, the MORPHOLOGICAL LEVEL, and the SENTENTIAL LEVEL.[2] The lexical level of language makes contact with the categorial structure of the world (Rosch, 1975). Lexical items (simple words) designate concrete objects, abstract concepts, actions, properties, and logical connectives. The basic form of a simple lexical item consists of a phonological representation that specifies the segmental elements (phonemes) of the word and their organization into metrical structures (e.g., syllables) (Halle & Vergnaud, 1980). The form of a word can also be represented orthographically (Henderson, 1982). The morphological level of language allows the meaning associated with a simple lexical item to be used as a different syntactic category (Selkirk, 1982) (e.g., noun formation with the suffix *-tion* allows the semantic values associated with a verb to be used nominally, as in the word *destruction*

---

[2] Other levels of language structure exist, but will not be considered here. There are different reasons for our exclusion of different levels of language structure from the present discussion. For instance, the discourse level is excluded because its processing is heavily interconnected with nonlinguistic processes, such as logical inference and retrieval of information from semantic memory; the level of sentential intonational contours is not discussed because very little is known about its neural basis.

derived from *destroy*) and thus avoids the need for an enormous number of elementary lexical items in an individual's vocabulary. The sentential level of language makes use of the syntactic categories of lexical items (e.g., noun, verb, etc.) to build hierarchically organized syntactic structures (e.g., noun phrase, verb phrase, sentence, etc.) that define relationships between words relevant to the propositional content of a sentence (Jackendoff, 1983). The propositional content of a sentence expresses aspects of meaning such as the-matic roles (who did what to whom), attribution of modification (which adjec-tives go with which nouns), the reference of pronouns and other referentially dependent categories, and so on. Propositional meanings make assertions that can be entered into logical and planning processes and that can serve as a means for updating an individual's knowledge of the world.

The major components of the language processing system for simple words are listed in Table I, and for derived words and sentences in Table II. Figure 1 presents a model indicating the sequence of activation of components of the lexical processing system. Figure 2 presents a similar model of the processing system for morphologically complex words and sentences. The model of the language processing system outlined in Tables I and II and Figures 1 and 2 represents the minimal decomposition of language processing functions that can serve as a first step toward a systematic, detailed model of the psycholinguistic processes underlying language use.[3] More general descriptions of language processing only refer to language tasks (e.g., speaking, comprehension, etc.) and give no indication of the nature and organization of the cognitive processes that allow these tasks to be accomplished. Our interest is therefore in the way the brain is organized to support components of the language processing system described in at least the level of detail captured in these tables and figures.

III. Methodological Approaches to the Functional Neuroanatomy of Language

There are two basic logical approaches to the study of the neural basis for language. The first is to correlate "positive" language phenomena with meta-bolic or physiological activity in the brain. The second is to correlate deficits in language functioning with lesions in the brain. In both cases, there is a set of criteria that must be met in order to relate a language function to the brain. In positive studies, a language function can be RELATED to metabolic or physio-logical activity in an area of the brain if and only if that activity is significantly correlated with the language function in question, and a language function can be EXCLUSIVELY RELATED to metabolic or physiological activity in an area of the brain if and only if that activity is significantly correlated with the language function in question and no other activity or location is so correlated. In deficit

---

[3] In terms of the features of language processing just described, the description of the language processing system provided in Tables I and II and Figures 1 and 2 is incomplete in at least three ways. First, it does not identify subprocesses within each of the components of the language processing system. Second, it does not capture the full extent of parallelism and interaction in the operation of language processing components. Third, it does not recognize feedback between components.

TABLE I
Summary of Components of the Language Processing System for Simple Words

Component	Input	Operation	Output
Auditory–Oral Modality			
Acoustic-phonological processing	acoustic waveform	matches acoustic properties to phonetic features	phonological segments (phonemes, allophones, syllables)
Input-side lexical access	phonological units	activates lexical items in long-term memory on basis of sound; selects best fit to stimulus	phonological forms of words
Input-side semantic access	words (represented as phonological forms)	activates semantic features of words	word meanings
Output-side lexical access	word meanings ("lemmas"; 12)	activates the phonological forms of words	phonological form of words
Phonological output planning	phonological forms of words (and nonwords)	activates detailed phonetic features of words (and nonwords)	speech
Written Modality			
Written lexical access	abstract letter identities	activates orthographic forms of words	orthographic forms of words
Lexical semantic access	orthographic forms of words	activates semantic features of words	word meanings
Accessing orthography from semantics	word meanings	activates orthographic forms of words	orthographic forms of words
Accessing lexical orthography from lexical phonology	phonological representations of words	activates orthographic forms of words from their phonological forms	orthographic forms of words
Accessing sublexical orthography from sublexical phonology	phonological units (phonemes, other units)	activates orthographic units corresponding to phonological units	orthographic units in words and nonwords
Accessing lexical phonology from whole-word orthography	orthographic forms of words	activates phonological forms of words from their orthographic forms	phonological forms of words
Accessing sublexical phonology from orthography	orthographic units (graphemes, other units)	activates phonological units corresponding to orthographic units	phonological units in words and nonwords

studies, a language function can be RELATED to an area of the brain if and only if (a) abnormal performance on a task is best interpreted as a result of a deficit in the language processing component in question and (b) the abnormal performance is significantly correlated with a lesion in a particular area of the brain. A language function can be EXCLUSIVELY RELATED to an area of the brain if and only if conditions (a) and (b) are met and the abnormal performance in

TABLE II
Summary of Components of the Language Processing System for Derived Words and Sentences (Collapsed over Auditory–Oral and Written Modalities)

Component	Input	Operation	Output
Processing Affixed Words			
Accessing morphological form	word forms	segments words into structural (morphological) units; activates syntactic features of words	morphological structure; syntactic features
Morphological comprehension	word meaning; morphological structure	combines word roots and affixes	meanings of morphologically complex words
Accessing affixed words from semantics	word meanings; syntactic features	activates forms of affixes and function words	forms of affixes and function words
Sentence Level Processing			
Lexico-inferential processing	meanings of simple and complex words; world knowledge	infers aspects of sentence meaning on basis of pragmatic plausibility	aspects of propositional meaning (thematic roles; attribution of modifiers)
Syntactic comprehension	word meanings; syntactic features	constructs syntactic representation and combines it with word meanings	propostional meaning
Construction of sentence form	word forms; propositional meaning	constructs syntactic structures; inserts word forms into structures	sentence form (including positions of lexical items)

question does not occur in association with other lesions (Von Eckardt, 1978). In both positive and lesion studies, the issue of the units of description—how to describe language functions and brain states—is crucial. To advance a model of the functional neuroanatomy of psycholinguistically justified components of the language processing system, activation and deficit data must be interpretable in terms of components of the language processing system (such as those outlined in Tables I and II), and brain regions must be similarly defined in justifiable neuroanatomical terms (Caplan, 1982).

IV. CORTICAL STRUCTURES AND LANGUAGE

Clinical studies (Luria, 1970; Russell & Esper, 1961; Basso et al., 1985; Weisenberg & McBride, 1935; Brown, 1972; Pick, 1973) indicate that the association cortex in the region of the Sylvian fissure—specifically, the posterior half of the pars triangularis and the pars opecularis of the third frontal convolution (Broca's area), the association cortex in the opecular area of the pre- and post-

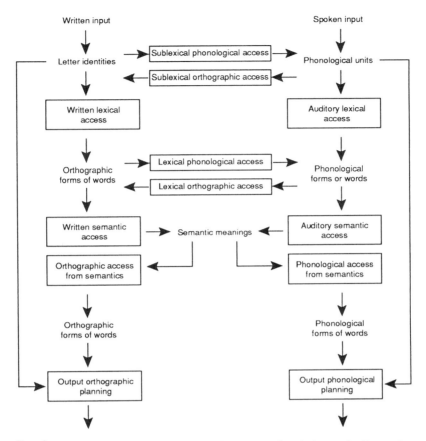

FIG. 1 A model of the language processing system for single words. Processing components, indicated in boxes, activate linguistic representations in the sequences indicated by arrows. (Reprinted with permission from D. Caplan, *Language: Structure, processing, and disorders*, Cambridge, MA, MIT Press, 1992).

central gyri, the supramarginal and angular gyri of the parietal lobe, the first temporal gyrus from the supramarginal gyrus to a point lateral to Heschl's gyrus (Wernicke's area), and possibly a portion of the adjacent second temporal gyrus—are responsible for language processing. On the basis of present knowledge, there is no other cortical area that can be confidently thought to subserve language functions. The supplementary motor area is the only other cortical structure that has been suggested to play a role in language processing. However, its primary function in language tasks appears to be to initiate vocalization, not to activate linguistic representations through subserving a component of the language processing system per se (Masdeu et al., 1978).

Two general classes of theories of the relationship of portions of the perisylvian association cortex to components of the language processing system have been developed, one based on "holist" or distributed views of neural function (Jackson, 1878; Freud, 1891; Marie, 1906; Head, 1926; Mohr et al., 1978) and one based on localizationist principles (Luria, 1970, 1973; Broca, 1861; Wernicke, 1874; Dejerine, 1892; Lichtheim, 1885; Henschen, 1920; Nielson, 1936; Geschwind, 1965; Damasio & Damasio, 1980). Though theories within

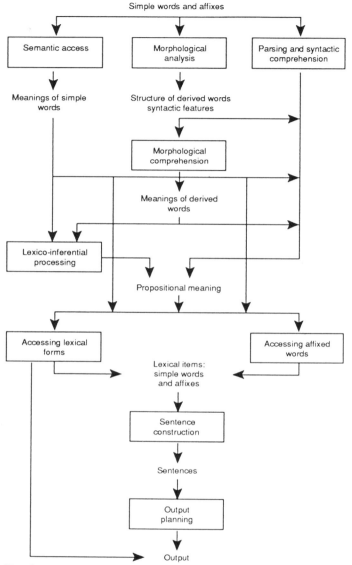

FIG. 2 A model of the language processing system for derived words and sentences. Processing components, indicated in boxes, activate linguistic representations in the sequences indicated by arrows. (Reprinted with permission from D. Caplan, *Language: Structure, processing, and disorders,* Cambridge, MA, MIT Press, 1992).

each of these two major groupings vary, there are a number of features common to theories within each class.

The basic tenet of holist/distributed theories of the functional neuroanatomy for language is that linguistic representations are distributed widely and that specific stages of linguistic processing recruit widely scattered areas of perisylvian association cortex. Lashley (1929, 1950) identified two functional features of holist/distributed models that determine the effects of lesions on perfor-mance: EQUIPOTENTIALITY (every portion of a particular brain region can carry out a specific function in every individual) and MASS ACTION (the larger the neuronal pool that carries out a particular function, the more efficiently that function is accomplished). The features of equipotentiality and mass action jointly entail that lesions of similar sizes anywhere in a specified brain region have equivalent effects on function, and that the magnitude of any functional deficit is directly proportional to the size of a lesion in this specified area. More recently, models of lesions in parallel distributed processing (PDP) simula-tions of language and other cognitive functions have provided a mathemati-cal basis for these properties of these systems (McClelland & Rumelhart, 1986b).

All the traditional theories that postulate localization of components of the language processing system maintain the view that, discounting lateralization, the localization of components of the language processing system is invariant across the normal adult population. Thus, all the traditional localizationist theories have as a corollary that lesions in particular areas of the perisylvian association cortex interrupt the same language processing components in all individuals. Many localizationist theories also maintain that the specific localiza-tion of language processing components results from a computational advantage inherent in juxtaposing particular language processing components to each other or to cortex supporting arousal, sensory, and motor processes (Luria, 1970, 1973; Geschwind, 1965; Caplan, 1987).

Because of the plethora of specific theories within each of these two general camps, it is impossible to critically review the empirical basis of all theories that have present-day adherents (for a partial review, see Caplan, 1987a). I shall focus on the most widely cited theories, as examples of each class.

A. Holist Theories

Unlike narrow localizationist theories, there is no one holist model that has emerged as the major example of this class of theories. However, several lines of evidence are adduced as evidence for holist theories, and all holist theories suffer from similar inadequacies in accounting for certain empirical findings.

The first line of evidence supporting holist theories consists of the ubiquity of general factors in accounting for the performance of aphasic patients. For instance, factor analyses of the performances of groups of patients both on general aphasia tests (Goodglass & Kaplan, 1982; Schuell, 1957) and on tests of specific language abilities (Caplan et al., 1985) almost always result in first eigenvectors (usually accounting for more than half the variance in performance) that are roughly equally weighted for most of the subtests used to test the population. Such vectors are usually taken to reflect disruption of a single factor that affects performance on all measures, such as a limited amount of mental resources available for psycholinguistic computations. The existence of such factors would be the immediate consequence of a system in which functions were disruptable by lesions in a variety of locations, and they have therefore been widely taken as evidence for a distributed basis for language functions. A second finding supporting holist theories is the frequent observation of so-called "graceful degradation" of performance within specific language domains after brain damage. An example of such degradation is the strong tendency of certain dyslexic patients to read irregularly spelled words according to a regularization strategy (e.g., *pint* is read with a short *i*), a tendency which is inversely proportional to the frequency of the word (Bub et al., 1985). Graceful degradation reflects the preservation of the simplest (in many cases, the most commonly occuring) aspects of language processing after brain damage. Modern work with PDP models, which provide formal models of holist concepts, indicate that such patterns of performance can arise following focal lesions in systems in which information is represented and processed in massively parallel, distributed forms (McClelland & Rumelhart, 1986b; Seidenberg & McClelland, 1989). A third source of empirical support for holist theories comes from the finding of an effect of lesion size on the overall severity of functional impairments in several language spheres (Knopman et al., 1983, 1984; Selnes et al., 1983, 1984). This would follow from the principle of mass action (Lashley, 1929). These results therefore are consistent with some form of holism in the neural basis for linguistic representations and processes.

Against the complete adequacy of any holist model is the finding that multiple individual language deficits arise in patients with small perisylvian lesions, often in complementary functional spheres. For instance, studies of acquired dyslexia have documented patients who cannot read by a whole-word route [i.e., by using the entire form of a written word to gain access to the mental representation of that word (Shallice & McCarthy, 1985)] and others who cannot read by the application of spelling–sound correspondences at the letter and grapheme level (Beauvois & Désrouésne, 1979). In our studies of syntactic comprehension, we have documented patients who have trouble finding the referent of a reflexive form (e.g., *himself*) but perform normally on pronouns (e.g., *him*), and vice versa (Caplan & Hildenbrandt, 1988). The existence of these isolated complementary deficits in different single cases indicates that at least one abnormal performance cannot result from the relative complexity of processing required by one of these tasks. Double dissociations of this sort abound in the contemporary psycholinguistic aphasiological literature (Warrington & Shallice, 1984, 1988; see Shallice, 1988 for discussion). They indicate that the mode of organization of language in the brain must be one that allows focal lesions to disrupt specific aspects of psycholinguistic processing, not simply a mode of organization that produces complexity effects and degrades gracefully. Though some selective disruptions of function can occur when "lesions" are produced in simulated language processing systems that operate in parallel and distributed fashion (Wood, 1982; Gordon, 1982), to date no mechanism of lesioning a distributed neural system has been shown to produce the range of specific patterns of language breakdown observed in patients.[4]

---

[4] One hypothesis with much current appeal is that the entire perisylvian area is organized into multiple (possibly partially overlapping) neural nets, each responsible for a particular language process, each of which is organized as a parallel distributed processing system. In effect, this approach views each component (or subcomponent) of the language processing system as a stochastic process best modeled by a holist/distributed system but maintains the localizationist view that different areas of cortex are specialized for different components of the system.

B. Classical Localizationist Theories

Though many localizationist models exist, the "Connectionist" model of language representation and processing in the brain revived by Geschwind and his colleagues (1965) in the 1960s and 1970s probably remains the best known localizationist model of the functional neuroanatomy of language, at least in medical circles in North America.[5] This model is based on observations of aphasic patients and the interpretation of those observations that were first made over a century ago (Broca, 1861; Wernicke, 1874; Dejerine, 1892; Lichtheim, 1885).

Figure 3 represents the basic "Connectionist" model of auditory–oral language processing and its relation to areas within the dominant perisylvian cortex. This model postulates three basic "centers" for language processing, all in cerebral cortex. The first (A), located in Wernicke's area, stores the permanent representations for the sounds of words (what psycholinguists would now call a PHONOLOGICAL LEXICON). The second (M), located in Broca's area, houses the mechanisms responsible for planning and programming speech. The third (B), diffusely localized in cortex in the 19th century models, stores the representations of concepts. A major innovation proposed by Geschwind is in the location of one aspect of the concept center (Geschwind, 1970). Geschwind proposed that the inferior parietal lobule—the supra-marginal and angular gyri—are the location at which the fibers projecting from somesthetic, visual, and auditory association cortices all converge, and that as a consequence of this convergence, associations between word sounds and the sensory properties of objects can be established in this area. Geschwind argued that these associations are critical aspects of the meanings of words and that their establishment is a prerequisite of the ability to name objects.

Language processing in this model involves the activation of linguistic representations in these cortical centers and the transfer of these representations from one center to another, largely via white matter tracts. For instance, in auditory comprehension, the representations of the sound patterns of words are accessed in Wernicke's area following auditory presentation of language stimuli. These auditory representations of the sounds of words in turn evoke the concepts associated with words in the CONCEPT CENTER. Accessing the phonological representations of words and the subsequent concepts associated with these representations constitutes the function of comprehension of auditory language. In spoken language production, concepts access the phonological representations of words in Wernicke's area, which are then transmitted to the motor programming areas for speech in Broca's area. In most versions of this

---

[5] The term "Connectionist" is widely used to refer to the models of functional neuroanatomy for language championed by Geschwind, and related models. It derives from the nature of these models, which see language processing as being carried out in cortical centers "connected" by white matter tracts. The term "connectionist" is also used to refer to PDP models. In this case, the term is derived from the fact that activation in these models depends on the strength of connections between neuron-like entities. Since PDP models are generally regarded as examples of the holist approach to modeling language processing, these different uses of the term—which arose in scientific circles that were separate from each other—are potentially confusing. Many writers capitalize "Connectionist" when referring to the Geschwind-type models and use lower case when refering to PDP models as "connectionist." I follow this usage.

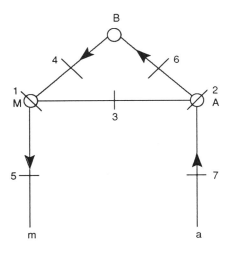

Fɪɢ. 3 The classical Connectionist model (after Lichtheim, 1885). *A* represents the auditory center for word processing. *M* represents the motor center for speech planning. *B* represents the concept center. Information flow is indicated by arrows. Numbers indicate the location of lesions said to produce the classic clinical aphasic syndromes.

model, the proper execution of the speech act also depends upon Broca's area receiving input directly from the concept center. Repetition, reading, and writing are modeled as involving similar sequences of activation of centers via connections.

The principal evidence in favor of this model is said to be the occurrence of specific syndromes of language disorders that can be accounted for by lesions of these centers and the connections between them, shown in Table III. The database supporting this model originated at the same time as the theory, in the late 19th century (Broca, 1861; Wernicke, 1874; Dejerine, 1892; Lichtheim, 1885). A lesion in Broca's area was associated with "Broca's aphasia," a severe expressive language disturbance without concomitant disturbances of auditory comprehension (Broca, 1861). A lesion of Wernicke's area was associated with the combination of fluent speech with erroneous choices of the sounds of words (phonemic paraphasias) and an auditory comprehension disturbance (Wernicke, 1874). A lesion of the input pathway to Wernicke's area was associated with pure word deafness, in which spontaneous speech is normal but comprehension and repetition are disturbed. A lesion in the outflow pathway from Broca's area was associated with pure anarthria or dysarthria, in which both repetition and spontaneous speech are misarticulated but comprehension is preserved. A lesion between the concept center and Broca's area was associated with "transcortical motor aphasia," in which spontaneous speech is reduced but repetition is intact. A lesion of the pathway between the concept center and Wernicke's area was associated with "transcortical sensory aphasia," a comprehension disturbance without a disturbance of repetition. Finally, a lesion of the pathway connecting Wernicke's and Broca's area was associated with a disturbance in spontaneous speech and repetition without a disturbance in auditory comprehension, termed "conduction aphasia." All these syndromes were claimed to have been discovered in relatively pure form by Lichtheim

TABLE III
The Classic Aphasic Syndromes

Sydrome	Clinical manifestations	Hypothetical deficit	Classical lesion location
A. Syndromes Attributed to Disturbances of Cortical Centers			
Broca's aphasia	Major disturbance in speech production with sparse, halting speech, often misarticulated, frequently missing function words and bound morphemes	Disturbances in the speech planning and production mechanisms	Primarily posterior aspects of the third frontal convolution and adjacent inferior aspects of the precentral gyrus
Wernicke's aphasia	Major disturbance in auditory comprehension; fluent speech with disturbances of the sounds and structures of words (phonemic, morphological, and semantic paraphasias)	Disturbances of the permanent representations of the sound structures of words	Posterior half of the first temporal gyrus and possibly adjacent cortex
Anomic aphasia	Disturbance in the production of single words, most marked for common nouns with variable comprehension problems	Disturbances of the concepts and/or the sound patterns of words	Inferior parietal lobe or connections between parietal lobe and temporal lobe
Global aphasia	Major disturbance in all language functions	Disruption of all language processing components	Large portion of the perisylvian association cortex
B. Syndromes Attributed to Disruptions of Connections between Centers			
Conduction aphasia	Disturbance of repetition and spontaneous speech (phonemic paraphasias)	Disconnection between the sound patterns of words and the speech production mechanism	Lesion in the arcuate fasciculus and/or corticocortical connections between temporal and frontal lobes
Transcortical aphasia	Disturbance of spontaneous speech similar to Broca's aphasia with relatively preserved repetition	Disconnection between conceptual representations of words and sentences and the motor speech production system	White matter tracts deep to Broca's area
Transcortical sensory aphasia	Disturbance in single word comprehension with relatively intact repetition	Disturbance in activation of word meanings despite normal recognition of auditorily presented words	White matter tracts connecting parietal lobe to temporal lobe or in portions of inferior parietal lobe
Isolation of the language zone	Disturbance of both spontaneous speech (similar to Broca's aphasia) and comprehension, with some preservation of repetition	Disconnection between concepts and both representations of word sounds and the speech production mechanism	Cortex just outside the perisylvian association cortex

(Lichtheim, 1885) and to have resulted from lesions in the appropriate cortical and subcortical areas of the brain. Recent studies using modern imaging technology have been said to support the Wernicke–Lichtheim–Geschwind theory by providing additional evidence of the correlation of these lesion sites with these aphasic syndromes (Basso et al., 1985; Damasio & Damasio, 1980; Kertesz, 1979; Kertesz et al., 1979, 1982; Naeser & Hayward, 1978; Naeser et al., 1979, 1981; Barat et al., 1978; Hayward et al., 1977; Mazzocchi & Vignolo, 1980; Noel et al., 1977; Yarnell et al., 1976; Benson & Patton, 1967).

Despite this accumulation of data, there are many inadequacies in the database that supports this theory of the functional neuroanatomy of language. On the neurological side, problems exist with several aspects of the published data. Lesion sites are often only reported for patient groups, not individual patients (Kertesz, 1979), precluding the investigation of variability in lesion sites across patients in these reports (see below). Lesions have often been described in very general terms (Basso, Lecours, Moraschini, & Vanier, 1985; Naeser & Hayward, 1978). The techniques used to localize lesions are often imprecise and have at times been inconsistently applied to imaging data (Kertesz et al., 1982). Ignoring these technical problems, the correlations between lesion sites and aphasic syndromes are far from perfect even in vascular cases, and they become less reliable in other neurological conditions (Kertesz, 1979). As early as 1908, François Moutier documented large numbers of stroke patients with lesions in Broca's area without Broca's aphasia and patients with the syndrome with lesions elsewhere (Moutier, 1908; Lecours & Joanette, 1984). Recent work has confirmed the failure of small Broca's area lesions to produce Broca's aphasia (Mohr et al., 1978), leading to various modifications of the simplest version of the Connectionist localizationist model (Levine & Sweet, 1982). The variability in lesions associated with Wernicke's aphasia has been strikingly documented in a recent review (Bogen & Bogen, 1976).

From the psycholinguistic point of view, the principal problem with this correlational evidence for the classical localizationist theory is its dependence on the interpretation of the clinical aphasic syndromes. These syndromes reflect the relative ability of patients to perform language tasks (speaking, comprehension, etc.), not the integrity of specific components of the language processing system. In all cases, these syndromes cross-classify patients with respect to their underlying functional deficits in language processing components and reflect disturbances of different language processing components in different patients (Schwartz, 1984). For instance, Broca's aphasia can represent any one of a number of language production impairments, ranging from a mild agrammatism to severe apraxia of speech. Most researchers now think of Wernicke's aphasia as a complex disorder in which the deficit affects either phonological or lexical semantic representations or both (Goodglass et al., 1966, 1970), and a variable number of other processing components (Lecour et al., 1983). There are at least two major deficits that underlie "conduction aphasia," one affecting word production and one affecting verbal short-term memory (Shallice & Warrington, 1977). Conversely, identical deficits occur in different syndromes (for instance, an anomia that reflects a disturbance of the ability to activate the phonological forms of words can occur in any aphasic syndrome). For these reasons, knowing that a particular aphasic syndrome tends to be associated with a lesion in a particular part of the perisylvian cortex does not tell us what components of the language processing system are located in that area of cortex and does not guarantee that these same components are not also damaged by lesions in different cortical areas (that are associated with different syndromes).

These problems with the interpretation of the classic aphasic syndromes are a reflection and a consequence of basic conceptual limitations of the Connectionist model of the functional neuroanatomy of language. It (and related models) are satisfied with a description of language processing that includes both components of the language processing system (e.g., a storehouse for the sound patterns of words that is activated in word recognition and word production) and entire language tasks (e.g., planning speech production). This mixture of components and tasks in the basic Connectionist model limits the detail and specificity of the model and leads to a polythetic classification of patients. To explore the neural organization of the components of the language processing system, we must begin with a justifiable componential model of the system such as that outlined in Section II and search for the neural correlates of the components so specified.

C. Localization of Specific Components of the Language Processing System: The Issue of Individual Variability

Lesion–deficit correlations have been studied in patients with more specific functional impairments than are captured by the classic aphasic syndromes [e.g., semantic memory (Warrington, 1987); whole-word writing and the conversion of sounds to their corresponding orthographic units (Roeltgen & Heilman, 1984); short-term memory (Shallice & Vallar, 1990); word comprehension (Coslett et al., 1987)]. These correlations have often not been consistent with the classical Connectionist model. For instance, semantic memory (word meaning) appears to be disrupted after temporal, not inferior parietal, damage (Warrington, 1987) and auditory–verbal short-term memory after parietal, not temporal, lesions (Shallice & Vallar, 1990).

An important aspect of the database relating specific language functional deficits to lesions is the finding that individual components of the language processing system can be either affected or spared following lesions in particular parts of the perisylvian association cortex. This variability in the effects of lesions at particular sites ranges across all areas of the perisylvian association cortex and is true of components of the language processing system responsible for activating any of the types of linguistic representations described in Section II (i.e., lexical, morphological, and sentential representations). At the lexical level, Blumstein et al. (1977a) reported no differences in phoneme discrimination in natural speech real word stimuli in 25 patients as a function of lesion site (anterior and posterior). Basso and her colleagues (1977) reported a similar result using synthetic speech stimuli in 50 aphasic patients with left hemisphere perisylvian lesions. Blumstein et al. (1977b) reported equal rates of disturbed and retained abilities to discriminate and identify synthetic stop consonants in 16 aphasic patients with either anterior or posterior lesions. A series of papers by Knopman and his associates documented considerable individual variability in localization of the lesions responsible for the comprehension of single words

(Knopman et al., 1983, 1984; Selnes et al., 1983, 1984). Similar disturbances in the production of morphological forms have been described in patients with agrammatism (with more anterior lesions) and paragrammatism [with more posterior lesions (Caplan, 1989)]. Knopman's work also documents variability in the lesion sites associated with aspects of sentence comprehension (Selnes et al., 1983). Caplan (1987b; Caplan et al., 1985) reported great variability in lesion sites in patients with different degrees and types of syntactic comprehension deficits. Our studies identifying computer tomography (CT) lesion sites in patients with a particular form of acquired dyslexia ["surface dyslexia" (Vanier & Caplan, 1985)] and agrammatism (Vanier & Caplan, 1990) have shown similar variability. In other work [e.g., the production of phonemic errors by conduction aphasics and Broca's aphasics in spontaneous speech (Blumstein, 1973), picture naming (Kohn, 1984), and repetition and reading (Nespoulous et al., 1984)], though the data are more subject to a variety of interpretations, extensive similarities in pathological performances have been reported in different clinical aphasic groups, suggesting similar deficits in groups of patients who, in aggregate, are known to have different central tendencies with respect to lesion sites within the perisylvian cortical area.

Our study of CT lesion sites in patients with a particular form of impaired sentence production, agrammatism, is illustrative of the basic pattern of localization of lesions in a disturbance of a relatively restricted type (Vanier & Caplan, 1990). We examined CT scan lesions in 20 agrammatic patients. Large lesions, affecting the entire territory supplied by the middle cerebral artery, were found in five cases. These lesions are not informative regarding the area of the left hemisphere responsible for the aspects of sentence production disrupted in agrammatism, but they indicate that other areas of the left hemisphere or the right hemisphere can take over the sentence production functions spared in this condition. Middle-sized lesions resulting from occlusion of several terminal branches of the middle cerebral artery (MCA) but not the entire territory of the MCA occurred in seven cases. Two of these lesions were similar to those described by Mohr et al. (1978) in cases of Broca's aphasia and were almost exclusively localized to the "upper bank" of the MCA. However, the five other middle-sized lesions affected variable amounts of temporal lobe as well as areas above the Sylvian fissure, and one of these cases showed complete sparing of Broca's area. Small lesions, resulting from occlusion of a single terminal branch of the middle cerebral artery, occured in several cortical and subcortical locations. Four small lesions were frontal. One, in a right hemisphere case (i.e., a crossed dextral aphasic), involved only pars triangularis of the third frontal convolution. One showed the opposite pattern in the frontal lobe, involving pars opercularis and the precentral opercular association cortex and sparing pars triangularis. Two small lesions in the frontal lobe involved both Broca's area and the precentral opercular cortex. Three small lesions were entirely subcortical, involving the insula, the arcuate fasciculus, and the corona radiata. Finally, one small lesion was entirely located in the inferior parietal and superior temporal region and spared the frontal lobe entirely. Overall, the lesions showed a tendency to involve frontal and insular cortex but considerable variability in size and location. On the assumption that agrammatism represents a deficit in a stage in language processing involving the construction of the syntactic form of a sentence (Caplan, 1986), these data suggest that this stage of sentence planning is accomplished by quite different areas of the association cortex in the perisylvian area in different individuals.[6]

The conclusion that the localization of specific language processing operations varies across the population also emerges from electrocortical stimulation studies. This procedure usually leads to interference with language functioning, and its use can been seen as inducing a geographically and temporally limited lesion. Ojemann (1983; Ojemann et al., 1989) has reported the largest number of studies of the effects of intra-operative stimulation on language functions. He has found that complete or partial interference following such stimulation occurs in tests of phoneme discrimination, picture naming, sentence comprehension, and other language functions. Each of these language tasks was most likely to be interrupted with stimulation in particular regions of the perisylvian cortex across the entire set of patients he studied, but considerable variation in sites associated with interruption of each task was also noted. For instance, phoneme discrimination was interrupted by stimulation throughout the entire central region of the perisylvian association cortex (itself a fairly large portion of the entire "language zone") in about 80% of cases, and in sites within the language zone that are a little further removed from the Sylvian fissure (such as the more dorsal regions of the inferior parietal lobule) in the remaining 20% of cases. Ojemann's own interpretation of his findings is that the perisylvian association cortex is organized into concentric zones along a radius extending out from the center of the Sylvian fissure, each of which is responsible for more abstract aspects of language processing (phonemic processing, syntactic processing, and verbal memory are said to be located in three consecutive zones). Close inspection of his data, however, shows nontrivial numbers of exceptions to this generalization for each of the tasks for which data are reported. To the extent that impaired performance on Ojemann's tasks can be taken to reflect disturbances in different components of the language processing system, these results provide support for the view that there are both central tendencies and considerable variability in the localization of these language processing components within the perisylvian cortex.

Recently, positron emission tomography (PET) scanning has been used to investigate the localization of language processing. The use of PET scanning to define lesions shows large, overlapping areas of hypometabolism in association with each of the clinical aphasic syndromes (Metter et al., 1984, 1986, 1989), making it difficult to identify the areas of abnormality responsible for each syndrome. PET has also been used to study the regions of cortex that are activated during the performance of a number of language tasks by normal

---

[6] Discerning a disturbance of a given language processing component is not simple. For instance, the assumption that agrammatism represents a deficit in a single language processing component has been questioned on the grounds that agrammatic patients vary with respect to the grammatical elements and syntactic structures they can produce (Badecker & Caramazza, 1985; Miceli et al., 1989). However, this variability can represent impairments of different operations within a single component of the sentence production system (Caplan, 1986, 1987a). At the least, the variability of lesion sites in agrammatic patients indicates that closely related sentence structure building operations can be disrupted following lesions in a variety of perisylvian locations. In general, disturbances such as agrammatism and the other impairments cited above are not simply attributable to disruptions of entire language tasks, but reflect deficits defined in terms of processing components that group together sets of related psycholinguistic operations at some level of the language processing hierarchy.

subjects (Peterson et al., 1988; Posner et al., 1988). Some of the published results have been somewhat unexpected. For instance, semantic functions appear to activate frontal cortex, and the dominant inferior parietal lobe has shown no activation in any language test in the published studies. These particular PET activation results are incompatible with the results of deficit–lesion correlations (and are not in keeping with the predictions of the classical Connectionist theory). Activation PET studies have also not shown the degree of individual variability in localization of language processing components suggested by deficit–lesion correlational studies. These contradictions between the results of PET activation studies and other approaches to language–brain relationships may be resolvable.[7] For the moment, though the potential of PET and other metabolic scanning methods to elucidate aspects of the functional neuroanatomy of language and other cognitive processes is evident, we must exercise caution in integrating these new results into models of functional neuroanatomy based on other approaches.

In summary, data available from several sources suggest that language processing components tend to be located in specific portions of the perisylvian association cortex, but that at least 20% of normal adults (and often many more) show significant deviations from these central localizationist tendencies, for each language processing component. This pattern is incompatible with models that postulate invariant localization of language processing components and with the holist principles of equipotentiality and mass action. The implications of this pattern for the determinants of the functional neuroanatomy for language and for clinical aphasiology will be discussed after I review the role of subcortical structures in language and the issue of hemispheric specialization and lateralization.

V. SUBCORTICAL STRUCTURES AND LANGUAGE

In considering the role of subcortical mechanisms in language functioning, we must distinguish between the functions of white matter tracts and subcortical gray matter nuclei in language. White matter tracts are not thought to accomplish computations; they transmit representations from one area to another. Subcortical gray matter structures may carry out language processing operations; several theories have been proposed that specify roles in language processing for these structures.

There are conflicting reports regarding the language disorders that follow white matter lesions. According to some reports, the aphasic syndromes that follow white matter lesions do not differ from those that occur with perisylvian cortical lesions, and the classical aphasic syndromes correlate with subcortical

---

[7] For instance, the absence of individual variability in these studies may reflect the lack of sufficiently large numbers of trials in single subjects in the experiments carried out so far. Similarly, unpublished studies do show activation of temporal and parietal lobes by lexical semantic processing (M. Raichle, D. Bub, personal communication). However, problems in interpretation of PET still exist. For instance, the reasons for the failure of temporal and parietal lobes to be activated by passive visual presentation of words in the original studies remain unclear and this failure points to as yet unresolved questions about the sensitivity of the PET technique and the interpretation of its findings.

lesion sites (Naeser et al., 1982; Alexander et al., 1987; Cappa et al., 1983). A study by Basso and her colleagues (1987), however, reports that the language disorders seen with subcortical CT lesions are not easily classified as any of the standard aphasic syndromes, that language disturbances of all sorts occur with lesions in all subcortical areas, and that total sparing of language functions can follow lesions in identical subcortical areas. The literature on language disorders in multiple sclerosis (M.S.) has stressed the relative sparing of language functions in this disease [for review, see Rao (1986), who expresses surprise over the paucity of aphasic symptoms and other disconnection syndromes in M.S. patients]. This may be because M.S. lesions do not affect white matter tracts in a manner needed to interrupt language processes.

The pattern of language impairments following white matter lesions has implications for theories of the functional neuroanatomy for language of the overlying perisylvian cortex. The pattern of deficits seen after white matter lesions speaks to the nature of the transfer of representations from one cortical area to another or to and from subcortical and other nuclei (Wernicke, 1874; Lichtheim, 1885; Geschwind, 1965; Dejerine & Klumpke, 1908). The number of such transfers will be proportional to the number of computationally sequential language processing stages that take place in nonadjacent areas of cortex connected by deep white matter fibers. Unfortunately, the conflicting results in the literature preclude any firm conclusions being drawn regarding the organization of cortex on the basis of language disturbances that follow lesions in white matter tracts. The fact that multiple language processing disturbances occur following subcortical strokes (Naeser et al., 1982; Alexander et al., 1987; Cappa et al., 1983; Basso et al., 1987) is consistent with the existence of many information transfers carried out by white matter fibers, suggesting that many of the areas of cortex and/or subcortical nuclei that carry out sequential language processing operations are not contiguous. If it is true that lesions in identical white matter areas may affect any or no linguistic functions (Basso et al., 1987), we must conclude that the representations transferred by particular tracts vary across individuals, consistent with the conclusion reached above that localization of language processing components varies across the population.

Uncertainties also exist regarding the consequences of lesions in the deep gray matter nuclei for language. Several studies report aphasic disturbances following strokes in these locations (Alexander et al., 1987; Damasio et al., 1982; Mohr et al., 1975), but studies of other diseases affecting the same nuclei fail to show significant language impairments. For instance, Damasio et al. (1982) report aphasias following caudate strokes, but language disorders are minimal in patients with Huntington's disease, even at a stage of the illness at which memory impairments are readily documented (Butters et al., 1978). The language disturbances seen after lesions in the central gray nuclei are of importance in determining the neural systems that underlie language. One interpretation of the published data is that subcortical gray matter structures play roles in core language processing (Damasio et al., 1982; Mohr et al., 1975; Crosson, 1985). If this is the case, the theory that core language functions depend entirely on neocortical structures must be revised (Damasio & Geschwind, 1984). Alternatively, it is possible that the aphasic symptoms seen after deep gray matter lesions reflect the effects of disturbances in other cognitive functions on language. For instance, the fluctuation between neologistic jargon and virtual mutism seen after some thalamic lesions corresponds to a more general fluctuation between states of delirium and near akinetic mutism (Mohr et al., 1975) and most likely reflects the effects of some thalamic lesions upon arousal, alerting, and motivational functions, some of which are seen in the sphere of language. Intra-operative stimulation studies of the interference with language functions following dominant thalamic stimulation also suggest that the language impairments seen in at least some thalamic cases are due to disturbances of attentional mechanisms (Ojemann, 1983).

Perhaps the most important consideration regarding language disorders following subcortical lesions is the question of whether they result from altered physiological activity in the overlying cortex, not disorders of the subcortical structures themselves. The availability of patients with focal strokes that are visible only subcortically on CT scans, in whom metabolic scanning is used to assess lesion site and size in both cortical and subcortical structures, provides an opportunity to investigate the role that both cortical and subcortical structures play in language. The most important fact in the literature to date is that, across all the published cases, there is a one-to-one correspondence between the presence or absence of cortical hypometabolism or hypoperfusion and the presence or absence of aphasic impairments in patients with focal strokes visible only subcortically on CT scans (Perani et al., 1987; Olsen et al., 1986). Moreover, studies correlating the degree of hypometabolism measured cortically and subcortically with the degree of language impairment indicate a much higher correlation of language impairments with the indices of cortical hypometabolism (Metter et al., 1983, 1987, 1988; Kempler et al., 1988). There is not a single published case in which an aphasia has been documented in a patient in whom metabolic scanning, blood flow studies, and physiological measures have all shown a normally functioning perisylvian association cortex. The conclusion that is suggested by this pattern is that subcortical structures play no essential role in core language processes themselves but serve only to activate the language processing system and to transfer the results of psycholinguistic computations from one part of the perisylvian association cortex to another. Language processing may be carried out only in perisylvian association cortex.

VI. LATERALIZATION OF LANGUAGE PROCESSES

Lateralization of language functions can be seen as a broad form of localization—the localization of a function in one of the two cerebral hemispheres. Lateralization for language processing varies as a function of handedness profiles. In about 98% of familial strong right-handers, the left perisylvian association cortex accomplishes most if not all language processing functions (Luria, 1970; Milner, 1974; Milner et al., 1964). In individuals with anomalous dominance handedness profiles (Geschwind & Galaburda, 1985, 1987; Annett, 1985), core language functions are far more likely to involve the corresponding regions of the right hemisphere (Luria, 1970; Russell & Esper, 1961; Goodglass & Quadfasel, 1954), with different likelihoods of right and left hemispheric involvement in language functions in different subgroups within this population (Subirana, 1964). The data on differential lateralization as a function of sex are controversial (McGlone, 1980).

A potentially important point is that many aphasic syndromes that follow either left or right hemisphere lesions in subjects with anomalous dominance are often mild. To the extent that they reflect disturbances of isolated components of the language processing system, their occurrence indicates that many individual language processing components can be located in either hemisphere. Whether these language processing components are located in a given hemisphere in isolation from others can only be resolved by studies that establish whether remaining intact language components are based in the intact portions of the lesioned hemisphere or in the undamaged hemisphere of patients with mild aphasias. In some cases (Kinsbourne, 1971), intracarotid amytal injections (Wada studies) indicate that the latter appears to be the case. This would suggest separate control of lateralization for individual language processing components, but very few data are available on this point.

These facts suggest intriguing similarities between the phenomena of localization and lateralization of language. In both the case of localization and lateralization, the location of a particular language processing component varies across the adult population as a whole. In both cases, however, there are central tendencies with respect to the location of particular language processing components—there appear to be preferred sites for particular language processing functions within the perisylvian region, and there is a strong preference for language processing components to be left-hemisphere based. In the case of lateralization, these central tendencies are profoundly affected (though never statistically reversed) by handedness profiles. There are no data regarding differences in intrahemispheric localization of language processing components as a function of handedness. The data regarding sex differences in intrahemispheric localization of language processing components as a function of sex are controversial (Kimura, 1983; Kertesz & Benke, 1986), as are those regarding sex differences in language lateralization (McGlone, 1980).

VII. DETERMINANTS OF TELENCEPHALIC ORGANIZATION FOR LANGUAGE: A SKETCH OF A GENERAL THEORY OF THE BIOLOGICAL BASIS FOR LANGUAGE

Stated in their most succinct form, the basic facts that I have presented regarding the neural substrate for language processes are that: (a) language processing is carried out only in the perisylvian association cortex; (b) language processing components may be localized in either hemisphere and in any part of the perisylvian cortex of the left hemisphere; (c) despite this variation, there are strong tendencies for most components of the language processing system to be located in the left hemisphere and for particular language processing components to be localized in particular areas of the left perisylvian cortex; and (d) a phenotypic characteristic associated with genetic load [handedness profiles (Annett, 1985)] serves to define subpopulations in whom the tendency for language processing components to be located in the left hemisphere differs.

These data suggest that the basic determinants of language lateralization and localization are genetic. The invariant role of the perisylvian association cortex in language must be due to elements and organization of that cortex that are required for normal language development and processing. These must be invariant across the species and cannot be so much affected by normally present, variable endogenous influences (such as sex hormone levels) that they can no longer support language in a significant group of humans. Such features are most likely directly determined by the genetic code (Rakic, 1988). The fact that lateralization of language processing varies as a function of a genetically determined phenotypic feature (handedness) strongly suggests that genetic variation plays an important role in determining the variability in the lateralization of components of the language processing system. The simplest model would postulate that, at the initial stage of language development, any area of either perisylvian association cortex is capable of supporting any subcomponent of the language processing system [a state termed LOCAL GENETIC EQUIPOTENTI-ALITY by Caplan (1988)] and that different areas of cortex assume particular language processing roles as a function of their intrinsic, genetically determined, developmental patterns. Since the human genome codes for basically similar patterns of brain development in all normal humans, there are central tendencies in localization and lateralization of language processing components. However, since the human genome also codes for variation in local neural development, the functional neuroanatomy for language differs to some extent across individuals. Some of this variation is systematically related to identifiable genetic load (e.g., that related to handedness), and some reflects individual genetic differences (as seen in crossed dextral aphasics and "exceptions" to localization tendencies in right-handers). This theory makes several predictions: that there would be more variability in the intrahemispheric localization of language processing subcomponents in the anomalous dominance population than in the right-handed population (if the genetic factors that affect the degree of variability of language lateralization apply in the same way to the intrahemispheric organization of language); that the functional neuroanatomy of language will be similar in identical twins; and others. Such findings would provide strong support for the model.

Influences other than directly genetically encoded patterns of cortical development are also likely to play some role in determining localization and lateralization for language. For instance, sex hormones (themselves a result of the expression of genetically determined development of sexual organs) may play some role in determining language lateralization and even localization. The development of certain language skills, such as the acquisition of a second language or the mastery of a writing system, could also affect cortical organization for language (see Weisel, 1982, for an example of the effects on cerebral organization of environmental factors). In general, however, these factors appear to play secondary roles in determining GROSS cerebral organization for language (as is also true of other systems, such as vision). I indicated above that the evidence supporting the existence of sex differences in localization and lateralization of language functions is unconvincing. The data suggesting that the cerebral structures responsible for auditory–oral use of first languages are affected by factors such as the acquisition of a second language or the mastery of a writing system are also weak and controversial (Paradis, 1977; Obler, 1984).

The genetic model just outlined overlaps in some respects with models of the functional neuroanatomy of language and its determinants suggested by other researchers. It incorporates Geschwind and Galaburda's (1985, 1987) suggestions that differences in patterns of local cortical development determine the allocation of language processing components to different regions of the brain, and that the documented interhemispheric variability in the size of different areas of the perisylvian association cortex across individuals is related to the variability of lateralization of components of the language processing system. The model presented here extends these concepts to the intrahemispheric organization of language. It recognizes individual variability in the intrahemispheric localization of components of the language processing system and suggests that it is due to individual differences in cortical development within the perisylvian region. The model presented here differs from Geschwind and Galaburda's theory in the emphasis it places on the importance of direct genetic control of cortical development in determining the functional neuroanatomy of the language, as opposed to indirect genetic effects mediated by sex hormones [for comments on this aspect of Geschwind and Galaburda's theory, see Caplan (1987c)].[8]

The theory presented here contrasts sharply with the classical Connectionist theory and many other localizationist models that maintain that language functions are located in particular areas of perisylvian cortex because of the relationship of these areas to cortical structures supporting aspects of sensory and motor functions (Geschwind, 1965, 1970, 1979; Luria, 1970; Broca, 1861; Wernicke, 1874; Dejerine, 1892; see Caplan, 1987a for discussion).[9] The present theory holds that language processing components are primarily under direct genetic control with respect to their localization. At one level, the two accounts simply differ with respect to what they take to be the primary pattern of neural organization for language that needs to be explained. The present theory maintains that individual variation in the localization of language processing components is an important feature of the functional neuroanatomy of language, and that it cannot be explained by any model that considers the relationship of language-devoted cortex to sensory- and motor-devoted cortex to be the primary determinant of localization of a component of the language processing system. However, the differences between the two theories go deeper than this disagreement over the extent and significance of variability in localization of language processing components. They also reflect substantially different views of the nature of language and language processing.

The concept of language that we are attempting to relate to the brain has been developed in modern linguistics, psycholinguistics, and cognitive science. It views language processing as largely consisting of the activation of abstract linguistic codes and of computational processes applying to the representations specified in these codes. This view of language is naturally allied to the notion that the ability of an area of cortex to represent certain linguistic forms or to support particular types of computations is due to its intrinsic structural and physiological properties, which are largely genetically determined. This is true

---

[8] Lenneberg's (1967) pioneering work emphasized the genetic basis for language functions and discussed many of the topics presented here in a slightly different framework.

[9] These theories differ in how they relate language cortex to other brain structures. Geschwind (1965) emphasizes the connectivity of auditory association cortex to visual and somesthetic association cortex. Luria (1970) emphasizes the continuity of language-devoted cortex with cortex devoted to high-level motor control (in frontal lobe) and spatial and temporal discrimination (in parietal and temporal lobes). These different specific models all have in common the effort to relate language localization to the localization of some aspects of motor and/or sensory processes.

whether or not the localization of language processing components varies across individuals. The traditional theory does not view language in these formal computational terms. Rather, it is heavily influenced by models that tend to see language processing as emerging from sensory–motor function. Determination of localization of language functions on the basis of juxtaposition of language processing components to sensory and motor areas of the brain is naturally allied to the traditional model.

These different conceptual approaches to language have often given rise to vigorous debate in the neurolinguistic literature (Kimura, 1976; Zurif, 1982). Many considerations speak in favor of the view of language that arises in contemporary cognitive science and therefore support the genetic model over traditional accounts. Key postulates of traditional models—the idea that language processing is an elaboration of motor and sensory functions, that language acquisition is based on simple stimulus–response learning, that word meanings primarily reflect cross-modal associations, and so on—are now discredited (Chomsky, 1985; Fodor, 1985). The rationale for postulating that language localization is determined by the relationship of language-devoted cortex to motor- and sensory-devoted cortex is rendered less powerful by the observation that, in other systems (e.g., the motor system), widely scattered gray matter structures are effectively coordinated to produce integrated functional activity. The inability of traditional models to explain individual variation in the localization of components of the language processing system is just one basis for preferring a neurolinguistic model that is more closely linked to an information processing view of language.

If the genetic model is correct for the determinants of the functional neuroanatomy of language, it is of interest to ask whether it might pertain to other cognitive functional spheres. I have argued that variability of localization of a function within a limited cerebral area that is uninfluenced by endogenous factors (such as sex hormones) and that varies with genetic load (as evidenced by, e.g., handedness profile) is evidence for a major role for direct genetic influences on the gross functional neuroanatomy of that function. There are data that suggest that at least some central computational aspects of other cognitive functions show variability in their localization (Riddoch & Humphreys, 1986), though not enough data are available to know whether the entire picture resembles that which I have presented for language. One speculation is that variable localization, with central tendencies for localization and lateralization of specific components of cognitive functions, is the mode of organization of cortex with respect to any function that has no topographic mapping; that is, for the abstract computational components of all human cognitive functions. Invariant localization may only characterize the topographic mapping of cortical areas onto the body itself and the external world, as Henry Head suggested over 60 years ago (Head, 1926).

VIII. CLINICAL IMPLICATIONS

To characterize a language disorder, a clinician must attempt to identify the major language processing components that are intact and disrupted in a patient (the ability to activate the form and meaning of words, derived words, and sentences, and to produce these linguistic structures, in both the auditory–oral and written modalities). Simply classifying patients into the traditional aphasic syndromes does not achieve this goal, because the classical clinical aphasic syndromes are all heterogeneous with respect to the disturbances of language processes they specify. The psycholinguistic approach to characterizing language impairments recognizes multiple language processing deficits in most aphasic patients. It is important for medical and other health care professionals to identify these deficits because they are the targets of increasingly successful, focused therapeutic efforts (Byng, 1988). The neurolinguistic theory presented here, which denies any invariant relation between psycholinguistic processes and areas of cortex, implies that knowing the neuroanatomical location of a patient's lesions will provide only limited help in the effort to characterize his deficits in language processing components. If there is considerable variability in localization of language processing components, lesions in particular parts of the language zone will be associated with many different groupings of disturbed and intact language processing components.

The theory presented here has implications regarding the nature of the classic aphasic syndromes. Despite the variability in localization of language processing subcomponents, there are central tendencies for particular language processing components to be localized in particular areas of perisylvian cortex. Therefore, there will be patterns of co-occurrence of impaired and spared language processing components following lesions in particular areas of the language zone that are relatively common. At least some of the classical aphasic syndromes might correspond to these patterns. However, another possibility is that the classic aphasic syndromes reflect nothing more than co-occurrence of different language processing impairments with disruptions of motor speech production. It may be that a patient with a motor disorder affecting speech is a global aphasic if he has many language processing deficits, or a Broca's aphasic or a patient with apraxia of speech or transcortical motor aphasia if he has relatively few language processing impairments. A patient without a motor disorder affecting speech may be a Wernicke's aphasic if he has many language processing deficits, and may fall under one or another minor category of fluent aphasia (such as anomia, conduction aphasia, transcortical sensory aphasia) if he has relatively few language processing impairments. The clinical syndromes may reflect the co-occurrence of language processing deficits with disturbances of motor output processes, not commonly occurring constellations of language processing deficits. The relationship of the classic syndromes to neural areas may be due to the relatively constant localization of lesions producing motor speech disturbances (Alexander, 1987; Naeser et al., 1989).

IX. CONCLUSIONS

I have presented a model of the functional neuroanatomy of language and its determinants that differs in several key respects from many models that are widely accepted today. The model I have developed is a direct response to data regarding language, language disorders, and neural correlates of language and language disorders that have accumulated in the past decade. Our newly acquired abilities to identify specific language processing deficits in patients, to characterize lesions with modern imaging techniques, and to use technologies such as intra-operative electrocortical stimulation, event-related potentials, and metabolic scanning to study the neural basis for language position us to investigate the neural basis for language at a level of detail previously unattainable. Research using these techniques is likely to continue to change our ideas of the way the human brain supports language functions.

ACKNOWLEDGMENTS

This work was supported by a grant from the National Institute for Neurological Disease and Stroke (NS29101-01A1). I wish to thank Dan Bub, Verne Caviness, Harold Goodglass, Nancy Hildebrandt, Andrew Kertesz, Steven Kosslyn, and Edgar Zurif for stimulating discussions of the ideas presented here.

REFERENCES

Alexander, M. P., Naeser, M. B., & Palumbo, C. L. (1987). Correlations of subcortical CT lesion sites in aphasia profiles. *Brain, 110*, 961–991.

Annett, M. (1985). *Left, right, hand and brain: The right shift theory*. London: Erlbaum.

Badecker, W., & Caramazza, A. (1985). On considerations of method and theory governing the use of clinical categories in neurolinguistics and neuropsychology: The case against agrammatism. *Cognition, 20*, 97–125.

Barat, M., Constant, P. H., Mazaux, J. M., Caille, J. M., & Arne, L. (1978). Correlations anatomo-cliniques dans l'aphasie. Apport de la tomodensitometrie. *Rev. Neurol. 134*, 611–617.

Basso, A., Casati, G., & Vignolo, L. A. (1977). Phonemic identification defect in aphasia. *Cortex, 13*, 85–95.

Basso, A., Della Sala, S., & Farabola, M. (1987). Aphasia arising from purely deep lesions. *Cortex, 23*, 29–44.

Basso, A., Lecours, A. R., Moraschini, S., & Vanier, M. (1985). Anatomoclinical correlations of the aphasias as defined through computerized tomography: Exceptions. *Brain and Language, 26*, 201–229.

Beauvois, M. F., & Désrouésne, J. (1979). Phonological alexia: Three dissociations. *J. Neurol. Neurosurg. Psychiatry, 42*, 1115–1124.

Benson, D. F. (1979). *Aphasia, alexia, and agraphia*. New York: Churchill Livingstone.

Benson, D. F., & Patten, D. H. (1967). The use of radioactive isotopes in the localization of aphasia-producing lesions. *Cortex, 3*, 258–271.

Blumstein, S. (1973). *A phonological investigation of aphasic speech*. The Hague: Mouton.

Blumstein, S., Baker, W. E., & Goodglass, H. (1977a). Phonological factors in auditory comprehension in aphasia. *Neuropsychologia, 15*, 19–30.

Blumstein, S., Cooper, W. E., Zurif, E. B., & Caramazza, A. (1977b). The perception and production of voice-onset time in aphasia. *Neuropsychologia, 15*, 371–383.

Bogen, J. E., & Bogen, G. M. (1976). Wernicke's region: Where is it? *Ann. N. Y. Acad. Science 280*, 834–843.

Broca, P. (1861). Rémarques sur le siège de la faculté de la parole articulée, suives d'une observation d'aphémie (perte de parole). *Bulletin de la Societé d'Anatomie, 36*, 330–357.

Brown, J. (1972). *Aphasia, apraxia, and agnosia—Clinical and theoretical aspects*. Springfield, IL: Thomas.

Bub, D., Cancelliere, A., & Kertesz, A. (1985). Whole word and analytic translation of spelling to sound in a non-semantic reader. In K. Patterson, M. Coltheart, & Marshall, J. C. (Eds.), *Surface dyslexia* (pp. 15–34). London: Lea & Febiger.

Butters, N., Sax, D., Montgomery, K., & Tarlow, S. (1978). Comparison of the neuropsychological deficits associated with early and advanced Huntington's disease. *Arch. Neurol. 35*, 585–589.

Byng, S. (1988). Sentence comprehension deficit: Theoretical analysis and remediation. *Cognitive Neuropsychology, 5*, 629–676.

Caplan, D. (1982). Reconciling the categories: Representation in neurology and in linguistics. In M. Arbib, D. Caplan, & J. C. Marshall (Eds.), *Neural models of language processes* (pp. 411–427). New York: Academic Press.

Caplan, D. (1986). In defense of agrammatism. *Cognition, 24,* 263–276.

Caplan, D. (1987a). *Neurolinguistics and linguistic aphasiology.* Cambridge, UK: Cambridge University Press.

Caplan, D. (1987b). Discrimination of normal and aphasic subjects on a test of syntactic comprehension. *Neuropsychologia, 25,* 173–184.

Caplan, D. (1987c). Review of N. Geschwind & A. M. Galaburda, Cerebral lateralization: Biological mechanisms, associations, and pathology. *Nature (London), 328,* 484–485.

Caplan, D. (1988). The biological basis for language. In F. Newmeyer (Ed.), *Linguistics: The Cambridge survey, vol. 3, Language: Psychological and biological aspects* (pp. 237–255). Cambridge, U.K: Cambridge University Press.

Caplan, D., Baker, C., & Dehaut, F. (1985). Syntactic determinants of sentence comprehension in aphasia. *Cognition, 21,* 117–175.

Caplan, D., & Hildebrandt, N. (1988). *Disorders of syntactic comprehension.* Cambridge, MA: MIT Press.

Cappa, S. F., Cavalotti, G., Guidotti, N., Papagno, C., & Vignolo, L. A. (1983). Subcortical aphasia: Two clinical-CT scan correlation studies. *Cortex, 19,* 227–241.

Chomsky, N. (1985). *Knowledge of language.* New York: Praeger.

Coslett, H. B., Roeltgen, D. P., Rothi, L. G., & Heilman, K. M. (1987). Transcortical sensory aphasia: Evidence for subtypes. *Brain and Language, 32,* 362–378.

Crosson, B. (1985). Subcortical functions in language: A working model. *Brain and Language, 25,* 257–292.

Damasio, A., Damasio, H., Rizzo, M., Varney, N., & Gersch, F. (1982). Aphasia with nonhemorrhagic lesions in the basal ganglia and internal capsule. *Arch. Neurol. 39,* 15–20.

Damasio, A., & Geschwind N. (1984). The neural basis of language. *Annual Review of Neurosciences, 7,* 127–147.

Damasio, H., & Damasio, A. R. (1980). The anatomical basis of conduction aphasia. *Brain, 103,* 337–350.

Dejerine, J. J. (1892) Contribution à l'étude anatomo-pathologique et clinique des différentes variétés de cécité verbale. *Mémoire Societé Biologique, 4,* 61–90.

Dejerine, J. J., & Klumpke, A. (1908). Discussion sur l'Aphasie, *Rev. Neurol., 16,* 611–636.

Fodor, F. A. (1985). *Representations.* Cambridge, MA: MIT Press.

Fodor, J. A. (1983). *The modularity of mind.* Cambridge, MA: MIT Press.

Freud, S. (1891). *On aphasia.* Leipzig: Deuticke.

Furth, H. (1966). *Thinking without language: Psychological implications of deafness.* New York: Free Press.

Geschwind, N. (1965). Disconnection syndromes in animals and man. *Brain, 88,* 237–294; 585–644.

Geschwind, N. (1970). The organization of language and the brain. *Science, 170,* 940–944.

Geschwind, N. (1979). Language and the brain. *Scientific American, 241,* 180–199.

Geschwind, N., & Galaburda, A. M. (1985). Cerebral lateralization: Biological mechanism, associations and pathology i–iii: A hypothesis and a program for research. *Arch. Neurol. 42,* 428–459, 421–452, 634–654.

Geschwind, N., & Galaburda, A. M. (1987). *Cerebral lateralization: Biological mechanisms, associations, and pathology.* Cambridge, MA: MIT Press.

Goodglass, H., Gleason, J. B., & Hyde, M. R. (1970). Some dimensions of auditory language comprehension in aphasia. *J. Speech Hear. Research, 14,* 595–606.

Goodglass, H., & Kaplan, E. (1982). *The assessment of aphasia and related disorders, 2nd edition.* Philadelphia: Lea & Febiger.

Goodglass, H., Klein, B., Carey, P., & Jones, K. (1966). Specific semantic word categories in aphasia. *Cortex, 2,* 74–89.

Goodglass, H., & Quadfasel, F. A. (1954). Language laterality in left-handed aphasics. *Brain, 77,* 521–548.

Gordon, B. (1982). Confrontation naming: Computational model and disconnection simulation. In M. A. Arbib, D. Caplan, & J. C. Marshall (Eds.), *Neural models of language processes,* (pp. 511–529). New York: Academic Press.

Halle, M., & Vergnaud, J.-R. (1980). Three dimensional phonology. *Journal of Linguistic Research, 1,* 83–105.

Hayward, R., Naeser, M. A., & Zatz, L. M. (1977). Cranial computer tomography in aphasia. *Radiology, 123,* 653–660.

Head, H. (1926). *Aphasia and kindred disorders of speech.* Cambridge, UK: Cambridge University Press.

Henderson, L. (1982). *Orthography and word recognition in reading.* London: Academic Press.

Henschen, S. E. (1920). *Klinische und anatomische beitrage zür pathologie des gehirns.* Stockholm: Nordische Bokhandler.

Jackendoff, R. (1983). *Semantics and cognition.* Cambridge, MA: MIT Press.

Jackson, J. H. (1878). On affections of speech from disease of the brain. *Brain, 1,* 304–330; *2,* 203–222, & 323–356.

Kempler, D., Metter, E. J., Jackson, C. A., Hanson, W. R., Riege, W. R., Mazziotta, J., & Phelps, M. E. (1988). Disconnection and cerebral metabolism: The case of conduction aphasia. *Arch. Neurol. 45,* 275–279.

Kertesz, A. (1979). *Aphasia and associate disorders.* New York: Grune and Stratton.

Kertesz, A., & Benke, T. (1986). *The sexual mystique of intrahemispheric language organization.* Nashville: Academy of Aphasia.

Kertesz, A., Harlock, W., & Coates, R. (1979). Computer tomographic localization, lesion size, and prognosis in aphasia and nonverbal impairment. *Brain and Language, 8,* 34–50.

Kertesz, A., Sheppard, A., & MacKenzie, R. (1982). Localization in transcortical sensory aphasia. *Arch. Neurol. 39,* 475–478.

Kimura, D. (1976). The neural basis of language qua gesture. In H. Whitaker & H. A. Whitaker (Eds.), *Studies in neurolinguistics, Vol. 2.* New York: Academic Press.

Kimura, D. (1983). Sex differences in the functional cerebral organization for speech and praxic functions. *Canadian Journal of Psychology, 37,* 19–35.

Kinsbourne, M. (1971). The minor cerebral hemisphere as a source of aphasic speech. *Arch. Neurol. 25,* 302–306.

Knopman, D. S., Selnes, O. A., Niccum, N., & Rubens, A. B. (1984). Recovery of naming in aphasia: Relationship to fluency comprehension and CT findings. *Neurology 34,* 1461–1470.

Knopman, D. S., Selnes, O. A., Niccum, N., Rubens, A. B., Yock, D., & Larson, D. (1983). A longitudinal study of speech fluency in aphasia: CT correlates of recovery and persistent nonfluency. *Neurology, 33,* 1170–1178.

Kohn, S. E. (1984). The nature of the phonological disorder in conduction aphasia. *Brain and Language, 23,* 97–115.

Lashley, K. S. (1929). *Brain mechanisms and intelligence.* Chicago, IL: University of Chicago Press.

Lashley, K. S. (1950). In search of the engram. *Symp. Soc. Exp. Biol. 4,* 454–482.

Lecours, A.-R., & Joanette, Y. (1984). Francois Moutier. Or "From folds to folds," *Brain Cognition, 3,* 198–230.

Lecours, A. R., Lhermitte, F., & Bryans, B. (1983). *Aphasiology.* London: Ballière Tindall.

Lenneberg, E. H. (1967). *Biological foundations of language.* New York: Wiley.

Levelt, W. J. M. (1989). *Speaking: From intention to articulation.* Cambridge, MA: MIT Press.

Levine, D. N., & Sweet, E. (1982). The neuropathological basis of Broca's aphasia and its implications for the cerebral control of speech. In M. A. Arbib, D. Caplan, & J. C. Marshall (Eds.), *Neural models of language processes* (pp. 29–326). New York: Academic Press.

Lichtheim, L. (1885). On aphasia. *Brain, 7,* 433–484.

Lieberman, P. (1984). *The biology and evolution of language.* Cambridge, MA: Harvard University Press.

Luria, A. R. (1970). *Traumatic aphasia.* The Hague: Mouton.

Luria, A. R. (1973). *The working brain.* New York: Basic Books.

Marie, P. (1906). Révision de la question de l'aphasie: La troisième circonvolution frontale gauche ne joue aucun rôle spécial dans la fonction du langage. *Semaine Médicale, 26,* 241–247.

Marr, D. (1982). *Vision.* San Francisco: W. H. Freeman.

Marslen-Wilson, W. (1973). Linguistic structure and speech shadowing at very short latencies. *Nature (London), 244,* 522–523.

Masdeu, J. C., Schoene, W. C., & Funkenstein, H. (1978). Aphasia following infarction of the left supplementary motor area: A clinicopathological study. *Neurology, 28,* 1220–1223.

Mazzocchi, F., & Vignolo, L. A. (1980). Localization of lesions in aphasia: Clinical-CT scan correlations in stroke patients. *Cortex, 15,* 627–654.

McClelland, J. L., & Rumelhart D. E. (Eds.). (1986a). *Parallel distributed processing*. Cambridge, MA: MIT Press.

McClelland, J. L., & Rumelhart, D. E. (1986b). Amnesia and distributed memory. In J. L. McClelland & D. E. Rumelhart (Eds.), *Parallel distributed processing* (pp. 503–528). Cambridge, MA: MIT Press.

McGlone, J. (1980). Sex differences in human brain asymmetry: A critical survey. *Behavioral and Brain Sciences, 3,* 215–263.

Metter, E. J., Kempler, D., Jackson, C. A., et al. (1987). Cerebellar glucose metabolism and chronic aphasia. *Neurology, 37,* 1599–1606.

Metter, E. J., Kempler, D., Jackson, C. A., Hanson, W. R., Mazziotta, J. C., & Phelps, M. E. (1986). Cerebral glucose metabolism: Differences in Wernicke's, Broca's, and conduction aphasia. *Clinical Aphasiology, 16,* 97–104.

Metter, E. J., Kempler, D., Jackson, C. A., Hanson, W. R., Mazziotta, J. C., & Phelps, M. E. (1989). Cerebral glucose metabolism in Wernicke's, Broca's, and conduction aphasia. *Arch. Neurol, 46,* 27–34.

Metter, E. J., Riege, W. H., Hanson, W. R., et al. (1983). Comparison of metabolic rates, language and memory, and subcortical aphasias. *Brain and Language, 19,* 33–47.

Metter, E. J., Riege, W. H., Hanson, W. R., Camras, L. R., Phelps, M. E., & Kuhl, D. E. (1984). Correlations of glucose metabolism and structural damage to language function in aphasia. *Brain and Language, 21,* 187–207.

Metter, E. J., Riege, W. H., Hanson, W. R., Jackson, C. A., Kempler, D., & VanLancker, D. (1988). Subcortical structures in aphasia: An analysis based on (F-18)-fluorodoxyglucose positron emission tomography, and computed tomography. *Arch. Neurol. 45,* 1229–1234.

Miceli, G., Silveri, M. C., Romain, C., & Caramazza, A. (1989). Variation in the pattern of omissions and substitutions of grammatical morphemes in the spontaneous speech of so-called agrammatic patients. *Brain and Language, 36,* 447–492.

Milner, B. (1974). Hemispheric specialization: Its scope and limits. In F. O. Schmidt & F. G. Warden (Eds.), *The neurosciences: Third study program* (pp. 75–89). Cambridge, MA: MIT Press.

Milner, B., Branch, C., & Rasmussen, T. (1964). Observations on cerebral dominance. In A. de Reuck & M. O'Conner (Eds.), *Disorders of language* (pp. 200–214). London: Churchill.

Mohr, J. P., Pessin, M. S., Finkelstein, S., Funkenstein, H. H., Duncan, G. W., & Davis, K. R. (1978). Broca aphasia: Pathologic and clinical. *Neurology, 28,* 311–324.

Mohr, J. P., Watters, W. C., Duncan, G. W. (1975). Thalamic hemorrhage and aphasia. *Brain and Language, 2,* 3–17.

Moutier, F. (1908). *L'Aphasie de broca*. Paris: Steinheil.

Naeser, M. A., Alexander, M. P., Helm-Estabrooks, N., Levine, H. L., Laughlin, S., & Geschwind, N. (1982). Aphasia with predominantly subcortical lesion sites: Description of three capsular/putaminal aphasia syndromes. *Arch. Neurol, 39,* 2–14.

Naeser, M. A., & Hayward, R. W. (1978). Lesion localization in aphasia with cranial computed tomography and the Boston diagnostic aphasia examination. *Neurology, 28,* 545–551.

Naeser, M. A., Hayward, R. W., Laughlin, S., & Zatz, L. M. (1979). Quantitative CT scans studies in aphasia. I. Infarct size and CT numbers. *Brain and Language, 12,* 140–164.

Naeser, M. A., Hayward, R. W., Laughlin, S., Decker, J. M. T., Jernigan, T., & Zatz, L. M. (1981). Quantitative CT scan studies in aphasia. II. Comparison of the right and left hemispheres. *Brain and Language, 12,* 165–189.

Naeser, M. A., Palumbo, C. L., Helm-Estabrooks, N., Stiassny-Eder, D., & Albert, M. L. (1989). Severe non-fluency in aphasia: Role of the medial subcallosal fasciculus and other white matter pathways in recovery of spontaneous speech. *Brain, 112,* 1–38.

Neilson, J. M. (1936). *Agnosia, apraxia, aphasia*. New York: Holber.

Nespoulous, J. L., Joanette, Y., Ska, B., Caplan, D., & Lecours, A. R. (1984). Phonological disturbances in aphasia: Is there a "markedness" effect in aphasic phonemic errors? In F. C. Rose (Ed.), *Progress and aphasiology, Vol. 42*. New York: Raven Press.

Noel, G., Collard, M., Dupont, H., & Huvelle, R. (1977). Nouvelles possibilités de correlations anatomo-cliniques en aphasiologie grace à la tomodensitometrie cerebrale. *Acta Neurologica Belgica, 77,* 351–362.

Obler, L. (1984). The neuropsychology of bilingualism. In D. Caplan, A. R. Lecours, & A. Smith, (Eds.), *Biological perspectives on language*. Cambridge, MA: MIT Press.

Ojemann, G. (1983). Brain organization for language from the perspective of electrical stimulation mapping. *Behavioural and Brain Sciences, 6,* 189–230.

Ojemann, G., Ojemann, J., Lettich, E., & Berger, M. (1989). Cortical language localization in left, dominant hemisphere. *Journal of Neurosurgery, 71,* 316–326.

Olsen, T. S., Bruhn, P., & Oberg, R. G. E. (1986). Cortical hypertension as a possible cause of subcortical aphasia. *Brain, 109,* 393–410.

Paradis, M. (1977). Bilingualism and aphasia. In H. Whitaker & H. A. Whitaker (Eds.), *Studies in Neurolinguistics, Vol. 3* (pp. 65–122). New York: Academic Press.

Perani, D., Vallar, G., Cappa, S., Messa, C., & Fazio, F. (1987). Aphasia and neglect after subcortical stroke. A clinical/cerebral study. *Brain, 110,* 1211–1229.

Peterson, S. E., Fox, P. T., Posner, M. I., Mintun, M., & Raichle, M. E. (1988). Positron emission tomographic studies of the cortical anatomy of single-word processing. *Nature (London), 331,* 585–589.

Pick, A. (1973). *Aphasia.* Translated and edited by J. Brown. Springfield, IL: Thomas.

Poizner, H., Klima, E. S., & Bellugi, U. (1989). *What the hands reveal about the brain.* Cambridge, MA: MIT Press.

Posner, M. I., Peterson, S. E., Fox, P. T., & Raichle, M. E. (1988). Localization of cognitive operations in the human brain. *Science, 240,* 1627–1632.

Pylyshyn, Z. (1984). *Computation and cognition: Toward a foundation for cognitive science.* Cambridge, MA: MIT Press.

Rakic, P. (1988). Specification of cerebral cortical areas. *Science, 241,* 170–176.

Rao, S. M. (1986). Neuropsychology of multiple sclerosis: A critical review. *J. Clin. Exp. Neuropsych. 8,* 503–542.

Riddoch, J., & Humphreys, G. W. (1986). Neurological impairments of object constancy: The effects of orientation and size disparities. *Cognitive Neuropsychology, 3,* 207–244.

Roeltgen, D., & Heilman, K. M. (1984). Lexical Agraphia: Further support for the two system hypothesis of linguistic agraphia. *Brain, 107,* 811–827.

Rosch, E. (1975). Cognitive representations of semantic categories. *Journal of Experimental Psychology: General, 104,* 192–233.

Russell, W. R., & Esper, M. L. E. (1961). *Traumatic aphasia.* London: Oxford University Press.

Schuell, H. (1957). *Minnesota test for the differential diagnosis of aphasia.* Minneapolis: University of Minnesota Press.

Schwartz, M. (1984). What the classical aphasia categories can't do for us, and why. *Brain Language 21,* 1–8.

Seidenberg, M., & McClelland, J. (1989). A distributed, developmental model of word recognition and naming. *Psychology Review, 96,* 523–568.

Selkirk, E. (1982). *The syntax of words.* Cambridge, MA: MIT Press.

Selnes, O. A., Knopman, D., Niccum, N., Rubens, A. B., & Larson, D. (1983). CT scan correlates of auditory comprehension deficits in aphasia: A prospective recovery study. *Neurology, 13,* 558–566.

Selnes, O. A., Niccum, N., Knopman, D., & Rubens, A. B. (1984). Recovery of single word comprehension: CT scan correlates. *Brain and Language, 21,* 72–84.

Shallice, T. (1988). *From neuropsychology to mental structure.* Cambridge, UK: Cambridge University Press.

Shallice, T., & McCarthy, R. (1985). Phonological reading: From patterns of impairment to possible procedures. In K. Patterson, M. Coltheart, & J. C. Marshall (Eds.), *Surface dyslexia* (pp. 335–360). London: Lea & Febiger.

Shallice, T., & Vallar, G. (1990). The short term memory syndrome. In T. Shalice & G. Vallar (Eds.), *Neuropsychological studies of short term memory.* Cambridge, UK: Cambridge University Press.

Shallice, T. & Warrington, E. (1977). Auditory-verbal short-term memory and conduction aphasia. *Brain and Language, 4,* 479–491.

Shiffrin, R. M., & Schneider, W. (1977). Controlled and automatic human information processing: II. Perceptual learning, automatic attending, and a general theory. *Psychology Review, 84,* 127–190.

Slobin, D. (Ed). (1985). *The crosslinguistic study of language acquisition.* Hillsdale, NJ: Erlbaum.

Subirana, A. (1964). The relationship between handedness and language function. *International Journal of Neurology, 4,* 215–234.

Vanier, M., & Caplan, D. (1985). CT scan correlates of surface dyslexia. In K. Patterson, M. Coltheart, & J. C. Marshall (Eds.), *Surface dyslexia* (pp. 509–522). London: Erlbaum.

Vanier, M., & Caplan, D. (1990). CT-scan correlates of agrammatism. In L. Menn & L. Obler (Eds.), *Agrammatic aphasia* (pp. 37–114). Amsterdam: Benjamins.

Von Eckardt, B. (1978). Inferring functional localization from neuropsychological evidence. In E. Walker (Ed.), *Explorations in the biology of language* (pp. 27–66). Montgomery, VT: Bradford.

Wanner, E. and Maratsos, M. (1978). An ATN approach to comprehension. In M. Halle, J. Bresnan, & G. A. Miller (Eds.), *Linguistic theory and psychological reality* (pp. 119–161). Cambridge, MA: MIT Press.

Warrington, E. (1987). Localization of lesions associated with impairments of semantic memory. Presentation at European Cognitive Neuropsychology Society, Bressanone, Italy.

Warrington, E. K., & Shallice, T. (1969). The selective impairment of auditory-verbal short-term memory. *Brain, 92,* 885–896.

Warrington, E. K., & Shallice, T. (1984). Category specific semantic impairments. *Brain, 102,* 43–63.

Weisel, T. (1982). Postnatal development of the visual cortex and the influence of the environment. *Nature (London), 299,* 583–591.

Weisenberg, T., & McBride, K. (1935). *Aphasia.* New York: Commonwealth Fund.

Wernicke, C. (1874). *The aphasic symptom complex: A psychological study on a neurological basis.* Breslau: Kohn and Weigert. Reprinted in: Cohen, R. S., & Wartofsky, M. W. (Eds.) (1974). *Boston studies in the philosophy of science, Vol. 4.* Boston: Reidel.

Wood, C. (1982). Implications of simulated lesion experiments for the interpretation of lesions in real nervous systems. In M. A. Arbib, D. Caplan, & J. C. Marshall (Eds.), *Neural models of language processes* (pp. 485–509). New York: Academic Press.

Yarnell, P. R., Monroe, M. A., & Sobel, L. (1976). Aphasia outcome in stroke: A clinical and neuroradiological correlation. *Stroke, 7,* 516–522.

Zurif, E. B. (1982). The use of data from aphasia in constructing a performance model of language. In M. A. Arbib, D. Caplan, & J. C. Marshall (Eds.), *Neural models of language processes* (pp. 203–207). New York: Academic Press.

Chapter 32

The Neuropsychology of Language

Edgar Zurif and David Swinney

I. Introduction

This chapter presents an account of the neurological organization of human language processing. It relies largely on studies of language disorder arising from brain damage—that is, on studies of aphasia. And within this research domain, we focus primarily on the fate of sentence comprehension. Recent findings suggest that linguistic inquiry and neuroscience most readily converge at the sentence level—that it is at this level that the relations between language structure, processing resources, and brain architecture are most apparent.

    The studies that illuminate these connections build on aspects of clinical descriptions first provided in the 1870s, at the start of the modern era of aphasia research. We begin by briefly reviewing these early descriptions and continue in a roughly chronological fashion, pointing out along the way some false starts and controversies.

II. Language Activities and Cerebral Organization: Research in the 1870s

The enduring clinical descriptions of the late 19th century (e.g., Lichtheim, 1885; Wernicke, 1874/1977)—the so-called "classical" descriptions—turn on two distinct kinds of language failure and the relation of each to a specific region of brain damage. One of these is most usually referred to as Broca's aphasia, after the 19th century neurologist Paul Broca who first brought attention to the disorder. It typically results from damage to at least the lower part of the left frontal lobe (Broca's area).[1] Although patients with this form of aphasia show relatively good comprehension at the conversational level, they produce little speech and do so slowly, with effort and poor articulation. Also, their speech is telegraphic or AGRAMMATIC: They tend to omit articles, connective words, and grammatical inflections and they produce, at best, only simple syntactic forms (e.g., Goodglass & Kaplan, 1972; Lecours, Lhermitte, & Bryans, 1983).

The second of these classical aphasias, Wernicke's aphasia (attributed to Carl Wernicke's original observations), usually results from a lesion in the posterior region of the left hemisphere, specifically, to the area adjacent to that involved in hearing. Patients with damage to this area (Wernicke's area) produce a form of speech strikingly different from that of patients with Broca's aphasia, one that is rapid and effortless, with a superficially normal syntactic appearance. Yet their speech is remarkably empty of content and often contains errors of word choice (e.g., *boy* or *girl*). Moreover, patients with Wernicke's aphasia show a very apparent comprehension deficit at the sentence and conversational levels (Goodglass & Kaplan, 1972; Lecours et al., 1983).

Actually, sentence-level phenomena were hardly considered in the classical descriptions. That came later. Reflecting the theoretical ambiance of the time, the initial focus was on the individual word, and crucially on the distinction between MOTOR memory images of words and their SENSORY memory images—that is, on the processes used for producing words and for understanding them. Specifically, given the two kinds of aphasias and the brain site each implicated, Wernicke theorized that the brain organized language in the form of anatomically discrete interconnected centers: Broca's area was claimed to be the center for the memory representations implicated in producing words (for the storage of "rules" by which words were coded into articulatory form) and Wernicke's area was argued to be the center for the sensory memories of words (comprehension). These two centers were hypothesized to be connected to each other, and each, in turn, connected to a general conceptual center (Geschwind, 1970; Lichtheim, 1885; Wernicke, 1874/1977).

Notwithstanding the formal typology of aphasia that it generated, Wernicke's theory was criticized from its inception for, among other matters, its failure to do justice to the complexity of aphasic phenomena—most notably for its failure to account for disruptions of the capacity to "propositionalize" (Jackson, 1884). But given the comparatively restricted linguistic theorizing of the time, early attempts to shift analyses of aphasia from the word to the sentence level—to focus on such features as agrammatism—remained unsystematic and largely underdeveloped. Indeed, on some accounts agrammatism

---

[1] The pathologic lesion in Broca's aphasia was initially (and incorrectly) described by Broca as being confined to the pars opercularis of the third frontal convolution of the left hemisphere. It is now recognized, however, that lesions typically responsible for persisting Broca's aphasia as described here are more extensive. Such lesions occupy indeterminately sizable amounts of the area of supply of the upper division of the left middle-cerebral artery (Mohr, 1976). Although early workers, including Wernicke, seem to have accepted the original formulation, our own occasional use in this chapter of the term Broca's area should be taken to signify this larger territory, which is, nonetheless, distinguishable from the posterior Sylvian territory implicated in Wernicke's aphasia.

was considered to be the result only of a nonlinguistic disruption to the motor implementation of speech—a means of economizing effort. (See Goodglass, 1976, and DeBleser, 1987, for detailed reviews of this early work.)

III. LANGUAGE COMPETENCE AND CEREBRAL ORGANIZATION: RESEARCH IN THE 1970S

The shift in focus from word to sentence level phenomena began in earnest in the 1970s—about 100 years after Wernicke—with a number of studies of comprehension in Broca's aphasia (e.g., Caramazza & Zurif, 1976; Goodglass, 1968; Heilman & Scholes, 1976; Zurif, Caramazza, & Myerson, 1972). Given the prevailing influence of linguistic theorizing in the 1960s and its emphasis on the centrality of knowledge structures in the determination of both speaking and listening, these comprehension studies were impelled by the possibility that agrammatic output was something other than just an economizing effort; rather, that it was the most public manifestation of a disruption to syntactic knowledge or competence. If so, the reasoning went, careful observation should also reveal syntactic disruptions in comprehension. After all, although Wernicke's theory stressed the distinction between input and output centers, very few clinicians—even those of a decidedly classical bent—actually ever claimed the comprehension of Broca's aphasic patients to be entirely normal; the working phrase was always "relatively normal comprehension" (Geschwind, 1970).

To assess syntactic competence, these studies typically used a sentence–picture matching paradigm in which aphasic patients were presented with a sentence and asked to demonstrate their understanding of it by pointing to its correct depiction embedded in a multiple-choice array of pictures. By systematically manipulating the availability of semantic and pragmatic cues, these studies documented the Broca's patients' abnormal reliance on such cues and their corresponding inability to carry out normal syntactic analysis. At least this was so for sentences cast in noncanonical (non–active voice) form (e.g., Caramazza & Zurif, 1976). So, for example, even though they could interpret the passive sentence *The mouse was chased by the cat,* they could not interpret the passive sentence *The boy was chased by the girl;* it seems that this was so because in the former case there was only one pragmatically likely organization of the words, while in the second case there were no pragmatic constraints to help the Broca's patients decide who was the chaser and who was chased.

Other experiments demonstrated the Broca's patients' difficulty in situations in which interpretation depended on the processing of the article *the* (Goodenough, Zurif, & Weintraub, 1977; Heilman & Scholes, 1976). Thus, Heilman and Scholes (1976) observed that the patients were not able to distinguish the meaning of *He showed her baby the pictures* from the meaning of *He showed her the baby pictures*.

Taken together, these various analyses suggested important parallels between production and comprehension. Just as the Broca's patients' speech was syntactically simplified and relatively devoid of function words, so, too, they appeared unable to process syntax normally during comprehension and to use function words for phrasal segmentation. In the sweeping terms used at the time, Broca's patients were said to be as agrammatic in listening as in speaking, and left anterior brain damage was claimed to produce an overarching syntactic limitation, even as it spared the capacity to carry out semantic inference (e.g., Caramazza & Zurif, 1976; Zurif & Blumstein, 1978).

Moreover, this seemed to be true only of Broca's aphasia and the brain tissue it implicated. Wernicke's aphasic patients appeared to be different. They made semantic errors and sentence-level errors; but, unlike the Broca's patients, their comprehension limitations could not be assigned solely to a syntactic component; rather, the Wernicke's problem also seemed importantly rooted to their inability to retrieve precise lexical semantic units (e.g., Heilman & Scholes, 1976; Zurif & Blumstein, 1978).

It appeared at that time, then, that Wernicke and his colleagues had (approximately) correctly localized the language centers in the brain and that further research would serve simply to redefine their functions. Thus, by the mid 1970s Broca's area (see footnote 1) appeared to be a syntactic center—a center for the rules and representations defining syntactic competence and, optimistically, it seemed that Wernicke's area would be discovered to sustain semantic inference.

IV. CURRENT ISSUES: CONTROVERSY CONCERNING THE CLASSICAL CATEGORIES

The position that Broca's aphasic patients have an overarching syntactic limitation was soon challenged on empirical grounds. This came in the form of several case reports: several individually studied patients who showed a production impairment clinically categorized as agrammatism, yet who had no detectable sentence comprehension impairment (Miceli, Mazzucchi, Menn, & Goodglass, 1983; Kolk, VanGrunsven, & Keyser, 1985; Nespoulous, Dordain, Perron, Ska, Bub, Caplan, Mehler, & Lecours, 1988).[2] In the light of these three reports, the characterization of an overarching agrammatism patently did not apply to all Broca's patients.

But there was more. Even the homogeneity of agrammatic output was soon questioned. The evidence here was in the form of an analysis of speech samples of agrammatic (Broca's) aphasics—an analysis that revealed great quantitative variation across patients in their omission of grammatical morphemes (Miceli,

---

[2] Actually, most of the exceptional cases diverge noticeably from typical agrammatic Broca's patients in production, too. Case 1 of Miceli et al. (1983) was able to repeat and read aloud without any agrammatic limitation, and case 2 showed normal fluency and normal phrase length as did Kolk et al.'s (1985) patient. So it is not at all clear that these patients ought to even be counted as Broca's to begin with.

Silveri, Romani, & Caramazza, 1989).[3] For some, these data led to the view that not only was the overarching agrammatism notion unreliable, but also that there was not even a homogeneous category of agrammatic Broca's aphasics.

This view has since been enlarged and hardened by Caramazza and his colleagues into a philosophical stance—the SINGLE CASE ONLY position—that denies the legitimacy of any research that seeks to elaborate on a theory of a cognitive capacity and that uses clinically defined groups for this purpose (Badecker & Caramazza, 1985; Caramazza, 1986; Caramazza & McCloskey, 1988). The single case only position has received great play in the literature and warrants consideration here. Its linchpin is that the procedures in cognitive neuropsychology differ in a fundamental way from typical experimental procedures in other sciences. As Caramazza and his colleagues state it, in contrast to scientists in other domains, cognitive neuropsychologists cannot control all relevant experimental manipulations; brain-damaged subjects are experiments of nature in which one experimental condition (the "functional" lesion) cannot be determined in advance, but rather must be inferred from the individual patient's performance. Caramazza and his colleagues take this to indicate that the a priori classification of patients into clinical categories is theoretically arbitrary and that the only nonarbitrary classification of patients possible is, thus, a posteriori. That is, in their account, the only classification that is possible is one that is based after the fact on those theoretically relevant performance characteristics that allow the identification of a functional lesion in a cognitive system. And this, they hold, is equivalent to the claim that patient classification cannot play any significant role independent of the single-patient research projects that are required to determine that each of the patients in question has the appropriate functional lesion for a posteriori classification. In short, "The basic unit of analysis in cognitive neuropsychology must be the individual patient" (Caramazza & Badecker, 1989).

There are a number of points about this general position that we think are highly problematic, however. The first is that the contrast made by Caramazza and colleagues of the "ideal" of experimental method as portrayed for other sciences compared with cognitive neuropsychology is far from realistic. Even when the "manipulated" variable (the strength of the scientific experimental method) is manipulable, as in standard experimentation, it is always an open question whether the experimenter has the right theory about that which he is manipulating. It is a truism of the philosophy of method that the theory of the experimental manipulation, as well as the theory that the experiment is designed

---

[3] We note that the Miceli et al. (1989) report refers to substitutions as well as omissions of inflectional morphemes, whereas we have characterized the disorder of agrammatic output only in terms of omissions. This difference corresponds to the fact that we have based our description on the performance of English-speaking patients, while Miceli et al. dealt with Italian-speaking Broca's. This cross-linguistic difference is accountable as follows: substitutions of inflectional morphemes are observed only if their omission violates lexical well-formedness. In this respect, omission is almost always an option in English, but much less so in Italian (still less in Hebrew, where even the phonological status of a word presupposes inflection). In effect, the same underlying problem in the production of bound grammatical morphemes is manifested differently in the output of different languages. [A detailed account of such cross-linguistic variation is beyond the scope of this chapter, but can be found in Grodzinsky (1990).]

to test, can, in principle, be revised in the face of recalcitrant data. (This is an immediate consequence of the Duhem (1962)/Quine (1961) thesis, which argues that, in principle, any statement of a theory is revisable in the face of recalcitrant data.) The fact that the scientist claims, in all sincerity, to have performed a certain manipulation does not entail that he has actually done so. In this sense, then, the experimental conditions that are manipulated can never be "determined in advance" (i.e., in advance of the best explanation of the experimental outcome). So it is not at all clear, as Caramazza and his supporters would have it, that there is a principled difference between neuropsychology and other cognitive sciences with respect to control over experimental manipulations.

A more important consideration, however, has to do with the consequences of theoretically arbitrary a priori classification. Even where there is no prior theory to justify a particular taxonomy, there need be no impediment to rational inquiry. Our point here is that taxonomies in cognitive neuropsychology do not have to be theoretically motivated; they have to be empirically motivated. And this brings us to the heart of the matter: Cognitive neuropsychology, like, for example, astronomy, is an observational science. Its practitioners get by without actively manipulating functional lesions or, for that matter, brain lesions. In this framework, syndromes (even loosely defined ones like nonfluent, agrammatic Broca's aphasia) are what the world gives us; they are there to constrain theory and, to this end, to allow groups to be formed for research purposes. And the basic questions in this observational enterprise necessarily concern only empirical matters (e.g., Zurif, Swinney, & Fodor, 1991).

Thus, the only question that can count in this approach to science is whether the data do or do not sustain the classification of Broca's aphasia. In particular, the issue comes down to whether we ought to retain the category of Broca's aphasia for research purposes in the face of the two empirical challenges mentioned earlier: (a) the failure to find an overarching agrammatism in all cases of Broca's aphasia, and (b) the quantitative variation in agrammatic output. Of the two, the point about patient quantitative variation is without merit. The numerical values Miceli et al. (1989) cite are simply irrelevant to the issue of categorizing this patient group for the exploration of most linguistic and psycholinguistic issues. By examining whether agrammatic output in Broca's aphasia can be characterized as a quantifiable entity, they end up entering the factor of severity which most theories of processing and structure necessarily abstract over. They also enter some critical statistical issues. [See Bates, Appelbaum & Allard (1991) for a critique of Miceli et al. along statistical lines which appears to prove their particular analysis to misrepresent the situation.] But perhaps most importantly, by focusing on differences among agrammatic Broca's patients, they miss the point that these patients nonetheless share grammatical output features that allow categorization in the first place—features that allowed categorization even for their own study. They miss the point that every Broca's patient they examined showed abnormal control of grammatical morphemes. And this is one of the crucial qualitative features that define the category of Broca's aphasia—indeed, the syndrome is really only defined qualitatively (Grodzinsky, 1991).

The other empirical challenge—the challenge that not all Broca's patients show an overarching agrammatism—cannot be so easily dismissed. On the contrary, it is an important one. It establishes that the observation of agrammatic output in Broca's aphasia need not entail a co-occurring syntactic limitation in their comprehension. But that said, it remains the case that the number of Broca's patients that do show syntactic comprehension problems (the patients included in the group studies) far outweigh the few that have been reported not to. In effect, the small number of exceptional cases must be considered as checks that cannot yet be cashed. They may be anomalous (outlier) subjects, perhaps because of some subtly different lesion properties that we cannot yet detect. (After all, very little is known of the precise nature of the lesions implicated in Broca's and Wernicke's aphasia, other than that they are grossly differentiable.) Or, they might constitute an important disproof of the notion that lesions that cause agrammatic output also cause parallel syntactic problems in comprehension (Zurif et al., 1991).

Partly as a response to this last possibility, very few, if any, researchers still focus on the notion of an overarching agrammatism, an agrammatism that implicates the same structures in speaking and listening. Another reason is the fact that the ingredients from the production side of the equation are not in place. In the realm of syntax, models of the production system are far less detailed than those worked out for comprehension (Bock, 1991). For example, whereas levels of representation specified in modern generative grammars seem in certain respects to constitute exactly the targets that real-time comprehension processes compute (Swinney & Fodor, 1989), this kind of relation cannot yet even be gauged for the production system; the data are not available. And this asymmetry is nowhere more apparent than in aphasia research, where characterizations of linguistic and processing features of the comprehension problem are far more theoretically focused than are descriptions of production patterns in aphasia.

Yet, even if for these reasons the question concerning parallelism of linguistic deficits in production and comprehension remains open, Broca's aphasia and Wernicke's aphasia continue to serve research. In effect, these syndromes exist apart from what we make of them; they continue to be mined for answers to other aspects of brain–language relations. Currently, this focuses on evidence bearing on the neurological organization of the comprehension system alone.

In what follows, our discussion of recent research in comprehension treats descriptive generalizations concerning representational limitations and analyses of real-time processing disruptions separately. But we seek to account for the former in terms of the latter.

V. CURRENT ISSUES: REPRESENTATIONAL LIMITATIONS IN APHASIC COMPREHENSION

One view of the representational limitation as it applies to agrammatic comprehension is that, for whatever reason, the patients are virtually incapable of constructing any aspect of a syntactic representation. This view, a legacy of research of the 1970s and of work detailed by Caplan in his "lexical" hypothesis (1983), holds that agrammatic Broca's patients retain no syntactic capacities other than the ability to identify syntactic categories at the word level. In this view, in the absence of any semantic and/or pragmatic constraints, the patients rely solely on the nongrammatical strategy of assigning thematic roles to linear strings of noun–verb sequences. Most importantly, they rely on the strategy of assigning AGENCY to the first encountered noun (Bever, 1970).

Unfortunately, this claim does not appear to comport well with the data. Setting aside the few uncashed checks—the few cases that show agrammatic production and normal comprehension—the pertinent fact is that for noncanonical structures (e.g., the passive, in which the first noun is the patient, not the agent, of the action) the Broca's patients perform roughly at chance levels (Ansell & Flowers, 1982; Caplan & Futter, 1986; Caramazza & Zurif, 1976; Grodzinsky, 1986, 1989; Grodzinsky, Finkelstein, Nicol, & Zurif, 1988; Wulfeck, 1988). Caplan's lexical hypothesis founders on this fact. Although it correctly predicts good interpretation for active-voice sentences (wherein first nouns are agents), it predicts not random performance for passives, but performance that is, at the least, significantly below chance. That is, on Caplan's account, the Broca's patients should show a systematic inversion of thematic role assignment, always incorrectly interpreting the first noun as agent in the passive.

Grodzinsky (1986; 1990) has provided a generalization that is somewhat more compatible with the performance levels that are actually observed. Before turning to his account, however, we note that the active–passive contrast is part of a larger pattern. Specifically, although Broca's patients show uncertain comprehension for semantically reversible object-relative sentences (e.g., *The girl whom the boy is pushing is tall*)—that is, they are not sure who is doing the pushing—they perform well with corresponding subject-relatives (e.g., *The boy who is pushing the girl is tall*) (e.g., Caramazza & Zurif, 1976). And again, even as they have difficulty assigning thematic roles when faced with object-cleft sentences (e.g., *It is the girl whom the boy is pushing*), they have little difficulty when faced with subject-clefts (e.g., *It is the boy who is pushing the girl*) (Caplan & Futter, 1986). As with the contrast between passives and actives, the first-mentioned construction of each pair yields chance performance, the second yields performance significantly above chance.

Grodzinsky's account of this pattern is that Broca's aphasic patients have a problem understanding any sentence in which a transformation has been applied to move a phrasal constituent from a nonagentive position. This account is grounded in government-binding theory (GB; Chomsky, 1981). According to this (and other transformational) theory(s), movement of a constituent leaves a trace (an abstract, phonologically unrealized marker) in the vacated position in S(urface)-structure. Traces are held to be crucial for maintaining interpretative identity between D(eep) and transformed S(urface) structures. They are involved, among other things, in the assignment of thematic roles in a sentence. If a thematic position is filled with a lexical noun phrase, then it receives its thematic role directly; but if a thematic position contains a trace, then the trace is assigned the thematic role and the moved constituent that left the trace (e.g., the first noun phrase in a passive) gets its role only indirectly, by being co-indexed to the trace.

Attendant on this theoretical feature, Grodzinsky's characterization of the comprehension limitation in Broca's aphasia is that, although patients of this type appreciate hierarchical syntactic organization, they cannot represent traces and, therefore, cannot gramatically assign thematic roles to moved constituents. Faced with a thematically unassigned noun phrase, the Broca's patient applies an agent-first strategy—the same strategy outlined in Bever (1970) and in Caplan's (1983) lexical hypothesis. But in contrast to Caplan's account, the strategy is claimed to apply in the context of an otherwise elaborated syntactic representation. Thus, when a constituent is moved from object position, the strategy yields two agent noun phrases for the same sentence. One is assigned grammatically (via the *by*-phrase), the other is incorrectly assigned by the nongrammatical strategy. Faced with two agents (on a sentence–picture matching task), the patient is forced into a guessing situation, which leads to random performance.

This explanation accounts for the data, both the failures and the successes. The constructions that yield chance performance—passives, object-relatives, and object-clefts—contain S-structure traces in object position, whereas the constructions that yield good performance—actives, subject-relatives, and subject-clefts—either do not have a trace in their S-structure representation (as in the active) or if there is a trace, it appears in the subject position. And in these latter instances, the agent-first strategy works—were grammatical capacity normal, it would yield the same solution.[4]

Grodzinsky's account has not gone unchallenged. Consider in this respect, two recent reports, one by Martin, Wetzel, Blossom-Stach, and Feher (1989) and one by Badecker, Nathan, & Caramazza (1991).

Martin et al. (1989) examined comprehension for full and truncated passives (respectively, *The boy was pushed by the girl* and *The boy was pushed*). On the basis of Grodzinsky's theory, one should predict that for the latter sentence type, agrammatic patients should not show random performance but systematic inversion of thematic role assignment: They should assign agency to the initial noun phrase, and in the absence of a countervailing force provided by a *by*-phrase, thereby consistently misassign the thematic role. But this is not what Martin et al. observed. Contrary to Grodzinsky's formulation, they found that for both types of passives, the truncated as well as the full, their patients assigned thematic roles at chance level.

However, as pointed out in a response by Grodzinsky (1991), there are some problematic aspects to Martin et al.'s challenge. On the production task used initially to assign patients to the agrammatic Broca's category, only one of the three patients tested fit within the investigators' own definition of agrammatism. The other two patients performed virtually normally on all the morphological indices in the task and in addition showed much greater articulatory agility than is usually observed in Broca's aphasia. These patients were aphasic, but it is not at all clear that they were Broca's aphasics. (A fourth patient, who

---

[4] Grodzinsky has not relied uncritically on GB theory (Chomsky, 1981). He has also tested the "neurological adequacy" of competing linguistic theories (Grodzinksy & Pierce, 1987). To state his findings very briefly, he has observed that although Broca's patients have problems interpreting verbal passives (e.g., *Tom was pushed by Mary*, and see text above), they perform significantly above chance with adjectival passives (e.g., *Tom was interested in Mary*). This distinction is statable within GB theory (Chomsky, 1981), but not within lexical functional grammar (Bresnan, 1982). In the former, verbal passives are transformationally derived in the manner described in the text above, whereas adjectival passives are derived by lexical rule. By contrast, in lexical functional grammar, all passives are lexical. From the standpoint of breakdown compatibility on this set of data alone, therefore, GB theory is perhaps to be preferred; of course this only holds if one believes that the entire issue is one of competence and not performance, and that the current state of these competence theories is immutable.

could not be tested on the standard production test used for classification but was tested on a picture description test, also yielded some morphological data that approximated normal levels.) Similarly, the particular use of the comprehension task may have confounded the interpretation of the results. In all, it is not at all clear that this work has refuted the theory.

Badecker et al.'s (1991) empirical challenge, in the form of data from a single agrammatic patient, is even more difficulty to evaluate. Quite simply, the patient's performance was inconsistent. With respect to his comprehension of active and passive sentences, the only pattern that is at all discernible is that the task seemed to make a difference: he performed mostly at chance for both the active and passive constructions in a sentence–picture matching situation, but tended to show above chance performance for both constructions when the task was one of figure manipulation. And with respect to the cleft sentences, he performed at chance on subject-clefts and above chance on object-clefts—the reverse pattern of all previous findings reported for these constructions. Given that the authors make no effort to reconcile their data with those of others, nor even to account for the mysterious patterns within their own experiment (chance on sentence–picture matching, improvement on the figure manipulation task for the same patient and for the same sentence types), it is not clear how or whether these data bear on the hypothesis at stake.

There have been other examinations of Grodzinsky's generalization that have sought to broaden the descriptive adequacy of Grodzinsky's account (Cornell, Fromkin, & Mauner, 1989; Hickok, 1992; Mauner, Cornell, & Fromkin, 1990). The fact is that Broca's aphasic patients have problems, not only with intrasentence dependency relations involving traces, but also with dependency relations involving overt anaphors, in particular, pronouns (Caplan & Hildebrandt, 1988; Grodzinsky, 1990; Grodzinsky, Wexler, Chien, Marakovitz, & Solomon, 1992). So, for example, given sentences of the sort *John bandaged him,* patients perform at chance level, often taking *him* to refer to *John.* And while Grodzinsky's formulation adequately accounts for the Broca's patients' comprehension pattern observed for active, passive, relative, and cleft constructions, it does not cover the Broca's problem with overt pronoun anaphors.

An analysis formulated by Hickok (1992) does, however, provide a unified account for dependency relations involving both traces and overt anaphors. Hickok has revised Grodzinsky's trace-deletion notion to incorporate a recent aspect of syntactic theory termed the verb phrase–internal subject hypothesis (Burton & Grimshaw, 1992; Kitagawa, 1986; Koopman & Sportiche, 1988). The suggestion here is that the grammatical subject (even in simple active sentences) does not receive its thematic role directly from the verb. Rather, the subject noun phrase originates within the verb phrase and occupies its surface position only by undergoing movement and leaving a trace behind. The assignment of a thematic role to the moved subject noun phrase is, therefore, mediated by the trace. Only unmoved object noun phrases are directly assigned thematic roles. On the basis of this hypothesis, Hickok proposes that Broca's patients never assign thematic roles to subject noun phrases in normal grammatical fashion, but instead resort to a nongrammatical strategy. The latter is not the agent-first strategy that figures in Grodzinsky's account, but a fill-in strategy—a strategy whereby in a sentence–picture situation, the moved subject noun phrase is given the thematic role that has not yet been grammatically assigned and that makes sense in terms of the depiction. This fill-in strategy works for active constructions, subject-relatives, and subject-clefts for which only one noun phrase is available for interpretation as a given unsatisfied argument—that is, remains to be filled in. But the strategy does not work for passive, object-relative, and object-cleft constructions for which, according to the verb phrase–internal subject hypothesis, no argument is directly assigned.

To illustrate, consider some examples provided in Hickok's analysis. These are representations for subject-cleft and object-cleft constructions as specified by the verb phrase–internal subject hypothesis: Respectively, *It was the boy$_i$ that* [VP(t)$_i$ *kissed the girl*] and *It was the boy$_i$* [*that the girl$_j$* [VP(t)$_j$ *kissed* (t)$_i$]]. For the subject-cleft construction, the internal argument *the girl* is in object position; it has not undergone movement and therefore receives its thematic role (as the person being kissed) directly from the verb. Accordingly, the thematic role for the noun phrase *the boy* (which has been moved from subject position) can be filled in—it can be assigned the one remaining role that fits in with a depiction of the sentence. By contrast, for the object-cleft sentence, both the noun phrases have undergone movement. The noun phrase *the boy* has been moved from object position (as indicated by subscript$_i$), and the noun phrase *the girl*, this time being in subject position, has also been moved (as indicated by subscript$_j$). Both thematic role assignments must thus be mediated by traces. And since Broca's patients cannot capture antecedent–trace links for the purpose of comprehension, they cannot narrow down their options—they cannot fill in. So they guess.

Although Hickok's account clearly makes use of the defining characteristic of Grodzinsky's trace-deletion hypothesis—namely, that traces are deleted in S-structure—it also offers an important contrast. In Grodzinsky's view, Broca's patients are capable of grammatically assigning thematic roles to subject noun phrases. In Hickok's revision, chance performance results from completely unspecified thematic assignment—the patients make no thematic assignments whatsoever for passives, object-relatives, and object-clefts. Hickok's variation also accounts for the Broca's comprehension of pronoun anaphors. The verb phrase–internal subject hypothesis holds that the governing category of a pronoun is the verb phrase which entails that it is within this category that the pronoun must be free (Kitagawa, 1986).[5] In this respect, consider the example *John bandaged him*. Its representation under the verb phrase–internal hypothesis is *John* [VP(t) *bandaged him*]—again, the subject noun phrase has undergone movement, leaving a trace. Since the trace of *John* is inside the verb phrase and since the verb phrase is hypothesized to be the governing category, the pronoun *him* cannot refer to John; it must be free. But Broca's aphasic patients cannot link antecedents and traces; they cannot, therefore, apply the binding principle to block co-reference of *him* and *John*. That is, without the trace, nothing in their representation of the sentence specifies what the pronoun *him* refers to—or, more to the point, cannot refer to—and so they guess.

Our account of Grodzinsky's trace-deletion hypothesis and Hickok's reworking of the trace-deletion hypothesis has glossed over a number of clever and

---

[5] All versions of GB theory (Chomsky, 1981) consider pronouns to be free within their governing category. What is at issue is the identity of the category, the new formulation shifting it from the inflectional phrase (essentially, the sentence level) to the verb phrase.

interesting details of these representational accounts of language dysfunction in aphasia. Still, even from our partial description, it should be apparent that both investigators agree on what is particularly problematic for Broca's patients: namely, their inability to represent intrasentence dependency relations involving traces. Indeed, in Hickok's formulation, the Broca's problem with traces is invoked even to account for their poor performance with dependencies involving overt anaphors.

A final point: The accounts we have covered—Grodzinsky's, Hickok's, and Caplan's before them—all constitute an attempt to describe what can and cannot be syntactically represented. What they do not address is the source of the representational limitations: in particular, the source of the Broca's problem with intrasentence dependency relations.

It is to this issue that we now turn. And, as we show in the next section, the evidence points not to a competence limitation (i.e., not to a partial loss of knowledge that somehow erases traces or the like) but to a disruption to the processes that IMPLEMENT syntactic knowledge in real time.

VI. CURRENT ISSUES: PROCESSING DISRUPTIONS IN APHASIC COMPREHENSION

There are, basically, two competing ideas concerning the nature of the processing disruption that underlies the sentence comprehension limitation in Broca's aphasia—that yield the problems described above. One idea is that there is a failure of mapping between syntactic representations and thematic roles. The other is that there is a disruption in the initial construction of the syntactic representation, a disruption that can be traced to the non-normal operation of lexical access mechanisms.

A. A Mapping Failure

This hypothesis is rooted to data from experimental tasks involving grammaticality judgments. Specifically, Linebarger, Schwartz, and Saffran (1983) observed that agrammatic Broca's aphasics who showed noticeable syntactic limitations in comprehension were, nonetheless, able to detect a wide variety of grammatical deformations in a grammaticality judgment task, including those that required an awareness of syntactic dependencies involving traces. What emerges from this is a picture of agrammatic aphasic patients in which they can be seen to carry out quite complex syntactic judgments yet lack the ability to exploit this sensitivity for comprehension.

As pointed out by Sproat (1986), these judgment data indicate that the failure to specify empty categories, or traces, makes little sense except in processing terms. Sproat's reasoning turns on the fact that in GB theory, the presence of a trace follows directly from the projection principle. This principle states that representations at each syntactic level are projected from the lexicon, each level thereby observing the allowable syntactic environments of lexical items. This means, in effect, that by not representing traces, agrammatic Broca's patients build syntactic structures that violate a core grammatical principle. And if this deficit is one of competence—if the projection principle is no longer a part of retained knowledge—then the patients ought to have been insensitive to the syntactic deformations provided by Linebarger et al. But since the patients WERE sensitive to these deformations, it follows that their inability to represent traces must be due to some defect in the system that converts the input stream into an interpreted structure. So again the data gained by Linebarger et al. argue for a processing explanation of agrammatic comprehension. But of what sort?

Linebarger et al. (1983) opt for a mapping explanation. In the words of Saffron and Schwartz (1988), the problem arises "not from a failure to parse sentences for their grammatical functions, but rather from a difficulty in assigning those functions the appropriate thematic roles" (p. 390).

Several points about this hypothesis warrant consideration. The first is that it is not clear that the Linebarger et al. data compel any sort of mapping hypothesis. The task of making grammaticality judgments about a sentence need not depend on the normal construction of a coherent syntactic representation. We do not suggest under this view that there need to be different analyzers for comprehension and for grammaticality judgment. Rather, it is simply that it is one thing to notice the absence of an empty position in a deformed "sentence" and make a "non-normal" judgment to it, and quite another matter to fill that position in a nondeformed sentence with the correct antecedent during the strict time constraints of the initial structure-building process. Sensitivity in the first instance will yield good performance on a grammaticality judgment task, but only the latter capacity will yield a normally complete syntactic representation that can support subsequent thematic mapping (Wulfeck, 1988; Zurif & Grodzinsky, 1983).

Further, however, it is not inconceivable to suggest that grammaticality judgments may actually be made by a processing device that is not normally involved in ongoing sentence comprehension. Baynes and Gazzaniga (1987; Gazzaniga, 1989) report that the right hemisphere of split-brain patients can support correct grammaticality judgments, but that this same hemisphere "is severely limited in its capacity to use syntactic information in comprehension," such that the patients have "difficulty understanding semantically reversible active and passive sentences." An interesting possibility is that, although the processing of sentences is left hemispheric, the right hemisphere in aphasic patients may be called into play for grammaticality judgment tasks but is unable to aid normal comprehension.

In addition, it should be noted that if there were to be a mapping problem, it is clearly not an undifferentiated one—one that arises for all syntactic types. Schwartz and her colleagues acknowledge this by pointing to what they term a THEMATIC TRANSPARENCY EFFECT, that agrammatic Broca's patients have noticeably more difficulty in mapping moved noun phrases than in mapping noun phrases directly in thematic positions (Schwartz, Saffran, Linebarger, & Pate, 1987). In effect, they restate in mapping terms the distinction that is at the heart of the various versions of the trace-deletion hypothesis (Cornell et al., 1989; Grodzinsky, 1986, 1990; Hickok, 1992; Mauner et al., 1990).

As the current experimental basis for their theory may have alternative explanations rooted in processes that are independent from the comprehension data they are intended to illuminate, the theory itself needs further empirical definition. And finally, we note that by failing to provide either an independent theory of parsing or any evidence for the selective disruption of processing modules in terms of their real-time operating characteristics, Linebarger et al. have little basis for distinguishing mapping failures from prior parsing (structural processing) failures. Indeed, as we show below, when real-time processing properties are revealed through the application of on-line analysis, parsing is observed not to be normally intact in Broca's aphasia.

B. Disruptions of Structure Building

The notion that the parser itself is the weak link in Broca's aphasia arises from a recently completed analysis of the ability of aphasic patients to establish intrasentence dependency relations in real time (Zurif, Swinney, Prather, Solomon, & Bushell, in preparation). The analysis is based on observations of early-stage lexical activation characteristics.

Some background: Over the past 11 years, researchers have consistently observed that Wernicke's aphasics have normal lexical access functions and that Broca's do not. The data supporting this generalization come from studies of lexical priming (Blumstein, Milberg, & Shrier, 1982; Katz, 1986; Milberg & Blumstein, 1981; Milberg, Blumstein, & Dworetsky, 1987; Prather, Shapiro, Zurif, & Swinney, 1991; Swinney, Zurif, & Nicol, 1989). Priming in this case refers to the finding that processing a lexical item (e.g., deciding whether or not a string of letters forms a word) is faster for target words when these are immediately preceded by semantically related words than when preceded by unrelated words. This pattern of results is taken to indicate that the meaning of the preceding related prime has been present to aid the recognition of the subsequent word (Meyer, Schavenveldt & Ruddy, 1975). So, to state the matter directly in terms of the relevant data, Wernicke's patients but not Broca's patients show the normal pattern of faster word recognition in semantically facilitating contexts (priming).

That noted, we hasten to emphasize that Broca's patients are not completely insensitive to prime–target relations—they are not, after all, disbarred from activating lexical meanings. Rather, for Broca's, priming seems to be temporally protracted, or more to the point, lexical contact and activation, as revealed by priming, seems to have a slower than normal time course (Prather et al., 1991; Swinney et al., 1989).

The effects of this form of aberrant lexical access may reasonably be supposed to ramify throughout the comprehension system. Consider just one of its likely effects—that concerning syntactic processing in the case involving the linking of antecedents and traces. Crucially, traces have real-time processing consequences. We refer here to what has come to be known as gap-filling, the demonstration based on priming patterns that in normal subjects, antecedents and traces are actually linked during the course of ongoing comprehension, and that the antecedents actually fill the gap left by their movement at the point when that gap is encountered by the listener. (See Swinney and Fodor, 1989, and Swinney and Osterhout, 1990, for reviews of this work.) This is an operation that is implemented under strict time constraints. And this being so, the inability of Broca's aphasic patients to represent antecedent–trace relations can be viewed in real-time terms as the inability to reactivate the moved constituent at the normal time in the processing sequence—in time, that is, to fill the gap left by its movement (and indexed by the trace).

We have lately tested the possibility of this scenario by assessing gap-filling in Broca's patients, Wernicke's patients, and elderly neurologically intact subjects (Zurif et al., in preparation). We used subject-relative constructions of the sort *The gymnast loved the professor$_i$ from the northwestern city who (t)$_i$ complained about the bad coffee.* As shown by this example, movement from subject position is hypothesized.

We chose this construction because it offered the possibility of revealing whether the brain areas implicated in Broca's and Wernicke's aphasia are distinguishable in terms of their functional commitments to sentence processing. The relevant point in this respect is that Broca's and Wernicke's differ not only in terms of lexical access characteristics, but also in their ability to understand the subject-relative construction. Broca's patients, as already indicated, show relatively normal comprehension for this construction. But Wernicke's patients are unpredictable, more often than not showing chance comprehension (Grodzinsky, 1984; Shankweiler, personal communication, February, 1992). So, do Broca's patients show normal parsing, as Linebarger et al. (1983) would have it? Or does their slower than normal lexical access pattern disallow normal gap-filling, requiring, in consequence, an abnormal reliance on one or another nongrammatical heuristic for thematic assignment? And to consider a reverse scenario, do Wernicke's aphasics show normal gap-filling even though they often fail ultimately to achieve a normal level of comprehension for this sentence type?

Our assessment of gap-filling and the range of possibilities just outlined turned on the use of an on-line task termed cross-modal lexical priming (CMLP) (Swinney, Onifer, Prather, & Hirshkowitz, 1979). Some particulars are warranted here, both about what we mean by on-line and about the nature of the task itself.

By an on-line analysis we mean an analysis that reveals aspects of processes that operate during the course of comprehension. Such an analysis is intended to reveal something of the fixed operating characteristics of these processes, and/or the nature of their real-time interaction, and/or their dependence on processing resources such as memory capacity. And the use of reaction time measures alone does not guarantee this perspective (cf. Berndt, 1990). Several recent incorporations of reaction time measures in grammaticality judgment tasks impel us to emphasize this last point. Either these studies have served to confirm what is known from off-line tasks [e.g., Baum's (1989) demonstration that Broca's patients are relatively insensitive to violations involving gaps] or, at best, they bear only upon very general architectural features [e.g., Shankweiler et al.'s (1989) demonstration that Broca's patients, like normals, reduce their structural options as more of the input is made available]. And again, the finding that a patient notices a structural error in a deformed sentence, even if he does so quickly, does not necessarily indicate that the patient has incorporated all the lexical items into a fully specified structure. In particular, and to return to the present concern, the patient's ability to notice the absence of a gap where one should exist is not necessarily based on the ability to fill that gap with the structurally correct antecedent on-line.

Our use of a CMLP task did, however, reveal whether gaps were filled at the appropriate (normal) time. The features of the task were these: subjects listened to a sentence over earphones (delivered uninterruptedly and at a normal speaking rate) and at one point, while listening to the sentence, were required to make a lexical decision for a visually presented letter string flashed on a screen in front of them.

What we sought to discover was whether a letter-string probe forming a word related to the moved constituent (the antecedent) was primed at the gap. Such priming would indicate that the moved constituent was reactivated, or filled, at the gap (thus providing the prime). So, for each of our experimental sentences we recorded lexical decision times either for antecedent-related probes or for letter string probes that were semantically unrelated control words. For the example given earlier, *The gymnast loved the professor$_i$ from the northwestern city*^{*1} *who*^{*2} *(t)$_i$ complained about the bad coffee,* the probes were *teacher* (the probe for the antecedent, *professor*) and *address* (the control probe).

As indicated by the superscripts *1 and *2, priming was examined at two points, at the gap indexed by the trace (superscript *2) and at a pre-gap position (superscript *1). The latter served as a measure of any residual activation from the earlier appearance of the antecedent (*professor*); that is, it allowed an examination of any nonsyntactic priming effects. Of course, in each instance priming was determined by comparing the lexical decision time for the related probe to that for the unrelated probe.

The data that we gained are straightforward. The elderly normal subjects and the Wernicke's patients showed gap-filling; the Broca's patients did not. Specifically, the neurologically intact and the Wernicke's aphasic subjects showed priming (that is, relative facilitation in lexical decisions) for antecedents at gap sites but not at pre-gap sites. The Broca's patients did not show priming at either position.

The finding that Wernicke's patients show gap-filling for sentences that they have problems understanding suggests that the syntactic (parsing) operation that links a trace to its antecedent constituent is separable from the operation of thematic assignment to that constituent. Indeed, the finding that Wernicke's patients are not sensitive to the availability of argument structure entries for a verb in real time (Shapiro & Levine, 1990) strengthens this separation. These findings suggest that gap-filling is syntactically driven, not thematically driven. [See also Hickok (1991) and Fodor (1989) for the same conclusion based on studies of normal parsing.] And they suggest that left posterior cortex—the cortical region implicated in Wernicke's aphasia—is not critically involved in this syntactic process.

Left anterior cortex—the cortical region usually implicated in Broca's aphasia—does seem to be involved in the operation of gap-filling, however. Contrary to Linebarger et al.'s (1983) speculations on the matter, Broca's aphasic patients do have a parsing problem—a problem that explains structural limitations statable in the abstract terms of GB theory and that can itself by explained in a way that allows us to approach the basic resources from which the syntactic system is constructed—that is, in terms of a fairly elementary lexical access system. In this view, left anterior cortex is not the locus of syntactic representations per se, but rather seems to sustain fast-acting access systems that are, in turn, necessary for building such representations in real time.

VII. Concluding Remarks

The differences between Broca's aphasia and Wernicke's aphasia serve research as much now as they did over 100 years ago. This said, we do not claim yet to understand the significance of all of the individual features constituting the syndromes, nor to understand the significance of feature variability, nor to understand the significance of anomalous cases within the nonfluent, agrammatic Broca's group. For that matter, it is our hope that models that are currently being developed will eventually do away with the need even to grapple with the clinical signs of these aphasias—that they will allow us to form groups directly on the basis of lesion site. But for the present, however much our classification of Broca's aphasia and Wernicke's aphasia depends on a curious mix of production and comprehension factors and lesion localization considerations, the fact remains that such classification is possible and helpful for theoretical work.

Acknowledgments

The writing of the manuscript and some of the research reported in it were supported in part by NIH grants DC 00081 and AG 10496 and by AFOSR-91-0225.

References

Ansell, B., & Flowers, C. (1982). Aphasic adults' use of heuristic and structural linguistic cues for analysis. *Brain and Language, 26,* 62–72.

Badecker, W., & Caramazza, A. (1985). On considerations of method and theory governing the use of clinical categories in neurolinguistics and cognitive neuropsychology: The case against agrammatism. *Cognition, 20,* 97–126.

Badecker, W., Nathan, P., & Caramazza, A. (1991). Varieties of sentence comprehension deficits: A case study. *Cortex, 27,* 311–322.

Bates, E., Appelbaum, M., & Allard, L. (1991). Statistical constraints on the use of single cases in neuropsychological research. *Brain and Language, 40,* 295–329.

Baum, S. (1989). On-line sensitivity to local and long-distance syntactic dependencies in Broca's aphasia. *Brain and Language, 37,* 327–338.

Baynes, K., & Gazzaniga, M. (1987). In F. Plum (Ed.), *Language communication and the brain* (pp. 95–151). New York: Raven.

Berndt, R. S. (1990). Sentence processing in aphasia. In M. T. Sarno (Ed.), *Acquired aphasia.* New York: Academic Press.

Bever, T. G. (1970). The cognitive basis of linguistic structures. In J. R. Hayes (Ed.), *Cognition and the development of language.* New York: Wiley.

Blumstein, S., Milberg, W., & Shrier, R. (1982). Semantic processing in aphasia: Evidence from an auditory lexical decision task. *Brain and Language, 17,* 301–315.

Bock, K. (1991). A sketchbook of production problems. *Journal of Psycholinguistic Research (Special Issue on Sentence Processing), 20,* 141–160.

Bresnan, J. (1982). The passive in lexical theory. In J. Bresnan (Ed.), *The mental representation of grammatical relations.* Cambridge, MA: MIT Press.

Burton, S., & Grimshaw, J. (1992). Active–passive coordination and the VP–internal-subjects hypothesis. *Linguistic Inquiry, 23,* 305–313.

Caplan, D. (1983). Syntactic competence in agrammatism—a lexical hypothesis. In M. Studdert-Kennedy (Ed.), *Psychobiology of language.* Cambridge, MA: MIT Press.

Caplan, D., & Futter, C. (1986). Assignment of thematic roles by an agrammatic aphasic patient. *Brain and Language, 27,* 117–135.

Caplan, D., & Hildebrandt, N. (1988). *Disorders of syntactic comprehension.* Cambridge, MA: MIT Press.

Caramazza, A. (1986). On drawing inferences about the structure of normal cognitive systems from the analysis of impaired performance: The case for single-patient studies. *Brain and Cognition, 5,* 41–66.

Caramazza, A., & Badecker, W. (1989). Patient classification in neuropsychological research: A response. *Brain and Cognition, 10,* 256–295.

Caramazza, A., & McCloskey, M. (1988). The case for single-patient studies. *Cognitive Neuropsychology, 5,* 517–528.

Caramazza, A., & Zurif, E. B. (1976). Dissociation of algorithmic and heuristic processes in language comprehension: Evidence from aphasia. *Brain and Language, 3,* 572–582.

Chomsky, N. (1981). *Lectures on government and binding.* Dordrecht: Foris.

Cornell, T., Fromkin, V., & Mauner, G. (1989). A computational model of linguistic processing: Evidence from aphasia. *Paper presented at Academy of Aphasia,* Santa Fe, NM.

DeBleser, R. (1987). From agrammatism to paragrammatism: German aphasiological traditions and grammatical disturbances. *Cognitive Neuropsychology, 4,* 187–256.

Duhem, P. (1962). *The aim and structure of physical theory.* New York: Athenium.

Fodor, J. D. (1989). Empty categories in sentence processing. *Language and Cognitive Processes, 4,* 155–209.

Gazzaniga, M. (1989). Organization of the human brain. *Science, 245,* 947–951.

Geschwind, N. (1970). Organization of language and the brain. *Science, 170,* 940–944.

Goodenough, C., Zurif, E. B., & Weintraub, S. (1977). Aphasics' attention to grammatical morphemes. *Language and Speech, 20,* 11–19.

Goodglass, H. (1968). Studies in the grammar of aphasics. In S. Rosenberg and J. Koplin (Eds.), *Developments in applied psychological research.* New York: Macmillan.

Goodglass, H. (1976). Agrammatism. In H. Whitaker & H. A. Whitaker (Eds.), *Studies in neurolinguistics,* Vol. 1. New York: Academic Press.

Goodglass, H., & Kaplan, E. (1972). *The assessment of aphasia and related disorders.* Philadelphia: Lea and Febiger.

Grodzinsky, Y. (1984). Language deficits and linguistic theory. Unpublished doctoral dissertation, Brandeis University, Waltham, MA.

Grodzinsky, Y. (1986). Language deficits and the theory of syntax. *Brain and Language, 27,* 135–159.

Grodzinsky, Y. (1989). Agrammatic comprehension of relative clauses. *Brain and Language, 31,* 480–499.

Grodzinsky, Y. (1990). *Theoretical perspectives on language deficits.* Cambridge, MA: MIT Press.

Grodzinsky, Y. (1991). There is an entity called agrammatic aphasia. *Brain and Language, 41,* 555–564.

Grodzinsky, Y., Finkelstein, D., Nicol, J., & Zurif, E. B. (1988). Agrammatic comprehension and the thematic structure of verbs. *Paper presented at the Academy of Aphasia,* Montreal.

Grodzinsky, Y., & Pierce, A. (1987). Neurolinguistic evidence for syntactic passive. *Proceedings of the 17th annual meeting, NELS.* GLSA, University of Massachusetts, Amherst, MA.

Grodzinsky, Y., Wexler, K., Chien, Y.-C., Marakovitz, S., & Solomon, J. (1992). The breakdown of binding relations. Manuscript, Aphasia Research Center, Boston, MA.

Heilman, K., & Scholes, R. (1976). The nature of comprehension errors in Broca's, conduction, and Wernicke's aphasics. *Cortex, 12,* 258–265.

Hickok, G. (1991). Gaps and garden-paths: Studies on the architecture and computational machinery of the human sentence processor. Unpublished doctoral dissertation, Brandeis University, Waltham, MA.

Hickok, G. (1992). Agrammatic comprehension. Manuscript, MIT, Cambridge, MA.

Jackson, J. H. (1884). Evolution and dissolution of the nervous system. *Popular Science Monthy, 25,* 171–180.

Katz, W. (1986). An investigation of lexical ambiguity in Broca's aphasics using an auditory lexical priming technique. Manuscript, Brown University, Providence, RI.

Kitagawa, Y. (1986). Subjects in Japanese and English. Unpublished doctoral dissertation, University of Massachusetts, Amherst, MA.

Kolk, H., Van Grunsven, J., & Keyser, A. (1985). On parallelism between production and comprehension in agrammatism. In M. L. Kean (Ed.), *Agrammatism*. New York: Academic Press.

Koopman, H., & Sportiche, D. (1988). Subjects. Manuscript, UCLA, Los Angeles, CA.

Lecours, A.-R., Lhermitte, F., & Bryans, B. (1983). *Aphasiology*. London: Bailliere Tindall.

Lichtheim, K. (1885). On aphasia. *Brain, 7*, 433–484.

Linebarger, M., Schwartz, M., & Saffran, E. (1983). Sensitivity to grammatical structure in so-called agrammatic aphasics. *Cognition, 13*, 361–393.

Martin, R., Wetzel, W., Blossom-Stach, C., & Feher, E. (1989). Syntactic loss versus processing deficits: An assessment of two theories of agrammatism and syntactic comprehension deficits. *Cognition, 32*, 157–191.

Mauner, G., Cornell, T., & Fromkin, V. (1990). Explanatory models of agrammatism. Paper presented at the Academy of Aphasia, Montreal.

Meyer, D., Schvaneveldt, R., & Ruddy, M. (1975). Loci of contextual effects on visual word recognition. In P. Rabbit & S. Dornic (Eds.), *Attention and performance, Vol. V*. New York: Academic Press.

Miceli, G., Mazzucchi, A., Menn, L., & Goodglass, H. (1983). Contrasting cases of Italian agrammatic aphasia without comprehension disorder. *Brain and Language, 19*, 65–97.

Miceli, G., Silveri, M., Romani, C., & Caramazza, A. (1989). Variation in the pattern of omissions and substitutions of grammatical morphemes in the spontaneous speech of so-called agrammatic patients. *Brain and Language, 36*, 447–492.

Milberg, W., & Blumstein, S. (1981). Lexical decision and aphasia: Evidence for semantic processing. *Brain and Language, 14*, 371–385.

Milberg, W., Blumstein, S., & Dworetsky, B. (1987). Processing of lexical ambiguities in aphasia. *Brain and Language, 31*, 138–150.

Mohr, J. (1976). Broca's area and Broca's aphasia. In H. Whitaker and H. A. Whitaker (Eds.), *Studies in neurolinguistics, Vol. 1*. New York: Academic Press.

Nespoulous, J.-L., Dordain, M., Perron, C., Ska, B., Bub, D., Caplan, D., Mehler, J., & Lecours, A.-R. (1988). Agrammatism in sentence production without comprehension deficits: Reduced availability of syntactic structures and/or of grammatical morphemes? A case study. *Brain and Language, 33*, 273–295.

Prather, P., Shapiro, L., Zurif, E., & Swinney, D. (1991). Realtime examinations of lexical processing in aphasics. *Journal of Psycholinguistic Research (Special Issue on Sentence Processing), 20*, 271–281.

Quine, W. (1961). Two dogmas of empiricism. In W. Quine (Ed.): *From a logical point of view* (2nd Ed.). Cambridge, MA: Harvard University Press.

Safran, E., & Schwartz, M. (1988). Agrammatic comprehension it's not. *Aphasiology, 2*, 389–394.

Schwartz, M., Linebarger, M., Saffran, E., & Pate, D. (1987). Syntactic transparency and sentence interpretation in aphasia. *Language and Cognitive Processes, 2*, 85–113.

Shankweiler, D., Crain, S., Gorrell, P., & Tuller, B. (1989). Reception of language in Broca's aphasia. *Language and Cognitive Processes, 4*, 1–33.

Shapiro, L., and Levine, B. (1990). Verb processing during sentence comprehension in aphasia. *Brain and Language, 38*, 21–47.

Sproat, R. (1986). Competence, performance and agrammatism: A reply to Grodzinksy. *Brain and Language, 70*, 160–167.

Swinney, D., & Fodor, J. D. (Eds.) (1989). *Journal of Psycholinguistic Research (Special Issue on Sentence Processing), 18*(1).

Swinney, D., Onifer, W., Prather, P., & Hirshkowitz, M. (1979). Semantic facilitation across sensory modalities in the processing of individual words and sentences. *Memory and Cognition, 7*, 159–165.

Swinney, D., & Osterhout, L. (1990). Inference generation during auditory language comprehension. In A. Graesser & G. Bower (Eds.), *Inferences and text comprehension*. San Diego: Academic Pres..

Swinney, D., Zurif, E. B., & Nicol, J. (1989). The effects of focal brain damage on sentence processing: An examination of the neurological organization of a mental module. *Journal of Cognitive Neuroscience, 1,* 25–37.

Wernicke, C. (1874). The aphasia symtom complex: A psychological study on an anatomical basis. Reprinted in G. Eggert (1977). *Wernicke's works on aphasia.* The Hague: Mouton.

Wulfeck, B. (1988). Grammaticality judgments and sentence comprehension in agrammatic aphasia. *Journal of Speech and Hearing Research, 31,* 72–81.

Zurif, E. B., & Blumstein, S. (1978). Language and the brain. In M. Halle, J. Bresnan, & G. A. Miller (Eds.), *Linguistic theory and psychological reality.* Cambridge, MA. MIT Press.

Zurif, E. B., Caramazza, A., & Myerson, R. (1972). Grammatical judgments of agrammatic aphasics. *Neuropsychologia, 10,* 405–417.

Zurif, E. B., & Grodzinsky, Y. (1983). Sensitivity to grammatical structure in agrammatic aphasics: A reply. *Cognition, 15,* 207–213.

Zurif, E. B., Swinney, D., & Fodor, J. A. (1991). An evaluation of assumptions underlying the single-patient-only position in neuropsychological research. *Brain and Cognition, 16,* 198–210.

Zurif, E. B., Swinney, D., Prather, P., Solomon, J., & Bushell, C. (1993). An on-line analysis of syntactic processing in Broca's and Wernicke's aphasia. *Brain and Language, 45,* 448–464.

Chapter 33

Working Memory Constraints in Comprehension

Evidence from Individual Differences, Aphasia, and Aging

Patricia A. Carpenter, Akira Miyake, and Marcel Adam Just

I. Introduction

Working memory plays a central role in all forms of complex thinking; however, its role in language is especially evident because both producing and comprehending language require the processing of a sequence of symbols over time. The linearity of language necessitates temporarily storing the intermediate and final products of a reader's or listener's computations as she/he constructs and integrates ideas from the stream of successive words in a text or spoken discourse. In addition, working memory plays a role in transforming language out of the less sequentially organized representation of thought. Working memory can be viewed as the pool of operational resources that perform the symbolic computations and thereby generate the intermediate and final products. These resources are limited, and the limitations manifest themselves in the patterns of errors or processing times for more demanding sentences or tasks. This chapter shows that such effects are found across a variety of different subject populations. Moreover, the effects can be explained by a model of working memory constraints that includes both storage and computational resources.

This chapter has four major sections. In Section II, we review theories of the nature of working memory, summarizing the traditional view that emphasizes its nature and role in terms of passive storage. In Section III, we describe how capacity constraints in comprehension are manifested in individual differences among normal adults and briefly present a model of capacity constraints that accounts for the effects. In Section IV, we extend the account to a variety of individual differences, including comprehension by aphasic patients, the effects of aging, and individual differences in comprehension among school-age readers. In the final section, we discuss alternative mechanisms that may underlie capacity constraints and several central issues that are raised by a capacity perspective.

II. CONCEPTIONS OF WORKING MEMORY

In this section, we argue that structural concepts of memory dominate models of working memory and working memory constraints. The assumption traces back to traditional memory models, but it is also accepted in many recent models of working memory. In addition, the same structural assumption underlies many recent models of sentence parsing. However, this structural assumption is inadequate for both empirical and theoretical reasons. Empirically, traditional measures of structural capacity, namely, digit span and word span, are not highly correlated with performance in everyday tasks, like language comprehension, which we argue makes extensive use of working memory. Theoretically, the structural assumption ignores the computational aspect that is also central to language comprehension and other everyday cognitive tasks.

A. Memory Models

For the past 100 years, research on working memory (or short-term memory) has been dominated by the traditional construct of MEMORY as a structural entity in ways that are not always recognized. The role of short-term memory has traditionally emphasized storage (see Klatzky, 1980, for a summary of these models). For example, psychology textbooks often describe its role as information maintenance for retrieval after a brief interval, such as remembering a telephone number between the time when the number is looked up in a phone directory and the time when it is dialed. Another, related function attributed to short-term memory was as a stepping stone on the path to long-term memory. In either case, there was little emphasis on the transformation of information, as occurs during language comprehension or production.

Recent models have challenged many of the tenets of the traditional model (e.g., Barnard, 1985; Cowan, 1988; Monsell, 1984; Schneider & Detweiler, 1987), but strikingly, most still maintain the structural view of capacity limitations. For example, in place of a single buffer, these models espouse multiple working memories, typically independent modules that are associated with different modalities and, in some cases, with different types of representations (phonological, lexical, and so on) or types of relations (spatial, serial, syntactic). Control and coordination typically involve a central executive (Cowan, 1988) or several central executives (Monsell, 1984), and at least one proposal eschews any centralized control (Barnard, 1985). In spite of their radical departures from the notion of a unitary buffer, the proposals primarily emphasize information storage as the function of working memory.

B. Parsing Models

Even sentence parsing models, whose primary concern is comprehension rather than memory per se, tend to assume a structural buffer of a fixed size as the primary constraint on working memory and, hence, on comprehension (Abney & Johnson, 1991). The goal of parsing models is to provide a general characterization of parsing that will also explain why certain syntactic structures are difficult to understand (Wanner & Maratsos, 1978) and why readers tend to prefer one interpretation of an ambiguity over another, sometimes leading to comprehension difficulty in garden path sentences such as *The horse raced past the barn fell,* in which the initially preferred interpretation is not the ultimately correct one.

The influential parsing model of Kimball (1973) was based on the assumption that there is a limit on the number of structural elements that can be maintained during parsing or on the complexity of the final tree. The model suggested that preferences for certain interpretations reflected preferences for a simpler geometry in the developing parse tree because simple trees may be more easily retained in working memory. One specific instantiation of such a preference was a heuristic that Kimball called MINIMAL ATTACHMENT—the preference to introduce the fewest possible new nodes in attaching a new item. According to this preference, a sentence such as *We told the girl that everyone liked the story* is more likely to be interpreted as *What we told the girl was that everyone liked the story* rather than *What we told the girl that everyone liked was the story,* because the first interpretation is structurally simpler, although either interpretation is logically possible. Indeed, listeners show a preference of about 6 : 1 in favor of the minimally attached interpretation (Wanner, 1987).

Other models of parsing were proposed after Kimball's influential analysis. In most of these proposals, the constraint on working memory is assumed to be a structural limit. In this way, these proposals share the structural assumptions of traditional memory research. For instance, the constraint on the complexity of the representation is sometimes manifested by a limit on the number of ambiguities that the parser can handle at any one time (Gibson, 1990). In other accounts, the constraint is on the number of unanalyzed words that can be retained. An example of such a limitation is a LOOK AHEAD buffer, such as the three-word buffer proposed by Marcus (1980) in order to reduce the occurrence of ambiguity, although the empirical observation that many readers, if not all, attempt to interpret words immediately argues against such a fixed buffer (Just & Carpenter, 1980, 1987). A more influential parsing model than Marcus's was the SAUSAGE MACHINE proposal, which, as its name suggested, segmented the incoming stream of words into more manageable segments (Frazier & Fodor, 1978). A primary motivation for the segmentation was the assumption of a limited store to maintain words that were syntactically analyzed only locally, at a phrasal level, and not yet organized into a larger structure. In sum, these parsing proposals convincingly argued that comprehension preferences are likely to reflect working memory constraints. However, many of the proposals simply adopt the store-like conception of traditional memory models, in which capacity limits are construed as an upper bound on the number of chunks that can be retained over a brief time.

C. Working Memory Span versus Traditional Span

In contrast to an exclusive focus on structure, the computational component of working memory is highlighted by an analysis of the task requirements of natural language processing (Carpenter & Just, 1989). Computations, such as syntactic parsing, thematic role assignment, comparison, integration of information, inference, referential assignment, and logical operations, are at the heart of comprehension. Moreover, the computations provide the rationale for information storage. Information storage is needed for maintaining the partial results of the running multilevel representation of the text that are generated during comprehension, as well as maintaining a representation of the earlier text (Kintsch & van Dijk, 1978; van Dijk & Kintsch, 1983). Thus, some emphasis on the computational component of working memory, in addition to its storage component, is a natural outgrowth of considering how language comprehension is accomplished.

A more computational view of working memory is also consistent with a variety of empirical studies of the nature of traditional span measures. A large step forward occurred with Baddeley's suggestion that traditional span measures are strongly influenced by a peripheral system that he termed the ARTICU-LATORY LOOP, which is hypothesized to include a phonological buffer and a subvocal rehearsal process that is sensitive to the duration of the rehearsed material (Baddeley, 1976, 1986; Reisberg, Rappaport, & O'Shaughnessy, 1984). Such a model accounts for a variety of empirical data on the effects of factors such as phonological similarity, word length, and articulatory suppression on word and digit spans. On the other hand, various studies have documented the lack of relation between such traditional span measures and performance in more complex cognitive tasks. For example, the retention of a small number of words does not markedly interfere with some simple processing tasks (Baddeley, 1986; Baddeley & Hitch, 1974; Klapp, Marshburn, & Lester, 1983). In the analysis of aphasic processing, it has been found that a severely restricted digit or word span (2 or 3 items) does not necessarily correlate with sentence comprehension impairment (Caplan & Waters, 1990; Martin, 1987). Moreover, simple span does not correlate highly with individual differences among children in their reading performance (Perfetti & Goldman, 1976). Similarly, there is relatively little decline in traditional span tasks with age, in spite of the substantial decrements that occur in more complex tasks that involve both processing and information storage (Babcock & Salthouse, 1990). The empirical lack of relation helped to motivate the development of alternative measures of working memory capacity.

The alternative tests that were devised to assess working memory capacity had pronounced computational components, in addition to the storage component of the traditional span tests. One such test is the READING SPAN test, which requires subjects to read a set of unrelated sentences, such as (1)–(2), and then recall the final word of each sentence in a set (in this case, *anger* and *lake*) (Daneman & Carpenter, 1980).

(1) *When at last his eyes opened, there was no gleam of triumph, no shade of anger.*
(2) *The taxi turned up Michigan Avenue where they had a clear view of the lake.*

The number of sentences in a set is gradually increased, using an ascending method of limits. The reading span measure is usually the maximum number of sentences per set for which the subject can recall all the sentence-final words or the mean number recalled from a fixed number of sets. Among college students, reading spans typically vary from 2 to 5.5 words for sentences of this type and are highly correlated with analogous listening spans ($r = .80$), suggesting that similar processes are involved in both (Daneman & Carpenter, 1980). In general, the reading span is systematically lower for more complex sentences, which is consistent with the hypothesis that the comprehension of complex sentences is more demanding of working memory resources (Carpenter & Just, 1989).

The reading span and listening span measures correlate highly with many other measures of reading comprehension, such as verbal SAT (0.5 to 0.6) (Daneman & Carpenter, 1980; Masson & Miller, 1983). More generally, tests that make both processing and storage demands often reveal systematic individual differences that are not so apparent with more traditional measures. Analogous results have been found for the effect of aging, comparing young and older adults (Babcock & Salthouse, 1990), and in the analysis of individual differences among school children (Daneman & Blennerhassett, 1984; Perfetti & Goldman, 1976). Both reading and listening span tasks are also useful in differentiating reading-impaired from average high school students (when IQ is equated) (Carr, 1991). The implication is that tasks that have both computational and storage components may reveal working memory constraints more clearly than traditional span tasks.

One unresolved issue is the specificity of the working memory capacity tapped by the reading span and listening span measures. These measures show positive but low correlations with analogous working memory span tests in other domains, such as arithmetic or spatial processing (Babcock & Salthouse, 1990; Baddeley, Logie, Nimmo-Smith, & Brereton, 1985; Daneman & Tardif, 1987; Turner & Engle, 1989). Although in psychometrics, positive correlations among ability tests are typically interpreted as indicative of a general factor, the extent of overlap across different domains is unclear. In this chapter, we restrict our attention to language processing, and "working memory capacity" refers to "working memory capacity for language". In the final section, we consider whether all language processing, including comprehension and production, draws on the same or different working memory capacities.

D. Plan for the Chapter

In the following sections, we show that working memory constraints are most apparent in demanding comprehension tasks. Moreover, the time course and details of the processing effects are suggestive of the particular working memory mechanisms that may be responsible. In most of the cases we discuss, comprehension is made more demanding by varying the complexity of the sentence to be processed, for example by introducing ambiguity or syntactic complexity; in some studies, demand is manipulated by varying the text distance over which subjects must retain relevant information or by introducing an extraneous memory load; in other cases, demand is manipulated through the constraints put on the time allowed for processing.

A second dimension to our analysis is a consideration of population differences, broadly construed. In pursuing this dimension, we evaluate several population differences in terms of their profile of sentence processing under a variety of demanding conditions. Our analysis begins with individual differences among normal college-age students. In later sections, we describe sentence processing by aphasic patients with different degrees of severity in their impairments, the comprehension performance of older adults compared to younger adults, and individual differences among school-age children. In many cases, the effects of demanding tasks are strikingly similar, which suggests that a small number of mechanisms may provide a useful account of language processing constraints across a range of individuals, even though the biological mechanisms that may be responsible for the variability are likely to differ from population to population.

Before presenting the data on individual differences, it is worthwhile to acknowledge the problem that correlational data are open to alternative causal interpretations. In some cases, an analysis of these patterns suggests a causal explanation that can be experimentally examined through task variation. Nevertheless, many results to be discussed are solely correlational. In spite of the inherent limitation, correlational data provide an important window on a dimension of variation—the differences among people—that is of both practical importance and theoretical usefulness in analyzing the nature of working memory.

III. CAPACITY CONSTRAINTS IN COMPREHENSION

A central argument of this chapter is that the language comprehension shows systematic effects of working memory constraints. In this section, we first show that such capacity constraints, as measured by working memory span, account for systematic differences among a relatively homogeneous population, such as college students, in the time course and accuracy of their language processing. These differences are particularly apparent when the sentence is highly demanding, either because of its structural complexity or because of temporal constraints during processing. Then, in the second part of the section, we describe a particular model that instantiates capacity constraints on both processing and storage. In this model, called CC READER, both maintenance and computation are mediated by activation (Just & Carpenter, 1992). The capacity limitation is implemented as a constraint on the total amount of activation available to the system. The model makes quantitative predictions about the time course of working memory constraints that are consistent with the results we present next.

A. Individual Differences among Normal Adults

1. Syntactic Complexity

One of the factors that strongly influence capacity demands is the structural complexity of the sentence to be comprehended. Correspondingly, structural complexity has large effects on performance. For example, reading span is smaller when the sentences used in the reading span test are more complex (Carpenter & Just, 1989). The effects of structural complexity, however, manifest themselves in a more specific, localized manner.

One syntactic structure that is known to be difficult even for a skilled comprehender and that has attracted researchers' attention is a sentence that contains a center-embedded clause. An example is the sentence *The student that the teacher questioned passed the course,* in which the relative clause (i.e. *that the teacher questioned*) is embedded within a main clause (i.e. *the student passed the course*). In part, center-embedded sentences are capacity-demanding because the embedded clause interrupts the constituents in the main clause, and the initial noun phrase must be maintained in working memory while the comprehender is processing the embedded clause. Several studies have shown, however, that not all center-embedded sentences are equally capacity-demanding; object-relative sentences like (3) are found to be more difficult than subject-relative sentences like (4).

(3) *The reporter that the senator attacked admitted the error.*
(4) *The reporter that attacked the senator admitted the error.*

Readers spent more time reading object-relative than subject-relative sentences in a self-paced, word-by-word reading experiment (Ford, 1983). An eye fixation study (conducted in French) reported that object-relative sentences produced more regressive fixations as well as longer reading times (Holmes & O'Regan, 1981). In addition, extrinsic memory loads (a list of five names) impaired readers' comprehension and recall of the memory items more seriously on object-relative than subject-relative sentences (Wanner & Maratsos, 1978). Such differential difficulty of object-relative and subject-relative constructions appears to derive from at least two sources. First, the first noun (*reporter*) plays two different thematic roles in the main and embedded clauses, namely the thematic roles of agent and patient. Associating a single concept with two different roles simultaneously is a computationally demanding process (Bever, 1970; Sheldon, 1974). Second, the order in which thematic roles are assigned in the object-relative clause is not canonical because the agent of the relative clause is assigned after the patient, rather than in the more usual agent-first order. In general, sentences with noncanonical thematic role orders are more difficult than equivalent sentences with canonical orders (Caplan & Hildebrandt, 1988; Schwartz, Linebarger, Saffran, & Pate, 1987). Supporting this analysis, the studies cited above all showed that the performance differences between the two constructions were particularly large on or around the two verbs, the words that trigger a large number of computations (Ford, 1983; Holmes & O'Regan, 1981; Wanner & Maratsos, 1978).

Using sentences like (3) and (4), a recent study examined how working memory capacity constrains the syntactic comprehension of normal adults (King & Just, 1991). In this study, readers with different working memory spans read center-embedded sentences in a self-paced, word-by-word reading paradigm (Just, Carpenter, & Woolley, 1982). According to the capacity theory, each individual's working memory capacity will influence the relative difficulty of the sentences. Although all readers are expected to find object-relative sentences more difficult to comprehend than subject-relative sentences, readers with a lower capacity are likely to have more difficulty with object-relative sentences than those with a higher capacity, particularly in the regions where demanding computations are performed.

The results supported these predictions, as shown in Figure 1. First, all three groups of readers took more time to process object-relative sentences than subject-relative sentences. There were, however, large individual differences in

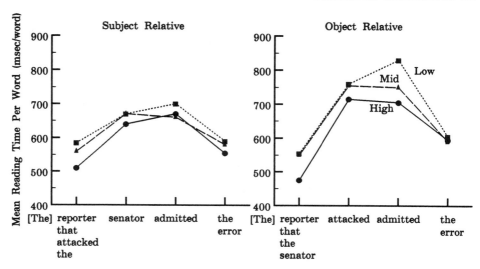

FIG. 1   Reading time per word for successive areas of subject-relative and object-relative sentences, for high span (*circles*), mid span (*triangles*), and low span (*squares*) readers. The differences among the span groups are greater for the more complex object-relative sentences than for the subject-relative sentences. In addition, the differences are greater at the verbs, which are points of processing difficulty that are expected to stress working memory capacity. The reading times for parenthesized words are not included in the plotted points. The figure is from "A capacity theory of comprehension: Individual differences in working memory" by Just and Carpenter (1992, p. 130). Copyright 1992 by American Psychological Association. Reprinted by permission.

reading times, and these differences were primarily localized to the object-relative sentences (*right panel*). The finding that the intergroup differences were larger on the more demanding object-relative sentences suggests that working memory constraints are manifested primarily when processing demands exceed capacity. Second, the word-by-word reading times localized much of the processing difficulty of object-relative clauses to the point at which the critical syntactic information becomes available. The subjects showed a selective increase in reading time at the verb of the embedded relative clause (*attacked*) and at the verb of the main clause (*admitted*). Moreover, the increase was larger for subjects with smaller spans, so the curves diverge in the right panel at the location where the processing load is at its peak. The timing of the major individual differences parallels the effects of other task complexity manipulations described earlier and suggests that working memory constraints are most evident when demands are high and resources are depleted.

2. Linguistic Ambiguity

Another facet of language that could generate demand for additional resources is linguistic ambiguity, lexical or syntactic, in the absence of a preceding context to guide interpretation. Representing and maintaining multiple possible interpretations would clearly demand additional capacity. The hypothesis that high span readers are more able to maintain multiple interpretations has been supported by two recent studies of syntactic and lexical ambiguity (MacDonald, Just, & Carpenter, 1992; Miyake, Just, & Carpenter, in press b).

The ability to maintain multiple lexical interpretations was examined by constructing sentences that contained a homograph preceded by neutral introductions (Miyake et al., in press b). The homograph was only disambiguated much later, as in (5)–(6).

(5) *Since Ken really like the boxer, he took a bus to the nearest sports arena to see the match.*

(6) *Since Ken really like the boxer, he took a bus to the nearest pet store to buy the animal.*

Note that the target homograph *boxer* can be interpreted either as a 'pugilist' (the dominant meaning) or as a 'short-haired dog' (the subordinate meaning) and that readers cannot be sure how to resolve the ambiguity until eight words later at the disambiguating phrase, *sports arena* or *pet store*. A number of previous studies have repeatedly demonstrated that both meanings of a homograph are activated immediately after its occurrence, even when the preceding context strongly favors only one interpretation (e.g., Seidenberg, Tanenhaus, Leiman, & Bienkowski, 1982; Swinney, 1979; Tanenhaus, Leiman, & Seidenberg, 1979; but see Simpson & Krueger, 1991). The question here is how different readers deal with those activated multiple meanings when, as in (5) and (6), the disambiguation comes much later in the sentence.

If low span readers have a small pool of resources, their working memory will be taxed by the demands of maintaining and elaborating multiple mental representations for an ambiguity. As a result, the subordinate interpretation is likely to be "forgotten" from working memory, because it has a lower initial activation level than the dominant interpretation in the absence of preceding contextual cues (Carpenter & Daneman, 1981, 1983; Gorfein & Bubka, 1989). Consequently, low span readers are expected to have difficulty and to show increased reading time when they encounter the subordinate resolution, as in (6), but not the dominant resolution, as in (5). The results supported these predictions. As shown in Figure 2, low span readers (*top*) spent a similar amount of time reading the ambiguous sentences and the unambiguous controls for the dominant resolution. For the subordinate resolution, however, these readers showed a large effect of ambiguity (much longer reading times for ambiguous than unambiguous sentences), particularly at the last word of the sentence. In contrast, the theory posits that high span readers, who supposedly have a larger pool of working memory resources, are more likely to maintain multiple interpretations of a homograph until the disambiguating word occurs. Consistent with this prediction, the high span readers (*bottom*) did not show reading time increases for either the dominant or subordinate resolution. Moreover, the magnitude of the ambiguity effect varied as a function of working memory capacity; as the working memory capacity of the reader increases from small to medium to large, the effects of ambiguity decrease for the subordinate resolution. Further supporting the capacity theory of lexical ambiguity resolution, a follow-up study that varied the number of words over which the ambiguity had to be maintained demonstrated that mid span readers were able to maintain multiple interpretations for a shorter distance.

The mechanisms underlying the resolution of temporary lexical ambiguity elucidated by the Miyake et al. (in press b) study may apply to the processing of syntactic ambiguity also. Using one of the most prevalent syntactic ambigu-

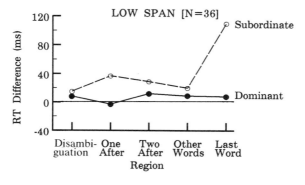

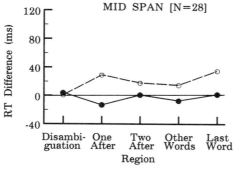

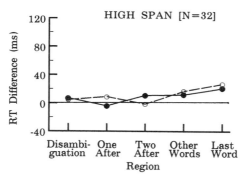

FIG. 2   The differences between the average reading time per word for the ambiguous and unambiguous sentences, for low-span, mid-span, and high-span readers, for both the dominant (*filled circles*) and subordinate (*open circles*) resolutions. The five regions of the x-axis refer to the disambiguating word and subsequent words after it. None of the three groups of readers has difficulty processing the sentences ending with the dominant resolution. For the subordinate resolution, however, the ambiguity effect decreases as a function of the reader's working memory capacity. The figure is based on data from "Working memory constraints on the resolution of lexical ambiguity: Maintaining multiple interpretations in neutral contexts" by Miyake et al. (in press b). Copyright 1994 by Academic Press. Reprinted by permission.

ities in English, MacDonald et al. (1992) demonstrated that working memory plays a role in the maintenance of multiple syntactic interpretations. In their study, high span and low span subjects read the following types of sentences, again in a self-paced, word-by-word paradigm.

(7) *The experienced soldiers warned about the dangers before the midnight raid.*

(8) *The experienced soldiers warned about the dangers conducted the midnight raid.*

Note that the two sentences are temporarily ambiguous because the first verb, *warned,* can be interpreted either as a main verb, as in (7), or as a past participle in a reduced relative construction, as in (8).

The capacity theory assumes that multiple syntactic representations are initially constructed by all comprehenders on first encountering the ambiguity (Gorrell, 1987; Kurtzman, 1985). As is the case with lexical ambiguity resolution, it proposes that the comprehender's working memory capacity influences the amount of intervening text over which she/he can maintain multiple syntactic representations. Consistent with this view, the results indicated that low span readers, who had less than sufficient capacity to maintain the two interpretations, abandoned the less preferred interpretation (in this case, the reduced relative interpretation) and showed great difficulty if the disambiguation turned out to be consistent with it. By contrast, the reading time and error profile for high span readers supported the hypothesis that they were able to maintain the subordinate interpretation over a longer distance, but only at the expense of postponing higher level processing (MacDonald et al., 1992).

3. Text Processing and Text Distance

Our focus so far has been on the role of working memory in the comprehension of single sentences. However, the comprehension of text presents an additional opportunity to examine the effects of working memory constraints. One problem to be faced is how to accommodate the numerous demands of an extended text. Because a text can contain an indefinitely large number of sentences whose storage could eventually consume any finite capacity, there must be countervailing mechanisms that reduce the storage demands. One mechanism is forgetting or purging certain types of information, such as lexical and syntactic representations, after the end of a sentence (Huey, 1908; Jarvella, 1971, 1979; Potter & Lombardi, 1990; Sachs, 1967). Other mechanisms selectively retain representations of only the most recent and most central clauses of the preceding text (Glanzer, Fischer, & Dorfman, 1984; Kintsch & van Dijk, 1978; van Dijk & Kintsch, 1983) and/or the most relevant aspects of world knowledge (Kintsch, 1988). Storage demands are also minimized through the immediacy of processing, the tendency to semantically interpret each new word or phrase as far as possible when the word is first encountered, in contrast to a wait-and-see strategy that imposes additional storage demands (Carpenter & Just, 1983; Just & Carpenter, 1980). In spite of this economy, texts still do present considerable demands, and readers must cope with these demands while constructing a representation of the text as well as a representation of the situations and events being described (Bransford & Johnson, 1973; Johnson-Laird, 1983; Just & Carpenter, 1987; Kintsch & van Dijk, 1978). Maintaining the appropriate information, particularly over longer distances, while processing the text is the kind of demanding task that reveals individual differences.

In several studies, readers with larger working memory spans were better at interconstituent or intersentential integration, presumably because they were able to maintain more information in an activated state. One study found a strong relation between a subject's reading span and the text distance over which she/he could find an antecedent for a pronoun (Daneman & Carpenter, 1980). The experiment manipulated the number of sentences that intervened between the last mention of the referent and the pronoun. Readers with larger reading spans were more accurate at answering comprehension questions that asked the identity of the pronoun. More precisely, the maximal distance across

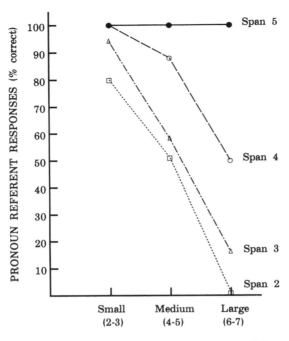

FIG. 3 The proportion of correct interpretations of a pronoun as a function of its distance from the preceding anaphoric reference for readers with different reading span scores. Readers with highest span have no difficulty interpreting a pronoun, even if its referent occurred six or seven sentences before. By contrast, readers with the lowest reading span are only moderately successful if the referent occurred more than three sentences earlier. The figure is adapted from "Individual differences in working memory and reading" by Daneman and Carpenter (1980, p. 456). Copyright 1980 by Academic Press. Reprinted by permission.

which readers could correctly interpret the pronoun was highly correlated with their reading spans, as Figure 3 indicates. When only a few words intervened between the target pronoun and its antecedent, all readers performed well. Large individual differences emerged, however, when six or seven sentences separated the two referential elements. Readers with a reading span of 5 were still able to identify the correct antecedent with 100% accuracy, but the performance of readers with a span of 2 went down to 0%.

Text comprehension, more than isolated sentence comprehension, may also reveal ways in which readers can accommodate to resource limitations that are extended over time. Such accommodation was found in a study of how high and low span college readers differentially coped with a demanding passage (Whitney, Ritchie, & Clark, 1991). These passages were written with vaguely specified referents and actions (e.g., *things, do*) so that the overall topic and the specific events and referents could not be inferred easily (such as the "washing clothes" passage developed by Bransford & Johnson, 1973). The readers provided thinking-out-loud protocols of their emerging interpretations as they read the passage (see Olson, Duffy, & Mack, 1984). Low span readers produced significantly more elaborations of individual sentences than high span readers, and their elaborations were relatively evenly distributed throughout the passage. But low span readers faced a trade-off between constructing a globally coherent passage representation and maintaining local sentence-to-sentence coherence. Some low span readers, therefore, committed themselves to a particular (usually wrong) interpretation early in the passage and forced the remaining text to fit into it; others focused on sentence-to-sentence connections and frequently changed their global interpretations as they read, without being able to figure out what the entire passage was about. By contrast, high span readers produced more elaborations toward the end of the passage, maintaining more cues and delaying their commitment to a final interpretation. As was the case with MacDonald et al.'s (1992) syntactic ambiguity and Miyake et al.'s (in press b) lexical ambiguity studies, high span readers were able to entertain multiple interpretations for a longer time, even throughout a longish text.

In sum, the effects of text distance provide evidence of working memory limitations. Computations over longer distances are particularly difficult for individuals with lower working memory capacities. In addition, the larger capacity of high span readers permits them to avoid the premature commitment to a specific interpretation that some low span readers make to cope with their capacity limitations in processing lengthy texts.

4. Extrinsic Memory Load

The availability of working memory resources has often been manipulated through the introduction of an extrinsic memory load, such as a series of words or digits that are to be retained during comprehension. The presence of interference suggests shared resources. However, the amount of interference depends on the task. If the task is primarily retrieval from memory, loads of four or five digits increase a base response time of 1.5 s by about 200 ms (Baddeley, 1986; Baddeley, Eldridge, Lewis, & Thomson, 1984), and the interference may primarily arise from the rehearsal processes (Klapp et al., 1983). By contrast, if the task makes larger computational demands, the effects of an extrinsic load are much larger. An extrinsic load of six digits increases the time to verify an active sentence by about 600 ms (approximately 25%), whereas it increases the time for passive, negative sentences by almost 2.5 s (approximately 70%) (Baddeley, 1976; Baddeley & Hitch, 1974; see also Wanner & Maratsos, 1978). The intereference under demanding conditions suggests that in those cases, resources are already consumed by comprehension and, consequently, cannot be expended to initiate or control rehearsal.

Interference from even a small extrinsic load was observed for some subjects, in the syntactic complexity experiment described earlier involving sentences with subject-relative and object-relative clauses (King & Just, 1991). When the subjects were required to retain one or two unrelated words while reading the sentence, their ability to answer a subsequent comprehension question was lower than in a condition in which there was no extrinsic load. In addition, the effect of the load was particularly apparent for the high span readers who, in the absence of a load, had sufficient capacity to comprehend the object-relative sentences with high accuracy. By contrast, low span readers were less affected by the load, primarily because even without an additional extrinsic load, half the low span readers had comprehension accuracy rates that were indistinguishable from chance. In sum, an extrinsic load depletes resources in a way that mimics the natural variation that occurs among individuals with different working memory capacities.

5. Time Constraints

Yet another factor that leads to systematic individual differences in comprehension accuracy involves temporal restrictions on processing, produced by a rapid presentation of the text or speech. Several studies, using compressed speech (e.g., Chodorow, 1979) or the rapid serial visual presentation (RSVP) technique (e.g., Forster, 1970; Juola, Ward, & McNamara, 1982; Potter, 1984), have demonstrated that comprehenders have difficulty processing structurally complex sentences under such capacity-demanding situations. In general, very fast input rates may prevent the successful completion of some analyses that are critical to the comprehension tasks.

One RSVP study compared readers' immediate memory of sentences with a center embedded clause (e.g., *The lawyer she wants is busy elsewhere*) with that of sentences of the same length without any embeddings (e.g., *The wealthy child attended a private school*) (Forster & Ryder, 1971). The words of a sentence were presented one at a time, centered on a screen, at the rate of 62.5 ms per word. Recall was better for one-clause sentences than for the center-embedded sentences. Specifically, the embedded relative clause was recalled less well for the two-clause sentences; the words from the main clause were remembered as well as the words from a single-clause sentence. These results suggest that the difficulty of determining the syntactic structure of the embedded clause and assigning the correct case roles to the relevant nouns within such severe time constraints prevented readers from perceiving and storing the words from the embedded clause as well as they would otherwise have.

A more recent RSVP study in our lab examined the ability of readers with different working memory capacities to comprehend sentences of different structural complexity at two different presentation rates (Miyake, Carpenter, & Just, in press a). The results (which are to be reported more fully in the section on aphasic language comprehension) indicated that both the time constraints imposed by the rapid presentation and the capacity demands imposed by structural complexity had particularly detrimental effects on low span readers relative to high span readers. The data are consistent with the hypothesis that low span readers have less working memory capacity and so are more vulnerable to both structural complexity and temporal demands on processing.

6. Summary of Results

In this section, we have reviewed recent studies that reported systematic individual differences in reading, in terms of each of the four factors associated with processing demands and constraints. Comprehension speed and accuracy generally decline with an intrinsic memory load (such as syntactic complexity or ambiguity), text distance, an extrinsic load (such as unrelated memory items), or temporal restrictions induced by rapid presentation rates. Moreover, these conditions tend to show larger performance decrements for individuals with smaller working memory spans.

Interestingly, these four factors have analogous effects on the comprehension performance of people other than college students. As we review in later sections, parallel effects are found among aphasic patients with different degrees of severity, adults of different ages, and children with different levels of reading skill. Table I summarizes the analogous findings obtained with these different populations by citing representative studies for each of the four capacity-demanding factors. Before discussing the parallel findings in these three populations, however, we first describe a computer simulation model that provides a coherent account of processing mechanisms behind the individual differences in language comprehension among normal college-age adults. This model offers mechanisms that may also account for the other categories of individual differences.

B. The Model: CC READER

Central to the current account is the idea that a common resource, namely activation, mediates both information maintenance and computation, and that working memory constraints exist in the amount of activation available or its allocation between storage and computation. The account is instantiated in a simulation model called CC READER; its initials refer to Capacity Constrained, and its patronym reflects its relation to an earlier CAPS/READER model of reading comprehension (Just & Carpenter, 1987; Thibadeau, Just, & Carpenter, 1982).

TABLE I

Representative Studies That Indicate Working Memory Capacity Constraints in Language Comprehension

Population	Complexity/ ambiguity	Text distance	Extrinsic memory load	Temporal restrictions
Adult/college students	King and Just (1991) MacDonald et al. (1992) Miyake et al. (in press b)	Daneman and Carpenter (1980)	King and Just (1991)	Miyake et al. (in press a)
Aphasics	Caplan et al. (1985) Naeser et al. (1987)			Blumstein et al. (1985)
Elderly adults	Emery (1985) Kemper (1986) Obler et al. (1991)	Light and Capps (1986)	Gick et al. (1988) Tun et al. (1991)	Stine et al. (1986) Stine and Wingfield (1987)
School-age children	Macaruso et al. (1989) Smith et al. (1989)	Yuill et al. (1989)		

CC READER, like the original READER model, is an ACTIVATION-BASED production system. It parses a limited number of sentence constructions from left to right, constructing a syntactic and semantic representation as fully as possible as it goes (Carpenter & Just, 1983; Just & Carpenter, 1980). The number of processing cycles that CC READER expends on the successive words of the sentence correlates with the time human readers spend reading those words. As is the case with conventional production systems, the procedural knowledge in CC READER consists of a set of units called productions, each of which is a condition–action contingency that specifies what symbolic manipulation should be made when a given information condition arises in working memory. For example, a typical condition is that "if the current word is a determiner (e.g., *the*)," then the action is to "expect that one is processing a noun phrase." The execution of the manipulation can change the contents of working memory, thereby enabling another production to operate (i.e., fire). CC READER, however, deviates in many important ways from conventional production systems by incorporating mechanisms that are common to activation-based parallel connectionist models (Cottrell, 1989; St. John & McClelland, 1990; Waltz & Pollack, 1985).

First, each element, which can represent a word, phrase, grammatical structure, or thematic structure, has an associated activation level, such that the element can have varying degrees of activation. The condition part of a production, thus, specifies not just the presence of an element but also the minimum activation level, the threshold, at which the element satisfies the condition. If the activation level of an element is above its threshold, it is part of the working memory and, consequently, is available to initiate other computational processes. Second, productions change the activation level of an element by propagating activation from a source element to that output element. Third, productions can fire reiteratively over successive cycles so that the activation levels of the output elements become gradually incremented until they reach some threshold. In other words, the symbolic manipulation occurs as a repeated action with cumulative effects. Finally, CC READER allows multiple productions to fire in parallel on a given cycle, as long as their conditions are met. The processor, hence, can work on different levels of language comprehension (such as syntactic, semantic, and referential) simultaneously and generate new partial computational products from different levels at the same time. Hence, processing is done in a single pass (Wanner, 1987), rather than in two passes as in parsers that have a first-pass syntactic analysis followed by a second-pass semantic and pragmatic analysis (Berwick & Weinberg, 1984; Frazier & Fodor, 1978; McRoy & Hirst, 1990).

Within this framework, activation underlies all the activities that take place in working memory. For example, consider the processing of a center-embedded sentence, such as (9).

(9) *The reporter that the senator attacked admitted the error.*

To comprehend the relative clause of this sentence, the reader must first retain the noun *reporter* in working memory until the occurrence of the verb *attacked* and then assign the correct thematic role to that noun. In CC READER, maintaining the element *reporter* in working memory means keeping its activation level above a threshold. Similarly, the assignment of a thematic role to a noun (in this case, the assignment of the patient role to *reporter*) involves propagating activation to a new element (i.e., a proposition that *reporter* plays the patient role) and incrementing its activation level above the threshold. Thus, the storage and computations that constitute comprehension are expressed in terms of the maintenance and manipulation of activation.

The constraint on capacity is operationally defined as the maximum amount of activation that the system has available conjointly for maintenance and processing purposes. The capacity limitation is realized under an allocation scheme that has the potential to trade off between maintenance and processing. Briefly stated, CC READER keeps the total activation within a maximum bound. If, on a given cycle, the activation propagation of production firings would exceed the activation maximum, then CC READER deallocates the activation being used for the maintenance and processing functions. One such allocation scheme limits both functions proportionately, akin to an across-the-board cut. This scaling back of activation has important consequences for both the time course and the content of language processing. First, the deallocation of the activation to computation can slow down processing by increasing the number of cycles required for an element to reach the threshold. Second, the deallocation of activation to the maintenance of earlier elements induces forgetting because the activation levels of some of the elements are continuously decremented with each new cycle of processing that exceeds the activation quota. An allocation parameter determines the relative extent to which computation or information maintenance suffers when the activation quota is about to be exceeded. Theoretically, the allocation scheme could permit a trading relation between speed and accuracy of processing, where accuracy refers to maintaining and later using partial products appropriately. More generally, the allocation scheme elicited by tasks with different characteristics is an important research issue that is highlighted by the model (see Haarmann & Kolk, in press, for a related discussion).

The CC READER model succeeded in simulating reasonably well the processing time profile of readers in the King and Just (1991) study described earlier. Figure 4 shows the word-by-word profile of the number of processing cycles that CC READER takes to process such sentences. Like college readers, CC READER spent relatively more cycles on the verbs of the object-relative sentence than in the other regions, because more computations were needed on the verbs to allow different constituents in the sentence (such as subjects and direct objects) to coalesce. Individual differences in working memory capacity (high span vs. low span readers) were implemented by varying the maximum amount of activation available to the system. An important result is that the number of the cycles the model needed in order to process the two verbs was larger when the activation maximum was set low (to simulate low span readers) than when it was set high (to simulate high span readers). The high–low capacity difference emerged in the simulation because when the available quota was small, the activation pool had been somewhat depleted by the time the model encountered the two verbs *attacked* and *admitted*. Hence, the system deallocated activation and slowed down the processing. As a consequence, the model ended up spending more cycles on the two demanding verbs when the activation maximum was low than when it was high. Additional points of similarity to the human data are that the model spent more cycles on the main verb and on the

SIMULATION

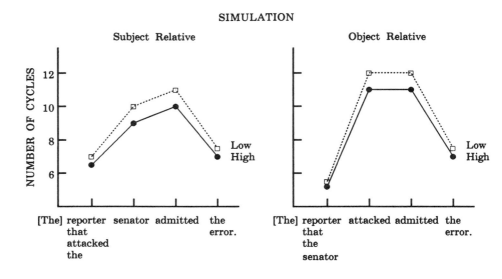

HUMAN DATA

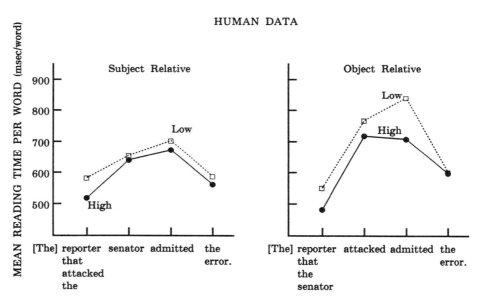

FIG. 4   The number of cycles expended on various parts of subject-relative and object-relative sentences when the simulation, CC READER, is operating with a higher or lower activation quota, to simulate the human data for the high span and low span readers (repeated from Fig. 1 in the bottom graphs). The figure is reprinted from "A capacity theory of comprehension: Individual differences in working memory" by Just and Carpenter (1992, p. 140). Copyright 1992 by American Psychological Association. Reprinted by permission.

last word of the subordinate clause than on other parts of the sentence, and that the model took longer on object-relative than on subject-relative sentences.

In addition to accounting for these data, the simulation model provides a detailed account of the quantitative results of the effect of complexity and individual differences in a variety of studies (Just & Carpenter, 1992). In summary, the performance of CC READER can be explained in terms of the resource demands that arise during the course of language comprehension and the consequences of the demands not being met due to the capacity constraints.

IV. CAPACITY CONSTRAINTS IN OTHER POPULATIONS

This section extends the theory to suggest that a slowing down of processing and a loss of old elements from working memory may account for the breakdown of syntactic comprehension in aphasic patients, for the localized effects of aging on comprehension, and for individual differences in some aspects of comprehension among school children.

A. Capacity Effects in Aphasic Comprehension

The capacity theory of language comprehension has implications for the disorders of syntactic comprehension in aphasic patients. Syntactic comprehension is often a source of processing difficulty in aphasic patients, a point frequently documented ever since a seminal study on Broca's aphasics found that they were unable to use syntax, without semantic or pragmatic cues, to successfully comprehend complex center-embedded sentences such as *The boy that the girl is hitting is tall* (Caramazza & Zurif, 1976). A plurality of the theories proposed so far to account for the mechanism underlying such deficits assumes, in one form or another, a loss of either structural (syntactic) or procedural knowledge that is critical to perform complete syntactic analyses (e.g., Berndt & Caramazza, 1980; Bradley, Garrett, & Zurif, 1980; Caplan, 1985; Grodzinsky, 1986; Kean, 1977; Linebarger, Schwartz, & Saffran, 1983). The working memory capacity approach, however, can offer an alternative view of syntactic comprehension deficits without assuming any loss of specific pieces of knowledge crucial for syntactic analysis (Miyake et al., in press a; also Frazier & Friederici, 1991; Friederici, 1988; Gigley, 1983; Haarmann & Kolk, 1991a; Kolk & van Grunsven, 1985).

According to the theory, the disorders of syntactic comprehension originate, at least in part, from reductions in patients' working memory resources. Stated from the perspective of the CC READER model, the theory assumes that, while the lexicon and the production rules in the system are still intact, the maximum amount of activation available for the storage and processing of linguistic information is far more severely limited in the aphasic system than in the normal system. Due to this emphasis on the quantitative rather than qualitative differences between aphasic patients and normal adults, all the basic principles and mechanisms of the CC READER model still hold in the aphasic system. Thus, when the activation quota is about to be exceeded, the same activation allocation scheme as the normal system takes effect to deal with the various resource demands. The theory proposes that the two major consequences of the triggering of this scheme, namely loss of old elements from working memory and processing slowdown, conjointly make aphasic patients' syntactic comprehension highly error-prone.

Within the CC READER framework, when the system cannot meet the newly imposed processing demands a deallocation of the activation currently used to sustain the activation levels of old elements takes place. The more often the system has to accommodate the over-budget demands for resources, the larger the decrement for the activation levels. Such gradual "forgetting" of old elements affects patients' syntactic comprehension performance in two related but conceptually separable ways. First, when the activation used for maintenance purposes is repeatedly decremented, the activation levels of some of the oldest elements might be rendered lower than a predetermined threshold value. This implies that some representations constructed earlier may be lost from working memory and hence will not be available for further processes. Within the framework of the CC READER model, this type of comprehension failure manifests itself as the failure of some critical production(s) to fire at some appropriate time(s). Second, even if a certain production rule successfully fired at an appropriate time, the computational product of the production firing might be lost from working memory by the time the end of the sentence has been reached.

Another consequence of the triggering of the activation allocation scheme is a slowing down of computational processes. When the system cannot meet the processing demands, a scaling back of the activation being currently propagated takes place and increases the number of cycles that the new element needs in order to reach the threshold. The larger the difference between the current demands and the available quota, the more cycles must be spent to bring the activation level of that element above threshold. According to the current theory, this mechanism is highly responsible for auditory syntactic comprehension failures in aphasic patients.

Despite the fact that the auditory mode is typically used to test patients' language comprehension abilities, auditory comprehension tends to impose more computational demands on patients than reading comprehension, because the former must generally operate under much stronger temporal restrictions than the latter. Unlike a reader, a listener cannot spend as much time as she/he wants on a given word or phrase, nor can they go back to reprocess any previous parts of the text. This means that a listener does not have any control over the presentation rate to match the internal processing rate. If their processing is so slow that not all the necessary computations are completed within certain time limits, a comprehension error is likely. A particularly crucial computation, given the type of sentences that are frequently used to test patients, is case-role assignment, determining which noun phrase plays the agent role or patient role, and so on. By making the time constraints in auditory comprehension still more severe, a slowing down of parsing processes can have severe consequences for syntactic comprehension by aphasic patients.

This aspect of the theory is supported by the frequent observation that a slower speech rate often improves patients' auditory comprehension. First, a significant proportion of complaints made by aphasic patients about their everyday lives concerns their perception that other people talk "too fast" (Skelly, 1975). This difficulty underlies the remarks of aphasic patients, such as "That goes in, and before I figure it out, it's gone" and "You speak in books, and I can only understand in pages," which suggest that some patients are unable to keep up with the pace of natural speech (Rosenbek, LaPointe, & Wertz, 1989, p. 154). In addition, several studies have demonstrated that slower speech or longer pauses facilitate syntactic and discourse comprehension in aphasic patients (e.g., Blumstein, Katz, Goodglass, Shrier, & Dworetsky, 1985; Lasky, Weider, & Johnson, 1976; Nicholas & Brookshire, 1986; Pashek & Brookshire, 1982). For example, longish silent pauses between constituent boundaries (e.g., *The boy* [1 s] *who hit* [500 ms] *the girl* [1 s] *chased* [500 ms] *the dog*) were found to be especially helpful to those aphasic patients who had difficulty comprehending such speech at normal rates (180 words per minute) (Blumstein et al., 1985). This result is consistent with the current theory because heavy computational demands seem to arise usually at the end of major constituent phrases (refer to the reading time data from the King and Just, 1991, study in Fig. 1). Relatively long pauses at such places might provide patients with the opportunity to perform all the necessary computations that would not otherwise be completed within the normal time limits.

More general support for the view that reductions in working memory resources are implicated in the disorders of syntactic comprehension comes from the observation that the severity of the deficits interacts with the structural complexity of the stimulus sentences (Haarmann & Kolk, 1991a). Aphasic patients can usually comprehend simple sentences without much difficulty, suggesting that they have enough working memory resources available to sustain the processing and storage activities. If, however, the sentence requires more processing/storage capacity than they can afford, their performance starts to deteriorate rapidly.

One of the most striking demonstrations of the interaction of severity and structural complexity comes from a clinically oriented group study (Naeser et al., 1987). The study investigated the auditory syntactic comprehension abilities of 60 aphasic patients, who were assessed as belonging to different clinical syndromes and having differential degrees of severity, based on the results from the Boston Diagnostic Aphasia Examination (BDAE). The patients were given a sentence–picture matching task called the Palo Alto Syntax Test (PAST), which was created to test the patients' ability to discriminate ten different syntactic contrasts (such as negative/affirmative, plural/singular). For example, one of the stimulus sentences for the subject/object reversible pairs was *The boy is following the dog.* The patients' task was to choose a picture that correctly depicted the event or state described in the sentence from among four alternatives. The alternatives include (1) the correct picture (a boy following a dog), (2) a syntactic foil (a dog following a boy), (3) and (4) two lexical foils (a picture of a girl following a dog and a picture of a dog following a cat). Figure 5 presents the comprehension accuracy data, that is, the proportion of the trials in which the correct picture was chosen, from the Naeser et al. study, excluding the two most severe groups (who performed poorly on even the simplest syntactic contrasts). In the graph, data points are represented by a letter designating the first word of the syndrome name. The ten syntactic contrasts are ordered along the *x*-axis in terms of increasing difficulty, based on the mean comprehension scores from the 60 patients. The straight lines drawn in the figure are the linear regression lines calculated for each syndrome group, treating the difficulty ordering of the ten syntactic contrasts as if it were a ratio scale (i.e., M/F as 1, O/U as 2, etc.). Although this application of regression equations to the Naeser et al. data is unjustified from a statistical point of view, the regression lines provide a useful index of the general effect of syntactic complexity on comprehension for different syndrome groups at different severity levels.

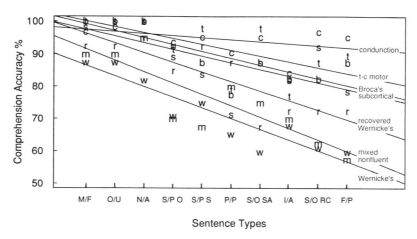

FIG. 5 Comprehension performance of seven clinical syndrome groups of aphasic patients with different degrees of severity for ten different syntactic contrasts. The ten contrasts are: Male/ Female (M/F), On/Under (O/U), Negative/Affirmative (N/A), Singular/Plural Object (S/P O), Singular/Plural Subject (S/P S), Past/Present Progressive Tense (P/P), Subject/Object in Simple Active Sentences (S/O SA), Is/Are (I/A), Subject/Object Relative Clause (S/O RC), and Future/ Present Progressive Tense (F/P). The straight lines are the best fitting linear regressions, which treat the difficulty ordering of syntactic contrasts as though it were a ratio scale. The diverging lines suggest that more difficult contrasts require more resources. Although all groups are able to discriminate the easiest syntactic contrast, the groups with more severe deficits have numerous errors as the difficulty level of the syntactic contrast increases. The graph is based on data reported in "Auditory syntactic comprehension in nine aphasia groups (with CT scans) and children: Differences in degree but not order of difficulty observed" by Naeser et al. (1987, Table III, p. 368).

First, the results suggest that patients found some syntactic contrasts more difficult than others. The Spearman rank-order correlations for the order of difficulty were high among the seven aphasia subgroups, suggesting that a syntactic contrast that was difficult for one group was also difficult for other groups of patients. Second, the nine clinical syndrome groups differed from each other in their overall comprehension accuracy. The patient's overall degree of severity (as assessed by the BDAE) was a highly reliable predictor of her/ his performance on the specific test of auditory comprehension. A correlation as high as +.91 was obtained with the BDAE auditory comprehension sub-score[1] and +.88 with the Token Test score.[2] Note, however, that the effects of complexity and severity are not simply additive, as shown by the seven regression lines which gradually diverge as the difficulty level of the syntactic

---

[1] In BDAE, auditory comprehension is examined by four subtests: (a) word recognition, (b) body part identification, (c) comprehension of simple commands, and (d) comprehension of complex ideational material requiring yes–no responding. Note that none of these subtests directly assesses the patient's syntactic comprehension capabilities.

[2] The major purpose of this frequently used test is to assess auditory comprehension of commands of increasing complexity. The patients' task is to manipulate tokens, according to the commands such as *Take the white square and the green circle* and *Put the red circle between the yellow square and the green square.*

contrasts increases. While all the groups performed well on the easiest syntactic contrasts, they exhibited large group differences for the most difficult ones. This severity by complexity interaction suggests that some patients still had sufficient working memory resources to comprehend the most challenging contrasts on the PAST, whereas others had a minimal amount of resources that enabled them to comprehend only the simplest ones.

A similar interaction between degrees of severity and structural complexity was obtained in a series of group studies conducted by Caplan and his colleagues (Caplan, Baker, & Dehaut, 1985; see also Caplan & Hildebrandt, 1988). They tested a large number of aphasic patients on their ability to comprehend nine different syntactic constructions. Table II lists these nine, along with two other constructions. In additon to sentence length, several factors may underlie complexity, as pointed out by Caplan et al. and other researchers who have investi-

TABLE II

Factors That Contribute to the Difficulty of Sentences Used in the Caplan et al. (1985) and Miyake et al. (in press a) Studies

	Contributing factor[a]				
Sentence type	(a) Three roles	(b) Two verbs	(c) Order canonical	(d) Retain noun	(e) Different roles
Active (A): *The rat hit the dog.*					
Cleft subject (CS): *It was the rat that hit the dog.*					
Passive (P): *The rat was hit by the dog.*			X		
Dative (D): *The rat gave the dog to the cow.*	X				
Cleft object (CO): *It was the rat that the dog hit.*			X		
Right-branching subject relative (RBS): *The rat hit the dog that hugged the cow.*		X			X
Conjoined (C): *The rat hit the dog and hugged the cow.*		X		X	
Dative passive (DP): *The rat was given to the dog by the cow.*	X		X		
Center-embedded subject relative (CES):[b] *The rat that hit the dog hugged the cow.*		X		X	
Right-branching object relative (RBO):[b] *The rat hit the dog that the cow hugged.*		X	X		
Center-embedded object relative (CEO): *The rat that the dog hit hugged the cow.*		X	X	X	X

[a] Contributing factors: (a) Three vs. two thematic roles; (b) Two vs. one verb; (c) Noncanonical vs. canonical order of thematic roles; (d) Need vs. no need to retrieve the first noun in a subsequent clause; (e) One constituent has the same vs. different thematic roles.
[b] These sentence types were used only in the Miyake et al. (in press a) study.

gated some of these sentences (see the discussion in Section III,A,1). These factors include: (a) the number of thematic roles (two or three) associated with a single verb; (b) the number of verbs (one or two) or, as a correlated factor, the number of pairs of thematic roles (the agent role and the patient role) within the sentence; (c) whether or not the order of thematic roles is canonical (the agent role precedes other roles); (d) the need to retain the first noun phrase while another set of thematic roles is computed; and (e) whether the noun plays the same thematic role in two clauses. Sentences with more of these factors are more structurally complex than those with fewer factors.

Performance is highly influenced by the factors that contribute to structural complexity. Caplan et al. used an object manipulation task, in which patients acted out the event described in the sentence, using animal dolls, to indicate the actions and roles of the participants. For example, to act out a sentence like *The elephant kicked the monkey*, the patient would have to pick up the elephant from among a group of animal dolls and touch the monkey. In spite of the differences in task and sentence construction, the data from Caplan et al.'s study showed the same basic pattern that was found by Naeser et al. The comprehension performance of the aphasic patients was highly influenced by the structural complexity of different sentence types. Figure 6 summarizes the

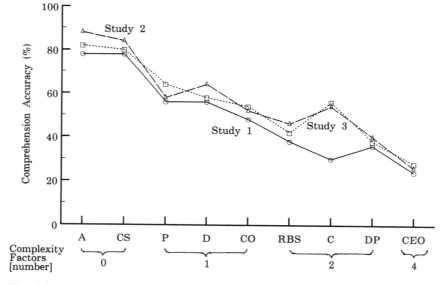

FIG. 6 Mean comprehension performance on nine sentence types in three studies of aphasic patients. The nine sentence types are: Active (A), Cleft subject (CS), Passive (P), Dative (D), Cleft object (CO), Right-branching subject relative (RBS), Conjoined (C), Dative Passive (DP), and Center-embedded object relative (CEO) sentences. The three studies reveal almost the same ordering of difficulty for the nine sentence types, an ordering that is consistent with the complexity metric in Table II. The same ordering also emerges when the sentences are presented rapidly to normal college students, as shown in Figure 7. The graph is based on data reported in *Disorders of syntactic comprehension* by Caplan and Hildebrandt (1988, Table 4.19, p. 122).

effects of structural complexity in terms of the mean comprehension accuracy obtained in each of three studies involving 56, 37, and 49 aphasic patients, respectively. Replicating each other's results, the three studies yielded almost the same ordering of difficulty for the nine sentence structures.

As the graph suggests, complexity had substantial influences on average comprehension performance; overall, the mean decreases as the number of complexity factors increases. Caplan et al. performed cluster analyses and statistically classified patients into subgroups according to how well the patient comprehended each of the nine sentence constructions. Supporting the resource reduction view of syntactic comprehension disorders, the results from subsequent principal component analyses revealed that the most important determinant of the group classification was the patient's overall performance in the task. This factor, which Caplan et al. interpreted as the "success" or "severity" factor, accounted for approximately 60% of the variance in each of the three studies. The analysis showed that whereas most subgroups comprehended the simplest sentences (almost) perfectly, there was large variability in their comprehension accuracy for the most difficult ones. One explanation of the data is that more complex constructions require more resources; hence, it may primarily be a reduction in working memory resources, rather than the loss of a specific piece of syntactic knowledge, that underlies the larger variance with the more structurally complex constructions. Whereas capacity limitations certainly do not account for all the performance deficits in aphasia, these types of data suggest that such general deficits should be evaluated before concluding that a deficit is due to the loss of some specific piece of syntactic knowledge.

This conclusion is further supported by a recent study that attempted to simulate aphasic patients' performance among normal college-age adults who supposedly possess intact structural and procedural knowledge necessary for parsing (Miyake et al., in press a). According to the capacity theory, one important consequence of capacity limitation is a slowing down of comprehension processes. Under severe time restrictions (as in auditory comprehension), patients cannot fully process linguistic inputs and fail to comprehend the sentence accurately, even though they might have the knowledge necessary to perform syntactic analyses. If this is the case, normal adults should perform more like aphasic patients, when severe time constraints are imposed by rapidly presenting stimulus sentences and thereby limiting the amount of time they can spend processing each word.

Using the rapid serial visual presentation (RSVP) paradigm, Miyake et al. (in press a) presented 11 different types of sentences, including 9 which were used in the Caplan et al. study, to normal college-age subjects with different working memory spans. Sentences were presented at the center of a computer screen, one word at a time, at two rapid rates, either 200 ms per word (called "slow") or 120 ms per word (called "fast"). This speed of presentation manipulation and the working memory span of the subject are expected to conjointly constrain processing in a way that might approximate the severity dimension of aphasic patients' comprehension. Subjects were asked to answer a true/false question after the presentation of each sentence (e.g., *Did the actor kick the comedian?* after the sentence *The comedian that the actor kicked ignored the pianist*). The questions assessed whether subjects correctly understood the case-role relationships among different participants in the sentence. In that respect, the paradigm resembled the picture-matching task used in the Naeser et al. (1987) study described earlier.

The results from the RSVP study, presented in Figure 7, show some important parallels to the pattern of performance that was observed for aphasic patients (see Fig. 5). First, the two factors that were supposed to mimic the severity level of aphasic patients (i.e., working memory span and the presentation speed) each had a significant impact on the comprehension accuracy. Second, the complexity of the sentence also significantly affected the subject's performance. The ordering of difficulty of 11 constructions (averaged across subjects) was almost identical to the ordering found in three studies reported by Caplan et al. (1985) (see Fig. 6). Finally and most important, the severity factors interacted with the structural complexity of the sentences, with the more complex sentences leading to more variability among different severity levels. This pattern of comprehension data elicited from normal adults supports the hypothesis that severe temporal restrictions in the face of reduced resources are likely to be a major cause of syntactic comprehension failures of aphasic patients, too. More generally, resource limitations and resource allocation may account for a variety of deficits in the comprehension performance of aphasic patients.

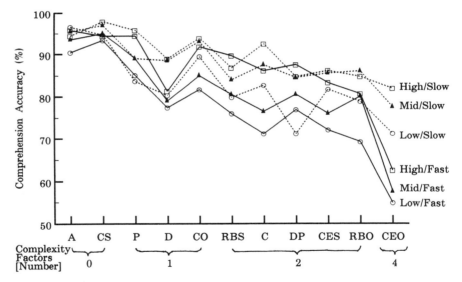

FIG. 7 Syntactic comprehension performance of normal college-age adults with different working memory spans under two rapid presentation rates (labeled slow and fast) for 11 sentence types, nine from Caplan et al. (1985), plus Center-embedded subject relative (CES) and Right-branching object relative (RBO) sentences. The working memory span of the reader and the presentation speed do not affect comprehension performance for the simplest sentence constructions. As the complexity level of the sentence increases, however, the two factors exert increasingly stronger detrimental effects on comprehension accuracy, affecting lower span/faster presentation groups to a greater extent than higher span/slower presentation groups. The data are from *A capacity approach to syntactic comprehension disorders: Making normal adults perform like aphasic patients* by Miyake et al. (in press a). Copyright 1994 by Lawrence Erlbaum Associates, Ltd. Reprinted by permission.

B. Capacity Effects in Aging

Among a wide array of human cognitive capabilities, language functions are commonly believed to be the least likely to deteriorate with normal aging. This common belief, however, is contradicted by evidence that has accumulated in recent studies in cognitive gerontology (for a comprehensive review, see Kemper, 1992). In certain contexts comprehension declines with age, and the decline is not entirely due to the peripheral visual and auditory impairments commonly observed in elderly adults (Rupp, 1980). One important feature of the age-related decline is that it is not general, nor does it appear to be attributable to the loss of some specific linguistic computation. Rather, the age-related performance decrements are observable with the same kind of language tasks and syntactic constructions that are considered to make large demands on the working memory capacities of college-age students. Consequently, one major hypothesis to account for the circumscribed decline in language performance in elderly adults attributes it to reductions in working memory capacity, and several variations of this hypothesis have been proposed (Craik & Byrd, 1982; Salthouse, 1990, 1991). The specific hypothesis that there is a reduction in the activation available for information maintenance and computation or in the allocation of resources to these functions is consistent with many of the empirical results.

Older adults are frequently found to have smaller working memory spans, as measured by the reading or listening span tests. Tables III and IV summarize the results from all the published studies (to the best of our knowledge) that administered the reading/listening span test to a wide range of subjects (including people older than 60) and reported either the mean scores for different age groups or the correlation between age and working memory span. Table III shows the mean working memory span scores for young (mostly, college students) and old adults (aged 60 or older), along with the ratio of old adults' to young adults' span scores. The general result is that old adults have smaller

TABLE III
Mean Working Memory Span Scores for Young and Old Adults

Study	Modality	Young	Old	O/Y[a]
Gick et al. (1988)[b]	Reading	2.41	1.49	0.62**
Hartley (1986)	Reading	2.88	2.88	1.00
Hartley (1988)	Reading	2.67	2.67	1.00
Light and Anderson (1985, Experiment 1)	Reading	3.60	3.08	0.86*
Light and Anderson (1985, Experiment 2)	Reading	3.25	2.95	0.91
Marmurek (1990)	Reading	2.78	2.13	0.77**
Pratt and Robins (1991)	Reading	2.70	2.32	0.86*
Stine and Wingfield (1987)	Listening	4.00	2.46	0.62**
Stine and Wingfield (1990)	Listening	3.33	2.38	0.71**
Tun et al. (1991)	Composite[c]	3.89	2.57	0.66**
Wingfield, Stine, Lahar, Aberdeen (1988)	Listening	4.00	2.43	0.61**

[a] O/Y = ratio of old adults' to young adults' scores.
[b] Span scores are based on paced, five-sentence trials.
[c] Composite of reading span and listening span scores.
* and ** indicate that the group difference is significant at $p < .05$ and $p < .01$ levels, respectively.

TABLE IV
Correlations between Age and Working Memory Span Scores

Study	Modality	Correlation r
Hartley (1986)	Reading	.01
Pratt and Robins (1991)	Reading	− .29*
Salthouse (1992, Study 1)	Reading	− .42**
Salthouse (1992, Study 2)	Reading	− .32**
Salthouse and Babcock (1991, Study 1)	Listening	− .52**
Salthouse and Babcock (1991, Study 2)	Listening	− .41**
Stine and Wingfield (1987)	Listening	− .72**
Stine, Wingfield, and Myers (1990)	Reading	− .44**
Stine, Wingfield, and Myers (1990)	Listening	− .66**
Tun et al. (1991)	Composite	− .69**

* and ** indicate that the correlation is significant at $p < .05$ and $p < .01$ levels, respectively.

working memory spans (by 15–40%) than young adults, irrespective of the testing modality, with the exceptions of two studies (Hartley, 1986, 1988). Similarly, Table IV summarizes the correlations between age and working memory spans. Again, although there are some exceptions (Hartley, 1986; Pratt & Robins, 1991), the moderately high correlations between age and reading/ listening spans (ranging from − .40 to − .70) suggests that age or some correlate of age is implicated in the decline of working memory span. By contrast, traditional digit span is more resistant to aging effects. Most studies do not find systematic declines, although some studies have found statistically smaller digit spans among older adults than younger adults (e.g., Kemper, 1988). In general, the old-to-young ratio in simple digit span ranges from 0.80 to 1.0 (see Babcock & Salthouse, 1990).

Further supporting evidence for the working memory hypothesis in cognitive aging is that age-related decrements in language comprehension do not occur in an across-the-board manner. In general, while older adults rival or sometimes even outperform young adults on tasks that simply tap accumulated knowledge (or CRYSTALLIZED intelligence), age-related declines are prevalent on tasks that assess processing aspects of cognition (or FLUID intelligence) if the task imposes severe processing or storage demands on working memory (Babcock & Salthouse, 1990; Salthouse, Mitchell, Skovronek, & Babcock, 1989; Salthouse & Skovronek, 1992). As expected, given this framework, the kinds of manipulations or linguistic factors that we reviewed earlier in the context of normal young adults and aphasic patients have stronger impacts on elderly adults than on younger adults.

One such factor is the syntactic complexity of a sentence; age-related declines in comprehension and production become evident only as the complexity of the sentence increases. In one set of studies, subjects across a wide range of ages were given a variety of language comprehension tests to assess their ability to comprehend structurally complex sentences (i.e., Token Test, Emery Test for Syntactic Complexity, and Chomsky Test of Syntax) (Emery, 1985, 1986). While no group difference was present on simpler and easier tests (e.g., most of the Boston Diagnostic Aphasia Examination subtests), older adults (aged 75–93) performed significantly worse than younger adults (aged 30–42) on all language tests that involved syntactically complex sentences. Moreover, the group differences in the comprehension performance were larger on the more structurally complex and difficult subsections.

A similar interaction between age and structural complexity was observed in a more recent study on auditory syntactic comprehension (Obler, Fein, Nicholas, & Albert, 1991). In this study, four groups of adults with different ages (30s, 50s, 60s, and 70s) listened to sentences of varying difficulty and answered a true–false comprehension question after each sentence. Figure 8 summarizes the main results of the study. As was the case with the studies reviewed in the section on comprehension by aphasic patients (Caplan et al., 1985; Miyake et al., in press a; Naeser et al., 1987), the group differences in comprehension accuracy were minimal for simple active sentences (e.g., *The fierce wolf attacked the lost sheep in the woods*) but were larger for more complex sentences, such as double embedded sentences (e.g., *The doctor who helped the patient who was sick was healthy*) and double negative sentences (e.g., *The bureaucrat who was not dishonest refused the bribe*). This pattern of results suggests that reductions in working memory resources are implicated in age-related differences.

Stronger effects of syntactic complexity in older adults than young adults were found in a sentence imitation (repetition) task (Kemper, 1986). In this experiment, young adults (aged 30–49) and elderly adults (aged 70–89) repeated a sentence that they had just heard. When the sentence contained a grammatical error, they were encouraged to reproduce a grammatically correct imitation. Young and elderly adults did not differ when the sentences were short; both

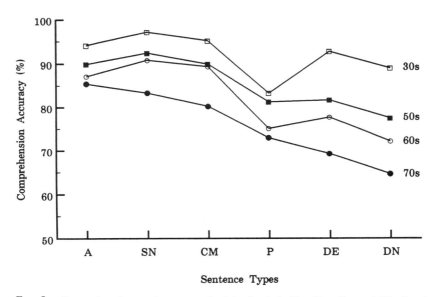

FIG. 8 Comprehension performance of adults in their 30s, 50s, 60s, and 70s for six different sentence types: Simple active (A), Simple negative (SN), Comparative (CM), Passive (P), Doubly embedded (DE), and Double negative (DN). The simpler sentences show little age-related difference in comprehension. However, as the structural complexity increases, older adults have more difficulty. The graph is based on data presented in "Auditory comprehension and aging: Decline in syntactic processing" by Obler et al. (1991, Table 5, p. 442).

groups produced grammatically correct imitations on most of the trials, regardless of the grammaticality of the original sentences. However, elderly adults showed a large disadvantage when long sentences were involved, particularly when they were structurally complex and contained grammatical errors (e.g., *What I have took out of the oven interested my grandchildren*). When only this sentence type was concerned, young adults were able to produce grammatically corrected imitations or paraphrases 94% of the time. Elderly adults, however, had considerable difficulty and produced a satisfactory response on only 8% of the trials. They instead produced grammatically correct but incomplete imitations (51%) or semantically distorted or otherwise totally irrelevant responses (41%). These results suggest that reduced working memory resources in elderly adults may limit their capabilities to simultaneously retain, monitor, and manipulate structurally complex sentences in working memory. Also, in the case of language production, Kemper and her colleagues have found that elderly people tend to use simpler syntactic constructions than young people in both spontaneous speech and writing (Cheung & Kemper, 1992; Kemper, 1987, 1988; Kemper, Kynette, Rash, O'Brien, & Sprott, 1989; Kynette & Kemper, 1986).

Second, there is some evidence that a long intervening text has a more detrimental effect for elderly adults than for young adults. Although old adults generally have more problems determining pronoun antecedents than young adults (e.g., G. Cohen, 1979; Pratt, Boyes, Robins, & Manchester, 1989), young and old adults do not differ reliably when there are no intervening sentences between the pronoun and its antecedent. As the number of intervening sentences increases, age-related differences clearly emerge (Light & Capps, 1986; but see Light & Anderson, 1985). This disadvantage of elderly adults, however, seems to be present only when the topics of the discourse were not foregrounded due to a topic change. As long as the topics are foregrounded, old adults appear to be as adept as young adults in identifying the correct referent of an ambiguous pronoun (Zelinsky, 1988).

Third, language processing capabilities of old adults are more easily taxed by extrinsic processing or storage loads than those of young adults (Wright, 1981). One study that compared the performance of younger adults (average age, 30 years) and older adults (average age, 68 years) involved a modified version of the reading span test, in which subjects verified successive sentences in a set (Gick, Craik, & Morris, 1988). When simple positive sentences were used (e.g., *Cats usually like to hunt mice*), there were only small age-related differences; the error rate for the semantic verification task increased from about 4% to 6% for young adults and from 3% to 9% for older adults, as the memory load increased from zero to four. In contrast, large group differences emerged when more complex, negative sentences were used (e.g., *Bookcases are not usually found by the sea*). While the error rates for young adults did not change much as a function of the memory loads (15% for no load and 13% for the four-word load), those for older adults showed a large increase even when the extrinsic load was minimum (19% for no load, 31% for the one-word load, and 30% for the four-word load). Similarly, the recall of the memory loads was similar across the two groups when the set involved positive sentences but revealed large differences when the set involved negative sentences, with older adults recalling fewer words (0.75 words out of 5) than young adults (2.15 words). These results suggest that older adults are more vulnerable to extrinsic memory loads if the internal capacity demands are high.

The results of a recent dual task study also support the notion of age-related reductions in working memory resources (Tun, Wingfield, & Stine, 1991). Young (aged 18–20) and elderly (aged 60–80) adults listened to spoken passages for immediate recall while performing a secondary reaction time task. The latencies in this secondary task were interpreted as an index of the working memory resources that were not being consumed by the primary language processing task. A major finding was that age-related differences in the reaction time measures were larger when the secondary task was complex (choice reaction time) than when it was simple (simple reaction time), suggesting that the reserve capacity available to older subjects while processing spoken passages was so limited that they were able to perform the secondary task as quickly as young adults only when it was simple enough. Further supporting the capacity reduction view, these age differences in reaction time data disappeared when the analysis included only subsets of young and older subjects who had equivalent working memory spans (as measured by the listening span test).

Furthermore, an increased rate of speech input has been shown to be particularly detrimental to elderly adults when compared to young adults. For example, when relatively long sentences (16–18 words in length) were presented auditorily, the immediate recall of the sentences by older adults (aged 61–80) did not differ much from that of young adults (aged 17–32), as long as the speech rate was within the normal range (e.g., 200 words per minute). Age differences in immediate recall performance systematically increased, however, once the speech rate went beyond normal limits (e.g., 300 and 400 words per minute). This differential effect of input rates was present even when elderly adults had slightly more education and higher verbal ability (Stine, Wingfield, & Poon, 1986). A similar immediate recall study showed that an increased presentation rate was particularly detrimental to elderly adults when it was combined with the removal of prosodic cues (Stine & Wingfield, 1987). The capacity reduction view of cognitive aging was further supported in this study because correlational analyses revealed that listening span scores were highly correlated with age ($r = -.72$; see Table IV) and by themselves accounted for 44% of the total variance in determining the immediate recall performance.

In summary, individual operations of language processing show little evidence of age-related decline when the total processing load is small. However, when the capacity demands are high, performance does deteriorate more for elderly adults than for young adults, suggesting an age-related decrease in the overall working memory capacity for language. Although some studies reported a lack of such interactive effects between age and the task demands (e.g., Light, 1991; Light & Anderson, 1985), there is a considerable amount of evidence supporting the view that reductions in working memory capacity are implicated, at least in part, in age-related decline in language comprehension.

C. Capacity Effects in Children's Comprehension

The problems of children with specific reading disability are not always specific to word decoding because some children have difficulty in comprehending complex spoken sentences as well. Of particular relevance to the current chapter are several recent studies on spoken language comprehension that suggest that a reduced working memory capacity for language may be a source of difficulty for these children.

One reason to suspect that working memory problems are implicated in these children is that their comprehension markedly improves when the task is designed to minimize working memory demands. In a study featuring an object manipulation task similar to Caplan et al.'s (1985), 3rd grade poor readers made significantly more errors than good readers of the same age in comprehending structurally complex sentences, such as center-embedded relative clause sentences (Mann, Shankweiler, & Smith, 1984). However, a follow-up study elicited much higher comprehension performance from poor readers by introducing several methodological changes to reduce the processing demands (Smith, Macaruso, Shankweiler, & Crain, 1989). First, the number of relations among animate noun phrases that needed to be determined and acted out was reduced by replacing a third animate noun with an inanimate noun that could not be the potential agent of any verb in the sentence. Second, the sentences all depicted highly plausible events, thus limiting the number of possible agent–patient pairs to a minimum. Finally, the situation was altered to satisfy the pragmatic presuppositions that are usually associated with the use of restrictive relative clauses. For example, the center-embedded sentence *The boy who the girl pushed tickled the crown* presupposes that there was more than one boy at the scene. Providing more than one boy doll makes the act-out task more natural and hence may allow children to focus on the comprehension of the relative clause per se rather than the pragmatic constraints that are irrelevant to the task at hand (Hamburger & Crain, 1982). The improved performance of the poor readers in this less demanding situation suggests that they already possess the knowledge of relative clause structure, but that limitations in working memory resources prevent them from attaining the same high level of language proficiency as good readers. Similar effects of task demands were also found in a related study that tested 2nd grade good and poor readers for their comprehension of spoken sentences with the temporal terms *before* and *after* (Macaruso, Bar-Shalom, Crain, & Shankweiler, 1989).

Furthermore, greater facility in integrating information over distances in a text characterized young readers (aged 7 and 8) who had larger working memory spans, as assessed by a modified version of the reading span test that involved digit repetition and recall (Yuill & Oakhill, 1991; Yuill, Oakhill, & Parkin, 1989). Two groups of children were selected who had similar levels of word decoding skill and vocabulary knowledge but who differed in overall language comprehension measures. They were given a comprehension test that required them to integrate two pieces of information in a story. For example, one piece of information was an adult's reaction that was inconsistent with a norm, such as blaming a boy for sharing sweets with his little brother. The resolution (for example, information that the little brother was on a diet) was either adjacent or separated from the anomaly by two sentences. The two groups of children were similar in their ability to comprehend passages when the information was adjacent, indicating that both groups of children understood the task and could perform it comparably in the absence of a large working memory demand. However, the children with smaller working memory capacities performed worse than those with larger capacities when the two sources of information were separated by some text. These results for children converge with the individual differences data for young adults and the age-related differences data to suggest that working memory capacity is related to the ability to retain text information that facilitates the comprehension of subsequent sentences. These studies suggest that some individual differences among children in their language comprehension skill parallel the kinds of data found among college-age adults; these parallels, in turn, suggest that variation in working memory capacity may explain aspects of their comprehension performance.

D. Summary

Across the four factors that impose heavy processing demands or constraints, we have described systematic differences found in different populations. As is the case with normal college-age adults that we have reviewed earlier, comprehension performance generally declines with an increase in intrinsic complexity, the presence of an extrinsic memory load, or temporal constraints on processing. The impact of each of these factors on comprehension speed and/or accuracy is greater for those who have smaller capacities, sometimes as assessed by a working memory span task. That is, severe aphasic patients, elderly adults, and children with poor comprehension skills are more disrupted by extra demands or constraints than mild aphasics, younger adults, and children with good comprehension skills, respectively. The working memory capacity perspective provides a useful framework which allows us to capture the parallelism among data from quite different populations.

V. ALTERNATIVE ACCOUNTS AND CENTRAL ISSUES

A working memory capacity perspective shifts the scientific schema within which language and language behavior have been studied to focus on the dynamics of language processing, in addition to its structural aspects. This focus has provided the basis of our account of individual differences in comprehension as it is broadly construed as variation among normal adults, among children, between young and elderly adults, and in aphasic patients. In this section, we describe and evaluate alternative accounts of capacity constraints and then consider other issues that are raised by the capacity perspective.

A. Alternative Mechanisms

Across the broad spectrum of individual differences, including aphasia, aging, and development, several mechanisms have been suggested to account for systematic performance deficits in tasks that make large demands on both processing and storage. In this section, we describe these mechanisms and their likely role in the larger domain of tasks and population differences that we have discussed.

1. Total Capacity and Efficiency

We have argued that the notion of CAPACITY traditionally has been interpreted as a structural limit on the number of simultaneously active representations that could be maintained in working memory. In symbolic models, the representations are conceptualized as chunks (Miller, 1956). In network models, an analogous concept would be a limit on the number of simultaneously activated nodes. The assumption that capacity has a representational facet is widely held, as we discussed in the introduction. One goal of the current paper has been to argue that the conception of capacity should be extended to include computation. The limitation on activation, as instantiated in CC READER, can impact on either the maintenance of previously activated representations or on the computation of new information.

In addition, the model also provides a precise framework in which to express a different but frequently hypothesized source of deficit—processing speed or efficiency. The efficiency concept can apply to several computational aspects of comprehension—the time course with which information is activated from long-term memory, the time course of computing new information, and the time course of information decay (Haarmann & Kolk, 1991a). A generalized efficiency hypothesis has been suggested to explain the deficit among some young readers, whose decoding and lexical access skill may be slow and consume "resources" needed by other processes (Frederiksen, 1982; Perfetti, 1985). A related version of this hypothesis is that individual differences reside in the allocation or management of resources, rather than in the efficiency of the system in general or the efficiency of some specific process. The efficiency hypothesis is implicated by data showing differences in the temporal parameters of specific processes for some aphasics in various priming and judgment tasks; some studies suggest slower activation in aphasics than in normals (Haarmann & Kolk, 1991b), and others suggest faster decay of activation (Friederici & Kilborn, 1989; Haarmann & Kolk, in press). A comparison of studies suggest that aphasics may have different resource allocation schemes in different tasks, resulting in some cases in relatively slower activation and in other cases in decreased maintenance (Haarmann, 1993). In the domain of aging, the speed of information activation, not decay, has been hypothesized as a source of working memory limitation, based on a statistical analysis of the covariance between working memory span tasks and speeded perceptually based tasks as a function of age (Salthouse, 1992).

Changes in total resources and in efficiency are not mutually exclusive, although they differ in their intuitive appeal as explanations across various domains. The types of generalized performance changes induced by fatigue, extreme age, or concentration seem compatible with the concept of total available activation (Kahneman, 1973). By contrast, a change in processing efficiency may be more specific to a particular process (J. D. Cohen, Dunbar, & McClelland, 1990; also Schneider & Shiffrin, 1977). Moreover, both constructs may be appropriate and useful in accounting for the effects induced by brain trauma (Kolk & van Grunsven, 1985).

2. Inhibition

Another mechanism that could contribute to reductions in the effective capacity of working memory is the generation and maintenance of irrelevant information, due to a lack of efficient inhibitory mechanisms. These activities would effectively reduce the resources for more relevant processing. Evidence for a lack of inhibition is most convincing in studies that show systematic intrusions and interference from inappropriate associations in output responses (Dempster, 1992). But versions of the inhibition hypothesis have been put forward to explain developmental deficits in tasks that have inhibitory components (Bjorklund & Harnishfeger, 1990; Dempster, 1992), comprehension deficits in aging (Hamm & Hasher, 1992; Hasher & Zacks, 1988), individual differences in comprehension among college-age students (Gernsbacher, Varner, & Faust, 1990), and deficits associated with frontal lobe damage (Dempster, 1992).

In one form, the inhibition hypothesis is closely related to the concept of resource allocation. In this view, the deficit arises because inappropriate information is maintained, rather than forgotten or actively suppressed. Hence, inhibition becomes highly related to the issue of total capacity, as well as efficiency, as described above. In another view, the inhibition hypothesis refers to the active recruitment of inappropriate information. Intuitively, this latter version seems most appealing as a potential explanation for deficits in domains such as text comprehension, which are richer and less constrained and may provide more opportunity for irrelevant or inappropriate associations (Hamm & Hasher, 1992; Hasher & Zacks, 1988) than the sentence processing tasks that have been the focus of the current discussion. The inhibition hypothesis would need more specification to account for the precise time course of capacity effects in the comprehension of sentences, such as those described in the section on syntactically complex sentences.

3. Strategic Processes

The establishment and tracking of subgoals may be a crucial factor in organizing performance in complex tasks. Thus, such strategic processes may be a source of performance deficit either because a person lacks the knowledge base to enable the construction of an effective strategy or because of resource limitations that interfere with constructing, maintaining, and updating it (Carpenter & Just, 1989). The role of these strategic processes is most evident in more complex tasks, such as the comprehension of literary texts, where a primary source of individual differences lies in problem solving, rather than language comprehension per se. This hypothesis would need considerable development to account for the precise pattern of effects found in the more routine sentence comprehension tasks that have been of primary concern in this chapter.

4. Long-Term Knowledge

An alternative to the hypothesis that working memory is a source of individual differences in performance is the hypothesis that the variance arises from differences in long-term knowledge. The idea is that experts, compared to novices, have a richer, more organized knowledge base that can be activated in the course of processing. Moreover, the activation of larger chunks of knowledge from long-term memory may give the appearance of increased working memory capacity, but the operative mechanism is the richness and organization of knowledge in long-term memory. The long-term knowledge hypothesis has proven to be particularly illuminating in complex domains, such as mnemonic expertise (e.g., Chase & Ericsson, 1982) and problem solving (Chase & Simon, 1973; Chi, Glaser, & Farr, 1988; de Groot, 1965), and it has also been supported in the domain of memory development, as an explanation for children's improved performance in traditional span tasks (Chi, 1976).

In the domain of language processing, a version of the knowledge hypothesis is that expertise resides in a richer, better organized vocabulary, perhaps as a result of more extensive reading and exposure. However, assessments of the contribution of vocabulary suggest that variation in vocabulary does not entirely account for differences in working memory span tasks (Daneman & Green, 1986; Dixon, LeFevre, & Twilley, 1989; Engle, Nations, & Cantor, 1990). Knowledge-based explanations are less useful in accounting for the on-line processing profile of comprehension. Moreover, the potential role of vocabulary and knowledge is not so salient in sentence processing tasks, in which the structure and vocabulary are familiar and restricted. The long-term knowledge hypothesis is also not compatible with the general effects found in aging, given that older adults often do have greater vocabulary knowledge (and other crystallized knowledge) but show systematic decrements in tasks that have high processing components (Salthouse, 1988).

5. Summary

Reductions in effective working memory capacity may arise from a variety of sources. The evidence for each of these sources often comes from tasks that differ greatly in their complexity, their susceptibility to interference or strategies, or their reliance on domain knowledge. It is dangerous to ignore such dimensions of difference in assessing the potential contribution of these various processes to working memory deficits. The total capacity and efficiency explanations provide good accounts of the systematic deficits in sentence comprehension described in this chapter, but the other mechanisms may contribute in more complex, less structured domains. What the present model offers, however, is a relatively precise instantiation of exactly what is meant by deficits in capacity, in terms of the total resources available for both maintenance and computation.

A more general concern, raised by Navon (1984), is that capacity theories are often vague and only positive evidence is considered relevant. But the detailed account given by CC READER of sentence processing in various populations, for various sentence structures, and in various tasks provides an example of a process theory of capacity limitations that transcends the shortcomings of previous theories. Navon also suggested several specific alternative interpretations of resource limitations. For example, he pointed out that an effect of task difficulty does not necessarily implicate capacity limitations, if, for example, the task's difficulty arises because the sensory information is poor. Such an alternative explanation is not viable in the studies of normal sentence processing. Moreover, where the point might be applicable, in the case of aphasics and elderly people, the role of peripheral sensory problems can be assessed to evaluate their contribution to the processing difficulty. Navon also pointed out that complexity effects do not necessarily entail a resource limitation, unless processing is thought to be done in parallel; however, parallel processing is assumed in CC READER, as well as many other activation-based models. The capacity theory we have proposed provides a mechanistic account for a wide variety of phenomena, by specifying a precise computational mechanism within which resources (activation), storage, and processing are all well defined. By virtue of this specification, the theory can explain a variety of phenomena without the vacuity against which Navon cautioned.

B. How Many Capacities?

The capacity perspective raises the issue of how many capacities there are, and, if there is more than one capacity, how they are distributed. This question has often been framed in the context of cognitive functioning more generally, as in the issue of whether language processing shares resources with spatial or arithmetic processing (Baddeley et al., 1985; Daneman & Tardif, 1987; Turner & Engle, 1989). In this section, we explore the issue much more locally, by examining the evidence about shared capacities between language processes. The correlation data suggest that the comprehension of different languages acquired by a bilingual draws on shared resources. By contrast, when language comprehension and production are compared, it looks likely that speaking and listening may involve different working memory capacities. However, because the data are almost entirely correlational, their interpretation is inherently ambiguous and the interpretations are only suggestive at this point.

1. Second Language Acquisition

Recent studies of individual differences in working memory performance in processing a bilingual's second language (L2) are remarkably parallel to the results for individual differences in the first language (L1). Specifically, individual differences in L2 reading skill are highly correlated with L2 working memory span (Harrington & Sawyer, 1992). In that study, 32 native speakers of Japanese who were learning English as their second language completed an English and a Japanese version of the reading span test, along with the grammar and the reading/vocabulary subsections of the Test of English as a Foreign Language (TOEFL). Correlational analyses revealed that readers with higher L2 reading span scores did better on both subsections of the TOEFL, resulting in the correlation coefficients of $+.57$ (the grammar section) and $+.54$ (the reading/vocabulary section), respectively ($p < .01$). As was the case with the L1 research, a simple word span or digit span was not as good a predictor of L2 reading ability ($r = +.20$ to $+.25$). Other findings also suggest that L2 reading is often associated with less efficiency than L1 reading and, consequently, that second language learners may not have many resources left to allocate for higher level processing and/or the storage of intermediate products of comprehension. Such studies have found that word meanings are activated more slowly and decay more quickly in L2 than in L1 (Favreau & Segalowitz, 1983; Segalowitz, 1986; Segalowitz & Hebert, 1990). Furthermore, less skilled L2 readers tend to focus on lower level aspects of reading (e.g., orthographic aspects), at the expense of higher level semantic and inferential processes (McLeod & McLaughlin, 1986). As is the case with L1 reading, less efficient (or less well developed) L2 component processes may rob other processes not just of good data (Perfetti, 1985) but also of cognitive resources available (Frederiksen, 1982).

An interesting question that arises from this similarity between L1 and L2 is to what extent working memory resources are shared by the two languages, as indicated by correlations between spans in the two languages. One study that found a high correlation administered a Japanese and two English versions of the reading span test to 32 native speakers of Japanese (Osaka & Osaka, 1992). The college students were all majoring in English and were highly proficient in it. There was a high correlation between the Japanese and English reading spans (+.72 and +.84). (The Harrington and Sawyer, 1992, study reports a significant but lower correlation between L1 and L2 reading spans, $r = +.39$.) Given the proficiency level of the participants in the study, the results suggest that, at least in highly skilled second language users, the processing of L2 may share the same pool of working memory resources as the processing of L1.

This conclusion is in agreement with a number of correlational studies demonstrating that, in both children and adults, L2 proficiency is at least moderately correlated with L1 proficiency ($r = +.30$ to $+.80$; see Cummins, 1991, for a review). For example, a recent study with adult ESL learners reports moderate correlations of $+.37$ (Chinese learners) and $+.51$ (Japanese learners) between their L1 and L2 reading abilities (Carson, Carrell, Silberstein, Kroll, & Kuehn, 1990). Similarly, the data collected by the California State Department of Education (1981) revealed a strong correlation between L1 and L2 reading skills ($r = +.60$ to $+.74$) among Hispanic children (cited in Cummins, 1991). These correlations increase as children acquire proficiency in L2. A longitudinal study relating L1 (Spanish) and L2 (English) proficiency among Hispanic children found that the correlation went from essentially zero to $+.68$ between kindergarten and the third grade (Hakuta & Diaz, 1985, cited in Cummins, 1991). These data suggest that L1 proficiency may determine an upper limit to L2 proficiency. Moreover, the working memory capacity for L1 may influence the speed of L2 acquisition. In a recent study, basic English was taught for 20 hours to Japanese 6th graders who had no previous exposure to English, using the traditional, grammar-oriented approach (Ando et al., 1992). The results indicated that the children's listening and reading spans in L1 before instruction strongly correlated with their post-test performance in L2 ($r = .60$ for reading span and $r = .72$ for listening span).

Of course, these correlations could be due to other factors, such as differences in learning approaches or motivation. While acknowledging the ambiguity in interpreting such correlational data, it is also the case that overall, the high correlations among various measures of L1 and L2 performance in second language learners are consistent with the hypothesis that comprehension in the two languages draws on the same capacity.

2. Speech Production

Although we have focused on the role of working memory in language comprehension, clearly the demands for concurrent computation and storage are equally crucial in language production. Speakers must plan what to say and temporarily store their plans while retrieving words and phrases and concurrently articulating what was planned moments earlier (Clark & Clark, 1977; Levelt, 1989). Speech production, thus, involves a highly complex and skillful management of processing and storage requirements in real time, just like reading or listening comprehension (Power, 1985, 1986). The issue we examine is the evidence that comprehension and production draw on different working memory resources.

Some evidence that speaking and comprehension do not involve the same resources comes from the analysis of individual differences in the two domains. A speaking span test, analogous to the reading span test, has been used to examine individual differences in the speed and ease with which people produce language (Daneman, 1991; Daneman & Green, 1986). In this test, subjects are presented increasingly longer sets of unrelated words, one word at a time, and at the end of each set, they have to generate a sentence containing each of the words in the set. The maximum number of words for which meaningful and grammatical sentences are generated defines that subject's speaking span. Thus, the test involves the usual planning and execution demands of sentence production, plus the additional component of storing words concurrently with producing semantically and syntactically acceptable sentences. Working memory capacity, as measured by the speaking span test, appears to be an important source of individual differences in verbal fluency. College students with greater speaking spans are faster than lower span subjects in providing a contextually appropriate completion when given a sentence frame such as *The politician delivered his speech with great* . . . ($r = -.56$); by contrast, reading span did not significantly correlate with performance in this task ($r = -.33$) (Daneman & Green, 1986). Speaking span also correlates with performance on a number of other tasks that assess verbal fluency, such as generating a speech about a picture and reading aloud a prose passage (Daneman, 1991). These results corroborate the close relationship between working memory capacity and verbal fluency.

The finding that reading span did not predict the subject's speech production performance well (with the exception of the oral reading task), however, suggests that working memory for language is not a general system with a unitary capacity (Daneman, 1991). Instead, working memory resources may relate to the person's capacity or resource allocation with respect to specific types of processes (Daneman & Tardif, 1987). Although this task-specific view of working memory capacity has been controversial (e.g., Turner & Engle, 1989), there is additional evidence, irrespective of the span test literature, that suggests a functional separation of comprehension and production mechanisms.

In aphasiology, a number of AGRAMMATIC patients have been described who produce extremely slow, effortful speech devoid of grammatical morphemes but demonstrate normal (or near-normal) syntactic comprehension (e.g., Caramazza & Hillis, 1989; Kolk, van Grunsven, & Keyser, 1985; Miceli, Mazzucchi, Menn, & Goodglass, 1983; Nespoulous et al., 1988). The opposite dissociation has been suggested to exist in some patients with conduction aphasia who have relatively intact production coupled with comprehension problems (Howard, 1985). These two dissociations may imply that language comprehension and production capabilities can be separately impaired. However, any strong inferences from this literature await more careful analysis of the nature of the impairments in various case studies.

One last piece of evidence comes from a large-scale correlational study on individual differences in first language acquisition which suggests that the two components of language, comprehension and production, can come apart at the seams and develop quite independently of each other at different rates in different children (Bates, Bretherton, & Snyder, 1988). This finding is also consistent with the hypothesis that working memory resources in producing language are not identical to those in language comprehension. Nevertheless, this issue, as well as the more general question concerning the relation between resources for language and those used in cognition, have not yet been conclusively answered by correlational studies.

C. Syntactic Modularity

Capacity constraints provide an interesting new perspective on the interrelation-ships among different levels of language processes. The controversy concerning the modularity of language is one such example (see Garfield, 1987). An interest-ing conjecture offered by Fodor (1983) states that the syntactic level of language processing is performed by a cognitive module, namely, a fast, domain-specific set of processes that is mandatory and informationally encapsulated. The last property of a cognitive module, informational encapsulation, is probably the single most distinguishing property. It refers to the module's activities and outputs being uninfluenced by certain classes of information that may exist elsewhere in the system. The issue of whether parsing operations are informa-tionally encapsulated or not has been subjected to empirical scrutiny (e.g., Britt, Perfetti, Garrod, & Rayner, 1992; Crain & Steedman, 1985; Rayner, Carlson, & Frazier, 1983; Taraban & McClelland, 1988). A number of studies focused on structurally ambiguous sentences in which readers could avoid being led down a garden path only by making immediate use of nonsyntactic information. One influential study in favor of the modularity of syntax used sentences with a temporary ambiguity, such as *The evidence examined by the lawyer shocked the jury* (Ferreira & Clifton, 1986). Surprisingly, readers showed garden path effects on the disambiguating *by*-phrase, in spite of the potential availability of one's knowledge that an inanimate head noun, such as *evidence,* could not be the agent of the verb *examined.* That is, the first-pass fixation times on the *by*-phrase were as long as when no such prior disambiguating information was present, as in *The defendant examined by the lawyer . . . .* Because the cue was pragmatic rather than syntactic, its lack of influence on the syntactic processing was attributed to the encapsulation of the syntactic module.

A capacity account offers a contrasting view, namely, that interactive pro-cesses, such as those that require the integration of syntactic and pragmatic information, may require more resources and consequently may manifest indi-vidual differences. Supporting this capacity view, when the Ferreira and Clifton (1986) experiment was rerun, only low span readers showed garden path effects, failing to use the pragmatic information immediately to guide their parsing (Just & Carpenter, 1992). People with a smaller working memory may not have the capacity to entertain (keep activated and propagate additional activation from) nonsyntactic information during the syntactic computations, or at least not to the degree that the nonsyntactic information can influence the syntactic processing. In contrast, high span readers showed no such effects, suggesting that they had enough capacity to take the inanimacy of the head noun into account in initially interpreting the syntactic ambiguity.

This pattern of results is most easily explained in terms of a capacity difference between the two groups of subjects. The modularity explanation does not fit this pattern of results unless one postulates that the syntactic processing of low span readers is modular and the syntactic processing of high span readers is interactive. But modularity was originally construed as a hypothesis about a universal functional architecture, a construal that is violated by a finding of individual differences (Fodor, 1983). In contrast, the capacity theory simply postulates that interaction requires capacity, so only those readers with greater capacity have the resources to support immediate interaction.

VI. SUMMARY

In this chapter, we have argued that a variety of individual differences and task effects can be illuminated by a theory of capacity-constrained comprehension. Across a range of tasks, constraints are most prominent in tasks that impose large storage and computation demands. Beyond the generalized deficits, the time course of the effects within sentence comprehension tasks are often localizable to points that make particularly heavy processing demands. Such effects can be explained by a theory of working memory that entails constraints on both processing and storage. As an instantiation of such a theory, we presented the CC READER model. By giving the concept of "working" equal status with the concept of "memory," the theoretical framework outlined in this chapter brings theories of WORKING MEMORY into closer alignment with the dynamics involved in on-line language processing.

ACKNOWLEDGMENTS

The research described in this paper was partially supported by National Institute of Mental Health Grant MH29617 and Research Scientist Development Awards MH-00661 and MH-00662.

REFERENCES

Abney, S. P., & Johnson, M. (1991). Memory requirements and local ambiguities of parsing strategies. *Journal of Psycholinguistic Research, 20,* 233–251.

Ando, J., Fukunaga, N., Kurahashi, J., Suto, T., Nakano, T., & Kage, M. (1992). A comparative study on the two EFL teaching methods: The communicative and the grammatical approach. *Japanese Journal of Educational Psychology, 40,* 247–256. (in Japanese)

Babcock, R. L., & Salthouse, T. A. (1990). Effects of increased processing demands on age differences in working memory. *Psychology and Aging, 5,* 421–428.

Baddeley, A. D. (1976). *The psychology of memory.* New York: Basic Books.

Baddeley, A. D. (1986). *Working memory.* New York: Oxford University Press.

Baddeley, A. D., Eldridge, M., Lewis, V., & Thomson, N. (1984). Attention and retrieval from long-term memory. *Journal of Experimental Psychology: General, 113,* 518–540.

Baddeley, A. D., & Hitch, G. (1974). Working memory. In G. H. Bower (Ed.), *The psychology of learning and motivation* (Vol. 8, pp. 47–89). New York: Academic Press.

Baddeley, A. D., Logie, R., Nimmo-Smith, I., & Brereton, N. (1985). Components of fluent reading. *Journal of Memory and Language, 24,* 119–131.

Barnard, P. (1985). Interacting cognitive subsystems: A psycholinguistic approach to short-term memory. In A. W. Ellis (Ed.), *Progress in the psychology of language* (Vol. 2, pp. 197–258). London: Erlbaum.

Bates, E., Bretherton, I., & Snyder, L. (1988). *From first words to grammar: Individual differences and dissociable mechanisms.* New York: Cambridge University Press.

Berndt, R. S., & Caramazza, A. (1980). A redefinition of the syndrome of Broca's aphasia: Implications for neuropsychological model of language. *Applied Psycholinguistics, 1,* 225–278.

Berwick, R. C., & Weinberg, A. S. (1984). *The grammatical basis of linguistic performance.* Cambridge, MA: MIT Press.

Bever, T. G. (1970). The cognitive basis for linguistic structures. In J. R. Hayes (Ed.), *Cognition and the development of language* (pp. 279–362). New York: Wiley.

Bjorklund, D. F., & Harnishfeger, K. K. (1990). The resources construct in cognitive development: Diverse sources of evidence and a theory of inefficient inhibition. *Developmental Review, 10,* 48–71.

Blumstein, S. E., Katz, B., Goodglass, H., Shrier, R., & Dworetsky, B. (1985). The effects of slowed speech on auditory comprehension in aphasia. *Brain and Language, 24,* 246–265.

Bradley, D. C., Garrett, M. F., & Zurif, E. B. (1980). Syntactic deficits in Broca's aphasia. In D. Caplan (Ed.), *Biological studies of mental processes* (pp. 269–286). Cambridge, MA: MIT Press.

Bransford, J. D., & Johnson, M. K. (1973). Considerations of some problems of comprehension. In W. G. Chase (Ed.), *Visual information processing* (pp. 383–438). New York: Academic Press.

Britt, M. A., Perfetti, C. A., Garrod, S., & Rayner, K. (1992). Parsing in discourse: Context effects and their limits. *Journal of Memory and Language, 31,* 293–314.

California State Department of Education. (1981). *Schooling and language minority students: A theoretical framework.* Los Angeles: California State University.

Caplan, D. (1985). Syntactic and semantic structures in agrammatism. In M.-L. Kean (Ed.), *Agrammatism* (pp. 125–152). Orlando, FL: Academic Press.

Caplan, D., Baker, C., & Dehaut, F. (1985). Syntactic determinants of sentence comprehension in aphasia. *Cognition, 21,* 117–175.

Caplan, D., & Hildebrandt, N. (1988). *Disorders of syntactic comprehension.* Cambridge, MA: MIT Press.

Caplan, D., & Waters, G. S. (1990). Short-term memory and language comprehension: A critical review of the neuropsychological literature. In G. Vallar & T. Shallice (Eds.), *Neuropsychological impairments of short-term memory* (pp. 337–389). New York: Cambridge University Press.

Caramazza, A., & Hillis, A. E. (1989). The disruption of sentence production: Some dissociations. *Brain and Language, 36,* 625–650.

Caramazza, A., & Zurif, E. B. (1976). Dissociation of algorithmic and heuristic processes in language comprehension: Evidence from aphasia. *Brain and Language, 3,* 572–582.

Carpenter, P. A., & Daneman, M. (1981). Lexical retrieval and error recovery in reading: A model based on eye fixations. *Journal of Verbal Learning and Verbal Behavior, 20,* 137–160.

Carpenter, P. A., & Just, M. A. (1983). What your eyes do while your mind is reading. In K. Rayner (Ed.), *Eye movements in reading: Perceptual and language processes* (pp. 275–307). New York: Academic Press.

Carpenter, P. A., & Just, M. A. (1989). The role of working memory in language comprehension. In D. Klahr & K. Kotovsky (Eds.), *Complex information processing: The impact of Herbert A. Simon* (pp. 31–68). Hillsdale, NJ: Erlbaum.

Carr, A. G. (1991). *Theoretical considerations of the Daneman and Carpenter paradigm for the study of working memory span.* Unpublished doctoral dissertation, New School for Social Research, New York.

Carson, J. E., Carrell, P. L., Silberstein, S., Kroll, B., & Kuehn, P. A. (1990). Reading–writing relationships in first and second language. *TESOL Quarterly, 24,* 245–266.

Chase, W. G., & Ericsson, K. A. (1982). Skill and working memory. In G. H. Bower (Ed.), *The psychology of learning* (Vol. 16, pp. 1–58). New York: Academic Press.

Chase, W. G., & Simon, H. A. (1973). Perception in chess. *Cognitive Psychology, 4,* 55–81.

Cheung, H., & Kemper, S. (1992). Competing complexity metrics and adults' production of complex sentences. *Applied Psycholinguistics, 13,* 53–76.

Chi, M. T. H. (1976). Short-term memory limitations in children: Capacity or processing deficits? *Memory & Cognition, 4,* 559–572.

Chi, M. T. H., Glaser, R., & Farr, M. J. (1988). *The nature of expertise.* Hillsdale, NJ: Erlbaum.

Chodorow, M. (1979). Time compressed speech and the study of lexical and syntactic processing. In W. Cooper & E. Walker, (Eds.), *Sentence processing* (pp. 87–111). Hillsdale, NJ: Erlbaum.

Clark, H. H., & Clark, E. V. (1977). *The psychology of language.* New York: Harcourt Brace Jovanovich.

Cohen, G. (1979). Language comprehension in old age. *Cognitive Psychology, 11,* 412–429.

Cohen, J. D., Dunbar, K., & McClelland, J. L. (1990). On the control of automatic processes: A parallel distributed processing account of the Stroop effect. *Psychological Review, 97,* 332–361.

Cottrell, G. W. (1989). *A connectionist approach to word sense disambiguation.* London: Pitman.

Cowan, N. (1988). Evolving conceptions of memory storage, selective attention, and their mutual constraints within the human information-processing system. *Psychological Bulletin, 104,* 163–191.

Craik, F. I. M., & Byrd, M. (1982). Aging and cognitive deficits: The role of attentional resources. In F. I. M. Craik & S. Trehub (Eds.), *Aging and cognitive processes* (pp. 191–211). New York: Plenum.

Crain, S., & Steedman, M. (1985). On not being led up to the garden path: The use of context by the psychological syntax processor. In D. R. Dowty, L. Karttunen, & A. M. Zwicky (Eds.), *Natural language processing* (pp. 320–358). Cambridge: Cambridge University Press.

Cummins, J. (1991). Interdependence of first- and second-language proficiency in bilingual children. In E. Bialystok (Ed.), *Language processing in bilingual children* (pp. 70–89). New York: Cambridge University Press.

Daneman, M. (1991). Working memory as a predictor of verbal fluency. *Journal of Psycholinguistic Research, 20,* 445–464.

Daneman, M., & Blennerhassett, A. (1984). How to assess the listening comprehension skills of prereaders. *Journal of Educational Psychology, 76,* 1372–1381.

Daneman, M., & Carpenter, P. A. (1980). Individual differences in working memory and reading. *Journal of Verbal Learning and Verbal Behavior, 19,* 450–466.

Daneman, M., & Carpenter, P. A. (1983). Individual differences in integrating information between and within sentences. *Journal of Experimental Psychology: Learning, Memory and Cognition, 9,* 561–584.

Daneman, M., & Green, I. (1986). Individual differences in comprehending and producing words in context. *Journal of Memory and Language, 25,* 1–18.

Daneman, M., & Tardif, T. (1987). Working memory and reading skill re-examined. In M. Coltheart (Ed.), *Attention and performance XII: The psychology of reading* (pp. 491–508). London: Erlbaum.

de Groot, A. (1965). *Thought and choice in chess.* The Hague: Mouton.

Dempster, F. N. (1992). The rise and fall of the inhibitory mechanism: Toward a unified theory of cognitive development and aging. *Developmental Review, 12,* 45–7●.

Dixon, P., LeFevre, J., & Twilley, L. C. (1989). Word knowledge and working memory as predictors of reading skill. *Journal of Educational Psychology, 80,* 465–472.

Emery, O. B. (1985). Language and aging. *Experimental Aging Research (Monograph), 11,* 3–60.

Emery, O. B. (1986). Linguistic decrement in normal aging. *Language and Communication, 6,* 47–64.

Engle, R. W., Nations, J. K., & Cantor, J. (1990). Is "working memory capacity" just another name for word knowledge? *Journal of Educational Psychology, 82,* 799–804.

Favreau, M., & Segalowitz, N. (1983). Automatic and controlled processes in reading a second language. *Memory & Cognition, 11,* 565–574.

Ferreira, F., & Clifton, C. (1986). The independence of syntactic processing. *Journal of Memory and Language, 25,* 348–368.

Fodor, J. A. (1983). *The modularity of mind.* Cambridge, MA: Bradford Books.

Ford, M. (1983). A method for obtaining measures of local parsing complexity throughout sentences. *Journal of Verbal Learning and Verbal Behavior, 22,* 203–218.

Forster, K. I. (1970). Visual perception of rapidly presented word sequences of varying complexity. *Perception & Psychophysics, 8,* 215–221.

Forster, K. I., & Ryder, L. A. (1971). Perceiving the structure and meaning of sentences. *Journal of Verbal Learning and Verbal Behavior, 10,* 285–296.

Frazier, L., & Fodor, J. D. (1978). The sausage machine: A new two-stage parsing model. *Cognition, 6,* 291–325.

Frazier, L., & Friederici, A. D. (1991). On deriving properties of agrammatic comprehension. *Brain and Language, 40,* 51–66.

Frederiksen, J. R. (1982). A componential theory of reading skills and their interactions. In R. J. Sternberg (Ed.), *Advances in the psychology of human intelligence* (Vol. 1, pp. 125–180). Hillsdale, NJ: Erlbaum.

Friederici, A. D. (1988). Agrammatic comprehension: Picture of a computational mismatch. *Aphasiology, 2,* 279–282.

Friederici, A. D., & Kilborn, K. (1989). Temporal constraints on language processing: Syntactic priming in Broca's aphasia. *Journal of Cognitive Neuroscience, 1,* 262–272.

Garfield, J. L. (Ed.), (1987). *Modularity in knowledge representation and natural-language understanding.* Cambridge, MA: MIT Press.

Gernsbacher, M. A., Varner, K. R., & Faust, M. (1990). Investigating differences in general comprehension skill. *Journal of Experimental Psychology: Learning, Memory, and Cognition, 16,* 430–445.

Gibson, E. (1990). Recency preferences and garden-path effects. In *Proceedings of the twelfth annual conference of the Cognitive Science Society* (pp. 372–379). Hillsdale, NJ: Erlbaum.

Gick, M. L., Craik, F. I. M., & Morris, R. G. (1988). Task complexity and age differences in working memory. *Memory & Cognition, 16,* 353–361.

Gigley, H. M. (1983). HOPE—AI and the dynamic process of language behavior. *Cognition and Brain Theory, 6,* 39–88.

Glanzer, M., Fischer, B., & Dorfman, D. (1984). Short-term storage in reading. *Journal of Verbal Learning and Verbal Behavior, 23,* 467–486.

Gorfein, D. S., & Bubka, A. (1989). A context-sensitive frequency-based theory of meaning achievement. In D. S. Gorfein (Ed.), *Resolving semantic ambiguity* (pp. 84–106). New York: Springer-Verlag.

Gorrell, P. G. (1987). *Studies of human syntactic processing: Ranked-parallel versus serial models.* Unpublished doctoral dissertation, University of Connecticut, Storrs.

Grodzinsky, Y. (1986). Language deficits and the theory of syntax. *Brain and Language, 15,* 143–160.

Haarmann, H. J. (1993). *Agrammatic aphasia as a timing deficit.* Unpublished doctoral dissertation, Nijmegen Institute for Cognition and Information, Nijmegen, The Netherlands.

Haarmann, H. J., & Kolk, H. H. J. (1991a). A computer model of the temporal course of agrammatic sentence understanding: The effects of variation in severity and sentence complexity. *Cognitive Science, 15,* 49–87.

Haarmann, H. J., & Kolk, H. H. J. (1991b). Syntactic priming in Broca's aphasics: Evidence for slow activation. *Aphasiology, 5,* 247–263.

Haarmann, H. J., & Kolk, H. H. J. (in press). On-line sensitivity to subject–verb agreement violations in Broca's aphasics: The role of syntactic complexity and time. *Brain and Language.*

Hakuta, K., & Diaz, R. M. (1985). The relationship between degree of bilingualism and cognitive ability: A critical discussion and some new longitudinal data. In K. E. Nelson (Ed.), *Children's language* (Vol. 5). Hillsdale, NJ: Erlbaum.

Hamburger, H., & Crain, S. (1982). Relative acquisition. In S. Kuczaj, II (Ed.), *Language development: Vol. 1. Syntax and semantics* (pp. 245–274). Hillsdale, NJ: Erlbaum.

Hamm, V. P., & Hasher, L. (1992). Age and the availability of inferences. *Psychology and Aging, 7,* 56–64.

Harrington, M., & Sawyer, M. (1992). L2 working memory capacity and L2 reading skill. *Studies in Second Language Acquisition, 14,* 25–38.

Hartley, J. T. (1986). Reader and text variables as determinants of discourse memory in adulthood. *Psychology and Aging, 1,* 150–158.

Hartley, J. T. (1988). Aging and individual differences in memory for written discourse. In L. L. Light & D. M. Burke (Eds.), *Language, memory, and aging* (pp. 36–57). New York: Cambridge University Press.

Hasher, L., & Zacks, R. (1988). Working memory, comprehension, and aging: A review and a new view. In G. H. Bower (Ed.), *The psychology of learning and motivation* (Vol. 22, pp. 193–225). San Diego, CA: Academic Press.

Holmes, V. M., & O'Regan, J. K. (1981). Eye fixation patterns during the reading of relative clause sentences. *Journal of Verbal Learning and Verbal Behavior, 20,* 417–30.

Howard, D. (1985). Agrammatism. In S. Newman & R. Epstein (Eds.), *Current perspectives in dysphasia* (pp. 1–31). London: Churchill-Livingstone.

Huey, E. B. (1908). *The psychology and pedagogy of reading.* New York: Macmillan.

Jarvella, R. J. (1971). Syntactic processing of connected speech. *Journal of Verbal Learning and Verbal Behavior, 10,* 409–416.

Jarvella, R. J. (1979). Immediate memory and discourse processing. In G. H. Bower (Ed.), *The psychology of learning and motivation* (Vol. 13). New York: Academic Press.

Johnson-Laird, P. N. (1983). *Mental models.* Cambridge, MA: Harvard University Press.

Juola, J. F., Ward, N., & McNamara, T. (1982). Visual search and reading rapid serial presentations of letter strings, words, and text. *Journal of Experimental Psychology: General, 111,* 208–227.

Just, M. A., & Carpenter, P. A. (1980). A theory of reading: From eye fixations to comprehension. *Psychological Review, 87,* 329–354.

Just, M. A., & Carpenter, P. A. (1987). *The psychology of reading and language comprehension.* Newton, MA: Allyn & Bacon.

Just, M. A., & Carpenter, P. A. (1992). A capacity theory of comprehension: Individual differences in working memory. *Psychological Review, 99,* 122–149.

Just, M. A., Carpenter, P. A., & Woolley, J. D. (1982). Paradigms and processes in reading comprehension. *Journal of Experimental Psychology: General, 111,* 228–238.

Kahneman, D. (1973). *Attention and effort*. Englewood Cliffs, NJ: Prentice-Hall.

Kean, M.-L. (1977). The linguistic interpretation of aphasic syndromes: Agrammatism in Broca's aphasia, an example. *Cognition, 5,* 9–46.

Kemper, S. (1986). Imitation of complex syntactic constructions by elderly adults. *Applied Psycholinguistics, 7,* 277–287.

Kemper, S. (1987). Life-span changes in syntactic complexity. *Journal of Gerontology, 42,* 323–328.

Kemper, S. (1988). Geriatric psycholinguistics: Syntactic limitations of oral and written language. In L. L. Light & D. M. Burke (Eds.), *Language, memory, and aging* (pp. 58–76). New York: Cambridge University Press.

Kemper, S. (1992). Language and aging. In F. I. M. Craik, & T. A. Salthouse (Eds.), *The handbook of aging and cognition* (pp. 213–270). Hillsdale, NJ: Erlbaum.

Kemper, S., Kynette, D., Rash, S., O'Brien, K., & Sprott, R. (1989). Life-span changes to adults' language: Effects of memory and genre. *Applied Psycholinguistics, 10,* 49–66.

Kimball, J. P. (1973). Seven principles of surface structure parsing in natural language. *Cognition, 2,* 15–47.

King, J., & Just, M. A. (1991). Individual differences in syntactic processing: The role of working memory. *Journal of Memory and Language, 30,* 580–602.

Kintsch, W. (1988). The use of knowledge in discourse processing; A construction–integration model. *Psychological review, 95,* 163–182.

Kintsch, W., & van Dijk, T. A. (1978). Toward a model of text comprehension and production. *Psychological Review, 85,* 363–394.

Klapp, S. T., Marshburn, E. A., & Lester, P. T. (1983). Short-term memory does not involve the "working memory" of information processing: The demise of a common assumption. *Journal of Experimental Psychology: General, 112,* 240–264.

Klatzky, R. L. (1980). *Human memory: Structures and processes* (2nd ed.). San Francisco: Freeman.

Kolk, H. H. J., & van Grunsven, M. M. F. (1985). Agrammatism as a variable phenomenon. *Cognitive Neuropsychology, 2,* 347–384.

Kolk, H. H., van Grunsven, M., & Keyser, A. (1985). On parallelism between production and comprehension in agrammatism. In M.-L. Kean (Eds.), *Agrammatism* (pp. 165–206). Orlando, FL: Academic Press.

Kurtzman, H. (1985). *Studies in syntactic ambiguity resolution*. Doctoral dissertation, Massachusetts Institute of Technology, Cambridge. Distributed by Indiana University Linguistics Club.

Kynette, D., & Kemper, S. (1986). Aging and the loss of grammatical forms: A cross-sectional study of language performance. *Language and Communication, 6,* 43–49.

Lasky, E. Z., Weider, W. E., & Johnson, J. P. (1976). Influence of linguistic complexity, rate of presentation, and interphrase pause time on auditory–verbal comprehension of adult aphasic patients. *Brain and Language, 3,* 386–395.

Levelt, W. J. M. (1989). *Speaking: From intention to articulation*. Cambridge, MA: MIT Press.

Light, L. L. (1991). Memory and aging: Four hypotheses in search of data. *Annual Review of Psychology, 42,* 333–376.

Light, L. L., & Anderson, P. A. (1985). Working-memory capacity, age, and memory for discourse. *Journal of Gerontology, 40,* 737–747.

Light, L. L., & Capps, J. L. (1986). Comprehension of pronouns in young and older adults. *Developmental Psychology, 22,* 580–585.

Linebarger, M. C., Schwartz, M. F., & Saffran, E. M. (1983). Sensitivity to grammatical structure in so-called agrammatic aphasics. *Cognition, 13,* 361–392.

Macaruso, P., Bar-Shalom, E., Crain, S., & Shankweiler, D. (1989). Comprehension of temporal terms by good and poor readers. *Language and Speech, 32,* 45–67.

MacDonald, M. C., Just, M. A., & Carpenter, P. A. (1992). Working memory constraints on the processing of syntactic ambiguity. *Cognitive Psychology, 24,* 56–98.

Mann, V. A., Shankweiler, D., & Smith, S. T. (1984). The association between comprehension of spoken sentences and early reading ability: The role of phonetic representation. *Journal of Child Language, 11,* 627–643.

Marcus, M. P. (1980). *A theory of syntactic recognition for natural language*. Cambridge, MA: MIT Press.

Marmurek, H. H. (1990). The dissociation of impression formation and person memory: The effects of processing resources and trait favorableness. *Journal of Research in Personality, 24,* 191–205.

Martin, R. C (1987). Articulatory and phonological deficits in short-term memory and their relation to syntactic processing. *Brain and Language, 32,* 159–192.

Masson, M. E. J., & Miller, J. A. (1983). Working memory and individual differences in comprehension and memory of text. *Journal of Educational Psychology, 75,* 314–318.

McLeod, B., & McLaughlin, B. (1986). Restructuring of automaticity? Reading in a second language. *Language Learning, 36,* 109–124.

McRoy, S. W., & Hirst, G. (1990). Race-based parsing and syntactic disambiguation. *Cognitive Science, 14,* 313–353.

Miceli, G., Mazzucchi, A., Menn, L., & Goodglass, H. (1983). Contrasting cases of Italian agrammatic aphasia without comprehension disorder. *Brain and Language, 19,* 65–97.

Miller, G. A. (1956). The magical number seven, plus or minus two: Some limits on our capacity for processing information. *Psychological Review, 63,* 81–97.

Miyake, A., Carpenter, P. A., & Just, M. A. (in press a). A capacity approach to syntactic comprehension disorders: Making normal adults perform like aphasic patients. *Cognitive Neuropsychology.*

Miyake, A., Just, M. A., & Carpenter, P. A. (in press b). Working memory constraints on the resolution of lexical ambiguity: Maintaining multiple interpretations in neutral contexts. *Journal of Memory and Language.*

Monsell, S. (1984). Components of working memory underlying verbal skills: A "distributed capacities" view. In H. Bouma & D. G. Bouwhuis (Eds.), *Attention and performance X: Control of language processes* (pp. 327–350). Hillsdale, NJ: Erlbaum.

Naeser, M. A., Mazurski, P., Goodglass, H., Peraino, M., Laughlin, S., & Leaper, W. C. (1987). Auditory syntactic comprehension in nine apshasia groups (with CT scans) and children: Differences in degree but not order of difficulty observed. *Cortex, 23,* 359–380.

Navon, D. (1984). Resources—A theoretical soup stone? *Psychological Review, 91,* 216–234.

Nespoulous, J.-L., Dordain, M., Perron, C., Ska, B., Bub, D., Caplan, D., Mehler, J., & Lecours, A. R. (1988). Agrammatism in sentence production without comprehension deficits: Reduced availability of syntactic structures and/or of grammatical morphemes? A case study. *Brain and Language, 33,* 273–295.

Nicholas, L. E., & Brookshire, R. H. (1986). Consistency of the effects of rate of speech on brain-damaged adults' comprehension of narrative discourse. *Journal of Speech and Hearing Research, 29,* 462–470.

Obler, L. K., Fein, D., Nicholas, M., & Albert, M. L. (1991). Auditory comprehension and aging: Decline in syntactic processing. *Applied Psycholinguistics, 12,* 433–452.

Olson, G., Duffy, S. A., & Mack, R. L. (1984). Thinking-out-loud as a method for studying real-time comprehension processes. In D. E. Kieras & M. A. Just (Eds.), *New methods in reading comprehension research* (pp. 253–286). Hillsdale, NJ: Erlbaum.

Osaka, M., & Osaka, N. (1992). Language-independent working memory as measured by Japanese and English reading span tests. *Bulletin of the Psychonomic Society, 30,* 287–289.

Pashek, G. V., & Brookshire, R. H. (1982). Effects of rate of speech and linguistic stress on auditory paragraph comprehension of aphasic individuals. *Journal of Speech and Hearing Research, 25,* 377–383.

Perfetti, C. A. (1985). *Reading ability.* New York: Oxford University Press.

Perfetti, C. A., & Goldman, S. R. (1976). Discourse memory and reading comprehension skill. *Journal of Verbal Learning and Verbal Behavior, 14,* 33–42.

Potter, M. C. (1984). Rapid serial visual presentation (RSVP): A method for studying language processing. In D. E. Kieras & M. A. Just (Eds.), *New methods in reading comprehension research* (pp. 91–118). Hillsdale, NJ: Erlbaum.

Potter, M. C., & Lombardi, L. (1990). Regeneration in the short-term recall of sentences. *Journal of Memory and Language, 29,* 633–654.

Power, M. J. (1985). Sentence production and working memory. *Quarterly Journal of Experimental Psychology, 37A,* 367–385.

Power, M. J. (1986). A technique for measuring processing load during speech production. *Journal of Psycholinguistic Research, 15,* 371–382.

Pratt, M. W., Boyes, C., Robins, S. L., & Manchester, J. (1989). Telling tales: Aging, working memory, and the narrative cohesion of story retellings. *Developmental Psychology, 25,* 628–635.

Pratt, M. W., & Robins, S. L. (1991). That's the way it was: Age differences in the structure and quality of adults' personal narratives. *Discourse Processes, 14,* 73–85.

Rayner, K., Carlson, M., & Frazier, L. (1983). The interaction of syntax and semantics during sentence processing: Eye movements in the analysis of semantically biased sentences. *Journal of Verbal Learning and Verbal Behavior, 22,* 358–374.

Reisberg, D., Rappaport, I., & O'Shaughnessy, M. (1984). Limits of working memory: The digit digit-span. *Journal of Experimental Psychology: Learning, Memory, and Cognition, 10,* 203–221.

Rosenbek, J. C., LaPointe, L. L., & Wertz, R. T. (1989). *Aphasia: A clinical introduction.* Austin, TX: Pro-Ed.

Rupp, R. R. (1980). Speech input processing, hearing loss, and aural rehabilitation with the elderly. In L. K. Obler & M. L. Albert (Eds.), *Language and communication in the elderly: Clinical and therapeutic approaches* (pp. 159–180). Lexington, MA: D. C. Heath.

Sachs, J. S. (1967). Recognition memory for syntactic and semantic aspects of connected discourse. *Perception & Psychophysics, 2,* 437–442.

Salthouse, T. A. (1988). Initiating the formalization of theories of cognitive aging. *Psychology and Aging, 3,* 3–16.

Salthouse, T. A. (1990). Working memory as a processing resource in cognitive aging. *Developmental Review, 10,* 101–124.

Salthouse, T. A. (1991). *Theoretical perspectives on cognitive aging.* Hillsdale, NJ: Erlbaum.

Salthouse, T. A. (1992). Influence of processing speed on adult age differences in working memory. *Acta Psychologia, 79,* 155–170.

Salthouse, T. A., & Babcock, R. L. (1991). Decomposing adult age differences in working memory. *Developmental Psychology, 27,* 763–776.

Salthouse, T. A., Mitchell, D. R. D., Skovronek, E., & Babcock, R. L. (1989). Effects of adult age and working memory on reasoning and spatial abilities. *Journal of Experimental Psychology: Learning, Memory, and Cognition, 15,* 507–516.

Salthouse, T. A., & Skovronek, E. (1992). Within-context assessment of age differences in working memory. *Journal of Gerontology: Psychological Sciences, 47,* 110–120.

Schneider, W., & Detweiler, M. (1987). A connectionist/control architecture for working memory. In G. H. Bower (Ed.), *The psychology of learning and motivation* (Vol. 21, pp. 53–119). Orlando, FL: Academic Press.

Schneider, W., & Shiffrin, R. M. (1977). Controlled and automatic human information processing: I. Detection, search, and attention. *Psychological Review, 84,* 1–66.

Schwartz, M. F., Linebarger, M. C., Saffran, E. M., & Pate, D. S. (1987). Syntactic transparency and sentence interpretation in aphasia. *Language and Cognitive Processes, 2,* 85–113.

Segalowitz, N. (1986). Skilled reading in a second language. In J. Vaid (Ed.), *Langauge processing in bilinguals: Psycholinguistic and neuropsychological perspectives* (pp. 3–19). Hillsdale, NJ: Erlbaum.

Segalowitz, N., & Hebert, M. (1990). Phonological recoding in the first and second language reading of skilled bilinguals. *Language Learning, 40,* 503–538.

Seidenberg, M. S., Tanenhaus, M. K., Leiman, J. M., & Bienkowski, M. (1982). Automatic access of the meanings of ambiguous words in context: Some limitations of knowledge-based processing. *Cognitive Psychology, 14,* 489–537.

Sheldon, A. (1974). The role of parallel function in the acquisition of relative clauses in English. *Journal of Verbal Learning and Verbal Behavior, 13,* 272–281.

Simpson, G. B., & Krueger, M. A. (1991). Selective access of homograph meanings in sentence context. *Journal of Memory and Language, 30,* 627–643.

Skelly, M. (1975). Aphasic patients talk back. *American Journal of Nursing, 75,* 1140–1142.

Smith, S. T., Macaruso, P., Shankweiler, D., & Crain, S. (1989). Syntactic comprehension in young poor readers. *Applied Psycholinguistics, 10,* 429–454.

Stine, E. A. L., & Wingfield, A. (1987). Process and strategy in memory for speech among younger and older adults. *Psychology and Aging, 2,* 272–279.

Stine, E. A. L., & Wingfield, A. (1990). How much do working memory deficits contribute to age differences in discourse memory? *European Journal of Cognitive Psychology, 2,* 289–304.

Stine, E. A. L., Wingfield, A., & Myers, S. D. (1990). Age differences in processing information from television news: The effects of bisensory augmentation. *Journal of Gerontology: Psychological Sciences, 45,* 1–8.

Stine, E. A. L., Wingfield, A., & Poon, L. W. (1986). How much and how fast: Rapid processing of spoken language in later adulthood. *Psychology and Aging, 4,* 303–311.

St. John, M. F., & McClelland, J. L. (1990). Learning and applying contextual constraints in sentence comprehension. *Artificial Intelligence, 46*, 217–257.

Swinney, D. A. (1979). Lexical access during sentence comprehension: (Re)consideration of context effects. *Journal of Verbal Learning and Verbal Behavior, 18*, 645–659.

Tanenhaus, M. K., Leiman, J. M., & Seidenberg, M. S. (1979). Evidence for multiple stages in the processing of ambiguous words in syntactic contexts. *Journal of Verbal Learning and Verbal Behavior, 18*, 427–440.

Taraban, R., & McClelland, J. L. (1988). Constituent attachment and thematic role assignment in sentence processing: Influences of content-based expectation. *Journal of Memory and Langauge, 27*, 597–632.

Thibadeau, R., Just, M. A., & Carpenter, P. A. (1982). A model of the time course and content of reading. *Cognitive Science, 6*, 157–203.

Tun, P. A., Wingfield, A., & Stine, E. A. L. (1991). Speech-processing capacity in young and older adults: A dual-task study. *Psychology and Aging, 6*, 3–9.

Turner, M. L., & Engle, R. W. (1989). Is working memory capacity task dependent? *Journal of Memory and Language, 28*, 127–154.

van Dijk, T. A., & Kintsch, W. (1983). *Strategies of discourse comprehension.* New York: Academic Press.

Waltz, D. L., & Pollack, J. B. (1985). Massively parallel parsing: A strongly interactive model of natural language interpretation. *Cognitive Science, 9*, 51–74.

Wanner, E. (1987). The parser's architecture. In F. Kessel (Ed.), *The development of language and language researchers: Essays in Honor of Roger Brown* (pp. 79–96). London: Erlbaum.

Wanner, E., & Maratsos, M. (1978). An ATN approach to comprehension. In M. J. Halle, J. Bresnan, & G. A. Miller (Eds.), *Linguistic theory and psychological reality* (pp. 119–161). Cambridge, MA: MIT Press.

Whitney, P., Ritchie, B. G., & Clark, M. B. (1991). Working-memory capacity and the use of elaborative inferences in text comprehension. *Discourse Processes, 14*, 133–145.

Wingfield, A., Stine, E. A. L., Lahar, C. J., & Aberdeen, J. S. (1988). Does the capacity of working memory change with age? *Experimental Aging Research, 14*, 103–107.

Wright, R. D. (1981). Aging, divided attention, and processing capacity. *Journal of Gerontology, 36*, 605–614.

Yuill, N. M., & Oakhill, J. V. (1991). *Children's problems in text comprehension.* New York: Cambridge University Press.

Yuill, N. M., Oakhill, J. V., & Parkin, A. (1989). Working memory, comprehension ability and the resolution of text anomaly. *British Journal of Psychology, 80*, 351–361.

Zelinsky, E. M. (1988). Integrating information from discourse: Do older adults show deficits? In L. L. Light & D. M. Burke (Eds.), *Language, memory, and aging* (pp. 117–132). New York: Cambridge University Press.

CHAPTER 34

FUTURE DIRECTIONS

ALAN GARNHAM

Men must pursue things which are just in present, and leave the future to divine Providence.

Francis Bacon, *The Advancement of Learning,* II.xxi.11

So long as a man rides his hobby-horse peaceably and quietly along the king's highway, and neither compels you or me to get up behind him,—pray, Sir, what have either you or I to do with it.

Laurence Sterne, *Tristram Shandy,* vol. 1, chap. 7.

I. INTRODUCTION

There is nothing more foolish than trying to predict the future. Even prophecies that seem reasonable at the time are apt to be made ridiculous by future events. More sensible is to say what one thinks ought to happen, for even if it does not, one can always claim that it, nevertheless, should have. In this final chapter I identify what seem to me some of the most interesting and important psycholinguistic developments in recent years, and hence, either explicitly or implicitly, I suggest topics on which research might profitably be pursued in the coming years. Inevitably my presentation reflects my own interests and will appear hobby-horsical, more so to some than to others. Those who disagree with me are welcome to ride their own hobby horses into the future. In my survey I follow, though sometimes only roughly, the organization of the handbook itself.

II. HISTORY

In the textbooks of a mature discipline history is rewritten, so that the state of the art can be presented in a coherent manner. Real history is written separately, and by historians. This handbook makes a start by separating out the history. We await the historians.

III. Methodology

A. The Research Environment

I begin this section with a hope that will almost certainly not be fulfilled. There are pressures on psycholinguists, and in particular young psycholinguists, that make it almost impossible to think deeply about difficult issues. They have to write grant proposals that allow them to carry out a substantial program of research in three years. And they have to ensure that they publish a reasonable number of important papers, first to get a job, then to get tenure, then to get promoted. Of course, there is something to be said for the discipline and devotion to duty that this regime entails, but it has become too protracted and too much of a game. It gets people into the habit of doing safe research—research that will attract the funds and lead, almost inexorably, to the publications.

B. Insularity

It might seem surprising to say that we still need to be less insular—that we need, as psycholinguists, to be more familiar with work in other disciplines, in particular linguistics. After all, modern psycholinguistics grew from George Miller's introduction of Chomskyan linguistics into psychology. And much psycholinguistic research, particularly that in developmental psycholinguistics, has been carried out in linguistics departments. Nevertheless, the hold of generative grammar on research into the language production and, more particularly, the language comprehension of ordinary adults was broken in the late 1960s and it has never been wholly regained (see Reber, 1987). Linguists certainly believe we are still too insular (e.g., N. Smith, 1991).

Of course the derivational theory of complexity was a naive theory, at least it seems so in retrospect. But just because it was never cast in a testable form (see Garnham, 1983) does not mean that the idea of basing a psychological theory on a linguistic one was mistaken. And even if it is, knowing about the theories, and more particularly the detailed debates, of linguistics increases one's sensitivity to the way language works.

This notion of sensitivity raises, however, an interesting point. Linguistic analyses of phenomena above the sentential level have suffered from linguists imposing two set types of analysis on them, one theoretical, the other based on "linguistic intuitions" (often the two are linked). I have always felt that the notion of a linguistic intuition is a confused one. And Bever (1970) pointed out long ago that it bears an unsatisfactory relation, from a psychological point of view, to the competence/performance distinction. The justification for the use of "linguistic intuitions" is that native speakers can often verify data about their own language for themselves. The trick is for them to know when they might be wrong. Of course, anyone who knows a syntactician knows that even in this core area of linguistics, linguists don't trust their "intuitions"—they are forever bugging people about whether they think this sentence is ok, or which of these two they think is worse. There are so many ("performance") factors that can affect such judgments that one has to take great care to make sure the data are correct. Unfortunately, such care is not always taken outside the syntactic arena. In any case, meticulous checking with other linguists is not always enough.

One interesting example of what can go wrong with "linguistic intuitions" comes from our own work on interpreting anaphoric expressions (Garnham & Oakhill, 1987, 1988, 1989). Our starting point was Hankamer and Sag's (1976; Sag & Hankamer, 1984) distinction between two types of anaphoric device: deep, or model-interpretive, anaphors and surface anaphors or ellipses. The distinction is supported by a series of seemingly uncontroversial judgments about when certain types of anaphor can and cannot be used felicitously. For example, it is ok to say (1), but it is infelicitous to say (2); compare (3).

(1) *The carpet needed beating, so John did it.*
(2) *The carpet needed beating, so John did.*
(3) *Someone needed to beat the carpet, so John did.*

The explanation is that *do it* is a model-interpretive anaphor that takes its meaning from a conceptual representation in which the wording of the antecedent (active vs. passive) is unimportant, whereas the proform *do* (often analyzed as the result of *do*-support following verb phrase ellipsis, see, e.g., Bresnan, 1976) is a surface anaphor whose interpretation is mediated by a superficial representation of the antecedent, which does preserve the active/passive distinction.

However, despite the apparent clarity of the linguistic judgments, there are reasons to doubt whether ordinary language users are as sensitive to the distinctions that underlie them as they are to, for example, straightforward syntactic errors, such as the omission of obligatory function words. Even sophisticated language users, among whom we hope we can include ourselves without too much immodesty, often fail to notice violations of the conditions that Hankamer and Sag lay down for the felicitous use of, in particular, surface anaphors. The most straightforward illustration of this fact is that, when we were compiling our corpus of anaphoric expressions (described briefly in Garnham & Oakhill, 1989), we often went through phases when we only collected a few startlingly aberrant anaphors. Nevertheless, when we set ourselves to find "interesting examples," we inevitably found more. Many supposedly infelicitous uses of anaphors simply pass the ordinary reader by.

We are, of course, somewhat cautious in the conclusions we draw from this observation. Simple syntactic errors can also be missed. For example, failures of subject–verb agreement may pass unnoticed, if a noun phrase of a different number intervenes between subject and object (e.g., Bock & Miller, 1991). Nevertheless, judgments of well-formedness at the level of discourse are considerably more fragile than those at the sentence level.

Just to close this section, if psycholinguists could be less insular, so could those who study language in other branches of cognitive science. There is, for example, room for much more sensitivity to the need for psychological techniques to answer questions that are genuinely psychological.

C. Data Analysis

Psycholinguists, like most other psychologists, are inherently conservative in their approach to data analysis. In much of adult psycholinguistics, for example, traditional factorial designs (though often using within-subject or within-material designs that are frowned on by some statisticians) coupled with ANOVA remain the norm. Although standard significance levels are often replaced by exact probabilities, this change is more a reflection of modern statistics packages than of a more sophisticated approach to statistics.

Although one sometimes despairs about the possibility of psychologists making wider use of statistical techniques developed after 1940, there has always been a modest proportion of statistically sophisticated psycholinguists, and their potential effect on the discipline is enormous. The clearest precedent is Clark's seminal 1973 paper "The language-as-fixed-effect fallacy," in which he introduced the notion of by-items analyses and the min F' statistic. Although there is a move away from reporting min F', the importance of analyses that treat items as random effects, in addition to analyses that treat subjects as random effects (or of some related procedure), cannot be stressed too strongly, given the hypotheses that psycholinguists are usually interested in testing—hypotheses about classes of linguistic items of which their experimental materials are supposed to be representative. It is, therefore, worrying that one still encounters serious misconceptions about by-items analyses and questions about whether they are worth carrying out, particularly given that there have been many arguments against them, including a number that have appeared in print (e.g., Cohen, 1976; Keppel, 1976; J. K. Smith, 1976; Wike & Church, 1976). It is necessary to distinguish between arguments against the min F' statistic itself (e.g., too conservative in certain instances), arguments for alternative techniques of checking whether findings generalize to other materials, and arguments against the whole Clark package, most of which are cases of special pleading. Failure to find an effect by items does not mean that an effect is restricted to the set of materials used in the experiment under discussion, as is sometimes still argued; it almost certainly means that it is restricted to just a few of those items. Given this restriction, it is probable that the items that produce the effect have some special properties that the experimenter has not noticed. In this connection, it is regrettable that innumeracy among social scientists (taken to include psychologists) has been identified as a serious problem, at least in the United Kingdom (Economic and Social Research Council, 1987).

Given that psycholinguists are, for a variety of reasons, producing more and more complex data sets, one of the most important lessons they could learn from recent advances in statistics is the importance of the techniques devised by John Tukey (see especially 1977), which he refers to as exploratory data analysis (EDA). Data sets should not simply be fed into the latest and fastest ANOVA package, but should be looked at using a variety of graphical (and other) techniques, many of which will now run quickly on a PC or Macintosh on data sets that are large for psycholinguistics. To give a simple example, distributions can be displayed and examined for multimodality or for long tails. Techniques of this kind led us to develop our regression contingent analysis of eye-movement (Altmann, Garnham, & Dennis, 1992), when we noticed that two conditions with different means had similar distributions, except that the one with the higher mean had a longer, fatter tail.

There are, of course, many other "newer" statistical techniques that psycholinguistics might at least consider exploring more thoroughly. Another obvious example is multivariate analysis of variance, in which several dependent variables are included in the same analysis. The technique is most likely to produce new insights when the dependent variables are not too highly correlated. It has potential applications, for example, in the analysis of reading-time experiments, where the dependent variables could include reading times for various frames, question answering times, and question answering accuracy, and in the analysis of eye-movement monitoring experiments, where different measures may reflect different processes and so need not be highly correlated.

IV. SPEECH

Research on speech—with its use of signal processing techniques such as Fourier analysis—has always had a strong engineering flavor. With the advent of cheap computer processing power (and very high power available at a price), this research has become even more technology-oriented. In the UK, for example, much research on speech falls under the head of speech and language technology (SALT), which to a psychologist at least seems an influential body with the power to lobby for (again from a psychological point of view) big money.

To some extent, psychologists, and, I gather, linguists too, feel that speech research has been hijacked by those who want to process large corpora using large computers. Much of this work is driven by the desire to produce technological products that recognize real speech (large vocabularies, many speakers). The approach taken means that the spinoffs are more likely to be for computer science (algorithms for processing large databases) than for psycholinguistics. This research may have psycholinguistic implications, but it is not yet apparent what they are.

Much of this analysis of large corpora is statistics-based—looking for recurrent patterns across large numbers of utterances. This aspect of the research suggests the possibility of neural network analysis, since neural networks are good at extracting statistical patterns from large (or large-ish) databases. If a pattern-based analysis is the only way that machines can be made to recognize speech, perhaps people use a similar technique, and perhaps the mechanism they use to do it is a neural network (and not just a neural network simulating a von Neumann machine). Research that pursued this possibility might effect a link between psychological and technological research on speech processing.

Despite the attempted hijacking, psycholinguistically oriented speech research still thrives (see Kluender; Massaro; and Remez, all this volume). There can be no question of the linguistic sophistication of this research (see, in particular, Kluender, this volume, and cf. comments above). In addition, the attempt to apply general theories of categorization to phoneme learning has already produced some interesting results (see Kluender, this volume) and seems certain to generate neural network models of this process. Identification of phonemes will initially be modeled in a single speech stream; however, the problem of segmenting an acoustic stream into sounds from different sources is one that remains to be fully solved, and the Gestalt principles incorporated into auditory scene analysis (see Remez, this volume) show that the desire to "do a Marr" on speech is far from dead. At a slightly "higher" level, as Massaro's (this volume) discussion shows, ideas about speech perception will have to be better integrated with models of auditory word identification.

V. WORD RECOGNITION

Word recognition, and in particular visual word recognition, has generated, and continues to generate, an enormous research literature. The sheer density of information in Balota's chapter (this volume) gives some indication of the size of that literature, even though it is far from comprehensive. Despite this effort, many fundamental issues remain unresolved: the role, if any, of sublexical units, and the existence of certain types of context effect, for example, or the role of context in the processing of ambiguous words (see Simpson, this volume). In recent years, connectionist models of both spoken and written word recognition have been hugely influential, though there is some indication that this work has reached an impasse. Balota suggests that some issues (e.g., the role of sublexical units) may be resolved when connectionist models are scaled up. Such a development would be a welcome one, since the field certainly needs better theories, rather than further uninterpretable data. However, as Balota also points out, there are other problems—from the dyslexic literature, for example—for connectionist models, and these problems will have to be resolved if such models are to retain their influence in this area.

Another issue that will not go away, but which, again, might be resolved in scaled-up neural network models, is that of phonological encoding in visual word recognition. Although it has been clear for some time that many of the standard findings can be explained by postlexical recoding, the still unresolved question, and the one that connectionist research might answer, is whether there is prelexical phonological recoding.

Methodological issues, too, continue to prove particularly stubborn in word identification, though they are likely to become so in other fields, too, as the questions addressed become more specific. Analysis of the processes that might contribute, for example, to lexical decision is useful, at least in protecting against unwarranted conclusions. However, my own feeling is that what is really needed is a theory that is well enough supported that it can provide some "top-down" input to the interpretation of results from experimental paradigms.

VI. WORD MEANING

Questions about word meaning have a checkered history in psycholinguistics. Indeed, there is some debate about whether they should rightly be addressed within psycholinguistics or whether they should be studied under the head of conceptualization as part of the psychology of thinking (they are not, for example, covered in any great detail in this volume). In the late 1960s and early 1970s network theories did battle with feature theories and both strove to fend off prototype theories, as typicality effects came to assume central importance. There then followed a lean period, at least in psycholinguistics, in which the network vs feature controversy was seen to be unresolvable and the prototype theory too vague. In any case, none of the theories seemed able to deal with words other than the simplest concrete common nouns.

More recently, there have been two important developments. First, exemplar theories and connectionist pattern abstraction theories have vied with better formulated versions of prototype theory and have often been found empirically superior (e.g., Gluck & Bower, 1988; Nosofsky, 1986). Second, it has been argued that conceptualization and categorization can only be explained on the assumption that concepts are defined by their place within a theory, and that even everyday concepts are embedded in mentally represented folk theories of the appropriate domains (Carey, 1985; Markman, 1989; Murphy & Medin, 1985). One problem is whether and how these two ideas can be reconciled. Connectionist networks can effectively abstract patterns that correspond to commonalities among instances of a concept, but folk theories would appear to have just the kind of structure that connectionist models have difficulty handling.

A problem shared by these accounts is that both, at least potentially, make it hard to say what a particular concept is. However, the difficulty of formulating satisfactory definitions (e.g., Fodor, Garrett, Walker, & Parkes, 1980) may provide a partial vindication for this aspect of the theories. An advantage of these accounts is that both might at least partially explicate the relation between language and perception. For example, the types of general relation (spatial, temporal, intentional, causal, moral) identified by Miller and Johnson-Laird (1976) could be part of the folk psychology and naive physics that ground our everyday concepts.

The theory-based account of concepts, though probably not the connectionist one, might usefully be supplemented with increasingly sophisticated ideas about word meaning that are emerging in linguistics. This integration should be facilitated by the fact that such approaches (e.g., Jackendoff's, 1990, conceptual semantics) have been developed in a cognitive science tradition that recognizes the importance of psychological considerations.

VII. LEARNING TO READ

I suppose that all psychologists who work on reading have the same wish: that educationalists would take them more seriously. This wish is not grounded on the belief that psychologists know how children should be taught to read, but on the belief that they do not, and that they know they do not. Some educationalists, however, do not know that they do not know the best way of teaching reading. And those that are charismatic can have an undue and, from a psychologist's point of view, unjustifiable influence on teaching practice.

Psychologists can, however, be reasonably certain of some of the things about reading. One of those is that, for skilled readers reading easy or moderately difficult texts, reading is not a "psycholinguistic guessing game." The work of Stanovich (e.g., 1980), in particular, has shown that two uses of context must be clearly distinguished. Good readers are better than poor readers at cloze tasks—they can use their knowledge to "guess" what word has been omitted from a text. But in ordinary reading good readers rely more on perceptual information to identify words—they are so good at this task that they do not need to guess what the word might be. Indeed, contextual information becomes available too slowly to have much influence on the skilled identification of common words. Poor readers, on the other hand, make more use of context to identify words as they read, which is bad news for them, as they are not very good at doing so.

Followers of F. Smith (1988) and Goodman and Goodman (1979) argue against the explicit teaching of traditional "decoding" skills. Indeed, this idea underlies a method of teaching reading that has become popular recently both in the USA and in the UK, the "apprenticeship" or "real books" approach. The method is based on the sound observation that children are more likely to want to read books that interest them, and on the unsound idea that learning to read should be like learning to speak. Thus, it converts a piece of common sense into the doctrine that children will pick up reading skills simply from being exposed to books that they like. However, all the evidence suggests that methods of teaching reading that include a systematic element of phonics work best. Unfortunately, much of what is said about how phonics works—about the role of blending, for example—is either speculative or incorrect (see Oakhill & Garnham, 1988, Chap. 4), thus providing opponents of phonics with the opportunity to produce plausible arguments against its use. Research into how and why phonics works would, therefore, have important applied, as well as theoretical, consequences.

It might be argued that psychological research on reading has been dominated too much by cognitive considerations. We have found out, for example, that the phonological awareness of 4-year-olds predicts how good they will be at reading a few years later (Bradley & Bryant, 1983). However, looked at from a broader perspective, these effects are small, and those who work with children know that far more important in determining progress in reading are aspects of the home environment, the availability of books, interest in letters and rhymes—interest, indeed, in language in general. If these influences really are straightforward effects of aspects of the environment, it will be much easier to show, at least in principle, how we can help children from poor environments learn to read.

We have argued elsewhere (Oakhill & Garnham, 1988) that, in the study of learning to read and its problems, two main sets of processes should be distinguished: decoding and comprehension. Often a poor reader will have problems in both domains, but the skills of decoding and comprehension are different enough that some children who are good at one will be poor at the other. Decoding problems have had more than their fair share of attention, though, as noted above, there is still much to be found out about how decoding skills are learned. However, there is a growing recognition that children have to learn to comprehend written language, and that their skills in comprehending spoken language do not necessarily transfer to the domain of print. Reading researchers need to know why those skills sometimes do not transfer smoothly, and what can be done to help.

VIII. PARSING

Although a comparatively small research field, work on syntactic processing has produced some of the most interesting results, and some of the fiercest controversy, of the last 15 years. The results of this work also bear on the more general issue of modularity. For about a decade from the late 1970s what has become known as the garden path (GP) theory (see Mitchell, this volume) went virtually unchallenged in the psycholinguistic literature. However, recent studies from a number of labs have produced results that are difficult for the GP theory to accommodate (e.g., Altmann et al., 1992; Boland, Tananhaus, & Garnsey, 1990; Taraban & McClelland, 1988; Trueswell & Tanenhaus, 1991). These studies demonstrate the effect of nonsyntactic factors on parsing. The crucial issue, however, is when these factors have their effect. Is it on the initial stages of analysis, as opponents of the GP theory would argue, or is it at a stage of reanalysis, as proponents of the GP theory would claim?

The GP theory was quickly elaborated to include a so-called THEMATIC PROCESSOR, which deals with many aspects of reanalysis (e.g., Rayner, Carlson, & Frazier, 1983) and which has been invoked, on the assumption that it is fast-acting, in an attempt to accommodate some of the recalcitrant experimental findings. A crucial question in the coming years will, therefore, be whether further refined versions of the GP theory are empirically distinguishable from alternative theories, which claim that nonsyntactic factors have a more direct effect on syntactic processing. To put this question another way: When does fast reanalysis become empirically indistinguishable from initial analysis? More generally still, is the idea that the language processing system is modular a testable one?

At this point readers of a certain age (like me) will probably experience a feeling of déjà vu. When I first entered graduate school, as a budding psycho-linguist, the burning question in sentence processing was that of syntactic–semantic interaction–an issue that ended the 1970s with the label "unresolv-able" firmly attached to it. However, modern experimental techniques, and in particular eye-movement monitoring, allow a more precise determination of which issues are unresolvable. An attractive idea, which has some of the proper-ties of a middle way between the GP theory and its rivals, is that of minimal commitment in the initial analysis (see Mitchell, this volume). However, this idea has still to be worked out in a form that is both viable and compatible with the empirical evidence.

Another important issue in parsing research is whether gaps (and their corresponding empty categories) are psychologically real. This issue is related to a debate in linguistics about the use of empty categories in describing the phrase structure of natural language sentences. Although psycholinguistic stud-ies of the processing of sentences with empty categories have often produced inconclusive results, Pickering and Barry (1991) have recently made a series of observations that appear to favor a gap-free account of processing, in which "moved" constituents are linked directly to the constituents (usually verbs) that subcategorize for them, rather than indirectly via an empty category in the "canonical" sentence position for the moved constituent. If this account receives support from sentence processing experiments, it will have important implications for theories of parsing and, possibly, for linguistic analysis.

This account would also mesh well with ideas about the importance of thematic roles in sentence processing. Thematic roles are typically assigned to elements that are subcategorized for in syntactic structure. In the theory pro-posed by Pickering and Barry, a potential (thematic) role filler is linked directly to the element that subcategorizes for it and, hence, assigns it a role. There is no need to wait for the gap until the role is assigned. This idea would be consistent with evidence for the immediate use of thematic role information in parsing (Tanenhaus, Carlson, & Trueswell, 1989).

The notion of thematic roles is a problematic one. In government and binding theory (GB), thematic roles are treated as part of the grammar, but many of the phenomena that thematic roles are supposed to account for might be better explained by people's knowledge about the world and how it influences their comprehension of sentences (see, e.g., Ladusaw & Dowty, 1988). Fortunately, much of this debate is irrelevant to the psychological questions. Whether thematic roles are assigned directly or indirectly via the role of the corresponding object (or whatever) in an event, state or process does not much matter to questions about parsing. The status of thematic roles is, however, more important for an account of how lexical information is mentally represented and used in sentence processing and, more generally, for the question of modularity. In GB, the roles associated with a subcategorizer are encoded in a THEMATIC GRID. This grid may be abstracted from world knowledge about the actions, states, or processes that correspond to the relevant verb (the subcategorizer) and stored in the mental lexicon, or it may be constructed on the fly, using knowledge about the world, each time the verb is encountered.

IX. FIGURATIVE LANGUAGE

Psycholinguistics has tended to shun the idea that figurative language might be central to its concerns. The psycholinguistic question about figurative language has been: Is figurative language interpreted directly, or indirectly by conversational implicatures, as proposed by Grice (1975) and applied by him (Grice, 1978) to figurative language? The hoped-for answer was that the comprehension of figurative language is parasitic on the comprehension of literal language. The weight of evidence now goes against this Gricean view (Cacciari & Glucksberg, this volume; Gibbs, this volume), as do some recent pragmatic treatments of figurative language (e.g., Sperber & Wilson, 1986). However, even if there is a consensus that the Gricean view is wrong, there is no clear agreement about the detailed content of the alternative view. There is an urgent need to specify in more detail this view that both literal and figurative language are understood by the same mechanism, using contextual support. Gibbs (this volume) suggests that in spelling out this view, psycholinguists will find that some of the questions they must answer are not questions about immediate on-line comprehension of the kind that many of them are happiest with. For example, one crucial disagreement is about the psycholinguistic import of, and hence the role in a processing account of, Lakoff's (1987; Lakoff & Johnson, 1980) provocative views on metaphor. One possibility is that Lakoff's views have direct processing consequences. Another is that they are best viewed as a metalevel description of (part of) the content of our conceptual systems.

X. TEXT COMPREHENSION

A. Mental Models

People, psycholinguists included, find it difficult to think sensibly about text comprehension. The mental models theory provides a framework in which this thinking becomes less difficult. Unfortunately, the term "mental model" is used in different ways by different people. Indeed, the popularity of the notion has resulted in it becoming ill defined. The problem in psychology is not so acute as in human–computer interaction, where the term seems to have lost any meaning it once had, but there is nevertheless a problem. Many people associate the term "mental model" with highly elaborated representations of the content of texts, often spatial in nature. However, mental models do not represent only spatial information, they do not represent (other) information only spatially, and they need not be highly elaborated. What must be brought back to the center of attention is the set of concerns that mental models theory was originally intended to highlight. These concerns include the incremental nature of text comprehension and the importance of questions about reference and coreference. They are concerns that tend to be overlooked in studies motivated by questions of the form: Does this or that manipulation of a text make it more difficult to understand? More generally, the mental models theory focuses on the detailed mental processes that construct and manipulate representations of the content of texts and on the information that is encoded into such representations.

B. Anaphora

A major achievement of the mental models theory is that it provides a framework in which a conceptually coherent account of anaphor interpretation can be formulated. In this respect its links with modern versions of model theoretic semantics, such as discourse representation theory (Kamp, 1981), file change semantics (Heim, 1983), and situation semantics (Barwise & Perry, 1983) is clear. Nevertheless, a detailed psychological theory of anaphor interpretation, within the mental models framework, remains to be developed.

As we have argued in several places (e.g., Garnham & Oakhill, 1989), Johnson-Laird's original suggestion (1983, pp. 393ff)—that Sag and Hankamer's (1984) account of anaphor processing should be adopted as a starting point—was a plausible one. On this account, anaphors are divided into two main groups, model interpretive anaphors, which include most definite and indefinite pronouns and definite noun phrase anaphors; and ellipses, which include most verbal elliptical forms. These two types of anaphor are interpreted directly from a mental model, and indirectly via a representation of the surface form of the text, respectively. Nevertheless, we have also argued that the theory does not work. Mental models are implicated in the interpretation of ellipses (e.g., Garnham & Oakhill, 1987), and representations of surface form are implicated in the interpretation of model theoretic anaphors (e.g., Carreiras, Garnham, & Oakhill, 1993). These results should inform a more accurate theory of anaphor interpretation, within the mental models framework.

C. Inference

Questions about inference-making in text comprehension will continue to be central, despite the apparently insurmountable difficulties in answering them (see Singer, this volume). Maybe the questions need reformulating. I made some suggestions to this effect in a recent overview of four *wh*-questions about inference making (what, when, why and how; Garnham, 1989). In particular, in answer to the question of when inferences are made, I suggested that the mental processing that contributes to inference-making occurs when the text is being mentally encoded, while its representation(s) are being stored, and when information about the text is being retrieved. I was not merely claiming that some inferences are made at encoding and some at retrieval, but that processes at encoding, storage, and retrieval could contribute to the same inference. This idea was based on an earlier observation (Garnham, 1982) about the correct account of why implicit and highly probably explicit case fillers (e.g., instruments) are confused in memory. My OMISSION THEORY suggests that both kinds of case filler are left out of the representation of the content of a text, to be reconstructed at retrieval, if required (see also Spiro & Esposito, 1981). I showed that this theory made the same predictions for memory experiments as the theory that highly probable implicit instruments are immediately inferred and encoded during reading, but was to be preferred on a priori grounds. The predictions of the theory that inferences are deferred until the memory test did not fit the data.

The omission theory relates, albeit indirectly, to the perennial question of how much inference-making people engage in as they read or listen—indirectly, since it provides an alternative perspective on evidence in favor of immediate, and perhaps extensive, inference-making. Thinking on this topic has changed dramatically over the last 25 years. Bransford and others argued for extensive on-line inference-making, almost entirely from memory experiments. This indirect evidence for inference during comprehension had an alternative, retrieval-based explanation, which was supported by a number of elegant empirical studies, most notably those of Corbett and Dosher (1978). These ideas led to the distinction between inferences necessary to produce a coherent interpretation of a text and those that are merely elaborative.

The idea that only necessary inferences are made during normal comprehension (whatever that is) has seemed counterintuitive to many—though it may be no worse for that—and from one perspective, the work of the 1980s can be viewed as an attempt to discover which, if any, inferences, other than necessary ones, are made during comprehension (see Sanford & Garrod, this volume). As I have already mentioned, the mental models approach to text comprehension is sometimes taken to claim that elaborative inference-making is part of normal text comprehension. For example, in his preface to a recent edited volume on inference-making (Graesser & Bower, 1990) Graesser described a situation model, usually regarded as equivalent to a mental model, as "a FULLY ELABORATED representation about a specific experience or situation, with information about the spatial setting, characters, activities, events, and state of affairs suggested by the text" (p. xviii, emphasis added). Part of the reason is that mental model theorists explicitly acknowledge their debt to Bransford, and their broad acceptance of his view that comprehension is both an INTEGRATIVE and a CONSTRUCTIVE process. McKoon and Ratcliff (1992) have recently contrasted a mental models, or constructivist, view with their own minimalist view of inference, according to which "only the two classes of inferences, those based on easily available information and those required for local coherence, are encoded during reading, unless a reader adopts special goals or strategies" (p. 2). However, this contrast is based on a misunderstanding of what is meant by constructivism and of what is entailed more generally by the mental models approach.

To say that text comprehension is a constructive process is to say that information explicit in the text must be combined with information from long-term memory to construct a representation of the text. Constructive processes are required even for simple inferences that establish local coherence, for example Haviland and Clark's (1974) justly famous "beer is a likely component of (Californian) picnic supplies." Even if a position something like McKoon and Ratcliff's minimalist one is correct, comprehension is a constructive process.

It follows that, even if the mental models theory subscribes to Bransford's view of comprehension as integrative and constructive, it need not be committed to the view that elaborative inferences are made willy-nilly during comprehension. Indeed, McKoon and Ratcliff's minimalist hypothesis has a remarkably familiar ring to it (see Garnham, 1989, p. 169). The crucial assumptions of the mental models theory lie elsewhere from what it has to say about elaborative inference-making (e.g., Garnham & Oakhill, 1993).

McKoon and Ratcliff's characterization of the minimalist position raises an important question about what counts as an inference necessary to establish the coherence of a text. Their focus is on the local links widely studied by psycholinguists since Haviland and Clark. However, there are other inferences that do not necessarily establish local links but without which a text cannot be properly understood (see also Singer, this volume, on distal causal bridging inferences). For example, Gernsbacher, Goldsmith, and Robertson (1992; Gernsbacher & Robertson, 1992) have shown that readers will often infer the emotional states of characters even if those emotional states are not directly mentioned in the text. And although the inference to an emotional state may not link sentences locally, it is impossible to get the point of a story about Tom's friend Joe being fired from a job in a 7–11 store as a result of Tom's stealing money from the cash register while Joe was in the storage room, without inferring Tom's feeling of guilt. Of course it remains an empirical question whether such inferences are made—Gernsbacher's results suggest they are—but there is nevertheless a clear sense in which such inferences are crucial to the point of the story. Other types of "necessary," but nonlocal, inferences deserve investigation.

Constructive inferences require information from long-term memory, so what happens when people do not have the required knowledge? The answer that immediately suggests itself is that they cannot make the inference. However, closer consideration shows that this answer is too simple. There is a crucial distinction between textual signals that show that an inference is required and the particular piece of knowledge that underlies the inference. So, for example, in the Haviland and Clark "beer" inference, the occurrence of a definite noun phrase *the beer* signals the need for an inference, whereas the underlying knowledge is about the connection between beer and Californian picnic supplies. Psycholinguists have usually studied inference-making in cases where people both recognize the textual signals—which they do as competent speakers of their native language—and have the requisite piece of knowledge. However, Noordman and Vonk (1992) have recently investigated what happens when people do not have the necessary knowledge. In such cases they obviously recognize such textual cues for inferences as *because* (causal inference, evidential inference, inference to person's reasons) and *but* (inference to some relevant contrast). Often, in the absence of the right background knowledge, that knowledge can be reconstructed from the text, together with its inferential signal. For example, from (4) it can be deduced that not reacting with other substances is a property that a propellant should have.

(4) *Chlorine compounds are frequently used as propellants, because they do not react with other substances.*

Nevertheless, Noordman and Vonk found that people who did not have this information did not derive it as they read the sentence, though they presumably registered that *because* signaled a causal link between the information in the two clauses. Conversely—and this suggestion fits with McKoon and Ratcliff's idea that inferences "based on easily available information" are made—Noordman and Vonk suggest, although they admit their evidence here is much weaker, that elaborative inference may be made when they are strongly suggested.

XI. INDIVIDUAL DIFFERENCES

Individual differences used to mean psychometrics, and in many areas of psycholinguists that topic is barely beginning to recover from the bad press that "psychometrics" has come to mean. One area to have suffered less than others is aphasiology, where the importance of treating patients, as opposed to studying them, naturally leads to a focus on individual cases. Indeed, some aphasiologists (e.g., Caramazza & McCloskey, 1988) and other neuropsychologists (e.g., Shallice, 1979) argue that single case studies are crucially important, and Caramazza, in particular, argues that pooling data across subjects can be grossly misleading.

While Caramazza's position may be too extreme (see Caplan, this volume), pooling data, even in laboratory experiments with normal subjects, can lead to the wrong conclusions. Thus, Carpenter, Miyake and Just's (this volume) suggestion that differences in working memory capacity can lead to qualitative differences in parsing performance is a welcome one. Whether this particular theory is correct or not, it alerts us to the kind of difference that we should bear more strongly in mind in future psycholinguistic research.

XII. CROSS-LINGUISTIC APPROACHES

Like linguists before them, psycholinguists have gradually come to realize that, if they are to make universal claims, in this case about language processing mechanisms, they should not restrict themselves to the study of English. However, although there has been a growing number of cross-linguistic studies in all the domains of psycholinguistics, the full potential of such studies remains to be exploited. Our own work on pronouns illustrates both the linguistic and psycholinguistic problems that can arise in theories that are designed primarily with English in mind. Sag and Hankamer's (1984) idea that pronouns are interpreted from a mental model ignores the fact that in languages other than English, pronouns that refer to inanimate objects take the arbitrary nonsyntactic gender of the noun used to introduce their referent into a text, or with the noun that would most naturally have been used. In such languages it is easy to construct sentences in which the pronouns can only be interpreted by using a gender match. Furthermore, our experimental research in Spanish (Carreiras, Garnham, & Oakhill, 1993) and in French (in collaboration with Marie-France Ehrlich) has shown that even when a gender match is not needed to resolve a pronoun it still speeds processing. If pronouns are interpreted directly from mental models, the account of what information is included in a mental model will have to be revised.

XIII. LANGUAGE ACQUISITION

Early modern work on language acquisition (e.g., Brown, 1973) was driven by hypotheses from linguistics. It was, however, followed by a period in which, on the one hand, reports of observational research became more descriptive and, on the other hand, theoretical analyses of language acquisition, mainly carried out by linguists, were largely divorced from empirical data. One of the most welcome recent developments in research on language acquisition has been the beginning of a rapprochement between the theoretical and empirical approaches, notably in the work of Pinker (e.g., 1989). This development should be assisted by the wide availability of the CHILDES database, which will allow language acquisition researchers to test predictions from their theories without having to collect huge new corpora of data.

Studies of the development of phonology are now highly sophisticated (see Gerken, this volume). As Gerken points out, one question that is bound to attract increasing attention is the role of suprasegmental cues in the acquisition of syntax. Another, given the astonishing abilities of the neonate, is the role, if any, of in utero influences on language development. For obvious reasons, these influences will almost inevitably be phonological.

XIV. PRODUCTION

Compared with comprehension, production has always been a neglected aspect of language processing within psycholinguistics. One surprising lacuna has been that the substantial body of research on production in pragmatics, sociolinguistics, and ethnomethodology has, with the exception of the work of Clark and his colleagues (see Clark, this volume), inspired little psycholinguistic research. However, the attempt to formulate precise psycholinguistic research questions, based on these ideas from related disciplines, immediately suggests a possible reason: It is difficult to produce testable ideas!

Work on the mechanics of constructing sentences has long been dominated by Garrett's model (e.g., 1975, for an early version), though many of its specific assumptions have been challenged. Levelt, in his 1989 book *Speaking*, presents a detailed working out of a model in the spirit of Garrett's, though he stresses the importance of computer modeling and of the use of data from sources other than speech errors (see also Bock & Levelt, this volume). It is to be hoped that the emphasis on theory in this work, before much of the data is in, will ensure that some of the problems that have arisen in the study of comprehension will not be repeated in the study of production.

XV. LANGUAGE AND BRAIN

Psycholinguists have always had a stand-offish relationship with neuropsychologists. Most of psycholinguistics adopts the traditional symbolic approach to cognition, according to which mental representations and processes should be characterized and studied at an abstract level, independent of neural mechanisms. Traditional neuropsychology has discovered much about aphasia, but this work has had almost no influence in thinking about such topics as word identification, syntactic analysis, interpretation, and language production. However, neurolinguistic research itself has been increasingly influenced by linguistic analysis, so that theories about aphasic deficits now make reference to the fine details of GB theory. However, the (still largely implicit) link with normal language processing remains at an abstract level: If this (GB) framework is a useful one for studying language deficits, it ought to be useful for describing language processing in normals. A more exciting idea would be that research on aphasia should tell us something new about models of sentence processing to choose the area that Zurif and Swinney focus on. However, drawing conclusions about normal psychological functioning on the basis of grossly pathological cases has always been fraught with problems, and there is no reason to believe that these problems have been solved.

Zurif and Swinney end their chapter with the hope that aphasics will eventually be classified by lesion site. This idea, coming from an increasingly cognitive approach to neurolinguistics, is a surprising one and conflicts with conclusions drawn by advocates of other cognitive approaches to neuropsychology, particularly those that have their origins in the UK. These approaches have had much closer links with psycholinguistics, particularly in the area of word identification, but have largely eschewed specific questions about the brain. Even where these approaches have led to connectionist models, which can make appeal to a general similarity with the functioning of the brain, the specifics of language and brain have been set aside.

In principle, a complete cognitive science of language processing should integrate analyses at the three levels identified by Marr (e.g., 1982): computational theory, representation and algorithm, and neural implementation. Marr shows how the three levels of analysis fit together into a complete picture in his analysis of low-level vision. The nature of the algorithm that computes boundaries in an image is, for example, reflected in the neural architecture on which it is implemented. Marr does not, however, claim that the algorithm (or for that matter the computational theory) can be derived by considering the neural architecture. Indeed, he argues that the function of the neural architecture cannot be understood except in the light of the computational theory. On this view, then, psycholinguists should continue with their work at the levels of computational theory and of algorithm and representation and only in the longer term seek an integration of their results with those of brain researchers. All the indications are that integration at this level of detail will only be achieved in the long term.

Working from the other end, as it were, brain imaging techniques will, where money allows, help to map out, initially at a coarse level, the areas of the brain that are important in language processing. As in other areas of cognitive functioning, questions about the involvement of subcortical structures are likely to become increasingly important, as they already have in some areas of psycholinguistics (e.g., speech production, see Lieberman, 1991).

XVI. COMPUTATIONAL WORK

A. Computer Modeling

Psychological theories are often vaguely formulated, so it is not possible to extract precise predictions from them. One of the virtues of artificial intelligence (AI) was supposed to be that it forced researchers to be more explicit about the processing they hypothesised as underlying, say, language comprehension. However, from a psychological point of view, traditional AI research suffered from two defects. First, because the goal was often a working system, and a working system with reasonably broad coverage, many AI programs had ad hoc patches that were of no psychological interest and that were only included to make the system work. Worse, many of these patches disguised fundamental problems in modeling aspects of language processing. Second, because of the differences in the underlying architecture (von Neumann machine vs. massively parallel brain), it was difficult to use AI programs to model data collected in psycholinguistic experiments, even though those programs were supposed to model the mental processes that produced the data.

The existence of such AI programs almost certainly contributed to psycholinguists' reluctance to engage in their own computer modeling. This reluctance is regrettable, because computer modeling can force a psycholinguist both to formulate a theory in such a way that it makes explicit predictions, and to produce a program that can model data from experiments. Once a theory is embodied in a computer model, its predictions are often seen to be different from those that appear to follow from armchair contemplation. Indeed, Broadbent (1987) argues that such cases are the most interesting. A few psycholinguists have regularly proclaimed the virtues of this kind of computer modeling—Johnson-Laird is a prime example—but it has only really blossomed with the advent of connectionism.

B. Connectionism

One of the hardest things to predict is the future role of connectionism in psycholinguistic research. Connectionist models, back to the interactive activation model (McClelland & Rumelhart, 1981; Rumelhart & McClelland, 1982) and its precursors, have made a dramatic impact on research into word-level processes. However, the explanations that neural network models provide can be difficult to discern, particularly when the nets have learned their tasks rather than being hard-wired. Against this disadvantage, such models are usually fully implemented, and hence their predictions are easy to derive and test.

Despite this advantage, at the higher syntactic and message levels, the influence of neural network models has been minimal, occasional claims to the contrary notwithstanding. A glance at the literature confirms this feeling. It is scarcely possible to write about auditory word recognition without mentioning TRACE (McClelland & Elman, 1986), or about the identification of written words without mentioning the Seidenberg and McClelland (1989) model. But most papers on syntactic analysis and discourse processing end without mentioning connectionism (but see Kintsch, this volume).

Even at the word level, something of an impasse seems to have been reached, as in connectionist modeling in cognitive science in general. This impasse manifests itself both in a stagnation in connectionist research—for example, in the domain of spoken word identification there has been no significant development since TRACE—and in the rhetoric. The arguments of Fodor and Pylyshyn (1988), Pinker and Prince (1988), and others suggest that connectionist models as they stand are fundamentally inadequate to the task of modeling our linguistic abilities. Fodor and Pylyshyn's (1988) critique seems to rule out connectionist models, at least as presently defined, of syntactic and semantic processes, whereas Pinker and Prince's (1988) attack is on a specific (and particularly weak—no hidden units) model of one aspect of lexical processing, and their critique does not generalize so readily. English spelling-to-sound "rules," in the modeling of which connectionist models have had their real successes, may only be statistical regularities, even if the rules of the past tense system are not. Nevertheless, both types of argument suggest that, if the connectionist framework is to contribute to the modeling of high-level cognitive processes, it needs to be extended. Connectionist research, at least within psychology, tends to be carried out within strictly defined boundaries, defined largely by the connectionist "Bible" (Rumelhart, McClelland, & the PDP Research Group, 1986; McClelland, Rumelhart, & the PDP Research Group, 1986). Development of neural network techniques has largely passed into the hands of people who are mathematically more sophisticated than most psychologists. New kinds of models may emerge that do not fit the Rumelhart/McClelland/Hinton definition, and that may not, indeed, be purely associationist.

One conclusion that might be drawn from Fodor and Pylyshyn's arguments against connectionism, and McClelland, Rumelhart, and Hinton's (1986) arguments for, is that some amalgam of the symbolic and subsymbolic approaches is necessary. One suggestion that is often made informally is that a symbolic system should, in some sense, "sit on top of" a connectionist one. While this suggestion is superficially attractive, systems of this kind have not been forthcoming and, indeed, it is unclear what "sitting on top of" would mean in practice. Other kinds of hybridization seem more plausible, though within the connectionist framework they seem to be regarded as archaic. Thus, the interactive activation model and TRACE models can be thought of as hybrid models, since the units in these systems represent features (of letters at particular positions), letters at particular positions, and words (again, in TRACE at least, at particular positions). Typically, however, such models do not learn; thus they lose one of the great advantages of connectionist modeling.

Of course, there are models in other branches of cognitive science that combine some of the advantages of traditional symbolic models with some of the advantages of connectionist models (most importantly, multiple simultaneous constraint satisfaction). Waltz's (1975) filtering algorithm for finding interpretations of line drawings of BLOCKSWORLD scenes is an early example. The prototypical example is Marr's work on vision. This latter research has often been subjected to hijack attempts by connectionists, but, despite his emphasis on massively parallel processing, their is no doubt that Marr (1982) was deeply committed to symbolic representations. In an area somewhat closer to psycholinguistics, Holyoak and Thagard (1989, 1990) have recently suggested an approach that they label "symbolic connectionism." However, since they too appeal to constraint satisfaction, their amalgam of symbolic and connectionist ideas is not as new as they imply.

XVII. THE REAL FUTURE?

I said at the beginning that it is foolish to attempt to predict the future. What I have done is to highlight a range of issues that, in my view, could lead to interesting and productive research programs. I have admitted to being hobbyhorsical, and I do not expect other readers of this handbook to concur with my judgment, or to condone my relative ignorance of what has been happening in some branches of psycholinguistics. One thing, however, is certain. There are more than enough important and difficult questions about language processing to keep all of us and more busy for the foreseeable future. There is no doubt about the future of psycholinguistics or that there will be far more material to cover in the second edition of this Handbook.

ACKNOWLEDGMENTS

I would like to thank Jane Oakhill and Morton Gernsbacher for comments on previous versions of this chapter. The author's work is supported by grants C00232439 "Mental models and the interpretation of anaphora" from the ESRC, SPG 8920151 "Parsing in context" from the ESRC/MRC/SERC Joint Initiative on Human Computer Interaction and Cognitive Science, and CRG.890527 "A cross-linguistic study of anaphor interpretation" from NATO.

REFERENCES

Altmann, G. T. M., Garnham, A., & Dennis, Y. (1992). Avoiding the garden path: Eye movements in context. *Journal of Memory and Language, 31,* 685–712.

Barwise, J., & Perry, J. (1983). *Situations and attitudes.* Cambridge, MA: MIT Press/Bradford Books.

Bever, T. G. (1970). The cognitive basis of linguistic structures. In J. R. Hayes (Ed.), *Cognition and the development of language* (pp. 279–362). New York: Wiley.

Bock, K., & Miller, C. A. (1991). Broken agreement. *Cognitive Psychology, 23,* 45–93.

Boland, J. E., Tanenhaus, M. K., & Garnsey, S. M. (1990). Evidence for immediate use of verb control information in sentence processing. *Journal of Memory and Language, 29,* 413–432.

Bradley, L., & Bryant, P. E. (1983). Categorising sounds and learning to read: A causal connection. *Nature (London), 301,* 419–421.

Bresnan, J. W. (1976). On the form and functioning of transformations. *Linguistic Inquiry, 7,* 3–40.

Broadbent, D. E. (1987). Simple models for experimentable situations. In P. Morris (Ed.), *Modelling cognition* (pp. 169–185). Chichester, Sussex: John Wiley & Sons.

Brown, R. (1973). *A first language: The early stages.* Cambridge, MA: Harvard University Press.

Caramazza, A., & McCloskey, M. (1988). The case for single-patient studies. *Cognitive Neuropsychology, 5,* 517–528.

Carey, S. (1985). *Conceptual change in childhood.* Cambridge, MA: MIT Press/Bradford Books.

Carreiras, M., Garnham, A., & Oakhill, J. V. (1993). The use of superficial and meaning-based representations in interpreting pronouns: Evidence from Spanish. *European Journal of Cognitive Psychology, 5,* 93–116.

Clark, H. H. (1973). The language-as-fixed-effect fallacy: A critique of language statistics in psychological research. *Journal of Verbal Learning and Verbal Behavior, 12,* 335–359.

Cohen, J. (1976). Random means random. *Journal of Verbal Learning and Verbal Behavior, 15,* 261–262.

Corbett, A. T., & Dosher, B. A. (1978). Instrument inferences in sentence encoding. *Journal of Verbal Learning and Verbal Behavior, 17,* 479–491.

Economic and Social Research Council. (1987). *Horizons and opportunities in the social sciences.* London: Economic and Social Research Council.

Fodor, J. A., Garrett, M. F., Walker, E. C. T., & Parkes, C. H. (1980). Against definitions. *Cognition, 8,* 263–369.

Fodor, J. A., & Pylyshyn, Z. W. (1988). Connectionism and cognitive architecture: A critical analysis. *Cognition, 28,* 3–71.

Garnham, A. (1982). Testing psychological theories about inference making. *Memory & Cognition, 10,* 341–349.

Garnham, A. (1983). Why psycholinguists don't care about DTC: A reply to Berwick and Weinberg. *Cognition, 15,* 263–269.

Garnham, A. (1989). Inference in language understanding: What, when, why and how. In R. Dietrich & C. F. Graumann (Eds.), *Language processing in social context* (pp. 153–172). Asterdam: North-Holland.

Garnham, A., & Oakhill, J. V. (1987). Interpreting elliptical verb phrases. *Quarterly Journal of Experimental Psychology, 39A,* 611–627.

Garnham, A., & Oakhill, J. V. (1988). "Anaphoric islands" revisited. *Quarterly Journal of Experimental Psychology, 40A,* 719–735.

Garnham, A., & Oakhill, J. V. (1989). The everyday use of anaphoric expressions: Implications for the "mental models" theory of text comprehension. In N. E. Sharkey (Ed.), *Models of cognition: A review of cognitive science* (pp. 78–112). Norwood, NJ: Ablex.

Garnham, A., & Oakhill, J. V. (1993). Modèles mentaux et compréhension du langage. In M.-F. Ehrlich, H. Tardieu, & M. Cavazza (Eds.), *Les modèles mentaux: Approche cognitive des représentations* (pp. 23–46). Paris: Masson.

Garrett, M. F. (1975). The analysis of sentence production. In G. H. Bower (Ed.), *The psychology of learning and motivation 9* (pp. 133–177). New York: Academic Press.

Gernsbacher, M. A., Goldsmith, H. H., & Robertson, R. R. W. (1992). Do readers mentally represent characters' emotional states? *Cognition and Emotion, 6,* 89–111.

Gernsbacher, M. A., & Robertson, R. R. W. (1992). Knowledge activation versus sentence mapping when representing fictional characters' emotional states. *Language and Cognitive Processes, 7,* 353–371.

Gluck, M. A., & Bower, G. H. (1988). Evaluating an adaptive network model of human learning. *Journal of Memory and Language, 27,* 166–195.

Goodman, K. S., & Goodman, Y. M. (1979). Learning to read is natural. In L. B. Resnick & P. A. Weaver (Eds.), *Theory and practice of early reading* (Vol. 1, pp. 137–154). Hillsdale, NJ: Erlbaum.

Graesser, A. C., & Bower, G. H. (Eds.). (1990). *Inferences in text comprehension: The psychology of learning and motivation* (Vol. 25). San Diego, CA: Academic Press.

Grice, H. P. (1975). Logic and conversation. In P. Cole & J. Morgan (Eds.), *Syntax and semantics 3: Speech acts* (pp. 41–58). New York: Academic Press.

Grice, H. P. (1978). Further notes on logic and conversation. In P. Cole (Ed.), *Syntax and semantics 9: Pragmatics* (pp. 121–152). New York: Academic Press.

Hankamer, J., & Sag, I. A. (1976). Deep and surface anaphora. *Linguistic Inquiry, 7,* 391–428.

Haviland, S. E., & Clark, H. H. (1974). What's new? Acquiring new information as a process in comprehension. *Journal of Verbal Learning and Verbal Behavior, 13,* 512–521.

Heim, I. (1983). File change semantics and the familiarity theory of definiteness. In R. Bauerle, C. Schwarze, & A. von Stechow (Eds.), *Meaning, use, and interpretation of language* (pp. 164–189). Berlin: de Gruyter.

Holyoak, K. J., & Thagard, P. R. (1989). Analogical mapping by constraint satisfaction. *Cognitive Science, 13,* 295–355.

Holyoak, K. J., & Thagard, P. R. (1990). A constraint-satisfaction approach to analogue retrieval and mapping. In K. J. Gilhooly, M. T. G. Keane, R. H. Logie, & G. Erdos (Eds.), *Lines of thinking: Reflections of the psychology of thought* (Vol. 1, pp. 205–220). Chichester, Sussex: Wiley.

Jackendoff, R. S. (1990). *Semantic structures.* Cambridge, MA: MIT Press.

Johnson-Laird, P. N. (1983). *Mental models: Towards a cognitive science of language, inference, and consciousness.* Cambridge: Cambridge University Press.

Kamp, H. (1981). A theory of truth and semantic representation. In J. Groenendijk, T. Janssen, & M. Stokof (Eds.), *Formal methods in the study of language* (pp. 255–278). Amsterdam: Mathematical Centre Tracts.

Keppel, G. (1976). Words as random variables. *Journal of Verbal Learning and Verbal Behavior, 15,* 263–265.

Ladusaw, W. A., & Dowty, D. R. (1988). Toward a nongrammatical account of thematic roles. In W. Wilkins (Ed.), *Syntax and semantics 21: Thematic roles* (pp. 62–73). San Diego, CA: Academic Press.

Lakoff, G. (1987). *Women, fire and dangerous things: What categories reveal about the mind.* Chicago: University of Chicago Press.

Lakoff, G., & Johnson, M. (1980). *Metaphors we live by.* Chicago: University of Chicago Press.

Levelt, W. J. M. (1989). *Speaking: From intention to articulation.* Cambridge, MA: MIT Press.

Lieberman, P. (1991). *Uniquely human: The evolution of speech, thought and selfless behavior.* Cambridge, MA: Harvard University Press.

Markman, E. M. (1989). *Categorization and naming in children: Problems of induction.* Cambridge, MA: MIT Press/Bradford Books.

Marr, D. (1982). *Vision: A computational investigation into the human representation and processing of visual information.* San Francisco: Freeman.

McClelland, J. L., & Elman, J. L. (1986). The TRACE model of speech perception. *Cognitive Psychology, 18,* 1–86.

McClelland, J. L., & Rumelhart, D. E. (1981). An interactive activation model of context effects in letter perception: Part 1. An account of the basic findings. *Psychological Review, 88,* 375–407.

McClelland, J. L., Rumelhart, D. E., & Hinton, G. E. (1986). The appeal of parallel distributed processing. In J. L. McClelland, D. E. Rumelhart, & the PDP Research Group (Eds.), *Parallel distributed processing: Explorations in the microstructure of cognition: Vol. 1. Foundations.* Cambridge, MA: MIT Press/Bradford Books.

McClelland, J. L., Rumelhart, D. E., & the PDP Research Group (Eds.). (1986). *Parallel distributed processing: Explorations in the microstructure of cognition: Vol. 1. Foundations.* Cambridge, MA: MIT Press/Bradford Books.

McKoon, G., & Ratcliff, R. (1992). Inference during reading. *Psychological Review, 99,* 440–666.

Miller, G. A., & Johnson-Laird, P. N. (1976). *Language and perception.* Cambridge: Cambridge University Press.

Murphy, G. L., & Medin, D. L. (1985). The role of theories in conceptual coherence. *Psychological Review, 92,* 289–316.

Noordman, L. G. M., & Vonk, W. (1992). Reader's knowledge and the control of inferences in reading. *Language and Cognitive Processes, 7,* 373–391.

Nosofsky, R. M. (1986). Attention, similarity, and the identification–categorization relationship. *Journal of Experimental Psychology: General, 115,* 39–57.

Oakhill, J. V., & Garnham, A. (1988). *Becoming a skilled reader.* Oxford: Basil Blackwell.

Pickering, M., & Barry, G. (1991). Sentence processing without empty categories. *Language and Cognitive Processes, 6,* 229–259.

Pinker, S. (1989). *Learnability and cognition: The acquisition of argument structure.* Cambridge, MA: MIT Press.

Pinker, S., & Prince, A. (1988). On language and connectionism: Analysis of a parallel distributed processing model of language acquisition. *Cognition, 28,* 73–193.

Rayner, K., Carlson, M., & Frazier, L. (1983). The interaction of syntax and semantics during sentence processing. Eye movements in the analysis of syntactically biased sentences. *Journal of Verbal Learning and Verbal Behavior, 22,* 358–374.

Reber, A. S. (1987). The rise and (surprisingly rapid) fall of psycholinguistics. *Synthese, 72,* 325–339.

Rumelhart, D. E., & McClelland, J. L. (1982). An interactive activation model of context effects in letter perception: Part 2. The contextual enhancement effect and some tests and extensions of the model. *Psychological Review, 89,* 60–94.

Rumelhart, D. E., McClelland, J. L., & the PDP Research Group (Eds.). (1986). *Parallel distributed processing: Explorations in the microstructure of cognition: Vol. 2. Psychological and biological models.* Cambridge, MA: MIT Press/Bradford Books.

Sag, I. A., & Hankamer, J. (1984). Toward a theory of anaphoric processing. *Linguistics and Philosophy, 7,* 325–345.

Seidenberg, M., & McClelland, J. L. (1989). A distributed, developmental model of word recognition and naming. *Psychological Review, 96,* 523–568.

Shallice, T. (1979). Case-study approach in neuropsychological research. *Journal of Clinical Neuropsychology, 1,* 183–211.

Smith, F. (1988). *Understanding reading: A psycholinguistic analysis of reading and learning to read* (4th ed.). Hillsdale, NJ: Erlbaum.

Smith, J. K. (1976). The assuming-will-make-it-so fallacy. *Journal of Verbal Learning and Verbal Behavior, 15,* 262–263.

Smith, N. (1991). Review of Laura: A case for the modularity of language. *Mind and Language, 6,* 390–396.

Sperber, D., & Wilson, D. (1986). *Relevance: Cognition and communication.* Oxford: Basil Blackwell.

Spiro, R. J., & Esposito, J. (1981). Superficial processing of explicit inferences in text. *Discourse Processes, 4,* 313–322.

Stanovich, K. E. (1980). Toward an interactive–compensatory model of individual differences in the development of reading fluency. *Reading Research Quarterly, 16,* 32–71.

Tanenhaus, M. K., Carlson, G., & Trueswell, J. C. (1989). The role of thematic structures in interpretation and parsing. *Language and Cognitive Processes, 4,* SI 211–SI 234.

Taraban, R., & McClelland, J. L. (1988). Constituent attachment and thematic role assignment in sentence processing: Influences of content-based expectations. *Journal of Memory and Language, 27,* 597–632.

Trueswell, J., & Tanenhaus, M. K. (1991). Tense, temporal context and syntactic ambiguity resolution. *Language and Cognitive Processes, 6,* 303–338.

Tukey, J. W. (1977). *Exploratory data analysis.* Reading, MA: Addison-Wesley.

Waltz, D. (1975). Understanding line drawings of scenes with shadows. In P. H. Winston (Ed.), *The psychology of computer vision* (pp. 19–92). Cambridge, MA: MIT Press.

Wike, E. L., & Church, J. D. (1976). Comments on Clark's "The language-as-fixed-effect fallacy." *Journal of Verbal Learning and Verbal Behavior, 15,* 249–255.

INDEX

A

Abortion, 666–667
ABR, *see* Auditory brainstem response
Acoustic signal, 231
Activation concept, 3, 22
  interpretation in decision testing, 16
  measurement, 4
  memory, working versus long-term, 16
  nodes and, 4
  sentence processing, 47
  strength, 16
Adaptive resonance theory, 295
Affricate, 187
Aging
  working memory capacity
    activation reduction hypothesis, 1101,
      1105
    auditory syntactic complexity, 1103
    crystallized intelligence, 1102
    fluid intelligence, 1102
    intervening text, 1104
    sentence syntactic complexity, 1102–1103
    speech rate, 1105
    storage load, 1104
Agrammatism, 1036, 1038–1039, 1056
  Broca's aphasia, 1058, 1061–1070
Allophones, speech perception, 148–149
Alpha suppression, mental activity, 84
Altherman, Nathan, 440
Alveolar, place of articulation, 177, 794–796
  voiced stop consonants, 198, 203
  voice onset time, 186
American Family, The, 411
American Sign Language, 158, 462
  N400 ERP component, 107, 116–117
AN, *see* Auditory nerve
Anacruses, 950
Analogies, 447
Anaphoric links, 829–830
Anaphoric reference, 19–21, 23
  narrative characters, 706

Anaphoric relations, 540–541, 549–551
  leading edge model, 550
Anaphoric resolution, 487, 630, 694
  comprehension and, 559–560, 574
Anaphors, 558–560
  activation modulation, 559
  antecedent–anaphor semantic relatedness,
    679
  antecedent identifiability, 679
  bonding, 694
  conceptual, 429–430
  definite descriptions, 678–681, 684
    referent to role assignment, 681
    role restriction constraints, 689–690
  discourse context, 677
  linguistic constraints, 41
  parallel backward memory search, 559–560
  referential, 677
    cohesion devices, 678
    hierarchy, 678–679, 688, 695–696
  semantic, 40–41
  temporal, 40–41
Anger metaphor, 423
Anna Karenina, 541, 573
ANOVA, 1125–1126
Antonyms, 439–440
Aperiodic energy, 185
Aphasia, 116–117, 1055–1071; *see also* Boston
  Diagnostic Aphasia Examination
  Broca's, *see* Broca's aphasia
  conduction, 1034–1036
  holist neural function, 1031
  multiple language deficits, 1032
  transcortical motor, 1034–1035
  transcortical sensory, 1034–1035
  Wernicke's, *see* Wernicke's aphasia
  word finding, 950
Aphasic comprehension
  processing disruptions, 1066–1070
    cross-modal lexical priming, 1069–1070
    grammaticality judgement, 1066–1067
    intrasentence dependency relations, 1068

P

ISBN 0-12-280890-8

90065